INVINCIBLE

TRUEMAN'S *Specific* Series®

NTA

UGC-NET/SET

For JRF and Eligibility Test for Assistant Professor

(and Ph.D/M.Phil Entrance Exams)

Code No. : 17

MANAGEMENT

New Syllabus

With Previous Years' Papers

By

M. SHIVANI

Authentic & Dependable

Produced and Published by
Danika Publishing Company
(Publishers of Trueman's *Specific* Series)
4352/4C, Ansari Road,
Daryaganj, New Delhi - 110002
Ph.: 011-23242482, 41501988
e-mail: danikabooks@yahoo.com

Can be had from
Invincible Publishers
2nd Floor, SAS Tower, Medicity, Sector 38,
Gurugram (Haryana)

ISBN : 9788189301927

New Edition : 2027

Price : Rs. 850/-

Data Processing :
Inhouse

Printed at :
Dhruv Printers
New Delhi.

Subject to New Delhi Jurisdiction only

PUBLISHERS' NOTE

The present work is a humble attempt to satisfy the needs of students appearing for UGC NET/SET Examinations. Syllabus and Guidelines for Paper II have been given in the book. After theory and MCQs, model papers are provided for practice. We have also incorporated questions asked in previous NET examinations. The book in the present form shall serve as a reliable evocative book for those preparing for NET/SET examinations.

Any suggestions for the improvement shall be thankfully acknowledged.

— With Best Wishes

CONTENTS

UGC-NET New Syllabus

The Test will consist of two papers as given below:

Paper	Marks	Number of Questions	MCQs	Duration
I	100	50	The questions will be generic in nature, intending to assess the teaching/research aptitude of the candidate. It will primarily be designed to test reasoning ability, comprehension, divergent thinking and general awareness of the candidate.	03 hours All the questions will be compulsory.
II	200	100	This will be based on the subject selected by the candidate.	

The Test will be conducted in Computer Based Test (CBT) mode only.

The candidates who desire to appear in the test may see the detailed **Information Bulletin** for UGC-NET which will be available on the website **www.nta.ac.in**.

SYLLABUS

UNIT – I

Management – Concept, Process, Theories and Approaches, Management Roles and Skills

Functions – Planning, Organizing, Staffing, Coordinating and Controlling.

Communication – Types, Process and Barriers.

Decision Making – Concept, Process, Techniques and Tools

Organisation Structure and Design – Types, Authority, Responsibility, Centralisation, Decentralisation and Span of Control

Managerial Economics – Concept & Importance

Demand analysis – Utility Analysis, Indifference Curve, Elasticity & Forecasting

Market Structures – Market Classification & Price Determination

National Income – Concept, Types and Measurement

Inflation – Concept, Types and Measurement

Business Ethics & CSR

Ethical Issues & Dilemma

Corporate Governance

Value Based Organisation

UNIT – II

Organisational Behaviour – Significance & Theories

Individual Behaviour – Personality, Perception, Values, Attitude, Learning and Motivation

Group Behaviour – Team Building, Leadership, Group Dynamics

Interpersonal Behaviour & Transactional Analysis

Organizational Culture & Climate
Work Force Diversity & Cross Culture Organisational Behaviour
Emotions and Stress Management
Organisational Justice and Whistle Blowing
Human Resource Management – Concept, Perspectives, Influences and Recent Trends
Human Resource Planning, Recruitment and Selection, Induction, Training and Development
Job Analysis, Job Evaluation and Compensation Management

UNIT – III

Strategic Role of Human Resource Management
Competency Mapping & Balanced Scoreboard
Career Planning and Development
Performance Management and Appraisal
Organization Development, Change & OD Interventions
Talent Management & Skill Development
Employee Engagement & Work Life Balance
Industrial Relations: Disputes & Grievance Management, Labour Welfare and Social Security
Trade Union & Collective Bargaining
International Human Resource Management – HR Challenge of International Business
Green HRM

UNIT – IV

Accounting Principles and Standards, Preparation of Financial Statements
Financial Statement Analysis – Ratio Analysis, Funds Flow and Cash Flow Analysis, DuPont Analysis
Preparation of Cost Sheet, Marginal Costing, Cost Volume Profit Analysis
Standard Costing & Variance Analysis
Financial Management, Concept & Functions
Capital Structure – Theories, Cost of Capital, Sources and Finance
Budgeting and Budgetary Control, Types and Process, Zero base Budgeting
Leverages – Operating, Financial and Combined Leverages, EBIT–EPS Analysis, Financial Breakeven Point & Indifference Level.

UNIT – V

Value & Returns – Time Preference for Money, Valuation of Bonds and Shares, Risk and Returns
Capital Budgeting – Nature of Investment, Evaluation, Comparison of Methods; Risk an Uncertainly Analysis
Dividend – Theories and Determination
Mergers and Acquisition – Corporate Restructuring, Value Creation, Merger Negotiations, Leveraged Buyouts, Takeover
Portfolio Management – CAPM, APT

Derivatives – Options, Option Payoffs, Option Pricing, Forward Contracts & Future Contracts

Working Capital Management – Determinants, Cash, Inventory, Receivables and Payables Management, Factoring

International Financial Management, Foreign exchange market

UNIT – VI

Strategic Management – Concept, Process, Decision & Types

Strategic Analysis – External Analysis, PEST, Porter's Approach to industry analysis, Internal Analysis – Resource Based Approach, Value Chain Analysis

Strategy Formulation – SWOT Analysis, Corporate Strategy – Growth, Stability, Retrenchment, Integration and Diversification, Business Portfolio Analysis - BCG, GE Business Model, Ansoff's Product Market Growth Matrix

Strategy Implementation – Challenges of Change, Developing Programs Mckinsey 7s Framework

Marketing – Concept, Orientation, Trends and Tasks, Customer Value and Satisfaction

Market Segmentation, Positioning and Targeting

Product and Pricing Decision – Product Mix, Product Life Cycle, New Product development, Pricing – Types and Strategies

Place and promotion decision – Marketing channels and value networks, VMS, IMC, Advertising and Sales promotion

UNIT – VII

Consumer and Industrial Buying Behaviour: Theories and Models of Consumer Behaviour

Brand Management – Role of Brands, Brand Equity, Equity Models, Developing a Branding Strategy; Brand Name Decisions, Brand Extensions and Loyalty

Logistics and Supply Chain Management, Drivers, Value creation, Supply Chain Design, Designing and Managing Sales Force, Personal Selling

Service Marketing – Managing Service Quality and Brands, Marketing Strategies of Service Firms

Customer Relationship Marketing – Relationship Building, Strategies, Values and Process

Retail Marketing – Recent Trends in India, Types of Retail Outlets.

Emerging Trends in Marketing – Concept of e-Marketing, Direct Marketing, Digital Marketing and Green Marketing

International Marketing – Entry Mode Decisions, Planning Marketing Mix for International Markets

UNIT – VIII

Statistics for Management: Concept, Measures Of Central Tendency and Dispersion, Probability Distribution – Binominal, Poison, Normal and Exponential

Data Collection & Questionnaire Design

Sampling – Concept, Process and Techniques

Hypothesis Testing – Procedure; T, Z, F, Chi-square tests

Correlation and Regression Analysis

Operations Management – Role and Scope

Facility Location and Layout – Site Selection and Analysis, Layout – Design and Process

Enterprise Resource Planning – ERP Modules, ERP implementation

Scheduling; Loading, Sequencing and Monitoring

Quality Management and Statistical Quality Control, Quality Circles, Total Quality Management – KAIZEN, Benchmarking, Six Sigma; ISO 9000 Series Standards

Operation Research – Transportation, Queuing Decision Theory, PERT / CPM

UNIT – IX

International Business – Managing Business in Globalization Era; Theories of International Trade; Balance of payment

Foreign Direct Investment – Benefits and Costs

Multilateral regulation of Trade and Investment under WTO

International Trade Procedures and Documentation; EXIM Policies

Role of International Financial Institutions – IMF and World Bank

Information Technology – Use of Computers in Management Applications; MIS, DSS

Artificial Intelligence and Big Data

Data Warehousing, Data Mining and Knowledge Management – Concepts

Managing Technological Change

UNIT – X

Entrepreneurship Development – Concept, Types, Theories and Process, Developing Entrepreneurial Competencies

Intrapreneurship – Concept and Process

Women Entrepreneurship and Rural Entrepreneurship

Innovations in Business – Types of Innovations, Creating and Identifying Opportunities, Screening of Business Ideas

Business Plan and Feasibility Analysis – Concept and Process of Technical, Market and Financial Analysis

Micro and Small Scale Industries in India; Role of Government in Promoting SSI

Sickness in Small Industries – Reasons and Rehabilitation

Institutional Finance to Small Industries – Financial Institutions, Commercial Banks, Cooperative Banks, Micro Finance.

UNIT 1

SYLLABUS

- Management – Concept, Process, Theories and Approaches, Management Roles and Skills
- Functions – Planning, Organizing, Staffing, Coordinating and Controlling.
- Communication – Types, Process and Barriers.
- Decision Making – Concept, Process, Techniques and Tools
- Organisation Structure and Design – Types, Authority, Responsibility, Centralisation, Decentralisation and Span of Control
- Managerial Economics – Concept & Importance
- Demand analysis – Utility Analysis, Indifference Curve, Elasticity & Forecasting
- Market Structures – Market Classification & Price Determination
- National Income – Concept, Types and Measurement
- Inflation – Concept, Types and Measurement
- Business Ethics & CSR
- Ethical Issues & Dilemma
- Corporate Governance
- Value Based Organisation

MEANING OF MANAGEMENT

Management is an individual or a group of individuals that accept responsibilities to run an organisation. They Plan, Organise, Direct and Control all the essential activities of the organisation. Management does not do the work themselves. They motivate others to do the work and co-ordinate (*i.e.,* bring together) all the work for achieving the objectives of the organisation.

Management brings together all **Six Ms** *i.e.,* Men and Women, Money, Machines, Materials, Methods and Markets. They use these resources for achieving the objectives of the organisation such as high sales, maximum profits, business expansion, etc.

Management is the process of conducting a set of functions (planning, organising, staffing, directing and controlling) to get the work done in an efficient and effective manner.

Management is the art of knowing what you want to do and then seeing that they do it in the best and the cheapest way.

In other words, "Management is the process of planning, organising, leading, and controlling the efforts of organisation members and of using all other organisational resources to achieve stated organisational goals".

According to **Theo Heimann**, management has three different meanings, viz.,

1. **Management as a Noun.** refers to a Group of Managers.
2. **Management as a Process.** refers to the Functions of Management *i.e.*, Planning, Organising, Directing, Controlling, etc.
3. **Management as a Discipline.** refers to the Subject of Management.

Definition of Management

- According to **D.J. Clough,** "Management is the art and Science of decision-making and leadership."
- According to **Henry L. Sisk,** "Management is the coordination of all resources through the process of planning, organising, directing and controlling in order to attain stated goals."
- According to **George R. Terry,** "Management is a distinct process consisting of planning, organising, actuating and controlling performed to determine and accomplish stated objectives by the use of human being and other resources."
- According to **C.W. Wilson,** "Management is a process of releasing and directing human energies towards attaining a definite goal.
- According to **B.O. Wheeler,** "Business management is a human activity which directs and controls the organisation and operations of business enterprise."
- According to **Mary Parker Follet,** "Management is the art of getting things done through people."
- According to **Peter F. Drucker,** "Management is a multi-purpose organ that manages business and manages managers and manages workers and work." This definition of management was given by Peter Drucker in his book "*The Principles of Management*".
- According to **Henry Fayol**, "To manage is to forecast and to plan, to organise, to command, to co-ordinate and to control." Henry Fayol gave this definition of management in his book "*Industrial and General Administration*".

Some other Definitions

- Management consists in guiding human and physical resources into dynamic, hard-hitting organisation unit that attains its objectives to the satisfaction of those served and with a high degree of morale and sense of attainment on the part of those rendering the service.

  – Lawrence A. Appley
- Management is principally the task of planning, coordinating, motivating, and controlling the efforts of others towards specific objective. *– James L. Lundy*
- Management is the art and science of organising and directing human efforts applied to control the forces and utilise the materials of nature for the benefit of man.

  – American Society of Mechanical Engineers
- Management is the art of knowing what you want to do and then seeing that it is done in the best and cheapest way. *– F.W. Taylor*
- Management is the function of executive leadership anywhere. *– Ralph C. Davis*
- Management is concerned with seeing that the job gets done, its tasks all centre on planning and guiding the operations that are going on in the enterprise. *– E.F.L. Breach*

Features of Management

1. **Continuous and never ending process.** Management is a Process. It includes four main functions, viz., Planning, Organising, Directing and Controlling. The manager has to Plan and Organise all the activities. He had to give proper Directions to his subordinates. He also has to Control all the activities. The manager has to perform these functions continuously. Therefore, management is a continuous and never ending process.
2. **Getting things done through people.** The managers do not do the work themselves. They get the work done through the workers. The workers should not be treated like slaves. They should not be tricked, threatened or forced to do the work. A favorable work environment should be created and maintained
3. **Result oriented science and art.** Management is result oriented because it gives a lot of importance to "**Results**". Examples of Results like, increase in market share increase in profits, etc. Management always wants to get the best results at all times.
4. **Multi-disciplinary in nature.** Management has to get the work done through people. It has to manage people. This is a very difficult job because different people have different emotions, feelings, aspirations, etc. Similarly, the same person may have different emotions at different times. So, management is a very complex job. Therefore, management uses knowledge from many different subjects such as Economics, Information Technology, Psychology, Sociology, etc. Therefore, it is Multi-disciplinary in nature.
5. **A group and not an individual activity.** Management is not an individual activity. It is a group activity. It uses group (employees) efforts to achieve group (owners) objectives. It tries to satisfy the needs and wants of a group (consumers). Nowadays, importance is given to the team (group) and not to individuals
6. **Follows established principles or rules.** Management follows established principles; such as division of work, discipline, unity of command, etc. These principles help to prevent and solve the problems in the organisation.
7. **Situational in nature.** Management makes plans, policies and decisions according to the situation. It changes its style according to the situation. It uses different plans, policies, decisions and styles for different situations. The manager first studies the full present situation. Then he draws conclusions about the situation. Then he makes plans, decisions, etc., which are best for the present situation. This is called **Situational** Management.
8. **Both an art and science.** Management is result-oriented. Therefore, it is an Art. Management conducts continuous research. Thus, it is also a Science.
9. **Management is all pervasive.** Management is necessary for running a business. It is also essential for running business, educational, charitable and religious institutions. Management is a must for all activities, and therefore, it is all pervasive.
10. **Management is intangible.** Management is intangible, *i.e.,* it cannot be seen and touched, but it can be felt and realised by its results. The success or failure of management can be judged only by its results. If there is good discipline, good productivity, good profits, etc., then the management is successful and vice-versa.
11. **Dynamic in nature.** Management is dynamic in nature. That is, management is creative and innovative. An organisation will survive and succeed only if it is dynamic. It must continuously bring in new and creative ideas, new products, new product features, new ads, new marketing techniques, etc.

Process of Management

Management process is a process of setting goals, planning and/or controlling the organizing and leading the execution of any type of activity, such as:

- a project (project management process) or
- a process (process management process, sometimes referred to as the process performance measurement and management system).

An organisation's senior management is responsible for carrying out its management process. However, this is not always the case for all management processes, for example, it is the responsibility of the project manager to carry out a project management process.

A brief discussion of each of these functions can be explained as follow:

Planning. Planning is deciding in advance what is to be done, how and when it is to be done. It is concerned with projecting the future course of action for the business as a whole and the different sections within it. Planning is the foremost and the primary function of management. It involves the determination of objectives and selecting the best course of action which will lead to the achievement of the predetermined objectives. Planning is the preparatory step for actions and helps in bridging the gap between the present and the future. Planning provides the solution to the various problems like:

- What are the necessary actions for the achievements of the predetermined objectives?
- What are the reasons for these necessary actions?
- When will these actions take place?
- How will these actions take place?
- Who should be made responsible for these actions?

PROCESS OF PLANNING

- Determination of the objectives of the organisation
- Forecasting or anticipating the future courses of actions
- Choosing the best course of action or decision making
- Formulation of policies, programmes, budget etc. for the achievement of the predetermined objectives.
- Laying down the procedures and standards of performance.

Basically planning is concerned with the determination of the following: Objectives, Policies, Procedures, Rules, Programme, Budget & Strategie.

Organising. To divide the work, rights, and liability among the personnel engaged in the achievement of the objectives and establishing the formal relationship among them is called organising. It is concerned with development of a structure of authority and responsibility among the personnel, so that they can effectively perform their work. Thus, Organising is the process of establishing harmonious relationship among the members of the enterprise.

Organising basically consists of the following steps:

- Determination of the activities of the enterprise keeping in view its objectives.
- Classification of such activities into convenient groups for the purpose of division.
- Assignment of these groups of activities to the individuals.
- Delegation of authority and fixing of responsibility for carrying out the assigned duties.
- Coordination of these activities and authority relations throughout the organisation.

So, division of work among people and coordination of their efforts to achieve specific objectives are the fundamental aspects of organising.

Staffing. Organisation as a function of management helps the executive to establish positions and lay down their functional relation to each other whereas through staffing function, the different positions in the organisation structure are kept manned. Staffing involves manning of various positions created by the organising process. So staffing is the process of filling all positions in the organisation with qualified and adequate personnel. Staffing is a continuous function. A new enterprise needs to employ people to fill positions established in the organisation. In an established concern also such factors like death, retirement, resignation, termination, promotion, demotion, transfer etc. necessitate continuous performance of this function.

Staffing involves the finding of right person for the right job and placing him at the right place, doing the right job at the right time. Steps involved in the process of staffing:

- Estimate the size and the makeup of the future manpower needs (Manpower Planning).
- Acquiring the most competent and qualified applicants to meet the manpower needs (Recruitment).
- Evaluating the applicants for different positions, choosing the best candidates, and assigning them to the right jobs (Selection and Placement).
- To arrange training and development of the employees to secure efficiency of operation.
- Periodic evaluation of the performance of employees (Performance appraisal).
- Promotion and transfer of employees (Job changes).

The importance of staffing as a function of management arises from the importance of human resources in an organisation. Staffing involves manning the organisation structure through proper and effective recruitment, selection, training, development and appraisal of personnel to fill the roles designed into structure. Staffing ensures the availability of the required human resources at all times.

Directing. In addition to planning, organising and staffing every manager must also direct his subordinates. Directing is thus the initiating function of management that actuates plans and the organisation. Directing is an important function of management which involves communicating and providing leadership to the subordinates and motivating them to continue to the best of their capability for the achievement of organisational objectives. It is concerned with influencing the behaviour of human resources for the accomplishment of organisational objectives. It is therefore the life spark of an organisation as it is through directing that actual performance of the employees is guided towards common goals.

Important elements of Directing. The main elements of directing are :

- *Supervision.* Supervision is the main element of directing. The term supervision is made up of two words super and vision which means expert overseeing of employees at work. It involves direct personal contact with the subordinates. Supervision converts plans into action. Further the supervisor serves as a link between the workers and the management. It is necessary at all levels of management and throughout the chain of command; each superior supervises the work performance of his subordinates.
- *Motivation.* Motivation is an impulse drive or urge to move in specific direction to reduce a need. It is an act of understanding the motives and satisfying them to direct and sustain behaviour towards the accomplishment of organisational goals. Thus, motivation is an act of stimulating people to get desired course of action. Motivation is a psychological concept. It is concerned with the intrinsic forces operating within an individual which impel him to act or not to act in a particular way.
- *Communication.* Communication is an important element of direction. In fact superior subordinate relationship cannot thrive without effective and meaningful communication. Effective communication is defined as the exchange of thoughts, facts, opinions, or information by two or more persons so as to bring mutual understanding or confidence. Communication can be done through words, symbols, letters, or actions. So communication is the transfer of information or understanding from one person to another.

- *Leadership.* Leadership is one of the important aspects of managing. It is an interpersonal process of influencing the behaviour of individual and the group so that defined objectives are accomplished willingly and enthusiastically. A leader is the individual with the major influence in the group and whose main role is to get others to the organisational goals. A leader directs and motivates members of the group. He also represents the group to the outside world and the outside world to the group.

Controlling. Control is a fundamental function of management that usually follows the other functions. It is a continuing process of management. Controlling means the measurement and correction of performance of activities of subordinates in order to ensure that predetermined objectives can be achieved. So control guides the activities of the employees towards the predetermined goals. It is the process of ensuring that events confirm to the plans as closely as possible. It is the application of corrective measures to remove the deviations if actual performance does not meet the standards.

Controlling is the last but the most important function of management. Objective of every organisation is to use scarce resources in a best possible way. Plans are framed to achieve better results. Control is the process of checking whether the plans are being adhered to or not, keeping a record of progress, then taking corrective measures, if there is any deviation. Control is one of the important managerial functions which bring the actual results closer to the desired results.

PROCESS OF CONTROLLING

- Setting of goals and standards.
- Appraisal of performance.
- Determining the reasons of deviations.
- Taking Corrective Action.

Thus, controlling is the process under which actual performance is compared with the fixed standards, deviations are discovered, the reasons are analyzed, and corrective action is taken so that repetition of such mistakes in future can be avoided.

THEORIES AND APPROACHES

Stages in the History of Development of Management Thought

I. The Classical Approach
1. Bureaucratic model introduced by Max Weber around 1900.
2. Scientific management concepts introduced by F.W. Taylor around 1910.
3. Functional and administrative theory advanced by Henry Fayol around 1910.

II. The Neo Classical Approach
1. Human relation movement was propagated by Elton Mayo and Roethlisberger around 1930.
2. Behavioural Sciences movement was introduced by A. Maslow, McGregor around 1940.

III. The Modern Approach
1. Quantitative approach or operation research analysis.
2. System approach was propounded by Boulding, Johnson and others after 1950.
3. Contingency Approach was developed by Lorsch, Lawrence and others.

Classical Scientific Management

The classical management theory, developed during the Industrial Revolution when new problems related to the factory system began to appear. Managers were unsure of how to train employees (many of them non-english speaking immigrants) or deal with increased labour dissatisfaction, so they began to test solutions.

As a result, the classical management theory developed from efforts to find the "one best way" to perform and manage tasks. This school of thought is made up of two branches: classical scientific and classical administrative.

The **classical scientific branch** arose because of the need to increase productivity and efficiency. The emphasis was on trying to find the best way to get the most work done by examining how the work process was actually accomplished and by scrutinising the skills of the workforce.

The classical scientific school owes its roots to several major contributors, including Fredrick Taylor, Henry Gantt, Frank and Lillian Gilbert.

Meaning of Scientific Management

The concept of scientific management was introduced by Fredrick Winslow Taylor in U.S.A in the beginning of 20th Century. This concept was further carried on by Frank and Lillian, Edward Fellen etc. Scientific management was basically concerned with the improvement in the operational efficiency of the shop floor workers.

In a broad sense, scientific management implies the application of scientific methods of study and analysis to the problems of management. It is a systematic and thoughtful approach to the job of management as compared to the rule-of-thumb, or hit and miss, or trial and error approaches. It is concerned with the scientific bent of mind and is more than merely a set of techniques for improving efficiency. It implies substitution of exact scientific investigation and knowledge for individual judgement or opinion in all matters undertaken in the establishment.

Definition of Scientific Management

- According to **F.W. Taylor**, "Scientific management is concerned with knowing exactly what you want men to do and then see in that they do it in the best and cheapest way".
- According to **Drucker**, "The cost of scientific management is the organised study of work, the analysis of work into its simplest elements and the systematic management of the workers, performance of each element".

Principles of Scientific Management

Taylor's philosophy consists of the following principles which constitute the cornerstone of scientific management:

1. **Science, not rule of thumb.** According to this principle, scientific investigation should be applied in the scientific management, which will replace the rule of thumb. Taylor had made study of every job and fixed the method and timing for performing the job so that the worker should know that what, when, and how is required to perform the job. This principle is the starting point that distinguishes scientific management with the traditional management. Further, this principle eliminates the trend of go on trying, failing, wasting the resources, and finally perfecting the job. For this purpose Taylor had developed the various studies like; method study, time study, motion study etc.
2. **Harmony, not discord.** This principle states that there should be cooperation between the management and the workers. In order to achieve the best possible results from the business operations, it is essential that there should be harmonious relations between the management and the workers. According to this principle, attempts should be made to obtain the harmony in the group action rather than discord. Workers should have sense of belongingness towards the organisation.

3. **Mental Revolution.** The technique of Mental revolution involves a change in the attitude of workers and management towards each other. Both should realize the importance of each other and should work with full cooperation. Management as well as the workers should aim to increase the profits of the organisation.

   For this the workers should put in their best efforts so that the company makes profit and on the other hand management should share part of profits with the workers. Thus, mental revolution requires a complete change in the outlook of both management and workers. There should be a spirit of togetherness between workers and management.

4. **Cooperation, Not Individualism.** This principle is an extension of principle of 'Harmony, not discord' and lays stress on mutual cooperation between workers and the management. Cooperation, mutual confidence, sense of goodwill should prevail among both, managers as well as workers. The intention is to replace internal competition with cooperation.

5. **Development of each and every person to his or her greatest efficiency and prosperity.** According to this principle the right men is placed on the right job. The jobs are determined first for which the workers are required and then the qualifications required for the job are determined. On the basis of these standards the employees are selected. So procedure for the selection of the members is designed scientifically. Further, management is responsible for the development and training of the workers. In scientific management, all workers should be developed to the fullest extent possible for their own as well as for the company's prosperity.

Techniques of Scientific Management

1. **Functional Foremanship.** Functional foremanship involves the supervision of the workers by several specialist foremen. Taylor evolved the concept of functional foremanship on the basis of specialisation and provided the importance to the supervision. He advocated the appointment of specialist foreman for the specific jobs. In this system eight persons are involved to direct the activities of the workers at the job. These eight persons are divided in two:

   Production department : Four persons
   - **Speed boss.** Maintaining the planned speed of production.
   - **Inspector.** Matching that work done is according to the standards.
   - **Maintenance Foreman.** Maintenance of machines and equipments.
   - **Gang Boss.** Making arrangement of machines, material, and men for the job.

   Planning department : Four persons
   - **Route Clerk.** Determine the process of job.
   - **Instruction Card Clerk.** Laying down the instructions for the workers.
   - **Time and Cost Clerk.** Setting the time table and cost budget for the job.
   - **Disciplinarian.** Maintaining proper discipline in the factory.

2. **Motion Study.** Motion study is designed to eliminate unnecessary motions and to reinforce necessary motions. It is a close observation of analyzing the body movements of the worker performing the job. This study helps in analyzing that if any element of the job can be eliminated or not. This study helps in:
   - Finding and eliminating the unnecessary motions of the workers on the job.
   - Increasing the efficiency of the workers by reducing the fatigue and manual labour.
   - Increasing the production and the productivity of the worker.

3. **Time study.** This study helps in determining the time required by an average skill worker to efficiently perform a particular job. Time study helps in determining the standard time for the

job. This standard time is then fixed for the workers for performing the job. So, time study is used to measure precisely the time required in doing every element of a job with the purpose of deciding the fair day's work. This study helps in:

- Determine scientifically the standard time required to perform the job.
- Creating time consciousness among the workers.
- Measuring the efficiency of the workers.
- Restricting the carelessness of the employees.
- Differentiating between efficient and inefficient workers.

4. **Differential Piece Wage System.** According to the Taylor, the efficient worker should be paid more than the inefficient one. Financial incentives motivate the workers to put their maximum efforts and according to Taylor are the provision exists in the company to earn higher wages by putting the extra effort, worker will be motivated to work more. Based on this Taylor evolved the Differential Piece Rate System. Under this system there are two piece rates:
   - Higher piece rate for those who produce standard quantity or more.
   - Lower piece rate for those who produce less than standard quantity.
5. **Standardisation.** Taylor emphasized that standardisation should be maintained in respect of product, raw material, machines, equipments, methods, and working conditions. These things should be planned in advance on the basis of job analysis and the elements of cost that involved in the performance of the job. So according to Taylor the maximum objectives can be achieved only when the labour, raw material, machine etc. should be standardised and not to be left on hit and trial. Standardisation is required for:
   - **Standardisation of raw material.** Raw material used in the production of the product should be standardised and also predetermined.
   - **Standardisation of product.** Product produced should also be standardised in their design, weight, shape, and size.
   - **Standardisation of machines and equipments.** Machines and equipments on which the job is performed by the workers should also be standardised.
   - **Standardisation of methods.** Method and the techniques of production should be determined in advance after proper job analysis and the research.
   - **Standardisation of working conditions.** Working conditions under which the worker has to perform the job should be standardised and all the requirements for the job to be made available to the workers.
6. **Work Study.** The critical examination of efficiency of the various operations in an organisation is called work study. The overall objective of the scientific management is to achieve maximum output at the minimum cost. For the purpose of the achievement of this objective it is required to examine the efficiency of every factor which affects the production for the purpose of bringing improvement in the operations. Work study is the generic term given to those techniques which are used for analyzing the human work and systematic investigation of all factors which affect the efficiency and effectiveness of the operations. The following studies are included in the work study :

   (a) **Method Study.** Method study is conducted to know the standardised method of doing the job in the best manner. Method study helps in efficiently performing the job by:
   - Simplifying the use of tools and equipments.
   - Integrating similar activities.
   - Eliminating unnecessary actions.
   - Reducing the distance between the place of storing and consumption of raw material.

(b) **Scientific Selection and Training of workers.** According to Taylor, management should design scientific method for selecting the suitable workers, and for determining the training needs of the workers. Further, worker should be given work for which the worker is competent and suitable. Proper emphasis should be given on the training of the workers to make them efficient for the job, which they have to perform.

(c) **Fatigue Study.** When a worker works continuously his efficiency in the work goes on diminishing and he becomes tired. So fatigue in the work is natural and obvious. Fatigue has an adverse effect on the ability and efficiency of the worker. Scientific management determines the standard time of the job and the time after which the worker will require the rest. Fatigue study helps in

- Reducing the fatigue among the workers
- Increasing the efficiency of the worker.
- Maintains the operational efficiency of the worker.

(d) **Mental Revolution.** Taylor emphasized the mutual cooperation between the workers and the management as the human element comprising of worker and management is essentially a very sensitive factor of production. The basic idea behind the mental revolution is to change the mental attitude of the workers and the management towards each other. Mental revolution requires that there should be perfect cooperation and coordination between the efforts of labour and the management. The basic objectives of mental revolution are:

- To encourage the workers to put maximum efforts for the increase in production.
- Creation of mutual trust and confidence.
- Making the relations between the management and workers harmonious.
- Developing the scientific attitude towards the business problems and issues.
- Relationship between Fayol's and Taylor's Principles of Management.

Advantages of Scientific Management

Scientific management provide the following advantages to the management:

1. Enhanced production
2. Ability to control
3. Decreased inaccuracy
4. Decreased autocracy
5. Cost of production is reduced
6. Pay system
7. Quick decision making
8. Benefit to customers
9. Efficiency increased
10. Best use of resources and development
11. Beneficial to the nation
12. Less production time
13. Work is carried out in a systematic manner
14. A proper atmosphere for working and conditions
15. Beneficial for owners and investors
16. Avoids labour and management disputes.

Disadvantages of Scientific Management

Following are the limitations of scientific management:

1. Requires huge capital
2. Management takes control
3. Planning reduces productivity
4. Demotivating approach
5. Overly bureaucratic
6. Mechanistic
7. Not suitable for teams
8. Work division
9. Avoids bargaining
10. Loss

11. Unemployment
12. Adverse effects
13. Stress
14. Wrong assumption
15. Follows narrow application
16. Time consuming.

Classical Administrative School

Whereas scientific management focused on the productivity of individuals, the classical administrative approach concentrates on the total organisation. The emphasis is on the development of managerial principles rather than work methods.

Contributors to this school of thought include Max Weber, Henri Fayol, Mary Parker Follett, and Chester I. Barnard. These theorists studied the flow of information within an organisation and emphasized the importance of understanding how an organisation operated.

In the late 1800s, **Max Weber** disliked that many European organisations were managed on a "personal" family-like basis and that employees were loyal to individual supervisors rather than to the organisation. He believed that organisations should be managed impersonally and that a formal organisational structure, where specific rules were followed, was important. In other words, he didn't think that authority should be based on a person's personality. He thought authority should be something that was part of a person's job and passed from individual to individual as one person left and another took over. This no personal, objective form of organisation was called a **bureaucracy.**

Elements of Bureaucracy

Weber has provided a number of features in bureaucratic organisation. These are given below :

- **Hierarchy.** Hierarchy is a way of ranking positions in descending order from top to bottom of an organisation. All positions within a bureaucracy are structured in a way that permits the higher positions to supervise and control the lower positions. This clear chain of command facilitates control and order throughout the organisation.
- **Rules, regulations and procedures.** Standard operating procedures govern all organisational activities to provide certainty and facilitate coordination.
- **Division of work.** All responsibilities in an organisation are specialised so that each employee has the necessary expertise to do a particular task.
- **Impersonal relationships.** Managers should maintain an impersonal relationship with employees so that favouritism and personal prejudice do not influence decisions.
- **Competence.** Competence, not "who you know," should be the basis for all decisions made in hiring, job assignments, and promotions in order to foster ability and merit as the primary characteristics of a bureaucratic organisation.
- **Records.** Proper records have to be kept for everything. A bureaucracy needs to maintain complete files regarding all its activities.

Human Relations School

Functional and Administrative Management

Henry Fayol (1841-1925) started his career as a junior engineer in a coal mine company in France and become its general manager in 1880. He not only saved a large coal and steel company from bankruptcy, but also led to crowning success.

His ideas on management have been summed up as the **Administrative Management Theory,** which later evolved into the management process school. Fayol contribution to management can be discussed under the following heads:

1. Division of Industrial Activities

Fayol observed the organisational functioning from manager's point of view

He found that all activities of the industrial enterprise could be divided into six groups :

(i) Technical (relating to production)
(ii) Commercial (buying, selling and exchange)
(iii) Financial (Search for capital and its optimum use)
(iv) Security (protection of property and person)
(v) Accounting (preparation of various statements, accounts, return etc.) and
(vi) Managerial (Planning, organisation, command, coordination and control)

2. Qualities of an Effective Manager

Henry Fayol was the first person to recognise the different qualities for managers.

According to him these qualities are :

(i) **Physical** (health, vigour, and address)
(ii) **Mental** (ability to understand and learn judgement, mental vigour, and adaptability)
(iii) **Moral** (energy, firmness, willingness to accept responsibility)
(iv) **Educational** (acquaintance with matters related to general functioning)
(v) **Technical** (peculiar to the functions being performed)
(vi) **Experience** (arising out of the work)

3. Functions of Management

Fayol classified the elements of management into five and all such elements were considered by him as the functions of management.

According to him following are the functions of management:

(i) Planning
(ii) Organising
(iii) Commanding
(iv) Co-ordinating
(v) Controlling

4. Principles of Management

Henri Fayol, a French mining engineer, developed 14 principles of management based on his management experiences. These principles provide modern-day managers with general guidelines on how a supervisor should organise her department and manage her staff. Although later research has created controversy over many of the following principles, they are still widely used in management theories.

- **Division of Work.** Division of work in the management process produces more and better work with the same effort. Various functions of management like planning, organising, directing and controlling cannot be performed efficiently by a single proprietor or by a group of directors. They must be entrusted to specialists in related fields.
- **Authority and Responsibility.** As the management consists of getting the work done through others, it implies that the manager should have the right to give orders and power to exact obedience. A manager may exercise formal authority and also personal power. Formal authority is derived from his official position, while personal power is the result of intelligence, experience, moral worth, ability to lead, past service, etc. Responsibility is closely related to authority and it arises wherever authority is exercised. An individual who is willing to exercise authority, must also be prepared to bear responsibility to perform the work in the manner desired. However, responsibility is feared as much as authority is sought after.
- **Discipline.** Discipline is absolutely essential for the smooth running of business. By discipline we mean, the obedience to authority, observance of the rules of service and norms of performance,

respect for agreements, sincere efforts for completing the given job, respect for superiors, etc. The best means of maintaining discipline are (a) good supervisors at all levels, (b) clear and fair agreements between the employees and the employer, and (c) judicious application of penalties. In fact, discipline is what leaders make it.

- **Unity of Command.** This principle requires that each employee should receive instructions about a particular work from one superior only. Fayol believed that if an employee was to report to more than one superior, he would be confused due to conflict in instructions and also it would be difficult to pinpoint responsibility to him.
- **Unity of Direction.** It means that there should be complete identity between individual and organisational goals on the one hand and between departmental goals *inter se* on the other. They should not pull in different directions.
- **Subordination of Individual Interest to General Interest.** In a business concern, an individual is always interested in maximising his own satisfaction through more money, recognition, status, etc. This is very often against the general interest which lies in maximising production. Hence the need to subordinate the individual interest to general interest.
- **Remuneration.** The remuneration paid to the personnel of the firm should be fair. It should be based on general business conditions, cost of living, productivity of the concerned employees and the capacity of the firm to pay. Fair remuneration increases workers" efficiency and morale and fosters good relations between them and the management.
- **Centralisation.** If subordinates are given more role and importance in the management and organisation of the firm, it is decentralisation. The management must decide the degree of centralisation or decentralisation of authority on the basis of the nature of the circumstances, size of the undertaking, the type of activities and the nature of organisational structure. The objective to pursue should be the optimum utilisation of all faculties of the personnel.
- **Scalar Chain.** Scalar chain means the hierarchy of authority from the highest executive to the lowest one for the purpose of communication. It states superior-subordinate relationship and the authority of superiors in relation to subordinates at various levels. As per this principle, the orders or communications should pass through the proper channels of authority along the scalar chain. But in case there is need for swift action, the proper channels of authority may be short-circuited by making direct contact (called gang plank) with the concerned authority.
- **Order.** To put things in an order needs effort. Disorder does not need any effort. It evolves by itself. Management should obtain orderliness in work through suitable organisation of men and materials. The principle of "right place for everything and for every man" should be observed by the management. To observe this principle, there is need for scientific selection of competent personnel, correct assignment of duties to personnel and good organisation.
- **Equity.** Equity means equality of fair treatment. Equity results from a combination of kindness and justice. Employees expect management to be equally just to everybody. It requires managers to be free from all prejudices, personal likes or dislikes. Equity ensures healthy industrial relations between management and labour which is essential for the successful working of the enterprise.
- **Stability of Tenure of Personnel.** In order to motivate workers to do more and better work, it is necessary that they should be assured security of job by the management. If they have fear of insecurity of job, their morale will be low and they cannot give more and better work. Further, they will not have any sense of attachment to the firm and they will always be on the lookout for a job elsewhere.
- **Initiative.** Initiative means freedom to think out and execute a plan. The zeal and energy of employees are augmented by initiative. Innovation which is the hallmark of technological progress is possible only where the employees are encouraged to take initiative. According to

Fayol. Initiative is one of the keenest satisfactions for an intelligent man to experience, and hence, he advises managers to give their employees sufficient scope to show their initiative. Employees should be encouraged to make all kinds of suggestions to conceive and carry out their plans, even when some mistakes result.

Differences between Fayol and Taylor Contribution

Similarities between Taylor's and Fayol's point of view:

- Point of views of both has systematically attempted to overcome the managerial problems.
- Principles of both can be applied in solving the managerial problems.
- Both have concluded that sound principles are required for the effective management decisions.
- Both have emphasized that training is necessary for developing the managerial qualities among the personnel's.
- For the achievement of organisational goals both have emphasized the cooperation and mutual trust among the workers and the management.

Basis	Henry Fayol	F.W Taylor
Place	France	America
Period	1841-1925	1856-1915
Level	Higher Management Level	Shop Floor Level
Scope	Wider as principles are applicable to all types of management.	Narrower, as is applied to factory level only.
Emphasizes	Overall efficiency can be achieved by observing principles.	Efficiency through work simplification and standardisation.
Results	Personal experiences translated into universal truths.	Scientific observation and measurement.
Concern	Efficiency of managers	Asks, workers, and supervisors
Achievement	Administrative management	Scientific management
Status	Father of modern management	Father of scientific management
Orientation	Managerial functions	Production and engineering

Behavioural School

Behavioural management theory was developed in response to the need to account for employee behaviour and motivation. The shift moved management from a production orientation (classical leadership theory) to a leadership style focussed on the workers, human need for work related satisfaction and good working conditions.

The **behavioural science approach** developed as a natural evolution from the Hawthrone experiment. The behavioural science approach applies the knowledge of the behavioural science – psychology, sociology, and anthropology –to managing people.

The **behavioural management theory** is often called the human relations movement because it addresses the human dimension of work. Behavioural theorists believed that a better understanding of human behaviour at work, such as motivation, conflict, expectations, and group dynamics, improved productivity. The theorists who contributed to this school viewed employees as individuals, resources, and assets to be developed and worked with — not as machines, as in the past. Several individuals and experiments contributed to this theory.

Elton Mayo's contributions came as part of the *Hawthorne studies,* a series of experiments that rigorously applied classical management theory only to reveal its shortcomings. The Hawthorne experiments consisted of two studies conducted at the Hawthorne Works of the Western Electric

Company in Chicago from 1924 to 1932. The first study was conducted by a group of engineers seeking to determine the relationship of lighting levels to worker productivity. Surprisingly enough, they discovered that worker productivity increased as the lighting levels decreased — that is, until the employees were unable to see what they were doing, after which performance naturally declined.

A few years later, a second group of experiments began. Harvard researchers Mayo and F. J. Roethlisberger supervised a group of five women in a bank wiring room. They gave the women special privileges, such as the right to leave their workstations without permission, take rest periods, enjoy free lunches, and have variations in pay levels and workdays. This experiment also resulted in significantly increased rates of productivity.

In this case, Mayo and Roethlisberger concluded that the increase in productivity resulted from the supervisory arrangement rather than the changes in lighting or other associated worker benefits. Because the experimenters became the primary supervisors of the employees, the intense interest they displayed for the workers was the basis for the increased motivation and resulting productivity. Essentially, the experimenters became a part of the study and influenced its outcome. This is the origin of the term *Hawthorne effect,* which describes the special attention researchers give to a study's subjects and the impact that attention has on the study's findings.

The general conclusion from the Hawthorne studies was that human relations and the social needs of workers are crucial aspects of business management. This principle of human motivation helped revolutionise theories and practices of management.

The Following are the important aspect of the behavioral science approach:

(i) **Communication.** Communication plays a vital role in human behavior school. A better understanding develops between the management and workers, because of the reduced channel of communication in an organisation.

(ii) **Employee development.** It is concerned with the continued upgrading of employee skill and managerial skill.

(iii) **Leadership.** This school also underlines the role of the personal leadership of management. The scope of this school includes study of human relations and how the managers can grasp their implication, study of managers as a leaders and the way he should lead and study of successful and unsuccessful managerial behaviour.

(iv) **Employee motivation.** This includes a determination of the factors that lead to high productivity and high morale.

(v) **Organisation as social system.** It includes the study of role, status symbol as well as the function of the informal organisation.

Contributions of Behavioural Scientists

Abraham Maslow, James March and Herbert Simon, Douglas McGregor, Victor Vroom, Fredrick Herzberg, Chester Barnard, etc., made important contributions to the behavioural science approach.

Assumptions of Behavioral Science Approach

Basic assumptions and **propositions** of Behavioral Science Approach are :

1. In an organisation conflicts are unavoidable.
2. Different people have different perceptions, attitudes, needs and values. These differences must be found out and recognised by management.
3. Personal goals and Organisational goals must be joined together.
4. Work and interpersonal behaviour of people in the organisation is influenced by many factors.
5. Organisations are socio-technical systems. The management must integrate both the systems.
6. Employees are motivated not only by physiological needs but also by social and psychological needs.

Abraham Maslow's Hierarchy of need Theory

Abraham Maslow. A practising psychologist, developed one of the most widely recognised **need theories,** a theory of motivation based upon a consideration of human needs. His theory of human needs had three assumptions:

- Human needs are never completely satisfied.
- Human behavior is purposeful and is motivated by the need for satisfaction.
- Needs can be classified according to a hierarchical structure of importance, from the lowest to highest.

Maslow divided hierarchy of needs into five specific areas:

- **Physiological needs.** Maslow grouped all physical needs necessary for maintaining basic human well-being, such as food and drink, into this category. After the need is satisfied, however, it is no longer is a motivator.
- **Safety needs.** These needs include the need for basic security, stability, protection, and freedom from fear. A normal state exists for an individual to have all these needs generally satisfied. Otherwise, they become primary motivators.
- **Belonging and love needs.** After the physical and safety needs are satisfied and are no longer motivators, the need for belonging and love emerges as a primary motivator. The individual strives to establish meaningful relationships with significant others.

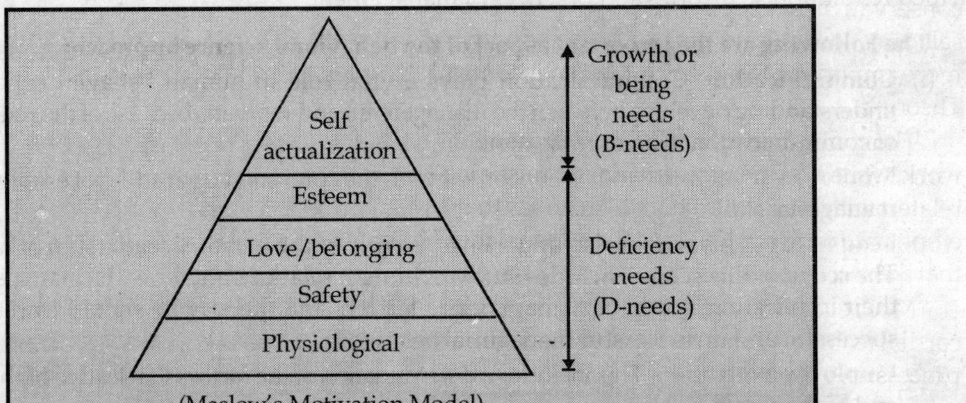

(Maslow's Motivation Model)

- **Esteem needs.** An individual must develop self-confidence and wants to achieve status, reputation, fame, and glory.
- **Self-actualisation needs.** Assuming that all the previous needs in the hierarchy are satisfied, an individual feels a need to find himself.

Douglas McGregor's (1906-1964) Theories X and Y

In 1960, Douglas McGregor formulated Theory X and Theory Y suggesting two aspects of human behavior at work, or in other words, two different views of individuals (employees): one of which is negative, called as Theory X and the other is positive, so called as Theory Y. According to McGregor, the perception of managers on the nature of individuals is based on various assumptions.

Assumptions of Theory X

- An average employee intrinsically does not like work and tries to escape it whenever possible.
- Since the employee does not want to work, he must be persuaded, compelled, or warned with punishment so as to achieve organisational goals. A close supervision is required on part of managers. The managers adopt a more dictatorial style.
- Many employees rank job security on top, and they have little or no aspiration/ ambition.

- Employees generally dislike responsibilities.
- Employees resist change.
- An average employee needs formal direction.

Assumptions of Theory Y

- Employees can perceive their job as relaxing and normal. They exercise their physical and mental efforts in an inherent manner in their jobs.
- Employees may not require only threat, external control and coercion to work, but they can use self-direction and self-control if they are dedicated and sincere to achieve the organisational objectives.
- If the job is rewarding and satisfying, then it will result in employees' loyalty and commitment to organisation.
- An average employee can learn to admit and recognise the responsibility. In fact, he can even learn to obtain responsibility.
- The employees have skills and capabilities. Their logical capabilities should be fully utilised. In other words, the creativity, resourcefulness and innovative potentiality of the employees can be utilised to solve organisational problems.

The assumptions in Theory X and Theory Y are fundamentally distinct. Theory X is static, rigid, conservative and pessimistic. Theory Y is optimistic, dynamic, flexible and progressive. It suggests self direction and the integration of individual needs with organisational needs. On the other hand, more importance is given to external control imposed by the superior on the subordinate in the Theory X.

Thus, we can say that Theory X presents a pessimistic view of employees' nature and behavior at work, while Theory Y presents an optimistic view of the employees' nature and behavior at work. If correlate it with Maslow's theory, we can say that Theory X is based on the assumption that the employees emphasize on the physiological needs and the safety needs; while Theory X is based on the assumption that the social needs, esteem needs and the self-actualisation needs dominate the employees.

McGregor views Theory Y to be more valid and reasonable than Theory X. Thus, he encouraged cordial team relations, responsible and stimulating jobs, and participation of all in decision-making process.

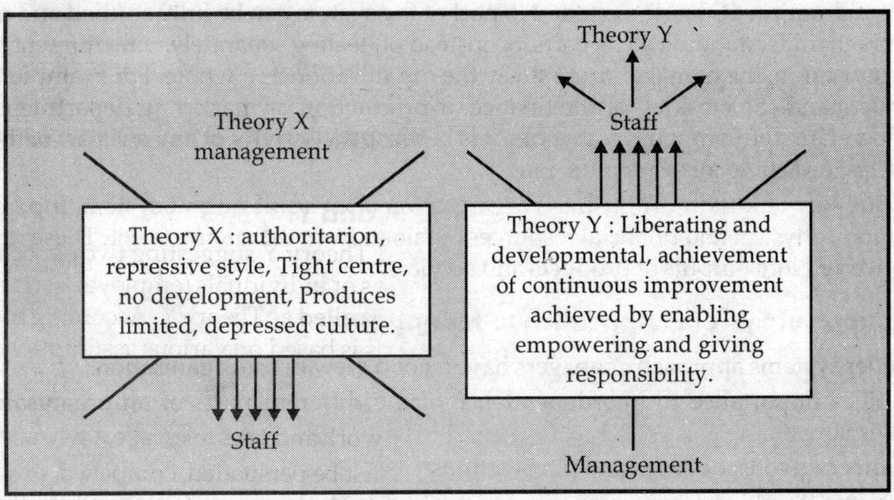

System Approach

The word **System** is taken from a Greek language which means to bring together or to combine. A system is a set of inter-related parts, which work together to achieve certain goals.

Ludwig von Bertalanffy is called the Father of the Systems Approach.

Definition

According to Ludwig von Bertalanffy, "In order to understand an organised whole, we must know both the parts as well as the relation between them."

Concepts of System Approach to Management

A system approach has the following key concepts:

1. **Open or Closed Systems.** Systems may be either open or closed. An open system is one, which depends on the outside environment for survival. A closed system does not interact with the environment.
2. **Sub-system.** The full system is made up of many parts. Each part is called sub-systems. A system may be a sub-system of a larger system. For e.g. A department is a sub-system of a plant. A plant is a sub-system of a company.
3. **Synergy.** Synergy means that the whole is greater than the sum of its parts. In an organisation, when different departments co-operate and interact, they become more productive. This is called synergy.
4. **Defined boundaries.** Each system has a boundary that separates it from its environment. In case of a closed system, the system boundary is rigid. However, in an open system, the boundary is flexible. A business organisation has boundaries with many external systems like creditors, suppliers, customers, government agencies, etc. The system is inside the boundary, the environment is outside the boundary.
5. **Feedback mechanism.** A system can adjust itself to the changing environment through the feedback mechanism. Feedback helps the system to find out and correct its mistakes.
6. **Multi-disciplinary.** Management system uses information from many fields such as psychology, sociology, ecology, economics, mathematics, statistics, operations research, systems analysis, etc. Therefore, it is Multi-disciplinary.
7. **Consideration of whole system.** No part of the system can be fully studied and understood without understanding all its parts. So instead of dealing separately with different parts of one organisation, the manager must study the organisation as a whole. For example, in order to understand the working of the finance or production or marketing departments, he must understand the company as a whole. It is because the activity of any one part of the company affects the activity of every other part.
8. **Input output system.** A business organisation is an input-output system. Inputs consist of human, physical and financial resources obtained from the environment. These resources are converted into outputs of products and services.

Contributions of Systems Approach to Management

- Under systems approach, managers have a good view of the organisation.
- It gives importance to interdependence of the different parts of an organisation and its environment.
- It forecasts consequences and plans actions.
- Systems' thinking warns managers against adopting piecemeal approach to the problem-solving.

Contingency School of Management

The contingency school of management can be summarised as an "it all depends" approach. The appropriate management actions and approaches depend on the situation. Managers with a contingency view use a flexible approach, draw on a variety of theories and experiences, and evaluate many options as they solve problems.

- Contingency management recognises that there is no one best way to manage. In the contingency perspective, managers are faced with the task of determining which managerial approach is likely to be most effective in a given situation. For example, the approach used to manage a group of teenagers working in a fast-food restaurant would be very different from the approach used to manage a medical research team trying to find a cure for a disease.
- Contingency thinking avoids the classical "one best way" arguments and recognises the need to understand situational differences and respond appropriately to them. It does not apply certain management principles to any situation. Contingency theory is a recognition of the extreme importance of individual manager performance in any given situation. The contingency approach is highly dependent on the experience and judgement of the manager in a given organisational environment.

Quantitative School of Management

During World War II, mathematicians, physicists, and other scientists joined together to solve military problems. The quantitative school of management is a result of the research conducted during World War II. The **quantitative approach** to management involves the use of quantitative techniques, such as statistics, information models, and computer simulations, to improve decision making. This school consists of several branches following.

Management Science

The management science school emerged to treat the problems associated with global warfare. Today, this view encourages managers to use mathematics, statistics, and other quantitative techniques to make management decisions. Managers can use computer models to figure out the best way to do something – saving both money and time. Managers use several science applications.

- Mathematical forecasting helps to make projections that are useful in the planning process.
- Inventory modelling helps control inventories by mathematically establishing how and when to order a product.
- Queuing theory helps allocate service personnel or workstations to minimise customer waiting and service cost.

Operation Management

Operations management is a narrow branch of the quantitative approach to management. It focuses on managing the process of transforming materials, labour, and capital into useful goods and/or services. The product outputs can be either goods or services; effective operations management is a concern for both manufacturing and service organisations. The resource inputs, or factors of production, include the wide variety of raw materials, technologies, capital information, and people needed to create finished products. The transformation process, in turn, is the actual set of operations or activities through which various resources are utilised to produce finished goods or services of value to customers or clients. Operations management today pays close attention to the demands of quality, customer service, and competition. The process begins with attention to the needs of customers: What do they want? Where do they want it? When do they want it? Based on the answers to these questions, managers line up resources and take any action necessary to meet customer expectations.

Management Information System

Management information systems (MIS) is the most recent subfield of the quantitative school. A management information system organises past, present, and projected data from both internal and external sources and processes it into usable information, which it then makes available to managers at all organisational levels. The information systems are also able to organise data into usable and accessible formats. As a result, managers can identify alternatives quickly, evaluate alternatives by using a spreadsheet program, pose a series of "what-if" questions, and finally, select the best alternatives based on the answers to these questions.

Quality School of Management

The quality school of management is a comprehensive concept for leading and operating an organisation, aimed at continually improving performance by focusing on customers while addressing the needs of all stakeholders. In other words, this concept focuses on managing the total organisation to deliver high quality to customers.

The quality school of management considers the following in its theory:

- **Organisation makeup.** Organisations are made up of complex systems of customers and suppliers. Every individual, executive, manager, and worker functions as both a supplier and a customer.
- **Quality of goods and services.** Meeting the customers' requirements is a priority goal and presumed to be a key to organisational survival and growth.
- **Continuous improvement in goods and services.** Recognising the need to pinpoint internal and external requirements and continuously strive to improve. It is an idea that says, "the company is good, but it can always become better."
- **Employees working in teams.** These groups are primary vehicles for planning and problem solving.
- **Developing openness and trust.** Confidence among members of the organisation at all levels is an important condition for success.

Quality management involves employees in decision making as a way to prevent quality problems. The **Kaizen** (pronounced *ky*-zen) approach uses incremental, continuous improvement for people, products, and processes. The re-engineering approach focuses on sensing the need to change, seeing change coming, and reacting effectively to it when it comes.

MANAGEMENT ROLES

A manager wears many hats. Not only is a manager a team leader, but he or she is also a planner, organiser, cheerleader, coach, problem solver, and decision maker — all rolled into one. And these are just a few of a manager's roles.

In his classic book, **The Nature of Managerial Work, Henry Mintzberg** describes a set of ten roles that a manager fills. These roles fall into three categories:

- **Interpersonal.** This role involves human interaction.
- **Informational.** This role involves the sharing and analyzing of information.
- **Decisional.** This role involves decision making.

Table contains a more in-depth look at each category of roles that help managers carry out all five functions described in the preceding "Functions of Managers".

Mintzberg's Set of Ten Roles

Category	Role	Activity
Informational	Monitor	Seek and receive information; scan periodicals and reports; maintain personal contact with stakeholders.
	Disseminator	Forward information to organisation members via memos, reports, and phone calls.
	Spokesperson	Transmit information to outsiders via reports, memos, and speeches.
Interpersonal	Figurehead	Perform ceremonial and symbolic duties, such as greeting visitors and signing legal documents.
	Leader	Direct and motivate subordinates; counsel and communicate with subordinates.
	Liaison	Maintain information links both inside and outside organisation via mail, phone calls, and meetings.
Decisional	Entrepreneur	Initiate improvement projects; identify new ideas and delegate idea responsibility to others.
	Disturbance handler	Take corrective action during disputes or crises; resolve conflicts among subordinates; adapt to environments.
	Resource allocator	Decide who gets resources; prepare budgets; set schedules and determine priorities.
	Negotiator	Represent department during negotiations of union contracts, sales, purchases, and budgets.

SKILLS NEEDED BY MANAGERS

Not everyone can be a manager. Certain **skills**, or abilities to translate knowledge into action that results in desired performance, are required to help other employees become more productive. These skills fall under the following categories:

- **Technical Skills.** This skill requires the ability to use a special proficiency or expertise to perform particular tasks. Accountants, engineers, market researchers, and computer scientists, as examples, possess technical skills. Managers acquire these skills initially through formal education and then further develop them through training and job experience. Technical skills are most important at lower levels of management.
- **Human Skills.** This skill demonstrates the ability to work well in cooperation with others. Human skills emerge in the workplace as a spirit of trust, enthusiasm, and genuine involvement in interpersonal relationships. A manager with good human skills has a high degree of self-awareness and a capacity to understand or empathise with the feelings of others. Some managers are naturally born with great human skills, while others improve their skills through classes or experience. No matter how human skills are acquired, they're critical for all managers because of the highly interpersonal nature of managerial work.
- **Conceptual Skills.** This skill calls for the ability to think analytically. Analytical skills enable managers to break down problems into smaller parts, to see the relations among the parts, and to recognise the implications of any one problem for others. As managers assume ever-higher responsibilities in organisations, they must deal with more ambiguous problems that have long-term consequences. Again, managers may acquire these skills initially through formal education and then further develop them by training and job experience. The higher the management level, the more important conceptual skills become. Although all three categories contain skills essential for managers, their relative importance tends to vary by level of managerial responsibility.

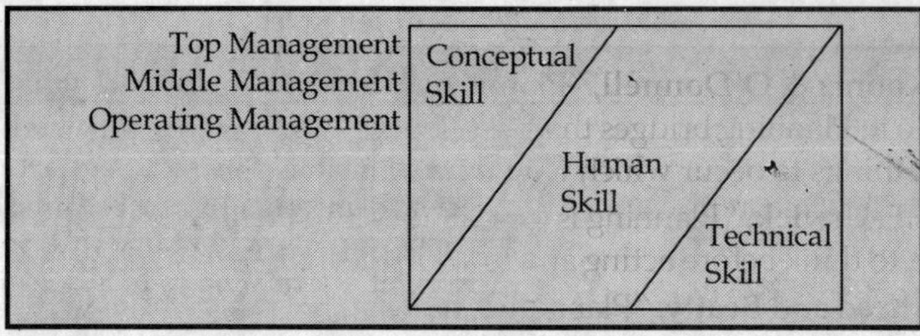

Managerial Skills at Various Levels

Business and management educators are increasingly interested in helping people acquire technical, human, and conceptual skills, and develop specific competencies, or specialised skills that contribute to high performance in a management job. Following are some of the skills and personal characteristics :

- **Leadership** – ability to influence others to perform tasks
- **Self-objectivity** – ability to evaluate yourself realistically
- **Analytic thinking** – ability to interpret and explain patterns in information
- **Behavioural flexibility** – ability to modify personal behaviour to react objectively rather than subjectively to accomplish organisational goals
- **Oral communication** – ability to express ideas clearly in words
- **Written communication** – ability to express ideas clearly in writing
- **Personal impact** – ability to create a good impression and instil confidence
- **Resistance to stress** – ability to perform under stressful conditions
- **Tolerance for uncertainty** – ability to perform in ambiguous situation

FUNCTIONS OF MANAGEMENT

PLANNING

A plan is a course of action to be taken in future. It is a predecided course of action. Planning is the process of deciding in advance what is to be done, how it is to be done, where, when and by whom. It involves determination of objectives to be achieved as well as the activities required to achieve the objectives. For example, a trader decides to increase his sales. In order to achieve this objective he should examine various alternatives e.g. advertising, price cut, better service to customers, etc. and choose the most appropriate course of action.

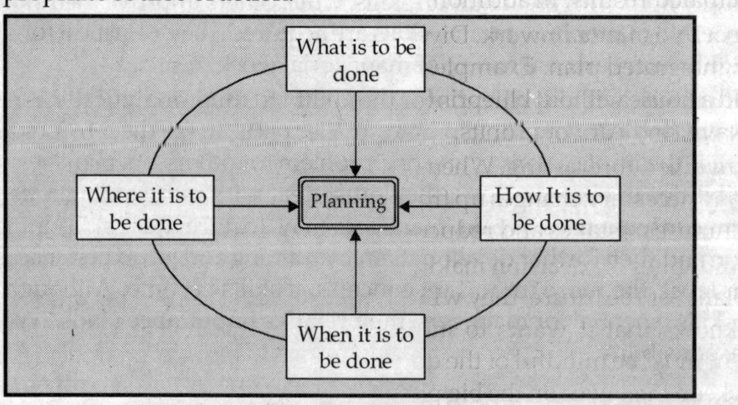

Meaning of Planning

Definition

- According to **Koontz & O'Donnell,** "Planning is deciding in advance what to do, how to do and who is to do it. Planning bridges the gap between where we are to, where we want to go. It makes possible things to occur which would not otherwise occur".
- According to **L.F. Urwick,** "Planning is fundamentally a mental predisposition to do things in an orderly way, to think before acting and to act in the light of the facts rather than of guesses."
- According to **Alfred and Beatty**, "Planning is the thinking process, the organised foresight, the vision based on facts and experience that is required for intelligent action."
- According to M.E. Hurley, "Planning is deciding in advance what is to be done. It involves the selection of objectives, policies, procedures and programmes from among alternatives."

The word **planning** incorporates both ideas: It means determining the organisation's goals and defining the means for achieving them. Planning allows managers the opportunity to adjust to the environment instead of merely reacting to it. Planning increases the possibility of survival in business by actively anticipating and managing the risks that may occur in the future.

In short, planning is preparing for tomorrow, today. It's the activity that allows managers to determine what they want and how they will achieve it.

Not only does planning provide direction and a unity of purpose for organisations, it also answers six basic questions in regard to any activity:

- What needs to be accomplished?
- When is the deadline?
- Where will this be done?
- Who will be responsible for it?
- How will it get done?
- How much time, energy, and resources are required to accomplish this goal?

Advantages of Planning

The advantages of planning are numerous. Planning fulfils the following objectives:

- **Gives an organisation a sense of direction.** Without plans and goals, organisations merely react to daily occurrences without considering what will happen in the long run. For example, the solution that makes sense in the short term doesn't always make sense in the long term. Plans avoid this drift situation and ensure that short-range efforts will support and harmonise with future goals.
- **Focuses attention on objectives and results.** Plans keep the people who carry them out focused on the anticipated results. In addition, keeping sight of the goal also motivates employees.
- **Establishes a basis for teamwork.** Diverse groups cannot effectively cooperate in joint projects without an integrated plan. Examples are numerous: Plumbers, carpenters, and electricians cannot build a house without blueprints. In addition, military activities require the coordination of Army, Navy, and Air Force units.
- **Planning involved forecasting.** When management plans, it can help forecast future problems and make any necessary changes up front to avoid them. Planning for these potential problems helps to minimise mistakes and reduce the "surprises" that inevitably occur.
- **Provides guidelines for decision making.** Decisions are future-oriented. If management doesn't have any plans for the future, they will have few guidelines for making current decisions. If a company knows that it wants to introduce a new product three years in the future, its management must be mindful of the decisions they make now. Plans help both managers and employees keep their eyes on the big picture.

- **Serves as a prerequisite to employing all other management functions.** Planning is primary, because without knowing what an organisation wants to accomplish, management can't intelligently undertake any of the other basic managerial activities: organising, staffing, leading, and/or controlling.

Types of Planning

1. **Corporate Planning.** Drucker has defined corporate planning as the continuous process of making present risk-taking decision systematically and with the greatest knowledge of their futurity: organising systematically the efforts needed to carry out these decision, and measuring the result of these decision against the expectations through organised and systematic feedback.
2. **Strategic Planning.** A **strategic planning** is an outline of steps designed with the goals of the entire organisation as a whole in mind, rather than with the goals of specific divisions or departments. Strategic planning begins with an organisation's mission.
3. **Tactical Planning Or Operational Planning.** Operational planning is defined as the process of deciding the most effective use of the resources already located and to develop a control mechanism to assure effective implementation to the desired action.

   A tactical planning is concerned with what the lower level units within each division must do, how they must do it, and who is in charge at each level. Tactics are the means needed to activate a strategy and make it work.

   An operational plan is annual work plan. Tactical plans are concerned with shorter time frames and narrower scopes than are strategic plans. These plans usually span one year or less because they are considered short-term goals. Long-term goals, on the other hand, can take several years or more to accomplish. Normally, it is the middle manager's responsibility to take the broad strategic plan and identify specific tactical actions.
4. **Functional Planning.** The planning that is carried out to ensure smooth working of the organisation taking into consideration the requirement of each and every department. The goal of functional planning is to promote standardised management practice for corporate function in the department decentralised corporate management structure.
5. **Proactive and Reactive Planning. Proactive planning** is based on the anticipation of the future outcomes and state of affairs that would affect the working in an organisation. Such a planning has to be broad based, highly flexible and creative in nature.

   Reactive planning as the name suggest the reactive planning is not based on the anticipation of the future outcomes but becomes active only when the problem is confronted and occurred.
6. **Formal And Informal.** Formal planning exists in the formal hierarchy of the organisation and always carried out in the step wise process. This type of planning is done at large scale and is based on logical thinking.

   On the other hand the informal planning is usually carried out in very small organisation where the formal organisation structure may or may not exist. The planning is usually intuitive in nature and short term.
7. **Contingency Plans.** Intelligent and successful management depends upon a constant pursuit of adaptation, flexibility, and mastery of changing conditions. Strong management requires a "keeping all options open" approach at all times — that's where contingency planning comes in. **Contingency planning** involves identifying alternative courses of action that can be implemented if and when the original plan proves inadequate because of changing circumstances. Keep in mind that events beyond a manager's control may cause even the most carefully prepared alternative future scenarios to go awry. Unexpected problems and events

frequently occur. When they do, managers may need to change their plans. Anticipating change during the planning process is best in case things don't go as expected. Management can then develop alternatives to the existing plan and ready them for use when and if circumstances make these alternatives appropriate.

Steps in Planning Process

Planning function of management involves following steps:

1. **Establishment of objectives**
   - Planning requires a systematic approach.
   - Planning starts with the setting of goals and objectives to be achieved.
   - Objectives provide a rationale for undertaking various activities as well as indicate direction of efforts.
   - Moreover objectives focus the attention of managers on the end results to be achieved.
   - As a matter of fact, objectives provide nucleus to the planning process. Therefore, objectives should be stated in a clear, precise and unambiguous language. Otherwise the activities undertaken are bound to be ineffective.
   - As far as possible, objectives should be stated in quantitative terms. For example, Number of men working, wages given, units produced, etc. But such an objective cannot be stated in quantitative terms like performance of quality control manager, effectiveness of personnel manager.
   - Such goals should be specified in qualitative terms.
   - Hence objectives should be practical, acceptable, workable and achievable.
2. **Establishment of Planning Premises**
   - Planning premises are the assumptions about the lively shape of events in future.
   - They serve as a basis of planning.
   - Establishment of planning premises is concerned with determining where one tends to deviate from the actual plans and causes of such deviations.
   - It is to find out what obstacles are there in the way of business during the course of operations.
   - Establishment of planning premises is concerned to take such steps that avoid these obstacles to a great extent.
   - Planning premises may be internal or external. Internal includes capital investment policy, management labour relations, philosophy of management, etc. Whereas external includes socio- economic, political and economical changes.
   - Internal premises are controllable whereas external are non- controllable.
3. **Choice of alternative course of action**
   - When forecast are available and premises are established, a number of alternative course of actions have to be considered.
   - For this purpose, each and every alternative will be evaluated by weighing its pros and cons in the light of resources available and requirements of the organisation.
   - The merits, demerits as well as the consequences of each alternative must be examined before the choice is being made.
   - After objective and scientific evaluation, the best alternative is chosen.
   - The planners should take help of various quantitative techniques to judge the stability of an alternative.

4. **Formulation of derivative plans**
   - Derivative plans are the sub plans or secondary plans which help in the achievement of main plan.
   - Secondary plans will flow from the basic plan. These are meant to support and expedited the achievement of basic plans.
   - These detail plans include policies, procedures, rules, programmes, budgets, schedules, etc. For example, if profit maximisation is the main aim of the enterprise, derivative plans will include sales maximisation, production maximisation, and cost minimisation.
   - Derivative plans indicate time schedule and sequence of accomplishing various tasks.
5. **Securing Co-operation**
   - After the plans have been determined, it is necessary rather advisable to take subordinates or those who have to implement these plans into confidence.
   - The purposes behind taking them into confidence are :
     i. Subordinates may feel motivated since they are involved in decision making process.
     ii. The organisation may be able to get valuable suggestions and improvement in formulation as well as implementation of plans.
     iii. Also the employees will be more interested in the execution of these plans.
6. **Follow up/Appraisal of plans**
   - After choosing a particular course of action, it is put into action.
   - After the selected plan is implemented, it is important to appraise its effectiveness.
   - This is done on the basis of feedback or information received from departments or persons concerned.
   - This enables the management to correct deviations or modify the plan.
   - This step establishes a link between planning and controlling function.
   - The follow up must go side by side the implementation of plans so that in the light of observations made, future plans can be made more realistic.

Characteristics of Planning

1. **Planning is goal-oriented.**
   - Planning is made to achieve desired objective of business.
   - The goals established should general acceptance otherwise individual efforts & energies will go misguided and misdirected.
   - Planning identifies the action that would lead to desired goals quickly & economically.
   - It provides sense of direction to various activities. E.g. Maruti Udhyog is trying to capture once again Indian Car Market by launching diesel models.
2. **Planning is looking ahead.**
   - Planning is done for future.
   - It requires peeping in future, analyzing it and predicting it.
   - Thus planning is based on forecasting.
   - A plan is a synthesis of forecast.
   - It is a mental predisposition for things to happen in future.
3. **Planning is an intellectual process.**
   - Planning is a mental exercise involving creative thinking, sound judgement and imagination.

- It is not a mere guesswork but a rotational thinking.
- A manager can prepare sound plans only if he has sound judgement, foresight and imagination.
- Planning is always based on goals, facts and considered estimates.

4. **Planning involves choice & decision making.**
    - Planning essentially involves choice among various alternatives.
    - Therefore, if there is only one possible course of action, there is no need planning because there is no choice.
    - Thus, decision making is an integral part of planning.
    - A manager is surrounded by no. of alternatives. He has to pick the best depending upon requirements & resources of the enterprises.
5. **Planning is the primary function of management / Primacy of Planning.**
    - Planning lays foundation for other functions of management.
    - It serves as a guide for organising, staffing, directing and controlling.
    - All the functions of management are performed within the framework of plans laid out.
    - Therefore planning is the basic or fundamental function of management.
6. **Planning is a Continuous Process.**
    - Planning is a never ending function due to the dynamic business environment.
    - Plans are also prepared for specific period of time and at the end of that period, plans are subjected to revaluation and review in the light of new requirements and changing conditions.
    - Planning never comes into end till the enterprise exists issues, problems may keep cropping up and they have to be tackled by planning effectively.
7. **Planning is all Pervasive.**
    - It is required at all levels of management and in all departments of enterprise.
    - Of course, the scope of planning may differ from one level to another.
    - The top level may be more concerned about planning the organisation as a whole whereas the middle level may be more specific in departmental plans and the lower level plans implementation of the same.
8. **Planning is designed for efficiency.**
    - Planning leads to accomplishment of objectives at the minimum possible cost.
    - It avoids wastage of resources and ensures adequate and optimum utilisation of resources.
    - A plan is worthless or useless if it does not value the cost incurred on it.
    - Therefore planning must lead to saving of time, effort and money.
    - Planning leads to proper utilisation of men, money, materials, methods and machines.
9. **Planning is Flexible.**
    - Planning is done for the future.
    - Since future is unpredictable, planning must provide enough room to cope with the changes in customer's demand, competition, govt. policies etc.
    - Under changed circumstances, the original plan of action must be revised and updated to make it more practical.

Advantages of Planning

1. **Planning facilitates management by objectives.**
    - Planning begins with determination of objectives.

- It highlights the purposes for which various activities are to be undertaken.
- In fact, it makes objectives more clear and specific.
- Planning helps in focusing the attention of employees on the objectives or goals of enterprise.
- Without planning an organisation has no guide.
- Planning compels manager to prepare a Blue-print of the courses of action to be followed for accomplishment of objectives.
- Therefore, planning brings order and rationality into the organisation.

2. **Planning minimise uncertainties.**
   - Business is full of uncertainties.
   - There are risks of various types due to uncertainties.
   - Planning helps in reducing uncertainties of future as it involves anticipation of future events.
   - Although future cannot be predicted with cent percent accuracy but planning helps management to anticipate future and prepare for risks by necessary provisions to meet unexpected turn of events.
   - Therefore with the help of planning, uncertainties can be forecasted which helps in preparing standbys as a result, uncertainties are minimised to a great extent.
3. **Planning facilitate co-ordination.**
   - Planning revolves around organisational goals.
   - All activities are directed towards common goals.
   - There is an integrated effort throughout the enterprise in various departments and groups.
   - It avoids duplication of efforts. In other words, it leads to better co-ordination.
   - It helps in finding out problems of work performance and aims at rectifying the same.
4. **Planning improves employee's moral.**
   - Planning creates an atmosphere of order and discipline in organisation.
   - Employees know in advance what is expected of them and therefore conformity can be achieved easily.
   - This encourages employees to show their best and also earn reward for the same.
   - Planning creates a healthy attitude towards work environment which helps in boosting employees moral and efficiency.
5. **Planning helps in achieving economies.**
   - Effective planning secures economy since it leads to orderly allocation of resources to various operations.
   - It also facilitates optimum utilisation of resources which brings economy in operations.
   - It also avoids wastage of resources by selecting most appropriate use that will contribute to the objective of enterprise. For example, raw materials can be purchased in bulk and transportation cost can be minimised. At the same time it ensures regular supply for the production department, that is, overall efficiency.
6. **Planning facilitate controlling.**
   - Planning facilitates existence of certain planned goals and standard of performance.
   - It provides basis of controlling.
   - We cannot think of an effective system of controlling without existence of well thought out plans.
   - Planning provides pre-determined goals against which actual performance is compared.
   - In fact, planning and controlling are the two sides of a same coin. If planning is root, controlling is the fruit.

7. **Planning provide competitive edge.**
   - Planning provides competitive edge to the enterprise over the others which do not have effective planning. This is because of the fact that planning may involve changing in work methods, quality, quantity designs, extension of work, redefining of goals, etc.
   - With the help of forecasting not only the enterprise secures its future but at the same time it is able to estimate the future motives of its competitor which helps in facing future challenges.
   - Therefore, planning leads to best utilisation of possible resources, improves quality of production and thus the competitive strength of the enterprise is improved.
8. **Planning encourage innovations.**
   - In the process of planning, managers have the opportunities of suggesting ways and means of improving performance.
   - Planning is basically a decision making function which involves creative thinking and imagination that ultimately leads to innovation of methods and operations for growth and prosperity of the enterprise.

Disadvantages of Planning

Internal Limitations. There are several limitations of planning. Some of them are inherit in the process of planning like rigidity and other arise due to shortcoming of the techniques of planning and in the planners themselves.

1. **Rigidity**
   - Planning has tendency to make administration inflexible.
   - Planning implies prior determination of policies, procedures and programmes and a strict adherence to them in all circumstances.
   - There is no scope for individual freedom.
   - The development of employees is highly doubted because of which management might have faced lot of difficulties in future.
   - Planning therefore introduces inelasticity and discourages individual initiative and experimentation.
2. **Misdirected Planning**
   - Planning may be used to serve individual interests rather than the interest of the enterprise.
   - Attempts can be made to influence setting of objectives, formulation of plans and programmes to suit ones own requirement rather than that of whole organisation.
   - Machinery of planning can never be freed of bias. Every planner has his own likes, dislikes, preferences, attitudes and interests which is reflected in planning.
3. **Time consuming**
   - Planning is a time consuming process because it involves collection of information, its analysis and interpretation thereof. This entire process takes a lot of time specially where there are a number of alternatives available.
   - Therefore planning is not suitable during emergency or crisis when quick decisions are required.
4. **Probability in planning**
   - Planning is based on forecasts which are mere estimates about future.
   - These estimates may prove to be inexact due to the uncertainty of future.
   - Any change in the anticipated situation may render plans ineffective.

- Plans do not always reflect real situations in spite of the sophisticated techniques of forecasting because future is unpredictable.
- Thus, excessive reliance on plans may prove to be fatal.

5. **False sense of security**
   - Elaborate planning may create a false sense of security to the effect that everything is taken for granted.
   - Managers assume that as long as they work as per plans, it is satisfactory.
   - Therefore they fail to take up timely actions and an opportunity is lost.
   - Employees are more concerned about fulfillment of plan performance rather than any kind of change.
6. **Expensive**
   - Collection, analysis and evaluation of different information, facts and alternatives involves a lot of expense in terms of time, effort and money
   - According to Koontz and O'Donell, 'Expenses on planning should never exceed the estimated benefits from planning.'

ORGANISING

Organising, the second of the universal management functions, is the process of establishing the orderly use of resources by assigning and coordinating tasks. The organising process transforms plans into reality through the purposeful deployment of people and resources within a decision-making framework known as the organisational structure. The organisational structure is defined as

- The set of formal tasks assigned to individuals and departments
- The formal reporting relationships, including lines of authority, decision responsibility, number of hierarchical levels, and span of managerial control
- The design of systems to ensure effective coordination of employees across departments

The organisational structure provides a framework for the hierarchy, or *vertical structure,* of the organisation. An **organisational chart** is the visual representation of this vertical structure.

DEFINITION OF ORGANISING

- According to **Henri Fayol**, "To organise a business means to provide it everything useful to its functioning–raw materials, tools, capital & personnel."
- According to **George R. Terry**, "Organising is the process of establishing effective authority relationship among selected works, persons and work places in order for the group to work together efficiently."
- According to **Haney**, "Organisation is harmonious adjustment of the specialised parts for the accomplishment of some common purpose or purposes."
- According to **Mc Farland**, "An identifiable group of people contributing their efforts for the attainment of the common goals is called organisation."
- According to **Urwick,** "To determine the activities necessary to complete any work and distribution of those activities among persons is called organisation."

The Organisation Process

Organising, like planning, must be a carefully worked out and applied process. This process involves determining what work is needed to accomplish the goal, assigning those tasks to individuals, and arranging those individuals in a decision-making framework (organisational structure). The end result of the organising process is an **organisation** – a whole consisting of unified parts acting in harmony to execute tasks to achieve goals, both effectively and efficiently.

A properly implemented organising process should result in a work environment where all team members are aware of their responsibilities. If the organising process is not conducted well, the results may yield confusion, frustration, loss of efficiency, and limited effectiveness.

In general, the organisational process consists of six steps (a flowchart of these steps shown in Figure):

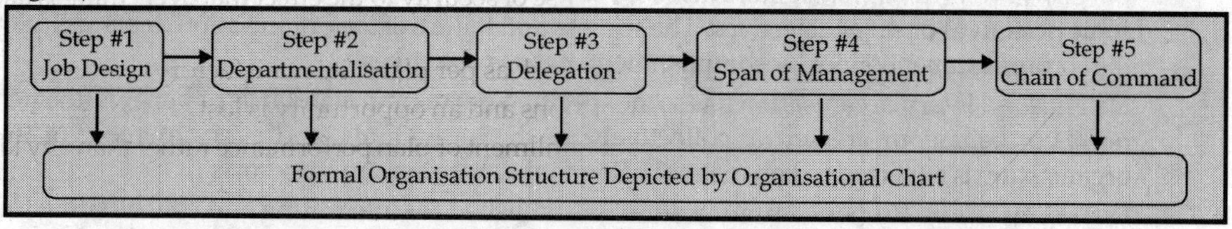

Figure. The organisational process.

- **Clearly defined objectives.** Objectives are the specific activities that must be completed to achieve goals. Plans shape the activities needed to reach those goals. Managers must examine plans initially and continue to do so as plans change and new goals are developed.
- **Determine the work activities.** Although this task may seem overwhelming to some managers, it doesn't need to be. Managers simply list and analyze all the tasks that need to be accomplished in order to reach organisational goals.
- **Assigning duties.** A manager can group activities based on four models of departmentalisation: functional, geographical, product, and customer.
- **Delegate authority.** Managers assign the defined work activities to specific individuals. Also, they give each individual the authority (right) to carry out the assigned tasks.
- **Providing physical facilities and right environment.** The success of an organisation depends upon the providing physical facilities and right environment. Whereas its important right person in the right job. It is equally important to have right working environment.
- **Design a hierarchy of relationships.** A manager should determine the vertical (decision-making) and horizontal (coordinating) relationships of the organisation as a whole. Next, using the organisational chart, a manager should diagram the relationships.

Features of Organising

Organisation has the following features:

1. **Group of Persons.** Organisation is concerned with the group of persons working together for the achievement of the common objectives. This group can be large or small. Further, cooperative relationship between two or more persons is known as organisation.
2. **Division of Work.** Organisation follows the Fayol's principle of division of work. An organisation comes into existence when the total work is divided among the different employees. This is not because that one person cannot perform the whole task but due to the reason it's the only way of ensuring specialisation in business.
3. **Common Objectives.** Every organisation has common objectives separated from the personal objectives of the individuals in the organisation. Organisation is directed towards the achievement of the common goals which is the basis of cooperation among the members.
4. **Cooperative Effort.** For the achievement of the common goals cooperative relationships are established both vertically and horizontally among different departments of the organisation. The members of the organisation help each other for the achievement of the common goals.

5. **Central and Top Authority.** There is a central and top authority in every organisation and this authority controls and directs the efforts of the groups or departments for the achievement of the organisational objectives. Further the chain of command is also established, which defines the authority and responsibility of every individual in the organisation.
6. **Purposive Creation.** The organisation is a purposive creation that is all the organisations have some objectives or set of objectives. The success and failure of the organisation depends upon the accomplishment or non-accomplishment of these objectives.
7. **Rationality.** Every organisation has some specified norms and standards of behaviour, such norms of behaviour are set up collectively by the individuals, and every member of the organisation is expected to behave according to these norms and standards.
8. **Communication.** Proper communication is established for integrating and coordinating the efforts of the personnel's. The structure can be such that personnel can perform their work effectively.

Authority

Authority is the formal and legitimate right of a manager to make decisions, issue orders, and allocate resources to achieve organisationally desired outcomes. A manager's authority is defined in his or her job description.

Organisational authority has three important underlying principles:

- Authority is based on the organisational position, and anyone in the same position has the same authority.
- Authority is accepted by subordinates. Subordinates comply because they believe that managers have a legitimate right to issue orders.
- Authority flows down the vertical hierarchy. Positions at the top of the hierarchy are vested with more formal authority than are positions at the bottom.

Delegation

Delegation of Authority. To delegate is to give, offer, confer, and allot a part of authority to subordinates. Large scale and complex nature are the important features of the modern organisations. Due to this management cannot perform all its tasks and thus they share their work with their subordinates. So this shared task along with the corresponding authority is called delegation of authority. Delegation of authority is the essence of management. It is one of the important factors in the process of organising and facilitates the existence of the formal organisation. With the help of the delegation manager calls his subordinates to render their help in accomplishing the organisational objectives. So, the practice of granting authority to a subordinate for getting things done from him is known as delegation of authority.

Elements of Delegation of Authority

Following are the elements of delegation of authority:

1. **Responsibility.** The basic essence of the responsibility is obligation. Responsibility is the obligation of the subordinate to complete the work which is assigned to him. The responsibility is always in relation to a person and in relation to a thing and the basis of responsibility is the superior-subordinate relationship that exists in the organisation. So the duty to perform the assigned organisational tasks, functions, and assignments is called responsibility.

   According to Haimann, "Responsibility is the obligation of a subordinate to perform the duty as required by his superior."

According to Koontz, "Responsibility may be defined as the obligation of a subordinate to whom the duty has been assigned to perform."

2. **Authority.** Authority is the term packed with variety of meanings by theorists and management practitioners. In everyday life authority is commonly understood as rightful power or right to command. Authority is the attribute of the job and not of man. Thus, Mr. A, as office superintendent derives authority over his subordinates not because he is Mr. A but because he is office superintendent. Authority gives the legitimate right to the superior to command over his subordinates and get the work done from them.

   According to Henry Fayol, "Authority is the right to give orders to and the power to extract obedience from the subordinates."

   According to Allen, "Authority is the sum of powers and rights entrusted to make possible the performance of the work delegated."

3. **Accountability.** Accountability denotes answerability for the accomplishment of the task assigned by the superior to his subordinates. It is to be noted that the process of delegation is not at all complete with just assigning the duty and delegating appropriate authority for the accomplishment of the task. The process of delegation becomes complete only by making the delegate answerable to the superior for his functioning. For example if the publicity manager of a company is assigned with the task of formulating and implementing a mass publicity plan for a new product, he is answerable for its effectiveness. So accountability is the obligation of an individual to keep his superior informed of his use of authority and accomplishment of the assigned tables.

Basis	Authority	Responsibility
Meaning	It is the right of the manager to command his subordinates.	It is the obligation of the subordinate to complete the assigned work.
Origin	It arises due to the position of superior.	It arises due to superior-subordinate relationship.
Flow	It flows from top to bottom.	It flows from bottom to top.
Period	It has longer period as compared to responsibility.	It gets completed with the completion of the task so has the shorter period.
Nature	Authority is power.	Responsibility is the duty.
Delegation	Authority can be delegated to others.	Responsibility cannot be delegated.

According to Peterson, "To be accountable is to be answerable for one's conduct in respect to obligation fulfilled or unfulfilled."

DIRECTION

Directing is said to be a process in which the managers instruct, guide and oversee the performance of the workers to achieve predetermined goals. Directing is said to be the heart of management process. Planning, organising, staffing have got no importance if direction function does not take place.

Directing initiates action and it is from here actual work starts. Direction is said to be consisting of human factors. In simple words, it can be described as providing guidance to workers is doing work. In field of management, direction is said to be all those activities which are designed to encourage the subordinates to work effectively and efficiently. According to Human, "Directing consists of process or technique by which instruction can be issued and operations can be carried out as originally planned" Therefore, Directing is the function of guiding, inspiring, overseeing and instructing people towards accomplishment of organisational goals.

Importance of Directing Function

Directing or Direction function is said to be the heart of management of process and therefore, is the central point around which accomplishment of goals take place. A few philosophers call Direction as *"Life spark of an enterprise"*. It is also called as on actuating function of management because it is through direction that the operation of an enterprise actually starts.

Being the central character of enterprise, it provides many benefits to a concern which are as follows:

- **It Initiates Actions.** Directions is the function which is the starting point of the work performance of subordinates. It is from this function the action takes place, subordinates understand their jobs and do according to the instructions laid. Whatever are plans laid, can be implemented only once the actual work starts. It is there that direction becomes beneficial.
- **It Integrates Efforts.** Through direction, the superiors are able to guide, inspire and instruct the subordinates to work. For this, efforts of every individual towards accomplishment of goals are required. It is through direction the efforts of every department can be related and integrated with others. This can be done through persuasive leadership and effective communication. Integration of efforts bring effectiveness and stability in a concern.
- **Means of Motivation.** Direction function helps in achievement of goals. A manager makes use of the element of motivation here to improve the performances of subordinates. This can be done by providing incentives or compensation, whether monetary or non - monetary, which serves as a "Morale booster" to the subordinates Motivation is also helpful for the subordinates to give the best of their abilities which ultimately helps in growth.
- **It Provides Stability.** Stability and balance in concern becomes very important for long term sun survival in the market. This can be brought upon by the managers with the help of four tools or elements of direction function -- judicious blend of persuasive leadership, effective communication, strict supervision and efficient motivation. Stability is very important since that is an index of growth of an enterprise. Therefore a manager can use of all the four traits in him so that performance standards can be maintained.
- **Coping up with the changes.** It is a human behavior that human beings show resistance to change. Adaptability with changing environment helps in sustaining planned growth and becoming a market leader. It is directing function which is of use to meet with changes in environment, both internal as external. Effective communication helps in coping up with the changes. It is the role of manager here to communicate the nature and contents of changes very clearly to the subordinates. This helps in clarifications, easy adoptions and smooth running of an enterprise. For example, if a concern shifts from handlooms to power looms, an important change in technique of production takes place. The resulting factors are less of manpower and more of machinery. This can be resisted by the subordinates. The manager here can explain that the change was in the benefit of the subordinates. Through more mechanisation, production increases and thereby the profits. Indirectly, the subordinates are benefited out of that in form of higher remuneration.
- **Efficient Utilisation of Resources.** Direction finance helps in clarifying the role of every subordinate towards his work. The resources can be utilised properly only when less of wastages, duplication of efforts, overlapping of performances, etc. doesn't take place. Through direction, the role of subordinates become clear as manager makes use of his supervisory, the guidance, the instructions and motivation skill to inspire the subordinates. This helps in maximum possible utilisation of resources of men, machine, materials and money which helps in reducing costs and increasing profits.

Elements of Direction Includes

The are four elements of direction. They are:

(a) Supervision (b) Leadership (c) Motivation (d) Communication

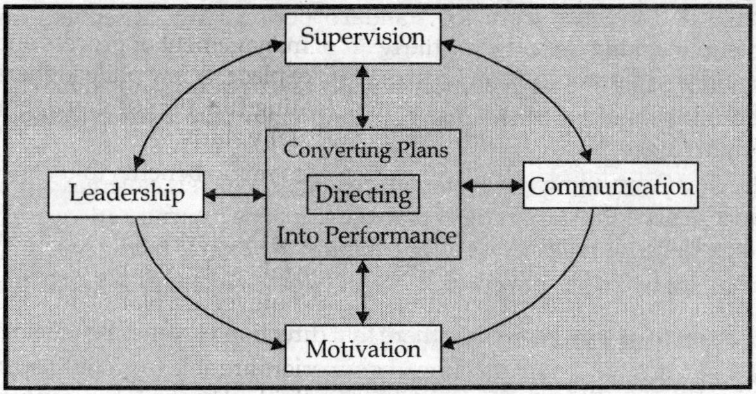

Elements of Directing

Supervision. *"Guiding and directing efforts of employees and other resources to accomplish stated work outputs"* **- Terry and Franklin.**

Supervision is an element of direction. *"Day-to-day relationship between an executive and his immediate assistant and covers training, direction, motivation, coordination, maintenance of discipline, etc."* **- Newman and Warren.**

Supervision denotes the functions performed by the supervisors.

Motivation. *"Motivation is the complex force starting and keeping a person at work in an organisation. Motivation is something that moves the person to action, and continues him in the course of action already initiates."* **- Dubin.**

Motivation is the core of management. Technically, the term motivation can be traced to the Latin word movere, which means 'to move'. Motivating is a term which implies that one person induces another, to engage in action by ensuring that a channel to satisfy the motive becomes available to the individual. Motive is energizer of action, motivating is the channelisation and activation of motives, motivation is the work behavior itself. Motivation depends on motives and motivating. It is a complex process.

Leadership. *"Leadership is essentially a continuous process of influencing behavior. A leader breathes life into the group and motivates it towards goals. The lukewarm desires for achievement are transformed into burning passion for accomplishment"* **- George R. Terry.**

Leadership is the process of influencing the behavior of others to work willingly and enthusiastically for achieving predetermined goals. It is an essential ingredient for successful organisation. The successful organisation has one major attribute that sets it apart from unsuccessful organisation that is dynamic and effective leadership.

Communication. *"Communication is the transfer of information from one person to another person. It is a way of reaching others by transmitting ideas, facts, thoughts, feeling sand values."* **- Newstrom and Davis.**

Communication is regarded as basic to the functioning of the organisation, in its absence; the organisation would cease to exist. It is the process through which two or more persons come to exchange ideas and understanding among themselves.

CONTROLLING

Concept and Definition

Controlling consists of verifying whether everything occurs in conformities with the plans adopted, instructions issued and principles established. Controlling ensures that there is effective and efficient utilisation of organisational resources so as to achieve the planned goals. Controlling measures the deviation of actual performance from the standard performance, discovers the causes of such deviations and helps in taking corrective actions.

According to Donnell, "Just as a navigator continually takes reading to ensure whether he is relative to a planned action, so should a business manager continually take reading to assure himself that his enterprise is on right course."

According to Brech, "Controlling is a systematic exercise which is called as a process of checking actual performance against the standards or plans with a view to ensure adequate progress and also recording such experience as is gained as a contribution to possible future needs."

Controlling has got two basic purposes: 1. It facilitates co-ordination and 2. It helps in planning

Features of Controlling Function

Following are the characteristics of controlling function of management :

1. **Controlling is a dynamic process.** Since controlling requires taking reviewable methods, changes have to be made wherever possible.
2. **Controlling is forward looking.** Because effective control is not possible without past being controlled. Controlling always look to future so that follow-up can be made whenever required.
3. **Controlling is related with planning.** Planning and Controlling are two inseparable functions of management. Without planning, controlling is a meaningless exercise and without controlling, planning is useless. *Planning presupposes controlling and controlling succeeds planning.*
4. **Controlling is an end function.** A function which comes once the performances are made in conformities with plans.
5. **Controlling is a pervasive function.** which means it is performed by managers at all levels and in all type of concerns.

The Control Process

The control process involves carefully collecting information about a system, process, person, or group of people in order to make necessary decisions about each. Managers set up control systems that consist of four key steps:

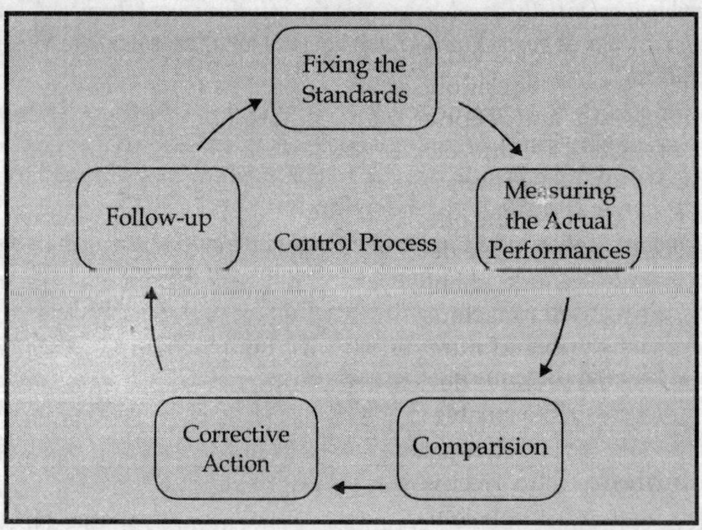

1. **Fixing the Control Standards.** A standard is a criterion (base) which is used to measure the performance of the subordinates. Standards may be of two types, *i.e.,* Quantitative Standards and Qualitative Standards. **Quantitative Standard** can be easily defined and measured. For e.g. number of products, number of customers, cost, net profit, time limits, etc. **Qualitative Standard** cannot be easily defined and measured. For e.g. measurement of morale, measurement of job satisfaction, measurement of effect of a training programme, advertisement programme, etc. It is better to have quantitative standards because they are measurable. However, today there are many new techniques for measuring qualitative standards. The standards should be as clear as possible. It should be easily understood by both superiors and subordinates. The responsibility of each individual should also be clearly defined *i.e.,* everyone should be responsible for achieving a particular goal, objective, target, etc. For e.g. The marketing department fixes a standard – *"We will sell 2,000 units of product X in one month"*. So here the standard is 2,000 units.
2. **Measuring the Actual Performances.** The second major step in controlling is to measure the performance. Finding out deviations becomes easy through measuring the actual performance. Performance levels are sometimes easy to measure and sometimes difficult. Measurement of tangible standards is easy as it can be expressed in units, cost, money terms, etc. Quantitative measurement becomes difficult when performance of manager has to be measured. Performance of a manager cannot be measured in quantities. It can be measured only by :
   a. Attitude of the workers,
   b. Their morale to work,
   c. The development in the attitudes regarding the physical environment, and
   d. Their communication with the superiors.

   It is also sometimes done through various reports like weekly, monthly, quarterly, yearly reports.
3. **Comparison of actual and standard performance.** The actual performances of the subordinates are compared with established standards, and then the deviations are found out. The deviations which are found out may be positive or negative.

   Positive Deviation means that the actual performances are better than the established standards. Positive deviations should be appreciated. Negative Deviation means that the actual performance is less than the established standards. The management should pay special attention to the negative deviation. They should find out the causes of negative deviations. Generally, minor (small) deviations are ignored. However, major deviations should be immediately addressed and reported to the top management. PERT, Budgetary Control, Observation, Inspection, Reports, etc. are some of the methods used for comparison. For e.g. 10,000 units (Standard) - 9,000 units (Actual Performance) = 1,000 units (Negative Deviation).
4. **Corrective Action.** After finding out the negative deviations and their causes, the managers should take steps to correct these deviations. Corrective actions should be taken promptly. Corrective action may include, changing the standards, providing better motivation, giving better training, using better machines, etc. The management should take essential steps to prevent these deviations in the future.

   For e.g. The cause of the negative deviation was less advertising and untrained salesmen. So, the company must spend reasonable money on advertising and training.
5. **Follow-up.** After taking corrective action, the management must do a follow-up. Follow-up is done to find out whether the corrective actions are taken properly. It also finds out whether the deviations and their causes are removed. If follow-up is done properly, then the actual performance will be equal to or better than the established standards.

Organisational Control Techniques

Control techniques provide managers with the type and amount of information they need to measure and monitor performance. The information from various controls must be tailored to a specific management level, department, unit, or operation.

To ensure complete and consistent information, organisations often use standardised documents such as financial, status, and project reports. Each area within an organisation, however, uses its own specific control techniques, described in the following sections.

1. **Financial controls.** After the organisation has strategies in place to reach its goals, funds are set aside for the necessary resources and labour. As money is spent, statements are updated to reflect how much was spent, how it was spent, and what it obtained. Managers use these financial statements, such as an income statement or balance sheet, to monitor the progress of programs and plans. **Financial statements** provide management with information to monitor financial resources and activities. The **income statement** shows the results of the organisation's operations over a period of time, such as revenues, expenses, and profit or loss. The *balance sheet* shows what the organisation is worth (assets) at a single point in time, and the extent to which those assets were financed through debt (liabilities) or owner's investment (equity).

   Financial audits, or formal investigations, are regularly conducted to ensure that financial management practices follow generally accepted procedures, policies, laws, and ethical guidelines. Audits may be conducted internally or externally. **Financial ratio analysis** examines the relationship between specific figures on the financial statements and helps explain the significance of those figures:

   - **Liquidity ratios** measure an organisation's ability to generate cash.
   - **Profitability ratios** measure an organisation's ability to generate profits.
   - **Debt ratios** measure an organisation's ability to pay its debts.
   - **Activity ratios** measure an organisation's efficiency in operations and use of assets.

   In addition, *financial responsibility centres* require managers to account for a unit's progress toward financial goals within the scope of their influences. A manager's goals and responsibilities may focus on unit profits, costs, revenues, or investments.

2. **Budget controls.** A budget depicts how much an organisation expects to spend (expenses) and earn (revenues) over a time period. Amounts are categorised according to the type of business activity or account, such as telephone costs or sales of catalogues. Budgets not only help managers plan their finances, but also help them keep track of their overall spending.

   A budget, in reality, is both a planning tool and a control mechanism. Budget development processes vary among organisations according to who does the budgeting and how the financial resources are allocated. Some budget development methods are as follows:

   - **Top-down budgeting.** Managers prepare the budget and send it to subordinates.
   - **Bottom-up budgeting.** Figures come from the lower levels and are adjusted and coordinated as they move up the hierarchy.
   - **Zero-based budgeting.** Managers develop each new budget by justifying the projected allocation against its contribution to departmental or organisational goals.
   - **Flexible budgeting.** Any budget exercise can incorporate flexible budgets, which set "meet or beat" standards that can be compared to expenditures.

3. **Marketing controls. Marketing controls** help monitor progress toward goals for customer satisfaction with products and services, prices, and delivery. The following are examples of controls used to evaluate an organisation's marketing functions:

   (i) **Market research** gathers data to assess customer needs—information critical to an organisation's success. Ongoing market research reflects how well an organisation is meeting customers' expectations and helps anticipate customer needs. It also helps identify competitors.

(ii) **Test marketing** is small-scale product marketing to assess customer acceptance. Using surveys and focus groups, test marketing goes beyond identifying general requirements and looks at what (or who) actually influences buying decisions.

(iii) **Marketing statistics** measure performance by compiling data and analyzing results. In most cases, competency with a computer spreadsheet program is all a manager needs. Managers look at *marketing ratios,* which measure profitability, activity, and market shares, as well as *sales quotas,* which measure progress toward sales goals and assist with inventory controls.

Unfortunately, scheduling a regular evaluation of an organisation's marketing program is easier to recommend than to execute. Usually, only a crisis, such as increased competition or a sales drop, forces a company to take a closer look at its marketing program. However, more regular evaluations help minimise the number of marketing problems.

4. **Human resource controls.** Human resource controls help managers regulate the quality of newly hired personnel, as well as monitor current employees' developments and daily performances.

   On a daily basis, managers can go a long way in helping to control workers' behaviours in organisations. They can help direct workers' performances toward goals by making sure that goals are clearly set and understood. Managers can also institute policies and procedures to help guide workers' actions. Finally, they can consider past experiences when developing future strategies, objectives, policies, and procedures.

   Common control types include performance appraisals, disciplinary programs, observations, and training and development assessments. Because the quality of a firm's personnel, to a large degree, determines the firm's overall effectiveness, controlling this area is very crucial.

5. **Computers and information controls.** Almost all organisations have confidential and sensitive information that they don't want to become general knowledge. Controlling access to computer databases is the key to this area. Increasingly, computers are being used to collect and store information for control purposes. Many organisations privately monitor each employee's computer usage to measure employee performance, among other things. Some people question the appropriateness of computer monitoring. Managers must carefully weigh the benefits against the costs – both human and financial – before investing in and implementing computerised control techniques.

6. **Management Audit.** Management Audit is an evaluation of the management as a whole. It critically examines the full management process, *i.e.,* planning, organising, directing, and controlling. It finds out the efficiency of the management. To check the efficiency of the management, the company's plans, objectives, policies, procedures, personnel relations and systems of control are examined very carefully. Management auditing is conducted by a team of experts. They collect data from past records, members of management, clients and employees. The data is analysed and conclusions are drawn about managerial performance and efficiency

7. **Management Information System (MIS).** In order to control the organisation properly the management needs accurate information. They need information about the internal working of the organisation and also about the external environment. Information is collected continuously to identify problems and find out solutions. MIS collects data, processes it and provides it to the managers. MIS may be manual or computerised. With MIS, managers can delegate authority to subordinates without losing control.

8. **PERT and CPM Techniques.** Programme Evaluation and Review Technique (PERT) and Critical Path Method (CPM) techniques were developed in USA in the late 50's. Any programme consists

of various activities and sub-activities. Successful completion of any activity depends upon doing the work in a given sequence and in a given time.

CPM / PERT can be used to minimise the total time or the total cost required to perform the total operations. Importance is given to identifying the critical activities. Critical activities are those which have to be completed on time otherwise the full project will be delayed. So, in these techniques, the job is divided into various activities / sub-activities. From these activities, the critical activities are identified. More importance is given to completion of these critical activities. So, by controlling the time of the critical activities, the total time and cost of the job is minimised.

9. **Self-Control.** Self-Control means self-directed control. A person is given freedom to set his own targets, evaluate his own performance and take corrective measures as and when required. Self-control is especially required for top level managers because they do not like external control.

   The subordinates must be encouraged to use self-control because it is not good for the superior to control each and everything. However, self-control does not mean no control by the superiors. The superiors must control the important activities of the subordinates.

10. **Break Even Analysis.** Break Even Analysis or Break Even Point is the point of no profit, no loss. For e.g. When an organisation sells 50K cars it will break even. It means that, any sale below this point will cause losses and any sale above this point will earn profits. The Break-even analysis acts as a control device. It helps to find out the company's performance. So the company can take collective action to improve its performance in the future. Break-even analysis is a simple control tool.

11. **Return on Investment (ROI).** Investment consists of fixed assets and working capital used in business. Profit on the investment is a reward for risk taking. If the ROI is high then the financial performance of a business is good and vice-versa. ROI is a tool to improve financial performance. It helps the business to compare its present performance with that of previous years' performance. It helps to conduct inter-firm comparisons. It also shows the areas where corrective actions are needed.

12. **Management Audit.** Management Audit is an evaluation of the management as a whole. It critically examines the full management process, i.e., planning, organising, directing, and controlling. It finds out the efficiency of the management. To check the efficiency of the management, the company's plans, objectives, policies, procedures, personnel relations and systems of control are examined very carefully. Management auditing is conducted by a team of experts. They collect data from past records, members of management, clients and employees. The data is analyzed and conclusions are drawn about managerial performance and efficiency.

13. **Management Information System (MIS).** In order to control the organisation properly the management needs accurate information. They need information about the internal working of the organisation and also about the external environment. Information is collected continuously to identify problems and find out solutions. MIS collects data, processes it and provides it to the managers. MIS may be manual or computerised. With MIS, managers can delegate authority to subordinates without losing control.

COORDINATION

Meaning

Coordination as a function of the management refers to the tasks of integrating the activity of separate units of an organisation to accomplish the goals efficiently. It permeates all levels and all department of the management hence it is regarded as the essence of the management.

Definition of Coordination

According to the Mcfarland, "Coordination is the process whereby an executive develops an orderly pattern of group efforts among his subordinate and secure unity of the action in the pursuit of a common purpose".

According to E.F.L Breach, "Coordination is the balancing and keeping together, the team by ensuring a suitable allocation of tasks to various members and seeing that the tasks are performed with due harmony among the members themselves".

According to Henry Fayol, "To coordinate is to harmonise all the activities of a concern so as to facilitate its working and its success".

According to George terry, "The orderly synchronisation of efforts to provide the proper amount timing and directly of execution resulting harmonious and unified action to stated objectives".

According to Haimann, "Coordination is not a separate activity of management. It is the organ of all other managerial functions like – planning, organising, staffing, directing, and controlling".

According to Mooney and Railey, "Coordination is the achievement or group efforts and the unity of action of the pursuit of a common purpose".

Features of Coordination

1. **Function.** Coordination is not a separate function of management. It is the part and essence of management.
2. **Responsibility.** Coordination is the basic responsibility of all managers and it can be only achieved through managerial function. This cannot be avoided by any manager and whenever people work together for the common objective, coordination is required.
3 **Unity.** The main aspect of coordination is the unity of effort and action, which includes the predetermining the timing and method of the performance of the various activities so that efforts of individual are blended into group efforts.
4. **Requirement.** Coordination is required in the group efforts and not in the individual efforts. It is not required when an individual works alone but when the group is working for the common objective then their efforts needs to be coordinated.
5. **Integration.** Higher the degree of integration higher the coordination is required, further lower the degree of integration, lower level of coordination is required.
6. **Continuous and dynamic.** Coordination is a continuous and dynamic process. It is continuous as it is achieved through the performance of functions. It is dynamic as it changes with the changes in the functions.
7. **Purpose.** Coordination has the purpose to achieve the organisational objectives.
8. **Elements.** Balancing, timing, and integration are the three main elements of the coordination.

Difference Between Coordination and Cooperation

Basis	Coordination	Cooperation
Scope	It has the wider scope and cooperation is the part of it.	It has limited scope and it is the part of the coordination.
Nature	It is practical and professional in nature.	It is emotional in nature.
Principle	Direct Contact and Continuity of efforts	Voluntary association
Relationship	Formal and informal both	Informal only
Objective	Synchronisation of efforts of individual.	Protecting the interest of members.

Types of Coordination

Coordination can be classified into following categories:

- **Vertical Coordination.** Vertical coordination exists between the departments where the department heads are asked to coordinate the work of the employees Principles of coordination
- **Horizontal Coordination.** Horizontal coordination takes place sideways. It exists between different departments such as production, sales, purchasing, finance etc.
- **Internal Coordination.** Coordination among the employees of the same department or section and among the employees at different levels is called internal coordination.
- **External Coordination.** Coordination with the outside parties with whom the organisation has the business connections like government, suppliers, customers etc. is called external coordination.

Following are the Principles of Coordination

- **Principle of early introduction.** Coordination must be visualised right from the early stages of planning and policy-making. At the time of preparation of the plan, mutual cooperation, consultation, give and take become the necessity. In case the plan is prepared without coordination then it becomes difficult to supply the required materials or results in the misallocation of the duties.
- **Principle of continuity.** According to this principle, coordination should be followed in the organisation on continuous basis and it should be taken as a regular activity. Managers should treat coordination as the never ending exercise.
- **Principle of Direct Contact.** According to the principle of direct contact, coordination can only be established through the direct contact of the parties whose activities are to be coordinated. As through direct contact the parties can discuss the methods, plans, actions, activities and work for the achievement of overall organisational goals.
- **Principle of mutual relation.** This principle states that every employee should understand the problems faced by the other employees and try to solve them. For the purpose of coordination, there should be perfect adjustment and sense of fellow feeling among the employees placed under them.

COMMUNICATION

It is the process of passing ideas, emotions, feelings, informations or messages from one person to another. It is the exchange of verbal or written information. It means the conveying of a message by one person to another so that another person may understand the message in the same sense, follow and implement the message. It is the sum of all the things one person does when he wants to create understanding in the mind of another. It involves a systematic and continuous process of telling, listening and understanding.

Characteristics

(a) Communication involves at least two persons - Nobody wants to communicate with himself. As it involves at least two persons, one will be the sender and other will be the receiver.

(b) It is the transmission of facts, ideas, opinions, feelings, emotions, message from one person to another *i.e.,* something which is to be communicated is must.

(c) There is a need of media for communication like speech, writing or gestural communication which can be there.

(d) It is a two way process. It includes feedback. If the receiver has received the message, he must give feedback about what he has understood.

(e) The main purpose of communication is to motivate response from the receiver.
(f) It includes all those means and efforts which one adopts to create understanding in the minds of others.
(g) It may travel from up and down, from side to side, that means communication may be horizontal, vertical or diagonal.
(h) It is the base for action and co-operation.
(i) It is required at all the levels of management and at all times.

Communication Process

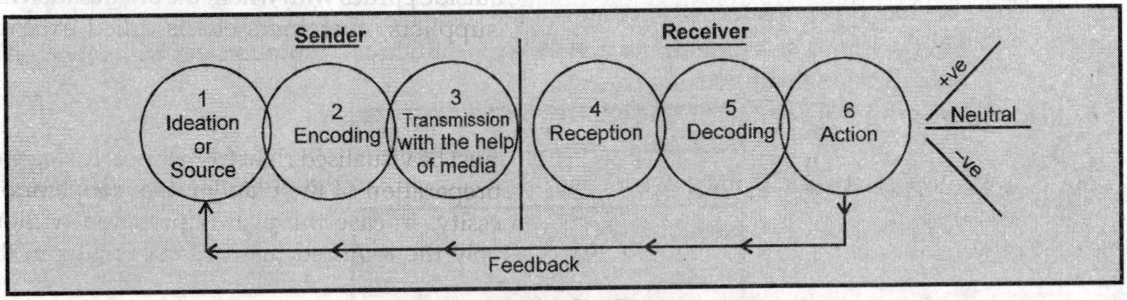

Communication Process

(a) **Ideation.** Communication starts when one has got an idea, opinion, suggestion or problem etc. It is a thinking stage. According to Davis, "Don't start talking until you begin thinking."
(b) **Encoding.** It means when the ideas, feelings, thoughts of sender are put in the form of a logical sequence of sentences. It is the selection of words, dialogues, symbols and models.
(c) **Transmission with media.** The communicator has to decide about the appropriate means of communication *i.e.*, whether face to face or through e-mail or any other medium. While deciding about the appropriate mean the psychological, physiological, financial and emotional aspect should be considered.
(d) **Reception.** At this stage the message is received for whom the message is meant. In reception only listening by the receiver is not enough, his willingness is also must.
(e) **Decoding.** It means understanding of the message by the receiver. After receiving the message, the receiver analyses the message to know its contents. He translates the symbols, figures so that he could properly understand the message.
(f) **Action.** It means the response shown by the receiver on receiving the message communicated by the communicator.

In final stage, there is feedback. The sender receives the feedback from receiver. This may help the sender to evaluate the effectiveness of his message so that sender can modify his subsequent message.

Communication Network

In an organisation, there are a number of channels or paths connecting various positions for purposes of communication. The sum-total of these channels is referred to as 'communication network'. This is made up of two types of channels which are interrelated and interdependent, viz., formal and informal.

A. **Formal Channel.** The formal channel is the deliberately created, officially prescribed path for flow of communication between the various positions in the organisation. It is the deliberate attempt to regulate the flow of organisational communication so as to make it orderly and thereby to ensure that information flows smoothly, accurately and timely to the points to which it is required. Further, it is also intended to prescribe for filtering of the information to various points to ensure that information does not flow unnecessarily thereby causing the problem of overload.

B. **Informal Channel or Grapevine.** The informal channel of communication, also known as 'grapevine' is the result not of any official action, but of the operation of social forces at work-place. The term grapevine arose during the days of U.S. civil war. At that time, intelligence telephone lines were strung loosely from tree to tree in the manner of a grapevine, and the message thereon was often distorted; hence any rumour was said to be the form of grapevine. Today the term applies to all informal communication. While formal communication exists to meet the utilitarian needs of the organisation, informal communication is the method by which people carry on social, non-programmed activities within the formal boundaries of the system. It, thus, exists outside the official network, though continuously interacting with it.

There are four types of informal communication channels

(i) **Single Strand.** In single strand network, the individual communicates with other individuals through intervening persons.

(ii) **Gossip network.** In the gossip network, the individual communicates non-selectively.

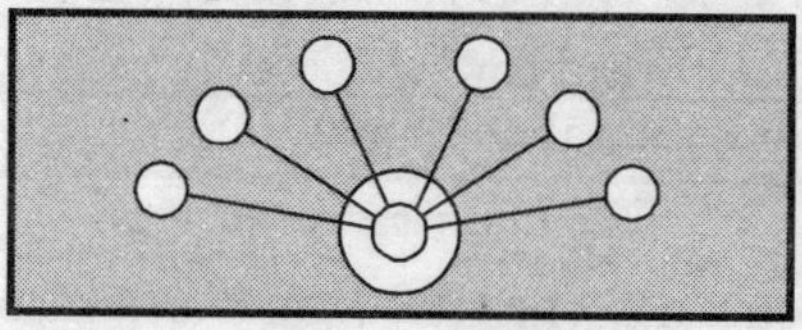

(iii) **Probability network.** In probability network, the individual communicates randomly with other individuals according to the law of probability.

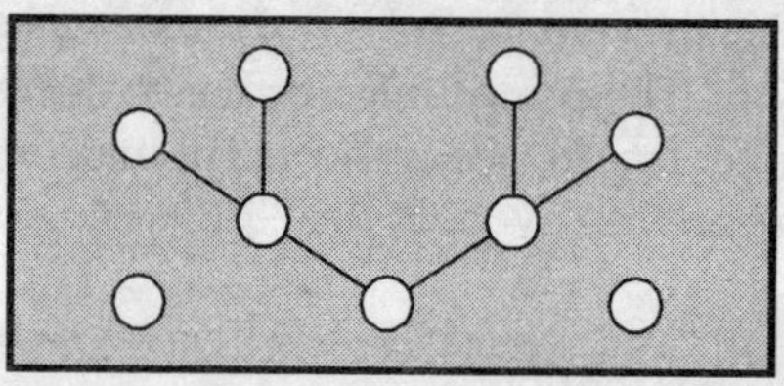

(iv) **Cluster network.** In the cluster network, the individual communicates with only those individuals whom he trusts.

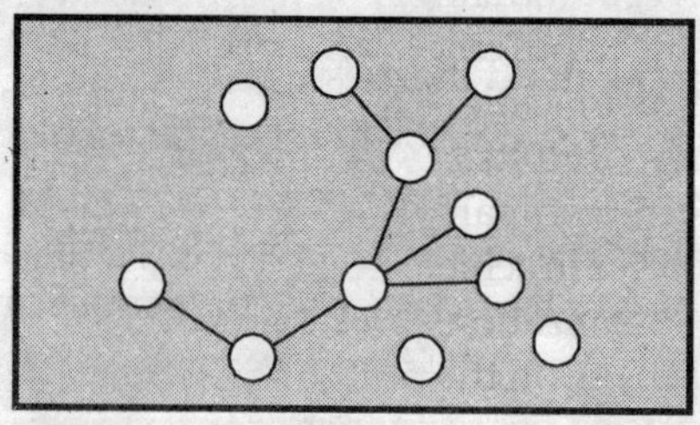

(v) **Y-Pattern.** It is highly centralised, two persons are closer to the centre of the network. Person 1 and 2 are closer to leader A.

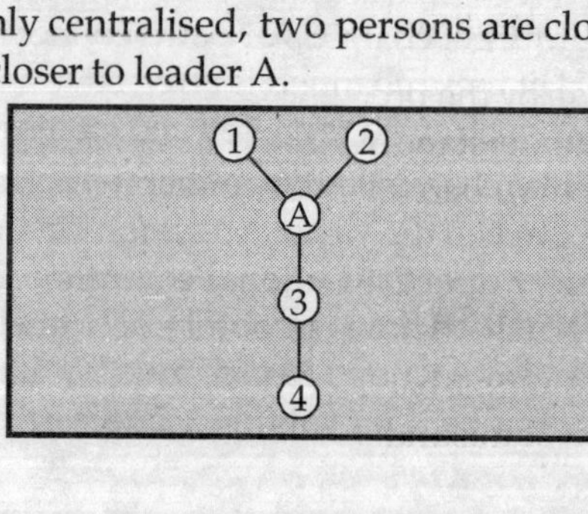

Direction of Communication

A. Downward Communication. Downward communication within the organisation flows from a superior either in the same line of command or in the different one. It stands out as a great force for controlling, influencing and initiating activities of organisation members. Communication in this category includes:

(i) orders and instructions about job.
(ii) directions about understanding of job and its relationships with other jobs.
(iii) organisational policies and procedures.
(iv) feedback of subordinate's performance.
(v) reprimands, criticisms etc.
(vi) questions inviting upward communication.

In the organisation, people at lower levels have a high degree of fear and regret towards such communication which leads to high degree of acceptance of such communication. Coordination, distortion and resistance are three important problems that characterise the downward communication process.

B. Upward Communication. Upward communication flows from a subordinate position to a superior position. It includes information about:

(i) subordinate's work performance.
(ii) problems relating to work.
(iii) performance appraisal of their subordinates.
(iv) feedback of understanding of orders, instructions, etc.
(v) clarifications of orders, etc.
(vi) opinion, attitude, feeling, etc.
(vii) procedures, methods, practices followed in doing the work.
(viii) criticisms.
(ix) new ideas and suggestions.
(x) personal and family problems.

C. Horizontal Communication. It is the flow of information between persons of the same hierarchical level. Formal organisation provides for horizontal communication by means of right of persons at any level to consult or work with others at the same level. Communication among peers, in addition to providing task coordination, also furnishes emotional and social support to the individual. Horizontal communication is impeded in the organisation that overstresses functional departmentalisation. The creation of functional departments or units creates problems of coordination and communication between members of such units. Some companies develop committee structure near the top level of the organisation to assist the chief executive in achieving coordination and better horizontal communication in terms of control function in the organisations. Horizontal communication, if in operation at various levels in an organisation, is a real check on the power of the top leaders.

Barriers in Communication

This far we have seen what we mean by the process of communication. But, at times even after taking care of every other detail some misunderstandings arise. So, to eliminate these misunderstandings, we have to understand the most common barriers to effective communication. Let us see what these Barriers of Communication are!

Barriers to Effective Communication

The process of communication has multiple barriers. The intended communique will often be disturbed and distorted leading to a condition of misunderstanding and failure of communication. The Barriers to effective communication could be of many types like linguistic, psychological, emotional, physical, and cultural etc.

Linguistic Barriers

The language barrier is one of the main barriers that limit effective communication. Language is the most commonly employed tool of communication. The fact that each major region has its own language is one of the Barriers to effective communication. Sometimes even a thick dialect may render the communication ineffective.

As per some estimates, the dialects of every two regions changes within a few kilometres. Even in the same workplace, different employees will have different linguistic skills. As a result, the communication channels that span across the organization would be affected by this.

Thus keeping this barrier in mind, different considerations have to be made for different employees. Some of them are very proficient in a certain language and others will be ok with these languages.

Psychological Barriers

There are various mental and psychological issues that may be barriers to effective communication. Some people have stage fear, speech disorders, phobia, depression etc. All of these conditions are very difficult to manage sometimes and will most certainly limit the ease of communication.

Emotional Barriers

The emotional IQ of a person determines the ease and comfort with which they can communicate. A person who is emotionally mature will be able to communicate effectively. On the other hand, people who let their emotions take over will face certain difficulties.

A perfect mixture of emotions and facts is necessary for effective communication. Emotions like anger, frustration, humour, can blur the decision-making capacities of a person and thus limit the effectiveness of their communication.

Physical Barriers to Communication

They are the most obvious barriers to effective communication. These barriers are mostly easily removable in principle at least. They include barriers like noise, closed doors, faulty equipment used for communication, closed cabins, etc. Sometimes, in a large office, the physical separation between various employees combined with faulty equipment may result in severe barriers to effective communication.

Cultural Barriers of Communication

As the world is getting more and more globalized, any large office may have people from several parts of the world. Different cultures have a different meaning for several basic values of society. Dressing, Religions or lack of them, food, drinks, pets, and the general behaviour will change drastically from one culture to another.

Hence it is a must that we must take these different cultures into account while communication. This is what we call being culturally appropriate. In many multinational companies, special courses are offered at the orientation stages that let people know about other cultures and how to be courteous and tolerant of others.

Organisational Structure Barriers

As we saw there are many methods of communication at an organizational level. Each of these methods has its own problems and constraints that may become barriers to effective communication. Most of these barriers arise because of misinformation or lack of appropriate transparency available to the employees.

Attitude Barriers

Certain people like to be left alone. They are the introverts or just people who are not very social. Others like to be social or sometimes extra clingy! Both these cases could become a barrier to communication. Some people have attitude issues, like huge ego and inconsiderate behaviours.

These employees can cause severe strains in the communication channels that they are present in. Certain personality traits like shyness, anger, social anxiety may be removable through courses and proper training. However, problems like egocentric behaviour and selfishness may not be correctable.

Perception Barriers

Different people perceive the same things differently. This is a fact which we must consider during the communication process. Knowledge of the perception levels of the audience is crucial to effective communication. All the messages or communique must be easy and clear. There shouldn't be any room for a diversified interpretational set.

Physiological Barriers

Certain disorders or diseases or other limitations could also prevent effective communication between the various channels of an organization. The shrillness of voice, dyslexia, etc are some examples of physiological barriers to effective communication. However, these are not crucial because they can easily be compensated and removed.

Technological Barriers & Socio-religious Barriers

Other barriers include the technological barriers. The technology is developing fast and as a result, it becomes difficult to keep up with the newest developments. Hence sometimes the technological advance may become a barrier. In addition to this, the cost of technology is sometimes very high.

Most of the organizations will not be able to afford a decent tech for the purpose of communication. Hence, this becomes a very crucial barrier. Other barriers are socio-religious barriers. In a patriarchal society, a woman or a transgender may face many difficulties and barriers while communicating.

DECISION MAKING

A decision is the selection from among alternatives. In the words of MacFarland, "A decision is an act of choice wherein an executive forms a conclusion about what must be done in a given situation. A decision represents a course of behaviour chosen from a number of possible alternatives." The way an executive acts or decides the course of action from among various alternatives is an act of decision-making.

Characteristics

Following are the characteristics of decision-making:

1. Decision-making is based on rational thinking. The manager tries to foresee various possible effects of a decision before taking a particular one.
2. It is a process of selecting the best from among alternatives available.
3. It involves the evaluation of various alternatives available. The selection of best alternative will be made only when pros and cons of all of them are discussed and evaluated.
4. Decision making is the end product because it is preceded by discussions and deliberations.
5. Decision-making is aimed to achieve organisational goals.
6. It also involves certain commitment. Management is committed to every decision it takes.

Types of Decisions

The Managerial decisions may be classified as follows:

1. **Organisational and Personal Decisions.** When a person takes a decision in the organisation as an executive it will be an organisational decision.

   An executive can also take decisions about himself. Such decisions are known as personal decisions.
2. **Routine and Strategic Decisions.** Routine decisions are made repetitively following certain established rules, procedures, policies etc. These are taken at middle and lower level management.

   Strategic decisions relate to policy matters and need the development and analysis of alternatives and are taken by top management.
3. **Programmed and Non-programmed Decisions.** Programmed decisions are of a routine nature and are taken within the specified procedures.

   Non-repetitive decisions are on the other hand non-programmed decisions.
4. **Policy and Operative Decisions.** Policy decisions determine the basic policies of the organisation and are taken at top level management.

   Operative decisions, on the other hand, are less important and are related with day-to-day operations of the business. These decisions are taken in the light of policies decided by the top management.
5. **Individual and Group Decisions.** If the decision is taken by one person it is known as individual decision. In small concerns only the owner takes all important decisions.

   Group decisions are taken by a group of persons. The decisions of Board of Directors or Committees come under this category. These are, generally, important decisions and relate to policy matters.

Decision Making Process

Decision making is the process of making choices by identifying a decision, gathering information, and assessing alternative resolutions.

Using a step-by-step decision-making process can help you make more deliberate, thoughtful decisions by organizing relevant information and defining alternatives. This approach increases the chances that you will choose the most satisfying alternative possible.

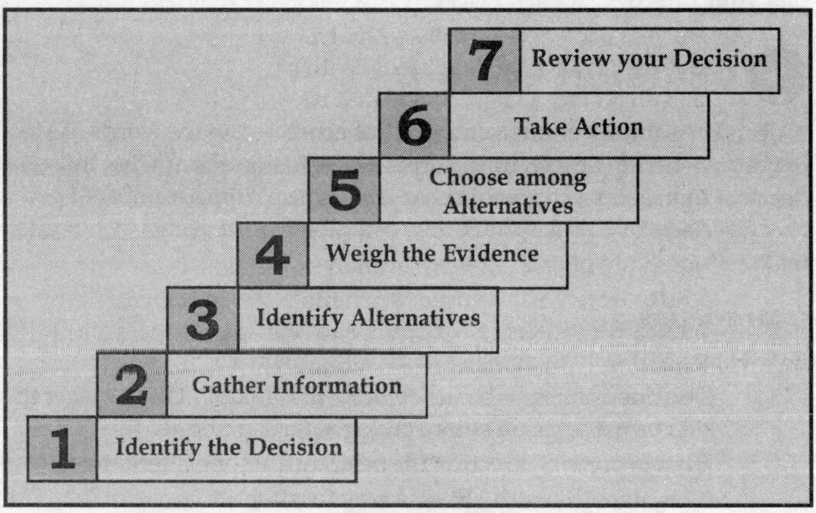

Seven Steps to Effective Decision Making

Step 1: Identify the decision. You realize that you need to make a decision. Try to clearly define the nature of the decision you must make. This first step is very important.

Step 2: Gather relevant information. Collect some pertinent information before you make your decision: what information is needed, the best sources of information, and how to get it. This step involves both internal and external "work." Some information is internal: you'll seek it through a process of self-assessment. Other information is external: you'll find it online, in books, from other people, and from other sources.

Step 3: Identify the alternatives. As you collect information, you will probably identify several possible paths of action, or alternatives. You can also use your imagination and additional information to construct new alternatives. In this step, you will list all possible and desirable alternatives.

Step 4: Weigh the evidence. Draw on your information and emotions to imagine what it would be like if you carried out each of the alternatives to the end. Evaluate whether the need identified in Step 1 would be met or resolved through the use of each alternative. As you go through this difficult internal process, you'll begin to favor certain alternatives: those that seem to have a higher potential for reaching your goal. Finally, place the alternatives in a priority order, based upon your own value system.

Step 5: Choose among alternatives. Once you have weighed all the evidence, you are ready to select the alternative that seems to be best one for you. You may even choose a combination of alternatives. Your choice in Step 5 may very likely be the same or similar to the alternative you placed at the top of your list at the end of Step 4.

Step 6: Take action. You're now ready to take some positive action by beginning to implement the alternative you chose in Step 5.

Step 7: Review your decision & its consequences. In this final step, consider the results of your decision and evaluate whether or not it has resolved the need you identified in Step 1. If the decision has not met the identified need, you may want to repeat certain steps of the process to make a new decision. For example, you might want to gather more detailed or somewhat different information or explore additional alternatives.

Decision-making Tools and Techniques

While the basic principles might be the same, there are dozens of different techniques and tools that can be used when trying to make a decision. Here are some of the more popular options, many of which use graphs, models or charts. You may want to use a combination of these techniques to arrive at your final decisions.

- **Decision matrix.** A decision matrix is used to evaluate all the options of a decision. When using the matrix, create a table with all of the options in the first column and all of the factors that affect the decision in the first row. Users then score each option and weigh which factors are of more importance. A final score is then tallied to reveal which option is the best.
- **T-Chart.** This chart is used when weighing the plusses and minuses of the options. It ensures that all the positives and negatives are taken into consideration when making a decision.
- **Decision tree.** This is a graph or model that involves contemplating each option and the outcomes of each. Statistical analysis is also conducted with this technique.
- **Multivoting.** This is used when multiple people are involved in making a decision. It helps whittle down a large list options to a smaller one to the eventual final decision.
- **Pareto analysis.** This is a technique used when a large number of decisions need to be made. This helps in prioritizing which ones should be made first by determining which decisions will have the greatest overall impact.
- **Cost-benefit analysis.** This technique is used when weighing the financial ramifications of each possible alternative as a way to come to a final decision that makes the most sense from an economic perspective.
- **Conjoint analysis.** This is a method used by business leaders tc determine consumer preferences when making decisions.
- **SWOT Analysis.** SWOT stands for strengths, weaknesses, opportunities and threats, which is exactly what this planning tool assesses.

- **PEST Analysis.** An acronym for political, economic, social and technological, PEST can improve decision-making and timing by analyzing external factors. This method considers present trends to help predict the future ones.

ORGANISATION STRUCTURE AND DESIGN

Organisation structure is a basic framework within which the managers' decision-making behaviour takes place. Structure basically deals with relationships. It is an important scientific concept. All sciences try to discover the structural relationships in the phenomena in which they are interested. For example, biologist wants to know the structure of cells; the astronomer wants to know the structure of the universe, the physicist studies the structure of the atom or molecule; the economist seeks to discover the structure of a labour market or of money-flow patterns. Similarly in management, we need to understand how organisations are structural and how these structures are created and maintained.

Concept of Organisation Structure

In a simple term, structure is the pattern in which various parts or components are interrelated or interconnected. Thus organisation structure is the pattern of relationships among various components or parts of the organisation. This prescribes the relationships among various activities and positions. Since these positions are held by various persons, the structure is the relationship among people in the organisation.

The organisation structure, being abstract, is not visible in the same way as a biological or mechanical structure, though it can be inferred from the actual operations and behaviour of the organisation. The biological or mechanical system, such as organism and machine, can be identified even when it is not working because it has both anatomy and physiology. The study of the anatomy is basically the study of the structure of the organism whereas the physiology deals with functions of living organism. The biological and mechanical systems can be studied in both these terms – structure as well as functioning. However, this is not the case with social systems which do not have both anatomy and physiology. As such, it is very difficult to study the organisation's structure separately from its functioning. For example; Katz and Khan observe as follows in this context: "*A Social system is a structuring of events or happenings rather than of physiological parts and it, therefore, has no structure apart from its functioning.*"

Organizational Structure Types

(1) **Hierarchical Structure.** The hierarchical model is the most popular organizational chart type. There are a few models that are derived from this model.

In a hierarchical organization structure, employees are grouped with every employee having one clear supervisor. The grouping is done based on a few factors, hence many models derived from this. Below are few of those factors:

- **Function** employees are grouped according to the function they provide. The below image shows a functional org chart with finance, technical, HR and admin groups.
- **Geography** employees are grouped based on their region. For example in USA employees might be grouped according to the state. If it's a global company the grouping could be done according to countries.
- **Product.** If a company is producing multiple products or offering different services it can be grouped according to the product or service.

This is the dominant mode of organization among large organizations. For example Corporations, Governments, and organized religions are hierarchical organizations with different levels of management, power or authority.

(2) **Matrix Structure.** In a Matrix organizational structure, the reporting relationships are set up as a grid, or matrix, rather than in the traditional hierarchy. It is a type of organizational management in which people with similar skills are pooled for work assignments, resulting in more than one manager to report to (sometimes referred to as solid line and dotted line reports, in reference to traditional business organization charts).

For example, all engineers may be in one engineering department and report to an engineering manager. But these same engineers may be assigned to different projects and might be reporting to those project managers as well. Therefore some engineers might have to work with multiple managers in their job role.

(3) **Horizontal/Flat Structure.** This is an organizational chart type mostly adopted by small companies and start-ups in their early stage. It's almost impossible to use this model for larger companies with many projects and employees.

The most important thing about this structure is thát many levels of middle management are eliminated. This enables employees to make decisions quickly and independently. Thus a well-trained workforce can be more productive by directly getting involved in the decision-making process.

This works well for small companies because work and effort in a small company are relatively transparent. This does not mean that employees don't have superiors and people to report. Just that decision making power is shared and employees are held accountable for their decisions.

So in summary, when deciding on a suitable organizational chart, it is important to have an understanding of the current organizational structure of your company.

(4) **Network Structure.** Network organizational structure helps visualize both internal and external relationships between managers and top-level management. They are not only less hierarchical but are also more decentralized and more flexible than other structures.

The idea behind the network structure is based on social networks. Its structure relies on open communication and reliable partners; both internal and external. The network structure is viewed as agiler than other structures because it has few tires, more control and bottom flow of decision making.

Using a Network organizational structure is sometimes a disadvantage because of its complexity. The below example of network org chart shows the rapid communication between entities.

(5) **Divisional Structure.** Within a divisional structure, each organizational function has its own division which corresponds to either products or geographies. Each division contains the necessary resources and functions needed to support the product line and geography.

Another form of divisional org chart structure is the multi-divisional structure. It's also known as M-form. It's a legit structure in which one parent company owns several subsidiary companies, each of which uses the parent company's brand and name.

The main advantage of the divisional structure is the independent operational flow, that failure of one company does not threaten the existence of the others.

It's not perfect either. There can be operational inefficiencies from separating specialized functions. Increase in accounting taxes can be seen as another disadvantage.

(6) **Line Organizational Structure.** Line organizational structure is one of the simplest types of organizational structures. Its authority flows from top to bottom. Unlike other structures, specialized and supportive services do not take place in these organizations.

The chain of command and each department head has control over their departments. The self-contained department structure can be seen as its main characteristic. Independent decisions can be taken by line officers because of its unified structure.

The main advantage of a line organizational structure can be identified as the effective communication that brings stability to the organization.

(7) **Team-based Organizational Structure.** Team-based organizational structures are made of teams working towards a common goal while working on their individual tasks. They are less hierarchical and they have flexible structures that reinforce problem-solving, decision-making and teamwork.

Team organization structures have changed the way many industries work. Globalization has allowed people in all industries around the world to produce goods and services cooperatively. Especially, manufacturing companies must work together with the suppliers around the globe while keeping the cost to a minimum while producing high-quality products.

AUTHORITY AND RESPONSIBILITY

Authority

Authority, in simple words, is the right way of commanding subordinates, issuing orders and instructions, and exacting obedience from the team. It is also the right of the manager to make decisions. Also, to act or not to act depends on how he perceives the objectives of the organization.

Henri Fayol, who designed the administrative theory of 14 principles of management, defined authority as 'the right to give orders and exact obedience'. He also recognized that any official authority vested in the job was often ineffective.

He further added that the presence of leadership qualities and traits like intelligence, experience, etc., usually, enhance authority. However, as an important key to the manager's job, authority is the power to command others and decide to act or refrain from acting to achieve the organization's goals.

A manager needs authority. It makes his position real and gives him the power to order his subordinates and get them to comply. When there is a chain of superior-subordinate relations in an organization, it is the authority which binds and provides a basis for responsibility.

James Mooney specified that coordination is the primary principle of an organization. Therefore, it must have its own principle and foundation in Authority or the supreme coordinating power.

Coordination is the all-inclusive principle of organization, it must have its own principle and foundation in Authority or the supreme coordinating power.

Always, in every form of organization, this supreme coordinating authority must rest somewhere, else there would be no directive for any truly coordinated effort. Without authority, there will be no relations between subordinates and superiors and the organization will be in chaos.

Official and Personal Authority

The authority that a manager enjoys due to his position is the official authority or authority of position. Apart from the official authority, a manager might influence the behavior of other people in the organization.

This is the personal authority of the manager. A manager with both official and personal authority is very effective. Authority is not unlimited power and consists of specific rights and permissions to act for the organization in specified areas.

Responsibility

Responsibility has different meanings in management. The most common description is the obligation on the manager to perform the task himself. The essence of responsibility is 'obligation'.

Anyone who accepts a task must be held responsible for its performance too. In the context of hierarchical relations in an organization, responsibility is the obligation of a subordinate to perform the tasks assigned.

Therefore, responsibility is relative to the person. Also, it emanates from the subordinate-superior relations in an organization. Hence, the manager can get the assigned duty done by his subordinate.

He also needs to ensure a proper discharge of the duty. Therefore, in an organization, authority and responsibility move as follows - authority flows downwards, whereas responsibility is exacted upwards.

Sometimes, informal leadership emerges in an organization. This can create problems in the clear definition of responsibilities of the subordinates. However, the responsibility towards the seniors does not change.

Accountability

Every employee is answerable to his superior for the accomplishment of the task assigned to him. This is accountability. When a manager delegates a task, he assigns duties and delegates the required authority so that his subordinates can accomplish the task.

However, the process is not complete unless the subordinate is answerable to the superior for his functioning. Therefore, authority goes downward and makes everyone accountable for the duties assigned.

CENTRALISATION AND DECENTRALISATION

Apart from delegation, another important factor leading to effective organisation is the degree of centralisation or decentralisation of authority.

The two terms 'centralisation' and 'decentralisation' refer to a philosophy of organisation and management that focuses on either the selective concentration (centralisation) or the dispersal (decentralisation) of authority within the structure of an organisation. In fact, the question of where authority resides with such a structure is of crucial importance for organisational effectiveness.

This question is sought to be resolved through an operational philosophy of management - either to concentrate authority for decision-making in the hands of only one individual or a handful of people or force it down the organisation structure into the hands of quite a large number of people.

Like the concept of delegation the concept of centralisation has to with the degree to which authority is concentrated or dispersed. Just as authority can be delegated from one individual to another, organisations also develop patterns of authority across a wide variety of positions and departments. 'Delegation' is a narrow concept.

In general, it refers to the extent to which individuals delegate authority and responsibility to people reporting directly to them. On the other hand, 'decentralisation' is a much broader concept. It usually refers to the extent to which top-level management delegates authority downward to divisions, branches, or lower-level organisational units.

In others words, it refers to the extent to which power and authority are systematically delegated throughout the organisation to middle and lower-level managers. General Electric, for example, has historically allowed middle and lower level managers to make decisions regulating the area of responsibility.

In short, centralisation refers to concentrating the power and authority near the top, or in the head, of an organisation or the extent to which powers and authority are systematically retained by higher-level managers. Hence a decentralised organisation is one in which decision-making power and authority are delegated as far down the chain of command as possible. Conversely, in a decentralised organisation, decision-making power and authority are retained at the higher levels of management. This distinction is made clear in figure.

It may be noted in this context that both centralization and decentralization are relative concepts, when applied to organisations. For instance, the upper management may decide to centralize all decision making: purchasing, staffing, and operations.

Alternatively it may decide to set monetary limits on what can be purchased at each level, decentralise the hiring decisions to first-level management for clerical workers (retaining authority for managerial decisions); and permit operational (e.g., production) decisions be made where appropriate.

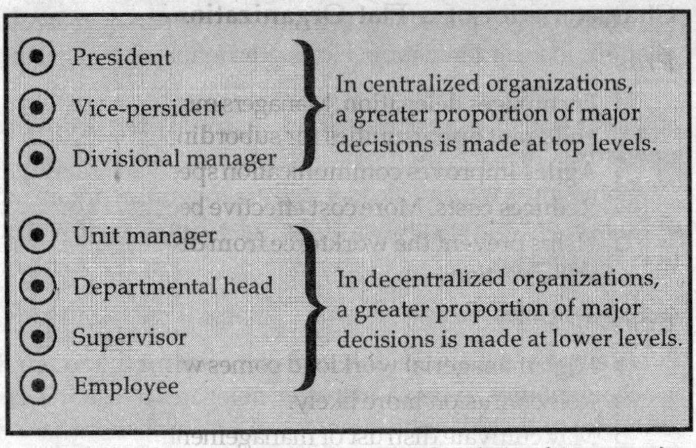

Centralization-decentralization and the Chain of Command

It may be noted that no organisation is ever completely centralised or completely decentralised. Some firms position themselves toward one end of the continuum, while some lean the other way. Empirical study reveals that the extent of either ranges along a continuum from high centralisation to high decentralization.

SPAN OF CONTROL

What is Span of Control and Organizational Structure?

It is very important to understand span of control and organizational structure when describing an organization. Simply, span of control refers to the number of subordinates under the manager's direct control. As an example, a manager with five direct reports has a span of control of five. To many or to few direct reports is a good way to view how efficent an organization is as long as it looked at in the context of the companys organizational structure.

How many direct reports can a manager have?

Is there an optimal number? What needs to be considered is the nature of the work that subordinates are performing and how much attention each requires. For example a Call Center, the span of control can be numbers over 100, while executive functions - with high degrees of collaboration and interaction - could productively tolerate no more than three or four. So the nature of the work being performed, and how much attention it requires should govern the assignment of personnel to a manager, and not some industry ideal goal.

Expanding on the Concept of Span of Control

While we are addressing span of control, let's also broaden our understanding to see it in the context of the organizational structure levels of hierarchy.

- **Width.** Organization structures can be described as wide (with larger span of control) or narrow (with smaller span of control.)
- **Height.** As there are levels of management, or hierarchy, an organization may be tall (with many levels) or flat (with fewer levels.)

Flat organizations have a 'wide' span of control and Tall organizations have a 'narrow' span of control. While there are pros and cons with both tall and flat structures, a company's structure must be designed to suit the business (the customer and markets) and in a way that fits with the workforce's capability.

Characteristics of a Flat Organizational Structure (Wide Span of Control)

Pros

- **Encourages delegation.** Managers must better delegate to handle larger numbers of subordinates, and grant opportunities for subordinates to take on responsibilities.
- **Agile.** Improves communication speed and quality.
- **Reduces costs.** More cost effective because of fewer levels, thus requiring fewer managers.
- Helps prevent the workforce from disengaging by focusing on empowerment, autonomy and self-direction.

Cons

- High managerial workload comes with high Span of Control.
- Role confusion more likely.
- May cultivate distrust of management.

Characteristics of a Tall Organizational Structure (Narrow Span of Control)

Pros

- More rapid communication between small teams.
- Groups are smaller and easier to control/manage.
- There's a greater degree of specialization and division of labor.
- More and better opportunities for employee promotion.

Cons

- Communication can take too long, hampering decision-making.
- Silos may develop and prevent cross-functional problem solving.
- Employees may feel lost and powerless.

MANAGERIAL ECONOMICS

Introduction

Managerial Economics is defined as 'consisting of the use of economic modes of thought to analyse business situations.' Managerial Economics had its beginning in the early part of 1950's. It has progressively displaced the term business economics. It refers to the firm's decision making process. It may be taken as economics applied to problems of choice of alternatives of economic nature and allocation of the scarce resources by the firms.

Managerial Economics is more of an "Applied Economics" used in decision making. It bridges the gap between economic theory and managerial practices. It emphasises the use of economic analysis in clarifying problems, in organising and evaluating information and comparing alternative courses of action. To some, managerial economics is applied economics plus the application of economic theory and methodology to business administration practices. It uses the tools and techniques of economic analysis to solve business problems. It provides the link between traditional economics and the managerial decision making.

Economics is defined as the study of allocation of scarce resources among unlimited ends, whereas managerial economics is the study of allocation of the resources available to a firm or management. It is concerned with choice. It is goal-oriented and prescriptive and aims at maximising the achievement of objectives. Economic theory deals with a number of concepts relating to profit, demand, cost, pricing,

"*Managerial Economics consists of the use of economic model of thought to analyze business situation.*"

–Malcoln E. Mc-Nair and Richard S.

"*The purpose of managerial economics is to show how economic analysis can be used in formulating business policies.*"

–Joel Dean

"*Managerial Economics is a study of the behaviour of firms in theory and practice.*"

–Bates and Parkinson

"*Managerial economics is the integration of economic theory with business practice for the purpose of facilitating decision making and forward planning by management.*"

–Milton H. Spencer

"*Price theory in the service of business executives.*" **–Watson**

"*The application of economic theory and methodology to business administration practice.*"

–Brigham and Pappas

"*A fundamental academic subject which seeks to understand and to analyse the problems of business decision-making.*"

–Hague

business cycles, national income etc., and aided by accounting, statistics, operations research for solving problems of business management. The manner through which economic analysis is used to solve business problems constitutes the subject matter of managerial economics. Managerial economics can also be defined as normative micro-economics, which deals with smallest units, like individual consumers, single producer or a factor of production.

Managerial Economics derives tools and techniques from decision sciences to analyse business problems. To achieve pre-determined established goals, the managerial economics draws from the area of optimisation techniques and statistical tools are made use of for estimating relationship among important economic variables in decision making problems. Financing, production and sales are very important factors and their inter-relationships are to be studied and operation research provides the company with the necessary models.

In a sense, managerial economics provides a link between traditional economics and the decision sciences for managerial decision making.

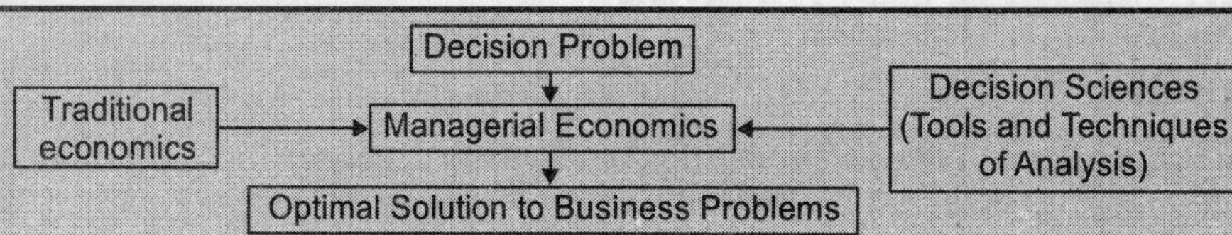

Nature of Managerial Economics

The nature of managerial economics consists of the following points :

(1) Identification of the problems and decision to be made.

(2) A statement of alternative solutions to the problems.

(3) A determination of what data is relevant to the decisions and an analysis of that data relative to the alternative solutions.

(4) Choosing the best solution consistent with the firm's or agency's objectives.

Chief Characteristics of Managerial Economics

(1) Managerial economics is micro-economic in character as it concentrates only on the study of the firm and not on the working of the economy.

(2) Managerial economics takes the help of macro-economics to understand and adjust to the environment in which the firm operates.

(3) Managerial economics is normative rather than positive in character.
(4) It is both conceptual and metrical.
(5) The contents of managerial economics are based mainly on the 'theory of firm'.
(6) Knowledge of managerial economics helps in making wise choices.

Scope of Managerial Economics

Managerial Economics has a wide scope and covers the following :

A. Demand Analysis and Forecasting
B. Production and Cost Analysis
C. Pricing decisions, Policies and Practices
D. National Income Analysis
E. Profit Management
F. Capital Management
G. Business Cycles (Economic Fluctuations) etc.

A. Demand Analysis and Forecasting

The business involves accurate estimation of demand both in the present and future. Demand analysis and forecasting form an integral part of managerial economics. The market demand schedule needs the study of individual demand of consumers. Consumer behaviour is an important part of demand analysis, which identifies various factors affecting demand, like price, incomes, substitutes, tastes, likes and dislikes, habits etc. On this basis, demand forecasting is made for specified period. A business firm is an economic organism, which transforms productive resources into goods to be sold in the market. A forecast of future sales and demand is very necessary for the preparation of production schedules. The forecast is also important for the firm for maintaining or strengthening market position and improving profits. Accuracy in demand forecasting is necessary for the firm to produce the required quantities and to arrange the various infrastructure in advance.

B. Production and Cost Analysis

The study of production and cost of firm is an essential part of managerial economics. Profit depends upon the total output and cost of production. To achieve maximum profits, the firms have to arrive at maximum output at minimum cost. Analysis of production and cost behaviour enables the business to take right decision to fulfill the objectives of maximum profits. The manager has to determine the optimum output where the cost of production is minimum. The cost estimates are useful for management decisions. Discovering economic cost and be able to measure them are necessary steps for more effective profit planning. Production analysis is in physical terms, while the cost analysis is in monetary terms. Cost concepts and classifications, cost-output relationships, economies and diseconomies of scale and production functions are some of the points constituting cost and production analysis.

C. Pricing Decisions, Policies and Practices

Pricing is the basis of revenue of a firm and it is price that is fixed that determines the profits and in turn the success of a business enterprise. Price determination; pricing methods; pricing policies; profit line pricing and price forecasting are important factors that constitute pricing decisions. Price of the product, other things remaining constant, determines the level of profits. The firm's decisions about price depend upon the market structure. Once the market structure is provided, the firm is free to follow any method or price fixation that will be equal to the cost or more.

D. National Income Analysis

The economic environment prevailing in a country decides the profits earned by a business firm. The economic conditions determine the demand for a product and the working operations of factors. A detailed analysis and study of the trends of national income and its components are very essential for managerial economics. Besides national income analysis, the nature and causes of trade cycles are also important factors to be studied.

E. Profit Management

Profit is consequence and causation factors are many like maximum output; cost minimisation; involvement of science and technology; good industrial relations etc. Profit making is the Universal objective of any firm. Production and profit always go together. There is always an element of uncertainty about profit due to variation in cost and revenues caused by internal and external factors. Thus, a study and nature of profits and theories of profits form the subject matter of managerial economics.

F. Capital Management

One of the major inputs in the productive process is capital and a very scarce factor of production. The future and prospects of business depend upon capital. It is the responsibility of the business firm to mobilise enough capital to the optimum point. A proper capital management includes efficient planning and control of capital expenditure. The most complex problem of a business enterprise is to find out sufficient capital investments. Cost of capital, rate of return and selection of projects are important factors.

G. Business Cycles (Economic Fluctuations)

Business conditions rarely stand still. Prosperity may be followed by panic or crash. National income, employment and production fall. Price and profits decline, and men are thrown out of work. Eventually the bottom is reached and revival begins. The recovery may be slow or fast. It may be incomplete or it may be strong as to lead to a boom. The new prosperity may represent a long, sustained plateau of brisk business demand and plentiful jobs, buoyant prices and increased living standards or it may represent a quick, inflationary flaring up of prices and speculation to be followed by another disastrous slump. This in brief is called Business cycles.

The economic progress of capitalistic economics has been marked by occasional fluctuations in the tempo of economic activity in the investment, in output, in income and in employment. The ideal equilibrium among the various economic magnitudes is never realised in practice. The dynamic forces operating in the economy create various kinds of business or economic fluctuations. Some fluctuations are sudden, isolated and discontinuous. Some are continuous for long periods in the same direction, while some others are rhythmic and recurring in nature. These economic fluctuations are as follows.

(i) Secular trends (ii) Seasonal trends (iii) Cyclical trends (iv) Random trends

Managerial economics can point out the role of business firms to improve the society's benefits. It helps the society in making the best use of scarce economic resources. Managers are helped to solve their problems of profit making and business promotions. Profit is the difference between total revenue and total cost. A manager can increase his profits either by decreasing cost or by increasing the revenue or both. 'The law of diminishing returns' and 'Returns to scale' help the managers to determine the level of output at which the unit cost is the minimum. Depending upon the models of price determination under various market conditions, the manager can sell the product at the highest profit level. Economics theory helps in determining the equilibrium point at which the firm can get maximum profits. Managerial economics also covers other disciplines like Mathematics, Statistics, Psychology, Sociology and Politics, which helps the manager to manage the firm efficiently and effectively. Mathematics helps to understand production techniques. Statistics helps to study the trends of cost, demand and prices. Politics helps to understand the political environment which can influence economic conditions in which the organisation has to operate. The business has to operate within the laws and regulations imposed by government.

The managerial economist can help the management relating to decision making and forward planning by supplying skills and techniques. Big 'Industrial Houses' make use of the services of managerial economists to determine the methodology and models that are necessary to improve the operational efficiency of their firms. A managerial economist can contribute effectively to the external and internal factors that affect the working operations of a business firm. The volume of trade, national income, output and price affect every organisation. The outlook of national economy, the demand prospects, the prices of raw materials and finished products, the government economic policies etc., all have an impact on the business firm. The managements seek the advise of managerial economists in meeting the situation. Even with regard to internal factors like sales and profit budgets, the wage and price structures, market research, capital projects, production programmes etc., the managerial economists can help.

Functions of Managerial Economics

As per K.J. Alexander and G.K. Alexander :

(1) Sale forecasting
(2) Industrial Market Research
(3) Economic Analysis of Competing Companies
(4) Pricing Problems of Industries
(5) Capital Projects
(6) Production Programmes
(7) Investment Analysis
(8) Forecasting
(9) Advice on Trade and Public Relations
(10) Advice on Foreign Exchange
(11) Advice of Primary Commodities
(12) Economic Analysis of Agriculture
(13) Analysis of under-development Economics
(14) Environmental Forecasting

DEMAND ANALYSIS

Concept of Demand

In managerial economics, we are concerned with demand for a commodity faced by the firm. This depends upon the size of the total market or industry demand for the commodity, k, which in turn is the sum of the demands for the commodity of the individual consumers in the market. Thus we begin by examining the theory of consumer demand in order to learn about the market demand on which the demand for the product faced by a particular firm depends.

Demand is one of the crucial requirements for the existence of any business enterprise. A firm is interested in its own profit and/or sales, both of which depend partially upon the demand for its product. The decision which management makes with respect to production, advertising, cost allocation, pricing etc., call for an analysis of demand.

Demand for a commodity refers to the quantity of the commodity which an individual household is willing to purchase per unit of time at a particular price.

Demand for a commodity implies:

- Desire to acquire it,
- Willingness to pay for it, and
- Ability to pay for it

Mere desire to buy a product is not demand. A miser's desire for and his ability to pay for a car is not demand because he does not have the necessary will to pay for it. Similarly, poor man's desire for and his willingness to pay for a car is not demand because he lacks the necessary purchasing power. One can also conceive of a person who possesses both the will and purchasing power to pay for a commodity, yet this is not demand for that commodity if he does not have desire to have that commodity.

Demand for a commodity has to be stated with reference to time, its price and that of related commodities, consumer's income and taste etc. Demand varies with fluctuations in these factors. Further it also depends on quality because if the quality changes it can be deemed as another commodity.

Determinants of Demand

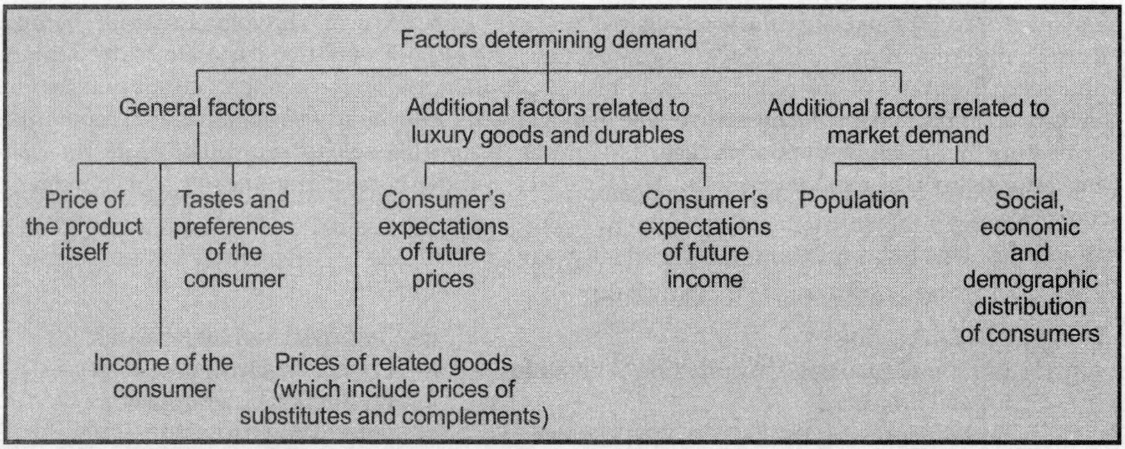

Let us discuss these demand determinants

(i) **Price of the Commodity.** We often find that a consumer buys more of a commodity when its price declines, and vice-versa. Thus, we can say that for a normal good the price of a commodity and its demand vary inversely, determinants other than the price of the commodity remaining constant. A fall in the price of a normal good leads to rise in consumer's purchasing power. He can, therefore, buy more of it (*Substitution effect*). Similarly, an increase in price will reduce his purchasing power and, thereby reducing demand for the commodity (*Income Effect*).

(ii) **Income of the Consumer.** With an increase in income, a household buys increased amount of most of the commodities in his consumption bundle though the extent of the increase may differ between commodities. Normally both the quantity demanded of a good and income of the household move in the same direction (shown as Oa curve in Fig.). However, in case of certain commodities like foods, fruits, vegetables, etc., the amount demanded increases with an increase in income, but beyond a certain level of income the amount demanded of the good remains unchanged even when income changes (Ob in Fig.). There are still some other commodities in whose case, beyond a point, the amount demanded even starts decreasing with further increases in income (Oc in Fig.). Such commodities in case of which amount demanded decreases with an increase in income and increases with a decrease in income after a particular level of income, are called *inferior goods.* The term inferior is not used here in the context of the quality of the commodity; it simply refers to the case of an exception to the normal income-demand relationship.

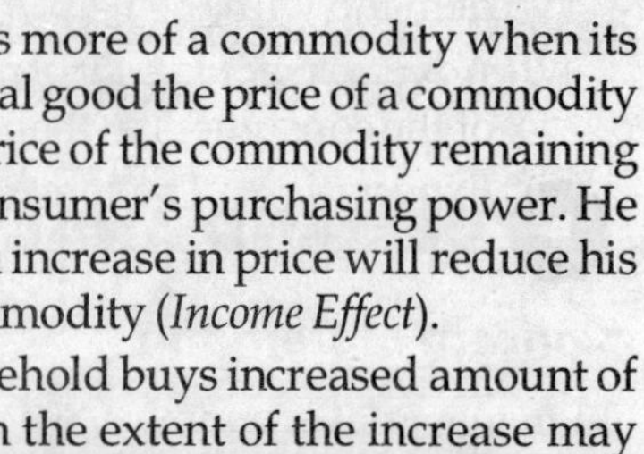

Income-Demand Relationship

(iii) **Prices of Related Goods.** When a change in the price of one commodity influences the demand of the other commodity, we say that the two commodities are related. These related commodities are of two types : substitutes and complements. When the price of one commodity and the quantity demanded of the other commodity move in the same direction (i.e., both increase together or decrease together), the two goods are called substitutes, e.g., apple and pears, tea and coffee, rail and road transport services, etc.

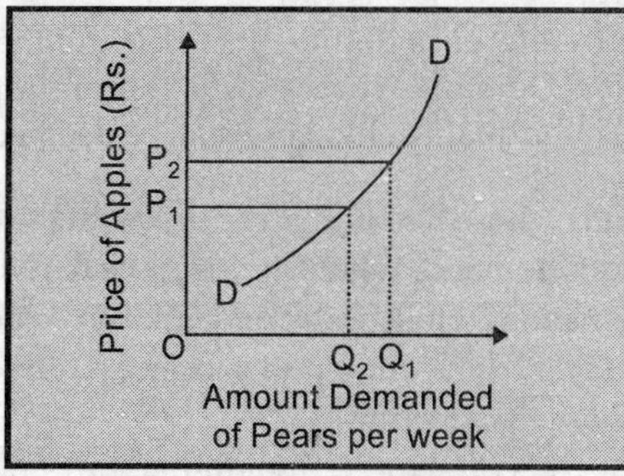

Substitute Goods Case.

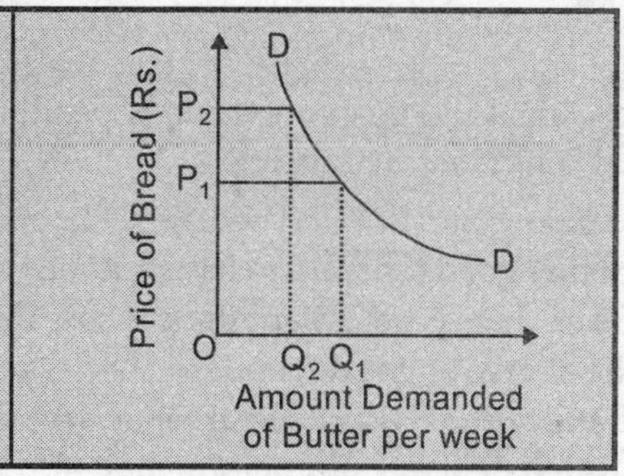

Complementary Goods case.

On the other hand, when price of one commodity and quantity demanded of the other commodity move in opposite direction, then the two commodities are said to be complementary to each other, e.g., bread and butter, pen and ink, petrol and automobiles, tea and sugar, etc.

(iv) **Tastes and Preferences.** We know it quite well that the change in tastes and preferences of a consumer in favour of a commodity results in greater demand for the commodity, while if this change is against the commodity it results in smaller demand for the commodity. For example, if jeans catch the fancy of consumers, the firms selling jeans will have greater demand now than before. Opposite will be the case if jeans go out of fashion. Modern business firms not only try to adjust to changes in market trends and fancies, they also try to influence the market demand with the help of their sales campaigns.

(v) **Advertisement.** A lot of money is spent on advertisement to influence the tastes and preferences of the consumers in their favour. This increases their sales.

(vi) **Expectations.** The consumers make two kinds of expectations:

(a) related to their future income; and

(b) related to future prices of the good and its related goods.

In case the consumer expects a higher income in future, he spends more at present, and thereby the demand for the good increases. Opposite will be the case, if he expects lower income in future. Similarly, if the consumer expects future prices of the good to increase, he would rather like to buy the commodity now than later. This will increase the demand for the commodity. Opposite holds good when it is expected that prices in future will come down.

Type of Demand

For a purposeful demand analysis for managerial decisions, it is necessary to classify the large number of goods and services available in every economy. Policy decisions are also facilitated by an understanding of demand at various levels of aggregation. A classification in these respects is as follows:

1. **Consumer goods and producer goods.** Goods and services used for final consumption are called consumer goods. These include, those consumed by human-beings, animals, birds etc. Producer goods refers to the goods used for production of other goods, like plant and machines, factory buildings, services of employees, raw materials etc.
2. **Perishable and durable goods.** Perishable goods become unusable after sometime, others are durable goods. Precisely, perishable goods are those which can be consumed only once while in durable goods, their services are only consumed. Durable goods pose more complicated problems for demand analysis than non-durables. Sales of non-durables are made largely to meet current demand which depends on current conditions. In contrast, sales of durable goods

go partly to satisfy new demand and partly to replace old items. Further, the latter set of goods are generally more expensive than the former set, and their demand alone is subject to preponement and postponement, depending on current market conditions vis-à-vis expected market conditions in future.

3. **Autonomous and derived demand.** The goods whose demand is not tied with the demand for some other goods are said to have autonomous demand, while the rest have derived demand. However, there is hardly anything whose demand is totally independent of any other demand. But the degree of this dependence varies widely from product to product. Thus, the autonomous and derived demand vary in degree more than in kind.
4. **Individual demand and market demand.** Market demand is the summation of demand for a good by all individual buyers in the market. For example, if the market of good X has, say only three buyers, then individual and market demand (monthly) could be as follows:

Demand of X.

Price of X	Buyer 1	Buyer 2	Buyer 3	All Buyers Market Demand
8	5	10	0	15
7	8	12	4	24
6	12	15	7	34
5	20	19	12	57
4	30	25	20	75
3	45	30	30	105

This can be shown by a graph as:

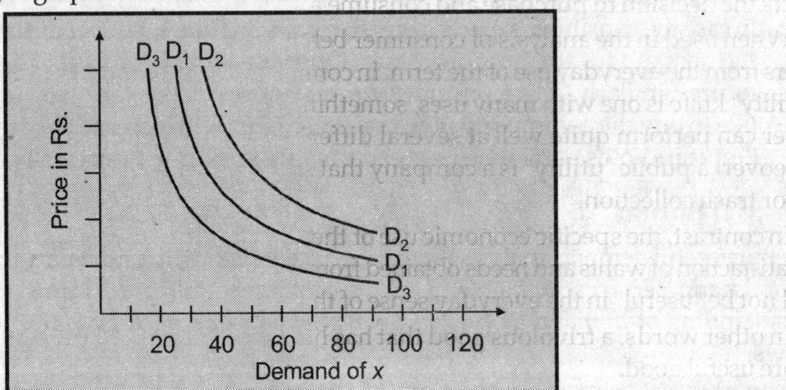

Individual Demand and Market Demand.

In Fig. D_1D_1 represents demand curve of buyer 1, D_2D_2 of buyer 2, D_3D_3 of buyer 3 and DD that of all three of them called the market demand curve. The market demand curve is thus the horizontal summation of individual demand curves. A firm would be interested in the market demand for its products while each consumer would be concerned basically with only his own individual demand.

5. **Firm and industry demand.** Goods are produced by more than one firm and so there is a difference between the demand facing an individual firm and that facing an industry. (All firms

producing a particular good constitute an industry engaged in the production of that good). For example, demand for Fiat car alone is a firm's demand and demand for all kinds of cars is industry's demand.

6. **Demand by market segments and by total market.** If the market is large in terms of geographical spread, product uses, distribution channels, customer sizes or product varieties, and if any one or more of these differences were significant in terms of product price, profit margins, competition, seasonal patterns or cyclical sensitivity, then it may be worthwhile to distinguish the market by specific segments for a meaningful analysis. In that case, the total demand would mean the total demand for the product from all market segments while a particular market segment demand would refer to demand for the product in that specific market segment.

UTILITY ANALYSIS

A subset of consumer demand theory that analysis consumer behavior and market demand using total utility and marginal utility. The key principle of utility analysis is the law of diminishing marginal utility, which offers an explanation for the law of demand and the negative slope of the demand curve.

Utility analysis, a subset of consumer demand theory, provides insight into an understanding of market demand and forms a cornerstone of modern microeconomics. In particular, this analysis investigates consumer behavior, especially market purchases, is based on the satisfaction of wants and needs (that is, utility) generated from the consumption of a good.

Utility analysis is primarily taught in introductory courses. A more sophisticated version of consumer demand theory relies on the analysis of indifference curves and is more commonly found at the intermediate course level and above.

Utility and Satisfaction

The primary focus of utility analysis is on the satisfaction of wants and needs obtained by the consumption of goods. This is technically termed utility. The utility generated from consumption affects the decision to purchase and consume a good.

When used in the analysis of consumer behavior, utility assumes a very precise meaning, which differs from the everyday use of the term. In common use, the term utility means "useful." For example, a "utility" knife is one with many uses, something that is handy to have around. In baseball, a "utility" player can perform quite well at several different positions and is thus useful to have on the team. Moreover, a public "utility" is a company that supplies a useful product, such as electricity, natural gas, or trash collection.

In contrast, the specific economic use of the term utility in the study of consumer behavior means the satisfaction of wants and needs obtained from the consumption of a commodity. The good consumed need not be "useful" in the everyday sense of the term. It only needs to provide satisfaction.

In other words, a frivolous good that has little or no practical use, can provide as much utility as a more useful good.

- An Omni Open Deluxe Can Opener is extremely useful, especially when a sealed can needs to be opened.
- An autographed photo of Brace Brickhead, Medical Detective, is not very useful. It does nothing but rest peacefully in a picture frame.

Both items, however, provide utility. Both items satisfy wants and needs. The OmniOpen Deluxe Can Opener obviously makes it possible to open cans of food which satisfy the hunger need. The autographed photo of Brace Brickhead provides the owner with a warm, fuzzy feeling and a reminder of the time spent enjoying the thrilling exploits of Brace Brickhead, Medical Detective.

The Law of Demand

The primary focus of utility analysis is an understanding of market demand and the law of demand. The law of demand, which gives rise to a negatively-sloped demand curve, is an essential principle underlying market analysis. Modern microeconomic theory, among other topics, is concerned with understanding and explaining the law of demand.

The explanation of the law of demand using utility analysis is relatively simple. Consumers purchase goods that satisfy wants and needs, that is, generate utility. Those goods that generate more utility are more valuable to consumers and thus buyers are willing to pay a higher price. The key to the law of demand is that the utility generated declines as the quantity consumed increases. As such, the demand price that buyers are willing to pay decreases as the quantity demanded increases.

Total Utility

Utility analysis begins with the total utility derived from the consumption of different quantities of a good. Total utility is simply a measure of the total satisfaction of wants and needs obtained from the consumption or use of a good or service. It is often convenient to present total utility for a range of quantities in a table such as the one displayed to the right.

Total Utility	
Rides	**Total Utlity (Util)**
0	0
1	11
2	20
3	27
4	32
5	35
6	36
7	35
8	32

Utility analysis is based on the presumption that the amount of utility generated from the consumption of a good can be explicitly measured. The standard hypothetical measurement unit is "utils."

Suppose, for example, that Edgar Millbottom spends a day riding the Monster Loop Death Plunge roller coaster at the Shady Valley Amusement Park, then records the amount of total utility achieved at the end of each ride. The two columns presented in the table measure the number of rides and the total utility accumulated by Edgar at the end of each ride (in utils).

- Before his first ride, Edgar receives no utility. No activity, no utility.
- Edgar's first ride generates 11 utils of utility.
- The total utility generated if Edgar takes 8 rides is 32 utils.
- Edgar's utility increases for the first 6 rides, reaching a high of 36 utils, before declining back to 32 utils for the 8th ride.
- Presumably Edgar's utility continues to decline after the 8th ride.
- Edgar obtains the highest total utility from 6 rides on the roller coaster.

The motivation that guides Edgar's roller coaster riding is to maximize utility, that is, to consume the quantity of the good that generates the highest level of utility. In this example, utility is maximized at 6 rides.

In many situations, however, the consumption of a good faces constraints. Edgar, for example, might face a time constraint because he plans to attend a live concert of the rock-and-roll group, Live Headless Squirrels, that prevents him from riding more than 4 times. Or he might face an income constraint because the amusement park charges $1 per ride and he has only $5 in his pocket.

In these situations Edgar, as well as other consumers, might pursue constrained utility maximization. This means achieving the highest possible utility, given certain restrictions that prevent the highest overall level of utility from being achieved.

Marginal Utility

Total utility is used as a starting point for utility analysis. However, a great deal of additional insight is gained from marginal utility. Marginal utility is the additional utility, or extra satisfaction of wants and needs, obtained from the consumption or use of an additional unit of a good or service. Marginal utility is, in other words, the extra satisfaction gained from an extra unit of good.

Marginal utility is specified as:

$$\text{Marginal utility} = \frac{\text{Change in total utility}}{\text{Change in quantity}}$$

If, for example, total utility increases from 20 to 27 utils, then marginal utility is 7 utils.

The far right column of this table presents marginal utility values derived from each ride Edgar undertakes. Marginal utility from the first ride is 11 utils. The extra utility generated by the second ride is 9 utils. The third ride provides another 7 utils. The remaining numbers in the right column are interpreted in a similar manner.

Marginal Utility

Rides	Total Utlity (Util)	Marginal Utlity (Util)
0	0	
1	11	11
2	20	9
3	27	7
4	32	5
5	35	3
6	36	1
7	35	–1
8	32	–3

Marginal utility provides a direct link between utility analysis and demand. The demand price a buyer is willing to pay for a given good is based on the marginal utility derived from consuming the good. In this example, Edgar is most likely willing is to pay more for the first ride than the fifth ride, in that the first ride generates 11 utils of satisfaction, but the fifth ride generates only 3 utils.

The Law of Diminishing Marginal Utility

A clear pattern is displayed by the marginal utility values in the far right column. Marginal utility decreases as Edgar takes more rides. This decreasing marginal utility reflects the law of diminishing marginal utility. The law of diminishing marginal utility states that marginal utility, or the extra utility obtained from consuming a good, decreases as the quantity consumed increases. In essence, each additional good consumed is less satisfying than the previous one. This law is particularly important for insight into market demand and the law of demand.

If each additional unit of a good is less satisfying, then a buyer is willing to pay less. As such, the demand price declines. This inverse law of demand relation between demand price and quantity demanded is a direct implication of the law of diminishing marginal utility.

Utility Maximization

The process or goal of obtaining the highest level of utility from the consumption of goods or services. The goal of maximizing utility is a key assumption underlying consumer behavior studied in consumer demand theory. Consumers are assumed to make choices, especially concerning the purchase of goods, such that they obtain the highest possible level of satisfaction. Utility maximization can be achieved at the peak of the total utility curve.

Utility maximization is the guiding notion underlying consumer choices analyzed with consumer demand theory and utility analysis. It makes sense to think that people are generally motivated to do what is best for them, to purchase the most satisfying goods, to make the decisions that do more good than harm, to improve their overall living standards and well-being, that is, to maximize their utility.

Working through the logical consequences of this assumption, when combined with other principles of consumer behavior especially the law of diminishing marginal utility, makes it possible to gain insight into such things market demand and the law of demand.

The Scarcity Connection

The utility maximization goal is based on the seemingly obvious presumption that people prefer more to less. This presumption is tied to the unlimited wants and needs aspect of scarcity. In other words, because people have unlimited wants and needs, satisfying those wants and needs is a desirable thing to do. Someone like Duncan Thurly would rather have a full belly than an empty one. He would rather live in a cozy, climate-controlled house than in a cardboard box under a bridge.

Of course, if wants and needs are unlimited, can anyone actually maximize utility? That is, can Duncan ever achieve the absolute pinnacle of satisfaction? Can he actually maximize utility. In terms of the scarcity problem, probably not. He might be able to boost utility a little higher by satisfying another unfulfilled want or need. But he is unlikely to maximize utility totally and completely. This is one reason why it is reasonable to think of utility maximization as a process of seeking what is ultimately unreachable.

However, in the analysis of consumer demand theory, utility maximization has a more pragmatic interpretation--obtaining the highest possible satisfaction from consuming a given good or undertaking a specific activity. While Duncan might not be able to maximize his OVERALL utility, he can maximize the utility obtained from eating Hot Momma Fudge Bananarama Ice Cream Sundaes. It is this pragmatic interpretation of utility maximization that pervades the study of economics.

Utility Analysis

The accompanying table can be used to illustrate utility maximization. The numbers indicate the total utility obtained by Edgar Millbottom while riding the Monster Loop Death Plunge roller coaster at the Shady Valley Amusement Park. The right-hand column is the accumulated satisfaction Edgar receives from riding the Monster Loop Death Plunge roller coaster 8 times during his day at the amusement park.

Roller Coaster Utility

Rides	Total Utlity (Util)
0	0
1	11
2	20
3	27
4	32
5	35
6	36
7	35
8	32

The numbers indicate that Edgar receives the greatest total utility, 36 utils, by riding the Monster Loop Death Plunge roller coaster 6 times. Click the [Utility Max] button to highlight this quantity. Taking 5 trips around the Monster Loop Death Plunge roller coaster track generates only 35 utils. Likewise, 7 rides generate only 35 utils. Maximum utility comes from 6 rides and only 6 rides. Anything else comes in less.

The Peak of the Curve

Utility maximization can be visually identified with a total utility curve, such as the one presented in this exhibit. In this case the maximum level of utility obtained by Edgar riding the Monster Loop Death Plunge roller coaster is relatively obvious. The total utility curve reaches its highest point for 6 roller coaster rides. the curve increases up to the sixth ride, then declines for subsequent rides.

Real World Constraints

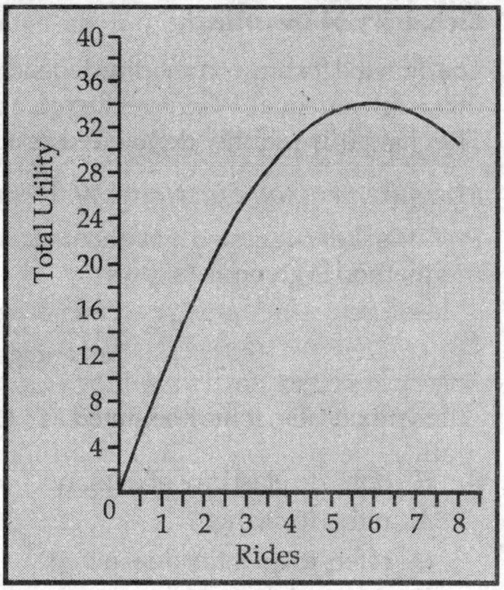

Total Utility Curve

In the real world, the goal of utility maximization often encounters obstacles that prevent obtaining the highest overall level of utility. In many circumstances, consumers are unable to reach the peak of the total utility curve. Under these circumstances, consumers face a constrained utility maximization.

The constraints could be physical or legal. For example, Edgar might not be able to ride the Monster Loop Death Plunge roller coaster 6 times because a bolt of lightning struck the track destroying a large section or perhaps the Shady Valley Amusement Park obtained a court order preventing Edgar for entering the park.

However, the constraints facing most consumers most of the time are economic--that is, they have limited income and cannot afford to buy as much of a good as they want. If Edgar is charged $1 per ride and has only $5 of cash, then he is not able to achieve the utility maximizing 6 rides.

The Essence of Life

While regular, everyday, noneconomist folks seldom use the term utility maximization, it is a powerful motivation force underlying a great deal (if not all) of the decisions people make and the actions they take. Again make note of the close connection between utility maximization, unlimited wants and needs, and the pervasive problem of scarcity.

While Duncan might buy a freshly prepared Hot Momma Fudge Bananarama Ice Cream Sundae because it just "sounds tasty," what he is really trying to do is to raise his utility level to its maximum. He is motivated to eat the hot fudge sundae because it adds more to his utility total. And if he can add to his utility total, then he is not AT the maximum.

Utility Measurement

A quantification of the satisfaction of wants and needs achieved through the consumption of goods and services. In principle, utility measurement can take one of two forms: (1) cardinal, which is based on numerical values (1, 2, 3, etc.) and (2) ordinal which is based on rankings (first, second, third, etc.). While the hypothetical instructional analysis of utility relies on cardinal utility, ordinal utility is a more realistic way to measure satisfaction.

Utility measurement provides a basis for discussing the satisfaction of wants and needs derived from consumption, which then enables an understanding of the role utility plays in market demand. When economists began looking into the influence utility has on price in the 1800s, they presumed that utility was a characteristic, like height and weight, that could be measured in a cardinal manner.

However, as the study of consumer demand theory progressed, economists realized that cardinal utility was both unlikely and unneeded. Ordinal utility, the ranking or preferences, was not only more realistic, it also provided a sufficient theoretical basis for analyzing the connection between utility and market demand.

Cardinal Utility

Cardinal utility is the measurement of satisfaction using numerical values (1, 2, 3, etc.) that are comparable and based on a benchmark or scale. Height and weight are common cardinal measures.

Elasticity of Demand

The demand for any commodity depends upon the price of the commodity, with the condition that other things remain equal. Whenever there is a change in price, there is also a change in the quantity demanded. The change in quantity demanded as a result of change in price is known as elasticity of demand.

Measurement of Elasticity of Demand

Prof. Marshall suggested a mathematical method for measuring elasticity of demand. The formula for this method is given as follows :

$$E = \frac{\text{Percentage change in demand for a product}}{\text{Percentage change in the price of the product}}$$

Symbolically, it may be stated as : $E = \dfrac{\Delta Q/Q}{\Delta Z/Z} = \dfrac{\Delta Q}{\Delta Z} \cdot \dfrac{Z}{Q}$

E refers to elasticity of demand

Δ refers to change

Q refers to quantity demanded

Z demand determinant which may be one of the following :

(i) current price of the commodity (P_x), (ii) current price of related good (P_R),
(iii) current income (Y), (iv) the expected price of the commodity (EP_x), and
(v) Advertisement expenditure (A), etc.

The formula states that the elasticity of demand refers to the percentage change in demand as a result of a percentage change in price. The percentage change in demand for a product is expressed as:

$$\frac{\text{Change in Demand}}{\text{Original Demand}} \times 100$$

Likewise, the percentage change in price for product is expressed as : $\dfrac{\text{Change in Price}}{\text{Original Price}} \times 100$

The elasticity formula is thus rewritten as follows :

$$E = \frac{\dfrac{\text{Change in Demand}}{\text{Original Demand}} \times 100}{\dfrac{\text{Change in Price}}{\text{Original Price}} \times 100}$$

$$E = \frac{\text{Change in Demand}}{\text{Original Demand}} \times \frac{\text{Original Price}}{\text{Change in Price}}$$

By re-arranging this formula, we will get

$$E = \frac{\text{Change in Demand}}{\text{Change in Price}} \times \frac{\text{Original Price}}{\text{Original Demand}}$$

Factors Determining Elasticity of Demand

The Elasticity of demand is based on :

(1) Nature of commodity
(2) Extent of use
(3) Range of substitutes
(4) Income level
(5) Proportion of income spent on the commodity
(6) Urgency of demand
(7) Durability of the commodity
(8) Influence of price
(9) Joint demand
(10) Government policy

ARC and Point Elasticity Measurements

There are two kinds of elasticity measurement: (1) Point elasticity; (2) Arc elasticity.

Point elasticity of demand relates to the elasticity at a particular point on the demand curve, while arc elasticity of demand is the average elasticity over a segment of the demand curve, *i.e.*, average of the demand curve.

Point Elasticity. The formula of elasticity of demand for point elasticity is

$$\varepsilon = \frac{\Delta Q}{\Delta Z} \cdot \frac{Z}{Q}$$

If ΔZ is taken as very small, $\Delta Q/\Delta Z$ approximates to the slope of the demand curve in the neighbourhood of original Z and Q. In other words, when ΔZ approaches its limit of zero, then $\lim_{\Delta Z \to 0} \frac{\Delta Q}{\Delta Z}$ becomes $\frac{dQ}{dZ}$. Thus

$$\varepsilon = \frac{dQ}{dZ} \cdot \frac{Z}{Q}$$

Arc Elasticity. If instead of measuring elasticity by taking $\Delta Z \to 0$ (as we do in case of point elasticity), we measure it over larger segment of the demand curve, we get arc elasticity measure. The arc elasticity is the measure of average elasticity, *i.e.*, it is the elasticity at the mid-point of the chord that connects the initial and new point on the demand curve (Fig.). In the figure the end points of the arc are (P_1, Q_1) and (P_2, Q_2).

Coordinates of mid-point would, therefore, be $\left(\frac{P_1 + P_2}{2}, \frac{Q_1 + Q_2}{2}\right)$. The change between the end points would be ΔP and ΔQ. The elasticity at the mid-point of the arc (*i.e.*, Arc Elasticity) would be:

$$E = \frac{\Delta Q}{\left(\frac{Q_1 + Q_2}{2}\right)} \div \frac{\Delta P}{\left(\frac{P_1 + P_2}{2}\right)} = \frac{\Delta Q}{(Q_1 + Q_2)} \cdot \frac{(P_1 + P_2)}{\Delta P}$$

$$= \frac{\Delta Q}{\Delta P} \cdot \frac{P_1 + P_2}{Q_1 + Q_2}$$

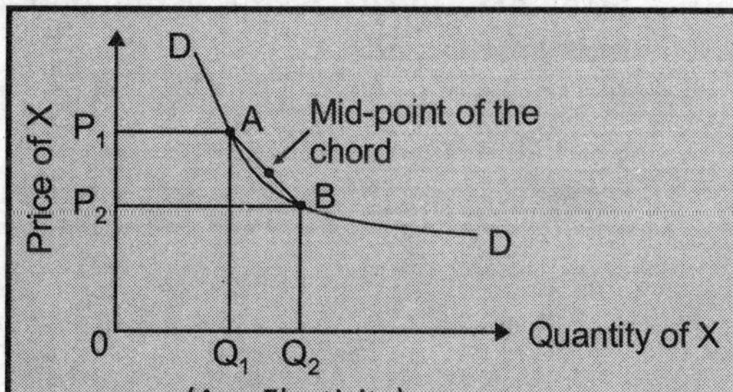

(Arc Elasticity)

Types of Elasticity of Demand

1. Price Elasticity of Demand. The elasticity (or responsiveness) of demand in a market is great or small, as the amount demanded increases more or less for a given fall in price and diminishes much or less for a given rise in price. It can be computed by:

$$e_p = \frac{\frac{\text{Change in the Quantity Demand}}{\text{Quantity Demand}}}{\frac{\text{Change in Price}}{\text{Price}}}$$

$$= -\frac{(Q_2 - Q_1)/Q_1}{(P_2 - P_1)/P_1}$$

$$= -\frac{\Delta Q/Q_1}{\Delta P/P_1} = -\frac{\Delta Q}{Q_1} \cdot \frac{P_1}{\Delta P} = -\frac{\Delta Q}{\Delta P} \cdot \frac{P_1}{Q_1}$$

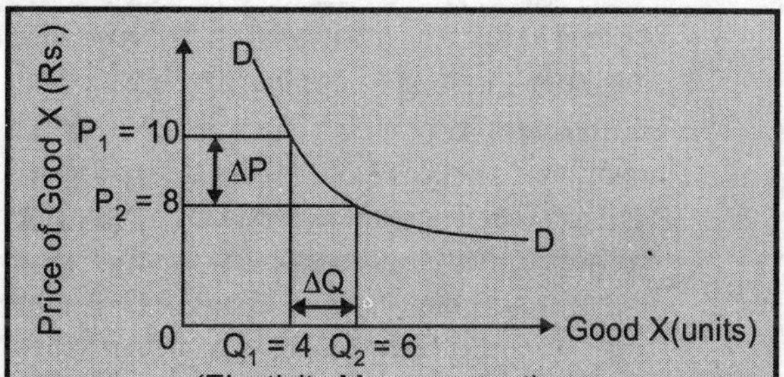

(Elasticity Measurement)

In figure, DD is the demand curve for a consumer for good X. At price = Rs. 10, 4 units of good X are demanded. When price goes down to Rs 8, quantity demanded increases to 6. So $\Delta P = 8 - 10 = -2$, and $\Delta Q = 6 - 4 = 2$, and

$$E = -\frac{\Delta Q}{\Delta P} \cdot \frac{P}{Q} = -\left(\frac{2}{-2}\right)\left(\frac{10}{4}\right) = 2.5$$

Higher the elasticity of demand, greater will be the percentage change in quantity demanded for every percentage change in price.

(i) **Perfect Elastic Demand** ($E = \infty$). This is a situation where no reduction in price is needed to cause an increase in demand.

(ii) **Perfect Inelastic Demand** ($E = 0$). In this situation a change in price causes no change in quantity demanded. When the quantity demanded of a commodity remains the same, irrespective of any rise or fall in price of a commodity, then the demand is perfectly inelastic.

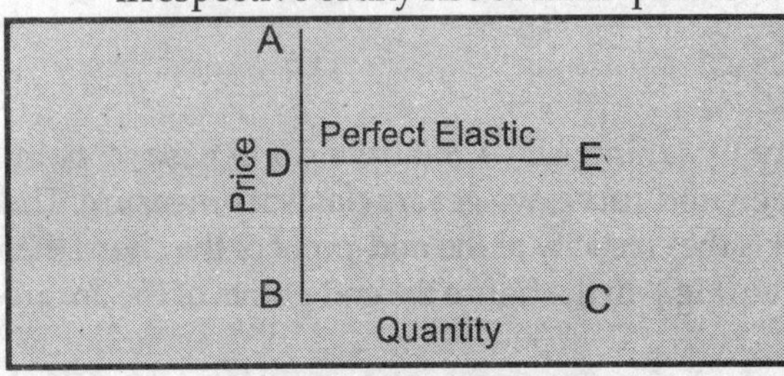

Perfect Elastic Demand.

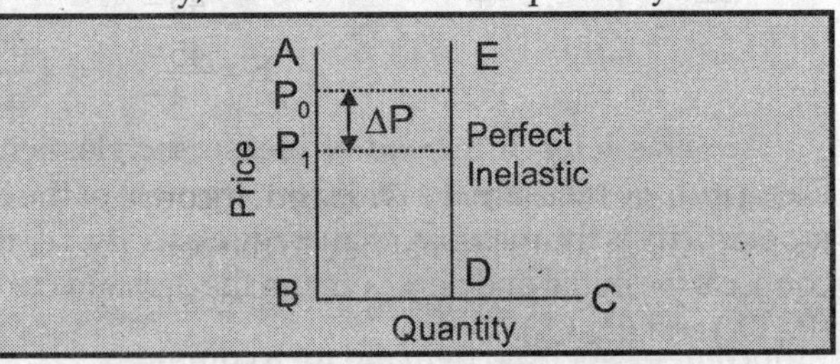

Perfect Inelastic Demand.

(iii) **Unit Elastic Demand** ($E = 1$). This is a situation when a given proportionate change in price causes equal proportionate change in the quantity demanded. If the price of commodity A goes up by 20%, and if it results in the contraction of demand by exactly 20%, demand curve slopes from left to right.

(iv) **Relatively More Elastic Demand** ($E > 1$). This is a situation when reduction in a price leads to more than proportionate change in demand. A proportionate fall in price accompanied by a relatively large proportionate increase in the quality demanded and vice-versa.

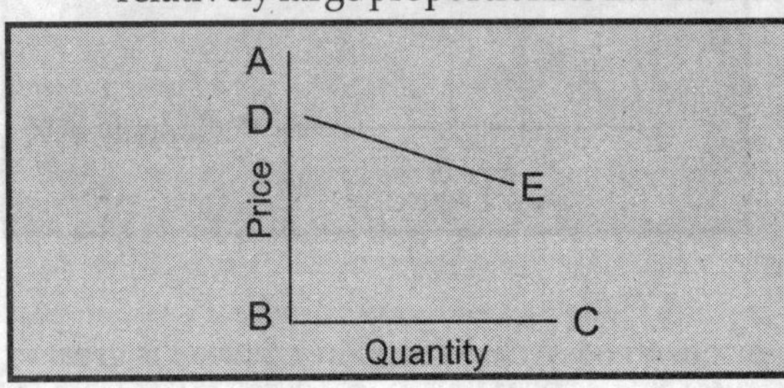

Unity of Elasticity Demand.

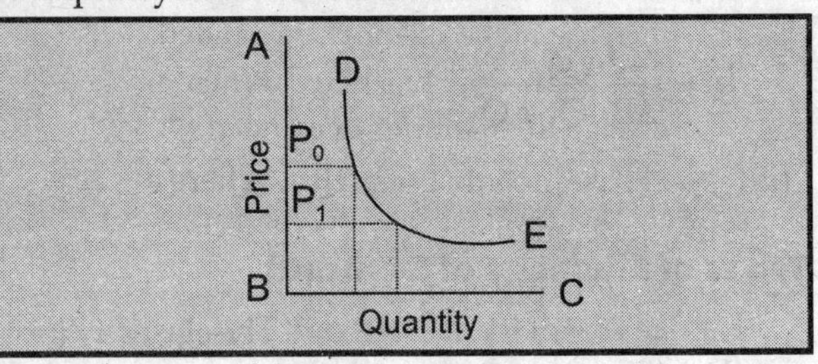

Relatively More Elastic Demand.

Demand is more sensitive to price changes and change in price brings about a large distortion in demand. The demand curve would be more inclined to appear like horizontal curve.

(v) **Relatively Inelastic Demand** ($E < 1$). This is a situation when a reduction in price leads to less than proportionate change in demand. Demand is in-elastic when a given proportionate fall in the price of a commodity causes a relatively small proportionate increase in the quantity demanded and vice-versa. In such a situation, the demand curve would be inclined to look vertical and look more parallel to AB axis.

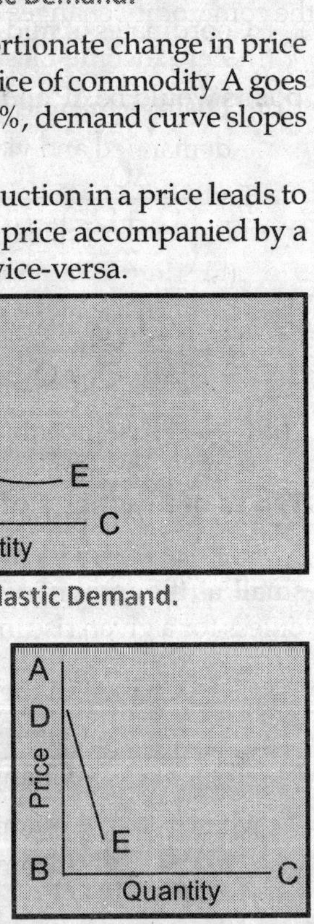

Relatively Inelastic Demand.

If the prices go-up by 50%, the demand reduces by less than 50%.

Example. Find Price elasticity of demand at price Rs 7, when price and quantity demanded behave in the following manner:

Price (P) (Rs per kg)	9	8	7	6	5	4	3	2	1
Quantity demanded (Q) (kgs)	5	15	20	30	36	45	55	70	90

Solution. The point elasticity of demand with price change from Rs 7 to Rs 6 (*i.e.*, $P_1 = 7$ and $P_2 = 6$) is

$$E = -\frac{\Delta Q}{\Delta P}\cdot\frac{P}{Q} = -\frac{10}{-1}\times\frac{7}{20} = \frac{7}{2} = 3.5$$

The arc elasticity of demand, for example, with $P_1 = 7$ and $P_2 = 4$ (*i.e.*, when price change is appreciable)

$$E = \frac{\frac{45-20}{45+20}}{\frac{4-7}{4+7}} = -\frac{25}{65}\times\frac{11}{-3} = 1.4$$

2. Income Elasticity of Demand. Income elasticity of demand means the ratio of the percentage change in the quantity demanded to the percentage change in income. The income elasticity measures the responsiveness of demand to changes in income.

Income elasticity of demand for a commodity shows the extent to which a consumer's demand for the commodity changes as a result of the change in his income.

(i) **Zero Income Elasticity.** When a change in income has no effect on the quantities demanded.

(ii) **Positive Income Elasticity.** Where an increase in income may lead to an increase in quantities demanded and vice versa.

(a) **Unit Elasticity.** When the increase in income brings about a proportionate change in the quantities demanded.

(b) **More than unit Elasticity.** When an increase in income brings about more than proportionate increase in the quantity demanded.

(c) **Less than unit Elasticity.** When an increase in income brings about less than proportionate change in quantities demanded.

(iii) **Negative Income Elasticity.** Where an increase in income may lead to a reduction in the quantity demanded.

It can be expressed as:

$$e_y = \frac{\frac{\text{Change in the Quantity Demand}}{\text{Quantity Demand}}}{\frac{\text{Change in Income}}{\text{Income}}}$$

or,

$$e_y = \frac{\Delta q_x}{q_x} \Big/ \frac{\Delta y}{y} = \frac{\Delta q_x}{\Delta y} \Big/ \frac{y}{q_x}$$

where q_x = quantity demanded of X, and

y = income level of consumer

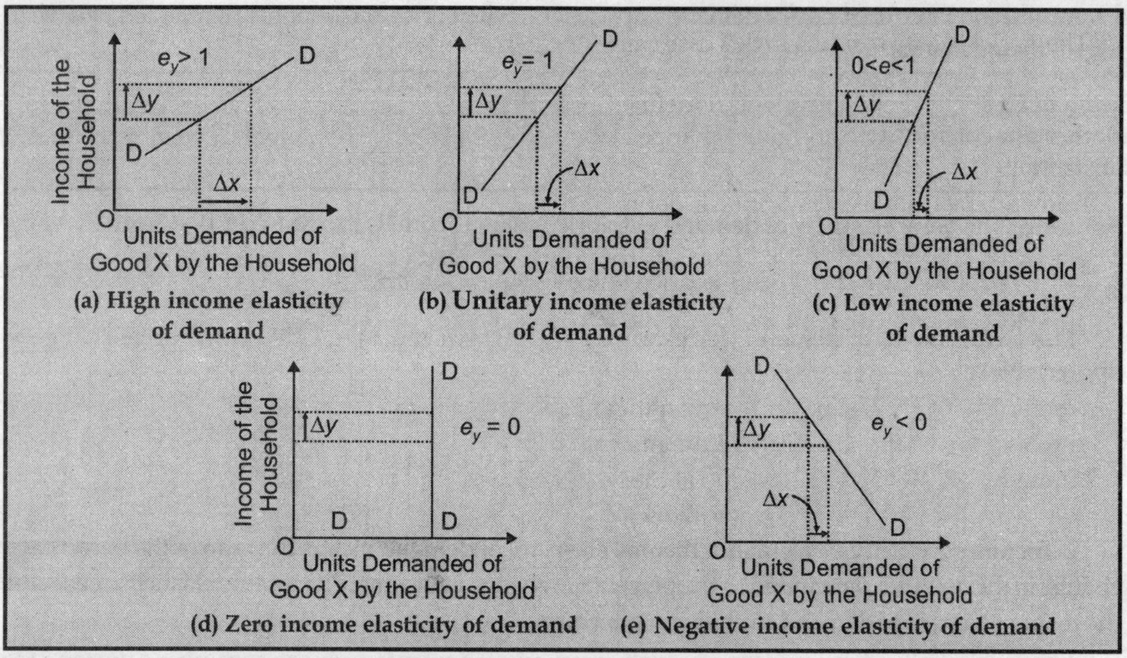

Types of Income Elasticities of Demand.

3. Cross Elasticity of Demand. The cross elasticity of demand refers to a change in the demand for a product due to the changes in the price of a related product (which could be a substitute or complimentary). If the cross elasticity is positive, the related commodity is a "substitute" and if the cross elasticity is "negative" the related commodity is 'complimentary'. Thus, the price of one commodity is the independent variable, where as the quantity of another commodity is a dependent variable.

It is defined as the ratio of the percentage change in demand for one good due to a change in the price of some other related good. Once we assume that two commodities X and Y are related, the expression of cross elasticity of demand would be:

$$e_{xy} = \frac{\Delta q_x}{q_x} \div \frac{\Delta p_y}{p_y} = \frac{\Delta q_x}{\Delta p_y} \times \frac{p_y}{q_x}$$

e_{xy} will have +ve sign if two goods are substitutes

e_{xy} will have –ve sign if two goods are substitutes

For substitutes $o < e_{xy} < \infty$

For complements $-\infty < e_{xy} < 0$

4. Advertising Elasticity. The responsiveness of demand to change in advertising or rather promotional expenses is known as advertising elasticity. It can be expressed as :

$$e_a = \frac{\dfrac{\text{Change in Sales}}{\text{Sales}}}{\dfrac{\text{Change in Advertisment Expenditure}}{\text{Advertisment Expenditure}}}$$

$$e_a = \frac{\Delta Q}{\Delta A} \cdot \frac{A}{Q}$$

where Q = quantity of good × sold, and A = units of advertising expenditure on good X.

The Arc elasticity formula in this case can be written as: $e_a = \dfrac{(Q_2 - Q_1)(A_2 + A_1)}{(Q_2 + Q_1)(A_2 - A_1)}$

Demand Elasticity of Substitution. It is defined as the degree to which one good can be substituted for another as a consequence of a given change in their price ratio, if the consumer is to enjoy the same satisfaction.

Demand elasticity of substitution is defined as

$$\sigma = \frac{\text{Proportionate change in the quantity ratios of goods X and Y}}{\text{Proportionate change in the price ratios of goods X and Y}}$$

$$= \frac{\Delta(Q_x / Q_y)}{(Q_x / Q_y)} \div \frac{\Delta(P_x / P_y)}{(P_x / P_y)}$$

where, (Q_x/Q_y) is the ratio of the quantities of goods Q_x and Q_y
and $\Delta(Q_x/Q_y)$ is the change in the quantity ratio.
Similarly, (P_x/P_y) is the price ratio of the two goods and
$\Delta(P_x/P_y)$ is the change in the price ratio.
ForInfinite substitution elasticity $(\sigma = \infty)$
Zero substitution elasticity $(\sigma = 0)$; High and low substitution elasticity $(0 < \sigma_s < \infty)$

Demand Forecasting

"Demand forecasting is an estimate of sales in monetary or physical units for a specified future period under a proposed marketing plan or programme and under an assumed set of economic and other forces outside the unit for which the forecast is made."

Steps Involved in Forecasting

The following steps are necessary to have an efficient forecast of demand :

Step I. Identification of objective. It is necessary to be clear about what does one want to get from the forecast. The purpose of the exercise may be the estimation of one or more than one aspect, like quantity and composition of demand, price to be quoted, sales planning, inventory control, etc. The approach to the problem will accordingly differ.

Step II. Determining the nature of goods under consideration. Different category of goods have their own distinctive demand patterns. It is, therefore, necessary to determine the class in which the good falls; these being broadly : the capital goods, consumer durables and non-durables. This will help us in identifying the approach of the forecasting exercise and in determining the variables to be considered for forecasting.

Step III. Selecting a proper method of forecasting. The selection of an appropriate method of forecasting is related to the objective of forecasting, type of data available, period for which the forecasting is to be made, etc. For example, if the data shows cyclic fluctuations, the use of linear trend will not be suitable. Similarly, general trend may be more useful for long-run forecasting, while seasonal patterns will be more important for the short-run forecasts.

Step IV. Interpretation of results. Mere preparation of forecasts does not lead the management anywhere. Interpretation of results is of equal importance. Efficiency of a forecast depends, to a large extent, upon the efficiency in the interpretation of its results. Most of the times, the forecasted results are to be well-supported by the background factors (like government policy, general business environment, international economic and political scene, etc.), which have not entered the exercise of forecasting. Further, we need to frequently revise the forecasts in the light of changing circumstances because forecasts are, in the first instance, made on the assumption of continuation of past events.

Factors of Demand Forecasting

(1) Period of estimating
(2) Level of forecasting
(3) Adjustment
(4) Specific factors
(5) Age of commodity
(6) Nature of commodity

Methods of Demand Forecasting

(1) Evolutionary Method
(2) Substitute Method
(3) Growth Curve Method
(4) Opinion Polling Method
(5) Sales Experience Approach
(6) Correlation Method
(7) Controlled Experiments
(8) Economic Indicators Methods

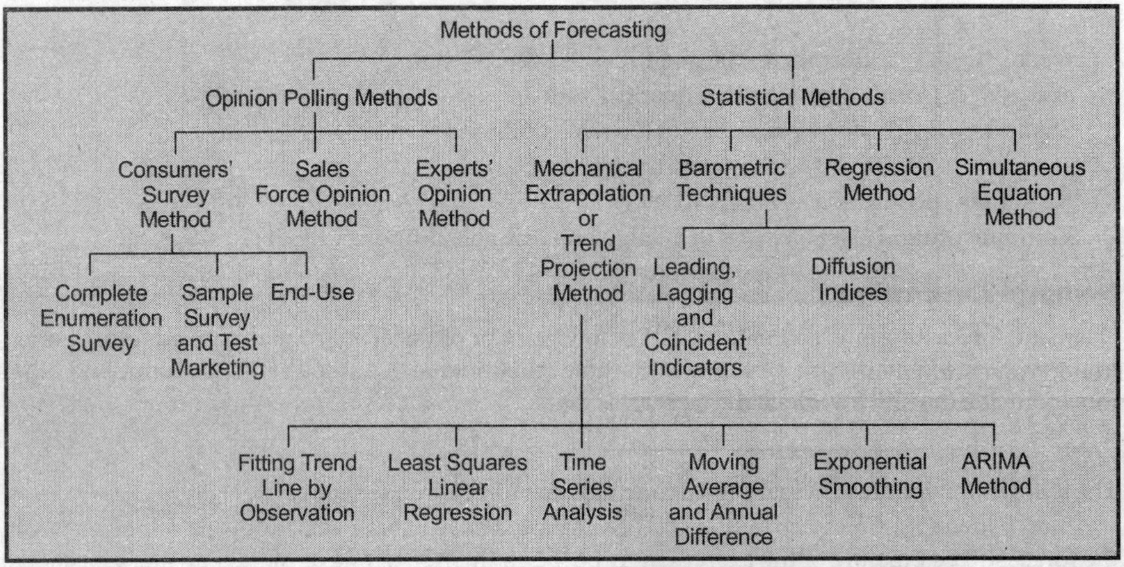

Indifference Curve Analysis

This approach has been developed by the economists like Hicks and Allen. Assuming ordinal measurement of utility and relatedness of goods and relaxing the assumption of constant marginal utility of money, the technique of indifference analysis has been developed.

Derivation of the Demand Curve using Indifference curve Teaching

Let us assume that there is only a single good X and that the consumer has an income of Rs 500 which he can spend on this good. So, the consumer has a choice to spend the entire or a part of his income on good X. As he spends less income he consumes lesser amount of X but saves some money. In the limit, when he spends nothing he gets no X at all. By joining all such combinations of money income and good X, we can get a budget line.

As the price of X declines the budget line shifts outwards from A_1B_1 to A_2B_2 and to A_3B_3. With every shift in the budget line we get a new equilibrium point (E_1, E_2 and E_3). At E_1 the consumer buys 40 units of X and has Rs 100 left with him. In other words, the consumer spends Rs 400 (= Rs 500 – Rs 100) to buy 40 units of X *i.e.*, P_x = Rs 400/40 = Rs 40. In a similar manner we can find that at equilibrium E_2 the consumer buys 50 units of X at P_x = Rs 7; at equilibrium E_3 he buys 60 units of X at price of Rs 5. When we plot combinations of quantity demanded and price of good X and join these points by a line, we get a demand curve (DD).

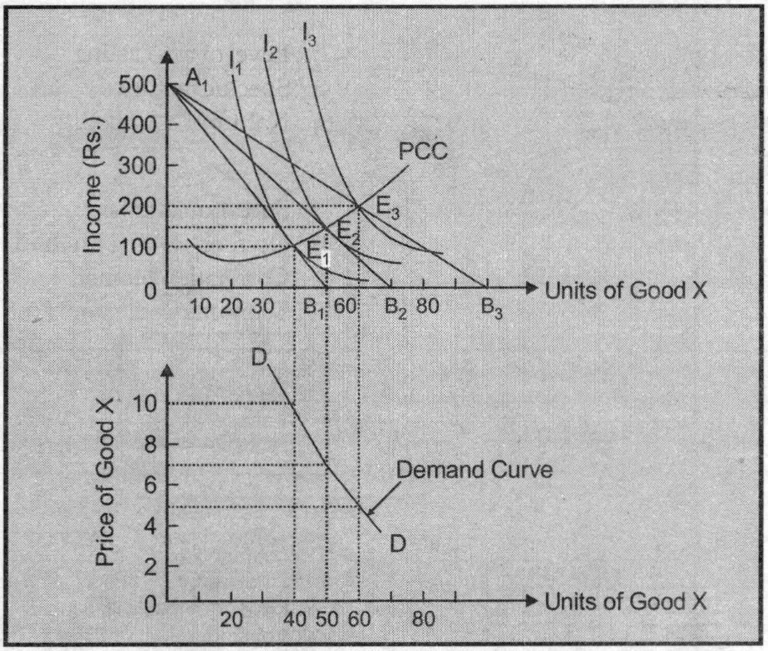

Figure. Derivation of a Demand Curve.

Trend Projection

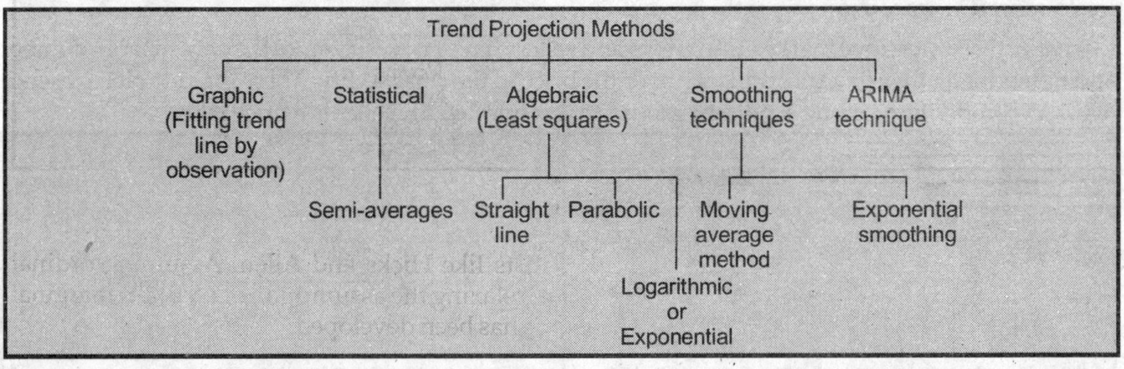

MARKET STRUCTURES

According to Prof. Sidgwick, "A market is a body of persons in such commercial relations that each can easily acquaint himself with the rate at which certain kinds of exchange of goods and services are from time to time made by the other."

Market structure refers to the number and size distribution of buyers and sellers in the market for goods or services.

Classification

A market consists of all firms and individuals who are willing and able to buy or sell a particular product. This includes firms and individuals currently engaged in buying and selling and potential entrants. Markets are traditionally divided into four basic classifications, like :

(1) Perfect competition
(2) Perfect monopoly
(3) Monopolistic competition
(4) Oligopoly

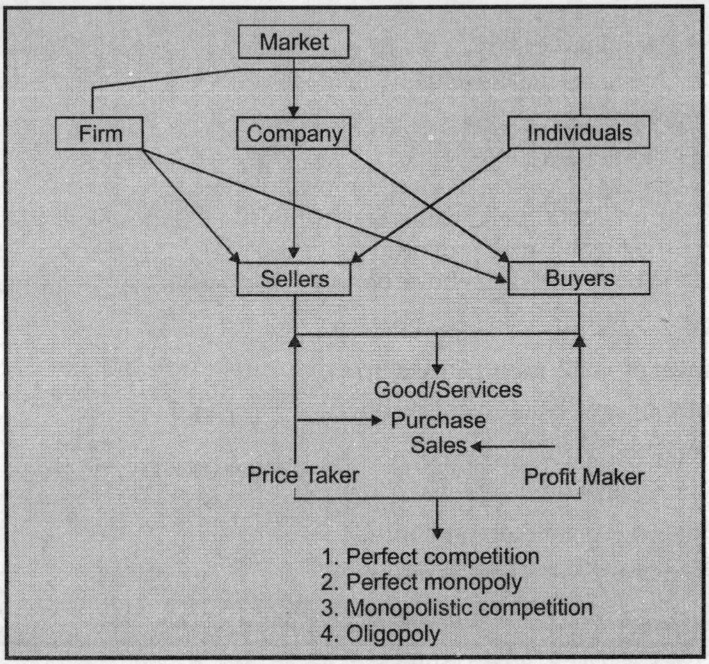

Market Structure.

A. Perfect Competition

In a perfectly competitive market, the buyers and sellers have no rivalry since they are in large number and individually they have no influence over the price of the commodity. There is a complete absence of direct competition among economic group. In this market, the seller is a price taker.

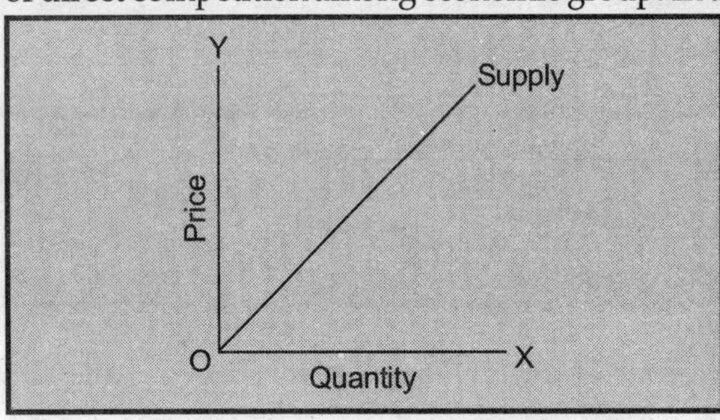

Supply Curve in Perfect Competition.

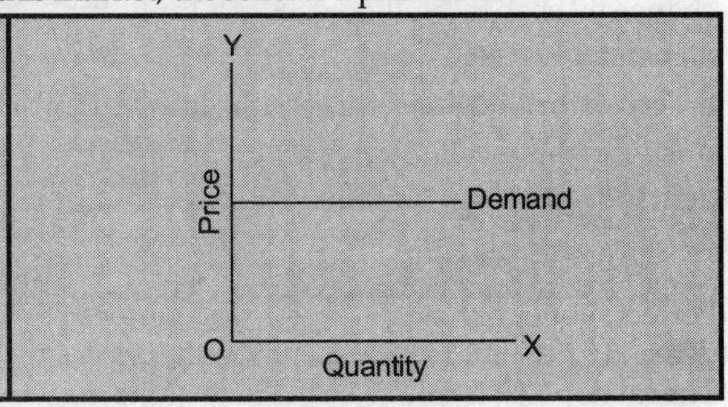

Demand Curve in Perfect Competition.

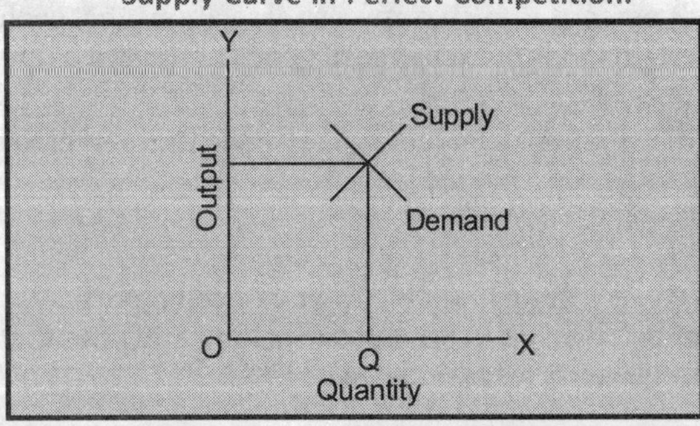

Market Price determination Perfect Competition.

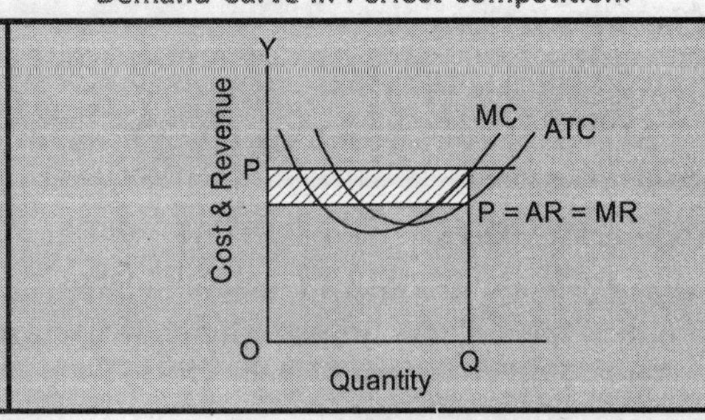

Price Output Competition.

where

MC = Marginal Cost

ATC = Average Total Revenue

P = Price

MR = Marginal Revenue

According to *Mrs. Joan Robinson,* "Perfect competition prevails when the demand for the output of each producer is perfect elastic. This entails, first that the number of sellers is large, so that the output of any one seller is a negligibly small proportion of the total output of the commodity, and second, that buyers are all alike in respect of their choice between rival sellers, so that the market is perfect."

Characteristics

(i) Large number of small, un-organised firms

(ii) Large number of small, un-organised buyers.

(iii) Existence of homogeneous products.

(iv) Free entry and exit of firms.

(v) Perfect knowledge of market conditions.

(vi) The goods and services as well as resources are to be perfectly mobile between firms.

(vii) All the firms should enjoy easy access to the market.

(viii) There should be absence of government or artificial restriction on the working of the firms.

Pricing under Perfect Competitions

Price under perfect competition is determined by the laws of supply and demand. The action and the inter-action of the forces of demand and supply determine price under perfect competition. Prices will be fixed at a point where the supply and demand are at an equilibrium, and this equilibrium will change by changes in the forces of supply and demand. The demand side is governed by the law of demand based on marginal utility of the commodity to the buyers; and the supply side is governed by the cost of production. So to say, the interaction of marginal supply and marginal demand decides the price and this is called equilibrium price and at this point, the buyers and sellers are satisfied and the demand and supply are equal.

B. Perfect Monopoly

Perfect monopoly means absence of competition. Under monopoly the cross elasticity is zero. The demand for a commodity depends on the prices of related goods, which are substitutes and complements. The monopolist is said to be the king of the market. He rules the market with his price.

Characteristics

(i) A perfect monopoly is a combination of several producers and they agree to produce a given output and to charge a given price.

(ii) Perfect monopoly avoids cut-throat competition and its attendant evils.

(iii) It possesses strong bargaining powers to purchase commodities at low prices.

(iv) It enjoys the benefit of large scale marketing.

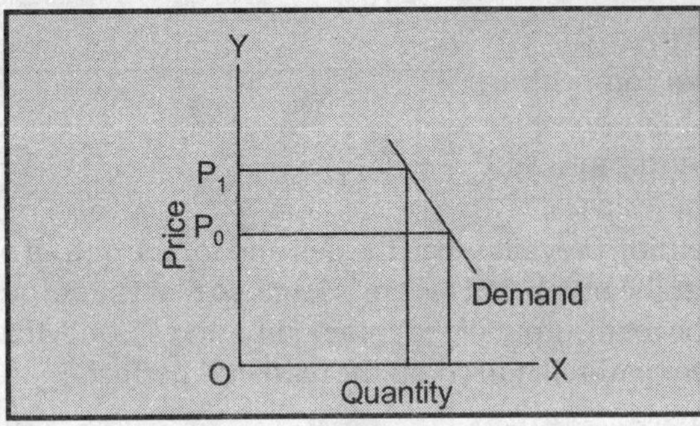

The Firm's Demand Carve and Monopoly

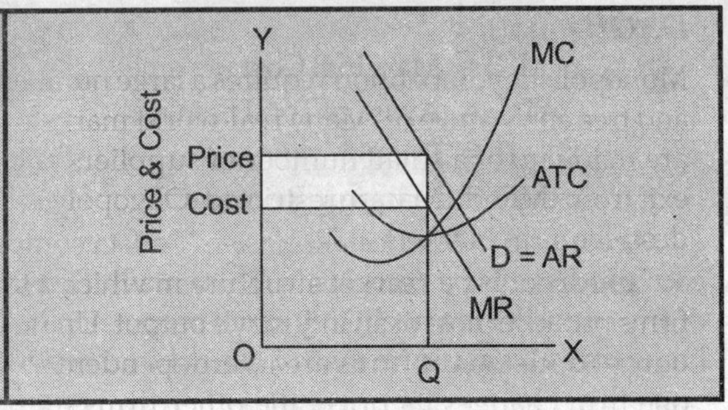

Price Output Decision under Monopoly

C. Monopolistic Competition

Monopolistic competition refers to markets in which there are a large number of firms competing supplying product which consumers believe are close but not complete substitutes. Monopolistic competition is analogous to perfect competition expect for the element of product differentiation.

According to Leftwithch, "Monopolistic competition is a market situation in which there are many sellers of a particular product but the product of each seller is in some way differentiated in the minds of consumers from the product of every other seller."

Monopolistic competition is a market structure quite similar to pure competition but distinguished from it by the fact that consumers perceive difference among the products of different firms. Firms have some control over the prices at which they sell their products. As in pure competition, above normal profit are attainable only in the short run.

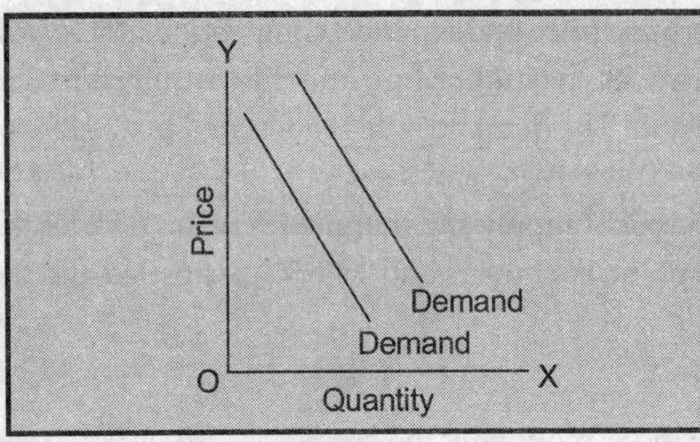

Relationship between Product Differentiation and Demand.

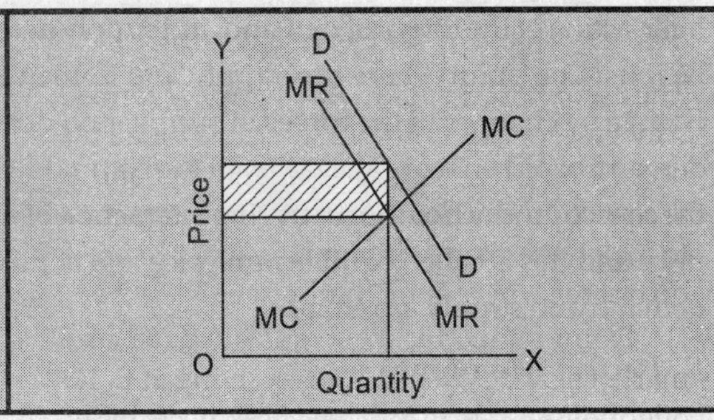

Elasticity O'- Equality of Marginal Cost and Marginal Revenue.

Characteristics

(1) Single seller or producer

(2) No close substitutes

(3) Effective check on the entry of new firms in industry

(4) One firm one industry

(5) Inelastic demand curve

(6) Complete control over the supply of commodity

(7) Profit in the long period

(8) A large number of buyers

D. Oligopoly

Monopolistic competition requires a large number of competitors and free entry and exit. Many real-world markets today, however are made up of a small number of suppliers and entry into and exit from the industry are restricted. Oligopoly is the term used to describe such markets.

Oligopoly is a market structure in which a small number of firms produce most of an industry's output. Under oligopoly, price output decisions of firms are interdependent in the sense that if one firm changes its price, the other firms may react, and this knowledge is incorporated into the price/output decision problem. In oligopoly, as in the case of monopoly, barriers to entry can be substantial and it may be possible for firms to earn above normal profits, even in the long run. In other instances, competition among a few firms can be rigorous, and above normal profits may only be observed in the short run. The demand curve under oligopoly is given as follows in figure.

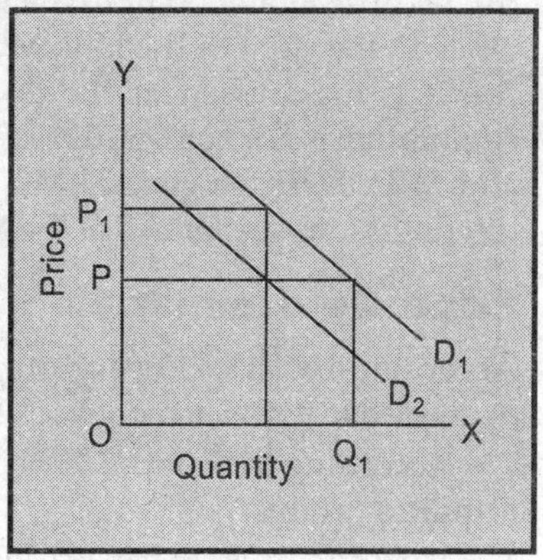

Demand Curve under Oligopoly.

Characteristics

(1) Few sellers
(2) Homogeneous or Differentiated products
(3) Conflicting attitudes of firms
(4) Indeterminateness of demand curve
(5) Interdependence
(6) Advertisement
(7) Sale promotion
(8) Price rigidity
(9) Elements of monopoly

Sweezy's Kinky Demand Model

The assumption behind the theory of kinked demand is that each oligopolist will act and react in a way that keeps conditions tolerable for all members of the industry. Such a situation is most likely to occur where products are quite similar and, therefore, their prices also the same. If one firm is selling at a price lower than that of its competitors, these competitors will be compelled to reduce their prices to match this firm's price on the other hand, if one firm decides to sell at a higher price its competitors do not react by raising their prices.

Figure shows the individual demand curve dd′ and the firm's market share curve DD′ intersecting at E. It is believed that if an oligopolist reduces his price he expects his competitors to follow his price he expects his competitors to follow suit, while no competitor will follow him when he raises the price. The relevant demand curve for the firm is, therefore, dED′ (with a kink at E). For price reduction below P, the share of the market-demand curve, D′E, is relevant as the countermoves by the rivals will keep the market share of the firm constant. And, for price increases above P, the firm goes alone and, therefore, the relevant demand curve for the firm is its own demand curve dE. Such a kinked demand curve is shown in second figure. The upper part of the demand curve has a higher price elasticity than the lower part. Due to the kink in the demand curve of the oligopolist, his MR curve is discontinuous at the level of output corresponding to the kink. The MR curve in second figure has two parts : the part dA corresponding to the upper part of the demand curve (dE) and BMR corresponding to the lower part of demand curve, ED′.

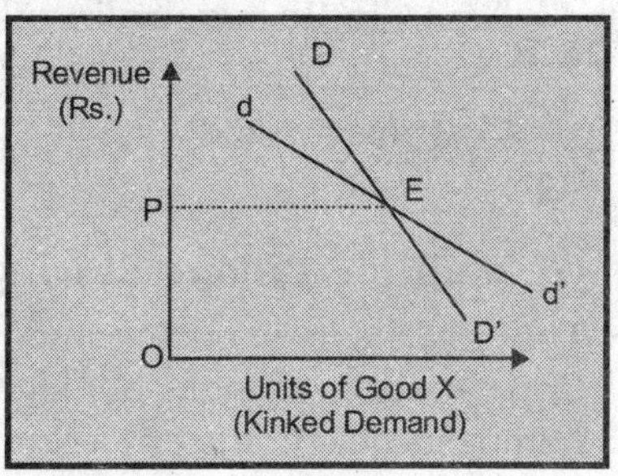

In second figure, equilibrium is defined by the point at the kink (E), because at any point to the left of the kink MC is below MR, while to the right of the kink MC is higher than MR. Thus, total profit is maximised at the point of the kink. However, the equilibrium is not necessarily defined by the intersection of the MC and MR curves. In general MC passes somewhere through the discontinuous section AB of the MR curve.

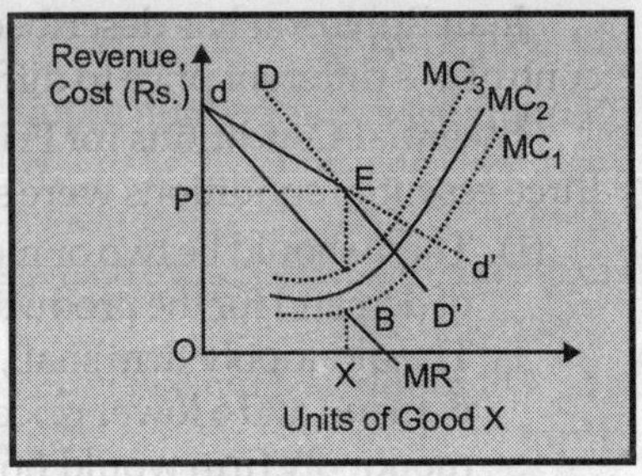

Stickiness of Price

Price Determination

According to Clark, "Price of an article or service is its market value expressed in terms of money."

According to Stanton, "Price is the amount of money and/or other item with utility needed to acquire a product."

Modern corporation may produce various products. When the demand for products is interrelated, the firm should take this interdependence into account. When a firm produces complementary goods, the output rate of each goods should be greater than if no demand interrelationship existed; for substitutes, output rates should be less than if the goods are independent.

There are a number of pricing strategies like:

(1) Cost Plus Pricing

Cost plus pricing is widely used by business firms. This practice involves setting price on average cost plus a mark-up designed to provide a target rate of return. Advantages of cost plus pricing include stable prices, a simple formula for pricing and a clear justification for pricing and a clear justification for pricing changes.

$$\text{Price} = \text{Average variable cost} + \text{Average variable margin}$$

or $$AVC = \frac{TVC}{Q}$$

and $$AFC = \frac{TFC}{Q}$$

$$\text{Formula of Mark-up of cost} = \frac{\text{Price} - \text{Cost}}{\text{Cost}}$$

According to marginalist rule:

$$\text{Price} = \text{Cost}(1 + \text{mark-up})$$

Cost plus method

$$\text{Price} = \text{Per unit cost} + \text{Expected profit in percent}$$

(2) Multiple Product Pricing

The price theory or microeconomic models of price determination are based on the assumption that a firm produces a single, homogenous product. In actual practice, however, production of a single homogeneous product by a firm is an exception rather than a rule.

Price Discrimination

Price discrimination is also known as differential pricing. Sometimes, a monopolist charges different prices for the same article or from the different buyers at the same time or at different times. It is profitable to monopolist to do so. According to J.S. Bain, "Price discrimination refers strictly to the practice by seller of changing different prices from different buyers of the same good".

Joan Robinson has described it as "the act of the selling the same article produced under single control at a different price to different buyers."

Essential Conditions for Price Discrimination. Price discrimination would not be possible unless three essential conditions were satisfied :

(1) There should be two or more than two markets for the monopoly product. Further the elasticity of demand for the product should be different in the different markets at single monopoly price. The monopoly firm shall, then be in a position to fix a higher price in the market with inelastic demand and a lower price in the market with elastic demand. It should be remembered that the monopoly firm would not be able to resort to price discrimination if the elastic ties of demand in the various markets at single monopoly price are equal because it cannot be expected to increase total profit by transferring output from one market to the other. Additional revenue in one market is bound to be less than the loss of revenue in the other.

(2) There should not be any possibility of resale of the monopoly product from the consumers in the low priced market to the consumers in the high priced market. The two types of markets should be segregated from each other. In case they are not, the consumers in the low priced market will buy the commodity to sell into the consumers in the high priced market. The price discrimination policy will then break down in practice.

(3) The price discrimination is not possible under perfect competition. It is possible under other forms of imperfect competition only if there is some tacit or explicit understanding on the part of all the firms with regard to the price of the product.

Following organisation may used price discrimination type of price:

(1) Railway company
(2) Road transport company
(3) Electricity supply company
(4) Postal department
(5) Gas supply company
(6) Mobile company (network)

Factors influencing Price Differentials

(1) Trade status of the buyer
(2) Amount of his purchase
(3) Location of the purchaser
(4) Promptness of payment
(5) Time of purchase
(6) Personal situation

Objects of Price Differentials

(1) Implementation of Marketing strategy
(2) Market segmentation
(3) Market expansion
(4) Competitive adaptation
(5) Reduction in product cost
(6) Marketing sealing

Analysis of Price Discrimination. Price discrimination occurs when variation in price of product sold in different markets does not correspond to difference in costs. The three conditions for successful price discrimination are markets, power, variation in the elasticity of demand and separable markets. First degree price discrimination involves charging each consumer the maximum amount that he or she is willing to pay. Second degree discrimination separates markets in terms of elasticity of demand. The segmentation may be based on location, use or personal characteristics, usually higher prices are charged when demand is less elastic. The below degree can be drawn by different curves:

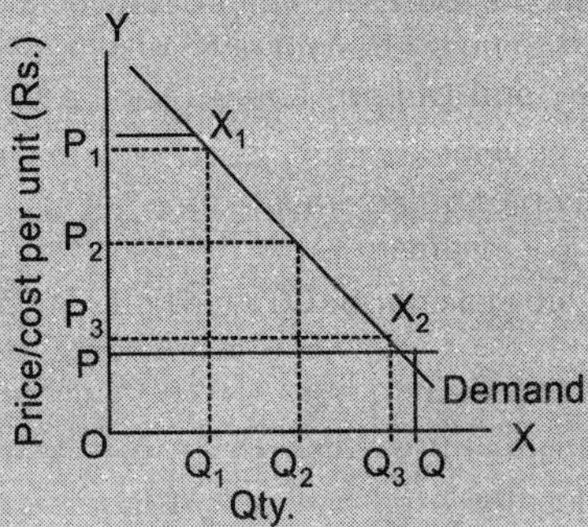

First Degree Price Marginal Cost = Average Cost.

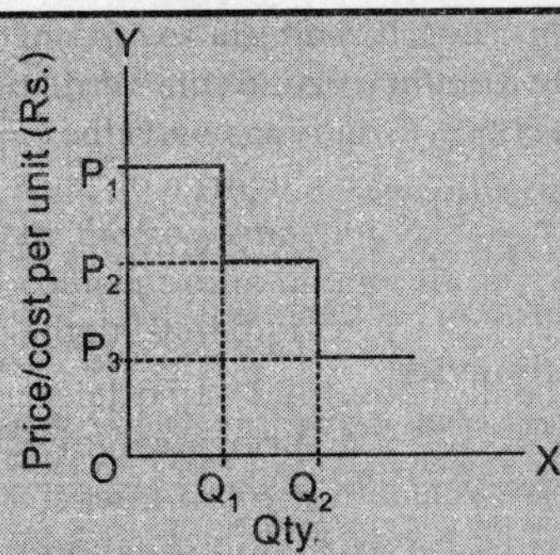

Second Degree Price.

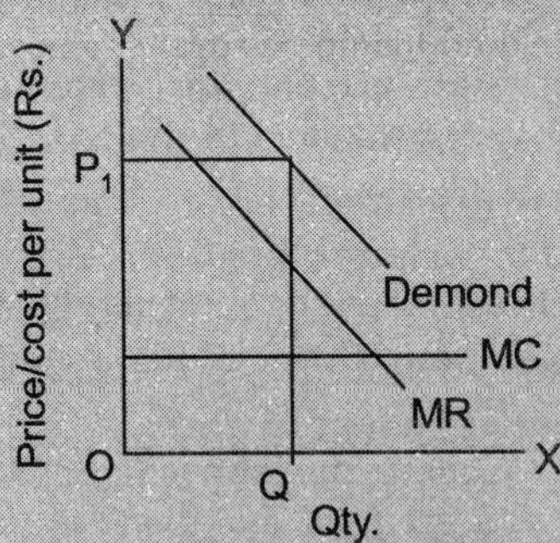

Here :
D = Demand
MR = Marginal Reveune
MC = Marginal Cost

Market 'A' under Second Degree.

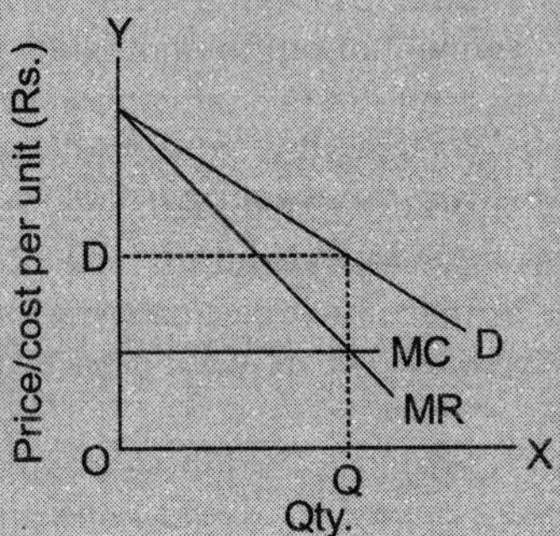

Here :
D = Demand
MR = Marginal Reveune
MC = Marginal Cost

Market 'B' under Second Degree.

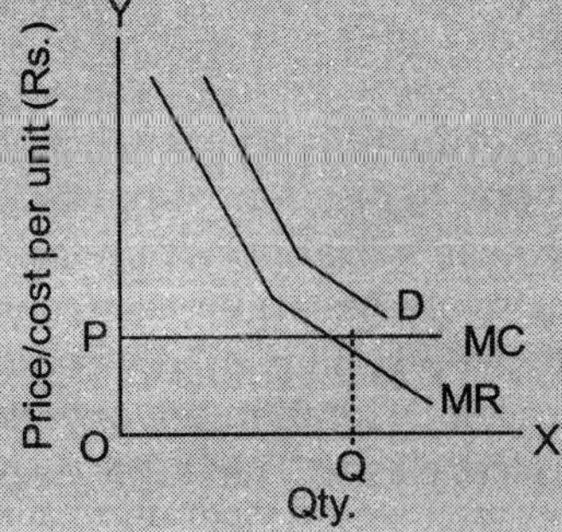

Here :
D = Demand
MR = Marginal Reveune
MC = Marginal Cost

Market 'A' + 'B'.

(3) Pricing in Life Cycle

According to Kotler and Armstrong, "Product life cycle is the course of a product's sales and profit over its life time".

It includes:

(1) Product
(2) Product life cycle
(3) Variation in price and profit
(4) Market
(5) Production
(6) Marketing
(7) Consumer taste

The life cycle of a product is a process which begins from the research and development of a new product, till it comes to final output.

Pricing in life cycle of products can be expressed by this curve :

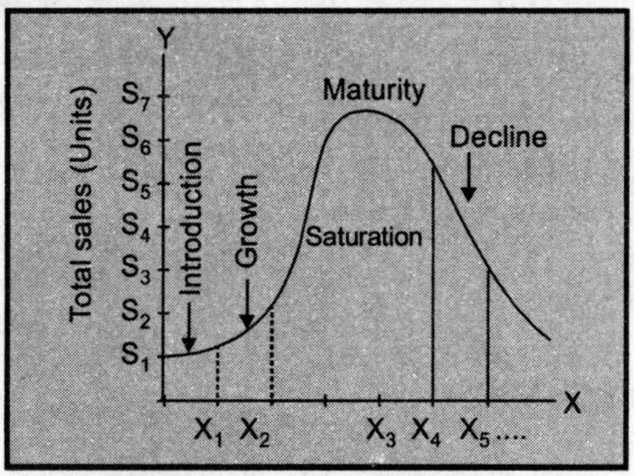

Life Cycle of Products.

The life cycle of a product is generally divided into five stages, like :

(1) **Introduction.** The introduction phase is the period taken to introduce the product to market.
(2) **Growth.** It is a successful trail during which the product gains popularity among the consumers and sales increase at an increasing rate.
(3) **Maturity:** Maturity is the stage in which sales continue to increase but at a lower rate and the total sales eventually become constant.
(4) **Saturation period.** The stage which is neutral viz. neither increase nor decrease in the sales volume.
(5) **Decline.** The stage in which sales volume is continuously falling.

(4) Transfer Pricing

If a parent division buys the product of its subsidiaries, such a firm faces the problem of determining an appropriate price for the product transferred from one division or subsidiaries to the other. Specifically the problem is of determining the price of product produced by one division of the same firm. Thus problem becomes much more different when each division has a separate profit function to maximise. Pricing to inter firm transfer products is referred to as transfer pricing.

Factors Influencing the Price

Two categories of factors - Internal and external influence the pricing decisions of any enterprise. They are as under:

(I) **Internal factors.** Various internal factors affecting the price decisions of a firm are :

(1) Corporate and marketing objectives of the firm.
(2) The image sought by the firm through pricing.

(3) The characteristics of the product.
(4) Price elasticity of demand of the product.
(5) The stage of the product in the product life cycle.
(6) Use pattern and turn around rate of the product.
(7) Costs of manufacturing and marketing.
(8) Extent of distinctiveness of the product and extent of product differentiation practiced by the firm.
(9) Other elements of the marketing mix of the firm and their interaction with pricing.
(10) Composition of the product line of the firm.

(II) External factors. These are:
(1) Market characteristics.
(2) Buyer behaviour in respect of the given product.
(3) Bargaining power of major customers.
(4) Bargaining power of major suppliers.
(5) Competitors' pricing policy.
(6) Government regulations and control.
(7) Legal aspects.
(8) Social considerations.

NATIONAL INCOME

Concepts

National income means the total value of goods and services produced annually in a country. The total amount of income accruing to a country from economic activities in a year's time, is known as national income. It includes payments made to all resources in the form of wages, interest, rent and profits.

According to Marshall, "the labour and capital of a country acting on its natural resources produce annually a certain net aggregate of commodities, material and immaterial including services of all kinds. This is the true net annual income or revenue of the country or national dividend." In this definition, the word 'net' refers to deductions from the gross national income in respect of depreciation and wearing out of machines. And to this must be added income from abroad.

Types of National Income

A. Gross National Product

It is the total measure of the flow of goods and services at market value resulting from current production during a year in a country, including net income from abroad. It includes four types of final goods and services :

(i) Consumer goods and services to satisfy the immediate wants of the people.
(ii) Gross private domestic investment in capital goods consisting of fixed capital formation, residential construction and inventories of finished and unfinished goods.
(iii) Goods and services produced by the government.
(iv) Net exports of goods and services *i.e.* the difference between the value of exports and imports of goods and services, known as net income from abroad.

There are certain factors to be taken into consideration.

(a) In GNP, all kinds of goods and services in a country during one year are measured in terms of money at current prices and then added together.

(b) Second, in estimating GNP of the economy, the market price of only the final products should be taken into account.

(c) Third, goods and services rendered free of charge are not included in GNP, because it is not possible to have a correct estimate of their market prices. For example, the bringing up of a child by the mother, imparting instructions to his son by a teacher, recitals to his friends by a musician, sculpturing as a hobby by a sculptor, etc.

(d) Fourth, the transactions which do not arise from the produce of current year or which do not contribute in any way to production, are not included in GNP.

(e) Fifth, the profits earned or losses incurred on account of changes in capital assets as a result of fluctuations in market prices, are not included in the GNP if they are not responsible for current production or economic activity.

(f) Last, the income earned through illegal activities is not included in the GNP.

Three Approaches to GNP

1. **Income Approach to GNP.** It consists of the remuneration paid in terms of money to the factors of production annually in a country. Thus, GNP is the sum total of the following items :

   (i) Wages and salaries
   (ii) Rents
   (iii) Interests
   (iv) Dividends
   (v) Undistributed corporate profits
   (vi) Mixed incomes
   (vii) Direct taxes
   (viii) Indirect taxes
   (ix) Depreciation
   (x) Net income earned from abroad.

2. **Expenditure Approaches to GNP.** It is the sum total of expenditure incurred on goods and services during one year in a country. It includes :

   (i) Private Consumption Expenditure
   (ii) Gross Domestic Private Investment
   (iii) Net Foreign Investment
   (iv) Government Expenditure on goods and services

3. **Value Added Approach to GNP.** Another method of measuring GNP is by value added. In calculating GNP, the money value of final goods and services produced at current prices during a year is taken into account. This is one of the ways to avoid double counting. But it is difficult to distinguish properly between a final product and an intermediate product. So, to avoid duplication, the value of intermediate products used in manufacturing final products must be subtracted from the value of total output of each industry in the economy. Thus the difference between the value of material outputs and inputs at each stage of production is called the value added.

B. GNP at Market Prices

When we multiply the total output produced in one year by their market prices prevalent during that year in a country, we get the Gross National Product at market prices. Thus GNP at market prices means the gross value of final goods and services produced annually in a country plus net income from abroad.

C. GNP at Factor Cost

GNP at factor cost is the sum of the money value of the income produced by and accruing to the various factors of production in one year in a country. GNP at factor cost is the income which the factors of production receive in return for their services alone. It is the cost of production. Therefore, in order to arrive at GNP at factor cost, we deduct indirect taxes from GNP at market prices. GNP at Factor Cost = GNP at Market Prices – Indirect Taxes + Subsidies.

D. Net National Product (NNP)

GNP includes the value of total output of consumption goods and investment goods. But the process of production uses up a certain amount of fixed capital. Some fixed equipment wears out, its other components are damaged or destroyed, and still others are rendered obsolete through technological changes. All this process is termed as depreciation or capital consumption allowance. In order to arrive at NNP, we deduct depreciation from GNP. The word 'net' refers to the exclusion of that part of total output which represents depreciation. So NNP = GNP – Depreciation.

E. NNP at Marketing Prices

Net National Product at market prices is the net value of final goods and services evaluated at market prices in the course of one year in a country. If we deduct depreciation from GNP at market prices, we get NNP at market prices. So NNP at Market Prices = GNP at Market Prices - Depreciation.

F. NNP at Factor Cost

Net National Product at factor cost is the net output evaluated at factor prices. It includes income earned by factors of production through participation in the product process such as wages and salaries, rents, profits, etc. It is also called National Income. This measure differs from NNP at market prices in that indirect taxes are deducted and subsidies are added to NNP at market prices in order to arrive at NNP at factor cost.

Thus NNP at Factor Cost = NNP at Market Prices – Indirect taxes + Subsidies.
= GNP at Market Prices – Depreciation – Indirect taxes + Subsidies.
= National Income

G. Domestic Income or Product

Income generated (or earned) by the factors of production within the country from its own resources is called domestic income or domestic product. Domestic income includes:

(i) wages and salaries,
(ii) rents, including imputed house rents,
(iii) interest,
(iv) dividends,
(v) undistributed corporate profits, including surpluses of public sector undertakings,
(vi) mixed incomes consisting of profits of unincorporated firms, self-employed persons, partnerships, etc., and
(vii) direct taxes.

Since domestic income does not include income earned from abroad, it can also be shown as : Domestic Income = National Income – Net Income earned from abroad.

H. Private Income

Private income is income obtained by private individuals from any source, productive or otherwise, and the retained income of corporations. Private Income = National Income (or NNP at Factor Cost) + Transfer Payments + Interest on Public Debt – Social Security – Profits and Surpluses of Public Undertakings.

I. Personal Income

Personal Income is the total income received by the individuals of a country from all sources before direct taxes in one year.

Personal income differs from private income in that it is less than the latter because it excludes undistributed corporate profits. Thus

Personal Income = Private Income – Undistributed Corporate Profits – Profit Taxes.

J. Disposable Income

Disposable income or personal disposable income means the actual income which can be spent on consumption by individuals and families.

Disposable Income = Personal Income – Direct Taxes

K. Real Income

Real income is national income expressed in terms of a general level of prices of a particular year taken as base. National income is the value of goods and services produced as expressed in terms of money at current prices. But it does not indicate the real state of the economy.

In order to find out the real income of a country, a particular year is taken as base year when the general price level is neither too high nor too low and the price level for that year is assumed to be 100. Now the general level of the prices of the given year for which the national income (real) is to be determined is assessed in accordance with the prices of the base year. For this purpose the following formula is employed :

$$\text{Real NNP} = \text{NNP for the Current Year} \times \frac{\text{Base Year Index (-100)}}{\text{Current Year Index}}$$

L. Per Capita Income

The average income of the people of a country in a particular year is called Per Capita Income for that year. This concept also refers to the measurement of income at current prices and at constant prices. For instance, in order to find out the per capita income for 2018, at current prices, the national income of a country is divided by the population of the country in that year.

$$\text{Per Capita Income for 2018} = \frac{\text{National Income for 2018}}{\text{Population in 2018}}$$

Similarly, for the purpose of arriving at the Real Per Capita Income also, this very formula is employed.

$$\text{Real Per Capita Income for 2018} = \frac{\text{Real National Income for 2018}}{\text{Population in 2018}}$$

National Income Measurement

The national income of a country can be measured by three alternative methods: (1) Product Method (2) Income Method, and (3) Expenditure Method.

(1) **Product Method.** In this method, national income is measured as a flow of goods and services. We calculate money value of all final goods and services produced in an economy during a year. Final goods here refer to those goods which are directly consumed and not used in further production process.

Goods which are further used in production process are called intermediate goods. In the value of final goods, value of intermediate goods is already included therefore we do not count value of intermediate goods in national income otherwise there will be double counting of value of goods.

To avoid the problem of double counting we can use the value-addition method in which not the whole value of a commodity but value-addition (i.e. value of final good value of intermediate good) at each stage of production is calculated and these are summed up to arrive at GDP.

The money value is calculated at market prices so sum-total is the GDP at market prices. GDP at market price can be converted into by methods discussed earlier.

(2) **Income Method.** Under this method, national income is measured as a flow of factor incomes. There are generally four factors of production labour, capital, land and entrepreneurship. Labour gets wages and salaries, capital gets interest, land gets rent and entrepreneurship gets profit as their remuneration.

Besides, there are some self-employed persons who employ their own labour and capital such as doctors, advocates, CAs, etc. Their income is called mixed income. The sum-total of all these factor incomes is called NDP at factor costs.

(3) **Expenditure Method.** In this method, national income is measured as a flow of expenditure. GDP is sum-total of private consumption expenditure. Government consumption expenditure, gross capital formation (Government and private) and net exports (Export-Import).

INFLATION

Inflation is often defined in terms of its supposed causes. Inflation exists when money supply exceeds available goods and services. Or inflation is attributed to budget deficit financing. A deficit budget may be financed by the additional money creation. But the situation of monetary expansion or budget deficit may not cause price level to rise. Hence the difficulty of defining 'inflation'.

Inflation may be defined as 'a sustained upward trend in the general level of prices' and not the price of only one or two goods. G. Ackley defined inflation as 'a persistent and appreciable rise in the general level or average of prices'. In other words, inflation is a state of rising prices, but not high prices.

It is not high prices but rising price level that constitute inflation. It constitutes, thus, an overall increase in price level. It can, thus, be viewed as the devaluing of the worth of money. In other words, inflation reduces the purchasing power of money. A unit of money now buys less. Inflation can also be seen as a recurring phenomenon.

While measuring inflation, we take into account a large number of goods and services used by the people of a country and then calculate average increase in the prices of those goods and services over a period of time. A small rise in prices or a sudden rise in prices is not inflation since they may reflect the short term workings of the market.

It is to be pointed out here that inflation is a state of disequilibrium when there occurs a sustained rise in price level. It is inflation if the prices of most goods go up. Such rate of increases in prices may be both slow and rapid. However, it is difficult to detect whether there is an upward trend in prices and whether this trend is sustained. That is why inflation is difficult to define in an unambiguous sense.

Let's measure inflation rate. Suppose, in December 2007, the consumer price index was 193.6 and, in December 2008, it was 223.8. Thus, the inflation rate during the last one year was

223.8- 193.6/ 193.6 x 100 = 15.6

As inflation is a state of rising prices, deflation may be defined as a state of falling prices but not fall in prices. Deflation is, thus, the opposite of inflation, i.e., a rise in the value of money or purchasing power of money. Disinflation is a slowing down of the rate of inflation.

Types of Inflation

As the nature of inflation is not uniform in an economy for all the time, it is wise to distinguish between different types of inflation. Such analysis is useful to study the distributional and other effects of inflation as well as to recommend anti-inflationary policies. Inflation may be caused by a variety of factors. Its intensity or pace may be different at different times. It may also be classified in accordance with the reactions of the government toward inflation.

Thus, one may observe different types of inflation in the contemporary society:

A. On the Basis of Causes

(i) Currency inflation

This type of inflation is caused by the printing of currency notes.

(ii) Credit inflation

Being profit-making institutions, commercial banks sanction more loans and advances to the public than what the economy needs. Such credit expansion leads to a rise in price level.

(iii) Deficit-induced inflation

The budget of the government reflects a deficit when expenditure exceeds revenue. To meet this gap, the government may ask the central bank to print additional money. Since pumping of additional money is required to meet the budget deficit, any price rise may the be called the deficit-induced inflation.

(iv) Demand-pull inflation

An increase in aggregate demand over the available output leads to a rise in the price level. Such inflation is called demand-pull inflation (henceforth DPI). But why does aggregate demand rise? Classical economists attribute this rise in aggregate demand to money supply. If the supply of money in an economy exceeds the available goods and services, DPI appears. It has been described by Coulborn as a situation of "too much money chasing too few goods."

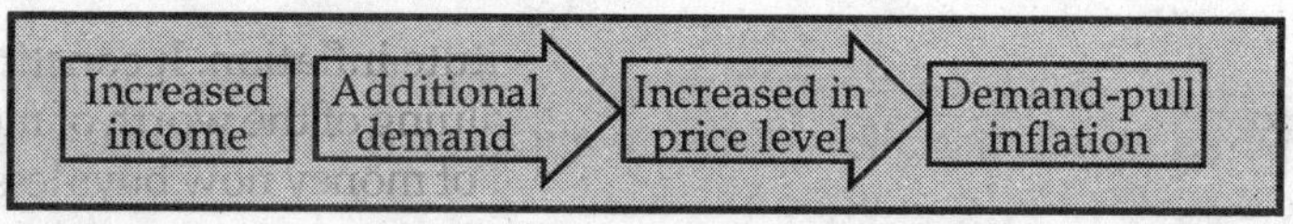

Keynesians hold a different argument. They argue that there can be an autonomous increase in aggregate demand or spending, such as a rise in consumption demand or investment or government spending or a tax cut or a net increase in exports (i.e., C + I + G + X – M) with no increase in money supply. This would prompt upward adjustment in price. Thus, DPI is caused by monetary factors (classical adjustment) and non-monetary factors (Keynesian argument).

DPI can be explained in terms of above figure, where we measure output on the horizontal axis and price level on the vertical axis. In Range 1, total spending is too short of full employment output, Y_F. There is little or no rise in the price level. As demand now rises, output will rise. The economy enters Range 2,

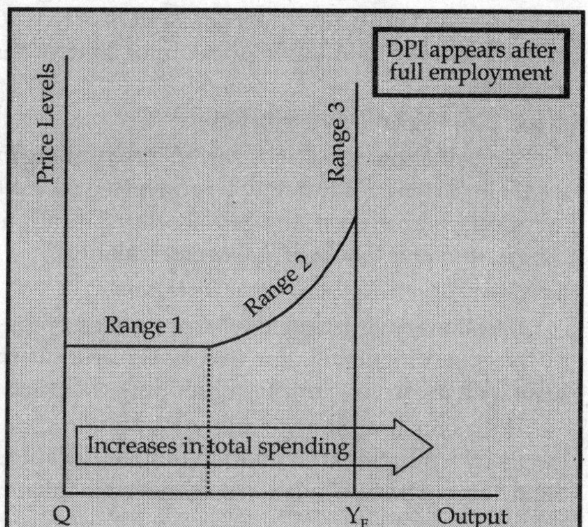

Demand-pull Inflation

where output approaches towards full employment situation. Note that in this region price level begins to rise. Ultimately, the economy reaches full employment situation, i.e., Range 3, where output does not rise but price level is pulled upward. This is demand-pull inflation. The essence of this type of inflation is that "too much spending chasing too few goods."

Cost-push inflation

Inflation in an economy may arise from the overall increase in the cost of production. This type of inflation is known as cost-push inflation (henceforth CPI). Cost of production may rise due to an increase in the prices of raw materials, wages, etc. Often trade unions are blamed for wage rise since wage rate is not completely market-determinded. Higher wage means high cost of production. Prices of commodities are thereby increased.

A wage-price spiral comes into operation. But, at the same time, firms are to be blamed also for the price rise since they simply raise prices to expand their profit margins. Thus, we have two important variants of CPI wage-push inflation and profit-push inflation.

Anyway, CPI stems from the leftward shift of the aggregate supply curve:

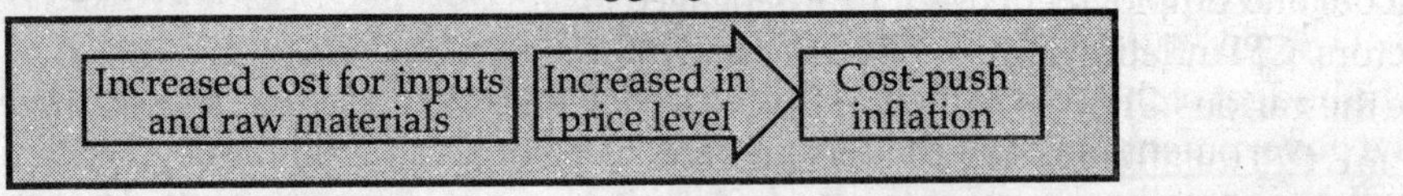

B. On the Basis of Speed or Intensity

(i) Creeping or Mild Inflation:

If the speed of upward thrust in prices is slow but small then we have creeping inflation. What speed of annual price rise is a creeping one has not been stated by the economists. To some, a creeping or mild inflation is one when annual price rise varies between 2 p.c. and 3 p.c. If a rate of price rise is kept at this level, it is considered to be helpful for economic development. Others argue that if annual price rise goes slightly beyond 3 p.c. mark, still then it is considered to be of no danger.

(ii) Walking Inflation:

If the rate of annual price increase lies between 3 p.c. and 4 p.c., then we have a situation of walking inflation. When mild inflation is allowed to fan out, walking inflation appears. These two types of inflation may be described as 'moderate inflation'.

Often, one-digit inflation rate is called 'moderate inflation' which is not only predictable, but also keep people's faith on the monetary system of the country. Peoples' confidence get lost once moderately maintained rate of inflation goes out of control and the economy is then caught with the galloping inflation.

(iii) Galloping and Hyperinflation

Walking inflation may be converted into running inflation. Running inflation is dangerous. If it is not controlled, it may ultimately be converted to galloping or hyperinflation. It is an extreme form of inflation when an economy gets shattered ."Inflation in the double or triple digit range of 20, 100 or 200 p.c. a year is labelled "galloping inflation".

(iv) Government's Reaction to Inflation

Inflationary situation may be open or suppressed. Because of anti-inflationary policies pursued by the government, inflation may not be an embarrassing one. For instance, increase in income leads to an increase in consumption spending which pulls the price level up.

If the consumption spending is countered by the government via price control and rationing device, the inflationary situation may be called a suppressed one. Once the government curbs are lifted, the suppressed inflation becomes open inflation. Open inflation may then result in hyperinflation.

Measurement of Inflation

There are two main set of inflation indices for measuring price level changes in India – the Wholesale Price Index (WPI) and the Consumer Price Index (CPI). The WPI, where prices are quoted from wholesalers, is constructed by Office of Economic Affairs, Ministry of Commerce and Industries. In the case of CPI (prices quoted from retailers), there are several indices to measure it: CPI for industrial labourers (CPI-IL), agricultural labourers (CPI-AL) and rural labourers (CPI-RL) besides an all India CPI.

In addition, Gross Domestic Product (GDP) deflator and Private Final Consumption Expenditure (PFCE) deflator from the National Accounts Statistics (NAS) provide an implicit economy-wide inflation estimate.

1. Consumer Price Index

Two Ministries - Ministry of Statistics and Programme Implementation (MOSPI) and Ministry of Labour and Employment (MOLE) are engaged in the construction of different CPIs for different groups/ sectors. CPI inflation is also called as retail inflation as the prices are quoted from retailers. Following are the various CPIs.

(a) CPI for all India or CPI combined.
(b) CPI for Agricultural Labourers (AL)
(c) CPI for Rural Labourers (RL); and
(d) CPI for Industrial Workers (IW)

(i) **CPI by MOSPI (CSO).** The CSO, which comes under MOSPI, is constructing the rural, urban and the combined CPIs. They are published from 2011 onwards. Of these, the CPI combined is the most important of all the CPIs as it is relevant for all categories of people.

In April 2014, the RBI has selected the all India CPI (of CSO) as the inflation index to target inflation under its new inflation targeting monetary policy framework. RBI's decision has made the CPI as the prime inflation index.

(ii) **CPIs by MOLE (Labour Bureau).** The Labour Bureau, Ministry of Labour and Employment (MOLE) is preparing different indices for various categories of people. These were CPI for Rural Laborares (CPI-RL), CPI for Agricultural Laborares (CPI-AL) and CPI for Industrial Workers (CPI-IW). There was a CPI For Urban Non-Manual Employees (CPI-UME), but it was discontinued from April 2010.

Since these CPIs were for specific categories of workers, it lacked the quality of an all India index.

Different price indices in India

Index	Agency	Base Year	Number of Commodities
WPI	Office of Economic Affairs, Ministry of Commerce and Industries	2011-12	697
CPI All India, CPI -Urban and Rural	CSO, Ministry of Statistics and Programme Implementation	2012	448 (rural) 460 (urban)
CPI-AL	Labour Bureau, Ministry of Labour and Employment	1986-87	
CPI-RL		1986-87	
CPI-IW		2001	

On the other hand, the first three indices are for specific occupational categories. The CPI compiled and released at national level by MOLE reflect fluctuations in retail prices relating to specific segments of population in the country like industrial Workers (CPI-IW), agricultural laborers (CPI-AL) and rural labourers (CPI-RL).

What is the difference between the various CPIs?

Difference between the various CPIs is not just that they measure price level changes for different sectors or groups. In addition to such a sector specific price level measurement; these indices differ in terms of their geographical coverage, commodities included, weights assigned to the different commodity groups and the base year on the basis of which price level changes are compared.

2. The Wholesale Price Index (WPI)

The WPI is published by the Office of Economic Adviser, Ministry of Commerce and Industry. It is in use since 1942 and is being published from 1947 regularly. It has a long history for serving as the nationwide inflation indicator till the emergence of the combined CPI in 2011. An important feature of the WPI which separate it from the CPI is that prices are collected from wholesalers.

BUSINESS ETHICS AND CSR

Business Ethics

The study and examination of moral and social responsibility in relation to business practice and decision making in business is known as "Business Ethics".

The term "business" is commonly referred to the commercial activities achieved at making profit. But gradually there is a substantial change in the way in which people viewed the business.

In the past primary objective of a business was profit maximization but the present perspectives on business objectives are not maximization.

It is profit maximization in long run besides fulfilling the ethics in the business. A business is regarded as social institution forming integral part of social systems .The business is viewed as subsystem to the social system.

This is because any type of social system is influenced by

1. The way the business functions.
2. The organization of the business.
3. Innovations.
4. Transmission and diffusion of information.
5. New ideas etc.

Need and Importance of Business Ethics

The following points explain the need for and importance of business ethics:

I. **Protection of Consumer rights.** Consumer is the centre of all business activities. In fact, business is essentially meant for satisfaction of consumer wants. Unfortunately, consumers are the most neglected and exploited group. The application of business ethics will help to confer and implement consumer rights. Business ethics can be used to check malpractices like adulteration, unfair trade practices and to make the working of business consumer oriented.

II. **Social Responsibility.** Business ethics is a means of making business socially responsible for its actions. Exploitation of consumers, employees, discriminate use of natural resources, etc.; is quite common in all types of business. Compliance to ethical standards will ensure (a) protection of consumer rights, (b) public accountability, (c) protection of worker's interests, and (d) proper utilization of natural resources.

III. **Concept of Socialism.** The concept of socialism in business states that gains of a business must be shared by all and just by the owner of business. Profit is a sing of business skill and talent.

Profit is also a result of group efforts. Employees, shareholders, consumers, Suppliers and others contribute to the success of the business. Therefore, success should be shared by all concerned.

IV. **Interest of Industry.** Business ethics are necessary to safeguard the interests of small scale business firms.

The tendency of big business firms is always to dominate the market and drive away the small scale industries out of the market. Small scale units can establish their position and fight for their rights if the industry follows a code of ethics.

V. **Consumer Movement.** The growth in consumer movement is also another important factor that has necessitated the need for business ethics. The spread of education and awareness among consumers about their rights has made the business community to conduct business on ethical principles.

VI. **Better Relations with the Society.** Business ethics is needed to develop good relations between business and society. The relationship of business with society has various dimensions such as its relations with shareholder, employees, consumers, distributors, competitors and government. Business ethics will help to promote and protect the interest to various groups.

VII. **Buyer's Market.** There has been a structural change in the concept of business. The concept of profit has been gradually taken over by consumer satisfaction. The large scale production and increased competition in the market has changed the business scene from a seller's market to a buyer's market. In a changed situation, business ethics is needed to redefine the traditional concept of profit and replace it by a balance between profit and consumer satisfaction.

VIII. **Beneficial to Business and Society.** Ethics suggests what is good and bad, right and wrong, ethical and unethical, etc.; to businessmen. It also brings an element of honesty, sincerity, fairness, and human touch to business activities. Society is also benefited by the introduction of business ethics. It ensures healthy and competitive business atmosphere, consumer and labor welfare, and improvement in social, economic and cultural values of the society. They have either direct or indirect effect on the society.

Important ethical principles that should be followed :

(a) Do not deceive or cheat customers by selling substandard or defective products, by under - measurement or by any other means.
(b) Ensure sincerity and accuracy in advertising, labelling and packaging
(c) Do not resort to hoarding, black marketing or profiteering.
(d) Do not destroy or distort competition
(e) Do not tarnish the image of competitors by unfair practices.
(f) Make accurate business records available to all authorised persons.
(g) Ensure payment of fair wages to and fair treatment of employees.
(h) Refrain from secret kickbacks or payoffs to customers, suppliers, administrators, politicians, etc.
(i) Do not form cartel agreements, even informal, to control production, price, etc., to the common detriment.
(j) Pay taxes and discharge other obligations promptly.

There are two theories which are pertinent about the nature of ethics :

(i) The *theory of moral unity* essentially advocates the principle that business actions should be judged by the general ethical standards of society. There exists only one ethical standard which applies to business and to non-business situations.

(ii) The *theory of amorality*, which argues that business can be amoral, and the actions of businessmen need not be guided by general ethical standards. Managers may act selfishly because the market mechanism distills their actions into benefits to shareholders and society at large. Adam Smith argued that the 'invisible hand' of the market assures that by "*pursuing his own interest* (a merchant) *frequently promotes that of the society more effectively than when he really intends to promote it.*" In this way, capitalism provides moral justification for the pursuit of profit through behaviour which is not purposefully ethical.

However, the theory of amorality is not acceptable to anybody. Everyone agrees that business actions should be subject to the same ethical standards as the one applicable to the society in general.

Promotion of Business Ethics. Trade associations can promote business ethics in three important ways:

(i) **Education and persuasion.** Trade associations can promote business ethics by educating the members in the importance of, and the need for, having business ethics, and persuading them to give due regard to ethical principles in the conduct of their business. The members should understand that if every business man follows business ethics, everyone of them would be benefited and there would be an improvement in the general image of the business community in the eyes of the public.

(ii) **Code of ethics.** Trade associations can formulate a code of conduct for their members. Such a code of conduct should also contain the code of ethics. The code of conduct will not only guide but also regulate the conduct of business by the members.

(iii) **Moral sanctions.** 'Sanctions' refer to the ways in which moral conduct is rewarded, or misconduct is punished. Such incentives and punishments should be expected to promote business ethics. Fear of punishment might prompt members to refrain from unfair business practices. On the other hand, public recognition and reward for high moral standard in business might give a positive inducement to them to practise business ethics.

3D of Ethics

- **Unitarian view of Ethics**; business is a part of moral structure and moral ethics.
- **Separatists views of Ethics**; Adam smith, Milton Friedman, says business in order to flourish should concentrate on its goals of profit maximization; it is influence by the government and market systems. Morality and ethics has no role in business. Society and law deals with ethics and morality.
- **Integrated view of Ethics**; ethical behavior and business should be integrated in a new era called business ethics. Intersection of business and morality and ethics. Talbot parsons views are that Business and morality are interrelated and are guided by factors such government and market system and law and society. The interrelated dimensions enhance the sense of belongingness.

CSR

Corporate Social Responsibility

In recent years, many organizations have embraced corporate social responsibility (CSR), a philosophy (introduced in Why Ethics Matter,) in which the company's expected actions include not only producing a reliable product, charging a fair price with fair profit margins, and paying a fair wage to employees, but also caring for the environment and acting on other social concerns. Many corporations work on prosocial endeavors and share that information with their customers and the communities where they do business. CSR, when conducted in good faith, is beneficial to corporations and their stakeholders. This is especially true for stakeholders that have typically been given low priority and little voice, such as the natural environment and community members who live near corporate sites and manufacturing facilities.

CSR in its ideal form focuses managers on demonstrating the social good of their new products and endeavors. It can be framed as a response to the backlash corporations face for a long track record of harming environments and communities in their efforts to be more efficient and profitable. Pushback is not new. Charles Dickens wrote about the effects of the coal economy on nineteenth-century England and shaped the way we think about the early industrial revolution. The twentieth-century writer Chinua Achebe, among many others, wrote about colonization and its transformative and often painful effect on African cultures. Rachel Carson first brought public attention to corporation's chemical poisoning of U.S. waterways in her 1962 book Silent Spring.

Betty Friedan's The Feminine Mystique (1963) critiqued the way twentieth-century industrialization boxed women into traditional roles and limited their agency. Kate Chopin's novel The Awakening (1899) and the nineteenth-century novels of Jane Austen had already outlined how limited options were for women despite massive social and economic shifts in the industrializing West. Stakeholder communities left out of or directly harmed by the economic revolution have demanded that they be able to influence corporate and governmental economic practices to benefit more directly from corporate growth as well as entrepreneurship opportunities. The trend to adopt CSR may represent an opportunity for greater engagement and involvement by groups mostly ignored until now by the wave of corporate economic growth reshaping the industrialized world.

CSR and the Environment

Corporations have responded to stakeholder concerns about the environment and sustainability. In 1999, Dow Jones began publishing an annual list of companies for which sustainability was important. Sustainability is the practice of preserving resources and operating in a way that is ecologically responsible in the long term.

The Dow Jones Sustainability Indices "serve as benchmarks for investors who integrate sustainability considerations into their portfolios."

There is a growing awareness that human actions can, and do, harm the environment. Destruction of the environment can ultimately lead to reduction of resources, declining business opportunities, and lowered quality of life. Enlightened business stakeholders realize that profit is only one positive effect of business operations. In addition to safeguarding the environment, other ethical contributions that stakeholders could lobby corporate management to make include establishing schools and health clinics in impoverished neighborhoods and endowing worthwhile philanthropies in the communities where companies have a presence.

Other stakeholders, such as state governments, NGOs, citizen groups, and political action committees in the United States apply social and legal pressure on businesses to improve their environmental practices. For example, the state of California in 2015 enacted a set of laws, referred to as the California Transparency in Supply Chains Act, which requires firms to report on the working conditions of the employees of their suppliers. The law requires only disclosures, but the added transparency is a step toward holding U.S. and other multinational corporations responsible for what goes on before their products appear in shiny packages in stores. The legislators who wrote California's Supply Chains Act recognize that consumer stakeholders are likely to bring pressure to bear on companies found to use slave labor in their supply chains, so forcing disclosure can bring about change because corporations would rather adjust their relationships with supply-chain stakeholders than risk alienating massive numbers of customers.

As instances of this type of pressure on corporations increase around the world, stakeholder groups become simultaneously less isolated and more powerful. Firms need customers. Customers need employment, and the state needs taxes just as firms need resources. All stakeholders exist in an interdependent network of relationships, and what is most needed is a sustainable system that enables all types of key stakeholders to establish and apply influence.

ETHICAL ISSUES AND DILEMMA

Ethical Issues

1. **Ethical Issues Related to Society.** At the societal level, we ask questions about the basic institutions in a society. The problem of apartheid in South Africa as a societal-level question: Is it ethically correct to have a social system in which a group of people – indeed, the majority – is systematically denied basic rights? Although recent changes in South Africa have ended the apartheid system, it is difficult to project how smoothly the transition to equality will go. Companies wishing to do business there still face a complex set of issues as political, economic, and social dynamics change; the situation can still present an ethical conundrum for many companies.

   Another societal-level question concerns the merits of capitalism. Is capitalism a just system for allocating resources? What role should the government play in regulating the marketplace? Should we tolerate gross inequalities of wealth, status, and power? For some people, the relatively huge increases in executive compensation in the past decade or so in the United States are part of this issue. For example, in the United States from 1980 to 1990, while worker pay increased 53 per cent and corporate profits 78 per cent, CEO pay rose by 212 per cent. In 1980 the chief executive's average pay was $624,247 in total pay–57 times what factory workers earned. By way of contrast, in Japan CEOs make less than 32 times as much as the rank-and-file. In 1992 there were only eight Japanese CEOs whose compensation was over a million dollars.

   Societal-level questions usually represent an ongoing debate among major competing institutions. As managers and individuals, each of us can try to shape that debate. Andrew Carnegie (along with other early theorists of corporate social responsibility) worked at this level when he argued that the proper role of a business such as his own U.S. Steel was to apply the principles of charity to assist the poor and unfortunate.
2. **Ethical Issues Related to Stakeholders.** The second kind of ethical questions concerns stakeholders–suppliers, customers, shareholders, and the rest. Here we ask questions about how a company should deal with the external groups affected by its decisions, as well as how the stakeholders should deal with the company.

   There are many stakeholder issues. Insider trading is one; another is company's obligation to inform its customers about the potential dangers of its products. What obligations does a company have to its suppliers? To the communities where it operates? To its stockholders? How should we attempt to decide such matters? Kinko's managers face the ethical question of whether to respect the rights of copyright holders as stakeholders.
3. **Internal Policy.** A third category of ethics might be called "internal policy." Here we ask questions about the nature of company's relations with its employees. What kind of employment contract is fair? What are the mutual obligations of managers and workers? What rights do employees have? These questions, too, pervade the workday of a manager. Layoffs, benefits, work rules, motivation, and leadership are all ethical concerns here.
4. **Personal Issues.** Here we ask questions about how people should treat one another within an organization. Should we be honest with one another whatever the consequences? What obligations do we have–both as human beings and as worker who fill specific work roles–to our bosses, our employees, and our peers? These questions deal with the day-to-day issues of life

in any organization. Behind them lie two broader issues: Do we have the right to look at other people primarily as means to our ends? Can we avoid doing so?

One example of meeting ethical obligations is Kidd & Co. When a fire destroyed family-owned Kidd & Co.'s Nevada marshmallow factory, vice president John Kidd and his older brother Charlie decided to pay all 63 employees while they were rebuilding, honoring an obligation to employees and other stakeholders. In turn, the employees performed community service work.

Ethical Dilemma

An ethical dilemma (ethical paradox or moral dilemma) is a problem in the decision-making process between two possible options, neither of which is absolutely acceptable from an ethical perspective. Although we face many ethical and moral problems in our life, most of them come with relatively straightforward solutions.

On the other hand, ethical dilemmas are extremely complicated challenges that cannot be easily solved. Therefore, the ability to find the optimal solution for ethical dilemmas is critical to everyone.

Every person can encounter an ethical dilemma in almost every aspect of his life, including personal, social, and professional.

How to Solve an Ethical Dilemma?

The biggest challenge of ethical dilemma is that it does not offer an obvious solution that would comply with ethical norms. Throughout the history of humanity, people always faced ethical dilemmas, and philosophers aimed and worked to find solutions to the problems.

By far, the following approaches to solve an ethical dilemma were deduced:

- **Refute the paradox (dilemma).** The situation must be carefully analyzed. In some cases, the existence of the dilemma can be logically refuted.
- **Value theory approach.** Choose the alternative that offers the greater good and the lesser evil.
- **Find alternative solutions.** In some cases, the problem can be reconsidered, and the new alternative solutions may arise.

Examples of Ethical Dilemmas

Some examples of ethical dilemmas examples include:

- Taking credit for others' work.
- Offering a client a worse product for your own profit.
- Utilizing inside knowledge for your own profit.

Ethical Dilemmas in Business

Ethical dilemmas are especially significant in professional life as they frequently occur in the workplace. Some companies and professional organizations (e.g., CFA) adhere to their own codes of conduct and ethical standards. Violation of the standards may lead to disciplinary sanctions.

Almost every aspect of the business can become a possible ground for ethical dilemmas. It may include the relationships with the co-workers, management, clients, and business partners.

The people's inability to determine the optimal solution for ethical dilemmas in the professional setting may result in serious consequences for businesses and organizations. The situation may be common in companies that value results the most.

In order to solve ethical problems, companies and organizations should develop strict ethical standards for their employees. Every company must demonstrate its concerns regarding the ethical norms within the organization. In addition, the companies may provide ethical training for their employees.

CORPORATE GOVERNANCE AND ETHICS

Corporate governance is the overall control of activities in a corporation. It is concerned with the formulation of long-term objectives and plans and the proper management structure (organisation, systems and people) to achieve them. At the same time, it entails making sure that the structure functions to maintain the corporation's integrity and responsibility to its various constituencies.

The structure to ensure corporate governance, for our purpose, includes the board of directors, top management, shareholders, creditors and others. Role of each of these stakeholders is crucial in guaranteeing responsible corporate performance.

Corporate governance addresses three basic issues :

- Ethical issues
- Efficiency issues, and
- Accountability issues.

Ethical issues are concerned with the problem of fraud, which is becoming wide spread in capitalist economies.

Efficiency issues are concerned with the performance of management.

"Accountability issues" emerge out of the stakeholders need for transparency of management in the conduct of business.

Factors Influencing Corporate Governance

(a) **The Ownership Structure.** The structure of ownership of a company determines how a corporation is managed and controlled. The ownership structure can be either dispersed among individual and institutional shareholders or can be concentrated in the hands of a few large shareholders.

Our corporate sector is characterised by the co-existence of state owned, private and multinational enterprises. The shares of these enterprises (except those belonging to the public sector) are held by institutional as well as small investors. Specifically, shares are held by (i) the term-lending institution (ii) institutional investors, comprising government owned mutuals funds, Unit Trust of India and the government owned insurance corporations (iii) corporate bodies (iv) directors and their relatives and (v) foreign investors.

Large shareholders tend to be active in corporate governance either through their representatives on company boards or through their active participation in annual general body meetings. This has been demonstrated by Reliance Industries. Ltd. which has the highest number of equity shareholders spread across the country.

(b) **The Structure of Company Boards.** Along with the structure of ownership, the structure of company boards has considerable influence on the way the companies are managed and controlled. The board of directors is responsible for establishing corporate objectives, developing broad policies and selecting top-level executives to carry out those objectives and policies. The board also reviews management's performance to ensure that the company is run well and shareholder's interests are protected.

(c) **The Financial Structure.** The financial structure of the company *i.e.*, proportion between debt and equity, has implications for the quality of governance. Banks as creditors, for example, can perform the important function of screening and monitoring companies as banks are better informed than other investors. Banks, because of the close financial relationships, foster with the companies to which they lend and because of their nominees on company boards, are considered to play a more favourable role than other investors in reducing the costs of financial distress.

(d) **The Institutional Environment.** Corporate governance mechanisms are economic and legal institutions and often the outcome of political decisions. For example, the extent to which shareholders can control the management depends on their voting rights as defined in company law, the extent to which creditors will be able to exercise financial claims on a bankrupt unit will depend on bankruptcy laws and procedures and the extent to which the market for corporate control efficiency operates to discipline under performing management will depend on take-over regulations.

Mechanisms Ensuring Corporate Governance

The fundamental institutions of corporate governance in our country have been in existence for a long time. Compared to many developing countries, mechanisms of corporate governance in India are much more institutionalized. In our country, there are six mechanisms to ensure corporate governance.

1. **Companies Act, 1956.** Companies Act is one of the biggest legislations with 658 sections and 14 schedules. Through the consolidation of many successive amendments, and a large number of statutory rules and regulations, the Act aims at not only ensuring that the interests of all stakeholders are adequately protected but purports to go beyond. The Act seeks to translate into action Articles 38 and 39 in Part IV of the Constitution, by which the State was directed that the ownership and control of the material resources of the community are so distributed as to subserve the common good and the operation of the economic system does not result in the concentration of wealth and means of production to the common detriment.

   To ensure corporate governance, the Act confers legal rights to shareholders to (a) vote on every resolution placed before an annual general meeting; (b) to elect directors who are responsible for specifying objectives and laying down policies; (c) determine remuneration of directors and the CEO; (d) removal of directors and (e) take active part in the annual general meetings.

   The Companies Bill, 1997 and the recently promulgated Ordinance on Companies (Amendment) Bill, 1997, have amended several provisions of the Act and introduced new provisions incorporating some internationally accepted corporate governance practices aimed at strengthening corporate democracy, protecting the interests of minority shareholders and providing maximum flexibility to the companies in responding to the market needs.

2. **Securities Law.** The primary securities law in our country is the SEBI Act. Since its inception in 1992, the Board has taken a number of initiatives towards investor protection.

   One such initiative is to mandate information disclosure both in prospectus and in annual accounts. SEBI Act has added substantially in an attempt to make these documents more meaningful. One of the most valuable is the information relating to the performance of other companies in the same group, particularly those companies which have accessed the capital market in the recent past.

   The Board constituted a Committee under the chairmanship of Kumaramangalam Birla to suggest ways to promote and raise the standards of corporate governance in listed companies. The Board, in its meeting held on January 25, 2000, considered the recommendations of the Committee and decided to make amendments to the listing agreements by adding a new clause, namely clause 49, to the listing agreement.

   The clause 49 provides for the optimum composition of executive and non-executive directors; setting up of a qualified and independent audit committee; remuneration of directors; Management Discussion and Analysis Report to form part of annual report to the shareholders; a separate section on Corporate Governance in the annual reports of the company; for information to be furnished in the report on corporate governance; and auditor's compliance certificate tot he effect that all the conditions of corporate governance have been complied with.

3. **Discipline of the Capital Market.** Capital market has considerable impact on corporate governance. Herein lies the role the minority shareholders can play effectively. They can refuse to subscribe to the capital of a company in the primary market and in the secondary market, they can sell their shares, thus depressing the share prices. A depressed share price makes the company an attractive take-over target.

In a well functioning capital market, there is a strong incentive for corporate managements themselves to voluntarily adopt transparent processes and subject themselves to external monitoring to reassure potential investors. What makes capital market discipline so much more attractive than regulatory intervention is that unlike the regulator, the market is very good at micro level judgements and decisions. Infact, the market is taking micro-decisions all the time. Unlike the regulator, the market is not bound by broad rules and can exercise business judgement. It therefore makes sense for the regulator to pass on as much of the burden of ensuring corporate governance to the markets as possible. The regulator can then concentrate on making the markets more efficient at performing this function.

4. **Nominees on Company Boards.** Development banks hold large blocks of shares in companies. They are equally big debt-holders too. Being equity holders, these investors have their nominees in the boards of companies. These nominees can effectively block resolutions which may be detrimental to their interests. FIS have been asked to take full responsibility for corporate governance in companies where they have substantial stakes. The objective is to boost investor confidence and pop up the capital market. The government has issued a four point directive to FIS asking them to insist on :
   (a) making adequate disclosures
   (b) moving towards internationally accepted accounting standards
   (c) maintaining distance between the CEO and chairman where applicable
   (d) holding regular board meeting with proper recording and dissemination of proceedings.

   FIs are in the process of revising guidelines for nominee directors. The IDBI is coordinating the process, and the norms will be drawn up in consultation with the Ministry of Finance and the RBI. Among the norms under consideration is one making it mandatory for FI nominee directors on boards of companies to attend specific board meetings, especially those related to finalization of accounts.

   FIs are insisting on setting up of audit sub-committees comprising 'adequate' number of non-executive independent directors of the company board in each and every large and medium corporate to strengthen internal control structures and safeguard shareholder interests. Constitution of an audit sub-committee, according to the FIs, would help bring in substantial financial discipline on the part of management and check against executive malpractice.
5. **Statutory Audit.** Statutory audit is yet another mechanism directed to ensure good corporate governance. Auditors are the conscience-keepers of shareholders, lenders and others who have financial stakes in companies.

   Auditing enhances the credibility of financial reports prepared by an enterprise. The auditing process ensures that financial statements are accurate and complete, thereby enhancing their reliability and usefulness for making investment decisions. Credible financial statements are essential for business enterprises to raise capital and for society to have trust in limited companies. Obviously, good corporate governance depends, in part, on good auditing.
6. **Codes of Conduct.** The code is based on checks and balances, especially at the level of the board of directors and the chief executive, to guard against undue concentration of power, and, adequate disclosure to enable those entitled to have the information they need, in order to exercise their rights. It comprises four sections:
   - **Role of the Board of Directors.** It was proposed that the ('inside') executive directors be balanced by adequate number of ('outside') non-executive directors, with the posts of the board, chairman and chief executive being separated.
   - **Role of Non-executive Directors.** It was emphasized that the majority of the Board should be 'independent' (in the sense of being free of any business relation which could materially interfere with the exercise of independent judgement), that non-executive directors

should be appointed only for a specific term and there should be a formal process for their appointment involving the board as a whole.

- **Executive Directors.** The main concern was with their remuneration that there should be a full and clear disclosure of directors' emoluments, and that pay should be set by a Remuneration Committee, consisting mainly of non-executive directors.
- **Financial Reporting and Controls.** It was recommended that properly constituted Audit Committees of the Board be appointed, and that non-executive directors report regularly on the effectiveness of systems and internal financial control.

MODELS OF CORPORATE GOVERNANCE

Generally, there are following types of models prevalent in today's business environment, which are as follows:

- **Single Tier System.** There is a single board comprising of 10-15 members. It is followed in countries like Canada, UK and US. In countries like India, Korea, Japan there are more than 30 members in these boards.
- **Two Tier Systems.** There are dual boards or two boards comprising of management board and supervisory board. They are practiced by Taiwan, Indonesia, China and European countries.
- **Independent Board.** There is an emerging concept of independent board which implies that there should be an independent board which does not have any material interest in the functioning of the organisation. They do not have any personal motive to favour the company. It comprises of outside directors who have no association or minimal dealings with the other key directors of the company. This enhances the quality of governance.

On the basis of above said points, following are the models:

American Model or Anglo Saxon Model

- It is followed in the countries such as UK, US and Australia.
- It is governed by the Sarbanes Oxley Act (SOX). The individual shareholders and the independent person has more say and dominance in the company.
- The management is accountable to the shareholders and BOD. The countries following common law follow this model.
- Compensations are highly based on performance.
- There is a separation of proprietorship from the use of independent BOD, stock finance and control.
- The Weakness of this model lies in the volatility of the market.
- The strength is the dynamic market, internationalisation and fluid capital. There is high importance given to the bond and stock market. It comprises of a single tier system.
- There is a low concentration in ownership, that is a high number of individual shareholders are there.
- Hence, shareholders exert pressure on managerial decisions.

German Model

- This country is known for industrialisation and Wealthy families. There are the small number of shareholders and a very high concentration of ownership. Pew individuals hold a large percentage of shares.
- This model is market-oriented and relatively influenced by the linkage of banks, families and shareholders (oligarchic).

- This model is practised in regions like Finland, Norway, Netherlands, Austria, Sweden, Denmark, Germany.
- The concept of the firm is institutional. A firm is considered as an economic autonomous unit which is built by a union of customers, shareholders, managers and suppliers.
- It follows a two-tier board system where the supervisory board monitors, appoints or dismisses the executives that are management.
- The organisations are highly pressurised by the banks and shareholders.
- Hence, industrial -banks exert pressure on managerial decisions.

Clause 49 Listing Agreement of Stock Exchange

Various reforms were taken and Clause 49 was inserted in listing agreement. Some of the provisions of this are:

- Any company with an executive chairman, must have atleast 50% independent directors in board.
- CEO and CFO must maintain internal controls.
- Company must obtain a certificate of compliance from company secretaries and auditors.
- One of the member of audit committee should be financially literate.
- It came into force in, 26th August, 2003.
- It recommended by Kumarmanglam Birla committee in 2000.

Role of Minority Shareholders

They can refuse to subscribe to the capital of a company in the primary market and in the secondary market, they can sell their shares, thus depressing the share prices. A depressed share price makes the company an attractive takeover target. The market force in itself govern the conduct of business.

Statutory Audit

Statutory audit is yet another mechanism directed to ensure good corporate governance. Auditors are the conscious keepers of shareholders, lenders and others who have financial stakes in companies.

Auditing enhances the credibility of financial reports prepared by any enterprise. The auditing process ensures that financial statements are accurate and complete, thereby enhancing their reliability and usefulness for making investment decisions.

It is only through statutory audit that the external world learns about the financial operations of the company.

VALUE BASED ORGANISATION

"Our people are our most important asset." You've heard these words many times if you work in an organization. Yet how many organizations act as if they really believe these words? Not many. These words are the clear expression of a value, and values are visible through the actions people take, not their talk.

Values form the foundation for everything that happens in your workplace. If you are the founder of an organization, your values permeate the workplace. You naturally hire people who share your values. Whatever you value, will largely govern the actions of your workforce.

Sample Workplace Value-based Actions

If you value integrity and you experience a quality problem in your manufacturing process, you honestly inform your customer of the exact nature of the problem. You discuss your actions to eliminate the problem, and the anticipated delivery time the customer can expect. If integrity is not a fundamental value, you may make excuses and mislead the customer.

If you value and care about the people in your organization, you will pay for health insurance, dental insurance, retirement accounts, and provide regular raises and bonuses for dedicated staff. If you value equality and a sense of family, you will wipe out the physical trappings of power, status, and inequality such as executive parking places and offices that grow larger by a foot with every promotion.

Whatever You Value is what you Live in Your Organization

You know, as an individual, what you personally value. However, most of you work in organizations that have already operated for many years. The values, and the subsequent culture created by those values are in place, for better or worse.

If you are generally happy with your work environment, you undoubtedly selected an organization with values congruent with your own. If you're not, watch for the disconnects between what you value and the actions of people in your organization.

As an HR professional, you will want to influence your larger organization to identify its core values and make them the foundation for its interactions with employees, customers, and suppliers. Minimally, you will want to work within your own HR organization to identify a strategic framework for serving your customers that is firmly value-based.

Strategic Framework

Every organization has a vision or picture of what it desires for its future, whether foggy or crystal clear. The current mission of the organization or the purpose for its existence is also understood in general terms. The values that members of the organization manifest in daily decision making, and the norms or relationship guidelines which informally define how people interact with each other and customers, are also visible. But are these usually vague and unspoken understandings enough to fuel your long-term success?

I don't think so

Every organization has a choice. You can allow these fundamental underpinnings of your organization to develop on their own with each individual acting in a self-defined vacuum. Or, you can invest the time to proactively define them to best serve members of the organization and its customers. Many successful organizations agree upon and articulate their vision, mission or purpose, values, and strategies so all organization members can enroll in and own their achievement.

Want the background about why values are important in an organization? See the impact that identifying organizational values can have. Values are traits or qualities that are considered worthwhile; they represent an individual's highest priorities and deeply held driving forces.

Value statements are grounded in values and define how people want to behave with each other in the organization. They are statements about how the organization will value customers, suppliers, and the internal community. Value statements describe actions that are the living enactment of the fundamental values held by most individuals within the organization.

Vision is a statement about what the organization wants to become. The vision should resonate with all members of the organization and help them feel proud, excited, and part of something much bigger than themselves. A vision should stretch the organization's capabilities and image of itself. It gives shape and direction to the organization's future.

Mission/Purpose is a precise description of what an organization does. It should describe the business the organization is in. It is a definition of "why" the organization exists currently. Each member of an organization should be able to verbally express this mission. Strategies are the broadly defined four or five key approaches the organization will use to accomplish its mission and drive toward the vision. Goals and action plans usually flow from each strategy.

One example of a strategy is employee empowerment and teams. Another is to pursue a new worldwide market in Asia. Another is to streamline your current distribution system using lean management principles. I recommend that you start developing this strategic framework by identifying your organization's values. Create an opportunity for as many people as possible to participate in this process. All the rest of your strategic framework should grow from living these.

What Values Are

The following are examples of values. You might use these as the starting point for discussing values within your organization:

- ambition
- integrity
- respect
- enjoyment/fun
- innovativeness
- empowerment
- collaboration
- courage
- challenge
- friendliness
- optimism
- competency
- service
- dedication
- loyalty
- teamwork
- quality
- stewardship
- wisdom
- influence
- discipline/order
- dependability
- individuality
- responsibility
- diversity
- credibility
- excellence
- efficiency
- empathy
- independence
- learning
- generosity
- flexibility
- equality
- accuracy
- improvement
- honesty
- accountability
- dignity
- accomplishment
- security
- compassion
- persistence

Identifying and Establishing Values

Effective organizations identify and develop a clear, concise and shared meaning of values/beliefs, priorities, and direction so that everyone understands and can contribute. Once defined, values impact every aspect of your organization. You must support and nurture this impact or identifying values will have been a wasted exercise. People will feel fooled and misled unless they see the impact of the exercise within your organization. If you want the values you identify to have an impact, the following must occur.

- People demonstrate and model the values in action in their personal work behaviors, decision making, contribution, and interpersonal interaction.
- Organizational values help each person establish priorities in their daily work life.
- Values guide every decision that is made once the organization has cooperatively created the values and the value statements.
- Rewards and recognition within the organization are structured to recognize those people whose work embodies the values the organization embraced.
- Organizational goals are grounded in the identified values.
- Adoption of the values and the behaviors that result is recognized in regular performance feedback.
- People hire and promote individuals whose outlook and actions are congruent with the values.
- Only the active participation of all members of the organization will ensure a truly organization-wide, value-based, shared culture.

MULTIPLE CHOICE QUESTIONS

1. What is the primary function of management?
   (a) Planning (b) Organizing
   (c) Leading (d) Controlling
2. Which of the following is not a key element of the management process?
   (a) Decision making (b) Communication
   (c) Delegation (d) Marketing
3. What is the first step in the planning process?
   (a) Implementation (b) Evaluation
   (c) Setting objectives (d) Controlling
4. Which of the following is a characteristic of effective delegation?
   (a) Micromanagement
   (b) Lack of trust
   (c) Accountability
   (d) Centralized decision-making
5. Which management function involves monitoring and measuring performance to ensure that goals are being met?
   (a) Planning (b) Organizing
   (c) Leading (d) Controlling
6. SWOT analysis is a tool used in which phase of the planning process?
   (a) Setting objectives
   (b) Environmental scanning
   (c) Implementation
   (d) Controlling
7. Which leadership style is characterized by a high level of task orientation and low relationship orientation?
   (a) Autocratic (b) Democratic
   (c) Laissez-faire (d) Transformational
8. What is the primary focus of organizational culture?
   (a) Profitability
   (b) Employee satisfaction
   (c) Customer satisfaction
   (d) Values and beliefs
9. Which management function involves arranging resources and tasks to achieve organizational goals?
   (a) Planning (b) Leading
   (c) Controlling (d) Organizing
10. Which of the following is an example of an operational plan?
    (a) Annual budget
    (b) Strategic plan
    (c) Long-term vision
    (d) Mission statement
11. Which of the following is a key component of the controlling function in management?
    (a) Employee motivation
    (b) Feedback and measurement
    (c) Goal setting
    (d) Delegation
12. Who is considered the father of modern management and introduced the concept of scientific management?
    (a) Peter Drucker (b) Frederick Taylor
    (c) Henry Fayol (d) Max Weber
13. What is the purpose of a Gantt chart?
    (a) Risk assessment
    (b) Employee motivation
    (c) Project scheduling
    (d) Quality control
14. Which of the following is not one of the five functions of management identified by Henri Fayol?
    (a) Planning (b) Organizing
    (c) Staffing (d) Negotiating
15. Which management theory emphasizes the importance of understanding the individual needs and motivations of employees?
    (a) Classical management
    (b) Human relations theory
    (c) Contingency theory
    (d) Total quality management
16. Which type of power is based on a person's formal position within an organization?
    (a) Referent power
    (b) Expert power

(c) Legitimate power
(d) Coercive power

17. In the context of decision-making, what does the acronym SWOT stand for?
(a) Strengths, Weaknesses, Opportunities, Threats
(b) Sales, Workflow, Objectives, Timelines
(c) Strategies, Workflows, Objectives, Tasks
(d) Skills, Weaknesses, Opportunities, Targets

18. What is the key principle of the Hawthorne effect in management?
(a) Increased productivity due to improved lighting
(b) Increased productivity due to employee participation
(c) Increased productivity due to strict supervision
(d) Increased productivity due to automation

19. Which of the following is a component of Maslow's Hierarchy of Needs theory?
(a) Job enrichment
(b) Self-actualization
(c) Profit maximization
(d) Competitive analysis

20. Which stage of the decision-making process involves generating a range of possible solutions?
(a) Evaluation
(b) Implementation
(c) Identification of alternatives
(d) Monitoring

21. Which management function involves motivating and guiding employees to achieve organizational goals?
(a) Planning (b) Organizing
(c) Leading (d) Controlling

22. What is the primary purpose of a mission statement for an organization?
(a) To outline the company's financial goals
(b) To describe the organization's core purpose and values
(c) To list the names of all employees
(d) To provide a detailed marketing plan

23. Which type of control focuses on preventing problems from occurring in the first place?
(a) Feedback control
(b) Feed forward control
(c) Concurrent control
(d) Post-action control

24. Which of the following is not one of the four functions of management as described by Peter Drucker?
(a) Planning (b) Leading
(c) Organizing (d) Innovating

25. Which of the following is a characteristic of a matrix organizational structure?
(a) Clear hierarchy and chain of command
(b) Functional departments operate independently
(c) Employees report to multiple managers
(d) Centralized decision-making

26. Who is often considered the father of modern management and introduced scientific management?
(a) Peter Drucker (b) Max Weber
(c) Frederick Taylor (d) Henry Fayol

27. Which management theory emphasizes the importance of understanding the individual needs and motivations of employees?
(a) Classical management
(b) Contingency theory
(c) Human relations theory
(d) Total quality management

28. What management approach is characterized by the idea that organizations are like machines that can be fine-tuned for efficiency?
(a) Systems theory
(b) Contingency theory
(c) Scientific management
(d) Human relations theory

29. The SWOT analysis is often associated with which management approach?
(a) Bureaucratic management
(b) Total quality management
(c) Contingency theory
(d) Strategic management

30. Who developed the hierarchy of needs theory in management?
(a) Max Weber (b) Frederick Taylor
(c) Abraham Maslow (d) Elton Mayo

31. Which management approach focuses on the development of a strong organizational culture?
(a) Bureaucratic management
(b) Total quality management
(c) Contingency theory
(d) Human relations theory

32. The concept of "span of control" is closely associated with which management approach?
(a) Scientific management
(b) Total quality management
(c) Contingency theory
(d) Bureaucratic management

33. Who introduced the concept of the "Theory X and Theory Y" styles of management?
(a) Douglas McGregor
(b) Frederick Taylor
(c) Elton Mayo
(d) Peter Drucker

34. Which management approach emphasizes that there is no one-size-fits-all solution and that the best approach depends on the situation?
(a) Bureaucratic management
(b) Total quality management
(c) Contingency theory
(d) Scientific management

35. The TQM (Total Quality Management) approach focuses on what aspect of management?
(a) Maximizing employee turnover
(b) Reducing product quality
(c) Achieving customer satisfaction and quality improvement
(d) Streamlining bureaucracy

36. Who is known for his work on management by objectives (MBO)?
(a) Peter Drucker (b) Max Weber
(c) Frederick Taylor (d) Elton Mayo

37. The Hawthorne studies, which had a significant impact on management theory, were conducted at which organization?
(a) Ford Motor Company
(b) General Electric
(c) Hawthorne Works of Western Electric
(d) IBM

38. What management approach focuses on aligning an organization's goals with its social and environmental responsibilities?
(a) Sustainable management
(b) Scientific management
(c) Classical management
(d) Bureaucratic management

39. Which management approach is often associated with the concepts of empowerment and self-managed teams?
(a) Scientific management
(b) Total quality management
(c) Human relations theory
(d) Contingency theory

40. The PESTEL analysis is a tool used in which management approach?
(a) Strategic management
(b) Scientific management
(c) Bureaucratic management
(d) Total quality management

41. Which management approach emphasizes the importance of top-down control and a formal hierarchy?
(a) Human relations theory
(b) Total quality management
(c) Bureaucratic management
(d) Contingency theory

42. Who introduced the concept of the Five Functions of Management?
(a) Henry Fayol
(b) Max Weber
(c) Abraham Maslow
(d) Douglas McGregor

43. Which management approach focuses on continuous improvement and the reduction of waste in processes?
(a) Classical management
(b) Contingency theory
(c) Scientific management
(d) Lean management

44. Who is associated with the development of the 14 Principles of Management?
(a) Peter Drucker (b) Max Weber
(c) Frederick Taylor (d) Henry Fayol

45. The contingency theory of management suggests that
(a) There is one best way to manage in all situations.
(b) Management principles are timeless and universal.
(c) Management practices should be adapted to fit the specific situation.
(d) Managers should always follow a strict chain of command.

46. Which management approach emphasizes the importance of employee involvement, teamwork, and open communication?
(a) Scientific management
(b) Classical management
(c) Human relations theory
(d) Bureaucratic management

47. What is the main focus of the classical management approach?
(a) Human resources and employee satisfaction
(b) Efficiency and productivity
(c) Innovation and creativity
(d) Environmental sustainability

48. Which management approach places a strong emphasis on rules, procedures, and adherence to a formal hierarchy?
(a) Human relations theory
(b) Total quality management
(c) Bureaucratic management
(d) Lean management

49. Who is known for developing the concept of the "Four Ps" in marketing, which is also applicable to management?
(a) Max Weber (b) Henry Fayol
(c) Peter Drucker (d) Philip Kotler

50. The Balanced Scorecard is a management tool often used in which management approach?
(a) Sustainable management
(b) Classical management
(c) Strategic management
(d) Scientific management

51. Which management approach is often associated with a focus on reducing costs and improving efficiency through systematic analysis of processes?
(a) Scientific management
(b) Total quality management
(c) Human relations theory
(d) Lean management

52. The Deming Cycle, also known as the PDCA cycle, is a key component of which management approach?
(a) Scientific management
(b) Total quality management
(c) Classical management
(d) Sustainable management

53. Which management approach encourages a participative leadership style and values employee input in decision-making?
(a) Scientific management
(b) Classical management
(c) Human relations theory
(d) Bureaucratic management

54. Who is known for the theory of bureaucratic management, which emphasizes a formal, hierarchical structure with clear rules and procedures?
(a) Frederick Taylor
(b) Max Weber
(c) Douglas McGregor
(d) Elton Mayo

55. The contingency theory of management suggests that the effectiveness of a management style depends on
(a) The personality of the manager.
(b) The situation or context in which it is applied.
(c) The size of the organization.
(d) The level of technology used.

56. What is the primary focus of the sustainable management approach?
(a) Maximizing profits at any cost
(b) Achieving social and environmental goals alongside financial objectives
(c) Minimizing employee turnover
(d) Implementing rigid bureaucratic procedures

57. Who introduced the concept of "emotional intelligence" and its importance in leadership and management?
(a) Frederick Taylor
(b) Abraham Maslow
(c) Daniel Goleman
(d) Douglas McGregor

58. Which management approach focuses on improving employee morale and creating a more positive work environment?
(a) Scientific management
(b) Classical management
(c) Human relations theory
(d) Lean management

59. The Contingency Theory argues that there is no one-size-fits-all management style, and the most effective approach depends on the specific circumstances of the organization and its environment.
(a) True (b) False
(c) Both (a) and (b) (d) None of these

60. Which management approach emphasizes the importance of decentralization, empowerment, and giving employees more decision-making authority?
(a) Bureaucratic management
(b) Classical management

(c) Total quality management
(d) Contingency theory

61. Which of the following is one of the primary roles of a manager, as identified by Henry Mintzberg?
(a) Decisional (b) Informational
(c) Interpersonal (d) Technical

62. Interpersonal roles of a manager include
(a) Negotiating with suppliers
(b) Making strategic decisions
(c) Setting performance goals
(d) Building relationships with subordinates

63. The "figurehead" role of a manager involves
(a) Being a symbolic head of the organization
(b) Handling day-to-day operational tasks
(c) Making important strategic decisions
(d) Developing long-term organizational goals

64. The role of a manager as a "liaison" involves
(a) Making important financial decisions
(b) Building relationships with external contacts and stakeholders
(c) Creating organizational policies
(d) Solving technical problems

65. Informational roles of a manager include
(a) Monitoring employee performance
(b) Negotiating with suppliers
(c) Handling customer complaints
(d) Disseminating information both inside and outside the organization

66. What is the key role of a manager when they act as a "monitor"?
(a) Decision making
(b) Gathering and distributing information
(c) Motivating employees
(d) Conducting performance appraisals

67. The "disseminator" role of a manager involves
(a) Providing technical guidance to subordinates
(b) Communicating information to employees and external contacts
(c) Negotiating with labor unions
(d) Setting long-term organizational goals

68. The "spokesperson" role of a manager involves
(a) Representing the organization to the media and public
(b) Acting as a technical expert within the organization
(c) Making operational decisions
(d) Handling customer complaints

69. Decisional roles of a manager include
(a) Communicating information to employees
(b) Handling customer complaints
(c) Negotiating with suppliers
(d) Making important choices for the organization

70. The "entrepreneur" role of a manager involves
(a) Solving technical problems
(b) Generating and implementing new ideas and projects
(c) Handling employee conflicts
(d) Managing day-to-day operations

71. When a manager acts as a "disturbance handler," they are typically
(a) Making strategic decisions
(b) Resolving conflicts and crises
(c) Building relationships with external contacts
(d) Setting performance goals

72. The role of a manager as a "resource allocator" involves
(a) Building relationships with suppliers
(b) Allocating organizational resources, such as budget and staff
(c) Handling employee complaints
(d) Making important strategic decisions

73. A manager acting as a "negotiator" is primarily involved in
(a) Motivating employees
(b) Communicating with external stakeholders
(c) Making operational decisions
(d) Settling disputes and making agreements

74. Which of the following skills is considered a key interpersonal skill for managers?
(a) Technical expertise
(b) Strategic planning
(c) Leadership
(d) Financial analysis

75. Technical skills are most important for which level of management?
(a) Top management
(b) Middle management
(c) First-line management
(d) All levels of management equally

76. Conceptual skills are most crucial for
(a) First-line managers
(b) Middle managers
(c) Top managers
(d) Non-managerial employees

77. Which management skill involves the ability to work with and through other people to achieve organizational goals?
(a) Technical skills
(b) Human skills
(c) Conceptual skills
(d) Decision-making skills

78. Which skill is essential for effectively interpreting financial reports and analyzing budgets?
(a) Human skills
(b) Conceptual skills
(c) Technical skills
(d) Interpersonal skills

79. Which level of management typically requires the most developed conceptual skills?
(a) Top management
(b) Middle management
(c) First-line management
(d) Supervisory management

80. Which of the following is an example of a technical skill?
(a) Leadership
(b) Financial analysis
(c) Conflict resolution
(d) Team building

81. The ability to see the organization as a whole and understand how its various parts interact is an example of which skill?
(a) Technical skills
(b) Conceptual skills
(c) Human skills
(d) Decision-making skills

82. Which skill is vital for effectively motivating and leading teams?
(a) Technical skills
(b) Conceptual skills
(c) Interpersonal skills
(d) Decision-making skills

83. A manager who is skilled in decision-making is most likely to possess
(a) Technical skills
(b) Conceptual skills
(c) Human skills
(d) Problem-solving skills

84. Which skill is essential for resolving conflicts and building positive relationships with employees?
(a) Technical skills
(b) Conceptual skills
(c) Human skills
(d) Decision-making skills

85. The ability to analyze complex issues, think critically, and make sound decisions is associated with which skill?
(a) Interpersonal skills
(b) Technical skills
(c) Conceptual skills
(d) Problem-solving skills

86. What is the first step in the planning process?
(a) Implementation
(b) Setting objectives
(c) Controlling
(d) Leading

87. What type of planning involves setting broad, long-term goals for an organization?
(a) Strategic planning
(b) Tactical planning
(c) Operational planning
(d) Contingency planning

88. Which of the following is an example of a short-term planning horizon?
(a) 5 years (b) 1 year
(c) 10 years (d) 20 years

89. Which planning technique involves identifying potential future scenarios and preparing for them?
(a) Strategic planning
(b) Contingency planning
(c) Tactical planning
(d) Operational planning

90. Organizing, as a management function, involves
(a) Setting goals and objectives
(b) Allocating resources and arranging tasks
(c) Motivating employees
(d) Measuring performance

91. The organizing function includes
(a) Establishing the organizational culture
(b) Recruiting and hiring employees
(c) Setting financial goals
(d) Providing feedback to employees

92. What is the purpose of an organizational chart?
    (a) To define the organization's mission
    (b) To allocate financial resources
    (c) To represent the structure of the organization
    (d) To set performance standards
93. In the organizing function, the process of allocating resources and tasks is often referred to as
    (a) Controlling (b) Leading
    (c) Delegation (d) Coordination
94. What is the primary focus of the staffing function in management?
    (a) Allocating resources
    (b) Setting objectives
    (c) Recruiting and selecting employees
    (d) Controlling operations
95. Which of the following is not a key component of the staffing process?
    (a) Training and development
    (b) Performance appraisal
    (c) Motivation
    (d) Job analysis
96. What is the term for the process of attracting qualified individuals to fill job openings?
    (a) Delegation (b) Recruitment
    (c) Controlling (d) Coordination
97. What type of interview involves asking open-ended questions to assess a candidate's qualifications and fit for a position?
    (a) Structured interview
    (b) Unstructured interview
    (c) Behavioral interview
    (d) Stress interview
98. The coordinating function in management involves
    (a) Setting objectives and goals
    (b) Allocating resources
    (c) Ensuring that activities are harmoniously integrated
    (d) Measuring performance
99. Which role in the organization is primarily responsible for coordinating the activities of different departments?
    (a) First-line managers
    (b) Middle managers
    (c) Top managers
    (d) Non-managerial employees
100. Coordinating involves ensuring that
    (a) Employees work in isolation to maximize efficiency
    (b) Resources are allocated without any planning
    (c) Activities are synchronized and aligned with organizational goals
    (d) The organization operates without control mechanisms
101. What is the primary purpose of a project manager in the context of coordinating activities?
    (a) Allocating resources
    (b) Setting objectives
    (c) Ensuring that the project is completed on time and within budget
    (d) Conducting performance appraisals
102. The controlling function in management involves
    (a) Setting objectives and goals
    (b) Allocating resources
    (c) Monitoring and measuring performance
    (d) Coordinating activities
103. Which of the following is not a step in the control process?
    (a) Setting objectives
    (b) Measuring performance
    (c) Comparing results to standards
    (d) Taking corrective action
104. In the control process, what is the purpose of comparing results to standards?
    (a) To identify deviations from the plan
    (b) To set performance goals
    (c) To motivate employees
    (d) To make resource allocation decisions
105. Which of the following is an example of an external control mechanism?
    (a) Budgeting
    (b) Benchmarking
    (c) Performance appraisal
    (d) Market competition
106. Which type of control occurs while a project or activity is in progress?
    (a) Feedback control
    (b) Feedforward control
    (c) Concurrent control
    (d) Post-action control
107. What is the primary purpose of feedback control?
    (a) Preventing problems before they occur

(b) Identifying and correcting deviations from the plan
(c) Setting performance standards
(d) Allocating resources

108. Which of the following is an example of a qualitative performance measurement?
(a) Number of units produced
(b) Sales revenue
(c) Customer satisfaction rating
(d) Employee attendance

109. The control function helps organizations to
(a) Set objectives and goals
(b) Allocate resources
(c) Adapt to changing circumstances and achieve their objectives
(d) Coordinate activities

110. A balanced scorecard is a tool used in which management function?
(a) Planning (b) Organizing
(c) Staffing (d) Controlling

111. Which type of communication occurs within the organization and involves interactions between employees and management?
(a) External communication
(b) Downward communication
(c) Horizontal communication
(d) Informal communication

112. When a manager communicates with subordinates to provide instructions or feedback, it is an example of
(a) Upward communication
(b) Downward communication
(c) Horizontal communication
(d) Informal communication

113. What is the term for communication that occurs between individuals or groups at the same hierarchical level in an organization?
(a) Upward communication
(b) Downward communication
(c) Horizontal communication
(d) Diagonal communication

114. When an organization communicates with its customers, suppliers, or the general public, it is engaging in
(a) Upward communication
(b) Downward communication
(c) External communication
(d) Informal communication

115. Which of the following is the first step in the communication process?
(a) Encoding (b) Feedback
(c) Decoding (d) Message

116. The process of converting the message into understandable symbols or language is known as
(a) Encoding (b) Feedback
(c) Decoding (d) Channel

117. In the communication process, the medium or method used to transmit the message is referred to as the
(a) Encoding (b) Feedback
(c) Channel (d) Noise

118. What is the final step in the communication process?
(a) Encoding (b) Feedback
(c) Decoding (d) Message

119. Which of the following is an example of a semantic barrier to communication?
(a) Using jargon or technical language
(b) Cultural differences
(c) Emotional barriers
(d) Lack of feedback

120. What type of barrier to communication can result from language differences and misunderstandings?
(a) Noise
(b) Physical barriers
(c) Semantic barriers
(d) Psychological barriers

121. What is the term for communication barriers that arise from a person's emotional state or emotional response to the message?
(a) Noise
(b) Physical barriers
(c) Semantic barriers
(d) Psychological barriers

122. Which of the following is not a psychological barrier to effective communication?
(a) Prejudice and stereotypes
(b) Anxiety and fear
(c) Lack of information
(d) Defensive behavior

123. Physical barriers to communication include
(a) Language differences
(b) Cultural differences
(c) Noise and distractions
(d) Lack of feedback

124. Which type of barrier to communication can result from a noisy or crowded environment?
(a) Noise
(b) Physical barriers
(c) Semantic barriers
(d) Psychological barriers

125. What is the term for communication barriers that arise from differences in values, beliefs, and norms among individuals or groups?
(a) Noise
(b) Physical barriers
(c) Semantic barriers
(d) Cultural barriers

126. Which of the following is an example of a cultural barrier to communication?
(a) Using technical language
(b) Interrupting the speaker
(c) Misinterpreting nonverbal cues
(d) Speaking too softly

127. Which type of communication involves listening and seeking to understand the perspective of the speaker?
(a) Nonverbal communication
(b) Active listening
(c) Written communication
(d) Informal communication

128. When a manager asks for clarification during a conversation and paraphrases what the speaker said, they are demonstrating
(a) Nonverbal communication
(b) Active listening
(c) Written communication
(d) Informal communication

129. What is the term for nonverbal communication through facial expressions, body language, and gestures?
(a) Verbal communication
(b) Written communication
(c) Active listening
(d) Nonverbal communication

130. Which of the following is an example of written communication?
(a) An email
(b) A face-to-face conversation
(c) Active listening
(d) A phone call

131. Which of the following is a key principle of effective communication?
(a) Interrupting the speaker to ask questions
(b) Avoiding eye contact to reduce tension
(c) Using language that is clear and easy to understand
(d) Providing one-word responses to speed up the conversation

132. What is the term for the process of conveying information or ideas through written words, symbols, or visuals?
(a) Nonverbal communication
(b) Active listening
(c) Written communication
(d) Informal communication

133. Which communication channel is most suitable for conveying complex technical information or detailed instructions?
(a) Face-to-face communication
(b) Written communication
(c) Telephone communication
(d) Email communication

134. Which communication channel is often preferred for conveying sensitive or emotionally charged messages?
(a) Face-to-face communication
(b) Written communication
(c) Telephone communication
(d) Email communication

135. Email, instant messaging, and video conferencing are examples of which communication channel?
(a) Face-to-face communication
(b) Written communication
(c) Electronic communication
(d) Telephone communication

136. Why is feedback important in the communication process?
(a) It ensures that the sender is always right.
(b) It provides a chance to interrupt the speaker.
(c) It helps confirm that the message was understood and received.
(d) It is not important in the communication process.

137. Which of the following is not a benefit of receiving feedback in the communication process?
(a) Clarification of misunderstandings
(b) Confirmation of the message's receipt
(c) Ensuring that the speaker's perspective is the only one considered
(d) Validation of the message's effectiveness

138. In the communication process, feedback can be both verbal and
   (a) Visual
   (b) Nonverbal
   (c) Written
   (d) Interrupting

139. Which type of feedback is nonverbal and involves nodding, eye contact, or body language?
   (a) Verbal feedback
   (b) Written feedback
   (c) Nonverbal feedback
   (d) Interrupting feedback

140. What is the key to overcoming language barriers in communication?
   (a) Avoiding communication with individuals from different cultures
   (b) Using technical and complex language
   (c) Being aware of language differences and adapting communication
   (d) Speaking faster to convey more information

141. To overcome psychological barriers to communication, it is important to
   (a) Encourage defensive behavior in others
   (b) Ignore emotional responses to the message
   (c) Create a supportive and non-judgmental environment
   (d) Avoid eye contact

142. Cultural barriers to communication can be overcome by
   (a) Ignoring cultural differences
   (b) Making assumptions about the other person's culture
   (c) Being culturally sensitive and adapting communication
   (d) Speaking louder to ensure understanding

143. To overcome physical barriers to communication, one should
   (a) Use noisy environments for important conversations
   (b) Eliminate any distractions or background noise
   (c) Speak softly to avoid disruptions
   (d) Provide written communication only

144. What is the term for the process of verifying that the message has been correctly understood by the receiver?
   (a) Feedback (b) Encoding
   (c) Decoding (d) Noise

145. Which of the following is an effective strategy to overcome noise as a communication barrier?
   (a) Increasing the use of technical language
   (b) Ignoring distractions in the environment
   (c) Using nonverbal communication exclusively
   (d) Clearly articulating the message and verifying understanding

146. Decision making is the process of
   (a) Generating ideas
   (b) Solving problems
   (c) Taking action from alternatives
   (d) Communicating with others

147. In decision making, a choice is made from among two or more
   (a) Ideas (b) Problems
   (c) Alternatives (d) Questions

148. The concept of "bounded rationality" in decision making suggests that
   (a) Decision makers have unlimited time and resources
   (b) Decision makers have access to all information
   (c) Decision makers make rational choices within certain limits
   (d) Decision makers always choose the optimal solution

149. Which type of decision making is characterized by a systematic and rational process with a clear objective?
   (a) Intuitive decision making
   (b) Programmed decision making
   (c) Non-programmed decision making
   (d) Collaborative decision making

150. What is the first step in the decision-making process?
   (a) Implementing the decision
   (b) Identifying the problem or opportunity
   (c) Evaluating alternatives
   (d) Gathering information

151. In the decision-making process, what comes after generating and evaluating alternatives?
   (a) Implementing the decision
   (b) Identifying the problem or opportunity
   (c) Gathering information
   (d) Making the decision

152. The final step in the decision-making process is

(a) Gathering information
(b) Identifying the problem or opportunity
(c) Making the decision
(d) Evaluating alternatives

153. The decision-making process that is used for recurring or routine decisions with well-established procedures is known as
(a) Intuitive decision making
(b) Non-programmed decision making
(c) Programmed decision making
(d) Collaborative decision making

154. The SWOT analysis is a tool used in decision making to assess an organization's
(a) Marketing strategy
(b) Strengths, weaknesses, opportunities, and threats
(c) Financial performance
(d) Customer satisfaction

155. What decision-making technique involves listing and comparing the pros and cons of each alternative?
(a) Brainstorming
(b) SWOT analysis
(c) Force field analysis
(d) Decision matrix

156. In decision making, the Delphi technique is often used to
(a) Make quick, intuitive decisions
(b) Generate creative ideas
(c) Obtain consensus from a group of experts
(d) Rank alternatives based on cost-effectiveness

157. The technique of "Force Field Analysis" was developed by
(a) Abraham Maslow
(b) Kurt Lewin
(c) Douglas McGregor
(d) Frederick Taylor

158. What tool involves visually representing the relationship between multiple variables in a decision-making process?
(a) Decision tree
(b) SWOT analysis
(c) Force field analysis
(d) Pareto chart

159. The decision tree is a visual tool that helps decision makers
(a) Identify strengths and weaknesses
(b) Compare pros and cons
(c) Analyze the potential outcomes of various decisions
(d) Prioritize tasks

160. Which decision-making technique encourages group members to generate as many creative ideas as possible without criticism?
(a) Nominal group technique
(b) Brainstorming
(c) Delphi technique
(d) Decision matrix

161. The Pareto chart is a tool used in decision making to
(a) Prioritize tasks or problems based on their significance
(b) Generate creative ideas
(c) Compare pros and cons
(d) Analyze financial data

162. Groupthink is a decision-making challenge that can result from
(a) Diverse perspectives
(b) Open and honest communication
(c) A desire for consensus and harmony
(d) An objective evaluation of alternatives

163. Confirmation bias in decision making refers to
(a) A tendency to seek out information that confirms one's existing beliefs
(b) An open-minded approach to problem solving
(c) A preference for consensus in group decision making
(d) A focus on the most critical issues

164. Escalation of commitment is a decision-making challenge that involves
(a) Consistently seeking new information
(b) Continuing to invest resources in a failing course of action
(c) Avoiding risks and uncertainties
(d) Seeking consensus in group decisions

165. "Analysis paralysis" in decision making is characterized by
(a) A quick and efficient decision-making process
(b) Overanalyzing a situation and delaying a decision
(c) Seeking confirmation from others
(d) Relying on intuition for decision making

166. Ethical dilemmas in decision making often involve a conflict between

(a) Personal interests and professional interests
(b) Legal requirements and personal preferences
(c) Organizational values and individual values
(d) Traditional methods and innovative methods

167. In decision making, the term "group polarization" refers to the tendency of a group to
(a) Seek out diverse perspectives
(b) Move toward a more extreme position after discussing an issue
(c) Reach a quick consensus
(d) Avoid making a decision

168. What is a key element of effective decision making?
(a) Ignoring the input of others
(b) Relying solely on intuition
(c) Seeking input from diverse sources
(d) Making decisions in isolation

169. In group decision making, what is the value of diversity in perspectives and backgrounds?
(a) It often leads to conflict and confusion
(b) It can enhance creativity and problem-solving
(c) It slows down the decision-making process
(d) It ensures consensus and harmony

170. A structured and systematic approach to decision making can help reduce
(a) Confirmation bias
(b) Ethical dilemmas
(c) Analysis paralysis
(d) Escalation of commitment

171. In a functional organizational structure, employees are grouped based on
(a) Geographic location
(b) Product lines or services
(c) Project teams
(d) Customer segments

172. A matrix organizational structure combines elements of both
(a) Functional and divisional structures
(b) Functional and network structures
(c) Network and divisional structures
(d) Functional and hierarchical structures

173. In a divisional organizational structure, each division operates as a
(a) Standalone business unit
(b) Functional department
(c) Project team
(d) Research and development center

174. A network organizational structure relies on
(a) Centralized decision making
(b) A traditional hierarchy
(c) Interconnected relationships with external partners
(d) Strict functional departments

175. Authority in an organization refers to
(a) The number of employees reporting to a manager
(b) The right to give orders, make decisions, and enforce compliance
(c) The amount of work assigned to an employee
(d) The level of responsibility assigned to a manager

176. Responsibility in the context of organization structure is related to
(a) The number of employees in a department
(b) The authority to make decisions
(c) The obligations and duties associated with a position
(d) The number of divisions in an organization

177. Which type of authority is based on a manager's position within the organizational hierarchy?
(a) Line authority
(b) Staff authority
(c) Functional authority
(d) Delegated authority

178. Staff authority is often associated with
(a) Direct control over operations
(b) Support and advisory roles
(c) The production of goods and services
(d) High levels of decentralization

179. Centralization is the degree to which
(a) Decision-making authority is distributed throughout the organization
(b) Decision-making authority is concentrated at the top of the hierarchy
(c) Line and staff authority are balanced
(d) Functional and divisional structures are integrated

180. Decentralization is typically associated with
(a) Faster decision making

(b) More hierarchical organizations
(c) Lower levels of responsibility
(d) Narrow spans of control

181. In a highly centralized organization, decision-making authority is primarily vested in
(a) Top management
(b) Middle management
(c) Front-line employees
(d) Support staff

182. The level of centralization or decentralization in an organization can affect its
(a) Productivity
(b) Size
(c) Legal status
(d) Marketing strategy

183. Span of control refers to the number of
(a) Managers reporting to top management
(b) Employees reporting to a manager
(c) Divisions in an organization
(d) Functional departments in an organization

184. A narrow span of control implies that a manager
(a) Has fewer subordinates
(b) Has more subordinates
(c) Has a balanced number of subordinates
(d) Has a fixed number of subordinates

185. What is one of the advantages of a wide span of control?
(a) Enhanced communication and closer supervision
(b) Greater efficiency and cost savings
(c) More opportunities for career advancement
(d) Reduced responsibility for managers

186. A span of control that is too wide may result in
(a) Slower decision making
(b) Overburdened managers
(c) Centralized authority
(d) Increased organizational complexity

187. Organization design involves
(a) Choosing the organization's products or services
(b) Creating an organizational chart
(c) Determining the span of control
(d) Structuring the organization to achieve its objectives

188. An organization's structure should align with its
(a) Financial resources
(b) Size
(c) Strategy and goals
(d) Market share

189. When designing an organization, managers need to consider factors such as the organization's environment, technology, and
(a) Employee turnover
(b) Budget constraints
(c) Resource allocation
(d) Competitive strategy

190. A mechanistic organization design is characterized by
(a) A flat hierarchy
(b) Flexibility and adaptability
(c) Centralized decision making
(d) Wide spans of control

191. An organic organization design is typically associated with
(a) Formalized rules and procedures
(b) Hierarchical decision making
(c) Collaboration, flexibility, and decentralized authority
(d) Narrow spans of control

192. What is one of the key considerations when determining the appropriate structure for an organization?
(a) Employee job titles
(b) Employee diversity
(c) Organizational culture and goals
(d) Industry trends

193. An organization's structure should facilitate
(a) Quick and reactive decision making
(b) Bureaucratic processes
(c) Rigidity and standardization
(d) Close supervision of employees

194. What is a potential drawback of a highly centralized organizational structure?
(a) Slower response to changes in the environment
(b) Enhanced adaptability and flexibility
(c) Increased delegation of authority
(d) Stronger alignment with local markets

195. An organization's structure can influence its
(a) Employee benefits
(b) Marketing budget
(c) Communication flow, efficiency, and overall performance
(d) Financial statements

196. Managerial economics is primarily concerned with
(a) Maximizing profits
(b) Achieving social welfare
(c) Allocative efficiency
(d) Government regulations

197. Managerial economics integrates concepts and methods from which two fields?
(a) Microeconomics and macroeconomics
(b) Psychology and sociology
(c) Marketing and finance
(d) Statistics and engineering

198. The objective of managerial economics is to help managers make decisions that
(a) Maximize sales
(b) Minimize production costs
(c) Maximize shareholder wealth
(d) Minimize competition

199. Managerial economics applies economic concepts and principles to solve
(a) Economic policy issues
(b) Short-term financial problems
(c) Managerial problems and decisions
(d) Ethical dilemmas

200. One of the key functions of managerial economics is to provide a framework for
(a) Forecasting stock market trends
(b) Analyzing historical data
(c) Decision making and problem-solving
(d) Calculating taxes

201. Managerial economics helps in optimizing
(a) Social welfare
(b) Government regulations
(c) Limited resources
(d) Competition in the market

202. The use of managerial economics can lead to improved
(a) Employee morale
(b) Short term profits
(c) Decision-making effectiveness
(d) Legal compliance

203. Which of the following is a benefit of using managerial economics in decision making?
(a) Reducing the importance of ethics in business decisions
(b) Eliminating the need for cost analysis
(c) Enhancing the efficiency and effectiveness of decisions
(d) Minimizing government regulations

204. Managerial economics is particularly important in industries with
(a) Perfect competition
(b) No external stakeholders
(c) Monopoly power
(d) No profit motive

205. One of the key aspects of managerial economics is the consideration of
(a) Economic variables only
(b) Short-term objectives only
(c) Social and ethical considerations
(d) Managerial decisions unrelated to economics

206. In managerial economics, decision making often involves trade-offs between
(a) Profits and ethics
(b) Short-term and long-term objectives
(c) Government regulations and market forces
(d) Total revenue and total cost

207. Which of the following is an example of a microeconomic decision that managers often face?
(a) Setting the national interest rate
(b) Deciding on the country's trade policies
(c) Determining the selling price of a product
(d) Managing the national budget

208. Managerial economics helps managers analyze how changes in market conditions and company strategies affect
(a) Government regulations
(b) Social welfare
(c) Total profit
(d) Business objectives

209. Managerial economics is particularly useful for understanding and managing issues related to
(a) Political campaigns
(b) International diplomacy
(c) Business operations and strategies
(d) Non-profit organizations

210. The analysis of demand, cost, and pricing falls under which area of managerial economics?
(a) Strategic management
(b) Macroeconomics
(c) Microeconomics
(d) Social responsibility

211. Managerial economics is often applied in areas such as
(a) Perfect competition

(b) Decision making, forecasting, and pricing
(c) Environmental protection
(d) Ethical dilemmas

212. A key application of managerial economics is the analysis of the impact of
(a) Short-term objectives on long-term objectives
(b) Government regulations on market competition
(c) Taxes on corporate profits
(d) Ethics on decision making

213. Managerial economics can be used to analyze the effect of advertising on
(a) Managerial salaries
(b) Government regulations
(c) Sales and revenue
(d) Ethics in business

214. Which of the following industries would not benefit from applying managerial economics?
(a) Manufacturing (b) Healthcare
(c) Education (d) Technology

215. The application of managerial economics can lead to better decision making by
(a) Eliminating the need for forecasting
(b) Providing managers with complete information
(c) Enhancing the decision-making process through systematic analysis
(d) Minimizing the importance of ethics in business decisions

216. In the context of demand analysis, utility refers to
(a) The amount of a good that consumers purchase
(b) The satisfaction or benefit consumers derive from consuming a good
(c) The total revenue generated by the sale of a good
(d) The price consumers are willing to pay for a good

217. Total utility is the
(a) Satisfaction derived from consuming one additional unit of a good
(b) Total satisfaction or benefit derived from consuming a quantity of a good
(c) Price at which consumers are willing to purchase a good
(d) Amount of money spent on a good

218. The law of diminishing marginal utility suggests that
(a) As a consumer consumes more of a good, the total utility remains constant
(b) As a consumer consumes more of a good, the marginal utility decreases
(c) As a consumer consumes more of a good, the marginal utility increases
(d) As a consumer consumes more of a good, the total utility increases

219. A consumer reaches consumer equilibrium when
(a) Marginal utility is zero
(b) Total utility is maximized
(c) Marginal utility is equal to price
(d) Total utility is zero

220. In indifference curve analysis, an indifference curve represents
(a) The consumer's preferences and choices
(b) The budget constraint of a consumer
(c) The law of diminishing marginal utility
(d) The demand curve for a good

221. An indifference curve that is farther from the origin represents
(a) Lower levels of satisfaction
(b) Higher levels of satisfaction
(c) The budget constraint of the consumer
(d) Equal levels of satisfaction

222. Indifference curves are typically
(a) Concave to the origin
(b) Convex to the origin
(c) Linear
(d) Straight lines

223. The concept of the marginal rate of substitution (MRS) represents
(a) The rate at which a consumer can trade one good for another while remaining indifferent
(b) The total utility derived from a good
(c) The price elasticity of demand
(d) The consumer's budget constraint

224. Price elasticity of demand measures the
(a) Change in quantity demanded in response to changes in income
(b) Responsiveness of quantity demanded to changes in price
(c) Responsiveness of quantity demanded to changes in the quantity supplied
(d) Total revenue generated by a good

225. If the price elasticity of demand is greater than 1, the demand is considered

(a) Perfectly elastic
(b) Inelastic
(c) Elastic
(d) Unitary elastic

226. If the price elasticity of demand is less than 1, the demand is considered
(a) Perfectly inelastic
(b) Elastic
(c) Inelastic
(d) Unitary elastic

227. Cross elasticity of demand measures the responsiveness of the quantity demanded of one good to changes in the price of
(a) A complementary good
(b) An inferior good
(c) A substitute good
(d) An inelastic good

228. Income elasticity of demand measures the responsiveness of the quantity demanded to changes in
(a) The price of the good
(b) Consumer preferences
(c) Income
(d) Advertising

229. Demand forecasting is important for businesses because it helps with
(a) Maximizing production costs
(b) Predicting macroeconomic trends
(c) Inventory management and production planning
(d) Reducing advertising expenses

230. Qualitative methods of demand forecasting typically involve
(a) Statistical data analysis
(b) Expert opinions and market research
(c) Mathematical models
(d) Historical sales data

231. Time-series analysis in demand forecasting involves
(a) Gathering data on consumer preferences
(b) Analyzing historical data to identify patterns and trends
(c) Using expert opinions to predict future demand
(d) Conducting surveys of potential customers

232. The Delphi method in demand forecasting relies on
(a) Expert opinions
(b) Mathematical modeling
(c) Regression analysis
(d) Historical data

233. Which demand forecasting method uses a combination of various forecasting techniques to improve accuracy?
(a) Time-series analysis
(b) Causal modeling
(c) Delphi method
(d) Composite forecasting

234. In demand forecasting, the difference between the forecasted value and the actual value is known as
(a) Standard deviation
(b) Forecasting error
(c) Margin of error
(d) Regression coefficient

235. A forecasting error is considered "positive" when the forecasted value is
(a) Greater than the actual value
(b) Less than the actual value
(c) Equal to the actual value
(d) Negative

236. Which of the following is a measure of forecasting accuracy that calculates the absolute differences between forecasted and actual values?
(a) Mean absolute percentage error (MAPE)
(b) Mean absolute deviation (MAD)
(c) Standard error of the estimate
(d) Correlation coefficient

237. A forecasting method with a small MAD is generally considered
(a) Less accurate
(b) More accurate
(c) Suitable for long-term forecasting
(d) Suitable for short-term forecasting

238. The mean squared error (MSE) is calculated by
(a) Taking the square root of the MAD
(b) Squaring the absolute differences between forecasted and actual values
(c) Dividing the MAD by the sample size
(d) Finding the absolute differences between forecasted and actual values

239. Which of the following measures forecasting accuracy in percentage terms?
(a) Mean absolute deviation (MAD)
(b) Mean squared error (MSE)

(c) Mean absolute percentage error (MAPE)
(d) Correlation coefficient

240. In demand forecasting, a MAPE value of 5% indicates
(a) A high level of forecasting accuracy
(b) A low level of forecasting accuracy
(c) Perfect accuracy
(d) A negative forecasting error

241. A market in which there are many buyers and sellers, homogeneous products, and perfect information is known as
(a) A monopoly
(b) A perfectly competitive market
(c) An oligopoly
(d) A monopolistic competition

242. In a monopolistic competition, products are
(a) Perfect substitutes
(b) Homogeneous
(c) Differentiated
(d) Identical

243. An industry with a small number of firms, each of which has the ability to influence market prices, is known as
(a) A perfectly competitive market
(b) A monopoly
(c) An oligopoly
(d) A monopolistic competition

244. In a monopolistic competition, firms engage in product differentiation to
(a) Achieve a perfect monopoly
(b) Increase market power
(c) Produce homogeneous products
(d) Create a perfectly competitive market

245. A market structure in which a single firm is the sole producer of a good with no close substitutes is called
(a) A perfectly competitive market
(b) A monopoly
(c) An oligopoly
(d) A monopolistic competition

246. An industry characterized by high barriers to entry, few firms, and differentiated products is most likely
(a) A perfectly competitive market
(b) A monopoly
(c) An oligopoly
(d) A monopolistic competition

247. In a perfectly competitive market, the price is determined by
(a) The government
(b) Individual firms
(c) The interaction of supply and demand
(d) The largest firm in the market

248. In a monopoly, the monopolist has
(a) No control over the price
(b) Complete control over the price
(c) Partial control over the price
(d) No ability to influence demand

249. The demand curve facing a perfectly competitive firm is
(a) Vertical
(b) Downward-sloping
(c) Upward-sloping
(d) Horizontal

250. In a monopolistic competition, each firm faces a demand curve that is
(a) Perfectly elastic (b) Perfectly inelastic
(c) Downward-sloping
(d) Horizontal

251. In an oligopoly, firms often engage in price wars and non-price competition to
(a) Raise prices
(b) Maintain high barriers to entry
(c) Maximize profits
(d) Gain a competitive advantage

252. Price leadership is a common practice in which type of market structure?
(a) Perfectly competitive market
(b) Monopoly
(c) Oligopoly
(d) Monopolistic competition

253. A kinked demand curve is typically associated with which market structure?
(a) Perfectly competitive market
(b) Monopoly
(c) Oligopoly
(d) Monopolistic competition

254. In a perfectly competitive market, the demand curve for the individual firm is
(a) Vertical
(b) Downward-sloping
(c) Upward-sloping
(d) Horizontal

255. In a monopolistic competition, firms have some control over price because they can
(a) Set any price they desire
(b) Influence consumer preferences

(c) Engage in price discrimination
(d) Differentiate their products

256. The equilibrium price and quantity in a perfectly competitive market are determined by the point at which
(a) Total revenue equals total cost
(b) Marginal cost equals marginal revenue
(c) Average total cost is minimized
(d) Supply and demand intersect

257. A firm operating in a perfectly competitive market can increase its output by hiring more labor until the point at which
(a) Marginal cost exceeds marginal revenue
(b) Marginal cost is minimized
(c) Total cost is maximized
(d) Average variable cost equals marginal revenue

258. In an oligopoly, firms often engage in collusion to
(a) Increase competition
(b) Lower prices
(c) Raise prices
(d) Promote perfect competition

259. In a monopolistic competition, firms have some market power due to
(a) Homogeneous products
(b) Perfect information
(c) Product differentiation
(d) Perfect substitutes

260. In a perfectly competitive market, a firm's long-run equilibrium occurs when it
(a) Maximizes profits
(b) Incurs losses
(c) Sets a price above market equilibrium
(d) Operates at the minimum average total cost

261. Price discrimination is a pricing strategy often employed in which market structure?
(a) Perfectly competitive market
(b) Monopoly
(c) Oligopoly
(d) Monopolistic competition

262. A natural monopoly occurs when
(a) A single firm is the most efficient producer
(b) There are many firms in the industry
(c) Firms engage in price wars
(d) Market demand is perfectly elastic

263. In monopolistic competition, firms often face a downward-sloping demand curve because
(a) Their products are perfect substitutes
(b) Firms have no market power
(c) Consumers have perfect information
(d) Products are differentiated

264. In a, perfectly competitive market, firms can earn
(a) Economic profits in the long run
(b) Normal profits in the long run
(c) Monopoly profits in the short run
(d) Negative profits in the short run

265. In a perfectly competitive market, individual firms are
(a) Price makers
(b) Price takers
(c) Price leaders
(d) Price followers

266. National income is a measure of
(a) The total wealth of a nation
(b) The economic well-being of individuals
(c) The economic performance of a country over a period
(d) The number of people living in a nation

267. Gross National Product (GNP) includes
(a) Only the production of domestic residents
(b) The production of domestic residents and foreign residents
(c) The production of foreign residents
(d) The production of foreign residents and exports

268. Net National Product (NNP) is calculated by subtracting
(a) Depreciation from GNP
(b) Taxes from GNP
(c) Government spending from GNP
(d) Imports from GNP

269. Gross Domestic Product (GDP) measures
(a) The total output of a nation's residents and businesses within its borders
(b) The income of a nation's residents
(c) The total output of a nation's residents and businesses outside its borders
(d) The total output of a nation's businesses within its borders

270. Personal income is
(a) The total income of a nation's government
(b) The total income of a nation's residents
(c) The total income of a nation's businesses
(d) The total income of a nation's exports

271. Disposable income is calculated by subtracting which of the following from personal income?
(a) Personal taxes
(b) Government spending
(c) Savings
(d) Imports

272. Which of the following is NOT a component of the national income of a country?
(a) Wages and salaries
(b) Interest income
(c) Corporate profits
(d) Personal savings

273. Transfer payments, such as social security and welfare, are included in which type of national income?
(a) Personal income
(b) Disposable income
(c) National income
(d) Gross Domestic Product

274. The expenditure approach to measuring GDP includes
(a) Consumption, investment, and government spending
(b) Imports and exports
(c) Personal income and corporate profits
(d) Savings and investments

275. Which of the following is considered an investment in the context of measuring GDP?
(a) Purchasing stocks and bonds
(b) Building a new factory
(c) Buying a new car for personal use
(d) Paying off a mortgage

276. The income approach to measuring GDP calculates it as the sum of
(a) Personal income, corporate profits, and transfer payments
(b) Wages, interest, rent, and corporate profits
(c) Imports and exports
(d) Consumption and government spending

277. The value-added approach to measuring GDP involves
(a) Calculating the total value of imports
(b) Summing up the value added by each firm in the production process
(c) Determining the final selling price of goods and services
(d) Analyzing income and expenditure data

278. Gross National Product (GNP) measures the total production of
(a) Domestic residents
(b) Foreign residents
(c) Government
(d) Exports and imports

279. Gross Domestic Product (GDP) is equal to GNP minus
(a) Personal income
(b) Corporate profits
(c) Net factor income from abroad
(d) Savings

280. The term "real GDP" is used to describe GDP that has been adjusted for changes in
(a) Nominal income
(b) Taxes
(c) Inflation
(d) Interest rates

281. The Consumer Price Index (CPI) is used to calculate the
(a) Unemployment rate
(b) Inflation rate
(c) Exchange rate
(d) Balance of trade

282. A decrease in the unemployment rate is associated with which of the following?
(a) An increase in inflation
(b) Economic growth
(c) A decrease in government spending
(d) A trade deficit

283. The Lorenz curve is used to visualize and analyze
(a) The distribution of income within a country
(b) The inflation rate
(c) The balance of trade
(d) The national debt

284. Which of the following economic indicators is NOT a measure of economic performance?
(a) Gross Domestic Product (GDP)
(b) Inflation rate
(c) Balance of trade
(d) Unemployment rate

285. A country's Gross National Product (GNP) is equal to its Gross Domestic Product (GDP) plus
(a) Net factor income from abroad
(b) Personal income
(c) Government spending
(d) Corporate profits

286. Inflation is best described as
(a) A decrease in the overall level of prices
(b) The rate at which a currency appreciates
(c) An increase in the overall level of prices
(d) A stagnant economy with no price changes

287. Hyperinflation is characterized by
(a) Mild price increases over time
(b) Extremely rapid and uncontrollable price increases
(c) Stable prices
(d) Price decreases

288. Which of the following is a consequence of moderate inflation?
(a) Encouragement of saving
(b) Reduced uncertainty in the economy
(c) Erosion of purchasing power
(d) Increased real wages

289. Cost-push inflation is caused by
(a) An increase in aggregate demand
(b) A decrease in the money supply
(c) An increase in production efficiency
(d) Rising production costs, such as wages and raw materials

290. Demand-pull inflation is typically associated with
(a) A decrease in consumer spending
(b) A decrease in aggregate demand
(c) Excess demand for goods and services
(d) A recession

291. Built-in inflation, also known as wage-price spiral, is characterized by
(a) Sustained decreases in wages and prices
(b) Workers demanding higher wages to keep up with rising prices
(c) Falling demand for goods and services
(d) A stable economy

292. Demand-pull inflation is said to occur when
(a) There is a shortage of goods and services
(b) Aggregate supply exceeds aggregate demand
(c) Government spending decreases
(d) Aggregate demand exceeds aggregate supply

293. Which of the following is an example of cost-push inflation?
(a) Increased consumer spending
(b) A decrease in the money supply
(c) A surge in oil prices leading to higher production costs
(d) A reduction in taxes

294. Inflation resulting from an excessive growth of the money supply is referred to as
(a) Demand-pull inflation
(b) Cost-push inflation
(c) Monetarist inflation
(d) Stagflation

295. The Consumer Price Index (CPI) measures changes in the
(a) Total income of a country
(b) Aggregate supply of goods and services
(c) Cost of a fixed basket of consumer goods and services
(d) Exchange rate of a currency

296. Core inflation excludes which of the following from its calculations?
(a) Energy and food prices
(b) Housing costs
(c) Wages and salaries
(d) Transportation expenses

297. The Producer Price Index (PPI) measures changes in the prices of goods at what stage of production?
(a) Final stage
(b) Retail stage
(c) Wholesale stage
(d) Intermediate stage

298. The GDP deflator measures changes in the
(a) Consumer Price Index (CPI)
(b) Gross Domestic Product (GDP)
(c) Producer Price Index (PPI)
(d) Exchange rate

299. If the GDP deflator for a country increases from 120 to 130, this suggests
(a) Deflation (b) Hyperinflation
(c) Inflation (d) Stagflation

300. Inflation measured by the GDP deflator reflects price changes in
(a) Consumer goods and services only
(b) Final goods and services produced within a country
(c) Intermediate goods and services used in production
(d) The prices of foreign goods and services

301. Business ethics is concerned with
(a) Maximizing shareholder wealth

(b) Legal compliance only
(c) Ethical behavior in business activities
(d) Government regulations

302. Which ethical theory suggests that actions are morally right when they promote the greatest good for the greatest number?
(a) Virtue ethics (b) Deontology
(c) Utilitarianism (d) Rights-based ethics

303. Ethical dilemmas in business often arise when there is a conflict between
(a) Profit and revenue
(b) Legal and ethical standards
(c) Short-term and long-term goals
(d) Supply and demand

304. The concept of corporate social responsibility (CSR) suggests that businesses should
(a) Focus solely on maximizing profits
(b) Be accountable only to shareholders
(c) Consider the impact of their actions on various stakeholders
(d) Ignore the well-being of employees

305. A company that engages in ethical behavior is more likely to
(a) Maximize profits in the short term
(b) Attract and retain customers and employees
(c) Face legal challenges
(d) Ignore the interests of shareholders

306. CSR involves a company's responsibility to
(a) Maximize profits at all costs
(b) Only consider the interests of shareholders
(c) Balance economic, social, and environmental concerns in its operations
(d) Avoid government regulations

307. Which of the following is NOT a common area of CSR focus for businesses?
(a) Environmental sustainability
(b) Economic growth
(c) Social responsibility
(d) Ethical labor practices

308. Sustainable business practices often involve
(a) Maximized resource consumption
(b) Ignoring social and environmental concerns
(c) Balancing profit generation with long-term environmental and social well-being
(d) Strict adherence to legal standards

309. The "triple bottom line" approach to CSR evaluates a company's performance in terms of
(a) Profit, profit, and profit
(b) People, planet, and profit
(c) Profit, ethics, and government regulations
(d) Financial, ethical, and social metrics

310. The United Nations Global Compact encourages businesses to adopt principles related to
(a) Short-term profit maximization
(b) Environmental sustainability
(c) Government regulations
(d) Ignoring the interests of employees

311. The first step in ethical decision-making for businesses is often
(a) Maximizing profits
(b) Identifying the stakeholders involved
(c) Ignoring potential consequences
(d) Avoiding ethical dilemmas

312. Whistleblowing is the act of
(a) Ignoring unethical behavior
(b) Reporting unethical behavior within an organization
(c) Encouraging unethical behavior
(d) Engaging in insider trading

313. When a company makes ethical decisions to enhance its public image or reputation, this is often referred to as
(a) Greenwashing
(b) CSR-washing
(c) Whistleblowing
(d) Ethical leadership

314. Ethical leadership in business typically involves
(a) Encouraging unethical behavior within the organization
(b) Setting a positive example and promoting ethical behavior
(c) Focusing solely on maximizing shareholder wealth
(d) Avoiding social responsibility

315. Stakeholder theory suggests that businesses should consider the interests of
(a) Shareholders only
(b) Customers and employees only
(c) All parties that may be affected by their actions
(d) Government regulators

316. Ethical issues in business often involve conflicts between
(a) Profit and competition
(b) Legal and ethical standards
(c) Short-term and long-term goals
(d) Marketing and advertising

317. A conflict of interest occurs when
(a) Employees have similar personal interests
(b) Employees have opposing personal interests
(c) Employees have no personal interests
(d) Employees are not involved in decision-making

318. Intellectual property theft, such as copyright infringement, raises ethical issues related to
(a) Employee salaries
(b) Product quality
(c) Privacy
(d) Fair competition

319. The concept of ethical relativism suggests that
(a) There is a single set of universally applicable ethical principles
(b) Ethical standards can vary depending on the culture or context
(c) Ethical issues can only be resolved through legal means
(d) Ethics and morals are unrelated in business

320. Ethical issues related to discrimination in the workplace often involve factors such as
(a) Employee job titles
(b) Age, race, gender, and sexual orientation
(c) Employee job performance
(d) Social media usage

321. An ethical dilemma is a situation in which
(a) There is a clear choice between right and wrong
(b) A decision must be made between two or more equally undesirable options
(c) There are no consequences to consider
(d) Legal standards apply, and ethics are irrelevant

322. A common ethical dilemma in business involves balancing the interests of
(a) Employees and shareholders
(b) Shareholders and competitors
(c) Customers and government regulators
(d) Owners and customers

323. Whistleblowing is often considered an ethical dilemma because it involves
(a) Reporting unethical behavior, potentially harming one's career
(b) Ignoring unethical behavior and protecting one's job
(c) Encouraging unethical behavior within the organization
(d) Promoting transparency and accountability

324. In the "trolley problem" ethical dilemma, a person must decide whether to
(a) Stay on the trolley track and let it hit five people or divert it to hit one person
(b) Do nothing and let the trolley hit five people
(c) Save themselves and let the trolley hit five people
(d) Take no action and let the trolley hit one person

325. An ethical dilemma that involves the choice between honesty and loyalty is often called
(a) The "trolley problem"
(b) The "prisoner's dilemma"
(c) The "whistleblower's dilemma"
(d) The "tug of war"

326. When resolving ethical dilemmas, the "Golden Rule" suggests
(a) Focusing on self-interest
(b) Treating others as you would like to be treated
(c) Prioritizing profits above all else
(d) Ignoring the interests of others

327. The ethical principle of "utilitarianism" suggests making decisions that
(a) Maximize profits for the organization
(b) Promote the greatest good for the greatest number
(c) Benefit only a select group of stakeholders
(d) Avoid legal consequences

328. "Deontological ethics" is an ethical approach that focuses on
(a) The consequences of actions
(b) The intrinsic moral value of actions
(c) Profits and shareholder wealth
(d) Business competition

329. "Virtue ethics" emphasizes
(a) Legal standards and compliance

(b) The development of good character traits
(c) Profit maximization
(d) Strict adherence to government regulations

330. An ethical decision-making framework that involves assessing the potential consequences of actions, considering alternatives, and making a decision based on the least harmful outcome is known as
(a) Ethical relativism
(b) The categorical imperative
(c) The "trolley problem"
(d) Ethical reasoning

331. Corporate governance refers to the system by which companies are directed and controlled. It primarily involves
(a) Maximizing shareholder wealth
(b) Ensuring legal compliance
(c) Balancing the interests of various stakeholders
(d) Minimizing government regulations

332. The board of directors of a company is responsible for
(a) Day-to-day management of the organization
(b) Maximizing short-term profits
(c) Providing oversight and strategic guidance
(d) Ignoring shareholder interests

333. The concept of separation of ownership and control in corporate governance relates to
(a) Shareholders having direct control over the company's operations
(b) Shareholders owning a majority of the company's assets
(c) The board of directors overseeing management, who may not be the company's owners
(d) Government regulations governing shareholder rights

334. A key principle of corporate governance is transparency, which refers to
(a) Keeping corporate information confidential
(b) Providing clear, accurate, and timely information to stakeholders
(c) Avoiding public disclosures
(d) Minimizing corporate reporting

335. The primary responsibility of the audit committee within a company's board of directors is to
(a) Maximize shareholder profits
(b) Ensure the company's compliance with legal regulations
(c) Set executive compensation packages
(d) Manage the company's daily operations

336. Shareholder activism in corporate governance typically involves
(a) Encouraging shareholders to vote on corporate decisions
(b) Ignoring shareholder interests
(c) Excessive executive compensation
(d) Promoting government regulations

337. The "say on pay" principle in corporate governance is related to
(a) CEO compensation and shareholder approval
(b) Government regulations on executive pay
(c) The rights of employees
(d) Shareholder voting rights

338. One of the primary roles of external auditors in corporate governance is to
(a) Maximize shareholder profits
(b) Ensure the accuracy of the company's financial statements
(c) Manage shareholder meetings
(d) Influence executive compensation

339. Whistleblower protection is an important corporate governance mechanism because it
(a) Encourages employees to report unethical behavior without fear of retaliation
(b) Discourages employees from reporting unethical behavior
(c) Promotes excessive government regulations
(d) Maximizes executive compensation

340. The "board independence" principle in corporate governance refers to
(a) Directors being related to the company's top executives
(b) Directors being free from conflicts of interest and not being employees or relatives of the company's top executives
(c) Directors having full control over company operations
(d) Government regulations on director qualifications

341. The OECD Principles of Corporate Governance provide guidelines for corporate governance in
(a) The United States only
(b) Europe only
(c) All OECD member countries
(d) Developing nations only

342. The Sarbanes-Oxley Act is a U.S. law that was enacted to
(a) Promote shareholder activism
(b) Strengthen corporate governance and financial reporting
(c) Maximize executive compensation
(d) Eliminate government regulations

343. The term "corporate social responsibility" (CSR) is often associated with corporate governance and refers to a company's responsibility to
(a) Maximize profits
(b) Focus solely on shareholder interests
(c) Balance economic, social, and environmental concerns in its operations
(d) Ignore the well-being of employees

344. The Global Reporting Initiative (GRI) provides standards for
(a) Shareholder activism
(b) Transparency and sustainability reporting
(c) Executive compensation
(d) Government regulations

345. The International Corporate Governance Network (ICGN) is an organization that focuses on
(a) Shareholder activism
(b) Developing global corporate governance standards
(c) Minimizing government regulations
(d) Promoting executive compensation

346. A value-based organization is primarily focused on
(a) Maximizing short-term profits
(b) Maximizing shareholder wealth
(c) Aligning its activities and decisions with core values
(d) Minimizing employee benefits

347. The core values of a value-based organization typically reflect
(a) Only the interests of shareholders
(b) Social and environmental concerns
(c) Government regulations
(d) Short-term profit goals

348. Which of the following is a key characteristic of a value-based organization?
(a) Frequent changes in core values
(b) Consistent adherence to ethical principles
(c) Ignoring the interests of employees
(d) Emphasizing government regulations

349. The process of embedding values in all aspects of an organization's operations is known as
(a) Shareholder activism
(b) Value creation
(c) Value alignment
(d) Cost minimization

350. In a value-based organization, employees are encouraged to make decisions that are
(a) Most profitable for shareholders
(b) Consistent with the organization's core values
(c) In line with government regulations
(d) Minimally disruptive to the company's operations

351. Leadership in a value-based organization often involves
(a) Ignoring the organization's core values
(b) Setting a positive example and promoting ethical behavior
(c) Focusing solely on short-term profits
(d) Maximizing shareholder wealth

352. An organization's culture is shaped by
(a) Strict adherence to government regulations
(b) The personal values and behaviors of its leaders and employees
(c) Constant changes in core values
(d) Maximizing employee benefits

353. The role of values in shaping an organization's culture is to
(a) Align it with government regulations
(b) Guide behaviors and decision-making
(c) Ensure compliance with ethical standards
(d) Minimize employee satisfaction

354. In a value-based organization, leaders are expected to
(a) Ignore the interests of employees
(b) Prioritize profits over values
(c) Lead by example, promoting ethical behaviors and values
(d) Focus solely on shareholder interests

355. The "tone at the top" refers to
(a) A focus on short-term profit goals

(b) The ethical behavior and values demonstrated by top leadership
(c) Strict adherence to government regulations
(d) Maximizing shareholder wealth

356. In a value-based organization, decision-making is guided by
(a) The pursuit of government regulations
(b) Ethical principles and core values
(c) Maximizing employee benefits
(d) Short-term profit goals

357. When facing a difficult decision, employees in a value-based organization are encouraged to
(a) Disregard the organization's core values
(b) Follow government regulations
(c) Seek guidance from leaders and colleagues
(d) Prioritize their own interests over those of the organization

358. The process of considering the ethical implications of decisions and actions is known as
(a) Ethical relativism
(b) Ethical reasoning
(c) Maximizing shareholder wealth
(d) Government regulations

359. A key benefit of value-based decision-making is
(a) Maximizing short-term profits
(b) Enhanced corporate reputation and trust
(c) Ignoring the interests of employees
(d) Focusing solely on government regulations

360. The practice of value-based organizations measuring and reporting their ethical and sustainable performance is often referred to as
(a) Ethical relativism
(b) CSR-washing
(c) Transparency and sustainability reporting
(d) Maximizing shareholder wealth

ANSWER KEY

1. (a) **2.** (d) **3.** (c) **4.** (c) **5.** (d) **6.** (b) **7.** (a) **8.** (d) **9.** (d) **10.** (a)
11. (b) **12.** (b) **13.** (c) **14.** (d) **15.** (b) **16.** (c) **17.** (a) **18.** (b) **19.** (b) **20.** (c)
21. (c) **22.** (b) **23.** (b) **24.** (d) **25.** (c) **26.** (c) **27.** (c) **28.** (c) **29.** (d) **30.** (c)
31. (d) **32.** (d) **33.** (a) **34.** (c) **35.** (c) **36.** (a) **37.** (c) **38.** (a) **39.** (b) **40.** (a)
41. (c) **42.** (a) **43.** (d) **44.** (d) **45.** (c) **46.** (c) **47.** (b) **48.** (c) **49.** (d) **50.** (c)
51. (a) **52.** (b) **53.** (c) **54.** (b) **55.** (b) **56.** (b) **57.** (c) **58.** (c) **59.** (a) **60.** (c)
61. (a) **62.** (d) **63.** (a) **64.** (b) **65.** (d) **66.** (b) **67.** (b) **68.** (a) **69.** (d) **70.** (b)
71. (b) **72.** (b) **73.** (d) **74.** (c) **75.** (c) **76.** (c) **77.** (b) **78.** (c) **79.** (a) **80.** (b)
81. (b) **82.** (c) **83.** (d) **84.** (c) **85.** (c) **86.** (b) **87.** (a) **88.** (b) **89.** (b) **90.** (b)
91. (b) **92.** (c) **93.** (c) **94.** (c) **95.** (c) **96.** (b) **97.** (b) **98.** (c) **99.** (b) **100.** (c)
101. (c) **102.** (c) **103.** (a) **104.** (a) **105.** (d) **106.** (c) **107.** (b) **108.** (c) **109.** (c) **110.** (d)
111. (b) **112.** (b) **113.** (c) **114.** (c) **115.** (a) **116.** (a) **117.** (c) **118.** (b) **119.** (a) **120.** (c)
121. (d) **122.** (c) **123.** (c) **124.** (b) **125.** (d) **126.** (c) **127.** (b) **128.** (b) **129.** (d) **130.** (a)
131. (c) **132.** (c) **133.** (b) **134.** (a) **135.** (c) **136.** (c) **137.** (c) **138.** (b) **139.** (c) **140.** (c)
141. (c) **142.** (c) **143.** (b) **144.** (a) **145.** (d) **146.** (c) **147.** (c) **148.** (c) **149.** (b) **150.** (b)
151. (d) **152.** (d) **153.** (c) **154.** (b) **155.** (d) **156.** (c) **157.** (b) **158.** (a) **159.** (c) **160.** (b)
161. (a) **162.** (c) **163.** (a) **164.** (b) **165.** (b) **166.** (a) **167.** (b) **168.** (c) **169.** (b) **170.** (a)
171. (a) **172.** (a) **173.** (a) **174.** (c) **175.** (b) **176.** (c) **177.** (a) **178.** (b) **179.** (b) **180.** (a)
181. (a) **182.** (a) **183.** (b) **184.** (a) **185.** (b) **186.** (b) **187.** (d) **188.** (c) **189.** (d) **190.** (c)
191. (c) **192.** (c) **193.** (a) **194.** (a) **195.** (c) **196.** (a) **197.** (a) **198.** (c) **199.** (c) **200.** (c)
201. (c) **202.** (c) **203.** (c) **204.** (c) **205.** (c) **206.** (b) **207.** (c) **208.** (d) **209.** (c) **210.** (c)
211. (b) **212.** (a) **213.** (c) **214.** (c) **215.** (c) **216.** (b) **217.** (b) **218.** (b) **219.** (c) **220.** (a)
221. (b) **222.** (b) **223.** (a) **224.** (b) **225.** (c) **226.** (c) **227.** (c) **228.** (c) **229.** (c) **230.** (b)
231. (b) **232.** (a) **233.** (d) **234.** (b) **235.** (a) **236.** (b) **237.** (b) **238.** (b) **239.** (c) **240.** (a)
241. (b) **242.** (c) **243.** (c) **244.** (b) **245.** (b) **246.** (c) **247.** (c) **248.** (b) **249.** (d) **250.** (c)
251. (d) **252.** (c) **253.** (c) **254.** (d) **255.** (d) **256.** (d) **257.** (a) **258.** (c) **259.** (c) **260.** (d)
261. (b) **262.** (a) **263.** (d) **264.** (b) **265.** (b) **266.** (c) **267.** (a) **268.** (a) **269.** (a) **270.** (b)
271. (a) **272.** (d) **273.** (a) **274.** (a) **275.** (b) **276.** (b) **277.** (b) **278.** (a) **279.** (c) **280.** (c)
281. (b) **282.** (b) **283.** (a) **284.** (c) **285.** (a) **286.** (c) **287.** (b) **288.** (c) **289.** (d) **290.** (c)
291. (b) **292.** (d) **293.** (c) **294.** (c) **295.** (c) **296.** (a) **297.** (c) **298.** (b) **299.** (c) **300.** (b)
301. (c) **302.** (c) **303.** (b) **304.** (c) **305.** (b) **306.** (c) **307.** (b) **308.** (c) **309.** (b) **310.** (b)
311. (b) **312.** (b) **313.** (a) **314.** (b) **315.** (c) **316.** (b) **317.** (b) **318.** (d) **319.** (b) **320.** (b)
321. (b) **322.** (a) **323.** (a) **324.** (a) **325.** (d) **326.** (b) **327.** (b) **328.** (b) **329.** (b) **330.** (d)
331. (c) **332.** (c) **333.** (c) **334.** (b) **335.** (b) **336.** (a) **337.** (a) **338.** (b) **339.** (a) **340.** (b)
341. (c) **342.** (b) **343.** (c) **344.** (b) **345.** (b) **346.** (c) **347.** (b) **348.** (b) **349.** (c) **350.** (b)
351. (b) **352.** (b) **353.** (b) **354.** (c) **355.** (b) **356.** (b) **357.** (c) **358.** (b) **359.** (b) **360.** (c)

UNIT 2

SYLLABUS

- Organisational Behaviour – Significance & Theories
- Individual Behaviour – Personality, Perception, Values, Attitude, Learning and Motivation
- Group Behaviour – Team Building, Leadership, Group Dynamics
- Interpersonal Behaviour & Transactional Analysis
- Organizational Culture & Climate
- Work Force Diversity & Cross Culture Organisational Behaviour
- Emotions and Stress Management
- Organisational Justice and Whistle Blowing
- Human Resource Management – Concept, Perspectives, Influences and Recent Trends
- Human Resource Planning, Recruitment and Selection, Induction, Training and Development
- Job Analysis, Job Evaluation and Compensation Management

ORGANISATIONAL BEHAVIOUR

The field of organisational behaviour has already developed and matured as an academic discipline. As with any other relatively new academic endeavour, however, there have been some rough spots and sidetracks in its development. Besides the healthy academic controversies over theoretical approach or research finding, perhaps the biggest problem that organisation behaviour has had to face in an identify crisis. Exactly what is meant by organisational behaviour? It is an attempt to replace all management with behavioural science concepts and techniques? How, if at all does it differ from good old applied or Industrial Psychology? Fortunately these questions have now largely been answered to the satisfaction of most management academicians, behavioural scientists and management practitioners. Such relation can be drawn as follows.

Characteristics of Organisational Behaviour

It consists of the following characteristics:

(1) **Large size.** It employs hundreds and thousands of employees.

(2) **Organisation**

(3) **Human resources**

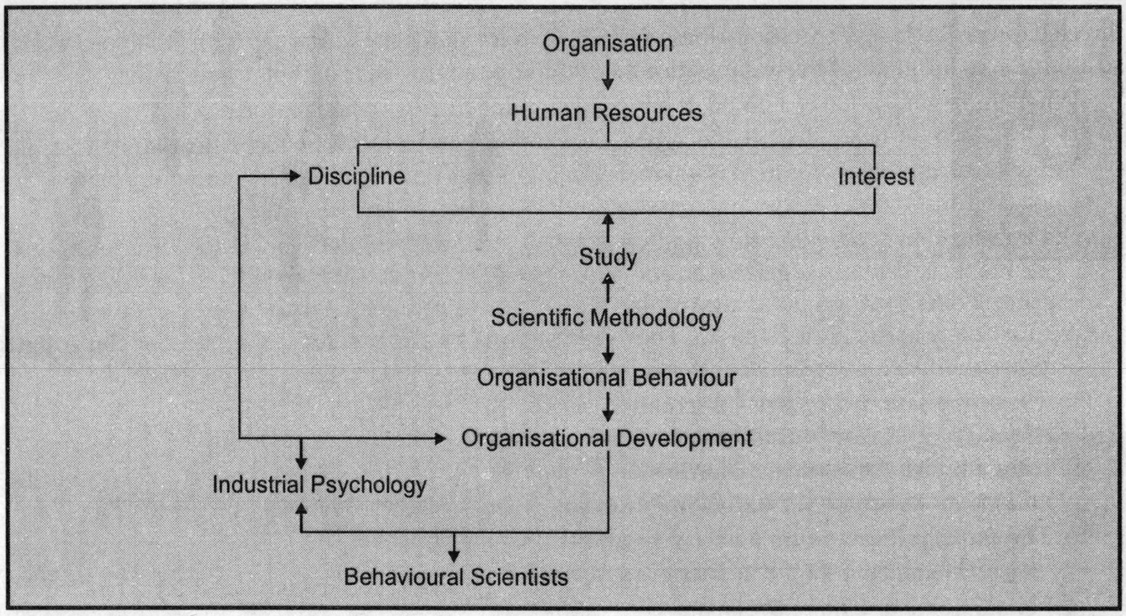

Organisational Behaviour Relation.

(4) **Complexity.** It involves huge investment and complicated technology, their management and operation is a complex affair.

(5) **Conscious rationality**

(6) **Co-ordination**

(7) **Pattern of behaviour.** There is a system of working in all organisations like hierarchical levels, a chain of command, rules and procedures.

(8) **Psychological industry**

(9) **Discipline**

(10) **Differentiation**

Concept of Organisational Behaviour

The concept of organisational goals, like concept of power, authority or leadership has been unusually resistant to precise, unambiguous definition. Yet a definition of goal is necessary and unavoidable in organisational analysis. Organisations are established to do something, they perform work directed toward some end. We must examine the end or goal if we are to analyse organisational behaviour. In other words, the concept of organisational behaviour is based on Goal.

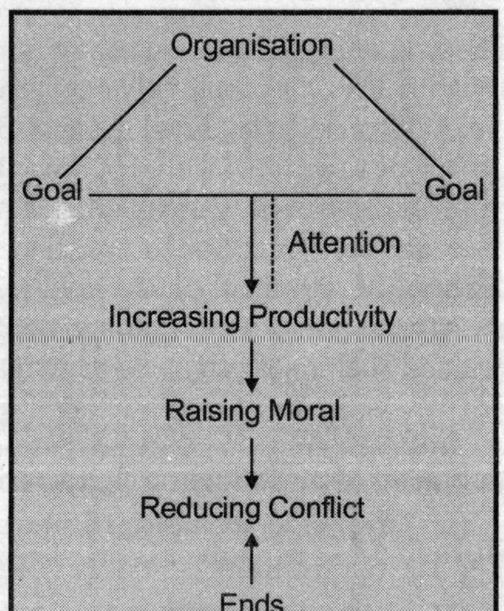

Organisational Analysis.

When research concerns the behaviour of group or individuals who happen to function within a organisation, attention to the goal of the organisation as a whole is not necessary. Much investigation that goes under the name of organisational behaviour is of this type. It is really concerned how groups or individuals function in certain settings.

It is assumed that increasing productivity, raising morale, and reducing conflict are legitimate goals, and attention is directed towards whatever promotes these ends. But we are ultimately concerned with group processes, so attention to the goals of the organisation as a whole, or some major part of it is necessary.

When the organisation is defined, it has the following distinguished features :

(1) Organisation is an identifiable aggregation of human beings. The identification is possible because human organisation is not merely a number of persons collected at random, but it is an organisation of the persons who are interrelated.

(2) Organisation is a deliberately and consciously created human organisation. It implies that relationship between organisation and its members is contractual. They enter in the organisation through the contract and can be replaced also, that is, unsatisfactory persons can be removed and others assigned their tasks. The organisation can also recombine its personnel through promotion, demotion and transfers.

(3) The organisation is a purposive creation, that is, all the organisations have some goals or set of goals. The goals are mutually agreed upon by the members of the organisation.

(4) In the organisation, there is a coordination of closely relevant activities of the members. The coordination is necessary because all the members contribute to achieve commonly agreed goals.

(5) The coordination of human activities requires a structure wherein various individuals are fitted. The structure provides for power centres which coordinate and control concerned effects of the organisation and direct them towards its goal.

(6) There is rationality in coordination of activities or behaviour. Every organisation has some specified norms and standards of behaviour – such norms and standards of behaviour are set up collectively by the individuals and every member of the organisation is expected to behave according to these norms and standards.

Organisation-people Interinfluence

It suggests that an organisation and people working in it interact. In this interaction process, organisation and people influence each other. This influence can be seen through two processes : fusion process and inducement – contribution process.

Fusion Process.

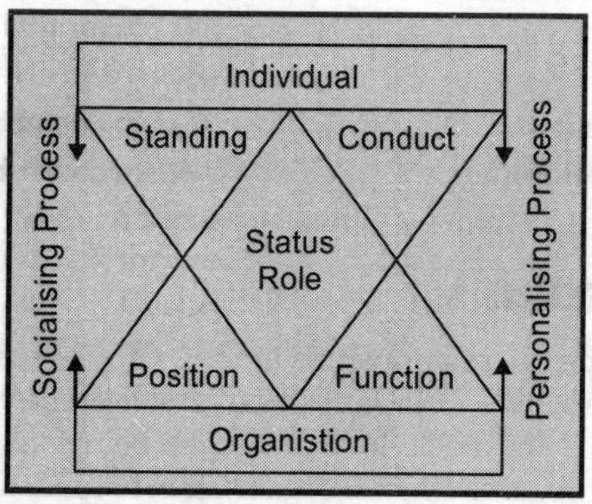

Inducement Contribution Process. In this each member of the organisation gets inducements for the contributions which he makes to the organisation.

Significance of Organisational Behaviour

Organisational behaviour represents the behavioural approach to management, not the whole of management. Other recognised approaches to management include the process quantitative systems and contingency approaches. In other words, organisational behaviour does not intend to protract the whole of management. The charge the old wine (applied or industrial Psychology) has merely been poured into a new bottle (organisational behaviour) has proved to be groundless. Although it is certainly true that the behavioural sciences make a significant contribution to both the theoretical and the research foundation of organisational behaviour, it is equally true that applied or industrial Psychology should not be equated with organisational behaviour. For example, organisational structure and management process have an integral, direct role in organisational behaviour, but have at most an indirect role in applied or industrial Psychology. Basically, organisations have grown in size because of three reasons : limitations of individuals, social reasons and material reasons.

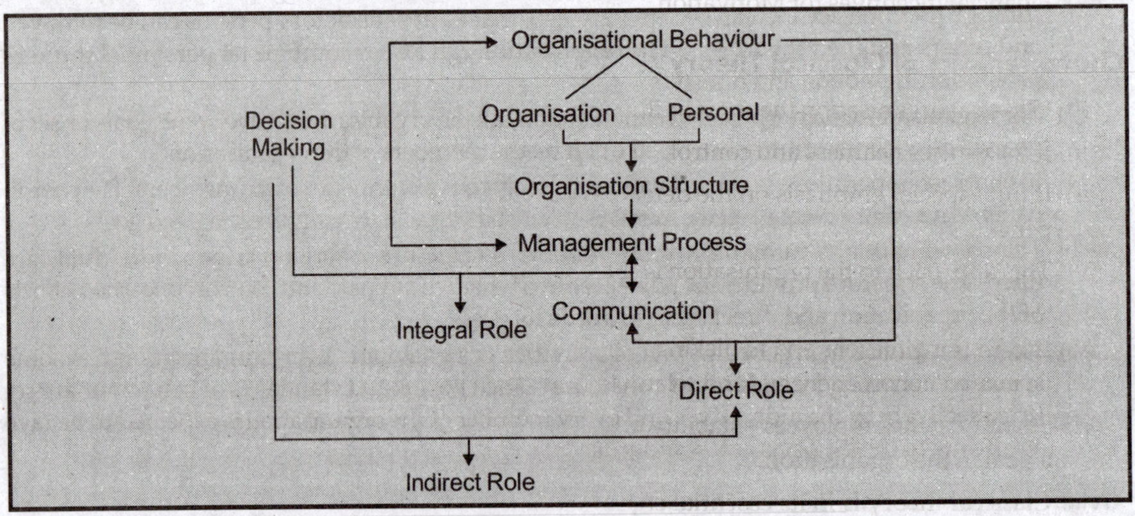

Significance of Organisational Behaviour.

The organisational behaviour plays a very vital role in the following areas as well:

(1) In making effective organisational structure
(2) In defining authority, power and status of an employee in the organisation
(3) In making group
(4) In motivation
(5) In leadership
(6) In effective communication
(7) In conflict management
(8) In organisational change
(9) In organisational development
(10) In control
(11) In effectiveness
(12) In project selection

ORGANISATION THEORIES

Organisation theories describe the relationships among variables in the organisation. It is a set of variables describing the parameters of organisation which predict the effect of certain structural arrangements on performance and behaviour of human beings in the organisation. Organisation theory can be treated as a macro examination of organisation because it analyses the whole organisation as a unit.

Organisation theory has been classified into three groups : classical, neo classical and modern.

A. Classical Organisation Theory

The term 'Classical' means something traditional or long established. According to classical writers, organisation is a machine and human beings are different components of that machine. This theory focuses on human beings and their behaviour.

According to this approach, more importance is laid on input-output mediators and less importance to facilitating and constraining factors in the external environment. Therefore, this theory has been termed as 'Machine Theory', 'Structural Theory' or 'Physiological Theory'.

Classical approach of organisational behaviour has the following implications :

(1) Interrelated management functions

(2) Guiding Principles

(3) Rigid Organisation Structure

(4) Financial Incentives for Motivation

Characteristics of Classical Theory

(i) Classical organisation theory is built on an accounting model.

(ii) It maximises neatness and control.

(iii) It puts special emphasis on the detection of errors and their correction after they have happened.

(iv) This approach to the organisation is the classical embodiment of the extra pair of hands concept.

(v) In designing the jobs and in picking these extra pair of hands, classical theory assumes man to be relatively homogeneous and relatively unmodifiable.

(vi) Stability of the employees – stability in the sense of minimising change with the employees – is a goal in the organisation.

(vii) Classical theory is in its essential character centralised, and the integration of the system is achieved through the authority and control of the central mechanism.

It may be quite interesting to note how these propositions have been developed. Among classical writers, few have emphasised the technological aspect of the organisation and have concentrated on how each individual in the organisation can be made more efficient. On the other hand, many writers have emphasised the structural aspects of the organisation so that individuals collectively can be made more efficient. Thus classical organisation theory presents two distinct theories :

(1) Scientific Management Theory

Though some attempts were made earlier to study organisational problems, particularly its engineering problems, the real study in an organised way is recorded through the Scientific Management, with which *Taylor, Frank Gilbraith, Lillian Gilbraith, Henry Gnatt and Harrington Emerson* are associated. They have investigated the effective use of human beings in industrial organisations and studied primarily the use of human beings as adjuncts to machines in the performance of routine tasks. The area of human behaviour in organisations investigated by them is quite narrow and the theories in human behaviour in this approach encompass primarily physiological variables. As such this is also referred to as physiological organisation theory.

The Scientific Management group has been most concerned with the kind of tasks that are performed on the production floor or at the operative levels. These tasks are quite different from other tasks in the organisations. First, they are largely repetitive so that the daily activity of an individual worker can be divided into a large number of cyclical repetition of essentially the same, or closely related, activities. Secondly, the tasks do not require complex problem-solving activity by those workers who handle them. Thus more attention is required towards the standardisation of working methods. This is what

Scientific Management group has done. Taylor, on the basis of his experiments of Midvale and Bethlehem, perceived several new functions of managers. These are

(i) replacing rule-of thumb method with scientific determination of each element of a man's job.
(ii) scientific selection and training of workmen.
(iii) co-operation of management and labour to accomplish work in accountability between managers and workmen.

Taylor has given various principles of scientific management as follows:

1. Separation of planning from doing;
2. Function foremanship of supervision, having eight different supervisors to give instructions in their respective fields;
3. Job analysis, based on time, motion, and fatigue studies to determine fair amount of work;
4. Standardisation of tools, period of work, working conditions, and cost of production.
5. Scientific selection and training of workmen, and
6. Financial incentives to motivate workmen.

Most of other persons who were mostly contemporary of Taylor attempted on similar lines with very few variations. For example, Frank and Lillian Gilbraith advocated three positions plan apart from carrying on experiments on time, motion and fatigue studies. Gnatt developed a Gnatt chart to be used in production control. Emerson suggested an improved method of wage payment as well as the concept of line-staff relationship instead of functional foremanship. These findings suggest that although the various individuals engaged in scientific management have given some different things, their approach was basically the same.

Critical Analysis of the Scientific Management Theory. Although the principles of scientific management were intended for broad application, as claimed by the contributors, the emphasis was not beyond the improvement at the shop levels. They were more concerned about the efficiency of workers at actual work place and had left the principles which could be applied to other functions of the organisation. Similarly, they emphasised the physiological variables affecting human behaviour at work place both in term of work efficiency and methods of motivating the workers. As such, the scientific management is more relevant to mechanisation and automation, technical aspect of efficiency than to the broader aspects of human behaviour in organisation. March and Simon observe that Taylor's contribution was not a set of general principles for organising work efficiently, but a set of operating procedures that could be efficient in that situation to secure their application.

Machine model visualised organisational constancy as a right and static arrangement of parts, although maintenance is a dynamic process of preserving patterns of relationships by constant adjustments. Consequently, machine theory was sometimes wrong and sometimes right in its basic tenets, but it was always inadequate in dealing with the complexities of organisational structure and functioning. It lacked the power of open-system theory to deal with significant organisational variables.

The major reasons for the opposition of scientific management were as follows:

(1) There were many of the followers of Taylor who took aggressive mechanical view of production and sidelined human aspect at the workplace. This created aggressive attitudes among workers.
(2) The work used to be performed under close and strict supervision based on authoritarian approach. Workers were not allowed to raise their voice even for genuine grievances.
(3) There was lack of scientific standardization of work and whether standard used to be set by the management, the workers had to follow strictly. Such standards often used to raise production norm without taking into consideration the factors affecting such a norm.
(4) The most crucial element which was under contention was the differential piece rate system. The workers, even the efficient ones, and their unions opposed this system on the plea that it

was a new method of exploiting workers by the industrialists. It may be mentioned that trade unions were quite popular at that time.

(2) Administrative Theory

Scientific management group was primarily concerned with problems at the operative level and did not emphasise managerial organisation and process. The administrative theorists-Weber, Fayol, Gulick, Shelden, Mooney and Reiley and Urwick have viewed the central problem as being one where there must be identification of tasks necessary for achieving the general purpose of the organisation and of the grouping or departmentation to take place to fulfil those functions most effectively. As such, this approach is referred to as departmentalisation. The similarity between Scientific management and administrative management theories is found in the context that both treat organisation as a closed system; however, there are differences between the two. March and Simon observe that they (Scientific Management and administrative management theorists) share, particularly in their more formal versions, a preoccupation with the simpler neurophysiological properties of humans and the simpler kinds of tasks that are handled in organisations. However, the administrative management theorists tended to carry their analysis, at least at the level of wisdom and insight, beyond the boundaries set by their formal models.

Henry Fayol divided his approach of studying management into three parts: (1) managerial qualities (physical, mental, moral, educational, technical and experience); (2) elements of management (planning, organisation, commanding, coordination and controlling; and (3) general principles of management.

Max Weber's Theory

The Bureaucratic Model was developed by Max Weber in 1900's. His work was first time translated from German to English in the 1940's. He was a social scientist. He is the father of the concept of the bureaucracy.

Weber specified several characteristics of his ideal organisation structure. The ten major ones are the following :

(1) Specialisation
(2) Division of labour
(3) Positions arranged in hierarchy
(4) A system of abstract roles
(5) Impersonal relationship
(6) Expert training
(7) More or less stable
(8) More or less exhaustive rules and regulations
(9) Promotion
(10) Selection based on technical competence

Fayol, Gulik and Urwick

Henery Fayol, a French mining engineer, is regarded as the father of management theory. The General and Industrial Administration was written by him in 1916. His fourteen principles were :

(1) Division of work
(2) Authority and responsibility
(3) Discipline
(4) Unity of command
(5) Unity of direction
(6) Initiative
(7) Subordination of individual interests to general interests
(8) Fair remuneration
(9) Centralisation
(10) Scalar chain
(11) Order
(12) Equity and a sense of justice
(13) Stability of tenure of personnel
(14) Esprit de corps leading to team work and maintenance of interpersonal relationship.

Gulick and **Urwick** edited papers on the science of administration published by the Institute of Public Administration at Columbia University in 1937. The paper contains the following principles of organisational theories :

(1) Fitting people to the organisational structure
(2) Recognising one top executive as source of authority
(3) Unity of command
(4) Line and staff
(5) Departmental
(6) Delegating and utilising the exception principle
(7) Responsibilities
(8) Spans of control

Dissimilarity between Contributions of Taylor and Fayol

Basis of difference	Taylor	Fayol
1. Perspective	Shop floor level	Higher management level
2. Focus	Efficiency through work simplification and standardization	Overall efficiency by observing certain principles
3. Orientation	Production and engineering	Managerial functions
4. Results	Scientific observation and measurement	Personal experiences translated into universal truths
5. Overall contributions	Basis for accomplishment on the production line	Systematic theory of management

Major Factors of Classical Theory

(a) **Division of labour.** It means that work is divided to obtain clear cut specialisation and the main aim is to improve the performance of individuals in the organisation. The classical approach rests firmly on the assumption that the more a particular job is broken into its simplest component parts, the more specialised a worker can become in carrying out his part of the job. The more specialised a worker becomes in fulfilling his particular job, the more efficient the whole organisation will be.

For division of labour, it is necessary to identify the various activities to be performed. Such identification can be done at various levels in a large organisation because a major activity is to be fragmented into subactivities; these subactivities into further sub-subactivities, and so on. This process leads to differentiating the tasks necessary to accomplish an objective. Each differentiated task can be handled separately either by different individuals at the same time or by the same individuals at different times.

(b) **Scalar and functional processes.** It takes into consideration that there is a chain of command throughout the organisation. It is called scalar process because it provides a scale or grading of duties according to degree of authority and responsibility. Scalar process generates superior - subordinate relationships in the organisation. Functional process refers to the division of organisation into specialised parts and the regrouping of the parts into compatible units. Thus each unit of the organisation may be functionally different than others; for example, marketing unit is different than production unit. Thus while scalar process deals with the vertical growth of the organisation, functional process deals with the horizontal growth. When both scalar and functional processes are superimposed on each other, superior-subordinate positions are created in various departments and functions. There are five basic components of scalar and functional processes: departmentation, coordination by hierarchy, unity of command, delegation of authority, and line and staff relationship.

(i) **Departmentation.** Division of work or specialisation is usually accomplished through departmentation. Departmentation is the process of dividing the work of the organisation into various units or departments. The basic problem of departmentation is to find out the ways in which to group the tasks into individual jobs or to group into individual administrative units, to group units into larger units, and finally to establish the department at the top level so that costs involved in carrying out these organisational work are minimum.

(ii) **Coordination by Hierarchy.** With jobs specialised and divided among units, coordination becomes necessary. Coordination can be achieved mainly through hierarchy or chain of command. The chain of command principle implies that every one from bottom to the top should have a superior to whom he is accountable. Therefore, coordination can be achieved in better way if this chain of command is defined properly in the organisation.

(iii) **Unity of Command.** Unity of command means that a person in the organisation should receive orders from only one superior. The more completely an individual has a reporting relationship to a single superior, the less is the problem of conflict in instructions and greater is the feeling of personal responsibility for results.

(iv) **Delegation of Authority.** Since assignment of activity to a person makes him responsible for achieving the results, he should be delegated authority to carry out his work. Delegation of authority means authorisation to an individual for making decisions. Through the process of delegation and re-delegation, the authority is distributed at various points in the organisation.

(v) **Line and Staff Relationships.** Classical theory differentiates between line and staff relationship. Line relationship exists between superior and his subordinate in which a superior can direct the activities of his subordinate. He can give order and subordinate is obliged to carry the order. On the other hand, staff relationship involves tendering the advice by staff personnel to line managers. It is not obligatory on the part of the line managers to carry the work according to the advice. Line and staff relationships exist because of the functional process in the organisation.

(c) **Structure.** It means the relationships among various tasks, activities and people in the organisation. Therefore, there should be logical and rational structure. Basic structural element in the classical theory is the position. Each position is made up of several expectations that others hold about the appropriate behaviour for the holder of the position. Various positions in the organisation are grouped in various ways – horizontally, vertically, or both. Each position holder is then sanctioned a certain amount of authority to perform organisational functions in a certain way. Depending on the distribution of authority, the organisational structure may be centralised or decentralised. In the case of centralisation, authority is concentrated in the higher positions and in the case of decentralisation, relevant authority is delegated to the lowest positions in the organisation.

(d) **Span of Control.** It means number of subordinates under one superior. And it takes into consideration that to enable one superior to control the subordinates effectively, span of control should be limited for a superior.

Criticism of Principles of Classical Theories

A major contribution of classical theorists is the formulation of various principle of organisation. Though various writers have their own view on these principle and there is great amount of difference in these principles, they have emphasised that these principles disclosed otherwise. The main criticisms of classical principles are as follows :

(i) Lack of Empirical Research.

(ii) Lack of Universality.

B. Neo-Classical Organisation Theory

The behavioural approach emphasises on the task of complementing for some of the deficiencies in classical doctrine. Though the behavioural approach takes the postulates of classical school regarding the pillars of organisation as given, these postulates are regarded as modified by people acting independently or within the content of the informal organisation. Thus it views organisation as a combination of both formal and informal forms of organisation. The latter form was missing in classical approach. Another contribution of behavioural approach is the introduction of behavioural science in analysing the nature of organisation. Through the use of this science, behavioural writers have demonstrated how the pillars of classical doctrines – division of labour, specialisation, structure and scalar and functional processes are affected and modified by human actions. Since this approach has suggested only modifications in the basic postulates of classical theory, it is referred to as neo-classical theory.

The main characteristics are :

(i) The organisation is a social system.

(ii) The social environment of the job affects people and is also affected by them and not by management alone.

(iii) In the formal organisation, informal organisation also exists with it and it affects and is affected by the formal organisation.

(iv) A conflict between individual and organisational objectives which increases the importance of integration between individuals and organisation.

(v) Human being is interdependent and his behaviour can be predicted in terms of social and psychological factors.

(vi) Human being has diverse motivational pattern and he tries to fulfil different types of needs.

(vii) Human being approach is not always rational; often he behaves irrationally in terms of rewards which he seeks from the works.

(viii) Communication is necessary as it carries information necessary for organisational functioning and conveys the feelings and sentiments of people who work in the organisation.

(ix) Team-work is essential for co-operation and sound organisational functioning. This is not achieved automatically but achieved through behavioural approach.

This theory basically lays emphasis on the following factors:

1. **Flat Structure.** Neoclassical theory suggests flat structure as against tall structure. Neoclassicists feel that tall structure is against the human beings. It suffers from the following problems: communication problem, increased differentiation between decision makers and implementers, lack of motivation to people, and is expensive because too many levels are added in the organisation. As against this, flat structure with wide span of control is more suitable for motivating human beings in the organisation; communication chain is shorter; and it is free from hierarchical control.
2. **Decentralisation.** Neoclassical theory suggests decentralisation in organisation structure. Decentralisation is closely related to flat structure as wide span of control will result into horizontal increase of people. The decentralised structure offers various advantages and is in accordance with the various characteristics of human beings as identified by the neoclassicists.
3. **Informal Organisation.** A major departure of neoclassical theory from the classical theory is that the former recognises that in every formal organisation, informal organisation also exists. Formal organisation structure represents as closely as possible the deliberate intention of its framers for the purpose of interactions that are expected to take place among its members. The informal organisation, on the other hand, is created because of the limitations of the formal

organisation to fulfil the members' needs, particularly the psychological needs. In an organisation, the behaviour of members is determined with interaction of formal and informal organisations. Since a manager cannot control the informal organisation, he should make the best use of this in achieving the organisational objectives.

C. Modern Organisation Theory

Modern Organisation Theory (MOT) was developed in early 1960s. It is an integrative theory and combines the valuable concepts of classical models with the social and behavioural sciences (human and behavioural models). It is an amorphous aggregation of these models in the meaningful way to enable us to understand organisations. MOT truly represents a theoretical breakthrough in the organisational analysis. However, it is not entirely a new approach or idea but it is the integration of various models. MOT has been evolved on the pattern of general system theory (GST). GST studies the various parts of a system in an integrated way; it considers the interaction of the system with its environment, it considers the interaction of various subsystems of the system; and it takes into account the problems of growth and stability of the system. MOT does the same thing for the organisation system. While GST is relevant for the study of any system, MOT has relevance for organisational study.

HUMAN RELATIONS APPROACH

Human relations approach of organisational behaviour was developed out of the reaction to classical approach with Hawthorne experiments during 1924-32 at the Hawthorne plant of General Electric Company USA.

SOCIAL SYSTEM APPROACH

Social systems approach of management extended the implications of human relations approach further. This approach was introduced by Vilfredo Pareto, a sociologist. The major features of this approach are as follows :

- Organisation is a social system, a system of cultural relationships.
- Relationships exist among the external environments of the organisation.
- Cooperation among group members is necessary for the achievement of organisational objectives.
- For effective management, efforts should be made for establishing harmony between the goals of the organisation and the various groups therein.

Features of Modern Organisation (Theory)

Modern organisation theory has a number of features which differentiate it from other organisation theories.

These characteristics are as follows :

1. **Open System View.** MOT takes organisation as an open system. It implies that the organisation continuously interacts with its environment for its survival and growth. Thus, an organisation has different elements: input, transformation, process, output, feedback and environment. This is where MOT differs from classical theory which treats organisation as a close system.
2. **Adaptive.** MOT takes organisation as an adaptive system. Organisation being an open system, its survival and growth in a dynamic environment demands an adaptive system which can continuously adjust to changing environment. Organisation tends to achieve environmental constancy by bringing the external world under control, or bringing internal modification of organisational functioning to meet the needs of the changing world. Since there is a provision of feedback mechanism, it can evaluate its performance and take corrective actions.
3. **Dynamic.** Organisation as a system is dynamic. It suggests that organisation attempts at achieving equilibrium. However, this equilibrium is not static as happens in mechanical system.

Organisation moves towards growth and expansion by preserving some of the energy. Organisational effectiveness depends on this energy exchange. Therefore, it is not only the internal management process that determines the effectiveness of management but also how it interacts with the changing environment in terms of taking inputs and giving output.

4. **Probabilistic.** MOT is probabilistic and not deterministic. A deterministic model always specifies the use of model in a condition with predetermined results. Therefore, the outcome of an action can be predicted accurately. For example, if one wants to get the total of 250 and 500, he can use a calculator and gets 750. This is possible because the outcome is certain. In case of probabilistic model, the outcome can be assigned only probability and not certainty. For example; if a coin is tossed, the probability of getting a head is 0.5. But one cannot say with certainty that there will be 50 heads out of tossing of a coin 100 times. MOT being probabilistic points out only the probability and never the certainty of the performance and consequent results. Management has to function in the face of many dynamic variables and there cannot be absolute predictability of these variables. For example, we make forecast of future events but the forecast is relevant to a certain degree only and not to the level of certainty. This is what MOT takes into account.
5. **Multilevel and Multidimensional.** MOT points out the multilevel and multidimensional features of organisation. It has both macro and micro approach. At macro level, it can be applied to supersystem, say a business system as a whole. At micro level, it can be applied to an organisation. It can even be applied to a subsystem of an organisation. However, it has the same characteristics at all these levels: supersystem level, system level, and subsystem level. Thus both parts and whole are equally important.
6. **Multivariable.** MOT is multivariable and involves taking into account many variables simultaneously. This suggests that there is no simple cause effect phenomenon, rather an event may be the result of so many variables which themselves are interrelated and interdependent. This interrelatedness and interdependence makes managing quite a complex process. Thus it realises the complexity of modern organisations.
7. **An Integrated Approach.** MOT takes an integrated view. It identifies the reason for a phenomenon in its wider context taking into account the total factors affecting the phenomenon. In other approaches, a particular phenomenon has been explained in terms of a single factor or cluster of factors. MOT tries to integrate the various factors to find out the reasons behind a phenomenon. It emphasises on how the management of one subsystem of the organisation should be taken in relation with others because other subsystems become environment for the given system. Thus, the problem in one subsystem should not be traced into the subsystem only but in a much wider context.

McKinsey 7S Framework

It is a Value Based Management (VBM) model developed by well-known business consultants Waterman and Peters (who also developed the MBWA—"Management By Walking Around", and authored "In Search of Excellence").

This was a strategic vision for groups to include businesses, business units, and teams. The 7S are structure, strategy, systems, skills, style, staff and shared values. The theory also defines hard and soft elements which are as follows:

Hard Elements

They are easier to define or identify and management can directly influence them. These are strategy statements, organisation charts and reporting lines and formal processes and IT systems. These are

S1-Strategy. Plans for the allocation of firm's scarce resources to reach identified goals in time.

S2-Structure. The way the organisation's units relate to each other. Centralised, functional divisions (top-down), decentralised (large holdings), matrix, network.

S3-System. Procedures, processes and routines that characterises how work is to be done, financial systems, hiring procedure, information systems, performance appraisal.

Soft Elements

It can be more difficult to describe and are less tangible and more influenced by culture. However, these soft elements are as important as the hard elements, if the organisation to be successful. These are:

S4-Shared Values. What does the organisation stands for and what it believes in central beliefs and attitudes.

S5-Staff. Numbers and types of personnel within the organisation.

S6-Style. Cultural style of organisation and how key managers behave in achieving goals.

S7-Skill. Distinctive capabilities of personnel or of the organisation as a whole.

Organisational Behaviour Models

A model is an abstraction of reality, a simplified representation of some real-world phenomenon. Models are developed to provide framework about 'how people will be treated in an organisation.' For developing an OB model, various variables are divided into two groups – dependent variables and independent variables.

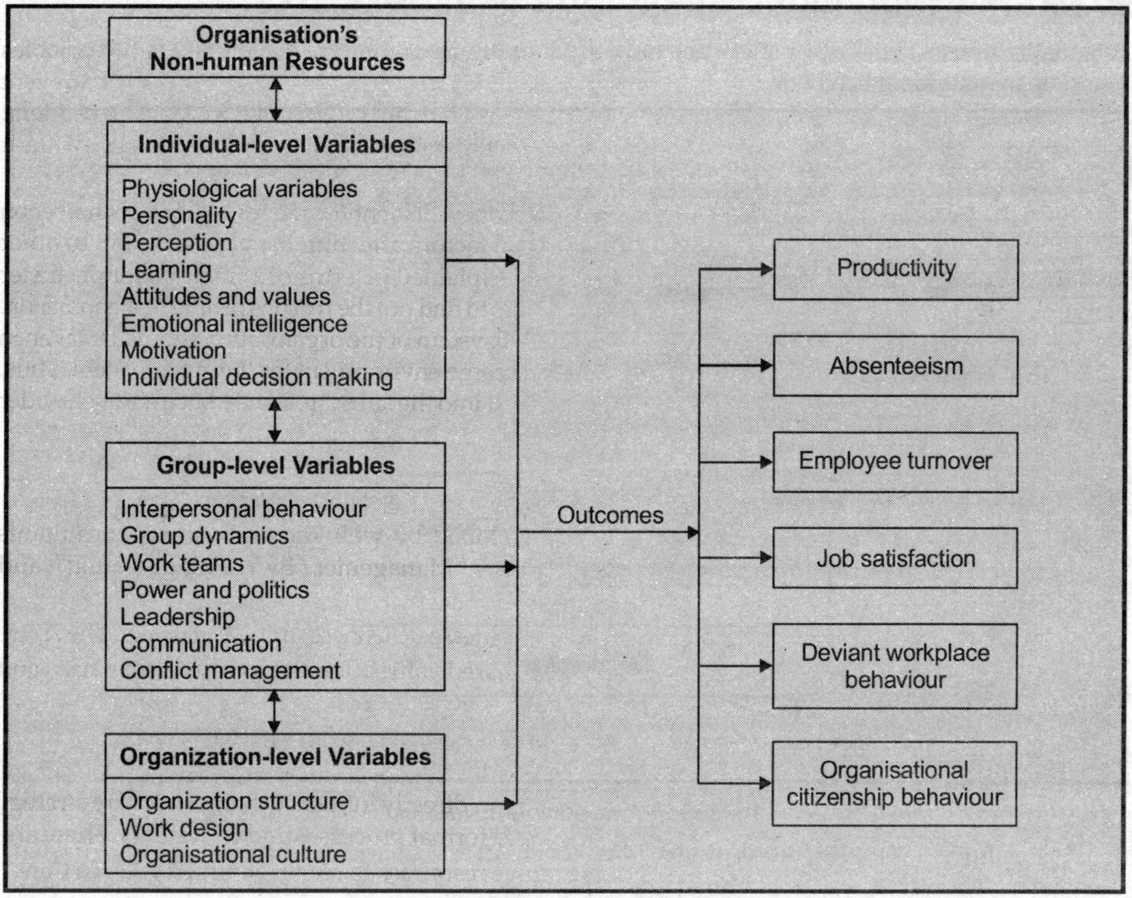

Basic Model of Organisational Behaviour.

Models of Organisational Behaviour

	Autocratic	Custodial	Supportive	Collegial
Basic of model	Power	Economic resources	Leadership	Partnership
Managerial orientation	Authority	Money	Support	Teamwork
Employee orientation	Obedience	Security and benefits	Job performance	Responsible behaviour
Employee psychological result	Dependence on boss	Dependence on organisation	Participation	Self-discipline
Employee needs met	Subsistence	Security	Status and recognition	Self-actualization
Performance result	Minimum	Passive cooperation	Awakened drives	Moderate enthusiasm

INDIVIDUAL BEHAVIOUR PERSONALITY - PERCEPTION - VALUES - ATTITUDES - LEARNING - MOTIVATION

MANAGING INDIVIDUAL BEHAVIOUR PERSONALITIES

Personality means the adjustment of the individual to his environment. Personality is the unique aspect of an individual behaviour.

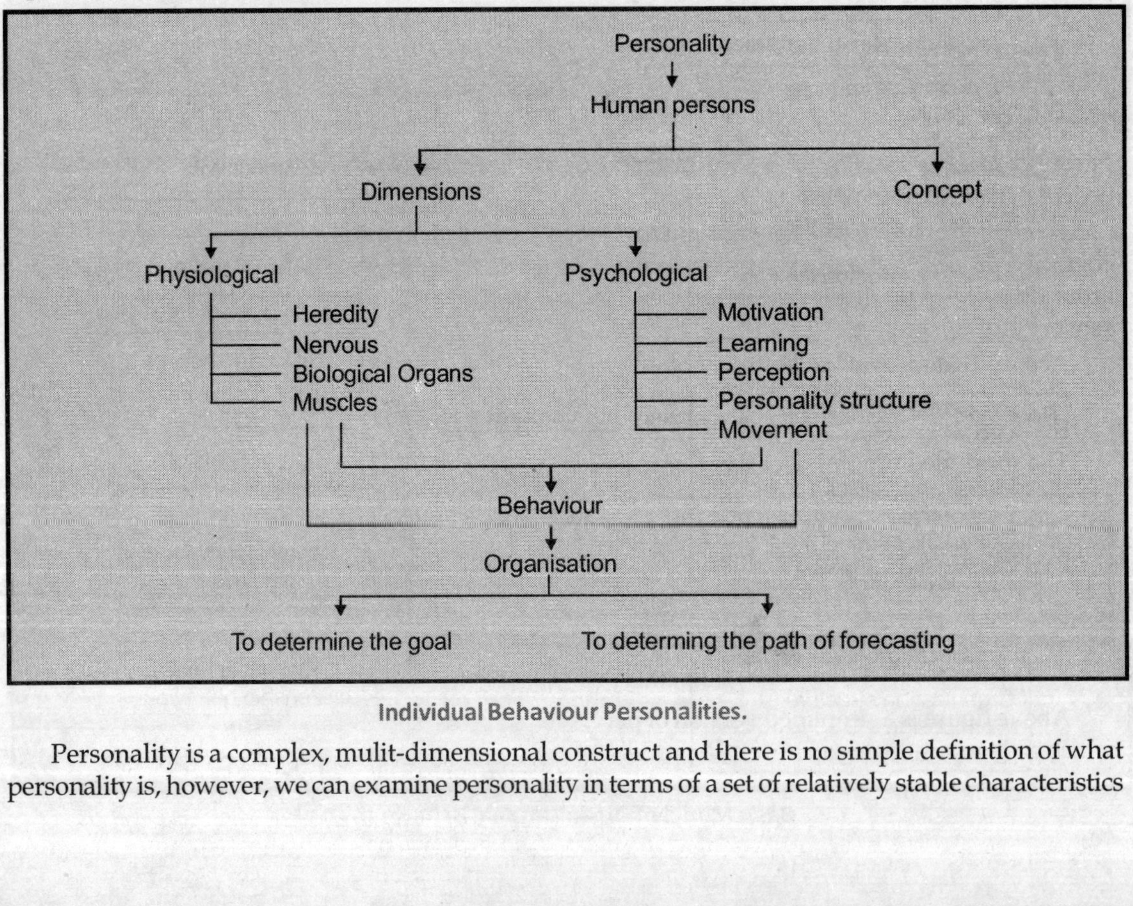

Individual Behaviour Personalities.

Personality is a complex, mulit-dimensional construct and there is no simple definition of what personality is, however, we can examine personality in terms of a set of relatively stable characteristics and tendencies that determine our thoughts, feelings, and behaviour and which have same continuity or consistency over time.

Determination of Personalities

Many factors affect the shaping of our personalities. Chief among these are heredity, cultural, learning, muscles, family and others.

According to *Luthans*, these are :

(i) Biological contribution
(ii) Cultural contribution
(iii) Contribution from the family
(iv) Situation

According to *J. Kelly*, these are:

(i) Heredity
(ii) Physique
(iii) Environmental effects
(iv) Childhood experiences
(v) Feelings
(vi) Learning

Major Determinants of Personality

The following factors determine the personality of a human person :

(1) Heredity
(2) Physique
(3) Environmental effects
(4) Family
(5) Social environment
(6) Entertainment facility
(7) Background
(8) Childhood experiences
(9) Expression - Body movements
(10) Cultural values
(11) Experience in life
(12) Nervous System
(13) Biological organs - skills
(14) Muscles and glands
(15) Perception
(16) Learning
(17) Motivation
(18) Personality structure
(19) Living standard
(20) Status

PERCEPTION

Perception is a process by which an individual organises and interprets his sensory impressions in order to give meaning to his environment.

Perception takes place whenever you have human sensation which gives rise to perceptual process, cognitive process – analytical process in the brain to have the knowledge about what is happening around us. It is a process of receiving, selecting, organising, interpreting, checking and reacting to sensory stimuli and data.

According to *Uday Parekh*, "perception process is something which comprises of 6 organs.

Receiving → Selecting → Organising → Response → Checking → Interpreting

The simplified process of perception is presented in figure.

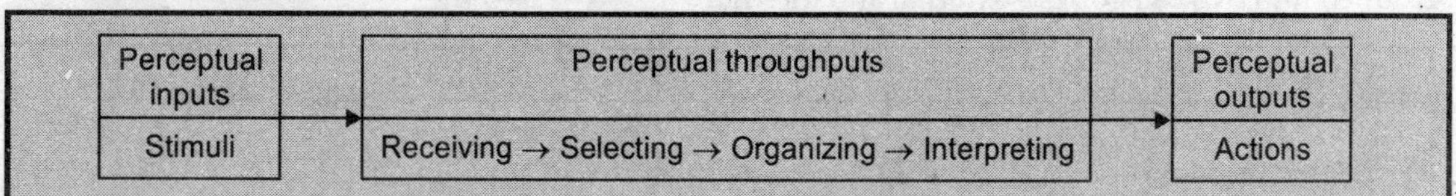

Simplified Process of Perception.

Above figure is a simplified version of perceptual process. It does not represent the whole factors which go in input-throughput-output process of perception. Figure 15 presents a comprehensive view of process of perception.

Perception can be negative or positive. For positive perception, there are five main attributes.

(i) Develop your attitude
(ii) Free communication
(iii) Be empathetic
(iv) Avoid perceptual distortions
(v) Improve self image

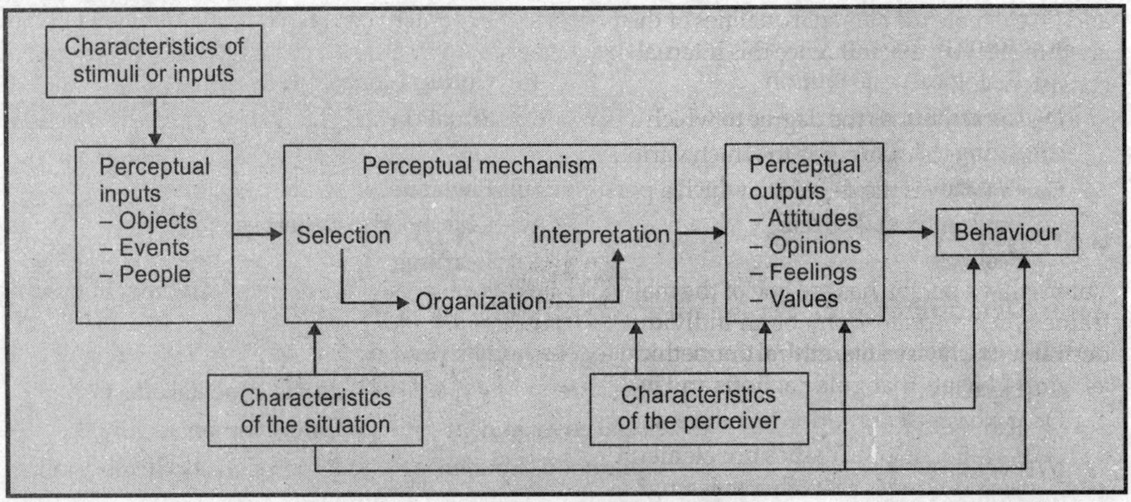

Complex Process of Perception.

Importance of Perception

Perception affects the outcome of behaviour. This is so because people act on the basis of what they see. Hence, in understanding behaviour, the managers must recognize that facts people do not perceive meaningful usually will not influence their behaviour, whereas the things they believe to be real, even though factually incorrect or non-existent, will influence it. Thus, the understanding of human perception, particularly in the organisational setting is important in understanding and controlling the behaviour. In an organisational setting, perception is important in various activities. However, there are three major areas which require special attention so far as the perceptual accuracy is concerned. These are :

(1) Interpersonal working relationship, (2) Selection of new employees, (3) Performance appraisal

Perceptual Selectivity

By selection, certain aspects of stimuli are screened out and others are admitted. Those which are admitted remain in the awareness of the people and those which are screened out fall below the threshold. This is known as perceptual selectivity. This is caused by a variety of factors which may be grouped into two categories – external and internal.

External Factors	Internal Factors
1. Size	1. Self concept
2. Intensity	2. Beliefs
3. Repetition	3. Expectations
4. Novelty and Familiarity	4. Inner Needs
5. Contrast	5. Response Disposition
6. Motion	6. Response Salience
	7. Perceptual Defence

Attribution

In general, attribution means assigning cause to an event. In the case of person perception, it is the act of assigning cause to why a person has behaved in a particular way. Based on this theme, attribution theory has been developed which aids in perceptual interpretation by focussing on how people attempt to (1) understand the causes of an event, (2) assess responsibility for the outcomes of the event, and (3) evaluate the personal qualities of the people in the event. According to attribution theory, there are three factors that influence this internal or external determination : distinctiveness, consensus and consistency.

Distinctiveness is the degree to which a person shows consistent behaviour in different situations.

Consensus is the degree to which various persons behave similarly in a given situation.

Consistency is the degree to which a person shows the same behaviour over time.

VALUES

Values that a person has are one of the major forces shaping behaviour. Values are convictions and a frame work of philosophy of an individual on the basis of which he judges what is good or bad, desirable or undesirable, ethical or unethical. Rokeach, a noted socio-psychologist, has defined values as "global beliefs that guide actions and judgements across a variety of situations.

On the basis of definition of values, we can infer its following characteristics.

(1). **Part of Culture.** Values are elements of culture, and culture is the complex blend of values, ideas, attitudes and other meaningful symbols to shape human behaviour in the society. Every society has its own culture and people in that society adhere to culture requirements.

(2) **Learned responses.** Human behaviour represents learned phenomenon. Unlike other animals, human beings have to learn almost everything about how to be human from experience. This is because human beings live in a society having certain culture characteristics which prescribe to behave in a particular way. Cultural field represents a set of stimuli to an individual and also a set of responses appropriate to those stimuli. The individual either is directly rewarded for adopting those responses or indirectly associated them with other stimulus situations that are rewarding. Cultural items learned early in the life tend to resist change more strongly than those learned late in life. This fact is very important from organisational behaviour point of view.

(3) **Inculcated.** Values are inculcated and are passed through generation to generation by specific groups and institutions. Such transmission starts from the family from where the socialisation process starts. Apart from family, educational, religious and ethnic institutions also transmit cultural values from one generation to another.

(4) **Social Phenomenon.** Values are a social phenomenon, that is, cultural habits are shared by aggregates of people living in organised society. An individual's way of thinking and behaving is not culture, rather group behaviour constitutes culture. Group is developed and reinforced through social pressure upon those who are interacting with one another.

(5) **Gratifying Responses.** Values exist to meet the biological and other needs of the individuals in the society. Thus, elements in the culture become extinguished when they no longer are gratifying the members of the society. The society rewards behaviours which are gratifying for its members.

(6) **Adaptive Process.** Culture is adaptive, either through a dialectical process or evolutionary process. Dialectical or sharply discontinuous change occurs, when the value system of a culture becomes associated with the gratification of only one group or class in the environment. In such a case, other classes of the society reject the logic of the value system and replace it with a new value system.

VALUES AND ATTITUDES

Some researchers see values as consisting of large sets of related attitudes. For example, Fishbein and Ajzen have included three components in attitudes – informational (ideas, beliefs and values, and information), emotional (feelings of likes and dislikes or positive and negative), and behavioural (tendency to behave). Thus they have taken values as a part of attitudes. However, some differences exist between values and attitudes. Attitudes are specific and related to distinct objects, people, or ideas; values are more general and are not related to any object or situation. In addition to being more general than attitudes, values often contain statements of goodness or badness associated with the attitudes which people hold. Values are, then, beliefs about which attitudes we should have or how we should behave.

Attitudes. The importance of attitude in understanding Psychological Phenomenon was given formal recognition early in the history of social Psychology. From the time of the concept's entry into the language of Psychology until now, interest in attitudes has been strong and growing. However, over the years, attitudes have been studied with differing emphasis and methods.

Attitudes and Behaviour

Attitude have been thought as serving four functions and thereby influencing the behaviour. These are : (1) utilitarian or instrumental, (2) ego-defensive, (3) value-orientation, (4) knowledge.

Attitude is a persistent tendency to feel and behave in a particular way towards some object. Attitude comprises of three components :

(i) **Emotional attitude.** The feeling towards object or individual. Businessman has positive attitude towards customer but has negative attitude towards income tax.

(ii) **Informational component.** The belief, opinions and informations. Personnel manager is having a belief that employees of an organisation should be sent for training for their mental development.

(iii) **Behavioural Component.** Like perception this is exposed and if personal manager actually sends employees on training, then this is behavioural component.

Attitudes can be formed and there are so many factors for the formation of attitudes. They are:

(i) The family and peer group
(ii) Economic & Social status
(iii) Direct experiences
(iv) Classical conditioning
(v) Mass Media

Theories of Attitude Formation

(1) Cognitive Consistency Theories : (i) Balance theory, (ii) Congruity theory, (iii) Affective cognitive consistency theory, (iv) Cognitive dissonance theory
(2) Functional Theory
(3) Social Judgement Theory

Factors in Attitude Formation

(1) Group Factors : (i) Family, (ii) Reference groups, (iii) Social classes
(2) Personality Factors

Developing Positive Attitudes by Individuals

(1) Identification of attitudes
(2) Looking for positive
(3) Building positive self-esteem
(4) Setting challenging targets
(5) Avoiding procrastination
(6) Continuous learning

LEARNING

According to the dictionary of psychology, learning means 'the process of acquiring the ability to respond adequately to a situation which may or may not have been previously encountered.

Sanford has defined learning as a relatively enduring change in behaviour brought about as a consequence of experience. In the context of organisational behaviour too, learning is defined in this way. Mitchell has defined learning as follows:

"Learning is the process by which new behaviours are acquired. It is generally agreed that learning involves changes in behaviour, practising new behaviours, and establishing permanency in the change."

We take learning as a relatively enduring change in behaviour due to experience.

Nature of Learning

Based on the definition of Learning, the nature of learning is as follows:

1. Learning involves a change in behaviour, though this change is not necessarily an improvement over previous behaviour. Learning generally has the connotation of improved behaviour, but bad habits, prejudices, stereotypes and work restrictions are also learned.
2. The behavioural change must be relatively permanent. Any temporary change in behaviour due to fatigue or any reason is not a part of learning.
3. The behavioural change must be based on some form of practice or experience.
4. The practice or experience must be reinforced in order for learning to occur.

Elements of Learning

Learning consists of the following elements :

(1) Learning involves changes in the activity
(2) Permanent change
(3) Learning is an organisation
(4) Learning is a form of experience
(5) Confirmation
(6) Learning is a continuous process
(7) Learning is a universal activity
(8) Learning is a development

Factors of Development

(1) Goal-oriented
(2) Motivation
(3) Stimulus
(4) Reaction
(5) Perception → Direct knowledge
(6) Reinforcement → Self desire
(7) Reward
(8) Change

Type of Learning

(1) Sensor motor learning
(2) Intellectual learning
(3) Motor learning
(4) Perceptual learning
(5) Conceptual learning → Through, Logic and Imagination
(6) Associative learning
(7) Attitudinal learning

According to Dalton, there are six antecedents for creating a learning organisation :

(1) There is a shift in the relative importance of factors of production, from physical and financial resources to human resources.
(2) There is acceptance of the fact that knowledge is prime source of competitive advantage.
(3) There is increasingly rapid pace of change in business environment.
(4) There is dissatisfaction with the existing management practices as these are not able to meet the needs of changing environment.

(5) There is increasingly, competitive business environment which is putting pressure on business.
(6) There are increasingly demanding customers who place high demands on business.

MOTIVATION

Motivation means a process of stimulating people to accomplish desired goals. Motivation comes from motives which are the expression of human needs by a human being. The need can be defined as feeling of lackness for something and human being tries to get lackness removed (satisfaction). So motivation is the way in which urges, drives, desires, aspirations, striving, needs, directly explain the behaviour of human beings.

Motivation has few characteristics :

(a) **Motivation is an internal feeling.** Motivation is a psychological phenomenon which generates within an individual.
(b) **Person in totality, not in part, is motivated.** Each individual in the organisation is a self-contained and inseparable unit and all his needs are inter-related.
(c) Motivation is the product of anticipated values from an action and the perceived probability that these values will be achieved by the action.

Factors Affecting Individual Performance

Observations show that : (1) various individuals perform differently in the same work situations and (2) the same individual performs differently in different work situations.

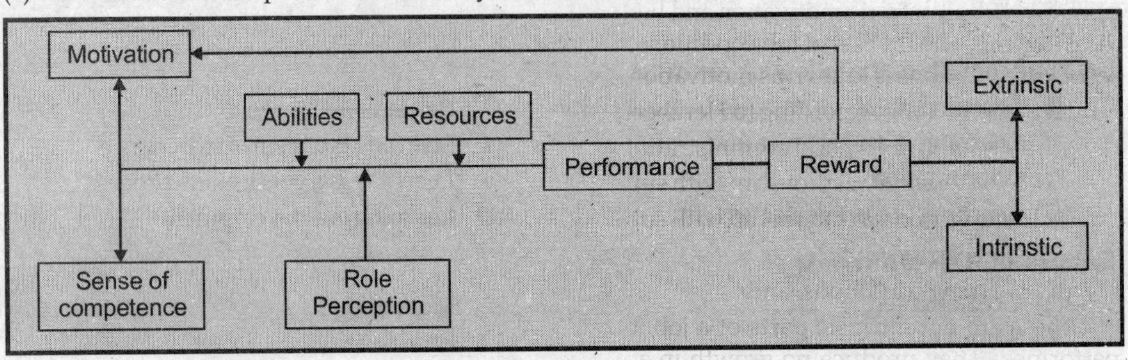

Factors Affecting Individual Performance.

In consequence to various people having been engaged in finding out the answer to the question relating to what motivates people, a number of theories concerning motivation have resulted. They are as follows:

A. Maslow's need Hierarchy

The behaviour of an individual at a particular moment is usually determined by his strongest need. As the more basic needs are satisfied, an individual seeks to satisfy the higher needs. It forms a hierarchy like:

(i) **Physiological needs.** The physiological needs are shown at the top of the hierarchy because they tend to have the highest strength until they are reasonably satisfied. Until these needs are satisfied to the degree needed for the efficient operation of the body, the majority of a person's activities will probably be at this level, and the other levels will provide him with little motivation.
(ii) **Safety needs.** Once the physiological needs are satisfied to a reasonable level – it is not necessary that they are fully satisfied and degree of reasonableness is subjective – other levels of needs

become important. In this hierarchy comes the needs for safety, that is need for being free of physical danger or self-preservation. In the industrial society, safety needs may take considerable importance in the context of the dependent relationship of employees to employers. Organisation can influence these security needs either positively – through pension plan, insurance plan etc. or negatively by arousing fears of being fired or laid off, demoted.

(iii) **Social needs.** Since man is a social being, he has a need to belong and to be accepted by various groups. When social needs become dominant, a person will strive for meaningful relations with others.

(iv) **Esteem needs.** The esteem needs are concerned with self-respect, self-confidence, a feeling of personal worth, feeling of being unique and recognition. Satisfying these needs produces feelings of self confidence, prestige, power and control.

(v) **Self actualisation needs.** Self-actualisation is the need to maximise one's potential, whatever it may be. This is related with the development of intrinsic capabilities which lead people to seek situations that can utilise their potential. This includes competence which implies control over environmental factors, both physical and social, and achievement.

B. Herzberg's Motivation – Hygiene Theory

This theory characterises the types of behaviour. It is directed towards achieving certain desirable positive goals or avoiding other undesirable consequences. The findings of this theory are that there are some job conditions which operate primarily to dissatisfy employees when the conditions are absent, their presence does not motivate them in a strong way. Another set of job conditions operates primarily to build strong motivation and high job satisfaction but their absence rarely proves strongly dissatisfying. The first set of job conditions is known as maintenance or hygiene factors and second set of job conditions is known as motivational factors.

Hygiene Factors. According to Herzberg, there are ten maintenance or hygiene factors. These are

(i) company policy and administration
(ii) technical supervision
(iii) interpersonal relationship with supervisors
(iv) interpersonal relationship with peers
(v) interpersonal relationship with subordinates
(vi) salary
(vii) job security
(viii) personal life
(ix) working conditions, and
(x) status.

These are not intrinsic parts of a job, but they are related to conditions under which a job is performed. They produce no growth in a worker's output; they only prevent losses in workers' performance due to work restrictions. These maintenance factors are necessary to maintain a reasonable level of satisfaction in employees. Any increase beyond this level will not provide any satisfaction to the employees; however, any cut below this level will dissatisfy them. As such, these are also called as dissatisfiers. Since any increase in these factors will not affect employee's level of satisfaction, these are of no use for motivating them.

Motivational Factors. These factors are capable of having a positive effect on job satisfaction often resulting in an increase in one's total output. Herzberg includes six factors that motivate employees. These are:

(i) achievement
(ii) recognition
(iii) advancement
(iv) work itself
(v) possibility of growth, and
(vi) responsibility.

Most of these factors are related with job contents. An increase in these factors will satisfy the employees; however, any decrease will not affect their level of satisfaction. Since these increase the level of satisfaction in the employees, these can be used in motivating them for higher output.

C. McClelland's needs Theory

McClelland has identified three types of basic motivating needs. He classified these as need for power, need for affiliation and need for achievement. Considerable research work was done by McClelland and his associates in this respect particularly on achievement motive.

Power Motive. The ability to induce or influence behaviour is power. Power motive has been formally recognised and studied for a relatively long time. The leading advocate of the power motive was Alfred Adler. Adler developed the concepts of inferiority complex and compensation. Accordingly, the individual's life style is characterised by striving to compensate for the feelings of inferiority which are combined with the innate drive for power. McClelland and his associates have found that people with a high power need have a great concern for exercising influence and control. Such individuals are generally seeking positions of leadership; they are forceful, outspoken, hard headed, and demanding.

Affiliation Motive. Since people are social animals, most individuals like to interact and be with others in situations where they feel they belong and are accepted. Sometimes affiliation is equated with social motives.

However, the affiliation motive is not so broad. Affiliation plays a very complex but vital role in human behaviour. The study of affiliation is complicated by the fact that some behavioural scientists believe that it is an unlearned motive. However, the fact is partly true. McClelland has suggested that people with high need for affiliation usually derive pleasure from being loved and tend to avoid the pain of being rejected. They are concerned with maintaining pleasant social relationships, enjoying a sense of intimacy and understanding, and enjoy consoling and helping others in trouble.

Achievement Motive. Over the years, behavioural scientists have observed that some people have an intense desire to achieve. McClelland's research has led him to believe that the need for achievement is a distinct human motive that can be distinguished from other needs. It can also be isolated and assessed in any group. McClelland has identified four basic characteristics of high achievers.

(i) *Moderate risks.* Taking moderate risks is probably the simple most descriptive characteristic of the person possessing high achievement need. This is against the commonsense that a high achiever would take high risks.

(ii) *Immediate feedback.* Person with high achievement motive desires activities which provide immediate and precise feedback information on how he is progressing toward a goal.

(iii) *Accomplishment.* Person with high achievement motive finds accomplishing a task intrinsically satisfying in and of itself, or he does not expect or necessarily want the accompanying material rewards. Though he likes to earn a lot of money but not for the usual reason of wanting money for its own sake or for the material benefits that it can buy.

(iv) *Preoccupation with the tasks.* Once a high achiever selects a goal, he tends to be totally preoccupied with the task until it is successfully completed. He will not feel satisfied unless he has put his maximum effort in completing the task. This type of dedicated commitment often reflects on his outward personality, which frequently has a negative effect on those who come in contact with him.

D. Vroom's Valence Expectancy Theory

Vroom has presented a theory, which is based on motivation process. Various theories which are based on motivation process are more concerned with the cognitive antecedents that go into motivation or effort and the way they relate to each other :

Motivation (force) = Valence × Expectancy × Instrumentality

Valence is the strength of an individual's preference to a particular outcome.

Expectancy is the probability that a particular action will lead to the outcome.

Valence. According to Vroom, valence means the strength of an individual's preference to a particular outcome. Other terms equivalent to valence used in various theories of motivation are incentive, attitude, and expected utility. In order for the valence to be positive for individual, he must prefer attending the outcome to not attending it; a valence of zero occurs when the individual is indifferent toward the outcome; and the valence is negative when the individual prefers not attaining the outcome to attaining it. Another major input into the valence is the instrumentality of the first level outcome in obtaining a derived second outcome.

Expectancy. Another factor in determining the motivation is expectancy, that is, the probability that a particular action will lead to the outcome. Expectancy differs from instrumentality in that it relates efforts to first-level outcomes whereas instrumentality relates first and second-level outcomes to each other. Thus, expectancy is the probability that a particular action will lead to a particular first-level outcome. The strength of motivation to perform a certain act will depend on the sum of the products of the values for the outcomes times the expectancies.

E. Porter and Lawler Model of Motivation

This model explains the complex relationship that exists between job attitudes and job performance. This is based on the assumption that there is positive relationship between satisfaction and performance. The various elements of this model are :

(i) **Effort.** Effort refers to the amount of energy exerted by an employee on a given task. Perceived-reward probability refers to the individual's perception of the probability that differential rewards depend upon differential amounts of effort. These two factors - value of reward and perception of effort-reward probability - determine the amount of effort that the employee will put in.

(ii) **Performance.** Effort leads to performance but both of these may not be equal, rather, performance is determined by the amount of effort and the ability and role perception of the individual. Thus, if an individual has little ability and / or inaccurate role perception, his performance may be ineffective in spite of his putting great efforts.

(iii) **Rewards.** Performance is seen as leading to intrinsic rewards (such as a sense of accomplishment and actualisation) and extrinsic rewards (such as working conditions and status). However, the intrinsic rewards are much more likely to produce attitudes about satisfaction that are related to performance. In addition, the perceived equitable rewards vitally affect the performance-satisfaction relationship. They reflect the fair level of rewards that the individual feels should be given for a given level of performance.

(iv) **Satisfaction.** Satisfaction is derived from the extent to which actual rewards fall short, meet or exceed the individual's perceived level of equitable rewards. If actual rewards meet or exceed perceived equitable rewards, the individual will feel satisfied; if these are less than equitable rewards, he will be dissatisfied. Thus this provides two implications. First, satisfaction is only in part determined by actual rewards. Second, satisfaction is more dependent on performance than performance is on satisfaction. Only through the less direct feedback loops will satisfaction affect performance. This is a marked departure from the traditional analysis of the satisfaction-performance relationship.

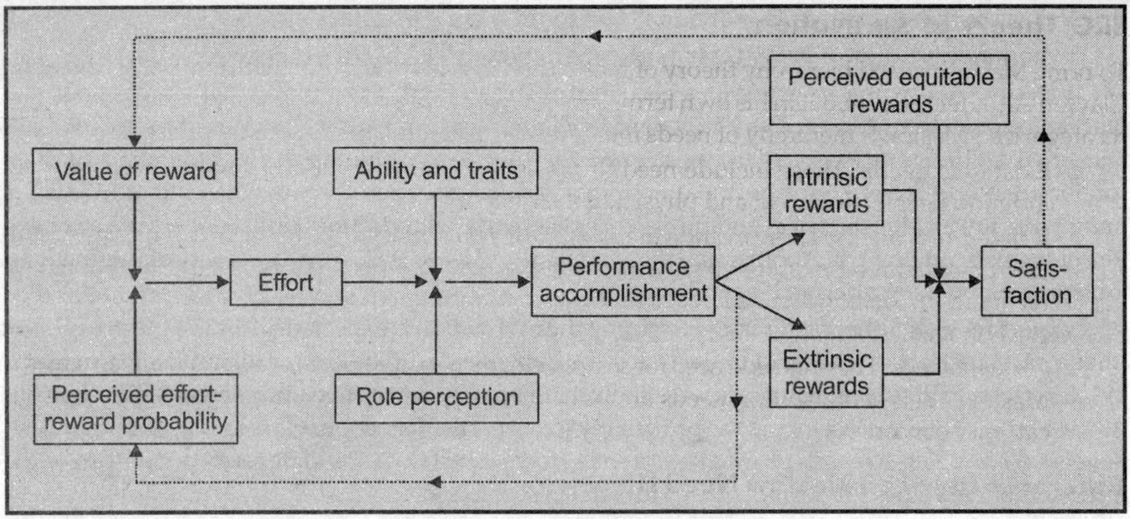

Porter-Lawler Motivation Model.

F. Carrot and Stick Approach

It comes from the old story that the best way to make donkey move is to put a carrot out in front of him or job him with a stick from behind. The carrot is the reward for moving and the stick is the punishment for not moving. In motivating people for behaviour that is desirable, some carrots, rewards, are used such as money, promotion and other financial and non-financial factors. Some sticks, punishments, are used to push the people for desired behaviour or to refrain from undesired behaviour.

In order to make the stick to work more effectively, following points should be taken into consideration while using it :

1. Punishment is effective in modifying the behaviour if it forces the person to select a desirable alternative behaviour.
2. If the above does not occur, the behaviour will be only temporarily suppressed and will reappear when the punishment is removed. Furthermore, the suppressed behaviour may cause the person to be fearful and anxious.
3. Punishment is more effective if applied at the time when the undesirable behaviour is actually performed.
4. Punishment must be administered with extreme care so that it does not become reward for undesirable behaviour. A punishment from one point of view, may become a reward for the person concerned.

The mixture of both carrot and stick should be used judiciously so that both have positive effects on the motivational profile of the people in the organisation.

G. Equity Theory

Equity Theory of work motivation is based on the social exchange process. This theory has been around just as long as the expectancy theories of motivation. However, Adams has crystallised in a more formal way. Basically, the theory points out that people are motivated to maintain fair relationship between their performance and reward in comparison to others. Assumptions of this theory are :

1. Individuals make contribution (inputs) for which they expect certain rewards (outcomes).
2. Individuals decide whether or not, a particular exchange is satisfactory, by comparing their inputs and outcomes with those of others and try to rectify any inequality.

ERG Theory of Motivation

To bring Maslow's need hierarchy theory of motivation in synchronization with empirical research, Clayton Alderfer redefined it in his own terms. His rework is called as ERG theory of motivation. He recategorized Maslow's hierarchy of needs into three simpler and broader classes of needs:

- **Existence needs.** These include need for basic material necessities. In short, it includes an individual's physiological and physical safety needs.
- **Relatedness needs.** These include the aspiration individual's have for maintaining significant interpersonal relationships (be it with family, peers or superiors), getting public fame and recognition. Maslow's social needs and external component of esteem needs fall under this class of need.
- **Growth needs.** These include need for self-development and personal growth and advancement. Maslow's self-actualization needs and intrinsic component of esteem needs fall under this category of need.

Difference between Maslow Need Hierarchy Theory and Alderfer's ERG Theory

- ERG Theory states that at a given point of time, more than one need may be operational.
- ERG Theory also shows that if the fulfillment of a higher-level need is subdued, there is an increase in desire for satisfying a lower-level need.
- According to Maslow, an individual remains at a particular need level until that need is satisfied. While according to ERG theory, if a higher- level need aggravates, an individual may revert to increase the satisfaction of a lower- level need. This is called frustration- regression aspect of ERG theory. For instance- when growth need aggravates, then an individual might be motivated to accomplish the relatedness need and if there are issues in accomplishing relatedness needs, then he might be motivated by the existence needs. Thus, frustration/ aggravation can result in regression to a lower-level need.
- While Maslow's need hierarchy theory is rigid as it assumes that the needs follow a specific and orderly hierarchy and unless a lower-level need is satisfied, an individual cannot proceed to the higher-level need; ERG Theory of motivation is very flexible as he perceived the needs as a range/variety rather than perceiving them as a hierarchy. According to Alderfer, an individual can work on growth needs even if his existence or relatedness needs remain unsatisfied. Thus, he gives explanation to the issue of "starving artist" who can struggle for growth even if he is hungry.

Implications of the ERG Theory

Managers must understand that an employee has various needs that must be satisfied at the same time. According to the ERG theory, if the manager concentrates solely on one need at a time, this will not effectively motivate the employee. Also, the frustration- regression aspect of ERG Theory has an added effect on workplace motivation. For instance- if an employee is not provided with growth and advancement opportunities in an organization, he might revert to the relatedness need such as socializing needs and to meet those socializing needs, if the environment or circumstances do not permit, he might revert to the need for money to fulfill those socializing needs. The sooner the manager realizes and discovers this, the more immediate steps they will take to fulfill those needs which are frustrated until such time that the employee can again pursue growth.

Theory X and Theory Y

Theory X and Theory Y were first explained by McGregor in his book, "The Human Side of Enterprise," and they refer to two styles of management - authoritarian (Theory X) and participative (Theory Y).

If you believe that your team members dislike their work and have little motivation, then, according to McGregor, you'll likely use an authoritarian style of management. This approach is very "hands-on" and usually involves micro-managing people's work to ensure that it gets done properly. McGregor called this Theory X.

On the other hand, if you believe that your people take pride in their work and see it as a challenge , then you'll more likely adopt a participative management style. Managers who use this approach trust their people to take ownership of their work and do it effectively by themselves. McGregor called this Theory Y.

The approach that you take will have a significant impact on your ability to motivate your team members. So, it's important to understand how your perceptions of what motivates them can shape your management style.

We'll now take a more in-depth look at the two different theories, and discover how and when they can be useful in the workplace.

Theory X

Theory X managers tend to take a pessimistic view of their people, and assume that they are naturally unmotivated and dislike work. As a result, they think that team members need to be prompted, rewarded or punished constantly to make sure that they complete their tasks.

Work in organizations that are managed like this can be repetitive, and people are often motivated with a "carrot and stick" approach. Performance appraisals and remuneration are usually based on tangible results, such as sales figures or product output, and are used to control staff and "keep tabs" on them.

This style of management assumes that workers:

- Dislike their work.
- Avoid responsibility and need constant direction.
- Have to be controlled, forced and threatened to deliver work.
- Need to be supervised at every step.
- Have no incentive to work or ambition, and therefore need to be enticed by rewards to achieve goals.

According to McGregor, organizations with a Theory X approach tend to have several tiers of managers and supervisors to oversee and direct workers. Authority is rarely delegated, and control remains firmly centralized. Managers are more authoritarian and actively intervene to get things done.

Although Theory X management has largely fallen out of fashion in recent times, big organizations may find that adopting it is unavoidable due to the sheer number of people that they employ and the tight deadlines that they have to meet.

Theory Y

Theory Y managers have an optimistic, positive opinion of their people, and they use a decentralized, participative management style. This encourages a more collaborative , trust-based relationship between managers and their team members.

People have greater responsibility, and managers encourage them to develop their skills and suggest improvements. Appraisals are regular but, unlike in Theory X organizations, they are used to encourage open communication rather than control staff.

Theory Y organizations also give employees frequent opportunities for promotion.

This style of management assumes that workers are:

- Happy to work on their own initiative.

- More involved in decision making.
- Self-motivated to complete their tasks.
- Enjoy taking ownership of their work.
- Seek and accept responsibility, and need little direction.
- View work as fulfilling and challenging.
- Solve problems creatively and imaginatively.

Theory Y has become more popular among organizations. This reflects workers' increasing desire for more meaningful careers that provide them with more than just money.

It's also viewed by McGregor as superior to Theory X, which, he says, reduces workers to "cogs in a machine," and likely demotivates people in the long term.

GROUP BEHAVIOUR AND INTERPERSONAL BEHAVIOUR

A. GROUP BEHAVIOUR

Groups exist in every organisation and they affect the behaviour of their members. They not only affect the behaviour of their members rather they have impact on other groups and the organisation as a whole. Such groups are created by the organisation as well as by organisation members for their own satisfaction.

Group behaviour is concerned with the interactions and forces between group members in a social situation. When the concept is applied in organisational behaviour, the focus is on the dynamics of members of formal or informal groups in the organisation. Group behaviour is based upon few factors.

(i) **Two or More Persons.** To form a group, there should be at least two persons because a single individual cannot interact. However, there cannot be any specific limit on the maximum number of persons in a group but the size of the group will be determined by rules and regulations of the organisation in this context, or meaningful interaction among the members in the case of informal groups.

(i) **Collective Identity.** Group behaviour can be determined if the members of the group are aware about their membership of the group. It is the awareness of each other that most clearly differentiates a group from an aggregation of individuals.

(ii) **Interaction.** Members of the group interact among themselves. Interaction means that each member shares his ideas with others through communication and this communication can take place face to face, in writing, over the telephone, across a computer network, or in any other manner which allows communication among group members.

(iii) **Shared Goal Interest.** Members of the group should subscribe to the attainment of some common objectives. However, it is not necessary that each member subscribes to or agrees with all the objectives of the group. If a group has a variety of objectives or interests, each member of the group must share at least one of the group's concerns.

The group determines the nature and patterns of reinforcement the members receive in the course of their interaction with one another. Therefore, the behaviour of individual members in a group may be different than their behaviour outside the group situation. In group behaviour, the factors that should be analysed are group norms, group cohesion and group decision-making.

(i) **Group Norms.** Group members tend to form and conform to norms. Norms are rules of behaviour or proper ways of action which are accepted as legitimate by group members. Group norms perform two functions. First, norms help the group to accomplish its goals. Second, norms help the group maintain itself as a group.

(ii) **Group Cohesiveness.** It may be characterised by the group situation in which all members work together for a common goal, or where everyone is ready to take responsibility for group chores. If group cohesion is high, the interaction between members of the group is high and the amount of agreement in group opinion is high.

(iii) **Group Decision Making.** It is an activity based on the old saying "two heads are better than one". It permits many persons simultaneously to interact and to arrive at a decision. In group decision making, there can be either co-members among the members of the group or the decision can be arrived at through simple majority unless the group prescribes any other mode of majority.

B. INTERPERSONAL BEHAVIOUR

It can be divided into two types :

(a) **Interpersonal co-operative behaviour.** When the interaction between two persons is mutually gratifying, it is co-operative behaviour. In this case, both persons are engaged in complementary transactions. Out of this interaction, both persons get satisfied over the objectives of mutual interaction.

(b) **Interpersonal conflicting behaviour.** Because of several reasons like personality differences, different value systems, interest conflict, role ambiguity etc., interpersonal conflict may arise in the organisation. This type of behaviour may not be good for the organisation.

Interpersonal behaviour can be better understood with the help of transactional analysis.

Transaction analysis (TA) is a model of personality and the dynamics of self and its relationship to others that makes possible a clear and meaningful discussion of behaviour. When people interact, there is social transaction in which one person responds to another. The study of these transactions between people is called transactional analysis. TA was originally developed by Eric Berne for psychotherapy in 1950. TA involves analysis of awareness, structural analysis (ego states), analysis of transactions, script analysis, and games analysis.

(i) **Self Awareness.** Self is the core of personality pattern which provides interaction. It includes the model as follows:

This model is made up of four different quadrants that together represent total person in relation to others on the basis of awareness of behaviour, feeling and motivation.

(ii) **Ego States.** People interact with each other in terms of three psychological positions or behavioural patterns, known as ego states. Thus, ego states are a person's way of thinking, feeling and behaving at any time. These ego states are : parent, adult and child.

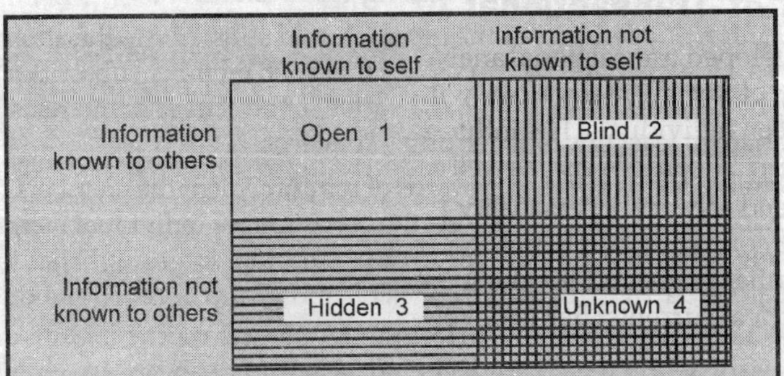

Self Awareness Model (Johari Window).

Parent Ego state incorporates the attitudes and behaviours of all emotionally significant people who serve as parent figure when an individual was a child.

Adult ego state is based upon reasoning, seeking and providing information.

Child Ego includes creativity, conformity, depression, anxiety, dependence, fear and hate.

Behavioural Responses with different ego states

Parent ego	Adult ego	Child ego
Rules and laws	Rationality	Seeing, hearing, touching
Do's and don'ts	Estimation	Experiencing joy/frustration
Truths	Evaluation	Creating
How to	Storing data	Wishing/fantasizing
Tradition	Figuring out	Feeling internally
Teaching	Exploring	Impulsive
Demonstrating	Testing	Spontaneous

(iii) **Script Analysis.** When confronted with a situation, a person acts according to his script which is based on what he expects or how he views his life position. In TA, a person's life is compared to a play and the script in the text of that play. A person's psychological script is a life plan, a drama which he writes and then feels compelled to live out.

According to Berne

"Berne is a complete plan of living, offering both structures – structure of injections, prescription and permissions, and structure which makes and winner or losser in life."

(iv) **Stroking.** It is an important part of TA. It is any act implying recognition of another's presence. People seek recognition in interaction with others.

(v) **Psychological Games.** People usually learn their game patterns right since their childhood. They learn to believe certain things about themselves and about others and act accordingly.

TRANSACTIONAL ANALYSIS

Transactional analysis, developed by psychiatrist Eric Berne, is a form of modern psychology that examines a person's relationships and interactions. Berne took inspiration from Sigmund Freud's theories of personality, combining them with his own observations of human interaction in order to develop transactional analysis. In therapy, transactional analysis can be used to address one's interactions and communications with the purpose of establishing and reinforcing the idea that each individual is valuable and has the capacity for positive change and personal growth.

Development of Transactional Analysis

Dr. Eric Berne developed transactional analysis in the last 1950s, using "transaction" to describe the fundamental unit of social intercourse, with "transactional analysis" being the study of social interactions between individuals. His influences included contemporaries such as René Spitz, Erik Erikson, Paul Federn, Edoardo Weiss, as well as Freud and Wilder Penfield, a Canadian neurosurgeon.

Inspired by Freud's theory of personality-primarily his belief that the human psyche is multifaceted and that different components interact to produce a variety of emotions, attitudes and complex behaviors-and Penfield's ground breaking experiments involving the stimulation of specific brain regions with electrical currents, Berne developed an approach that he described as both neo- and extra-Freudian.

Discerning the need to build upon the philosophical concepts Freud introduced with observable data, Berne developed his own observable ego states of Parent, Adult, and Child, following Freud's proposal of the existence of the Id (emotional and irrational component), Ego (rational component), and Superego (moral component) as different and unobservable factions of personality.

Berne also took special note of the complexities of human communication. He highlighted the fact that facial expressions, gestures, body language, and tone may be regarded as more important by the receiver than any spoken words. In his book Games People Play, he noted that people may sometimes communicate messages underpinned with ulterior motives.

Examining the Ego States of Transactional Analysis

Like Freud, Berne posited that each individual possesses three ego states. His ego states-the Parent, the Adult, and the Child-do not directly correspond to Freud's Id, Ego, and Superego, however. Instead, these states represent an individual's internal model of parents, adults, and children. An individual may assume any of these roles in transactions with another person or in internal conversation. These roles are not directly associated with their typical English definitions but can be described as follows:

Parent consists of recordings of external events observed and experienced by a child from birth through approximately the first five years of life. These recordings are not filtered or analyzed by the child; they are simply accepted without question. Many of these external events are likely to involve the individual's parents or other adults in parent-link roles, which led Berne to call this ego state "the Parent." Examples of external events recorded in this state:

- Do not play with matches.
- Remember to say "please" and "thank you."
- Do not speak to strangers.

Child represents all brain recordings of internal events (feelings or emotions) that are directly linked to the external events observed by the child during the first five years of life. Examples of events recorded in this state may include:

- I feel happy when Mom hugs me.
- Dad's late night movie was very scary.
- I feel sad when Mom is sad.

Adult, the final ego state, is the period in which a child develops the capacity to perceive and understand situations that are different from what is observed (Parent) or felt (Child). The Adult serves as a data processing center that utilizes information from all three ego states in order to arrive at a decision. One important role of the Adult is to validate data which is stored in the Parent:

- I see that Suzie's house was burnt down. Mom was right-I should not play with matches.

Communication Using Transactional Analytic Theory

Any indication (speech, gestures or other nonverbal cues) that acknowledges the presence of another person is called a transactional stimulus. All transactions are initiated via the use of a transactional stimulus. When two individuals encounter each other and the receiver reacts in a manner related to the transactional stimulus, that individual has performed a transactional response. The key to successful person-to-person communication generally lies in identifying which ego state (in the speaker) initiated the transactional stimulus and which ego state (in the receiver) provided the transactional response.

Due to the typically rational and reasonable nature of the Adult, Berne believes that the easiest and simplest transactions occur between Adult ego states, but transactions may occur between any of the three ego states. In a complementary transaction, the transaction response from the receiver is directed to the sending ego state in the speaker. For example, if the Adult in the speaker sends a transactional stimulus to the Child in the receiver, then the transaction will be complementary if the

Child in the receiver then sends the transactional response to the Adult in the speaker. According to Berne, communication will continue if the transactions remain complementary.

A crossed transaction occurs when an ego state that did not receive the transactional stimulus sends the transactional response. Crossed transactions may lead to breakdowns in communication, which may sometimes be followed by conflict. For example, the Adult state in an individual may send a transactional stimulus to the Adult in another individual, asking "Have you seen my coat?" But the Child in the second individual may instead send the transactional response to the Parent in the first individual by replying, "You always blame me for everything!"

Not only is communication considered to be an important aspect of everyday life, it is also thought to be an integral part of being human. Even newborns exhibit the need to be recognized and acknowledged. Research conducted by Spitz showed that infants who received less cuddling, handling, and touching were more likely to experience physical and emotional challenges. Berne described this innate need for social recognition as recognition-hunger, defining the fundamental unit of social action or recognition as a stroke.

From Berne's perspective, the adversely affected children in Spitz's studies exhibited physical and emotional deficits due to a lack of strokes. Berne applied this theory to adults, theorizing that men and women also experience recognition-hunger and a need for strokes. However, while infants may desire strokes that are primarily physical, an adult may be contented with other forms of recognition, such as nods, winks, or smiles.

While strokes may be positive or negative, Berne theorized that it is better to receive a negative stroke than no stroke at all. When one person asks another out on a date, for example, and receives a flat refusal, that person may find the refusal to be less damaging than a complete lack of acknowledgment.

TRANSACTIONAL ANALYSIS IN THERAPY

The goal of transactional analysis is help the individual in therapy gain and maintain autonomy by strengthening the Adult state. Typically, the individual and the therapist will establish a contract that outlines the desired outcome they wish to achieve in therapy. This may contribute to the person in therapy taking personal responsibility for events that take place during treatment. The individual will generally then become more able to rely on their Adult ego states to identify and examine various thoughts, behaviors, and emotions which might hinder the ability to thrive.

The atmosphere that supports transactional analysis is one of comfort, security, and respect. When a positive relationship is forged between the therapist and the person seeking treatment, this often provides a model for subsequent relationships developed outside of the therapy arena. Analysts who practice this form of therapy generally use a broad range of tools gathered from many disciplines including psychodynamic, cognitive behavioral, and relational therapies.

Who can Benefit from Transactional Analysis?

Transactional analysis is frequently applied in the areas of medicine, communications, education, and business management as well as therapy. The mainstream appeal of this technique has attracted parents, professionals, social workers, and others who strive to achieve maximum personal development. Transactional analysis is considered to be one effective method of enhancing relationships with oneself and with others.

Studies show that transactional analysis, often used by counselors and clinicians to address issues currently faced by the person in treatment, can be an effective tool in the treatment of emotional and relationship difficulties that may develop as a result of chronic health challenges.

Transactional analysis is used widely in the educational arena, and this method can serve as a vessel through which educational principles and philosophy can be incorporated into the daily lives of students. This type of therapy can be administered to children and adults of all ages, regardless of social circumstances.

Johari Window Model

It is necessary to improve self-awareness and personal development among individuals when they are in a group. The 'Johari' window model is a convenient method used to achieve this task of understanding and enhancing communication between the members in a group. American psychologists Joseph Luft and Harry Ingham developed this model in 1955. The idea was derived as the upshot of the group dynamics in University of California and was later improved by Joseph Luft. The name 'Johari' came from joining their first two names. This model is also denoted as feedback/disclosure model of self-awareness.

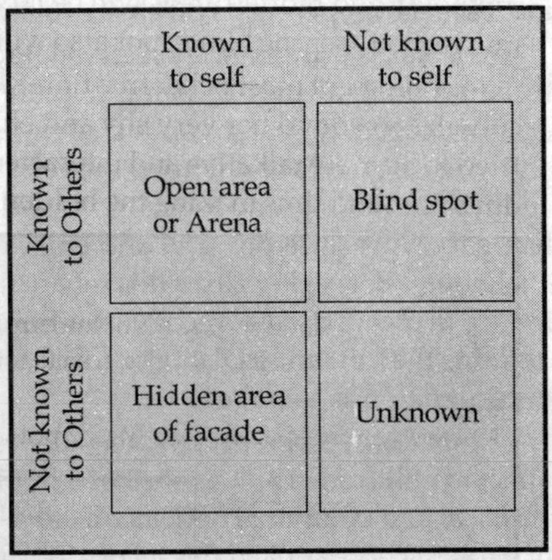

The Johari window model is used to enhance the individual's perception on others. This model is based on two ideas- trust can be acquired by revealing information about you to others and learning yourselves from their feedbacks. Each person is represented by the Johari model through four quadrants or window pane. Each four window panes signifies personal information, feelings, motivation and whether that information is known or unknown to oneself or others in four viewpoints.

The method of conveying and accepting feedback is interpreted in this model. A Johari is represented as a common window with four panes. Two of these panes represent self and the other two represent the part unknown to self but to others. The information transfers from one pane to the other as the result of mutual trust which can be achieved through socializing and the feedback got from other members of the group.

1. **Open/self-area or arena.** Here the information about the person his attitudes, behaviour, emotions, feelings, skills and views will be known by the person as well as by others. This is mainly the area where all the communications occur and the larger the arena becomes the more effectual and dynamic the relationship will be. 'Feedback solicitation' is a process which occurs by understanding and listening to the feedback from another person. Through this way the open area can be increased horizontally decreasing the blind spot. The size of the arena can also be increased downwards and thus by reducing the hidden and unknown areas through revealing one's feelings to other person.
2. **Blind self or blind spot.** Information about yourselves that others know in a group but you will be unaware of it. Others may interpret yourselves differently than you expect. The blind spot is reduced for an efficient communication through seeking feedback from others.
3. **Hidden area or facade.** Information that is known to you but will be kept unknown from others. This can be any personal information which you feel reluctant to reveal. This includes feelings, past experiences, fears, secrets etc. we keep some of our feelings and information as private as it affects the relationships and thus the hidden area must be reduced by moving the information to the open areas.
4. **Unknown area.** The Information which are unaware to yourselves as well as others. This includes the information, feelings, capabilities, talents etc. This can be due to traumatic past

experiences or events which can be unknown for a lifetime. The person will be unaware till he discovers his hidden qualities and capabilities or through observation of others. Open communication is also an effective way to decrease the unknown area and thus to communicate effectively.

Example

Linda got a job in an organization. Her co-workers knew a little about her and in this context the unknown and hidden areas will be larger and the open area will be small. As the others don't know much about her the blind spot also will be smaller and the model will be as shown in Figure A.

Linda spent most of her free time sketching in the office which was her preferred pastime and her co-workers found her very shy and elusive. With that evaluation she got the idea how she was and tried to be more talkative and interacted more with other co-workers. This helped her to increase her open area and thus making the hidden and unknown areas smaller. (Figure B).

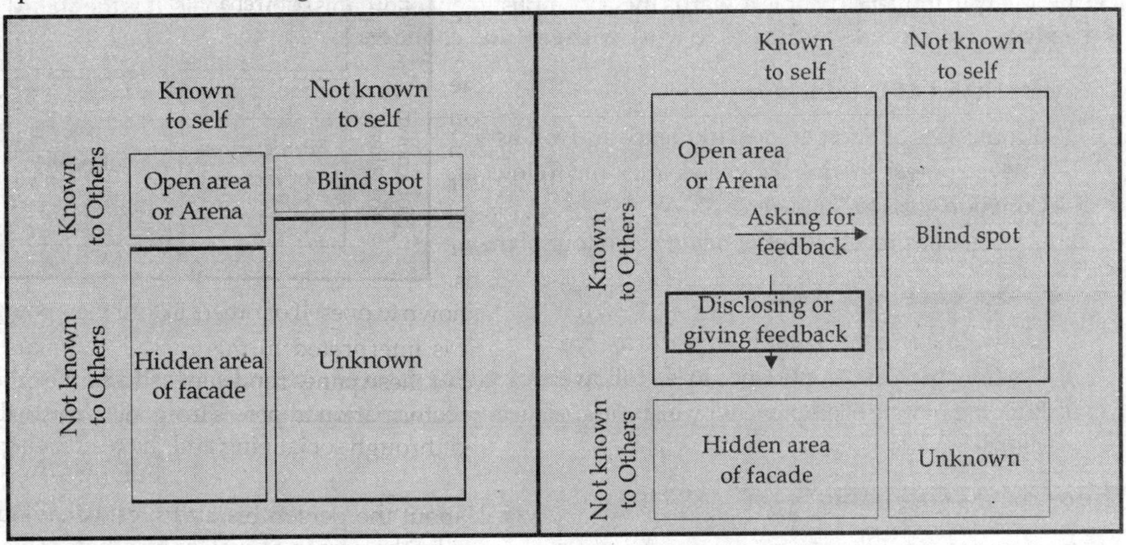

(A) (B)

TEAM BUILDING

Work group comprises of people who interact with each other. However, Work teams are defined as a work group working together and achieving synergy as an output of collective efforts.

Types of Team Building

- **Problem Solving Teams.** They are temporary in nature and are formed to find the solution to specific problems.
- **Self Managed Work Teams.** They are groups of employees (typically 10 to 15 in number) who perform highly related or interdependent jobs 'and take on many of the responsibilities of their former supervisors. They deal with operations, planning scheduling etc.
- **Cross Functional Teams.** This team comprises of members from different functions such as representatives from finance, HR, marketing etc.
- **Virtual Teams.** These types are physically dispersed but work through internet and computer technology.

Process of Team Building

- **Selecting.** The management must hire individuals with abilities and skills to work in team. The candidates must be able to play the technical roles and team roles.
- **Training.** Management can train the selected employees and enhance their team building skills. Frequent workshops should be organised for the individuals so that they improve their communication skills and enhance their negotiation, coaching skills, problem solving skills and conflict management skills.
- **Rewarding.** The company must be the team players. Hence, this gives a message that be the company promotes cooperation rather than individualism. Individuals who work cooperatively with the teams should be given recognition, pay rises and promotions.

LEADERSHIP

It is the ability to influence people towards the accomplishment of organisational goals. It is the ability of a manager to induce subordinates to work with zeal and confidence.

Characteristics of Leadership

- It comprises of interpersonal influence and followers.
- Uneven power sharing between leader and followers.
- Common goals for followers.
- Continuous process of influencing behaviour of members.

Importance of Leadership

- Motivating employees for high performance.
- Creating trust and confidence in his followers by giving them advice and suggestions.
- Building morale of employees by inspiring, securing cooperation and providing good working climate.

Theories of Leadership

Transactional vs Transformational Leaders

According to James Burns, there are two types of leaders:

- **Transactional Leaders.** Leaders clarify subordinate's role, job requirements, rewards to subordinates. His focus is on achieving organisational results. He takes pride in keeping things to run smoothly, he emphasis impersonal and unemotional aspects. He conforms to organisational norms and value systems. They are practical planners.
- **Transformational Leaders.** These leaders recognise and satisfy the needs of his followers while elevating them into high levels of motivation and morality. They provide a sense of vision and feeling of pride, faith and respect to the employees. They have charismatic as well as intellectual power, e.g., J.F. Kennedy, Jawaharlal Nehru.

Charismatic Theory/Great Man Theory

'Charisma' is a Greek word which means 'gift'. This theory considers that a leader has some charisma which is a god-gifted attribute which acts as a influence. These leaders, irrespective of situation, have personal vision and energy to influence its followers.

This theory assumes and implies that leaders are born and not developed. Since, these qualities are naturally gifted, they cannot be acquired by way of training. These qualities are personal and cannot be shared. Situational factors do not have any influence.

Trait Theory

The trait theory emphasises that leaders are made because of their own personal traits. These traits are of two types:

- **Innate Qualities.** These are god-gifted, e.g. Physical features like height, weight, physique, health, vigour, appearance, intelligence.
- **Acquirable Qualities.** These can be acquired and enhanced through training methods, e.g. Social skills communications skills, technical skills etc.

Leadership Continuum

Tannenbaum and Schmidt have depicted a broad range of leadership styles between two extremes, i.e. Autocratic and Free-rein.

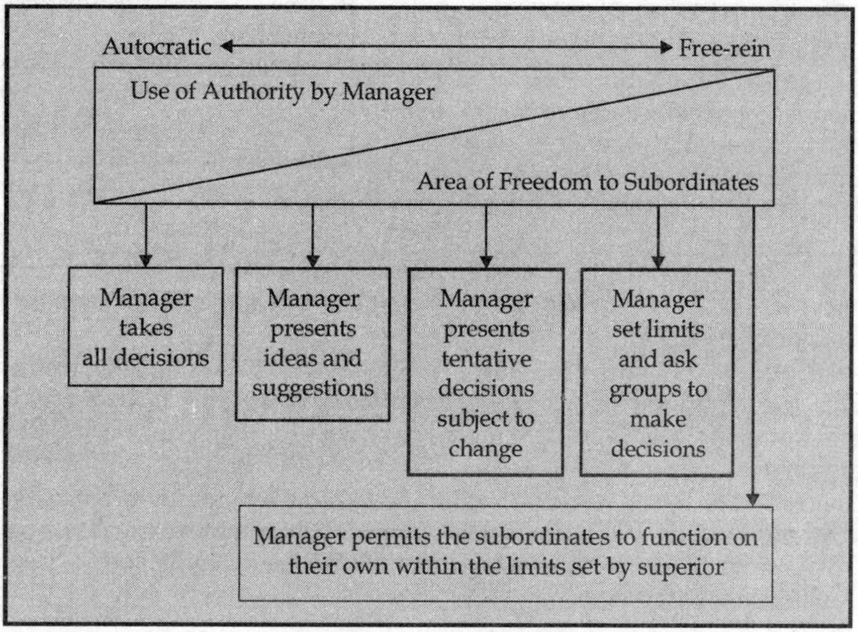

Managers who are production oriented use autocratic style of leadership to get the work done. They treat employees as tools for accomplishing the jobs and focus on output.

Managers who are employee-oriented use participative or free-rein style of leadership. They emphasises that every individual is important and take interest in views and suggestions of employees. They work with the team.

Managerial Grid

Managerial grid is most effective practical contribution made by 'Blake and Mouton' which assumes that a manager shows either task-oriented behaviour or relation-oriented behaviour.

Managers are concerned for people or production or a balance of two.

Managerial grid identifies five leadership styles which are as follows:

(1, 1) Impoverished. Manager put little efforts to get work done and sustain morale of employees.

(1, 9) Country Club. Manager show great concern for employees and make good organisational climate for work.

(9, 1) Task. Manager gets little involvement of employees in setting work, he is more structural and technical in approach.

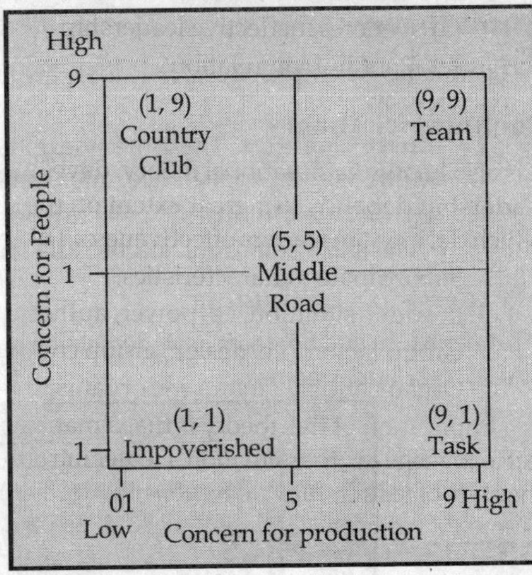

(5, 5) Middle Road. A good balance of work requirements and maintaining satisfactory morale leads to adequate performance.

(9, 9) Team. Work is accomplished by a team or committed people with interdependence through a common stake in organisation, gaining trust, respect and resulting productivity.

Likert's Management System

'Rensis Likert' has developed four models of management known as management systems on the basis of goal-setting, decision making, communication related strategies. These are as follows:

- **Exploitative Autocratic.** These in one way communication with minimum participation in decision-making. The superior has stiff relations with his subordination. He rewards for attaining objectives while punishes for failure.
- **Benevolent Autocratic.** The leader adopts a paternalistic approach towards his subordinate. The goals are centralised and subordinates are given little freedom to carry out their tasks within the limit. There is a distrust, suspicion and fear in the relationship between superior and subordinate.
- **Consultative/Participative.** Employees are involved in decision-making but major decisions are taken at the top and subordinates freely discuss work with managers, it promotes two way communication. There is greater emphasise on rewards than punishment, alongwith flexible control system.
- **Democratic.** Managers maintain cordial and friendly relations with subordinates with high decentralisation. There is active participation of subordinates in goal-setting. The manager acts like a guide, mentor, counselor and there is transparent communication. Here, self-appraisal and self-control is important.

Behavioural Theory

Michigan researchers emphasises that strong leadership comes from effective role behaviour rather than his personality traits. Researches found that to operate effectively, manager need to perform two major functions.

- **Task Related.** These functions provide solutions to the task related problems faced by employees in their performing job.
- **Group Maintenance.** This is also called social function, relates to actions of mediating disputes and ensuring that individuals feel valued in the organisation.

The person who performs both these functions successfully, would be an effective leader. To perform both these functions, a manager can show two types of behaviours:

- **Functional Behaviour**
  - (a) Motivate subordinates
  - (b) Setting clear goals for subordinates
  - (c) Building high morale to perform
  - (d) Team spirit in employees
  - (e) Open communication with subordinates

- Dyfunctional Behaviour
  - (a) Denotes ineffective leadership
  - (b) Display of emotional immaturity
  - (c) Poor human relation
  - (d) Inability to involve employees

Contingency Theory

It is also known as situational theory, developed by Fiedler. This theory proposes that effectiveness of leadership depends to a great extent on the situation around. There are some situational variables which decides the leaders effectiveness. These are as follows:

- Subordinate's characteristics.
- Leader's situation, i.e. power, authority and relationship with subordinate.
- Group factors, i.e. design, group composition, cohesiveness.
- Organisational factors, i.e. organisational culture.

Implication of this theory is that a manager can be a successful leader in one situation and he may fail to manage in other situation. Fiedler introduced Least Preferred Co-worker (LPC) scale to determine the style of leadership.

GROUP DYNAMICS

Concept of Group Dynamics. The term group dynamics contains two terms : group and dynamics. Group is basically a collectively of two or more persons. Dynamics comes from Greek word meaning force. Thus group dynamics refers to the interaction of force between group members in a social situation. However, the term group dynamics is defined in different ways. One view is that group dynamics describes how a group should be organised and operated. This includes democratic leadership, participation and cooperation. Another view takes group dynamics as a set of techniques, such as role playing brainstorming, leaderless group, group therapy, sensitivity training etc. According to the third view, group dynamics is viewed from the internal nature of groups, their formation structure and process, and the way they affect individual members, other groups, and the organisation. This view is more prevalent. The determinants of group dynamics are as follows :

1. External conditions of the group.
2. Group member resources.
3. Group structure – composition, size, roles, leadership, norms, cohesiveness and status.
4. Group processes.

ORGANISATIONAL CULTURE AND CLIMATE

Elements of Organisational Culture

- **Innovation and Taking Risks.** It describes the degree to which the individuals of an organisation are motivated to take risks and be innovative.
- **Detailed Attention.** It describes the amount of degree expected by the employees to show attention, analysis and precision in the organisation.
- **Outcome Orientation.** Organisational culture also focuses on what are the outcomes or results and not how these outcomes have been derived, *i.e.*, processes, tools and techniques.
- **People Orientation.** Organisational culture defines how cautious and considerate the management becomes while making decisions. It keeps in mind how these decisions will impact the employees. Thus, the culture is oriented towards it's people.

- **Team Orientation.** It defines the extent to which the work is planned with the teams and not individuals. Thus, organisational culture also defines whether the organisation promotes teamwork or individual effort.
- **Aggressiveness.** It refers to the extent to which the employees are competitive and aggressive about their work rather than being unconcerned or easy going.
- **Stability.** It refers to the level to which the organisation focuses in maintaining stability or 'status quo' with reference to progress and growth.

Layers of Organisational Culture

Schein has defined three levels of organisational culture which are as follows:

- **Observable Artifacts of Culture (Top Most Layer).** These are the visible, tangible symbols of the organisation that are accessible. They are present in the social and physical environment of the organisation, e.g. language, material symbols and practices. They comprise of the following:
  - *Cultural Symbols.* Here, the values and beliefs of the A organisation are manifested in an unspoken manner such as large cabins for top leaders, dress-code, uniform, office layout, slogans etc.
  - *Organisational Heroes.* The behaviour of the top level management reflects the ideology of the institution. The top leaders live with the organisational values and reinforce them in the organisation and promote the organisational culture that is expected from the employees. Thus, here the practice of the top organisation becomes a visible symbol.
  - *Ceremonies and Rites.* These refer to events that are performed frequently on special occasions which reflect the culture of the organisation. E.g. Farewell to retiring staff, organisational trips, celebration on various festivals. Thus, these ceremonies clearly manifest the culture of the organisation and also bind the organisation together.
  - *Stories.* These comprise about the myths or stories about the heroes of the organisation. They help in reinforcing the cultural values especially when a new employee is orientated. The stories retell the individuals why they are expected to perform their work in a specified manner.
- **Shared Values (Middle Layer).** This is the second layer and deeper level as values determine the behaviour of the individual, 'they shape the thinking and behaviour of the person. Values are learnt through families, socialisation, peer influence, religion etc. Thus, Peters and Waterman suggest that "every institution should develop a dominant and coherent set of shared values', so that all members will have a predictable behaviour pattern which is consistent with the organisational philosophy and group cohesion is enhanced." E.g. Making employees learn particular software.
- **Common Assumptions (Base Layer).** They are deepest and fundamental layer of culture. These beliefs are deeply held and are not observable. However, they are strongly manifested by the behaviour of the employee so much that their violation is impossible. It represents the core of the culture. E.g. All people are good, hence such organisation runs on the belief of presence of mutual trust. Thus, these values develop the nature of the individuals and of the organisation in totality.

Types of Organisational Culture

Clan Culture

Here, the working atmosphere is amiable. There are commonalities among the people and the entire organisation is equivalent to a large family. The leaders seems as fatherly figures while loyalty and traditions holds the organisation together. The sense of unity binds the organisation together. There is strong peer pressure.

The leader here is a team builder and a facilitator. The values that drive the organisation are development, communication and commitment. Various theories like participation and human resource development prove effective. The leader uses strategies lie open communication, HRD, empowerment etc. to improve the quality.

Adhocracy Culture

Here, the working environment is creative and dynamic. The leaders are innovative whereas the individuals take risks. The culture supports innovations and experiments and the future goal is to create resources and grow. Invention of new services or products is considered as a success. Thus, this organisational culture promotes freedom and initiation within the organisation.

Here, the leader is an entrepreneur and visionary. The drivers are agility, transformation and innovative outputs. The measures to improve quality include creating different standards and evolving continuously to find creative solutions.

Market Culture

This organisational structure focuses on results and getting outputs and finishing the work. Here, employees are focussed on the outcomes and are competitive. Leaders are rivals, producers and hard drivers alongwith being tough. They have high expectations from the individuals. Success, win and reputation is the primary objective in such culture. The sense of winning binds the organisation together.

Here, the leader is competitive and hard driver. Profitability, goal achievement and market share are the values that drive the organisation. Effectiveness is achieving by motivating the employees to focus on the goals and customers. Improvements are made by creation of external partnership, involving suppliers and customers, measurement of preference of the client etc.

Hierarchy Culture

It is the most formalised organisational culture. There are procedures that define the behaviour and work of the individuals. Leaders focus only coordination that results into efficiency The formal policies and rules bind the organisation together Success is defined with low cost arising out of smooth planning It is also known as bureaucratic culture.

Here, the leader is a coordinator, organiser and a monitor The key value drivers are uniformity, dependability timeliness and effectiveness Effectiveness is achieved with control The leader uses following strategic to increase the quality of detection of errors, process control, quality tools, systematic problem solving.

Organisational Climate is helpful in the fulfilment of committed goals of an individual, organisation and society. It increases the capabilities and efficiency of an individual and is likely to reflect itself in the long run in the well-being of the individual, reputation of the institution and ultimately the well-being of the society. However, the nature of efforts and investments in developing human resources may vary from organisation to organisation depending on its need, nature of capabilities the organisation wants to build up and the size of the organisation etc. Payne and Monsfield viewed HRD climate as a conceptual linkage between organisations and individuals that intervenes between specific situation attributes or events and individual perceptions, attitudes and behaviour. Pritchard and Marasick define HRD climate as a relatively enduring quality of an organisation's internal environment, distinguishing it from other organisations, which:

(a) results from the behaviour and practice of members of the organisation especially in top management

(b) is perceived by members of the organisation
(c) serves as a basis for interpreting the situation and
(d) acts as a source of pressure for directing activity. The elements of HRD climate can be grouped into three-broad categories;
    (1) General climate
    (2) HRD culture and
    (3) Human Resource Development mechanisms. HRD culture is essential for facilitating HRD climate. The HRD culture deals with the extent to which Openness, Confrontation, Trust, Autonomy, Proactivity, Authenticity, Collaboration and Experimentation (OCTAPACE) are valued and promoted in the organisation.

Factors Affecting Organisational Climate

There are six factors given by Stringer and Litwin:

- **Organisational Structure.** How the individual perceives organisational regulations, rules, constraints and red tapes.
- **Individual Responsibility.** Whether the individual has a sense of autonomy or freedom of being one's own boss.
- **Support and Warmth.** Whether the individual has a feeling of helpfulness and good fellowship in the work environment.
- **Risk and Risk Taking.** What is the perception of the individual about the challenges and risks in his work situation.
- **Rewards.** Whether the individual is confident about appropriate, fair and adequate rewards.
- **Conflict and Tolerance.** This is the extent to which an employee is confident that the organisational climate will tolerate conflicting beliefs or opinions.

Levels of Organisational Climate

- **Psychological Climate.** It is an individual feature and comprises of individual's depiction of organisational policies and procedures.
- **Group Climate.** It is a subsystem climate which defines how the individuals perceive the atmosphere of a subsystem of a group within the organisation.
- **Organisational Climate.** It is an organisational feature which represents the average view/ perception of all the individuals giving collective description about the organisation.

Dimensions of Organisational Climate

- **Dominant Orientation.** If there are established rules then climate is controlling, if the aim is to achieve efficiency then it is characterised by accomplishment.
- **Conflict Management.** If conflicts are handled efficiently then climate is cooperative, if they are not then the climate will be non-cooperative and distrust.
- **Individual Autonomy.** If more freedom is given to employees then there is a lighter atmosphere as the burden shifts from superiors.
- **Control System in Organisation.** If there is rigid control, there will be bureaucratic/impersonal atmosphere if there is flexibility in control there will be a scope of self-regulation.
- **Organisational Structure.** If there is decentralisation, then the environment will be of participative decision-making, while in centralisation it will be authoritative.
- **Relation Oriented and Task Oriented.** If bosses are relation oriented, then climate will be supportive whereas, if superiors are task oriented then the employees may face punishment.

WORK FORCE DIVERSITY & CROSS CULTURE ORGANISATIONAL BEHAVIOUR

Managing workforce diversity implies creating an organisational climate in which a heterogeneous workforce performs to its best potential; without the organisation favouring / dis-favouring any particular segment of workforce with a view to facilitating the best attainment of organisational goals.

Some salient features of workforce diversity management are stated below:

(i) Workforce diversity management requires creation of an organisational climate, in which people from different cultural, social backgrounds and being diverse in many other respects (e.g. age, gender, education etc.) can co-exist and work, with full co-operation of one another.

(ii) Workforce diversity management aims at making people work to the best of their potential

(iii) Workforce diversity management rules out any discrimination among people, in any respect, whatsoever.

(iv) Work-force diversity management is expected to work towards the best attainment of organisational goals.

Some people dimensions of workforce diversity are described below:

(i) **Age.** People belonging to different age groups cause diversity in workforce. Young people may be enriched with health, merit, capacity for hard-work etc.; while elderly people may possess more maturity than their junior counterparts and are full of experiences of life.

(ii) **Gender.** Male workers are usually aggressive, bold and materialistic; while female workers possess sympathy for others and are more concerned with quality of life. What is important to observe is that people of both sex have material differences in outlook, nature, habits etc.; as differences between males and females are the design of God who created mankind.

(iii) **Education.** In an organisation people may range from less educated to highly educated. Educated people have a broad outlook and are open-minded. They are endowed with logic and rationality and usually dislike discrimination among individuals on petty grounds of caste, colour, religion etc.

(iv) **Culture.** Culture is a complex of race, religion, language, social traditions and values etc. People from different cultural backgrounds may have ethnic orientations, i.e., a sense of favouritism towards their nation, race or tribe, which they belong to.

(v) **Psychology.** (Psychology is the kind of mind that one has that makes one think or behaves in a particular way). In a organisation, there are people with different psychology. Some may be optimistic or pessimistic; some may be bold or timid or so on. Psychology may be a gift of nature or a manifestation of family background or social affiliations.

Types of Discrimination

The organisation faces following types of discrimination:

- **Discriminatory.** Policies or Practices It comprises of unequal rewards for same performance or practices/ actions of the organisations that does not give equal opportunity to the members.
- **Sexual Harassment.** Any verbal or nonverbal/Physical misconduct/advance of sexual nature which creates an offensive or hostile work atmosphere.
- **Exclusion.** Here, certain individuals are excluded from various discussions, social events, job opportunities and informal mentoring. This can take place intentionally or unintentionally.

- **Intimidation.** Here, the specific group of individuals are bullied or threatened, these are generally minority groups.
- **Insults.** This is a form of negative stereotypes and jokes thrown at employees. Sometimes the results of such actions are adverse.
- **Incivility.** Here, some of the employees are treated disrespectfully, interrupted or avoided or their opinions are ignored.

Thus, it is important to manage the workforce diversity so that there is a conducive work climate and there are no grounds of discrimination. Thus, managers are also recognising importance of managing workforce diversity as explained in upcoming section.

Techniques/Strategies for Managing Diversity

Diversity management sensitises individuals about the diversity in the organisation and respecting it. Following are the strategies for managing diversity:

- **Awareness.** Creating awareness about the diversity and the basis of such diversity such as culture, education, age etc. This helps the individuals in accepting diversity in rational manner.
- **Conditions for Shared Organisational Culture.** The training program must incorporate cross cultural segments and create such organisational climate which enables the members to work cooperatively.
- **Exceptional Programmes for the Diversity.** Special care for aged people, better work schedules for woman employees etc.
- **Avoiding Discrimination.** Enforcing policies and rules for non-discrimination among workforce and penalising any misconduct. E.g. Women should be given equal opportunity for promotions.
- **Career Enhancement Programmes.** Each individual must be given equal opportunity to grow and develop his career. Individuals should be respected for their different characteristics and should be given enough opportunities to gauge their weaknesses and strengths.
- **Preventing Sexual Harassment.** Clearly explaining the fine and punishment -for misconduct such as unwelcome teasing slurs, touching and even joking. Special cells should be created where such harassment can be reported. Abiding by laws of the nation such as Sexual Harassment of Women at Workplace (Prevention, prohibition and redressal) Act of 2013.
- **Special Committees.** The organisation must establish committees for members belonging to diversity so that they can express their complaints and sad experiences.

Significance of Workforce Diversity Management

Workforce diversity management is significant for the following reasons:

(i) **Ability to Deal with Diverse Market.** Culturally diverse workforce can better appreciate the needs, feedings, and attitudes of culturally diverse consumers. Thus workforce diversity increases the competence of a corporation to deal with a market, that consists of diverse consumer groups in respect of age, sex, culture etc.

(ii) **Better Decision-Making.** People from heterogeneous backgrounds may aid management in better decision-making, by offering suggestions from a wide range of perspectives and orientations. In fact, heterogeneous groups of people may be more creative and innovative; when they pool their knowledge and experiences and agree on a common solution to a tricky problem; which might aid management in making excellent decisions for the organisation.

EMOTIONS AND STRESS MANAGEMENT

Emotions exert an incredibly powerful force on human behavior. Strong emotions can cause you to take actions you might not normally perform or to avoid situations you enjoy. Why exactly do we have emotions? What causes us to have these feelings? Researchers, philosophers, and psychologists have proposed different theories to explain the how and why behind human emotions.

What is Emotion?

In psychology, emotion is often defined as a complex state of feeling that results in physical and psychological changes that influence thought and behavior. Emotionality is associated with a range of psychological phenomena, including temperament, personality, mood, and motivation. According to author David G. Meyers, human emotion involves "...physiological arousal, expressive behaviors, and conscious experience."

Theories of Emotion

The major theories of motivation can be grouped into three main categories: physiological, neurological, and cognitive.

1. Physiological theories suggest that responses within the body are responsible for emotions.
2. Neurological theories propose that activity within the brain leads to emotional responses.
3. Cognitive theories argue that thoughts and other mental activity play an essential role in forming emotions.

Evolutionary Theory of Emotion

It was naturalist Charles Darwin who proposed that emotions evolved because they were adaptive and allowed humans and animals to survive and reproduce. Feelings of love and affection lead people to seek mates and reproduce. Feelings of fear compel people to either fight or flee the source of danger.

According to the evolutionary theory of emotion, our emotions exist because they serve an adaptive role. Emotions motivate people to respond quickly to stimuli in the environment, which helps improve the chances of success and survival.

Understanding the emotions of other people and animals also plays a crucial role in safety and survival. If you encounter a hissing, spitting, and clawing animal, chances are you will quickly realize that the animal is frightened or defensive and leave it alone. By being able to interpret correctly the emotional displays of other people and animals, you can respond correctly and avoid danger.

The James-Lange Theory of Emotion

The James-Lange theory is one of the best-known examples of a physiological theory of emotion. Independently proposed by psychologist William James and physiologist Carl Lange, the James-Lange theory of emotion suggests that emotions occur as a result of physiological reactions to events.

This theory suggests that when you see an external stimulus that leads to a physiological reaction. Your emotional reaction is dependent upon how you interpret those physical reactions. For example, suppose you are walking in the woods and you see a grizzly bear. You begin to tremble, and your heart begins to race. The James-Lange theory proposes that you will interpret your physical reactions and conclude that you are frightened ("I am trembling. Therefore, I am afraid"). According to this theory of emotion, you are not trembling because you are frightened. Instead, you feel frightened because you are trembling.

The Cannon-Bard Theory of Emotion

Another well-known physiological theory is the Cannon-Bard theory of emotion. Walter Cannon disagreed with the James-Lange theory of emotion on several different grounds. First, he suggested, people can experience physiological reactions linked to emotions without actually feeling those emotions. For example, your heart might race because you have been exercising and not because you are afraid.

Cannon also suggested that emotional responses occur much too quickly for them to be simply products of physical states. When you encounter a danger in the environment, you will often feel afraid before you start to experience the physical symptoms associated with fear such as shaking hands, rapid breathing, and a racing heart.

Cannon first proposed his theory in the 1920s and his work was later expanded on by physiologist Philip Bard during the 1930s. According to the Cannon-Bard theory of emotion, we feel emotions and experience physiological reactions such as sweating, trembling, and muscle tension simultaneously.

More specifically, it is suggested that emotions result when the thalamus sends a message to the brain in response to a stimulus, resulting in a physiological reaction. At the same time, the brain also receives signals triggering the emotional experience. Cannon and Bard's theory suggests that the physical and psychological experience of emotion happen at the same time and that one does not cause the other.

Schachter-Singer Theory

Also known as the two-factor theory of emotion, the Schachter-Singer Theory is an example of a cognitive theory of emotion. This theory suggests that the physiological arousal occurs first, and then the individual must identify the reason for this arousal to experience and label it as an emotion. A stimulus leads to a physiological response that is then cognitively interpreted and labeled which results in an emotion.

Schachter and Singer's theory draws on both the James-Lange theory and the Cannon-Bard theory of emotion. Like the James-Lange theory, the Schachter-Singer theory proposes that people do infer emotions based on physiological responses. The critical factor is the situation and the cognitive interpretation that people use to label that emotion.

Like the Cannon-Bard theory, the Schachter-Singer theory also suggests that similar physiological responses can produce varying emotions. For example, if you experience a racing heart and sweating palms during an important math exam, you will probably identify the emotion as anxiety. If you experience the same physical responses on a date with your significant other, you might interpret those responses as love, affection, or arousal.

The Two-Factor Theory of Emotion

Cognitive Appraisal Theory

According to appraisal theories of emotion, thinking must occur first before experiencing emotion. Richard Lazarus was a pioneer in this area of emotion, and this theory is often referred to as the Lazarus theory of emotion.

According to this theory, the sequence of events first involves a stimulus, followed by thought which then leads to the simultaneous experience of a physiological response and the emotion. For example, if you encounter a bear in the woods, you might immediately begin to think that you are in great danger. This then leads to the emotional experience of fear and the physical reactions associated with the fight-or-flight response.

Facial-Feedback Theory of Emotion

The facial-feedback theory of emotions suggests that facial expressions are connected to experiencing emotions. Charles Darwin and William James both noted early on that sometimes physiological responses often had a direct impact on emotion, rather than simply being a consequence of the emotion. Supporters of this theory suggest that emotions are directly tied to changes in facial muscles. For example, people who are forced to smile pleasantly at a social function will have a better time at the event than they would if they had frowned or carried a more neutral facial expression.

What is a Healthy Job?

A healthy job is likely to be one where the pressures on employees are appropriate in relation to their abilities and resources, to the amount of control they have over their work, and to the support they receive from people who matter to them. As health is not merely the absence of disease or infirmity but a positive state of complete physical, mental and social well-being (WHO, 1986), a healthy working environment is one in which there is not only an absence of harmful conditions but an abundance of health-promoting ones.

These may include continuous assessment of risks to health, the provision of appropriate information and training on health issues and the availability of health promoting organisational support practices and structures. A healthy work environment is one in which staff have made health and health promotion a priority and part of their working lives.

What is Work-related Stress?

- Work-related stress is the response people may have when presented with work demands and pressures that are not matched to their knowledge and abilities and which challenge their ability to cope.
- Stress occurs in a wide range of work circumstances but is often made worse when employees feel they have little support from supervisors and colleagues, as well as little control over work processes.
- There is often confusion between pressure or challenge and stress and sometimes it is used to excuse bad management practice.

Pressure at the workplace is unavoidable due to the demands of the contemporary work environment. Pressure perceived as acceptable by an individual, may even keep workers alert, motivated, able to work and learn, depending on the available resources and personal characteristics. However, when that pressure becomes excessive or otherwise unmanageable it leads to stress. Stress can damage an employees' health and the business performance.

Work-related stress can be caused by poor work organisation (the way we design jobs and work systems, and the way we manage them), by poor work design (for example, lack of control over work processes), poor management, unsatisfactory working conditions, and lack of support from colleagues and supervisors.

Research findings show that the most stressful type of work is that which values excessive demands and pressures that are not matched to workers' knowledge and abilities, where there is little opportunity to exercise any choice or control, and where there is little support from others.

Employees are less likely to experience work-related stress when - demands and pressures of work are matched to their knowledge and abilities - control can be exercised over their work and the way they do it - support is received from supervisors and colleagues - participation in decisions that concern their jobs is provided.

What are Stress-related Hazards at Work?

Stress related hazards at work can be divided into work content and work context.

Work contents includes - job content (monotony, under-stimulation, meaningless of tasks, lack of variety, etc) – work load and work pace (too much or too little to do, work under time pressure, etc.) – working hours (strict or inflexible, long and unsocial, unpredictable, badly designed shift systems) – Participation and control (lack of participation in decision-making, lack of control over work processes, pace, hours, methods, and the work environment)

Work context includes - career development, status and pay (job insecurity, lack of promotion opportunities, under- or over-promotion, work of 'low social value', piece rate payment schemes, unclear or unfair performance evaluation systems, being over- or under-skilled for a job) - role in the organization (unclear role, conflicting roles) - interpersonal relationships (inadequate, inconsiderate or unsupportive supervision, poor relationships with colleagues, bullying/ harassment and violence, isolated or solitary work, etc) -organizational culture (poor communication, poor leadership, lack of behavioural rule, lack of clarity about organizational objectives, structures and strategies) - work-life balance (conflicting demands of work and home, lack of support for domestic problems at work, lack of support for work problems at home, lack of organizational rules and policies to support work-life balance).

Individual's and Organisational Approaches to Managing Stress

As we know that stress has got a number of negative consequences for the individuals, that is why every individual should take personal responsibility for reducing his or her stress level. There are a number of ways by which a person can either avoid stressful conditions, change them or learn to cope with them. Stress can be managed by an individual, which will enable him to regain control over his life.

Some of the stress reducing strategies from individual's point of view are :

1. **Knowledge About Stress.** In the first stage, an individual should become knowledgeable about stress. He should know about the process and effects of stress. He must find out the major sources of his stress. He must anticipate stressful periods and plan accordingly in advance. He must be honest with himself and decide what he can cope with what he cannot.
2. **Physiological Fitness.** Excercise in any form can help people in coping with the stress. Non competitive physical excercise such as aerobics, walking, jogging, swimming, riding a bicycle, playing softball or tennis have been recommended by physicians as a way to deal with excessive stress levels. There is evidence to suggest that individuals who excercise are much less likely to suffer from certain types of stress related exercises. With proper exercise, diet control and non-smoking habits, blood pressure and cholesterol become controlled and the body becomes more resistant to pressures. People are more likely to get physically sick or emotionally depressed if they are over weight or poorly nourished.
3. **Time Management.** Most of the people are very poor in managing their time. They don't know that what must be done and when it would be desirable to do so. The result of poor time management is feeling of work overload, skipped schedules and tension. A well organised person can often accomplish twice as much as the person who is poorly organised. Therefore, an individual must understand how to manage his time so that he can cope with tensions created by job demands. A few of the well known time management principles are :
   - Preparing a daily list of activities to be attended to.
   - Prioritizing activities by importance and urgency.

- Scheduling activities according to the priorities set.
- Knowing your daily schedule and handling the most demanding parts of a job when you are most alert and productive.

4. **Assertiveness.** An individual should become assertive. He should not say 'Yes' when he wants to say 'No'. He should start saying No to people or managers who demand too much of his time. Being assertive is an important factor in reducing stress.
5. **Social Support Network.** Every person should have people to turn to, talk to and rely upon. Good friends become highly supportive during times of stress and crisis. Social net work includes friends, family or work colleagues. Expanding your social support system can be a means for tension reduction because friends are there when needed and provide support to get the person through stressful situations.
6. **Readjust life Goals.** Every individual must know what he really wants to do. This should relate to not only the major decisions of the life but to all activities in our life. He must know what is important for him. Because of the severe competition in life to go ahead, most individuals set very high standards and goals for themselves. These high expectations and limited resources to reach such expectations result in stress. Accordingly, every person must readjust his goals and make sure he has the ability and resources to reach such goals. Perhaps the goals should be established after the resources have been analysed.
7. **Relaxation Techniques.** Every individual must teach himself to reduce tension through relaxation techniques such as Yoga, mediation, hypnosis and biofeedback. 15-20 minutes a day of deep relaxation releases tension and provides a person with pronounced sense of peacefulness. Deep relaxation conditions will bring significant changes in heart rate, blood pressure and other physiological factors. Yoga is probably the most effective remedy for stress. Studies have revealed that Yoga has cured several stress related diseases.
8. **Plan your life in Advance.** So many times, people create situations which induce stress because they either did not plan or did a bad job of planning. The traditional Indian attitude of "whatever will be, will be" a way of accepting the unexpected difficulties in life. This attitude may be relevant in those situations over which we do not have any control like death in the family, but for other events in life, it is better to plan in advance, so that we can confront them with confidence when they occur.

Individuals may design their own strategies to reduce stress, but it is a must for the organisations to develop programmes that will help the employees in reducing their stress. This will lead to less employee turnover, absenteeism and as a result productivity will improve.

Some of the measures which organisations can take are :

1. **Selection and Placement.** Individuals differ in their response to stress situations. We know that 'Type A' individuals are more prone to stress. On the other hand, in the organisations there are certain jobs which are more stressful as compared to other jobs. While doing the selection and placement of the employees, these factors must be kept in mind. The individuals who are more prone to stress should not be put on jobs which are stressful. The individuals who are less prone to stress may adapt better to high stress jobs and perform those jobs more effectively.
2. **Goal Setting.** Based on extensive amount of research it has been concluded that individuals perform better when they have specific and challenging goals and they receive feedback on how well they are progressing towards those goals. Goal setting can reduce stress as well as provide motivation. It will result in less employee frustration, role ambiguity and stress.

3. **Improved Communication.** Sometimes due to lack of effective communication from the superiors, the employees do not know what they have to do and how they have to do it. This result in role ambiguity. Similarly, when two or more persons have contradicting role demands from an employee, it leads to role conflict if there is lack of proper communication. Effective communication with employees reduces the uncertainty by lessening role ambiguity and role conflict.
4. **Redesigning Jobs.** Organisations should redesign the jobs in such a way as to give employees more responsibility, more meaningful work, more autonomy and increased feed back. This will help reduce the stress caused by monotony, routine work, work overload or underload and role ambiguity. Job redesigning enhances motivation, reduces the stress among the employees and enhances "Quality of work life".
5. **Participative Decision Making.** If the organisations give the employees participation in those decisions that directly affect them and their job performance, it can increase employee control and reduce the role stress. The main reason of role stress is that employees feel uncertain about their goals, expectations and how they will be evaluated. These uncertainties can be reduced by the management by giving the employees a right to participate in the decision making.
6. **Building Teamwork.** The management should try to create such work environment in which there is no provision for interpersonal conflict or inter group conflict. Such conflicts are the causes of stress, such should be prevented from building or eliminated if they develop. Accordingly such team work should be developed that groups and the members are mutually supportive and productive. Members of the group should consider themselves as members of the same family and seek social support from each other.
7. **Personal Wellness Programmes.** These personal wellness programmes focus on the employees total physical and mental condition. Organisations can provide facilities at their premises for physical fitness such as gyms, swimming pools, tennis courts etc. as well as psychological counselling. They should hold seminars or workshops to make the employees understand nature and sources of stress and the possible ways to reduce it. These workshops should help those individuals who are already under stress. Moreover, a supervisor can impact personal wellness of his subordinates through positive example, encouragement and by practising the basic concepts and techniques of human resource management.

ORGANISATIONAL JUSTICE

Organisational justice, first postulated by Greenberg in 1987, refers to an employee's perception of their organisation's behaviours, decisions and actions and how these influence the employees own attitudes and behaviours at work.

The term is closely connected to the concept of fairness; employees are sensitive to decisions made on a day-to-day basis by their employers, both on the small and large scale, and will judge these decisions as unfair or fair. These judgements influence an individual's behaviour and can, in cases where the actions have a personal effect on the employee and are judged as unfair, lead to workplace deviance.

Organisational justice is concerned with all matters of workplace behaviour, from treatment by superiors to pay, access to training and gender equality. It is originally derived from equity theory, which suggests individuals make judgements on fairness based on the amount they give (input) compared to the amount they get back (output).

Ensuring organisational justice should be a priority for organisation – it can reduce the incidence of workplace deviance, absence, disengagement and counterproductive workplace behaviours (CWB) and also encourage positive attributes like trust and progressive communication.

Organisational justice is sometimes discussed alongside corporate social responsibility (CSR), a form of societal justice.

Types of Organisational Justice

Distributive justice

When we think of distributive justice, one of the first things that come to mind is 'am I being paid fairly?'. Although how much we are paid is important for most people, distributive justice also covers who gets the exciting work and who gets the mundane tasks, who gets the better career opportunities and promotions, etc. In fact, distributive justice includes any aspect where something is distributed within the employment setting, even punishment.

Procedural justice

Much of the employment legislation focuses on establishing the minimum standards for what should happen in the employment setting. Factors such as consistency, free from bias, based on fact, correctable, democratic, ethical viewpoints, and legal considerations are all part of the process of making a fair decision. While this is an objective view of what organisational justice should be, how we perceive fairness in the workplace is more subjective. If we think a process is unfair, then we are more likely to think the outcome (whatever is distributed) is also unfair, but we are less likely to question the fairness of the process if we are happy with the amount received. Not surprisingly, we are more likely to perceive an outcome as being fair if we were involved in the process.

Interactional justice

Regardless of who we are in the organisation, we all expect to be treated with dignity and respect, as well as being trusted, but how outcomes are communicated, including the adequacy of the explanations and the timeliness of the communication, also shape our perceptions of what is fair in the work setting.

WHISTLEBLOWING

A whistleblower is a person who comes forward and shares his/her knowledge on any wrongdoing which he/she thinks is happening in the whole organisation or in a specific department. A whistleblower could be an employee, contractor, or a supplier who becomes aware of any illegal activities.

To protect whistleblowers from losing their job or getting mistreated there are specific laws. Most companies have a separate policy which clearly states how to report such an incident.

A whistleblower can file a lawsuit or register a complaint with higher authorities which will trigger a criminal investigation against the company or any individual department.

There are two types of whistleblowers: internal and external. Internal whistleblowers are those who report the misconduct, fraud, or indiscipline to senior officers of the organisation such as Head Human Resource or CEO.

External whistleblowing is a term used when whistleblowers report the wrongdoings to people outside the organisation such as the media, higher government officials, or police.

The crime or wrongdoing could be in the form of fraud, deceiving employees, corruptions, or any other act which misleads people. The Whistle Blowers Protection Act, 2011 lays down the complete framework to investigate alleged cases of wrongdoing.

There is one name which pops up in history whenever we talk about 'whistleblowers' and that is Edward Joseph Snowden. He was a former CIA employee who leaked classified and restricted information to the public from the United States National Security Agency in 2013.

HUMAN RESOURCE MANAGEMENT

Concept

The term 'human resources' may be defined as the total knowledge, talents and aptitudes of an organisation's workforce, as well as the values, attitudes, approaches and beliefs of the individuals involved in the affairs of the organisation. It is the sum, total or aggregate of inherent abilities, acquired knowledge and skills represented by the talents and aptitudes of the persons employed in an organisation.

Several terms have been used by various management thinkers to represent human resources. These includes 'personnel', 'people at work', 'human resource', 'staff' and 'employees'. Whatever may be the term used, the human resources of an organisation include all individuals engaged in various organisational activities at different levels. Leon C. Megginson says, "From the national point of view, human resources may be defined as the knowledge, skills, creative abilities, talents and aptitudes obtained in the population; whereas from the viewpoint of the individual enterprise, they represent the total of the inherent abilities, acquired knowledge and skills as exemplified in the talents and aptitudes of its employees". HRM is a process, which consists of four main activities, namely acquisitions, development, motivation, as well as maintenance of human resources.

According to the Institute of Personnel Management (U.K.), "Personnel management is an integral but distinctive part of management, concerned with people at work and their relationships within the enterprise. It seeks to bring together into an effective organisation the men and women who staff the enterprise, enabling each to make his/her best contribution to its success, both as a member of a working group and as an individual. It seeks to provide relationships within the enterprise that are conducive both to effective work and human satisfaction."

According to Flippo, "Personnel management is the planning, organising, compensation, integration and maintenance of people for the purpose of contributing to organisational, individual and societal goals.

According to Breach, "Personnel Management is that part which is primarily concerned with human resource of organisation.

Perspectives of Human Resource Management

The growth of human resource management in United State of America was evolutionary in nature. It took place because of the voluntary efforts of the employers. But in countries like India, human resource management grew because of compulsions made by the Government. In 1931, the Royal Commission on Labour recommended the abolition of Jobber system and the appointment of labour officers in the industries to look after recruitment and welfare of employees. In 1948, the Factories Act made it obligatory for certain industrial enterprises to appoint welfare officers.

The scope of human resource management has expanded considerably throughout the world. Over the last forty years or so, new techniques and styles of managing the human resources have been developed as a result of the researches and experiences in the field. The task of the human manager is not confined only to the recruitment of workers, but also to looking after their welfare and handling their grievances.

Under the influence of technological development, organisational complexities are growing. The impact on the work, working methods, work rules, tools, equipment, etc. is inevitable. Jobs have become more complex and need specialised skills and professionals. As a result of this, emphasis is being given to the training and development aspects. In order to meet the growing needs of such human resources, management institutes, universities and other bodies have started training and executive development programmes.

Human management is no longer restricted only to the wage earners in the factories. It has become equally important in offices, sales organisations, hospitals, research and development institutions and in the ranks of management itself. Human management is not needed by private industry alone. No-profit institutions, government departments and armed services also need human management for better employer-employee relations.

The other terms used frequently in discussion of personnel problems and techniques are "labour relations" and "industrial relations". Sometimes, these are used interchangeably with "personnel management or administration", but it is useful to distinguish between them. The term "labour relations" refers primarily to the relations between management and unionised labour. The subject matter of labour relations includes the negotiation of contracts with unions and day-to-day relations with union leaders and business agents in the handling of differences arising under the contract, arbitration and government regulations of the terms and conditions of employment.

The use of the term 'industrial relations' as synonymous with 'human resource/personnel management' has been very common in United States of America.

In India, the field of personnel management has three branches, viz. (i) personnel administration, (ii) industrial relations and (iii) labour welfare. Personnel administration deals with the administrative aspects of personnel functions such as recruitment, selection, placement, promotion, transfer, wages and incentives, etc. Industrial relations deals broadly with employer-employee relationship, negotiations and collective bargaining, settlement of grievance and disputes, joint consultation. Labour welfare programmes seek to improve the working and living conditions of the employees by the provision of facilities such as crèches, canteen, housing, recreation, education etc.

In the Indian context, these three areas have developed some kind of identity of their own and have been recognised as integral parts of the broad field of personnel management. However, these three are not watertight compartments. This kind of division has facilitated convenient grouping of personnel functions. It is worth noting that these three groups of personnel functions have been generally dealt with by officers with three different sets of designations. The first have been usually dealt with by officers designated as personnel officers, while the second and third are handled generally by those with designations of labour officer and welfare officer respectively.

Nature of Human Resource Management

The nature of the human resource management has been highlighted in its following features :

(1) Inherent part of management
(2) Pervasive function
(3) Basic to all functional areas
(4) People centred
(5) Personal activities of functions
(6) Continuous process
(7) Based on human relations

Objectives

The objectives of Human Resource Management are :

(a) To provide attractive, equitable incentives, rewards, benefits, social security measures, to ensure retention of competent employees.

(b) To provide, create, utilise and motivate employees to accomplish organisational goals.

(c) To maintain high morale, encourage value system and create environment of trust, mutuality of interests.

(d) To create opportunities, to provide facilities, necessary motivation to individuals and groups for their growth with the growth of the organisation by training and development.

(e) To secure integration of individuals and groups in securing organisational effectiveness.

(f) To ensure that, there is no threat of unemployment, inequalities, adopting a policy recognising merit and employee contribution and conditions for stability of employment.

(g) To provide opportunities for communication, expression, participation, appreciation, recognition and provide fair efficient leadership.

(h) To create a sense and feeling of belongingness, team spirit and encourage suggestions from employees.

(i) To develop dyadic relationship between each employee and every supervisor.

(j) To develop the overall health and self renewing capabilities.

Scope

All major activities in the working life of the employee from the time of his entry into the organisation until he leaves, come under the purview of human resource management.

The most important activities undertaken are :

(1) **Planning,** job design, job analysis, procurement, recruitment, selection, induction, placement, training and development.

(2) **Compensation,** rewards, benefits, retrial benefits, medical and health care.

(3) **Motivation.** Motivational aids, bonus, incentives, career development, growth, decision making, delegation of authority and power, promotion etc.

(4) **Employee Relations.** Grievance handling, participation, collective bargaining and other aspects of cordial relations conducive to mutual understanding and trust.

(5) Employee evaluation and performance improvement, Human Resource Audit and Human Resource Accounting.

(6) Appraisal of performance of employees and taking corrective steps such as transfer from one job to another.

(7) Social security and welfare of employees.

Influences and Recent Trends

1. Retaining your best talent – Make it your top priority

Gone are the days where recruiting good talent was enough, retaining that good talent is also imperative. Especially those employees who possess greater professional and technical knowledge are much in demand in the job market as such employees have the ability to keep their company ahead in the race. Such employees are invaluable assets for any company. Employee development and engagement, health and safety, recognition, flexible work timings, work-life balance are some examples of novel approaches that you could use to retain your employees.

2. Ensuring better employee productivity to maximise your profits

Maximizing profit and minimizing cost is the core of every business. Higher the in case it is due to inefficient employee, training the employee of eve staff could be a solution of finding alternative resources for sufficient inadequate resources are the case. HRM should manage on-site as was training for employees. Providing training and support to employees benefits the company but also helps the employees who take this round they are a vital part of the business.

3. Managing a diverse workforce : Unity in diversity is the new business

Composition of workforce is getting diverse at present situation. Divided and created by age, gender, educational background and religion but also personality and background of workers. However, with a more diversed some usual issues such as harassment of discrimination may arise. To instances, a company must formulate and implement strict rules.

4. Dealing with the 'New normal' - Globalization

We live in a global world today. In fact, mergers, acquisitions, collaborate takeovers are a common phenomenon. While internationalization of a firm is sign of success, it is also a challenge as with globalization, you also several challenges related to different language, work culture, manage approach, culture and tradition. You are also required to handle various such as scheduling meetings, managing holidays and out-sourcing of overcome these challenges.

5. Resistance to change-What if i am replaced by a machine in the future?

This is a common fear which plagues the mind of many employees. Especially the ones who consider change to be a threat and think that their roles within the company will be replaced by a machine or computer that can do the job cheaper or faster.

As with any change in the workplace, changes in technology could cause anxiety or even resistance among your employees. The role of the human resource manager would be to develop strategies to combat this resistance to change which begins by assuring employees of their worth for the business. They must be able to perceive the technology as an aid not an obstacle to their work.

6. Maintaining privacy and managing vital business information

As the technology within an organization advances, so do the privacy and security concerns connected with those technical changes. Ensuring that your employees are well trained in securing data and hence preventing privacy breaches Providing employee training on how to secure data and preventing any breach of privacy thus ensuring the safety of sensitive business information is a key challenge for human resources. Communicating with technology vendors and keeping up-to-date with the technical aspects of the company are some more ways for human resources managers to recognize and confront this challenge.

7. Maintaining discipline and ensuring successful achievement of business goals

Discipline is one of the key issues, lack of which can cause various problems impacting the productivity of the company. For instance, if discipline is not maintained; employees may neglect their tasks and duties or even procrastinate their tasks and misbehave with co-workers. The ultimate result of these activities is decreased productivity of your company.

You need to make your policies clear and inform every employee about your disciplinary procedures as well as let them know who they can appeal to. You must follow different processes depending on the severity of the employee's actions. There is a need to ascertain whether discipline is due to employee performance issue or if it is misconduct.

8. Embrace technology or get extinct

Any company must consider technological changes as the present day world demands every firm to move with the change, or else be left behind Technological changes influence the overall nature of work and businesses need to find employees that are able to adjust with the change.

During this process, unemployment as well as employment opportunities arise, creating new challenges for HRM. With new developments in technology as well as with the use of new tools, such as talent networks and internal social networks, there is the promise of increased flexibility and productivity.

9. Leadership Development and Succession Planning

Leadership development is one of the biggest challenges for human resource management. It needs to be a critical strategic initiative. HR professionals are expected to provide the essential structure, processes and tools to select the best and develop the future leaders of the organization.

Most such initiatives can also be successfully conducted with the use of a scientific approach through customised assessments. With online assessments on identifying the best talent, predicting success at your workplace as well as building the next set of leaders by evaluating them through this approach can be the best next steps.

HUMAN RESOURCE PLANNING

Human Resource Planning is the process by which a management determines how an organisation should move from its current human resource position to its desired human resource position. Through planning, a management strives to have the right number and the right kind of people at the right places, at the right time, to do things which result in both the organisation and the individual receiving the maximum long range benefits. Of all the "M.S." in management (*i.e.*, the management of materials, machines, methods, money, motive power) the most important is "M" for men or human resources. It is the most valuable asset of an organisation. It is in fact an important economic resource, covering all human resources – organised or unorganised, employed or capable of employment, working at all levels – supervisors, executives; government employees, 'blue' and 'white' collar workers, managerial, scientific, engineering, technical, skilled or unskilled persons, who are employed in creating, designing, developing, managing and operating productive and service enterprises and other economic activities.

1. **Coleman** has defined Human Resource Planning as "the process of determining manpower requirements and the mans for meeting those requirements in order to carry out the integrated plan of the organisation.
2. According to **Wikstrom**, Human Resource Planning consists of a series of activities, viz.
   (a) Forecasting future manpower requirements, either in terms of mathematical projections of trends in the economic environment and developments in industry, or in terms of judgemental estimates based upon the specific future plans of a company;
   (b) Making an inventory of present manpower resources and assessing the extent to which these resources are employed optimally;
   (c) Anticipating manpower problems by projecting present resources into the future and comparing them with the forecast of requirements to determine their adequacy, both quantitatively and qualitatively; and
   (d) Planning the necessary programmes of requirements, selection, training, development, utilisation, transfer, promotion, motivation and compensation to ensure that future manpower requirements are properly met.

Human resource planning is an important tool of Human Resources Management as it helps in the following ways :

1. Human resource planning results in reduced labour costs as it helps the management to anticipate shortages and /or surpluses of human resource and correct these imbalances before they become unmanageable and expensive.
2. It is a better basis for planning employee development that is designed to make optimum use of workers skills within the organisation.
3. It enables identification of the gaps of the existing human resource so that corrective training could be imparted. Thus, the training programme becomes more effective.
4. It leads to improvement in the overall business planning process.
5. It helps in formulating managerial succession plan as a part of the replacement planning process which is necessitated when job change plans for managers are formulated. Besides, this exercise would provide enough lead time for identifying and developing managers to move up the corporate ladder.
6. It leads to a greater awareness of the importance of sound human resource management throughout the organisation.
7. It serves as a tool to evaluate the effect of alternative human resource actions and policies.
8. It formulate transfer and promotion policies.

RECRUITMENT AND SELECTION, INDUCTION, TRAINING AND DEVELOPMENT

The selection procedure is concerned with securing relevant information about an applicant. The objective of selection process is to determine whether an applicant meets the qualifications for a specific job and to choose the applicant who is most likely to perform well in that job. It is a long process, commencing from the preliminary interview of the applicants and ending with the contract of employment.

Model Procedure for Effective Personnel Selection

Essentials of Selection Procedure

1. Nature of selection. Whether faculty or safe, because a faculty selection affects not only the training periods that may be needed, but also results in heavy expenditure on the new employee.
2. Policy of the company and attitude of the management. As a practice some companies usually hire more than the actual number needed with a view to removing the unfit person from the job.
3. The length of the probationary of the trial period. The longer the period, greater the uncertainty in the minds of the selected candidate about his future.
4. Presence of an authority for hire. The authority comes from employment requisition as developed by an analysis of the work load and work force.
5. There should be some standard or personnel with which a prospective employer may be compared.
6. There must be a sufficient number of applicants from whom the required number of employees may be selected.

Induction, Training and Development

Induction is a technique by which a new employee is rehabilitated into his surroundings and introduced to the practices, policies and purposes of the organisation. In other words, the idea is to welcome a newcomer, make him feel at home and generate in him a feeling that his own job, however small, is meaningful and has a significance as a part of the total organisation.

The purpose of induction is to introduce the new employee and the organisation to each other, to help them become acquainted and to help them accommodate each other. The newcomer is explained what is expected of him and for this, he is explained the rules, regulations, policies and procedures that directly affect him. He is made aware of how his job fits into the overall operation of the organisation, his own duties and responsibilities and to whom he should look for when he has any problem.

Induction Procedure

Each industry develops its own procedures as per its needs. The procedure should basically follow these steps :

First, the new person needs time and a place to report to work.

Second, it is very important that the supervisor or the immediate boss meet and welcome the employee to the organisation.

Third, administrative work should be completed. Such items as vacations, probationary period, medical absences, suggestion systems should be covered.

Fourth, the departmental orientation can be conducted. This should include a get - acquainted talk, introduction to the department, explanation of the functions of the department, and job instruction and to whom he should look for help when he has any problem.

Fifth, verbal explanations are supplemented by a wide variety of printed material, employee hand books, flyers, employee manuals, house-journals, picture stories, comics and cartoons, pamphlets, etc. alongwith short guided tour around the plant.

Typical Techniques of Induction Programs

A typical induction program should consist primarily of three steps :

(a) General orientation by the staff of the personnel department;

(b) Specific orientation by the job supervisor, or his representative; and

(c) Follow-up orientation by either the personnel department or the supervisor.

The first phase of the programme should ordinarily be conducted by the personnel department. This type of induction is general, because it gives the necessary general information about the history and operations of the firm - *the purpose of which is to help an employee to build up some pride and interest in the organisation*. Information is also given on specific employee services, such as pension, health and welfare plans, safety programmes etc. *The better policy is not to give everything in one day, but to administer smaller doses over a long period.*

At the second stage, induction should be conducted by the job supervisor. *Induction is specific and requires skill on the part of the foreman.* The employee is shown the department and his place of work, introduced to other employees, informed of the locations of the bathrooms, lavatories, canteens and time clock; and told about the organisation's specific practices and customs. The *purpose of specific induction is to enable an employee to adjust himself to his work and environment.*

Follow-up induction takes place within one week to six months from the time of the initial hiring and orientation. It is conducted either by a foreman or a specialist. *Its purpose is to find out whether the employee is reasonably well-satisfied with him.*

Training and Development

In a rapidly changing society, employee's training and development are not only an activity that is desirable but also an activity that an organisation must commit resources to if it is to maintain a viable and knowledgeable work force.

Training is a process of learning a sequence of programmed behaviour. It is application of knowledge. It gives people an awareness of the rules and procedures to guide their behaviour. It attempts to improve their performance on the current job or prepare them for an intended job. *Development* is a related process. It covers not only those activities which improve job performance but also those which bring about growth of their personality; help individuals in the progress towards maturity and actualisation of their potential capacities. In organisational terms, it is intended to equip persons to earn promotion and hold greater responsibility. Training a person for a bigger and higher job is development.

Training has been defined by different scholars of management. Some important definitions of training are as under:

- *According to Dale S. Beach*, "Training is the organised procedure in which people learn knowledge and skill for definite purpose".
- *According to Jucius*, "The term training is used here to indicate only process by which the aptitudes, skill and abilities of employees to perform specific jobs are increased".
- *In the words of Michael J. Jucius*, "Training is a process by which the aptitudes, skills and abilities of employees to perform specific jobs are increased."

Distinction between Training and Development

"*Training*" is short-term process utilising a systematic and organised procedure by which non-managerial personnel learn technical knowledge and skills for a definite purpose.... On the other hand Development is a long-term educational process utilising a systematic and organised procedure by which managerial personnel learn conceptual and theoretical knowledge for general purpose.

"*Training*" refers only to instruction in technical and mechanical operations, while "development" refers to philosophical and theoretical educational concepts. Training is designed for non-managers, while development involves managerial personnel.

> **FACTS**
>
> - We Need to Invest More in Training.
> - Employees Want More Training.
> - Convert Beliefs into Practice!
> - Employees Are Disengaged at Work; You Need to Engage them!
> - Invest in Onboarding Early On.
> - Make Retaining Your Employees a Priority.
> - Increase Learning Transfer
> - Take Learner Needs into Consideration.
> - Make Workplace Training More Fun.
> - Ineffective Training Costs Money.

Characteristics of Features of Training

1. Job related
2. Continuous
3. Provides benefit to employee and employer.
4. Training is different from development.
5. Training is different from education.
6. Training is needed at all levels.
7. All types of employees need training.

Differences Between Training and Development

Basis	Training	Development
Meaning	Training means learning skills and knowledge for the particular job.	Development means growth of an employee in all aspects
Use	Training is used for imparting specific Skills.	Development is used for the overall growth of the executives.
Nature	It is job related in nature.	It is career oriented in nature.
Perspective	It has short term perspective.	It has long term perspective.
Aim	The best possible performance on the specific job by the employee.	The best possible utilization of the employee capability.
Scope	Training is limited in scope and is the part of development.	Development is wider term and includes education, learning, and training.
Level of involved persons	It is imparted to lower level employees or junior managers.	The level of development is higher and concerns with senior managers.
Depth of knowledge	Deep Knowledge is provided.	Development does not provide deep knowledge and simply facilitates growth.
Initiative in learning	Initiative of learning is not on the employee and is on the organisation.	Initiative of learning is on the employee and not on the organisation.
Duration	It is imparted for the fixed period.	It is an unending practice in the company.

Steps in Training Programs

1. Discovering or Identifying Training Needs

A training program should be established only when it is felt that it would assist in the solution of specific operational problems. The most important step, in the first place, is to make a thorough analysis of the entire organisation, its operations and human resource resources available in order to find out "The trouble spots" where training may be needed.

2. Getting Ready for the Job

Under this step, it is to be decided who is to be trained – the newcomer or the older employee, or the supervisory staff or all of them selected from different departments.

The trainer has to be prepared for the job, for he is the key figure in the entire program.

3. Preparation of the Learner

This step consists : (i) In putting the learner at ease; (ii) in stating the importance and ingredients of the job and its relationship to work flow; (iii) in explaining why he is being taught; (iv) in creating interest and encouraging questions. Finding out what the learner already knows about his job or other jobs; (v) in explaining the 'why' of the whole job and relating it to some other job, the worker already knows; (vi) in placing the learner as close to his normal working position as possible; and (vii) in familiarising him with the equipments, materials, tools and trade terms.

4. Presentation of Operation and Knowledge

The trainer should clearly *tell show*, *illustrate* and *question* in order to put over the new knowledge and operations. The learner should be told of the sequence of the entire job and why each step in its performance is necessary. Instructions should be given clearly, completely and patiently; there should be an emphasis on key points, and one point should be explained at a time. For this purpose, the trainer should demonstrate or make use of audio-visual aids and should ask the trainee to repeat the operations. He should also be encouraged to ask questions in order to indicate that he really knows and understands the job.

5. Performance Try Out

Under this, the trainee is asked to go through the job several times slowly, explaining him each step. Mistakes are corrected and if necessary, some complicated steps are done for the trainee the first time. The trainee is asked to do the job, gradually building up skill and speed. As soon as the trainee demonstrates that he can do the job in a right way, he is put on his own, but not abandoned.

6. Follow-up

This step is undertaken with a view to testing the effectiveness of training efforts.

This consists in :

(a) Putting a trainee "on his own."

(b) Checking frequently to be sure that he has followed instructions; and

(c) Tapering off extra supervision and close follow-up until he is qualified to work with normal supervision.

Elements of Training

1. Trainee

The proper selection of trainers is of major importance of permanent and gainful results are to be obtained. A trainee should be trained for the kind of job he likes and is suitable to perform. In respect of this, training is closely related to the selection of personnel. Careful screening of conditions for training raises the effectiveness of the training work.

While giving training to an employer the first step is to place him at ease as most people are generally nervous when approaching an unfamiliar task. The trainee must be given the proper background information before he starts learning the new job skills and knowledge.

In case of suspensory training, it is better to include all suspensions and other employers considered suitable for promotion. Excluding the employers who do not need training or who are already doing their work satisfactorily is poor policy. The presence of outstanding persons benefits the less competent persons and they benefit themselves too.

2. Trainer

The trainer is the key figure in an effective training programme. Qualified instructions may be got from inside or outside the organisation. He must be able to divide the job into logical parts, so that he may teach one part at a time without losing the perspective of the whole. He must be tolerant and patient.

Training has to be based on the needs of the organisation and the trainer must have a clear cut idea about the requirements of the organisation. Very often training occurs in vacuums i.e. trainers organise courses which seem to be interesting or an agenda is developed in terms of some preconceived notion of what constitutes a body of useful information.

3. Training Period

The length of the training period depends upon the skill to be acquired, the trainers learning capacity and the training media used. The use of effective visual material usually helps to reduce the training time.

To maintain interest and to secure maximum accomplishment, no single session should last longer than two hours. The alternative to giving training during working hours which may effect production and the organisation, will have to compensate the time, is to organise training after the working hours when the employer may not be able to make full the use of training.

4. Training Methods

There are many methods and techniques for importing training among trainers. The choice of any method will depend upon:

- cost
- number of trainees
- background of the trainers
- time available
- depth of knowledge required

Various Training Techniques

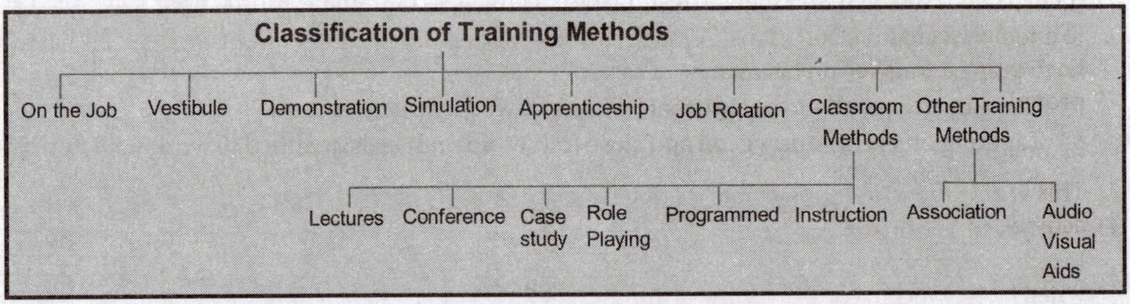

1. On-The-Job-Training

This is the most common and widely used, accepted form of training and is also the most necessary one. Trainers learn as they work under mechanic or craftsman, they receive immediate feedback, practice in the actual work environment and associate with the very same people they will work with after training. Under this training, an employee is placed in a new job and is told how it is performed.

2. Job Instruction Training

This method is very popular for preparing supervisors to train operatives. The instruction and training method requires skilled trainers, extensive job analysis, training schedules and prior assignment of the trainees job knowledge. This method is also known as 'training through step-by-step learning.' It involves listing all necessary steps in the job. This shows what is to be done, alongside is listed the corresponding 'key point' which shows how and why it is done.

3. Vestibule Training

It is a classroom training which is often imparted with the help of equipment and machines which are identical to those used at the place of work. This technique enables the trainee to concentrate on learning the new skill rather than on performing on actual job. Theoretical training is given in the class room, while the practical work is conducted on the production time.

4. Demonstrations and Examples

In this method the trainee describes and displays something by actually performing the activity himself and by going through on step by step explanation of why and what he is doing.

Demonstration are very effective in teaching because it is much easier to show a person how to do a job than to tell him or ask him to gather instruction from the reading material. Demonstrations are often used in combination with lectures, pictures, text materials and discussions.

Teaching by example is effective in mechanical operations or interpersonal relationships for job duties and responsibilities for informal group standards, supervisory explanations and the like.

5. Simulation

Simulation is a technique which duplicates as nearly as possible the actual conditions encountered on a job. The vestibule training method or the business game method are examples of business simulation.

6. Apprenticeship

For training in crafts, trades and in technical areas, this is the oldest and most commonly used method especially when proficiency in a job is the result of a relatively long training period of 2-3 years. The field in which apprenticeship training is offered are numerous and range from the job of a mechanist to a tool maker and electricians. A major part of training time is spent on-the-job productive work. Each practice is given a programme of assignments according to a pre-determined schedule which provides for efficient training in trade skills.

7. Lecture or Classroom Instruction

This is one of the methods of 'off-the-job training which means training is not part of everyday job activity.'

Lectures are regarded as one of the most single ways of imparting knowledge to the trainees, especially when facts, concepts or principles, attitudes, theories and problem solving abilities are to be taught. Lectures are formal organised talks by training specialists.

8. Conference Method

In this method the participating individuals confer to discuss points of common interest to each other. A conference is basic to most participative group centred methods of development. Its a formal meeting conducted in accordance with an organised plan in which the leader seeks to develop knowledge and understanding by obtaining a considerable amount of oral participation from the trainers. It lays stress on small group discussions, on organised subject matter and on active participation of members involved.

There are three types of conferences.

(i) **Directed discussions.** Where the trainee guides the discussion by explaining the facts, principles or concepts.

(ii) **Training conference.** Where the instruction gets the group to pool its knowledge and brings different parts of view to bear on the problem.

(iii) **Seminar conference.** The answer is bound to question or solution of a problem. Here the instructor defines the problem, encourages and ensures full participation.

9. Seminar or Team Discussion

This is an established way for training. A seminar can be conducted in many ways :

(i) It may be based on a paper prepared by one or more trainees on a subject selected in consultation with the person in charge of the seminar. The trainees read their papers and this is followed by a critical discussion. The chairman of the seminar summarises the contents of the paper and the discussions.

(ii) It may be based on a statement made by the person in charge of the seminar or on a document prepared by an expert who is invited to participate in the discussion.

(iii) The person in charge of the seminar distributes in advance the material to be analyzed in the form of required readings. The seminar compares the reactions of trainees, encourage discussion, defines the general trends and guides the participant to certain conclusions.

(iv) Valuable working material may be provided to the trainees by actual files. The trainees may consult the files and bring these to the seminar where they may study in detail the various aspects, specifications and complexities of a particular job or work or task.

10. Case Studies

This method was first developed in the 1880's by Christopher Langdell. The objective of this is to help students learn by themselves by independent thinking and by discovering principles and ideas which have lasting validity and general applicability. The object is to help them, develop skills in using their knowledge.

The case study is based on the belief that management competence can best be attained through the study, contemplation and discussion of concrete cases. The 'case' is a set of data written or oral miniature description and summary of such data that presents issues and problems calling for solutions or action on part of trainer. The trainees are given cases to analyse, they are asked to identify the problems and to recommend solutions.

In the case study the trainee is expected to:

(i) Master the facts and become acquainted with the content of the case.

(ii) Define the objectives sought in dealing with the issues of the case.

(iii) Identify the problems in case and uncover their probable causes.

(iv) Develop alternative courses of action

(v) Screen the alternatives using the objectives as criteria

(vi) Select the alternative that is most in keeping with the stated objectives.

(vii) Define the controls needed to make the action effective.

(viii) To role play the action, to test its effectiveness and find conditions that may limit it.

11. Role Playing

The method is also called as 'Role reversal', socio-drama or psychodrama, emphasises on learning human relation skills through practice and insight into ones own behaviour and its effect on others. It has been defined as, 'a method of human interactions which involves realistic behaviour in imaginary situations.' A role playing experience demonstrates the gap between thinking and doing. The idea of role playing involves action, doing and practice.

Role playing primarily involves employee-employer relationships – hiring, filling, discussing grievance procedure, conducting a post appraisal interview, disciplinary or a sales marketing situation.

12. Programmed Instruction

Also referred to as teaching by the machine method, it involves a sequence of steps which are often set up through the control panel of an electronic computer as it guides in the performance of a desired operation or series of operation. It incorporates a 'pre-arranged, proposed or desired course of proceedings pertaining to the learning or acquisition of some specific skills or general knowledge. A programmed instruction involves creating information down into meaningful units and then arranging these in a proper way to form a logical and sequential learning programme or package.

13. T-Group Training

Also called 'sensitivity training'. The aim is to improve the trainers in dealing with people. This method has a two fold function.

(a) to help the trainers learn how groups actually work.

(b) to give each member of the group a chance to discover how other people interpret and are affected by their own behaviour.

This training mainly consists of sitting around a table discussing for hours. A trainer usually a psychologist merely guides the discussion. As the member are free to criticise the behaviour of each other, thereby giving feedback which may be positive or negative.

14. Retraining

Retraining programmes are generally arranged for employers who have long been in the services of the organisation. The retraining programme may be necessitated by the following facts :

(a) Some employers are engaged in a confined phase of a particular task and lose their all around skills in a particular trade. To represent them active in are around skills, training is needed.

(b) During prolonged lay offs, employers on certain highly skilled jobs are given retraining when called back to work.

(c) Technological changes may make a particular job unnecessary and its beneficial to retrain the employer than discharging him.

(d) An employee due to illness, accident or incapacity may no longer be able to do his share of work which he performed when in normal health.

(e) Economic depression or cyclic variations in production create conditions in which employment stabilisation may be achieved by having a versatile force capable of performing more than one job.

15. Job Rotation

In this method the trainee moves from one job to another, so that he can know to work on all the seats. This type of training is common for the employees of general management positions. Under this method trainee understand the problems of the other seats while working on that seat. Such movement may be for the period ranging from 6 months to 2 years before a person is established in a particular job or department.

16. Internship Training

The training is basically provided to bring the balance between the theoretical knowledge and the practical skills required to do the job. This training is the combined effort of the educational institutions and business organisations. In this theoretical knowledge is imparted by educational institutions and practical knowledge is imparted through business organisations.

JOB ANALYSIS

Job analysis is a procedure by which pertinent information is obtained about a job, i.e., it is a detailed and systematic study of information relating to the operation and responsibilities of a specific job. An authority has defined job analysis as "the process of determining, by observation and study, and reporting pertinent information relating to the nature of a specific job... "It is the determination of the tasks which comprise the job and of the skills, knowledge, abilities and responsibilities required of the worker for a successful performance and which differentiate one job from all others".

Job analysis is a part of overall work planning also known as 'work design' which involves analysis, measurement, control, design and redesign of different jobs in the organisation. It is a primary tool in personnel management.

A job may be defined as a, "collection or aggregation of tasks, duties and responsibilities which as a whole, are regarded as a regular assignment to individual employees" and which is different from other assignments. In other words, when the total work to be done is divided and grouped into packages, we call it a "job". And when some information is required about this job, then job analysis comes into existence.

Purpose of Job Analysis

Job Analysis plays an important role in recruitment and selection, job evaluation, job designing, deciding compensation and benefits packages, performance appraisal, analyzing training and development needs, assessing the worth of a job and increasing personnel as well as organisational productivity.

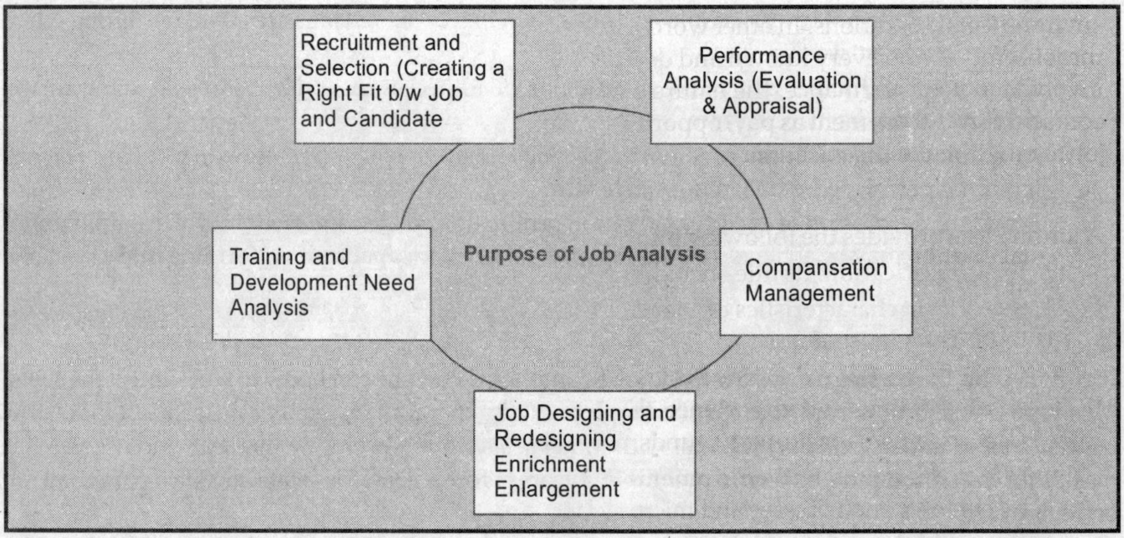

- **Recruitment and Selection.** Job Analysis helps in determining what kind of person is required to perform a particular job. It points out the educational qualifications, level of experience and technical, physical, emotional and personal skills required to carry out a job in desired fashion. The objective is to fit a right person at a right place.
- **Performance Analysis.** Job analysis is done to check if goals and objectives of a particular job are met or not. It helps in deciding the performance standards, evaluation criteria and individual's output. On this basis, the overall performance of an employee is measured and he or she is appraised accordingly.
- **Training and Development.** Job Analysis can be used to assess the training and development needs of employees. The difference between the expected and actual output determines the level of training that need to be imparted to employees. It also helps in deciding the training content, tools and equipments to be used to conduct training and methods of training.
- **Compensation Management.** Of course, job analysis plays a vital role in deciding the pay packages and extra perks and benefits and fixed and variable incentives of employees. After

all, the pay package depends on the position, job title and duties and responsibilities involved in a job. The process guides HR managers in deciding the worth of an employee for a particular job opening.

- **Job designing and Redesigning.** The main purpose of job analysis is to streamline the human efforts and get the best possible output. It helps in designing, redesigning, enriching, evaluating and also cutting back and adding the extra responsibilities in a particular job. This is done to enhance the employee satisfaction while increasing the human output. Therefore, job analysis is one of the most important functions of an HR manager or department. This helps in fitting the right kind of talent at the right place and at the right time.

After a job has been defined, it is analyzed *i.e.* each task is described in detail. Job analysis is a procedure and a tool for determining the specified tasks, operations and requirements of each job. In the process of getting information about jobs, especially, what the worker does, how he gets it done; why he does it, skill, education and training is required; relationship to other jobs; physical demands;

Job Analysis : Area of Application

environmental conditions. In other words, it refers to the anatomy of the job. It is a complete study of the job, embodying every known and determinable factor including the duties and responsibilities involved in its performance, the nature of the task, the qualities required in the worker, and such conditions of employment as pay, opportunities and privileges. It also emphasises the relation of one job to others in the organisation.

Contents of Job Analysis

A job analysis provides the following information:

(i) **Job identification.** Its title, including its code number.

(ii) **Significant characteristics of a job.** Its location, physical setting, supervision, union jurisdiction, hazards and discomforts.

(iii) **What the typical worker does.** Specific operation and tasks that make up an assignment, their relative timings and importance, their simplicity, routine or complexity, the responsibility or safety of others for property, funds, confidence and trust.

(iv) **Which materials and equipments a worker uses.** Metals, plastics, grains, yarns, milling machines, punch presses and micrometres; etc.

(v) **How a job is performed.** Nature of operation – lifting, handling, cleaning, washing, feeding, removing, drilling, driving, setting up and many others.

(vi) **Required personnel attributes.** Experience, training, apprenticeship, physical strength, co-ordination or dexterity, physical demands, mental capabilities, aptitudes, social skills.

(vii) **Job relationship.** Experience required, opportunities for advancement, patterns of promotions, essential co-operation, direction or leadership from and for a job.

The Steps in Job Analysis

There are five basic steps required for doing a job analysis, *viz.*,

Step 1. Collection of Background Information. The information about the job can be had by reviewing available background information such as organisation charts (which show how the job in question relates to other jobs and where they fit into the overall organisation); class specifications (which describes the general requirements of the class of job to which the job under analysis belongs); and the existing *job descriptions* which provide a starting point from which to build the revised job description.

Step 2. Selection of Representative Position to be Analysed. Since the analysis of all jobs would be time-consuming, flow representative positions should be analysed.

Step 3. Collection of Job Analysis Data. Job data on features of the job, required employee qualifications and requirements, should be collected either from the employees who actually perform a job; or from other employees (such as foremen or supervisors) who watch the workers doing a job and thereby acquire knowledge about it or from the outside persons, known as the *trade job analysts* who are appointed to watch employees performing a job.

The duties of such a trade job analyst are :

(i) to outline the complete scope of a job and to consider all the physical and mental activities involved in determining what the worker does. For this purpose, he studies the physical methods used by a worker to accomplish his task including the use of machinery, tools and his own movements and necessary mental facilities.

(ii) Find out why a worker does a job; and for this purpose he studies why each task is essential for the overall result.

(iii) The skill factor which may be needed in the worker to differentiate between jobs and establish to the extent of the difficulty of any job.

Step 4. Job Description. The information collected is to be developed in the form of a job description. This is a written statement that describes the main features of the job, as well as the qualifications/activities which the job incumbents must possess.

Step 5. Developing Job Specification. The last step is to convert the Job Description statement into Job Specifications *i.e.*, to specifically mention what personal qualities, traits, skills and background is necessary for getting the job done.

Techniques of Job Analysis Data

(i) **Personal Observation.** The materials and equipments used, the working conditions and probable hazards, and an understanding of what the work involves are the facts which should be known by an analyst. Direct observation is especially useful in jobs that consist primarily of physical ability like the jobs of draftsmen, mechanic, spinner.

(ii) **Sending Out Questionnaires.** The method is usually employed by engineering consultants. Properly drafted questionnaires are sent out to job-holders for completion and are returned to supervisors. However, the information received is often unorganised and incoherent. The idea in issuing questionnaire is to elicit the necessary information from job-holders so that any error may first be discussed with the employee and, after due corrections, may be submitted to the job analyst.

(iii) **Maintenance of Log Records.** The employee maintains a daily diary record of duties he performs, marking the time at which each task is started and finished. But, this system is incomplete, for it does not give us any desirable data on supervisor relationship, the equipment used, and working conditions. Moreover, it is time-consuming.

(iv) **Personnel Interviews.** May be held by the analyst with the employees and answers to relevant questions may be recorded.

(v) **Critical incidents.** In this method, job holder are asked to describe incidents concerning the job based on the past experiences. The incidents are so collected are analysed and classified according to the job areas described. A fairly clear picture of actual job requirement can be obtained by distinguishing between effective and ineffective behaviour of the job. The analyst requires the high degree of skill to analyses the content of descriptions given by the workers.

Quantitative Methods

1. **Position Analysis Questionnaire Model.** PAQ represents Position Analysis Questionnaire. This well-known and commonly used technique is used to analyze a job by getting the questionnaires filled by job incumbents and their superiors. Designed by a trained and experienced job analyst, the process involves interviewing the subject matter experts and employees and evaluating the questionnaires on those bases. The PAQ contain 194 items, each of which represent a basic elements that may or may not play an important role on the job. The job analyst decided Whether each item play a role on the job, if so to that extent.
   194 job elements covered by PAQ are grouped into six section.
   (i) Information input (ii) Mental processes
   (iii) Work output (iv) relationship
   (v) Job context (vi) Other job characteristics
2. **Management position analysis questionnaire (MPDQ).** MPDQ is a standardised instrument designed by specifically for use in analysing managerial jobs. The 274 items questionnaire contains 15 sections. It would take 2 ½ hours to complete the questionnaire .in most cases the respondent are asked to state how each item is to the positions
3. **Functional Job Analysis Model.** FJA is a worker oriented job analysis techniques that attempts to describe the whole person on the job .its tries to examine the fundamental components of data, people and thing.
   Functional Job Analysis and helps in collecting and recording job-related data to a deeper extent. It is used to develop task-related statements. Developed by Sidney Fine and his colleagues, the technique helps in determining the complexity of duties and responsibilities involved in a specific job. This work-oriented technique works on the basis of relatedness of job-data where complexity of work is determined on a scale of various scores given to a particular job. The lower scores represent greater difficulty.

Job Evaluation

Job evaluation is an attempt to determine and compare demands which the normal performance of a particular job makes on normal workers without taking into account the individual abilities or performance of the workers concerned.

The evaluation may be achieved through the assignment of points or the use of some other systematic methods for essential job requirements, such as skills, experience and responsibility.

It does not set the price of a job; it merely fixes its relative worth. It presents an effort to determine the relative value of every job in a plant and to determine what the fair basic wage for such a job should be. It is not evaluating the merit of the worker who is doing the work. It rates the job and not the qualities of the individual worker on the job, which is the task of employee rating.

Definitions of Job Evaluations

Below are given some important definitions of job analysis:

Job Evaluation involves determination of relative worth of each job for the purpose of establishing wage and salary differentials. Relative worth is determined mainly on the basis of Job Description and Job Specification only. Job Evaluation helps to determine wages and salary grades for all jobs. Employees need to be compensated depending on the grades of jobs they perform. Remuneration must be based on the relative worth of each job. Ignoring this basic principle results in inequitable compensation and attendant ill effects on employees' morale. A perception of inequity is a sure way of De-motivating an employee.

- In the words of **Dale Yoder,** *"Job evaluation is a practice which seeks to provide a degree of objectivity in measuring the comparative value of jobs within an organisation and among similar organisations."*
- According to **Bethel, Atwater and Smith et at,** *"Job evaluation as a personal term has both a specific and genetic meaning specifically, it means job rating or the grading of occupations in terms of duties ; generally it means the entire field of wages and salary administration along modern lines"*
- According to **Bureau of Labour Statistics,** *"Job evaluation is the evaluation or rating of job to determine their position in job hierarchy. The evaluation may be achievement through assignment of points or the use of some other systematic rating method for essential job requirements such as skill, experience and responsibility."*
- In the words of **Edwin B. Flippo.** *"Job evaluation is a systematic and orderly process of determining the worth of a job in relation to other jobs."*
- According to **International Labour Organisation,** *"Job evaluation may be defined as an attempt to determine and compare the demands which the normal performance of particular job makes on normal workers without taking account of the individual abilities or performance of the workers concerned."*
- According to **Kimball and Kimball Jr.**, *"Job evaluation represents an effort to determine the relative value of every job in a plant and to determine what the fair basic wage for such a job should be."*

Objectives of Job Evaluation

(i) To secure and maintain complete, accurate and impersonal descriptions of each distinct job or occupation in the entire plant;

(ii) To provide a standard procedure for determining the relative worth of each job in a plant;

(iii) To determine the rate of pay for each job which is fair and equitable with relation to other jobs in the plant, community or industry;

(iv) To ensure that like wages are paid to all qualified employees for advancement and transfer;

(v) To promote a fair and accurate consideration of all employees for advancement and transfer;

(vi) To provide a factual basis for the consideration of wage rates for similar jobs in a community and in an industry; and

(vii) To provide information for 'work organisation, employees' selection, placement, training and numerous other similar problems.

Procedure of Job Evaluation

(i) **Analyse and Prepare Job Description.** This requires the preparation of a job description and also an analysis of job requirements for successful performance.

(ii) **Select and Prepare a Job Evaluation Plan.** This means that a job must be broken down into its component parts, *i.e.*, it should involve the selection of factors, elements needed for the performance of all jobs for which money is paid, determining their value and preparing written instructions for evaluation.

(iii) **Classify Jobs.** This requires grouping for arranging jobs in a correct sequence in terms of value to the firm and relating them to the money terms in order to ascertain their relative value.

(iv) **Install the Program.** This involves explaining it to employees and putting it into operation.

(v) **Maintain the Program.** Jobs cannot continue without updating new jobs and job changes in obedience to changing conditions and situations.

Methods of Job Evaluation

A. Non-Quantitative Methods or Qualitative Methods.

1. Ranking Method. Under this system all the jobs are arranged or ranked in order of their importance from simplest to the hardest order, each job being higher than the previous one in the sequence. A committee of several executives is constituted, which evaluated the job descriptions and ranks them in order of importance. The committee does not have specific factors before it but the things like nature of job, working conditions, supervision needed, responsibilities involved etc. are kept in mind while ranking the job. These factors are not assigned any weight or points. Following steps are taken in ranking.

(a) **Preparation of Job Description.** The first step in job evaluation process is the preparation of job description. Though it is not essential to prepare job description under ranking system but it is better and helpful in this system. If more than one person is assigned the job of ranking then they will give different ranking to the jobs.

(b) **Selection of Raters.** The second step in the process of ranking is the selection of raters. The jobs may be ranked department wise or in cluster (factory jobs, clerical jobs, menial jobs). Factory jobs should not be compared with clerical jobs or menial jobs because of their different nature. Generally, a committee of raters is used for the purpose.

(c) **Selection of Rates and Key Jobs.** First of all certain key jobs are selected and then other jobs are compared with them. The key jobs are selected from major departments or main functions.

(d) **Ranking of All Jobs.** Each job is then compared with the other similar job to establish its exact ranking in the scale. All the jobs are then ranked from lowest to highest or vice-versa.

Advantages

- **Simple.** The system is quite simple. A company does not face any difficulty in installing this system.
- **Easy.** As the workers understand the process there is no problem in administering this system.
- **Less time.** Less time is taken in evaluating the jobs.
- **Suitable for smaller concern.** This system is suitable for smaller organisation where the rates are fully acquainted with all the existing jobs in the enterprise.

Disadvantages

- **No scientific approach.** As there is no standard for an analysis of the whole job position, different bases of comparison may occur. Importance of the job may be arbitrarily ranked resulting in differences in similar jobs and may be resented by the employees.
- **No fair judgement.** This method decides the ranks of the jobs on the basis of their importance but does not tell the reasons. So ranks judgements are subjective and the fairness of the judgement cannot be advocated.
- **Difficult for large organisation.** In a complex industrial organisation, it is not possible to be familiar with all the jobs and thus general description will not enable correct assessment of the relative importance of the jobs.

2. Job Grading Method. Under this system, a number of pre-determined grades or classifications are decided by the committee and each job is assigned to one of the grades of classes. With the help of job analysis, information about different jobs is collected and they are put under different grades as per their nature and importance. For each grade or class there is different rate of wage. The jobs may be graded as skilled, unskilled, clerical, administrative etc.

The following steps are involved in grading system.

(a) **Preparation of Grade Descriptions.** The first thing to be done in this method is to prepare grade description to evolve classifications of jobs. A number of grades, different from each other, are selected. The grading should be done by considering the nature of duties of the job, supervising responsibilities etc. Each job is then, attached to an appropriate grade. For grade description, information about various jobs is collected through job description.

(b) **Selection of Grades and Key Jobs.** A number of jobs are graded, normally between 10 to 20, are selected. Key jobs are selected from important functions and major departments.

(c) **Grading the key jobs.** Key jobs are assigned to an appropriate grade level and their relationship to each other studied.

(d) All the jobs are put in relevant grades or classification. For e.g., all menial jobs, put in one class, clerical jobs in another class, technical jobs in still other class and so on. The jobs in one class receive the same wage rates.

Following table is a brief description of such a classification in an office:

Grade	Description of Job-Classification
I. Grade Unskilled	This generally covers the jobs of clerical nature, which requires accuracy, reliability etc. So special training is required.
II. Grade Skilled	This also covers the job with the nature of clerical work. But under this personnel require training programmes. This may include: ***draftsman, ledger man, laboratory assistant etc.***
III. Grade Interpretative	This requires a special skill to perform the jobs. These may be of clerical or non-clerical nature. This includes: ***foremans, layout draftsman etc.*** This is also of non-supervisory nature.
IV. Grade Creative	This involves a high degree of creativity and special knowledge. This covers ***engineers, salesman, staff supervisor, designers etc.***
V. Grade Executive	This is related to the supervisory and creative jobs category. This generally covers the ***managers of all different departments.***
VI. Grade Administrative	This is related with a little bit policy formulation and implementation. They have to work with great sense of responsibility. This may include: ***division manager, district sales managers, works engineers and treasurer etc.***
VII. Grade Policy	Their position is of the top in a concern. They have to formulate the policies of a company. This cover the top management posts like ***directors, managers etc.***

3. Point System. It involves quantitative and analytical approach to the measurement of job worth. A number of important factors to be considered in each job are determined. The degree of each factor is also determined for assigning points. Various factors are assigned points and sum of them gives us an index for the relative significance of the jobs that are rated. The point system is based on these assumptions that important factors of each job can be determined for evaluating it. The point of different jobs are, later on, converted into money value or wage rates.

Following steps are taken for job evaluation :

(a) **Type of jobs to be evaluated.** There are a number of jobs in every organisation and these may range from top executive to unskilled one. Similar jobs should be put in the same category for evaluation purpose. There should be separate evaluation programme for each class because the factors influencing them will be different. The job requirement of supervisor will be different from that of an unskilled worker.

(b) **Number of factors to be used.** It is very difficult to select the number of factors to be used for evaluating a job. The number of factors should be such that all aspects of a job are evaluated. The number of factors to be used varies from company to company, ranking from 3 to as many as 50. The common factors to be selected are education, training, skills, physical ability, mental requirement, suspensibility, job conditions etc.

(c) **Determination of Degree.** Each factor if evaluation should be further sub-divided into degrees for example, experience which is commonly used factor in each job may be sub-divided into five degrees. The first degree may have experience of 3 to 6 months with 5 points, second degree points having experience from 6 months to 1 year with 10 points, 15 for experience between 1 to 2 years, 20 points for experience of 2 to 4 years and 25 points for experience of over 4 years.

(d) **Assigning of Weights.** Each factor may be assigned a weight as per as its importance. For executives, mental requirements will have more weight than physical requirements.

(e) **Assigning Money Values to points.** The points assigned to each factor are added up for finding out the value of job. The values of jobs are translated into terms of money with a pre-determined formula. The following types of formula may be used:

Point Range	Pay Scale Rs.	Grade
50–100	700–1600	1
100–150	1200–2000	2
150–250	1500–2500	3
200–250	2500–4000	4
250–300	3000–5000	5

4. Factor Comparison Method. This method is a combination of ranking and point system of job evaluation. Under this method the relative rank of the jobs is evacuated in relation of monetary scale. Some key jobs are selected at the first instance and then ranked by considering one factor at a time. In this method five factors are generally evaluated for each job; mental requirements, skill, physical requirements, responsibilities and working conditions.

Following steps are taken under factor comparison method.

(a) **Selecting factors to be used.** The first thing to be done under this method is the selection of factors to be used this method is the selection of factors to be used for evaluation. The persons writing job descriptions should be given the proper definitions of these factors. The universally used factors are:

(i) mental requirements (ii) physical requirements (iii) skill requirements (iv) stop usability (v) working conditions.

The number of factors may be more than five. Pay will be assigned in this method by compaining the weights of the factor required for each job, i.e., the present wages paid for key jobs may be divided among the factors weighted by importance. So the wages are assigned to the job in comparison to its ranking on each job factor.

(b) **Selection of key jobs.** They are to be taken as a standard and all other jobs are to be compared with key jobs evaluation. All key jobs should be exact and will understood and there should be no conflict between management and employees about them. The jobs so selected should cover the range from lowest to the lightest paid ones. Generally, 10 to 25 jobs are picked up as key jobs.

(c) **Ranking of key jobs.** All the members of job evaluation committee rank various jobs given earlier. A meeting of the committee is called to evolve a consensus on each job.
(d) **Valuing the factors.** Each factor of key job is then allocated a basic pay. The pay for such jobs should range from the lowest to the highest.
(e) **Comparison of jobs.** All jobs are compared with key job factor to determine their relative importance and position in the scale of jobs. The money value of jobs is also determined with this comparison.
(f) **Establishing wage structure.** By assigning money value to each factor of various jobs, a wage structure is determined by summing up these values.

COMPENSATION MANAGEMENT

In very simple terms, compensation is the results or rewards that the employees receive in return for their work. Compensation includes payments like bonuses, profit sharing, overtime pay, recognition rewards and sales commission, etc.

Compensation can also include non-monetary perks like a company-paid car, company-paid housing and stock opportunities. Compensation is a vital part of human resource management, which helps in encouraging the employees and improving organizational effectiveness.

From a manager's point of view, the compensation package offered to a company's employees is essential not only because it costs money, but because it is likely to be the primary reason the employees work for the firm.

Compensation packages with good pay and advantages can help attract and retain the best employees. A quick survey of employees about compensation is likely to expose an expectation that wages are fair and cover basic living expenses, keep up with inflation, leave some money for savings (perhaps for retirement) and leisure, increment over time.

A company's compensation scheme also informs a great deal about the firm's values and cultures. Employees often look at what a company pays rather than what it says. In many aspects, people behave as they are rewarded.

A compensation scheme projects what the company expects of its employees. For example, if quality is an essential value, then it should be implemented through some element of the total compensation system.

Objectives of Compensation Policy

The objectives of compensation policy are as follows:

- Allure suitable staff.
- Keep qualified personnel.
- Develop reward structures that are equitable with logical and fair pay relationships between differently valued jobs.
- Manage pay structures to mirror inflationary effects.
- Assure that rewards and salary costs handle changes in market rates or organizational change.
- Appraise performance, duty, and loyalty, and provide for progression.
- Abide with legal requirements.
- Maintain compensation levels and differentials under review and control salary or wage costs.

Importance of Compensation Management

A good compensation is a must for every business organization, as it gives an employee a reason to stick to the company.

An organization gains from a structured compensation management in the following ways:

- It tries to give proper refund to the employees for their contributions to the organization.
- It discovers a positive control on the efficiency of employees and motivates them to perform better and achieve the specific standards.
- It creates a base for happiness and satisfaction of the workforce that limits the labor turnover and confers a stable organization.
- It enhances the job evaluation process, which in return helps in setting up more realistic and achievable standards.
- It is designed to abide with the various labor acts and thus does not result in conflicts between the employee union and the management. This creates a peaceful relationship between the employer and the employees.
- It excites an environment of morale, efficiency and cooperation among the workers and ensures satisfaction to the workers.

In short, we can say that compensation management is required as it encourages the employees to perform better and show their excellence as well as provides growth and development options to the deserving employees.

Types of Compensations

We have learnt about what compensation and its importance is. However, when it comes to an organization, be it private or public, compensations are further divided into the following:

- **Direct Compensation.** It is naturally made up of salary payments and health benefits. The creation of salary ranges and pay scales for different positions within an organization are the central responsibility of compensation management staff.

  Direct compensation that is in line with the industry standards facilitates employees with the assurance that they are getting paid fairly. This helps the employer not to worry about the costly loss of trained staff to a competitor.
- **Indirect Compensation.** It focuses on the personal encouragements of each individual to work. Although salary is essential, people are most productive in jobs where they share the company's values and priorities.

  These benefits can include things like free staff development courses, subsidized day care, the chances for promotion or transfer within the company, public recognition, the ability to effect change or bring some changes in the workplace, and service to others.

  These are the two types of compensation that need to be managed and have its own contribution in the development of the organization. Moving forward, we will see the different components of compensation.
- **Components of Compensation.** Compensation as a whole is made up of different components that work as an aid for an employee after retirement or in case of some accident or injury. Now we shall see the key elements or components that make compensation.
- **Wages and Salary.** Wages mark hourly rates of pay, and salary marks the monthly rate of pay of an employee. It is irrelevant of the number of hours put in by an employee working in the firm. These are subject to annual increase.
- **Allowances.** Allowances can be defined as the amount of something that is allowed, especially within a set of rules and regulations or for a specified purpose. Various allowances are paid in addition to basic pay.

Some of these allowances are as follows:

- **Dearness Allowance.** This allowance is given to protect real income of an employee against price rise. Dearness allowance (DA) is paid as a percentage of basic pay.
- **House Rent Allowance.** Companies who do not provide living accommodation to their employees pay house rent allowance (HRA) to employees. This allowance is calculated as a percentage of salary.
- **City Compensatory Allowance.** This allowance is paid basically to employees in metros and other big cities where cost of living is comparatively more. City compensatory allowance (CCA) is normally a fixed amount per month, like 30 per cent of basic pay in case of government employees.
- **Transport Allowance/Conveyance Allowance.** Some companies pay transport allowance (TA) that accommodates travel from the employee's house to the office. A fixed amount is paid every month to cover a part of traveling expenses.
- **Incentives and Performance Based Pay.** Incentive compensation is performance-related remuneration paid with a view to encourage employees to work hard and do better.

  Both individual incentives and group incentives are applicable in most cases. Bonus, gain-sharing, commissions on sales are some examples of incentive compensation.
- **Fringe Benefits/Perquisites.** Fringe benefits include employee benefits like medical care, hospitalization, accident relief, health and group insurance, canteen, uniform, recreation and the likes.

  In recent years, a great deal of attention has been directed to the development of compensation systems that go beyond just money. We can say that all the components of compensation management play a very important role in the life of an employee.

  In particular, there has been a marked increase in the use of pay-for-performance (PrP) for management and professional employees, especially for executive management and senior managers. Compensation is a primary motivation for most employees.

MULTIPLE CHOICE QUESTIONS

1. Organizational Behavior (OB) is important be cause it helps organizations
   (a) Maximize shareholder wealth
   (b) Minimize employee satisfaction
   (c) Understand and manage human behavior within the organization
   (d) Ignore the impact of leadership
2. The study of OB is significant because it contributes to
   (a) Maximizing government regulations
   (b) Reducing employee benefits
   (c) Enhancing employee performance and well-being
   (d) Focusing solely on short-term profit goals
3. A key benefit of understanding OB is improved
   (a) Efficiency and productivity
   (b) Government regulations
   (c) Shareholder wealth
   (d) Employee conflicts
4. The "contingency approach" in OB recognizes that
   (a) There is a one-size-fits-all solution for managing employees
   (b) Organizational behavior principles are universal and apply in all situations
   (c) Effective management depends on the specific context and situation
   (d) Organizations should prioritize legal compliance over employee well-being
5. Studying OB helps organizations in
   (a) Minimizing leadership roles
   (b) Maximizing short-term profit goals
   (c) Achieving a balance between employee and organizational goals
   (d) Disregarding the interests of shareholders
6. The Hawthorne studies are known for their contribution to which theory of OB?
   (a) Classical management theory
   (b) Scientific management theory
   (c) Human relations theory
   (d) Contingency theory
7. The theory that focuses on the impact of group dynamics and informal social interactions on employee motivation and performance is
   (a) Scientific management theory
   (b) Classical management theory
   (c) Human relations theory
   (d) Contingency theory
8. Theory X and Theory Y, proposed by Douglas McGregor, are related to
   (a) Scientific management theory
   (b) Classical management theory
   (c) Employee motivation and management assumptions
   (d) Contingency theory
9. In the Equity Theory, individuals compare their own inputs and outcomes to those of others to evaluate
   (a) The effectiveness of scientific management
   (b) The organization's profit margin
   (c) The fairness of their treatment at work
   (d) Government regulations
10. According to Maslow's Hierarchy of Needs theory, the highest level of needs that individuals seek to satisfy are
    (a) Physiological needs
    (b) Safety needs
    (c) Self-actualization needs
    (d) Social needs
11. McGregor's Theory Y suggests that employees
    (a) Are inherently lazy and need to be closely monitored
    (b) Have a natural inclination to work and be creative
    (c) Can be motivated only by financial incentives
    (d) Prefer strict hierarchy and structure
12. Which OB theory emphasizes the importance of the social environment in the workplace and

the role of supportive relationships?
(a) Human relations theory
(b) Scientific management theory
(c) Classical management theory
(d) Contingency theory

13. The Expectancy Theory in OB suggests that individuals are motivated to perform well when they believe that
(a) Job security is guaranteed
(b) Their needs are met through job performance
(c) Government regulations are in place
(d) They are entitled to promotions

14. According to the Goal-Setting Theory, specific and challenging goals are more likely to
(a) Result in decreased employee motivation
(b) Lead to government regulations
(c) Improve employee performance and motivation
(d) Ignite conflicts among employees

15. The Leadership-Member Exchange (LMX) theory emphasizes
(a) Strict adherence to government regulations
(b) The role of formal organizational hierarchy
(c) The development of unique leader-follower relationships
(d) The importance of classical management principles

16. The Bureaucratic Theory of OB, associated with Max Weber, focuses on
(a) Employee motivation and human relations
(b) Scientific management principles
(c) The importance of a formal organizational structure and rules
(d) The impact of group dynamics on employee performance

17. The theory that explores the relationship between an individual's personality traits and their job satisfaction and performance is known as
(a) Maslow's Hierarchy of Needs theory
(b) Goal-Setting Theory
(c) Trait Theory
(d) Equity Theory

18. The Theory of Planned Behavior emphasizes that an individual's intention to perform a behavior is influenced by their
(a) Physiological needs
(b) Attitude toward the behavior, subjective norms, and perceived behavioral control
(c) Self-actualization needs
(d) Government regulations

19. In the Organizational Culture Theory, culture refers to
(a) Strict adherence to government regulations
(b) The set of shared values, beliefs, and norms within an organization
(c) Employee motivation and job satisfaction
(d) Scientific management principles

20. The theory that focuses on the role of cognitive processes in explaining employee motivation and behavior is known as
(a) Human relations theory
(b) Expectancy Theory
(c) Trait Theory
(d) Classical management theory

21. The Contingency Theory suggests that the effectiveness of various leadership styles depends on
(a) The level of government regulations in the industry
(b) The personality of the leader
(c) The specific situation and context in which the leader operates
(d) The organization's hierarchical structure

22. According to the Transactional Leadership Theory, leaders primarily
(a) Inspire and motivate employees through a shared vision
(b) Use rewards and punishments to influence employee behavior
(c) Emphasize employee autonomy and self-direction
(d) Focus on employee job satisfaction

23. The Path-Goal Theory of Leadership is concerned with
(a) The formal structure of organizations
(b) The importance of government regulations
(c) The relationship between a leader's behavior and employee motivation
(d) The impact of group dynamics on organizational culture

24. The Social Exchange Theory in OB explores the relationships between

(a) The organization's core values and employee motivation
(b) The employee and government regulations
(c) Employees and their organizations in terms of the exchange of resources and obligations
(d) The effects of scientific management principles

25. The Expectancy-Valence Theory is primarily concerned with
(a) Human relations in the workplace
(b) Employee motivation and satisfaction
(c) Employee perceptions of effort-reward relationships
(d) Government regulations on labor

26. Personality is best defined as
(a) A person's physical appearance
(b) A person's unique set of traits, characteristics, and behaviors
(c) A person's job title and responsibilities
(d) A person's ability to adapt to changes

27. The "Big Five" personality traits include
(a) Extraversion, openness, optimism, teamwork, and resilience
(b) Assertiveness, adaptability, agreeableness, diligence, and conscientiousness
(c) Extraversion, agreeableness, openness, conscientiousness, and neuroticism
(d) Assertiveness, creativity, determination, leadership, and flexibility

28. An individual high in conscientiousness is likely to be
(a) Organized and dependable
(b) Reserved and introverted
(c) Open to new experiences
(d) Emotionally unstable

29. A person with a high level of extraversion is likely to be
(a) Reserved and introverted
(b) Outgoing, sociable, and assertive
(c) Cautious and risk-averse
(d) Emotionally stable

30. The trait theory of personality suggests that
(a) Personality is primarily shaped by environmental factors
(b) Personality is a result of unconscious conflicts
(c) Personality can be described and understood through a set of distinct traits
(d) Personality is determined by early childhood experiences

31. Perception is the process of
(a) Ignoring sensory information
(b) Interpreting and organizing sensory information
(c) Suppressing emotions
(d) Avoiding social interactions

32. The perceptual process involves several stages, including
(a) Sensing, ignoring, and suppressing
(b) Attention, recognition, and memory
(c) Judgment, emotions, and intuition
(d) Rejection, avoidance, and denial

33. Stereotyping in perception refers to
(a) Providing detailed information about a person
(b) Categorizing individuals based on assumptions about a group they belong to
(c) Ignoring sensory information
(d) Having an unbiased perspective

34. Confirmation bias in perception is when individuals
(a) Seek out information that confirms their existing beliefs or stereotypes
(b) Avoid all forms of sensory input
(c) Actively suppress their emotions
(d) Exhibit emotional stability

35. The fundamental attribution error in perception occurs when
(a) Individuals underestimate the influence of internal factors and overestimate external factors when explaining the behavior of others
(b) Individuals overestimate the influence of internal factors and ignore external factors when explaining their own behavior
(c) Individuals accurately assess the factors that influence their own behavior
(d) Individuals prioritize government regulations when making decisions

36. Values are best described as
(a) Temporary beliefs that change frequently
(b) Personal preferences that are unrelated to behavior
(c) Stable, long-lasting beliefs about what is important to an individual
(d) Unconscious conflicts that shape behavior

37. Cognitive dissonance theory suggests that individuals experience discomfort when their
(a) Values align with their attitudes
(b) Values are clear and consistent
(c) Attitudes align with their behaviors
(d) Values are not in alignment with government regulations

38. Attitudes are composed of three main components, including
(a) Cognitive, emotional, and social components
(b) Personal, professional, and ethical components
(c) Cognitive, affective, and behavioral components
(d) Values, beliefs, and behaviors

39. Job satisfaction is an example of
(a) A cognitive attitude
(b) Affective attitude
(c) Behavioral attitude
(d) An unconscious attitude

40. The theory that suggests that attitudes are developed through a process of social learning and interaction is
(a) Cognitive dissonance theory
(b) Attribution theory
(c) Social cognitive theory
(d) Maslow's Hierarchy of Needs theory

41. Classical conditioning, as studied by Ivan Pavlov, involves
(a) Associating a neutral stimulus with an unconditioned stimulus to produce a conditioned response
(b) Reinforcing behavior through rewards and punishments
(c) Shaping behavior through observation and imitation
(d) Ignoring behavior and its consequences

42. Operant conditioning, as proposed by B.F. Skinner, focuses on
(a) The formation of conditioned responses through associations
(b) The role of internal factors in shaping behavior
(c) The consequences of behavior in reinforcing or extinguishing it
(d) The influence of government regulations on behavior

43. Observational learning, as described by Albert Bandura, involves
(a) Associating a neutral stimulus with an unconditioned stimulus
(b) Reinforcing behavior through rewards and punishments
(c) Shaping behavior through observation and imitation
(d) Ignoring the consequences of behavior

44. In the context of learning, reinforcement refers to
(a) A process of shaping behavior through observation
(b) Providing a stimulus or consequence to increase the likelihood of a behavior
(c) Associating a neutral stimulus with an unconditioned stimulus
(d) Ignoring behavior entirely

45. The concept of "self-regulation" in learning refers to an individual's ability to
(a) Avoid government regulations
(b) Set and monitor their own learning goals and behaviors
(c) Reinforce behaviors through rewards and punishments
(d) Ignore the influence of external factors on behavior

46. Motivation is best described as
(a) A state of rest and relaxation
(b) The process that initiates, guides, and sustains goal-directed behavior
(c) The absence of goals and desires
(d) A result of government regulations

47. Intrinsic motivation is driven by
(a) External rewards and punishments
(b) Internal factors such as personal interest and enjoyment
(c) The influence of government regulations
(d) The desire for monetary compensation

48. The "Hierarchy of Needs" theory, proposed by Abraham Maslow, suggests that individuals must satisfy their physiological and safety needs before they can pursue higher-level needs such as
(a) Self-actualization and esteem
(b) Government regulations and conformity
(c) Intrinsic motivation and self-determination
(d) Monetary rewards and job security

49. The Expectancy Theory of Motivation suggests that individuals are motivated when they
    (a) Believe their needs are met through job performance
    (b) Receive external rewards and recognition
    (c) Are driven by social pressure
    (d) Have no expectations of success
50. Equity theory in motivation suggests that individuals are motivated when they perceive
    (a) A fair balance between their input and outcomes in comparison to others
    (b) A lack of government regulations in the workplace
    (c) Intrinsic factors play a minimal role in motivation
    (d) Their salary is above industry standards
51. Team building is the process of
    (a) Isolating individuals to work independently
    (b) Ignoring the strengths and weaknesses of team members
    (c) Creating a cohesive and high-performing group of individuals
    (d) Promoting competition among team members
52. Which of the following is NOT a stage of team development in Tuckman's model?
    (a) Forming (b) Norming
    (c) Storming (d) Competing
53. In team building, "norms" refer to
    (a) Established guidelines and expectations for team behavior
    (b) Arguments and conflicts among team members
    (c) Strict adherence to government regulations
    (d) Isolating team members from each other
54. A successful team building process often involves
    (a) Encouraging open communication, trust, and collaboration
    (b) Promoting competition among team members
    (c) Ignoring the unique strengths and weaknesses of team members
    (d) Disregarding the team's goals and objectives
55. What is the primary focus of diversity and inclusion in team building?
    (a) Creating a team of individuals with identical backgrounds and experiences
    (b) Recognizing and valuing differences among team members
    (c) Ignoring the individual needs and preferences of team members
    (d) Strictly adhering to government regulations regarding diversity
56. Leadership is best defined as
    (a) The process of assigning tasks and monitoring their completion
    (b) The ability to enforce authority and control over subordinates
    (c) Influencing and guiding others to achieve a common goal
    (d) The process of assigning blame for failures
57. Transformational leadership is characterized by
    (a) Encouraging transactional exchanges between leaders and followers
    (b) Focusing solely on task completion and efficiency
    (c) Inspiring and motivating followers to exceed their own expectations
    (d) Strict adherence to government regulations
58. The situational leadership theory suggests that effective leadership depends on
    (a) A one-size-fits-all approach to leadership
    (b) The leader's charisma and charm
    (c) The specific situation and the readiness of followers
    (d) Strict hierarchical control over subordinates
59. Authentic leadership emphasizes
    (a) Concealing one's true self to maintain authority
    (b) The importance of leader-follower transactions
    (c) Gaining compliance through rewards and punishments
    (d) Leading with honesty, transparency, and self-awareness
60. Servant leadership focuses on
    (a) Leaders serving their own interests first
    (b) Maximizing government regulations
    (c) Leaders prioritizing the needs of followers and the greater good

(d) Strictly enforcing authority and control over followers

61. Group dynamics refers to the
(a) Number of members in a group
(b) Interactions, relationships, and processes within a group
(c) Competition among group members
(d) Group's ability to strictly adhere to government regulations

62. In-group and out-group dynamics often lead to
(a) Enhanced cooperation and trust within the group
(b) Favoritism and bias towards one's own group
(c) Excessive conformity and compliance with leaders
(d) Ignoring the influence of leadership in groups

63. Groupthink is a phenomenon where
(a) Group members encourage open and critical discussion of ideas
(b) The group is highly diverse and inclusive
(c) Group members prioritize consensus and harmony over critical evaluation
(d) Government regulations dictate group decisions

64. Conflict resolution within a group typically involves
(a) Avoiding any form of confrontation
(b) Ignoring the perspectives and concerns of group members
(c) Addressing and resolving differences or disagreements
(d) Promoting competition among group members

65. The Abilene Paradox is a concept related to group dynamics, which occurs when
(a) Group members are comfortable expressing their true opinions
(b) Group members collectively agree on a course of action they believe is against their individual interests
(c) Groups strictly adhere to government regulations
(d) Leadership in the group is ineffective

66. The "Social Loafing" phenomenon in group dynamics is characterized by
(a) Increased individual effort and contribution in a group
(b) Reduced individual effort and contribution in a group
(c) A strong sense of individual accountability in a group
(d) Strict adherence to government regulations in a group

67. The "Diversity Paradox" in group dynamics refers to
(a) The challenges of managing diverse groups
(b) The benefits of homogeneous groups
(c) The concept of group conformity
(d) The absence of government regulations in diverse groups

68. The "Group Polarization" phenomenon is when group discussions
(a) Lead to a moderation of initial views and opinions
(b) Reinforce and amplify the group's existing attitudes and beliefs
(c) Strictly adhere to government regulations
(d) Encourage conformity and uniformity

69. The role of a group leader in managing group dynamics often involves
(a) Ignoring the group's needs and conflicts
(b) Promoting competition among group members
(c) Facilitating open communication, resolving conflicts, and guiding the group toward its goals
(d) Enforcing strict control and authority

70. The "Social Identity Theory" in group dynamics explains how
(a) Groups prioritize government regulations over identity
(b) Groups shape individual identities and self-concept
(c) Individuals resist conforming to group norms
(d) Leadership is the sole determinant of group behavior

71. Interpersonal behavior refers to
(a) Individual behavior in isolation
(b) The behavior that occurs within social interactions
(c) Strict adherence to government regulations
(d) The internal thought processes of individuals

72. Effective interpersonal communication involves
(a) Avoiding active listening
(b) Ignoring the perspectives of others
(c) Communicating clearly and actively listening to others
(d) Strict adherence to one's own viewpoint

73. Nonverbal communication includes
(a) Spoken words and written messages
(b) The use of gestures, body language, and facial expressions
(c) Strict adherence to government regulations
(d) Ignoring the needs and emotions of others

74. Empathy in interpersonal behavior refers to
(a) The ability to manipulate and control others
(b) Understanding and sharing the feelings and perspectives of others
(c) Strict adherence to rules and regulations
(d) Ignoring the emotions and needs of others

75. Conflict resolution in interpersonal behavior often involves
(a) Avoiding any form of disagreement or confrontation
(b) Promoting competition and rivalry
(c) Addressing and resolving differences and disputes
(d) Strict adherence to one's own beliefs and values

76. Transactional Analysis (TA) is a psychological theory that focuses on
(a) Studying unconscious conflicts
(b) Analyzing government regulations
(c) Understanding social transactions and communication
(d) Ignoring interpersonal relationships

77. The three ego states in TA are
(a) Parent, child, and adult
(b) Dominant, submissive, and assertive
(c) Rigid, flexible, and neutral
(d) Strict, lenient, and adaptable

78. The "Parent" ego state in TA is associated with
(a) Nurturing and controlling behaviors
(b) Spontaneity and creativity
(c) Rational and logical thinking
(d) Adherence to government regulations

79. The "Adult" ego state in TA is characterized by
(a) Emotional reactions and impulsiveness
(b) Rational, objective, and analytical thinking
(c) Rebellious and nonconforming behavior
(d) Ignoring the influence of others

80. The "Child" ego state in TA includes
(a) Obedient and submissive behaviors
(b) Playful and spontaneous behaviors
(c) Compliance with government regulations
(d) Strict adherence to rules and authority

81. In TA, a "transaction" refers to
(a) Financial exchanges between individuals
(b) Social interactions and communication between ego states
(c) Legal contracts and agreements
(d) Ignoring interpersonal communication

82. A "complementary transaction" in TA occurs when
(a) The communication is inconsistent with ego states
(b) The communication is consistent with ego states, fostering effective communication
(c) The communication is confrontational and argumentative
(d) Government regulations dictate communication

83. A "crossed transaction" in TA occurs when
(a) The communication is consistent with ego states, fostering effective communication
(b) The communication is inconsistent with ego states, leading to misunderstandings
(c) The communication is manipulative and controlling
(d) Ignoring the needs and perspectives of others

84. A "game" in TA refers to
(a) Sporting events and recreational activities
(b) Recurring, unproductive patterns of interaction and communication
(c) Strict adherence to government regulations
(d) Ignoring the influence of ego states

85. The concept of "strokes" in TA relates to
(a) Physical contact and affection
(b) Positive or negative units of recognition or attention received from others
(c) Legal transactions and contracts
(d) Strict adherence to social norms

86. The "life positions" in TA describe an individual's fundamental attitude toward self and others. Which of the following life positions is characterized by a positive view of both self and others?
(a) "I'm Okay, You're Not Okay"
(b) "I'm Not Okay, You're Not Okay"
(c) "I'm Okay, You're Okay"
(d) "I'm Not Okay, You're Okay"

87. The concept of "script" in TA refers to
(a) A written plan for a movie or play
(b) Unconscious life plans and decisions made in childhood that influence behavior
(c) Strict adherence to government regulations
(d) Ignoring one's life experiences and choices

88. In TA, "rackets" refer to
(a) Sporting equipment
(b) Unconscious, manipulative patterns of behavior designed to gain strokes
(c) Government regulations related to gambling
(d) Ignoring the influence of ego states in communication

89. The goal of TA therapy is to help individuals
(a) Strictly adhere to societal norms
(b) Understand and change unproductive patterns of behavior and communication
(c) Maximize government regulations
(d) Suppress their emotions and needs

90. The concept of "ulterior transactions" in TA refers to
(a) Transactions that are open and honest
(b) Hidden or concealed motives behind communication
(c) Strict adherence to government regulations
(d) Ignoring the influence of ego states in transactions

91. Organizational culture is best described as
(a) The physical infrastructure of the organization
(b) The formal rules and regulations governing the organization
(c) The shared values, beliefs, and norms that shape behavior within the organization
(d) Ignoring the influence of leadership in an organization

92. The visible elements of organizational culture include
(a) Core values and beliefs
(b) Employee attitudes
(c) Artifacts, symbols, and rituals
(d) Government regulations

93. A "strong culture" in an organization typically means that
(a) The organization enforces strict rules and regulations
(b) Employees exhibit a wide range of values and beliefs
(c) There is a clear and consistent set of shared values and beliefs
(d) The organization is resistant to change

94. The "artifacts" of organizational culture refer to
(a) The tangible elements such as office layout, dress code, and company symbols
(b) The hidden values and beliefs of employees
(c) Strict adherence to government regulations
(d) The organization's financial assets

95. The "core values" in organizational culture are
(a) The official rules and policies of the organization
(b) The unwritten, underlying beliefs and norms that guide behavior
(c) Ignoring the perspectives of employees
(d) Government regulations imposed on the organization

96. Organizational climate is a concept related to
(a) The physical environment within the organization
(b) The atmosphere and the prevailing conditions in the workplace
(c) The structure of the organization
(d) The legal framework governing the organization

97. A positive organizational climate is typically characterized by
(a) Low employee morale and high turnover
(b) Employee dissatisfaction and conflicts
(c) Employee engagement, satisfaction, and a supportive work environment
(d) Ignoring the needs of employees

98. The concept of "psychological safety" in organizational climate relates to

(a) A work environment where employees are hesitant to speak up or share ideas
(b) Employee competition and rivalry
(c) A work environment where employees feel comfortable taking risks and expressing themselves
(d) The enforcement of strict government regulations in the workplace

99. Employee engagement in the organizational climate refers to
(a) Strict adherence to rules and regulations
(b) The level of commitment, motivation, and involvement of employees in their work
(c) Ignoring the influence of leadership
(d) The rate of employee turnover

100. A toxic organizational climate is characterized by
(a) Employee collaboration and support
(b) High levels of stress, hostility, and negativity
(c) A positive work atmosphere and effective communication
(d) Government regulations that protect employee well-being

101. When the organizational culture and climate are aligned, it typically leads to
(a) Employee dissatisfaction and conflicts
(b) Improved organizational performance and employee well-being
(c) Strict adherence to government regulations
(d) Ignoring the values and beliefs of the organization

102. The concept of "cultural congruence" in organizations relates to
(a) The existence of diverse cultures within the organization
(b) The alignment between the organizational culture and the climate
(c) A rigid, unchanging culture
(d) The influence of government regulations on culture

103. In a culture-climate misalignment, what might occur if the culture emphasizes teamwork and collaboration while the climate is characterized by competition and individualism?
(a) Enhanced employee engagement and satisfaction
(b) A harmonious work environment
(c) Conflicts, stress, and reduced performance
(d) Ignoring government regulations

104. The role of leadership in aligning culture and climate is to
(a) Promote competition among employees
(b) Ignore the values and beliefs of the organization
(c) Model and reinforce the desired culture and climate
(d) Enforce strict government regulations

105. The "values-practices gap" in organizational culture and climate alignment refers to
(a) The absence of any values or practices in the organization
(b) A misalignment between the stated values and actual practices within the organization
(c) The influence of government regulations on values and practices
(d) Ignoring the perspectives of employees

106. When an organization seeks to change its culture, it often involves
(a) Maintaining the status quo and resisting change
(b) Fostering openness and experimentation
(c) Strict adherence to government regulations
(d) Ignoring the influence of leadership

107. The process of "cultural integration" in organizational change refers to
(a) Maintaining separate, isolated cultures within the organization
(b) Merging diverse cultures into a single, cohesive culture
(c) The enforcement of government regulations
(d) Ignoring the influence of employees

108. A common reason for cultural change in organizations is to
(a) Reinforce the existing culture
(b) Enhance employee well-being and satisfaction
(c) Align the culture with evolving business goals or challenges
(d) Strictly adhere to government regulations

109. The "cultural artifact" in organizational change refers to
(a) Tangible elements like office layout and symbols that represent the new culture

(b) Unwritten beliefs and norms that are unchanged during the change process
(c) Ignoring the perspectives of employees
(d) The government regulations imposed during change

110. "Change agents" in cultural change are typically individuals responsible for
(a) Maintaining the status quo
(b) Enforcing government regulations
(c) Guiding and facilitating the cultural change process
(d) Ignoring the needs and concerns of employees

111. Workforce diversity refers to
(a) A homogenous group of employees with similar backgrounds
(b) The inclusion of individuals from different backgrounds and demographics in the workplace
(c) Strict adherence to government regulations
(d) Ignoring the influence of leadership in the workplace

112. The benefits of workforce diversity include
(a) Decreased creativity and innovation
(b) Enhanced problem-solving and creativity
(c) A reduction in employee turnover
(d) Ignoring the needs and perspectives of employees

113. Inclusion in the context of workforce diversity means
(a) Isolating employees from different backgrounds
(b) Ensuring that all employees have an equal opportunity to contribute and succeed
(c) Strict adherence to government regulations
(d) Suppressing diverse perspectives and experiences

114. Diversity dimensions may include
(a) A single demographic factor such as age or gender
(b) Multiple factors such as race, ethnicity, gender, and age
(c) Strict adherence to corporate policies
(d) Ignoring the influence of leadership

115. A "glass ceiling" in workforce diversity represents
(a) Transparent office architecture
(b) Invisible barriers that limit the advancement of underrepresented groups
(c) The enforcement of government regulations
(d) Ignoring the importance of leadership

116. Cross-cultural organizational behavior focuses on
(a) Studying the behavior of a single cultural group
(b) Understanding how culture influences behavior in a global context
(c) Adhering to a universal set of organizational principles
(d) Ignoring the influence of leadership

117. Cultural intelligence (CQ) in cross-cultural organizational behavior refers to
(a) The knowledge of specific cultural facts and data
(b) The ability to understand and adapt to different cultural contexts
(c) Strict adherence to government regulations
(d) Suppressing one's own cultural identity

118. The concept of "cultural dimensions" in cross-cultural organizational behavior, as proposed by Geert Hofstede, includes dimensions such as
(a) High and low context communication
(b) Power distance, individualism-collectivism, and uncertainty avoidance
(c) The enforcement of government regulations
(d) Ignoring the perspectives of employees

119. In a high power distance culture, there is typically
(a) A strong emphasis on equality and individualism
(b) A hierarchical structure with significant power differentials
(c) Little emphasis on cultural diversity
(d) An absence of government regulations

120. "Individualism" in cultural dimensions refers to
(a) A focus on group harmony and collectivism
(b) Emphasis on individual rights and autonomy
(c) The strict enforcement of group norms
(d) Ignoring the impact of leadership

121. The concept of "collectivism" is characterized by
(a) A focus on individual success and achievement
(b) A strong emphasis on group cohesion and shared goals
(c) Strict adherence to government regulations
(d) Ignoring cultural diversity

122. In a culture with high uncertainty avoidance, there is typically
(a) A tolerance for ambiguity and risk
(b) A strong desire for rules and structure
(c) A focus on cultural assimilation
(d) Ignoring the role of leadership

123. "Masculinity" in cultural dimensions is often associated with
(a) A focus on feminine values such as nurturing and empathy
(b) A focus on traditionally masculine values such as competition and assertiveness
(c) Strict adherence to government regulations
(d) Ignoring the influence of leadership

124. In a "feminine" culture, there may be an emphasis on values such as
(a) Competitive achievement and material success
(b) Nurturing, caring, and quality of life
(c) Compliance with cultural norms
(d) Suppressing individual aspirations

125. The concept of "long-term orientation" in cultural dimensions is related to
(a) A focus on short-term results and immediate gains
(b) A focus on values like persistence and thrift
(c) Strict adherence to government regulations
(d) Ignoring the values of different cultures

126. Managing diversity in organizations involves
(a) Creating a homogeneous workforce to avoid conflicts
(b) Fostering an inclusive and equitable workplace that values differences
(c) Strictly adhering to government regulations
(d) Suppressing diverse perspectives and experiences

127. The "cultural iceberg" concept in cross-cultural organizational behavior suggests that
(a) Most cultural differences are visible on the surface
(b) Only a small portion of cultural differences is visible, while the majority is hidden below the surface
(c) Cultural diversity is not a significant factor in organizations
(d) Ignoring the influence of leadership

128. In managing cross-cultural teams, it is important to
(a) Expect everyone to conform to a single, dominant culture
(b) Ignore cultural differences and focus solely on individual skills
(c) Foster communication, understanding, and cultural sensitivity
(d) Strictly adhere to government regulations

129. "Culture shock" refers to
(a) The excitement of experiencing new cultures
(b) The discomfort and disorientation experienced in a new cultural environment
(c) The enforcement of government regulations in foreign countries
(d) Ignoring the importance of leadership

130. Effective cross-cultural leadership often involves
(a) Enforcing a single, standardized leadership style across cultures
(b) Adapting leadership approaches to the cultural context
(c) Strict adherence to government regulations
(d) Suppressing the influence of cultural factors

131. Emotions are best defined as
(a) Rational thought processes
(b) Chemical reactions in the brain
(c) Complex psychological responses to stimuli
(d) Strict adherence to government regulations

132. Which of the following is NOT one of the basic emotions proposed by Paul Ekman?
(a) Joy (b) Sadness
(c) Envy (d) Anger

133. Emotional intelligence (EI) refers to
   (a) The ability to control and suppress emotions
   (b) The ability to recognize, understand, and manage one's own emotions and the emotions of others
   (c) Strict adherence to organizational policies
   (d) Ignoring the influence of leadership
134. The "emotional cycle" describes
   (a) The sequential occurrence of emotions in a specific order
   (b) Emotional patterns that repeat over time
   (c) The influence of government regulations on emotions
   (d) Suppressing one's emotions entirely
135. Emotional contagion refers to
   (a) The spread of infectious diseases caused by emotions
   (b) The phenomenon where one person's emotions can affect the emotions of others
   (c) Strict adherence to societal norms
   (d) Ignoring the perspectives of colleagues
136. Stress is best defined as
   (a) A state of complete relaxation
   (b) The body's response to a threat or demand, whether real or perceived
   (c) A heightened state of happiness
   (d) The enforcement of government regulations
137. The "fight-or-flight" response in stress is characterized by
   (a) A calm and rational assessment of the situation
   (b) Physiological changes that prepare the body to confront or flee from a threat
   (c) The suppression of all emotions
   (d) Ignoring the influence of leadership
138. Distress is a type of stress that is
   (a) Positive and beneficial
   (b) Harmful and negative
   (c) Strict adherence to government regulations
   (d) Ignoring one's own needs
139. Coping strategies for stress management may include
   (a) Ignoring the stressor and hoping it will go away
   (b) Seeking social support, problem-solving, and relaxation techniques
   (c) Strict adherence to personal preferences
   (d) Suppressing all emotions and thoughts
140. The term "burnout" in stress management refers to
   (a) The excessive use of vacation days
   (b) A state of emotional, mental, and physical exhaustion due to chronic stress
   (c) Strict adherence to government regulations
   (d) Ignoring the perspectives and needs of others
141. Mindfulness meditation is a stress management technique that involves
   (a) Ignoring the present moment
   (b) Focusing on the past and future
   (c) Paying attention to the present moment without judgment
   (d) Strict adherence to government regulations
142. Cognitive-behavioral therapy (CBT) is an approach that aims to
   (a) Eliminate all emotions and thoughts
   (b) Identify and change negative thought patterns and behaviors
   (c) Strictly enforce personal beliefs and values
   (d) Suppress the influence of emotions
143. Progressive muscle relaxation is a technique for stress management that involves
   (a) Exercising vigorously to release stress
   (b) Tensing and relaxing different muscle groups to reduce physical tension
   (c) Ignoring the physical manifestations of stress
   (d) Strict adherence to government regulations
144. Emotional self-regulation techniques aim to
   (a) Eliminate all emotions and thoughts
   (b) Recognize, understand, and manage one's own emotions
   (c) Suppress emotions and thoughts completely
   (d) Ignore the needs and perspectives of others
145. "Resilience" in the context of emotional and stress management refers to
   (a) The ability to avoid all stressful situations
   (b) The ability to bounce back and adapt to adversity

(c) Strict adherence to government regulations
(d) Ignoring the influence of leadership

146. The term "job burnout" is often associated with
(a) A high level of job satisfaction
(b) A state of chronic physical and emotional exhaustion
(c) Strict adherence to job descriptions
(d) Ignoring the perspectives and needs of colleagues

147. "Role overload" in the workplace refers to
(a) A lack of job responsibilities and tasks
(b) An excessive amount of job tasks and responsibilities
(c) Strict adherence to government regulations
(d) Ignoring one's role and responsibilities

148. "Work-life balance" is the concept of
(a) Separating work and personal life entirely
(b) Achieving equilibrium between the demands of work and personal life
(c) Strict adherence to corporate policies
(d) Suppressing all emotions in both work and personal life

149. The "psychological contract" in the workplace is often related to
(a) Legal contracts between employees and employers
(b) The unwritten expectations and obligations between employees and employers
(c) Strict adherence to government regulations
(d) Ignoring the values and needs of employees

150. Employee assistance programs (EAPs) in the workplace typically offer support for
(a) Career advancement and promotions
(b) Employee health and well-being, including stress management and counseling
(c) Strict adherence to organizational policies
(d) Ignoring the influence of leadership

151. Organizational justice refers to the perception of fairness in
(a) Employee compensation
(b) Organizational structure
(c) Organizational policies and procedures
(d) Strict adherence to government regulations

152. Distributive justice in organizations focuses on the fairness of
(a) Employee promotions and career development
(b) Employee-manager relationships
(c) Allocation of rewards and resources
(d) Ignoring employee needs

153. Procedural justice involves
(a) The distribution of rewards and punishments
(b) The fairness of decision-making processes
(c) Strict adherence to government regulations
(d) Ignoring the influence of leadership

154. Interactional justice is concerned with
(a) Employee interactions with customers
(b) Interactions among employees in the workplace
(c) The quality of interpersonal treatment in the organization
(d) Suppressing employee complaints

155. Retaliation against employees who raise concerns about organizational injustice is an example of
(a) Distributive justice
(b) Procedural justice
(c) Injustice
(d) Whistleblowing

156. Whistleblowing is the act of
(a) Participating in workplace conflicts
(b) Reporting unethical or illegal activities within an organization
(c) Strict adherence to government regulations
(d) Ignoring the perspectives of colleagues

157. The Whistleblower Protection Act in the United States is aimed at
(a) Protecting organizations from whistleblowers
(b) Protecting employees who report violations of the law by their employers
(c) Strictly enforcing corporate policies
(d) Suppressing employee concerns

158. Internal whistleblowing involves reporting concerns to
(a) Government authorities
(b) The media
(c) An organization's internal channels, such as a supervisor or ethics hotline
(d) Ignoring the influence of leadership

159. External whistleblowing typically means reporting concerns to
(a) The organization's legal department
(b) Government agencies or regulatory bodies
(c) Internal departments
(d) Strict adherence to corporate policies

160. The "motive" for whistleblowing can vary and may include
(a) A desire for financial rewards
(b) A genuine concern for ethics and compliance
(c) Strict adherence to government regulations
(d) Ignoring the values and needs of colleagues

161. The "code of ethics" in an organization typically outlines
(a) Legal regulations that employees must follow
(b) Ethical principles and guidelines for employee conduct
(c) Strict adherence to government regulations
(d) Suppressing any form of dissent

162. Whistleblower protection laws are intended to
(a) Punish whistleblowers for revealing confidential information
(b) Encourage and protect individuals who report wrongdoing within organizations
(c) Strictly enforce organizational rules
(d) Ignore the perspectives of employees

163. "Anonymous reporting" in the context of whistleblowing allows
(a) Complete transparency of the whistleblower's identity
(b) Whistleblowers to report concerns without revealing their identity
(c) Strict adherence to government regulations
(d) Suppressing the influence of leadership

164. The term "whistleblower retaliation" refers to
(a) Whistleblowers being rewarded for their actions
(b) Negative consequences faced by whistleblowers for their disclosures
(c) Strict adherence to corporate policies
(d) Ignoring the values and needs of colleagues

165. Ethical theories such as "utilitarianism" and "deontology" can be used to
(a) Ignore ethical dilemmas in the workplace
(b) Evaluate the moral implications of whistleblowing
(c) Strictly adhere to government regulations
(d) Suppress employee concerns

166. A "culture of silence" in an organization refers to
(a) An open and transparent organizational culture
(b) A culture where employees are encouraged to speak up about wrongdoing
(c) A culture where employees are discouraged from reporting concerns
(d) Ignoring government regulations

167. The "public interest disclosure" in whistleblowing involves reporting concerns that
(a) Benefit the organization's leadership
(b) Are in the best interest of the public or society as a whole
(c) Strictly adhere to organizational policies
(d) Suppressing the influence of employees

168. "Whistleblowing hotlines" are typically established by organizations to
(a) Encourage employees to share personal grievances
(b) Provide a confidential and anonymous channel for reporting concerns
(c) Strictly enforce government regulations
(d) Ignore the perspectives and needs of colleagues

169. A "whistleblower ombudsman" may be appointed within an organization to
(a) Promote employee dissent and confrontations
(b) Support and guide whistleblowers through the reporting process
(c) Strict adherence to corporate policies
(d) Suppress employee concerns

170. In fostering a culture that supports whistleblowing, organizations often emphasize
(a) Transparency, accountability, and protection for whistleblowers
(b) Strict adherence to government regulations
(c) Suppressing any form of dissent

(d) Ignoring the values and needs of colleagues

171. Human Resource Management (HRM) is best defined as
(a) The process of recruiting and hiring employees
(b) The management of an organization's workforce and personnel
(c) Strict adherence to government regulations
(d) Ignoring the influence of leadership in the workplace

172. HRM encompasses activities related to
(a) Inventory management and supply chain operations
(b) Managing the organization's financial resources
(c) Managing people within an organization
(d) Suppressing employee needs and perspectives

173. The primary goal of HRM is to
(a) Achieve high profitability
(b) Enhance employee well-being and satisfaction
(c) Strictly enforce corporate policies
(d) Ignore the values and needs of employees

174. Human Resource Planning (HRP) involves
(a) Monitoring employees' daily tasks
(b) Anticipating and planning for future staffing needs
(c) Adhering to government regulations
(d) Suppressing employee performance

175. Which of the following HRM functions deals with performance evaluations, feedback, and career development?
(a) Recruitment
(b) Compensation and Benefits
(c) Training and Development
(d) Performance Management

176. The "soft" approach to HRM emphasizes
(a) A strict adherence to rules and regulations
(b) The human side of employees and their well-being
(c) Ignoring the perspectives of employees
(d) Suppressing employee creativity

177. The "hard" approach to HRM focuses on
(a) Employee development and job satisfaction
(b) Maximizing employee potential and contribution
(c) Strict enforcement of government regulations
(d) Achieving short-term financial objectives

178. The "contingency perspective" in HRM suggests that
(a) One HRM approach fits all organizations
(b) HRM practices should be tailored to the unique needs and context of each organization
(c) Ignoring the influence of leadership
(d) Suppressing employee concerns

179. The "resource-based view" of HRM argues that
(a) Human resources are easily replaceable and not a source of competitive advantage
(b) Human resources can be a source of sustainable competitive advantage
(c) Strict adherence to government regulations
(d) Ignoring the values and beliefs of employees

180. The "stakeholder perspective" in HRM considers the interests of
(a) Only the organization's shareholders
(b) All parties involved, including employees, customers, and the community
(c) The enforcement of corporate policies
(d) Suppressing employee opinions

181. Labor unions can influence HRM through activities related to
(a) Employee performance evaluations
(b) Collective bargaining and negotiations on behalf of employees
(c) Strict adherence to government regulations
(d) Ignoring the influence of leadership

182. Government regulations impact HRM through laws related to
(a) Employee salaries and bonuses
(b) Equal employment opportunity, minimum wage, and workplace safety
(c) Adhering to corporate policies
(d) Suppressing employee concerns

183. Technological advances influence HRM by
(a) Reducing the need for human resources in the workplace
(b) Changing how HRM tasks are performed, such as using HR software and data analytics

(c) Strict adherence to corporate policies
(d) Ignoring the values and needs of employees

184. The globalization of business impacts HRM by
(a) Isolating organizations from international markets and employees
(b) Increasing the diversity of the workforce and requiring cross-cultural skills
(c) Suppressing employee contributions
(d) Strict enforcement of government regulations

185. Workplace diversity and inclusion initiatives in HRM focus on
(a) Excluding underrepresented groups from the workforce
(b) Fostering an inclusive and diverse work environment
(c) Strict adherence to government regulations
(d) Ignoring employee needs and perspectives

186. "Remote work" or "telecommuting" refers to
(a) Working on a remote island far from the office
(b) The practice of employees working from locations outside the traditional office
(c) Strict enforcement of office attendance
(d) Suppressing the influence of remote employees

187. "Agile HR" in recent HRM trends relates to
(a) The slow and rigid HR practices
(b) A flexible, responsive approach to HR that aligns with business needs
(c) Ignoring the values and needs of employees
(d) Strict adherence to government regulations

188. The use of "artificial intelligence (AI)" in HRM includes
(a) Replacing HR managers with AI robots
(b) Using AI to streamline HR tasks like resume screening and chatbots for employee support
(c) Suppressing employee creativity
(d) Strictly enforcing corporate policies

189. "Employee wellness programs" in recent HRM trends focus on
(a) Ignoring employee health and well-being
(b) Promoting the physical and mental health of employees
(c) Strict adherence to government regulations
(d) Suppressing employee morale

190. "Diversity, Equity, and Inclusion (DEI)" initiatives in HRM aim to
(a) Maintain a homogenous workforce
(b) Create an inclusive and equitable workplace that values differences
(c) Strictly enforce corporate policies
(d) Ignore the influence of leadership

191. "Sustainable HRM" involves considering the environmental and social impacts of HR practices, such as
(a) Maximizing resource consumption
(b) Promoting diversity and inclusion
(c) Strict adherence to government regulations
(d) Suppressing environmental concerns

192. The "triple bottom line" in sustainable HRM represents a focus on
(a) Maximizing profits and minimizing expenses
(b) Evaluating performance in terms of economic, environmental, and social outcomes
(c) Ignoring the perspectives of employees
(d) Strict enforcement of corporate policies

193. "Green HRM" practices in sustainable HRM may include efforts to
(a) Increase energy consumption
(b) Minimize environmental impact and promote sustainability
(c) Suppress employee opinions
(d) Strictly enforce government regulations

194. "Corporate social responsibility (CSR)" in HRM relates to
(a) Ignoring ethical and social obligations
(b) A commitment to conducting business ethically and contributing positively to society
(c) Strict adherence to government regulations
(d) Suppressing employee well-being

195. "Ethical sourcing" in sustainable HRM refers to
(a) Acquiring unethical and unsustainable resources
(b) Procuring products and services from suppliers that meet ethical and sustainability criteria

(c) Strict enforcement of corporate policies
(d) Ignoring the values and needs of colleagues

196. Human Resource Planning (HRP) involves
(a) Immediate hiring of employees to fill gaps
(b) Anticipating and planning for future staffing needs
(c) Strict adherence to government regulations
(d) Ignoring the influence of leadership

197. The primary goal of HRP is to
(a) Maximize short-term profits
(b) Ensure a diverse workforce
(c) Forecast and meet future HR needs
(d) Suppress employee performance

198. Demand forecasting in HRP refers to
(a) Predicting the demand for HR services based on historical data
(b) Estimating future staffing needs based on organizational goals and objectives
(c) Strictly enforcing corporate policies
(d) Ignoring employee needs and perspectives

199. Supply forecasting in HRP involves
(a) Predicting the number of candidates available in the job market
(b) Determining the exact number of employees required for each position
(c) Ignoring government regulations
(d) Suppressing employee morale

200. HR Planning typically takes into account factors like
(a) Government regulations and legal compliance
(b) Organizational values and culture
(c) Strict adherence to industry standards
(d) Ignoring the perspectives of employees

201. Recruitment is the process of
(a) Training new employees
(b) Identifying and attracting potential candidates to fill job vacancies
(c) Strict adherence to government regulations
(d) Suppressing employee creativity

202. The "job description" in the recruitment process typically outlines
(a) The qualities and qualifications of an ideal candidate
(b) The organization's corporate policies
(c) The enforcement of workplace regulations
(d) Ignoring employee expectations

203. In the selection process, "interviews" are used to
(a) Socialize new employees
(b) Assess a candidate's qualifications, skills, and suitability for a position
(c) Strictly enforce government regulations
(d) Suppress the influence of leadership

204. "Assessment centers" in selection may involve
(a) Physical fitness evaluations
(b) Simulated job-related exercises and assessments
(c) Ignoring industry standards
(d) Strict adherence to company guidelines

205. Reference checks in the selection process aim to
(a) Verify a candidate's education and experience
(b) Obtain personal information about candidates
(c) Strict adherence to industry standards
(d) Suppress employee diversity

206. Employee induction, or orientation, is typically conducted to
(a) Select the most qualified candidates
(b) Welcome and familiarize new employees with the organization
(c) Enforce government regulations
(d) Ignore the influence of leadership

207. During the induction process, new employees may be introduced to
(a) Organizational culture, values, and policies
(b) Legal requirements they need to ignore
(c) Strictly adhere to industry norms
(d) Suppress employee concerns

208. The primary goal of employee induction is to
(a) Make employees feel overwhelmed
(b) Ensure new employees feel comfortable, informed, and motivated
(c) Strictly enforce company policies
(d) Ignore the perspectives of colleagues

209. A well-structured induction program can help with
(a) Maximizing employee turnover
(b) Reducing employee engagement
(c) Improving employee retention and productivity
(d) Suppressing employee performance

210. "Buddy systems" or mentorship programs in induction involve
(a) Pairing new employees with experienced mentors for guidance
(b) Isolating new employees from existing colleagues
(c) Strict adherence to government regulations
(d) Ignoring the values and needs of employees

211. Training programs typically aim to
(a) Suppress employee skills and knowledge
(b) Enhance employee skills, knowledge, and job performance
(c) Strictly adhere to industry standards
(d) Ignore government regulations

212. "On-the-job training" (OJT) involves
(a) Learning through off-site workshops and courses
(b) Acquiring skills and knowledge while performing actual job tasks
(c) Ignoring industry norms
(d) Strictly enforcing company policies

213. "Needs assessment" in training and development is about
(a) Meeting the needs of the organization, not the employees
(b) Identifying the skills and knowledge gaps of employees
(c) Strict adherence to government regulations
(d) Suppressing employee creativity

214. Development programs typically focus on
(a) Improving existing job-related skills
(b) Preparing employees for future responsibilities and career advancement
(c) Strict adherence to corporate policies
(d) Ignoring the influence of leadership

215. "E-learning" or online training platforms are used to
(a) Replace in-person training entirely
(b) Supplement training options and provide flexibility
(c) Strictly enforce government regulations
(d) Suppress employee morale

216. Job analysis is the process of
(a) Determining employee training needs
(b) Identifying and documenting job-related information
(c) Strictly adhering to government regulations
(d) Suppressing employee performance

217. The primary goal of job analysis is to
(a) Maximize employee turnover
(b) Establish job classifications and descriptions
(c) Ignore the influence of leadership
(d) Ensure job security for all employees

218. Job analysis typically involves collecting data about
(a) Employee job satisfaction
(b) Job-related duties, responsibilities, and qualifications
(c) Adhering to company policies
(d) Ignoring employee needs and perspectives

219. "Job description" and "job specification" are two key outputs of job analysis. The job description primarily focuses on
(a) Employee qualifications and skills
(b) A summary of job duties and responsibilities
(c) Strict adherence to government regulations
(d) Suppressing employee morale

220. Which method of job analysis involves observing and recording employee behavior and actions?
(a) Questionnaires (b) Interviews
(c) Direct observation
(d) Job evaluation

221. Job evaluation is the process of
(a) Evaluating employee performance
(b) Assessing the monetary value of a job within an organization
(c) Strictly enforcing company policies
(d) Ignoring the influence of leadership

222. The "point-factor" method in job evaluation involves
(a) Assigning numerical values to job-related factors and characteristics
(b) Calculating employee performance ratings
(c) Strict adherence to government regulations
(d) Suppressing employee creativity

223. "Ranking" and "grading" are two common approaches to job evaluation. "Ranking" involves

(a) Assigning jobs to salary grades based on a predetermined hierarchy
(b) Ordering jobs from highest to lowest in terms of value or difficulty
(c) Ignoring industry standards
(d) Strictly enforcing corporate policies

224. "Job classification" is a job evaluation method that
(a) Determines pay based on employee qualifications
(b) Groups jobs into predefined classes or categories with similar pay scales
(c) Strict adherence to industry norms
(d) Suppressing employee opinions

225. The goal of job evaluation is to
(a) Ensure pay equity among all employees
(b) Maximize the organization's profits
(c) Strictly adhere to government regulations
(d) Ignore the perspectives of employees

226. Compensation management involves designing and administering
(a) Employee training programs
(b) The organization's pay and benefits structure
(c) Adherence to industry standards
(d) Suppressing employee needs and perspectives

227. The "total rewards" approach to compensation management includes
(a) Providing monetary rewards only
(b) Offering a comprehensive package of monetary and non-monetary rewards
(c) Strict adherence to government regulations
(d) Ignoring the influence of leadership

228. "Salary surveys" in compensation management aim to
(a) Reduce employee salaries
(b) Compare the organization's pay rates to those of other employers
(c) Suppress employee concerns
(d) Strictly enforce corporate policies

229. "Variable pay" or "incentive pay" is often used to
(a) Guarantee a fixed income for all employees
(b) Reward employees for exceptional performance or meeting specific goals
(c) Strict adherence to industry norms
(d) Ignore the values and needs of employees

230. "Benchmarking" in compensation management involves
(a) Comparing the organization's performance to industry standards
(b) Determining the lowest possible pay for employees
(c) Adhering to government regulations
(d) Suppressing employee performance

231. Base salary is primarily determined by
(a) Employee job satisfaction
(b) Employee qualifications, experience, and market rates
(c) Strict adherence to company policies
(d) Ignoring the influence of leadership

232. "Bonuses" and "incentives" are typically tied to
(a) Employee attendance and punctuality
(b) Employee performance, productivity, or achievement of specific goals
(c) Strictly enforcing government regulations
(d) Suppressing employee creativity

233. "Benefits" in compensation management can include items like
(a) Employee discounts at local restaurants
(b) Health insurance, retirement plans, and paid time off
(c) Ignoring industry standards
(d) Strict adherence to corporate policies

234. "Stock options" are often offered to
(a) New employees without experience
(b) Employees to purchase company stock at a specified price
(c) Suppressing employee opinions
(d) Strictly enforcing government regulations

235. "Perquisites" or "perks" are
(a) Additional responsibilities assigned to employees
(b) Extra benefits or privileges provided to certain employees, such as company cars or club memberships
(c) Adhering to government regulations
(d) Ignoring the values and needs of colleagues

ANSWER KEY

1. (c)	**2.** (c)	**3.** (a)	**4.** (c)	**5.** (c)	**6.** (c)	**7.** (c)	**8.** (c)	**9.** (c)	**10.** (c)
11. (b)	**12.** (a)	**13.** (b)	**14.** (c)	**15.** (c)	**16.** (c)	**17.** (c)	**18.** (b)	**19.** (b)	**20.** (b)
21. (c)	**22.** (b)	**23.** (c)	**24.** (c)	**25.** (c)	**26.** (b)	**27.** (c)	**28.** (a)	**29.** (b)	**30.** (c)
31. (b)	**32.** (b)	**33.** (b)	**34.** (a)	**35.** (b)	**36.** (c)	**37.** (a)	**38.** (c)	**39.** (b)	**40.** (c)
41. (a)	**42.** (c)	**43.** (c)	**44.** (b)	**45.** (b)	**46.** (b)	**47.** (b)	**48.** (a)	**49.** (a)	**50.** (a)
51. (c)	**52.** (d)	**53.** (a)	**54.** (a)	**55.** (b)	**56.** (c)	**57.** (c)	**58.** (c)	**59.** (d)	**60.** (c)
61. (b)	**62.** (b)	**63.** (c)	**64.** (c)	**65.** (b)	**66.** (b)	**67.** (a)	**68.** (b)	**69.** (c)	**70.** (b)
71. (b)	**72.** (c)	**73.** (b)	**74.** (b)	**75.** (c)	**76.** (c)	**77.** (a)	**78.** (a)	**79.** (b)	**80.** (b)
81. (b)	**82.** (b)	**83.** (b)	**84.** (b)	**85.** (b)	**86.** (c)	**87.** (b)	**88.** (b)	**89.** (b)	**90.** (b)
91. (c)	**92.** (c)	**93.** (c)	**94.** (a)	**95.** (b)	**96.** (b)	**97.** (c)	**98.** (c)	**99.** (b)	**100.** (b)
101. (b)	**102.** (b)	**103.** (c)	**104.** (c)	**105.** (b)	**106.** (b)	**107.** (b)	**108.** (c)	**109.** (a)	**110.** (c)
111. (b)	**112.** (b)	**113.** (b)	**114.** (b)	**115.** (b)	**116.** (b)	**117.** (b)	**118.** (b)	**119.** (b)	**120.** (b)
121. (b)	**122.** (b)	**123.** (b)	**124.** (b)	**125.** (b)	**126.** (b)	**127.** (b)	**128.** (c)	**129.** (b)	**130.** (b)
131. (c)	**132.** (c)	**133.** (b)	**134.** (a)	**135.** (b)	**136.** (b)	**137.** (b)	**138.** (b)	**139.** (b)	**140.** (b)
141. (c)	**142.** (b)	**143.** (b)	**144.** (b)	**145.** (b)	**146.** (b)	**147.** (b)	**148.** (b)	**149.** (b)	**150.** (b)
151. (c)	**152.** (c)	**153.** (b)	**154.** (c)	**155.** (c)	**156.** (b)	**157.** (b)	**158.** (c)	**159.** (b)	**160.** (b)
161. (b)	**162.** (b)	**163.** (b)	**164.** (b)	**165.** (b)	**166.** (c)	**167.** (b)	**168.** (b)	**169.** (b)	**170.** (a)
171. (b)	**172.** (c)	**173.** (b)	**174.** (b)	**175.** (d)	**176.** (b)	**177.** (d)	**178.** (b)	**179.** (b)	**180.** (b)
181. (b)	**182.** (b)	**183.** (b)	**184.** (b)	**185.** (b)	**186.** (b)	**187.** (b)	**188.** (b)	**189.** (b)	**190.** (b)
191. (b)	**192.** (b)	**193.** (b)	**194.** (b)	**195.** (b)	**196.** (b)	**197.** (c)	**198.** (b)	**199.** (a)	**200.** (b)
201. (b)	**202.** (a)	**203.** (b)	**204.** (b)	**205.** (a)	**206.** (b)	**207.** (a)	**208.** (b)	**209.** (c)	**210.** (a)
211. (b)	**212.** (b)	**213.** (b)	**214.** (b)	**215.** (b)	**216.** (b)	**217.** (b)	**218.** (b)	**219.** (b)	**220.** (c)
221. (b)	**222.** (a)	**223.** (b)	**224.** (b)	**225.** (a)	**226.** (b)	**227.** (b)	**228.** (b)	**229.** (b)	**230.** (a)
231. (b)	**232.** (b)	**233.** (b)	**234.** (b)	**235.** (b)					

UNIT 3

SYLLABUS

- Strategic Role of Human Resource Management
- Competency Mapping & Balanced Scoreboard
- Career Planning and Development
- Performance Management and Appraisal
- Organization Development, Change & OD Interventions
- Talent Management & Skill Development
- Employee Engagement & Work Life Balance
- Industrial Relations: Disputes & Grievance Management, Labour Welfare and Social Security
- Trade Union & Collective Bargaining
- International Human Resource Management – HR Challenge of International Business
- Green HRM

THE STRATEGIC ROLES OF HUMAN RESOURCE MANAGEMENT

An organization cannot form a good team of working professionals without the aid of a sound Human Resource Management. The key functions of Human Resource Management team comprised of recruiting the right people, providing them the right training, administering performance appraisal, motivating workers and the workplace communication plus the workplace safety and lots more.

Recruitment and Training are a few of the primary responsibilities of the human resource team. Human Resource managers create plans and strategies for hiring the appropriate individuals. They formulate the criteria that are most suited for a certain job description. Their other tasks connected to recruitment involve creating employee obligations as well as the scope of tasks assigned to her/him.

Founded on these two factors, the contract of a worker with the firm is prepared. When necessary, they also offer training to the workers in accordance to the requirements of the company or organization.

Therefore, the staff members obtain the chance to sharpen their present skills or enhance specialized skills which will eventually aid them to take up some other roles.

- Performance Appraisals. Human Resource Management motivates the individuals working within the organization to function in accordance to their potential and provides them recommendations which can aid them to bring development in it.

- **Sustaining work atmosphere.** This is a valuable aspect of Human resource Management since the performance of an individual within an organization is greatly directed by the work culture or work atmosphere which dominates at the workplace.
- **Handling disputes.** In an organization, there are many issues in which conflicts may emerge between the employers and the employees. You can say that disputes are nearly inevitable.
- **Developing Public relations.** The responsibility of building good public relations depends largely on Human Resource Management. They administer seminars, different official gatherings and business meetings on behalf of the firm so to establish relationships with other sectors of business. At times, the Human Resource department plays a vital role in preparing the marketing and business plans for the organization as well.

Any firm or organization without a suitable setup for Human Resource Management is constrained to suffer from serious complications while handling its regular activities. Due to this, at present, firms must place a lot of effort and exert more energy in establishing an effective and strong Human Resource Management.

Having an internal Human Resource function is deemed necessary. An in-house human resources expert or human resources staff can greatly aid maximize the understanding of how vital human capital is to the firm's core. For mini-sized businesses, specifically, human capital is crucial due to the fact that there are several smaller companies that have workers who execute cross-functional duties. With a smaller workforce, if just one individual leaves, it leaves the firm with a potential; threat and big gap to fill to the firm's profitability.

- **Unwavering principles.** Human resources guarantee the workforce grasps the firm's business principles and philosophy. From the point of view of a small enterprise, establishing a close-knit work environment is quite fundamental. The very first opportunity which human resources needs to attain is smart hiring decisions that determine the desirable professional attributes and on-boarding programs as well as the orientation.
- **Conflict Resolution.** Needless to say, workplace issues are inevitable given the distinction of levels of experience, personalities, backgrounds, work styles and the like. A staff person or human resources manager who is trained to manage worker relations plays a vital role since he/she can determine and resolve the issue between two workers or a manager and worker and regain positive or a more pleasant working relationship.
- **Employee Satisfaction.** Human resources experts often times are charged with the accountability of identifying the level of worker satisfaction- usually an unclear measurement at best. With thoroughly established focus groups, worker surveys and an exit interview strategy, human resources can clearly identify what governs worker dissatisfaction and addresses those problems in order to encourage workers.
- **Budget Control.** Human resources hampers excessive spending by enhancing methods for cutting down management costs that composed of negotiating more excellent rates for benefits like health care coverage. In line with this, human resources guarantees realistic and cut-throat wage-setting relied on studying the employment salary and trends analysis relied on job functions as well as studying the labor market. Because small enterprises have budget restrictions, this type of human resources function is absolutely useful.
- **Cost Savings.** The expense to hire replacement or new employees, including ramp-up time and training can be extravagant for employers particularly for the small businesses. Through a well-formed recruitment and selection procedure, the human resources function can reduce costs with regards to training new workers, advertising job postings, enrolling new workers in benefits plans.
- **Training and Development.** Human resources administers needs evaluations for the firm's present workforce to identify the kind of skills training and worker development required for

enhancing qualifications and skills. Firms at the start or growth stages can gain from determining training needs for current staff. It is much less costly as compared to the cost to hire more qualified candidates and additional staff. Indeed, it is a strategy which also can minimize turnover and enhance worker retention.

- **Sustaining business.** By means of succession planning which human resources develop, the firm identifies workers with the requisite and promise capabilities to sooner or later transform into leadership roles with the firm. This is a crucial function since it can ensure the firm's success and stability.
- **Performance Management.** Human resources develop performance management programs. Without a human resources staff to formulate a plan which evaluates performance, workers can wind in tasks or jobs which are not suitable for their expertise and skills. In addition to this, workers whose performance falls below the employer's expectations may continue on the payroll, in that, making wasted money on low-performing workers.
- **Corporate Image.** Enterprises prefer to be regarded as the employer of choice. These refer to the firms which receive recognition for the manner they treat their workers; they are the firms for whom people wish to work. Being an employer of choice only means to say that human resources stabilizes recruiting the most qualified candidates, choosing the most deserving candidates and retaining the most skilled workers.

COMPETENCY MAPPING

Competency Mapping is a process to identify key competencies for an organization and/or a job and incorporating those competencies throughout the various processes (i.e. job evaluation, training, recruitment) of the organization. A competency is defined as a behavior (i.e. communication, leadership) rather than a skill or ability.

The steps involved in competency mapping are presented below:

1. Conduct a job analysis by asking incumbents to complete a position information questionnaire (PIQ). This can be provided for incumbents to complete, or used as a basis for conducting one-on-one interviews using the PIQ as a guide. The primary goal is to gather from incumbents what they feel are the key behaviors necessary to perform their respective jobs.
2. Using the results of the job analysis, a competency based job description is developed. It is developed after carefully analyzing the input from the represented group of incumbents and converting it to standard competencies.
3. With a competency based job description, mapping the competencies can be done. The competencies of the respective job description become factors for assessment on the performance evaluation. Using competencies will help to perform more objective evaluations based on displayed or not displayed behaviors.
4. Taking the competency mapping one step further, one can use the results of one's evaluation to identify in what competencies individuals need additional development or training. This will help in focusing on training needs required to achieve the goals of the position and company and help the employees develop toward the ultimate success of the organization.

BALANCED SCOREBOARD

The Balanced Scorecard concept is a management and measurement system which enables organizations to clarify their vision and strategy and translate them into action. The goal of the balanced scorecard is to tie business performance to organizational strategy by measuring results in four areas: financial performance, customer knowledge, internal business processes, and learning and growth.

Four perspectives of the Balanced Scorecard

The Balanced Scorecard method of Kaplan and Norton is a strategic approach, and performance management system, that enables organizations to transiate a company's vision and strategy into implementation, working from four perspectives:

1. Financial perspective.
2. Customer perspective.
3. Business process perspective.
4. Learning and growth perspective.

The balanced scorecard forces managers to look at the business from four important perspectives. It links performance measures by requiring firms to address four basic questions:

1. How do customers see us? - Customer perspective.
2. What must we excel at? - Internal perspective.
3. Can we continue to improve and create value? - Innovation & learning perspective.
4. How do we look to shareholders? - Financial perspective.

BENEFITS OF THE BALANCED SCORECARD

Kaplan and Norton cite the following benefits of the usage of the Balanced Scorecard:

- Focusing the whole organization on the few key things needed to create breakthrough performance.
- Helps to integrate various corporate programs. Such as: quality, re-engineering, and customer service initiatives.
- Breaking down strategic measures towards lower levels, so that unit managers, operators, and employees can see what's required at their level to achieve excellent overall performance.

CAREER PLANNING AND DEVELOPMENT

CAREER PLANNING

Meaning & Definitions of Career Planning

Career planning is an ongoing process through which an individual sets career goals and identifies the means to achieve them. The process by which individuals plan their life's work is referred to as career planning.

"Career planning is a process of systematically matching career goals and individual capabilities with opportunities for their fulfillment." ***(Schermerhorn: 2002)***

"Career Planning is a deliberate process of becoming aware of self, opportunities, constraints, choices, and consequences; identifying career-related goals; and "career pathing" or programming work, education, and related developmental experiences to provide the direction, timing, and sequence of steps to attain a specific career goal." ***(McMahon and Merman: 1987)***

Career Anchors

Career anchors denote the basic drives that create the urge to take up a certain type of a career. These drives are as follows:

- **Managerial Competence.** Person having this drive seeks managerial positions that provide opportunities for higher responsibility, decision making, control and influence over others.
- **Technical Competence.** People having this anchor seek to make career choices based on the technical or functional content of the work. It provide continuous learning and updating one's

expertise in a technical or specialised area such as quality control, engineering, accounting, advertising, public relations etc.

- Security. If one's career anchor is security than he is willing to do what is required to maintain job security (through compliance with organisational prescriptions), a decent income and a stable future.
- Creativity. This drive provides entrepreneurial and innovative opportunities to the people. People are driven by an overwhelming desire to do something new that is totally of their own making.
- Autonomy. These people seek a career that provides freedom of action and independence.
- Career planning facilitates the employees to develop not only their career goals but also the ways to achieve these goals.
- It helps individuals to remain competitive in the labour market by constantly upgrading competences as part of goal fulfillment efforts.
- It acts as the basis or standard for tracing the career progression achieved by an employee throughout his work life.
- It forms the basis for succession planning in the organisation. It helps the organisation in its preparation for the future by identifying and developing people for critical positions.
- Through career planning, an organisation can attract and retain its best people for a relatively longer period of time.
- Career planning is viewed as an effective technique by the organisation to limit the labour turnover and achieve better employee efficiency and commitment.
- It provides an opportunity for the organisation to assess the strengths and weaknesses and also the area of development of the employees for the purpose of *career* planning and development.
- It forms the basis for determining the training and development requirements of each employee in the organisation.

The main purpose of career planning is to integrate individuals' and organisational growth needs.

- It helps to develop individuals and groups, provides opportunities and challenges and strengthens work cultures.
- To increase managerial competence.
- To attract competent person and retain them in the organisation.
- To provide suitable promotional opportunities.
- To enable the employees to develop and make them ready to meet the future challenges.
- To increase the utilization of managerial reserves within an organisation.
- To correct employee placement.
- To reduce employee dissatisfaction and turnover.
- To improve motivation and morale.

Nature of Career Planning

The following are the salient features of career planning:

- A Process. Career planning is a process of developing human resources rather than an event.
- Upward movement. It involve upward movement in the organisational hierarchy, or special assignments, project work which require abilities to handle recurring problems, human relations issued and so on.

- **Mutuality of Interest.** The individual's interest is served as his needs and aspirations are met to a great extent and the organisation's interest is served as each of its human resources is provided an opportunity to develop and contribute to the organisational goals and objectives to the optimum of its ability and confidence.
- **Dynamic.** Career planning is dynamic in nature due to an ever changing environment.

Functions of Career Planning

The following are the functions performed by career planning:

(i) It helps in determining the career paths for different types of employees.

(ii) Create positions of self-development for employees in an organisation.

(iii) Provide such career planning information system which works as a database of career path, promotions and replacement.

(iv) To boost up morale of the employees and remove frustration from their minds.

(v) To develop such an internal environment in which employees can develop their talents and give them a fair chance to go up and contribute the organisation.

(vi) To establish such career paths on which employee can promote himself.

(vii) To enable employees to discover, develop and use their full potential for the organisation.

Career Planning Process

The possibility of conflict between the individual and organisation objectives calls for career planning efforts which can help to identify areas of conflict and initiate such actions as necessary to resolve the conflict. Career planning, thus, involves matching of rewards and incentives offered by the career path and career structure with hopes and aspirations of different categories of employees regarding their own concept of progression. A general approach to career planning would involve the following steps:

(i) **Analysis of the characteristics of the rewards and incentives** offered by the prevailing career system needs to be done and made known to employees. Many individuals may not be aware of their own career progression paths as such information may be confined to only a selected group of managers.

(ii) **Analysis of the characteristics of the hopes and aspirations** of different categories of employees including identification of their career anchors must be done through objective assessment. Most organisations assume the career aspirations of individual employees which need not be in tune with the reality. The individuals may not have a clear idea of their short and long-term career and life goals, and may not be aware of their aspirations and career anchors.

(iii) **Mechanisms for identifying congruence between individual career aspirations** and organisational career systems must be developed so as to enable the organisation to discuss cases of mismatch or incongruence. On the basis of above analyses, it will be necessary to compare and identify specific areas of match and mismatch for different category of employees.

(iv) **Alternative strategies for dealing with mismatch** will have to be formulated.

Some of the strategies adopted by several organisations include the following:

(a) **Changes in the career system** by creating new career paths, new incentives, new rewards, by providing challenges through job redesign opportunities for lateral movement and the like.

(b) **Change in the employees' hopes** and aspirations by creating new needs, new goals, new aspirations or by helping the employees to scale down goals and aspirations that are unrealistic or unattainable for one reason or the other.

(c) Seek new basis of integration, compromise or other forms of mutual change on the part of both employees and organisation through problem-solving, negotiations or other devices.

The Need for Carrier Planning

Organisations can hope to achieve high quality of work from their employees and foster positive attitudes and loyalty among workers through career planning. Career planning ensures that goals of individuals and organisations are in synergy and consequently tries to keep the motivation of managers high. This implies that once the individual becomes aware of his capabilities and opportunities within the organisation, he chooses to develop himself in a direction that improves his chances of being able to handle new responsibilities.

Organisational Career Planning

Following activities should be included:

1. **Human Resource Forecasting and Planning.** This helps in identifying the number of people to be hired. Second, the organisations will be able to coordinate their selection procedure with the overall strategic goals.
2. **Career information.** This should he shared with employees and includes promotional policy and career paths. Role directions and critical attributes could he made available to employees for identifying possible career paths and competency requirements.
3. **Career Counselling.** Senior executives should have periodic discussions with their subordinates and offer career counselling to them.
4. **Career Patching.** Organisations nowadays plan job sequences for their employees by which transfers and promotions are done more systematically.
5. **Skill Assessment Training.** Three types of analysis should be performed – organisational analysis, job analysis and job manpower requirement analysis. Organisational analysis and job analysis are the first steps in the training process.
6. **Succession Planning.** Here organisations assure that competent candidates are available in succession for critical positions. HR subsystems like promotions, terminations, transfers, retirements, etc. also make succession planning necessary.

Limitations of Career Planning

Though career planning helps an organisation in numerous ways, it has a few limitations that undermine the importance and relevance of career planning.

These are:

- **Time Factor.** Career planning is usually a long-term and time-consuming process. It is based on the logic of suffering short-term pain to get long-term gains. However, organisations may not be ready to spend a lot of time and resources on a process that would prove beneficial only in the long term.
- **Unsuitable for Large Workforce.** It may not be possible for organisations with a large workforce to develop individual careèr plans breach and every employee of the organisation. This is because the career plan process requires an in-depth analysis of each employee's strengths and weaknesses on a sustained basis.
- **Lack of Objectivity.** Only those organisations which believe in strict observance of objectivity in promotion and transfers can succeed in career planning. In contrast, favoritism and nepotism in promotions often make career planning an unsuccessful exercise.
- **External Interventions.** Government rules and regulations can also affect the Grieve planning options of an organisation.

- Lack of Knowledge and Awareness. Career planning by an employee is essentially a self-management process. It requires the employees to be aware of the basics of career planning and management activities. However, the employees at the lower levels of the organisational hierarchy may not be familiar with the career planning process.
- Lack of Flexibility. Many organisations treat career planning as a ritualistic, rigid exercise. They often fail to consider the uncertainties caused to the career planning activities by the changes in the situation. In fact, the absence of dynamic career planning programmes may limit the applicability of the career plans in uncertain and changing situations.

CAREER DEVELOPMENT

Career development is the process of improving an individual's abilities in anticipation of future opportunities for achieving career objectives. A formal approach taken by an organisation to help its people acquire the skills and experiences needed to perform current and future jobs is termed as career development. Company's policies especially policies regarding promotion, counselling the employees, opportunities to excel in future help employees to develop their career. Career development consists of skills, education and experiences as well as behavioural modification and refinement techniques that allow individuals to work better and add value.

Career development is an ongoing organised and formalised effort that recognises people as a vital organisational resource. It differs from training in that it has a wider focus, longer time frame, and broader scope. The goal of training is improvement in performance; the goal of development is enrichment and more capable workers.

Recently, career development has come to be seen as a means for meeting both organisational and employee needs, as opposed to solely meeting the needs of the organisation as it had done in the past. Now, organisations see career development as a way of preventing job burnout, providing career information to employees, improving the quality of work lives and meeting affirmative action goals. That is, career development must be seen as a key business strategy if an organisation wants to survive in an increasingly competitive and global business environment.

Meeting the Challenges of Effective Career Development

Creative decision making is a must in designing and implementing an effective development program. The three phases of development often blend together in a real life program. These three phases include the assessment phase, the direction phase, and the development phase.

A. **The Assessment Phase.** The assessment phase involves activities ranging from self-assessment to organisationally provided assessment. The goal of both of these types of assessment is to identify employees' strengths and weaknesses.

B. **The Direction Phase.** This involves determining the type of career that employees want and the steps they must take to make their career goals a reality. It involves:
   - Individual career counseling
   - Information services

C. **The Development Phase.** The development phase is taking actions to create and increase skills to prepare for future job opportunities and is meant to foster this growth and self-improvement. The methods are :
   1. *Mentoring & Coaching*. It has become increasingly clear over the years that employees who aspire to higher management levels in the organisation often need the assistance and advocacy of someone higher up in the organisation. When senior employee takes an active role in guiding another individual, we refer to this activity as mentoring and coaching.

This can occur at any level and can be most effective when the two individuals do not have any type of reporting relationship.

2. *Job Rotation.* Involves moving employees from one job to another for the purpose of providing them with broader experience.
3. *Tuition Assistance Programs.* To help individuals plan their careers, organisations try to provide additional information in order to have better choice of the career.

PERFORMANCE MANAGEMENT AND APPRAISAL

Performance appraisal is a process of evaluating an employee's performance for a job in terms of its requirements.

According to Mc Gregor, "*Formal Performance appraisal plans are designed to meet three needs,* one of the organisation and the other two of the individual, namely:

(i) They provide systematic judgements to back up salary increases, transfers, demotions or terminations.

(ii) They are means of telling a subordinate how he is doing and suggesting needed changes in his behavioural attitudes, skills or job knowledge. They let him know 'where he stands' with the boss.

(iii) They are used as a base for coaching and counselling the individual by the superior.

Definitions

Performance appraisal has been defined by different scholars in various ways. Some of the important definitions are as follows:

- **Heyel,** "It is the process of evaluating the performance and qualifications of the employees in terms of the requirements of the job for which he is employed, for purposes of administration including placement, selection for promotions, providing financial rewards and other actions which require differential treatment among the members of a group as distinguished from actions affecting all members equally."
- **Dale S. Beach,** "Performance appraisal is systematic evaluation of the individual with respect to his or her performance on the job and his or her potential for development".
- **Dale Yoder,** "Performance appraisal includes all formal procedures used to evaluated personalities and contributions and potentials of group members in a working organisation. It is a continuous process to secure information necessary for making correct and objective decisions on employees."
- **Randall S. Schuler,** "Performance appraisal is a formal, structured system of measuring

THE SEVEN CRITERIA FOR ASSESSING PERFORMANCE

1. **Quality.** The degree to which the process or result of carrying out an activity approaches perfection.
2. **Quantity.** The amount produced, expressed in monetary terms, number of units, or number of completed activity cycles.
3. **Timeliness.** The degree to which an activity or a result produced.
4. **Cost Effectiveness.** The degree to which the use of the organisation's resources (*e.g.*, human, monetary, technology, material) is maximised in the sense of getting the highest gain.
5. **Need for Supervision.** The degree to which a job performer can carry out a job function without supervisory assistance.
6. **Interpersonal Impact.** The degree to which a performer promotes feelings of self-esteem, goodwill and co-operation among co-workers and subordinates.
7. **Training.** Need for training for improving his skill's knowledge.

and evaluating an employee's job, related behaviour and outcomes to discover how and why the employee is presently perfuming on the job and how the employee can perform more effectively in the future so that the employee, organisation, and society all benefit."

Approaches to Performance Appraisal

There is great degree of variation in the approaches, design and use of performance appraisal system and also in the formats. Generally, now a days, there are three approaches used in making performance appraisal.

(a) **The Traditional Approach.** This approach is highly systematic and takes into account the measurement of employees characteristics and/or their contribution or both. In this system all employees are rated in the same manner utilising the same approach so that the rating of separate personnel can be compared.

(b) **The Causal Approach.** This is an unsystematic use and often haphazard appraisal system which was commonly used in the past, but now it has given a place to more formal method, the main basis being seniority or quantitative measures of quantity and quality of output for rank and file personnel.

(c) **The Behavioural or Modern Approach.** This approach is based upon mutual goal setting and appraisal of progress by both appraisor and appraise. This lays emphasis on behavioural values of fundamental trust in goodness, capability and responsibility of human beings.

Methods of Performance Appraisal

1. Traditional Methods

(a) **Straight Ranking Methods.** This is the oldest and simplest method of performance appraisal. This yields a ranking from best to worst of all individuals comprising the group. The rater simply picks out the individual he considers best, the one he thinks next best etc. and ranks them in order on the basis of work. The ranks assigned by rater are then averaged and then relative ranking of each individual in the group are assigned/determined.

(b) **Paired Comparison.** By this technique, each employee is compared with all the persons in pairs one at a time. With this technique, the judgement is easier and simpler than ordinary ranking method. The number of times each individual is compared with another is tallied on a piece of paper. These numbers yield the rank order of the entire group. For example, if there are five persons in a group, then A's performance is compared to B's and a decision is arrived at A, B to whose is the better performance. Then A is compared to C, D and E in that order. Next B is compared with all the others in the group individually. Since he has already been compared with A, he is only compared with C, D and E. Similar comparison is made with respect to all the individuals. Thus by this method, we arrive at ten decisions and only two are involved in each decision. The results of decisions and comparisons are tabulated and a rank is assigned to each individual.

(c) **Man to Man Comparison.** In this method, certain factors are selected for the purpose of analysis such as leadership, dependability, initiative etc. and a scale is designed by the rater for each factor awarded.

(d) **Grading Method.** Under this system, the rater considers certain features and marks them accordingly to the scale. Certain categories of worth are carefully established and defined. The selected features may be analytical ability, co-operativeness, dependability, self experience job knowledge, judgement, leadership and organising ability etc. These may be rated (i) outstanding (ii) very good, (iii) good/average (iv) fair, (v) poor or any other scale. The actual performance of an employee is then compared with these grade definitions and he is allotted the grade which best describes his performance.

(e) **Graphic or Linear Rating Scale.** Under this system a printed form, one for each employee to be rated is filled. There are various factors to be checked and rated as per the performance and ability and as felt by the supervisors. The factors are of two type i.e. (i) Employer characteristics such initiative, leadership, co-operativeness, dependability, attitude, enthusiasm, loyalty etc. and (ii) employee's contribution e.g. quality and quantity of work, the responsibilities assumed, specific goals achieved, regularity of attendance, leadership offered, attitudes towards superiors and associates versatility etc. These traits are evaluated on a continuous scale or sometime a discontinuous scale is also used, consisting of appropriate boxes or squares which are to be ticked off.

(f) **Forced Choice Description Method.** This rating form prepares a series of item or statements which usually describe the degree of proficiency. The rater then chooses among the member of each group in terms of how will be believes the statements describing the individual being rated on various arrangements of items employed.

(g) **Check List.** Under this system, the rater does not evaluate an employer's performance. He supplies report information about it and the final rating is done by the personnel department. A series of questions are presented concerning an employee to his behaviour. The rater then checks to indicate if the answer to a question about an employee is positive or negative. The value of each question may be valued/weighed equally or certain questions may be weighed heavily than others.

The following are some of the sample questions in the check list

Is the employee really interested in the task assigned?	Yes/No
Is he respected by his colleagues (Co-workers)	Yes/No
Does he give respect to his superiors?	Yes/No
Does he follow instructions properly?	Yes/No
Does he make mistakes frequently?	Yes/No.

(h) **Free Essay Method.** In this method, the supervisor makes a free form, open ended appraisal of an employer in his own words and puts down his impression about the employer. The following factors are taken into account by supervisor.

(i) Relation with fellow supervisor and personnel assigned to him.
(ii) General organisation and planning ability
(iii) Job knowledge and potentials
(iv) Employee characteristics and attitudes
(v) Understanding and application of company policies and procedures
(vi) Production, quality and cost control
(vii) Physical conditions.
(viii) Development needs for future.

(i) **Critical Incident Method.** The basis of the method is the principle that 'there are certain significant acts in each employee's behaviour and performance which make all the difference between success and failure on the job'. The supervisor keeps a written record of the events that can be easily recalled/referred and used in the course of periodical or formal appraisal. Feedback is provided about the incidents during performance review session.

This method provides an objective basis for conducting a thorough discussion of an employee's performance. This method avoids recency bias (most recent incidents get too much emphasis).

Most frequently, the critical incidents technique of evaluation is applied to evaluate the performance of superiors rather than of peers of subordinates.

(j) **Group Appraisal Method.** Under this, employees are rated by an appraisal group, consisting of their supervisors and three or four supervisors who have some knowledge of employee's performance. The supervisor explains to the group the nature of his subordinate's job, the actual performance of job holder, the causes of their particular level of performance and offers suggestions for future improvement.

(k) **Field Review Method.** Under this method, a trained employer from personnel department interviews the line supervisor to evaluate their respective subordinates. The appraiser is fully equipped with definite test questions, usually memorised in advance, which he puts to supervisors. The supervisor is required to give his opinion about the progress of his subordinates, the level of performance of each subordinate, his weaknesses, his good points, outstanding ability, promotability and possible plans of action in cases requiring further consideration. The appraisal takes detailed notes of the answers, which are then approved by the supervisors and placed in employee's personal file.

2. Modern Methods of Appraisal

(a) **Appraisal by Results or Management by Objectives (MBO).** This has been evolved by Peter Drucker. MBO has been defined as a 'process where by superior and subordinate managers of an organisation jointly identify the goals which are common, define each individual's major area of responsibility and set the targets and results which are expected of them and use these as guide for unit operations and assessing, the contribution of each of its members.'

Some features of MBO are:

- MBO emphasizes participatively set goals that are tangible, verifiable and measurable.
- MBO focuses attention on what must be accomplished (goals) rather than how it is to be accomplished (Methods).
- MBO, by concentrating on key result areas translates the abstract philosophy of management into concrete phraseology. The technique can be put to general use (non specialist technique). Further it is a dynamic system which seeks to integrate the company's need to clarify and achieve its profit and growth targets with the manager's need to contribute and develop himself.'
- MBO is a systematic and rational technique that allows management to attain maximum results from available resources by focussing on achievable goals. It allows the subordinate plenty of room to make creative decisions on his own.

This process emphasises the value of present and the future instead of past and focuses attention on the results that are accomplished and not on personal traits.

(b) **Assessment Centre Method.** Under this method many evaluators join together to judge employee's performance in several situations with the use of a variety of criteria. The assessments are made/done with the help of couple of employees and involves a par and pencil test, interviews and situational exercises such as in basket exercise, business game, a role playing incident and leaderless group discussions.

(c) **Human Assets Accounting Method.** This method refers to the activity devoted to attaching money estimates to the nature of a firm's internal human organisation and the external customer goodwill. If able and will trained personnel leave the firm, the human organisation is worthless, if they join it, its human assets increase. If distrust and conflict prevails the human enterprise is devalued. If team work and high morale prevails, the human organisation is a very valuable asset.

(d) **Behaviourally Anchored Rating Scales.** The procedure for BARS is usually five stepped.

(i) Generate critical incidents
(ii) Develop performance dimensions
(iii) Reallocate incidents
(iv) Scale of incidents
(v) Develop final instrument

Potential Assessment

In most Indian organisations, people earn promotions on the basis of their past performance. The performance is considered a good indicator of future job success. This could be true, if the jobs to played by the promotee are similar. However, in actual practice, the roles that a role holder played in the past may not be the same that he is expected to play if he assumes a different job after his transfer or promotion to a new position. Past performance, therefore, may not be a good indicator of the suitability of an indicator for a higher role.

To overcome this inadequacy, organisations must think of a new system called potential appraisal. The objective of potential appraisal is to identify the potential of a given employee to occupy higher positions in the organisation hierarchy and under take higher responsibilities.

Potential assessment is required to :

(i) Inform employees about their future prospects;
(ii) Help the organisation chalk out of a suitable succession plan;
(iii) Update training efforts from time to time;
(iv) Advice employees about what they must do to improve their career prospects.

Steps to be followed while introducing a Good Potential Assessment System

The following are some of the steps required to be followed while introducing a potential assessment system:

- **Role Description.** Organisational roles and functions must be defined. To this end, job descriptions must be prepared for each job.
- **Qualities needed to Perform the Roles.** Bases on job descriptions, the roles to be played by people must be prepared (i.e., technical, managerial jobs and behavioural dimensions).
- **Rating Mechanism.** Besides listing the functions and qualities, the potential assessment system must list mechanisms of judging the qualities of employees such as:
  1. *Rating by others.* The potential of a candidate could be rated by the immediate supervisor who is acquainted with the candidate's work in the past, especially his technical capabilities.
  2. *Test.* Managerial and behavioural dimensions can be measured through a battery of psychological tests.
  3. *Games.* Simulation games and exercise (assessment centre, business games, in basket, role play etc.) could be used to uncover the potential of a candidate.
  4. *Records.* Performance records and ratings of a candidate on his previous jobs could be examined carefully on various dimensions such as initiative, creativity, risk taking ability, etc., which might play a key role in discharging his duties in a new job.
- **Organising the System.** After covering the above preliminaries, he must set up a system that will allow the introduction of the scheme smoothly giving answers to some puzzling questions:

  (i) How much weightage to merit in place of seniority in promotions?

(ii) How much weightage to each of the performance dimensions - technical, managerial, behavioural qualities.

(iii) What are the mechanisms of assessing the individual on different indicators of his potential and with what reliability?

- **Feedback.** The system must provide an opportunity for every employee to know the results of his assessment. "He should be helped to understand the qualities actually required for performing the role for which he thinks he has the potential, the mechanisms used by the organisations to appraise his potential and the results of such an appraisal".

ORGANISATIONAL DEVELOPMENT (OD)

Organisational development refers to a wide range of strategies for organisational improvement. It can be defined as a technique for bringing change in the entire aspect of the organisation, rather than focusing attention on individuals, so that change is easily absorbed. It has following characteristics

(a) It is an educational strategy for bringing planned change.

(b) It is related to real problems of the organisation.

(c) Laboratory training methods based on experienced behaviour are primarily used to bring change.

(d) Change agent applying OD technique for change is external.

(e) There are close working relationships between change agents and the people who are being changed. The relationships involve mutual trust, joint goals and means and mutual influence.

(f) The change agents share a social philosophy about human value. They are humanists seeking to get a humanistic philosophy in organisation.

Action Research Model of OD

The OD process can be conveniently presented in the form of action research model. OD emphasizes the process of problem solving, and trains the participants to identify and solve problems that are important to them. For this purpose, various steps of OD–problem identification and diagnosis, planning for change, interventions for change, and evaluation of change–are undertaken on continuous and cyclical basis. This cyclical process of using research to guide action, which generates new data as the basis for new actions, is known as action research. French *et al* have defined action as follows:

"Action research is the process of systematically collecting research data about an ongoing system relative to some objective, goal, or need of that system; feeding these data back into the system; taking actions by altering selected variables within the system based both on the data and on hypothesis; and evaluating the results of actions by collecting more data."

There are two major factors which have caused the use of OD as a technique for planned change. These are as follows :

(i) Training for change does not work properly only through reward structure on the job, unless there is a proper change in the environment of organisation in which people work. The old structures of the organisation do not support training adequately, and trained people even fail to bring the desired change. This requires a change in the organisation environment so that it supports training. This is the basic objective of OD.

(ii) In the dynamic environment, the change is extremely rapid. This requires a highly receptive and effective organisation so that changes are implemented and absorbed to help organisation survive and prosper. OD tries to make organisation receptive and effective, because it tries to free up communication tightness by increasing the amount, trust and candour of communication. It seeks to build problem-solving capacity by improving group dynamics and problem confrontation.

Besides, the two above factors necessitating the origin of OD, it brings some other factors like :

(i) emphasis on rationality and objectivity
(ii) focus on shared authority
(iii) creation of social organisation
(iv) emphasis on long range planning and strategy
(v) taking advantage of organisational conflicts, and
(vi) more widely dispersed improvement.

There are five steps in OD Programmes :

(i) studying the managerial grid as a theoretical framework to understand behaviour dynamics of organisation culture.
(ii) study of the dynamics of the actual work-team.
(iii) launching similar activities in different units engaging the top team.
(iv) implementing tactics for transforming the organisation into the above model.
(v) measurement of changes

Various activities involved in action research are presented in Figure.

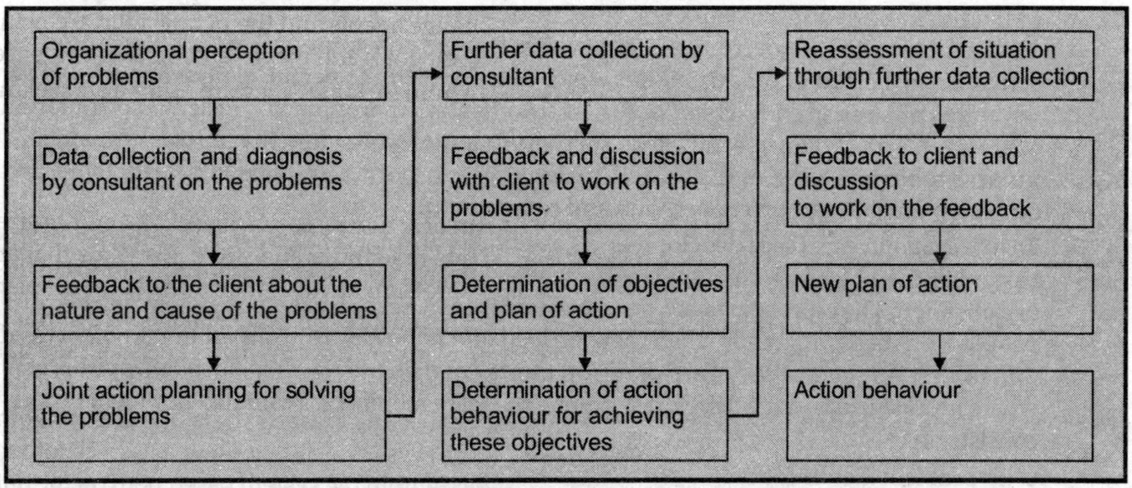

Action Research Model of OD.

These steps involve the following activities:

(i) *Problem identification and diagnosis.* OD programmes lead to meet a certain objective in the organisation because OD is a means and not an end in itself. The problem may be a gap between desired path of action and actual path of action, that is, the organisation fails to meet its objectives on a long-term basis. OD programmes start with the identification of the problem in the organisation.

(ii) *Planning strategy for change.* Attempts are made to transform diagnosis of the problem into a proper action plan involving the overall goals for change, determination of the basic approach for attaining these goals, and the sequence of detailed scheme for implementing the approach.

(iii) *Intervening in the system.* It refers to the planned programme activities during the course of an OD Programme. These planned activities bring certain changes in the system which is the basic objective of OD. There may be various methods like, education and laboratory training, process consultation, team development etc.

(iv) *Evaluation.* This step relates to evaluate the results of OD programmes so that suitable actions may be followed. There is an urgent need for careful monitoring to get precise feedback regarding what is going on as soon as an OD programme starts. For this, the use of critique sessions, systematic appraisal of change efforts, and pre and post-training behavioural patterns are quite effective.

Organisation Development Techniques

There are several techniques which are used in OD programmes depending on the individual requirement. These are:

1. *Sensitivity Training.* Sensitivity training is a method of changing behaviour through unstructured group interaction. It seeks to help individuals towards better relations with others. The primary focus is on reducing interpersonal friction through developing better interaction among individuals.
2. *Transactional Analysis.* Transactional analysis (TA) is another method to develop interpersonal communication and interaction. It aims at developing an ability among individuals to analyse the ego states involved in communication and interaction, development of positive values towards others, and interacting on the basis of mature personality.
3. *Process Consultation.* Process consultation is the process in which the consultant works with individuals and groups to help them to learn about human and social processes and learn to solve problems that stem from process events. Process consultation is defined as "the set of activities on the part of the consultant which help the client to perceive, understand, and act upon the process events which occur in the client's environment." Process consultation concentrates on certain specific areas such as communication, functional roles of members, group problem-solving and decision making, group norms and growth, leadership and authority, and intergroup cooperation and competition.
4. *Team Development.* Team development is essentially an intervention used at group level. The basic objective of team development is to increase effectiveness of various formal groups in the organisation. The essence of team development is to increase trust among members because people work better together when there is open and honest sharing about the problems and difficulties. As such, at the initial level, attempts are made to develop such an environment where mutual trust can be developed among the team members. Team development process consists of
   (i) problem identification
   (ii) examination of effect of differences in perception
   (iii) giving and receiving feedback about adverse feelings of members to overcome these feelings
   (iv) developing interactive skills
   (v) personal contact with team members to solve differences, and
   (vi) follow-up actions to review what has been learned and what the next step in team development should be.

These attempts bring cooperative and supportive feelings among members of the team. In order to bring these feelings on long-term basis, team exercises are undertaken continuously for long time.

5. *Grid Organisation Development.* Grid organisation development is a comprehensive and systematic OD programme. The programme aims at individuals, groups, and the organisation as a whole. It utilises considerable number of instruments enabling individuals and groups to assess their own strengths and weaknesses; focuses on skills, knowledge and processes necessary for effectiveness at the levels of individual, group, intergroup, and the total organisation. Normally, grid organisation development proceeds to change the various factors of the organisation in the following sequence :
   (i) At the first stage, it covers various aspects of managerial styles, problem-solving, communication skills, etc.
   (ii) The focus is turned to develop teamwork by analysing teamwork, traditions, and alike. Skills relating to planning, objective-setting, and problem-solving in these areas are developed.
   (iii) At the intergroup level, attempt is made to move groups from conflict to co-operation by undertaking exercises relating to analysis of group relationships and building co-operative group behaviour.
   (iv) At the total organisation level, the focus shifts to the total organisation and to develop skills necessary to develop organisational skills. Attempt is made to identify the characteristics of the ideal organisation and members are trained to achieve excellence.
   (v) Last stage involves critical evaluation and analysis of the various OD efforts made so that various efforts can be redesigned, if necessary.

OD INTERVENTIONS

On interventions refer to various activities which a consultant and client organisation perform for improving organisational performance through enabling organisational members better manage their behaviour, their work group, and organisational culture. OD interventions are also referred as *OD techniques* or *OD strategies* as they are designed to accomplish specific objectives.

PROCESS OF MBO

MBO is a system for achieving organisational objectives, enhancement of employee commitment and participation. Therefore, its process should facilitate translation of basic concepts into management practices. The MBO process is characterized by the emphasis on the rigourous analysis, the clarity and balance of objectives, and participation of the managers with accountability for results. The MBO process is not as simple as it appears to be. Managers need training and experience for developing the required skills.

TALENT MANAGEMENT AND SKILL DEVELOPMENT

Today, forward-thinking human resources (HR) executives and business leaders view learning as a strategic component of their overall strategic HR mission and are leveraging integrated talent applications to drive optimal employee performance. E-learning is widely considered to be the most efficient and cost effective way to deliver training to a workforce. However, the best way to truly prepare employees for meeting organizational objectives is to focus the training in three major areas of skill development. Using a learning solution that is capable of delivering optimal training for each type of skill and checking for comprehension by examining the outcomes from other HR processes will drive performance within the company as employees develop their soft, functional and compliance based skills.

This article explores each of these three critical skill areas and how to drive employee and organizational performance.

1. Soft-skill Development

Soft skill development targets the improvement of an individual's competencies and behaviors. These encompass the communication, negotiation, conflict resolution, personal effectiveness, creative problem solving, strategic thinking and team building skills that govern much of the interpersonal actions inside and outside of a company. E-learning offers a variety of training sessions and modalities, making it an optimal training method for soft skills development. Using short, self-paced learning modules, employees can view common scenarios and engage in periodic check points that asses their personal choices. Using HR solutions that integrate talent and analytics can help your organization link sales and customer satisfaction ratings from the field to specific soft skill development initiatives. These metrics will help your company determine which employees have high competency in certain areas and which should supplement their skill sets with more training.

2. Functional Skill Development

Functional skill development targets an employee's improvement of "hard skills" such as data analysis, equipment operation, or medical field certifications. An organization cannot produce or sell products or services if its employees do not maintain the appropriate tactical skills to efficiently perform their job requirements. Training for hard skills often takes place when an employee is onboarding for a new position or directly preceding a task that requires new skills. However, providing continuous development opportunities for hard skills will improve overall bench strength and allow organizations to immediately adapt to evolving business challenges. Because functional skills are quantifiable, companies can test their employees' competencies in these areas during hiring, recruiting and at regular intervals thereafter. As part of the performance review process, companies can compare an employee's knowledge of certain tasks on the job and their comprehension based on testing as recorded in an organization's learning solution.

3. Compliance Development

Compliance training includes topics ranging from regulatory and industry mandates to workplace safety to sexual harassment. While compliance skills may be rooted in soft or functional skills, compliance requirements tend to be company or industry specific. Several industries find themselves facing particularly detailed and stringent compliance regulations that require sufficient training and training management to prevent breaches of acceptable standards. Implementing a learning management system that supports compliance completion tracking as well as requirements around logging, auditing and validation can help ensure that the company has taken the proper procedures to prevent costly mistakes and breaches of law.

The Ideal Scenario for Developing Skills

The strategic approach to nurturing talent includes prioritizing and defining development plans based on the needs of both the individual and the organization. The ideal scenario takes into account the following:

- Key organizational objectives are cascaded across the enterprise
- Individual performance goals are linked to organizational objectives to ensure focused direction
- Competencies are defined and used as the basis for job profiles
- 360 feedback from peers and managers highlight competency gaps and additional focus for individual development
- Skill gaps identified from job profiles and talent profiles highlight other potential deficiencies
- E-learning includes personalized learning paths to provide the most needed development on demand (just in-time)

EMPLOYEE ENGAGEMENT AND WORK LIFE BALANCE

Employee management is one way to help turn an under performing employee around or prevent high-performing employees from becoming a weak performer. The concept of employee management is more than just making sure that people are doing their jobs; it's a variety of procedures and strategies that can help you measure, monitor, and interact with the workforce that plays a huge role in your company.

Employee management should play a role in every part of the employee life-cycle, starting with employee recruiting and training. A key part of this process is building a relationship with your employees. This involves adopting a few crucial tactics to allow your employees realize their full potential.

Effective communication is important for any company a survey of more than 1,000 employees, "81 percent of employees said they would rather join a company that values "open communication" than some other perks. That same survey also noted that "only 15 percent of employees are satisfied with the quality of communication within their companies."

Of course, good communication is more than just talk. It's important to set up practices that give employees a voice and allow you better means to listen to their thoughts, suggestions, and complaints. These include:

- **Being visible.** Make sure that your employees see you around the workplace and know that you're available to talk with them if they need anything.
- **Being transparent.** Share company information with your employees. This will help them stay informed and make them feel included.
- **Being open to criticism.** Make sure that there is a proper grievance system so that employees can make their opinions known. This feedback can be used to identify potential issues that may negatively impact your employees.

One way to help manage employees is to not micro manage them. Give them enough space so that they can work on their own and step in when they need help or to check in on progress. By giving them a level of independence within reason, you can build a sense of trust that can help motivate your employees.

Some ways to nurture growth include:

- Offering in-house training.
- Sending employees to conferences and trade shows.
- Allowing employees to adjust roles based on strengths and interests.

Work life balance is a method which helps employees of an organization to balance their personal and professional lives. Work life balance encourages employees to divide their time on the basis on priorities and maintain a balance by devoting time to family, health, vacations etc along with making a career, business travel etc. It is an important concept in the world of business as it helps to motivate the employees and increases their loyalty towards the company.

Working on a job for a company and making a career can be an extremely time consuming duty for any employee. Employees are busy at their offices throughout the day and sometimes even on weekends. This gives them very little time to interact with their family. Because of high pressure of work, often family members get neglected. Also, stressful jobs cause the health of employees to deteriorate. This is where work life balance come into the picture. Work life balance concept allows an employee to maintain a fine balance in the time he or she gives to work as well as to personal matters. By having a good balance, people can have a quality of work life. This helps to increase productivity at workplace as the employee is relaxed about his personal commitments. It also allows the employee to give quality time with family to spend vacations, leisure time, work on his/her health etc. Hence work life balance is extremely important for employees and increases their motivation to work for the company.

Benefits of work life balance

There are several advantage of work life balance. Some of them are discussed below:

1. Work life balance increases the motivation of employees and helps them perform better at job.
2. It helps people to relieve their stress as they can spend leisure time with their near and dear ones.
3. Companies can maximise productivity from an employee who is rejuvenated and refreshed as compared to a over worked employee.
4. Healthy lifestyles can be maintained by having a work life balance. This includes a good diet, regular exercises etc.
5. Employees who are highly motivated can help the business grow as they are more attached to their job and careers.

INDUSTRIAL RELATIONS AND TRADE UNIONS

INDUSTRIAL RELATIONS

Industrial relations are an integral aspect of social relations arising out of employer-employee interaction in modern industries, which are regulated by the state, the legal system and the workers' and employers' organisations at the institutional level; and of the patterns of industrial organisation (including management), capital structure (including technology), compensation of the labour force and a study of market forces – all at the economic level.

Definitions

The term 'industrial relations' has been variously defined :

- **J.T. Dunlop** defines industrial relations as "the complex interrelations among managers, workers and agencies of the governments".
- **According to International Labour Organisation**, Industrial relations comprise relationships between the state on one hand and the employer's and employee's organisation on the other, and the relationship among the occupational organisations themselves.
- Industrial Relation is a relation between employer and employees, employees and employers and employees and trade unions. - Industrial dispute Act 1947
- According to **Dale Yoder** "industrial relations is the process of management dealing with one or more unions with a view to negotiate and subsequently administer collective bargaining agreement or labour contract".

Industrial relations do not constitute a simple relationship, but are a set of functional, inter-dependent complexities involving historical, economic, social, psychological, demographic, technological, occupational, political, legal and other variables, and call for an inter-disciplinary approach to their study. If we make industrial disputes (the absence of positive industrial relations) the centre of the circle, it will have to be divided into various segments. A study of the conditions of work, mainly of the levels of wages and security of employment, comes under the purview of *economics*; their origin and development under *history*; the resultant social conflicts under *sociology*; the attitudes of the combatants, the government and the press under *social psychology*; their cultural interactions under *cultural anthropology*; state policies bearing on the issues involved in the conflict under political science; the legal aspects of disputes under *law*; the issues arising out of international aid (to combatants) under *international relations*; the technological aspects (for example, control of temperature and the introduction of rationalisation) of disputes under *technology*; and the quantitative assessment of losses incurred by the parties and the country's economy under *mathematics*.

It is obvious from these facts that industrial relations do not function in a vacuum but are multi-dimensional in nature; and they are conditioned by two sets of determinants – the institutional factors and economic factors.

Institutional factors includes matters as state policy; labour legislation; labourers' organisation and social institutions (community, caste and joint family, religions); attitudes to work; systems of power and status; motivation and influence; the system of industrial relations, etc. Under *economic factors* are included economic organisations (socialist, capitalist, individual ownership, company ownership, government ownership); capital structure, including technology; the nature and composition of the labour force and the sources of supply and demand in the labour market.

Features of Industrial Relations

The main Features of industrial relations system are:

- Industrial relation is an active associations among the workers, the management and the organisation of the workers *i.e.* trade union and the state.
- There are not simple relationship between the two or more parties but it is set of functions interdependent of numbers of factors like-historical, economical, technological, occupational, legal relationship are available in industry.
- Industrial relation broadly give emphasis on accommodations, adjustment and cooperation between the employer and employees.
- It aims at industrial peace and leads to industrials democracy.
- The government intervene to shape the industrials relations through laws, rules, agreement, terms and charters.
- The central and state government play a major role in the industrial Relation of the country. It influence and give proper shape of industrial relations through laws rules and regulations and different awards of the court of law.
- Several parties are involved in the Industrial relations system. The main parties are employers and their associations, employees and their unions and the government. These three parties interact within economic and social environment to shape the Industrial relations structure.
- Industrial relations are a dynamic and developing concept, not a static one. They undergo changes with changing structure and scenario of the industry as and when change occurs.
- Industrial relations include both individual relations and collective relationships.

Objectives of Industrial Relations

In addition to their primary objective of bringing about good and healthy relations between employers and employees, industrial relations are designed :

(a) To safeguard the interests of labour and of management by securing the highest level of mutual understanding and goodwill among all those sections in the industry which participate in the process of production.

(b) To avoid industrial conflict and develop harmonious relations, which are an essential factor in the productivity of workers and the industrial progress of a country.

(c) To raise productivity to a higher level in an era of full employment by lessening the tendency to high turnover and frequent absenteeism.

(d) To establish and nurse the growth of an Industrial Democracy based on labour partnership in the sharing of profits and of managerial decisions, so that an individual's personality may grow to its full stature for the benefit of the industry and of the country as well.

(e) To eliminate, as far as is possible and practicable, strikes, lockouts and gheraos by providing reasonable wages, improved living and working conditions and fringe benefits.

(f) To establish government control of such plants and units as are running at a loss or in which production has to be regulated in the public interest.

Principles for Industrial Discipline

1. A code of rules and regulations embodying the ideal pattern of behaviour in the work-place should be drawn-up. 'Where the process of consultation is well developed as a genuine element in the practice of management, discipline is nearly always better.'
2. The code of discipline must lay down the same standards for everyone so that it does not give rise to controversies and became a cause of indiscipline.
3. There must be an occasional evaluation and re-appraisal of all rules so that only those which are sensible, useful and appropriate are kept in force.
4. The employees must be kept fully informed about the rules and conditions of work as also about the penalties prescribed for breach of such conditions and enforcement.
5. The discipline policy should lay more emphasis on the prevention of the breach of discipline than on the administration of penalties.
6. The management should be extremely careful to ensure that the supervisors or the policies of the management do not encourage the breaking of rules.
7. The personnel manager should try to look deep into the causes that bend to the breach of a rule or the rules. This becomes absolutely necessary if the same rule is violated time and again by the employees.
8. The management should make provision for machinery for appeals against, and review of, all disciplinary action. Such machinery should as far as possible, be internal to the organisation concerned. Provision of this type can be made in the employee's handbook, collective agreements etc.

Dispute Resolution and Grievance Management

I. Dispute Resolution

The Industrial Disputes Act, 1947 defines an industrial dispute as "any dispute or difference between employers and employers or between employees and employees or between employers and employees, which is connected with the employment, or non-employment, or the terms of employment or with the conditions of work of any person."

Industrial disputes may take the form of strikes, go-slow tactics, taken strikes, sympathetic strikes, pen-down strikes, hunger strikes, bandhs, gheraos and lockouts.

Types of Disputes

Disputes are of two kinds they are :

(a) Disputes of Right, which relate to the application or interpretation of an existing agreement or contract of employment; and

(b) Disputes of Interest, which relate to claims by employees or proposals by a management about the terms and conditions of employment.

According to the Industrial Disputes Act, 1947 and the many judicial decisions which have been handed down by courts and tribunals, industrial disputes may be raised on any one of the following issues:

(i) Fairness of the Standing Orders;
(ii) Retrenchment of workers following the closing down of a factory, lay-offs, discharge or dismissal, reinstatement of dismissed employees and compensation for them;
(iii) Benefits of an Award denied to a worker; non-payment of personal allowance to seasonal employees; the demand of employees for medical relief for their parents;
(iv) Wages, fixation wages, and minimum rates, modes of payment and the right of an employee to choose one of the awards when two awards on wages have been given;
(v) Lockout and claim for damages by an employer because employees resorted to an illegal strike;
(vi) Payment of hours, gratuity, provident fund, pension and travelling allowance;
(vii) Disputes between rival unions; and
(viii) Disputes between employers and employers.

Methods and Machinery for the Settlement of Industrial Disputes

Preventions of Industrial Disputes

The consequences of an Industrial dispute will be harmful to the owners of industries, workers, economy and the nation as a whole, which results in loss of productivity, profits, market share and even closure of the plant. Hence, Industrial disputes need to be averted by all means.

Prevention of Industrial disputes is a pro-active approach in which an organisation undertakes various actions through which the occurrence of Industrial disputes is prevented. Like the old saying goes, "prevention is better than cure".

1. **Model Standing Orders.** Standing orders define and regulate terms and conditions of employment and bring about uniformity in them. They also specify the duties and responsibilities of both employers and employees thereby regulating standards of their behaviour. Therefore, standing orders can be a good basis for maintaining harmonious relations between employees and employers.

   Under Industrial Dispute Act, 1947, every factory employing 100 workers or more is required to frame standing orders in consultation with the workers. These orders must be certified and displayed properly by the employer for the information of the workers.
2. **Code of Industrial discipline.** The code of Industrial discipline defines duties and responsibilities of employers and workers. The objectives of the code are:
   - To avoid work stoppage.
   - To secure settlement of disputes by negotiation, conciliation and voluntary arbitration.
   - To promote constructive co-operation between the parties concerned at all levels.
   - To eliminate all forms of coercion, intimidation and violence.
   - To maintain discipline in the industry.
3. **Works Committee.** The Industrial Dispute Act, 1947 has provided for the establishment of works committees. In case of any industrial establishment in which 100 or more workers are employed, a works committee consisting of employees and workers is to be constituted; it shall be the duty of the Works Committee to promote measures for securing and preserving amity and good relations among the employees and workers.
4. **Joint Management Councils.** Under this system Joint Management Councils are constituted at the plant level. These councils were setup as early as 1958. These councils consist of equal number of representatives of the employers and employees, not exceeding 12 at the plant level.

The plant should employ at least 500 workers. The council discusses various matters relating to the working of the industry. This council is entrusted with the responsibility of administering welfare measures, supervision of safety and health schemes, scheduling of working hours, rewards for suggestions etc.

5. **Joint Councils.** The joint councils are constituted for the whole unit, in every Industrial Unit employing 500 or more workers; there should be a Joint Council for the whole unit. Only such persons who are actually engaged in the unit shall be the members of Joint Council. A joint council shall meet at least once in a quarter. The chief executive of the unit shall be the chairperson of the joint council. The vice-chairman of the joint council will be nominated by the worker members of the council. The decisions of the Joint Council shall be based on the consensus and not on the basis of voting.
6. **Collective Bargaining.** Collective Bargaining is a process in which the representatives of the employer and of the employees meet and attempt to negotiate a contract governing the employer-employee-union relationships. Collective Bargaining involves discussion and negotiation between two groups as to the terms and conditions of employment.
7. **Labour welfare officer.** The factories Act, 1948 provides for the appointment of a labour welfare officer in every factory employing 500 or more workers. The officer looks after all facilities in the factory provided for the health, safety and welfare of workers. He maintains liaison with both the employer and the workers, thereby serving as a communication link and contributing towards healthy industrial relations through proper administration of standing orders, grievance procedure etc.
8. **Tripartite bodies.** Several tripartite bodies have been constituted at central, national and state levels. The India labour conference, standing labour committees, Wage Boards and Industries Committees operate at the central level. At the state level, State Labour Advisory Boards have been set up. All these bodies play an important role in reaching agreements on various labour-related issues. The recommendations given by these bodies are however advisory in nature and not statutory.

Settlement of Disputes

1. **Collective Bargaining.** Collective bargaining is a process of discussion and negotiation between two parties, one or both of whom is a group of persons acting in concert. The resulting bargain is an understanding as to the terms or conditions under which a continuing service is to be performed. More specifically, collective bargaining is the procedure by which an employer or employers and a group of employees agree upon the conditions of work.
2. **Conciliation.** Conciliation is a process by which representations of workers and employers are brought together before a third party with a view to persuading them to arrive at an agreement by mutual discussion between them. The Industrial Disputes Act, 1947 and other state enactments authorise the government to appoint conciliators charged with the duty of mediating in and promoting the settlement of industrial disputes.
3. **Adjudication.** Adjudication means a mandatory settlement of industrial disputes by labour courts or industrial tribunals or national tribunals under the Industrial Disputes Act or under any other corresponding state statutes.
4. **Voluntary Arbitration.** Arbitration is a procedure in which a neutral third party studies the bargaining situation, listens to both the parties and gathers information, and then makes recommendations that are binding on the parties. The main ingredients of voluntary arbitration are :

   (i) the industrial dispute must exist or be apprehended;

(ii) the agreement must be in writing;

(iii) the reference to voluntary arbitration must be made before a dispute has been referred to a labour court, tribunal or national tribunal;

(iv) the name of arbitrator/arbitrators must be specified; and

(v) the arbitrator or arbitrators shall investigate the dispute and submit to the appropriate government the arbitration award signed by the arbitrator or all the arbitrators, as the case may be.

Grievance Management

Grievance is a complaint of one or more workers in respect of wages, allowances, conditions of work and interpretation of service stipulations, covering such areas as overtime, leave, transfer, promotion, seniority, job assignment and termination of service.

According to National Commission on Labour, "complaints affecting one or more individual workers in respect of wage payments, over time, leave, transfer, promotion, seniority, work assignment and discharges constitute grievances."

(i) Grievance is word which covers dissatisfaction and which has the following characteristic:

(a) It may be unvoiced or expressly stated by an employee;

(b) It may be written or verbal;

(c) It may be valid and legitimate, untrue or completely false or ridiculous; and

(d) It may arise out of something connected with the organisation or work.

(ii) An employee feels that an injustice has been done to him.

In other words, grievances are feelings, sometimes real, sometimes imagined, which an employee may have in regard to his employment situation.

Whenever there is any discontent among employees, it is bound to result in a turmoil which may affect the interests of the management very adversely. Grievances generally give rise to unhappiness, frustration, discontent, indifference to work, poor morale and they ultimately lead to the inefficiency of workers and low productivity. A personnel administrator should, therefore, see to it that grievances are redressed at the earliest possible moment.

Grievance Procedure Steps in Unionised Organisations

In an unionised organisation, the operation of the grievance procedure may contain the following steps :

Step 1. The aggrieved employee verbally explains his grievance to his immediate supervisor or in a conference or a discussion specifically arranged for the purpose. The employee seeks satisfaction from his supervisor. He may or may not be accompanied by his shop steward. The grievance can be settled if the supervisor has been properly trained for the purpose and if he adheres strictly to a basic problem-solving method.

Step 2. The second step begins when the grievance is not settled by the supervisor. In this case, it is sent to a higher level manager with a note in which he mentioned the time, place and nature of the action to which the employee objects. The higher level manager is generally the chief business manager, a superintendent or an Industrial Relations Officer who goes into the grievance and gives his decision on the matter.

Step 3. This means that the grievance is to be submitted to the Grievance Committee since the decisions of the supervisor and of the higher level manager have not solved the problem. This committee, which is composed of some fellow-employees, the shop steward or a combination of union and management representatives, considers the record and may suggest a possible solution.

Step 4. If the decision or suggestion of the Grievance Committee is not accepted by the grievant, he may approach the management or the corporate executive. This is the *fourth step* in the grievance handling procedure.

Step 5. The final step is taken when the grievance is referred to an arbitrator who is acceptable to the employee as well as the management. They may agree beforehand that the arbitrator's award will be final and binding on both the parties.

Labour Welfare and Social Security Measures

According to Arthur James Todd, "Labour welfare means anything done for the comfort and improvement, intellectual and social, of the employees over and above the wages paid which is not a necessity of the industry."

According to Industrial Labour Organisation (ILO), "Labour welfare may be understood and includes, such services facilities and amenities which may be established in vicinity of undertaking to perform their work in healthy and congenial environment and to avail of facilities which improve their health and bring high morale."

Labour is one of the most important factor to run the business. It is required at every step. Without this anybody cannot even think of starting and expanding his business. The co-operation between employer and employee, can only be there if the response from both sides is equal. If the boss expects that the labour should work according to him, then he should also do something for the labour. The importance of labour welfare has increased because of large scale industrialisation in which human beings are subject to mechanical, chemical, electrical and radiation hazards. Besides modern industry is characterised by complicated mechanisms, intricate job requirements and fast moving production lines. One of the important consequence of all this is increased dangers to human life, through accidents. So the measures should be taken for the welfare of the labour and also to provide them with social security.

Objectives of Labour Welfare

Several objectives of Labour welfare are mentioned below:

1. Labour welfare provides social comfort to employees.
2. It provides intellectual improvement of employees.
3. To develop sense of responsibility and belongingness among employees.
4. To ensures that the working conditions for employees are of higher standard.
5. To build stable work force.
6. To reduce absenteeism and labour turnover.
7. To make employees lives good and worth living.
8. To boost productivity and efficiency at the workplace.
9. To provide healthy and proper working conditions.
10. To ensure well being of employees and families.

Approaches or Theories of Labour Welfare

There are some theories which constitutes the conceptual frame framework of the labour welfare, describe these theories. Several theories constituting the conceptual framework of labour welfare have so far been outlined these are :

1. **Policy theory.** This theory is based on the contention that a minimum standard of welfare is necessary for workers. The assumption on which the theory is based is the without compulsion,

supervision and fear of punishment, no employer will provide even the barest minimum of welfare facilities for workers this theory is based on the assumption that man is selfish and self –centered, and always tries to achieve his own ends, even at the cost of the welfare of others. According to this theory, owners and managers of industrial undertakings make use of every opportunity to engage in this kind of exploitation. The sate has therefore to step in to prevent exploitation by enacting stiff laws to coerce industrialists into offering a minimum standard of welfare to their workers. Such interference it is felt is in the interests of the progress and welfare of the state as well. Laws are enacted to compel management to provide minimum wages, congenial working conditions and reasonable hours of work and social security.

The policy theory involves several stages of implementation :

- Enactments
- Periodical supervision
- Punishment

2. **Religious theory.** The religion theory has two connotations, namely, the investment and atonement aspects. The investment aspect of the religion theory implies that the fruits of today's deeds will be reaped tomorrow. Any action, good or bad, is therefore treated as an investment. Inspired by this belief, some employers plan and organise canteens and creches. The atonement aspect of the religion theory implies that the present disabilities of a person are the result of the sins committed by him/her previously. He/she should undertake to do good deeds now to atone or compensate for his/her sins. There is the story of a big Jain employer who firmly held the belief that the provision of welfare facilities for workers was outside the duties of the management. Whatever he did provide was under government compulsion and supervision. It so happened, however, that the children born to him died as soon as they were born. Later, his own health suffered. He felt that, as a compensation, or expiration or even as an investment in a good deed (punyam), he should liberally contribute to the creche in the factory (as well as to other child-welfare institutions), and also to medical services for his workers. Consequently, in this particular factory, there came to exist an excellent creche and a well-organised dispensary.
3. **Philanthropic theory.** Philanthropy means affection for mankind. The philanthropic theory of labour welfare refers to the provision of good working conditions, creches and canteens out of pity on the part of the employers who want to remove the disabilities of the workers. Robert Owen of England was a philanthropic employer, who worked for the welfare of his workers. The philanthropic theory is more common in social welfare. Student hostels, drinking water facilities, the rehabilitation of crippled persons, donations to religious and educational institutions, and so forth are examples of philanthropic deeds.
4. **Trusteeship theory.** In this theory it is held that the industrialists or employers holds the total industrial estate, properties and profits accruing form them in trust for the workmen, for himself, and for society. It assumes that the workmen are like minors and are not able to look after their own interests that they are ignorant because of lack of education. Employers therefore have the moral responsibility to look after the interests of their wards, who are the workers.
5. **Paternalistic Theory.** According to the paternalistic theory, also called the trusteeship theory, of labour welfare, the industrialist or the employer holds the total industrial estate, properties and the profits accruing from them, in trust. The property which he/she can use or abuse as he/she likes is not entirely his/her own. He/she holds it for his/her use, no doubt, but also for the benefit of his/her workers, if not for the whole society. For several reasons, such as low wages, lack of education, and so forth the workers are at present unable to take care of themselves. They are, therefore, like minors, and the employers should provide for their well-being out of funds in their control. The trusteeship is not actual and legal, but it is moral and, therefore, not less real.

6. **Placating theory.** As labour groups are becoming better organised and are becoming demanding and militant, being more conscious of their rights and privileges that even before, their demand for higher wages and better standards increases. The placing theory advocates timely and periodical acts of labour welfare to appease the workers.
7. **Public Relations Theory.** According to this theory, welfare activities are provided to create a good impression on the minds of the workers and the public, particularly the latter. Clean and safe working conditions, a good canteen, creche and other amenities, make a good impression on the workers, visitors and the public. Some employers proudly take their visitors round the plant to show how well they have organised their welfare activities.
8. **Functional Theory.** Also known as the efficiency theory of labour welfare, the functional theory implies that welfare facilities are provided to make the workers more efficient. If workers are fed properly, clothed adequately and treated kindly, and if the conditions of their work are congenial, they will work efficiently. Welfare work is a means of securing, preserving and increasing the efficiency of labour.
9. **Social Theory.** The social obligation of an industrial establishment has been assuming great significance these days. The social theory implies that a factory is morally bound to improve the conditions of the society in addition to improving the condition of its employees. Labour welfare, as mentioned earlier, is gradually becoming social welfare.

Safety Programme

Safety programme deals with the prevention of accidents and with minimising the resulting loss and damage to persons and property. Five basic principles must govern the safety program of an organisation. These are :

1. Industrial accidents result from a multiplicity of factors, but these have to be traced to their root causes, which are usually faults in the management system arising from poor leadership from the top, inadequate supervision, insufficient attention to the safety design into the system, an unsystematic approach to the identification, analysis and elimination of hazards and poor training facilities.
2. The most important function of safety program is to identify potential hazards and provide effective safety facilities and equipments and to take prompt remedial action.
3. The safety policies of the organisation should be determined by the managements who must be continuously involved in monitoring safety performance and in ensuring that corrective action is taken when necessary.
4. Management and supervision must be made fully accountable for safety performance in the work places they control.
5. All employees should be given thorough training in safe methods of work and should receive continuing education and guidance on eliminating safety hazards and of the prevention of accidents.

(a) **Safety Organisation.** A safety director and a safety committee be set up by an organisation. The following facts should be given due consideration in any safety organisation program:
   (i) Safety programmes must have top management approval, sanction and support.
   (ii) Responsibility for safety must rest with the supervisory personnel.
   (iii) Safety must be given equally important consideration with that of other factors of production.

(iv) Provision must be made for prompt action in the elimination of mechanic and personal hazards.

(v) A definite safety program must be developed to educate all employees safety and to secure their active cooperation in the effort to eliminate accident.

(vi) Safety must be included in all phases of planning, purchasing, supervision and operation.

(b) **Appraisal of Employees Attitude to Safety Programs.** A knowledge of the attitude of the employees to the safety programs developed for them and the specific measures adopted for that purpose – such as the setting up of bulletin boards, displays of safety measures, pamphlets, booklets, posters, magazines and motion pictures which highlight them – would help the safety director in presenting safety information to the employees of an organisation.

(c) **Safety Engineering.** The adoption of proper engineering procedures to minimise and, if possible, eliminate work hazards is fundamental to any organised safety program. New products, processes and machines are designed, and full attention is paid to safety engineering in design, layout and installation.

(d) **Safety Education and Training.** Safety education for all levels of management personnel and for employees is vital for any successful safety program. The goal of safety education is two-fold : to develop safety consciousness among employees and build up a favourable attitude on their part towards safety measures and precautions; and, secondly, to ensure safe work performance on the part of each employee by developing his skill in the use and operation of safety equipments.

(e) **Safety Contests.** Some companies encourage safety competitions among their departments with a view to bringing about a reduction in the number of accidents.

(f) **Disciplinary Action.** To enforce plant rules governing safety, employees are reprimanded, fined, laid off or even discharged if they are found guilty of any violations.

(g) **Accident Analysis and Tabulation.** The safety director must investigate and report on every accident. He should, moreover, periodically summarise all the injuries which have been sustained by employees during a particular period of time and classify them plant-wise, department-wise, and shift-wise. He should also classify the causes and kinds of those injuries and mention whether they were disabling or not.

Protection Against Health Hazards

An industrial establishment should protect its employees against health hazards:

(i) By substituting a less toxic substance for the hazardous chemical, by isolating the process, or by providing protective clothing, handling and warning devices and by providing safety education.

(ii) By ensuring that firms using radiation in their manufacturing process insist that their employees wear badges which indicate the amount of radiation they have been exposed to.

(iii) By controlling noise in factories, by the use of vibration - absorbing material at certain points. The employee may be asked to wear ear-coverings or ear-plugs.

(iv) By devoting adequate attention to lighting, temperature and atmospheric conditions, by controlling dust, fumes and gases and by providing protective devices, clothing, goggles and shields.

Social Security

Statutory Welfare Schemes

The statutory welfare schemes include the following provisions:

1. **Drinking Water.** At all the working places safe hygienic drinking water should be provided.
2. **Facilities for sitting.** In every organisation, especially factories, suitable seating arrangements are to be provided.
3. **First aid appliances.** First aid appliances are to be provided and should be readily assessable so that in case of any minor accident initial medication can be provided to the needed employee.
4. **Latrines and Urinals.** A sufficient number of latrines and urinals are to be provided in the office and premises and are also to be maintained in a neat and clean condition.
5. **Canteen facilities.** Cafeteria or canteens are to be provided by the employer so as to provide hygienic and nutritious food to the employees.
6. **Spittoons.** In every work place, such as ware houses, store places, in the dock area and office premises spittoons are to be provided in convenient places and same are to be maintained in a hygienic condition.
7. **Lighting.** Proper and sufficient lights are to be provided for employees so that they can work safely during the night shifts.
8. **Washing places.** Adequate washing places such as bathrooms, wash basins with tap and tap on the stand pipe are provided in the port area in the vicinity of the work places.
9. **Changing rooms.** Adequate changing rooms are to be provided for workers to change their cloth in the factory area and office premises. Adequate lockers are also provided to the workers to keep their clothes and belongings.
10. **Rest rooms.** Adequate numbers of restrooms are provided to the workers with provisions of water supply, wash basins, toilets, bathrooms, etc.

Non-statutory Schemes

Many non-statutory welfare schemes may include the following schemes:

1. **Personal Health Care (Regular medical check-ups).** Some of the companies provide the facility for extensive health check-up.
2. **Flexi-time.** The main objective of the flex-time policy is to provide opportunity to employees to work with flexible working schedules. Flexible work schedules are initiated by employees and approved by management to meet business commitments while supporting employee personal life needs
3. **Employee Assistance Programs.** Various assistant programs are arranged like external counseling service so that employees or members of their immediate family can get counseling on various matters.
4. **Harassment Policy.** To protect an employee from harassments of any kind, guidelines are provided for proper action and also for protecting the aggrieved employee.
5. **Maternity & Adoption Leave.** Employees can avail maternity or adoption leaves. Paternity leave policies have also been introduced by various companies.
6. **Mediclaim Insurance Scheme.** This insurance scheme provides adequate insurance coverage of employees for expenses related to hospitalisation due to illness, disease or injury or pregnancy
7. **Employee Referral Scheme.** In several companies employee referral scheme is implemented to encourage employees to refer friends and relatives for employment in the organisation.

TRADE UNIONS

A trade union is any combination of persons, whether temporary or permanent, primarily for the purpose of regulating the relations between workers and employers or between workers and workers, and for imposing restrictive conditions on the conduct of any trade or business and includes the federation of two or more trade unions.

It may be observed that the trade union is an association, either of employees or employers or of independent workers. *Secondly*, it is a relatively permanent combination of workers and is not temporary a casual. *Thirdly*, it is an association of workers engaged in securing economic benefits for its members. Fourthly, the character of trade union has been constantly changing. *Finally*, its origin and growth has been influenced by a number of ideologies.

Definition

According to Webb's, a trade union is a continuous association of wage earners for the purpose of maintaining and improving the conditions of their working lives.

(De Cenzo & Robbins, 1993), A more recent and non-legislative definition of a union is "an organisation of workers acting collectively who seek to protect and promote their mutual interests through collective bargaining".

Forms of Trade Union

Classical. A trade union's main objective is to collectively protect the interests of its members in given socio-economic-political system. Trade Unions are the expressions of the needs, aspirations and wishes of the working class.

Neo-classical. It goes beyond classical objectives and tries to improve up other wider issues like tax-reliefs, raising saving rates etc.

Revolutionary. Change in the system. Establishing the rule of working class even through violence and use of force etc.

Principles of Trade Unionism

Trade unions function on the basis of three cardinal principles. If any one of them is threatened or is in jeopardy, they would fight back. These principles are :

(i) *Unity is strength.*

"All your strength is in your union,
All your danger is in your discord;
Therefore, be at peace henceforward,
And, as brothers, live together."

(ii) *Equal pay for equal work or for the same job.*

"Men and women should receive equal remuneration for work of equal value."

(iii) *Security of service,* which enjoins upon trade unions that they ensure social and economic security for their members.

Objectives of Trade Union

1. Wages and Salaries
2. Working conditions
3. Discipline
4. Personnel Policies

5. Welfare
6. Employee-employer relation
7. Negotiating machinery
8. Safeguarding organisational health and the interest of the industry.

Functions of Trade Unions

1. Militant functions.
2. Fraternal functions
3. Social functions.

Essentials of a Successful Trade Union

(i) Should be an enlightened one, so that it may be able to guide and direct the trade union movement properly.

(ii) Should have a solid foundation, so that it may be strong enough to achieve success in the realisation of its objectives.

(iii) Should have clearly enunciated objectives and a coherent and well-conceived policy; and it should consider itself as a business organisation which requires careful planning and sound organisational methods for its success.

(iv) Should be run by the members for the members; that is, its leadership should come from the rank and file of its members and it should be subject to their support or rejection.

(v) Should have honesty and integrity of purpose; that is, it should be honest not only in financial matters; its integrity should be all-inclusive and should extend to its relationship with employers, to the formulation of its policies and the evaluation of its performance and to what it says to its own members.

(vi) Should look beyond its own horizon and recognise and fulfil its proper role in the life of the nation and of the community in the midst of which it lives and functions.

(vii) Should have a sense of responsibility; that is, it is necessary that:

(a) It should be internally strong so that it may be effective in protecting the interests of the workers;

(b) It should use its economic power in a careful and responsible way; that is, it should be aware of the existing realities in terms of the opportunities. It has to bring about an improvement in the living conditions of its members; and

(c) It should be democratic so that the workers' right of self-government acquires a reality.

Theories of Trade Unionism

The Important theories of trade unionism are as follows :

1. **Karl Marx theory Classless society.** This theory is also called anti-capitalism approach. Karl marx represented trade union as an instrument for destroying the capitalist class. The trade unionism become necessary to bring about revolunatry and fundamental changes in the social order of the workers. Marx considered trade union as an instrument to overthrow capitalism. He Believed that the capitalism develop three tendency.

   (i) The tendency of heavy conservations of wealth in the hands of few of the largest capitalists.

   (ii) The tendency towards a steady depression of wages and growing misery of the wage earners keep revolutionary order alive.

(iii) The inevitable and frequent economic crisis under capitalism lead the working class towards destruction. In his view, it was imperative for the workers of the world to collects in an international.

2. **Webb's Theory of Industrial Democracy or Non-Revolutionary.** Webb's book 'Industrial democracy' is the Bible of trade unionism. According to Webb, trade unionism is an extension of democracy from political sphere to industrial sphere. Webb agreed with Marx that trade unionism is a class struggle and modern capitalist state is a transitional phase which will lead to democratic socialism. He considered collective bargaining as the process which strengthens labour.
3. **Cole's Theory of Union Control of Industry.** Cole's views are given in his book "World of Labour" 1913. His views are somewhere in between Webb and Marx. He agrees that unionism is class struggle and the ultimate is the control of industry by labour and not revolution as predicted by Marx. As per cole, the ultimate objective of the trade union is to have control of the workers over the industry, although the immediate objectives may be realizations of higher wages and better condition of employment for the workers.
4. **Perlman's Theory of the "Scarcity Consciousness" of Manual Workers.** He rejected the idea of class consciousness as an explanation for the origin of the trade union movement but substituted it with what he called job consciousness.

   According to him, 'working people in reality felt an urge towards collective control of their employment opportunities, but hardly towards similar control of industry.' Perlman observed that three dominant factors emerged from the rich historical data:

   (i) The capacity or incapacity of the capitalist system to survive as a ruling group in the face of revolutionary attacks (e.g., failure in Russia).

   (ii) The source of the anti-capitalist influences being primarily from among the intellectuals in any society.

   (iii) The most vital factor in the labour situation was the trade union movement. Trade unionism, which is essentially pragmatic, struggles constantly not only against the employers for an enlarged opportunity measure in income, security and liberty in the shop and industry, but struggles also, whether consciously or unconsciously, actively or passively, against the intellectual who would frame its programmes and shape its policies.

   But Perlman also felt that a theory of the labour movement should include a theory of the psychology of the labouring man. For instance, there was a historical continuity between the guilds and trade unions, through their common fundamental psychology; the psychology of seeking a livelihood in the face of limited economic opportunity. It was when manual workers became aware of a scarcity of opportunity, that they banded together into unions for the purpose of protecting their jobs and distributing employment opportunities among themselves equitably, and to subordinate the interests of the individual to the whole labour organism. Unionism was ruled thus by this fundamental scarcity consciousness (Perlman, 1970).
5. **Hoxie's Social psychological approach.** He classified Unionism on the basis of their functions. His classification were Business Unionism for protecting the interest of various **craftsmen**, "Uplift unionism" for the purpose of contributing better life such as association of sales engineers etc. "Revolutionary Unionism" which is eager to replace existing social order, "Predatory Unionism" which rests on these support of others.

In other words workers are not divergent in temperament and training but are similar situated at economic and social levels, they have common interpretations of their social situation to their problem of living, so that unite into a union.

6. **Tannenbaum's Theory of capitalism approach or Man Vs. Machine.** He traces the rise of union to the industrial revolution and the workers reaction to the philosophy of individualism. He believed that the fundamental cause of exploitation of workers in the use of machines. The machines threatens the security of the individual workers and they react in self defence, through the union, to attempt to control of machines.

   According to him Union is formed in reaction to alienation and loss of community in an individualistic and unfeeling society. In his words, the union returns to the workers his society, which he left behind him when he migrated from a rural background to the anonymity of an urban industrial location. The union gives the worker a fellowship and a value system that he shares with others like him. Institutionally, the trade union movement is an unconscious effort to harness the drift of our time and reorganise it around the cohesive identity that men working together always achieve Reasons for Joining Trade Union.

7. **Common's Environment Theory.** He was sceptical of generalisations and believed only that which could be proved by evidence. He agreed that collective bargaining was an instrument of class struggle, but he summarised that ultimately there will be partnership between employers and employees.

8. **Mitchell's Economic Protection Theory of Trade Unionism.** Mitchell, a labour leader, completely rejected individual bargaining. According to him unions afford economic protection to.

9. **Simons Theory of Monopolistic.** He denounced trade unionism as monopoly founded on violence. And he claimed monopoly power has no use save abuse.

10. **Sarvodaya Approach of Gandhi.** Mahatma gandhi approach to the growth of trade union was contrary to those of karl marx. Gandhiji philosophy is based upon the sarvodaya principle of truth, trusteeship and non violence. He believed trade union as economic institutions in which capital and labour are not antagonistic but are supplementary to each others. In gandhiji words, "My ideals is that capital and labour should supplement and help each other. They should be a great family living in unity and harmony. Capital not only looking material welfare of the labourers but their moral welfare also-capitalist being trustee of the welfare of the labouring classes under them.

Collective Bargaining

Good relations between the employer and employees are essential for the success of industry. In order to maintain good relations, it is necessary that industrial disputes are settled quickly and amicably. One of the efficient methods of resolving industrial disputes and deciding the employment conditions is ***Collective Bargaining***. Industrial disputes essentially refer to differences or conflicts between employers and employees.

Collective Bargaining is a process in which the management and employee representatives meet and negotiate the terms and conditions of employment for mutual benefit. Collective bargaining involves discussion and negotiation between two groups as to the terms and conditions of employment. It is termed Collective because both the employer's negotiators and the employees act as a group rather than individuals. It is known as Bargaining because the method of reaching an agreement involves proposals and counter-proposals, offers and counter offers. There should be no outsiders involved in the process of collective bargaining.

According to Walton and McKersie the process of Collective Bargaining consists of four types of activities:

1. **Distributive Bargaining.** It involves haggling over the distribution of surplus. Various activities involved in this activity are wages, salaries, bonus and other financial issues. In this activity, both the parties face a win/lose situation.
2. **Integrative Bargaining.** Also known as Interest-Based Bargaining, issues which are not damaging to either party are discussed. It is a negotiation strategy in which both the parties collaborate to find a win-win solution to their problems. This strategy focuses on developing mutually beneficial agreements based on the interests of the disputants. Issues brought up may be better job evaluation procedures, better performance appraisal methods or training programmes etc.
3. **Attitudinal structuring.** Attitudinal structuring refers to efforts by negotiators to shape their opponents' perceptions about the nature of the issues to be negotiated. By cultivating an atmosphere of friendliness, mutual respect, trust, and cooperation, negotiators can encourage their opponents to view issues largely in integrative terms and participate in joint problem solving. This activity involves shaping and reshaping some perceptions like trust/distrust, friendliness/hostility, co-operative/non-cooperative between the labour and management. When there is a backlog of bitterness between both the parties, attitudinal structuring is required to maintain smooth and harmonious industrial relations.
4. **Intra-Organisational Bargaining.** It is a type of manoeuvreing to achieve consensus among the workers and management. Even within the union there may be differences between different groups as may be the case with the management. Intra-organisational consensus is required for the smooth acceptance of the outcome of Collective Bargaining.

Objectives of Collective Bargaining

1. To maintain cordial relations between the employer and employees.
2. To protect the interests of the workers through collective action and by preventing unilateral actions from being taken by the employer.
3. To ensure the participation of trade unions in industry.
4. To avoid the need for government intervention as collective bargaining is a voluntary collective process.
5. To promote Industrial democracy.

Characteristics of Collective Bargaining

1. It is a group or collective action as opposed to individual action. It is initiated through the representatives of the employees.
2. It is a flexible and dynamic process where no party adopts a rigid attitude.
3. It is a continuous process, which provides a mechanism for continuous negotiations and discussions between management and the trade unions.
4. It is a voluntary process without any third-party intervention. Both workers and management voluntarily participate in the negotiations, discuss and arrive at a solution. That is why it is known as a bipartite process where workers' representatives and management get an opportunity for clear, face-to-face communication.
5. It ensures industrial democracy at the workplace; it is a self-run government in action.
6. It is a two-way process. It is a mutual give and take rather than a ***take home all*** method of arriving at a solution to a dispute.

Process of Collective Bargaining

1. **Preparation for Negotiation.** Preparation for negotiation in Collective Bargaining is as important as the negotiation process itself. Upto 83% of the outcomes are influenced by pre-negotiation process. Such preparation is required for both management as well as the union representatives. From the management's point of view, pre-negotiation preparation is required as:
   - Management should decide when and how to open the negotiations/dialogue.
   - Management must choose the representatives to negotiate at the negotiation table.
   - Draft for likely decisions should be prepared in advance so that the final agreement draft can be prepared as soon as the negotiation process is over.
   - From the employees' side also, preparation is required for the following reasons:
     (i) The union should collect the information related to the financial position of the company and their ability to pay the employees.
     (ii) The union must also be aware of the various practices followed by other companies in the same region or industry.
     (iii) The union must assess the attitudes and expectations of the employees over concerned issues so that the outcome of negotiations does not face any resistance from them.
2. **Identifying issues for Bargaining.** The second step in bargaining process is the determination of issues which will be taken up for negotiations. The different types of issues are:
   - *Wage-related issues.* Include wage or salary revision, allowance for meeting increased cost of living like Dearness Allowance (D.A.), financial perks, incentives etc.
   - *Supplementary economic benefits.* These include pension plans, gratuity plans, accident compensation, health insurance plans, paid holidays etc.
   - *Administrative issues.* Include seniority, grievance procedures, employee health and safety measures, job security and job changes.

   The wage and benefits issues are the ones which receive the greatest amount of attention on the bargaining table.
3. **Negotiation.** When the first two steps are completed, both parties engage in actual negotiation process at a time and place fixed for the purpose. There are two types of negotiations:
   - *Boulwarism.* In this method, the management themselves takes the initiative to find out through comprehensive research and surveys the needs of the employees. Based on the analysis of the findings, the company designs its own package based on the issues to be bargained. Thereafter, a change is incorporated only when new facts are presented by the employees or their unions.
   - *Continuous Bargaining.* Involves parties to explore particular bargaining problems in joint meetings over a long period of time, some throughout the life of each agreement. The basic logic behind this method is that all persistent issues can be addressed through continuous negotiation over a period of time. The success of negotiations depends on the skills and abilities of the negotiators.
4. **Initial negotiated agreement.** When two parties arrive at a mutually acceptable agreement either in the initial stage or through overcoming negotiation breakdown, the agreement is recorded with a provision that the agreement will be formalized after the ratification by the respective organisations.
5. **Ratification of agreement.** Ratification of negotiated agreement is required because the representatives of both the parties may not have ultimate authority to decide various issues

referred to for collective bargaining. The ratification of agreement may be done by the appropriate manager authorized for the purpose in the case of management, or trade executives in the case of the employees. Ratification is also required by the Industrial Disputes Act. It is important that the agreement must be clear and precise. Any ambiguity leads to future complications or other such problems.

6. **Implementation of agreement.** Signing the agreement is not the end of collective bargaining, rather it is the beginning of the process when the agreement is finalized, it becomes operational from the date indicated in the agreement. The agreement must be implemented according to the letter and spirit of the provisions made by the agreement agreed to by both parties. The HR manager plays a crucial role in the day-to-day administration, implementation of the agreement.

INTERNATIONAL HUMAN RESOURCE MANAGEMENT

IHRM can be defined as set of activities aimed managing organizational human resources at international level to achieve organizational objectives and achieve competitive advantage over competitors at national and international level. IHRM includes typical HRM functions such as recruitment, selection, training and development, performance appraisal and dismissal done at international level and additional activities such as global skills management, expatriate management and so on.

In simple terms, IHRM is concerned about managing human resources at Multinational Companies (MNC) and it involves managing three types of employees namely:

1. **Home country employees.** Employees belonging to home country of the firm where the corporate head quarter is situated.
2. **Host country employees.** Employees belonging to the nation in which the subsidiary is situated.
3. **Third country employees.** These are the employees who are not from home country/host country but are employed at subsidiary or corporate head quarters. As an example a American MNC which has a subsidiary at India may employ a French person as the CEO to the subsidiary. The Frenchman employed is a third country employee.

Differences between domestic HRM and International HRM (IHRM) are summarized below:

- Domestic HRM is done at national level and IHRM is done at international level.
- Domestic HRM is concerned with managing employees belonging to one nation and IHRM is concerned with managing employees belonging to many nations (Home country, host country and third country employees)
- Domestic HRM is concerned with managing limited number of HRM activities at national level and IHRM has concerned with managing additional activities such as expatriate management.
- Domestic HRM is less complicated due to less influence from the external environment. IHRM is very complicated as it is affected heavily by external factors such as cultural distance and institutional factors.

Challenges/Issues in Staffing Policy in IHRM

Development of an effective staffing policy poses a significant challenge for IHRM (International Human Resource Management). The ability of a firm to attract, recruit, and maintain qualified, skilled, and committed workforce handles the success of any company. One of the primary challenges is the geographical barrier between the head offices and the overseas branches which make it practically hard to implement a day-to-day relationship.

Several other factors affect the staffing policy in IHRM as summarized below:

Political Factors

Certain political risk factors in the overseas countries serve to create an air of uncertainty and an environment of suspicion in IHRM. As such human resource managers live with the fear of unknown; consequently, the fail to make strategic decision owing to their long-term nature for fear of what will transpire.

Legal Factors

Undoubtedly, the host country's legal system serves as the main determinant of the staffing policy to be adopted by an organization. As such, most international firms face a challenge where the host country sets the minimum representation of the local employees in the multinational firms.

Economic Factors

Several economic factors such as the economic development and position concerning the investment made by the MNCs have a huge impact on the staffing policy adopted by multinational firms. The international human resource managers must take into account the differing purchasing as well as prosperity powers. For instance, escalating costs in many developing countries have forced MNCs to replace the expatriates with the local managers. Moreover, as a result of the scarcity of managerial talent in most developing countries MNCs have experienced huge transaction costs as they 'import' managerial staffs from other countries.

Socio-cultural Factors

Cultural distance serves as one of the main determinants of the staffing philosophy and impacts immensely on IHRM. Among the most complex challenges facing international human resource managers is cross-culture communication. Culture refers to a 'software of the mind' that directs the pattern of thinking and behavior thus influencing how a particular people live and how they associate with others. Cultural differences inarguably handle the performance of the company. Some cultures may support particular types of organization and reject others.

Demographic Diversity

Most countries in the developing countries in Africa are characterized by a dwindling youth population and high unemployment rates. Consequently, such countries experience a severe skilled labor shortage given the fact that most of the youths have limited skills. Research have established that more than half of Africa's population comprise of youths below the age of 25 years most of whom are still students. Currently, the only solution to solve the problem of a limited skilled workforce is by the company filling the gap with older skilled workers and bringing more women into the workforce.

Recommendations to Solve the Challenge of International Staffing

Given the fact that human resource managers face an array of challenges when deciding on the appropriate staffing policy, the following solutions would assist in solving the problems associated with international staffing

Effective Cross-cultural Management

Irrespective of the good will that might exist in any firm, miscommunication will more often than not occur owing to the differences in culture between the communicators. However, cross-cultural management serves as the leading solution to cross-cultural conflicts. Multicultural companies can adopt several strategies to overcome the blocks of behavior, emotions, culture, and race. Such strategies include the transfer and dissemination of knowledge and bicultural skills.

Short-term international Assignments

Short-term assignments serve as the most appropriate form of the non-standard tasks. Such assignments involve a temporary/short-term (less than a year) transfer of the staffs/employees to a foreign subsidiary. Such assignment would assist the firm to solve the challenge associated with talent shortage in the host country and managerial development. Short-term assignments also come with additional benefits which include increased effectiveness, flexibility, and simplicity.

Commuter and Rotational Assignments

Such an assignment involves an employee working in one country for a week or two and then transferring to another workstation in another country and so on. Such an arrangement enables to solve the challenge of cross-culture communication and increased flexibility.

Training and Development

International human resource managers face a range of challenges in their efforts to create and develop a high-caliber workforce. An important point to note in training and development is that the HR manager should not only focus a lot of attention on quality training but must also make sure that the training is effective and engaging. The following are the challenges faced in training and development.

Green HRM

Green HR is the use of HRM policies such a way to promote sustainable use of resources in business organizations to make ecofriendly and promote environmental economical sustainability practices to keep healthier environment by increasing employee awareness and commitments on the issues of sustainability.

The HR function can become the driver of environmental sustainability within the organization by aligning its practices and policies with sustainability goals representing ecofriendly which can contribute to organizational goals. It involves undertaking environment-friendly HR initiatives resulting in:

1. Greater efficiencies with motivation, and
2. Lower costs and better employee engagement and retention.

Green management initiatives can be an important factor in forward thinking business organizations around the world. Green HR initiatives help companies find alternative ways to cut cost without losing their talent & important resources etc.

Now a days, there is a growing need for strategic Green HRM – the integration of environmental management into HRM in the perspective of the question of environment pollution in the world. HR professionals can indicate that encouraging employees to be more environmentally friendly in the workplace is the top practice for their organizations. This means organizations can encourage their employees to perform activities such as early morning office time, making double-sided photocopies, powering down computers after a few minutes of inactivity, using energy efficient bulbs can be the top environmentally responsible practices in initial stage of Green HR.

Nowadays companies are implementing EMS (Environmental Management System) a strategic tool to gain competitive advantage. This system provides better control of firm's environmental impacts. It includes commitment, policy, planning, implementation, measurement and evaluation, review and improvement of HR systems that fit with organization's culture and long-term goals.

Improved employee morale, stronger public image, increased consumer/ customer confidence, employee loyalty and brand recognition, position as an employer of choice, increased workforce productivity, efficiency, motivation and employee retention are few of the many advantages and benefits an organization can have by implementing and developing such Green HRM techniques.

Steps taken by companies to start Go Green practice:

1. Power Saving by early morning office startup.
2. Conduct an internal environment & energy audit in the organization.
3. Conduct ecofriendly or Go Green Surveys.
4. Go paperless by using apps, software & e-hr.
5. Recycle waste.
6. Reduce business travel - Teleconference instead of travelling.
7. Save water - Monitor sinks and toilets for leaks that waste water.
8. Explore opportunities for implementing alternative energy sources.

MULTIPLE CHOICE QUESTIONS

1. The strategic role of Human Resource Management (HRM) involves aligning HR practices with
   (a) Organizational goals and objectives
   (b) Employee preferences
   (c) Strict adherence to government regulations
   (d) Suppressing employee creativity
2. HR as a strategic partner means that HR professionals
   (a) Only focus on administrative tasks
   (b) Are actively involved in shaping the organization's strategic direction
   (c) Strictly enforce corporate policies
   (d) Ignore the influence of leadership
3. Strategic HRM helps organizations to gain a competitive advantage by
   (a) Reducing employee salaries
   (b) Attracting and retaining top talent
   (c) Ignoring industry standards
   (d) Suppressing employee morale
4. The concept of "human capital" emphasizes that
   (a) Employees are valuable assets that can contribute to an organization's success
   (b) Employees are replaceable and their value is low
   (c) Strict adherence to government regulations
   (d) Ignoring the perspectives of employees
5. HR's role in workforce planning and talent management includes
   (a) Ignoring employee performance
   (b) Attracting, developing, and retaining a skilled workforce
   (c) Strict adherence to industry norms
   (d) Suppressing employee concerns
6. Strategic HR planning begins with a clear understanding of
   (a) Employee preferences
   (b) Strict adherence to government regulations
   (c) Ignoring the influence of leadership
   (d) The organization's long-term goals and objectives
7. SWOT analysis in HR planning involves assessing
   (a) Employee satisfaction levels
   (b) The organization's strengths, weaknesses, opportunities, and threats
   (c) Suppressing employee creativity
   (d) Strict enforcement of company policies
8. Strategic HR planning includes developing strategies for
   (a) Ignoring industry standards
   (b) Attracting, retaining, and developing talent
   (c) Adhering to government regulations
   (d) Suppressing employee performance
9. HR forecasting methods aim to predict future HR needs based on
   (a) Employee job descriptions
   (b) Strictly enforcing corporate policies
   (c) Organizational objectives and market trends
   (d) Ignoring the values and needs of employees
10. Succession planning involves
    (a) Ensuring that employees always work in their current positions
    (b) Identifying and preparing employees for key leadership roles
    (c) Strict adherence to industry norms
    (d) Suppressing employee morale
11. In strategic recruitment, organizations aim to attract candidates who
    (a) Are willing to work for the lowest possible salary
    (b) Have the skills and qualities that align with the organization's strategic goals
    (c) Ignore the influence of leadership

(d) Strictly adhere to government regulations

12. "Employer branding" in recruitment refers to
(a) Providing branding and marketing services to other organizations
(b) Suppressing employee opinions
(c) Ignoring the perspectives of colleagues
(d) How an organization is perceived as an employer and its reputation in the job market

13. Recruitment channels in strategic HR include
(a) Only internal promotions
(b) A mix of internal and external sources to attract diverse talent
(c) Strict adherence to industry standards
(d) Ignoring industry trends

14. "Talent pipelines" in strategic recruitment involve
(a) Building a pool of qualified candidates for future needs
(b) Developing pipelines for transporting physical goods
(c) Strictly enforcing corporate policies
(d) Suppressing employee needs and perspectives

15. "Diversity and inclusion" in strategic recruitment emphasize
(a) Excluding candidates from diverse backgrounds
(b) Attracting a diverse workforce and creating an inclusive workplace
(c) Adhering to government regulations
(d) Ignoring the influence of leadership

16. Strategic HR development focuses on
(a) Ignoring employee training needs
(b) Enhancing the skills and capabilities of the workforce to achieve organizational goals
(c) Strict adherence to industry norms
(d) Suppressing employee performance

17. "Leadership development programs" aim to
(a) Ensure all employees have leadership roles
(b) Strict enforcement of company policies
(c) Identify and develop future leaders within the organization
(d) Ignore the values and needs of employees

18. In strategic HR development, "succession planning" involves
(a) Replacing all employees with new hires
(b) Identifying and preparing employees for key leadership roles in the future
(c) Suppressing employee creativity
(d) Strict adherence to government regulations

19. "Cross-functional training" in HR development means
(a) Training employees to work in isolation within their departments
(b) Ignoring industry standards
(c) Adhering to corporate policies
(d) Providing training that equips employees to work effectively in different functional areas

20. "Career development paths" in strategic HR development help employees
(a) Stay in the same role indefinitely
(b) Plan and progress in their careers within the organization
(c) Suppressing employee concerns
(d) Strictly enforcing industry norms

21. In strategic compensation management, pay is linked to
(a) Employee preferences
(b) Organizational goals and performance
(c) Strict adherence to government regulations
(d) Ignoring the influence of leadership

22. "Variable pay" or "incentive pay" is designed to reward employees based on
(a) Their years of service
(b) Their performance, achievements, or specific goals
(c) Suppressing employee morale
(d) Their job titles

23. "Pay-for-performance" systems in strategic compensation involve
(a) Providing fixed salaries regardless of performance
(b) Rewarding employees based on their job titles
(c) Ignoring industry standards
(d) Tying pay to individual or team performance

24. "Equity theory" in compensation management is concerned with
(a) Suppressing employee performance
(b) Ensuring everyone receives the same pay
(c) Strict adherence to industry norms
(d) Ensuring fairness in compensation by com-

paring employees' inputs and outcomes

25. "Total rewards" in strategic compensation encompass both
    (a) Employee job descriptions and qualifications
    (b) Monetary and non-monetary rewards that employees receive
    (c) Strict enforcement of corporate policies
    (d) Ignoring the values and needs of employees
26. Competency mapping is a process used to identify and manage
    (a) Employee salaries
    (b) Employee skills, knowledge, and abilities
    (c) Strict adherence to government regulations
    (d) Ignoring the influence of leadership
27. The goal of competency mapping is to
    (a) Suppress employee creativity
    (b) Ignore the values and needs of employees
    (c) Develop and align employee competencies with organizational objectives
    (d) Ensure all employees have the same competencies
28. "Competency models" are typically developed to
    (a) Determine employee job titles
    (b) Describe the desired skills and behaviors for specific roles
    (c) Strictly enforce company policies
    (d) Suppress employee performance
29. Competency mapping is often used for purposes such as
    (a) Reducing employee turnover
    (b) Recruitment, training, and performance management
    (c) Ignoring industry standards
    (d) Strict adherence to industry norms
30. "Behavioral interviews" in competency mapping assess candidates' competencies by
    (a) Suppressing employee concerns
    (b) Focusing on their job titles and education
    (c) Asking about past experiences and behaviors related to specific competencies
    (d) Adhering to government regulations
31. The Balanced Scorecard is a strategic management framework that looks at an organization's performance from four key perspectives, which are
    (a) Financial, Customer, Internal Processes, and Learning and Growth
    (b) Employee satisfaction, Market share, Productivity, and Regulations
    (c) Ignoring the influence of leadership
    (d) Strict adherence to industry norms
32. The "Financial Perspective" of the Balanced Scorecard focuses on
    (a) Employee compensation and benefits
    (b) Financial metrics such as revenue, profit, and return on investment
    (c) Suppressing employee morale
    (d) Adhering to company policies
33. "Customer Perspective" in the Balanced Scorecard measures
    (a) Employee performance and productivity
    (b) Customer satisfaction, loyalty, and retention
    (c) Strict adherence to government regulations
    (d) Ignoring employee needs and perspectives
34. The "Internal Processes Perspective" examines
    (a) Ignoring industry standards
    (b) Employee training and development
    (c) The efficiency and effectiveness of an organization's processes
    (d) Strictly enforcing corporate policies
35. "Learning and Growth Perspective" in the Balanced Scorecard focuses on
    (a) Employee salaries and bonuses
    (b) The organization's ability to innovate, learn, and develop its workforce
    (c) Suppressing employee performance
    (d) Ignoring the values and needs of colleagues
36. Key Performance Indicators (KPIs) in the Balanced Scorecard are
    (a) Specific financial metrics only
    (b) Strict adherence to government regulations
    (c) Adhering to industry norms
    (d) A set of measures used to track performance in each perspective
37. In the Financial Perspective, a KPI might be
    (a) Employee engagement
    (b) Return on investment (ROI)
    (c) Strictly enforcing company policies
    (d) Ignoring the influence of leadership

38. In the Customer Perspective, a KPI could be
    (a) Customer satisfaction score (e.g., Net Promoter Score)
    (b) Employee retention
    (c) Suppressing employee creativity
    (d) Strict adherence to industry norms
39. In the Internal Processes Perspective, a KPI might measure
    (a) Employee attendance
    (b) Process cycle time or error rate
    (c) Ignoring industry standards
    (d) Adhering to government regulations
40. The Learning and Growth Perspective may include KPIs related to
    (a) Employee job titles and descriptions
    (b) Ignoring the values and needs of employees
    (c) Reducing employee salaries
    (d) Employee training and development programs
41. The process of implementing the Balanced Scorecard typically starts with
    (a) Creating a strict set of company policies
    (b) Developing a strategy map and defining strategic objectives
    (c) Suppressing employee morale
    (d) Ignoring employee performance
42. Cascading the Balanced Scorecard means
    (a) Restricting access to scorecard data
    (b) Aligning departmental and individual objectives with the overall strategy
    (c) Strict adherence to government regulations
    (d) Adhering to industry norms
43. The Balanced Scorecard is often communicated and shared with
    (a) Employees at lower levels of the organization only
    (b) Ignoring the influence of leadership
    (c) All employees throughout the organization
    (d) Strictly enforcing corporate policies
44. "Scorecard review meetings" in the Balanced Scorecard process involve
    (a) Suppressing employee concerns
    (b) Regular discussions to review progress and address issues
    (c) Adhering to government regulations
    (d) Ignoring the values and needs of colleagues
45. Continuous improvement in the Balanced Scorecard involves
    (a) Regularly updating objectives and measures to adapt to changing conditions
    (b) Employee job descriptions and qualifications
    (c) Strict adherence to industry norms
    (d) Reducing employee morale
46. Measuring the alignment of strategic objectives with the Balanced Scorecard involves
    (a) Ignoring industry standards
    (b) Assessing whether performance measures support the achievement of objectives
    (c) Strictly enforcing company policies
    (d) Suppressing employee creativity
47. "Strategy execution" in the context of the Balanced Scorecard refers to
    (a) Implementing a rigid set of corporate policies
    (b) Aligning actions and processes to achieve strategic objectives
    (c) Ignoring the influence of leadership
    (d) Adhering to government regulations
48. "Strategic initiatives" may include projects and actions aimed at
    (a) Achieving strategic objectives
    (b) Increasing employee salaries
    (c) Ignoring employee needs and perspectives
    (d) Strict adherence to government regulations
49. The "cause-and-effect" relationships in the Balanced Scorecard help to
    (a) Suppress employee performance
    (b) Show how achieving one objective impacts others and supports the strategy
    (c) Adhere to industry norms
    (d) Ignore the values and needs of employees
50. "Alignment maps" or "strategy maps" are used to
    (a) Guide employees to strictly adhere to company policies
    (b) Visually depict the cause-and-effect relationships between objectives
    (c) Strictly enforce government regulations
    (d) Suppress employee morale
51. Career planning and development is a proactive process that involves

(a) Assigning job titles to employees
(b) Managing employee performance
(c) Setting personal and professional goals and strategies
(d) Suppressing employee creativity

52. The primary goal of career planning is to
(a) Restrict employees to their current roles
(b) Help individuals choose a career path and develop the skills and knowledge needed to succeed
(c) Strict adherence to government regulations
(d) Ignore the influence of leadership

53. The career development process often includes self-assessment, which involves
(a) Evaluating the performance of coworkers
(b) Ignoring industry standards
(c) Strictly enforcing corporate policies
(d) Reflecting on one's own strengths, weaknesses, interests, and values

54. "Career goals" are typically
(a) Defined by employers for employees
(b) Personal objectives related to an individual's career aspirations
(c) Suppressing employee morale
(d) Adhering to industry norms

55. "Mentoring" and "coaching" are strategies used in career development to
(a) Dictate employee job titles
(b) Provide guidance and support to individuals in their careers
(c) Strict adherence to industry norms
(d) Ignore the values and needs of employees

56. Career readiness assessments often evaluate factors such as
(a) Skills, knowledge, interests, and personal attributes
(b) Employee job titles and qualifications
(c) Adhering to government regulations
(d) Suppressing employee performance

57. A "gap analysis" in career readiness identifies
(a) Opportunities for pay raises
(b) Discrepancies between current skills and those needed for career goals
(c) Ignoring the influence of leadership
(d) Strict enforcement of company policies

58. "Career anchors" refer to
(a) Rigid job titles
(b) Ignoring industry standards
(c) Stable and consistent career preferences and values
(d) Strictly adhering to corporate policies

59. In career readiness, "transferable skills" are those that can be
(a) Applied only within a specific job or industry
(b) Utilized across different jobs and industries
(c) Suppressing employee creativity
(d) Ignoring the perspectives of colleagues

60. Career planning workshops" and "self-assessment tools" can help individuals with
(a) Setting unrealistic job title goals
(b) Identifying their strengths, weaknesses, and career interests
(c) Adhering to government regulations
(d) Strictly enforcing industry norms

61. Career transitions may include changes such as
(a) Moving to a new job or industry, or pursuing further education
(b) Receiving employee bonuses
(c) Ignoring employee performance
(d) Suppressing employee morale

62. "Reskilling" and "upskilling" are strategies used during career transitions to
(a) Restrict employees to their current roles
(b) Acquire new skills or enhance existing ones to remain employable
(c) Strict adherence to government regulations
(d) Ignore the influence of leadership

63. "Career development centers" or "career counselors" provide guidance and support in
(a) Dictating employee job titles
(b) Strictly adhering to corporate policies
(c) Ignoring industry standards
(d) Assisting individuals with their career choices, transitions, and development

64. The psychological response to a career transition, often characterized by anxiety or excitement, is known as
(a) Employee job descriptions
(b) Career adjustment or transition shock
(c) Suppressing employee needs and perspectives
(d) Strict adherence to industry norms

65. "Networking" during a career transition involves
    (a) Isolating oneself from others
    (b) Building and maintaining professional relationships to access opportunities and support
    (c) Ignoring the values and needs of employees
    (d) Adhering to company policies
66. In organizations, "career paths" or "ladders" typically show
    (a) The shortest route to reach the CEO position
    (b) A series of job titles and roles an employee can follow within the organization
    (c) Suppressing employee creativity
    (d) Strictly enforcing government regulations
67. A "career plateau" in an organization may occur when
    (a) All employees receive a promotion simultaneously
    (b) Strict adherence to industry norms
    (c) An employee feels stuck in their current position with limited opportunities for advancement
    (d) Ignoring the influence of leadership
68. "Job rotation" is a career development practice that involves
    (a) Forcing employees to stay in one role for their entire career
    (b) Moving employees through various roles to develop their skills and knowledge
    (c) Adhering to corporate policies
    (d) Ignoring industry standards
69. "High-potential" or "hi-po" employees are typically identified for
    (a) Reducing employee salaries
    (b) Fast-track development and potential leadership roles
    (c) Suppressing employee concerns
    (d) Strict adherence to company policies
70. "Succession planning" is a process that focuses on
    (a) Identifying and preparing employees for future leadership roles in the organization
    (b) Ignoring the perspectives of colleagues
    (c) Adhering to government regulations
    (d) Strictly adhering to industry norms
71. Career development challenges may include issues such as
    (a) Giving all employees equal pay
    (b) Balancing work-life demands and career aspirations
    (c) Ignoring industry standards
    (d) Strictly enforcing government regulations
72. The "glass ceiling" is a career development challenge that pertains to
    (a) All employees reaching the highest levels of leadership
    (b) Barriers that prevent certain groups, often women or minorities, from reaching top positions
    (c) Suppressing employee performance
    (d) Ignoring the values and needs of employees
73. "Career burnout" is a condition often caused by
    (a) Continuous career advancement
    (b) Prolonged job stress, overwork, or a lack of job satisfaction
    (c) Strict adherence to corporate policies
    (d) Ignoring the influence of leadership
74. "Impostor syndrome" in career development refers to
    (a) Employees pretending to be something they are not
    (b) A feeling of inadequacy despite evidence of competence and success
    (c) Adhering to company policies
    (d) Suppressing employee morale
75. Organizations can address career development challenges by
    (a) Dictating employee job titles and roles
    (b) Providing support, training, and mentorship programs
    (c) Strictly enforcing industry norms
    (d) Ignoring employee performance
76. What is the primary purpose of performance appraisal?
    (a) Employee development
    (b) Employee selection
    (c) Employee discipline
    (d) Employee recruitment
77. Which of the following is NOT a step in the performance appraisal process?
    (a) Goal setting
    (b) Performance evaluation
    (c) Compensation negotiation
    (d) Feedback and coaching

78. Which performance appraisal method assesses an employee's performance based on specific behaviors and competencies?
   (a) Graphic rating scale
   (b) 360-degree feedback
   (c) Behaviorally anchored rating scale (BARS)
   (d) Forced distribution

79. In a 360-degree feedback appraisal, who provides feedback on an employee's performance?
   (a) Only the immediate supervisor
   (b) Only HR department
   (c) Peers, subordinates, and superiors
   (d) External consultants

80. Which type of performance appraisal rating scale requires managers to rate employees on a scale from "exceeds expectations" to "needs improvement"?
   (a) Likert scale
   (b) Graphic rating scale
   (c) Forced ranking
   (d) Behavioral observation scale

81. The purpose of a self-assessment in performance appraisal is
   (a) To allow employees to evaluate their own performance
   (b) To minimize manager's effort
   (c) To reduce feedback discussions
   (d) To avoid conflict

82. What is the primary goal of a performance improvement plan (PIP)?
   (a) To terminate the employee
   (b) To identify areas for employee growth and development
   (c) To determine a promotion plan
   (d) To reduce the workload of the employee

83. Which of the following is an advantage of continuous performance feedback over annual reviews?
   (a) Reduced administrative burden
   (b) Increased employee motivation
   (c) More accurate assessment of long-term performance
   (d) Decreased employee engagement

84. The "Halo Effect" in performance appraisal refers to
   (a) Providing overly positive evaluations to all employees
   (b) Letting employees self-assess their performance
   (c) Allowing for bias in the appraisal process
   (d) Letting one positive trait or action overshadow an overall evaluation

85. What is the purpose of a performance management system?
   (a) To facilitate employee discipline
   (b) To establish a formal complaint process
   (c) To align individual performance with organizational goals
   (d) To provide job training

86. Which of the following is NOT a common source of performance appraisal bias?
   (a) Gender bias
   (b) Age bias
   (c) Job satisfaction bias
   (d) Recency bias

87. Which performance appraisal method forces managers to categorize employees into predetermined performance groups, such as "top performers" and "poor performers"?
   (a) Graphic rating scale
   (b) Critical incident method
   (c) Forced ranking
   (d) Self-assessment

88. What is the purpose of a calibration meeting in the performance appraisal process?
   (a) To calibrate the scores and feedback given to employees
   (b) To select employees for termination
   (c) To celebrate top performers
   (d) To review the company's financial performance

89. What is the role of HR in the performance appraisal process?
   (a) To directly appraise employee performance
   (b) To mediate conflicts between employees and managers
   (c) To design and manage the performance appraisal system
   (d) To set individual performance goals

90. Which type of appraisal focuses on employee performance over the entire performance period and encourages ongoing feedback?
   (a) Annual appraisal
   (b) Quarterly appraisal
   (c) Continuous appraisal
   (d) 360-degree appraisal

91. Which of the following is NOT a common performance appraisal error?
(a) Central tendency
(b) Leniency bias
(c) Stereotyping
(d) Timeliness

92. The term "SMART" goals in performance management stands for
(a) Specific, Measurable, Attainable, Relevant, Time-bound
(b) Subjective, Manageable, Ambiguous, Relevant, Timeless
(c) Strategic, Measurable, Actionable, Reliable, Tangible
(d) Significant, Measurable, Achievable, Realistic, Temporary

93. Which approach to performance appraisal emphasizes employee self-assessment and reflection?
(a) Manager-centered
(b) Employee-centered
(c) Peer-centered
(d) 360-degree

94. Which of the following is a potential consequence of a poorly conducted performance appraisal?
(a) Increased employee motivation
(b) Enhanced team collaboration
(c) Decreased employee morale
(d) Improved communication

95. Which step in the performance appraisal process involves setting clear expectations and performance standards?
(a) Evaluation
(b) Feedback
(c) Planning
(d) Documentation

96. The practice of ranking employees in order of their performance levels is known as
(a) 360 degree feedback
(b) Behaviorally anchored rating
(c) Forced ranking
(d) Graphic rating scale

97. What is the purpose of a mid-year review in the performance appraisal process?
(a) To determine annual bonuses
(b) To provide feedback and coaching
(c) To establish disciplinary actions
(d) To complete the final evaluation

98. Which of the following is a potential benefit of a well-implemented performance management system?
(a) Reduced employee turnover
(b) Decreased communication
(c) Increased absenteeism
(d) Lower productivity

99. Which performance appraisal method emphasizes specific, observable, and measurable behaviors and outcomes?
(a) Graphic rating scale
(b) Critical incident method
(c) Management by objectives (MBO)
(d) Peer appraisal

100. Who is typically responsible for conducting the performance appraisal for an employee?
(a) The employee themselves
(b) The employee's peers
(c) The employee's manager or supervisor
(d) The HR department

101. What is the primary goal of Organization Development (OD)?
(a) Maximizing short-term profits
(b) Improving employee job satisfaction
(c) Achieving long-term strategic goals
(d) Reducing organizational complexity

102. Which of the following is a key principle of OD?
(a) Maintaining the status quo
(b) Minimizing employee involvement
(c) Continuous improvement and adaptation
(d) Centralized decision-making

103. Which stage in the change process involves creating a sense of urgency and building a guiding coalition, according to the Kotter's Eight-Step Model?
(a) Diagnosing the problem
(b) Establishing a vision for change
(c) Creating short-term wins
(d) Sustaining the change

104. In the Lewin's Three-Step Model of change, what is the second stage?
(a) Unfreeze
(b) Refreeze
(c) Change
(d) Evaluate

105. Which type of change is typically more incremental and involves improving existing processes and systems?

(a) Radical change
(b) Continuous change
(c) Transformational change
(d) Reactive change

106. What does the acronym "SWOT" stand for in the context of organizational analysis?
(a) Strengths, Weaknesses, Opportunities, Threats
(b) Sales, Workforce, Operations, Technology
(c) Strategic, Workflow, Objectives, Targets
(d) Staffing, Workload, Optimization, Timelines

107. Which OD intervention focuses on improving communication and relationships within an organization?
(a) Process consultation
(b) Team building
(c) Strategic planning
(d) Six Sigma

108. What does the "Force-Field Analysis" technique help identify in the change process?
(a) The driving forces for change and restraining forces against change
(b) The costs associated with change
(c) The change management team
(d) The timeline for implementing change

109. Which type of OD intervention focuses on improving individual job performance and skills?
(a) Process consultation
(b) Team building
(c) Training and development
(d) Total quality management

110. Which stage of the ADKAR model (Awareness, Desire, Knowledge, Ability, Reinforcement) deals with creating a desire for change among employees?
(a) Awareness
(b) Desire
(c) Knowledge
(d) Ability

111. What is the purpose of a "Gap Analysis" in the context of organizational change?
(a) Identifying the current state and desired future state
(b) Analyzing the competition
(c) Assessing employee morale
(d) Evaluating financial performance

112. What is the primary focus of the "Appreciative Inquiry" OD intervention?
(a) Identifying weaknesses and problems
(b) Exploring an organization's positive attributes and strengths
(c) Reducing resistance to change
(d) Eliminating hierarchy within the organization

113. Which type of change typically results from external factors and requires a reactive response?
(a) Planned change
(b) Transformational change
(c) Unplanned change
(d) Incremental change

114. Which step in the Kotter's Eight-Step Model involves communicating the vision for change to all employees?
(a) Diagnosing the problem
(b) Establishing a guiding coalition
(c) Creating a vision for change
(d) Communicating the vision

115. What is the primary goal of a "SWOT analysis"?
(a) To eliminate weaknesses
(b) To exploit opportunities
(c) To prepare a budget
(d) To assess employee performance

116. Which of the following is an example of a "hard" OD intervention?
(a) Team building
(b) Leadership development
(c) Process reengineering
(d) Employee counseling

117. In the context of OD, what is "Action Research"?
(a) A specific type of data analysis
(b) A method for collecting customer feedback
(c) A research approach that involves collaboration between researchers and practitioners
(d) A tool for budgeting

118. What does the "Lewin's Force Field Analysis" seek to balance in the change process?
(a) Driving forces and restraining forces
(b) External and internal factors
(c) Resistance and acceptance
(d) Leadership and followership

119. Which OD intervention is focused on resolving conflicts and disputes within an organization?
(a) Coaching

(b) Mediation
(c) Six Sigma
(d) Process consultation

120. Which of the following is a potential benefit of a well-planned change management process?
(a) Increased employee resistance
(b) Lower employee morale
(c) Enhanced organizational agility
(d) Decreased innovation

121. Which stage in the change process involves monitoring the change to ensure it is sustained?
(a) Diagnosis
(b) Implementation
(c) Evaluation
(d) Planning

122. What is the primary purpose of a "Force-Field Analysis" in the change management process?
(a) To identify all possible solutions to a problem
(b) To weigh the pros and cons of a proposed change
(c) To identify factors that support and oppose the desired change
(d) To assess employee competencies

123. Which OD intervention is designed to improve leadership skills and behaviors within an organization?
(a) Team building
(b) Leadership development
(c) Process reengineering
(d) Survey feedback

124. In Kotter's Eight-Step Model, what is the final step in the change process?
(a) Create a guiding coalition
(b) Sustain the change
(c) Establish a vision for change
(d) Diagnose the problem

125. What does the "ADKAR" model primarily focus on in the change process?
(a) Identifying driving and restraining forces
(b) Assessing organizational culture
(c) Managing resistance to change
(d) Individual change adoption and awareness

126. What is the primary goal of talent management?
(a) Reducing employee turnover
(b) Maximizing short-term profits
(c) Developing and retaining top talent
(d) Decreasing workforce diversity

127. Which of the following is NOT a component of the talent management process?
(a) Recruitment
(b) Compensation management
(c) Performance management
(d) Employee engagement

128. What is succession planning in talent management?
(a) Identifying and developing future leaders within an organization
(b) Filling vacant positions with external candidates
(c) Evaluating employee performance annually
(d) Setting short-term performance goals

129. Which term refers to the process of attracting and retaining a diverse workforce?
(a) Workforce optimization
(b) Affirmative action
(c) Talent acquisition
(d) Diversity and inclusion

130. What does the acronym "L&D" stand for in the context of skill development?
(a) Learning and Development
(b) Labor and Discipline
(c) Leadership and Diversity
(d) Logistics and Delivery

131. Which type of training is designed to improve specific job-related skills and knowledge?
(a) Onboarding training
(b) Leadership development
(c) Soft skills training
(d) Compliance training

132. What is the purpose of a "360-degree feedback" process in skill development?
(a) To evaluate an employee's performance using multiple supervisors
(b) To provide feedback from customers only
(c) To assess technical skills
(d) To rank employees based on seniority

133. Which of the following is NOT a common method of skill assessment and development?
(a) Job rotation
(b) Competency modeling
(c) Self-assessment
(d) Employee termination

134. What is the primary goal of an "Individual Development Plan" (IDP)?

(a) Identifying employees for layoffs
(b) Promoting a competitive work environment
(c) Tailoring skill development for each employee
(d) Reducing workforce diversity

135. Which of the following is a soft skill often targeted in skill development programs?
(a) Coding
(b) Time management
(c) Data analysis
(d) Technical writing

136. What is the primary goal of a "Mentorship Program" in skill development?
(a) Creating competition among employees
(b) Pairing experienced employees with less experienced ones for learning and development
(c) Evaluating employee performance
(d) Reducing employee engagement

137. Which type of skill development program focuses on developing leadership and management skills?
(a) Technical training
(b) Onboarding
(c) Leadership development
(d) Compliance training

138. In the context of skill development, what is "Blended Learning"?
(a) Learning that involves mixing various forms of training, such as in-person and online
(b) Learning exclusively through books and manuals
(c) Learning through peer-to-peer training
(d) Learning through simulations and games

139. Which approach to skill development emphasizes learning by doing and solving real-world problems?
(a) Experiential learning
(b) Classroom training
(c) Web-based training
(d) Compliance training

140. What is the primary goal of a "Skill Gap Analysis"?
(a) Identifying areas where employees have too many skills
(b) Identifying areas where employees lack the necessary skills for their roles
(c) Reducing employee turnover
(d) Maximizing short-term profits

141. Which of the following is a potential benefit of investing in skill development for employees?
(a) Increased employee turnover
(b) Improved job satisfaction and performance
(c) Decreased employee engagement
(d) Reduced workforce diversity

142. Which term refers to the process of aligning an organization's learning and development initiatives with its strategic goals?
(a) Competency modeling
(b) Needs analysis
(c) Strategic alignment
(d) Employee termination

143. What is the primary purpose of "Cross-Training" in skill development?
(a) Preparing employees for layoffs
(b) Enhancing employee work-life balance
(c) Expanding employees' skill sets to perform multiple roles
(d) Reducing workforce diversity

144. What is "Gamification" in the context of skill development?
(a) A method of evaluating employees through games
(b) The process of terminating employees through gamified challenges
(c) Using game elements and principles in learning and development programs
(d) A tool for tracking employee attendance

145. Which type of training is typically required to ensure employees are compliant with legal and regulatory requirements?
(a) Soft skills training
(b) Technical training
(c) Compliance training
(d) Leadership development

146. What does the term "ROI" stand for in the context of skill development?
(a) Return on Investment
(b) Rate of Innovation
(c) Reach of Instructors
(d) Reduction of Incidents

147. Which of the following is a key component of a successful skill development program?
(a) One-size-fits-all approach
(b) Lack of support from management

(c) Regular evaluation and adjustment of the program
(d) Avoiding technology and e-learning

148. Which stage of the "Training Needs Analysis" process involves identifying performance gaps and learning objectives?
(a) Assess
(b) Design
(c) Implement
(d) Evaluate

149. What is the primary goal of "Onboarding" in skill development?
(a) Terminating employees who don't meet expectations
(b) Assimilating new employees into the organization and providing them with necessary skills and knowledge
(c) Reducing employee turnover
(d) Enhancing employee work-life balance

150. In the context of skill development, what is the primary goal of a "Skill Development Plan"?
(a) Identifying areas where employees have too many skills
(b) Tailoring skill development for each employee
(c) Promoting a competitive work environment
(d) Reducing workforce diversity

151. What is employee engagement?
(a) The number of employees in a company
(b) The emotional commitment and connection employees have with their organization
(c) The number of hours employees work each week
(d) The level of employee satisfaction with their salary

152. Which of the following is NOT a key factor contributing to employee engagement?
(a) Compensation and benefits
(b) Job satisfaction
(c) Career growth opportunities
(d) Workplace culture and relationships

153. What is the primary goal of an employee engagement survey?
(a) To assess employee productivity
(b) To evaluate the financial performance of the company
(c) To measure employee morale and satisfaction
(d) To identify the best time for employee vacations

154. Which of the following is a common strategy for increasing employee engagement?
(a) Reducing communication with employees
(b) Encouraging workaholic behavior
(c) Providing regular feedback and recognition
(d) Eliminating training and development programs

155. What is the role of leadership in fostering employee engagement?
(a) Creating a toxic work environment
(b) Minimizing employee involvement in decision-making
(c) Leading by example and promoting a positive workplace culture
(d) Isolating themselves from employees

156. What does the term "Employee Recognition" refer to?
(a) The process of downsizing or layoffs
(b) Acknowledging and appreciating employees' contributions and achievements
(c) Mandatory overtime
(d) Annual performance appraisals

157. Which of the following is NOT a common driver of employee engagement?
(a) Clear communication
(b) Career development opportunities
(c) Lack of job security
(d) Fair compensation

158. In the context of employee engagement, what is "Job Enrichment"?
(a) Reducing an employee's workload
(b) Adding more administrative tasks to a job
(c) Redesigning a job to include more meaningful and challenging tasks
(d) Decreasing employee responsibilities

159. Which of the following is a potential benefit of high employee engagement?
(a) Increased absenteeism
(b) Decreased employee morale
(c) Improved productivity and performance
(d) Higher turnover rates

160. What is the primary goal of a "Stay Interview" in employee engagement?

(a) To assess employee knowledge and skills
(b) To gather information on why employees are leaving or considering leaving the organization
(c) To provide performance feedback
(d) To determine the best time for employee vacations

161. What is the role of HR in promoting employee engagement?
(a) Ensuring strict control over employees' personal lives
(b) Implementing policies that discourage employee well-being
(c) Creating programs and initiatives that support employee engagement
(d) Increasing the workload of employees

162. In the context of employee engagement, what is "Employee Voice"?
(a) Employees are not allowed to express their opinions
(b) The process of actively seeking and listening to employees' opinions and ideas
(c) Employees are required to sing at work
(d) A type of employee recognition program

163. What is the primary goal of an "Engagement Action Plan"?
(a) To reduce employee engagement
(b) To create more stressful work environments
(c) To outline strategies for improving employee engagement
(d) To assess employee health

164. Which type of employee engagement program focuses on improving employees' health and well-being?
(a) Wellness programs
(b) Overtime programs
(c) Mandatory training programs
(d) Disciplinary programs

165. What is the role of feedback in employee engagement?
(a) To criticize and blame employees
(b) To provide constructive input and recognize employees' efforts
(c) To discourage employees from sharing their ideas
(d) To assess employee knowledge and skills

166. What is work-life balance?
(a) Spending more time at work than at home
(b) Achieving an equal distribution of work and personal life
(c) Focusing solely on one's career and ignoring personal life
(d) A lack of job security

167. Which of the following is NOT a common consequence of poor work-life balance?
(a) Increased stress and burnout
(b) Decreased job performance
(c) Enhanced personal relationships
(d) Higher employee turnover

168. What is telecommuting?
(a) A type of commuting to work
(b) Working remotely from a location other than the office, often from home
(c) A form of public transportation
(d) A type of job rotation

169. Which of the following is a potential benefit of flexible work hours for employees?
(a) Reduced autonomy
(b) Improved work-life balance
(c) Increased stress
(d) Reduced compensation

170. What is the primary goal of a "Compressed Workweek" schedule?
(a) Increasing the number of work hours
(b) Reducing job satisfaction
(c) Allowing employees to work longer hours each day but fewer days per week
(d) Eliminating vacation time

171. What is "Job Sharing" in the context of work-life balance?
(a) Two employees performing the same job simultaneously
(b) Sharing personal problems with coworkers
(c) Working long hours without breaks
(d) Increasing the workload of employees

172. Which term refers to the practice of employees taking unpaid leave for personal or family reasons?
(a) Sabbatical
(b) Overtime
(c) Job rotation
(d) Mandatory training

173. What is "Flextime" in the context of work-life balance?
(a) Rigid and inflexible working hours

(b) A set schedule for all employees
(c) Allowing employees to choose their work hours within certain limits
(d) A form of job elimination

174. What does the "9/80 Work Schedule" entail?
(a) Working 90 hours per week
(b) A compressed workweek with 9-hour workdays and every other Friday off
(c) Working 80 hours per week
(d) Working 9 days a week

175. What is the primary goal of a "Remote Work Policy"?
(a) To discourage remote work
(b) To specify the expectations and guidelines for remote work
(c) To eliminate work-life balance
(d) To increase employee stress

176. What does the term "industrial relations" refer to?
(a) Relations between competing companies
(b) Relations between employers and employees within an organization
(c) Relations between suppliers and customers
(d) Relations between government agencies and businesses

177. In industrial relations, what is a "collective bargaining agreement"?
(a) An agreement between the government and labor unions
(b) An agreement between employers and individual employees
(c) An agreement between labor unions and employees
(d) An agreement negotiated between employers and labor unions that outlines terms and conditions of employment

178. What is the purpose of a "grievance procedure" in an organization?
(a) To prevent employees from filing complaints
(b) To address and resolve employee complaints and disputes
(c) To promote strikes and protests
(d) To avoid government regulation

179. hat is a "wildcat strike" in the context of industrial relations?
(a) A strike that occurs during regular working hours
(b) A strike organized by a labor union
(c) An unauthorized and unofficial strike by employees
(d) A strike involving only union leaders

180. Which term refers to the process of bringing in a neutral third party to help resolve a labor dispute?
(a) Mediation
(b) Arbitration
(c) Adjudication
(d) Collective bargaining

181. What does the "Labor Relations Board" typically oversee?
(a) Employee recruitment and selection
(b) Workplace safety
(c) Labor disputes and unfair labor practices
(d) Employee benefits

182. In the context of labor relations, what is "workplace discrimination"?
(a) Firing employees for valid reasons
(b) Treating all employees equally
(c) Treating employees unfairly based on protected characteristics
(d) Providing equal pay for equal work

183. Which of the following is a common step in the grievance resolution process?
(a) Ignoring employee complaints
(b) Holding a public hearing
(c) Investigating the grievance
(d) Negotiating a collective bargaining agreement

184. What is "shop stewards" in the context of labor relations?
(a) Managers responsible for shop layout
(b) Elected or appointed union representatives who help address employee grievances
(c) HR personnel responsible for hiring
(d) A type of workplace mentor

185. In labor disputes, what is "strike pay"?
(a) Extra pay for employees working during a strike
(b) Compensation paid to employees who are on strike
(c) A type of incentive bonus
(d) Additional compensation for overtime work

186. What is the purpose of "conciliation" in labor relations?
(a) To intensify labor disputes

(b) To facilitate negotiations and assist parties in reaching an agreement
(c) To escalate labor conflicts
(d) To file legal actions against unions

187. Which term refers to the practice of employers using temporary workers to replace striking employees?
(a) Sympathy strike
(b) Lockout
(c) Closed shop
(d) Picketing

188. What is a "cooling-off period" in labor disputes?
(a) A period when employees receive extra paid vacation
(b) A period when all employees must remain at work
(c) A period of suspended labor action to allow negotiations and tensions to subside
(d) A break during which employees can address grievances

189. In industrial relations, what does "yellow-dog contract" refer to?
(a) An agreement to hire only unionized employees
(b) A contract that prohibits employees from joining or supporting labor unions
(c) A contract that establishes a profit-sharing plan
(d) A contract that requires employers to provide dog-friendly workplaces

190. What is "child labor"?
(a) A form of labor done by children for fun
(b) Any work performed by children
(c) The use of children in work that is harmful to their physical and mental development
(d) Training programs for children

191. What is "maternity leave" in labor welfare?
(a) Leave for fathers after childbirth
(b) Leave for expectant mothers to prepare for childbirth
(c) Leave for mothers to care for their newborns
(d) Leave for fathers after their child's birth

192. What does the term "pension" refer to in social security?
(a) A government payment to all citizens
(b) A financial account for emergency expenses
(c) A retirement plan that provides a regular income after retirement
(d) A form of unemployment insurance

193. What is the purpose of "unemployment insurance"?
(a) To provide financial assistance to those who are involuntarily unemployed
(b) To encourage people to quit their jobs
(c) To pay for employee benefits
(d) To fund social programs

194. Which term refers to a government program that provides financial assistance to individuals with low income and limited resources?
(a) Social security
(b) Welfare
(c) Retirement plan
(d) Labor union

195. What is the primary goal of "workers' compensation"?
(a) To provide paid vacations to workers
(b) To ensure employers can terminate employees without cause
(c) To provide financial compensation to employees who are injured or become ill on the job
(d) To fund employee training programs

196. What is "elderly care" in labor welfare?
(a) Care provided by the elderly to young children
(b) Care provided to elderly individuals to support their physical and mental well-being
(c) A government program for elder care
(d) Care provided to elderly employees by employers

197. What does "Social Security" typically include?
(a) Retirement benefits, disability benefits, and survivor benefits
(b) Employer-paid social events
(c) Public transportation for employees
(d) Subsidized housing for low-income workers

198. What is the primary goal of a "family and medical leave" program?
(a) To provide extended vacation for employees

(b) To ensure employees work longer hours
(c) To provide employees with job-protected leave for family or medical reasons
(d) To reduce employee benefits

199. In the context of social security, what is "disability benefits"?
(a) Benefits for employees who choose not to work
(b) Benefits for employees with disabilities who are unable to work
(c) Benefits for highly skilled workers
(d) Benefits for unionized workers

200. What is "catastrophic leave" in labor welfare?
(a) Leave granted to employees who experience personal catastrophes
(b) Leave for extended vacations
(c) Leave for new parents
(d) Leave for employees facing disciplinary actions

201. What is a trade union?
(a) A group of business owners
(b) An organization of workers formed to protect their rights and interests
(c) A government regulatory agency
(d) A financial institution

202. What is the primary purpose of a trade union?
(a) To maximize company profits
(b) To provide training programs for employees
(c) To protect and promote the interests of its members
(d) To enforce labor laws

203. What is a "shop steward" in a trade union?
(a) A union member who organizes strikes
(b) An employee responsible for shop maintenance
(c) A union representative who assists and represents members in a workplace
(d) A government inspector

204. What does the term "strike" refer to in the context of trade unions?
(a) A negotiation session between union leaders and employers
(b) A tactic used by employers to increase production
(c) A work stoppage by employees to put pressure on employers for better terms
(d) A trade union meeting

205. What is the primary purpose of "picketing" during a strike?
(a) To block access to the workplace
(b) To provide security to the workplace
(c) To demonstrate support for management
(d) To communicate the reasons for the strike to the public

206. In trade union terminology, what is a "closed shop"?
(a) A business that only serves union members
(b) A workplace where all employees are required to join the union
(c) A shop that is not open to the public
(d) A workplace with flexible membership rules

207. What is a "union organizer" in the context of trade unions?
(a) A person responsible for company organization
(b) An employee who manages union finances
(c) An individual who recruits and encourages workers to join a union
(d) A mediator in labor disputes

208. In labor relations, what does "certification" of a union mean?
(a) A document that certifies a company's financial stability
(b) The process of verifying an employee's qualifications
(c) Official recognition of a union as the exclusive bargaining agent for a group of employees
(d) The approval of a strike by the government

209. What does the term "arbitration" mean in trade union negotiations?
(a) A form of workplace discipline
(b) A labor strike strategy
(c) A process where a neutral third party makes a binding decision to resolve disputes
(d) A government inspection

210. What is "collective action" in the context of trade unions?
(a) Individual efforts to resolve workplace issues
(b) A type of worker protest

(c) Coordinated efforts by employees to achieve common goals, often through a trade union
(d) A government regulation

211. What is collective bargaining?
(a) Negotiating the purchase of goods in bulk
(b) A group of employees negotiating individually with an employer
(c) The process of negotiation between a labor union and an employer to reach an agreement on employment terms
(d) The process of firing employees for misconduct

212. What does "bargaining unit" refer to in collective bargaining?
(a) A group of employees eligible to vote in a union election
(b) A list of bargaining proposals
(c) A document outlining employer policies
(d) A description of the company's products and services

213. What is a "strike vote" in the context of collective bargaining?
(a) A vote to increase employee wages
(b) A vote to unionize a workplace
(c) A vote by union members to authorize a strike if negotiations fail
(d) A vote on company policies

214. What does "good-faith bargaining" mean in collective bargaining?
(a) Negotiating in a sincere and honest manner
(b) Negotiating with aggressive tactics
(c) Refusing to engage in negotiations
(d) Hiding information from the other party

215. In collective bargaining, what is a "no-strike clause" in a labor contract?
(a) A clause that encourages employees to strike
(b) A clause that prohibits union members from voting on strike action
(c) A clause that prohibits employees from striking during the term of the contract
(d) A clause that prevents employers from making changes to working conditions

216. What does "mediation" mean in the context of collective bargaining?
(a) A process in which a neutral third party helps parties reach an agreement but doesn't make a binding decision
(b) A form of strike action
(c) Negotiating with hostility and aggression
(d) A government inspection

217. What is "a lockout" in collective bargaining?
(a) A tactic used by unions to pressure employers
(b) A work stoppage by employees
(c) A tactic used by employers to prevent employees from working during a labor dispute
(d) A type of strike

218. What is the "strikebreaker" or "replacement worker" in collective bargaining?
(a) A union organizer
(b) An employee who crosses the picket line during a strike
(c) A government mediator
(d) A labor economist

219. In labor negotiations, what does "ratification" mean?
(a) The act of presenting a proposal for negotiation
(b) The process of approving or accepting an agreement by the members or parties involved
(c) A form of worker protest
(d) The act of breaking off negotiations

220. What is a "concession" in the context of collective bargaining?
(a) A form of workplace discipline
(b) A demand made by the employer
(c) A contract provision that provides extra benefits to employees
(d) A reduction in benefits or terms offered by the employer

221. What is International Human Resource Management (IHRM)?
(a) A specialized form of marketing
(b) The management of human resources in a global context
(c) A branch of finance
(d) A type of employee training program

222. What is the primary challenge in international HR management related to cultural differences?
(a) Language barriers
(b) Compliance with international laws
(c) Managing diverse teams and understanding cultural norms
(d) Economic challenges

223. What is "expatriate management" in international HR?
(a) Managing employees who work in their home country
(b) Managing employees who work in a different country than their home country
(c) Managing employees who work remotely
(d) Managing seasonal workers

224. What is "global mobility" in international HR management?
(a) The ability to travel to different countries
(b) The movement of employees across borders for work assignments
(c) Employee vacations
(d) An international trade agreement

225. In the context of international HR management, what is a "host country national"?
(a) An employee who is on a long vacation
(b) An employee who is a citizen of the home country
(c) An employee who is a citizen of the country where they are working
(d) A global HR manager

226. Which of the following is a key challenge in international HR management related to compensation and benefits?
(a) Providing the same compensation package to all employees
(b) Adhering to the laws of the home country only
(c) Understanding and complying with different tax and benefit regulations in multiple countries
(d) Offering generous compensation to all employees

227. What is the primary purpose of "repatriation" in international HR management?
(a) Sending employees on an extended overseas assignment
(b) Bringing expatriates back to their home country and ensuring a smooth transition
(c) Terminating employees
(d) Facilitating international mergers and acquisitions

228. In international HR management, what is the main challenge in recruitment and selection?
(a) Limited pool of potential candidates
(b) Cultural diversity
(c) Language barriers
(d) Currency exchange rates

229. What does "diversity and inclusion" mean in the context of international HR management?
(a) Focusing on homogeneity in the workplace
(b) Embracing differences and ensuring equal opportunities for employees from diverse backgrounds
(c) Promoting a single global corporate culture
(d) Discriminating against employees from different cultural backgrounds

230. What does "ethnocentrism" refer to in international HR management?
(a) A management approach that values diversity
(b) A tendency to evaluate other cultures based on the standards of one's own culture
(c) A preference for hiring only expatriates
(d) An international HR training program

231. What is "global talent management" in international HR management?
(a) Focusing on local talent only
(b) Identifying and developing a global pool of talented employees
(c) Exclusively recruiting expatriates
(d) Terminating underperforming employees

232. What is "cross-cultural training" in international HR management?
(a) Training employees to become experts in cross-border trade
(b) Preparing employees to work in a culturally diverse environment
(c) Providing technical skills training to employees
(d) Training employees to become fluent in a foreign language

233. What is "cultural intelligence" (CQ) in international HR management?
(a) The ability to adapt to any culture effortlessly
(b) The ability to speak multiple languages fluently
(c) The capacity to understand and work effectively in culturally diverse settings
(d) A measure of financial performance

234. In the context of international HR management, what does "local adaptation" mean?
(a) Implementing the same HR policies and practices globally

(b) Adapting HR practices to local cultural and legal contexts
(c) Promoting expatriate assignments
(d) A management approach that values diversity

235. What is the primary goal of "global workforce planning" in international HR management?
(a) Ensuring a uniform workforce worldwide
(b) Strategically managing the deployment of human resources across international locations
(c) Implementing local HR practices in every country
(d) Maximizing turnover

236. What is "geocentric staffing" in international HR management?
(a) A hiring strategy that focuses on recruiting employees from the home country only
(b) A strategy that hires employees from the host country exclusively
(c) A strategy that emphasizes hiring the best person for the job, regardless of nationality
(d) A strategy that exclusively hires expatriates

237. In international HR management, what is "globalization"?
(a) The process of becoming a more local organization
(b) The process of adapting to a single global culture
(c) The process of expanding and operating in multiple countries
(d) The process of eliminating cultural diversity

238. What is "expatriate failure" in international HR management?
(a) The inability to attract expatriates
(b) The inability to terminate employees
(c) The inability of an expatriate to adapt and succeed in a foreign assignment
(d) The inability to manage global workforce planning

239. What does "compensation parity" mean in international HR management?
(a) Paying the same salary to all employees, regardless of location
(b) Ensuring that expatriates are compensated the same as local employees
(c) Adjusting compensation to account for differences in living costs and economic conditions between locations
(d) Ignoring compensation as a factor in HR management

240. In international HR management, what is "the war for talent"?
(a) A literal military conflict
(b) The competition among countries to attract highly skilled professionals
(c) A strategy to avoid hiring talented individuals
(d) A type of training program

241. What does the term "global ethics" refer to in international HR management?
(a) Conducting business without adhering to any ethical standards
(b) Embracing the ethical values of the home country
(c) Adhering to consistent ethical standards and values across all international locations
(d) Allowing employees to determine their own ethical standards

242. In international HR management, what is "expatriate compensation"?
(a) Compensation that only expatriates receive
(b) The financial package provided to expatriate employees, which may include salary, benefits, and allowances
(c) Compensation for expatriates' home country employment
(d) Compensation that is identical in every country

243. What is "reverse culture shock" in international HR management?
(a) A shock experienced when returning to one's home country after an international assignment
(b) A shock experienced when traveling to a new country
(c) A type of workplace training
(d) A management strategy for adapting to different cultures

244. What is the primary challenge in international HR management related to labor laws and regulations?
(a) Simplification of international labor laws

(b) Ensuring compliance with the labor laws of all countries in which an organization operates
(c) Avoiding labor laws altogether
(d) Restricting employee rights

245. What is "corporate social responsibility" (CSR) in international HR management?
(a) A strategy for reducing business expenses
(b) A focus on maximizing short-term profits
(c) A commitment to ethical and sustainable business practices that benefit society
(d) A strategy for minimizing employee turnover

246. What does Green HRM primarily aim to integrate into HR practices?
(a) Financial management
(b) Environmental sustainability
(c) Employee diversity
(d) Technological innovation

247. Which of the following is a key focus of Green HRM?
(a) Maximizing energy consumption
(b) Minimizing employee benefits
(c) Reducing the carbon footprint of the organization
(d) Expanding office space

248. In the context of Green HRM, what is "environmental sustainability"?
(a) Ensuring that HR policies do not change over time
(b) Maintaining the status quo in HR practices
(c) Managing resources in a way that minimizes harm to the environment and ensures long-term ecological balance
(d) Continuously increasing resource consumption

249. What is the purpose of a "green recruitment process" in Green HRM?
(a) Focusing on hiring candidates with the highest salary expectations
(b) Selecting candidates based on their environmental activism
(c) Reducing environmental impacts associated with recruitment activities
(d) Expanding the hiring process

250. How can Green HRM contribute to reducing an organization's carbon footprint?
(a) By increasing business travel for meetings
(b) By using non-recyclable office supplies
(c) By implementing remote work policies and reducing office space
(d) By promoting frequent printing of documents

251. What is "green onboarding" in Green HRM?
(a) A process of introducing new employees to the company's eco-friendly products
(b) A process that involves rehiring former employees who are environmentally conscious
(c) An onboarding process that emphasizes the organization's environmental values and practices
(d) A process that encourages employees to share eco-friendly memes

252. In the context of Green HRM, what is the significance of "green training and development"?
(a) Training employees to use excessive amounts of paper
(b) Providing training on energy-wasting practices
(c) Offering training and development programs that promote environmental awareness and sustainable practices
(d) Training employees to avoid sustainable behaviors

253. What is the primary goal of "green compensation and benefits" in Green HRM?
(a) Offering extravagant compensation packages
(b) Providing benefits that encourage wasteful behaviors
(c) Aligning compensation and benefits with eco-friendly practices and values
(d) Cutting all employee benefits

254. How does Green HRM contribute to fostering a culture of environmental responsibility in the workplace?
(a) By ignoring the impact of HR practices on the environment
(b) By promoting wasteful practices among employees
(c) By integrating sustainability values into HR policies and encouraging eco-friendly behavior
(d) By discouraging employees from engaging in environmental initiatives

255. What is the primary purpose of a "green performance management system" in Green HRM?

(a) Evaluating employees based on their energy consumption
(b) Tracking employees' non-environmental performance metrics
(c) Assessing employees' contributions to sustainability and rewarding environmentally responsible behavior
(d) Ignoring employee performance

256. What is "eco-friendly employee engagement" in Green HRM?
(a) Encouraging employees to increase energy consumption
(b) Incentivizing employees to use single-use plastics
(c) Promoting employee involvement in eco-friendly initiatives and sustainable practices
(d) Excluding employees from decision-making processes

257. In Green HRM, what does "green supply chain management" refer to?
(a) Managing supply chains without any environmental considerations
(b) Focusing on supply chains that are green in color
(c) Integrating environmental sustainability into supply chain operations
(d) Discontinuing the supply chain

258. What is the primary goal of "green employee relations" in Green HRM?
(a) Promoting conflicts and disputes among employees
(b) Maintaining a divisive workplace environment
(c) Ensuring harmonious relationships between employees and promoting sustainable practices
(d) Ignoring employee relations altogether

259. What does "sustainable leadership" mean in the context of Green HRM?
(a) A leadership style that prioritizes profit over sustainability
(b) A leadership style that encourages wasteful behaviors
(c) Leadership that sets an example by promoting and practicing sustainability principles
(d) Leadership that emphasizes avoiding sustainability initiatives

260. In Green HRM, what is "green innovation"?
(a) Encouraging employees to avoid innovation
(b) Fostering a culture of innovation without any environmental considerations
(c) Promoting and supporting innovation that contributes to environmental sustainability
(d) Halting all innovation efforts

ANSWER KEY

1. (a)	**2.** (b)	**3.** (b)	**4.** (a)	**5.** (b)	**6.** (d)	**7.** (b)	**8.** (b)	**9.** (c)	**10.** (b)
11. (b)	**12.** (d)	**13.** (b)	**14.** (a)	**15.** (b)	**16.** (b)	**17.** (c)	**18.** (b)	**19.** (d)	**20.** (b)
21. (b)	**22.** (b)	**23.** (d)	**24.** (d)	**25.** (b)	**26.** (b)	**27.** (c)	**28.** (b)	**29.** (b)	**30.** (c)
31. (a)	**32.** (b)	**33.** (b)	**34.** (c)	**35.** (b)	**36.** (d)	**37.** (b)	**38.** (a)	**39.** (b)	**40.** (d)
41. (b)	**42.** (b)	**43.** (c)	**44.** (b)	**45.** (a)	**46.** (b)	**47.** (b)	**48.** (a)	**49.** (b)	**50.** (b)
51. (c)	**52.** (b)	**53.** (d)	**54.** (b)	**55.** (b)	**56.** (a)	**57.** (b)	**58.** (c)	**59.** (b)	**60.** (b)
61. (a)	**62.** (b)	**63.** (d)	**64.** (b)	**65.** (b)	**66.** (b)	**67.** (c)	**68.** (b)	**69.** (b)	**70.** (a)
71. (b)	**72.** (b)	**73.** (b)	**74.** (b)	**75.** (b)	**76.** (a)	**77.** (c)	**78.** (c)	**79.** (c)	**80.** (a)
81. (a)	**82.** (b)	**83.** (b)	**84.** (d)	**85.** (c)	**86.** (c)	**87.** (c)	**88.** (a)	**89.** (c)	**90.** (c)
91. (d)	**92.** (a)	**93.** (b)	**94.** (c)	**95.** (c)	**96.** (c)	**97.** (b)	**98.** (a)	**99.** (c)	**100.** (c)
101. (c)	**102.** (c)	**103.** (b)	**104.** (c)	**105.** (b)	**106.** (a)	**107.** (b)	**108.** (a)	**109.** (c)	**110.** (b)
111. (a)	**112.** (b)	**113.** (c)	**114.** (d)	**115.** (b)	**116.** (c)	**117.** (c)	**118.** (a)	**119.** (b)	**120.** (c)
121. (c)	**122.** (c)	**123.** (b)	**124.** (b)	**125.** (d)	**126.** (c)	**127.** (b)	**128.** (a)	**129.** (d)	**130.** (a)
131. (d)	**132.** (a)	**133.** (d)	**134.** (c)	**135.** (b)	**136.** (b)	**137.** (c)	**138.** (a)	**139.** (a)	**140.** (b)
141. (b)	**142.** (c)	**143.** (c)	**144.** (c)	**145.** (c)	**146.** (a)	**147.** (c)	**148.** (a)	**149.** (b)	**150.** (b)
151. (b)	**152.** (d)	**153.** (c)	**154.** (c)	**155.** (c)	**156.** (b)	**157.** (c)	**158.** (c)	**159.** (c)	**160.** (b)
161. (c)	**162.** (b)	**163.** (c)	**164.** (a)	**165.** (b)	**166.** (b)	**167.** (c)	**168.** (b)	**169.** (b)	**170.** (c)
171. (a)	**172.** (a)	**173.** (c)	**174.** (b)	**175.** (b)	**176.** (b)	**177.** (d)	**178.** (b)	**179.** (c)	**180.** (a)
181. (c)	**182.** (c)	**183.** (c)	**184.** (b)	**185.** (b)	**186.** (b)	**187.** (b)	**188.** (c)	**189.** (b)	**190.** (c)
191. (b)	**192.** (c)	**193.** (a)	**194.** (b)	**195.** (c)	**196.** (b)	**197.** (a)	**198.** (c)	**199.** (b)	**200.** (a)
201. (b)	**202.** (c)	**203.** (c)	**204.** (c)	**205.** (d)	**206.** (b)	**207.** (c)	**208.** (c)	**209.** (c)	**210.** (c)
211. (c)	**212.** (a)	**213.** (c)	**214.** (a)	**215.** (c)	**216.** (a)	**217.** (c)	**218.** (b)	**219.** (b)	**220.** (d)
221. (b)	**222.** (c)	**223.** (b)	**224.** (b)	**225.** (c)	**226.** (c)	**227.** (b)	**228.** (b)	**229.** (b)	**230.** (b)
231. (b)	**232.** (b)	**233.** (c)	**234.** (b)	**235.** (b)	**236.** (c)	**237.** (c)	**238.** (c)	**239.** (c)	**240.** (b)
241. (c)	**242.** (b)	**243.** (a)	**244.** (b)	**245.** (c)	**246.** (b)	**247.** (c)	**248.** (c)	**249.** (c)	**250.** (c)
251. (c)	**252.** (c)	**253.** (c)	**254.** (c)	**255.** (c)	**256.** (c)	**257.** (c)	**258.** (c)	**259.** (c)	**260.** (c)

UNIT

4

SYLLABUS

- Accounting Principles and Standards, Preparation of Financial Statements
- Financial Statement Analysis – Ratio Analysis, Funds Flow and Cash Flow Analysis, DuPont Analysis
- Preparation of Cost Sheet, Marginal Costing, Cost Volume Profit Analysis
- Standard Costing & Variance Analysis
- Financial Management, Concept & Functions
- Capital Structure – Theories, Cost of Capital, Sources and Finance
- Budgeting and Budgetary Control, Types and Process, Zero base Budgeting
- Leverages – Operating, Financial and Combined Leverages, EBIT–EPS Analysis, Financial Breakeven Point & Indifference Level.

ACCOUNTING PRINCIPLES AND STANDARDS, PREPARATION OF FINANCIAL STATEMENTS

Business Entity Concept. Accountants treat a business as distinct from the persons who own it; it then becomes possible to record transactions of the business with the proprietor, also without such a distribution, the affairs of the firm will be all mixed up with the private affairs of the proprietor and the true picture of the firm will not be available.

This concept has now been extended to accounting separately for various divisions for a firm in order to ascertain the result for each division separately. It has been of immense value in determining results by each responsibility center - Responsibility Accounting.

Money Measurement Concept. This assumption implies that only those transactions and events are recorded in accounting which can be expressed in monetary terms. An event, even though important like a quarrel between the production manager and the sales manager, will not be recorded unless its monetary effect can be measured with a fair degree of accuracy. It should be remembered that money enables various things of diverse nature to be added up together and dealt with. The use of a building and the use of clerical services can be aggregated only through money values and not otherwise.

Cost Concept. Transactions are entered in books of account at the moments actually involved. Suppose a firm purchases a piece of land for Rs. 150000 but considers it as worth Rs. 300000. The purchase of land will be recorded at Rs. 150000 and not any more. This is one of the most important concepts, it prevents arbitrary values being put on transactions chiefly those resulting in acquisition of assets. Of course, sometimes accountants have necessarily to be satisfied with an estimate only. If we take an example of machinery: The amount of depreciation has to be charged to accounts each year in respect of machinery . The amount has to be an estimate since the future life of the machinery cannot be known precisely.

Going Concern Concept. It is assumed that the business will exist for the foreseeable future and transactions are recorded from this point of view. It is this that necessitates distinction between expenditure that will render benefit over a long period and that whose benefit will be exhausted quickly, say within the year. Of course, if it is certain that the business will exist only for a limited time, the accounting record will keep the expected life in the view.

A firm is said to be a going concern when there is neither the intention nor the necessity to wind up its affairs or curtail substantially the scale of its operations. In other words, it should continue to operate at its present scale.

Dual - Aspect Concept. Each transaction has two aspects; if a business has acquired an asset, it must have resulted in one of the following:

(i) some other asset has been given up;

(ii) the obligation to pay for it has arisen

(iii) There has been a profit, leading to an increase in the amount that the business owes to the proprietor or

(iv) the proprietor has contributed money for the acquisition of the asset.

The reverse is also true. If, for instance, there is an increase in the money owed to others, there must have been an increase in assets or a loss. At any time

Assets = Liabilities + Capital or

Capital = Assets - liabilities

In other words, capital, *i.e.* the owner's share of the assets of the firm is always what is left out of asset after paying off outsiders.

A transaction must affect one of the things mentioned above.

Income or profits arises only when there has been an increase in the owners share of the assets of the firm (called owner's equity) but not if the increase has resulted from money contributed by the owners himself. Any increase in the owner's equity is called revenue and anything that reduces the owner's equity is expense (or loss); profit results only where the total of revenues exceeds the total of expenses or losses.

Realisation Concept. Accounting is a historical record of transaction; it records what has happened. It does not anticipate events, though anticipated adverse effect of events that have already occurred are usually recorded. This is of great importance in stopping business firms from inflating their profits by recording sales and incomes that are only likely to accrue unless money has been realised either cash has been received or a legal obligation to pay has been assumed by the customer no sale can be said to have taken place and no profits or income can be said to have arisen.

Accrual Concept. When an event takes place or a transaction is entered into, its consequences are bounded to follow. For example, if one borrows Rs. 100000 @ 15% P.A. at the end of the year Rs. 15000 will become due as interest. If the amount is paid, the record will certainly show it. If, however, the amount is not yet paid, there is the liability to pay the amount and there being no corresponding increase in the total assets, the capital will stand reduced. This must be brought into the record. The accrual concept demands that all transactions or events, not yet settled in cash, must be taken into account.

Periodicity Postulate. Truly speaking the measurement of income of a business entity can be accurately made only when it is liquidated. But the going concern postulate assumes the continuity of business for many years. The owners, investors, Government *etc.* are impatient and unwilling to wait till the business is terminated. They are interested in regular reports and accounts at proper intervals to know "how things are going?" This means that the financial statements must be prepared on a periodic basis rather than waiting until the business is liquidated.

To facilitate the preparation of financial statements on a periodic basis, accountants follow periodic postulate. According to this postulate, the life of the business is divided into appropriate segments for understanding the result shown by the business. Such a segment or time interval is called 'accounting period', which is usually of one year. Accounting period is the interval of time at the end of which income or revenue statement and balance sheets are prepared in order to show the result of operations and change in resources.

Matching Concept. It is based on periodic postulate. The primary objective of a business is to earn profit. It is for this reason that major share of attention of the accountant is absorbed involving technique for measuring profit. In order to measure the profits for the period, revenues should be matched with the costs (expenses) of that period. Thus matching concept implies the matching expenses against related revenues.

Basically matching concept involves two questions (a) what criteria should be used as a basis for associating costs with present and future periods and (b) how shall the expiration of products and service factors be measured.

The various bases used for determining the period in which the revenue is realised are sales basis, cash basis and the production basis. The second step is to find out the costs and expenses to be matched with revenues. Accountant must estimate the life span of the asset and allocate a part of the expired cost occur during that accounting period until its useful life is ended. Matching concept also requires the application of personal judgement in making the estimates for doubtful debts, discounts etc.

Capital and Revenue Transactions

The transactions in accounting may be classified into:

1. **Capital transactions.** The transactions which provide benefits or supply services to a business unit for more than one year or one operating cycle of business are known as capital transactions.
2. **Revenue transactions.** The transactions which provide benefit or supply services to a business unit for one accounting period only are known as revenue transactions.

These transactions are further divided into expenditures and receipts as shown below:

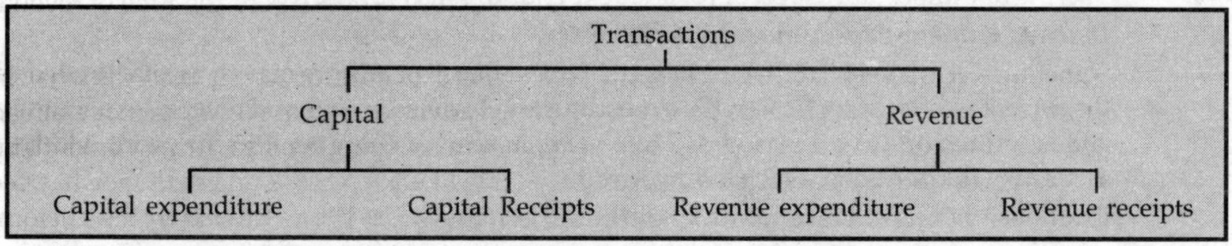

(a) **Capital Expenditure.** The capital expenditure is that expenditure the benefits of which is enjoyed or consumed not in one year only but over many years. It is the expenditure incurred which results in the purchase or acquisition of asset and properties which may be used for many years. Such an expenditure is of a non-recurring nature. The following expenditures are usually treated as capital expenditure.

(i) Any expenditures which results in the acquisition of fixed assets such as land, buildings, plant and machinery, furniture, plants *etc.*

(ii) Any expenditure incurred in connection with the acquisition of any asset, its transportation, its erection *etc.* such as brokerage paid in buying land, the freight or cartage paid to workers for installing the machine.

(iii) Any expenditure incurred in connection for the extension or improvement of any assets.

(iv) Expenditure which increases the revenue earning capacity of business, such as cost of making additions on the building or the amount spent on renovation of the old machinery.

(v) Expenditure incurred to acquire the right to carry on business, such as preliminary expenses, cost of patent.

(vi) Legal charges incurred in connection with acquiring or defending suits for protecting fixed assets, right *etc.*

All items of a capital nature are shown in the Balance Sheet. The main purpose of incurring such expenditure is to earn income over a period of years or increase the earning capacity of the business concern with the aid of such expenditure.

(b) **Revenue Expenditure.**

When the benefits of an expenditure is limited to the year in which it is incurred, it is treated as revenue expenditure. So all expenses which are incurred during the regular course of business are regarded as revenue expenditure. In other words, any expenditure which is not a capital expenditure and which is incurred for carrying the day to day business activities is called revenue expenditure. The following types of expenses are treated as revenue expenditure:

(i) Expenses that are incurred in day to day running of business such as wages, salaries, rent, postage, insurance etc.

(ii) Expenditure incurred for buying goods for resale.

(iii) Expenditure incurred for maintaining the assets such as repairs.

(iv) Depreciation on fixed assets.

(v) Interest on loan taken for running the business.

All items of revenue nature are shown in profit and loss account. The purpose of incurring such expenditure is to maintain the business. The amount spend is relatively small, but not always the benefit of such an expenditure is exhausted in a short period, in any case not more than a year.

There is one important aspect of revenue expenditure. It is as follows:

Deferred Revenue Expenditure. It is as follows:

Sometimes, it is perceived that the benefit of a revenue expenditure may be available beyond the current period. In such cases, the expenditure is classified as deferred revenue expenditure and is written off over a period of 3 to 4 years instead of charging it to the profit and loss account of the period in which it is incurred.

Examples of Deferred revenue expenditure are as follows :

(i) Discount allowed on issue of debentures.

(ii) Development expenditure of mines and minerals.

(iii) Expenditures on an advertisement campaign or a scientific expenditure.

(c) **Capital receipts.** Receipts of any amount is a capital receipt, if :

(i) It is realized from the sale of fixed assets such as plant and machinery, furniture, land, *etc.*

(ii) It is received by way of loan, capital (including premium in issue of shares) or contribution to capital fund of non-profit organizations, such as specific donation of life membership fees paid by members to the club.

(iii) It accrues in view to some sources of income.

(d) **Revenue Receipts.** A receipt would be revenue receipt, if:

(i) It accrues on account of sale of goods and services.

(ii) It is of commercial nature and yields some income to the business on a regular basis, such as royalty, consultancy fee *etc.*

(iii) It is of recurring nature such as interest on investments, dividend, rent of property, commission earned *etc.*

Distinction between Capital expenditure and Revenue expenditure

Capital expenditure	Revenue expenditure
1. It is incurred for acquisition of fixed assets.	1. It is incurred for running the business.
2. These are incurred in increasing the value of fixed assets.	2. They do not increase the value of fixed assets.
3. They increase the earning capacity of the business.	3. They are incurred to maintain the earning capacity of the business.
4. The benefit of such expenditure extends to more than one year.	4. The benefits is limited to one year only.
5. These expenses are of a non-recurring nature.	5. These expenses are of a recurring nature.
6. They are shown in the Balance Sheet.	6. They are shown in trading and P& L A/C.

The expenditure is capital or revenue expenditure can be explained with the following example :

Example.

Which of the following expenditures are capital, revenue and deferred revenue expenditure?

(a) Cost of air-conditioning in the office of the General Manager.

(b) Cost of overhauling and painting a second hand truck newly purchased.

(c) Cost of the annual taxes paid and the annual insurance premium paid on the truck mentioned above.

(d) Wages paid to workers for installation of machinery.

(e) Cost of making more exits in a cinema hall under orders of the Government.

(f) Cost of re-decorating a cinema hall.

(g) Cost of putting up a gallery in a theatre hall.

(h) Cost of acquiring the goodwill of an old firm.

(i) Cost of heavy advertisements for a new product and removal of works to a new and better site.

(j) Temporary rooms constructed for storing raw materials for the construction of a big building.

(k) A machinery costing Rs. 5000 has to be sold. It realises Rs. 3000. A new machine is purchased for Rs. 9000.

Solution.

(a) This is capital expenditure because the benefit of this expenditure will be available for a number of years. In any case, the machine which has been installed will be there and can be disposed of whenever desired.

(b) When a second hand machine is purchased, all expenditure incurred in the beginning to make it fit for working is treated as capital expenditure. The value of the machine is increased by the amount spent. Therefore, the cost of overhauling and painting the truck will be capital expenditure.

(c) Annual taxes and annual premium paid on the truck are revenue expenditures because they do not add to the value of the truck and their benefit will be exhausted within the year.
(d) This is capital expenditure because it is, necessary to put the machine in working condition.
(e) Making more exits in a cinema hall does not increase the capacity of the hall and therefore, it should be treated as revenue expenditure.
(f) Cost of re-decorating a cinema hall is also not capital expenditure because it does not add to the capacity of the hall. But the cost is fairly heavy and the benefit will be there for a number of years. Therefore, the cost of re-decoration should be treated as deferred revenue expenditure.
(g) When a new gallery is put up, it will increase the number of seats in the hall. Therefore, this cost should be treated as capital expenditure.
(h) This is capital expenditure because the use of that firm's name will benefit the purchaser for a long time.
(i) This expenditure is heavy but not of capital nature because no new asset is acquired. But since the benefit of the expenditure will be available for a number of years, it should be treated as deferred revenue expenditure.
(j) The cost of construction of temporary rooms should be treated as capital expenditure because it is necessary for the construction of the main building. The cost of the rooms will be added to the cost of the building.
(k) There is a loss of Rs. 2000 on sale of the old machinery. This is revenue loss. Rs. 9000 has been spent on acquiring a new machinery. It is capital expenditure.

ACCOUNTING STANDARDS

An accounting standard is a common set of principles, standards and procedures that define the basis of financial accounting policies and practices. Accounting standards improve the transparency of financial reporting in all countries. In the United States, the Generally Accepted Accounting Principles form the set of accounting standards widely accepted for preparing financial statements. International companies follow the International Financial Reporting Standards, which are set by the International Accounting Standards Board and serve as the guideline for non-U.S. GAAP companies reporting financial statements.

List of Indian Accounting Standards (AS 1~29)

List of Mandatory Accounting Standards of ICAI (as on 1 July 2017 and onwards), is as under:

1. **AS 1 Disclosure of Accounting Policies.** This Standard deals with the disclosure of significant accounting policies which are followed in preparing and presenting financial statements.
2. **AS 2 Valuation of Inventories.** This Standard deals with the determination of value at which inventories are carried in the financial statements, including the ascertainment of cost of inventories and any write-down thereof to net realisable value.
3. **AS 3 Cash Flow Statements.** This Standard deals with the provision of information about the historical changes in cash and cash equivalents of an enterprise by means of a Cash Flow Statement which classifies cash flows during the period from operating, investing and financing activities.
4. **AS 4 Contingencies and Events Occurring After Balance Sheet Date.** This Standard deals with the treatment of contingencies and events occurring after the balance sheet date.
5. **AS 5 Net profit or Loss for the period, Prior Period Items and Changes in Accounting Policies.** This Standard should be applied by an enterprise in presenting profit or loss from

ordinary activities, extraordinary items and prior period items in the Statement of Profit and Loss, in accounting for changes in accounting estimates, and in disclosure of changes in accounting policies.

6. **AS 7 Construction Contracts.** This Standard prescribes the accounting for construction contracts in the financial statements of contractors.
7. **AS 9 Revenue Recognition.** This Standard deals with the bases for recognition of revenue in the Statement of Profit and Loss of an enterprise. The Standard is concerned with the recognition of revenue arising in the course of the ordinary activities of the enterprise from: a) Sale of goods; b) Rendering of services; and c) Interest, royalties and dividends.
8. **AS 10 Property, Plant and Equipment.** The objective of this Standard is to prescribe the accounting treatment for property, plant and equipment (PPE).
9. **AS 11 The Effects of Changes in Foreign Exchange Rates.** AS 11 lays down principles of accounting for foreign currency transactions and foreign operations, i.e., which exchange rate to use and how to recognise in the financial statements the financial effect of changes in exchange rates.
10. **AS 12 Government Grants.** This Standard deals with accounting for government grants. Government grants are sometimes called by other names such as subsidies, cash incentives, duty drawbacks, etc.
11. **AS 13 Accounting for Investments.** This Standard deals with accounting for investments in the financial statements of enterprises and related disclosure requirements.
12. **AS 14 Accounting for Amalgamations.** This Standard deals with accounting for amalgamations and the treatment of any resultant goodwill or reserves.
13. **AS 15 Employee Benefits.** The objective of this Standard is to prescribe the accounting treatment and disclosure for employee benefits in the books of employer except employee share-based payments. It does not deal with accounting and reporting by employee benefit plans.
14. **AS 16 Borrowing Costs.** This Standard should be applied in accounting for borrowing costs. This Standard does not deal with the actual or imputed cost of owners' equity, including preference share capital not classified as a liability.
15. **AS 17 Segment Reporting.** The objective of this Standard is to establish principles for reporting financial information, about the different types of segments/ products and services an enterprise produces and the different geographical areas in which it operates.
16. **AS 18 Related Party Disclosures.** This Standard should be applied in reporting related party relationships and transactions between a reporting enterprise and its related parties. The requirements of this Standard apply to the financial statements of each reporting enterprise and also to consolidated financial statements presented by a holding company.
17. **AS 19 Leases.** The objective of this Standard is to prescribe, for lessees and lessors, the appropriate accounting policies and disclosures in relation to finance leases and operating leases.
18. **AS 20 Earnings Per Share.** AS 20 prescribes principles for the determination and presentation of earnings per share which will improve comparison of performance among different enterprises for the same period and among different accounting periods for the same enterprise.
19. **AS 21 Consolidated Financial Statements.** The objective of this Standard is to lay down principles and procedures for preparation and presentation of consolidated financial statements. These statements are intended to present financial information about a parent and its subsidiary(ies) as a single economic entity to show the economic resources controlled by the group, obligations of the group and results the group achieves with its resources.

20. **AS 22 Accounting for Taxes on Income.** The objective of this Standard is to prescribe accounting treatment of taxes on income since the taxable income may be significantly different from the accounting income due to many reasons, posing problems in matching of taxes against revenue for a period.
21. **AS 23 Accounting for Investments in Associates.** This Standard should be applied in accounting for investments in associates in the preparation and presentation of consolidated Financial Statements (CFS) by an investor.
22. **AS 24 Discontinuing Operations.** The objective of AS 24 is to establish principles for reporting information about discontinuing operations, thereby enhancing the ability of users of financial statements to make projections of an enterprise's cash flows, earnings generating capacity, and financial position by segregating information about discontinuing operations from information about continuing operations. AS 24 applies to all discontinuing operations of an enterprise.
23. **AS 25 Interim Financial Reporting.** This Standard applies if an entity is required or elects to publish an interim financial report. The objective of AS 25 is to prescribe the minimum content of an interim financial report and to prescribe the principles for recognition and measurement in complete or condensed financial statements for an interim period.
24. **AS 26 Intangible Assets.** AS 26 prescribes the accounting treatment for intangible assets (i.e. identifiable non-monetary asset, without physical substance, held for use in the production or supply of goods or services, for rental to others, or for administrative purposes).
25. **AS 27 Financial Reporting of Interests in Joint Ventures.** The objective of AS 27 is to set out principles and procedures for accounting for interests in joint ventures and reporting of joint venture assets, liabilities, income and expenses in the financial statements of venturers and investors.
26. **AS 28 Impairment of Assets.** The objective of AS 28 is to prescribe the procedures that an enterprise applies to ensure that its assets are carried at no more than their recoverable amount. The asset is described as impaired if its carrying amount exceeds the amount to be recovered through use or sale of the asset and AS 28 requires the enterprise to recognise an impairment loss in such cases. It should be noted that AS 28 deals with impairment of all assets unless specifically excluded from the scope of the Standard.
27. **AS 29 Provisions, Contingent Liabilities and Contingent Assets.** The objective of AS 29 is to ensure that appropriate recognition criteria and measurement bases are applied to provisions and contingent liabilities and that sufficient information is disclosed in the notes to the financial statements to enable users to understand their nature, timing and amount. The objective of this Standard is also to lay down appropriate accounting for contingent assets.

FINANCIAL STATEMENT ANALYSIS

A financial statement is a collection of data organised according to logical and consistent accounting procedures. Its purpose is to convey an understanding of some financial aspects of a business firm. It may show a position at a moment in time, as in the case of a balance sheet, or may reveal a series of activities over a given period of time, as in the case of an income statement. Thus the term *financial statements* refers to the two statements:

(i) The position statement or the balance sheet;
(ii) The income statement or the profit and loss account.

These statements are used to convey to management and other interested outsiders the profitability and financial position of a firm. According to John N. Myer, 'The financial statements are composed of data which are the result of a combination of:

(a) recorded facts concerning the business transaction,
(b) conventions adopted to facilitate the accounting technique,
(c) postulates or assumptions made to and
(d) personal judgements used in the application of the conventions and postulates.

The following points explain the nature of financial statements:

1. **Recorded Facts.** The term 'recorded facts' refers to the data taken out from the accounting records. The records are maintained on the basis of actual cost data. The original cost or historical cost is the basis of recording various transactions.

   The figures of various accounts such as cash in hand, cash at bank, bills receivables, sundry debtors, fixed assets *etc.* are taken as per the figures recorded in the accounting books. The assets purchased at different times and at different prices are put together and shown at cost prices. As recorded facts are not based on replacement costs, the financial statements do not show current financial condition of the concern.
2. **Accounting conventions.** Certain accounting conventions are followed while preparing financial statements. The convention of valuing inventory at cost or market price, whichever is lower, is followed. The valuing of assets at cost less depreciation principle for balance sheet purposes is followed. The convention of materiality is followed in dealing with small things like pencils, pens, postage stamps, *etc.* These items are treated as expenditure in the year in which they are purchased even though they are assets in nature. The stationary is valued at cost and not on the principle of cost or market price whichever is less. The use of accounting conventions makes financial statements comparable, simple and realistic.
3. **Postulate.** The accountant makes certain assumptions while making accounting records. One of these assumptions is that the enterprise is treated as a going concern. The other alternative to this postulate is that the concern is to be liquidated, this is untenable if management shows an intention to liquidate the concern. So the assets are shown on a going concern basis. Another important assumption is to present that the value of money will remain the same in different periods. Though there is a drastic change in purchasing power of money the assets purchased at different times will be shown at the amount paid for them. While preparing profit and loss account, the revenue is treated in the year in which the sale was undertaken even though the sale price may be received in a number of years. The assumption is known as realisation postulate.
4. **Personal judgement.** Even though certain standard accounting conventions are followed in preparing financial statements but still personal judgement of the accountant plays an important part. For example, in applying the cost or market value whichever is less to inventory valuation the accountant will have to use his judgement in computing the cost in a particular case. There are a number of methods for valuing stock *viz.* last in first out, first in first out, average cost method, standard cost, base stock method, *etc.* The accountant will use one of these methods for valuing materials. The selection of depreciation method, to use one of the several methods for estimating uncollectable debts, to determine the period for writing off intangible assets are some of the examples where judgement of the accountant will play an important role in choosing the most appropriate course of action.

Objectives of Financial Statements

(i) To provide reliable financial information about economic resources and obligations of a business firm.
(ii) To provide other needed information about changes in such economic sources and obligations.
(iii) To provide reliable information about charges in net resources (resources less obligations) arising out of business activities.

(iv) To provide financial information that assists in estimating the earning potential of business.
(v) To disclose, to the extent possible, other information related to the financial statements that is relevant to the needs of the users of these statements.

Types of Financial Statements

Generally Accepted Accounting Principles (GAAP) specify that a complete set of financial statements must include;

(i) A balance sheet.
(ii) An income statement.
(iii) A statement of changes in owner's accounts.
(iv) A statement of changes in financial position.

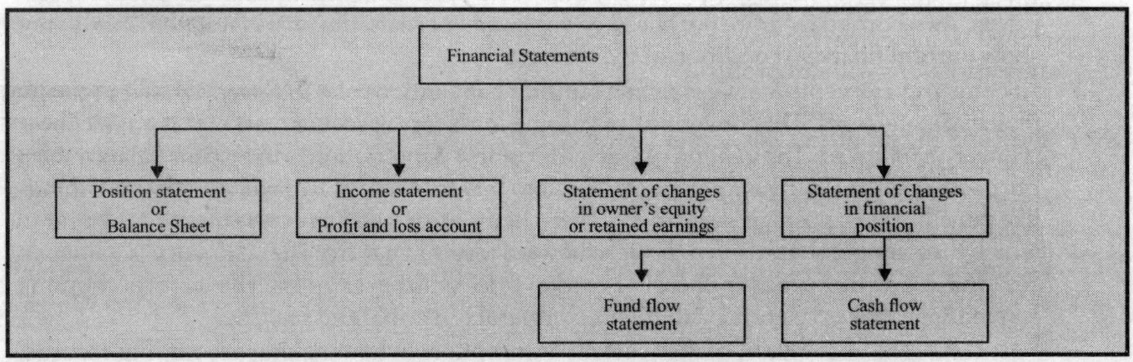

1. **Balance Sheet.** The balance sheet is one of the important statements depicting the financial strength of the concern. It shows on the one hand the properties that it utilises and on other hand the sources of those properties. The balance sheet shows all the assets owned by the concern and all the liabilities and claims it owes to owners and outsiders. The balance sheet is prepared on a particular date. The right hand side shows properties and assets and the liabilities are shown on the left hand side. Normally there is no particular sequence for showing various assets and liabilities. The companies Act, 1956 has prescribed a particular form for showing assets and liabilities in the balance sheet for companies registered under this act. These companies are also required to give figures for the previous year alongwith the current year's figures.
2. **Income statement (or Profit and Loss Account).** Income statement is prepared to determine the operational position of the concern. It is a statement of revenues earned and the expenses incurred for earning that revenue. If there is excess of revenues over expenditures it will show a profit and if the expenditures are more than the income then there will be a loss. The income statement is prepared for a particular period, generally a year. When income statement is prepared for the year ending on 31st December 1996 then all revenues and expenditures falling due in that year will be taken into account irrespective of their receipt or payment.
   The income statement may be prepared in the form of a Manufacturing Account to find out the cost of production, in the form of trading account to determine gross profit or gross loss, in the form of a profit and loss account to determine net profit or net loss. A statement of Retained Earnings may also be prepared to show the distribution of profits.
3. **Statement of Changes in Owner's Equity (or Retained Earnings).** The term owners equity refers to the claims of the owners of the business (shareholders) against the assets of the firm. It consists of two elements; (i) paid-up share capital, *i.e.* the initial amount of funds invested by the shareholders and (ii) retained earnings/reserves and surplus representing

undistributed profits. The statement of changes in owners equity simply shows the beginning balance of each owner's equity account, the reason for increase and decrease in each and its ending balance. However, in most-cases, the only owner's equity account that changes significantly is Retained Earnings and hence the statement of changes in owner's equity becomes a statement of retained earnings.

A statement of retained earnings is also known as Profit and Loss Appropriation Account or income disposal statement. As the name suggests it shows appropriations of earnings. The previous year's balance is first brought forward. The net profit during the current year is added to this balance. On the debit side, appropriations like interim dividend paid, proposed dividend on preference and equity share capital, amounts transferred to debenture redemption fund, capital redemption funds, general reserve, *etc.* are shown. The balance in this account will show the amount of profit retained in hand and carried forward. The appropriations cannot be more than the profits so this account will not have a debit balance. There can not be appropriations without profits.

4. **Statement of Changes in Financial Position.** The basic financial statements, *i.e.* the balance sheet and the profit and loss account or income statement of a business reveal the set effect of the various transactions on the operational and financial position of the company. The balance sheet gives a static view of the resources of a business and the uses to which these resources have been put at a certain point of time. The profit and loss account in a general way indicates the resources provided by operations. But there are many transactions that do not operate through profit and loss account. Thus, for a better understanding another statement called statement of changes in financial position has to be prepared to show the changes in assets and liabilities from the end of one period to the end of another part of time. The objective of this statement is to show the movement of funds (working capital or cash) during particular period. The statement of changes in financial position may take any of the following two forms:

   (a) *Funds flow statement.* The funds flow statement is designed to analyse the changes in the financial condition of a business enterprise between two periods. The word fund is used to denote working capital.

   This statement will show the sources from which the funds are received and the uses to which these have been put. This statement enables the management to have an idea about the sources of funds and their use for various purposes. This statement help the management in policy formulation and performance appraisal.

   (b) *Cash flow statement.* A statement of changes in the financial position of a firm on cash basis is called cash flow statement. It summarises the causes of changes in cash position of a business enterprise between dates of two balance sheets. This statement is very much similar to the statement of changes in working capital *i.e.* funds flow statement. A cash flow statement focuses attention on cash changes only. It describes the sources of cash and its uses.

Final Account

Preparation of final accounts is the last step in the accounting cycle. Final accounts are prepared to achieve the objectives of accountancy. In order to know the profit or loss earned by a firm 'trading and profit and loss account' *i.e.* income statement is prepared. Balance sheet or financial position statement will show the financial condition of the firm on a particular date. These two statements are prepared to give the final results of the business. That is why, both these are collectively called as 'final Accounts'.

Thus, final accounts include :

(i) Trading and profit and loss account or income statement and

(ii) Balance sheet or position statement.

Final accounts are the means of conveying to management, owners and interested outsiders a picture of profitability and financial position of the business. The preparation of final accounts is the end product of the accounting process which gives a concise accounting information of the accounting period after the accounting period is over. These accounts summarise all accounting information recorded in the subsidiary books and the ledger running into thousands of pages.

Procedure. Once the trial Balance is prepared traders prepares final accounts *i.e.* trading account, profit and loss account and balance sheet. Trading and profit and loss account are prepared by transferring from the trial balance, all revenues accounts and expenses accounts and accounts concerning goods by passing closing entries. All remaining account *i.e.* assets accounts, liabilities accounts and capital accounts are shown in Balance Sheet.

Trading Account

Income statement is made up of two accounts *i.e.* trading account and profit and loss account. Trading concerns *i.e.* those concern which purchase goods from one market and sell it in another market, prepare trading account. This account is prepared to know the trading results of the business *i.e.* how much profit the business has earned from buying and selling during a particular period. Trading account shows 'Gross profit' or 'Gross Loss' *i.e.* difference between net proceeds of sale and cost of goods sold.

Format of Trading Account

Trading Account for the year ending

Dr. Cr.

Particulars	Amount Rs.	Particulars	Amount Rs.
To opening stock		By sale	
To purchase A/C		Less sales	
Less–Purchases returns		return	
Less–Discount on purchases		By closing	
To direct expenses		stock	
To wages			
To carriage and Cartage			
To Manufacturing expenses			
To Coal, water & freight			
To factory lighting			
To fuel & Power			
To Motive Power			
To carriage & freight			
To wages & salaries			
To Octroi			
To factory, rent & taxes			
To duty on imported goods			
To Gross profit/loss			

Closing Entries in Respect of Trading Account

The accounts written in the trading account are closed with the help of passing closing entries in journal. Accounts having debit balance are closed by crediting them and accounts having credit balance are closed by debiting them. Following are the closing entries in respect of Trading Account.

(i) For transferring the accounts on the debit side of trading account.

Trading Account Dr.
To stock (Opening) A/C.
To Purchases A/C
To sales return A/C
To factory fuel and power A/C
To Freight and carriage A/C
To Manufacturing expenses A/C.

(ii) For transferring the account on the credit side of trading account.

Sales Account Dr.
Purchases return account Dr.
Stock (closing) Account Dr.
To trading Account

(iii) At this stage the trading account will reveal the gross profit or loss. For transferring the gross profit-

Stock (closing) Account Dr.
To profit and loss A/C
For transferring gross loss
Profit and loss Account Dr.
To trading Account

Profit and Loss Account

Profit and Loss account is prepared to calculate the net profit of the business. Net Profit is the surplus remaining after charging against gross profit all the expenses, including depreciation and other provisions, properly attributable to the normal activities of the particular business. The objectives of preparing profit and loss account can be summed up as under;

(i) Provides information about net profit.

(ii) Comparison of Current years income with that of the previous years can be made.

(iii) Concrete steps may be taken to increase the net profit in future through analysis of expenses.

(iv) Proper allocation of net profit can be made among partners and provisions for various types of Reserves as also for research and development programmes can be made.

Format of Profit and Loss Accounts for the year ending

Particular	Rs.	Particular	Rs.
To Gross loss b/d		By Gross Profit b/d	
To selling & distribution expenses.		By interest Received	
Advertisement		By discount	
Travelling, salaries		By commission	
Expenses & commission		By rent from tenants	
Bad debts		By income from invest-ment	
Godown rent			
Export expenses		By apprenticeship-premium	
Carriage outward			
Bank charges		By interest on debenture	
Agents commission			
B/f			
C/f			
Unkeep of Motor lorries		By income from any other sources	
To Management Expenses			
Rent, Rate and taxes		By Miscellaneous revenue	
Heating and lighting			
Office salaries		By Receipts	
Printing & Telegrams		By Net Loss transferred to capital A/C.	
Telephone charges			
Legal charges			
Audit fees			
Insurance			
General expenses			
To Depreciation and Maintenance			
Depreciation			
Repairs & Maintenance			
To financial expenses			
Discount allowed			
Interest on Capital			
Interest on loans			
Discount on Bills			
To Extra ordinary expenses			
Loss by fire (not covered by insurance)			
Cash defecations			
To net profit transferred to capital A/C			

Closing Entries in Respect of profit and Loss Account

1. The gross profit or loss is transferred to profit and loss account and thus profit and loss account is opened by gross profit or gross loss.

   Where there is gross profit:

   Trading Account Dr.

   To profit and Loss Account

   When there is gross loss:

   Profit and loss Account Dr.

   To trading Account.

2. Profit and loss account is debited with all indirect expenses and losses. For transfer of various expenses and losses following entry is passed :

   Profit and loss Account Dr.

   To various expenses A/C

   To various losses A/C

3. Profit and loss account is credited with miscellaneous incomes accounts. For transfer of various incomes, following entry is passed :

   Various Incomes Accounts Dr.

   To Profit and Loss accounts

4. The results of the account is either net profit or net loss. The profit and loss account is closed by transferring the net profit or net loss to capital A/C.

   When these is net profit:

   Profit and Loss A/C Dr.

   To capital A/C

   When there is net loss:

   Capital account Dr.

   To Profit and Loss A/C

Balance Sheet

Balance sheet is basically a simple statement about a business enterprise. It is a 'sheet' of all those ledger 'Balances' pertaining to the assets owned and liabilities owned by the business on a particular day. Balance sheet is prepared with a view to measure the correct financial position of a business in a systematic standard form.

The Committee on Technology of American Institute of Certified Public Accountant (AICPA) defines the balance sheet as 'list of balances in the assets and liability accounts. This list depicts the position of assets and liabilities of a specific business at a specific point of time.'

Balance sheet and trial balance both are statements and are prepared by almost all enterprises. Inspite of differences, they resemble in following :

(1) Both contain the cash balance.

(2) Both are prepared from the ledger.

(3) Both are not accounts but statements.

(4) Accounts having no balance do not appear in either of the two.

Important Adjustments

(i) **Closing Stock.** Closing stock means unsold or unused stock of goods remaining at the end of the accounting period. Closing stock needs adjustments at the time of preparing final account.

The adjustment entry for closing stock is as under :

Closing stock account Dr.

To trading account.

The impact of this entry will be that closing stock becomes an asset and appears in the balance sheet and the trading A/C is credited with closing stock.

(ii) **Outstanding Expenses.** 'Those expenses which have been incurred and are due for payment *i.e.* not paid as yet, are called outstanding expenses'. For example, Rs. 1000 p.m. is paid as a salary to an employee but during the year 1988, only Rs. 10000 are paid as salary. Two months salary *i.e.* Rs. 2000 which is due but not paid is outstanding salary. All such expenses must be accounted for in that accounting year in which they are accrued irrespective of the fact whether they are paid or not. In order to bring this fact into books of account, following adjusting entry will be passed at the end of the year.

Salary A/C Dr.

To outstanding salary A/C

The two fold effect of the above adjustment entry will be :

(a) Outstanding expenses will be shown on the debit side of the trading or profit & loss account by way of addition to the expenses.

(b) Outstanding expenses account represents liability and it will be shown on the liabilities side of the balance sheet.

(iii) **Prepaid or unexpired expenses.** There are certain expenses which are paid in advance or paid for the future period which is not set over or not yet expired since such expenses are already paid, they are also recorded in books of accounts of that period for which they do not relate. Therefore such prepaid expenses must be adjusted in the books of accounts to arrive at the true results. Generally insurance, taxes, telephone rent *etc.* are paid in advance. For *e.g.*, if a fire insurance policy is taken for a year paying Rs. 1000 as insurance premium on 1st April 1988, the policy will expire on 31st March 1989. If accounts are closed on 31st Dec. 1988, premium from Ist Jan, 1989 to 31st March 1989, will be prepaid expenses i.e. Rs. 250 will be prepaid expenses. The following adjustment entry will be passed :

Prepaid insurance A/C Dr.

To insurance A/C

The two fold effect of this entry will be :

(a) Prepaid expenses will be shown in the trading A/C or profit and loss account by way of deduction from the expenses.

(b) Prepaid expenses represents benefit receivable i.e. an asset and therefore it will be shown on the assets side of the balance sheet.

(iv) **Accrued Incomes.** That income which has been carried but not received during the accounting year is called accrued income. Income like interest on investments, rent of property, sublet *etc.* are many a time earned by the business during a particular accounting period but actually not received during that period. For example, if the business has invested Rs. 10000 in 5% securities on 1st Jan. 1988 but during the year Rs. 350 has been received as interest on securities, then Rs. 150 interest on securities will be accrued interest for the year 1988. The following adjustment entry will be passed :

Accrued interest A/C Dr.

To interest A/C

The two fold effect of above entry will be

(a) accrued income will be shown on the credit side of profit and loss account by way of addition to the income.

(b) It will be a benefit receivable *i.e.* an asset to the business and therefore, it will be shown on the assets side of the balance sheet.

(v) **Unearned incomes or income received in advance:** Income received but not earned during the accounting year is called as income received in advance. It is the income received in advance for which business in responsible, for example building has been given to a tenant on Rs. 200 p.m. but during the year Rs. 3000 has been received. Then Rs. 600 will be unearned income, for unearned income following adjustment entry will be passed :

Rent A/C Dr.
To unearned rent A/C

The effect of this entry will be:

(a) It is shown on the credit side of profit and loss account by way of deduction from the income.

(b) Unearned income will be shown on the liabilities side of the Balance sheet.

(vi) **Depreciation.** Depreciation is permanent decrease or reduction in the value of the assets. When an asset is employed for earning purpose, it is necessary that depreciation must be charged to the profit of the year in order to show correct profit or loss and to show the asset at its correct value in the balance sheet.

Generally, depreciation is charged at some percentage on the value of an asset, for example, if a machine is purchased for Rs. 10000 on Ist Jan. 1988 and depreciates at 10% p.a.. Following entries will be passed to adjust depreciation.

Depreciation A/C Dr.
To Machinery A/C

The two fold effect of this entry will be :

(a) Depreciation is shown on the debit side of the profit & loss account.

(b) Depreciation is shown on the asset side by way of deduction from the value of asset.

(vii) **Interest on capital and Drawings.** Charging interest on capital is based on the argument that the same amount of capital were invested else where the proprietor would have received interest thereon. In order to ascertain the efficiency it is a common practice to charge interest on capital employed by the proprietors. The adjusting entry will be :

Interest an capital A/C Dr.
To capital A/C

(a) Interest on capital like an expense, will be shown on the debit side of the profit & loss account.

(b) Interest on capital will be shown on the liability side of the Balance sheet by way of addition to the capital.

The proprietors may also realise that when he draws money for private use, the firm losses interest therefore the proprietor may be debited with the interest on the money drawn by him. Interest will depend on the amount and the data of drawings. The adjusting entry will be :

Capital A/C Dr.
To Interest or drawing A/C

The two fold effect of this entry will be:

(a) Interest on drawings like a revenue will be shown on the credit side of the profit and loss A/C.

(b) Interest on Capital will be shown on the liabilities side of the Balance sheet by way of reduction in the capital.

(viii) **Reserves for Bad and Doubtful Debts.** It is very difficult to carry on a business only by making cash sales. Sometimes it becomes necessary to sell goods on credit also. When goods are sold on credit the amounts receivable from all debtors may not be recovered fully. Some debts may become irrecoverable due to many reasons like death, insolvency, insanity or dishonesty of the debtor. Such debts are called as 'Bad debts'. It is loss for the business. Therefore, it is one shown on the debit side of profit and loss A/C and secondly, shown as a deduction from the amount of sundry debtors in balance sheet. The following entry is passed for its adjustment.

Bad debts A/C To concerned debtor A/C (Being adjustment entry passed for irrecoverable debts).	Dr.	xxx

The bad debt A/C is closed by transferring its balance to profit and loss A/C by a closing entry. The concerned debtor A/C gets reduced to the extent of the bad debts.

Doubtful Debts

Debts created by selling goods on credit in an accounting year may not become bad in the same year. They may become bad in the subsequent year. In such cases the bad debts arising on account of selling goods on credit in one year fall upon the next year or subsequent year. So it is advised to ascertain the amount of debts which may become bad out of the debts of a year before preparing final accounts of the year. Such debts are called as 'Doubtful debts'. These are calculated or estimated by a trader on the basis of past experience. It is generally calculated at a fixed percentage on the total debtors of a trader at the end of an accounting period. The amount of doubtful debts is once placed on the debt side of profit and loss A/C and secondly it is shown as a deduction from the amount of sundry debtors in Balance sheet. The following entry is passed for adjustment.

Profit and Loss A/C Dr.	xxx
To provision for doubtful debts	xxx
(Being a provision is made towards doubtful debts)	

The debt to the profit and loss account will reduce the year's profit suitably for the possible loss and the amount will be carried forward to the next year. Next year when bad debts actually occur and are written off, the bad debts accounts will be debited to the provision for bad debts account, the amount of bad debts will be debited to the profit and loss account since debit was already given to it last year. It should be noted that the customer account on sundry debtors account is not affected by creation of the provision for bad debts. The provision for bad and doubtful debts account are deducted from the amount of book debts in the balance sheet but the two accounts are separate.

Sometimes, the balance in the provision for bad and doubtful debts account is more than sufficient to meet the bad debts and the new provision required. The remaining amount then is credited to the profit and loss account.

(ix) **Reserve for Discount on debtors and creditors.** Debtors are sometimes allowed a discount to induce them for a prompt payment. The traders maintains a reserve for them which is called reserve for discount on sundry debtors. It is shown on the debit side of profit and loss A/C and deducted from the sundry debtors in the balance sheet. It should be kept in mind that while calculating the reserve for discount the reserve for bad debts should be deducted from the sundry debtors in the balance sheet. For *e.g.*, debtors own Rs. 10000, reserve for discount is Rs. 500. A reserve for bad debts @ 5% will not be calculated on Rs. 10000 but on Rs. 9500 (Rs. 10000- Rs. 500).

When discount is allowed, following journal entry is passed :

Discount A/C Dr.
To debtor's personal A/C

Following entry is passed to create a provision for discount on debtors.

Profit & Loss A/C Dr.
To Provision for discount on debtors A/C.

The discount allowed will be transferred to the provision for discount on debtors account by passing following entry:

Provision for discount on debtors A/C Dr
To discount A/C

Such provision will be shown on the debt side of profit and loss A/C. The provision will be shown by way of deduction from sundry debtors (after deduction of further bad debts and provision for doubtful debts) on the assets side of the balance sheet.

RATIO ANALYSIS

Ratio, broadly speaking is the numerical relationship between two numbers. And hence ratio analysis of statement stands for the process of determining and presenting the relationship of items and groups of items in the statements. When relations among various accounting data supplied by financial statements are worked out, they are termed as accounting ratios. Ratio may be expressed in the following three ways:

(a) **Ratio.** Specially the simple division of one number by another *e.g.*, current asset to current liability ratio is 2:1.

(b) **Rate.** The ratio between two numerical facts, usually over a period of time *e.g.*, stock turnover is three times a year.

(c) **Percentage.** A special type of rate which expresses the relation in hundredth *e.g.*, gross profit is 25% on sale. While determining a ratio it is well to understand. It is desirable to divide the "more favourable" one by the "less favourable".

Nature of Ratio Analysis

An accounting ratio shows the mathematical relationship between two figures that have a meaningful relation with each other e.g., net sales and profit, and current assets and current liabilities. No meaning can be attached to the ratio between two figures that are unrelated to each other. Ratio analysis uses financial ratios indicating a quantitative relationship to make qualitative judgements on various aspects of the business.

Interpretation of Ratios

The technique of interpretation of ratios involves the comparisons of existing ratios against defined standards. The standards of comparison may consist of the following:

(i) Ratios calculated from the past financial statements of the same company.

(ii) Ratio evolved using the projected financial expectations from the company in the future. These would help corrective action to be initiated in the present.

(iii) Ratios of a few carefully identified competitors, who have similar operations as a reflection on the company's relative performance.

(iv) Ratio of the industry of which the firm is a member.

Classification of Ratios

Classification of ratios depends upon the objective for which they are calculated. It may also depend upon the availability of data. Analysis of financial statement is made with a view to ascertain the efficiency and financial soundness of the company as such ratios can be classified on the basis of profitability, turnover and financial capability. On the basis of purpose, ratios may be classified as under:

A. Profitability Ratios
   - (a) Gross profit ratio
   - (b) Net profit ratio and operating net profit ratios
   - (c) Expenses ratios
   - (d) Operating ratio
   - (e) Net profit to net worth ratio
   - (f) Net profit to fixed assets ratio
   - (g) Return on investment or capital employed
   - (h) Return on equity capital
   - (i) Earning per share

B. Activity or Performance or Turnover Ratio
   - (a) Stock or inventory turnover ratio
   - (b) Total capital turnover ratio
   - (c) Fixed assets turnover ratio
   - (d) Working capital turnover ratio
   - (e) Debtors turnover ratio

C. Financial Ratios
   - (a) Liquid ratios or short term financial or solvency ratios
     - (i) Current ratio
     - (ii) Liquid ratio
   - (b) Solvency ratios or long term financial ratios
     - (i) Debt equity ratio
     - (ii) Total debt ratio
     - (iii) Interest coverage or debt service ratio
     - (iv) Fixed assets ratio
     - (v) Proprietary ratio

(vi) Solvency ratio or debt to total funds ratio

(vii) Capital gearing ratio.

Significance of Return on Investment - (ROI)

Return on investment ratio measures, the operational efficiency and borrowing policy of the enterprise. It also shows how effectively the capital employed in the business is used. It shows the earning capacity of the net assets of the business. The ratio judges the performance of the business. It can be used for comparing the performance of even dissimilar business or different departments of the same business.

Uses of Return on Investment - (ROI)

1. It measures overall profitability of the business
2. Return on investment is a very significant ratio for measuring operational efficiency of the management.
3. It is used for comparing the performance of the different departments and sections of the enterprise.
4. Return on investment helps in making investment decisions.
5. Return on investment helps in determining the price of the product.

Use and Significance of Ratio Analysis

The ratio analysis is one of the most powerful tools of financial analysis. It is used as a device to analyse and interpret the financial health of enterprise. Just like a doctor examines his patient by recording his body temperature, blood pressure *etc.*, before making his conclusion regarding the illness and before giving his treatment. A financial analyst analyses the financial statements with various tools of analysis before commenting upon the financial health or weaknesses of enterprise. 'A ratio known as a symptom like blood pressure, the pulse rate or the temperature of an individual.' It is with help of ratios that the financial statements can be analysed more clearly and decisions made from such analysis.

The use of ratios is not confined to financial managers only. As discussed earlier, there are different parties interested in the ratio analysis for knowing the financial position of a firm for different purposes. The supplier of goods on credit, banks, financial institutions, investors, shareholders and management all make use of ratio analysis as a tool in evaluating the financial position and performance of a firm for granting credit, providing loans or making investments in the firm. With the use of ratio analysis one can measure the financial condition of a firm and can point out whether the condition is strong, good, questionable or poor. The conclusions can also be drawn as to whether the performance of the firm is improving or deteriorating. Thus, ratios have wide applications and are of immense use today.

(a) **Managerial Uses of Ratio Analysis**

(i) ***Helps in decision-making.*** Financial statements are prepared primarily for decision making. But the information provided in financial statements is not an end in itself and no meaningful conclusion can be drawn from these statements alone. Ratio analysis helps in making decisions from the information provided in these financial statements.

(ii) ***Helps in financial forecasting and planning.*** Ratio Analysis is of much help in financial forecasting and planning. Planning is looking ahead and the ratios calculated for a number of years work as a guide for the future. Meaningful conclusions can be drawn for future from these ratios. Thus, ratio analysis helps in forecasting and planning.

(iii) *Helps in communicating.* The financial strength and weakness of a firm are communicated in a more easy and understandable manner by the use of ratios. The information contained in the financial statements is conveyed in a meaningful manner to the one for whom it is meant. Thus, ratios help in communication and enhance the value of the financial statements.

(iv) *Helps in co-ordination.* Ratios even help in co-ordination which is of utmost importance in effective business management. Better communication of efficiency and weakness of an enterprise results in better co-ordination in the enterprise.

(v) *Helps in Control.* Ratio analysis even helps in making effective control of the business. Standard ratios can be based upon proforma financial statements and variances or deviations, if any, can be found by comparing the actual with the standards so as to take a corrective action at the right time. The weaknesses or otherwise, if any, come to the knowledge of the management which helps in effective control of the business.

(vi) *Other Uses.* These are so many other uses of the ratio analysis. It is essential part of the budgetary control and standard costing. Ratios are of immense importance in the analysis and interpretation of financial statements as they bring the strength or weakness of a firm.

(b) **Utility to Shareholders/Investors.** An investor in the company will like to assess the financial position of the concern where he is going to invest. His first interest will be the security of his investment and then a return in the form of dividend or interest. For the first purpose he will try to assess the value of fixed assets and the loans raised against them. The investor will feel satisfied only if the concern has sufficient amount of assets. Long-term solvency ratios will help him in assessing financial concern. Profitability ratios, on the other hand, will be useful to determine profitability position. Ratio analysis will be useful to the investor in making up his mind whether the present financial position of the concern warrants further investment or not.

(c) **Utility to Creditors.** The creditors or suppliers extend short-term credit to the concern. They are interested to know whether financial position of the concern warrants their payments at a specified time or not. The concern pays short-term creditors out of its current assets. If the current assets are quite sufficient to meet current liabilities then the creditor will not hesitate in extending credit facilities. Current and acid-test ratios will give an idea about the current financial position of the concern.

(d) **Utility to Employees.** The employees are also interested in the financial position of the concern especially profitability. Their wage increases and amount of fringe benefits are related to the volume of profits earned by the concern. The employees make use of information available in financial statements. Various profitability ratios relating to gross profit, operating profit, net profit *etc.* enable employees to put forward their viewpoint for the increase in wages and other benefits.

(e) **Utility to Government.** Government is interested to know the overall strength of the industry. Various financial statements published by industrial units are used to calculate ratios for determining short-term, long-term and overall financial position of the concerns. Profitability indexes can also be prepared with the help of ratios. Government may base its future policies on the basis of industrial information available from various units. The ratios may be used as indicators of overall financial strength of public as well as private sector. In the absence of the reliable economic information, governmental plans and policies may not prove successful.

SUMMARY OF RATIOS

Objective of Analysis (1)	Ratios to be computed (2)	Basic Components (3)
(a) Short-term Financial Position or Test of Liquidity	1. Current Ratio	$\frac{\text{Current Assets}}{\text{Current Liabilities}}$
	2. Quick or Acid Test or Liquid Ratio (for immediate solvency)	$\frac{\text{Liquid/Quick Assets}}{\text{Current Liabilities}}$
	3. Absolute Liquid Ratio	$\frac{\text{Absolute Liquid Assets}}{\text{Current Liabilities}}$
(b) Current assets Movement or Efficiency or Activity Ratios	1. Inventory/Stock Turnover Ratio	$\frac{\text{Cost of Goods sold}}{\text{Average Inventory at Cost}}$
	2. Debtors or Receivables Turnover Ratio/Velocity	$\frac{\text{Net Credit Annual Sales}}{\text{Average Trade Debtors}}$
	3. Average Collection Period	$\frac{\text{Total Trade Debtors}}{\text{Sales per day}}$
	4. Creditors/payables Turnover Ratio/velocity	$\frac{\text{Net Credit Annual Purchase}}{\text{Average Trade Creditors}}$
	5. Average Payment Period	$\frac{\text{Total Trade Creditors}}{\text{Average Daily Purchases}}$
	6. Working Capital Turnover Ratio	$\frac{\text{Cost of Sales}}{\text{Net Working Capital}}$
(c) Analysis of Long-term Financial Position or Test of Solvency	1. Debt-Equity Ratio	$\frac{\text{Outsider's Funds}}{\text{Shareholders' Funds}}$ OR $\frac{\text{External Equities}}{\text{Internal Equities}}$
	2. Funded Debt to Total Capitalisation Ratio	$\frac{\text{Funded Debt}}{\text{Total Capitalisation}} \times 100$
	3. Ratio of Long-term Debt to Shareholders, Funds (Debt-Equity)	$\frac{\text{Long-term Debt}}{\text{Shareholders' Funds}}$

	4. Proprietary or Equity Ratio	$\frac{\text{Shareholder's Funds}}{\text{Total Assets}}$
	5. Solvency Ratio	$\frac{\text{Total Liabilities to Outsiders}}{\text{Total Assets}}$
	6. Fixed Assets Net Worth Ratio	$\frac{\text{Fixed Assets (after depreciation)}}{\text{Shareholders' funds}}$
	7. Fixed Assets Ratio or Fixed Assets to Long-term Funds	$\frac{\text{Fixed Assets (after depreciation)}}{\text{Total Long-term Funds}}$
	8. Ratio of Current Assets to Proprietors' Funds	$\frac{\text{Current Assets}}{\text{Shareholders' Funds}}$
	9. Debt-Service, or Interest Coverage Ratio	$\frac{\text{Net Profit (before interest \& taxes)}}{\text{Fixed Interest Charges}}$
	10. Total Coverage, or Fixed-Charge Coverage	$\frac{\text{EBIT}}{\text{Total Fixed Charges}}$
	11. Preference Dividend Coverage Ratio	$\frac{\text{Net Profit (before interest \& Income tax)}}{\text{Preference Dividend}}$
	12. Cash to Debt-Service Ratio or Debt Cash Flow Coverage	Annual Cash flow (before interest & Income tax) $\frac{CF}{1+\frac{\text{Interest on debt}}{1-\text{Tax rate}}} = \frac{CF}{1+\frac{SFD}{1-T}}$
(d) Analysis of Profitability (i) General Profitability	1. Gross Profit Ratio	$\frac{\text{Gross Profit}}{\text{Net Sales}}\times 100$
	2. Operating Ratio	$\frac{\text{Operating Cost}}{\text{Net Sales}}\times 100$
	3. Expense Ratio	$\frac{\text{Particular Expenses}}{\text{Net Sales}}\times 100$
	4. Net Profit Ratio	$\frac{\text{Net Profit after tax}}{\text{Net Sales}}\times 100$

	5. Operating Profit Ratio	$\frac{\text{Operating Profit}}{\text{Net Sales}} \times 100$
(ii) Overall Profitability	1. Return on Shareholders' Investments or Net Worth (ROI)	$\frac{\text{Net Profit (after interest \& tax)}}{\text{Shareholders' Funds}} \times 100$
	2. Return on Equity Capital	$\frac{\text{NetProfit after tax - Preference Div.}}{\text{Paid-up Equity Capital}} \times 100$
	3. Earnings Per Share (E.P.S.)	$\frac{\text{NetProfit after tax - Preference Div.}}{\text{Number of Equity Share}}$
	4. Return on Gross Capital Employed	$\frac{\text{Adjusted Net Profit}}{\text{Gross Capital Employed}} \times 100$
	5. Return on Net Capital Employed	$\frac{\text{Adjusted Net Profit}}{\text{Net Capital Employed}} \times 100$
	6. Capital Turnover Ratio	$\frac{\text{Sales or Cost of Sales}}{\text{Capital Employed}}$
	7. Dividend Yield Ratio	$\frac{\text{Dividend Per Share}}{\text{Market value per share}}$
	8. Dividend Pay-out Ratio or Pay-out Ratio	$\frac{\text{Dividend Per Equity Share}}{\text{Earnings per share}}$
	9. Price-Earning Ratio (P/E Ratio)	$\frac{\text{Market Price per Equity Share}}{\text{Earnings per share}}$
(e) Analysis of Capital Structure or Leverage	1. Capital Gearing Ratio	$\frac{\text{Eq. Share Capital + Reserves \& Surplus}}{\text{Pref. Capital + Long-term debt bearing fixed interest}}$
	2. Total Investment to long-term Liabilities	$\frac{\text{Shareholders' funds + Long-term Liabilities}}{\text{Long-term Liabilities}}$
	3. Debt Equity Ratio	$\frac{\text{Outsiders' Funds}}{\text{Shareholders'Funds}}$

4. Ratio of Fixed Assets to Funded Debt $\dfrac{\text{Fixed Assets}}{\text{Funded Debt}}$
5. Ratio of Current Liabilities to Proprietors Funds $\dfrac{\text{Current Liabilities}}{\text{Shareholders' Funds}}$
6. Ratio of Reserves to Equity Capital $\dfrac{\text{Reserves}}{\text{Equity Share Capital}} \times 100$
7. Financial Leverage $\dfrac{\text{Int. \& Tax (EBIT)}}{\text{EBIT – Inter \& Pref. Divd.}}$
8. Operating Leverage $\dfrac{\text{Contribution}}{\text{EBIT}}$

FUND FLOW

The Funds Flow Statement is a statement which shows the movement of funds and is a report of the financial operations of the business undertaking. It indicates various means by which funds were obtained during a particular period and the ways in which these funds were employed. In simple words, it is a statement of sources and applications of funds.

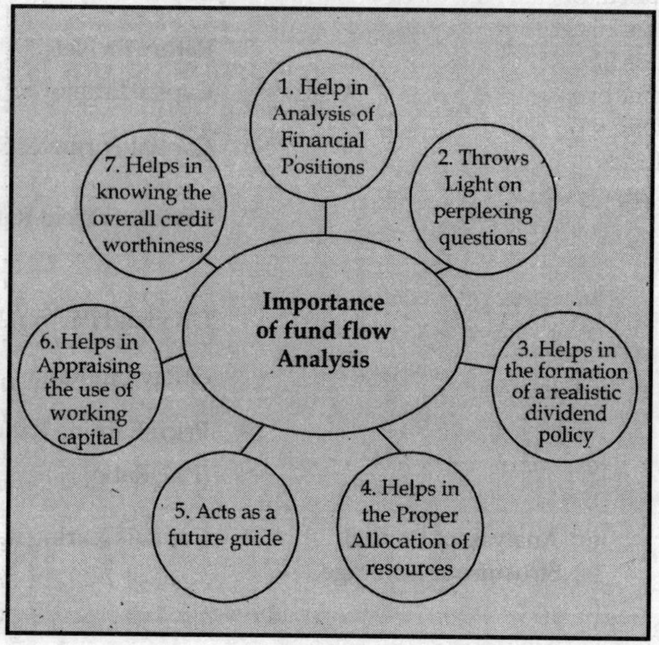

In a **narrow sense**, it means cash only and a funds flow statement prepared on this basis is called a cash flow statement. Such a statement enumerates net effects of the various business transactions on cash and takes into account receipts and disbursements of cash.

In a **broader sense**, the term 'funds' refers to money values in whatever form it may exist. Here 'funds' means all financial resources, used in business whether in the form of men, material, money, machinery and others.

In a **popular sense**, the term 'funds' means working capital *i.e.*, the excess of current assets over current liabilities. The working capital concept of funds has emerged due to the fact that total resources of a business are invested partly in fixed assets in the form of fixed capital and partly kept in the form of liquid or near liquid form as working capital.

The term 'flow' means movement and includes both 'inflow' and 'outflow'. The term 'flow of funds' means transfer of economic values from one asset of equity to another. Flow of funds is said to have taken place when any transaction makes changes in the amount of funds available before happening of the transaction. If the effect transactions results in the increase of funds, it is called as a source of funds and if it results in the decrease of funds, it is known as an application of funds. Further, in case the transactions does not change funds, it is said to have not resulted in the flow of funds. According to the working capital concept of funds, the term 'flow of funds' refers to the movement of funds in the working capital. If any transactions results in the increase in working capital, it is said to be a source or inflow of funds and if it results in the decrease of working capital, it is said to be an application or out-flow of funds.

According to I.C.W.A., 'Fund flow Statement is a statement either prospective or retrospective setting out the sources and applications of the funds of an enterprises. The purpose of the statement is to indicate clearly the requirement of funds and how they are proposed to be raised and the efficient, utilisation and application of the same'.

Uses, Significance and Importance of Funds Flow Statement

A funds flow statement is an essential tool for the financial analysis and is of primary importance to the financial management. Now-a-days, it is being widely used by the financial analysts, credit granting institutions and financial managers. The basic purpose of a funds flow statement is to reveal the changes in the working capital on the two balance sheet dates. It also describes the sources from which additional working capital has been financed and the uses to which working capital has been applied. Such a statement is particularly useful in assessing the growth of the firm, its resulting financial needs and in determining the best way of financing these needs. By making use of projected funds flow statements, the management can come to know the adequacy or inadequacy of working capital even in advance. One can plan the intermediate and long-term financing of the firm, repayment of long-term debts, expansion of the business, allocation of resources *etc*. The significance or importance of funds flow statement can be well followed from its various uses given below:

(i) **It helps in the analysis of financial operations.** The financial statements reveal the net effect of various transactions on the operational and financial position of a concern. The balance sheet gives a static view of the resources of a business and the uses to which these resources have been put at a certain point of time. But it does not disclose the causes for changes in the assets and liabilities between two different points of time. The funds flow statement explains causes for such changes and also the effect of these changes on the liquidity position of the company. Sometimes a concern may operate profitably and yet its cash position may become more and more worse. The funds flow statement gives a clear answer to such a situation explaining what has happened to the profits of the firm.

(ii) **It throws light on many perplexing questions of general interest** which otherwise may be difficult to be answered, such as

(a) Why were the net current assets lesser in spite of higher profits and vice versa?
(b) Why more dividends could not be declared in spite of available profits?
(c) How was it possible to distribute more dividends than the present earnings ?
(d) What happened to the net profit? Where did they go?
(e) What happened to the proceeds of sale of fixed assets or issue of shares, debentures, etc.?
(f) What are the sources of the repayment of debt?
(g) How was the increase in working capital financed and how it will be financed in future?

(iii) **It helps in the formation of a realistic dividend policy.** Sometimes a firm has sufficient profits available for distribution as dividend but yet it may not be advisable to distribute dividend for lack of liquid or cash resources. In such cases, a funds flow statement helps in the formation of a realistic dividend policy.

(iv) **It helps in the proper allocation of resources.** The resources of a concern are always limited and it wants to make the best use of these resources. A projected funds flow statement constructed for the future helps in making managerial decisions. The firm can plan the deployment of its resources and allocate them among various applications.

(v) **It acts as a future guide.** A projected funds flow statement also acts as a guide for future to the management. The management can come to know the various problems it is going to face in near future for want of funds. The firm's future needs of funds can be projected well in advance and also the timing of these needs. The firm can arrange to finance these needs more effectively and avoid future problems.

(vi) **It helps in appraising the use of working capital.** A funds flow statement helps in explaining how efficiently the management has used its working capital and also suggests ways to improve working capital position of the firm.

(vii) **It helps in knowing the overall credit worthiness of a firm.** The financial institutions and banks such as State Financial Institutions, Industrial Development Corporation, Industrial Finance Corporation of India, Industrial Development Bank of India, *etc.*, all ask for funds flow statements constructed for a number of years before granting loans to know the credit worthiness and paying capacity of the firm. Hence, a firm seeking financial assistance from these institutions has no alternative but to prepare funds flow statements.

Procedure for Preparing a Funds Flow Statement

Funds Flow statement is a method by which we study changes in the financial position of a business enterprise between beginning and ending financial statements dates. Hence, the funds flow statement is prepared by comparing two balance sheets and with the help of such other information derived from the accounts as may be needed. Broadly speaking, the preparation of a funds flow statement consists of two parts :

A. Statement or Schedule of Changes in Working Capital

Working Capital means the excess of current assets over current liabilities. Statement of changes in working capital is prepared to show the changes in the working capital between the two balance sheet dates. This statement is prepared with the help of current assets and current liabilities derived from the two balance sheets.

As, Working Capital = Current Assets – Current Liabilities.

So,

(i) An increase in current assets increases working capital.

(ii) A decrease in current assets decreases, working capital.

(iii) An increase in current liabilities decreases working capital and

(iv) A decrease in current liabilities increases working capital.

The change in the amount of any current asset or current liability in the current balance sheet as compared to that of the previous balance sheet either results in increase or decrease in working capital. The difference is recorded for each individual current asset and current liability. In case a current asset in the current period is more than in the previous period, the effect is an increase in working capital and it is recorded in the increase column . But if a current liability in the current period is more than in the previous period, the effect is decrease in working capital and it is recorded in the decrease column or vice versa. The total increase and the total decrease are compared and the difference shows the net increase or net decrease in working capital. It is worth noting that schedule of changes in working capital is prepared only from current assets and current liabilities and the other information is not of any use for preparing this statement. A typical form of statement or schedule of changes in working capital is as follows:

STATEMENT OR SCHEDULE OF CHANGES IN WORKING CAPITAL

Particulars	Previous Year	Current Year	Effect on Working Capital	
			Increase	Decrease
Current Assets:				
Cash in hand				
Cash at bank				
Bills Receivable				
Sundry Debtors				
Temporary Investments				
Stocks/Inventories				
Prepaid Expenses				
Accrued Incomes				
Total Current Assets				
Current Liabilities:				
Bills Payable				
Sundry Creditors				
Outstanding Expenses				
Bank Overdraft				
Short-term advances				
Dividends Payable				
Proposed dividends				
Provision for taxation				
Total Current Liabilities				
Working Capital (CA-CL)				
Net Increase or Decrease in Working Capital				

B. Statement of Sources and Application of Funds

Funds flow statement is a statement which indicates various sources from which funds (working capital) have been obtained during a certain period and the uses or applications to which these funds have been put during that period. Generally, this statement is prepared in two formats:

(a) Report Form

(b) T-Form or An Account Form or Self Balancing Type.

SPECIMEN OF REPORT FORM OF FUNDS FLOW STATEMENT

	Rs.
Sources of Funds:	
Funds from Operations	
Issue of Share Capital	
Raising of long-term loans	
Receipts from partly paid shares, called up	
Sales of non current (fixed) assets	
Non-trading receipts, such as dividends received	
Sale of Investments (long-term)	
Decrease in Working Capital (as per schedule of changes in Working Capital)	
Total	
Applications or Uses of Funds:	
Funds Lost in Operations	
Redemption of Preference Share Capital	
Redemption of Debentures	
Repayment of long-term loans	
Purchase of non-current (fixed) assets	
Purchase of long-term Investments	
Non-trading payments	
Payments of dividends	
Payment of tax	
Increase in Working Capital (as per schedule of changes in Working Capital)	
Total	

T Form or An Account Form or Self Balancing Type FUNDS FLOW STATEMENT

(For the year ended..........)

Sources	*Rs.*	*Applications*	*Rs.*
Funds from Operations		Funds lost in Operations	
Issue of Share Capital		Redemption of Preference	
Issue of Debentures		Share Capital	
Raising of long-term loans		Redemption of Debentures	

Receipts from partly paid shares, called up		Repayment of long-term loans	
Sale of non-current (fixed) assets		Purchase of non-current (fixed) assets	
Non-trading receipts such as dividends		Purchase of long-term Investments	
		Non-trading payments	
Sale of long-term Investments		Payment of Dividends	
Net Decrease in Working Capital		Payment of tax	
		Net Increase in Working Capital	

Sources of Funds

The following are the sources from which funds generally flow (come), into the business :

(a) Funds from Operations or Trading Profits

Trading profits or the profits from operations of the business are the most important and major source of funds. Sales are the main source of inflow of funds into the business as they increase current assets (cash, debtors or bills receivable) but at the same time funds flow out of business for expenses and cost of goods sold. Thus, the net effect of operations will be a source of funds if inflow from sales exceeds the outflow for expenses and cost of goods sold and vice-versa. But it must be remembered that funds from operations do not necessarily mean the profit as shown by the profit and loss account of a firm, because there are many non-fund or non-operating items which may have been either debited or credited to profit and loss account. The examples of such items on the debit side of a profit and loss account are the following:

Amortization of fictitious and intangible assets such as goodwill, Preliminary expenses and Discount on issue of shares and debentures written off; Appropriation of Retained Earnings, such as Transfers to Reserves, *etc.*, Depreciation and depletion Loss on sale of fixed assets ; Payment of dividend, *etc.* The non-fund items are those which may be operational expenses but they do not affect funds of the business, *e.g.*, for depreciation charged to profit and loss account, funds really do not move out of business. Non-operating items are those which although may result in the outflow of funds but are not related to the trading operations of the business, such as loss on sale of machinery or payment of dividends. The methods of calculating funds from operations have been discussed in the following pages.

Basically, there are two methods of calculating funds from operations:

(1) **The first method** is to prepare the profit and loss account afresh by taking into consideration only fund and operational items which involve funds and are related to the normal operations of the business. The balancing figure in this case will be either funds generated from operations or funds lost in operations depending upon whether the income or credit side of profit and loss account exceeds the expense or debit side of profit and loss account or vice-versa.

(2) **The second method** (which is generally used) is to proceed from the figure of net profit or net loss as arrived at from the profit and loss account already prepared. Funds from operations by this method can be calculated as under:

CALCULATION OF FUNDS FROM OPERATION	
Closing Balance of P & L A/C or Retained Earnings (as given in the balance sheet)	Rs.
Add: Non-fund and Non-operating items which have been already debited to P & L A/C:	
(i) Depreciation and Depletion	
(ii) Amortization of fictitious and Intangible Assets such as:	
(a) Goodwill	
(b) Patents	
(c) Trade marks	
(d) Preliminary Expenses	
(e) Discount on Issue of Shares, etc.	
(iii) Appropriation of Retained Earnings, such as:	
(a) Transfer to General Reserve	
(b) Dividend Equalisation Fund	
(c) Transfer to Sinking Fund	
(d) Contingency Reserve, etc.	
(iv) Loss on Sale of any non-current (fixed) assets such as :	
(a) Loss on sale of land and building	
(b) Loss on sale of machinery	
(c) Loss on sale of furniture	
(d) Loss on sale of long-term investments, etc.	
(v) Dividends including:	
(a) Interim Dividend	
(b) Proposed Dividend (if it is an appropriation of profits and not taken as current liability)	
(vi) Provision for Taxation (if it is not taken as Current Liability)	
(vii) Any other non-fund/non-operating items which have been debited to P/L	
Total (A)	

Less Non-fund or Non-operating items which have already been credited to P & L A/C	
(i) Profit or Gain from the sale of non-current (fixed) assets such as:	
(a) Profit on sale of land and building	
(b) Profit on sale of plant & machinery	
(c) Profit on sale of long-term investments, etc.	

(ii) Appreciation in the value of fixed assets, such as increase in the value of land if it has been credited to P & L A/C	
(iii) Dividends Received	
(iv) Excess Provision re-transferred to P&L A/C or written off	
(v) Any other non-operating item which has been credited to P&L A/C	
(vi) Opening balance of P& L A/C or Retained Earnings (as given in the balance sheet)	
Total (B)	
Total (A) – Total (B) = Funds generated by operations	

Funds from operations can also be calculated by preparing Adjusted Profit and Loss Account as follows:

ADJUSTED PROFIT AND LOSS ACCOUNT

	Rs.		Rs.
To Depreciation & Depletion or amortization of fictitious and intangible assets, such as: Goodwill, Patents, Trade Marks, Preliminary Expenses *etc.*		By Opening Balance (of P & L A/C)	
To Appropriation of Retained Earnings, such as: Transfers to General Reserve, Dividend Equalisation Fund, Sinking Fund, *etc.*		By Transfers from excess provisions	
To Loss on Sales of any non current or fixed asset		By Appreciation in the value of fixed assets	
To Dividends (including interim dividend)		By Dividends received	
To Proposed Dividend (if not taken as a current liability)		By Profit on sale of fixed or non-current assets	
To Provision for taxation (if not taken as a current liability)		By Funds from Operations (balancing figure in case debit side exceeds credit side)	
To Closing balance (of P & L A/C)			
To Funds lost in Operations (balancing figure, in case credit side exceeds the debit side)			

(b) Issue of Share Capital

If during the year there is any increase in the share capital, whether preference or equity, it means capital has been raised during the year. Issue of shares is a source of funds as it constitutes inflow of funds. Even the calls received from partly paid shares constitutes an inflow of funds. It should also be remembered that it is the net proceeds from the issue of share capital which amounts to a source of funds and hence in case shares are issued at premium, even the amount of premium collected shall become a source of funds. The same is true when shares are issued at discount ; it will not be the nominal value of shares but the actual realisation after deducting discount that shall amount to inflow of funds. But sometimes shares are issued otherwise than in cash, the following rules must be followed:

(i) Issue of shares for making of partly paid shares as fully paid out of accumulated profits in the form of bonus shares is not a source of funds.

(ii) Issues of shares for consideration other than current assets such as against purchase of land, machines, *etc.* does not amount to inflow of funds.

(iii) Conversion of debentures or loans into shares also does not amount to inflow of funds.

In all the three cases mentioned above, both the amounts involved are non-current and do not involve any current assets or funds.

(c) Issue of Debentures and Raising of Loans, etc.

Issue of debentures or raising of loans (long-term), whether secured or unsecured results in the flow of funds into the business. The inflow of funds is the actual proceeds from the issue of such debentures or raising of loans, *i.e.*, including the amount of premium or excluding discount, if any. However, loans raised for consideration other than a current asset, such as for purchase of building, will not constitute inflow of funds because in that case the accounts involved are only fixed or non-current.

(d) Sale of Fixed (non-current assets) and Long-term or Trade Investments

When any fixed or non-current asset like land, building, plant and machinery, furniture, long-term investments, *etc.* are sold it generates funds and becomes a source of funds. However, it must be remembered that if one fixed asset is exchanged for another fixed asset, it does not constitute an inflow of funds because no current assets are involved.

(e) Non-Trading Receipts

Any non-trading receipt like dividend received, refund of tax, rent received, *etc.* also increases funds and is treated as a sources of funds because such an income is not included in the funds from operations.

(f) Decrease in Working Capital

If the working capital decreases during the current period as compared to the previous period, it means that there has been a release of funds from working capital and it constitutes a source of funds.

Application or Uses of Funds

(a) **Funds lost in operations.** Sometimes the result of trading in a certain year is a loss and some funds are lost during that period in trading operations. Such loss of funds in trading amounts to an outflow of funds and is treated as an application of funds.

(b) **Redemption of preference share capital.** If during the year any preference shares are redeemed, it will result in the outflow of funds and is taken as an application of funds. When the shares are redeemed at premium or discount, it is the net amount paid (including premium or excluding discount, as the case may be). However, if shares are redeemed in exchanges of some other type of shares or debentures, it does not constitute an outflow of funds as no current account is involved in that case.

(c) **Repayment of loans or redemption of debentures, etc..** In the same way as redemption of preference share capital, redemption of debentures or repayment of loans also constitute an application of funds.

(d) **Purchase of any non-current or fixed asset.** When any fixed or non-current asset like land, building, plant and machinery, furniture, long-term investments, etc. are purchased, funds outflow from the business. However, if fixed assets are purchased for a consideration of issue of shares or debentures or if some fixed asset is exchanged for another, it does not involve any funds and hence not an application of funds.

(e) **Payments of Dividends and Tax.** Payments of dividends and tax are also applications of funds. It is the actual payment of dividend (may be interim dividend) and tax which should be taken as an outflow of funds and not the mere declaration of dividend or creating of a provision for taxation.

(f) **Any other non-trading payment.** Any payment or expense not related to the trading operations of the business amounts to outflow of funds and is taken as an application of funds. The examples could be drawings in case of sole trader or partnership firms, loss of cash, *etc.*

CASH FLOW

Cash plays a very important role in the entire economic life of a business. A firm needs cash to make payments to its suppliers, to incur day-to-day expenses and to pay salaries, wages, interest and dividends, *etc.* In fact, what blood is to a human body, cash is to a business enterprise. It is very essential for a business to maintain an adequate balance of cash. But many a times, a concern operates profitably and yet it becomes very difficult to pay taxes and dividends. This may be because:

(i) although huge profits have been earned, yet cash may not have been received or

(ii) even if cash has been received, it may have drained out (used) for some other purposes. This movement of cash is of vital importance to the management.

A statement of changes in the financial position affirm on cash basis is called a cash flow statement. Such a statement enumerates net effects of the various business transactions on cash and takes into account receipts and disbursements of cash. A cash flow statement summarises the causes of changes in cash position of a business enterprise between dates of two balance sheets. This statement is very much similar to the statement of changes in financial position prepared on working capital basis, *i.e.*, a funds flow statement, except that a cash flow statement focuses attention on cash instead of working capital. It is called a cash flow statement because it describes the inflow (sources) and outflow (uses) of cash.

DIFFERENCE BETWEEN FUNDS FLOW STATEMENT AND CASH FLOW STATEMENT

	Basis of Difference	Funds Flow Statement	Cash Flow Statement
(i)	Basis of Concept	It is based on a wider concept of funds, *i.e.*, Working capital.	It is based on a narrower concept of funds *i.e.*, cash.
(ii)	Basis of Accounting	It is based on accrual basis of accounting.	It is based on cash basis of accounting.
(iii)	Schedule of change in working Capital	Schedule of changes in working capital is prepared to show the changes in current assets and current liabilities.	No such schedule of changes in working capital is prepared.

	Basis of Difference	Funds Flow Statement	Cash Flow Statement
(iv)	Method of Preparing	Fund Flow Statement reveals the sources and applications of funds. The net difference between sources and applications of funds represents net increase or decrease in working capital.	It is prepared by taking the opening balance of cash, adding to this all the inflows of cash and deducting the out flows of cash from the the difference represents the closing balance of cash.
(v)	Basis of Usefulness	It is useful in planning intermediate and long term financing.	It is more useful for short-term analysis and cash planning of the business.

Uses and Significance of Cash Flow Statement

Cash flow statement is of vital importance to the financial management. It is an essential tool of financial analysis for short-term planning. The chief advantages of cash flow statement are as follows:

(i) Since a cash flow statement is based on the cash basis of accounting, it is very useful in the evaluation of cash position of a firm.

(ii) A projected cash flow statement can be prepared in order to know the future cash position of a concern so as to enable a firm to plan and coordinate its financial operations properly. By preparing this statement, a firm can come to know as to how much cash will be generated into the firm and how much cash will be needed to make various payments and hence the firm can well plan to arrange for the future requirements of cash.

(iii) A comparison of the historical and projected cash flow statements can be made so as to find the variations and deficiency or otherwise in the performance so as to enable the firm to take immediate and effective action.

(iv) A series of intra-firm and inter-firm cash flow statements reveals whether the firm's liquidity (short-term paying capacity) is improving or deteriorating over a period of time and in comparison to other firms over a given period of time.

(v) Cash flow statement helps in planning the repayment of loans, replacement of fixed assets and other similar long-term planning of cash. It is also significant for capital budgeting decisions.

(vi) It better explains the causes for poor cash position inspite of substantial profits of a firm by throwing light on various applications of cash made by the firm. It further helps in answering some intricate questions like – what happened to the net profits ? Where did the profits go? Why more dividends could not be paid in spite of sufficient available profit ?

(vii) Cash flow analysis is more useful and appropriate than funds flow analysis for short-term financial analysis as for a very short period it is cash which is more relevant then the working capital for forecasting the ability of the firm to meet its immediate obligations.

Procedure for Preparing a Cash Flow Statement

Cash flow statement shows the impact of various transactions on cash position of a firm. It is prepared with the help of financial statements, *i.e.,* balance sheet and profit and loss account and some additional information. A cash flow statement starts with the opening balance of cash and balance at bank, all the inflows of cash are added to the opening balance and the out flows of cash are deducted from the total. The balance, *i.e.* opening balance of cash and bank balance plus in flows of cash minus outflows of cash is reconciled with the closing balance of cash. The preparation of cash flow statement involves the determining of:

(a) **Sources of Cash Inflows.** The main sources of cash inflows are

(i) Cash flow from operations;

(ii) Increase in existing liabilities or creation of new liabilities and
(iii) Reduction in or Sale of Assets;
(iv) Non-trading Receipts.

(b) **Application of Cash or Cash Outflows.**
(i) Cash lost in operations;
(ii) Decrease in or discharge of liabilities;
(iii) Increase in or purchase of assets and
(iv) Non–trading payments.

Generally, cash flow statement is prepared in two forms:
(a) Report form
(b) T–Form or an Account Form or Self Balancing Type

SPECIMEN OF REPORT FORM OF CASH FLOW STATEMENT

	Rs.
Cash balance in the beginning **Add:** Cash inflows: Cash flow from operations Sale of assets Issue of shares Issue of debentures Raising of loans Collection from debtors Non trading receipts such as: Dividend received Income tax refund	
Less: Applications or Outflows of cash: Redemption of Preference shares Redemption of debentures Repayment of loans Purchase of assets Payment of dividend Payment of taxes Cash lost in operations	
Cash Balance at the end	

T–FORM OR AN ACCOUNT FORM OF CASH FLOW STATEMENT

	Rs.		Rs.
Cash balance in the beginning **Add.** Cash inflows: Cash flow from operation Sale of Assets Issue of Shares Issue of Debentures Raising of Loans		Outflow of Cash: Redemption of Preference Shares Redemption of Debentures Repayment of Loans Purchase of Assets Payment of Dividends	

Collection from Debtors Dividends Received Refund of tax		Payment of Tax Cash lost in Operations Cash Balance at the end	

Sources of Cash Inflows

A. Cash from Operations or Cash from Operating Profit.

Cash from trading operations during the year is a very important source of cash inflows. The net effect of various transactions in a business during a particular period is either net profit or net loss. Usually, net profit results in inflow of cash and net loss in outflow of cash. But it does not mean that cash generated from trading operations in a year shall be equal to the net profit or that cash lost in operations shall be identical with net loss. It may either be more or less. Even, there may be a net loss in a business but yet there may be a cash inflow from operations. It is so because of certain non-operating (expenses or incomes) charged to the income statement, *i.e.*, Profit and Loss Account.

How to Calculate Cash from Operations or Cash from Operating Profit?

There are three methods of determining cash from operations:

(a) **From Cash Sales.** Cash from operations can be calculated by deducting cash purchases and cash operating expenses from cash sales, *i.e.*

Cash from Operations = (Cash Sales) – (Cash Purchases + Cash Operating Expenses)

Cash sales are calculated by deducting credit sales or increase in receivables from the total sales. From the cash sales, the cash purchases and cash operating expenses are to be deducted. In the absence of any information, all expenses may be assumed to be cash expenses. In case outstanding and prepaid expenses are known/given, any decrease in outstanding expenses or increase in prepaid expenses should be deducted from the corresponding figure. Thus, cash from operations under this method can be tabulated as follows:

(a) CALCULATION OF CASH FROM OPERATIONS

Sales	**Amount**
Less. Credit Sales or Increase in accounts receivables.	
Cash Sales	
Less. Cash Purchases (Purchases–Credit Purchases or increase in payables)	
Less. Cash from Operating expenses (after adjusting prepaid and Outstanding expenses)	
Cash from Trading Operations.	

(b) **From Net Profit/ Net Loss.** Cash from operations can also be calculated with the help of net profit or net loss. Under this method, net profit or net loss is adjusted for non-cash and non-operating expenses and incomes as follows:

(b) CALCULATION OF CASH FROM TRADING OPERATIONS

	Amount
Net Profit (as given) **Add:** Non cash and non-operating items which have already been debited to P & L A/C: Depreciation	

Transfer to Reserves	
Transfer to provisions	
Goodwill written off	
Preliminary expenses written off	
Other intangible assets written off	
Loss on sale or disposal of fixed assets	
Increase in Accounts Payable	
Increase in outstanding expenses	
Decrease in prepaid expenses	
Less: Non-cash and non-operating items which have already been credited to P & L A/C:	
Increase in Accounts Receivables	
Decrease in Outstanding Expenses	
Increase in Prepaid Expenses	
Cash from Operations	

(c) **Cash from Operating Profit.** Cash from operating profit is also calculated with the help of net profit or net loss. The difference in this method as compared to the above discussed method is that increase or decrease in accounts payable and accounts receivable is not adjusted while finding cash from operations and it is directly shown in the cash flow statement as an inflow or outflow of cash as the cash may be. The cash from operations so calculated is generally called operating profit.

CALCULATION OF CASH FROM OPERATING PROFIT

	Amount
Net Profit (as given) or Closing Balance of Profit and Loss A/C	
Add: Non-cash and non-operating items which have already been debited to P & L A/C:	
Depreciation	
Transfers to Reserves and Provisions	
Writing off intangible assets	
Outstanding Expenses (current year)	
Prepaid Expenses (previous year)	
Loss on Sale of fixed Assets	
Dividend Paid, etc.	
Less: Non-cash and non-operating items which have already been credited to P & L A/C:	
Profit on Sale or disposal of fixed assets	
Non-trading receipts such as dividend received, rent received, *etc.*	
Re-transfers from provisions (excess provisions charged back)	
Outstanding income (current year)	
Pre-received income (in previous year)	
Opening balance of P & L A/C	
Cash from Operating Profit	

(i) **Outstanding/Accrued Expenses.** The outstanding/accrued expenses represent those expenses which are although charged to profit and loss account but no cash is paid during the year. For this reason, outstanding/accrued expenses of the current year are added back while calculating cash from operating profit. However, if some outstanding expenses of the previous year are also given, these may be assumed to have been paid during the year and hence shown as an outflow of cash in the cash flow statement.

(ii) **Prepaid Expenses.** Prepaid expenses are those expenses which are paid in advance and hence result in the outflow of cash but are not charged to profit and loss account because they do not relate to the current period of profit and loss account. For this reason, prepaid expenses of the current year should be taken as an outflow of cash in the cash flow statement. But the expenses, if any, paid in the previous year do not involve outflow of cash in the current year but are charged to profit and loss account. Therefore, prepaid expenses of the previous year (related to the current year) should be added back while calculating cash from operating profit.

B. Increase in Existing Liabilities or Creation of New Liabilities

If there is an increase in existing liabilities or a new liability is created during the year, it results in the flow of cash into the business. The liability may be either a fixed long-term liability such as Equity Share Capital, Preference Share Capital, Debentures, long-term loans, *etc.* or a current liability such as sundry creditors, bills payable, *etc.*

The inflow of cash may be either Actual or Notional

There is an actual inflow of cash when cash is actually received and generally long-term liabilities result into actual inflow of cash, *e.g.*

For Issue of Shares, during the year, the journal entry shall be

Cash A/C ...Dr.

To Share Capital A/C

So, actual cash flows into the business. In the same manner, issue of debentures, raising of loans for cash, *etc.* result into actual inflows of cash. But when the fixed liabilities are created in consideration of purchase of assets, *i.e.*, other than cash, there is no inflow of actual cash. The journal entry for the issue of debentures in lieu of purchase of machinery is:

Plant and Machinery A/C ...Dr.

To Debentures A/C

(It does not involve actual flow of cash)

Usually, current liabilities result into inflow of notional cash. For example, increase in Sundry Creditors implies purchase of goods on credit. In this case, although no cash is actually received but we may say that creditors have given us loans which have been utilised in purchasing goods from them. Hence, increase in the current liabilities may be taken as a source of inflow of cash and decrease in current liabilities as an outflow of cash.

C. Reduction in or Sale of Assets

Whenever a reduction in or sale of any asset-fixed or current-takes place (otherwise than depreciation) it results into inflow of actual or notional cash. There is an actual inflow of cash when assets are sold for cash and notional cash flows in when assets are sold or disposed off on credit. Thus, sale of building, machinery or even reduction in current assets like stocks, debtors, *etc.* result in inflow of actual or notional cash.

D. Non-Trading Receipts

Sometimes, there may be non-trading receipts like dividend received, rent received, refund of tax, etc. such receipts or incomes are although non-trading in nature but they result into inflow of cash and hence taken in the cash flow statement.

Applications of Cash or Cash Outflows

A. **Cash lost in Operations.** Sometimes the net result of trading in a particular period is a loss and some cash may be lost during that period in trading operations. Such loss of cash in trading is called cash lost in operations and is shown as an outflow of cash in Cash Flow Statement.

B. **Decrease in or Discharge of Liabilities.** Decrease in or discharge of any liability, fixed or current, results in outflow of cash either actual or notional. For example, when redeemable preference shares are redeemed and loans are repaid, it will amount to an outflow of actual cash. But when a liability is converted into another, such as issue of shares for debentures, there will be a notional flow of cash into the business.

C. **Increase in or Purchase of Assets.** Just like decrease in or sale of assets is a source or inflow of cash, increase or purchase of any assets is a outflow or application of cash.

D. **Non-Trading Payments.** Payment of any non-trading expenses also constitute outflow of cash. For example, payment of dividends, payment of income-tax, *etc.*

DUPONT ANALYSIS

There are three major financial metrics that drive return on equity (ROE): operating efficiency, asset use efficiency and financial leverage. Operating efficiency is represented by net profit margin or net income divided by total sales or revenue. Asset use efficiency is measured by the asset turnover ratio. Financial leverage is equal to average assets divided by average equity.

ROE can be broken down into these three factors as follows:

$$\text{ROE} = \underbrace{\left(\frac{\text{Net Income}}{\text{Ave. Equity}}\right)}_{\text{ROE}} = \underbrace{\left(\frac{\text{Net Income}}{\text{Revenue}}\right)}_{\text{Profit Margin}} \times \underbrace{\left(\frac{\text{Revenue}}{\text{Ave. Assets}}\right)}_{\text{Asset Turnover}} \times \underbrace{\left(\frac{\text{Ave. Assets}}{\text{Ave. Equity}}\right)}_{\text{Financial Laverage}}$$

DuPont Analysis Components

DuPont analysis breaks ROE into its constituent components to determine which of these factors are most responsible for changes in ROE.

Net Margin

Net margin is the ratio of bottom-line profits compared to total revenue or total sales. This is one of the most basic measures of profitability. One way to think about net margin is to imagine a store that sells a single product for \$1.00. After the costs associated with buying inventory, maintaining a location, paying employees, taxes, interest and other expenses, the store owner keeps \$0.15 in profit from each unit sold. That means the owner's profit margin is 15%, which can be calculated as follows:

$$\text{Profit Margin} = \frac{\text{Net Income}}{\text{Revenue}} = \frac{\$.15}{\$1.00} = 15\%$$

The profit margin can be improved if costs for the owner were reduced or if prices were raised, which can have a large impact on ROE. This is one of the reasons that a company's stock will experience high levels of volatility when management makes a change to its guidance for future margins, costs and prices.

Asset Turnover Ratio

The asset turnover ratio measures how efficiently a company uses its assets to generate revenue. Imagine a company had $100 of assets and it made $1,000 of total revenue last year. The assets generated 10 times their value in total revenue, which is the same as the asset turnover ratio and can be calculated as follows:

$$\text{Asset Turnover Ratio} = \frac{\text{Revenue}}{\text{Ave. Assets}} = \frac{\$1,000}{\$100} = 10$$

A normal asset turnover ratio will vary from one industry group to another. For example, a discount retailer or grocery store will generate a lot of revenue from its assets with a small margin, which will make the asset turnover ratio very large. On the other hand, a utility company owns very expensive fixed assets relative to its revenue, which will result in an asset turnover ratio that is much lower than that of a retail firm.

The ratio can be helpful when comparing two companies that are very similar. Because average assets include components like inventory, changes in this ratio can signal that sales are slowing down or speeding up earlier than it would show up in other financial measures. If a company's asset turnover rises, its ROE will improve.

Financial Leverage

Financial leverage, or the equity multiplier, is an indirect analysis of a company's use of debt to finance its assets. Assume a company has $1,000 of assets and $250 of owner's equity. The balance sheet equation will tell you that the company also has $750 in debt (assets – liabilities = equity). If the company borrows more to purchase assets, the ratio will continue to rise. The accounts used to calculate financial leverage are both on the balance sheet, so analysts will divide average assets by average equity rather than the balance at the end of the period, as follows:

$$\text{Financial Leverage} = \frac{\text{Ave. Assets}}{\text{Ave. Equity}} = \frac{\$1,000}{\$250} = 4$$

Most companies should use debt with equity to fund operations and growth. Not using any leverage could put the company at a disadvantage compared with its peers. However, using too much debt in order to increase the financial leverage ratio – and therefore increase ROE – can create disproportionate risks.

Using DuPont Analysis

An investor has been watching two similar companies, SuperCo and GearInc, that have recently been improving their return on equity compared to the rest of their peer group. This could be a good thing if the two companies are making better use of assets or improving profit margins.

In order to decide which company is a better opportunity, the investor decides to use DuPont analysis to determine what each company is doing to improve its ROE and whether that improvement is sustainable.

As you can see in the table, SuperCo improved its profit margins by increasing net income and reduced its total assets. SuperCo's changes improved its profit margin and asset turnover. The investor can deduce from the information that SuperCo also reduced some of its debt since average equity remained the same.

Looking closely at GearInc, the investor can see that the entire change in ROE was due to an increase in financial leverage. This means GearInc borrowed more money, which reduced average equity. The investor is concerned because the additional borrowings didn't change the company's net income, revenue or profit margin, which means the leverage may not be adding any real value to the firm.

DuPont Analysis Summary

A DuPont Analysis is used to evaluate the component parts of a company's return on equity (ROE). This allows an investor to determine what financial activities are contributing the most to the changes in ROE. An investor can use an analysis like this to compare the operating efficiency of two similar firms. Managers can use DuPont analysis to identify strengths or weaknesses that should be addressed.

COST SHEET

A cost sheet is a report on which is accumulated all of the costs associated with a product or production job. A cost sheet is used to compile the margin earned on a product or job, and can form the basis for the setting of prices on similar products in the future. It can also be used as the basis for a variety of cost control measures. Despite the name, a cost sheet can be compiled and viewed on a computer screen, as well as being manually developed on paper. The costs listed on the report are usually aggregated into the following categories:

- Direct materials
- Direct labor
- Allocated factory overhead

In some situations, a cost sheet may also include a line item for allocated administrative overhead.

In addition, the following costs may also appear on a cost sheet in varying degrees of detail:

- Shipping and handling
- Supplies
- Outsourced costs

The costs listed on a cost sheet usually include charges for actual material and labor costs incurred. However, it is also possible that these costs are only listed at their standard costs, which are obtained by backflushing; this is the process of multiplying the number of units produced by bills of material and labor routings to arrive at the costs that should have been associated with a product or job.

The development of a cost sheet can be a major production, especially if it is compiled by hand. Even if it is drawn from a database of compiled costs, a cost accountant must still review it for duplicate, missing, or incorrect entries before issuing it. A cost sheet is normally issued along with an explanatory page that points out any unusual costs incurred or variances that management should be aware of.

The format of a cost sheet is usually a standard one that is either manually rolled forward from earlier reports, or else set up within the accounting system for automatic display when a report is printed.

An alternative purpose for the cost sheet concept is to use it as the basis for a quote to a customer, usually for the manufacture of a custom product. In this case, the cost sheet includes the best estimates of the company's estimators for the requested product, with details for each of the previously indicated expense line items.

MARGINAL COSTING

According to the Terminology of Cost Accountancy of the Institute of Cost and Management Accountants, London, Marginal Cost represents "the amount of any given volume of output by which aggregate costs are changed if the volume of output is increased by one unit". In practice, this is measured by the total variable costs attributable to one unit. In this concept unit may be a single article, a batch of articles, an order, a stage of Production capacity, a man-hour, a process or a department. It relates to the change in output in the particular circumstances under consideration.

We find that with the increase in one unit of output the total cost is increased and this increase in total cost from the existing to the new level is known as marginal cost.

For example the cost of production of 1,000 units of radios is Rs. 2,00,000 and that of 1001 units is Rs. 2,00,150 the marginal cost is Rs. 150, *i.e.*, 2,00, 150 – Rs. 2,00,000

Marginal cost may also be defined as "the aggregate of variable costs" or "prime cost plus variable overheads". Thus, if for the production of 1,000 units of a product the manufacturer has to incur Rs. 75,000 for materials, Rs. 50,000 for direct wages, Rs. 25,000 for variable overheads and Rs. 50,000 fixed overheads the marginal cost can be ascertained as follows:

	Total (1,000 units)	Per unit
	Rs.	Rs.
Direct materials	75,000	75
Direct Wages	50,000	50
Prime Cost	1,25,000	125
Variable Overheads	25,000	25
Marginal Cost	1,50,000	150

The Institute of Cost and Management Accountants, London, has defined Marginal Costing as "the ascertainment of marginal costs and of the effect on profit of changes in volume or type of output by differentiating between fixed costs and variable costs". "In this technique of costing only variable costs are charged to operations, processes or products, leaving all indirect costs to be written off against profits in the period in which they arise."

Basic Characteristics of Marginal Costing

The technique of marginal costing is based on the distinction between product costs and period costs. Only the variable costs are regarded as the costs of the products while the fixed costs are treated as period costs which will be incurred during the period regardless of the volume of output. The main characteristics of marginal costing are as follows

(a) It is a technique of analysis and presentation of costs which help management in taking many managerial decisions and is not an independent system of costing such as process costing or job costing.

(b) All elements of cost–production, administration and selling and distribution are classified into variable and fixed components. Even semi-variable costs are analysed into fixed and variable.

(c) The variable costs (marginal costs) are regarded as the costs of the products.

(d) Fixed costs are treated as period costs and are charged to profit and loss account for the period for which they are incurred.

(e) The stocks of finished goods and work-in-process are valued at marginal costs only.

(f) Prices are determined on the basis of marginal cost by adding 'contribution' which is the excess of sales or selling price over marginal cost of sales.

Assumptions of Marginal Costing

The technique of marginal costing is based upon the following assumptions:

(a) All elements of cost-production, administration and selling and distribution-can be segregated into fixed and variable components.
(b) Variable cost remains constant per unit of output irrespective of the level of output and thus fluctuates directly in proportion to changes in the volume of output.
(c) The selling price per unit remains unchanged or constant at all levels of activity.
(d) Fixed costs remain unchanged or constant for the entire volume of production.
(e) The volume of production or output is the only factor which influences the costs.

Contribution

Contribution is the difference between sales and variable cost or marginal cost of sales. It may also be defined as the excess of selling price over variable cost per unit. Contribution is also known as Contribution Margin or Gross Margin. Contribution being the excess of sales over variable cost is the amount that is contributed towards fixed expenses and profit.

If the selling price of a product is Rs. 20/- per unit and its variable cost is Rs. 15/- per unit, contribution per unit is Rs. 5/- (*i.e.* Rs. 20–15). Further, let us say that the fixed expenses are 50,000 and the total number of units sold is 8,000. This means that the total contribution is 8000 × 5 or Rs. 40,000 which is not sufficient even to meet the fixed expenses and the result is a loss of Rs. 10,000 (50,000–40,000). In case, the output is 10,000 units, then total contribution of Rs. 50,000 equals the fixed cost, and no amount is left for profit. The profit can be earned only when the amount of contribution exceeds the fixed costs. Hence, any output beyond 10,000 units, will give some profit *e.g.*, at a level of output of 15,000 units, the total contribution is 15,000 × 5 or Rs. 75,000 while the fixed costs remain Rs. 50,000, thus making a profit of Rs. 25,000.

Contribution can be represented as:

Contribution = Sales – Variable (Marginal) Cost

or Contribution (per unit) = Selling price – Variable (or marginal) cost per unit

or Contribution = Fixed Costs + Profit (–Loss)

Advantages of Contribution

The concept of contribution is a valuable aid to management in making managerial decisions. A few benefits resulting from the concept of contribution margin are given below :

(a) It helps the management in the fixation of selling prices.
(b) It assists in determining the break-even point.
(c) It helps management in the selection of a suitable product mix for profit maximisation.
(d) It helps in choosing from among alternative methods of production ; the method which gives highest contribution per limiting factor is adopted.
(e) It helps the management in deciding whether to purchase or manufacture a product or a component.
(f) It helps in taking a decision as regards to adding a new product in the market.

Marginal Cost Equation

For the sake of convenience, a marginal cost equation can be derived as follows :

$$\text{Sales} - \text{Variable cost} = \text{Contribution}$$

or, $\text{Sales} = \text{Variable cost} + \text{Contribution}$

or, $\text{Sales} = \text{Variable cost} + \text{Fixed Cost} \pm \text{Profit/Loss}$

or, $\text{Sales} - \text{Variable cost} = \text{Fixed cost} \pm \text{Profit/Loss}$

or, $S - V = F \pm P$

where,

'S' stands for Sales

'V' stands for Variable cost

'F' stands for Fixed cost

'P' stands for Profit/Loss

The marginal cost equation is very useful in the sense that if any three factors out of the four are known, the fourth can easily be found out.

Profit/Volume Ratio (P/V Ratio or C/S Ratio)

The Profit/volume ratio, which is also called the 'contribution ratio' or 'marginal ratio', expresses the relation of contribution to sales and can be expressed as under:

$$\text{P/V Ratio} = \frac{\text{Contribution}}{\text{Sales}}$$

Since Contribution = Sales – Variable Cost = Fixed Cost + Profit, P/V ratio can also be expressed as:

$$\text{P/V Ratio} = \frac{\text{Sales - Variable cost}}{\text{Sales}} \quad \textit{i.e.,} \quad \frac{S-V}{S}$$

or, $$\text{P/V Ratio} = \frac{\text{Fixed Cost + Profit}}{\text{Sales}} \quad \textit{i.e.,} \quad \frac{F+P}{S}$$

or, $$\text{P/V Ratio} = \frac{\text{Change in Profit or Contribution}}{\text{Change in Sales}}$$

This ratio can also be shown in the form of percentage by multiplying by 100. Thus, if selling price of a product is Rs. 20 and variable cost is Rs. 15 per unit, then

$$\text{P/V Ratio} = \frac{20-15}{20} \times 100$$

$$= \frac{5}{20} \times 100$$

$$= 25\%$$

The P/V ratio, which establishes the relationship between contribution and sales is of vital importance for studying the profitability of operations of a business. It reveals the effect on profit of changes in the volume. In the above example, for every Rs. 100 sales, Contribution of Rs. 25 is made towards meeting the fixed expenses and then the profit comparison for P/V ratios can be made to find out which product, department or process is more profitable. Higher the P/V ratio, more will be the profit and lower the P/V ratio, lesser will be the profit. Thus, every management aims at increasing the P/V ratio. The ratio can be increased by increasing the contribution. This can be done by:

(i) Increasing the selling price per unit

(ii) Reducing the variable or marginal cost.
(iii) Changing the sales mixture and selling more profitable products for which the P/V ratio is higher.

The concept of P/V ratio is also useful to calculate the break-even point, the profit at a given volume of sales, the sales volume required to earn a given (or desired) profit and the volume of sales required to maintain the present profits if the selling price is reduced by a specified percentage.

The formula for the sales volumes required to earn a given profit is:

$$\text{P/V ratio} = \frac{\text{Contribution}}{\text{Sales}}$$

or,

$$\text{P/V ratio} = \frac{\text{Fixed Cost + Profit}}{\text{Sales}}$$

or,

$$\text{Sales} = \frac{\text{Fixed Cost + Profit}}{\text{P/V ratio}}$$

$$= \frac{F + P}{\text{P/V ratio}}$$

Cost-volume-profit Analysis

Cost-Volume-Profit analysis is a technique for studying the relationship between cost, volume and profit. Profits of an undertaking depend upon a large number of factors. But the most important of these factors are the cost of manufacture, volume of sales and the selling prices of the products. In the words of Herman C. Heiser, "the most significant single factor in profit planning of the average business is the relationship between the volume of business, costs and profits". The CVP relationship is an important tool used for the profit planning of a business.

The three factors of CVP analysis *i.e.*, costs, volume and profit are interconnected and dependent on one another. For example, profit depends upon sales, selling price to a large extent depends upon cost and cost depends upon volume of production as it is only the variable cost that varies directly with production, whereas fixed cost remains fixed regardless of the volume produced. In cost-volume-profit analysis an attempt is made to analyse the relationship between variations in cost with variations in volume.

The cost-volume-profit relationship is of immense utility to management as it assists in profit planning, cost control and decision making. Cost-volume-profit analysis can be used to answer questions such as:

(a) How much sales should be made to avoid losses?
(b) How much should be the sales to earn a desired profit?
(c) What will be the effect of change in prices, costs and volume on profits?
(d) Which product or product mix is most profitable?
(e) Should we manufacture or buy some product or component? and so on.

Margin of Safety

The excess of actual or budgeted sales over the break-even sales is known as the margin of safety. It is the difference between actual sales minus the sales at break-even point. It represents the amount by which sales revenue can fall before a loss is incurred. As at break-even point there is no profit no loss, sales beyond the break-even point represent margin of safety because any sales above the break-even point will give some profit. Thus,

$$\text{Margin of Safety} = \text{Total Sales} - \text{Sales at Break-even Point}$$

Say, actual present sales are Rs. 5,00,000 and the break-even sales are Rs. 4,00,000, then margin of safety is equal to Rs. 1,00,000, *i.e.*, 5,00,000 – 4,00,000.

Margin of Safety can also be expressed in percentage. For example, if a company can break-even at 60 percent of the expected sales; then it has a margin of safety of (100 – 60) 40 percent. In the previous example, margin of safety in percentage can be calculated as:

$$\frac{100000}{500000} \times 100 = 20\%$$

Margin of safety calculated in percentage is also known as Margin of safety Ratio and can be expressed as :

$$\text{M.S. Ratio} = \frac{\text{M.S}}{\text{Sales}} \times 100$$

$$= \frac{\text{Actual Sales} - \text{Sales at B.E.P}}{\text{Sales}} \times 100$$

Margin of safety can also be calculated with the help of the following formula:

$$\text{Margin of safety (M/S)} = \frac{\text{Profit}}{\text{P/V Ratio}}$$

This is so because margin of safety is the volume of sales beyond break-even point and all sales above the break-even point give some profit which can be calculated as :

$$\text{Profit} = \text{Margin of Safety} \times \text{P/V Ratio}$$

or

$$\text{M.S.} = \frac{\text{Profit}}{\text{P/V Ratio}}$$

The size of the margin of safety is an important indicator of the strength of business. The large margin of safety indicates that the business is sound and even if there is a substantial fall in sales, there will be some profit. On the other hand, small margin of safety indicates that position of the business is comparatively weak and even a small decline in the sales would adversely effect the profit of the business and may result into losses.

The margin of safety can be improved by taking the following steps:

(a) By increasing the level of production
(b) By increasing the selling price
(c) By reducing the fixed cost
(d) By reducing the variable cost
(e) By substituting unprofitable products with profitable products
(f) By increasing contribution by changing the mix or by dropping unprofitable products.

Angle of Incidence

The angle of incidence is the angle between the sales line and the total cost line formed at the break-even point where the sales line and the total cost line intersect each other. The angle of incidence indicates the profit earning capacity of a business. A large angle of incidence indicates a high rate of profit and, on the other hand, a small angle of incidence indicates a low rate of profit. Usually, the angle of incidence and margin of safety are considered together to indicate the soundness of a business. A large angle of incidence with a high margin of safety indicates the most favourable position of a business.

Profit Volume Graph

It is a pictorial representation of the profit volume relationship. This graph shows profit and loss at different volumes of sales. It is said to be simplified form of break-even chart as it clearly represents the relationship of profit to volume of sales. A profit volume graph also called the P/V graph or profit graph can be constructed from any data relating to a business from which a break-even chart can be drawn. The profit volume graph may be preferred to a break-even chart because profits or losses can be directly read at different levels of activity.

Managerial Applications of Marginal Costing

Marginal costing technique is a valuable aid to management in taking many managerial decisions. It is a useful tool for making policy decisions, profit planning and cost control. The information supplied by the 'total cost method' is usually not sufficient to solve managerial problems. The following are some of the important managerial problems where marginal costing technique can be applied.

Pricing Decisions

Fixing of selling prices is one of the most important functions of management. Although prices are generally determined by market conditions and other economic factors yet marginal costing technique assists the management in the fixation of selling prices under various circumstances as:

(a) **Pricing Under Normal Condition.** Under normal circumstances, the prices are based upon total cost of sales so as to cover both fixed as well as variable cost and in addition to provide for certain desired margin of profit. But prices can also be fixed on the basis of marginal cost by adding a sufficiently high margin to marginal (variable) cost so as to cover the fixed cost and profits. However, under other circumstances, products may have to be sold at a price below the total cost. For example, in the days of stiff competition or to meet the situation arising due to trade depression, for accepting special bulk or additional orders for utilising idle capacity for exporting and exploring new markets *etc*. The products may have to be sold at a price below the total cost based upon absorption costing. In such circumstances, the prices should be fixed on the basis of marginal cost (and total cost) in such a manner so as to cover the marginal cost and contribute something towards the fixed expenses. Sometimes it may become necessary to reduce the selling prices to the level of marginal cost or even below the marginal cost.

(b) **Selling Price below the Marginal Cost.** The selling prices of products may be fixed even below the marginal cost in the following circumstances:

(i) To introduce a new product in the market.
(ii) To popularise a particular product.
(iii) To explore foreign markets.
(iv) To eliminate the competitor from-the market.
(v) To help the sale of joint products.
(vi) To avoid the retrenchment of workers.
(vii) To dispose off the product of perishable nature.
(viii) To utilise idle capacity.
(ix) To keep plant and machinery in the running conditions.
(x) To retain old customers and prevent loss of future orders.
(xi) To avoid extra losses by closing down the business.
(xii) To dispose off surplus stocks.

(c) **Pricing During Stiff Competition and Trade Depression.** During stiff competition, produces may have to be sold at a price below the total cost. In such circumstances, the price should be fixed on the basis of marginal cost in such a manner so as to cover the marginal (variable) cost and contribute something towards the fixed expenses. Sometimes, to eliminate the weaker competitors from the market, the price may be fixed even below the marginal cost.
During depression also products may be sold at a price below the total cost. There is a fall in the price as a result of depression. The prices can be safely reduced to an extent which covers the variable cost and contributes something towards the fixed cost. This is so because fixed expenses will be incurred even if the product is discontinued during depression for a short period. In case the product can be sold at something above the marginal cost, the total loss on account of fixed expenses shall reduce as sales will recover some of the fixed expenses. If there is a serious but temporary fall in the demand of the product, the minimum price that can be fixed is the marginal cost because selling below the marginal cost would mean more losses than the losses on closing down the business. Hence, if the product can be sold at a price equal to or more than the marginal cost, the business should be continued under such circumstances. This has been made clear with the help of the following example:
Suppose, marginal cost of a product is Rs. 5/- per unit and fixed expenses amount to Rs. 1,00,000. Selling price per unit is Rs. 6/- and 50,000 units can be sold at this price.

	Rs.
Marginal cost of 50,000 units @ Rs. 5 per unit	2,50,000
Fixed Expenses	1,00,000
Total Cost	3,50,000

$$\text{Cost per unit} = \frac{3,50,000}{50,000} = \text{Rs. } 7$$

Selling price of Rs. 6/- per unit is below the total cost of Rs. 7/- per unit, yet it is advantageous to sell the products at Rs. 6/- per unit as it is more than the marginal costs.

	Rs.
Sales value of 50,000 units @ Rs. 6/- per unit	3,00,000
Less: Total cost, calculated above	3,50,000
Loss	50,000
Loss due to fixed expenses, if product is discontinued	1,00,000
Loss reduced if the product is continued (1,00,000 – 50,000)	50,000

(d) **Accepting Special orders, Bulk orders, additional orders, export orders and exploring new markets.** Bulk orders, additional orders and orders from foreign or new markets, may be accepted at a price below the normal market price so as to utilise the idle capacity. Such orders are received usually asking for a price below the market price and hence a decision is to be taken to accept or reject the order. The order may be accepted at any price above the marginal cost because the fixed costs have to be incurred even otherwise. Any contribution resulting from the additional sales would mean an additional profit. But care must be taken to see that accepting an order below the market price does not affect the normal selling price adversely. For example, an order from a local merchant should not be accepted at a price below the normal market price because it will affect the relationships with other customers buying at a normal price. But, if it is a foreign order, it may be accepted at a price below the normal price keeping in view the additional costs of exporting, if any and direct and indirect benefits of exporting such as, goodwill, subsidies, quotas, *etc.*

Profit Planning and Maintaining a Desired Level of Profit

Marginal costing techniques can be applied for profit planning as well. Profit planning involves the planning of future operations to achieve maximum profits or to maintain a desired level of profits. The change in the sales price, variable cost and product mix affect the profitability of a concern. Absorption costing fails to bring out the effect of such changes on the profits of a concern due to the inclusion of fixed expenses in the total cost. With the help of marginal costing, the required value of sales for maintaining or attaining a desired level of profit may be ascertained as follows:

$$\text{Desired Sales} = \frac{\text{Fixed Cost + Desired Profit}}{\text{P/V Ratio}}$$

Advantages of Marginal Costing

The following are the important advantages of marginal costing:

(i) The technique of marginal costing is very simple to operate and easy to understand. Since, fixed costs are kept outside the unit cost, the cost statements prepared on the basis of marginal cost are much less complicated.

(ii) It does away with the need for allocation, apportionment and absorption of fixed overheads and hence removes the complexities of under-absorption of overheads.

(iii) Marginal cost remains the same per unit of output irrespective of the level of activity. It is constant in nature and helps the management in production planning.

(iv) It prevents the carry forward of current year's fixed overheads through valuation of closing stocks. Since fixed costs are not considered in valuation of closing stocks, there is no possibility of fictitious profits by over-valuing stocks.

(v) It facilitates the calculation of various important factors, viz., break-even point, expectations of profits at different levels of productions, sales necessary to earn a predetermined target of profit, effect on profit due to changes of raw materials prices, increased wages, change in sales mixture, etc.

(vi) It is a valuable aid to management for decision-making and fixation of selling prices, selection of a profitable product/sales mix, make or buy decision, problem of key or limiting factor, determination of the optimum level of activity, close or shut down decisions, evaluation of performance and capital investment decisions, etc.

(vii) It facilitates the study of relative profitability of different product lines, departments, production facilities, sales divisions, etc.

(viii) It is complementary to standard costing and budgetary control and can be used alongwith them to yield better results.

(ix) Since fixed costs are not controllable and it is only variable or marginal cost that is controllable, marginal costing, by dividing costs into controllable and non-controllable, help in cost control.

(x) It helps the management in profit planning by making a study of relationship between cost, volume and profits. Further, break-even charts and profit graphs make the whole problem easily understandable even to a layman.

(xi) It is very useful in management reporting, marginal costing facilitates 'management by exception' by focusing attention of the management towards more important areas than to waste time on problems which do not require urgent attention of the higher management.

STANDARD COSTING & VARIANCE ANALYSIS

The word 'standard' means a bench-mark or yardstick. The standard cost is a predetermined cost which determines in advance what each product or service should cost under given circumstances. It is the amount the firm thinks a product or the operation of a process for a period of time should cost, based upon certain assumed conditions of efficiency, economic conditions and other factors. The costing terminology of Chartered Institute of Management Accountants, London defines standard cost as "a predetermined cost which is calculated from the managements standards of efficient operation and the relevant necessary expenditure." They are "the predetermined costs based on technical estimate to material, labour and overhead for a selected period of time and for a prescribed set of working conditions."

The technique of using standard costs for the purposes of cost control is known as standard costing. Standard costing may be defined as "a technique of cost accounting which compares the standard cost of each product or service with actual cost to determine the efficiency so that any remedial action may be taken immediately."

Standard costing is a system of cost accounting which is designed to find out how much should be the cost of a product under the existing conditions. The actual cost can be ascertained only when production is undertaken. The pre-determined cost is compared to the actual cost and a variance between the two enables the management to take necessary corrective measures.

Steps Involved in Standard Costing

The technique of standard costing involves the determination of cost before hand. The cost is based on technical information after considering the impact of current conditions. Cost ascertainment is not based on a guess work. The impact of possible factors on cost is studied before setting the standards. The standards are set as per existing conditions of work. With the change in condition, the standard cost too can be modified so as to make it more realistic. The standards may be divided according to the elements of costs. The standard cost is divided into standards for materials, labour and overheads. The sub-division of standards will be more useful for cost control purposes. The actual cost is recorded when incurred. The standard cost is compared to the actual cost. The difference between the two costs is known as variance. The variances are calculated element-wise. The management can take corrective measures to set the things right.

From the above discussion it is clear that standard costing involves the following steps:

(a) The determination of standard cost.

(b) The recording of actual cost.

(c) The comparison between standard cost and actual cost.

(d) The finding out of variance.

(e) The reporting of variance so as to find out inefficiency and take necessary corrective measures.

The technique of standard costing is complementary to the ordinary costing system. The standard costs will be of no use if they are not compared with actual costs. The basic purpose of standard costing is to determine efficiency or inefficiency in manufacturing a particular product. This will be possible only if both standard costs and actual costs are given side by side. Though standard costing system will be useful for all types of commercial and industrial undertakings but it will be more useful in those undertakings where production is standardised. It will be of less use in job costing system because every job has different specifications and it will be difficult to determine standard costs for every job.

Standard Costs and Estimated Costs

Both the standard costs and estimated costs are used to determine price in advance. The purpose of both the systems is to control cost. The same accounting principles are used in standard cost and estimated cost. Despite similarities, standard cost and estimated cost differ in their objects and purpose. The following points of difference between standard cost and estimated cost are discussed as under:

(a) Estimated costs are based on historical accounting. It is an estimate of what the cost will be. It is a cost of guess work or reasonable estimate for the costs in future. On the other hand standard costs are based on scientific analysis and engineering studies. Standard costing determines what the cost should be.

(b) Standard costs are used as a device for measuring efficiency. The standards are predetermined and a comparison of standards with actual costs enables to determine the efficiency of the concern. Estimated costs cannot be used to determine efficiency. It only determines the expected costs. An effort is made that estimated cost should almost be near to actual costs.

(c) The purpose of determining estimated costs is to find out selling price in advance to take a decision whether to produce or to make and also to prepare financial budgets. Estimated costs do not serve the purpose of cost control. On the other hand standard costs are helpful in cost control. The analysis of variance enables to take corrective measures, if necessary.

(d) Standard costs are not easily changed. The standards are set in such a way that small changes in conditions do not require a change in standards. Estimated costs are revised with the change in conditions. They are made more realistic by incorporating changes in prices. Standard costs are more static than estimated costs.

(e) Estimated costs are used by the concern using historical costing. Standard costing is used by those concerns which use standard costing system. Standard costing is a part of cost accounting process while estimated cost are statistical in nature and as such they may not become a part of accounting.

Advantages of Standard Costing

Standard costing is not only useful for cost control purposes but it is also helpful in production planning and policy formulation. It allows 'management by exception'. In the light of various objectives of this system, following advantages may be derived from standard costing.

(a) **Measuring Efficiency.** Standard costing is a yardstick for measuring efficiency. The comparison of actual costs with standard costs enables the management to evaluate performance of various cost centres. In the absence of standard costing system actual costs of different periods may be compared to measure efficiency. It is not proper to compare costs of different periods because circumstances of both the periods may be different. Moreover, a decision about base period with which the comparison is to be made is also difficult to be make. Standard costing gives targets with which actual performance can be compared.

(b) **Formulation of Production and Price Policy.** Standard costing is helpful in formulating production policies. The standards are set by studying all existing conditions. It becomes easy to formulate production plans by taking into account standard costs. It is also helpful for finding prices of various products. In case tenders are to be submitted or prices are to be quoted in advance then standard costing produces necessary data for price fixation.

(c) **Determination of Variance.** By comparing actual costs with standard costs variances are determined. Management is able to spot out the place of inefficiencies. It can fix responsibility for deviation in performance. It is possible to take corrective measures at the earliest. A regular check on various expenditures is also ensured by standard costing system.

(d) **Reduction of Work.** In historical costing, records are maintained for detaining the costs. Standard costing reduces clerical work to a considerable extent and management is supplied with useful information. In this system only necessary information will be recorded and superfluous data are avoided. The report presentation is simplified and only required information is presented in such a form that management is able to interpret the information easily and usefully.

(e) **Management by Exception.** With the use of standard costing, the targets of different individuals are fixed. If the performance is according to predetermined standards then there is nothing to worry. The attention of management is drawn only when actual performance is less than the budgeted performance. Management by exception means that everybody is given a target to be achieved and management need not supervise each and everything. The responsibilities are fixed and every body tries to achieve his targets. If the things are going as per targets then management need not bother. Management devotes its time to other important things. So, management by exception is possible only when targets of work can be fixed. Standard costing enables the determination of targets.

(f) **Facilitates Cost Control.** Every costing system aims at cost control and cost reduction. Standard costing helps in achieving these aims. The standards are being constantly analysed and an effort is made to improve efficiency. Whenever a variance occurs the reasons are studied and immediate corrective measures are undertaken. The action taken in spotting weak points enables cost control system.

(g) **Eliminating Inefficiencies.** The setting of standard for different elements of cost requires a detailed study of different aspects. The standards are differently set for manufacturing, administrative and selling expenses. Improved methods are used for setting these standards. The determination of manufacturing expenses will require time and motion study for labour and effective material control devices for materials, etc. Similar studies will be needed for finding other expenses. All these studies will make it possible to eliminate inefficiencies at different steps. The whole effort will give an improved costing system and will enable better service to the consumer.

(h) **Helpful in taking important decisions.** Standard Costing provides useful information to the management in taking important decisions. The problem created by inflation, rising prices, *etc.* can be effectively tackled with the help of standard costing. It can also be used to provide incentive plans for employees, etc.

FINANCIAL MANAGEMENT

Nature and Scope of Financial Management

Finance has become so much important for every business undertaking that all managerial activities are connected with it. Financial viability of various propositions influence decision on them. Finance function has become so important that it has given birth to Financial Management as a separate subject. Financial management refers to that part of the management activity which is concerned with the planning and controlling of firm's financial resources. It deals with finding out various sources for raising funds for the firm. The sources must be suitable and economical for the needs of the business. The most appropriate use of such funds also forms a part of financial management.

Financial management is applicable to every type of organization, irrespective of its size, kind or nature. It is as useful to a small concern as to a big unit. A trading concern gets the same utility from its application as a manufacturing unit may expect. This subject is important and useful for all types of ownership organizations. Where there is a use of finance, financial management is helpful. Every management aims to utilize its funds in a best possible and profitable way.

Objectives of Financial Management or Goals of Business Finance

Financial management is concerned with procurement and use of funds. Its main aim is to use business funds in such a way that the earnings are maximized. There are various alternatives available for using business funds. The pros and cons of various decisions have to be looked into before making a final selection. The decisions will have to take into consideration for the commercial strategy of the business. The main objective of a business is to maximize the owner's economic welfare. This objective can be achieved by :

A. Profit Maximization

Profit earning is the main aim of every economic activity. A business being an economic institution must earn profit to cover its costs and provide funds for growth. No business can survive without earning profit. Profit is a measure of efficiency of a business enterprise. Profits also serve as a protection against risks which cannot be ensured. The accumulated profits enable a business to face risks like fall in prices, competition from other units, adverse government policies etc. Thus, profit maximisation is considered as the main objective of business. The following arguments are advanced in favour of profit maximisation as the objective of business :

(i) When profit-earning is the aim of business then profit maximisation should be the obvious objective.

(ii) Profitability is a barometre for measuring efficiency and economic prosperity of a business enterprise, thus, profit maximisation is justified on the grounds of rationality.

(iii) Economic and business conditions do not remain same at all the times. There may be adverse business conditions like recession, depression, severe competitions, etc. A business will be able to survive under unfavourable situation, only if it has some past earnings to rely upon. Therefore, a business should try to earn more and more when situation is favourable.

(iv) Profits are the main sources of finance for the growth of a business. So, a business should aim at maximization of profits for enabling its growth and development.

(v) Profitability is essential for fulfilling social goals also. A firm by pursuing the objective of profit maximization also maximises socio-economic welfare.

However, profit maximisation cannot be the sole objective of a company. It is at best a limited objective. If profit is given undue importance, a number of problems can arise. Some of these have been discussed below :

(i) **The term profit is vague.** It does not clarify what exactly it means. It conveys a different meaning to different people. For example, profit may be in short term or long term period; it may be total profit or rate of profit etc.

(ii) **Profit maximisation has to be attempted with a realisation of risks involved.** There is a direct relationship between risk and profit. Many risky propositions yield high profit. Higher the risk, higher is the possibility of profits. If profit maximisation is the only goal, then risk factor is altogether ignored. This implies that finance manager will accept highly risky proposals also, if they give high profits. In practice, however, risk is very important consideration and has to be balanced with the profit objective.

(iii) **Profit maximisation as an objective does not take into account the time pattern of returns.** Proposal A may give a higher amount of profits as compared to proposal B, yet if the returns of proposal A begin to flow say 10 years later, proposal B may be preferred which may have lower overall profit but the returns flow is more early and quick.

(iv) **Profit maximisation as an objective is too narrow.** It fails to take into account the social considerations as also the obligations to various interests of workers, consumers, society, as well as ethical trade practices. If these factors are ignored, a company cannot survive for long. Profit maximisation at the cost of social and moral obligations is a short sighted policy:

2. Wealth Maximisation

Wealth maximization is the appropriate objective of an enterprise. Financial theory assets that wealth maximization is the single substitute for a stockholder's utility. When the firm maximizes the stockholder's wealth, the individual stockholder can use this wealth to maximize his individual utility. It means that by maximizing stockholder's wealth, the firm is operating consistently towards maximizing stockholder's utility.

A stockholder's current wealth in the firm is the product of the number of shares owned, multiplied with the current stock price per share.

Stockholder's current wealth in a firm

Symbolically, = (Number of shares owned) × (Current stock price per share)

$= W_0 = NP_0$

Given number of shares that the stockholder owns, the higher the stock price per share the greater will be the stockholder's wealth. Thus, a firm should aim at maximizing its current stock price. This objective helps in increasing the value of shares in the market. The share's market price serves as a performance index or report card of its progress. It also indicates how well management is doing on behalf of the shareholder. We can conclude that :

Maximum Utility $\xrightarrow{\text{refers to}}$ Maximum stockholder's wealth $\xrightarrow{\text{refers to}}$ Maximum current stock price per share.

Using Ezra Solomon symbols and methods, the net present worth can be calculated as shown below :

(i) $W = V - C$

Where,

W = Net present worth;

V = Gross present worth;

C = Investment (equity capital) required to acquire the asset or to purchase the course of action.

(ii) $V = E/K$

Where,

E = Size of future benefits available to the suppliers of the input capital;

K = The capitalization (discount) rate reflecting the quality (certainty/uncertainty) and timing of benefit attached to E.

(iii) $E = G - (M+T+I)$

Where,

G = Average future flow of gross annual earnings expected from the course of action, before maintenance charges, taxes and interest and other prior charges like preference dividend.

M = Average annual reinvestment required to maintain G at the projected level;
T = Expected annual outflow on account of taxes;
I = Expected flow of annual payments on account of interest, preference dividend and other prior charges.

Nature of Financial Management

(1) **Financial Management is an essential part of Top Management.** In the modern business management the financial manager is one of the active members of top management team and day-by-day his role is becoming more significant in solving the complex management problems. This is because almost all kinds of business activities such as production, marketing etc. directly or indirectly involve the acquisition and use of finance.

(2) **Less Descriptive and More Analytical.** Financial management is less descriptive and more analytical. Due to the development of new statistical and accounting techniques of financial analysis, the financial management chooses the best alternative out of the many possible alternatives.

(3) **Continuous Function.** Financing is a continuous function. In addition to the raising of finance, there is a continuous need for planning and controlling the finance of an enterprise. A firm performs finance functions continuously in the normal course of the business.

(4) **Different from Accounting Function.** There are key difference between the accounting and finance function. Accounting generates information of data whereas in the finance function the data reanalysed and used for the purpose of decision making.

(5) **Wide Scope.** There is wide scope of financial management. It is concerned not only with the raising of finance but also with the allocation and efficient use of such finance.

(6) **Centralised Nature.** Financial management is centralized in nature. It is neither possible nor desirable to decentralize the financial responsibilities.

(7) **Measurement of Performance.** Financial management is concerned with the wise use of finance. It fixes certain norms and standards against which the benefits of an investment decisions are matched.

(8) **Inseparable Relationship between Finance and other Activities.** There exists an inseparable relationship between finance on the one hand and production, marketing and other activities on the other. All other activities are related to finance.

(9) **Applicable to All Types of Organisation.** It is applicable to all forms of organization whether corporate or non-corporate such as sole proprietorship and partnership firms etc.

Scope of Financial Management

A. Traditional Approach. The traditional approach to the scope of financial management refers to its subject matter in the academic literature in the initial stages of its evolution as a separate branch of academic study. The term 'corporate finance' was used to describe what is now known in the academic world as 'financial management'.

Under this approach, a study of the following three things was made for the procurement of funds:

1. Arrangement of funds from Financial Institutions.
2. Arrangement of funds through Financial Instruments like share, bonds etc.
3. Legal and accounting relationship between a business and its source of funds.

The notable feature of the traditional approach was the assumption that the duty of the finance manager was only to raise funds from external parties and that he was not concerned with taking the internal financial decisions. He was not responsible for the efficient use of funds.

Limitations of Traditional Approach

(i) **More Emphasis on Raising of Funds.** This approach places more emphasis on procurement of funds from external sources and neglects the issues relating to the efficient utilization of funds. Since it is concerned with the raising of funds, it attaches more importance to the viewpoint of external parties who provide funds to the business and completely ignores the internal persons who make financial decisions.

(ii) **Ignores the Financial Problems of Non-Corporate Enterprises.** It places more emphasis on the problems faced by corporate enterprises in procuring the funds. The non-corporate enterprise like sole proprietorship and partnership firms are considered outside its scope.

(iii) **Ignored Routine Problems.** This approach concentrates on the financial problems on the occurrence of special events such as merger, incorporation etc., and fails to consider the day-t-day financial problems of a normal firm.

(iv) **Ignored Working Capital Financing.** This approach gives more emphasis on the problems relating to long term financing and the problems relating to working capital financing are considered outside the purview of this approach.

B. Modern Approach. The modern approach views the term financial management in a broad sense and provides a conceptual and analytical framework for financial decision making. According to it, the finance function covers both acquisition of funds as well as their allocation. Thus, apart from the issues involved in acquiring external funds, the main concern of financial management is the efficient and wise allocation of funds to various use.

In the modern approach, the financial management is responsible for taking three decisions :

(1) **The Investment Decision.** Investment decision also known as Capital Budgeting' is related to the selection of long-term assets or projects in which investments will be made by the business. Long term assets are the assets which would yield benefits over a period of time in future.

(2) **The Financing Decision.** This function is related to raising of finance from different sources. For this purpose the financial manager is to determine the proportion of debt and equity.

In other words there are two sources of finance :

(i) **Debt.** Debt means long term loans and includes :

- Debentures
- Loan from Bank
- Loan from Financial Institutions
- Mortgage Loans

(ii) **Equity.** Equity refers to shareholder's funds and includes :

- Equity Share Capital.
- Preference Share Capital
- Reserve
- Accumulated Profits.

(3) **The Dividend Policy Decision.** The financial management has to decide as to which portion of the profits is to be distributed as dividend among shareholders and which portion is to be retained in the business. For this purpose the financial management should take into consideration the factors of dividend stability, bonus shares and cash dividends in practice.

CAPITAL STRUCTURE

The optimum capital structure may be defined as "that capital structure or combination of debt and equity that leads to the maximum value of the firm." Optimal capital structure maximizes the company's cost of capital. Thus, every firm should aim at achieving the optimal capital structure and then to maintain it.

The following considerations should be kept in mind while maximising the value of the firm in achieving the goal of optimum capital structure :

(i) If the return on investment is higher than the fixed cost of funds, the company should prefer to raise funds having a fixed cost, such as debentures, loans and preference share capital. It will increase earnings per share and market value of the firm. Thus, a company, should make maximum possible use of leverage.

(ii) When debt is used as a source of finance, the firm saves a considerable amount in payment of tax as interest is allowed as a deductible expense in computation of tax. Hence, the effective cost of debt is reduced, called tax leverage. A company should, therefore, take advantage of tax leverage.

(iii) The firm should avoid undue financial risk attached with the use of increased debt financing. If the shareholders receive high risk in using further debt-capital, it will reduce the market price of shares.

(iv) The capital structure should be flexible.

Theories of Capital Structure

Different kinds of theories have been propounded by different authors to explain the relationship between capital structure, cost of capital and value of the firm.

1. Net Income Approach

According to this approach, a firm can minimise the weighted average cost of capital and increase the value of the firm as well as market price of equity shares by using debt financing to the maximum possible extent. The theory propounds that a company can increase its value and reduce the overall cost of capital by increasing the proportion of debt in its capital structure. This approach is based upon the following assumptions :

(i) The cost of debt is less than the cost of equity.

(ii) There are no taxes.

(iii) The risk perception of investors is not changed by the use of debt.

2. Net Operating Income Approach

This theory as suggested by Durand is another extreme of the effect of leverage on the value of the firm. According to this approach, change in the capital structure of a company does not affect the market value of the firm and the overall cost of capital remains constant irrespective of the method of financing. It implies that the overall cost of capital remains the same whether the debt-equity mix is 50:50 or 20:80

or 0:100. Thus, there is nothing as an optimal capital structure and every capital structure is the optimum capital structure. This theory presumes that:

(i) the market capitalises the value of the firm as a whole ;

(ii) the business risk remains constant at every level of debt equity mix.

Graphic Presentation of Net Operating Income Approach. Net Operating Income approach is explained graphically as follows :

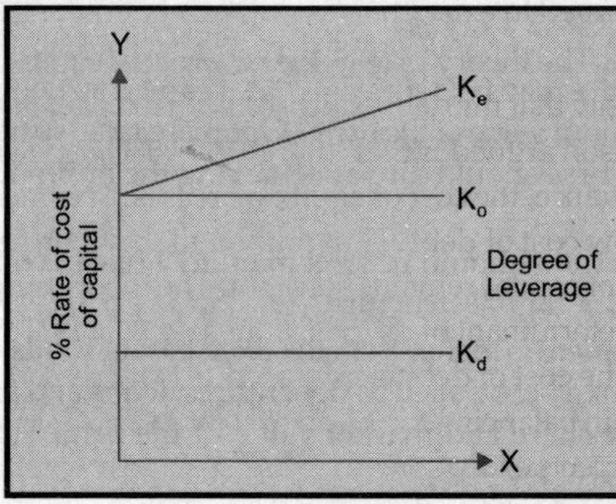

K_e = Cost of Equity

K_d = Cost of debt

K_o = Overall cost of capital

In the above figure, the degree of leverage is plotted along the X-axis, while the percentage rate of cost of capital is shown on Y-axis. The figure shows that K_e and K_d remain unchanged as the degree of leverage is increased. But with the increase in the leverage the cost of equity rises in such a manner so as to offset the advantage of using cheaper debt. As a result, K_0 and the value of firm (V) remain unchanged by the increase in the financial leverage.

Basic Terms

EBIT =	Earnings before Interest and Tax	S =	Value of Equity
B =	Value of Debt	V =	Value of firm
NI =	Net Income	K_d =	Cost of Debt
K_0 =	Overall Cost of Capital	K =	Cost of Equity

Basic Formulas :

$V = S + B$ $\qquad$ NI = EBIT – Interest

$$V = \frac{EBIT}{K} \qquad K_e = \frac{EBIT - I}{S} \times 100 \qquad K_0 = \frac{EBIT}{V} \times 100$$

3. The Traditional Approach

The traditional approach is also known as *Intermediate approach.* According to this theory, the value of the firm can be increased initially or the cost of capital can be decreased by using more debt as the debt is a cheaper source of funds than equity. Thus, optimum capital structure can be reached by a proper debt-equity mix. Beyond a particular point, the cost of equity increases because increased debt increases the financial risk of the equity shareholders. The advantage of cheaper debt at this point of capital structure is offset by increased cost of equity. After this there comes a stage, when the increased cost of equity cannot be offset by the advantage of low-cost debt. Thus, overall cost of capital, according to this theory, decreases upto a certain point, remains more or less unchanged for moderate increase in debt thereafter; and increases or rises beyond a certain point. Even the cost of debt may increase at this state due to increased financial risk.

4. Modigliani and Miller Approach

M & M hypothesis is identical with the Net Operating Income approach if taxes are ignored. However, when corporate taxes are assumed to exist, their hypothesis is similar to the Net Income Approach.

(a) **In the absence of taxes.** The theory proves that the cost of capital is not affected by changes in the capital structure or say that the debt-equity mix is irrelevant in the determination of the total value of a firm. The reason argued is that though debt is cheaper to equity, with increased use of debt as a source of finance, the cost of equity increases. This increase in cost of equity offsets the advantage of the low cost of debt. Thus, although the financial leverage affects the cost of equity, the overall cost of capital remains constant. The theory emphasises the fact that a firm's operating income is a determinant of its total value. The theory further propounds that beyond a certain limit of debt, the cost of debt increases (due to increased financial risk) but the cost of equity falls thereby again balancing the two costs. In the opinion of Modigliani and Miller, two identical firms in all respects except their capital structure cannot have different market values or cost of capital because of *arbitrage process.* In case two identical firms except for their capital structure have different market values or cost of capital arbitrage will take place and the investors will engage in personal leverage (*i.e.,* they will buy equity of the other company in preference to the company having lesser value) as against the corporate leverage'; and this will again render the two firms to have the same total value.

The M & M approach is based upon the following assumptions :

(i) There are no corporate taxes.
(ii) There is a perfect market.
(iii) Investors act rationally.
(iv) The expected earnings of all the firms have identical risk characteristics.
(v) The cut-off point of investment in a firm is capitalization rate.
(vi) Risk to investors depends upon the random fluctuations of expected earnings and the possibility that the actual value of the variables may turn out to different from their best estimates.
(vii) All earnings are distributed to the shareholders.

(b) **When the corporate taxes are assumed to exist.** Modigliani and Miller in their article of 1963 have recognized that the value of the firm will increase or the cost of capital will decrease with the use of debt on account of deductibility of interest charges for tax purpose. Thus, the optimum capital structure can be achieved by maximizing the debt mix in the equity of a firm.

According to the M & M approach, the value of a firm unlevered can be calculated as.

$$\text{Value of unlevered firm } (V_u) = \frac{\text{Earnings Before Interest \& tax}}{\text{Overall cost of capital}} \; i.e., \; \frac{\text{EBIT}}{K_0}(1-t)$$

and, the value of a levered firms is :

$V_L = V_u + tD$

where, V_u is value of unlevered firm

and, tD is the discounted present value of the tax savings resulting from the tax deductibility of the interest charges, t is the rate of tax and D is the quantum of debt used in the mix.

Limitations or Criticism of MM Approach

(1) **Risk Perceptions of personal and corporate leverages are different.** It is incorrect to assume that personal leverage is a perfect substitute for 'corporate leverage'. Liability of an investor is limited in corporate enterprises whereas the liability of an individual borrower is unlimited as even his personal property is liable to be used for payment to lenders. Hence, the risk to the individual borrower is higher.

(2) **Difference in cost of borrowing by the firm and individuals.** The assumption that firms and individuals can borrow at the same rate of interests does not hold good in practice.

(3) **Convenience.** The corporate borrowing is more convenient to the investor because the formalities and procedures in borrowing are to be observed by corporates.

(4) **Institutional Restrictions.** Institutional restrictions stand in the way of a smooth operation of arbitrage process.

COST OF CAPITAL

The cost of capital of a firm is the minimum rate of return expected by its investors. It is the weighted average cost of various sources of finance used by a firm. The capital used by a firm may be in the form of debt, preference capital, retained earnings and equity shares. A decision to invest in a particular project depends upon the cost of capital of the firm or the cut off rate which is the minimum rate of return expected by the investors. In case a firm is not able to achieve even the cut off rate, the market value of its shares will fall. In fact, cost of capital is the minimum rate of return expected by its investors which will maintain the market value of shares at its present level. Hence, to achieve the objective of wealth maximisation, a firm must earn a rate of return more than its cost of capital. Further, optimal capital structure maximizes the value of a firm and hence the wealth of its owners and minimizes the firm's cost of capital. The cost of capital of a firm or the minimum rate of return expected by its investors has a direct relation with the risk involved in the firm. Generally, higher the risk involved in a firm, higher is the cost of capital.

James C. Van Horne defines cost of capital as, "a cut-off rate for the allocation of capital to investments of projects. It is the rate of return on a project that will leave unchanged the market price of the stock."

According to Milton H. Spencer, "The cost of capital is the minimum rate of return which a firm requires as a condition for undertaking an investment."

According to M.J. Gordon, "The cost of capital is the rate of return a company must earn on an investment to maintain the value of the company."

Problems in Determination of Cost of Capital

1. **Historic Cost and Future Cost.** One major problem in the determination of cost of capital arises due to difference of opinion regarding the concept of cost itself. It is argued that book costs are historic costs and the calculation of cost of capital on the basis of such costs is irrelevant for decision making.
2. **Problems in Computation of Cost of Equity.** The computation of cost of equity capital depends upon the rate of return expected by equity shareholders. But it is very difficult to assess the expectation of equity shareholders because there are many factors which influence their expectations.

3. **Problems in computation of cost of retained earnings.** Sometimes it may appear that retained earning are free of cost because they have not been raised from outside.
4. **Problems in Assigning Weights.** Weights have to be assigned to various sources of finance to compute the weighted average cost of capital. The choice of using the book value weights or market value weights places another problem in the computation of cost of capital.

Three basic aspects of the concept of cost of capital are :-

(i) *Cost of capital is not a cost as such.* In fact, it is the rate of return that a firm requires to earn from its projects.

(ii) *It is the minimum rate of return.* Cost of capital of a firm is that minimum rate of return which will at least maintain the market value of the shares.

(iii) *It comprises of three components.* As there is always some business and financial risks is investing funds in a firm, cost of capital comprises of three components.

(a) the expected normal rate of return at zero risk level, say the rate of interest allowed by banks, (b) the premium for business risk and (c) the premium for financial risk on account of pattern of capital structure.

Cost of capital may be represented as :

$K = r_0 + b + f$

K = cost of capital

r_0 = Normal rate of return at zero risk level

b = Premium for business risks

f = Premium for financial risks

Classification of Cost

1. **History Cost and Future Cost.** Historical costs are book costs which are related to the past. Future costs are estimated costs for the future. In financial decisions future costs are more relevant than the historical costs. However, historical costs act as guide for the estimation of future costs.
2. **Specific Cost and Composite Cost.** Specific cost refers to the cost of specific source of capital while composite cost is combined cost of various sources of capital. It is the weighted average cost of capital. In case more than one form of capital is used in the business, it is the composite cost which should be considered for decision-making and not the specific cost. But where only one type of capital is employed the specific cost of that type of capital may be considered. In capital structure decisions, it is the weighted average cost of capital which should be given consideration.
3. **Explicit Cost and Implicit Cost.** An explicit cost is the discount rate which equates the present value of cash inflows with the present: value of cash outflows. In other words, it is the internal rate of return. The explicit cost of a specific sources of finance may be determined with the help of the following formula:

$$I_0 = \frac{O_1}{(1+k)} + \frac{O_2}{(1+k)^2} \cdots\cdots \frac{O_n}{(1+k)^n}$$

$$= \sum_{t=1}^{n} \frac{O_t}{(1+k)^t}$$

where, I_0, is the net cash inflow at zero point of time,

O_t is the outflow of cash in periods 1, 2 and n.

k is the explicit cost of capital.

Implicit cost also known as the opportunity cost is the cost of the opportunity foregone in order to take up a particular project. For example, the implicitly cost of retained earnings is the rate of return available to shareholders by investing the funds elsewhere.

4. **Average Cost and Marginal Cost.** An average cost refers to the combined cost of various sources of capital such as debentures, preference shares and equity shares. It is the weighted average cost of the costs of various sources of finance. Marginal cost of capital refers to the average cost of capital which has to be incurred to obtain additional funds required by a firm.

Computation of Cost of Capital

Computation of overall cost of capital of a firm involves:

A. Computation of cost of specific source of finance and

B. Computation of weighted average cost of capital.

A. Computation of Specific Source of Finance

Computation of each specific source of finance, viz., debt, preference share capital, equity share capital and retained earnings is discussed as below:

1. **Cost of Debt.** The cost of debt is the rate of interest payable on debt. For example, a company issues Rs. 1,00,000 for 10% debentures at par; the before-tax cost of this debt issue will also be 10%. By way of a formula, before-tax-cost of debt may be calculated as:

(i) $$K_{db} = \frac{I}{P}$$

where,

K_{db} = Before tax cost of debt

I = Interest

and P = Principal

In case the debt is raised at premium or discount, we should consider P as the amount of net proceeds received from the issue and not the face value of securities. The formula may be changed to

(ii) $$K_{db} = \frac{1}{NP}(1-t)$$

where,

NP = Net Proceeds

Further, when debt is used as a source of finance, the firm saves a considerable amount in payment of tax as interest is allowed as a deductible expense in computation of tax. Hence, the effective cost of debt is reduced. The After-tax cost of debt may be calculated with the help of following formula:

(iii) $$K_{da} = K_{db}(1-t) = \frac{D}{MP}$$

where,

K_{da} = After-tax cost of debt

t = Rate of tax.

Cost of Redeemable Debt. Usually, the debt is issued to be redeemed after a certain period during the life time of a firm. Such a debt issue is known as Redeemable debt. The cost of redeemable debt capital may be computed as:

(iv) Before-tax cost of debt:

$$K_{db} = \frac{1 + \frac{1}{n}(P - NP)}{\frac{1}{2}(P + NP)}$$

where,

I = Interest
N = Number of years in which debt is to be redeemed
P = Proceeds at par
NP = Net Proceeds

(v) After-tax cost of debt,

$$K_{da} = K_{db}\,(1 - t)$$

$$K_{da} = \frac{1 + \frac{1}{n}(P - NP)}{\frac{1}{2}(P + NP)}(1 - t)$$

2. **Cost of Preference Capital.** A fixed rate of divided is payable on preference shares. Though dividend is payable at the discretion of the Board of directors and there is no legal binding to pay dividend, yet it does not mean that preference capital is cost free. The cost of preference capital is a function of dividend expected by its investors, *i.e.*, its stated dividend. In case dividends are not paid to preference shareholders, it will affect the fund raising capacity of the firm. Hence, dividends are usually paid regularly on preference share except when there are no profits to pay dividends. The cost of preference capital which is perpetual can be calculated as:

$$K_p = \frac{D}{P}$$

where,

K_p = Cost of Preference Capital
D = Annual Preference Dividend
P = Preference Share Capital (Proceeds).

Further, if preference shares are issued at Premium or Discount or when costs of floatation are incurred to issue preference shares, the nominal or par value of preference share capital has to be adjusted to find out the net proceeds from the issue of preference shares. In such a case, the cost of preference capital can be computed with the following formula:

$$K_p = \frac{D}{NP}$$

It may be noted that as dividends are not allowed to be deducted in computation of tax, no adjustment is required for taxes

Sometimes Redeemable Preference Shares are issued which can be redeemed or cancelled on maturity date. The cost of redeemable preference share capital can be calculated as:

$$K_{pr} = \frac{D + \frac{MV - NP}{n}}{\frac{1}{2}(MV + NP)}$$

where,

K_{pr} = Cost of Redeemable Preference Shares

D = Annual Preference Dividend

MV = Maturity Value of Preference Shares

NP = Net Proceeds of Preference Shares.

3. **Cost of Equity Share Capital.** The cost of equity is the maximum rate of return that the company must earn on equity financed portion of its investments in order to leave unchanged the market price of its stock. The cost of equity capital is a function of the expected return by its investors. The cost of equity is not the out-of-pocket cost of using equity capital as the equity shareholders are not paid dividend at a fixed rate every year. Moreover, payment of dividend is not a legal binding. It may or may not be paid. But it does not mean that equity share capital is a cost free capital. Shareholders invest money in equity shares on the expectation of getting dividend and the company must earn this minimum rate so that the market price of the shares remains unchanged. Whenever a company wants to raise additional funds by the issue of new equity shares, the expectations of the shareholders have to be evaluated. The cost of equity share capital can be computed in the following ways:

(a) **Dividend Yield Method or Dividend Price Ratio Method.** According to this method, the cost of equity capital is the discount rate that equates the present value of expected future dividends per share with the net proceeds (or current market price) of a share. Symbolically.

$$K_e = \frac{D}{NP} \text{ or } \frac{D}{MP}$$

where,

K_e = Cost of Equity Capital

D = Expected dividend per share

NP = Net proceeds per share and

MP = Market Price per share

The basic assumptions underlying this method are that the investors give prime importance to dividends and risk in the firm remains unchanged. The dividend price ratio method does not seem to consider the growth in dividend, (i) it does not consider future earnings or retained earnings, and (ii) it does not take into account the capital gains. This method of computing cost of equity capital is suitable only when the company has stable earnings and stable dividend policy over a period of time.

(b) **Dividend yield plus growth in dividend method.** When the dividends of the firm are expected to grow at a constant rate and the dividend-pay-out ratio is constant this method may be used to compute the cost of equity capital. According to this method the cost of equity capital is based on the dividends and the growth rate.

$$K_e = \frac{D}{NP} + G$$

where,

K_e = Cost of Equity Capital

D = Expected dividend per share

NP = Net proceeds per share

G = Rate of growth in dividends.

Further, in case cost of existing equity share capital is to be calculated, the NP should be changed with MP (market price per share) in the above equation.

$$K_e = \frac{D}{NP} + G$$

(c) **Earning Yield Method.** According to this method, the cost of equity capital is the discount rate that equates the present values of expected future earnings per share with the net process (or, current market price) or a share. Symbolically:

$$K_e = \frac{\text{Earnings per share}}{\text{Net Proceeds}}$$

$$= \frac{EPS}{NP}$$

where, the cost of existing capital is to be calculated.

$$K_e = \frac{\text{Earnings per share}}{\text{Market Price per share}}$$

$$= \frac{EPS}{MP}$$

This method of computing cost of equity capital may be employed in the following cases:

(i) When the earnings per share are expected to remain constant.

(ii) When the dividend pay-out-ratio is 100 per cent, *i.e.* all the available profits are distributed as dividends.

(iii) When a firm is expected to earn an amount on new equity share capital, which is equal to the current rate of earning.

(iv) The market price of the share is influenced only by earnings per share.

(d) **Realised Yield Method.** One of the serious limitations of using dividend yield method or earnings yield method is the problem of estimating the expectations of the investors regarding future dividends and earnings. It is not possible to estimate future dividends and earnings correctly; both of these depend upon so many uncertain factors. To remove this drawback, realised yield method, which takes into account the actual average rate of return realised in the past, may be applied to compute the cost of equity share capital. To calculate the average rate of return realised, dividends received in the past alongwith the gain realised at the time of sale of shares should be considered. The cost of equity capital is said to be the realised rate of return by the shareholders. This method of computing cost of equity share capital is based upon the following assumption:

(a) The firm will remain in the same risk class over the period;

(b) The shareholders' expectations are based upon the past realised yield;

(c) The investors get the same rate of return as the realised yield even if they invest elsewhere and

(d) The market price of shares does not change significantly.

4. **Cost of Retained Earnings.** It is sometimes argued that retained earnings do not involve any cost because a firm is not required to pay dividends on retained earnings. However, the shareholders expect a return on retained profits. Retained earnings accrue to a firm only because of some sacrifice made by the shareholders in not receiving the dividends the dividends out of the available profits.

The cost of retained earnings may be considered as the rate of return which the existing shareholders can obtain by investing the after-tax dividends in alternative opportunity of equal qualities. It is thus the opportunity cost of dividends foregone by the shareholders. Cost of retained earnings can be computed with the help of following formula:

$$K_r = \frac{D}{NP} + G$$

where,

K_r = Cost of retained earnings
D = Expected dividend
NP = Net proceeds of share issue
G = Rate of growth.

Further, it is important to note that shareholders, usually, cannot obtain the entire amount of retained profits by way of dividends even if there is 100 per cent pay out ratio. It is so because the shareholders are required to pay tax on their dividend income. So, some adjustment has to be made for tax. However, tax adjustment in determining the cost of retained earnings is a difficult problem because all shareholders do not fall under the same tax bracket. Moreover, if the shareholders wish to invest their after-tax dividend income in alternative securities, they may have to incur some costs of purchasing the securities, such as brokerage Hence, the effective rate of return realised by the shareholders from the new investment will be somewhat lesser than their present retrain from the firm. To make adjustment in the cost in retained earnings for tax and costs of purchasing new securities, the following formula may be adopted

$$K_r = \left(\frac{D}{NP} + G\right) \times (1-t) \times (1-b)$$

or

$$K_r = K_e (1-t)(1-b)$$

where,

K_r = Cost of retained earnings
D – Expected dividend
G = Growth Rate
NP = Net Proceeds of Equity Issue
t = Tax rate
b = Cost of purchasing new securities or brokerage costs
K_e = Rate of return available to shareholders.

B. Computation of Weighted Average Cost of Capital

Weighted average cost of capital is the average cost of various sources of financing. Weighted average cost of capital is also known as composite cost of capital, overall cost of capital or average cost of capital. Once the specific cost of individual sources of finance is determined, we can compute the weighted average cost of capital by putting weights to the specific costs of capital in proportion of the various sources of funds to the total. The weights may be given either by using the book value of the source or marked value of the source The cost of capital calculated according to the market value weights is usually higher than the book value weights and market value weights are sometimes preferred to the book value weights because the market value represents the true value of the investors. However, the market value weights suffer from the following limitations:

(i) It is very difficult to determine the market values because of frequent fluctuations.

(ii) With the use of market value weights, equity capital gets greater importance.

For the above limitations, it is better to use book value which is readily available. Weighted average cost of capital can be computed as follows:

$$K_w = \frac{\Sigma XW}{\Sigma W}$$

where,

K_w = Weighted average cost of capital

X = Cost of specific source of finance

W = Weight, proportion of specific source of finance

BUDGETARY CONTROL

A budget is the monetary and quantitative expression of business plans and policies to be pursued in the future period of time. It is a pre-determined statement of management policy during a given period which provides a standard for comparison with the results actually achieved.

Budgetary control is the process of determining various budgeted figures for the enterprises for the future period and then comparing the budgeted figures with the actual performance for calculating variances, if any. First of all budgets are prepared and then actual results are recorded. The comparison of budgeted and actual figures will enable the management to find out discrepancies and take remedial measures at a proper time. The budgetary control is a continuous process which helps in planning and co-ordination. It provides a method of control too. A budget is a means and budgetary control is the end-result.

According to Brown and Howard, "Budgetary control is a system of controlling costs which includes the preparation of budgets, co-ordinating the department and establishing responsibilities, comparing actual performance with the budgeted and acting upon results to achieve maximum profitability." Budgeting Control involves the following:

(a) The objects are set by preparing budgets.

(b) The business is divided into various responsibility centres for preparing various budgets.

(c) The actual figures are recorded.

(d) The budgeted and actual figures are compared for studying the performance of different cost centres.

(e) If actual performance is less than the budgeted norms, a remedial action is taken immediately.

Thus, the three cardinal features of budgetary control are:

(i) Planning,

(ii) Co-ordination and

(iii) Control.

Objectives of Budgetary Control

Budgetary control is essential for policy planning and control. It also acts as an instrument of co-ordination. The main objectives of budgetary control are as follows :

(i) To ensure planning for future by setting up various budgets. The requirements and expected performance of the enterprise are anticipated.
(ii) To co-ordinate the activities of different departments.
(iii) To operate various cost centres and departments with efficiency and economy.
(iv) Elimination of wastes and increase in profitability.
(v) To anticipate capital expenditures for future.
(vi) To centralise the control system.
(vii) Correction of deviations from the established standards.
(viii) Fixation of responsibility of various individuals in the organisation.

Requisites for a Successful Budgetary Control System

For making a budgetary control system successful following requisites are required:

(a) **Clarifying objectives.** The budgets are used to realise objectives of the business. The objectives must be clearly spelt out so that budgets are properly prepared. In the absence of clear goals, the budgets will also be unrealistic.

(b) **Proper Delegation of Authority and Responsibility.** Budget preparation and control is done at every level of management. Even though budgets are finalised at top level but involvement of persons from lower levels of management is essential for their success. This necessitates proper delegation of authority and responsibility.

(c) **Proper Communication System.** An effective system of communication is required for a successful budgetary control. The flow of information regarding budgets should be quick so that these are implemented. The upward communication will help in knowing the difficulties in implementation of budgets. The performance reports of various levels will help top management in budgetary control.

(d) **Budget Education.** The employees should be properly educated about the benefits of budgeting system. They should be educated about their role in the success of this system. Budgetary control may not be taken only as a control device by the employees but it should be used as a tool to improve their efficiency.

(e) **Participation of All Employees.** Budgeting is done for every- segment of the business. It will also require the active participation and involvement of all employees. In practice the budgets are to be executed at upper levels of management. Those for whom the budgets are framed should be actively associated with their preparation and execution. The employees, on the basis of their past experience, may give more practical and useful suggestions. The success of budgetary control system depends upon the participation of all employees of the organisation.

(f) **Flexibility.** Flexibility in budgets is required to make them suitable under changed circumstances. Budgets are prepared for the future, which is always uncertain. Even though budgets are prepared by considering the future possibilities but still some occurrences later on may necessitate certain adjustments, flexibility will make the budgets more appropriate and realistic.

(g) **Motivation.** Budgets are to be implemented by human beings. Their successful implementation will depend upon the interest shown by the employees. All persons should be motivated to improve their working so that budgeting is successful. A proper system of motivation should be introduced for making this system a success.

Advantages of Budgetary Control

The budgetary control system help in fixing the goals for the organisation as a whole and concerted efforts are made for its achievements. It enables economies in the enterprise. Some of the advantages are:

(i) **Maximisation of Profit.** The budgetary control aims at the maximisation of profits of the enterprise. To achieve this aim, a proper planning and co-ordination of different functions is undertaken. There is a proper control over various capital and revenue expenditures. The resources are put to the best possible use.

(ii) **Co-ordination.** The working of different departments and sectors is properly co-ordinated. The budgets of different departments have a bearing on one another. The co-ordination of various executives and subordinates is necessary for achieving budgeted targets.

(ii) **Specific Aims.** The plans, policies and goals are decided by the top management. All efforts are put together to reach the common goal of the organisation. Every department is given a target to be achieved. The efforts are directed towards achieving some specific aims. If there is no definite aim then the efforts will be wasted in pursuing different aims.

(iv) **Tool for Measuring Performance.** By providing targets to various department, budgetary control provides a tool for measuring managerial performance. The budgeted targets are compared with actual results and deviations are determined. The performance of each department is reported to the top management. This system enables the introduction of management by exception.

(v) **Economy.** The planning of expenditure will be systematic and there will be economy in spending. The finances will be put to optimum use. The benefits derived for the concern will ultimately extend to industry and then to national economy. The national resources will be used economically and wastage will be eliminated.

(vi) **Determining Weaknesses.** The deviations in budgeted and actual performance will enable the determination of weak spots. Efforts are concentrated on those aspects where performance is less than the stipulated.

(vii) **Corrective Action.** The management will be able to take corrective measures whenever there is a discrepancy in performance. The deviations will be regularly reported so that necessary action is taken at the earliest. In the absence of a budgetary control system the deviations can be determined only at the end of the financial period.

(viii) **Consciousness.** It creates budget consciousness among the employees. By fixing targets for the employees, they are made conscious of their responsibility. Everybody knows what he is expected to do and he continues with his work uninterrupted.

(ix) **Reduces Costs.** In the present day competitive world budgetary control has a significant role to play. Every businessman tries to reduce the cost of production for increasing sales. He tries to have those combinations of products where profitability is more.

(x) **Introduction of Incentive Schemes.** Budgetary control system also enables the introduction of incentive schemes of remuneration. The comparison of budgeted and actual performance will enable the use of such schemes.

Classification and Types of Budgets

The budgets are usually classified according to their nature. The following are the types of budgets which are commonly used.

(A) Classification According to Time

(i) Long-term budgets.

(ii) Short-term budgets.

(iii) Current budgets.

(B) Classification on the Basis of Functions

(i) Operating Budgets

(ii) Financial Budgets

(iii) Master Budget

(C) Classification on the Basis of Flexibility

(i) Fixed budget.

(ii) Flexible budget

(A) Classification According to Time.

(i) *Long-Term Budgets.* The budgets are prepared to depict long term planning of the business. The period of long term budgets varies between five to ten years. The long term planning is done by the top level management; it is not generally known to lower levels of management. Long time budgets are prepared for some sectors of the concern such as capital expenditure, research and development, long term finances, *etc.* These budgets are useful for those industries where gestation period is long *i.e.*, machinery, electricity, engineering, etc.

(ii) *Short-term Budgets.* These budgets are generally for one or two years and in monetary terms. The consumers goods industries like sugar, cotton, textile, etc. use short-term budgets.

(iii) *Current Budgets.* The period of current budgets is generally of months and weeks, these budgets relate to the current activities of the business. According to I.C.W.A. London, "Current budget is a budget which is established for use over a short period of time and is related to current conditions."

(B) Classification on the Basis of Functions.

(i) *Operating Budgets.* These budgets relate to the different activities or operations of a firm. The number of such budgets depends upon the size and nature of business. The commonly used operating budgets are :

(a) Sales Budget

(b) Production Budget

(c) Production Cost Budget

(d) Purchase Budget

(e) Raw Material Budget

(f) Labour Budget

(g) Plant Utilisation Budget

(h) Manufacturing Expenses or Works Overhead Budget

(i) Administrative and Selling Expenses, Budget, etc.

The operating budget for a firm may be constructed in terms of programmes or responsibility areas and hence may consist of:

(1) Programme Budget and

(2) Responsibility Budget.

(1) *Programme Budget.* It consists of expected revenues and costs of various products or projects that are termed as the major programmes of the firm. Such a budget can be prepared for each product line or project showing revenues, costs and the relative profitability of the various programmes. Programme budgets are thus, useful in

locating areas where efforts may be required to reduce costs and increase revenues. They are also useful in determining imbalances and inadequacies in programmes so that corrective action may be taken in future.

(2) *Responsibility Budget.* When the operating budget of a firm is constructed in terms of responsibility areas it is called the responsibility budget. Such a budget shows the plan in terms of persons responsible for achieving them. It is used by the management as a control device to evaluate the performance of executives who are incharge of various cost centres. Their performance is compared to the targets (budgets), set for them and proper action is taken for adverse results, if any. The kinds of responsibility areas depend upon the size and nature of business activities and the organisational structure. However, responsibility areas may be classified under three broad categories:

(a) Cost Expense Centre
(b) Profit Centre
(c) Investment Centre.

We have discussed the concept and technique of responsibility budgeting in detail under a separate chapter on 'Responsibility Accounting' later in this book.

(ii) *Financial Budgets.* Financial budgets are concerned with cash receipts and disbursements, working capital, capital expenditure, financial position and results of business operations. The commonly used financial budgets are:

(a) Cash Budget
(b) Working Capital Budget
(c) Capital Expenditure Budget
(d) Income Statement Budget
(e) Statement of Retained Earnings Budget
(f) Budgeted Balance Sheet or Position Statement Budget.

(iii) *Master Budget.* Various functional budgets are integrated into master budget. This budget is prepared by the ultimate integration of separate functional budgets. According to I.C.W.A. London, "The Master Budget is the summary budget incorporating its functional budgets". Master budget is prepared by the budget officer and it remains with the top level management. This budget is used to co-ordinate the activities of various functional departments and also to help as a control device.

(C) Classification on the Basis of Flexibility

(i) *Fixed Budget.* The fixed budgets are prepared for a given level of activity, prepared before the beginning of the financial year. If the financial year starts in January then the budget will be prepared a month or two earlier, *i.e.*, November or December. The changes in expenditure arising out of the anticipated changes will not be adjusted in the budget. There is a difference of about twelve months in the budgeted and actual figures. According to I.C.W.A London, "Fixed budget is a budget which is designed to remain unchanged irrespective of the level of activity actually attained." Fixed budgets are suitable under static conditions. If sales, expenses and costs can be forecasted with greater accuracy then this budget can be advantageously used.

(ii) *Flexible Budgets.* A flexible budget consists of a series of budgets for different level of activity. It, therefore, varies with the level of activity attained. A flexible budget is prepared after taking into consideration unforeseen changes in the conditions of the business. A flexible budget is defined as a budget which by recognising the difference between fixed, semi-fixed and variable cost is designed to change in relation to the level of activity.

The flexible budgets will be useful where level of activity changes from time to time. When the forecasting of demand is uncertain and the undertaking operates under conditions of shortage of materials, labour *etc.*, then this budget will be more suited.

Sales Budget

A sales budget is an estimate of expected sales during a budget period. A sales budget is known as a nerve centre or backbone of the enterprise. The degree of accuracy with which sales are estimated will determine the practicability of operating budgets. A sales budget is the starting point on which other budgets are also based.

A sales budget lays down potential sales figures in value as well as in quantity. It lays down a comprehensive plan and programme for sales department. The sales manager is made responsible for preparing sales budget. He uses all possible information available from internal and external sources. The possible factors to be taken into account while preparing a sales budget are discussed as follows:

(a) *Past Sales Figures.* The sales forecasts are based on past sales figures. The sales figures of a number of years enable in the determination of trends of sales. The upward and downward sales trends will be of great use in fixing future sales. The actual past sales figures will be the most reliable criterion on which sales budgets should be based. The expected seasonal fluctuations, potential demand and position of trade cycles will also be helpful in preparing sales budgets.

(b) *Assessment and Reports by Salesman.* The salesman are the most appropriate persons for estimating future demand. They are in touch with the market and the customers. Their experience will enable them to forecast sales figures more realistically. The sales manager should cautiously scrutinise the figures of salesmen so as to eliminate their bias. The attitude and personal thinking of the salesmen may tempt them to underestimate or overestimate sales estimates. The sales manager gets an idea about the market situation from salesmen's estimates. He should wisely use these figures for incorporating them in sales budget.

(c) *Availability of Raw Materials.* The availability of raw materials is an important factor in preparing a sales budget. In some cases, raw material is a key factor. The quantum of raw materials available to the enterprise will enable the sales manager to anticipate sales figures. Moreover, the smooth supply of materials is necessary for achieving sales targets.

(d) *Seasonal Fluctuations.* The effect of seasonal fluctuations should also be considered while preparing a sales budget. The demand for goods may be more in some periods while they may be in less demand at other times. An effort should be made to reduce the seasonal effect by giving discounts or other concessions during off seasons.

(e) *Availability of Finances.* The availability of finances sometimes becomes a limiting factor. The finances will be required for purchasing various inputs. The sales budget is prepared alongwith the financial budget. The expansion of sales effort will need additional capital outlay. Financial aspect should be taken into consideration while preparing a sales budget.

(f) *Plant Capacity.* The goods will be sold only when they are produced, the capacity for producing goods should be taken into account. On the other hand, sales effort must ensure full utilisation of plant capacity.

Production Budget

The production budget is prepared in relation to the sales budget. Whatever is to be sold should be produced in time so that it is delivered to the customer. It is a forecast of the production for the budget period. Production budget is prepared for the number of units to be produced and also for the cost to be incurred on materials, labour and factory overheads.

Two important considerations are involved in the preparation of production budget:

(A) What is to be produced?

(B) When is it to be produced?

The preparation of production budget involves the following stages:

(a) **Production Planning.** A proper production planning schedule is essential for preparing production budget. The number of physical units to be produced is determined. The utilisation of optimum plant capacity and avoidance of bottlenecks due to shortage of materials and labour, *etc.* is considered while preparing a production plan. Production planning will ensure a smooth production schedule.

(b) **Consideration of Plant Capacity.** The number of units of different products to be produced should be determined and the capacity with which the plant will be able to work throughout the budgeted period should be decided. One should not fix the capacity either too high or too low. A normal plant capacity which will be a realistic estimate should be budgeted.

(c) **Stock Quantity to be Held.** The quantity of finished goods to be carried forward should be decided. This quantity will depend upon a number of factors like sales potential, storage facilities available and cost of the stock. While fixing production target, the required closing stock figures will be added to the estimated sales figures and opening stock figures will be deducted from it. The work in progress will also be taken into account while fixing a production target.

(d) **Considering Sales Budget.** The production budget is fixed with reference to sales budget. The sales budget will provide a guideline for production planning. If both the budgets are not co-ordinated then there may arise problems of either selling the whole stock or of producing it. In case the sales are not undertaken as per schedule then production should be reduced or vice-versa.

Cost of Production Budget

The production budget determines the number of units to be produced. When these units are expressed into monetary terms, it becomes a cost of production budget. The cost of production budget is the total amount to be spent on producing the units stipulated in the production budget. The physical units are broken into elements *i.e.*, material, quantity, labour, time and manufacturing overheads. The materials cost, labour cost and overheads required for manufacturing are totalled together to make it a cost of production budget.

Materials Budget

The material budget is concerned with determining the quantity of raw materials required for production. The programme for purchasing raw materials is adjusted according to the production budget. The materials are purchased as per the requirements of production department. The requirements of materials are determined product-wise. The rates of consumption of raw materials are also determined. The number of units to be produced multiplied by the rate of consumption (raw materials required for producing one unit) will give the figure of materials required. The stocks of materials required in hand at any time are added to the materials required for production. The opening stock of materials is deduced from the figures determined as above. In this way, the requirement of materials in units will be determined. The units of materials required multiplied by the rate per unit of raw material will give us a figure of material cost. The raw materials budget will serve the following purposes:

1. The Purchase Department will be able to plan the purchase of raw materials at different times.
2. It will enable the fixation of minimum stock level, maximum stock level and re-ordering level.

3. The raw materials purchase budget will be determined.
4. The budgeted cost of raw materials will be determined.

Direct Labour Budget

The labour required for production may be classified into direct and indirect labour. The labour required for manufacturing the product is known as direct labour. The labour which cannot be specified with production is called indirect labour. Though two budgets may be prepared, direct and indirect labour, but from costing point of view only direct labour budget is prepared because indirect labour is made a part of manufacturing overheads.

The labour content of each item is determined in terms of grades of workers required as per production budget. The labour time needed for each job, process and operation is determined with the help of time and motion study. The rates of pay including all allowances are multiplied by labour time for calculating labour cost. If labour incentive schemes are in operation then labour rates should be suitably increased. If piece-rate systems for paying wages is in operation then labour cost will be calculated by multiplying budgeted units by the labour rate per unit.

Labour budget is useful for anticipating labour time required for production. The personnel department is also able to make arrangements for recruitment of workers, *etc.*

Manufacturing Overheads Cost Budget

The manufacturing overheads cost is that part of works cost which arises from indirect labour, indirect materials, overheads and other factory expenses, manufacturing cost is excluded from direct material and direct labour. Manufacturing overhead cost may be classified into fixed cost, variable cost and semi-variable cost.

The fixed works overheads cost remains constant irrespective of output and it is estimated on the basis of past experience. The variable works overhead cost is determined per unit of cost and it is calculated by multiplying the rate per unit by the budgeted output. The semi-variable cost increases with the increase in output but the rate per unit decreases with the increase in output. While budgeting manufacturing overheads cost, management must consider the level of activity to be attained in future so that the expenses are estimated accurately.

Selling and Distribution Overhead Budget

This budget includes all expenses relating to selling, advertising and distribution of goods. These expenses may be analysed according to products, territories, salesmen, *etc.* The fixed expenses under this category may be estimated on the basis of past experience and anticipated changes. Variable selling and distribution overheads will vary with the anticipated sales figures. The responsibility for preparing this budget lies with the executives of sales departments. The volume of these expenses should be in direct proportion to expected sales figures. The future expectations estimated by the management, advertising policies, research programmes and nature of these expenses will influence the preparation of selling and distribution overhead budget.

Cash Budget

A cash budget is an estimate of cash receipts and disbursements during a future period of time. It proceeds various other budgets like materials budgets and research and development budget. "The cash budget is an analysis of flow of cash in a business over a future, short or long period of time. It is a forecast of expected cash intake and outlay".

The cash receipts from various sources are anticipated. The estimated cash collections for sales, debts, bills receivables, interests, dividends and other incomes and sale of investments and other assets will be taken into account. The amounts to be spent on purchase of materials, payment to creditors and meeting various other revenue and capital expenditure needs should be considered. Cash forecasts will include all possible sources from which cash will be received and the channels in which payments are to be made so that a consolidated cash position is determined.

The cash budget should be co-ordinated with other activities of the business. The functional budgets may be adjusted according to the cash budget. The available funds should be fruitfully used and the concern should not suffer for want of funds.

Capital Expenditure Budget

The budget lays down the amount of estimated expenditure to be incurred on fixed assets during the budget period. As the amount involved in capital expenditure is usually high this requires careful attention of the top management. The budget is based upon the annual forecasts of capital expenditure of various divisions or departments. Each division or department of an organisation sends the annual forecast of capital expenditure of its own department to Capital Expenditure Sanction Committee. The Committee after considering the profitabilities of the capital expenditure sanctions the expenditure and then the amount is incorporated in the budget.

Master Budget

The master budget is the summary of various functional budgets. It is prepared by integrating various budgets into one consolidated budget so as to represent the budgeted profit and loss account and the budgeted balance sheet as at the end of the budget period. In the words of Rowland and William H. Harr, the master budget is, "a summary of the budget schedules in capsule form made for the purpose of presenting in one report the highlights of the budget forecast." The Institute of Management Accountant, London, defines it as, "the summary budget, incorporating its component functional budgets and which is finally approved, adopted and employed."

The master budget is prepared by the budget officer and requires the approval of the Budget Committee before it is put into operation. This budget is used to co-ordinate the activities of various functional departments and also to serve as a control device.

The various steps involved in the preparation of this budget include the construction of :

(i) sales budget, as the starting point;
(ii) production budget
(iii) cost of production budget;
(iv) cash budget and
(v) the projected income statement and the balance sheet.

Performance Budgeting

Performance budget has been defined as a "budget based on functions, activities and projects." Performance budgeting may be described as the budgeting system in which input costs are related to the performance, *i.e.*, end results. It is a system of budgeting which provides for appraisal of performance as well as follow up measures.

Under conventional system of budgeting, a budget represents a statement of various amounts provided for different kinds of expenditures to be incurred. It takes the form of what is called as 'List of appropriations' and so long as expenses incurred by the concerned department do not exceed the budgeted amount, there is no apparent irregularity. Thus, the conventional budgeting lays emphasis only on the amount of expenses to be incurred. The performance budgeting, on the other hand, lays emphasis on the results achieved or the performance rather than the expenditure incurred. The performance budget as defined in the Report of the Estimates Committee on Budgetary reform reads as follows:

"The performance budget is a budget based on functions, activities and projects which focus attention on the accomplishment, the general and relative importance of the work to be done and the service to be rendered rather than upon the means of accomplishments such as personnel, service, supplies, equipment, *etc.* Under this system, the functions of various organisational units would be split into programmes of activities, sub-programmes and component schemes, *etc.* and estimates would be presented for each."

Performance budgeting seeks to establish relationship between inputs (costs) and their direct outputs. According to National Institute of Bank Management, performance budgeting is, "the process of analysing, identifying, simplifying and crystallising specific performance objectives of a job to be achieved over a period, in the framework of the organisational objectives, the purpose and objectives of the job. The technique is characterised by its specific direction towards the business objectives of the organisation."

Performance budgeting involves :

(i) development of performance criteria for various programmes;

(ii) assessment of performance of each programme and by each responsibility unit;

(iii) comparison of the actual performance with the budget and

(iv) undertaking periodic review of the programme with a view to make modifications as required.

Control Ratios

The management wants to know whether performance of its business going as per schedule or not. With this purpose in view, some control ratios are calculated. If the ratios are more than 100%, then the performance will be favourable but if these ratios are less than 100%, then the performance will be unfavourable or unsatisfactory. The following control ratios are calculated :

(i) $$\text{Capacity Ratio} = \frac{\text{Actual Hours Worked}}{\text{Budgeted Hours}} \times 100$$

This ratio indicates how-much budgeted hours have been actually utilised. If the ratio is 80%, then it means that 80% budgeted hours have been utilised and the remaining 20% capacity remains idle.

(ii) $$\text{Activity Ratio} = \frac{\text{Standard Hours for Actual Production}}{\text{Budgeted Hours}} \times 100$$

This ratio shows the level of activity attained during the period.

(iii) $$\text{Efficiency Ratio} = \frac{\text{Standard Hours for Actual Production}}{\text{Actual Hours Worked}} \times 100$$

This ratio shows the level of efficiency attained during a particular period. If this ratio is 130% then it shows that the efficiency is more by 30% or it has gone up by 30%.

(iv) $$\text{Calendar Ratio} = \frac{\text{Number of Actual Working Days in a Period}}{\text{Number of Working Days in the Budget Period}} \times 100$$

This ratio shows whether actual working days available are more or less than the budgeted working days. If the ratio is more than 100% then actual working days are more than the budgeted number of working days and vice versa if the ratio is less than 100%.

Zero-Base Budgeting (ZBB)

Zero base budgeting is the latest technique of budgeting and it has an increased use as a managerial tool. This technique was first used in America in 1962. The former President of America, Jimmy Carter used this technique when he was the Governor of Georgia for controlling State expenditure.

As the name suggests, it is starting from a 'scratch'. The normal technique of budgeting is to use previous year's cost levels as a base for preparing this year's budget. This method carries previous year's inefficiencies to the present year because we take last year as a guide and decide 'what is to be done this year when this much was the performance of the last year'. In zero base budgeting every year is taken as a new year and previous year is not taken as a base. The budget for this year will have to be justified according to present situation. Zero is taken as a base and likely future activities are decided according to the present situations. In the words of Peter A Pyher, "A planning and budgeting process which requires each manager to justify his entire budget request in detail from scratch (hence zero base) and shifts the burden of proof to each manager to justify why he should spend money at all. The approach requires that all activities be analysed in 'decision packages' which are evaluated by systematic analysis and ranked in order of importance."

In zero-base budgeting a manager is to justify why be wants to spend. The preference or spending on various activities will depend upon their justification and priority for spending will be drawn. It will have to be proved that an activity is essential and the amounts asked for are really reasonable taking into account the volume of activity.

Process of or Steps Involved in ZBB

The following steps are involved in zero base budgeting:

(i) The objective of budgeting should be determined. When the objective is clear, then efforts will be made to achieve that objective. Different organisations may have different objectives. One concern may try to reduce the expenditure on staff, another may try to discontinue one project in preference to another. So the first step will decide about the object and then other steps will be possible.

(ii) The extent to which zero base budgeting is to be applied should be decided. When should be used for all operational areas or it should be applied in some areas only should be decided beforehand.

(iii) The next step in ZBB is developing of 'decision packages'. A decision package is "a document that identifies a specific activity in such a manner that management can evaluate and rank it against other activities competing for limited resources and decide whether to approve or disapprove it."

(iv) Cost and benefit analysis should be undertaken. We should consider the cost involved and the likely benefits to accrue. Only those projects should be taken first where benefit is more as compared to the cost involved. Cost benefit analysis will help in fixing priority for various projects on the basis of their utility or ranking of decision packages.

(v) The final step involved in zero-based budgeting is concerned with selecting, approving decision packages and finalising the budget.

LEVERAGES

Leverage, as a business term, refers to debt or to borrowing funds to finance the purchase of inventory, equipment and other company assets. Business owners can use either debt or equity to finance or buy the company's assets. Using debt, or leverage, increases the company's risk of bankruptcy - but, it also can increase the company's profits and returns; specifically its return on equity. This is true because if debt financing is used rather than equity financing then the owner's equity is not diluted by issuing more shares of stock.

Borrowing in order to expand or invest is called leverage because the goal is to amplify the loan into a greater value for the firm or investors.

With debt financing, regardless if whether the interest charges are from a loan or line of credit, the interest payments are tax deductible. In addition, by making timely payments a company will establish a positive payment history and business credit rating.

Investors in a business prefer the business to use debt financing but only up to a point. Beyond a certain point, investors get nervous about too much debt financing as it drives up the company's default risk.

There are three types of leverage

Operating Leverage

Breakeven analysis shows us that there are essentially two types of costs in a company's cost structure – fixed costs and variable costs. Operating leverage refers to the percentage of fixed costs that a company has. Stated another way, operating leverage is the ratio of fixed costs to variable costs. If a business firm has a lot of fixed costs as compared to variable costs, then the firm is said to have high operating leverage. These firms use a lot of fixed costs in their business and are capital intensive firms.

A good example of capital intensive business firm are the automobile manufacturing companies. They have a huge amount of equipment that is required to manufacture their product - automobiles. When the economy slows down and fewer people are buying new cars, the auto companies still have to pay their fixed costs such as overhead on the plants that house the equipment, depreciation on the equipment, and other fixed costs associated with a capital intensive firm. An economic slowdown will hurt a capital intensive firm much more than a company not quite so capital intensive.

You can compare the operating leverage for a capital intensive firm, which would be high, to the operating leverage for a labor intensive firm, which would be lower. A labor intensive firm is one in which more human capital is required in the production process. Mining is considered labor intensive because much of the money involved in mining goes to paying the workers. Service companies that make up much of our economy, such as restaurants or hotels, are labor intensive as well. They all require more labor in the production process than capital costs.

In difficult economic times, firms that are labor intensive typically have an easier time surviving than capital intensive firms.

What does operating leverage really mean? It means that if a firm has high operating leverage, a small change in sales volume results in a large change in EBIT and ROIC, return on invested capital. In other words, firms with high operating leverage are very sensitive to changes in sales and it affects their bottom line quickly.

Business Risk

Business risk is just one portion of the risk that determines a business firm's future return on equity. Business risk is the risk that a firm's shareholders face if the firm has no debt. It is the risk inherent in the firm's operations. It rises from economic uncertainty which leads to uncertainty about future profits and capital requirements.

One component of business risk is variability in product demand. Customers always have to have food so in difficult economic times, the Public grocery store chain will have less product variability than Ford Motor Company. Customers don't have to buy new cars during periods of economic uncertainty. Most business firms also have variability in product sales prices and input costs. Firms that are slower to bring new products to market expose themselves to more business risk. Think of the American automobile companies.

Foreign car companies brought fuel efficient cars to market faster than American car companies, exposing them to more business risk.

If a business firm has high fixed costs and their costs do not decline as demand declines, then the firm has high operating leverage which means high business risk.

Financial Leverage

Financial leverage refers to the amount of debt in the capital structure of the business firm. If you can envision a balance sheet, financial leverage refers to the right-hand side of the balance sheet. Operating leverage refers to the left-hand side of the balance sheet - the plant and equipment side. Operating leverage determines the mix of fixed assets or plant and equipment used by the business firm. Financial leverage refers to how the firm will pay for it or how the operation will be financed.

As discussed earlier in this article, the use of financial leverage, or debt, in financing a firm's operations, can really improve the firm's return on equity and earnings per share. This is because the firm is not diluting the owner's earnings by using equity financing. Too much financial leverage, however, can lead to the risk of default and bankruptcy.

One of the financial ratios we use in determining the amount of financial leverage we have in a business firm is the debt/equity ratio. The debt/equity ratio shows the proportion of debt in a business firm to equity.

Combined Leverage

Combined, or total, leverage is the total amount of risk facing a business firm. It can also be looked at in another way. It is the total amount of leverage that we can use to magnify the returns from our business. Operating leverage magnifies the returns from our plant and equipment or fixed assets. Financial leverage magnifies the returns from our debt financing. Combined leverage is the total of these two types of leverage or the total magnification of returns. This is looking at leverage from a balance sheet perspective.

It is also helpful and important to look at leverage from an income statement perspective. Operating leverage influences the top half of the income statement and operating income, determining return from operations. Financial leverage influences the bottom half of the income statement and the earnings per share to the stockholders.

The concept of leverage, in general, is used in breakeven analysis and in the development of the capital structure of a business firm.

EBIT–EPS ANALYSIS

EBIT-EPS analysis is a technique used to determine the optimal capital structure in which the value of earnings per share (EPS) has the highest amount for a given amount of earnings before interest and taxes (EBIT). In other words, the objective of EBIT-EPS analysis is to determine the effect of using different sources of financing on EPS.

EBIT-EPS indifference point is an important tool used to choose between two alternative financing plans. The formula to calculate it is as follows:

$$\frac{(\text{EBIT}-1_A)(1-T)-PD_A}{S_A}=\frac{(\text{EBIT}-1_B)(1-T)-PD_B}{S_B}$$

where:

EBIT – earnings before interest and taxes

I_A – interest expense in financing plan A

I_B – interest expense in financing plan B

T – corporate income tax rate

PD_A – preferred dividends payable in financing plan A

PD_B – preferred dividends payable in financing plan B

S_A – amount of common stock outstanding in financing plan A

S_B – amount of common stock outstanding in financing plan B

The indifference point is the value of EBIT where both financing plans would bring the same EPS. In other words, there is no difference in the two alternative financing plans.

EBIT-EPS Graph

Let's assume that management of a company is considering two alternative capital structures.

Financing plan A with high financial leverage (debt financing)

Financing plan B with low financial leverage (equity financing)

The EBIT-EPS graph for both alternative capital structures is given in the figure below.

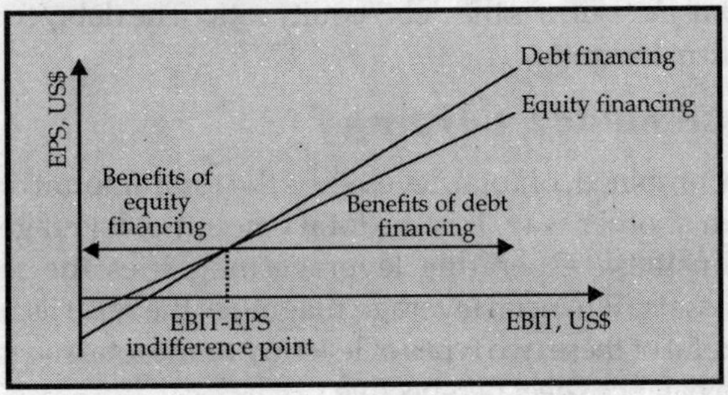

When EBIT reaches the EBIT-EPS indifference point, both financing plans generate equal EPS. However, if EBIT has a lower value, equity financing will generate higher EPS than debt financing. For any value of EBIT to the right of the indifference point, debt financing will give a higher value of EPS because of a higher degree of financial leverage.

Example

Management of Total S.E. Inc. is considering two alternative financing plans. The detailed information is given in the table below.

	Plan A	Plan B
Common stock	\$15,000,000	\$8,000,000
Preferred stock	\$3,000,000	\$2,000,000
Long-term debt	\$5,000,000	\$13,000,000

The par value of common stock is \$10, preferred stock has \$100 par value and 15% dividend, and long-term debt is presented by 10-year bonds of \$1,000 par value and a fixed annual coupon rate of 8%. The corporate income tax rate is 30%.

The first step of EBIT-EPS analysis is to find the indifference point. Thus, we have to calculate interest expense and preferred dividends for each financing plan.

$I_A = \$5,000,000 \times 8\% = \$400,000$

$I_B = \$13,000,000 \times 8\% = 1,040,000$

$PD_A = \$3,000,000 \times 15\% = \$450,000$

$PD_B = \$2,000,000 \times 15\% = \$300,000$

$S_A = \$15,000,000 \div 10 = 1,500,000$

$S_B = \$8,000,000 \div 10 = 800,000$

Let's make an equation using the data above.

$$\frac{(\text{EBIT} - \$400,000)(1-0.3) - \$450,000}{1,500,000} = \frac{(\text{EBIT} - \$1,040,000)(1-0.3) - \$300,000}{800,000}$$

Having solved this equation, we get an indifference point of $1,955,102, that is, for such a value of EBIT, each financing plan will give the same earnings per share of $0.4257. The EBIT-EPS graph is shown below.

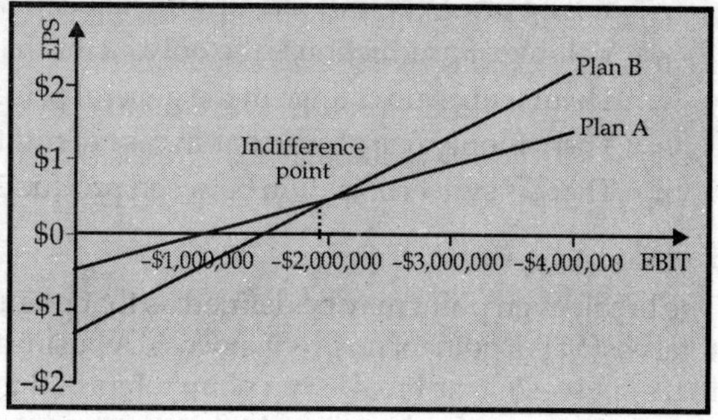

If the expected EBIT is lower than $1,955,102, financing plan A will demonstrate a higher EPS. Otherwise, the capital structure of financing plan B should be preferred.

Advantages and Disadvantages of EBIT-EPS Analysis

Advantages

- **Financial planning.** Applying EBIT-EPS analysis allows earnings per share to be maximized for any given value of earnings before interest and taxes. It helps to choose the best financing plan.
- **Comparative analysis.** Such analysis is possible not only for a company as a whole but also for a specific product, project, department, or market.
- **Determination of target capital structure.** Depending on the expected EBIT, management of a company is able to determine the target capital structure for maximizing EPS.

Disadvantages

- **Risk is not taken into account.** EBIT-EPS analysis does not take into account the risks associated with debt financing. In other words, a higher EPS associated with using financial leverage implies a higher risk that has to be taken into account by management.
- **Complexity.** The more alternative financing plans are considered, the higher the complexity of the calculations.
- **Limitations.** The technique does not account for limitations in raising various sources of financing.

Break-even Analysis

The study of cost-volume-profit analysis is often referred to as 'break-even analysis' and the two terms are used interchangeably by many. This is so, because break-even analysis is the most widely known form of cost-volume-profit analysis. The term 'break-even analysis' is used in two senses-narrow sense and broad sense. In its broad sense, break-even analysis refers to the study of relationship between costs, volume and profit at different levels of sales or production. In its narrow sense, it refers to a technique of determining that level of operations where total revenues equal total expenses, *i.e.*, the point of no profit, no loss.

Assumptions of Break-even Analysis

The break-even analysis is based upon the following assumptions:

(i) All elements of cost, *i.e.*, production, administration and selling and distribution can be segregated into fixed and variable components.

(ii) Variable cost remains constant per unit of output irrespective of the level of output and thus fluctuates directly in proportion to changes-in the volume of output.

(iii) Fixed cost remains constant at all volumes of output.

(iv) Selling price per unit remains unchanged or constant at all levels of output.

(v) Volume of production is the only factor that influences cost.

(vi) There will be no change in the general price-level.

(vii) There is only one product or in case of multi-products, the sales mix remains unchanged.

(viii) There is synchronisation between production and sales.

Break Even Point

The break-even point may be defined as that point of sales volume at which total revenue is equal to total cost. It is a point of no profit, no loss. A business is said to break-even when its total sales are equal to its total costs. The break-even point refers to that level of output which evenly breaks the costs and revenues and hence the name. At this point, contribution, i.e., sales minus marginal cost, equals the fixed costs and hence this point is often called as 'Critical Point', or 'Equilibrium Point, or 'Balancing Point' or no profit, no loss. If production/sales is increased beyond this level, there shall be profit to the organisation and if it is decrease from this level, there shall be loss to the organisation.

Break-even point can be stated in the form of an equation:

Sales revenue at break-even point = Fixed Costs + Variable Costs.

Computation of the Break-even Point

The break-even point can be computed by the following methods:

(i) The Algebraic Formula Method and

(ii) Graphic or Chart Method.

Algebraic Formula Method For Computing The Break-even Point

The break-even point can be computed in terms of:

(a) **Break-even Point in Units.** As the break-even point is the point of no profit, no loss, it is that level of output at which the total contribution equals the total fixed costs. It can be calculated with the help of following formula:

$$\text{Break - Even Point} = \frac{\text{Fixed Cost}}{\text{Selling Price per unit} - \text{Variable Cost per unit}}$$

$$= \frac{\text{Fixed Cost}}{\text{Contribution per unit}}$$

(b) **Break-even Point in terms of budget-total or money value**

At break-even point:

$$\text{Total Sales} = \text{Total Fixed Cost} + \text{Total Variable Cost}$$

or $$S = F + V$$

(where S = Sales, F = Fixed Cost and V = Variable cost)

or $$S - V = F$$

or $$\frac{S-V}{S-V} = \frac{F}{S-V} \quad \text{(Dividing both sides by S – V)}$$

or $$1 = \frac{F}{S-V}$$

or $$S \times 1 = \frac{F \times S}{S - V}$$ (Multiplying both sides by S)

Hence, break-even sales

$$= \frac{\text{Fixed Cost}}{\text{Sales} - \text{Variables Cost}} \times \text{Sales}$$

$$= \frac{\text{Fixed Cost}}{\text{Contribution}} \times \text{Sales}$$

With the use of P/V Ratio,

$$\text{B.E.P.} = \frac{\text{Fixed Cost}}{\text{P/V ratio}}$$

As, $$\frac{\text{Contribution}}{\text{Sales}} = \text{P/V ratio}$$

(c) **Break-even Point as a percentage of estimated capacity.** Break-even point can also be computed as a percentage of the estimated sales or capacity by dividing the break-even sales by the capacity sales. For example, if a firm has an estimated capacity of 1,00,000 units of products and its break-even point is reached at 50,000 units, then the break-even point is at 50% of capacity (1,00,000/50,000). If information as to total contribution at full capacity is available, the break-even point as a percentage of estimated capacity can be found as under:

$$\text{B.E.P (as \% age of capacity)} = \frac{\text{Fixed Cost}}{\text{Total Contribution}}$$

Cash Break-even Point

In the present competitive world of business, it may be difficult for new industrial units to achieve the break-even point in the initial years. Thus, the concept of cash break-even point has emerged. The cash break-even point may be defined as that point of sales volume at which total revenue is equal to total cash cost. At this point, cash contribution (which is calculated after making adjustment for variable portion of depreciation, *etc.*) equals the cash fixed cost, *i.e.*, fixed cost excluding depreciation and deferred expenses. This point enables the management to determine the level of activity below which the liquidity position of the firm would be adversely affected. Thus, cash break-even point may be calculated as below:

$$\text{Cash Break-Even Point (in Units)} = \frac{\text{Cash Fixed Cost}}{\text{Cash Contribution per unit}}$$

Composite Break-even Point

So far we have dealt with break-even point of firms producing single product. We can also calculate the composite break-even point for a firm producing several products, as below :

$$\text{Composite Break-Even} = \frac{\text{Total Fixed Cost}}{\text{Cash Contribution per unit}}$$

(in Sales value)

and, $$\text{Composite P/V Ratio} = \frac{\text{Total Contribution}}{\text{Total Sales}} \times 100$$

Graphic Method of Break-even Analysis or Break-even Chart

The break-even point can also be computed graphically. A break-even chart is a graphical representation of marginal costing. The break-even chart 'Portrays a pictorial view of the relationships between costs, volume and profits.' It shows the break-even point and also indicates the estimated profit or loss at various levels of output. The break-even point as indicated in the chart is the point at which the total cost line and the total sales line intersect.

Assumptions Underlying Break-even Charts

There are a number of assumptions which are made while drawing a break-even chart, such as:

(i) All costs can be separated into fixed and variable costs.
(ii) Fixed costs remain constant at all levels of activity.
(iii) Variable cost fluctuates directly in proportion to changes in the volume of output.
(iv) Selling prices per unit remain constant at all levels of activity.
(v) There is no opening or closing stock.
(vi) There will be no change in operating efficiency.
(vii) Product mix remains unchanged or there is only one product.
(viii) The volume of output or production is the only factor which influences the cost.

Advantages or Uses of Break-even Charts

Computation of break-even point or presentation of cost, volume and profit relationship by way of break-even charts has the following advantages:

(a) Information provided by the break-even chart is in a simple form and is clearly understandable even to a layman. The whole idea of the problem is presented at a glance.
(b) The break-even chart is very useful to the management for taking managerial decisions because the chart studies the relationship of cost, volume and profit at various levels of output. The effects of changes in fixed costs and variables costs at various levels of output and that of changes in the selling price on the profits can be depicted very clearly by way of break-even charts.
(c) The break-even charts help in knowing and analysing the profitability of different products under various circumstances.
(d) A break-even chart is very useful for forecasting (the costs and profits), planning and growth.
(e) The break-even chart is a managerial tool for control of costs as it shows the relative importance of fixed cost in the total cost of a product.
(f) Besides determining the break-even point, profits at various levels of output can also be determined with the help of break-even charts.
(g) The break-even charts can also be used to study the comparative plant efficiencies of business.

MULTIPLE CHOICE QUESTIONS

1. What is the fundamental accounting equation?
   (a) Assets = Liabilities + Revenue
   (b) Assets = Liabilities + Owner's Equity
   (c) Revenue = Expenses
   (d) Assets = Revenue – Expenses
2. Which accounting principle requires that financial information be recorded based on actual transactions and supported by source documents?
   (a) Matching Principle
   (b) Consistency Principle
   (c) Revenue Recognition Principle
   (d) Historical Cost Principle
3. According to the accrual basis of accounting, when should revenue be recognized?
   (a) When cash is received
   (b) When goods are delivered
   (c) When it is earned and realizable
   (d) When an invoice is issued
4. What is the purpose of the consistency principle in accounting?
   (a) To ensure that financial statements are free from errors
   (b) To maintain the same accounting methods from one period to the next
   (c) To record expenses in the same period as the related revenues
   (d) To match revenues with expenses
5. What accounting standard-setting body is responsible for creating Generally Accepted Accounting Principles (GAAP) in the United States?
   (a) International Financial Reporting Standards (IFRS)
   (b) Internal Revenue Service (IRS)
   (c) Financial Accounting Standards Board (FASB)
   (d) Generally Accepted Auditing Standards (GAAS)
6. Which financial statement provides a snapshot of a company's financial position at a specific point in time?
   (a) Income Statement
   (b) Cash Flow Statement
   (c) Balance Sheet
   (d) Statement of Retained Earnings
7. The Going Concern Assumption in accounting suggests that
   (a) Companies should always assume they are going out of business.
   (b) Companies should continue to operate indefinitely.
   (c) Companies should prepare for bankruptcy.
   (d) Companies should focus on short-term profitability.
8. Which accounting principle dictates that assets and liabilities should be initially recorded at their original purchase price?
   (a) Revenue Recognition Principle
   (b) Matching Principle
   (c) Historical Cost Principle
   (d) Materiality Principle
9. The income statement reports
   (a) A company's financial position at a specific date.
   (b) A company's cash flows from operating, investing, and financing activities.
   (c) A company's revenues, expenses, and net income over a specific period.
   (d) A company's equity at a specific date.
10. Which accounting principle requires that companies disclose all relevant information that could impact financial statement users' decisions?
    (a) Full Disclosure Principle
    (b) Materiality Principle
    (c) Going Concern Assumption
    (d) Consistency Principle
11. What financial statement shows a company's revenues and expenses over a specific period?
    (a) Balance Sheet
    (b) Statement of Retained Earnings

(c) Income Statement
(d) Cash Flow Statement

12. In the income statement, which of the following is calculated by subtracting expenses from revenues?
(a) Assets (b) Liabilities
(c) Net Income (d) Owner's Equity

13. What is the formula for calculating net income in the income statement?
(a) Net Income = Revenues - Expenses
(b) Net Income = Assets - Liabilities
(c) Net Income = Owner's Equity - Revenues
(d) Net Income = Liabilities - Expenses

14. The balance sheet equation is often expressed as
(a) Assets = Liabilities
(b) Assets - Owner's Equity = Liabilities
(c) Assets = Liabilities + Owner's Equity
(d) Liabilities = Owner's Equity

15. Which financial statement displays a company's assets, liabilities, and owner's equity at a specific point in time?
(a) Cash Flow Statement
(b) Statement of Retained Earnings
(c) Income Statement
(d) Balance Sheet

16. What is the primary purpose of the statement of cash flows?
(a) To report a company's financial position
(b) To disclose all relevant information
(c) To provide information about a company's cash inflows and outflows
(d) To summarize a company's revenues and expenses

17. The statement of retained earnings shows changes in
(a) A company's cash balance
(b) A company's income statement
(c) Owner's equity during a specific period
(d) A company's liabilities

18. The statement of cash flows is typically divided into three sections, which are
(a) Assets, Liabilities, and Owner's Equity
(b) Operating Activities, Investing Activities, and Financing Activities
(c) Revenues, Expenses, and Net Income
(d) Assets, Expenses, and Liabilities

19. Which section of the statement of cash flows includes cash flows related to the purchase and sale of long-term assets such as property and equipment?
(a) Operating Activities
(b) Investing Activities
(c) Financing Activities
(d) Reconciliation Activities

20. Which financial statement shows the change in owner's equity over a specific period?
(a) Income Statement
(b) Cash Flow Statement
(c) Balance Sheet
(d) Statement of Retained Earnings

21. What is the formula for calculating owner's equity in the balance sheet?
(a) Owner's Equity = Assets - Liabilities
(b) Owner's Equity = Liabilities - Assets
(c) Owner's Equity = Revenues - Expenses
(d) Owner's Equity = Net Income - Dividends

22. Which financial statement is used to reconcile the beginning and ending balances of retained earnings?
(a) Cash Flow Statement
(b) Income Statement
(c) Balance Sheet
(d) Statement of Retained Earnings

23. In the statement of cash flows, which section includes cash flows related to obtaining funds from investors and repaying those funds?
(a) Operating Activities
(b) Investing Activities
(c) Financing Activities
(d) Reconciliation Activities

24. What is the primary purpose of the notes to the financial statements in an annual report?
(a) To provide detailed explanations and additional information about the financial statements
(b) To summarize the income statement
(c) To disclose the company's cash flows
(d) To provide information about the company's organizational structure

25. The income statement, balance sheet, and statement of cash flows are collectively known as
(a) The financial statement trifecta
(b) The earnings reports
(c) The notes to the financial statements
(d) The statement of retained earnings

26. What does the current ratio measure?
(a) A company's ability to meet short-term obligations
(b) A company's profitability
(c) A company's long-term debt
(d) A company's market share

27. The debt-to-equity ratio is a measure of
(a) Liquidity (b) Profitability
(c) Financial leverage (d) Market value

28. What does the return on assets (ROA) ratio measure?
(a) A company's ability to generate profit from its assets
(b) A company's liquidity
(c) A company's debt level
(d) A company's market share

29. The quick ratio excludes which of the following from current assets?
(a) Cash (b) Inventory
(c) Accounts receivable
(d) Prepaid expenses

30. Which ratio indicates a company's ability to cover its interest expenses with operating income?
(a) Debt ratio
(b) Times interest earned
(c) Return on assets (d) Asset turnover

31. The price-to-earnings (P/E) ratio is used to assess
(a) Liquidity (b) Profitability
(c) Valuation (d) Financial leverage

32. What does the inventory turnover ratio measure?
(a) How quickly a company collects accounts receivable
(b) How efficiently a company manages its inventory
(c) The company's ability to pay off debt
(d) The company's overall profitability

33. The earnings per share (EPS) ratio is calculated as
(a) Net income divided by total assets
(b) Net income divided by total equity
(c) Net income divided by the number of outstanding shares
(d) Total assets divided by total equity

34. The current ratio is calculated as
(a) Current assets divided by current liabilities
(b) Total assets divided by total liabilities
(c) Net income divided by total assets
(d) Total assets divided by total equity

35. Which ratio measures a company's ability to generate profit relative to its revenue?
(a) Debt-to-equity ratio
(b) Return on equity (ROE)
(c) Asset turnover
(d) Price-to-earnings (P/E) ratio

36. What does a funds flow statement primarily explain?
(a) A company's income and expenses
(b) Changes in a company's financial position over time
(c) A company's cash inflows and outflows during a specific period
(d) A company's market share

37. In a cash flow statement, which section reports the cash generated or used by the company's core operating activities?
(a) Investing activities
(b) Financing activities
(c) Operating activities
(d) Non-operating activities

38. What does a positive cash flow from operating activities indicate?
(a) The company is generating cash from its core operations
(b) The company is incurring significant debt
(c) The company is investing heavily in new projects
(d) The company is experiencing a decline in sales

39. The indirect method of preparing a cash flow statement starts with which item from the income statement?
(a) Net income (b) Total revenue
(c) Total expenses (d) Earnings per share

40. What does free cash flow represent?
(a) Cash available to pay dividends to shareholders
(b) Cash available to invest in new projects or pay down debt
(c) Cash reserved for operating expenses
(d) Cash spent on non-operating activities

41. DuPont Analysis decomposes return on equity (ROE) into which two key components?
(a) Net income and revenue
(b) Profit margin and asset turnover
(c) Liquidity and solvency
(d) Debt and equity

42. What does the profit margin component of DuPont Analysis measure?
(a) A company's liquidity
(b) A company's efficiency in using assets
(c) A company's net income as a percentage of revenue
(d) A company's financial leverage

43. The asset turnover component of DuPont Analysis measures
(a) A company's ability to generate profit from its assets
(b) A company's net income as a percentage of revenue
(c) A company's liquidity
(d) A company's efficiency in using assets

44. DuPont Analysis helps to identify the key drivers of a company's
(a) Revenue (b) Profitability
(c) Total assets (d) Market share

45. In DuPont Analysis, how is return on equity (ROE) calculated?
(a) ROE = Profit margin × Asset turnover
(b) ROE = Net income ÷ Total equity
(c) ROE = Total assets × Total equity
(d) ROE = Current assets ÷ Current liabilities

46. What is the main purpose of preparing a cost sheet in accounting?
(a) To calculate profit
(b) To record revenue
(c) To estimate future costs
(d) To analyze cost elements

47. The total of direct material cost and direct labor cost is known as
(a) Variable cost (b) Prime cost
(c) Overhead cost (d) Total cost

48. Which of the following costs would typically be included in the prime cost?
(a) Manufacturing overhead
(b) Administrative expenses
(c) Direct materials
(d) Sales and marketing expenses

49. What is the formula for calculating the cost of goods manufactured (COGM)?
(a) Opening finished goods inventory + Purchases - Ending finished goods inventory
(b) Opening work in process inventory + Direct materials used + Direct labor + Manufacturing overhead - Ending work in pro cess inventory
(c) Opening raw materials inventory + Raw materials purchased - Ending raw materials inventory
(d) Sales - Gross profit

50. Indirect materials, indirect labor, and manufacturing overhead are typically classified as
(a) Variable costs (b) Prime costs
(c) Conversion costs (d) Direct costs

51. Marginal costing is also known as
(a) Absorption costing
(b) Variable costing
(c) Fixed costing (d) Direct costing

52. In marginal costing, which of the following costs are treated as fixed costs?
(a) Direct materials
(b) Direct labor
(c) Variable manufacturing overhead
(d) Fixed manufacturing overhead

53. The contribution margin is calculated as
(a) Sales revenue - Variable costs
(b) Sales revenue - Total costs
(c) Sales revenue - Fixed costs
(d) Gross profit - Variable costs

54. In marginal costing, which of the following costs are deducted to calculate the contribution margin?
(a) Variable costs (b) Fixed costs
(c) Total costs (d) Semi-variable costs

55. What is the break-even point in terms of sales revenue?
(a) The point at which total costs equal total revenue
(b) The point at which variable costs equal total costs
(c) The point at which fixed costs equal variable costs
(d) The point at which total costs equal zero

56. What is the main objective of cost-volume-profit (CVP) analysis?
(a) To calculate the break-even point
(b) To calculate the contribution margin
(c) To estimate future costs
(d) To prepare a cost sheet

57. The contribution margin ratio is calculated as
(a) Sales revenue ÷ Variable costs
(b) Variable costs ÷ Total costs
(c) Contribution margin ÷ Sales revenue
(d) Total costs ÷ Sales revenue

58. At the break-even point, the net profit is
(a) Zero (b) Negative
(c) Equal to fixed costs
(d) Equal to variable costs

59. In CVP analysis, which of the following is an assumption?
(a) Fixed costs change with changes in production
(b) Variable costs remain constant per unit

(c) Sales mix remains constant
(d) There is no selling price variance

60. What does the margin of safety represent in CVP analysis?
(a) The difference between actual sales and the break-even point
(b) The profit earned above the break-even point
(c) The difference between actual sales and the target sales
(d) The total sales revenue

61. If the contribution margin ratio is 40%, the variable cost ratio is
(a) 60% (b) 40%
(c) 20% (d) 100%

62. The degree of operating leverage (DOL) is calculated as
(a) Contribution margin ÷ Net profit
(b) Sales ÷ Contribution margin
(c) Net profit ÷ Contribution margin
(d) Contribution margin ÷ Fixed costs

63. What is the primary limitation of cost-volume-profit (CVP) analysis?
(a) It assumes fixed costs are constant
(b) It does not consider variable costs
(c) It does not account for changes in sales mix
(d) It is not applicable to service industries

64. What is the breakeven point in units?
(a) The number of units that need to be sold to cover all fixed costs
(b) The point at which total costs equal total revenue
(c) The point at which variable costs equal total costs
(d) The point at which total costs equal zero

65. In CVP analysis, the contribution margin is calculated as
(a) Sales revenue - Fixed costs
(b) Sales revenue - Variable costs
(c) Sales revenue - Total costs
(d) Gross profit - Fixed costs

66. What is standard costing?
(a) A cost accounting method for historical costs
(b) A system used to track actual costs
(c) A budgeting technique
(d) A predetermined cost for a unit of product or service

67. Which of the following is a key benefit of using standard costing?
(a) It simplifies accounting processes
(b) It encourages cost reduction efforts
(c) It eliminates the need for budgets
(d) It provides historical cost data

68. In standard costing, what is the "standard cost"?
(a) The actual cost incurred
(b) The projected cost
(c) The budgeted cost
(d) The predetermined cost

69. What is a "standard cost card" in the context of standard costing?
(a) A document that records actual costs
(b) A summary of actual expenses
(c) A record of historical data
(d) A document that contains standard costs for each element of production

70. Which of the following is not typically included in a standard cost for a product?
(a) Direct materials cost
(b) Direct labor cost
(c) Variable overhead cost
(d) Fixed overhead cost

71. What is a "cost variance" in the context of variance analysis?
(a) The actual cost incurred
(b) The difference between actual and standard costs
(c) The projected cost
(d) The standard cost

72. A "favorable variance" in variance analysis indicates that
(a) Actual costs exceeded standard costs
(b) Actual costs were equal to standard costs
(c) Actual costs were less than standard costs
(d) Standard costs were not established

73. What does the term "price variance" refer to in variance analysis?
(a) The difference between actual and budgeted prices
(b) The difference between actual and standard prices
(c) The difference between actual and projected prices
(d) The difference between actual and estimated prices

74. In variance analysis, the "efficiency variance" is also known as the
(a) Quantity variance (b) Rate variance
(c) Mix variance (d) Yield variance

75. What does the "total variance" in variance analysis represent?
(a) The sum of all variances
(b) The difference between actual and budgeted costs
(c) The difference between actual and standard costs
(d) The difference between actual and projected costs

76. The formula for calculating the total cost variance is
(a) Total Cost Variance = Actual Cost - Standard Cost
(b) Total Cost Variance = Standard Cost - Actual Cost
(c) Total Cost Variance = Budgeted Cost - Actual Cost
(d) Total Cost Variance = Actual Cost - Budgeted Cost

77. Which variance is calculated by comparing actual hours worked to standard hours allowed for the actual level of production?
(a) Direct materials efficiency variance
(b) Direct labor efficiency variance
(c) Variable overhead rate variance
(d) Fixed overhead volume variance

78. In a variance analysis report, what does the "variance analysis" section typically include?
(a) The actual costs incurred
(b) A comparison of actual to budgeted costs
(c) A breakdown of cost components
(d) The standard costs established for the year

79. What is the primary purpose of conducting variance analysis?
(a) To set standard costs for products
(b) To assess the financial performance of a company
(c) To allocate overhead costs
(d) To evaluate differences between actual and expected results

80. In variance analysis, what does a "mix variance" indicate?
(a) A difference in the quantity of materials used
(b) A difference in the rate of labor
(c) A difference in the cost of materials
(d) A difference in the volume of production

81. The "yield variance" in variance analysis is related to which of the following elements of production?
(a) Direct materials
(b) Direct labor
(c) Variable overhead
(d) Fixed overhead

82. What is the formula for calculating the materials quantity variance?
(a) Materials Quantity Variance = (Actual Quantity x Actual Price) - (Standard Quantity x Standard Price)
(b) Materials Quantity Variance = (Standard Quantity x Actual Price) - (Actual Quantity x Standard Price)
(c) Materials Quantity Variance = (Actual Quantity x Actual Price) + (Standard Quantity x Standard Price)
(d) Materials Quantity Variance = (Actual Quantity x Standard Price) - (Standard Quantity x Actual Price)

83. The formula for calculating the labor rate variance is
(a) Labor Rate Variance = (Actual Rate x Actual Hours) - (Standard Rate x Actual Hours)
(b) Labor Rate Variance = (Standard Rate x Actual Hours) - (Actual Rate x Actual Hours)
(c) Labor Rate Variance = (Actual Rate x Actual Hours) + (Standard Rate x Standard Hours)
(d) Labor Rate Variance = (Actual Rate x Standard Hours) - (Standard Rate x Actual Hours)

84. What is the formula for calculating the variable overhead spending variance?
(a) Variable Overhead Spending Variance = (Actual Overhead Rate x Actual Hours) - (Standard Overhead Rate x Actual Hours)
(b) Variable Overhead Spending Variance = (Standard Overhead Rate x Actual Hours) - (Actual Overhead Rate x Actual Hours)
(c) Variable Overhead Spending Variance = (Actual Overhead Rate x Actual Hours) + (Standard Overhead Rate x Standard Hours)
(d) Variable Overhead Spending Variance = (Actual Overhead Rate x Standard Hours) - (Standard Overhead Rate x Actual Hours)

85. In variance analysis, the fixed overhead volume variance is calculated as the difference between actual and budgeted
(a) Overhead costs
(b) Overhead hours

(c) Overhead rate
(d) Overhead allocation

86. What is the primary goal of financial management?
(a) Maximizing shareholder wealth
(b) Maximizing revenue
(c) Minimizing expenses
(d) Maximizing market share

87. Which financial management concept involves allocating resources among different investment opportunities?
(a) Capital budgeting
(b) Financial leverage
(c) Working capital management
(d) Risk management

88. Financial management encompasses which of the following areas?
(a) Marketing and sales
(b) Human resources
(c) Operations and production
(d) All of the above

89. The concept of time value of money is a fundamental principle in financial management. What does it refer to?
(a) The idea that money is worth more in the future than it is today
(b) The idea that money is worth less in the future than it is today
(c) The concept of compound interest
(d) The concept of simple interest

90. What is the role of a Chief Financial Officer (CFO) in an organization?
(a) Overseeing marketing activities
(b) Managing day-to-day operations
(c) Managing financial strategies and reporting
(d) Managing human resources

91. Which financial management function involves determining the company's capital structure?
(a) Capital budgeting
(b) Risk management
(c) Capital structure management
(d) Working capital management

92. Working capital management primarily deals with the management of
(a) Long-term investments
(b) Short-term assets and liabilities
(c) Debt financing
(d) Equity financing

93. Capital budgeting is a financial management function related to
(a) Managing day-to-day cash flows
(b) Making long-term investment decisions
(c) Managing short-term liabilities
(d) Monitoring financial ratios

94. Which financial management function is responsible for managing the company's credit policies and collections?
(a) Capital budgeting
(b) Risk management
(c) Capital structure management
(d) Accounts receivable management

95. Risk management in financial management involves
(a) Maximizing risks to achieve higher returns
(b) Minimizing risks to protect assets and investments
(c) Ignoring potential risks
(d) Speculating on volatile markets

96. The concept of "liquidity management" in financial management refers to
(a) Managing long-term investments
(b) Managing short-term assets and liabilities
(c) Managing marketing strategies
(d) Managing long-term debt

97. In financial management, what is the primary focus of capital structure management?
(a) Managing the company's investments
(b) Managing the company's short-term cash flows
(c) Determining the mix of debt and equity in the company's financing
(d) Managing the company's working capital

98. Which financial management function is associated with assessing and managing risks that may affect the company's financial performance?
(a) Capital budgeting
(b) Risk management
(c) Capital structure management
(d) Accounts payable management

99. The process of determining the financial needs of a company and acquiring the necessary capital is called
(a) Capital budgeting
(b) Risk management
(c) Financial planning
(d) Financial analysis

100. What is the primary purpose of financial analysis in financial management?
(a) To prepare financial statements
(b) To determine capital structure
(c) To assess the company's financial health and performance
(d) To calculate the time value of money

101. Which financial management function involves determining how the company will finance its operations and investments?
(a) Capital budgeting
(b) Risk management
(c) Capital structure management
(d) Accounts receivable management

102. In financial management, what does "capital budgeting" primarily focus on?
(a) Managing the company's cash flows
(b) Managing short-term investments
(c) Evaluating long-term investment projects
(d) Evaluating marketing strategies

103. Accounts payable management in financial management primarily deals with
(a) Managing long-term debt
(b) Managing short-term liabilities
(c) Managing marketing expenses
(d) Managing equity financing

104. What is the primary objective of working capital management?
(a) To maximize long-term investments
(b) To minimize short-term liabilities
(c) To maintain adequate liquidity for daily operations
(d) To maximize shareholder wealth

105. Which financial management function focuses on the management of day-to-day cash flows, such as collections and disbursements?
(a) Capital budgeting
(b) Risk management
(c) Capital structure management
(d) Cash flow management

106. According to the Modigliani and Miller Proposition I, in a world without taxes, the value of a firm is independent of its capital structure. What concept does this illustrate?
(a) The trade-off theory
(b) The pecking order theory
(c) The financial leverage theory
(d) The irrelevance theory

107. The trade-off theory of capital structure suggests that firms
(a) Should aim to have no debt in their capital structure
(b) Should use as much debt as possible to maximize value
(c) Should find an optimal balance between debt and equity
(d) Should rely solely on equity financing

108. According to the pecking order theory, firms prefer to finance new investments in the following order. What is the correct sequence?
(a) Debt, internal funds, equity
(b) Equity, debt, internal funds
(c) Equity, internal funds, debt
(d) Internal funds, equity, debt

109. The weighted average cost of capital (WACC) is calculated as the weighted sum of the cost of
(a) Equity financing
(b) Debt financing
(c) Both equity and debt financing
(d) Internal financing

110. The cost of debt is typically lower for a company if it
(a) Has a high credit rating
(b) Has a low credit rating
(c) Is a startup company
(d) Has no outstanding debt

111. Which of the following is NOT a component of a company's cost of equity?
(a) Dividend yield
(b) Risk-free rate
(c) Market risk premium
(d) Interest expense

112. The after-tax cost of debt is calculated by
(a) Multiplying the nominal interest rate by (1 - tax rate)
(b) Adding the nominal interest rate to the tax rate
(c) Subtracting the tax rate from the nominal interest rate
(d) Dividing the tax rate by the nominal interest rate

113. Which component of the cost of equity is based on the expected capital gains from holding the stock?
(a) Dividend yield (b) Risk-free rate
(c) Market risk premium
(d) Capital gains rate

114. Which source of finance allows a company to raise funds by selling a portion of the ownership in the company?

(a) Debt financing
(b) Equity financing
(c) Internal financing
(d) Hybrid financing

115. What is the primary advantage of issuing equity as a source of finance?
(a) It requires no repayment of principal or interest
(b) It is a tax-deductible expense
(c) It has a fixed maturity date
(d) It carries lower risk

116. Internal financing, also known as retained earnings, is obtained from
(a) Selling shares to the public
(b) Borrowing from banks
(c) The company's profits and savings
(d) Selling assets

117. The decision to invest in long-term assets and projects is referred to as
(a) Working capital management
(b) Capital budgeting
(c) Equity financing
(d) Debt restructuring

118. The capital structure decision involves determining the mix of
(a) Short-term and long-term debt
(b) Debt and equity financing
(c) Common and preferred stock
(d) Internal and external financing

119. In the context of financing decisions, what is meant by "capital rationing"?
(a) Restricting access to external financing sources
(b) Allocating capital to various projects based on a budget constraint
(c) Reallocating internal funds to new projects
(d) Paying off existing debt obligations

120. The decision to use a lease to acquire assets rather than purchasing them outright is an example of a
(a) Capital budgeting decision
(b) Capital structure decision
(c) Working capital management decision
(d) Dividend policy decision

121. The process of making financing decisions involves the determination of
(a) How to manage daily cash flows
(b) The company's dividend policy
(c) The company's overall financial strategy
(d) The company's day-to-day operations

122. In the context of financial distress, what is "bankruptcy"?
(a) The point at which a company is unable to meet its short-term liabilities
(b) The process of liquidating a company's assets
(c) A formal legal declaration that a company is insolvent
(d) The process of restructuring a company's debt

123. Which of the following statements is true regarding financial distress?
(a) Financial distress is always a result of poor management decisions.
(b) A company in financial distress can only choose between bankruptcy or liquidation.
(c) Financial distress can be resolved through restructuring or refinancing.
(d) Companies in financial distress are typically not impacted by declining stock prices.

124. What is the primary responsibility of a company's management when facing financial distress?
(a) Maximizing shareholder wealth at all costs
(b) Prioritizing the interests of creditors over shareholders
(c) Acting in the best interests of the company and all stakeholders
(d) Resigning from their positions

125. In the context of financial distress, which of the following is a common restructuring technique to avoid bankruptcy?
(a) Selling off profitable business divisions
(b) Liquidating all company assets
(c) Paying off all existing debt immediately
(d) Negotiating with creditors to extend repayment terms

126. What is the primary purpose of budgeting in an organization?
(a) To limit spending and reduce costs
(b) To track historical financial data
(c) To forecast future financial performance
(d) To eliminate the need for financial control

127. Budgetary control is a process that involves
(a) Creating budgets only for marketing activities
(b) Comparing actual performance to budgeted figures

(c) Reducing the budget for all departments
(d) Eliminating the need for financial reporting

128. Which of the following is NOT a key benefit of budgeting and budgetary control?
(a) Improved financial accountability
(b) Increased management control
(c) Enhanced decision-making
(d) Elimination of all financial risks

129. In the context of budgeting, what does the acronym "KPI" stand for?
(a) Key Performance Indicator
(b) Key Profit Indicator
(c) Key Planning Indicator
(d) Key Personnel Indicator

130. A static budget is one that
(a) Remains flexible and changes as the business environment changes
(b) Is based on historical data only
(c) Is created for a specific time period and does not change
(d) Is created without considering revenue projections

131. What type of budget is typically prepared for a period of one year or less and outlines expected revenues and expenses for each month?
(a) Master budget
(b) Rolling budget
(c) Cash budget
(d) Capital budget

132. A flexible budget is designed to
(a) Remain fixed and unchangeable
(b) Accommodate changes in activity levels
(c) Eliminate the need for budget revisions
(d) Project long-term financial performance

133. A capital budget primarily focuses on
(a) Short-term operational expenses
(b) Long-term investments in assets and projects
(c) Monthly cash flows
(d) Routine operating costs

134. What is the first step in the budgeting process?
(a) Monitoring and control
(b) Budget execution
(c) Budget preparation
(d) Budget review

135. During the budget preparation phase, what is the primary role of department heads and managers?
(a) Reviewing the final budget
(b) Setting targets and creating departmental budgets
(c) Approving the budget for the entire organization
(d) Conducting financial audits

136. Which phase of the budgeting process involves comparing actual results to budgeted figures and taking corrective actions?
(a) Budget preparation
(b) Budget execution
(c) Monitoring and control
(d) Budget review

137. The budget review process is often conducted by
(a) External auditors
(b) Shareholders
(c) Internal managers and executives
(d) The government

138. Zero-based budgeting (ZBB) is a budgeting approach that
(a) Assumes all expenses will be zero
(b) Starts with the previous year's budget and adjusts it
(c) Requires justifying all expenses from scratch
(d) Ignores historical financial data

139. In zero-based budgeting, what is the key question that must be answered for each expense item?
(a) How can we reduce this expense?
(b) Why was this expense incurred in the past?
(c) What is the industry average for this expense?
(d) Can we eliminate this expense entirely?

140. What is the main advantage of zero-based budgeting?
(a) It requires less effort than traditional budgeting
(b) It is based solely on historical data
(c) It promotes cost-consciousness and efficiency
(d) It eliminates the need for financial control

141. In zero-based budgeting, which of the following steps typically comes last in the process?
(a) Review and approval
(b) Cost-benefit analysis
(c) Priority setting
(d) Identification of decision packages

142. Operating leverage is related to changes in which financial metric?
(a) Earnings Before Interest and Taxes (EBIT)
(b) Earnings Per Share (EPS)
(c) Debt to Equity Ratio
(d) Net Income

143. Which of the following represents a high degree of operating leverage?
(a) A company with high fixed costs and low variable costs
(b) A company with low fixed costs and high variable costs
(c) A company with no fixed costs
(d) A company with high variable costs and low fixed costs

144. Operating leverage can lead to
(a) Increased risk due to fixed costs
(b) Decreased risk due to fixed costs
(c) No impact on risk
(d) Reduced fixed costs

145. The degree of operating leverage (DOL) can be calculated using which of the following formulas?
(a) DOL = EBIT / Net Income
(b) DOL = Contribution Margin / Fixed Costs
(c) DOL = Variable Costs / Fixed Costs
(d) DOL = Sales Revenue / EBIT

146. A high degree of operating leverage means that a company's profits are
(a) More sensitive to changes in sales
(b) Less sensitive to changes in sales
(c) Unaffected by changes in sales
(d) More sensitive to changes in variable costs

147. Financial leverage is related to changes in which financial metric?
(a) Earnings Before Interest and Taxes (EBIT)
(b) Earnings Per Share (EPS)
(c) Total Revenue
(d) Operating Income

148. Financial leverage is a result of
(a) High fixed operating costs
(b) High interest expenses
(c) High variable costs
(d) High depreciation expenses

149. The degree of financial leverage (DFL) can be calculated using which of the following formulas?
(a) DFL = EBIT / Net Income
(b) DFL = Contribution Margin / Fixed Costs
(c) DFL = EBIT / (EBIT - Interest Expense)
(d) DFL = Sales Revenue / EBIT

150. An increase in financial leverage leads to
(a) Increased risk due to fixed financial costs
(b) Decreased risk due to fixed financial costs
(c) No impact on risk
(d) Reduced interest expenses

151. Which of the following represents a high degree of financial leverage?
(a) A company with no debt
(b) A company with high equity financing
(c) A company with high interest expenses
(d) A company with high retained earnings

152. Combined leverage considers the impact of both operating leverage and
(a) Investment leverage
(b) Financing leverage
(c) Sales leverage
(d) Marketing leverage

153. The degree of combined leverage (DCL) can be calculated using which of the following formulas?
(a) DCL = DOL x DFL
(b) DCL = DOL / DFL
(c) DCL = DOL + DFL
(d) DCL = DOL - DFL

154. In the context of combined leverage, a DCL greater than 1 indicates
(a) A high degree of combined leverage
(b) No impact on financial performance
(c) A low degree of combined leverage
(d) No financial leverage

155. EBIT-EPS analysis is a tool used to
(a) Assess a company's level of operating leverage
(b) Determine the optimal level of earnings before interest and taxes
(c) Evaluate the impact of financing decisions on earnings per share
(d) Calculate the earnings before interest and taxes

156. In EBIT-EPS analysis, the indifference point is the level of EBIT at which
(a) Earnings per share (EPS) is maximized
(b) Interest expenses are eliminated
(c) There is no impact on EPS for different financing options
(d) The degree of operating leverage is highest

157. The break-even EBIT level represents the point at which
(a) The company starts making a profit
(b) EPS is maximized
(c) The degree of financial leverage is highest
(d) Interest expenses are lowest

158. A company's optimal capital structure is the one that
(a) Maximizes EBIT
(b) Minimizes interest expenses
(c) Maximizes EPS at the desired level of risk
(d) Minimizes operating leverage

159. The financial break-even point is the level of EBIT at which
(a) The company incurs no operating costs
(b) EPS is maximized
(c) Interest expenses are covered by EBIT
(d) Variable costs are covered by sales revenue

160. The financial break-even point is particularly important for
(a) Evaluating the impact of operating leverage
(b) Assessing the impact of taxes on earnings
(c) Determining the optimal level of EBIT
(d) Analyzing the impact of financing choices

161. The calculation of the financial break-even point considers
(a) Fixed operating costs and interest expenses
(b) Variable operating costs and taxes
(c) Variable operating costs and interest expenses
(d) Variable operating costs and depreciation expenses

162. The indifference point in EBIT-EPS analysis represents the level of EBIT where
(a) The company is indifferent between two financing options
(b) EBIT is maximized
(c) EPS is minimized
(d) Interest expenses are highest

163. The indifference level is important because it helps determine
(a) The optimal level of operating leverage
(b) The point at which taxes are minimized
(c) The level of risk in financing decisions
(d) The EBIT at which EPS is maximized for different financing options

ANSWER KEY

1. (b)	**2.** (d)	**3.** (c)	**4.** (b)	**5.** (c)	**6.** (c)	**7.** (b)	**8.** (c)	**9.** (c)	**10.** (a)
11. (c)	**12.** (c)	**13.** (a)	**14.** (c)	**15.** (d)	**16.** (c)	**17.** (c)	**18.** (b)	**19.** (b)	**20.** (d)
21. (a)	**22.** (d)	**23.** (c)	**24.** (a)	**25.** (a)	**26.** (a)	**27.** (c)	**28.** (a)	**29.** (b)	**30.** (b)
31. (c)	**32.** (b)	**33.** (c)	**34.** (a)	**35.** (b)	**36.** (b)	**37.** (c)	**38.** (a)	**39.** (a)	**40.** (b)
41. (b)	**42.** (c)	**43.** (d)	**44.** (b)	**45.** (a)	**46.** (d)	**47.** (b)	**48.** (c)	**49.** (b)	**50.** (c)
51. (b)	**52.** (d)	**53.** (a)	**54.** (a)	**55.** (a)	**56.** (a)	**57.** (c)	**58.** (a)	**59.** (c)	**60.** (a)
61. (a)	**62.** (a)	**63.** (c)	**64.** (a)	**65.** (b)	**66.** (d)	**67.** (b)	**68.** (d)	**69.** (d)	**70.** (d)
71. (b)	**72.** (c)	**73.** (b)	**74.** (a)	**75.** (a)	**76.** (a)	**77.** (b)	**78.** (b)	**79.** (d)	**80.** (d)
81. (a)	**82.** (d)	**83.** (b)	**84.** (a)	**85.** (d)	**86.** (a)	**87.** (a)	**88.** (d)	**89.** (b)	**90.** (c)
91. (c)	**92.** (b)	**93.** (b)	**94.** (d)	**95.** (b)	**96.** (b)	**97.** (c)	**98.** (b)	**99.** (c)	**100.** (c)
101. (c)	**102.** (c)	**103.** (b)	**104.** (c)	**105.** (d)	**106.** (d)	**107.** (c)	**108.** (d)	**109.** (c)	**110.** (a)
111. (d)	**112.** (a)	**113.** (d)	**114.** (b)	**115.** (a)	**116.** (c)	**117.** (b)	**118.** (b)	**119.** (b)	**120.** (a)
121. (c)	**122.** (c)	**123.** (c)	**124.** (c)	**125.** (d)	**126.** (c)	**127.** (b)	**128.** (d)	**129.** (a)	**130.** (c)
131. (c)	**132.** (b)	**133.** (b)	**134.** (c)	**135.** (b)	**136.** (c)	**137.** (c)	**138.** (c)	**139.** (d)	**140.** (c)
141. (a)	**142.** (a)	**143.** (a)	**144.** (a)	**145.** (d)	**146.** (a)	**147.** (b)	**148.** (b)	**149.** (c)	**150.** (a)
151. (c)	**152.** (b)	**153.** (a)	**154.** (a)	**155.** (c)	**156.** (c)	**157.** (a)	**158.** (c)	**159.** (c)	**160.** (d)
161. (a)	**162.** (a)	**163.** (d)							

UNIT 5

SYLLABUS

- Value & Returns – Time Preference for Money, Valuation of Bonds and Shares, Risk and Returns;
- Capital Budgeting – Nature of Investment, Evaluation, Comparison of Methods; Risk and Uncertainly Analysis
- Dividend – Theories and Determination
- Mergers and Acquisition – Corporate Restructuring, Value Creation, Merger Negotiations, Leveraged Buyouts, Takeover
- Portfolio Management – CAPM, APT
- Derivatives – Options, Option Payoffs, Option Pricing, Forward Contracts & Future Contracts
- Working Capital Management – Determinants, Cash, Inventory, Receivables and Payables Management, Factoring
- International Financial Management, Foreign exchange market

VALUE & RETURNS

The term value can mean different things to different people. Therefore major concepts of value are given below.

(a) **Liquidation value (LV) versus going concern value.** Liquidation value is the amount of money that could be realized if an asset or a group of assets is sold separately from its operating organisation. This value is in marked contrast to the going-concern value of a firm, which is the amount, the firm can sell as a continuing operating business. These two values are rarely equal, and sometimes a company is actually worth more dead them alive.

(b) **Book Value (BV) verses Market Value (MV).** The book value of an asset is the accounting value of the asset-the asset's cost minus its accumulated depreciation. The book value of a firm, on the other hand, is equal to its common stock equity (or alternatively, the dollar difference between the firm's total assets and its liabilities and preferred stock as listed on its balance sheet.). Because book value is based on historical values, it may bear little relationship to an asset's or firm's market value. In general, the market value of an asset is simply the market price of which the asset trades in an open market place. For a firm, market value reflects the company's risk and return as well as its future, their value is often viewed as being the higher of the firm's liquidation or going-concern value.

(c) **Market Value (MV) versus Intrinsic Value.** The market value of a security is the market price of the security. For an actively linked security, it would be the last reported price at which the security was sold. For an inactively traded security, an estimated market price would be needed. The intrinsic value of a security, on the other hand, is what the price of a security should be if properly priced based on the facts - assets, earnings, future prospects and management.

In short, the intrinsic value of a security is its economic value, if markets are reasonably efficient and informed, the current market price of a security should fluctuate closely around intrinsic value.

The valuation approach, is one of determining a security's intrinsic value what the security ought to be worth based on hard facts. This value is the present value of cash flow stream provided to the investor, discounted at a required rate of return appropriate for the risk involved.

BASIC VALUATION MODEL

Basically, the valuation model can be presented in terms of the cash flows, their timings and the required rate of return. The value of a security is determined by discounting the expressed cash flows to their present value at a discount rate commensurate with the risk-return prospective of the investor. So utilizing the present value technique, the value of financial asset can be expressed as follows :

$$V_0 = [cf_1/(1+k)^1] + [f_2/(1+k)^2] + [cf_3/(1+k)^n] ....(2)$$

Where

V_0 = value of the security
cf = cash flows expected at the end of year i
k = appropriate discount rate and
n = expected life of the asset

Thus the value of a security is the sum of discounted values of expected future cash inflows. For example, an investment is expected to provide an annual cash flow of Rs. 5000 p.m. for the next 5 years and the appropriate discount rate for the risk associated with the investment is 15% the valve of the investment may be found as follows :

$$V_0 = \sum_{i=1}^{n} 5000/(1+.15)^1$$

VALUATION OF BONDS AND SHARES

Bond Valuation

A bond or debenture is a debt security issued by a borrower and subscribed/purchased by a lender/investor. Bond is a usual form of long-term financing used by the firms, which upon issuing a bond, promise to make certain cash flows in future (in the form of interest and/or repayment) under clearly defined terms and conditions. In order to understand the valuation of bonds, the understanding of the following basic terms is required :

1. *Par value.* The par value (also called the face value or nominal value) of a bond is the principal amount of a bond and is stated on the face value of the bond is stated on the face of the bond security. The par value of a bond may be Rs. 100, Rs. 1000 or any amount. The issue price, however, may be less than, equal to or more than the par value.
2. *Coupon rate.* This is the rate at which interest on the par value of the bond is payable as per the payment schedule. The interest may be paid annually or even monthly. The coupon rate is

usually described as % rate and is applied to the par value to find out the periodic interest amount.

3. *Maturity.* The maturity of a bond refers to the period from the date of issue, after the expiry of which the redemption repayment will be made to the investor by the borrower firm. The value of a bond may be defined as the sum of the present values of the future interest payments plus the present value of the redemption repayment. The appropriate discount rate to find out the present value would be the required rate if the return k_d which depends upon the prevailing risk-free interest rate and the risk premium. The valuation model may be modified to find out the value of a bond as follows :

$$B_0 = \sum_{i=1}^{n} I_1/(1+k_d)^1 + RV/(1+k_d)^n$$

B_0 = value of bond at present.

I_1 = Annual interest payment starting one year from now till the end of the year n

RV = redemption repayment at the end of the year n

k_d = appropriate discount rate.

Preferred Stock Valuation. Most preferred stock pays a fixed dividend at regular intervals. Preferred stock has no stated maturity date and, given the fixed nature of its payments, is similar to a perpetual bond. All preferred stock issues have a call feature and many are eventually retired. When valuing a preferred stock that is expected to be called, we can apply a modified version of the formula used for valuing a bond with a finite maturity, the periodic preferred dividends replace the periodic interest payments and the 'call price' replaces the bond maturity value and all the payments are discounted at a rate appropriate to the preferred stock in question. Thus, the present value of a preferred stock is

$$v = Dp/Kp$$

where Dp is the stated annual dividend per share of preferred stock and Kp is the appropriate discount rate.

Common Stock Valuation. In recent years there has emerged growing acceptance of the idea that individual common stock be analyzed as part of a total portfolio of common stocks that the investor might hold.

In other words, investors are not as concerned with whether a particular stock goes up or down as they are with what happens to the overall value of their portfolios. This concept has important implications for determining the required rate of return on a security.

Valuation of Share

Preference share is a share which entitles the shareholder to receive (i) a dividend at a fixed rate for a given period (ii) a redemption amount at the time of preference share (in case of redeemable preference share) OR a dividend at the fixed rate perpetually till the liquidation of the company (in case of irredeemable preference share).

Assumptions. Two assumption are relevant while ascertaining the value of preference shares are as follows :

1. The dividend on preference share are received once a year and that the first dividend is received at the end of one year from the date of acquisition / purchase.
2. The company always intends to pay the preference dividend so that the stream of preference dividend is concerned to be known with certainty.

Redeemable preference share. The value of redeemable preference share may be defined as the present value of the cash flows expected from the company. The future cash flows associated with a redeemable preference share are (i) the stream of future dividends at a fixed rate of dividend (ii) the maturity payment at the time of redemption. These future cash flows are discounted at an appropriate rate to find out the value of the redeemable preference share as follows :

$$P_0 = [d_1/(1+k_p)^1] + [d_2/(1+k_p)^2]....[d_n/(1+k_p)^n + [RV/(1+k_p)^n....$$

$$P_0 = \sum_{i=1}^{n}[d_1/(1+k_p)^1] + [d_1/(1+k_p)^n]$$

where

P_0 = value of preference share
D_i = annual fixed dividend
RV = redemption value of preference share
n = life of the preference share.
k_p = required rate of return of the preference shareholders.

Irredeemable preference share. The value of irredeemable preference share may be defined as the present value of the perpetuity of the fixed, dividend on the preference shares. Symbolically, it may be defined as

$$P_0 = D/k_p$$

where

P_0 = value of the irredeemable preference share
D = fixed annual dividend
k_p = required rate of return of preference shareholders.

Valuation of Equity Shares

Conceptually, the valuation of the equity share is the most typical because of its residential ownership character. The equity shareholders receive the residential profit and also the residual assets in case of liquidation from the point of view of calculation also, the valuation of equity share is difficult for (i) the rate of dividend is not given, and (ii) unlike rate of interest or rate of preference dividend which remains constant over the life of the security. The rate of dividend on equity share maybe varying over the years. So the normal valuation model as applied for valuation of equity shares.

Assumptions. With ascertaining the value of equity share, different assumption are made regarding the company's future profits, the amount and the timing of dividends, the required rate of returns, etc. Different approaches have been developed for the valuation of equity shares. These different approaches, however, make the following assumptions regarding the basic characteristics of equity shares.

1. Equity shares does not have any redemption rate.
2. Equity share do not have any given redemption or liquidation value. In case of liquidation of the company, their claim is residual in nature and arising in the last (after paying all external liabilities and the preference shareholders).
3. Dividends on equity shares are neither guarantied nor compulsory. Further, neither the rate nor the timing of dividend is specified. So, the dividend can vary in any direction.

Broadly the value of equity share may be found by following either of the two approaches :

1. Valuation based on dividends.
2. Valuation based on earnings.

RISK AND RETURNS

Risk and Return Considerations

Risk refers to the variability of possible returns associated with a given investment. Risk, along with the return, is a major consideration in capital budgeting decisions. The firm must compare the expected return from a given investment with the risk associated with it. Higher levels of return are required to compensate for increased levels of risk. In other words, the higher the risk undertaken, the more ample the return – and conversely, the lower the risk, the more modest the return.

This risk and return tradeoff is also known as the risk-return spectrum. There are various classes of possible investments, each with their own positions on the overall risk-return spectrum. The general progression is: short-term debt, long-term debt, property, high-yield debt, and equity. The existence of risk causes the need to incur a number of expenses. For example, the more risky the investment the more time and effort is usually required to obtain information about it and monitor its progress. Moreover, the importance of a loss of X amount of value can be greater than the importance of a gain of X amount of value, so a riskier investment will attract a higher risk premium even if the forecast return is the same as upon a less risky investment. Risk is therefore something that must be compensated for, and the more risk the more compensation is required.

When a firm makes a capital budgeting decision, they will wish, as a bare minimum, to recover enough to pay the increased cost of investment due to inflation. Thus, inflation is a pivotal input in a firm's cost of capital. However, since interest rates are set by the market, it happens frequently that they are insufficient to compensate for inflation.

Risk aversion also plays an important role in determining a firm's required return on an investment. Risk aversion is a concept based on the behavior of firms and investors while exposed to uncertainty to attempt to reduce that uncertainty. Risk aversion is the reluctance to accept a bargain with an uncertain payoff rather than another bargain with a more certain, but possibly lower, expected payoff. For example, a risk-averse investor might choose to put his or her money into a bank account with a low but guaranteed interest rate, rather than into a stock that may have high expected returns, but also involves a chance of losing value. Risk aversion can be thought of as having three levels:

- Risk-averse or risk-avoiding
- Ri[illegible]
- Risk-loving or risk-seeking.

Beta is a measure firms can use in order to determine an investment's return sensitivity in relation to overall market risk. Beta describes the correlated volatility of an asset in relation to the volatility of the benchmark that said asset is being compared to. This benchmark is generally the overall financial market and is often estimated via the use of representative indices, such as the S&P 500. Beta is also referred to as financial elasticity or correlated relative volatility, and can be referred to as a measure of the sensitivity of the asset's returns to market returns, its non-diversifiable risk, its systematic risk, or market risk. Higher-beta investments tend to be more volatile and therefore riskier, but provide the potential for higher returns. Lower-beta investments pose less risk, but generally offer lower returns.

CAPITAL BUDGETING

Capital Budgeting Decisions – Risk Analysis

Capital budgeting is the process of making investment decisions in capital expenditures. Capital budgeting involves the planning and control of capital expenditure. It is the process of deciding whether or not to commit resources to a particular long term project whose benefits are to be realised over a period of time, longer than one year.

According to Milton H. Spencer, "Capital Budgeting involves the planning of expenditures for assets, the returns from which will be realized in future time periods."

Capital budgeting is concerned with the allocation of the firm scarce financial resources among the available market opportunities. The consideration of investment opportunities involves the comparison of the expected future streams of earnings from a project with the immediate and subsequent streams of earning from a project, with the immediate and subsequent streams of expenditures for it.

NATURE OF INVESTMENT

1. Funds are invested in long term assets.
2. Funds are invested in present times in anticipation of future profits.
3. The future profits will occur to the firm over a series of years.
4. Capital Budgeting decisions involve a high degree of risk because future benefits are not certain.

Importance of Capital Budgeting Decision

1. **Such Decision after the profitability of the Firm.** Capital Budgeting decision affect the long-term profitability of a firm. They enable a firm to produce finished goods which is ultimately sold for profit. Hence, a correct investment decision can yield large profits, whereas an incorrect decision can endanger the very survival of the firm.
2. **Long-Term Effects.** The consequence of capital expenditure decisions extend far into the future. To illustrate, if a company purchases a new plant to manufacture a new product, the company will have to incur a sizable amount of fixed costs, in terms of labour, supervisor's salary, insurance, rent of building etc., If, in future, the product turns out to be unsuccessful, the company will have to bear the burden of heavy fixed costs.
3. **Irreversible Decision.** Capital Budgeting decisions, once taken, are not easily reversible without heavy financial loss to the firm.
4. **Involvement of Large Amount of Funds.** Capital Budgeting decisions require large amount of funds and most of the firm have limited financial resources. Hence, it is absolutely necessary to take thoughtful and correct investment decisions.
5. **Risk.** Capital investment proposals have different degrees of risk.
6. **Most difficult to make.** These decisions are among the most difficult decisions to be taken by a firm. This is, because they require an assessment of future events which are uncertain and difficult to predict.

Difficulties

1. **Measurement Problems.** Identifying and measuring the costs and benefits of a capital expenditure proposals tend to be difficult. This is more so when a capital expenditure has a bearing on some other activities of the firm.
2. **Uncertainty.** A capital expenditure decision involves costs and benefits that extend fall into the future. It is impossible to predict exactly what will happen in the future. Hence, there is usually a great deal of uncertainty characterizing the cost and benefits of a capital expenditure decision.
3. **Temporal Spread.** The costs and benefits associated with a capital expenditure decision are spread out over a long period of time, usually 10-20 years for industrial projects and 20-50 years for infrastructural projects.

METHODS OF CAPITAL BUDGETING (EVALUATION AND COMPARISON OF METHODS)

A. Traditional Methods

1. **Pay-Back Period Method.** The 'Pay back' sometimes called as pay out or pay off period method represents the period in which the total investment in permanent assets pays back itself. This method is based on the principle that every capital expenditure pays itself back within a certain period out of the additional earnings generated from the capital assets. Thus, it measures the period of time for the original cost of a project to be recovered from the additional earnings of the project itself. Under this method, various investments are ranked according to the length of their pay back period in such a manner that the investment with a shorter pay back period is preferred to the one which has longer pay back period.

   In case of evaluation of a single project, it is adopted if it pays back for itself within a period specified by the management and if the project does not pay back itself within the period specified by the management then it is rejected.

   The pay-back period can be ascertained in the following manner:

   (i) Calculate annual net earnings (profits) before depreciation and after taxes; these are called annual cash inflows.

   (ii) Divide the initial outlay (cost) of the project by the annual cash inflow, where the project generates constant annual cash inflows.

   Thus, where the project generates constant cash inflows:

   $$\text{Pay-back period} = \frac{\text{Cash outlay of the project or Original cost of the asset}}{\text{Annual cash inflows}}$$

   (iii) **Where the annual cash inflows** (Profit before depreciation and after taxes) are unequal, the pay-back period can be found by adding up the cash inflows until the total is equal to the initial cash outlay of project or original cost of the asset.

2. **Improvements in traditional approach to pay back period method**

   (i) **Post Pay-back Profitability Method.** One of the serious limitations of Pay-back period method is that it does not take into account the cash inflows earned after pay-back period and hence the true profitability of the project cannot be assessed. Hence, and, improvement over this method can be made by taking into account the returns receivable beyond the pay-back period. These returns are called post pay-back profits.

   $$\text{Post Pay-back Profitability Index} = \frac{\text{Post Pay-back Profits} \times 100}{\text{Investment}}$$

   (ii) **Pay-back Reciprocal Method.** Sometimes, Pay-back Reciprocal method is employed to estimate the internal rate of return generated by a project. Pay-back Reciprocals can be calculated as under:

   $$\text{Pay back Reciprocal} = \frac{\text{Annual Cash Inflow}}{\text{Total Investment}}$$

   (This can also be calculated in percentage by multiplying the above by 100). However, this method should be used only when the following two conditions are satisfied:

   (i) Equal cash inflows are generated every year.

   (ii) The project under consideration has a long life which must be at least twice the pay-back period.

(c) **Post Pay-back Period Method.** One of the limitations of the pay-back period method is that is it ignores the life of the project beyond the pay-back period. Post Pay-back Period method takes into account the period beyond the pay-back method. This method is also known as Surplus Life over Pay-back method. According to this method, the project which gives the greatest post pay-back period may be accepted. The method can be employed successfully where the various projects under consideration do not differ significantly as to their size and the expected cash inflows are even throughout the life of the project.

(d) **Discounted Pay-back Method.** Another serious limitation of the pay-back period method is that it ignores the time value of money. Hence, an improvement over this method can be made by employing the discounted pay-back period method. Under this method the present values of all cash outflows and inflows are computed at an appropriate discount rate. The present values of all inflows are cumulated in order of time. The time period at which the cumulated present value of cash inflows equals the present value of cash outflows is known as Discounted Pay-back Period. The project which gives a shorter discounted pay-back period is accepted.

3. **Rate of Return Method.** This method takes into account the earnings expected from the investment over their whole life. It is known as Accounting Rate of Return method for the reason that under this method. The accounting concept of profit (net profit after tax and depreciation) is used rather than cash inflows. According to this method, various projects are ranked in order of the rate of earnings or rate of return. The project with the higher rate of return is selected as compared to the one with lower rate of return. This method can also be used to make decision as to accepting or rejecting a proposal. The expected return is determined and the project which has a higher rate of return than the minimum rate specified by the firm called the cut off rate, is accepted and the one which gives a lower expected rate of return than the minimum rate is rejected.

The return on investment method can be used in several ways as follows:

(a) **Average Rate of Return Method.** Under this method average profit after tax and depreciation is calculated and then it is divided by the total capital outlay or total investment in the project. In other words, it establishes the relationship between average annual profits to total investments.

Thus,

$$\text{Average Rate of Return} = \frac{\text{Total Profits (after depreciation and taxes)}}{\text{Net investment in the project} \times \text{No. of years of profits}} \times 100$$

or

$$= \frac{\text{Average annual profits}}{\text{Net investment in the project}} \times 100$$

(b) **Return per unit of Investment Method.** This method is small variation of the average rate of return method. In this method the total profit after tax and depreciation is dividend by the total investment, *i.e.*,

$$\text{Return per unit of Investment} = \frac{\text{Total Profit (after depreciation and taxes)}}{\text{Net investment in the project}} \times 100$$

(c) **Return on Average Investment Method.** In this method the return on average investment is calculated. Using of average investment for the purpose of return on investment is preferred because the original investment is recovered over the life of the asset on account of depreciation charges.

For example:

$$\text{The Return on Average Investment} = \frac{\text{Total Profit after depreciation and taxes}}{\dfrac{\text{Total Net investment}}{2}} \times 100$$

(d) **Average Return on Average Investment Method.** This is the most appropriate method of rate or return on investment. Under this method, average profit after depreciation and taxes is divided by the average amount of investment; thus:

Average Return on Average Investment

$$= \frac{\text{Average Annual Profit after dep. and taxes}}{\text{Average Investment}} \times 100$$

$$= \frac{\text{Average Annual Profit}}{\dfrac{\text{Net Investment}}{2}} \times 100$$

B. Time-adjusted or Discounted Cash Flow Methods

The traditional methods of capital budgeting *i.e.*, pay-back method as well as accounting rate of return method, suffer from the serious limitations that give equal weight to present and future flow of incomes. These methods do not take into consideration the time value of money, the fact that a rupee earned today has more value than a rupee earned after five years. The time-adjusted or discounted cash flow methods take into account the profitability and also the time value of money. These methods also called modern methods of capital budgeting are becoming increasingly popular day by day. Following are the discounted cash flow methods:

4. **Net present value method.** The net present value method is a modern method of evaluating investment proposals. This method takes into consideration the time value of money and attempts to calculate the return on investments by introducing the factor of time element. It recognises the fact that a rupee earned today is work more than the same rupee earned tomorrow. The net present values of all inflows and outflows of cash occurring during the entire life of the project is determined separately for each year by discounting these flows by the firm's cost of capital or a pre-determined rate. The following are the necessary steps to be followed for adopting the net present value method of evaluating investment proposals:

(i) First of all determine an appropriate rate of interest that should be selected as the minimum required rate of return called 'cut-off rate or discount rate'. The rate should be a minimum rate of return below which the investor considers that it does not pay him to invest. The discount rate should be either the actual rate of interest in the market on long-term loans or it should reflect the opportunity cost of capital of the investor.

(ii) Compute the present value of total investment outlay, *i.e.* cash outflows at the determined discount rate. If the total investment is to be made in the initial year, the present value shall be the same as the cost of investment.

(iii) Compute the present values of total investment proceeds, *i.e.*, cash inflows, (profit before depreciation and after tax) at the above determined discount rate.

(iv) Calculate the net present value of each project by substracting the present value of cash inflows from the present value of cash outflows for each project.

(v) If the net present value is positive or zero, *i.e.*, when present value of cash inflows either exceeds or is equal to the present value of cash outflows, the proposal may be accepted. But in case the present value of inflows is less than the present value of cash outflows, the proposal should be rejected.

(vi) To select between mutually exclusive projects, projects should be ranked in order of net present values, *i.e.* the first preference should be given to the project having the maximum positive net present value.

The present value of Re. 1 due in any number of years can be found with the use of the following mathematical formula:

$$PV = \frac{1}{(1+r)^n}$$

where, PV = present value

r = rate of interest/discount rate

n = number of years

The present value for all the cash inflows for a number of years is thus found as follows:

$$PV = \frac{A_1}{(1+r)} + \frac{A_2}{(1+r)^2} + \frac{A_3}{(1+r)^3} + \cdots + \frac{A_n}{(1+r)^n}$$

$A_1, A_2, A_3, \ldots\ldots A_n$ = Future net cash flows (profit after tax but before depreciation)

r = rate of interest

n = numbers of years

However as n becomes large, the calculations of $(I + r)^n$ becomes difficult. Present value can also be found by the use of Present value Tables.

5. **Internal Rate of Return Method.** The internal rate of return method is also a modern technique of capital budgeting that takes into account the time value of money. It is also known as 'time adjusted rate of return' 'discounted cash flow' 'discounted rate of return', 'yield method' and 'trial and error yield method'. In the net present value method the net present value is determined by discounting the future cash flows of a project at a predetermined or specified rate called the cut-off rate. But under the internal rate of return method, the cash flows of a project are discounted at a suitable rate by hit and trial method, which equates the net present value so calculated to the amount of the investment. Under this method, since the discount rate is determined internally, this method is called as the internal rate of return method. The internal rate of return can be defined as that rate of discount at which the present value of cash-inflows is equal to the present value of cash outflows. It can be determined with the help of the following mathematical formula.

$$C = \frac{A_1}{(1+r)} + \frac{A_2}{(1+r)^2} + \frac{A_3}{(1+r)^3} + \cdots + \frac{A_n}{(1+r)^n}$$

where,

C = Initial outlay at time zero.

$A_1, A_2, A_3, \ldots\ldots, A_n$ = Future net cash flows at different periods.

n = numbers of years

r = rate of discount of internal rate of return.

The internal rate of return can also be determined with the help of present value tables. The following steps are required to practice the internal rate of return method.

1. Determine the future net cash flows during the entire economic life of the project. The cash inflows are estimated for future profits before depreciation but after taxes.
2. Determine the rate of discount at which the value of cash inflows is equal to the present value of cash outflows. This may be determined as explained after step (4).
3. Accept the proposal if the internal rate of return is higher than or equal to the minimum required rate of return. *i.e.* ,the cost of capital or cut off rate and reject the proposal if the internal rate of return is lower than the cost of cut-off rate.
4. In case of alternative proposals select the proposal with the highest rate of return as long as the rates are higher than the cost of capital or cut-off-rate.

Determination of Internal Rate of Return (IRR)

(a) **When the annual net cash flows are equal over the life of the assets.** Firstly, find out present value Factor by dividing initial outlay (cost of the investment) by annual cash flow, *i.e.*,

$$\text{Present Value Factor} = \frac{\text{Initial Outlay}}{\text{Annual Cash Flow}}$$

The consult present value annuity tables with the number of years equal to the life of the asset and find out the rate at which the calculated present value factor is equal to the present value given in the table

(b) **When the annual cash flows are unequal over the life of the asset.** In case annual cash flows are unequal over the life of the asset, the internal rate of return cannot be determined according to the technique suggested above. In such cases, the internal rate of return is calculated by hit and trial and that is why this method is also known as hit and trial yield method. We may start with any assumed discount rate and find out the total present value of cash outflows which is equal to the cost of the initial investment where total investment is to be made in the beginning. The rate, at which the total present value of all cash inflows equals the initial outlay, is the internal rate of return. Several discount rates may have to be tried until the appropriate rate is found. The calculation process may be summed up as follows:

(i) Prepare the cash flow table using an arbitrary assumed discount rate to discount the net cash flows to the present value.

(ii) Find out the Net Present Value by deducting from the present value of total cash flows calculated in (i) above the initial cost of the investment.

(iii) If the Net Present Value (NPV) is positive, apply higher rate of discount.

(iv) If the higher discount rate still gives a positive net present value, increase the discount rate further until the NPV becomes negative.

(v) If the NPV is negative at this higher rate, the internal rate of return must be between these two rates.

Profitability Index Method or Benefit Cost Ratio

It is also a time – adjusted method of evaluating the investment proposals. Profitability index also called as benefit - Cost Ratio (B/C) or 'Desirability factor' is the relationship between present value of cash inflows and the present value of cash outflows. Thus,

$$\text{Profitability Index} = \frac{\text{Present value of cash inflows}}{\text{Present value of cash outflows}}$$

or

$$\text{P.I.} = \frac{\text{PV of cash inflows}}{\text{Initial cash outlay}}$$

The profitability index may be found for net present values of inflows.

$$\text{P.I. (Net)} = \frac{\text{NPV (Net Present Value)}}{\text{Initial cash outlay}}$$

The net profitability index can also be found as profitability index (gross) minus one.

The proposal is accepted if the profitability index is more than one and is rejected in case the profitability index is less than one. The various projects are ranked under this method in order of their profitability index, in such a manner that one with higher profitability index is ranked higher than the other with lower profitability index.

Risk and Uncertainty in Capital Budgeting

Risk Analysis. Risk in an investment refers to the variability that is likely to observed between the estimated returns and the actual returns form the proposal. The greater is the variability between the two returns, the more is the risk involved in the project, and vice versa.

Incorporation of the Risk in Investment Proposal. As stated earlier, risk is involved in every capital budgeting decision. As risk is involved in every capital budgeting proposal, the management of a firm must take the risk factor into account, while determining the returns or cash inflows and the profitability of a project for the purpose of capital budgeting.

All the techniques of capital budgeting require the estimation of future cash inflows and cash outflows. The future cash flows are based on the following factors :

1. Expected economic life of the project
2. Capacity of the project
3. Salvage value of the asset at the end of the economic life
4. Selling price of the product
5. Production cost
6. Depreciation rate
7. Rate of taxation
8. Future demand of the product etc.

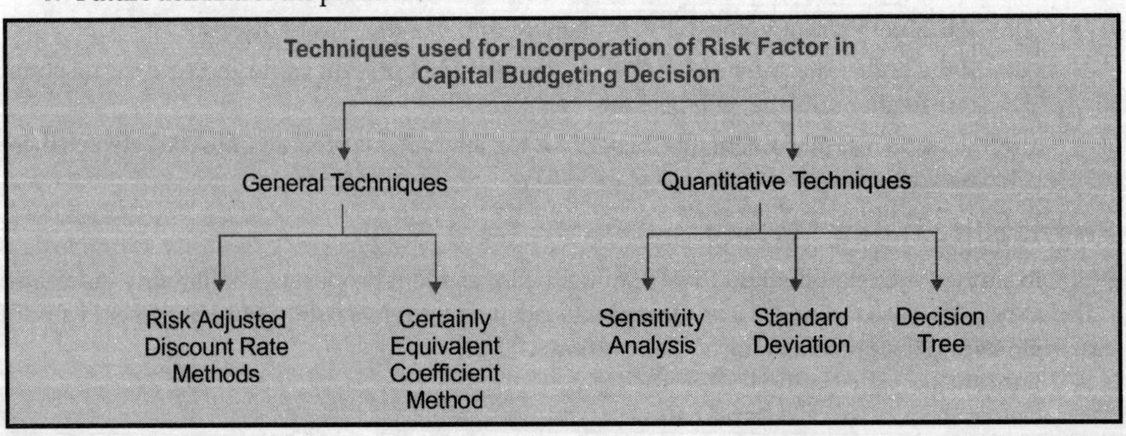

But due to uncertainties about the future, the estimates of demand, production sales, costs, selling prices etc., cannot be exact. For example, a product may become obsolete much earlier than anticipated due to unexpected technological developments. All these elements of uncertainty have to be taken into account in the form of forcible risk while taking a decision on investment proposals. It is perhaps the most difficult task while making an investment decision. But some allowances for the element of risk have to be provided.

The following methods are suggested for accounting for risk in capital budgeting :

(a) **Risk-Adjusted Discount Rate or Method of Varying Discount Rate.** The simplest method of accounting for risk in capital budgeting is to increase the cut-off rate or the discount factor by certain percentage on account of risk. The projects which are more risky and which have greater variability in expected returns should be discounted at a higher rate as compared to the projects which are less risky and are expected to have lesser variability in returns. The greatest drawback of this method is that it is not possible to determine the risk premium rate appropriately and moreover it is the future cash flow which is uncertain and requires adjustment and not the discount rate.

Merits.

(1) It is easy to understand and simple to calculate.

(2) The risk premium rate included in the risk adjusted rate takes care of the risk element in the future cash flows of the project.

(3) It takes into account the risk averse attitude of investors.

Demerits.

(1) The risk premium rates, determined under this method, are arbitrary. So this method may not give objective results.

(2) Under this method, the risk is compounded over time, since the risk premium is added to the discount rate. Which means, this method presumes that risk necessarily increases with the passage of time. But this may not happen in all situations or cases.

(3) This method presumes that investors are averse to risk I i.e., investors avoid facing risk). This may not be true in all cases. There are many investors who would like to take risk and are prepared to pay premium for taking risk.

(b) **Sensitivity Technique.** Where cash inflows are very sensitive under different circumstances, more than one forecast of the future cash inflows may be made. These inflows may be regarded as 'Optimistic', 'Most Likely' and 'Pessimistic'. Further cash inflows may be discounted to find out the net present values under these three different situations. If the net present values under the three situations differ widely it implies that there is a great risk in the project and the investor's decision to accept or reject a project will depend upon his risk bearing abilities.

(c) **Standard Deviation Method.** If two projects have the same cost and their net present values are also the same, standard deviations of the expected cash inflows of the two projects may be calculated to judge the comparative risk of the projects. The project having a higher standard deviation is said to be more risky as compared to the other.

(d) **Certainty Equivalent Method.** Another simple method of accounting for risk in capital budgeting is to reduce expected cash flows by certain amounts. It can be employed by multiplying the expected cash flows by certainly equivalent co-efficients as to convert the uncertain cash flows to certain cash flows.

Formula for Calculating Certainity Equivalent Coefficient. The certainity equivalent coefficient is the ratio of riskless cash flow to risky cash flow.

The certainty equivalent coefficient can be calculated with the help of the following formula :

$$\text{Certainty Equivalent Coefficient} = \frac{\text{Riskless Cash Flow}}{\text{Risky Cash Flow}}$$

(1) **Riskless Cash Flow.** Riskless cash flow means the cash flow which the management expects, when there is no risk in investment proposal.

(2) **Risky Cash Flow.** Risky cash flow means the cash flow which the management expects when there is risk in investment proposal.

Example. Suppose the risky cash flow is Rs. 200000 and the riskless cash flow is Rs. 140000.

$$\text{The Certainty Equivalent Coefficient} = \frac{140000}{200000} = 0.7$$

Steps Involved in Certainty Equivalent Coefficient Method. The various steps involved in the certainty equivalent coefficient method are :

(1) **First Step.** Firstly, the certainty equivalent coefficient has to be calculated for each year of a project.

(2) **Second Step.** Secondly, the risk-adjusted cash flow of a project for each year has to be calculated. The risk-adjusted cash flow of a year can be calculated as follows:
Risk-Adjusted Cash Flow = Estimated Cash flow for the year X Certainty Equivalent Coefficient.

(3) **Third Step.** Thirdly, we have to find out the present value of the capital project. The present value of the Capital Project can be found by adopting the following procedure. First, the risk-adjusted cash flow for each year should be multiplied by the present value factor or discount factor applicable to that year to get the present value of the risk-adjusted cash flow of each year.

(4) **Fourth Step.** Fourthly, we have to ascertain the net present value of the project. The net present value of the project will be :

Present Value of the Project	______
Less : Initial Investment on the Project	______
Net Present Value of the Project	______

(5) **Fifth Step.** After the NPV of a project is computed, decision is taken as to the selection of the project. The selection of a project, is, usually made on the following line :

(i) Generally, a project becomes acceptable, if it has a positive NPV.

(ii) If there are two or more mutually exclusive projects, generally, the project whose NPV is higher or highest is selected.

(e) **Probability Technique.** A probability is the relative frequency with which an event may occur in the future. When future estimates of cash inflows have different probabilities, the expected monetary values may be computed by multiplying cash inflow with the probability assigned. The monetary values of the inflows may further be discounted to find out the present values. The project that gives higher net present value may be accepted.

(f) **Coefficient of Variation Method.** Coefficient of variation is a relative measure of dispersion. If the projects have the same cost but different net present values, relative measure, *i.e.*, coefficient of variation should be computed to judge the relative position of risk involved. It can be calculated as :

$$\text{Coefficient of Variation} = \frac{\text{Standard Deviation}}{\text{Mean}} \times 100$$

(g) **Decision Tree Analysis.** In modern businesses, there are complex investment decisions which involve a sequence of decisions over time. Such sequential decisions can be handled by plotting decisions trees. A decision tree is a graphic representation of the relationship between a present decision and future events, future decisions and their consequences. The sequence of events is mapped out over time in a format resembling branches of a tree and hence the analysis is known as decision tree analysis. The various steps involved in a decision tree analysis are :

(i) Identification of the problem
(ii) Finding out the alternatives
(iii) Exhibiting the decision tree indicating the decision points, chance events and other relevant data
(iv) Specification of probabilities and monetary values for cash inflows; and
(v) Analysis of the alternatives.

DIVIDEND – THEORIES AND DETERMINATION

The term dividend refers to that part of profits of a company which is distributed by the company among its shareholders. It is the reward of the shareholders for investments made by them in the shares of the company. The investors are interested in earning the maximum return on their investments and to maximize their wealth. A company, on the other hand, needs to provide funds to finance its long-term growth. If a company pays out as dividend most of what it earns, then for business requirements and further expansion it will have to depend upon outside resources such as issue of debt or new shares. Dividend policy of a firm, thus affects both the long - term financing and the wealth of shareholders. As a result, the firm's decision to pay dividends must be reached in such a manner so as to equitably apportion the distributed profits and retained earnings. Since dividend is a right of shareholders to participate in the profits and surplus of the company for their investment in the share capital of the company, they should receive fair amount of the profits. The company should, therefore, distribute a reasonable amount as dividends (which should include a normal rate of interest plus a return for the risks assumed) to its members and retain the rest for its growth and survival.

DETERMINANTS OF DIVIDEND POLICY

The payment of dividend involves some legal as well as financial considerations. It is difficult to determine a general dividend policy which can be followed by different firms at different times because the dividend decision has to be taken into considering the special circumstances of an individual case. The following are the important factors which determine the dividend policy of a firm :

1. Legal Restrictions

Legal provisions relating to dividends are significant because they lay down a framework within which dividend policy is formulated. These provisions require that dividend can be paid only out of current profits or past profits after providing for depreciation or out of the moneys provided by the Government for the payment of dividends in pursuance of a guarantee given by the Government. The Companies (Transfer of Profits to Reserves) Rules, 1975 require a company providing more than ten percent dividend to transfer certain percentage of the current year's profits to reserves. Companies Act, further, provides that dividends cannot be paid out of capital, because it will amount to reduction of capital adversely affecting the security of its creditors.

2. Magnitude and Trend of Earnings

As dividends can be paid only out of present or past year's profits, earnings of a company fix the upper limits on dividends. The dividends should, generally, be paid out of current year's earnings only as the retained earnings of the previous years become more or less a part of permanent investment in the business to earn current profits. The past trend of the company's earnings should also be kept in consideration while making the dividend decision.

3. Desire and Type of Shareholders

Although, legally, the discretion as to whether to declare dividend or not has been left with the Board of Directors, the directors should give the importance to the desires of shareholders in the declaration of dividends as they are the representatives of shareholders. Desires of shareholders for dividends depend upon their economic status. Investors, such as retired persons, widows and other economically weaker persons view dividends as a source of funds to meet their day-to-day living expenses. To benefit such investors, the companies should pay regular dividends. On the other hand, a wealthy investor in a high income tax bracket may not benefit by high current dividend incomes. Such an investor may be interested in lower current dividends and high capital gains.

4. Nature of Industry

Nature of industry to which the company is engaged also considerably affects the dividend policy. Certain industries have a comparatively steady and stable demand irrespective of the prevailing economic conditions. For instance, people used to drink liquor both in boom as well as in recession. Such firms expect regular earnings and hence can follow a consistent dividend policy. On the other hand, if the earnings are uncertain, as in the case of luxury goods, conservative policy should be followed.

5. Age of the Company

The age of the company also influences the dividend decision of a company. A newly established concern has to limit payment of dividend and retain substantial part of earnings for financing its future growth and development, while older companies which have established sufficient reserves can afford to pay liberal dividends.

6. Government's Economic Policy

The dividend policy of a firm has also to be adjusted to the economic policy of the Government as was the case when the Temporary Restriction on Payment of Dividend Ordinance was in force. In 1974 and 1975, companies were allowed to pay dividends not more than 33 percent of their profits or 12 percent on the paid-up value of the shares, whichever was lower.

7. Taxation Policy

The taxation policy of the Government also affects the dividend decision of a firm. A high or low rate of business taxation affects the net earnings of company (after tax) and thereby its dividend policy. Similarly, a firm's dividend policy may be dictated by the income-tax status of its shareholders. If the dividend income of shareholders is heavily taxed being in high income bracket, the shareholders may forego cash dividend and prefer bonus shares and capital gains.

8. Inflation

Inflation acts as a constraint in the payment of dividends. When prices rise, funds generated by depreciation would not be adequate to replace fixed assets and hence to maintain the same assets and capital intact, substantial part of the current earnings would be retained. Otherwise, imaginary and inflated book profits in the days of rising prices would amount to payment of dividends much more than warranted by the real profits, out of the equity capital resulting in erosion of capital.

9. Requirement of Institutional Investors

Dividend policy of a company can be affected by the requirements of institutional investors such as financial institutions, banks insurance corporations, etc. These investors usually favour a policy of regular payment of cash dividends and stipulate their own terms with regard to payment of dividend on equity shares.

10. Stability of Dividends

Stability of dividends is another important guiding principle in the formulation of a dividend policy. Stability of dividends simply refers to the payment of dividends regularly and shareholders, generally, prefer payment of such regular dividends. Some companies follow a policy of constant dividend per share while others follow a policy of constant payout ratio and while there are some other who follow a policy of constant low dividend per share plus an extra dividend in the years of high profits.

11. Liquid Resources

The dividend policy of a firm is also influenced by the availability of liquid resources. Although, a firm may have sufficient available profits to declare dividends, yet it may not be desirable to pay dividends if it does not have sufficient liquid resources. Hence the liquidity position of a company is an important consideration in paying dividends.

If a company does not have liquid resources, it is better to declare *stock-dividend* i.e., issue of bonus shares to the existing shareholders. The issue of bonus shares also amounts to distribution of firm's earnings among the existing shareholders without affecting its cash position.

DIVIDEND THEORIES

1. Walter's Model

Professor James E. Walterargues that the choice of dividend policies almost always affects the value of the enterprise. His model shows clearly the importance of the relationship between the firm's internal rate of return (r) and its cost of capital (k) in determining the dividend policy that will maximise the wealth of shareholders.

Walter's model is based on the following assumptions:

1. The firm finances all investment through retained earnings; that is debt or new equity is not issued;
2. The firm's internal rate of return (r), and its cost of capital (k) are constant;
3. All earnings are either distributed as dividend or reinvested internally immediately.
4. Beginning earnings and dividends never change. The values of the earnings pershare (E), and the divided per share (D) may be changed in the model to determine results, but any given values of E and D are assumed to remain constant forever in determining a given value.
5. The firm has a very long or infinite life.

Walter's formula to determine the market price per share (P) is as follows:

$$P = D/K + r(E\text{-}D)/K/K$$

The above equation clearly reveals that the market price per share is the sum of the present value of two sources of income:

(i) The present value of an infinite stream of constant dividends, (D/K) and

(ii) The present value of the infinite stream of stream gains.

$$[r(E\text{-}D)/K/K]$$

2. Gordon's Model

One very popular model explicitly relating the market value of the firm to dividend policy is developed by Myron Gordon.

Assumptions

Gordon's model is based on the following assumptions.

1. The firm is an all Equity firm
2. No external financing is available
3. The internal rate of return (r) of the firm is constant.
4. The appropriate discount rate (K) of the firm remains constant.
5. The firm and its stream of earnings are perpetual
6. The corporate taxes do not exist.
7. The retention ratio (b), once decided upon, is constant. Thus, the growth rate (g) = br is constant forever.
8. K > br = g if this condition is not fulfilled, we cannot get a meaningful value for the share.

According to Gordon's dividend capitalisation model, the market value of a share (Pq) is equal to the present value of an infinite stream of dividends to be received by the share. Thus:

$$P_0 = \frac{E_1(1-b)}{K-br}$$

The above equation explicitly shows the relationship of current earnings (E,), dividend policy, (b), internal profitability (r) and the all-equity firm's cost of capital (k), in the determination of the value of the share (P_0).

3. Modigliani and Miller's Hypothesis

According to Modigliani and Miller (M-M), dividend policy of a firm is irrelevant as it does not affect the wealth of the shareholders. They argue that the value of the firm depends on the firm's earnings which result from its investment policy.

Thus, when investment decision of the firm is given, dividend decision the split of earnings between dividends and retained earnings is of no significance in determining the value of the firm. M – M's hypothesis of irrelevance is based on the following assumptions.

1. The firm operates in perfect capital market.
2. Taxes do not exist.
3. The firm has a fixed investment policy.
4. Risk of uncertainty does not exist. That is, investors are able to forecast future prices and dividends with certainty and one discount rate is appropriate for all securities and all time periods. Thus, r = K = Kt for all t.

Under M – M assumptions, r will be equal to the discount rate and identical for all shares. As a result, the price of each share must adjust so that the rate of return, which is composed of the rate of dividends and capital gains, on every share will be equal to the discount rate and be identical for all shares.

Thus, the rate of return for a share held for one year may be calculated as follows:

$$r = \frac{D+(P_1+P_0)}{P_0} = \frac{\text{Dividends} - \text{Capital gains (on loss)}}{\text{Purchase price}}$$

Where P^ is the market or purchase price per share at time 0, P, is the market price per share at time 1 and D is dividend per share at time 1. As hypothesised by M – M, r should be equal for all shares. If it is not so, the low-return yielding shares will be sold by investors who will purchase the high-return yielding shares.

This process will tend to reduce the price of the low-return shares and to increase the prices of the high-return shares. This switching will continue until the differentials in rates of return are eliminated. This discount rate will also be equal for all firms under the M-M assumption since there are no risk differences.

From the above M-M fundamental principle we can derive their valuation model as follows:

$$P_0 = \frac{D_1 + P_1}{(1+r)} \quad P_0 = \frac{D_1 + P_1}{(1+k)} \quad r = k$$

Multiplying both sides of equation by the number of shares outstanding (n), we obtain the value of the firm if no new financing exists.

$$V = nP_0 = \frac{N(D_1 + P_1)}{(1+k)}$$

If the firm sells m number of new shares at time 1 at a price of P^, the value of the firm at time 0 will be

$$nP_0 = \frac{ND_1 + (n+m)p_1 - mp_1)}{(1+k)}$$

The above equation of M – M valuation allows for the issuance of new shares, unlike Walter's and Gordon's models. Consequently, a firm can pay dividends and raise funds to undertake the optimum investment policy. Thus, dividend and investment policies are not confounded in M – M model, like waiter's and Gordon's models.

MERGERS AND ACQUISITIONS

A merger is a combination of two or more companies into one company. It means the merger of one or more companies with another company or merger of two or more companies to form one company in such a manner that :

(i) All the property of the amalgamating company or companies immediately before the amalgamation becomes the property of the amalgamated company by virtue of the amalgamation.

(ii) All the liabilities of the amalgamating company or companies immediately before the amalgamation become the liabilities of the amalgamated company by virtue of the amalgamation.

(iii) Shareholders holding not less than nine-tenths in value of the shares in the amalgamating company or companies (other than shares already held therein immediately before the amalgamation by or by a nominee for, the amalgamated company by virtue of the amalgamation.

Acquisition and Take–Over

An essential feature of merger through absorption as well as consolidation is the combination of the companies. The acquiring company takes over the ownership of one or more other companies and combine their operations. However, an acquisition does not involve combination of companies. It is simply an act of acquiring control over management of other companies. The control over management of another company can be acquired through either a 'friendly take-over' or through 'forced' or 'unwilling acquisition'. When a company takes-over the control of another company through mutual agreement, it is called acquisition or friendly take-over. On the other hand, if the control is acquired through unwilling acquisition, *i.e.*, when the take-over is opposed by the 'target' company, it is known as take-over.

Economics/Reasons of Mergers

1. **Economies of Scale.** An amalgamated company will have more resources at its command than the individual companies. This will help in increasing the scale of operations and the economies of large scale will be availed. These economies will occur because of more intensive utilisation of production facilities, distribution network, research and development facilities etc. These economies will be available in horizontal mergers (companies dealing in same line of products) where scope of more intensive use of resources is greater.
2. **Operating Economies.** A number of operating economies will be available with the merger of two or more companies. Duplicating facilities in accounting purchasing, marketing, etc. will be eliminated. Operating inefficiencies of small concerns will be controlled by the superior management emerging from the amalgamation.
3. **Synergy.** Synergy refers to the greater combined value of merged firms than the sum of the values of individual units. It is something like one plus one more than two. Operating economies are one of the various synergy benefits of merger or consolidation. The other instances which may result into synergy benefits include, strong R & D facilities of one firm merged with better organized production facilities of another.
4. **Growth.** A company may not grow rapidly through internal expansion merger or amalgamation enables satisfactory and balanced growth of a company.
5. **Diversification.** Two or more companies operating indifferent lines can diversify their activities through amalgamation. Since different companies are already dealing in their respective lines there will be less risk in diversification.
6. **Utilisation of Tax Shields.** When a company with accumulated losses merges with a profit making company, it is able to utilise tax shields. A company having losses will not be able to set off losses against future profits, because it is not a profit earning unit. On the other hand, if it merges with a concern earning profits then the accumulated losses of one unit will be set off against the future profits of the other unit. In this way, the merger or amalgamation will enable the concern to avail tax benefits.
7. **Increase in Value.** The value of the merged company is greater than the sum of the independent values of the merged companies. For example, if X Ltd. and Y Ltd. merge and form Z Ltd., the value of Z Ltd. is expected to be greater than the sum of the independent values of X Ltd. and Y Ltd.
8. **Eliminations of Competition.** The merger or amalgamation of two or more companies will eliminate competition among them. The companies will be able to save their advertising expenses thus enabling them to reduce their prices. The consumers will also benefit in the form of cheaper of goods being made available to them.
9. **Better Financial Planning.** The merged companies will be able to plan their resources in a better way. The collective finances of merged companies will be more and their utilization may be better than in the separate concerns. It may happen that one of the merging companies has short gestation period while the other has longer gestation period. The profits of the company with short gestation period will be utilised to finance the other company. When the company with longer gestation period starts earning profits then it will improve financial position as a whole.
10. **Economic Necessity.** Economic necessity may force the merger of some units. If there are two sick units, government may force their merger to improve their financial position and overall

working. A sick unit may be required to merge with a healthy unit to ensure better utilization of resources, improve returns and better management.

CORPORATE RESTRUCTURING

The Corporate Restructuring is the process of making changes in the composition of a firm's one or more business portfolios in order to have a more profitable enterprise. Simply, reorganizing the structure of the organization to fetch more profits from its operations or is best suited to the present situation.

The Corporate Restructuring takes place in two forms:

- **Financial Restructuring.** The Financial Restructuring may take place due to a drastic fall in the sales because of the adverse economic conditions. Here, the firm may change the equity pattern, cross-holding pattern, debt-servicing schedule and the equity holdings. All this is done to sustain the profitability of the firm and sustain in the market. Generally, the financial or legal advisors are hired to assist the firms in the negotiations.
- **Organizational Restructuring.** The Organizational Restructuring means changing the structure of an organization, such as reducing the hierarchical levels, downsizing the employees, redesigning the job positions and changing the reporting relationships. This is done to cut the cost and pay off the outstanding debt to continue with the business operations in some manner. The need for a corporate restructuring arises because of the change in company's ownership structure due to a merger or takeover, adverse economic conditions, adverse changes in business such as bankruptcy or buyouts, over employed personnel, lack of integration between the divisions, etc.

VALUE CREATION

Value creation is the primary aim of any business entity. Creating value for customers helps sell products and services, while creating value for shareholders, in the form of increases in stock price, insures the future availability of investment capital to fund operations. From a financial perspective, value is said to be created when a business earns revenue (or a return on capital) that exceeds expenses (or the cost of capital). But some analysts insist on a broader definition of "value creation" that can be considered separate from traditional financial measures. "*Traditional methods of assessing organizational performance are no longer adequate in today's economy,*" according to ValueBasedManagement.net. "*Stock price is less and less determined by earnings or asset base. Value creation in today's companies is increasingly represented in the intangible drivers like innovation, people, ideas, and brand.*"

When broadly defined, value creation is increasingly being recognized as a better management goal than strict financial measures of performance, many of which tend to place cost-cutting that produces short-term results ahead of investments that enhance long-term competitiveness and growth. As a result, some experts recommend making value creation the first priority for all employees and all company decisions.

The first step in achieving an organization-wide focus on value creation is understanding the sources and drivers of value creation within the industry, company, and marketplace. Understanding what creates value will help managers focus capital and talent on the most profitable opportunities for growth.

Although the intangible factors that drive value creation differ by industry, some of the major categories of intangible assets include technology, innovation, intellectual property, alliances, management capabilities, employee relations, customer relations, community relations, and brand value. According to Kaplan and Norton, the link between these intangible assets and value creation is corporate strategy. It is important to note that investments made to enhance intangible assets (research and development, employee training, and brand building, for example) usually provide indirect rather than direct benefits. In this way, focusing on value creation forces an organization to adopt a long-term perspective and align all of its resources toward future goals.

MERGER NEGOTIATIONS

Mergers and acquisitions (M&A) are transactions in which the ownership of companies, other business organizations, or their operating units are transferred or consolidated with other entities. As an aspect of strategic management, M&A can allow enterprises to grow or downsize, and change the nature of their business or competitive position.

From a legal point of view, a merger is a legal consolidation of two entities into one, whereas an acquisition occurs when one entity takes ownership of another entity's stock, equity interests or assets. From a commercial and economic point of view, both types of transactions generally result in the consolidation of assets and liabilities under one entity, and the distinction between a "merger" and an "acquisition" is less clear. A transaction legally structured as an acquisition may have the effect of placing one party's business under the indirect ownership of the other party's shareholders, while a transaction legally structured as a merger may give each party's shareholders partial ownership and control of the combined enterprise. A deal may be euphemistically called a merger of equals if both CEOs agree that joining together is in the best interest of both of their companies, while when the deal is unfriendly (that is, when the management of the target company opposes the deal) it may be regarded as an "acquisition".

LEVERAGED BUYOUTS

A leveraged buyout (LBO) is a financial transaction in which a company is purchased with a combination of equity and debt, such that the company's cash flow is the collateral used to secure and repay the borrowed money. The use of debt, which normally has a lower cost of capital than equity, serves to reduce the overall cost of financing the acquisition. The cost of debt is lower because interest payments often reduce corporate income tax liability, whereas dividend payments normally do not. This reduced cost of financing allows greater gains to accrue to the equity, and, as a result, the debt serves as a lever to increase the returns to the equity.

The term LBO is usually employed when a financial sponsor acquires a company. However, many corporate transactions are partially funded by bank debt, thus effectively also representing an LBO. LBOs can have many different forms such as management buyout (MBO), management buy-in (MBI), secondary buyout and tertiary buyout, among others, and can occur in growth situations, restructuring situations, and insolvencies. LBOs mostly occur in private companies, but can also be employed with public companies (in a so-called PtP transaction – Public to Private).

As financial sponsors increase their returns by employing a very high leverage (i.e., a high ratio of debt to equity), they have an incentive to employ as much debt as possible to finance an acquisition. This has, in many cases, led to situations in which companies were "over-leveraged", meaning that they did not generate sufficient cash flows to service their debt, which in turn led to insolvency or to debt-to-equity swaps in which the equity owners lose control over the business to the lenders.

PORTFOLIO MANAGEMENT

A portfolio refers to a collection of investment tools such as stocks, shares, mutual funds, bonds, cash and so on depending on the investor's income, budget and convenient time frame.

Following are the two types of Portfolio:

1. Market Portfolio
2. Zero Investment Portfolio

What is Portfolio Management ?

The art of selecting the right investment policy for the individuals in terms of minimum risk and maximum return is called as portfolio management.

Portfolio management refers to managing an individual's investments in the form of bonds, shares, cash, mutual funds etc so that he earns the maximum profits within the stipulated time frame.

Portfolio management refers to managing money of an individual under the expert guidance of portfolio managers.

In a layman's language, the art of managing an individual's investment is called as portfolio management.

Need for Portfolio Management

Portfolio management presents the **best investment plan** to the individuals as per their income, budget, age and ability to undertake risks.

Portfolio management **minimises the risks** involved in investing and also increases the chance of making profits.

Portfolio managers understand the client's financial needs and suggest the best and unique investment policy for them with minimum risks involved.

Portfolio management enables the portfolio managers to **provide customized investment solutions** to clients as per their needs and requirements.

Types of Portfolio Management

- **Active Portfolio Management.** As the name suggests, in an active portfolio management service, the portfolio managers are actively involved in buying and selling of securities to ensure maximum profits to individuals.
- **Passive Portfolio Management.** In a passive portfolio management, the portfolio manager deals with a fixed portfolio designed to match the current market scenario.
- **Discretionary Portfolio management services.** In Discretionary portfolio management services, an individual authorizes a portfolio manager to take care of his financial needs on his behalf. The individual issues money to the portfolio manager who in turn takes care of all his investment needs, paper work, documentation, filing and so on. In discretionary portfolio management, the portfolio manager has full rights to take decisions on his client's behalf.
- **Non-Discretionary Portfolio management services.** In non discretionary portfolio management services, the portfolio manager can merely advise the client what is good and bad for him but the client reserves full right to take his own decisions.

CAPITAL ASSET PRICING MODEL - CAPM

The Capital Asset Pricing Model (CAPM) describes the relationship between systematic risk and expected return for assets, particularly stocks. CAPM is widely used throughout finance for pricing risky securities and generating expected returns for assets given the risk of those assets and cost of capital.

The formula for calculating the expected return of an asset given its risk is as follows:

$ER_i = Rf + \beta_i (ER_m - R_g)$

ER_i = Expected return of investment

R_f = Risk-free rate

$\hat{a}_i$ = Beta of the investment

ER_m = Expected return of market

$(ER_m - R_f)$ = Market risk premium

Investors expect to be compensated for risk and the time value of money. The risk-free rate in the CAPM formula accounts for the time value of money. The other components of the CAPM formula account for the investor taking on additional risk.

The beta of a potential investment is a measure of how much risk the investment will add to a portfolio that looks like the market. If a stock is riskier than the market, it will have a beta greater than 1. If a stock has a beta of less than one, the formula assumes it will reduce the risk of a portfolio.

A stock's beta is then multiplied by the market risk premium, which is the return expected from the market above the risk-free rate. The risk-free rate is then added to the product of the stock's beta and the market risk premium. The result should give an investor the required return or discount rate they can use to find the value of an asset.

The goal of the CAPM formula is to evaluate whether a stock is fairly valued when its risk and the time value of money are compared to its expected return.

For example, imagine an investor is contemplating a stock worth \$100 per share today that pays a 3% annual dividend. The stock has a beta compared to the market of 1.3, which means it is riskier than a market portfolio. Also assume that the risk-free rate is 3% and this investor expects the market to rise in value by 8% per year.

The expected return of the stock based on the CAPM formula is 9.5%.

$$9.5\% = 3\% + 1.3\,(8\% - 3\%)$$

The expected return of the CAPM formula is used to discount the expected dividends and capital appreciation of the stock over the expected holding period. If the discounted value of those future cash flows is equal to \$100 then the CAPM formula indicates the stock is fairly valued relative to risk.

Problems with the CAPM

There are several assumptions behind the CAPM formula that have been shown not to hold in reality. Despite these issues, the CAPM formula is still widely used because it is simple and allows for easy comparisons of investment alternatives.

Including beta in the formula assumes that risk can be measured by a stock's price volatility. However, price movements in both directions are not equally risky. The look-back period to determine a stock's volatility is not standard because stock returns (and risk) are not normally distributed.

The CAPM also assumes that the risk-free rate will remain constant over the discounting period. Assume in the previous example that the interest rate on U.S. Treasury bonds rose to 5% or 6% during the 10-year holding period. An increase in the risk-free rate also increases the cost of the capital used in the investment and could make the stock look overvalued.

The market portfolio that is used to find the market risk premium is only a theoretical value and is not an asset that can be purchased or invested in as an alternative to the stock. Most of the time, investors will use a major stock index, like the S&P 500, to substitute for the market, which is an imperfect comparison.

The most serious critique of the CAPM is the assumption that future cash flows can be estimated for the discounting process. If an investor could estimate the future return of a stock with a high level of accuracy, the CAPM would not be necessary.

ARBITRAGE PRICING THEORY - APT

Arbitrage pricing theory (APT) is a multi-factor asset pricing model based on the idea that an asset's returns can be predicted using the linear relationship between the asset's expected return and a number of macroeconomic variables that capture systematic risk. It is a useful tool for analyzing portfolios from a value investing perspective, in order to identify securities that may be temporarily mispriced.

The arbitrage pricing theory was developed by the economist Stephen Ross in 1976, as an alternative to the capital asset pricing model (CAPM). Unlike the CAPM, which assume markets are perfectly efficient, APT assumes markets sometimes misprice securities, before the market eventually corrects and securities move back to fair value. Using APT, arbitrageurs hope to take advantage of any deviations from fair market value. However, this is not a risk-free operation in the classic sense of arbitrage, because investors are assuming that the model is correct and making directional trades - rather than locking in risk-free profits.

DERIVATIVES

A derivative is a contract between two parties which derives its value/ price from an underlying asset. The most common types of derivatives are futures, options, forwards and swaps.

OPTIONS

In finance, an option is a contract which gives the buyer (the owner or holder of the option) the right, but not the obligation, to buy or sell an underlying asset or instrument at a specified strike price prior to or on a specified date, depending on the form of the option. The strike price may be set by reference to the spot price (market price) of the underlying security or commodity on the day an option is taken out, or it may be fixed at a discount or at a premium. The seller has the corresponding obligation to fulfill the transaction - to sell or buy - if the buyer (owner) "exercises" the option. An option that conveys to the owner the right to buy at a specific price is referred to as a call; an option that conveys the right of the owner to sell at a specific price is referred to as a put. Both are commonly traded, but the call option is more frequently discussed.

The seller may grant an option to a buyer as part of another transaction, such as a share issue or as part of an employee incentive scheme, otherwise a buyer would pay a premium to the seller for the option. A call option would normally be exercised only when the strike price is below the market value of the underlying asset, while a put option would normally be exercised only when the strike price is above the market value. When an option is exercised, the cost to the buyer of the asset acquired is the strike price plus the premium, if any. When the option expiration date passes without the option being exercised, the option expires and the buyer would forfeit the premium to the seller. In any case, the premium is income to the seller, and normally a capital loss to the buyer.

The owner of an option may on-sell the option to a third party in a secondary market, in either an over-the-counter transaction or on an options exchange, depending on the option. The market price of an American-style option normally closely follows that of the underlying stock being the difference between the market price of the stock and the strike price of the option. The actual market price of the option may vary depending on a number of factors, such as a significant option holder may need to sell the option as the expiry date is approaching and does not have the financial resources to exercise the option, or a buyer in the market is trying to amass a large option holding. The ownership of an option does not generally entitle the holder to any rights associated with the underlying asset, such as voting rights or any income from the underlying asset, such as a dividend.

OPTION PAYOFFS

"Pay off diagrams" a good way to understand the profits and losses with a strategy.

A convenient way to envision what happens with option strategies as the value of the underlying asset changes is with the use of a profit and loss diagram, known as a "payoff diagram". A Payoff diagram is a graphical representation of the potential outcomes of a strategy. Results may be depicted at any point in time, although the graph usually depicts the results at expiration of the options involved in the strategy.

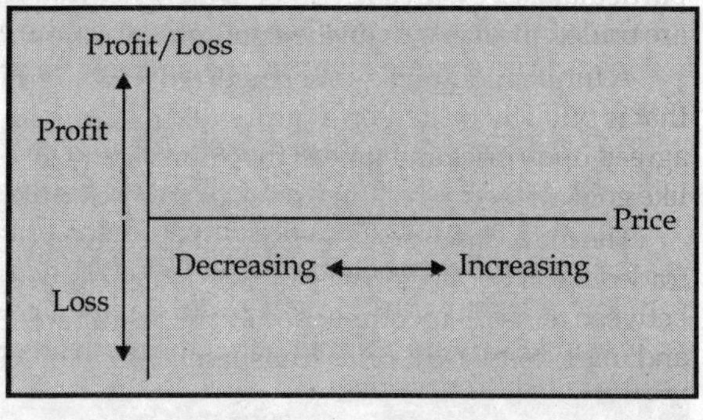

The vertical axis of the diagram reflects profits or losses on option expiration day resulting from particular strategy, while the horizontal axis reflects the underlying asset price on option expiration day. At expiration, there is no time value left, so the option will sell for its intrinsic value. By convention, the diagrams ignore the effect of commissions you have to pay.

OPTION PRICING

Option pricing theory uses variables (stock price, exercise price, volatility, interest rate, time to expiration) to theoretically value an option. Essentially, it provides an estimation of an option's fair value which traders incorporate into their strategies to maximize profits. Some commonly used models to value options are Black-Scholes, binomial option pricing, and Monte-Carlo simulation. These theories have wide margins for error due to deriving their values from other assets, usually the price of a company's common stock.

Understanding Option Pricing Theory

The primary goal of option pricing theory is to calculate the probability that an option will be exercised, or be in-the-money (ITM), at expiration. Underlying asset price (stock price), exercise price, volatility, interest rate, and time to expiration, which is the number of days between the calculation date and the option's exercise date, are commonly used variables that are input into mathematical models to derive an option's theoretical fair value.

Aside from a company's stock and strike prices, time, volatility, and interest rates are also quite integral in accurately pricing an option. The longer that an investor has to exercise the option, the greater the likelihood that it will be ITM at expiration. Similarly, the more volatile the underlying asset, the greater the odds that it will expire ITM. Higher interest rates should translate into higher option prices.

Marketable options require different valuation methods than non-marketable options. Real traded options prices are determined in the open market and, as with all assets, the value can differ from a theoretical value. However, having the theoretical value allows traders to assess the likelihood of profiting from trading those options.

The evolution of the modern-day options market is attributed to the 1973 pricing model published by Fischer Black and Myron Scholes. The Black-Scholes formula is used to derive a theoretical price for financial instruments with a known expiration date. However, this is not the only model. The Cox, Ross, and Rubinstein binomial options pricing model and Monte-Carlo simulation are also widely used.

FORWARD CONTRACTS & FUTURE CONTRACTS

A forward contract is a customized contractual agreement where two private parties agree to trade a particular asset with each other at an agreed specific price and time in the future. Forward contracts are traded privately over-the-counter, not on an exchange.

A futures contract — often referred to as futures — is a standardized version of a forward contract that is publicly traded on a futures exchange. Like a forward contract, a futures contract includes an agreed upon price and time in the future to buy or sell an asset — usually stocks, bonds, or commodities, like gold.

The main differentiating feature between futures and forward contracts — that futures are publicly traded on an exchange while forwards are privately traded — results in several operational differences between them. This comparison examines differences like counter party risk, daily centralized clearing and mark-to-market, price transparency, and efficiency.

	Forward Contract	Futures Contract
Definition	A forward contract is an agreement between two parties to buy or sell an asset (which can be of any kind) at a pre-agreed future point in time at a specified price.	A futures contract is a standardized contract, traded on a futures exchange, to buy or sell a certain underlying instrument at a certain date in the future, at a specified price.
Structure & Purpose	Customized to customer needs. Usually no initial payment required. Usually used for hedging.	Standardized. Initial margin payment required. Usually used for speculation.
Transaction method	Negotiated directly by the buyer and seller	Quoted and traded on the Exchange
Market regulation	Not regulated	Government regulated market (the Commodity Futures Trading Commission or CFTC is the governing body)
Institutional guarantee	The contracting parties	Clearing House
Risk	High counter party risk	Low counter party risk
Guarantees	No guarantee of settlement until the date of maturity only the forward price, based on the spot price of the underlying asset is paid	Both parties must deposit an initial guarantee (margin). The value of the operation is marked to market rates with daily settlement of profits and losses.
Contract Maturity	Forward contracts generally mature by delivering the commodity.	Future contracts may not necessarily mature by delivery of commodity.
Expiry date	Depending on the transaction	Standardized
Method of pre-termination	Opposite contract with same or different counter party. Counter party risk remains while terminating with different counter party.	Opposite contract on the exchange.
Contract size	Depending on the transaction and the requirements of the contracting parties.	Standardized
Market	Primary & Secondary	Primary

WORKING CAPITAL MANAGEMENT

Capital required for a business can be classified under two main categories *i.e.*,

(i) Fixed capital
(ii) Working capital

Every business needs funds for two purposes for its establishment and to carry out its day-to-day operations. Long term funds are required to create production facilities through purchase of fixed assets such as plant and machinery, land, building, furniture etc. Investments in these assets represent that part of firm's capital which is blocked on a permanent or fixed basis and is called fixed capital. Funds are also needed for short-term purposes for the purchase of raw materials, payment of wages and other day-to-day expenses, *etc.* these funds are known as working capital.

Working capital, in general practice, refers to the excess of current assets over current liabilities. Management of working capital is therefore concerned with the problems that arise in attempting to manage the current assets, the current liabilities and the inter-relationship that exists between them.

The basic goal of working capital management is to manage the current assets and current liabilities of a firm in such a way that a satisfactory level of working capital is maintained *i.e.* it is neither inadequate nor excessive. Working capital management is three dimensional in nature:

(i) Dimension I is concerned with the formulation of policies with regard to profitability, risk and liquidity.
(ii) Dimension II is concerned with the decisions about the composition and level of current assets.
(iii) Dimension III is concerned with the decisions about the composition and level of current liabilities.

Concepts of Working Capital

There are two concepts of working capital:

(i) Gross working capital
(ii) Net working capital

In the broad sense, the term working capital refers to the gross working capital and represents the amount of funds invested in current assets. Thus, *the gross working capital is the capital invested in total current assets of the enterprise.* Current assets are those assets which in the ordinary course of business can be converted into cash within a short period of normally one accounting year. Examples of current assets are given as under:

Constituents of Current Assets

1. Cash in hand and bank balances.
2. Bills Receivables.
3. Sundry Debtors (less provision for bad debts).
4. Short-term loans and advances.
5. Inventories of stocks, as:
   (a) Raw materials, (b) Work-in-process
   (c) Stores and spares, (d) Finished goods.
6. Temporary investments of surplus funds.
7. Prepaid Expenses.
8. Accrued Incomes.

In a narrow sense, the term working capital refers to the net working capital. *Net working capital is the excess of current assets over current liabilities*, or say:

Net working capital = Current Assets – Current liabilities

Net working capital may be positive or negative. When the current assets exceed the current liabilities the working capital is positive and the negative working capital results when the current liabilities are more than the current assets. Current liabilities are those liabilities which are intended to be paid in the ordinary course of business within a short period of normally one accounting year out of the current assets or the income of the business. Examples of current liabilities are given as under:

Constituents of Current Liabilities

1. Bills Payable.
2. Sundry Creditors or Accounts Payable.
3. Accrued or Outstanding Expenses.
4. Short-term loans, advances and deposits.
5. Dividends Payable.
6. Bank Overdraft.
7. Provision for taxation, if it does not amount to appropriation of profits.

The gross working capital concept is financial or going concern concept whereas net working capital is an accounting concept of working capital. These two concepts of working capital are not exclusive, rather both have their own merits. The gross concept is sometimes preferred to the net concept of working capital for the following reasons:

1. It enables the enterprise to provide correct amount of working capital at the right time.
2. Every management is more interested in the total current assets with which it has to operate than the sources from where it is made available.
3. The gross concept takes into consideration the fact that every increase in the funds of the enterprise would increase its working capital.
4. The gross concept of working capital is more useful in determining the rate of return on investments in working capital.

The net working capital concept, however, is also important for the following reasons:

1. It is a qualitative concept which indicates the firm's ability to meet its operating expenses and short-term liabilities.
2. It indicates the margin of protection available to the short-term creditors, *i.e.*, the excess of current assets over current liabilities.
3. It is an indicator of the financial soundness of an enterprise.
4. It suggests the need for financing a part of the working capital requirements out of permanent sources of funds.

To conclude, it may be said that, both gross and net, concepts of working capital are important aspects of the working capital management. The net concept of working capital may be suitable only for proprietary form of organisations such as sole-trader or partnership firms. But the gross concept is very suitable to the company form of organisation where there is a divorce between ownership, management and control.

However, it may be made clear that *as per the general practice, net working capital is referred to simply as working capital*. In the words of Hoagland, "Working capital is descriptive of that capital which is not fixed. But the more common use of the working capital is to consider it as the difference between the book value of the current assets and current liabilities."

Classification or Kinds of Working Capital

1. **Permanent or Fixed Working Capital.** Permanent or fixed working capital is the minimum amount which is required to ensure effective utilisation of fixed facilities and for maintaining the circulation of current assets. There is always a minimum level of current assets which is continuously required by the enterprise to carry out its normal business operations. For example, every firm has to maintain a minimum level of raw materials, work-in-process, finished goods and cash balance. This minimum level of current assets is called permanent or fixed working capital as this part of capital is permanently blocked in current assets. As the business grows, the requirements of permanent working capital also increase due to the increase in current assets. The permanent working capital can further be classified as regular working capital and reserve working capital required to ensure circulation of current assets from cash to inventories, from inventories to receivables and from receivables to cash and so on. Reserve working capital is the excess amount over the requirement for regular working capital which may be provided for contingencies that may arise at unstated periods such as strikes, rise in prices, depression, *etc.*
2. **Temporary or Variable Working Capital.** Temporary or variable working capital is the amount of working capital which is required to meet the seasonal demands and some special exigencies. Variable working capital can be further classified as seasonal working capital and special working capital. Most of the enterprises have to provide additional working capital to meet the seasonal and special needs. The capital required to meet the seasonal needs of the enterprise is called seasonal working capital. Special working capital is that part of working capital which is required to meet special exigencies such as launching of extensive marketing campaigns, for conducting research, *etc.*

   Temporary working capital differs from permanent working capital in the sense that it is required for short periods and cannot be permanently employed gainfully in the business. Figures given below illustrate the difference between permanent and temporary working capital.

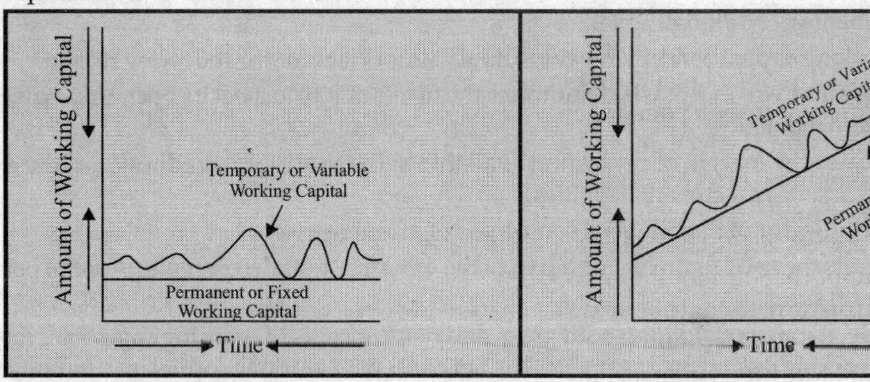

Fig. 1. Fig. 2

In Fig. 1, permanent working capital is stable or fixed over time while the temporary or variable working capital fluctuates. In Fig. 2, permanent working capital is also increasing with the passage of time due to expansion of business but even then it does not fluctuate as variable working capital which sometimes increases and sometimes decreases.

INTERNATIONAL FINANCIAL MANAGEMENT

At the Bretton Woods Conference in 1944 it was decided to establish a new monetary order that would expand international trade, promote international capital flows and contribute to monetary stability. The IMF and the World Bank were borne out of this Conference of the end of World War II. The World Bank was established to help the restoration of economies disrupted by War by facilitating the investment of capital for productive purposes and to promote the long-range balanced growth of international trade. On the other hand, the IMF is primarily a supervisory institution for coordinating the efforts of member countries to achieve greater cooperation in the formulation of economic policies. It helps to promote exchange stability and orderly exchange relations among its member countries. It is in this context that the present chapter reviews the purpose and working of some of the international financial institutions and the contributions made by them in promoting economic and social progress in developing countries by helping raise standards of living and productivity to the point of which development becomes self-sustaining.

International Sources of Finance

One major source of financing is international non-profit agencies. There are several regional development banks such as the Asian Development Bank, the African Development Bank and Fund and the Caribbean Development Bank. The primary purpose of these agencies is to finance productive development projects or to promote economic development in a particular region. The Inter-American Development Bank, for example, has the principal purpose of accelerating the economic development of its Latin American member countries. In general, both public and private entities are eligible to borrow money from such agencies as long as private funds are not available at reasonable rates and terms. Although the interest rate can vary from agency to agency, these loan rates are very attractive and very much in demand.

Of all the international financial organisations, the most familiar is the World Bank, formally known as the International Bank for Reconstruction and Development (IBRD). The World Bank has two affiliates that are legally and financially distinct entities, the International Development Association (IDA) and the International Finance Corporation (IFC). Exhibit 1 provides a comparison among IBRD, IDA and IFC in terms of their objectives, member countries, lending terms, lending qualifications as well as other details. All three organisations have the same central goals: to promote economic and social progress in poor or developing countries by helping raise standards of living and productivity to the point at which development becomes self-sustaining.

Toward this common objective, the World Bank, IDA and IFC have three interrelated functions and these are to lend funds, to provide advice and to serve as a catalyst in order to stimulate investments by others. In the process, financial resources are channelled from developed countries to the developing world with the hope that developing countries, through this assistance, will progress to a level that will permit them, in turn, to contribute to the development process of other less fortunate countries. Japan is a prime example of a country that has come full circle. From being a borrower, Japan is now a major lender to these three organisations. South Korea is moving in a direction similar to that of Japan nearly a quarter of a century ago.

International Monetary Fund

The International Monetary Fund (IMF) came into official existence on December 27, 1945, when 29 countries signed its Articles of Agreement (its Charter) agreed at a conference held in Bretton Woods, New Hampshire, USA, from July 1-22, 1944. The IMF commenced financial operations on March 1,

1947. Its current membership is 188 countries. Its Total Quotas are SDR 476 billion (about US$ 755.7 billion at the exchange rate), following a 45 per cent quota increase effective from January 22,1999.

- **Staff.** Approximately 2,700 from 110 countries.
- **Accounting Unit.** Special Drawing Right (SDR). As of August 23, 1999, SDR I equalled US $1.370280.

IMF is a cooperative institution that 182 countries have voluntarily joined because they see the advantage of consulting with one another on this forum to maintain a stable system of buying and selling their currencies so that payments in foreign currency can take place between countries smoothly and without delay. Its policies and activities are guided by its Charter known as the Articles of Agreement.

IMF lends money to members having trouble meeting financial obligations to other members, but only on the condition that they undertake economic reforms to eliminate these difficulties for their own good and that of the entire membership. Contrary to widespread perception, the IMF has no effective authority over the domestic economic policies of its members. What authority the IMF does possess is confined to requiring the member to disclose information on its monetary and fiscal policies and to avoid, as far as possible, putting restrictions on exchange of domestic for foreign currency and on making payments to other members.

There are several major accomplishments to the credit of the International Monetary System. For example, it

- sustained a rapidly increasing volume of trade and investment;
- displayed flexibility in adapting to changes in international commerce;
- proved to be efficient (even when there were decreasing percentages of reserves to trade);
- proved to be hardy (it survived a number of pre-1971 crises, speculative and otherwise, and the down-and-up swings of several business cycles);
- allowed for a growing degree or international cooperation;
- established a capacity to accommodate reforms and improvements.

To an extent, the fund served as an international central bank to help countries during periods of temporary balance of payments difficulties by protecting their rates of exchange. Because of that, countries did not need to resort to exchange controls and other barriers to restrict world trade.

Members and Administration

On joining the IMF, each member country contributes a certain sum of money called a 'quota subscription', as a sort of credit union deposit. Quotas serve various purposes.

- They form a pool of money that the IMF can draw from to lend to members in times of financial difficulty.
- They form the basis of determining the Special Drawing Rights (SDR).
- They determine the voting power of the member.

Statutory Purposes

The purposes of the International Monetary Fund are:

- To promote international monetary cooperation through a permanent institution that provides the machinery for consultation and collaboration on international monetary problems.
- To facilitate the expansion and balanced growth of international trade and to contribute, thereby, to the promotion and maintenance of high levels of employment and real income and to the development of the productive resources of all members as primary objectives of economic policy.

- To promote exchange stability, to maintain orderly exchange arrangements among members and to avoid competitive exchange depreciation.
- To assist in the establishment of a multilateral system of payments in respect of current transactions between members and in the elimination of foreign exchange restrictions which hamper the growth of world trade.
- To give confidence to members by making the general resources of the Fund temporarily available to them under adequate safeguards, thus providing them with opportunity to correct maladjustment in their balance of payments without resorting to measures destructive to national or international prosperity.
- In accordance with the above, to shorten the duration and lessen the degree of disequilibrium in the international balances of payments of members.

Financial Assistance

The IMF lends money only to member countries with balance of payments problems. A member country with a payments problem can immediately withdraw from the IMF the 25 per cent of its quota. A member in greater difficulty may request for more money from the IMP and can borrow up to three times its quota provided the member country undertakes to initiate a series of reforms and uses the borrowed money effectively. The frequently used mechanisms by the IMF to lend money are :

1. Standby Arrangements
2. Extended Arrangements
3. Structural Adjustment Mechanism (With low interest rates)

SDRs

As time passed, it became evident that the Fund's resources for providing short-term accommodation to countries in monetary difficulties were not sufficient. To resolve the situation, the Fund, after much debate and long deliberations, created new drawing rights in 1969. Special Drawing Rights (SDRs), sometimes called paper gold, are special account entries on the IMF books designed to provide additional liquidity to support growing world commerce. Although SDRs are a form of money not convertible to gold, their gold value is guaranteed, which helps to ensure their acceptability. Initially, SDRs worth $9.5 billion were created.

Participant nations may use SDRs as a source of currency in a spot transaction, as a loan for clearing a financial obligation, as a security for a loan, as a Swap against currency, or in a forward exchange operation. A nation with a balance of payments need may use its SDRs to obtain usable currency from another nation designated by the fund. A participant also may use SDRs to make payments to the Fund, such as repurchases. The Fund itself may transfer SDRs to a participant for various purposes including the transfer of SDRs instead of currency to a member using the Fund's resources.

By providing a mechanism for international monetary cooperation, working towards reducing restrictions to trade and capital flows and helping members with their short-term balance of payments difficulties, the IMF makes a significant and unique contribution to human welfare and improved living standards throughout the world.

Services

Besides supervising the international monetary system and providing financial support to member countries, the IMF assists its members by:

- Providing technical assistance in certain areas of its competence.

- Running an educational institute in Washington and offering training courses abroad.
- Issuing wide variety of publications containing valuable information and statistics that are useful not only to the member countries but also to banks, research institutes, university and the media.

The World Bank

The World Bank group is a multinational financial institution established at the end of World War II (1944) to help provide long-term capital for the reconstruction and development of member countries. The group is important to multinational corporations because it provides much of the planning and financing for economic development projects involving billions of dollars for which private businesses can act as contractors and suppliers of goods and engineering related services.

The purpose for the setting up of the Bank are :

- To assist in the reconstruction and development of territories of members by facilitating the investment of capital for productive purposes, including the restoration of economies destroyed or disrupted by war, the reconversion of productive facilities to peacetime needs and encouragement of the development or productive facilities and resources in less developed countries.
- To promote private foreign investment by means of guarantees or participation in loans and other investments made by private investors; and when private capital is not available on reasonable terms, to supplement private investment by providing, on suitable conditions, finance for productive purposes out of its own capital, funds raised by it and its other resources.
- To promote the long-range balanced growth of international trade and the maintenance of equilibrium in balance of payments by encouraging international investment for the development of the productive resources of members, thereby assisting in raising productivity, the standard of living and condition of labour in their territories.
- To arrange the loans made or guaranteed by it in relation to international loans through other channels so that the more useful and urgent projects, large and small alike, can be dealt with first.
- To conduct its operations with due regard to the effect of international investment on business conditions in the territories of members and, in the immediate post-war years, to assist in bringing about a smooth transition from a wartime to a peacetime economy.

The World Bank is the International Bank for Reconstruction and Development (IBRD) and the International Development Association (IDA). The IBRD has two affiliates, the International Finance Corporation (IFC) and the Multilateral Investment Guarantee Agency (MIGA). The Bank, the IFC and the MIGA are sometimes referred to as the "World Bank Group".

International Bank for Reconstruction and Development (IBRD)

The IBRD was set up in 1945 along with the IMF to aid in rebuilding the world economy. It was owned by the governments of 151 countries and its capital is subscribed by those governments; it provides funds to borrowers by borrowing funds in the world capital markets, from the proceeds of loan repayments as well as retained earnings. At its funding, the bank's major objective was to serve as an international financing facility to function in reconstruction and development. With Marshall Plan providing the impetus for European reconstruction, the Bank was able to turn its efforts towards the developing countries.

Generally, the IBRD lends money to a government for the purpose of developing that country's economic infrastructure such as roads and power generating facilities. Funds are directed towards developing countries at more advanced stages of economic and social growth. Also, funds are lent only to members of the IMF, usually when private capital is unavailable at reasonable terms. Loans generally have a grace period of five years and are repayable over a period of fifteen or fewer years.

International Development Association (IDA)

The IDA was formed in 1960 as a part of the World Bank Group to provide financial support to LDCs on a more liberal basis than could be offered by the IBRD. The IDA has 137 member countries, although all members of the IBRD are free to join the IDA. IDA's funds come from subscriptions from its developed members and from the earnings of the IBRD. Credit terms usually are extended to 40 to 50 years with no interest. Repayment begins after a ten-year grace period and can be paid in the local currency, as long as it is convertible. Loans are made only to the poorest countries in the world, those with an annual per capita gross national product of $480 or less. More than 40 countries are eligible for IDA financing.

International Finance Corporation (IFC)

The IFC was established in 1956. There are 133 countries that are members of the IFC and it is legally and financially separate from the IBRD, although IBRD provides some administrative and other services to the IFC. The IFC's main responsibilities are (i) To provide risk capital in the form of equity and long-term loans for productive private enterprises in association with private investors and management; (ii) To encourage the development of local capital markets by carrying out standby and underwriting arrangements; and (iii) To stimulate the international flow of capital by providing financial and technical assistance to privately controlled finance companies. Loans are made to private firms in the developing member countries and are usually for a period of seven to twelve years.

Asian Development Bank (ADB)

The Asian Development Bank is a multilateral developmental finance institution founded in 1966 by 31 member governments to promote social and economic progress of Asian and the Pacific region. The Bank gives special attention to the needs of smaller or less developed countries and gives priority to regional/non-regional national programmes.

In early 1960, the United National Economic Commission for Asia and Far East (UNECAFE) estimated that Asia and the Pacific region had an annual deficit of US $ one billion. The ADB was formed to fill this gap. The inaugural meeting was held in Tokyo and the newly named bank was installed in Manila (Philippines). The first President was Mr. Wanatanade and during his initial years the bank conducted regional surveys to develop a fuller understanding of the social and economic conditions of the Developing Member Countries (DMC).

In 1974, the Asian Development Fund was established to streamline the bank's means of financing. During 1972-76, the Banks' commitment to the DMCs increased from $316 million to 776 million. In the late 70s, the bank recognised the need to develop additional strategy to reduce poverty in the region, so they evolved the concept of multi-project loans which was a cost-effective means for funding projects too small for the Bank's involvement.

In 1978, the Asian Development Fund was increased to 2.15 billion. 1986 was a significant year for the Bank because the Peoples Republic of China joined the Bank and India received her first loan of $100 million to the ICICI (Investment Credit and Investment Corporation of India) for one lending to Private Sector enterprises. ADB achieved $ 22.9 billion operations in 2014 by leveraging $ 9.2 billion in cofinancing a record high for ACB with 13.7 billion.

On the borrowing front, in 1991, the Bank offered Dragon Bonds which was a US $ 300 million offering in the capital markets or Hong Kong, Singapore and Taipei.

The present President is Mr. Takechoko Nakao, who was Japan's former Vice Minister of Finance for International Affairs, before he took over in 28 April, 2013.

World Trade Organization (W.T.O.)

GATT was an international body having its headquarters at Geneva and was founded in 1947 by 23 member countries including India. The body now comprises of 162 member countries of which around two-thirds are developing nations.

According to the approved GAIT accord, a Preparatory Committee would be set up, which in turn would set up the World Trade Organization (WTO), to become operational in early 1995. The WTO will act as a permanent watchdog on the International Trade and will enjoy the status similar to that of UNIDO wherein each member nation will have single voting right.

GATT was converted from a provisional agreement into a formal international organisation called World Trade Organization (WTO) with effect from January 1, 1995. WTO will serve as a single institutional framework encompassing GATT and all the result of the Uruguay Round.

It will be directed by a Ministerial Conference that will meet at least once every two years and its regular business will be overseen by a General Council. The WTO is a more powerful body with enlarged functions than the GATT and is envisaged to play a major role in the world economic affairs.

Role of WTO in International Trade

(i) WTO's aim is to liberalise international trade.
(ii) WTO establishes rules regarding international trade and sees that these rules are obeyed.
(iii) 153 countries of the world are currently members of the WTO.
(iv) It is seen that the developed countries have unfairly retained trade barriers. On the other hand, WTO rules have forced developing countries to remove trade barriers.

Functions of WTO

The former GATT was not really an organisation; it was merely a legal arrangement. On the other hand, the WTO is a new international organisation set up as a permanent body. It is designed to play the role of a watchdog in the spheres of trade in goods, trade in services, foreign investment, intellectual property rights, etc. Article III has set out the following five functions of WTO;

(i) The WTO shall facilitate the implementation, administration and operation and further the objectives of this Agreement and of the Multilateral Trade Agreements, and shall also provide the frame work for the implementation, administration and operation of the Plurilateral Trade Agreements.
(ii) The WTO shall provide the forum for negotiations among its members concerning their multilateral trade relations in matters dealt with under the Agreement in the Annexes to this Agreement.
(iii) The WTO shall administer the Understanding on Rules and Procedures Governing the Settlement of Disputes.
(iv) The WTO shall administer Trade Policy Review Mechanism.
(v) With a view to achieving greater coherence in global economic policy making, the WTO shall cooperate, as appropriate, with the international Monetary Fund (IMF) and with the International Bank for Reconstruction and Development (IBRD) and its affiliated agencies.

Objectives of WTO

Important objectives of WTO are mentioned below:

(i) to implement the new world trade system as visualised in the Agreement;
(ii) to promote World Trade in a manner that benefits every country;
(iii) to ensure that developing countries secure a better balance in the sharing of the advantages resulting from the expansion of international trade corresponding to their developmental needs;
(iv) to demolish all hurdles to an open world trading system and usher in international economic renaissance because the world trade is an effective instrument to foster economic growth;
(v) to enhance competitiveness among all trading partners so as to benefit consumers and help in global integration;
(vi) to increase the level of production and productivity with a view to ensuring level of employment in the world;
(vii) to expand and utilize world resources to the best;
(viii) to improve the level of living for the global population and speed up economic development of the member nations.

INTERNATIONAL FINANCIAL MANAGEMENT

International Financial Management is a well-known term in today's world and it is also known as international finance. It means financial management in an international business environment. It is different because of the different currency of different countries, dissimilar political situations, imperfect markets, diversified opportunity sets.

International Financial Management came into being when the countries of the world started opening their doors for each other. This phenomenon is well known by the name of "liberalization". Due to the open environment and freedom to conduct business in any corner of the world, entrepreneurs started looking for opportunities even outside their country boundaries. The spark of liberalization was further aired by swift progression in telecommunications and transportation technologies that too with increased accessibility and daily dropping prices. Apart from everything else, we cannot forget the contribution of financial innovations such as currency derivatives; cross-border stock listings, multi-currency bonds and international mutual funds.

The resultant of liberalization and technology advancement is today's dynamic international business environment. Financial management for a domestic business and an international business is as dramatically different as the opportunities in the two. The meaning and objective of financial management do not change in international financial management but the dimensions and dynamics change drastically.

Four major facets which differentiate international financial management from domestic financial management are an introduction of foreign currency, political risk and market imperfections and enhanced opportunity set.

Foreign Exchange

It's an additional risk which a finance manager is required to cater to under an International Financial Management setting. Foreign exchange risk refers to the risk of fluctuating prices of currency which has the potential to convert a profitable deal into a loss-making one.

Political Risks

The political risk may include any change in the economic environment of the country viz. Taxation Rules, Contract Act etc. It is pertaining to the government of a country which can anytime change the rules of the game in an unexpected manner.

Market Imperfection

Having done a lot of integration in the world economy, it has got a lot of differences across the countries in terms of transportation cost, different tax rates, etc. Imperfect markets force a finance manager to strive for best opportunities across the countries.

Enhanced Opportunity Set

By doing business in other than native countries, a business expands its chances of reaping fruits of different taste. Not only does it enhances the opportunity for the business but also diversifies the overall risk of a business.

Just like domestic financial management, the goal of International Finance is also to maximize the shareholder's wealth. The goal is not only is limited to the 'Shareholders' but extends to all 'Stakeholders' viz. employees, suppliers, customers etc. No goal can be achieved without achieving welfare of shareholders. In other words, maximizing shareholder's wealth would mean maximizing the price of the share. Here again comes a question, whether in which currency should the value of the share be maximized? This is an important decision to be taken by the management of the organization.

International level initiatives like General Agreement on Trade and Tariffs (GATT), The North American Free Trade Agreement (NAFTA), World Trade Organization (WHO) etc has to give promoted international trade and given it a shape. All because of liberalization and those international agreements, we have a buzz word called "MNC" i.e. Multinational Corporations. MNCs enjoy an edge over other normal companies because of its international setting and best opportunities.

International Finance has become an important wing for all big MNCs. Without the expertise in International Financial Management, it can be difficult to sustain in the market because international financial markets have a totally different shape and analytics compared to the domestic financial markets. A sound management of international finances can help an organization achieve same efficiency and effectiveness in all markets.

Foreign Exchange Market

Foreign exchange, or Forex, is the conversion of one country's currency into that of another. In a free economy, a country's currency is valued according to factors of supply and demand. In other words, a currency's value can be pegged to another country's currency, such as the U.S. dollar, or even to a basket of currencies. A country's currency value also may be fixed by the country's government. However, most countries float their currencies freely against those of other countries, which keeps them in constant fluctuation.

The value of any particular currency is determined by market forces based on trade, investment, tourism, and geo-political risk. The foremost requirement of foreign exchange is in international trade. Also, every time a tourist visits a country, for example, he or she must pay for goods and services using the currency of the host country. Therefore, a tourist must exchange the currency of his or her home country for the local currency. Currency exchange of this kind is one of the demand factors for a particular currency. Another important factor of demand occurs when a foreign company seeks to do business with a company in a specific country. Usually, the foreign company will have to pay the local company in their local currency. At other times, it may be desirable for an investor from one country to invest in another, and that investment would have to be made in the local currency as well. All of these requirements produce a need for foreign exchange and are the reasons why foreign exchange markets are so large.

Foreign exchange is handled globally between banks and all transactions fall under the auspice of the Bank of International Settlements.

Exchange Rate

The rate at which one currency buys or exchanges for another currency is known as the rate of exchange.

The foreign-exchange rate between two currencies is the rate at which one currency will be exchanged for another. It is also regarded as the value of one country's currency in terms of another currency. For example, an inter-bank exchange rate of 91 Japanese yen (JPY, ¥) to the United States dollar (US$) means that ¥91 will be exchanged for each US$1 or that US$1 will be exchanged for each ¥91. The rate of exchange, therefore, expresses the external purchasing power of a currency. The rate of exchange is a price—the price of one currency in terms of another. Like any other price, the rate of exchange depends upon demand and supply of the local currency in terms of the foreign currency.

(i) **Spot Rate and Forward Rate.** The spot rate of exchange refers to the price of foreign exchange in terms of domestic money payable for the immediate delivery of particular foreign currency. It is an existing or day-to-day exchange rate.

There are several future transactions whose delivery would be made sometime in the future. The rates at which these transactions are consummated are called as forward rate of exchange. It is the rate fulfilling the agreement between two parties based on future delivery of goods. The forward rate is expressed at par, at premium and at a discount.

(ii) **Fixed, Flexible and Floating Exchange Rates.** Fixed exchange rate refers to the system under which the rate of exchange of a currency is fixed or pegged in terms of gold or in terms of another currency. Flexible exchange rate, on the other hand, involves keeping the exchange rate fixed over short periods and changing it from time to time according to need. Floating rate of exchange comes into existence when the currency unit of a country is free to fluctuate and find its own level, according to conditions of demand and supply in the foreign exchange market.

(iii) **Multiple Rates.** If a country adopts more than one rate of exchange for its currency, it is said to follow a system of multiple exchange rates. It may have one rate for exports and another for imports; or it may have one rate of exchange with some countries, and another rate with others.

(iv) **Two Tier Exchange Rate System.** A form of multiple exchange rate is known as the two-tier exchange rate system under which the Government maintains two rates – a higher rate for commercial transactions and a lower rate for capital transactions. Since 1971, France and Italy have adopted this system.

If a currency is free-floating, its exchange rate is allowed to vary against that of other currencies and is determined by the market forces of supply and demand. Exchange rates for such currencies are likely to change almost constantly as quoted on financial markets, mainly by banks, around the world. A movable or adjustable peg system is a system of fixed exchange rates, but with a provision for the devaluation of a currency. For example, between 1994 and 2005, the Chinese yuan renminbi (RMB) was pegged to the United States dollar at RMB 8.2768 to $1. China was not the only country to do this; from the end of World War II until 1967, Western European countries all maintained fixed exchange rates with the US dollar based on the Bretton Woods system.

The "real exchange rate" (RER) is the purchasing power of two currencies relative to one another. It is based on the GDP deflator measurement of the price level in the domestic and foreign countries, which is arbitrarily set equal to 1 in a given base year. Therefore, the level of the RER is arbitrarily set depending on which year is chosen as the base year for the GDP deflator of two countries. The changes of the RER are instead informative on the evolution over time of the relative price of a unit of GDP in the foreign country in terms of GDP units of the domestic country. If all goods were freely tradable, and foreign and domestic residents purchased identical baskets of goods, purchasing power parity (PPP) would hold for the GDP deflators of the two countries, and the RER would be constant and equal to one.

Arguments in Favour of and Against Flexible Exchange Rate

Arguments in Favour of a Floating Exchange Rate

(i) **Automatic balance of payments adjustment.** Any balance of payments disequilibrium will tend to be rectified by a change in the exchange rate. For example, if a country has a balance of payments deficit then the currency should depreciate. Conversely, a balance of payments surplus should be eliminated by an appreciation of the currency.

(ii) **Freeing internal policy.** With a floating exchange rate, balance of payments disequilibrium should be rectified by a change in the external price of the currency. However, with a fixed rate, curing a deficit could involve a general deflationary policy resulting in unpleasant consequences for the whole economy such as unemployment. The floating rate allows governments freedom to pursue their own internal policy objectives such as growth and full employment without external constraints.

(iii) **Absence of crises.** Fixed rates are often characterised by crises as pressure mounts on a currency to devalue or revalue. The fact that, with a floating rate, such changes are automatic should remove the element of crisis from international relations.

(iv) **Flexibility.** Post-1973 there were great changes in the pattern of world trade as well as a major change in world economics as a result of the OPEC oil shock. A fixed exchange rate would have caused major problems at this time as some countries would be uncompetitive given their inflation rate. The floating rate allows a country to re-adjust more flexibly to external shocks.

(v) **Lower foreign exchange reserves.** A country with a fixed rate usually has to hold large amounts of foreign currency in order to prepare for a time when they have to defend that fixed rate. These reserves have an opportunity cost.

Arguments Against Flexible Exchange Rate

(i) It creates uncertainty for exporters and importers as they remain unsure about the amount payable or receivable.

(ii) It discourages investment and borrowings due to uncertainty and thus hampers economic growth.

(iii) Under flexible exchange rate, macro-economic policies lose stability as they become prone to the wild fluctuations in the exchange rate

(iv) Flexible exchange rate may also give rise to irrational speculation that leads to destabilisation of the exchange rate.

(v) It also results in poor international co-operation since each country allows the exchange rate to be determined in the market that does not bind them to co-operate with other nations.

(vi) Flexible exchange rate is inflationary in nature as it results in frequent increase in prices due to depreciation of traded goods. Moreover, appreciation of goods does not bring about a parallel reduction in prices.

(vii) Under flexible exchange rate, depreciation of a currency may cause structural unemployment especially in developing countries.

To minimise these disadvantages, India has adopted the managed flexible exchange rate wherein the RBI selectively intervenes in the market to prevent wide fluctuations.

Exchange Market Intervention

Exchange Market Intervention' is defined as the sale or purchase of monetary authorities with the aim of changing the exchange rate of their own currency vis-a-vis one or more currencies.

If there is too much demand for foreign currency, that currency will appreciate too much and depreciate the domestic currency. At this point, the central bank intervenes by releasing the foreign currency (from its reserves) in the market to stabilize the exchange rate.

Similarly, if there is too less demand for foreign currency, that currency will depreciate and the domestic currency appreciates too much. At this point, the central bank intervenes by purchasing foreign currency from the market to stabilize exchange rate.

Arguments in favour of Exchange Rate Intervention

(i) **Appropriate exchange rate.** The central bank may be in a better position to gather all the relevant information than the other participants in the market. Hence it can appropriately predict the future course of policies and their implications on the exchange rate. So, it can plan its intervention in the market according to the situation and influence the exchange rate. In absence of intervention, the market may indulge in speculation due to lack of accurate information.

(ii) **Control over distortions in economic activities.** Exchange rate which deviate from the real exchange rate (in relation to the purchasing power parity) may lead to distortion in resource allocation between external and domestic sectors.

Undervaluation leads to inflationary pressure whereas overvaluation leads to higher rates of unemployment.

Either undervaluation or overvaluation brings in uncertainty and affects investment decisions. This can be controlled by intervention of the monetary authorities by making necessary adjustments in the exchange rates.

(iii) **Smoothens economic adjustment process.** A persistent surplus or deficit in the balance of payments leads to changes in the exchange rate to correct the disequilibrium.

These changes may result in disturbances in the domestic economic activities.

Intervention can reduce such disturbances and their effects.

(iv) **Others arguments**

- Managed flexibility facilitates economic growth due to proper flow of foreign trade.
- Higher economic growth increases employment and improves the standard of living of the people.
- Managed flexibility also facilitates higher investment due to growth potential which further boosts the economic growth of a nation.

Foreign Exchange Rate Management in India since Independence

India has undertaken various changes regard to its exchange rate management system. These changes have been brought about taking into consideration various changes taking place throughout the world that influence the foreign exchange market. At present, India has adopted the managed flexible exchange rate system that allows government intervention to bring the required stability in the exchange rate.

RBI and Exchange Rate

In India, the exchange rate policy at present is guided by principles of monitoring and management based on the underlying demand and supply conditions. The following are the objectives of RBI's intervention:

- Determining the exchange rate movements in an orderly manner.
- Reducing excess volatility.
- Preventing the occurrence of destabilising speculation.

In order to carry out these objectives, the RBI tries to maintain adequate foreign exchange reserves so that it can conduct the intervention operation.

Foreign Exchange Mechanism (Market)

The foreign exchange market consists of a number of banks, brokers and dealers engaged in selling foreign exchange and also the central bank of the country and the Treasury authorities. The last two may intervene in the market occasionally. However, in India, where there was strict exchange control system, there was no foreign exchange market as such. All exporters who secured foreign currency had to surrender it within a period of three months to the Reserve Bank of India and get rupees instead. All Indian importers had to secure the necessary foreign exchange from the Reserve Bank of India by supplying rupees.

Following are the functions of foreign exchange market:

(a) **Transfer Function.** The principal function of the foreign exchange market is to transfer money between countries. In the transfer of foreign exchange arising out of international trade, the bill of exchange is the instrument normally used. The bill of exchange may be a three-month bill or a sight bill or draft. The instrument most in use in foreign payments these days is the telegraphic transfer (T.T.). It is an instruction from one bank to its correspondent bank in a foreign country to pay a specific amount of foreign currency to a particular person or firm.

(b) **Credit Function.** The second function, viz., credit function, of the foreign exchange market may briefly be explained here. We have mentioned that the bill of exchange is an instrument used in the foreign exchange market. Since normally it has a maturity of 3 months, credit is required for that period. The three-month period is allowed so that the importer may be able to take possession of the goods, sell them and secure the amount to pay off the bill.

(c) **Hedging Function.** Finally, hedging function is performed by the foreign exchange market whenever there are exchange risks. When exchange rates are fixed and exchange controls are imposed, there is no risk involved in foreign exchange dealings. A business man can have rupees or pound-sterling, for rupees can be converted into the pound and back again. If, on the other hand, the rupee-sterling rate is subject to alteration, then a firm which has to receive or make payment in pound-sterling will have to take exchange risks.

MULTIPLE CHOICE QUESTIONS

1. Time preference for money is also known as
   (a) Time value of money
   (b) Present value of money
   (c) Future value of money
   (d) Net present value
2. In time value analysis, the idea that a certain amount of money today is worth more than the same amount of money in the future is based on
   (a) The risk-free rate of return
   (b) The law of diminishing returns
   (c) The principle of compounding
   (d) The principle of uncertainty
3. What is the present value of a future cash flow of $1,000 to be received in one year, assuming a discount rate of 10%?
   (a) $1,100
   (b) $909.09
   (c) $1,010
   (d) $1,000
4. Which of the following factors increases the present value of a future cash flow?
   (a) Higher interest rate
   (b) Longer time to receipt
   (c) Smaller cash flow amount
   (d) Lower risk
5. The concept of discounting is used to
   (a) Increase the future value of money
   (b) Calculate the present value of money
   (c) Determine the future value of money
   (d) Eliminate the effect of inflation
6. When valuing a bond, which of the following factors is NOT typically considered?
   (a) Face value of the bond
   (b) Coupon rate
   (c) Maturity date
   (d) Dividend yield
7. The current yield of a bond is calculated as
   (a) Annual coupon payment divided by the bond's face value
   (b) Annual coupon payment divided by the bond's market price
   (c) Bond's market price divided by its face value
   (d) Bond's maturity period in years
8. In stock valuation, the Gordon Growth Model is used to value
   (a) Preferred stocks
   (b) Common stocks
   (c) Bonds
   (d) Mutual funds
9. The Gordon Growth Model assumes that dividends will
   (a) Remain constant over time
   (b) Grow at a constant rate forever
   (c) Decline gradually
   (d) Be highly volatile
10. The Price-Earnings (P/E) ratio is commonly used to
    (a) Value bonds
    (b) Assess the risk of stocks
    (c) Evaluate the relationship between a stock's price and its earnings
    (d) Calculate the yield to maturity of a bond
11. Rik in financial investments is typically associated with
    (a) The potential for high returns
    (b) The certainty of returns
    (c) The absence of variability in returns
    (d) The potential for losses
12. Which of the following is NOT a common measure of investment risk?
    (a) Standard deviation
    (b) Beta
    (c) Return on investment (ROI)
    (d) Alpha
13. Beta is a measure of
    (a) Systematic risk
    (b) Total risk

(c) Unsystematic risk
(d) Absolute risk

14. An investment's alpha indicates its
(a) Total return
(b) Risk-adjusted return
(c) Market risk
(d) Systematic risk

15. A higher risk investment typically has
(a) Lower potential returns
(b) Higher potential returns
(c) No impact on potential returns
(d) Consistent returns

16. The total return on an investment includes which of the following components?
(a) Capital gains only
(b) Dividends only
(c) Capital gains and dividends
(d) Principal amount

17. The annualized return on an investment, taking into account the compounding effect, is known as the
(a) Nominal return
(b) Real return
(c) Risk-free return
(d) Compounded return

18. Which of the following measures the efficiency of an investment in generating returns?
(a) Earnings per share
(b) Price-to-earnings ratio
(c) Return on investment
(d) Dividend yield

19. Dividend yield is calculated as
(a) Dividend per share divided by stock price
(b) Stock price divided by earnings per share
(c) Market capitalization divided by book value
(d) Total assets divided by total liabilities

20. The Capital Asset Pricing Model (CAPM) is used to estimate
(a) The expected return on an investment
(b) The historical return on an investment
(c) The total assets of a company
(d) The earnings per share of a stock

21. What is the primary objective of capital budgeting?
(a) Maximizing revenue
(b) Minimizing expenses
(c) Maximizing long-term value
(d) Minimizing taxes

22. Capital budgeting decisions typically involve investments in
(a) Short-term assets
(b) Long-term assets
(c) Inventory management
(d) Daily operational expenses

23. The term "capital expenditure" refers to investments in
(a) Routine maintenance
(b) Short-term marketable securities
(c) Long-term assets with enduring benefits
(d) Day-to-day operational expenses

24. The decision to invest in new machinery for a manufacturing plant is an example of
(a) A capital budgeting decision
(b) A short-term investment decision
(c) A current asset management decision
(d) A financial budgeting decision

25. In the context of capital budgeting, "sunk costs" are
(a) Costs that can be recovered in the future
(b) Costs that are irrelevant to investment decisions
(c) Costs that have not yet been incurred
(d) Costs that impact the payback period

26. Payback period is a capital budgeting method that
(a) Focuses on the time it takes to recover the initial investment
(b) Calculates the net present value of a project
(c) Considers the accounting rate of return
(d) Evaluates the internal rate of return

27. Which capital budgeting method considers the time value of money and calculates the present value of future cash flows?
(a) Net present value (NPV)
(b) Payback period
(c) Accounting rate of return
(d) Return on investment (ROI)

28. The internal rate of return (IRR) is the discount rate that
(a) Equals the payback period
(b) Results in a positive net present value (NPV)
(c) Equals the accounting rate of return
(d) Always exceeds the cost of capital

29. The profitability index is calculated as
    (a) The present value of cash flows divided by the initial investment
    (b) The accounting rate of return divided by the initial investment
    (c) The payback period divided by the net present value
    (d) The internal rate of return divided by the accounting rate of return
30. The accounting rate of return (ARR) is also known as
    (a) The payback period
    (b) The return on investment (ROI)
    (c) The net present value (NPV)
    (d) The internal rate of return (IRR)
31. A project with a net present value (NPV) of $10,000 is considered
    (a) A profitable project
    (b) An unprofitable project
    (c) A project with no returns
    (d) A project with a negative payback period
32. The payback period method may be criticized for not considering
    (a) The time value of money
    (b) The initial investment
    (c) The profitability index
    (d) The internal rate of return
33. The profitability index is a useful method for
    (a) Comparing projects of different sizes
    (b) Calculating the payback period
    (c) Assessing a project's accounting rate of return
    (d) Evaluating the time value of money
34. In capital budgeting, the term "mutually exclusive" refers to
    (a) Projects that cannot be compared using the same methods
    (b) Projects that have the same payback period
    (c) Projects that are highly profitable
    (d) Projects that are not worth considering
35. Which capital budgeting method can lead to conflicts when evaluating mutually exclusive projects?
    (a) Net present value (NPV)
    (b) Payback period
    (c) Accounting rate of return
    (d) Profitability index
36. Sensitivity analysis in capital budgeting involves
    (a) Evaluating the project's sensitivity to changes in sales
    (b) Calculating the payback period
    (c) Assessing the project's risk of default
    (d) Determining the accounting rate of return
37. Monte Carlo simulation is a technique used in capital budgeting to
    (a) Determine the payback period
    (b) Assess the risk and uncertainty of a project
    (c) Calculate the profitability index
    (d) Evaluate the internal rate of return
38. Which of the following is NOT a source of risk in capital budgeting?
    (a) Market risk
    (b) Regulatory risk
    (c) Currency risk
    (d) Accounting risk
39. The certainty-equivalent approach in risk analysis converts uncertain cash flows into
    (a) Certain cash flows
    (b) Variable cash flows
    (c) Guaranteed cash flows
    (d) Constant cash flows
40. In the context of risk analysis, the risk-adjusted discount rate (RADR) is used to
    (a) Calculate the internal rate of return
    (b) Assess the payback period
    (c) Evaluate the project's expected returns
    (d) Account for the risk associated with a project
41. The Modigliani and Miller (MM) proposition argues that the value of a firm is determined by its
    (a) Dividend policy
    (b) Capital structure
    (c) Earnings per share
    (d) Profitability
42. According to the Bird-in-the-Hand Theory, investors prefer
    (a) High dividends to capital gains
    (b) Low dividends to capital gains
    (c) A mix of dividends and capital gains
    (d) No returns at all
43. The Residual Dividend Model suggests that dividends should be paid out of
    (a) Current earnings

(b) Retained earnings
(c) External borrowings
(d) Future earnings

44. The Dividend Irrelevance Theory proposed by MM suggests that, in a world without taxes and transaction costs
(a) Dividends are relevant to investors
(b) Dividends are irrelevant to investors
(c) Retained earnings have no value
(d) Dividends should always be maximized

45. The Signaling Theory of dividends suggests that an increase in dividends may signal
(a) Financial distress
(b) Strong future prospects
(c) Low profitability
(d) High debt levels

46. The Dividend Payout Ratio is calculated as
(a) Dividends per share divided by earnings per share
(b) Earnings per share divided by the dividend per share
(c) Total dividends paid divided by total earnings
(d) Market capitalization divided by book value

47. A company's Dividend Policy is influenced by factors such as
(a) Market demand for its products
(b) Employee salaries
(c) Government regulations
(d) Management's personal preferences

48. The Dividend Payment Date is also known as the
(a) Declaration date
(b) Record date
(c) Ex-dividend date
(d) Distribution date

49. The Dividend Yield is calculated as
(a) Dividends per share divided by market price per share
(b) Earnings per share divided by market price per share
(c) Dividends per share divided by earnings per share
(d) Market capitalization divided by book value

50. Dividends in the form of additional shares of stock are known as
(a) Cash dividends
(b) Stock dividends
(c) Preferred dividends
(d) Liquidating dividends

51. The Dividend Policy that focuses on paying out a consistent percentage of earnings as dividends is called
(a) Stable dividend policy
(b) Residual dividend policy
(c) Constant dividend policy
(d) Regular dividend policy

52. In the Gordon Growth Model (GGM), the formula for the expected dividend per share is given as
(a) $D1 = D0 / (1 - g)$
(b) $D1 = D0 \times (1 + g)$
(c) $D1 = D0 \times (1 - g)$
(d) $D1 = D0 / (1 + g)$

53. A high dividend yield is typically associated with
(a) A growth-oriented company
(b) A value stock
(c) A non-profit organization
(d) A speculative investment

54. The Declaration Date for dividends is when the company
(a) Pays the dividend to shareholders
(b) Sets the record date
(c) Declares the intention to pay dividends
(d) Sets the ex-dividend date

55. In the Dividend Discount Model (DDM), the discount rate used to determine the present value of future dividends is often the
(a) Dividend yield
(b) Dividend payout ratio
(c) Risk-free rate of return
(d) Market price per share

56. Corporate restructuring may involve activities such as mergers, acquisitions, divestitures, and
(a) Product development
(b) Market expansion
(c) Organizational redesign
(d) Marketing campaigns

57. The primary purpose of corporate restructuring is to
(a) Increase short-term profits
(b) Maximize market share
(c) Enhance shareholder value
(d) Eliminate competition

58. A spin-off is a corporate restructuring strategy that involves
(a) Combining two companies into one
(b) Separating a subsidiary into an independent entity
(c) Acquiring a competitor
(d) Selling off non-core assets

59. The concept of "synergy" in corporate restructuring refers to
(a) The combined value of two companies being greater than the sum of their individual values
(b) Eliminating competition through mergers
(c) Divestiture of unprofitable business units
(d) Reducing corporate taxes

60. In the context of corporate restructuring, a "white knight" refers to
(a) A friendly acquirer that rescues a target company from a hostile takeover
(b) A financial advisor hired to negotiate a merger
(c) A divestiture specialist
(d) An activist shareholder

61. The term "value creation" in the context of mergers and acquisitions (M&A) refers to
(a) Increasing the stock price of the acquiring company
(b) Maximizing the revenue of the merged entity
(c) Generating economic benefits for shareholders
(d) Reducing corporate costs

62. A value-creating merger is one that results in
(a) A decrease in shareholder wealth
(b) A decrease in stock price
(c) An increase in the combined firm's value
(d) A reduction in market share

63. In M&A, value is typically created through activities such as cost savings, revenue enhancement, and
(a) Increased competition
(b) Diversification
(c) Market volatility
(d) Regulatory compliance

64. The market-to-book ratio is a financial metric used to assess
(a) The market value of a company's assets relative to its book value
(b) The market price of a company's stock
(c) The revenue generated by a company
(d) The profitability of a company

65. Earnings before interest, taxes, depreciation, and amortization (EBITDA) is often used as a measure of
(a) Dividend yield
(b) Operating performance
(c) Stock price volatility
(d) Market capitalization

66. Due diligence in merger negotiations involves
(a) Negotiating the purchase price
(b) Investigating the target company's financial and operational condition
(c) Finalizing the merger agreement
(d) Setting post-merger integration plans

67. The negotiation stage in M&A typically includes discussions on price, financing, and
(a) Market share
(b) Cultural fit
(c) Regulatory approval
(d) Marketing strategies

68. In a friendly merger, the acquiring company and the target company
(a) Agree on the terms and conditions of the merger without opposition
(b) Engage in hostile takeover attempts
(c) Request government intervention
(d) Abandon the merger negotiations

69. The "golden parachute" is a provision in a merger agreement that benefits
(a) Shareholders of the target company
(b) The acquirer's management team
(c) Activist investors
(d) The legal advisors

70. The Hart-Scott-Rodino Antitrust Improvements Act is a U.S. federal law that requires companies to
(a) Seek regulatory approval for certain mergers and acquisitions
(b) Disclose financial statements
(c) Share proprietary information with competitors
(d) Notify employees of merger negotiations

71. In a leveraged buyout (LBO), the acquisition is primarily financed through
(a) Equity capital
(b) Bank loans and debt
(c) Preferred stock
(d) Grants and subsidies

72. Private equity firms are typically involved in
   (a) Hostile takeovers
   (b) Leveraged buyouts
   (c) Joint ventures
   (d) Spin-offs
73. The leveraged buyout (LBO) process often includes the restructuring of the target company's
   (a) Executive team
   (b) Product line
   (c) Debt structure
   (d) Marketing strategy
74. In a leveraged buyout, the leveraged refers to the use of
   (a) Debt financing to fund the acquisition
   (b) Equity financing to fund the acquisition
   (c) Government grants
   (d) Venture capital
75. A management buyout (MBO) is a type of LBO in which the acquisition is led by
   (a) External investors
   (b) The target company's board of directors
   (c) The target company's management team
   (d) A government agency
76. A hostile takeover is characterized by
   (a) The target company's consent to the acquisition
   (b) A friendly agreement between the acquirer and the target
   (c) Opposition from the target company's board of directors
   (d) Regulatory approval
77. The term "poison pill" in takeover defense refers to
   (a) A strategy used by the acquirer to sweeten the deal
   (b) A provision that makes the takeover target less attractive to the acquirer
   (c) A takeover offer that is too enticing to reject
   (d) A government intervention in the takeover process
78. In a "tender offer," the acquirer
   (a) Makes a public bid to purchase shares from the target's shareholders
   (b) Approaches the target company's management privately
   (c) Negotiates directly with the target company's board
   (d) Initiates a hostile takeover attempt
79. The "white squire" defense strategy involves
   (a) The target company acquiring a significant stake in the acquirer
   (b) The target company appointing an outside mediator
   (c) The acquirer withdrawing its takeover bid
   (d) A friendly agreement between the acquirer and the target
80. A "crown jewel" defense tactic involves
   (a) Selling off the target company's valuable assets to deter a hostile acquirer
   (b) The target company's management offering to resign
   (c) Government intervention to protect the target company
   (d) Appointing a new CEO from the acquirer's team
81. According to the CAPM, the expected return of a security is determined by its
   (a) Market risk premium
   (b) Total risk
   (c) Dividend yield
   (d) Coupon rate
82. The risk-free rate in the CAPM represents the return on an investment with
   (a) No risk (b) Low market risk
   (c) Low total risk (d) High total risk
83. The CAPM equation is expressed as
   (a) Expected return = Risk-free rate
   (b) Expected return = Market risk premium
   (c) Expected return = Risk-free rate + (Beta x Market risk premium)
   (d) Expected return = Total risk - Risk-free rate
84. The CAPM model assumes that investors are
   (a) Risk-averse
   (b) Risk-neutral
   (c) Risk-seeking
   (d) Indifferent to risk
85. Beta in the CAPM measures a security's
   (a) Market risk
   (b) Total risk
   (c) Non-systematic risk
   (d) Risk-free rate
86. The APT is an alternative model to the CAPM for determining
   (a) Expected returns on securities
   (b) Stock prices
   (c) Dividend yields
   (d) Book values

87. In the APT, the expected return of a security is a linear function of
 (a) Market risk premium
 (b) Dividend yield
 (c) Multiple factors
 (d) Stock price

88. How many factors does the APT typically consider in its model?
 (a) One (b) Two
 (c) Three (d) Unlimited

89. The APT assumes that differences in asset returns are primarily driven by
 (a) Market risk
 (b) Diversifiable risk
 (c) Systematic risk factors
 (d) Company-specific factors

90. Which of the following statements is true regarding the APT?
 (a) It requires an estimate of beta for each security
 (b) It is limited to a single factor model
 (c) It does not account for diversification benefits
 (d) It is primarily based on historical data

91. Diversification in a portfolio can
 (a) Increase returns and decrease risk
 (b) Decrease returns and decrease risk
 (c) Increase returns and increase risk
 (d) Decrease returns and increase risk

92. The efficient frontier represents a set of portfolios that
 (a) Maximize returns for a given level of risk
 (b) Minimize risk for a given level of returns
 (c) Are not feasible for investors
 (d) Maximize risk

93. Which of the following measures assesses the risk-adjusted performance of a portfolio?
 (a) Standard deviation
 (b) Beta
 (c) Sharpe ratio
 (d) Correlation coefficient

94. A portfolio with a positive alpha is considered to be
 (a) Overperforming (b) Underperforming
 (c) Efficient (d) Risk-free

95. The concept of "risk-free rate" in portfolio management represents the return on
 (a) Low-risk investments like Treasury bills
 (b) High-risk stocks
 (c) Real estate investments
 (d) Precious metals

96. In a well-diversified portfolio, unsystematic risk tends to be
 (a) High
 (b) Low
 (c) Equal to systematic risk
 (d) Constant

97. Systematic risk, also known as market risk, cannot be eliminated through
 (a) Diversification
 (b) Asset allocation
 (c) Portfolio optimization
 (d) Risk-free investments

98. The correlation coefficient measures the degree of relationship between the returns of two assets and can range from
 (a) –1 to 0
 (b) 0 to 1
 (c) 0 to 100
 (d) 1 to 2

99. An asset's standard deviation is a measure of
 (a) Its average returns
 (b) Its systematic risk
 (c) Its total risk
 (d) Its correlation with other assets

100. The Capital Market Line (CML) provides a graphical representation of the relationship between expected return and
 (a) Risk-free rate
 (b) Beta
 (c) Standard deviation
 (d) Sharpe ratio

101. The Sharpe ratio measures the
 (a) Total risk of a portfolio
 (b) Risk-adjusted return of a portfolio
 (c) Correlation of portfolio returns
 (d) Systematic risk of a portfolio

102. The Treynor ratio assesses a portfolio's
 (a) Total risk
 (b) Market risk
 (c) Systematic risk
 (d) Risk-adjusted return relative to the risk-free rate

103. The Jensen's Alpha measures a portfolio's performance relative to its
 (a) Expected return

(b) Market risk
(c) Expected beta
(d) Required rate of return

104. The concept of "risk aversion" among investors implies that they
(a) Prefer high-risk, high-return investments
(b) Prefer low-risk, low-return investments
(c) Are indifferent to risk
(d) Seek the highest returns without considering risk

105. In portfolio performance evaluation, a positive alpha indicates that the portfolio has
(a) Underperformed
(b) Outperformed expectations
(c) Negative returns
(d) High systematic risk

106. A call option gives the holder the right, but not the obligation, to
(a) Buy a security at a specified price before or on a specified date
(b) Sell a security at a specified price before or on a specified date
(c) Buy a security at a specified price after a specified date
(d) Sell a security at a specified price after a specified date

107. The maximum loss for a call option buyer is limited to
(a) The option premium paid
(b) The strike price
(c) The difference between the stock price and the strike price
(d) Unlimited

108. A put option gives the holder the right, but not the obligation, to
(a) Buy a security at a specified price before or on a specified date
(b) Sell a security at a specified price before or on a specified date
(c) Buy a security at a specified price after a specified date
(d) Sell a security at a specified price after a specified date

109. The profit for a put option buyer is maximized when the market price is
(a) Below the strike price
(b) Equal to the strike price
(c) Above the strike price
(d) Unpredictable

110. A covered call strategy involves
(a) Buying a call option and a put option on the same security
(b) Selling a call option and holding the underlying security
(c) Buying a call option and selling the underlying security
(d) Selling a put option and buying the underlying security

111. The Black-Scholes-Merton model is used to calculate the theoretical value of
(a) European call options
(b) American put options
(c) Asian options
(d) Barrier options

112. In the Black-Scholes-Merton model, the "volatility" parameter measures
(a) The rate of interest
(b) The dividend yield
(c) The expected price movement of the underlying asset
(d) The option's time to maturity

113. The "delta" of an option represents the sensitivity of the option price to changes in
(a) Time to expiration
(b) The stock's dividend yield
(c) The option's strike price
(d) The stock price

114. The "gamma" of an option measures the rate of change of the option's
(a) Theta (b) Vega
(c) Delta (d) Rho

115. The "theta" of an option represents the rate of change of the option's price with respect to
(a) Changes in interest rates
(b) Changes in stock price
(c) Changes in time to expiration
(d) Changes in volatility

116. A forward contract is a financial agreement between two parties to
(a) Buy or sell an underlying asset at a specified price on a future date
(b) Trade options on a stock exchange
(c) Execute immediate transactions
(d) Exchange currencies at the current spot rate

117. Unlike options, forward contracts have
(a) No expiration date
(b) A fixed strike price

(c) Exercisable features
(d) Maximum loss potential

118. A futures contract is a standardized and exchange-traded form of a
(a) Call option
(b) Put option
(c) Forward contract
(d) Swap agreement

119. In futures trading, the "margin" refers to
(a) The transaction cost
(b) The interest rate
(c) The upfront payment required to open and maintain a position
(d) The dividend payment

120. The main difference between a futures contract and a forward contract is that futures contracts are
(a) Customized to the needs of the parties involved
(b) Exchanged on a centralized exchange
(c) Settled in cash only
(d) Limited to financial assets

121. Hedging with options or futures is primarily used to
(a) Maximize profits
(b) Minimize losses
(c) Create leverage
(d) Increase market volatility

122. A speculator in the derivatives market
(a) Uses options and futures to protect against adverse price movements
(b) Assumes market risk in the hope of making a profit
(c) Hedges against potential losses
(d) Has no interest in price movements

123. An investor with a long stock position can use a futures contract to
(a) Lock in profits
(b) Hedge against a decline in stock price
(c) Increase dividend income
(d) Reduce capital gains tax

124. A put option can be used for
(a) Hedging a short stock position
(b) Speculating on an increase in stock price
(c) Generating dividend income
(d) Reducing the cost of an options strategy

125. A "straddle" is an options strategy that involves
(a) Buying both a call option and a put option with the same strike price and expiration date
(b) Selling a call option and buying a put option
(c) Writing covered calls
(d) Exercising options simultaneously

126. A "butterfly spread" is an options strategy that involves
(a) Buying three options with different strike prices
(b) Buying a call and a put option with the same strike price
(c) Writing covered calls
(d) Combining options and futures

127. An "iron condor" is an options strategy that aims to profit from
(a) A strong market trend
(b) Low market volatility
(c) High interest rates
(d) Currency fluctuations

128. A "strangle" is an options strategy that involves buying both a call and a put option with
(a) The same strike price
(b) Different strike prices
(c) The same expiration date
(d) No expiration date

129. A "collar" is an options strategy that combines
(a) A long call and a short put
(b) A long put and a short call
(c) A long stock position and a short stock position
(d) A long position in both call and put options

130. An "covered call" strategy involves
(a) Selling a call option without owning the underlying asset
(b) Buying a call option to protect a stock position
(c) Selling a call option and owning the underlying asset
(d) Writing a put option to profit from price decline

131. Which of the following is NOT a determinant of a company's working capital needs?
(a) Seasonal variations in demand
(b) Credit policy
(c) Fixed asset turnover
(d) Production cycle time

132. An increase in the credit period offered to customers typically leads to
(a) An increase in accounts receivable
(b) A decrease in accounts payable
(c) A decrease in cash reserves
(d) A decrease in the cash conversion cycle

133. The operating cycle of a company includes which of the following components?
(a) Cash cycle and debt cycle
(b) Cash conversion cycle and inventory conversion period
(c) Receivables turnover and payables turnover
(d) Equity cycle and accounts cycle

134. If a company extends its credit terms to customers, it is likely to experience
(a) A decrease in accounts receivable
(b) An increase in cash flow
(c) A shorter cash conversion cycle
(d) A longer collection period

135. External factors, such as inflation and changes in interest rates, can impact a company's working capital by affecting
(a) Credit policy
(b) Debtors' turnover
(c) The cost of goods sold
(d) Fixed asset turnover

136. Which of the following cash management techniques involves investing excess cash in short-term, low-risk securities?
(a) Lockbox system
(b) Float management
(c) Cash concentration
(d) Marketable securities

137. A company's "disbursement float" refers to the time delay between
(a) Depositing checks and having funds available
(b) Writing a check and the recipient's cashing of it
(c) Collecting accounts receivable and paying accounts payable
(d) Paying employees and paying suppliers

138. The primary goal of cash management is to
(a) Maximize cash holdings at all times
(b) Minimize cash holdings to reduce costs
(c) Balance cash inflows and outflows efficiently
(d) Keep all funds in interest-bearing accounts

139. A "lockbox system" is designed to
(a) Safeguard physical cash
(b) Concentrate cash receipts in a centralized location
(c) Monitor cash transactions in real-time
(d) Manage electronic funds transfers

140. Which cash management technique aims to reduce the collection time for accounts receivable?
(a) Concentration banking
(b) Float management
(c) Lockbox system
(d) Just-in-time inventory

141. The Economic Order Quantity (EOQ) model helps determine
(a) The reorder point for inventory
(b) The optimal order quantity that minimizes total inventory costs
(c) The maximum inventory level
(d) The safety stock level

142. Holding costs for inventory typically include expenses related to
(a) Ordering and setup costs
(b) Shortage costs
(c) Carrying costs and storage costs
(d) Stockouts and excess inventory

143. "Just-in-time" (JIT) inventory management aims to
(a) Maximize safety stock levels
(b) Minimize lead times for suppliers
(c) Reduce inventory levels to the minimum necessary
(d) Encourage overproduction

144. ABC analysis classifies inventory items into categories based on their
(a) Annual sales revenue
(b) Alphabetical order
(c) Physical size
(d) Order frequency

145. The inventory turnover ratio is calculated as
(a) Sales revenue divided by cost of goods sold
(b) Cost of goods sold divided by average inventory
(c) Average inventory divided by sales revenue
(d) Sales revenue divided by average inventory

146. Days Sales Outstanding (DSO) measures
(a) The average number of days it takes to collect accounts receivable
(b) The number of days inventory is held before sale
(c) The average payment period for accounts payable
(d) The average credit period offered to customers

147. The "aging of accounts receivable" is a technique used to
(a) Calculate the allowance for doubtful accounts
(b) Determine the credit terms offered to customers
(c) Identify slow-paying customers and estimate collectibility
(d) Accelerate the collection of accounts receivable

148. The credit policy of a company includes decisions related to
(a) Cash management strategies
(b) Inventory turnover
(c) Accounts payable management
(d) Credit terms, credit limits, and collection efforts

149. "Factoring" as a receivables management strategy involves
(a) Selling accounts receivable to a third party at a discount
(b) Offering longer credit terms to customers
(c) Reducing the credit limits for customers
(d) Paying suppliers earlier to secure discounts

150. The "bad debt expense" on the income statement represents the
(a) Amount of accounts receivable that is uncollectible
(b) Cash discounts offered to customers
(c) Interest expense on accounts payable
(d) Recovery of accounts previously written off as bad debt

151. The "payment float" in payables management refers to
(a) The time it takes for a check to clear the bank
(b) The time between the invoice date and the payment date
(c) The time it takes for accounts payable to be reconciled
(d) The time it takes to process employee payroll

152. The goal of effective payables management is to
(a) Maximize the payment float
(b) Minimize the credit terms offered to suppliers
(c) Optimize cash discounts
(d) Extend the time it takes to pay suppliers

153. "Trade credit" refers to
(a) The purchase of goods and services using a company credit card
(b) The extension of credit terms by suppliers to buyers
(c) The sale of goods and services on a cash basis
(d) The issuance of bonds to raise capital

154. "Early payment discounts" offered by suppliers can
(a) Encourage prompt payment by buyers
(b) Extend the time it takes to pay suppliers
(c) Increase accounts payable
(d) Reduce credit limits

155. The "accounts payable turnover ratio" measures
(a) The number of suppliers a company works with
(b) The frequency of purchases made on account
(c) The efficiency of inventory management
(d) The number of days it takes to pay suppliers

156. Factoring is a financial arrangement in which a company
(a) Borrows money from a bank to finance operations
(b) Sells its accounts receivable to a third party (factor) at a discount
(c) Invests in marketable securities to generate cash flow
(d) Pays off long-term debt

157. Factoring is often used by businesses to
(a) Increase inventory levels
(b) Reduce bad debt expense
(c) Speed up accounts payable payments
(d) Finance short-term working capital needs

158. In a non-recourse factoring arrangement, the factor assumes

(a) All the credit risk for the accounts receivable
(b) A percentage of the collection costs
(c) Responsibility for managing the company's cash flow
(d) Ownership of the accounts receivable

159. The factor's fee in a factoring agreement is typically based on
(a) The amount of accounts receivable sold
(b) The credit rating of the company
(c) The face value of the accounts receivable
(d) The cost of the company's products

160. One of the advantages of factoring is that it
(a) Increases the company's liability
(b) Reduces the need for credit management
(c) Provides a source of low-interest long-term financing
(d) Requires the company to retain ownership of accounts receivable

161. In the foreign exchange market, what does the term "spot exchange rate" refer to?
(a) The exchange rate for a future date
(b) The exchange rate for immediate delivery and settlement
(c) The exchange rate for commodity trading
(d) The exchange rate for options trading

162. A "currency pair" in the foreign exchange market represents
(a) Two different currency notes
(b) Two currencies used in the same country
(c) Two currencies being traded against each other
(d) Two denominations of the same currency

163. Which of the following is NOT considered a major currency in the foreign exchange market?
(a) Euro (EUR)
(b) Japanese Yen (JPY)
(c) Australian Dollar (AUD)
(d) Swiss Franc (CHF)

164. The foreign exchange market operates
(a) 24 hours a day, five days a week
(b) During standard business hours of major financial centers
(c) Only during banking hours in the home country
(d) Only on weekends

165. In the foreign exchange market, what does "forex" stand for?
(a) Foreign exploration
(b) Foreign expansion
(c) Foreign exchange
(d) Foreign exposure

166. In a direct exchange rate quotation, what is the domestic currency?
(a) The first currency listed
(b) The second currency listed
(c) The currency in the middle
(d) It depends on the market convention

167. If the EUR/USD exchange rate is 1.20, how many U.S. dollars are needed to buy 1 euro?
(a) \$0.20 (b) \$1.20
(c) \$12 (d) \$120

168. A cross rate is an exchange rate calculated between two currencies that are not the official currency of the country in which the rate is quoted. For example, if you see a EUR/JPY rate, where is this exchange rate most likely quoted?
(a) In the United States
(b) In Japan
(c) In the Eurozone
(d) In Australia

169. In a currency pair like GBP/USD, if the exchange rate goes from 1.30 to 1.35, what does this mean for the British pound (GBP)?
(a) It has depreciated
(b) It has appreciated
(c) It remains the same
(d) It's impossible to determine

170. Which exchange rate quotation would be more appropriate for a U.S. investor interested in the relative value of the U.S. dollar to the British pound?
(a) USD/GBP (b) GBP/USD
(c) GBP/EUR (d) EUR/GBP

171. The theory that exchange rates adjust to ensure that identical goods and services have the same real price in any two countries is known as
(a) The interest rate parity theory
(b) The purchasing power parity theory
(c) The international Fisher effect
(d) The efficient market hypothesis

172. If the nominal interest rate in the United States is 5% and the inflation rate is 2%, what is the real interest rate?
(a) 5% (b) 3%
(c) 2% (d) 7%

173. According to interest rate parity, if the interest rate in one country is higher than in another, what is expected to happen to the exchange rate between the two currencies?
(a) It will appreciate
(b) It will depreciate
(c) It will remain the same
(d) It is impossible to predict

174. If a country's current account is in surplus, what is the likely impact on its currency's exchange rate?
(a) It will appreciate
(b) It will depreciate
(c) It will have no impact
(d) It depends on other factors

175. The Big Mac Index is a humorous way to assess
(a) Inflation rates
(b) Interest rates
(c) Currency exchange rates
(d) Stock market performance

176. "Currency risk" refers to the potential impact of exchange rate movements on
(a) The prices of goods and services
(b) The timing of financial transactions
(c) The financial performance of a business or investment
(d) Government policies on currency trading

177. A U.S. company that exports goods to Europe and invoices its European customers in euros is exposed to
(a) Transaction risk (b) Translation risk
(c) Economic risk (d) Operating risk

178. Which of the following is a strategy for managing foreign exchange risk?
(a) Doing nothing and hoping for favorable exchange rate movements
(b) Entering into forward contracts to lock in exchange rates
(c) Ignoring financial reports and forecasts
(d) Reducing international business operations

179. A currency option contract gives the holder the
(a) Obligation to buy a specified amount of foreign currency
(b) Right, but not the obligation, to buy or sell a specified amount of foreign currency at a predetermined price
(c) Right to buy a currency only if the exchange rate is higher than the strike price
(d) Ability to sell a currency at any time, regardless of market conditions

180. "Hedging" in foreign exchange risk management involves
(a) Speculating on future exchange rate movements
(b) Eliminating all risks related to currency exchange
(c) Taking measures to offset potential losses from exchange rate movements
(d) Ignoring currency risk entirely

181. Large financial institutions that act as intermediaries in the foreign exchange market are known as
(a) Brokers
(b) Dealers
(c) Exchanges
(d) Regulators

182. A "speculator" in the foreign exchange market aims to
(a) Eliminate currency risk
(b) Earn a profit from exchange rate movements
(c) Engage in long-term investments
(d) Provide liquidity to the market

183. A "central bank" in a country typically has the authority to
(a) Speculate on currency exchange rates
(b) Regulate and oversee currency trading
(c) Print its own currency without limitations
(d) Engage in proprietary trading for profit

184. Retail foreign exchange traders, often individuals or small investors, access the foreign exchange market through
(a) Interbank trading
(b) Currency options
(c) Brokerage platforms
(d) Direct negotiations with central banks

185. "Arbitrage" in the foreign exchange market involves profiting from
(a) Differences in interest rates between two countries
(b) The purchase and sale of the same currency at different times
(c) Currency options trading
(d) Speculating on the long-term direction of a currency pair

ANSWER KEY

1. (a)	2. (c)	3. (b)	4. (d)	5. (b)	6. (d)	7. (b)	8. (b)	9. (b)	10. (c)
11. (d)	12. (c)	13. (a)	14. (b)	15. (b)	16. (c)	17. (d)	18. (c)	19. (a)	20. (a)
21. (c)	22. (b)	23. (c)	24. (a)	25. (b)	26. (a)	27. (a)	28. (b)	29. (a)	30. (b)
31. (a)	32. (a)	33. (a)	34. (d)	35. (a)	36. (a)	37. (b)	38. (d)	39. (a)	40. (d)
41. (b)	42. (a)	43. (b)	44. (b)	45. (b)	46. (c)	47. (d)	48. (d)	49. (a)	50. (b)
51. (c)	52. (b)	53. (b)	54. (c)	55. (c)	56. (c)	57. (c)	58. (b)	59. (a)	60. (a)
61. (c)	62. (c)	63. (b)	64. (a)	65. (b)	66. (b)	67. (c)	68. (a)	69. (a)	70. (a)
71. (b)	72. (b)	73. (c)	74. (a)	75. (c)	76. (c)	77. (b)	78. (a)	79. (d)	80. (a)
81. (a)	82. (a)	83. (c)	84. (a)	85. (a)	86. (a)	87. (c)	88. (d)	89. (c)	90. (a)
91. (a)	92. (a)	93. (c)	94. (a)	95. (a)	96. (b)	97. (a)	98. (a)	99. (c)	100. (c)
101. (b)	102. (d)	103. (d)	104. (b)	105. (b)	106. (a)	107. (a)	108. (b)	109. (a)	110. (b)
111. (a)	112. (c)	113. (d)	114. (c)	115. (c)	116. (a)	117. (d)	118. (c)	119. (c)	120. (b)
121. (b)	122. (b)	123. (b)	124. (a)	125. (a)	126. (a)	127. (b)	128. (b)	129. (b)	130. (c)
131. (c)	132. (a)	133. (b)	134. (d)	135. (c)	136. (d)	137. (b)	138. (c)	139. (b)	140. (c)
141. (b)	142. (c)	143. (c)	144. (a)	145. (b)	146. (a)	147. (c)	148. (d)	149. (a)	150. (a)
151. (a)	152. (d)	153. (b)	154. (a)	155. (d)	156. (b)	157. (d)	158. (a)	159. (a)	160. (b)
161. (b)	162. (c)	163. (c)	164. (a)	165. (c)	166. (d)	167. (b)	168. (a)	169. (b)	170. (b)
171. (b)	172. (b)	173. (b)	174. (a)	175. (c)	176. (c)	177. (a)	178. (b)	179. (b)	180. (c)
181. (b)	182. (b)	183. (b)	184. (c)	185. (a)					

UNIT 6

SYLLABUS

- Strategic Management – Concept, Process, Decision & Types
- Strategic Analysis – External Analysis, PEST, Porter's Approach to industry analysis, Internal Analysis – Resource Based Approach, Value Chain Analysis
- Strategy Formulation – SWOT Analysis, Corporate Strategy – Growth, Stability, Retrenchment, Integration and Diversification, Business Portfolio Analysis - BCG, GE Business Model, Ansoff's Product Market Growth Matrix
- Strategy Implementation – Challenges of Change, Developing Programs Mckinsey 7s Framework
- Marketing – Concept, Orientation, Trends and Tasks, Customer Value and Satisfaction
- Market Segmentation, Positioning and Targeting
- Product and Pricing Decision – Product Mix, Product Life Cycle, New Product development, Pricing – Types and Strategies
- Place and promotion decision – Marketing channels and value networks, VMS, IMC, Advertising and Sales promotion

STRATEGIC MANAGEMENT

Concept of Corporate Strategy

Corporate-level strategies are basically about the choice of direction that a firm adopts in order to achieve its objectives. There could be a small business firm involved in a single business or a large, complex and diversified conglomerate with several different businesses. The corporate strategy in both these cases is about the basic direction of the firm as a whole. In the case of the small firm it could mean the adoption of courses of action that would yield a better profit for the firm. In the case of the large firm the corporate-level strategy is also about managing the various businesses to maximize their contribution to the overall corporate objectives.

Corporate-level strategies are basically about decisions related to allocating resources among the different businesses of a firm, transferring resources from one set of businesses to others and managing and nurturing a portfolio of businesses in such a way that the overall corporate objectives are achieved. An analysis based on business definition provides a set of strategic alternatives that an organization can consider.

Strategic alternatives revolve around the question of whether to continue or change the business the enterprise is currently in or improve the efficiency and effectiveness with which the firm achieves its corporate objectives in its chosen business sector. There are four grand strategic alternatives: stability, expansion, retrenchment and any combination of these three. These strategic alternatives are termed as grand strategies.

Definition for Strategic Management

Strategic Management is defined as the dynamic process of formulation, implementation, evaluation and control of strategies to realize the organizations strategic intent.

Conceptual framework for the development of strategic management :

- Strategic Advantage
- Organisational capability
- Competencies
- Synergistic Effects
- Strengths and weaknesses
- Organisation Resources
- Organisational behaviour

Types of Strategic Management

A. Stability Strategies

It refers to attempt made by an organization at incremental improvement of functional performance. It is usually followed by small and medium sized firms. Stability strategies can be useful in the short run when such firms are satisfied with their current performance.

Stability strategy is adopted because :

1. It is less risky, involves fewer changes and people feel comfortable with things as they are
2. The environment faced is relatively stable.
3. Expansion may be perceived as being threatening.
4. Consolidation is sought through stabilizing after a period of rapid expansion.

B. Expansion Strategies

It is followed when an organization aims at high growth by substantially broadening the scope of one or more of its business in terms of their respective customer groups, customer functions and alternative technologies – singly or jointly – in order to improve its overall performance.

Expansion strategy is adopted because :

1. It may become imperative when environment demands increase in pace of activity.
2. Psychologically, strategists may feel more satisfied with the prospects of growth from expansion: chief executives may take pride in presiding over organizations perceived to be growth-oriented.
3. Increasing size may lead to more control over the market vis-a-vis competitors.
4. Advantages from the experience curve and scale of operations may accrue.

C. Retrenchment Strategy

It is followed when an organization substantially reduces the scope of its activity. This is done through an attempt to find out the problem areas and diagnose the cause of the problems. Next, steps are taken to solve the problem.

Retrenchment Strategy is adopted because

1. The management no longer wishes to remain in business either partly or wholly due to continuous losses and inviability.
2. The environment faced is threatening.
3. Stability can be ensured by reallocation of resources from unprofitable to profitable businesses.

D. Combination Strategy

These are a mixture of stability, expansion and retrenchment strategies applied either simultaneously (at the same time in different businesses) or sequentially (at different times in the same business).

Combination strategy is adopted because :

1. The organization is large and faces a complex environment.
2. The organization is composed of different businesses, each of which lies in a different industry requiring a different response.

STRATEGY ANALYSIS AND FORMULATION

Components of Strategy Formulation

1. **Quality.** Quality has become a unifying theme for many organizations, from Xerox to GE. Important to the success of total quality management, however, is linking the quality program to a few clear strategic goals. As Fortune magazine points out, "obsessing about quality is no replacement for a well-thought-out corporate strategy."

   At Johnson & Johnson, the quality program was redesigned with three targets in mind: boosting customer satisfaction, cutting costs, and reducing product introduction time. At J&J, a very intrapreneurial company where individual units are run like small businesses, each of the 168 units develops its own training program in keeping with these three unifying strategic goals.

   At Motorola, the quality program has two targets: defect prevention (with a goal of two defects per billion by the year 2000) and cycle time reduction – decreasing the amount of time it takes to complete a job. This quality goal does not just apply to manufacturing, but to departments such as finance as well. For instance, in 1988 it took Motorola 11 days to close its books each month, but by 1993 it took two days. This time difference translates to a considerable cost savings.

   Quality efforts should be clearly focused. In deciding how to tie quality to strategic plans, companies may want to listen to the advice of Motorola vice president Paul Noakes: "Identify three or four critical issues. You can't work on two dozen."

2. **Portfolio Approach.** In this approach, top management evaluates each of the corporation's various business units with respect to the marketplace and the corporation's internal makeup. When all business units have been evaluated, an appropriate strategic role is developed for each unit with the goal of improving the overall performance of the organization. The corporate portfolio approach is rational and analytical, is guided primarily by market opportunities, and tends to be initiated and controlled by top management only.

   One of the best-known examples of the corporate portfolio approach is the **portfolio framework** advocated by the Boston Consulting Group. This frame-work is also known as the *BCG Matrix.*

The BCG approach to analyzing a corporate portfolio of business focuses on three aspects of each particular business unit: its sales, the growth of its market, and whether it *absorbs* or *produces* cash in its operations. Its goal is to develop a balance among business units that use up cash and those that supply cash.

3. **"Five Forces" of Corporate Strategy.** Another well-known approach to corporate strategy is Michael Porter's "five forces" model. In Porter's view, an organization's technical and economic resources, as well as by five environmental "forces," each of which threatens the organization's venture into a new market. The strategic manager, says Porter, must analyze these forces and propose a program for influencing or defending against them. The aim is to find a lucrative and defensible niche for the organization.

   Five Forces Analysis assumes that there are five important forces that determine competitive power in a business situation. These are briefed as under :

   Supplier Power. Here we need to assess how easy it is for suppliers to drive up the prices. This is to determine how much pressure suppliers can place on a business. If one supplier has a large enough impact to affect a company's margins and volumes, then it holds substantial power. Here are a few reasons that suppliers might have power :

   - There are very few suppliers of a particular product.
   - Uniqueness of their product or service i.e. there are no substitutes.
   - Switching to another (competitive) product is very costly.
   - The product is extremely important to buyers – can't do without it.

   Buyer Power. In this factor we need to analyse how easy it is for buyers to drive prices down. This is to determine how much pressure customers can place on a business. If one customer has a large enough impact to affect a company's margins and volumes, then the customer holds a substantial power. Here are a few reasons that customers might have power.

   - Importance of each individual buyer to business, i.e. Small number of buyers.
   - Purchases large volumes
   - Switching to another (competitive) product is simple.
   - To product is not extremely important to buyers; they can do without the product for a period of time.
   - Customers are price sensitive.
   - Cost to them of switching from our products and services to those of someone else.

   Competitive Rivalry. What is important here is the number and capability of competitors. If business we are operating in has many competitors, and they offer equally attractive products and services, then we most likely have little power in the situation, because suppliers and buyers will go elsewhere if they don't get a good deal. On the other hand, if no-one else can do what we do, then we can often have tremendous strength. Highly competitive industries generally earn low returns because the cost of competition is high. A highly competitive market might result from :

   - Many players of about the same size; there is no dominant firm.
   - Little differentiation between competitor's products and services.
   - A mature industry with very little growth; companies can only grow by stealing customers away from competitors.

   Threat of Substitution. What is the likelihood that someone will switch to a competitive product or service? If the cost of switching is low, then this poses a serious threat. If substitution is easy and substitution is viable, then this weakness your power. Here are a few factors that can affect the threat of substitutes :

- The main issue is the similarity of substitutes. For example, if the price of coffee rises substantially, a coffee drinker may switch over to a beverage like tea.
- If substitutes are similar, it can be viewed in the same light as a new entrant.

Threat of New Entry. Power is also affected by the ability of people to enter the market. The easier it is for new companies to enter the industry, the more cutthroat competition there will be. Factors that can limit the threat of new entrants are known as barriers to entry. Some examples include :

- Existing loyalty to major brands.
- Incentives for using a particular buyer (such as frequent shopper programs)
- High fixed costs
- Scarcity of resources
- High costs of switching companies
- Government restrictions or legislation.

4. **Enterprise Strategies.** At least seven different enterprise strategies have been identified:
   (i) *Stockholder E-Strategy.* The corporation should maximize the interest of stockholders.
   (ii) *Managerial Prerogative E-Strategy.* The corporation should maximize the interests of management.
   (iii) *Restricted Stakeholder E-Strategy.* The corporation should maximize the interest of all stakeholders.
   (iv) *Unrestricted Stakeholder E-Strategy.* The corporation should maximize the interest of all stakeholders.
   (v) *Social Harmony E-Strategy.* The corporation should maximize social harmony.
   (vi) *Rawlsian E-Strategy.* The corporation should promote inequality among stakeholders only if inequality results in raising the level of the worst-off stakeholder.
   (vii) *Personal Projects E-Strategy.* The corporation should maximize its ability to enable corporate members to carry out their personal projects.

Examples of analytical methods used in strategic analysis include:

- SWOT analysis
- PEST analysis
- Porter's five forces analysis
- four corner's analysis
- value chain analysis
- early warning scans
- war gaming.

Analytical methods and tools are key to ensuring that consistency and an appropriate level of rigour is applied to the analysis.

Strategic Analysis

One of the key skills of a strategic analyst is in understanding which analytical tools or techniques are most appropriate to the objectives of the analysis. Below is an overview of some of the more commonly used strategic analysis tools.

SWOT ANALYSIS

A SWOT analysis is a simple but widely used tool that helps in understanding the strengths, weaknesses, opportunities and threats involved in a project or business activity.

It starts by defining the objective of the project or business activity and identifies the internal and external factors that are important to achieving that objective, strengths and weaknesses are usually internal to the organisation, while opportunities and threats are usually external. Often these are plotted on a simple 2×2 matrix.

SWOT Analysis Diagram

When using SWOT analysis, it should be ensured that:

Strengths • What does your organisation do better than others? • What are your unique selling points? • What do you competitors and customers in your market perceive as your strengths? • What is your organisations competitive edge?	**Opportunities** • What political, economic, social-cultural, or technology (PEST) changes are taking place that could be favourable to you? • Where are there currently gaps in the market or unfulfilled demand? • What new innovation could your organisation bring to the market?
Weakness • What do other organisations do better than you? • What elements of your business add little or no value? • What do competitors and customers in your market perceive as your weakness?	**Threats** • What political, economic, social-cultural, or technology (PEST) changes are taking place that could be unfavourable to you?• What restraints to you face? • What is your competition doing that could negatively impact you?

- Only specific, verifiable statements are used. An example might be 'price is £1.50 per unit lower than competition' rather than 'good value for money'.
- Internal and external factors are prioritised so that time is spent concentrating on the most significant factors. This should include a risk assessment to ensure that high risk or high impact threats and opportunities are clearly identified and are dealt with in priority order.
- Issues identified are retained for later in the strategy formation process.
- The analysis is pitched at the project or business activity level rather than at a total company level, which may be less actionable.
- It is not used in exclusivity. No one tool is likely to be completely comprehensive, so a mixture of option-generating tools should be used.

PEST ANALYSIS

PEST analysis is a scan of the external macro-environment in which an organisation exists. It is a useful tool for understanding the political, economic, socio-cultural and technological environment that an organisation operates in. It can be used for evaluating market growth or decline, and as such the position, potential and direction for a business.

Political factors. These include government regulations such as employment laws, environmental regulations and tax policy. Other political factors are trade restrictions and political stability.

Economic factors. These affect the cost of capital and purchasing power of an organisation. Economic factors include economic growth, interest rates, inflation and currency exchange rates.

Social factors. These impact on the consumer's need and the potential market size for an organisation's goods and services. Social factors include population growth, age demographics and attitudes towards health.

Technological factors. These influence barriers to entry, make or buy decisions and investment in innovation, such as automation, investment incentives and the rate of technological change.

PEST factors can be classified as opportunities or threats in a SWOT analysis. It is often useful to complete a PEST analysis before completing a SWOT analysis.

It is also worth noting that the four paradigms of PEST vary in significance depending on the type of business. For example, social factors are more obviously relevant to consumer businesses or a B2B business near the consumer end of the supply chain. Conversely, political factors are more obviously relevant to a defence contractor or aerospace manufacturer.

PORTER'S FIVE FORCES

Porter's five forces of competitive position analysis was developed in 1979 by Michael E. Porter of Harvard Business School as a simple framework for assessing and evaluating the competitive strength and position of a business organisation.

This theory is based on the concept that there are five forces which determine the competitive intensity and attractiveness of a market. Porter's five forces helps to identify where power lies in a business situation. This is useful both in understanding the strength of an organisation's current competitive position, and the strength of a position that an organisation may look to move into.

Strategic analysts often use Porter's five forces to understand whether new products or services are potentially profitable. By understanding where power lies, the theory can also be used to identify areas of strength, to improve weaknesses and to avoid mistakes.

The five forces are

1. Supplier power. An assessment of how easy it is for suppliers to drive up prices. This is driven by:
   - the number of suppliers of each essential input
   - the uniqueness of their product or service
   - the relative size and strength of the supplier
   - the cost of switching from one supplier to another.
2. Buyer power. An assessment of how easy it is for buyers to drive prices down. This is driven by:
   - the number of buyers in the market
   - the importance of each individual buyer to the organisation
   - the cost to the buyer of switching from one supplier to another.

   If a business has just a few powerful buyers, they are often able to dictate terms.
3. **Competitive rivalry.** The key driver is the number and capability of competitors in the market. Many competitors, offering undifferentiated products and services, will reduce market attractiveness.
4. **Threat of substitution.** Where close substitute products exist in a market, it increases the likelihood of customers switching to alternatives in response to price increases. This reduces both the power of suppliers and the attractiveness of the market.
5. **Threat of new entry.** Profitable markets attract new entrants, which erodes profitability. Unless incumbents have strong and durable barriers to entry, for example, patents, economies of scale, capital requirements or government policies, then profitability will decline to a competitive rate.

INTERNAL ANALYSIS – RESOURCE BASED APPROACH

The resource-based view (RBV) is a managerial framework used to determine the strategic resources a firm can exploit to achieve sustainable competitive advantage.

Barney's 1991 article "Firm Resources and Sustained Competitive Advantage" is widely cited as a pivotal work in the emergence of the resource-based view. However, some scholars argue that there was evidence for a fragmentary resource-based theory from the 1930s. RBV proposes that firms are heterogeneous because they possess heterogeneous resources, meaning firms can have different strategies because they have different resource mixes.

The RBV focuses managerial attention on the firm's internal resources in an effort to identify those assets, capabilities and competencies with the potential to deliver superior competitive advantages.

RBV and Strategy Formulation

Firms in possession of a resource, or mix of resources that are rare among competitors, are said to have a comparative advantage. This comparative advantage enables firms to produce marketing offerings that are either (a) perceived as having superior value or (b) can be produced at lower costs. Therefore, a comparative advantage in resources can lead to a competitive advantage in market position.

In the resource-based view, strategists select the strategy or competitive position that best exploits the internal resources and capabilities relative to external opportunities. Given that strategic resources represent a complex network of inter-related assets and capabilities, organisations can adopt many possible competitive positions. Although scholars debate the precise categories of competitive positions that are used, there is general agreement, within the literature, that the resource-based view is much more flexible than Porter's prescriptive approach to strategy formulation. Hooley et al. suggest the following classification of competitive positions:

- Price positioning.
- Quality positioning.
- Innovation positioning.
- Service positioning.
- Benefit positioning.
- Tailored positioning (one-to-one marketing).

VALUE CHAIN ANALYSIS

Before making a strategic decision, it is important to understand how activities within the organisation create value for customers. One way to do this is to conduct a value chain analysis.

Value chain analysis is based on the principle that organisations exist to create value for their customers. In the analysis, the organisation's activities are divided into separate sets of activities that add value. The organisation can more effectively evaluate its internal capabilities by identifying and examining each of these activities. Each value adding activity is considered to be a source of competitive advantage.

The three steps for conducting a value chain analysis are:

1. Separate the organisation's operations into primary and support activities. Primary activities are those that physically create a product, as well as market the product, deliver the product to the customer and provide after-sales support. Support activities are those that facilitate the primary activities.
2. Allocate cost to each activity. Activity cost information provides managers with valuable in-sight into the internal capabilities of an organisation.

3. Identify the activities that are critical to customer's satisfaction and market success. There are three important considerations in evaluating the role of each activity in the value chain.
   - Company mission. This influences the choice of activities an organisation undertakes.
   - Industry type. The nature of the industry influences the relative importance of activities.
   - Value system. This includes the value chains of an organisation's upstream and downstream partners in providing products to end customers.

ANSOFF'S GROWTH VECTOR

A company attempts to widen the scope of its business definition in such a manner that it results in serving the same set of customers. Integration basically means combining activities related to the present activity of a firm. Such a combination may be done on the basis of the value chain. Value chain is a set of interlinked activities performed by an organization right from the procurement of basic raw materials down to the marketing of finished products to the ultimate consumers. So a firm may move up or down the value chain to concentrate more comprehensively on the customer groups and needs than it is already serving.

Integration is also an expansion strategy as its adoption results in a widening of the scope of the business of a firm. Integration is also a subset of diversification strategies as it involves doing something different from what the firm has been doing previously. Several process-based industries, such as petrochemicals, steel, textiles or hydrocarbons, have integrated firms.

Ansoff has presented a matrix which explains different types of integration strategies:

New Products

	Related Technology	Unrelated technology
New functions		
Firm its own customer	Vertical integration	
Same type of product	Horizontal diversification	
Similar type of product	Marketing and technology-related diversification	Marketing related concentric diversification
New type of product	Technology-related concentric diversification	Conglomerate diversification

According to Ansoff, firms operate on the two dimensions of new products and new functions. New products could be made through related technology or unrelated technology. The new functions could range from the firm being its own customer to having an entirely new type of product. Based on these dimensions it is possible to have four types of integration and diversification strategies. Among the integration strategies there are two types : vertical and horizontal integration.

Vertical Integration. When an organization starts making new products that serve its own needs, vertical integration takes place. In other words, any new activity undertaken with the purpose of either supplying inputs (such as, raw materials) or serving as a customer for outputs (such as, marketing of firm's products) is vertical integration.

Vertical integration could be of two types backward and forward integration. **Backward integration** means retreating to the source of raw materials while **forward integration** moves the organization nearer to the ultimate customer.

Backward Integrations. Few practical illustrations used by the corporate world are as follows:-

(i) A steel making unit acquires an iron or mine.

(ii) A paper mill goes in for a massive fore station programme to get the raw materials required for paper making.

(iii) An automobile giant acquires a forge unit or a foundry to get its major raw materials in the form of castings and forgings.

Forward Integrations. Following are the illustrations:-

(i) A book publisher sets up a distribution network to improve its sales and ensure economies of scale.

(ii) A film producer acquired distribution rights in all the territories.

(iii) A manufacturer of consumer electronics goods (TV/radio) sets up retail outlets in all metro towns.

Horizontal integration. When an organization takes up the same type of products at the same level of production or marketing process, it is said to follow a strategy of horizontal integration. When a luggage company takes over its rival luggage company, it is horizontal integration (or a merger). Horizontal integration strategy may be frequently adopted with a view to expand geographically by buying a competitor's business, to increase the market share or to benefit from economies of scale.

B.C.G MODEL

Corporate portfolio analysis is defined as a set of techniques that help strategists in taking strategic decisions with regard to individual products or businesses in a firm's portfolio. It is primarily used for competitive analysis and corporate strategic planning in multi-product and multi-business firms. They may also be used in less diversified firms, if these consist of a main business and other minor complementary interests. For instance, a diversified company may decide to divert resources from its cash-rich businesses to the more prospective ones which hold the promise of a faster growth so that the company can achieve its corporate level objectives in an optimal manner.

There are a number of techniques that could be considered as corporate portfolio analysis techniques. The most popular is the Boston Consulting Group (B.C.G) matrix or product portfolio matrix.

B.C.G Matrix

The Boston Consulting Group (B.C.G) matrix, provides a graphic representation for an organization to examine the different businesses in its portfolio on the basis of their relative market shares and industry growth rates. As shown in the exhibit, businesses could be classified on the B.C.G matrix as either low or high according to their industry growth rate and relative market share. The vertical axis denotes the rate of growth in sales in percentage for a particular industry. The horizontal axis represents the relative market share, which is the ratio of a company's sales to the sales of the industry's largest competitor or market leader. The low and high market shares are separated by a vertical line set at 1.0. This means that a company would have a relative market share of less than 1.0 if it does not have the largest share. A relative market share of more than 1.0 would occur for companies that are the largest sellers in their various industries. Still, in order to get the maximum benefits out of the experience curve, the B.C.G matrix indicates that it is necessary to be the market leader. The four cells of the B.C.G matrix have been termed as stars, cash cows, question marks (or problem children), and dogs. Each of these cells represents a particular type of businesses.

Market growth is used as a measure of market's attractiveness. Markets experiencing high growth are ones where the total market is expanding meaning that it's relatively easy for businesses to grow their profits, even if their market share remains stable. While, competition in low growth markets is often bitter, and while you might have high market share now, it may be hard to retain that market share without aggressive discounting. This makes low growth markets less attractive.

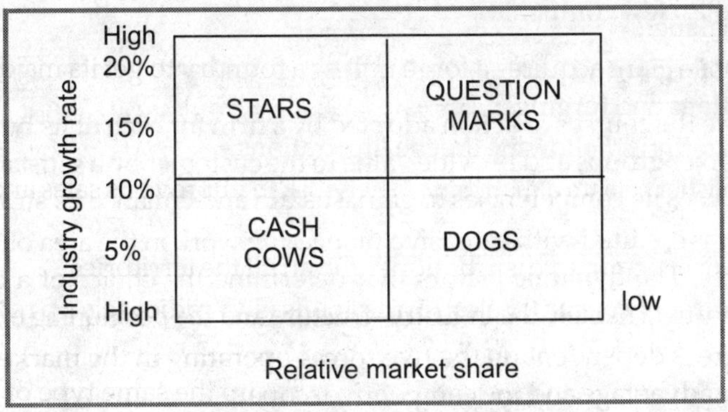

A Typical B.C.G Matrix.

Stars (High Market share / High Market Growth)

These are the SBU's having high share in a growth market. Stars are high-growth–high-market share businesses which may or may not be self-sufficient in terms of cash flow. This cell corresponds closely to the growth phase of the Product Life Cycle (P.L.C). A company generally pursues an expansion strategy to establish a strong competitive position with regard to a 'star' business. For instance, petrochemicals, electronics and telecommunications, fast foods, ceramic tiles, among others are some of the industries which have a very high growth rate.

Cash cows (High Market Share / Low Market Growth)

As the term indicates, cash cows are businesses which generate large amounts of cash but their rate of growth is slow. In terms of P.L.C, these are generally mature businesses which are reaping the benefits of the experience curve. The cash generation exceeds the reinvestment that could profitably be made into 'cash cows'. These businesses can adopt mainly stability strategies. Where long-term prospects are exceptionally bright limited expansion could be adopted. Scooters for Bajaj Auto, toothpaste for Colgate, decorative paints for Asian Paints are some of the 'cash cows' in the contemporary Indian market.

Question marks (Low Market Share / High Market Growth)

Businesses with the high industry growth but low market share for a company are 'question marks' or 'problem child'. These are also called as 'wild cat'. They require large amounts of dictates that the company obtaining an early lead can expect cost advantages and market leadership and can successfully create entry barriers. No single set of strategies can be recommended here. If the company feels that it can obtain a dominant market share, it may select expansion strategies, otherwise retrenchment may be a more realistic alternative. 'Question marks', therefore, may become 'stars' if enough investment is made or they may become 'dogs' if ignored. Holiday resorts, light commercial vehicles, home improvement products are a few of the examples.

Dogs (Low Market Share / Low Market Growth)

Those businesses which are related to slow-growth industries and where a company has a low relative market share are termed as 'dogs'. They neither generate nor require large amounts of cash. In terms of P.L.C, the 'dogs' are usually products in late maturity or a declining stage. The experience curve for the company shows that it faces cost disadvantages owing to a low market share. The only possibility for the company could be to gain market share at the expense of rival firms, a possibility that is remote owing to the high costs involved. So retrenchment strategies are normally suggested. Cotton textiles, jute, shipping, leasing, photocopiers are some of the products and services that have become 'dogs' for quite a few companies.

Porter's Generic Strategies

Business strategies are the courses of action adopted by a firm for each of its businesses separately to serve identified customer groups and provide value to the customer by a satisfaction of their needs. In the process, the firm uses its competencies to gain, sustain and enhance its strategic advantage.

Michael E. Porter is credited with extensive pioneering work in the area of business strategies or competitive strategies. The dynamic factors that determine the choice of a competitive strategy, according to Porter, are two, namely the industry structure and the positioning of a firm in the industry.

Industry structure is dependent on the five forces operating in the marketplace. Positioning is based on competitive advantage and the competitive scope.

Competitive advantage is derived from the two approaches of lower cost and differentiation. Competitive scope could be a broad target or a narrow target. When competitive advantage and competitive scope are juxtaposed what results is a matrix. Porter uses this matrix to suggest that there could be basically three types of competitive (or business) strategies.

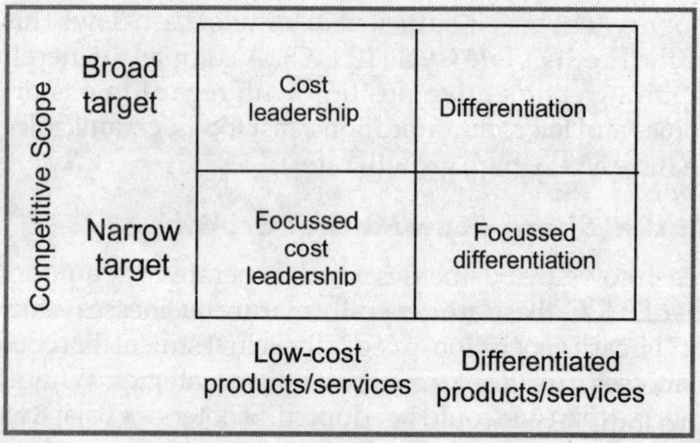

Competitive Advantage.

According to Porter, business strategies are of three types :

A. Cost leadership (lower cost/ broad target)

B. Differentiation (differentiation/broad target)

C. Focus (lower cost or differentiation/ narrow target)

A. Cost Leadership Business Strategy

When the competitive advantage of a firm lies in a lower cost of products or services relative to what the competitors have to offer, it is termed as cost leadership. The firm outperforms its competitors by offering products or services at a lower cost than they can. Customers prefer a lower cost product particularly if it offers the same utility to them as the comparable products available in the market have to offer. When all firms offer products at a comparable price, then the cost leader firm earns a higher profit owing to the low cost of its products. Cost leadership offers a margin of flexibility to the firm to lower price if the competition becomes stiff and yet earn more or less the same level of profit.

Example

- Gujarat Cooperative Milk Marketing Federation (G.C.M.M.F), the country's largest cooperative, probably known better by its brand name Amul, operates in the branded ice cream market on the lower-cost platform. It has the backing of about 180 cooperative dairy networks located across the country and an efficient supply-chain in place for the procurement of high-quality milk. Besides these, it has developed a cold chain for supplying its refrigerated products through an efficient distribution network.

B. Differentiation Business Strategy

When the competitive advantage of a firm lies in special features incorporated into the product/service, which are demanded by the customers who are willing to pay for those, then the strategy adopted is the differentiation business strategy. The firm outperforms its competitors who are not able or willing to offer the special features that it can and does. Customers prefer a differentiated product/service when it offers them a utility that they value and are willing to pay more for getting such a utility. A differentiated product/service stands apart in the market and is distinguishable by the customers for its special features and attributes.

Example

- Orient Fans, a Calcutta-based C.K Birla group company, offers premium ceiling fans based on product innovation and superior technology. The product attributes for differentiation are extra-wide blades, heavy duty motor, high velocity and maximum area coverage. Rivals in the fan market include market leader Crompton and others like Usha, Khaitan and Bajaj. More than 40 percent of the ceiling fan market is dominated by fragmented, low cost suppliers in the unorganised sector.

C. Focus Business Strategy

Focus business strategies essentially rely on either cost leadership or differentiation but cater to a narrow segment of the total market. The more commonly-used bases for identifying customer groups are the demographic characteristics (age, gender, income, occupation etc.), geographic segmentation (rural/urban or Northern India/Southern India) or life-style (traditional/modern).

Example

- Premiere, a high-priced film magazine from the Zee group, was launched in 1988 as a niche publication in a market dominated by cheap, glossy magazines which concentrated on gossip and the private lives of the film stars. It focussed on those readers who were bored with silly gossips and who were a new breed of serious film viewers generated by watching television at home. The differentiation was based on magazine features, such as, excellent visual presentation and features on the professional side of film personalities and on film history.

Competitor Analysis

Competitor analysis focuses on each company with which a firm competes directly. Competitor analysis, therefore, deals with the actions and reactions of individual firms within an industry or strategic group. It becomes specially important in the case of oligopolistic industries where there are a few powerful competitors and each needs to keep track of the strategic moves of the others.

The Porter's 5 Forces tool is a simple but powerful tool for understanding where power lies in a business situation. It helps to understand both the strength of present competitive position and the strength of a position one is willing to aspire. With a clear understanding of where power lies, one can take a fair advantage of the situation by improving a situation of weakness and avoid taking wrong steps. Conventionally, the tool is used to identify whether new products, services or businesses have the potential to be profitable.

According to Porter, the purpose of conducting a competitor analysis is to :

- Determine each competitor's probable reaction to the industry and environmental changes.
- Determine the response of each competitor to the likely strategic moves.
- Develop a profile of the nature and success of the possible strategic changes, each competitor might undertake.

Components of Competitors Analysis

A competitor response profile can be built on the basis of the four components of competitor analysis. These four components are :

(i) *Future goals of competitor* deals with questions such as these how do our goals compare to our competitors' goals ? Where will emphasis be placed in the future ? What is the attitude toward risk ?

(ii) *Current strategy of competitor* deals with questions such as these : How are we currently competing? Does this strategy support changes in the competition structure ?

(iii) *Key assumptions made by the competitor* deal with questions such as these : Do we assume that the future will be volatile ? Are we operating under a status quo ? What assumptions do our competitors hold about the industry and about themselves ?

(iv) *Capabilities of competitor* deal with questions such as these: What are our strengths and weaknesses ? How do we rate compared to our competitors ?

Based on a thorough analysis of these components, a response profile can be prepared for each competitor that can help predict their likely strategic moves which can be either of an offensive or defensive type. The response profile could be based on a firm posing questions such as these to itself; What will our competitors do in the future ? Where do we hold an advantage over our competitors ? And, how will this change our relationship with our competitors? The information collected in the response profile is a vital input for the purpose of business strategy formulation by any organization.

It is used profitably where competition is an important consideration in strategic choice. In India, competition is not new to industry but it has been particularly pronounced after the successive liberalization measures taken by the government after 1984. Supply has exceeded demand in industries and companies have overhauled their marketing strategies to be able to compete well in the market. The case of two-wheeler and four-wheeler industries are illustrations of the changing scenario of competitiveness. Waiting lists for scooters and cars were a common phenomenon a few years ago but now these markets have become highly competitive. Another case is of the F.M.C.G industry in general, where competitiveness in several subsectors such as soaps and detergents, cosmetics, bakery and confectionery products and others, has increased by leaps and bounds. It is in such a scenario that competitor analysis becomes relevant.

Competitor analysis is important because competitive forces shape the strategies adopted by rivals and because these strategies of rival firms, in turn, shape the competitive forces. It is useful for a firm, if it takes the results of competitor analysis into account while exercising a strategic choice.

STRATEGY IMPLEMENTATION

While some models of organizational effectiveness go in and out of fashion, one that has persisted is the McKinsey 7-S framework. Developed in the early 1980s by Tom Peters and Robert Waterman, two consultants working at the McKinsey & Company consulting firm, the basic premise of the model is that there are seven internal aspects of an organization that need to be aligned if it is to be successful.

The 7-S model can be used in a wide variety of situations where an alignment perspective is useful, for example, to help you:

- Improve the performance of a company.
- Examine the likely effects of future changes within a company.
- Align departments and processes during a merger or acquisition.
- Determine how best to implement a proposed strategy.

The McKinsey 7-S model can be applied to elements of a team or a project as well. The alignment issues apply, regardless of how you decide to define the scope of the areas you study.

The McKinsey 7-S model involves seven interdependent factors which are categorized as either "hard" or "soft" elements:

- **Hard.** Strategy, Structure, Systems.
- **Soft.** Shared Values, Skills, Style and Staff.

"Hard" elements are easier to define or identify and management can directly influence them: these are strategy statements; organization charts and reporting lines; and formal processes and IT systems.

"Soft" elements, on the other hand, can be more difficult to describe, and are less tangible and more influenced by culture. However, these soft elements are as important as the hard elements if the organization is going to be successful.

Let's look at each of the elements specifically:

- **Strategy** the plan devised to maintain and build competitive advantage over the competition.
- **Structure** the way the organization is structured and who reports to whom.
- **Systems** the daily activities and procedures that staff members engage in to get the job done.
- **Shared Values** called "superordinate goals" when the model was first developed, these are the core values of the company that are evidenced in the corporate culture and the general work ethic.
- **Style** the style of leadership adopted.
- **Staff** the employees and their general capabilities.
- **Skills** the actual skills and competencies of the employees working for the company.

The model is based on the theory that, for an organization to perform well, these seven elements need to be aligned and mutually reinforcing. So, the model can be used to help identify what needs to be realigned to improve performance, or to maintain alignment (and performance) during other types of change.

Whatever the type of change – restructuring, new processes, organizational merger, new systems, change of leadership, and so on – the model can be used to understand how the organizational elements are interrelated, and so ensure that the wider impact of changes made in one area is taken into consideration.

You can use the 7-S model to help analyze the current situation (Point A), a proposed future situation (Point B) and to identify gaps and inconsistencies between them. It's then a question of adjusting and tuning the elements of the 7-S model to ensure that your organization works effectively and well once you reach the desired endpoint.

Sounds simple? Well, of course not: changing your organization will likely not be simple at all! Whole books and methodologies are dedicated to analyzing organizational strategy, improving performance and managing change. The 7-S model is a good framework to help you ask the right questions – but it won't give you all the answers. For that, you'll need to bring together the right knowledge, skills and experience.

When it comes to asking the right questions, we've developed a Mind Tools checklist and a matrix to keep track of how the seven elements align with each other. Supplement these with your own questions, based on your organization's specific circumstances and accumulated wisdom.

Here are some of the questions that you'll need to explore to help you understand your situation in terms of the 7-S framework. Use them to analyze your current (Point A) situation first, and then repeat the exercise for your proposed situation (Point B).

Strategy

- What is our strategy?
- How do we intend to achieve our objectives?
- How do we deal with competitive pressure?
- How are changes in customer demands dealt with?
- How is strategy adjusted for environmental issues?

Structure

- How is the company/team divided?
- What is the hierarchy?
- How do the various departments coordinate activities?
- How do the team members organize and align themselves?
- Is decision making and controlling centralized or decentralized? Is this as it should be, given what we're doing?
- Where are the lines of communication? Explicit and implicit?

Systems

- What are the main systems that run the organization? Consider financial and HR systems as well as communications and document storage.
- Where are the controls and how are they monitored and evaluated?
- What internal rules and processes does the team use to keep on track?

Shared Values

- What are the core values?
- What is the corporate/team culture?
- How strong are the values?
- What are the fundamental values that the company/team was built on?

Style

- How participative is the management/leadership style?
- How effective is that leadership?
- Do employees/team members tend to be competitive or cooperative?
- Are there real teams functioning within the organization or are they just nominal groups?

Staff

- What positions or specializations are represented within the team?

- What positions need to be filled?
- Are there gaps in required competencies?

Skills

- What are the strongest skills represented within the company/team?
- Are there any skills gaps?
- What is the company/team known for doing well?
- Do the current employees/team members have the ability to do the job?
- How are skills monitored and assessed?

MARKETING

Marketing deals with identifying and meeting human and social needs. One of the shortest definitions of marketing is, "meeting needs profitably". Marketing is typically seen as the task of creating, promoting and delivering goods and services to consumers and business. Marketers are skilled in stimulating demand for a company's products, but this is too limited view of the tasks marketers perform. Marketing people are involved in marketing in 10 types of entities : goods, services, experiences, events, persons, places, properties, organizations, information and ideas. Thus, marketing is a societal process by which individuals and groups obtain what they need and want through creating, offering and freely exchanging products and services of value with others.

For *e.g.*, when Sony designed its walkman, when Nintendo designed its superior video game and when Toyata introduced its luxus automobiles, these manufacturers were swamped with orders because they had designed the 'right' product based on careful marketing network.

The American Marketing Association gives the following definition, "Marketing is the process of planning and executing the conception, pricing, promotion and distribution of ideas, goods and services to create exchanges that satisfy individual and organizational goals. Marketing management is an art and science of choosing target markets and getting, keeping and growing customers through creating, delivering and communicating superior customer values.

The Evolution of Marketing

Marketing has its origin in the fact that man is a creature of needs and wants. Needs and wants create a sense of discomfort in persons and they tend to get objects (i.e. products) those satisfy these needs and wants. The word marketing has been derived from market which may be looked upon as an arena for potential exchange, i.e. a place where products can be exchanged by money or anything else. Marketing includes the policy, techniques and methods necessary for selling and distribution.

The word 'Market' is derived from the Latin word 'Marcatus' meaning merchandise ware traffic, trade or a place where business is conducted.

CONCEPTS

To a layman, market means a place where goods are brought or sold. A market is a group of buyers and sellers interested in negotiating the terms of purchase/sale of goods and services. American Marketing Association defines 'market as the aggregate demand of the potential buyers for a product or service.' Philip Kotler defines market 'as an area for potential exchanges'. According to Pyle 'Marketing includes both place and region in which buyers and sellers are in free competition with one another'. Clark and Clark state, a market is a center about which or an area in which the forces leading to exchange of title to a particular product operate and towards which the actual goods tend to travel. Broadly, market is any region in which buyers and sellers are brought in contact with one another wherein the forces of demand and supply facilitate and exchange profess between them. Thus, exchange is an essence of marketing. Exchange takes place when there are two or more parties and each has something they desire to exchange for something else. Therefore, a market consists of a group of person or persons on one side having the goods they want to sell and on the other a group of prospective buyers who want to pay for and buy. It means that three points are interlinked namely, place, area and demand.

1. **Place.** A market is a convenient meeting place for buyers and sellers to gather together to effect the exchange of goods and services.
2. **Area.** A market develops in any area, where, there are:
   (i) Two or more individuals having unsatisfied wants,
   (ii) They have product(s) to exchange and
   (iii) They have some means of communication such as phone, teller, correspondence etc. With the means of communication, the forces of demand and supply freely operate and the informed buyers and sellers can strike the dealing without formal face to face meeting.
3. Demand. A market consists of people with needs to satisfy money to spend and the will to spend money to satisfy their wants.

The process of exchange represents the market where buyers (demand) and sellers (supply) exchange the product against money/other products. The means of communication assists the free flow of demand and supply which determines the price. Usually money acts as the medium of exchange. The act of exchange leads to transfer of ownership and possession from a seller to a buyer in the market. Feedback information indicates buyer's post purchase behaviour. If satisfied, buyer makes repeated purchases otherwise he switches to other brands.

CONCEPT OF MARKETING

A. Old Concept

This concept of marketing was popular when business was done on small scale and there was little or no competition. According to this concept, marketing consists of merely buying and selling activities that effect the transfer of ownership of goods and services.

According to Clark and Clark – Marketing consists of those efforts which effect transfer in the ownership of goods and services and which provide for physical distribution

According to American. Marketing Association – 'Marketing is the performance of business activities that direct the flow of goods and services from producer to consumer or user.

Characteristics of Old Concept of Marketing

1. It consists of only production, purchases and sales activities.
2. It is product oriented, i.e., it focuses attention only on product to be sold ignoring, consumer's interest and tastes.
3. Its activities come to an end on sale, i.e., it does not provide after sale services.
4. It does not give importance to consumer satisfaction.
5. It aims at earning maximum profits.

Criticism

1. It focuses only on production, purchases and sale activities and ignores other activities of marketing.

2. It ignores consumer research.
3. It is a product oriented concept.
4. It ignores after-sale activities.
5. Consumer satisfaction and social responsibility has no place in this concept.
6. It fails to point out close inter-relationship between product (supply) and market (demand).

B. New Concept

New concept of marketing is a broader concept which considers marketing as a continuous process of discovering and converting consumer wants into appropriate products and services by developing a product on the basis of marketing research, creating demand for these products through promotion and serving the demand through transport and storage with the help of channels of distribution such as wholesalers and retailers.

Marketing concept states that consumers want satisfaction is the economic and social justification of a firm's existence. Therefore, all the firm's activities in the areas of production, engineering, finance as well as marketing must be directed primarily to determine what the consumer's wants are and then satisfy these wants, though making a reasonable profits.

The new concept is consumer oriented. It considers consumer as the 'King' around which all business activities rotate. The concept is also founded on consumer satisfaction.

The concept says all business activities are integrated, i.e., marketing management cannot be an independent function. The management's functional areas are interdependent and not independent. The marketing function influences production, finance, personnel and in turn is influenced by these functions. This modern concept allows earning reasonable profits through consumer satisfaction.

According to William Stanton, 'Marketing is a total system of interacting business activities designed to plan, price, promote and distribute want satisfying products and services to present and potential customers'.

According to Council of Institute of Marketing, 'Marketing is the management function which organizes and directs all those activities involved in assessing and converting customer purchasing power into effective demand for a specific product or service and in moving the product or service to the final consumer or use so as to achieve the profit target or other objectives set by a company'.

According to Cundiff, Still and Govani, 'Marketing is the managerial process by which products are matched with markets and through which transfers of ownership are affected'.

Characteristics of New Concept of Marketing

1. It recognizes the consumer's supremacy as it is consumer oriented. Creation of satisfied customers is the main aim of marketing.
2. Modern marketing begins with consumers and it ends also with the consumers. Marketing research is starting point of marketing in-order to secure adequate information of current consumer needs. Offer of complete service and satisfaction including post-purchase satisfaction is the ending step of marketing.
3. Modern marketing begins before production as well as it succeeds production. Discovery of consumer needs and desires takes place before production with the help of marketing research. Product planning and development is undertaken before actual production. These are important marketing functions. Other marketing functions such as pricing, promotion, distribution, succeed production.

4. Modern marketing adopts the systematic approach to marketing. Such an approach provides a good basis for orderly and integrated analysis and planning of all business activities relating to product, pricing, promotion and distribution.
5. It aims at earning profit only by satisfying consumers.
6. It provides after sale services such as home delivery, guarantee etc.

This concept can be illustrated as under:

- Consumer Research • Purchase • Production • Storage
- Transport • Pricing • Promotion • Selling • After Sale Services

Merchandising, Selling and Marketing

Merchandising is only product planning. It aims at the internal planning relation to products or services for marketing at the right time, right price and in proper colour, qualities and sizes. Thus it is only a part of marketing study.

Selling is pre-occupied with the seller's need to convert his product into cash. It focuses on the needs of the seller. It seeks profits by 'pushing' the products on the buyers.

Selling is certainly a part of marketing. To quote Levitt, 'the difference between selling and marketing is more than semantic'.

Various Views Regarding Marketing Concept

(a) **Distribution of Goods and Services Concept.** According to this concept, marketing includes only those activities that assist in distribution of goods and services from the producer to the final consumer.

According to Tousley, Clark and Clark, 'Marketing consists of those efforts which effect transfers in the ownership of goods and services and which provide for physical (distribution)'.

According to American Marketing Association, 'Marketing is the performance of business activities that direct the flow of goods and services from producer to consumer or users.'

This concept has lost its significance in today's changed scenario. It is an indication of old concept and as such includes only three activities in marketing i.e., purchase, production and selling. Therefore, this concept is also criticized on some issues as the old concept.

(b) **Creation of Utilities Concept.** According to this concept, marketing is an activity concerned with generating utilities. According to Economists, marketing is a system which creates value in products by generating utilities in them. These utilities, according to Converse, Huegy and Mitchell are of three types – place, time and possession. But Richard Buskirk has added form utility also and therefore, according to him, there are four utilities. In fact, all the four utilities are effected by marketing activities. When the product is planned and developed and then this marketing activity creates form utility. When the products are sent to various places for sale through various means, place utility is created. Similarly, when the goods are stored by middleman much before its demand, there is creation of time utility. The marketing activity relating to advertisement and sales promotion creates possession utility where the consumer influenced by such promotion measures comes to purchase the product resulting in change of possession of ownership of product from producer to consumer. According to Richard Buskirk, 'Marketing is an integrated system of action that creates value in goods through its creation of form, place, time and ownership utilities'.

(c) **Delivery of Standard of Living Concept.** According to this concept, marketing is concerned with providing standard of living to the society. It is consumer oriented concept and it emphasizes on satisfying the desires. Therefore, product planning comes under its scope. In order, to provide the desired standard of living, it is necessary to make arrangements for the development of goods desired by society and to include all the features desired by them.

(d) **System Approach Concept.** According to this concept marketing refers to the total process by means of which goods and services are exchanged. It involves all business activities because these activities are mutually inter-related. Today the business environment is faced with mass production, stiff competition and complex channels of distribution, so there is need for proper system or process which will help the producer as well as consumer to overcome all the obstacles in the exchange of goods and services.

According to Stanton, 'Marketing system is an interacting set of institutions, activities and flows designed to facilitate exchange transactions between an organization (business or non-business) and its market'.

Philip Kotler says, 'The exchanges that take place in a society along with the facilitating institutions, make up its marketing system'.

In fact, the concept is based on new concept of marketing and as such it includes all the activities that start before production and continues even after sales. The first process of marketing process is assembling wherein inputs are gathered at a central place either for further processing or for sale. Then the goods are dispersed to consumers through wholesalers and retailers at profitable and reasonable price. But before dispersion, equalisation process is done to balance demand and supply through storage and transportation.

(e) **Societal Marketing Concept.** This concept concentrates on producing goods and services, which are beneficial to the society. It says that firm's task is to determine the needs and desires of consumers and to satisfy them more effectively than the competitors in a way that is beneficial both to the consumer and the society. It aims at balancing profits, consumer satisfaction and public interest. The marketing process is regarded as a means by which society meets its consumption needs. Here, the firm realizes its social responsibilities.

PRODUCT AND PRICING DECISION

PRODUCT MIX

Product mix or product assortment is a set of total number of products lines that a seller offers in the market to its buyers. The company may have one or several product lines and each product line may have several products. When these product lines get together are known as product mix of the company.

Width

Width or breath is the company's product mix that means the total number of product lines that a company offers to sell.

For instance, if a company offers milk and yogurts, this indicates the that its product mix has two lines. Similarly, a cosmetic company manufactures four different types of products – jewellery, cosmetics, fashion and household items. Its product mix width is 4.

Depth

Depth of product mix means the total number of products a company offers within a certain product line. There may be different variations in the product e.g. size, flavor, taste and many other characteristics. For example, Medicam toothpaste sells four sizes and two flavors mean it has a depth of eight.

Another thing I want to discuss is average depth of product line. Suppose a company first line depth is 8 and second one is 10 the average depth is 19.

Length

The length of product mix means total number of products within a company's product lines. For example, if a company has 10 product lines and each line has 3 product variations then product mix length is (10×3) = 30.

Length of the product mix refers to the total number of products in the mix. If a company has 5 product lines and 10 products under each product lines, the length of the mix will be 50 [5 × 10].

Consistency

At last, the consistency of a product mix is the close relationship between different product lines. The more product variation means less product consistency. For example, a dairy company has two product lines milk and yogurt. Both the lines have same users and distribution channels. Due to low product variation and high product mix consistency. Take another example of Philips Electronics with 7 product lines having high production mix variation and low consistency.

PRODUCT LIFE CYCLE

A new product progresses through a sequence of stages from introduction to growth, maturity, and decline. This sequence is known as the product life cycle and is associated with changes in the marketing situation, thus impacting the marketing strategy and the marketing mix.

The product revenue and profits can be plotted as a function of the life-cycle stages as shown in the graph below.

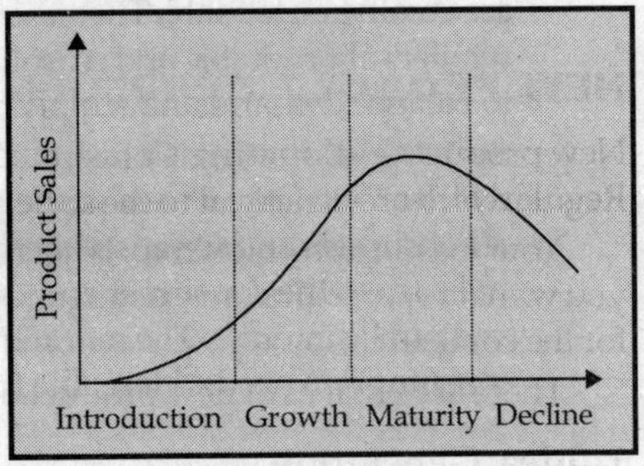

Introduction Stage

In the introduction stage, the firm seeks to build product awareness and develop a market for the product. The impact on the marketing mix is as follows:

- Product branding and quality level is established, and intellectual property protection such as patents and trademarks are obtained.
- Pricing may be low penetration pricing to build market share rapidly, or high skim pricing to recover development costs.
- Distribution is selective until consumers show acceptance of the product.
- Promotion is aimed at innovators and early adopters. Marketing communications seeks to build product awareness and to educate potential consumers about the product.

Growth Stage

In the growth stage, the firm seeks to build brand preference and increase market share.

- Product quality is maintained and additional features and support services may be added.
- Pricing is maintained as the firm enjoys increasing demand with little competition.
- Distribution channels are added as demand increases and customers accept the product.
- Promotion is aimed at a broader audience.

Maturity Stage

At maturity, the strong growth in sales diminishes. Competition may appear with similar products. The primary objective at this point is to defend market share while maximizing profit.

- Product features may be enhanced to differentiate the product from that of competitors.
- Pricing may be lower because of the new competition.
- Distribution becomes more intensive and incentives may be offered to encourage preference over competing products.
- Promotion emphasizes product differentiation.

Decline Stage

As sales decline, the firm has several options:

- Maintain the product, possibly rejuvenating it by adding new features and finding new uses.
- Harvest the product - reduce costs and continue to offer it, possibly to a loyal niche segment.
- Discontinue the product, liquidating remaining inventory or selling it to another firm that is willing to continue the product.
- The marketing mix decisions in the decline phase will depend on the selected strategy For example, the product may be changed if it is being rejuvenated, or left unchanged if it is being harvested or liquidated. The price may be maintained if the product is harvested, or reduced drastically if liquidated.

NEW PRODUCT DEVELOPMENT

New product development is a task taken by the company to introduce newer products in the market. Regularly there will arise a need in the business for new product development.

Your existing products may be technologically outdated, you have different segments to target or you want to cannibalize an existing product. In such cases, New product development is the answer for the company.

There are 7 stages of new product development and they are as follows.

1. Idea Generation

Idea generation in this you are basically involved in the systematic search for new product Ideas. A company has to generate many ideas in order to find one that is worth pursuing. The Major sources of new product ideas include internal sources, customers, competitors, distributors and suppliers.

Almost 55% of all new product ideas come from internal sources according to one study. Companies like 3M and Toyota have put in special incentive programs or their employees to come up with workable ideas.

Almost 28% of new product ideas come from watching and listening to customers. Customers: even create new products on their own, and companies can benefit by finding these products and putting them on the market.

2. Idea Screening

The second step in New product development is Idea screening. The purpose of idea generation is to create a large pool of ideas. The purpose of this stage is to pare these down to those that are genuinely worth pursuing. Companies have different methods for doing this from product review committees to formal market research.

It, is helpful at this stage to have a checklist that can be used to rate each idea based on the factors required for successfully launching the product in the marketplace and their relative importance.

Against these, management can assess how well the idea fits with the company's marketing skills and experience and other capabilities. Finally, the management can obtain an overall rating of the company's ability to launch the product successfully.

3. Concept Development and Testing

The third step in New product development is Concept Development and Testing. An attractive idea has to be developed into a Product concept. As opposed to a product idea that is an idea for a product that the company can see itself marketing to customers, a product concept is a detailed version of the idea stated in meaningful consumer terms.

This is different again from a product image, which is the consumers' perception of an actual or potential product. Once the concepts are developed, these need to be tested with consumers either symbolically or physically. For some concept tests, a word or a picture may be sufficient, however, a physical presentation will increase the reliability of the concept test.

After being exposed to the concept, consumers are asked to respond to it by answering a set of questions designed to help the company decide which concept has the strongest appeal. The company can then project these findings to the full market to estimate sales volume.

4. Marketing Strategy Development

This is the next step in new product development. The strategy statement consists of three parts: the first part describes the target market, the planned product positioning and the sales, market share and profit goals for the first few years.

The second part outlines the product's planned price, distribution, and marketing budget for the first year. The third part of the marketing strategy statement describes the planned long-run sales, profit goals, and the marketing mix strategy.

Business Analysis – Once the management has decided on the marketing strategy, it can evaluate the attractiveness of the business proposal.

Business analysis involves the review of projected sales, costs and profits to find out whether they satisfy a company's objectives. If they do, the product can move to the product development stage.

5. Product Development

Here, R&D or engineering develops the product concept into a physical product. This step calls for a large investment. It will show whether the product idea can be developed into a full- fledged workable product.

First, R&D will develop prototypes that will satisfy and excite customers and that can be produced quickly and at budgeted costs. When the prototypes are ready, they must be tested. Functional tests are then conducted under laboratory and field conditions to ascertain whether the product performs safely and effectively.

6. Test Marketing

If the product passes the functional tests, the next step is test marketing: the stage at which the product and the marketing program are introduced to a more realistic market settings. Test marketing gives the marketer an opportunity to tweak the marketing mix before the going into the expense of a product launch.

The amount of test marketing varies with the type of product. Costs of test marketing can be enormous and it can also allow competitors to launch a "me-too" product or even sabotage the testing so that the marketer gets skewed results. Hence, at times, management may decide to do away with this stage and proceed straight to the next one.

7. Commercialization

The final step in new product development is Commercialization. Introducing the product to the market – it will face high costs for manufacturing and advertising and promotion. The company will have to decide on the timing of the launch (seasonality) and the location (whether regional, national or international). This depends a lot on the ability of the company to bear risk and the reach of its distribution network.

Today, in order to increase speed to market, many companies are dropping this sequential approach to development and are adopting the faster, more flexible, simultaneous development approach. Under this approach, many company departments work closely together, overlapping the steps in the product development process to save time and increase effectiveness.

PRICING

Price is the only variable factor generating revenues. It is an important element which determines the success or failure of the concern. Price is the exchange value of a product or service expressed in monetary terms. Price is the money which the buyer pays to the seller for a product. The product does not mean only the physical aspect but it also includes services and benefits like warranty, repair facilities, free home delivery, credit facilities etc. The more the services, higher the price. Price is the amount for which a product, a service or an idea is exchanged regardless of its worth to the buyer. Thus, rent for house, tuition fees for education, consultancy fees for doctor, fare for bus, taxi or railway, salary to executive is the price in various forms. In short, 'price' is the amount of money to be paid in return for a bundle of utilities.

The term '*price*' need not be confused with the term '*pricing*'. Pricing is the function of translating into quantitative terms the value of the product or service or idea by the marketing manager before it is offered for sale to consumers. Pricing is the process of setting objectives, identifying the factors governing the price, formulating price policies and strategies setting prices, implementing them and controlling them.

Pricing policies provide the general framework within which pricing decisions are taken. It provides the guidelines without which pricing strategy is formulated and implemented. Following are few of them:

(a) **One Price Policy.** Under this policy, all the customers who are purchasing a particular quantity at a particular time are charged the same price, *i.e.*, the price is fixed and no changes are made in it.

(b) **Flexible Price Policy.** Under this policy different buyers are charged different prices for the same quantity purchased. The difference in pricing depends on bargaining power of buyer, his paying capacity, personal relationship between buyer and seller and many other such factors.

(c) **Meeting Competition Policy.** The companies adopting this policy adjust their prices according to that of the competitors. If the competitors lower their prices, they too do the same. On the other hand, if the competitors increase their price, they also follow suit.

(d) **Under the Market Policy.** It is a policy in which the company always keeps its prices less than those prevailing in the market.

(e) **Bait Pricing Policy.** The marketer keeps low priced and high priced goods. He attracts the consumer by showing low priced goods. Once the customer gets attracted towards the low priced goods, he is told about its drawbacks and is encouraged to purchase the other high priced product. Thus, low priced goods act as '*Bait*' for attracting the buyer.

(f) **Price Lining Policy.** The various products are priced according to their quality standards. The products may be classified as good, better and best.

(g) **Skimming Pricing Policy.** It is a policy, which aims at extracting maximum profits from the market and as such the manufacturer keeps high prices.

(h) **Uniform Delivery Pricing Policy.** It is one in which the firm bears full transportation cost irrespective of location of buyers.

(i) **Production Point Pricing Policy.** It is one in which the firm quotes ex-factory price. It does not bear the transportation cost. Such a policy may be '*ex-factory*' or '*free on rail*' (F.O.R).

(j) **Zonal Delivery Pricing Policy.** It is one where the firm divides the country into different zones and quotes uniform prices for each zone.

Pricing Methods

There are several methods of pricing & they can be grouped into few broad categories :

(1) **Cost Based Pricing.** Under the cost based pricing, different methods used are :

Mark-up Pricing. It refers to the pricing methods in which the selling price of the product is fixed by adding a margin to its cost price. The mark ups may vary depending on the nature of the product & the market. Usually, the higher the value of the product, the larger is the mark up. Again, the slower the turnaround of the product, the larger is the mark up. Mark-up pricing proceeds on the assumption that demand cannot be known accurately, but costs are known.

Absorption Cost Pricing. ACP rests on the estimated unit cost of the product at the normal level of production & sales. The method used standard costing techniques & works out the variable & fixed costs involved in manufacturing, selling & administering the product. By adding the costs of 3 operations, we get the total costs. The selling price of the product is arrived by adding the required margin towards profit to such total costs. The main merit of this method is that as long as the market can absorb the production at the determined price, the firm is assured of its profits without any risk & the main demerit is that the method simply assumes price to be a function of cost alone & this method becomes ineffective.

Target Rate of Return Pricing. It is similar to absorption cost pricing. The rate of return pricing uses a rational approach to arrive at the mark up. It is arrived in such a way that the ROI criteria of the firm is met in the process. But this process amounts to an improvement over absorption costing since it uses a rational basis for arriving at the mark up. Second, since the rate of return on the funds employed is a function of mark up as well as turnaround of capital employed, rate of return pricing constantly reminds the firm that there are 2 routes for profits - improvement in the capital turnover & increase in the mark up. The main limitation of the method is that the rate of return to the level of production & sales assumed.

Marginal Cost Pricing. It aims at maximizing the contribution towards fixed costs. Marginal costs include all the direct variable costs of the product. In marginal cost pricing, these direct variable costs are fully realized. In addition, a portion of the fixed costs is also realized under competitive market conditions marginal cost pricing is more useful. Moreover, when a firm has a number of product lines marginal cost pricing is useful. This method is also useful in quoting for competitive tenders & in export marketing.

On the demerits side, marginal costing makes certain assumptions, regarding cost & revenue behaviours which can turn out to be incorrect in some cases. Moreover, while marginal costing rests on a two fold classification of cost into fixed costs & variable costs, in reality there can be a third class of costs — The Semi variable costs.

(2) **Demand Based Pricing.** The following methods belong to the category of demand / market based pricing :

What the Traffic can Bear' Pricing. The seller takes the maximum price that the customers are willing to pay for the product under the given circumstances. This method is used more by retail traders than by manufacturing firms. This method brings high profits in the short term. But in the long run it is not a safe concept, chances of errors in judgement are very high.

Skimming Pricing. This method aims at high price & high profits in the early stage of marketing the product. It profitably taps the opportunity for selling at high prices to those segments of the market, which do not bother much about the price. This method is very useful in the pricing of new products, especially those that have a luxury or specialty elements.

Penetration Pricing. Penetration pricing seeks to achieve greater market penetration through relatively low price. This method is also useful in pricing of new products under certain circumstances. For e.g. when the new product is capable of bringing in large volume of sales, but it is not a luxury item & there is no affluent / price insensitive segment, the firm can choose the penetration pricing & make large size sales at a reasonable price before competitors enter the market with a similar product. Penetration pricing in such cases will help the firm have a good coverage of the market & keep competition out for some time.

In all demand based pricing methods, the price elasticity of demand is taken into account directly or indirectly. Price elasticity of demand refers to the relative sensitivity of demand for a product to change in its price in other words how significantly the sales of the product are affected when price is changed. If an increase or decrease in the price of the product results in significant decrease or increase the product is said to be price elastic conversely, if price change does not significantly affect the sales volume, a product is said to be price inelastic.

(3) **Competition Oriented Pricing.** In a competitive economy, competitive oriented pricing methods are common. The methods in this category rest on the principle of competitive parity in the matter of pricing. Three policy options are available to the firm under this pricing method:

- Premium Pricing
- Discount Pricing
- Parity Pricing

Premium pricing means pricing above the level adopted by competitors. Discount pricing means pricing below such level & parity pricing means matching competitors pricing.

(4) **Value Pricing.** Value pricing is a modern innovative & distinctive method of pricing. Value pricing rests on the premise that the purpose of pricing is not to recover costs, but to capture the value of the product perceived by the customer. Analysis will readily show that the following scenario are possible with the cost value price chain :

- Value > Price > Costs
- Price > Value > Costs
- Price > Costs > Value
- Price > Value > Costs

Under Scenario :

- Marketer recovers his costs through price, but fails to recover the value of his product.
- He recovers his costs as well as the value.
- The value that he passes on to the customer is still lesser.
- He matches the value & price & wins customer loyalty & since the value created is larger then his costs, he ensures his profits.

(5) **Product Line Pricing.** When a firm markets a variety of products grouped into suitable product lines, a special possibility in pricing arises. As the product in a given product line are related to each other, sales of one influence that of the others. They also have interrelated costs of manufacturing & distribution. It can fix the prices of the different product in such a manner

that the product line as a whole is priced optimally, resulting in optimal sales of all the products put together & optimal total profits from the line.

(6) **Tender Pricing.** Business firms are often required to fix the prices of their products on a tender basis. It is more applicable to industrial products & products purchased by Institutional customers. Such customers usually go by competitive bidding through sealed tenders. They seek the best price consistent with the minimum quality specification & thus bag the order.

(7) **Affordability Based Pricing.** The affordability based pricing is relevant in respect of essential commodities, which meet the basic needs of all sections of people. Idea here is to set prices in such a way that all sections of the population are in a position to buy & consume the products to the required extent.

(8) **Differentiated pricing.** Some firms charge different prices for the same product in different zones / areas of the market. Sometimes, the differentiation in pricing is made on the basis of customer class rather than marketing territory.

Price Determination Procedure

There is no specific procedure applicable to all firms for price determination. Usually, the following steps are adopted :

1. **Select Target Market.** The very first step is to select the segment or segments in which the company will pursue. The demographic and psychographic characteristics of the selected segment will affect the pricing decision. The buying motives, price sensitivity, paying capacity, location etc. have considerable affect on price.
2. **Determine Demand for the Product.** Each price level gives different levels of demand. Higher the price, lower will be the demand. Estimating the demand for an established product is easier than for a new product. There are two steps in demand estimation:
   (a) Knowing the expected price.
   (b) Determining sales volume at various prices.

   Expected price refers to the price range. Surveys may be conducted of potential buyers or competitors' prices may be studied or the product may be tested in limited area to know the expected price. After knowing the price range, sales volume at different prices are estimated. The product with elastic demand is usually priced lower than the product with an inelastic demand.
3. **Anticipate and Analyze the Competitive Reaction.** The competition has great influence on price. Competition may come from: (i) Similar products; (ii) Close substitute or even from; (iii) Unrelated products seeking the same consumer income. The marketer should study the competitor's product, price, promotional strategies and other marketing policies. The company tries to avoid potential competition by keeping prices as low as possible.
4. **Establish Expected Share of the Market.** The company intending to capture large market share, will opt for low prices. Large share of the market can also be captured by adopting promotional techniques and by going for non-price competition strategy. The company must consider its production capacity, plant extension cost etc. before deciding on market share.
5. **Select Pricing Strategy.** Normally, for pricing a new product, two alternatives are available- (a) Skimming price policy and (b) Penetration price policy.

   Skimming price policy is one in which prices are kept high with a view to skim the cream of demand. It is possible when the product has distinctive features or when there is no competition and the consumers are not price-sensitive. The firm can later, easily lower the prices and attract other segments of the market.

Penetration price policy on the other hand, is one in which prices are kept low with a view to capture large market share. This policy makes sense when buyers are price sensitive, there is fear of competition and the company's cost of production goes down with increase in scale of production.

6. **Consider Company's Marketing Policies.** The company's policies regarding product distribution and promotion affects the price:
   (i) **Product Policies.** The composition of product, its quality, durability, resistance to heat, light, water, breaking strength, shrinkage etc. affects its price. Perishable products which cannot be stored for long periods are priced low to facilitate its easy disposal. The change in fashion also forces the seller to price the products at a level so that they get disposed off before the fashion changes.
   (ii) **Distribution Policies.** The manufacturer may either sell the products directly or through intermediaries. The length and complexity of the distribution channel greatly influence the price. The long and more complex the channel, high will be the price in order to compensate the persons involved in it.
   (iii) **Promotion Policies.** The more the promotional activities undertaken, higher will be price. The price is set to cover all the promotional cost.
7. **Select the Specific Price.** After considering all the above facts ultimately a specific price is selected. The procedures used for setting specific prices vary under different market conditions. The prices may be determined through the forces of Demand and Supply or by cost of production or on the basis of competitor's prices. Commonly, there are three approaches to pricing: (a) Cost Based Pricing, (b) Demand Based Pricing, (c) Competition Based Pricing.

PLACE AND PROMOTION DECISION

MARKETING CHANNELS AND VALUE NETWORKS

Marketing Channels

Most producers do not sell their goods directly to the final users; between them stands a set of intermediaries performing a variety of functions. These intermediaries constitute a marketing channel (also called a trade channel or distribution channel). Formally, marketing channels are sets of interdependent organisations involved in the process of making a product or service available for use or consumption. They are the set of pathways a product or service follows after production, culminating in purchase and use by the final end user.

Some intermediaries such as wholesalers and retailers buy, take title to, and resell the merchandise; they are called merchants. Others brokers, manufacturers representatives, sales agents search for customers and may negotiate on the producers behalf but to not take title to the goods; they are called agents. Still others transportation companies, independent warehouses, banks, advertising agencies assist in the distribution process but neither take title to goods nor negotiate purchases or sales; they are called facilitators.

The Importance of Channels

A marketing channel system is the particular set of marketing channels employed by a firm. Decisions about the marketing channel system are among the most critical facing management. Marketing channels also represent a substantial opportunity cost. One of the chief roles of marketing channels is to convert potential buyers into profitable orders.

In managing its intermediaries, the firm must decide how much effort to devote to push versus pull marketing. A push strategy involves the manufacturer using its sales force and trade promotion money to induce intermediaries to carry, promote, and sell the product to end users. Push strategy is appropriate where there is low brand loyalty in a category, brand choice is made in the store, the product is an impulse item, and product benefits are well understood. A pull strategy involves the manufacturer using advertising and promotion to persuade consumers to ask intermediaries for the product, thus inducting the intermediaries to order it. Pull strategy is appropriate when there is high brand loyalty and high involvement in the category, when people perceive differences between brands, and when people choose the brand before they go to the store.

Channel Development

A new firm typically starts as a local operation selling in a limited market, using existing intermediaries. The number of such intermediaries is apt to be limited: a few manufacturers sales agents, a few wholesalers, several established retailers, a few trucking companies, and a few where houses. Deciding on the best channels might not be a problem; the problem might be to convince the available intermediaries to handle the firms line.

If the firm is successful, it might branch into new markets and use different channels in different markets. In smaller markets, the firm might sell directly to retailers; in larger markets, it might sell through distributors. In rural areas, it might work with general-goods merchants; in urban areas, with limited-line merchants. In one part of the country, it might grant exclusive franchises; in another, it might sell through all outlets willing to handle the merchandise. In one country it might use international sales agents; in another, it might partner with a local firm. In short, the channel system evolves in response to local opportunities and conditions.

Value Networks

A supply chain view of a firm sees markets as destination points and amounts to a linear view of the flow. The company should first think of the target market, however, and then design the supply chain backward from that point. This view has been called demand chain planning. North westerns Don Schultz says: A demand chain management approach doesn't just push things through the system. It emphasises what solutions consumers are looking for, not what products we are trying to sell them. Schultz has suggested that the traditional marketing four Ps be replaced by a new acronym. SIVA, which stands for solutions, information, value, and access.

An even broader view sees a company at the centre of a value network a system of partnerships and alliances that a firm creates to source, augment, and deliver its offerings. A value network includes a firms suppliers and its suppliers and its immediate customers and their end customers. The value network includes valued relations with others such as university researchers and government approval agencies.

A company needs to orchestrate these parties to enable it to deliver superior value to the target market. Palm, the leading manufacturer of handheld devices, consists of a whole community of suppliers and assemblers of semiconductor components, plastic cases, LCD displays, and accessories; of offline and online resellers; and of 2,75,000 developers who have created over 21,000 software programmes and 100 hardware add-ons for the Palm operating systems for hand-held computers and smartphones.

Demand chain planning yields several insights. First, the company can estimate whether more money is made upstream or downstream, in case it might want to integrate backward or forward. Second, the company is more aware of disturbances anywhere in the supply chain that might cause costs, prices, or supplies to change suddenly. Third, companies can go online with their business partners to carry on faster and more accurate communications, transactions, and payments to reduce costs, speed up information, and increase accuracy. With the advent of the Internet, companies are forming more numerous and complex relationships with other firms.

Managing this value network has required companies to make increasing investments in information technology and software. They have invited such software firms as SAP and Oracle to design comprehensive enterprise resource planning systems to manage cash flow, manufacturing, human resources, purchasing, and other major functions within a unified framework. They hope to break up department silos and carry out core business processes more seamlessly. Marketers, for their part, have traditionally focused on the side of the value network that looks toward the customer. In the future, they will increasingly participate in and influence their companies upstream activities and become network managers, not only product and customer managers.

Promotion Decisions - Promotion Mix

Sales Promotion consists of a diverse collection of incentive tools, mostly short term, designed to stimulate quicker or greater purchase of particular products or services by consumers or the trade.

Sales promotion includes tools for *consumer promotion* (samples, coupons, cash refund offers, prices off, premiums, prizes, free trials, warranties, tie-in promotions, cross-promotions, point-of-purchase displays and demonstrations); *trade promotion* (prices off, advertising, display allowances and free goods); and *business and sales-force promotion* (trade shows and conventions, contests for sales reps and specialty advertising). Sales promotion has been defined as, "those marketing activities, other than personal selling, advertising and publicity, that stimulate consumer purchasing and dealer effectiveness, such as displays, shows and demonstrations, expositions and various non current selling efforts, not in ordinary routine."

To accomplish promotion and marketing objectives combination of two or more promotional methods are applied for one product. This constitutes the promotion mix for that product. There is no ideal promotion mix for any firm. It depends largely on intention and judgement of the marketing manager because it is hard to measure the effect of one medium at a particular time for a particular product. The managerial decision about the promotional mix of a firm is influenced by the following factors :

1. **Nature of Product.** The selection of promotional method depends upon the nature of product. For example, *industrial goods* being highly complex and technical in nature require personal selling. Though, advertising and publicity may also have influence but just to provide general information. Whereas *convenience goods* depend on advertising and display as they are lowly priced and frequently purchased.
2. **Life Cycle of Product.** In the *introduction stage*, the consumers are unaware of the product, therefore, advertising is extensively used so as to stimulate primary demand. In addition to advertising emphasis is also placed on personal selling, trade shows, demonstrations, exhibitions, publicity etc. In the growth stage, consumer is aware of the uses and attributes of the product. Advertising is done to promote selective demand and to keep the buyer away from competitor's brand. During the *maturity stage*, creating brand preference and maintaining brand loyalty becomes utmost important. Therefore, emphasis is placed on advertising and sales promotion. In the *decline stage* promotional efforts are reduced to minimum. Only few concerns try to push up sales with high promotional advertisement.
3. **Size of Budget.** Selection depends on cost of media and availability of funds. A firm with huge promotional budget can undertake all promotional activities. Firm with low budget depends mainly on local newspapers, outdoor advertisements, wall writings etc.
4. **Nature of Competition.** The promotional efforts must match the level of competition. There is a general tendency to go for high advertising, sales promotion and personal selling when there is highly competitive environment.

5. **Promotional Strategy.** The choice of promotional tools depends whether a company adopts push or pull strategy. In case of push strategy, dealer is asked to promote the product line aggressively, for which they are granted high margins and exclusive dealership. Thus, here personal selling and sales promotion play a vital role. On the other hand, pull strategy stimulates demand of end-consumer so that they may ask retailers for the product.

Tools of Promotion Mix

(1) **Personal Selling.** It is the personal oral presentation of product to the customer for the purpose of making sales. It consists of interpretation of the benefits of product and services to the buyer and persuading him to buy right kind of the product. It aims at individual thus the sales person to tailor-make their messages according to the characteristics and need of the buyer. The sales person can also get immediate feedback. It helps to develop a personal relationship between the customer and salesman resulting in better understanding. It allows for demonstration of the product thereby enables the buyer to get intensive information.

The American Marketing Association defines personal selling as '*oral presentation in a conservation with one more prospective purchases for the purpose of making sales.*'

The tools of personal selling include – sales-presentation, sales meetings, salesman samples and Tele-marketing.

(2) **Advertising.** Advertising is a non-personal form of communication regarding goods and services from an identified source to large number of potential customers. It aims to sell goods and services, help the concern to face competition and create a favourable image of products and firm. The various media of advertising are – newspapers, magazines, catalogues, radio, T.V., billboards signs and posters etc. The recent trend is towards sponsorships like close-up Antakshri.

The American Marketing Association defines advertisement as, 'any paid form of non-personal presentation and promotion of goods, services or ideas by an identified sponsor.'

(3) **Sales Promotion.** Sales promotion is the device used to stimulate demand for the product. It consists of short term and temporary incentives to induce sales such as displays, demonstration, contests, gifts, premium packs, off season discounts, sampling, coupons, etc., e.g.,

(i) Fa soap advertises – Buy three soaps and get one free
(ii) Get 50 gm close-up toothpaste free with 160 ml clinic plus shampoo.
(iii) Get 100 gm Pepsodent paste free with 200 gm Pepsodent paste

American Marketing Association defines sales promotion as, '*those marketing activities, other than personal selling, advertising and publicity, that stimulate consumer purchasing and dealer effectiveness, such as displays, shows and demonstrations, expositions and various non current selling efforts, not in ordinary routine.*'

(iv) **Publicity and Public Relations.** Publicity is form of communication promoting to the mass market. It is not paid for. The tools of publicity include press conferences, speeches, annual reports, publication, donations and sponsorships (only that part which is not paid for).

Public relations is the firm's relationship with the public, e.g., customers, suppliers, stockholders, employees, government, general public and society. The purpose of such communication is to develop a favourable image of the product and the organization.

Factor Influencing Promotional Mix

To accomplish promotion and marketing objectives usually, combination of two or more promotional methods are applied for one product. This constitutes the promotion mix for the product. There is no ideal promotion mix for any firm. It depends largely on judgment of the marketing manager because it is hard to measure the effect of one medium at a particular time for a particular product. The managerial decision about the promotional mix of a firm is influenced by the following factors :

1. **Nature of Product.** The selection of promotional method depends upon the nature of product. For example, industrial goods being highly complex and technical in nature require personal selling. Though, advertising and publicity may also have influence but just to provide general information. Whereas convenience goods depend on advertising and display as they are lowly priced and frequently purchased. For shopping goods the consumer does not require much of prior knowledge. He purchases it after careful consideration of quality, price and durability, therefore the main emphasis is on personal selling together with advertising. Whereas in case of specially goods the consumer must have full knowledge. Such goods have high unit value and infrequently purchase, therefore, here the emphasis is on advertising, personal selling as well as sales promotion.
2. **Life Cycle of product.** In the introduction stage, the consumers are unaware of the product, therefore, advertising is extensively used so as to stimulate primary demand. In addition to advertising emphasis is also placed on personal selling, trade shows, demonstrations, exhibitions publicity etc. In the growth stage, consumer is aware of the uses and attributes of the product. Advertising is done to promote selective demand and to keep the buyer away from competitor's brand. During the maturity stage, creating brand preference and maintaining brand loyalty becomes utmost important. Therefore, emphasis is placed an advertising and sales promotion. In the decline stage promotional efforts are reduced to minimum. Only few concerns try to push up sales with high promotional advertisement. Aggressive personal selling programme may be taken at segments where demand for the product exists. In the obsolescence stage all-promotional efforts are stopped as the product is withdrawn from the market.
3. **Nature of the Market.**
   (a) *Kinds of Customers.* Final consumer - advertisement, personal selling and sales promotion.
   Industrial consumers - personal selling
   Wholesalers - personal selling
   Retailers - advertisement in trade magazines and newspaper, sales promotion.
   (b) *Geographical Area.* If it is local market - personal selling is possible. But if it is National/International market - advertisement and other promotional tools are applied.
   (c) *Concentration of Market.* If the customers are concentrated at one place personal selling is possible but if they are widely spread then advertisement and sales promotion is adopted.
4. **Size of budget.** Selection depends on cost of media and availability of funds. Firm with huge promotional budget can undertake all promotional activities. Firm with low budget depends mainly on local newspapers, outdoor advertisements, wall writing etc. because other means of promotion such as personal selling discounts, free gifts advertisement in trade magazines etc. involve high cost.
5. **Nature of Competition.** The promotional efforts must match the level of competition. There is a general tendency to go for high advertising, sales promotion and personal selling when there is highly competitive environment.
6. **Promotional Strategy.** The choice of promotional tools depends whether a company adopts push or pull strategy. In case of push strategy, dealer is asked to promote the product line aggressively, for which they are granted high margins and exclusive dealership. Thus, here personal selling and sales promotion play a vital role. On the

other hand, pull strategy stimulates demand of end-consumer so that they may ask retailers for the product.

Advertising

Advertising is the popular tool of promotion as it communicates in a persuasive manner about organization or products or services non-personally through paid media. In general term *Advertising* is to announce publicly. Advertising is derived from a Latin word '*adverto*', '*ad*' means towards and '*verto*' means I turn. Thus, advertising means to turn attention towards a specific thing. The advertisement should provide new information or support the information the audience already has in-order to capture their attention. It should be able to persuade them and influence their attitude and purchase behaviour.

According to William J. Stanton, "*Advertising consists of all the activities involved in presenting to a group a non-personal, oral or visual, openly sponsored message regarding a product, service* or *idea.*"

Profiles of Major Media Types

Medium	Advantages	Limitations
Newspapers	Flexibility; timeliness; good local market coverage; broad acceptance; high believability	Short life; poor reproduction quality; small 'pass along" audience
Television	Combines sight, sound, and motion; appealing to the senses; high attention; high reach	High absolute cost; high clutter; fleeting exposure; less audience selectivity
Direct mail	Audience selectivity; flexibility; no ad competition within the same medium; personalization	Relatively high cost; "junk mail" image
Radio	Mass use; high geographic and demographic selectivity; low cost	Audio presentation only; lower attention than television; non-standardized rates structures; fleeting exposure
Magazines	High geographic and demographic selectivity; credibility and prestige; high-quality reproduction; long life; good pass-along readership	Long ad purchase lead time; some waste circulation; no guarantee of position
Outdoor	Flexibility; high repeat exposure; low cost; low competition	Limited audience selectivity; creative limitations
Yellow Pages	Excellent local coverage; high believability; wide reach; low cost	High competition; long ad purchase lead time; creative limitations
Newsletters	Very high selectivity; full control; interactive opportunities; relative low costs	Costs could run away
Brochures	Flexibility; full control; can dramatize messages	Overproduction could lead to runaway costs
Telephone	Many Users; opportunity to give a personal touch	Relative high cost unless volunteers are used
Internet	High selectivity; interactive possibilities; relatively low cost	Relatively new media with a low number of users in some countries.

Several steps are involved in preparing an advertising campaign. The major steps are :

1. **Analysing Advertising Target.** The group of people to whom the advertisement is aimed at must be analysed thoroughly, with regard to their age, income, sex, occupation, education, location, buying habits, psychology etc. This helps in preparing effective advertising campaign. In addition to this, market situation, competition level, product features should also be studied. For this, research and interviews are conducted to know which benefits are most desired by the buyers. This leads to selection of an effective appeal for advertising message. For example, the most desired benefits by the purchaser of toothpaste may be ranked as follows on the basis of a survey – (i) decay, prevention, (ii) bright teeth, (iii) good taste and (iv) low price. This helps in deciding the contents of advertising message.
2. **Defining Advertising Goals.** The objectives of advertisement must be specifically and clearly stated as it provides direction to the campaign. For example if the firm aims at creating brand preference, it must clearly state that it wishes to establish brand preference for product among 50 lakh people within a year or if it wishes to increase sales, it must clearly state that 30% discount is offered for 15 days.

   The various goals of advertising can be :

   (i) **To Increase Sales.** Sales can be increased by following number of strategies, which are made known to buyer through advertising, e.g., offering discounts, free gifts, contests, extra services etc.

   (ii) **To Create Awareness.** The consumer can be informed about the type of products produced by the concern, benefits of the product, competitive superiority of the product, extra-feature not found in competition product, e.g., L.G.'s door cooling technology in refrigerators with patent right for 15 years is being used as an advertising message to create awareness among consumes.

   (iii) **To Enter New Markets.** To maximize profits, the concern may wish to explore new segments. Advertising may be used by the concern to lay down its background and portray a positive image of the concern.

   (iv) **To Introduce New Products.** Advertisement has the power to educate, stimulate and persuade the buyers and change their minds. Thus, it can be used as an effective force in creating demand for new products.

   (v) **To Build-up Image.** Advertising can be used to acquaint people about company's products packages, brands, sales efforts, sales, services, marketing programmes, achievements etc. and thus build up company's reputation in the minds of the people.
3. **Determining Advertising Budget.** Before actually carrying out the advertisement campaign, it is essential to decide about advertising appropriation. The advertising appropriation is the total amount of money which is allocated for advertising in a specific time period by the top management. Advertising budget is the amount spent on specific activities like media, men and other auxiliary services. There is no standard norms for deciding the amount of advertising budget. It varies from company to company, even within the same industry. Various factors like objectives of advertising, product class, stage of product life cycle, size of company, competition level, economic conditions etc. form the basis for deciding the size of budget. Deciding about the advertising budget is the most difficult question to be answered by the management because there is no formula to arrive at the right amount. The most commonly practiced methods followed for deciding the advertising budget are:

   (i) **Percentage of Sales Method.** Sales budget is set at a certain percentage either on gross sales or net sales volume of the last year or on the average sales volume for number of previous years or on the estimated future sales or estimate of sales may be combined with the average for more accuracy. The method simply expresses the relationship between advertising expenses and sales revenue.

Advertising appropriation = Rupee sales × pre-determined percentage

Instead of taking gross or net sales, the percentage can be calculated on gross or net profit. This prevents excessive investment of profits in advertising. Another approach is to spend a fixed sum per unit of product sold.

(ii) **Affordable Method.** The advertising budget is set at a level that the firm can afford. This means that the advertising expenditure will be done only when all other more important activities are met. This method is simple, practical and flexible but it is shortsighted. It does not realize the ability of advertising. It does not allow the firm to take advantage of market opportunities. Considering the competitive environment prevailing, this method cannot be applied in the long run.

(iii) **Competitive Parity Method.** The promotion budget is set at a level that is equivalent to that of the competitors. It is assumed that the competitors expenditure represents combined opinion of the industry and therefore, it is thought to be more appropriate.

(iv) **Objective and Task Method.** The promotion budget is based on the specific objectives to be attained through advertising, the task to be performed to achieve these objectives and the estimate cost of performing these tasks. The sum of these costs is the proposed advertising budget.

4. **Selecting Advertising Media.** Media selection refers to finding the most cost effective media to deliver the desired exposure to largest audience. For this, proper combination of reach, frequency and impact is sought. 'Reach' means the number of different persons exposed to a particular media, schedule at least once during the specified time period. 'Frequency' refers to the number of times within the specified time period than an average person is exposed to the message. 'Impact' is the qualitative value of an exposure through a given medium. Media planning and selection deals with identifying various media, considering factors governing media, evaluating each media, developing media-mix, appropriating media resources and phasing media. The advertiser has to know the capacity of major media types to deliver reach, frequency and impact. The major advertising media are–newspaper, magazines, direct mail, radio, television, cable, internet, posters, advertising boards, buses and train advertising and other outdoor means. A choice between these media is made after considering various variables like product, advertising objectives, message, market potential, distribution strategy, competition level, budget, media availability etc. In order to satisfy various consumer preferences, meet competitive pressures, adjust media availability and to maximize the message impact, the company goes for multimedia strategy. This strategy of media mix helps in optimum allocation of firm's advertising funds. The funds are so distributed over different media that the last rupee spent on any one media produces the same return as the last rupee spent on other medias.

5. **Deciding the Advertising Message.** The advertising message is conveyed to the prospects through advertisement copy. Advertisement copy is all written or spoken matter expressed in words, figures, pictures or symbols to convey the desired message to the target consumers. In print media, an advertisement copy consists of headlines, sub headline, body of the copy, picture or illustration, caption, slogan, brand name and a closing idea. Few people read body copy, therefore, headline and graphic must summarise the selling proposition. Advertisement copy involves lot of creativity and imagination. The advertisement copy is generally prepared by specialists - copywriters, artists and the layout men who have enough experience and knowledge to make the advertisement attractive and effective. The advertisement copy must

contain all relevant information about the product features, uses, benefits, prices, availability etc. For greater effect persuasive picture and proper colour combinations should be used without any exaggeration. Advertisement copy should be able to capture attention of prospects and encourage favourable response.

6. **Evaluating Advertising Effectiveness.** The effectiveness of advertising is measured to:
   (i) determine the optimum level of advertising expenditure,
   (ii) know whether the campaign accomplished its objective, or should the campaign be stopped, continued or improved, and
   (iii) Evaluate the need for changes in advertising message and media.

   There are mainly two measures of advertising effectiveness:
   (a) Communication Response and
   (b) Sales Response.

Personal Selling

Personal selling or salesmanship is the process of contacting the prospective buyers personally and persuading them to buy the products. In other words, it is an art of convincing customers to buy the given products or services. The objective is not only to sell the product but also to make permanent customers. This can be achieved by so presenting the product that the prospective buyers get convinced that the products being presented for sale can well satisfy their needs. For example, a company wants to sell a vacuum cleaner. For this purpose the company sends its salesman. The salesman, approaches a house lady to explain her how badly she needs a vacuum cleaner and then tells her about his product, its functions, how it is better than other brands, its price etc. Applying all his skills he is able to convince the lady that his product is the best one and persuades her to buy the product and books the order. This is salesmanship, *i.e.*, salesmanship is the ability to persuade people to buy and satisfy their needs. Following are the few steps :

(A) Prospecting and Qualifying

The first step in selling is to identify and qualify prospects. Historically, most companies have left it to their salespeople to find leads. Now, more companies are taking responsibility for finding and qualifying leads so that the salespeople can use their expensive time doing what they can do best selling. Companies can generate leads in the following way:

- Examining data sources (newspapers, directories, CD-ROMs) in search of names. Firms can acquire company and industry information from commercial list vendors.
- Putting up a booth at trade shows.
- Inviting current customers to suggest the names of prospects.
- Cultivating other referral sources, such as suppliers, dealers, non-competing sales representatives, bankers and trade association executives.
- Contacting organizations and associations to which prospects belong.
- Engaging in speaking and writing activities that will draw attention.
- Using the telephone, mail and the internet to find leads.

(B) Pre-approach

The salesperson needs to learn as much as possible about the prospect company (what it needs, who is involved in the purchase decision) and its buyers (their personal characteristics and buying styles). The salesperson can consult standard sources, acquaintances and others to learn about the company.

(C) Approach

The salesperson should know how to greet the buyer to get the relationship off to a good start. Show courtesy and attention to the buyer; and avoid distracting mannerisms, such as staring at the customer.

(D) Presentation and Demonstration

The salesperson now tells the product "story" to the buyer, following the A.I.D.A formula of gaining *attention*, holding *interest*, arousing desire, and obtaining action. The salesperson uses *features, advantages, benefits* and value approach (F.A.B.V). Features describe physical characteristics of a market offering. Advantages describe why the features provide an advantage to the customer. Benefits describe the economic, technical, service and social benefits delivered by the offering. Value describes the summative worth (often in monetary terms) of the offering.

Prospecting and qualifying → Preapproach → Approach → Presentation and demonstration → Overcoming objections → Closing → Follow-up and maintenance

(E) Overcoming Objections

Customers typically pose objections during the presentation or when asked for the order. To handle these objections, the salesperson maintains a positive approach, asks the buyer to clarify the objection, questions the buyer in a way that the buyer has to answer his or her own objections, denies the validity of the objection or turns the objection into a reason for buying.

(F) Closing

Now the salesperson attempts to close the sale. Some salespersons do not get to this stage or do not do it well. They lack confidence or feel uncomfortable about asking for the order or do not recognize the right psychological moment. Salespersons need to know how to recognize closing signs from the buyer, including physical actions, statements or comments and questions.

(G) Follow-up and Maintenance

Follow-up and maintenance are necessary if the salesperson wants to ensure customer satisfaction and repeat business. Immediately after closing, the salesperson should cement any necessary details on delivery time, purchase terms and other matters that are important to the customer.

Channel Management, Vertical Marketing Systems

Most producers do not sell their goods directly to final users. Between producers and final users stands one or more marketing channels, a host of marketing intermediaries performing a variety of functions. Marketing-channel decisions are among the most critical decisions facing management. The company's chosen channel(s) profoundly affect all other marketing decisions.

Companies use intermediaries when they lack the financial resources to carry out direct marketing, when direct marketing is not feasible, and when they can earn more by doing so. The use of intermediaries largely boils down to their superior efficiency in making goods widely available and accessible to target markets. The most important functions performed by intermediaries are information, promotion, negotiation, ordering, financing, risk taking, physical possession, payment, and title.

Producers generally do not sell their products directly to the final users. Between them and the final user stand a number of marketing intermediaries performing a variety of functions and bearing a variety of names. Each company usually confronts a member of alternative ways to make its product reach the market. They vary from direct selling (direct channel) to final user, to using one, two, three or more intermediaries. Channels of distribution refer to the exchange of ownership of the product until it reaches the final user.

Distribution channels are characterized according to the number of channel levels. Commonly used channels of distribution are :

(1) Manufacture --- Consumer

(2) Manufacturer --- Retailers --- Consumers

(3) Manufacturer --- wholesaler --- Retailer --- Consumer

(a) represents a two level distribution channel

(b) represents a three level distribution channel

(c) represents a four level distribution channel

It can be observed from the above discussion that goods are sold either.

1. direct from producer to consumer, or
2. from producer to consumer via. a middleman (e.g., a wholesaler, retailer or both).

1. The direct channel is very effective and profitable for goods which have a high profit margin, e.g., office machinery such as photo-copying machines, accounting machines, computers etc. Moreover, the more specialized or technical the product (e.g., machine tools), the better is to sell it directly, because the ordinary retailer is seldom in a position to give demonstration, etc. and specialized service later on. In direct selling, the producer has maximum control over selling practices and policies.
2. Selling through a middleman is known as indirect distribution. This method does vary well for products with a low profit margin, e.g., consumer goods – tooth paste, face views etc.

   Going through a middleman say a wholesaler usually results in larger orders. Middleman buys goods in bulk and thus enables a producer to avoid risks connected with stocking of goods. The risk may be in the form of a fall in price or physical deterioration of the goods. Middleman keep the producer informed about the prevalent market trends.

   Middleman such as wholesalers many times pay immediately to the producers the price of goods and thus help producers whose financial resources are not big.

Vertical Marketing System (V.M.S.)

A vertical marketing system (V.M.S) comprises the producer, wholesaler(s) and retailer(s) acting as a unified system. One channel member, the *channel captain*, owns the others or franchises them or has so much power that they all cooperate. The channel captain can be the producer, the wholesaler or the retailer. V.M.Ss arose as a result of strong channel members' attempts to control channel behaviour and eliminate the conflict that results when independent members pursue their own objectives. V.M.Ss achieve economies through size, bargaining power and elimination of duplicated services. There are three types of V.M.S : corporate, administered and contractual.

Corporate and Administered V.M.S.

A corporate V.M.S combines successive stages of production and distribution under single ownership. An administered V.M.S coordinates successive stages of production and distribution through the size and power of one of the members. Manufacturers of a dominant brand are able to secure strong trade cooperation and support from resellers. Thus Kodak, Gillette, Procter & Gamble and Campbell Soup are able to command high levels of cooperation from their resellers in connection with displays, shelf space, promotions and price policies.

Contractual V.M.S.

A *contractual* V.M.S consists of independent firms at different levels of production and distribution integrating their programs on a contractual basis to obtain more economies or sales impact than they could achieve alone.

Vendor Management System (VMS)

A vendor management system (VMS) is a Web-based application that allows an organization to secure and manage staffing services on a temporary, permanent or contract basis. It helps centralize the complex issues that surround the staffing.

A VMS generally involves the following:

- Job requisition or staff ordering
- Automatic billing
- Business intelligence (BI) functionality
- Management reporting
- Workflow engines
- Amenity tracking
- Service catalog, including standardized positions and skills

A VMS provides seamless access to cost-effective, qualified human resources, while facilitating efficient recruitment and long term growth. A VMS manages all staffing operations and management procedures and eliminates typical issues and inefficiencies of workforce management.

In a successful VMS program, clients work with top providers to recruit quality, affordable personnel in a timely manner.

VMS benefits include the following

- The complete process is significantly smoother and faster.
- Only accredited personnel are recruited.
- All vendors may participate in the bid process, which leads to competitive bidding.
- A buyer may create standardized job descriptions.
- Details about job candidates are accessible from a single location, and different systems have the ability to rank each application, per buyer requirements.
- A central, end-to-end work flow engine manages the process.
- Questions, interview processes and rejections are noted and monitored.
- Job rates are competitive.

Vendors benefit from the following

- Speedy approval for new hires
- Highly accurate invoicing that is uniformly delivered
- Reduced reporting errors
- Improved access to staffing requirements

Integrated Marketing Communications (IMC)

Integrated Marketing Communications is a simple concept. It ensures that all forms of communications and messages are carefully linked together.

At its most basic level, Integrated Marketing Communications, or IMC, as we'll call it, means integrating all the promotional tools, so that they work together in harmony.

Promotion is one of the Ps in the marketing mix. Promotions has its own mix of communications tools.

All of these communications tools work better if they work together in harmony rather than in isolation. Their sum is greater than their parts – providing they speak consistently with one voice all the time, every time.

This is enhanced when integration goes beyond just the basic communications tools. There are other levels of integration such as Horizontal, Vertical, Internal, External and Data integration.

Although Integrated Marketing Communications requires a lot of effort it delivers many benefits. It can create competitive advantage, boost sales and profits, while saving money, time and stress.

IMC wraps communications around customers and helps them move through the various stages of the buying process. The organisation simultaneously consolidates its image, develops a dialogue and nurtures its relationship with customers.

This 'Relationship Marketing' cements a bond of loyalty with customers which can protect them from the inevitable onslaught of competition. The ability to keep a customer for life is a powerful competitive advantage.

IMC also increases profits through increased effectiveness. At its most basic level, a unified message has more impact than a disjointed myriad of messages. In a busy world, a consistent, consolidated and crystal clear message has a better chance of cutting through the 'noise' of over five hundred commercial messages which bombard customers each and every day.

At another level, initial research suggests that images shared in advertising and direct mail boost both advertising awareness and mail shot responses. So IMC can boost sales by stretching messages across several communications tools to create more avenues for customers to become aware, aroused, and ultimately, to make a purchase

Carefully linked messages also help buyers by giving timely reminders, updated information and special offers which, when presented in a planned sequence, help them move comfortably through the stages of their buying process... and this reduces their 'misery of choice' in a complex and busy world.

IMC also makes messages more consistent and therefore more credible. This reduces risk in the mind of the buyer which, in turn, shortens the search process and helps to dictate the outcome of brand comparisons.

Un-integrated communications send disjointed messages which dilute the impact of the message. This may also confuse, frustrate and arouse anxiety in customers. On the other hand, integrated communications present a reassuring sense of order.

Consistent images and relevant, useful, messages help nurture long term relationships with customers. Here, customer databases can identify precisely which customers need what information when... and throughout their whole buying life.

Finally, IMC saves money as it eliminates duplication in areas such as graphics and photography since they can be shared and used in say, advertising, exhibitions and sales literature. Agency fees are reduced by using a single agency for all communications and even if there are several agencies, time is saved when meetings bring all the agencies together – for briefings, creative sessions, tactical or strategic planning. This reduces workload and subsequent stress levels – one of the many benefits of IMC.

Despite its many benefits, Integrated Marketing Communications, or IMC, has many barriers.

In addition to the usual resistance to change and the special problems of communicating with a wide variety of target audiences, there are many other obstacles which restrict IMC. These include: Functional Silos; Stifled Creativity; Time Scale Conflicts and a lack of Management know-how.

Take functional silos. Rigid organisational structures are infested with managers who protect both their budgets and their power base.

Sadly, some organisational structures isolate communications, data, and even managers from each other. For example the PR department often doesn't report to marketing. The sales force rarely meet the advertising or sales promotion people and so on. Imagine what can happen when sales reps are not told about a new promotional offer!

And all of this can be aggravated by turf wars or internal power battles where specific managers resist having some of their decisions (and budgets) determined or even influenced by someone from another department.

Here are two difficult questions: What should a truly integrated marketing department look like? And how will it affect creativity?

It shouldn't matter whose creative idea it is, but often, it does. An advertising agency may not be so enthusiastic about developing a creative idea generated by, say, a PR or a direct marketing consultant.

IMC can restrict creativity. No more wild and wacky sales promotions unless they fit into the overall marketing communications strategy. The joy of rampant creativity may be stifled, but the creative challenge may be greater and ultimately more satisfying when operating within a tighter, integrated, creative brief.

Add different time scales into a creative brief and you'll see Time Horizons provide one more barrier to IMC. For example, image advertising, designed to nurture the brand over the longer term, may conflict with shorter term advertising or sales promotions designed to boost quarterly sales. However the two objectives can be accommodated within an overall IMC if carefully planned.

But this kind of planning is not common. A survey in 1995, revealed that most managers lack expertise in IMC. But its not just managers, but also agencies. There is a proliferation of single discipline agencies. There appear to be very few people who have real experience of all the marketing communications disciplines. This lack of know how is then compounded by a lack of commitment.

MULTIPLE CHOICE QUESTIONS

1. Strategic management is best described as
   (a) A one-time decision-making process
   (b) A continuous and iterative process
   (c) A tactical approach to daily operations
   (d) A set of predefined rules and regulations
2. Which of the following statements is true regarding strategic management?
   (a) It focuses solely on the short-term goals of an organization
   (b) It involves setting objectives without considering external factors
   (c) It aligns an organization's goals with its internal and external environment
   (d) It doesn't require the involvement of top management
3. The ultimate goal of strategic management is to
   (a) Achieve profitability in the short term
   (b) Satisfy customers at any cost
   (c) Gain a competitive advantage and create long-term value
   (d) Minimize costs and overhead expenses
4. A company's mission statement should primarily address:
   (a) Short-term financial objectives
   (b) The organization's core values and purpose
   (c) The competition's weaknesses
   (d) Regulatory compliance
5. Strategic management involves which of the following key activities?
   (a) Daily task management
   (b) Crisis management
   (c) Setting objectives, crafting strategies, and implementing them
   (d) Employee supervision
6. The SWOT analysis in strategic management assesses:
   (a) Sales performance
   (b) Strengths, weaknesses, opportunities, and threats
   (c) Annual revenue
   (d) Customer satisfaction
7. Which stage of the strategic management process involves evaluating strategic alternatives and selecting the most appropriate strategies?
   (a) Strategy formulation
   (b) Strategy execution
   (c) Strategy assessment
   (d) Strategy identification
8. The BCG matrix classifies a company's business units based on:
   (a) Market share and market growth rate
   (b) Product quality and pricing
   (c) Historical performance and profitability
   (d) Number of employees and customer reviews
9. What is the primary purpose of setting strategic objectives in the strategic management process?
   (a) To create short-term action plans
   (b) To meet regulatory requirements
   (c) To provide guidance and direction to the organization
   (d) To assess employee performance
10. Which phase of the strategic management process involves tracking and adjusting strategies as necessary?
    (a) Strategy formulation
    (b) Strategy execution
    (c) Strategy assessment
    (d) Strategy identification
11. Rational decision-making in strategic management involves:
    (a) Intuitive judgments without data analysis
    (b) Making decisions based solely on gut feelings
    (c) A systematic and logical approach
    (d) Ignoring available information
12. In strategic decision-making, the "satisficing" approach involves:

(a) Maximizing the outcome by considering all possible alternatives
(b) Choosing the first acceptable solution that meets the minimum criteria
(c) Ignoring external factors
(d) Focusing on short-term results

13. Scenario planning in strategic decision-making aims to:
(a) Predict the future with certainty
(b) Analyze only the most likely future scenarios
(c) Identify and prepare for various possible future outcomes
(d) Ensure that past strategies are maintained

14. Which of the following is an example of a non-programmed decision in strategic management?
(a) Routine budget allocation
(b) Selecting a supplier from an approved vendor list
(c) Developing a new product line
(d) Employee performance evaluation

15. Group decision-making techniques in strategic management include:
(a) Avoiding brainstorming sessions
(b) Encouraging conformity and consensus
(c) Delphi technique, brainstorming, and nominal group technique
(d) Allowing one person to make all decisions

16. A cost leadership strategy aims to:
(a) Offer unique products or services at premium prices
(b) Differentiate products or services through innovation
(c) Achieve the lowest cost of production and become the low-cost provider
(d) Follow competitors' strategies closely

17. Differentiation strategy focuses on:
(a) Being the lowest cost provider in the industry
(b) Offering products or services with unique features and attributes
(c) Imitating the competition
(d) Ignoring customer preferences

18. A focused or niche strategy involves:
(a) Targeting a broad market segment with a standardized product
(b) Concentrating on a specific market segment or niche with specialized products or services
(c) Diversifying into unrelated industries
(d) Expanding operations globally

19. A retrenchment strategy in strategic management typically involves:
(a) Expanding into new markets
(b) Downsizing or divesting underperforming units or assets
(c) Acquiring competitors
(d) Increasing R&D investments

20. What is the primary objective of a turnaround strategy?
(a) To maintain the status quo
(b) To prepare for an IPO (Initial Public Offering)
(c) To reverse a company's declining performance and restore profitability
(d) To diversify the company's portfolio

21. In a PEST analysis, what does the "T" stand for?
(a) Technology (b) Tactics
(c) Teamwork (d) Time

22. The political factors in a PEST analysis refer to:
(a) Technological advancements
(b) Government policies and regulations
(c) Market trends
(d) Competitive strategies

23. Environmental factors in a PEST analysis include:
(a) Economic conditions
(b) Social media trends
(c) Ecological and sustainability issues
(d) Market demand

24. The social factors in a PEST analysis consider aspects such as:
(a) Legal regulations
(b) Cultural, demographic, and societal trends
(c) Technological advancements
(d) Market competition

25. Which of the following is an example of a potential "technological" factor in a PEST analysis?
(a) Increasing urbanization
(b) Changing consumer preferences
(c) Advancements in artificial intelligence
(d) Regulatory changes

26. Porter's Five Forces framework does NOT include which of the following forces?
(a) Threat of new entrants
(b) Bargaining power of suppliers

(c) Competitive rivalry among existing firms
(d) Bargaining power of customers

27. In Porter's Five Forces framework, the "threat of substitute products or services" relates to:
(a) The power of suppliers
(b) Competitive rivalry
(c) The power of customers
(d) Potential alternatives that customers can turn to

28. A high level of competitive rivalry among existing firms, as indicated by Porter's framework, typically results in:
(a) Lower profit potential for firms in the industry
(b) Higher prices for customers
(c) Fewer opportunities for innovation
(d) Decreased market share for leading companies

29. In Porter's framework, the "bargaining power of suppliers" is likely to increase when:
(a) There are numerous alternative suppliers available
(b) Suppliers offer unique and differentiated products
(c) The industry is characterized by high competition
(d) Suppliers have limited options for selling their products

30. The "threat of new entrants" in Porter's framework is higher when:
(a) Existing firms have strong brand recognition
(b) Capital requirements are low
(c) Economies of scale can be easily achieved
(d) Switching costs for customers are high

31. The resource-based approach to internal analysis focuses on identifying:
(a) External market conditions
(b) Financial statements and performance metrics
(c) Unique and valuable resources and capabilities
(d) PEST factors

32. In the context of the resource-based approach, a resource is considered valuable if it:
(a) Is easy to imitate by competitors
(b) Cannot be exploited by the organization
(c) Allows the organization to take advantage of opportunities or neutralize threats
(d) Has no impact on the organization's performance

33. The resource-based approach suggests that competitive advantage can be sustained when a firm possesses:
(a) Common and easily acquired resources
(b) Resources that are perfectly imitable
(c) Rare, valuable, non-substitutable, and inimitable (VRNI) resources
(d) A large quantity of resources

34. A valuable and rare resource that cannot be easily imitated by competitors is often referred to as a:
(a) Generic resource
(b) Temporary resource
(c) Core competency
(d) Non-core resource

35. According to the resource-based approach, a resource or capability that is non-substitutable means that:
(a) Competitors have easy access to similar resources
(b) It can be easily replaced by another resource
(c) It has no impact on the organization's performance
(d) There is no equivalent or alternative resource

36. Value chain analysis involves the examination of an organization's activities from:
(a) An external perspective
(b) A functional perspective
(c) A global perspective
(d) A competitive perspective

37. The primary activities in a value chain typically include:
(a) Research and development, human resources, and finance
(b) Inbound logistics, operations, outbound logistics, marketing and sales, and service
(c) Procurement, production, and distribution
(d) Strategic planning, risk management, and compliance

38. In the context of value chain analysis, "inbound logistics" refers to the:
(a) Process of delivering products to customers
(b) Activities related to receiving, warehousing, and managing inventory

(c) Promotion and advertising of products
(d) R&D and product design activities

39. Value chain analysis can help identify opportunities for cost reduction and differentiation by focusing on:
(a) Primary activities
(b) Support activities
(c) Both primary and support activities
(d) External factors only

40. "Human resources management" is typically considered a:
(a) Primary activity in a value chain
(b) Support activity in a value chain
(c) An external factor
(d) Non-essential function

41. What is the primary purpose of conducting a SWOT analysis in the context of strategic planning?
(a) To identify market trends
(b) To evaluate the organization's competitive advantage
(c) To eliminate weaknesses
(d) To avoid external threats

42. Which of the following is an example of a potential "opportunity" in a SWOT analysis?
(a) Declining customer demand
(b) New market segments
(c) Internal inefficiencies
(d) Regulatory changes

43. In the context of corporate strategy, what does "retrenchment" typically involve?
(a) Aggressively expanding into new markets
(b) Reducing the scope of operations and cutting costs
(c) Pursuing vertical integration
(d) Entering unrelated industries

44. "Growth strategies" in corporate strategy may include:
(a) Liquidation
(b) Downsizing
(c) Market penetration, market development, product development, and diversification
(d) Focusing solely on cost-cutting initiatives

45. Horizontal integration, as a corporate strategy, involves:
(a) Acquiring businesses at different stages of the supply chain
(b) Entering new geographic markets
(c) Expanding product lines
(d) Acquiring or merging with competitors

46. "Stability strategies" in corporate strategy aim to:
(a) Maintain or increase the size of an organization
(b) Pursue opportunities for innovation
(c) Reduce the scale of operations
(d) Exit the current industry

47. Diversification as a corporate strategy can be categorized into two main types: related and unrelated. Which of the following best describes "related diversification"?
(a) Entering new industries that are similar or have synergy with the current business
(b) Entering completely unrelated industries
(c) Exiting the current industry
(d) Staying focused on the current business without any diversification

48. The BCG Matrix classifies a company's business units based on:
(a) Market share and market growth rate
(b) Profit margins and market share
(c) Revenue and geographic location
(d) Customer satisfaction and employee turnover

49. In the BCG Matrix, a business unit that has a low market share in a high-growth market is typically categorized as a:
(a) Cash cow (b) Star
(c) Dog (d) Question mark

50. The BCG Matrix "cash cow" represents business units that:
(a) Are in high-growth markets with high market share
(b) Generate significant cash flow but have limited growth potential
(c) Have low market share in declining markets
(d) Are potential winners in emerging markets

51. Business units categorized as "question marks" in the BCG Matrix:
(a) Have high market share in mature markets
(b) Are highly profitable with limited growth prospects
(c) Require significant investments to capture market share

(d) Are in low-growth markets with low market share

52. The BCG Matrix is used for:
(a) Assessing the strengths and weaknesses of an organization
(b) Evaluating the external opportunities and threats in the market
(c) Portfolio analysis of a company's business units
(d) Conducting a SWOT analysis

53. The GE Business Model involves categorizing business units into how many quadrants?
(a) Two (b) Three
(c) Four (d) Five

54. In the GE Business Model, what does a "Strong Market Attractiveness" signify?
(a) A highly attractive market with significant growth potential
(b) A declining market with little growth opportunity
(c) A market with low competition
(d) A market with low customer demand

55. The GE Business Model assesses business units based on which two key dimensions?
(a) Market share and product quality
(b) Market attractiveness and competitive position
(c) Cost structure and revenue
(d) Employee satisfaction and customer loyalty

56. Business units in the "Selectivity" quadrant of the GE Business Model are typically considered:
(a) Strong performers with high market attractiveness
(b) Weak performers with low market attractiveness
(c) Marginal performers with high market attractiveness
(d) Cash cows with declining market attractiveness

57. According to the GE Business Model, business units in the "No Investment" quadrant should:
(a) Receive significant investments for growth
(b) Be monitored closely for changes in market conditions
(c) Be divested or liquidated
(d) Be considered for diversification

58. The Ansoff's Product Market Growth Matrix involves four growth strategies. Which one focuses on selling existing products to new markets?
(a) Market penetration
(b) Product development
(c) Market development
(d) Diversification

59. "Market development" in Ansoff's matrix involves:
(a) Developing new products for existing markets
(b) Selling existing products to new customer segments or geographic regions
(c) Expanding into unrelated industries
(d) Increasing market share in existing markets

60. The "diversification" strategy in Ansoff's matrix is considered the riskiest because it involves:
(a) Developing new products for existing markets
(b) Selling existing products to new markets
(c) Entering entirely new markets with new products
(d) Focusing on cost-cutting initiatives

61. "Product development" in Ansoff's matrix focuses on:
(a) Selling existing products in existing markets
(b) Entering new geographic markets
(c) Creating new products for existing customer segments
(d) Exiting the current industry

62. Which growth strategy in Ansoff's matrix aims to increase market share in existing markets by promoting and distributing products more effectively?
(a) Market penetration
(b) Product development
(c) Market development
(d) Diversification

63. What is the primary purpose of implementing a well-defined strategy in an organization?
(a) To increase shareholder value
(b) To reduce employee turnover
(c) To lower production costs
(d) To meet regulatory compliance

64. Which of the following is NOT a common challenge in strategy implementation?
    (a) Resistance to change
    (b) Lack of a clear vision
    (c) Excessive communication
    (d) Resource constraints

65. When implementing a strategic change, what is the primary reason for facing resistance from employees?
    (a) Lack of knowledge
    (b) Excessive enthusiasm
    (c) Fear of promotions
    (d) Compensation increases

66. Which element of the McKinsey 7S Framework refers to the core values and beliefs of an organization?
    (a) Strategy
    (b) Structure
    (c) Systems
    (d) Shared Values

67. In the McKinsey 7S Framework, what does "Staff" refer to?
    (a) The physical layout of the organization
    (b) The employees and their capabilities
    (c) The budget allocation for strategic initiatives
    (d) The legal structure of the organization

68. Which "S" in the McKinsey 7S Framework deals with the formal reporting structure within an organization?
    (a) Staff (b) Strategy
    (c) Structure (d) Systems

69. Which McKinsey 7S Framework element addresses the procedures and processes an organization uses to get things done?
    (a) Style (b) Structure
    (c) Systems (d) Strategy

70. What is the key role of the "Skills" component in the McKinsey 7S Framework?
    (a) Identifying the organization's target market
    (b) Evaluating the technical expertise of the staff
    (c) Assessing the competitive landscape
    (d) Ensuring the alignment of employee skills with the strategy

71. In the context of strategy implementation, what does "Alignment" mean?
    (a) Making all employees think the same way
    (b) Ensuring that all organizational elements are congruent and support the strategy
    (c) Reorganizing the company's structure
    (d) Focusing solely on financial targets

72. Which of the following is a common obstacle to successful strategy implementation?
    (a) Strong leadership and clear communication
    (b) A well-defined and flexible strategy
    (c) Employee empowerment and autonomy
    (d) Inadequate resource allocation and commitment

73. What is the primary role of a change management team during a strategic change initiative?
    (a) Define the strategy
    (b) Implement the new strategy
    (c) Manage resistance and facilitate adoption of the change
    (d) Monitor employee performance

74. Which of the following is NOT a phase in the typical change management process?
    (a) Planning and Analysis
    (b) Resistance Elimination
    (c) Implementation
    (d) Evaluation and Adaptation

75. What is the purpose of conducting a SWOT analysis during the strategic planning process?
    (a) To identify the strengths and weaknesses of competitors
    (b) To assess the internal and external factors that can impact the strategy
    (c) To create a detailed financial forecast
    (d) To define the company's mission and vision

76. Which component of the McKinsey 7S Framework focuses on the physical layout of the organization, including office spaces and facilities?
    (a) Style (b) Staff
    (c) Structure (d) Systems

77. In the McKinsey 7S Framework, what does "Style" refer to?
    (a) The leadership and management style within the organization
    (b) The fashion preferences of employees
    (c) The company's branding and design
    (d) The writing style of corporate documents

78. Why is it important to regularly review and update an organization's strategy?

(a) To confuse employees with constant changes
(b) To make the company appear dynamic to competitors
(c) To adapt to changing internal and external conditions
(d) To eliminate the need for performance evaluations

79. Which of the following is a component of the McKinsey 7S Framework that addresses the company's control systems and processes?
(a) Staff (b) Structure
(c) Style (d) Systems

80. What is a common challenge in the "Skills" component of the McKinsey 7S Framework?
(a) Inadequate financial resources
(b) Misalignment with the organization's strategy
(c) Lack of employee diversity
(d) Technological disruptions

81. In the context of strategy implementation, what is the primary function of the "Structure" element in the McKinsey 7S Framework?
(a) To define the company's core values
(b) To establish the reporting relationships and hierarchy
(c) To manage technology and processes
(d) To determine the compensation structure

82. Which of the following is a potential benefit of a well-implemented strategy?
(a) Increased employee resistance
(b) Higher customer churn
(c) Improved competitive advantage
(d) Decreased profitability

83. What is the primary objective of a change management plan?
(a) To create a detailed strategic plan
(b) To eliminate all resistance to change
(c) To ensure that the organization can adapt successfully to the changes
(d) To reduce the number of employees

84. Which of the following is a key factor for successful strategy implementation?
(a) Maintaining a rigid approach to the strategy
(b) Limited communication with employees
(c) Effective leadership and employee engagement
(d) Ignoring the external environment

85. In the context of the McKinsey 7S Framework, what does "Shared Values" represent?
(a) The company's financial performance
(b) The core values and guiding principles that shape the organization's culture
(c) The organizational chart
(d) The company's target market

86. What is the main purpose of the "Systems" component in the McKinsey 7S Framework?
(a) To align employee skills with the strategy
(b) To ensure that employees are rewarded for their performance
(c) To establish processes and procedures that support the strategy
(d) To define the company's style and culture

87. In the context of change management, which approach focuses on involving employees in decision-making and encouraging their active participation in the change process?
(a) Top-down approach
(b) Bottom-up approach
(c) Hierarchical approach
(d) Laissez-faire approach

88. What is the central focus of marketing?
(a) Maximizing short-term profits
(b) Satisfying customer needs and wants
(c) Reducing production costs
(d) Expanding the product line

89. A company that follows the production orientation believes in:
(a) Maximizing customer satisfaction
(b) Delivering high-quality products
(c) Producing efficiently and at low cost
(d) Customizing products for each customer

90. The marketing orientation emphasizes:
(a) Expanding production capacity
(b) Selling as many products as possible
(c) Customer needs and wants
(d) Reducing advertising expenses

91. Which marketing orientation focuses on building long-term customer relationships and delivering superior customer value?
(a) Product orientation
(b) Sales orientation
(c) Marketing orientation
(d) Production orientation

92. In societal marketing orientation, companies consider:
(a) Only their own interests

(b) Both the customer's and society's interests
(c) The interests of competitors
(d) Reducing product quality

93. What does the term "omnichannel marketing" refer to?
(a) Marketing products to children
(b) Using multiple marketing channels to reach customers
(c) Online marketing only
(d) Reducing marketing efforts

94. What is the primary goal of content marketing?
(a) Maximizing short-term sales
(b) Educating and engaging customers with valuable content
(c) Reducing advertising expenses
(d) Increasing production capacity

95. "Big data" in marketing refers to:
(a) The physical size of marketing materials
(b) Collecting and analyzing large volumes of data to gain insights
(c) Traditional marketing methods
(d) Reducing product diversity

96. Which of the following is a key element of influencer marketing?
(a) Targeting a broad audience
(b) Using only celebrity endorsements
(c) Leveraging individuals with influence to promote products or services
(d) Ignoring social media platforms

97. What does the term "green marketing" focus on?
(a) Sustainable and environmentally friendly products and practices
(b) Promoting unhealthy products
(c) Reducing product variety
(d) Maximizing short-term profits

98. What is the primary goal of personalized marketing?
(a) Treating all customers the same
(b) Delivering tailored and relevant messages to individual customers
(c) Reducing the product line
(d) Maximizing advertising expenses

99. Customer value is defined as:
(a) The lowest price available in the market
(b) The difference between the benefits a customer gains and the cost of acquiring the product
(c) The total number of customers a company has
(d) The number of products sold

100. In marketing, "customer satisfaction" is:
(a) A one-time event
(b) The perception of the product's price
(c) Meeting or exceeding customer expectations
(d) A metric not relevant to business success

101. A company that consistently delivers high customer value and satisfaction is more likely to achieve:
(a) Lower profitability
(b) Repeat business and customer loyalty
(c) Declining market share
(d) Reduced product quality

102. Which of the following is NOT a strategy for enhancing customer value and satisfaction?
(a) Offering high-quality products
(b) Building strong customer relationships
(c) Increasing prices to maximize profit
(d) Providing excellent customer service

103. Customer loyalty can lead to:
(a) Frequent customer complaints
(b) Increased marketing expenses
(c) Repeat business and positive word-of-mouth marketing
(d) A reduction in product quality

104. What is the primary purpose of market segmentation?
(a) Maximizing the number of products in the market
(b) Reducing production costs
(c) Dividing a heterogeneous market into smaller, more homogeneous segments
(d) Selling the same product to all customers

105. Demographic segmentation involves categorizing consumers based on:
(a) Their opinions and beliefs
(b) Age, gender, income, and other characteristics
(c) Their geographic location
(d) The benefits they seek from a product

106. Psychographic segmentation focuses on:
(a) Age and income
(b) Personality, lifestyle, and values
(c) Geographic location
(d) Demographic characteristics

107. Behavioral segmentation includes factors such as:
(a) Psychographic characteristics
(b) Geographic location
(c) Benefits sought, usage rate, and loyalty
(d) Income and occupation

108. A company that segments its market based on customers' loyalty and frequency of purchase is using:
(a) Demographic segmentation
(b) Psychographic segmentation
(c) Behavioral segmentation
(d) Geographic segmentation

109. Positioning refers to:
(a) The physical location of a store
(b) How customers perceive a product in relation to competitors
(c) The price of a product
(d) Reducing marketing expenses

110. A unique selling proposition (USP) is:
(a) A slogan that every company uses
(b) A distinct benefit that sets a product apart from competitors
(c) A legal requirement for all products
(d) A low price strategy

11. Perceptual mapping is a tool used in positioning to:
(a) Determine production costs
(b) Map the geographic location of customers
(c) Visually represent how customers perceive products in relation to one another
(d) Identify the demographic characteristics of customers

112. Which of the following is a characteristic of effective positioning?
(a) Being indistinguishable from competitors
(b) Providing inconsistent messaging
(c) Delivering a clear and compelling message to the target audience
(d) Avoiding differentiation

113. What is the purpose of repositioning a product?
(a) To keep marketing expenses low
(b) To maintain the same target audience
(c) To change how customers perceive the product in relation to competitors
(d) To reduce product quality

114. Targeting involves:
(a) Mass marketing to all potential customers
(b) Selecting specific customer segments to focus on
(c) Increasing product variety
(d) Reducing customer loyalty

115. What is a target market?
(a) The entire population
(b) A large and diverse group of customers
(c) A specific group of potential customers that a company aims to reach
(d) A limited group of existing customers

116. Which of the following is a consideration when selecting a target market?
(a) Targeting multiple markets simultaneously
(b) The size and growth potential of the market segment
(c) Ignoring market research
(d) Not considering customer needs

117. Differentiated marketing strategy involves:
(a) Targeting a single, homogeneous market segment
(b) Ignoring the competition
(c) Creating different marketing strategies for multiple market segments
(d) Reducing marketing efforts

118. Concentrated marketing strategy focuses on:
(a) Targeting a single, large market segment
(b) Targeting multiple market segments simultaneously
(c) Increasing product variety
(d) Selling to all customers indiscriminately

119. What is a product mix?
(a) The variety of products a company offers in the market
(b) The cost of producing a product
(c) The location of the production facility
(d) The number of employees in a company

120. Which stage of the product life cycle typically involves intense marketing efforts and investment in product development?
(a) Introduction (b) Growth
(c) Maturity (d) Decline

121. What does the "product width" refer to in a product mix?
(a) The number of product lines a company offers
(b) The physical width of the products
(c) The pricing of the products
(d) The weight of the products

122. Which product mix strategy involves adding more product lines to the existing ones?
(a) Product line extension
(b) Product line contraction
(c) Product line repositioning
(d) Product line elimination

123. A company that offers products that are related to each other but appeal to different customer groups is practicing:
(a) Product line filling
(b) Product line extension
(c) Product line stretching
(d) Product line trimming

124. In the product life cycle, which stage involves a rapid increase in sales and profit?
(a) Introduction (b) Growth
(c) Maturity (d) Decline

125. During the introduction stage of the product life cycle, what is the primary objective of a company?
(a) Maximize profits
(b) Gain market acceptance and awareness
(c) Reduce production costs
(d) Maintain low advertising expenses

126. What is the primary focus of the "idea generation" phase in the new product development process?
(a) Testing the product with consumers
(b) Generating potential product ideas
(c) Determining the final pricing strategy
(d) Analyzing the competition

127. What is the "concept testing" phase in the new product development process designed to do?
(a) Launch the product in the market
(b) Evaluate the technical feasibility of the product
(c) Gather feedback from potential consumers
(d) Set the product price

128. "Commercialization" in the new product development process involves:
(a) The final stage of product development before the product is launched in the market
(b) Developing the product concept
(c) Conducting market research
(d) Gathering ideas for new products

129. What is cost-plus pricing?
(a) Setting prices based on the production cost plus a markup
(b) Pricing products based on competitor prices
(c) Offering discounts to attract customers
(d) Pricing products randomly

130. What is dynamic pricing?
(a) Setting a fixed price for a product
(b) Adjusting prices based on real-time market conditions and demand
(c) Reducing prices during sales promotions
(d) Offering discounts for bulk purchases

131. What is price skimming?
(a) Pricing products low to gain market share
(b) Gradually reducing product prices
(c) Setting high initial prices for innovative products and gradually lowering them
(d) Matching competitor prices

132. Psychological pricing strategies often use prices ending in which numbers to make them appear lower?
(a) \$0.99 or \$0.95 (b) \$1.00
(c) \$0.50 (d) \$0.25

133. What is the primary goal of a penetration pricing strategy?
(a) Maximizing short-term profits
(b) Covering production costs
(c) Quickly gaining market share and customer acceptance
(d) Pricing products higher than the competition

134. What are marketing channels also referred to as?
(a) Value networks
(b) Sales promotion
(c) Marketing mix
(d) Market segmentation

135. A marketing channel helps in:
(a) Reducing production costs
(b) Getting products from producers to consumers
(c) Conducting market research
(d) Setting product prices

136. Which of the following is an example of a direct marketing channel?
(a) Manufacturer → Retailer → Consumer
(b) Manufacturer → Wholesaler → Retailer → Consumer
(c) Manufacturer → Agent/Broker → Consumer
(d) Manufacturer → Wholesaler → Agent/Broker → Consumer

137. What is the primary goal of a vertical marketing system (VMS)?
   (a) Minimizing marketing expenses
   (b) Maximizing short-term profits
   (c) Improving distribution efficiency and effectiveness
   (d) Reducing the number of products in the market

138. Which of the following best describes a horizontal marketing system?
   (a) A system where products are only sold online
   (b) A system where companies at the same level of the channel work together to expand their presence in the market
   (c) A system where products are distributed only through agents
   (d) A system where companies sell directly to consumers

139. What is the primary goal of Integrated Marketing Communication (IMC)?
   (a) Maximizing advertising expenses
   (b) Providing discounts to customers
   (c) Ensuring that all marketing messages are consistent and coordinated
   (d) Reducing customer loyalty

140. IMC involves coordinating various marketing communication tools, such as:
   (a) Production costs
   (b) Advertising, sales promotion, public relations, and personal selling
   (c) Pricing strategies
   (d) Reducing product quality

141. Which of the following is NOT a component of IMC?
   (a) Advertising
   (b) Sales promotion
   (c) Target market
   (d) Public relations

142. What is the purpose of a marketing communication plan in IMC?
   (a) To create a detailed budget for marketing activities
   (b) To outline how various communication tools will be used to deliver the message to the target audience
   (c) To evaluate production costs
   (d) To reduce competition in the market

143. In IMC, what does "touchpoint" refer to?
   (a) A type of advertising
   (b) A specific point of interaction between a brand and a customer
   (c) The price of a product
   (d) The production process

144. What is the primary goal of advertising in marketing?
   (a) Reducing customer loyalty
   (b) Maximizing short-term profits
   (c) Creating awareness and interest in a product or brand
   (d) Decreasing product variety

145. What is a "call-to-action" in advertising?
   (a) A request for a customer's feedback
   (b) A customer's response to an advertisement
   (c) A marketing channel
   (d) A type of sales promotion

146. Which of the following is a form of online advertising?
   (a) Direct mail
   (b) Billboard advertising
   (c) Pay-per-click (PPC) advertising
   (d) Radio advertising

147. Sales promotion techniques include:
   (a) TV commercials
   (b) Offering discounts, coupons, and contests to stimulate immediate sales
   (c) Social media marketing
   (d) Market research

148. What is the primary purpose of a sales promotion?
   (a) Building long-term customer relationships
   (b) Encouraging customers to make a purchase or take immediate action
   (c) Reducing production costs
   (d) Maximizing advertising expenses

ANSWER KEY

1. (b) **2.** (c) **3.** (c) **4.** (b) **5.** (c) **6.** (b) **7.** (a) **8.** (a) **9.** (c) **10.** (c)
11. (c) **12.** (b) **13.** (c) **14.** (c) **15.** (c) **16.** (c) **17.** (b) **18.** (b) **19.** (b) **20.** (c)
21. (a) **22.** (b) **23.** (c) **24.** (b) **25.** (c) **26.** (d) **27.** (d) **28.** (a) **29.** (b) **30.** (b)
31. (c) **32.** (c) **33.** (c) **34.** (c) **35.** (d) **36.** (d) **37.** (b) **38.** (b) **39.** (c) **40.** (b)
41. (b) **42.** (b) **43.** (b) **44.** (c) **45.** (d) **46.** (a) **47.** (a) **48.** (a) **49.** (d) **50.** (b)
51. (c) **52.** (c) **53.** (b) **54.** (a) **55.** (b) **56.** (c) **57.** (c) **58.** (c) **59.** (b) **60.** (c)
61. (c) **62.** (a) **63.** (a) **64.** (c) **65.** (a) **66.** (d) **67.** (b) **68.** (c) **69.** (c) **70.** (d)
71. (b) **72.** (d) **73.** (c) **74.** (b) **75.** (b) **76.** (c) **77.** (a) **78.** (c) **79.** (d) **80.** (b)
81. (b) **82.** (c) **83.** (c) **84.** (c) **85.** (b) **86.** (c) **87.** (b) **88.** (b) **89.** (c) **90.** (c)
91. (c) **92.** (b) **93.** (b) **94.** (b) **95.** (b) **96.** (c) **97.** (a) **98.** (b) **99.** (b) **100.** (c)
101. (b) **102.** (c) **103.** (c) **104.** (c) **105.** (b) **106.** (b) **107.** (c) **108.** (c) **109.** (b) **110.** (b)
111. (c) **112.** (c) **113.** (c) **114.** (b) **115.** (c) **116.** (b) **117.** (c) **118.** (a) **119.** (a) **120.** (a)
121. (a) **122.** (a) **123.** (b) **124.** (b) **125.** (b) **126.** (b) **127.** (c) **128.** (a) **129.** (a) **130.** (b)
131. (c) **132.** (a) **133.** (c) **134.** (a) **135.** (b) **136.** (a) **137.** (c) **138.** (b) **139.** (c) **140.** (b)
141. (c) **142.** (b) **143.** (b) **144.** (c) **145.** (b) **146.** (c) **147.** (b) **148.** (b)

UNIT

7

SYLLABUS

Consumer and Industrial Buying Behaviour: Theories and Models of Consumer Behaviour

Brand Management – Role of Brands, Brand Equity, Equity Models, Developing a Branding Strategy; Brand Name Decisions, Brand Extensions and Loyalty

Logistics and Supply Chain Management, Drivers, Value creation, Supply Chain Design, Designing and Managing Sales Force, Personal Selling

Service Marketing – Managing Service Quality and Brands, Marketing Strategies of Service Firms

Customer Relationship Marketing – Relationship Building, Strategies, Values and Process

Retail Marketing – Recent Trends in India, Types of Retail Outlets.

Emerging Trends in Marketing – Concept of e-Marketing, Direct Marketing, Digital Marketing and Green Marketing

International Marketing – Entry Mode Decisions, Planning Marketing Mix for International Markets

CONSUMER AND INDUSTRIAL BUYING BEHAVIOUR

ELEMENTS OF CONSUMER BEHAVIOUR

Consumer behaviour is psychological, social and physical behaviour of potential consumers. According to **Walter** and **Paul**, '*Consumer behaviour is the process whereby individuals decide whether what, when, where, how and from whom to purchase goods and services.*'

The study of consumer behaviour assumes that the consumers are actors in the marketplace. The perspective of role theory assumes that consumers play various roles in the marketplace. Starting from the information provider, from the user to the payer and to the disposer, consumers play these roles in the decision process.

The roles also vary in different consumption situations; for example, a mother plays the role of an influencer in a child's purchase process, whereas she plays the role of a disposer for the products consumed by the family.

The consumer behaviour can be studied with the help of stimulus response model. The buying process is made up of following stages, input-process-output-feedback. The potential consumers are subjected to various stimuli (input). Responding to these stimuli, they make certain purchases (output). After consumption, they convey their positive or negative responses.

Stimulus-Response Model

Outside Stimuli		Buyer's Black Box		Buyer's Purchase Decision
Marketing	Environment	Buyer's Characteristics	Buyer's Decision	
1. Product	1. Economic	1. Cultural	1. Problem recognition	1. Product choice.
2. Price	2. Technological →	2. Social recognition	2. Information research →	2. Brand choice
3. Place	3. Political	3. Personal	3. Evaluation	3. Dealer choice
4. Promotion	4. Cultural	4. Psychological	4. Decision.	4. Purchase timing
			5. Post Purchase behaviour	5. Purchase amount
Stimuli (Inputs)		Process (Processing)		Response (Output)

Stages in Buying Process

The buying process comprises of five stages :

1. **Need Recognition.** The decision to buy start with recognizing the need or desire for something which will give satisfaction on consumption. Such desire may arise either due to internal stimulus (*i.e.* desire for comfort, safety, prestige, conformity, curiosity etc.) Such stimulus acts as a cue for the marketer. The intensity of need determines the priority list of the consumer. He will make immediate purchases for the most urgent need and postpone other purchases because his means are limited. The marketer must search to know what aroused the need or desire of the consumer and how he proceeded to satisfy it.
2. **Information Search.** The recognized need can be satisfied promptly only when it is known what product or brand will best satisfy it and where is that product available. The consumer gathers such information either by recalling the relevant information stored in memory or by topping sources like friends, family, neighbour, colleagues or salespersons, dealers, advertisements, packaging, displays or mass media like newspaper, radio, television and consumer information centers.
3. **Evaluation of Alternatives.** The consumer assesses various alternative products or services and judges their want satisfying potential. In evaluating the alternatives many aspects are taken into consideration such as product attributes, utility function of each attribute, brand image, trade-off, concessions, convenience and facilities.

   As pointed in the above example, the consumer who wishes to buy a product may not be aware of the total number of product varieties available in the market. He may further not consider all the varieties that he is aware of because of the limitation of time, income, availability etc. Out of the consideration set, he lists out certain varieties on the basis of certain criteria. He then ultimately makes a decision regarding particular brand.
4. **Purchase Decision.** After evaluating the alternatives, the buyer buys the brand he likes the most. But, sometimes, his intention to purchase a particular brand is intervened by variables like – attitude of others, change in income, change in priority, dealer terms, availability and other unexpected situational factors. He may also postpone, modify or avoid a purchase due to perceived risk. The consumers are not certain about the purchase outcome and, therefore, they hesitate to take purchase action. The marketer should try to reduce the risk factor by

providing sufficient information, popularizing brands and giving warranties. Such actions on behalf of the marketer will boast up the confidence of the buyer.

5. **Post Purchase Reaction.** The consumer has certain expectations from the product. Such expectations are framed on the basis of message received from seller, friends and other sources. If the product performances match the expectations, the consumer feels satisfied and go for repeated purchase. He even speaks positive for it in public. But, if the product fails to come up to his expectations, he feels dissatisfied. He may then either simply stop buying the product or he may take action like talking negative about the product or launching complaint to the company or seeking help of other agencies that might help him or take legal action. It is for this reason that marketer should never exaggerate about product benefits. The marketer can minimize dissatisfaction by giving evidences of satisfied brand users, entertain customer suggestions, provide instructions of use and or communicate with buyers.

Types of Buying Behaviour

Buying behaviour vary with the type of product to be purchased. The more expensive and complex the product, more the efforts involved in its purchase. The buying behaviour can be classified as:

(a) **Complex Buying Behaviour.** Such behaviour on the part of consumers is found while purchasing an expensive, risky and infrequently product. The consumers are required to put in extra effort and time to compare brand differences. The buyer usually do not have much knowledge about the product and existing brands. He, therefore, first gathers information on the basis of which he develops his beliefs and attitudes and then after careful analysis makes the purchase choice. The marketer in-order to build brand preference must provide detailed information on product attributes and its competitive superiority.

(b) **Dissonance – Reducing Buying Behaviour.** When a consumer though highly involved in purchasing the product does not find much differences in brands, may take the decision quickly. He may either go for a price or convenient location or dealer relation as all the brands in the particular price range are more or less same. But after purchase he may find certain dissatisfying features or learn about better features of other brands or low price of apparently expensive product. The buyer feels restless and tends to reduce dissonance by either changing or justifying his views or altering his behaviour.

(c) **Habitual Buying Behaviour.** Such behaviour is found for inexpensive, frequently purchased product. The consumer do not make much effort in comparing brands. They usually purchase it on the basis of information received through advertisements without evaluating it on any significant aspect. The repetition of advertisement creates familiarity Of the brand name, which makes it easy for the consumer to select. The marketer of such products find price and sales promotion incentive as an effective tool in developing demand. They use catchy slogans and attractive pictures to make it easy for the consumer to recognize and remember the brand name.

(d) **Variety Seeking Buying Behaviour.** Such a behaviour is found for products characterizing low involvement on the part of consumer but having significant brand differences. The consumer purchases the product without much comparisons. They evaluate the product on use. Next time the consumer goes for change of brand just to have a variety and not due to dissatisfaction from the previous brand. The marketer of new brand encourages the consumer to seek variety by offering discounts, contest coupons, free samples, promoting as choice of new generation *etc.* whereas the marketer of existing brand promotes habitual buying by giving reminder advertisements, putting pressure on experienced trusted name in the field and ensuring continuous availability.

Determinants of Consumer Behaviour

The behaviour of consumers with regard to purchases are influenced by various uncontrollable variables. Most of these factors are interdependent and interrelated. The variables affect each consumer differently leading to different behaviour by consumers. Therefore, each of these factors should be analysed in detail.

(a) Economic	(b) Social	(c) Cultural	(d) Personal	(e) Psychological
1. Personal income	1. Family	1. Culture and subculture	1. Age and Life Cycle stage	1. Motivation
2. Family income	2. Reference groups	2. Social class	2. Occupation	2. Perception
3. Income expectations	3. Opinion leaders	3. Caste	3. Income	3. Learning
4 Liquid assets	4. Roles & status		4. Life-style	4. Beliefs & attitudes
5. Consumer credit			5. Personality	
6. Govt. policy				

THEORIES AND MODELS OF CONSUMER BEHAVIOUR

Theories of consumer behavior are a natural extension of human behavior theories. While no single theory is unifying, each one provides a unique piece of the puzzle in understanding the psychological processes of people and their patterns of consumption. Four theories stand out as influential for marketers.

Marshallian Economics

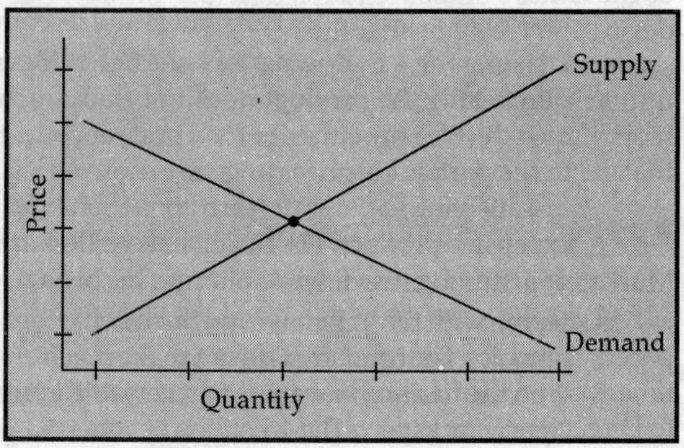

Alfred Marshall was an economist who believed that consumers buy their goods and services based on what offers the most personal satisfaction. Some have criticized this theory for being uninformative. (It is assumed that people buy what they like, if they can afford it.) However, the theory has given marketers several useful hypotheses. Some include:

- If a product's price is lower, the sales of that product will be higher.
- When there is a product and substitute of that product, sales of the substitute will be greater if its price is lower than the price of the original product.
- When the income of consumers is higher, sales of a product will therefore be higher, provided the product is not an inferior one.

The Marshallian Model

Ultimately, the Marshallian model offers a way for marketers to understand the behavior of consumers when they are making purchases that require rational consideration.

Psychoanalytic Theory

Psychoanalytic theory traces back to Sigmund Freud, the Austrian founder of psychoanalysis. Although he himself was not concerned with consumer behavior, his theories of human behavior were revolutionary. He believed that humans are not able to fully understand their own motivations because the psychological factors that shape them are largely unconscious. A major part of the unconscious mind is comprised of strong urges and desires. Since these desires can cause significant guilt and shame when they surface, people will repress them.

According to psychoanalytic theory, consumers respond to symbolic concerns as much as they respond to those of economics and function. Freud's work implies that external factors such as age and income cannot fully account for consumer behavior because motivations lay deep in the psyche. Instead, marketing messages that contain an emotional appeal to consumers' feelings, hopes, aspirations and fears are often more effective than rational appeals.

Pavlovian Theory

This theory comes from the work of Russian psychologist Ivan Pavlov. In a famous experiment, Pavlov discovered that if he rang a bell immediately prior to feeding a dog, he could eventually get the dog to salivate just by ringing it. He concluded that much of human behavior results from conditioned responses.

The Pavlovian Model

The Pavlovian theory can prove highly useful for marketers. When establishing or reinventing a brand, marketers can use this knowledge to help create or change consumer habits, or reinforce brand elements that are associated with positive customer experiences.

Veblenian Social-Psychological Model

Economist Thorstein Veblen suggested that humans are social creatures who conform to the standards of the culture and subgroups in which they live. He believed that people's individual needs and desires are created and influenced by group membership. Veblen focused his theory on members of society's "leisure class," whom he hypothesized were influenced by the desire for prestige rather than utilitarian need fulfillment. Although critics of Veblen's theory argue that it may be overstated in scope, the theory still proves useful. It suggests that marketers should understand the social influences that impact consumers in order to better comprehend product demand.

Applications of Consumer Behavior Theories

Marketers are now using these foundational theories of consumer behavior in innovative ways.

In keeping with the Veblenian model, for example, they are beginning to understand that our face-paced, technology-saturated culture means that consumers are placing an even higher value on their time. Marketers must find ways to make their advertisements both shorter and more impactful, according to Direct Marketing News (DMN). Other examples of changing consumer values include: decreasing tolerance for marketers who abuse personal data, rising expectations for interaction with brands and the desire to build long-term relationships with companies. The American Marketing Association adds that in order to move forward, marketing experts must begin to collect consumer data in far more intentional ways and increase their focus on advertising to a diverse, global audience.

The science of consumer behavior is always evolving, characterized by constant change and refinement. For those seeking to find their place at the forefront of the marketing profession, Husson University offers an online BSBA with a marketing concentration. The fully online program takes just one to two years to complete, giving students a fast track to achieving their career goals.

BRAND MANAGEMENT

A brand is a product or service which help the organisation differentiate their products or services from others. The role of brand come in critical for the organisation as it translates into loyalty and higher margins in the long run.

The differentiation of a brand can be:

1. Related to Product Performance : e.g. Gillette, Merck, Sony, 3M
   a. Functional
   b. Rational
   c. Tangible
2. Related to Brand Identity: e.g. Coca-Cola, Calvin Klein, Gucci, Tommy Hilfiger, Marlboro
   a. Symbolic
   b. Emotional
   c. Intangible

Building a Brand helps both the consumer and the manufacturer creating a win-win situation for both the parties.

Benefits of Brand for the Consumer

1. It helps to identify the source of manufacturer of the product and simultaneously assigns a responsibility towards an organization for the branded product.
2. Experience of customers with products of same brand help them to quickly decide whether they will want to go with their purchase decision or not making their decision easier.
3. Brands bring with them a certain level of quality assurance.

Benefits of Brand for the Firm

1. For a firm, the brand provides legal protection towards unique features or aspects of the product.
2. Brand loyalty helps organization to retain their existing customers when diversifying from one line of products to other. It provides security of demand and creates barrier for other manufactures to easily tap existing customers.
3. Firms can charge a premium for owning a brand boosting profit on every sale.
4. Product can be copied, but brand cannot. Once a brand is established, it's the invaluable asset for an organization.
5. A well established brand adds towards the overall value of the firm while calculating its net worth.

Scope of Branding

A brand is a perceptual entity that is rooted in reality but reflects the perceptions and perhaps even the idiosyncrasies of consumers. Ultimately a brand is something that resides in the minds of consumers. Therefore the scope of branding expands beyond boundaries.

To successfully brand a product it is necessary to teach consumers:

1. Who the product is.
2. What the product does.
3. Why consumers should choose that particular brand.

A branding strategy shall be considered successful only when the consumers have an answer to the above three questions which is strong enough to make them believe that there are significant differences in the products or services provided by a brand than others. Making sure the above three takes deep understanding of consumer and therefore the scope of branding becomes critical

The concept of branding can be applied to:

1. Physical Goods – e.g. Parle-G biscuits, Tata Tea, Maruti SX4 etc.

2. Services – e.g. Indigo Airlines, ICICI Bank etc.
3. Stores – e.g. Future Retail, Central, 99 Store, Amazon etc.
4. Person – e.g. Sachin Tendulkar, Amitabh Bacchhan etc.
5. Place – e.g. Gujrat Tourism, Incredible India etc.
6. Organization – e.g. The Rolling Stones
7. Idea – e.g abortion rights, free trade, or freedom of speech

BRAND EQUITY

Brand equity refers to a value premium that a company generates from a product with a recognizable name when compared to a generic equivalent. Companies can create brand equity for their products by making them memorable, easily recognizable, and superior in quality and reliability. Mass marketing campaignsalso help to create brand equity.

Brand equity has three basic components: consumer perception, negative or positive effects and the resulting value. Foremost, consumer perception, which includes both knowledge and experience with a brand and its products, builds brand equity. The perception that a consumer segment holds about a brand directly results in either positive or negative effects. If the brand equity is positive, the organization, its products and its financials can benefit. If the brand equity is negative, the opposite is true.

Finally, these effects can turn into either tangible or intangible value. If the effect is positive, tangible value is realized as increases in revenue or profits and intangible value is realized as marketing as awareness or goodwill. If the effects are negative, the tangible or intangible value is also negative. For example, if consumers are willing to pay more for a generic product than for a branded one, the brand is said to have negative brand equity. This might happen if a company has a major product recall or causes a widely publicized environmental disaster.

Brand Equity Example

A general example of a situation where brand equity is important is when a company wants to expand its product line. If the brand's equity is positive, the company can increase the likelihood that customers might buy its new product by associating the new product with an existing, successful brand. For example, if Campbell's releases a new soup, the company is likely to keep it under the same brand name rather than inventing a new brand. The positive associations customers already have with Campbell's make the new product more enticing than if the soup has an unfamiliar brand name.

Tracking a Company's Success with Brand Equity

Brand equity is a major indicator of company strength and performance, specifically in the public markets. Often, companies in the same industry or sector compete on brand equity. For example, an EquiTrend survey conducted on July 14, 2016, found that The Home Depot was the No. 1 hardware company in terms of brand equity. Lowe's Companies, Inc. came in second, with The Ace Hardware Corporation scoring below average. A large component of brand equity in the hardware environment is consumer perception of the strength of a company's e-commerce business. The Home Depot is an industry leader in this category. It was also found that, besides e-commerce, The Home Depot has the highest familiarity among consumers, allowing it to further penetrate the industry and increase its brand equity.

EQUITY MODELS

Aaker's Brand Equity Model

David Aaker defines brand equity as a set of assets and liabilities linked to a brand that add value to or subtract value from the product or service under that brand. He developed a brand equity model (also called Five Assets Model) in which he identifies five brand equity components:

Brand Loyalty

The following factors depict the extent to which customers are loyal to a brand:

- **Reduced Costs.** Maintaining loyal customers is cheaper than charming new ones.
- **Trade Leverage.** The loyal customers generate steady source of revenue.
- **Bringing New Customers.** Existing customers boost brand awareness and can bring new customers.
- **Competitive Threats Response Time.** Loyal customers take time to switch to a new product or service offered by other brand. Hence this buys time for the company to respond to competitive threats.

Brand Awareness

The following measures depict the extent to which a brand is widely known among consumers:

- **Association Anchors.** Depending upon the brand strength, associations can be attached to the brand which influence brand awareness.
- **Familiarity.** The consumers familiar with a brand will speak more about it and thus, influence brand awareness.
- **Substantiality.** Consumers' review on brand brings substantial and strong commitment towards the brand.
- **Consumer's Consideration.** At the time of purchasing, consumer looks for a particular brand.

Perceived Quality

It is the extent to which a brand is believed to provide quality products. It can be measured on the following criteria:

- **Quality.** The quality itself is the reason to buy.
- **Brand Position.** This is a level of differentiation as compared to competing brands. Higher the position, higher is the perceived quality.
- **Price.** When quality of the product is too complex to assess and consumer's status comes into picture, the consumer takes price as a quality indicator.
- **Wide Availability.** Consumers take widely available product as a reliable one.
- **Number of Brand Extensions.** The consumers tend to take a brand with more extensions as a measure of product guarantee.

Brand Associations

It is the degree to which a specific product/service is recognized within its product or service category. For example, a person asking for Xerox wants to actually make true copies of a paper document.

- **Information Retrieval.** It is the extent to which the brand name is able to retrieve or process the associations from consumer's memory.
- **Drive Purchasing.** This is the extent to which brand associations drive consumers to purchase.
- **Attitude.** This is the extent to which brand associations create positive attitude in the consumer's mind.

- Number of Brand Extensions. More the extensions, more the opportunity to add brand associations.

Proprietary Assets

They are patents, copyrights, trademarks, trade secrets, and other intellectual property rights. More the number of proprietary assets a brand has, greater is the brand's competency in the market.

Keller's Brand Equity Model

This model is developed by Kelvin Lane Keller, a marketing professor at Dartmouth College. It is based on the idea that the power of a brand lies in what the consumer has heard, learnt, felt, and seen as a brand over time. Hence this model is also termed as Customer Based Brand Equity (CBBE) model.

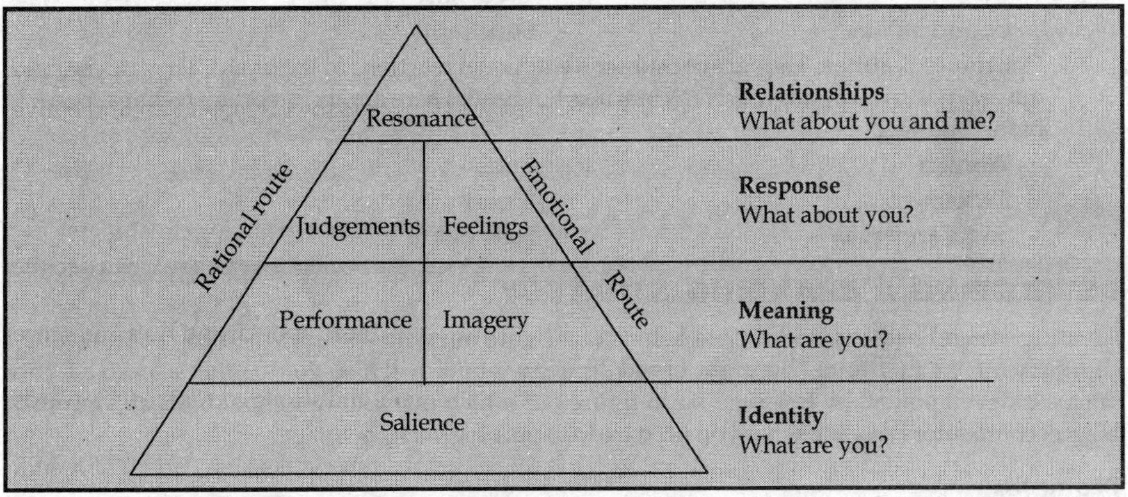

Customer Based Brand Equity.

According to CBBE model, it takes answers to four basic questions for building brand equity starting from the base of the pyramid shown above:

- Who are you? (Brand Identity)
- What are you? (Brand Meaning)
- What do I feel or think about you? (Brand Responses)
- What type and extent of association I would like to have with you? (Brand Relationships)

Brand Identity

It is not only how often and easily the consumer can recall or recognize the brand but also where and when he thinks of the brand. The key is to create brand salience to acquiring correct brand identity.

Brand Meaning

According to Keller, to make the brand meaningful it is essential to create a brand image and characteristics. Brand meaning arises out of brand associations, which can be imagery-related or function-related.

The imagery-related associations depict how well the brand meets social and psychological needs of the consumer. The function-related association such as product or service performance is what the consumer looks for primarily.

Regardless of the type of product or service, developing and delivering the product that completely satisfies the customer's needs and demands is the prime objective of making the brand meaningful. A brand with the right identity and meaning creates a sense of relevance in the consumer's mind.

Brand Responses

The companies must cater for the consumer's response. Keller segregates these responses into consumer's judgments and consumer's feelings.

- **Consumer Judgments.** They are consumer's personal opinions regarding the brand and how he has put imagery-related and performance-related associations together. There are four types of judgments crucial for creating a strong brand:
  - Quality
  - Credibility
  - Consideration
  - Superiority
- **Consumer Feelings.** They are consumer's emotional reactions to the brand. They can be mild, intense, positive, negative, driven from heart or head. There are six important feelings crucial in brand building:
  - Warmth
  - Fun
  - Excitement
  - Security
  - Social approval
  - Self-respect

DEVELOPING A BRANDING STRATEGY

Creating a brand strategy doesn't just help you to figure out who you are when you're launching a company for the first time. The right brand strategy model will also guide other aspects of your business development, by helping you to figure out which markets you should target, who your biggest competitors are, and what you need to do to nurture the right image.

Examples:

Samsung

Samsung hasn't always been as popular as it is today. This is a company that's struggled to keep up with the rest of the smartphone market, simply because it wasn't fully committed to any single identity. Samsung was so busy trying to compete on features and price, that it forgot one of the most important parts of any brand strategy – the personality. Now, after re-assessing its own brand strategy model, Samsung has emerged as the main competitor of the world's biggest tech brand – Apple Inc. In a quest to build an iconic identity, Samsung has focused its personality, marketing, and values on becoming an "innovator" in the eyes of its customers. "The New Normal" campaign has been carefully designed to appeal to a younger millennial audience of people ready to embrace a new level of technology. The campaign used VR, 360-degree cameras and more to show Samsung's commitment to becoming the next big thing.

L'Oréal

L'Oréal is another company that's struggled with its branding strategy over the years. Though its focus used to be on luxury and affordability, the company has rethought its approach recently to place greater importance on something that appeals to the younger generation: diversity.

The True Match foundation campaign in 2016 for L'Oréal Paris was the first makeup advertisement to target men. It highlighted a male makeup artist and blogger to reflect the fact that more men have begun to wear makeup.

L'Oréal is an excellent example of how a brand strategy can guide a company, but it needs to evolve and adapt over the years. By going back to its routes and remembering what it wanted to stand for, L'Oréal has been able to re-connect with its audience. In fact, the foundation mentioned above is now the best-selling foundation in the UK.

Your own Brand Strategy

A brand is more than just the features of your product or the colours on your website. It's something that's intangible, yet powerful at the same time. A brand is what you make someone feel - and that feeling should be the same no matter where someone encounters your company. Without a brand development strategy, it would be impossible for any company to cultivate the perfect image for their organisation over time. If you're still unsure whether you need a brand strategy, ask yourself:

- **Do you need to know your audience?** Many companies think they know their audience, but they run their business almost entirely on assumptions. By putting your guesses aside and using strategy to truly connect with your followers, you can convert anyone into a loyal advocate for your brand.
- **Does your business lack personality?** Today, emotions play an important part in decision making. Whether you're appealing to a teenager or a cynical CEO, everyone you talk to will be swayed by their emotions. If your company has no personality, then it won't make your prospects feel anything. A brand strategy can give your organisation the humanity it craves.
- **Are you consistent?** Branding is something that needs to develop slowly and continue to grow over time. As you gain exposure, your brand starts to imprint itself in the mind of your would-be customers. Without a brand strategy, you could end up sending a range of mismatched messages to your audience which leaves them confused and overwhelmed. Strategy ensures that your identity is clear, authentic, and easy-to-follow.

Ultimately, a brand strategy ensures that you're not just offering a product to your customers - but an experience. Your strategy will give you the tools to create a company that stands the test of time - building loyalty in your customers and making your identity truly unforgettable.

BRAND NAME DECISIONS

What name should be put on its product by a firm?

There are several alternatives as discussed below:

(i) **Individual Brand Name.** The manufacturer may give different names to each of its products. For example, Hindustan Lever Limited (HLL) has the policy of giving individual names to each of its products — Lifebuoy, Lux, Rexona, Surf, Vim, Rin, Liril, Wheel, Pears.
The main advantage of giving individual brand names to different products is that it does not tie its reputation with other products or its own name. Therefore, there is no effect of failure or low qualities of a brand on other brands. For example, HLL introduced Hina frozen peas in 1960s which failed because the Indian market was not mature enough to accept the product ideas of frozen peas. The failure of this brand did not affect the reputation of its company.

(ii) **Blanket Family Name.** The brand is used by the firm for all the products it offers, thus, overcoming the need for name research or heavy expenditure on brand building. For example, Himalaya is used for herbal healthcare products like Liv. 52, Tulsi, Neem, etc. and Sony is used for Televisions, CDs, Video Players, floppy drivers, etc. Similarly, Philips 7 uses its blanket name on all its products.

(iii) **Separate Family Names.** Here branding is carried out to substantially reduce the cost of advertising. For example, Reliance uses Vimal for sarees and suitings, Legacy for readymades, and harmony for curtains, etc. Each family name is limited to a particular product line.

(iv) **Company Trade Name Combined with Individual Product Name.** This policy may be used by a company to popularise own name and to individualise the product. This, Kellogg's uses

Kellogg's wheat flakes, Kellogg's cornflakes, Kellogg's chocos, etc. The House of Tatas is also using the combined name. Each product is promoted under the umbrella brand 'Tata', e.g., Tata Salt, Tata Tea, Tata Steel, Tata Safari and so on.

BRAND EXTENSIONS AND LOYALTY

Brand Extension

Brand extension is the use of an established brand name for a new product or new product category. It's sometimes known as brand stretching.

How Brand Extension Works?

A brand extension leverages the reputation and popularity of a well-known product to launch a new product. To be successful, there must be a logical association between the original product and the new item. A weak or nonexistent association can result in the opposite effect, brand dilution. This can even harm the parent brand.

Brand extension fails when the new product is unrelated to the original, or even creates a negative association, such as Colgate Lasagna.

Successful brand extensions allow companies to diversify their offerings, increase market share, and boost profits. The existing brand serves as an effective and inexpensive marketing tool for the new product.

Unsuccessful brand extensions are a mismatch and seem peculiar at a glance. Why would Arizona, the iced tea brand, bring out a line of nachos and cheese dip? Or consider a historic blunder in brand extension: Zippo perfume. Yes, it was a perfume bottle in the shape of a cigarette lighter, presumably for women who wanted to pretend they were lighting themselves on fire.

Examples of Brand Extension

Brand extension can be as obvious as offering the original product in a new form. For example, the Boston Market restaurant chain has launched a line of frozen dinners under its own name, offering similar fare.

Another form of brand extension combines two well-known products. Breyer's ice cream with Oreo cookie chunks is a matchup that relies on consumers' loyalty to either or both original brands.

Brand extension also may be applied to a different product category. Google's core business is a search engine, but it has attached its name to new products such as Google Wallet, the tap-to-pay app.

In the best examples, the brand extension is natural and arises from a recognized positive quality of the original product. Arm & Hammer produces a deodorizing cat litter under its brand name. Black & Decker makes a line of toy tools for children. Ghirardelli sells a brownie mix.

The creation of complementary products is a form of brand extension. The many varieties and flavors of Coca-Cola are an example.

Disadvantages of Brand Extension

The cost of introducing a product through brand extension is lower than the cost of introducing a new product that has no brand identity. The original brand communicates the message.

However, brand extensions fail when the product lines are a distinct mismatch. The brand name may even cast a disagreeable light on the new product. For example, Colgate, a brand synonymous with dental care products, once tried to extend its brand to a line of frozen dinners. Consumers just didn't want minty-fresh lasagna.

BRAND LOYALTY

Brand loyalty is the positive association consumers attach to a particular product, demonstrated by their repeat purchases of it even when given choices of competing alternatives. To marketing professionals, getting and maintaining brand loyalty for an established product are the ultimate achievements.

How Brand Loyalty Works?

Most established brand name products exist in a highly competitive market overwhelmed with new and old competing products, many of them barely distinguishable. Loyal customers are the ones who will purchase a brand regardless of convenience or price. They have found a product that meets their needs. They aren't interested in experimenting with another brand.

Companies employ many tactics to create and keep that brand loyalty. Marketing departments follow consumer buying trends closely and work to build relationships with their customers through active customer service. They spend their advertising budgets on messages targeted at the segment of the market that includes their loyal customers and like-minded people who could become loyal customers.

A brand loyalty campaign is most successful when it addresses the attributes that are crucial to its segment of the market. A Subaru will keep your kids safe. A Lincoln will make you as cool as Mathew McConaughey.

LOGISTICS AND SUPPLY CHAIN MANAGEMENT

The term "Supply Chain Management" was coined in 1982 by Keith Oliver of Booz, Allen and Hamilton Inc. But the discipline and practice has been in existence for centuries.

The terms Logistics and Supply Chain Management are used interchangeably these days, but there is a subtle difference that exists between the two.

'Logistics' has a military origin, and used to be associated with the movement of troops and their supplies in the battlefield. But like so many other technologies and terminologies, it entered into the business lexicon gradually and has now become synonymous with the set of activities ranging from procurement of raw materials, to the delivery of the final polished good to the end consumer.

In a typical business scenario, many organizations work in tandem (knowingly or unknowingly) to get the final product in hand of the end consumer. The supply chain is a network of these organizations that coalesce with each other (downstream or upstream) to make the final shipment successful.

A group of farmers, a cotton mill, a designer and a tailor is the least number of stakeholders you can expect from a regular shirt you wear every day.

Logistics is generally seen as a differentiator in terms of the final bottom line of a typical "hard and tangible goods" organization; enabling either a lower cost or providing higher value.

While a lower cost is mostly a one-time feel good factor and has been the traditional focus area in logistics, high value comes into the picture much later and may be tangible or intangible in a good's initial stages.

So while an organization like Zappos may look costly at a first glance, the extraordinary customer service due to robust policies is a value which more than offsets the slightly higher cost.

Logistics is concerned with both materials flow and information flow. While the materials flow from the supplier to consumer, the information flows the other way round. It is not only concerned with inventory and resource utilization, customer response also falls under the ambit of logistics.

In simple terms, logistics can be seen as a link between the manufacturing and marketing operations of a company. The traditional organizations used to think of them separately, but there is a definite value addition in integrating the two due to the interdependence and feedback channel between the two.

The level of coordination required to minimize the overall cost for the end consumer gets tougher to achieve as the number of participants in a supply chain increase, as an extremely efficient flow of material and information is required for optimization.

Logistics cover the following broad functional areas: *network design, transportation* and *inventory management*.

Manufacturing plants, warehouses, stores etc. are all facilities which form key components in the network design. Transportation: the cost and consistency (reliability) required out of the transportation network determines the type and mode of the movement of goods and also affects the inventory.

Buffer (or safety) stock is the reserve stock held to safeguard against shortages or unexpected surge in demand, to avoid "stock-outs". Fewer inventories with negligible stock-outs — the hallmark of an efficient logistical system.

Basic Concepts of Logistics and SCM

Inventory Planning

Organizations want to minimize the inventory levels due to its almost linear relationship with the cost. Yet if the demand is forecasted accurately, there would ideally be no need for inventory and the goods will move seamlessly from warehouses to customers.

- That would have been awesome, but it is deep into the ideal world zone. In the real world, the forecasted numbers can only take you so far and some inventory has to be maintained to satiate any surges in demand; the cost of unhappy consumers who are not serviced is often huge, and is immeasurable in most cases.
- Yet overstocks lead to increase in working capital requirements, insurance costs and blocked resources which could have been productive someplace else.
- Making a business forecast has largely been a gut-based process, but is changing rapidly in the era of data-based decision making. The forecast depends on the historical baseline for sales, seasonality (soft drinks have higher sales volume in May), recent trends (Samsung is losing out to competitors when it comes to phones, a declining trend), business cycles (economies go through expansion and contraction every few years), promotional offers (up to 50% off can drive the average fashionista mad) etc.

Transportation

The kind of transportation employed by an organization is a strategic decision (it usually accounts for around 1/3rd of the total logistics cost) based on the required level of risk exposure, customer service profiles, geographic area covered etc. Truck shipments take more time for delivery compared to air transport (customers with relaxed turnaround times); is cheaper but necessitates maintenance of higher inventory levels.

- Transportation serves the purpose of not just product movement, but storage as well (not very intuitive). Time spent for delivery means saved time for warehousing, and many times the cost to offload and reload shipments can be greater than the cost of letting the goods stay in the transportation vehicles itself.
- Two basic thumb rules apply for transportation decisions: truck load (TL) shipments are better than less-than-truckload (LTL) shipments as storage space is a perishable commodity (just like a commercial airline does not want to fly with empty seats), and the cost per kilometer decreases

as the distance increases (two 500 km shipments is usually more expensive than a single 1000 km shipment).

- The factors which determine the economies of transportation decisions include but are not limited to: distance between the starting and destination points, and density (higher density products take less space — space constraints outweigh weight constraints by a huge margin), stow ability (spherical packaging will lead to more empty spaces compared to cubical) and volume of the goods. Different modes of transport serve different strategic ends (rail, road, air, water etc).
- FlipKart has eKart for its logistical operations and warehousing, whereas smaller e-commerce players generally outsource their operations to specialized logistics players such BlueDart, DHL and now Delhivery.

Packaging

The end goals differ: can either be done for end consumers or for logistical considerations. The packaging will then depend on the end goal; form factor plays the lead role when packaging goods for the end consumers, while function plays the lead role in packaging for logistical operations.

Warehousing

It is the back-end building for storing goods. Based on the needs of the organization, it can be in-house or outsourced.

- Primary functions of a warehouse are product movement and storage. Activities such as offloading of the goods coming from the suppliers, the intermediate packaging (if required), and shipping to other destinations (retailers or end consumers) are handled in the warehouse. Similarly, they can also serve as a storage house for handing peak consumer demand to avoid stock out of items, and acts as a buffer between the starting point (usually manufacturing plant) and ending point (think about a typical retail outlet).
- Different distribution strategies can be adopted by an organization based on its needs and infrastructure in place, namely:
  - **Cross-Docking.** Relies on minimal processing at the warehouse level and facilitate seamless connection between "incoming" and "outgoing" goods through technologies such as bar code scanners; becoming increasingly important due to established structured communication between retailers and manufacturers; best for high velocity goods with predictable demand patterns.
  - **Milk Runs.** The delivery guy is out to deliver items from a single supplier to multiple retailers or to pick up items from multiple suppliers for a single retailer (An Indian Doodhwala can literally teach a thing or two about this, hence the naming we think).
  - **Direct Shipping.** A supplier directly ships to a particular retailer without any intermediaries. Mostly happens with big-name stores with huge good volumes, and very frequent replenishments. Big savings on time.
  - **Hub and Spoke Model.** Hub serves as the central node for nearby places, and the spokes depend on the hub for their needs (think of a metropolitan and various tier-2 cities in its proximity).
  - **Pooled Distribution.** Region is the most important factor driving this strategy. Delivers to every destination point in a geographical area, smart for handling peak time loads and LTL shipments. Plus one for the planet as a bonus!

Supply Chain Designing

It is important to recognize that a company's network determines its supply chain efficiency and customer satisfaction.

Designing an optimal supply chain network means the network must be able to meet the long term strategic objectives of the company.

Most business units or functional areas within a company are impacted by a network design project.

When designing a supply chain the following steps must be followed: 1) Define the business objectives, 2) The project scope must be defined, 3) The form of analyses to be done must be determined, 4) Determine what tools will be used, 5) Finally, Project completion, the best design.

Once the path forward is determined and the design approach has been completed correctly, the business will reap many significant benefits.

What Creates Real Economic Value?

Business and operations strategy - the formulation of strategies that drive investment, operations, and competitive positioning - is where all value begins.

There are five strategic questions that need to be answered:

1. What business is the CPG company in and why?
2. How should value be added to the business?
3. What are the target markets?
4. What are the products and why will customers buy from the CPG company?
5. What capabilities are needed to assure that the company adds value and differentiates?

Most companies develop strategies for target markets and products #3 and #4. Some at least consider #1 and #2. Few companies resolve #5 effectively.

This is generally because operations strategies are not developed or implemented with the same scenario plan or rigour that is given to the more often seemingly interesting issues of markets and products. The alignment of business and operations strategies is often weak or non-existent.

Mission and vision statements, plans, goals, objectives, and performance measures while important for driving execution, most often do not ensure that capabilities will be built for scenarios from the business strategies.

Therefore, companies do not always have carefully developed alternatives for customer demand, new channels, competition, supply risks, and product development.

Achieving clear and sustained alignment between operations execution and the plans derived from business strategies is challenging. Leadership understands the complexities involved, but are concerned that 90% of business strategies are not implemented as intended.

They are beginning to understand that supply chains are about more than logistics regarding the buying and selling of goods, they are about competitive differentiation and profitable business growth.

Sales Force

Sales force is linking between companies and customer. Therefore, companies have to be careful in designing and structuring sales force.

1. The first step is setting out an objective for sales force. Earlier companies had a single objective increasing sale making it objective also for sales people. Sales people are asked to perform a search for prospective clients or lead. Sales people are asked to balance time between a prospective customer and current customer. Effective communication of product and services

is essential to close the deal. Sales people also play an important role in after sales service and can make a difference for the company. Sales people are eyes and ears of the company in the market gathering information about competition and customer changing demands.

2. The second step is use sales people strategically. Sales people have to combine efforts with other team members to achieve the objective. Sales people should be aware how to analyze market data been provided and convert them into marketing strategies.
3. The third step is deciding the structure of the sales force. The structure of the sales is dependent on the strategy followed by the company. Common sales force structures are as follows:
   - **Territorial structure** is used where every sales representative is assigned specific geographical area. This structure is preferred for building relationships with locals.
   - **Product structure** is used for complex and un- related product portfolio. Here the sales people are directly associated with research and development of the products.
   - **Market structure** is used if the companies are operating different industry or market segments. Every sales force specializes in a definite market and helps push a product efficiently across the given market. However, the disadvantage would arise if customers are located over a wide geographical area.
   - **Complex structure** is used when companies are in business of selling complex product to different customer across a large geographical area. Here sales force structure is a combination of other structures discussed.
4. Once the structure is designed companies need to make a decision with respect to the size of the sales force. The size of the sales force is dependent on the market size and number of customers.
5. The next step is to design compensation for the sales force. Compensation plays a big motivational factor for sales people. Companies follow a structure of a fixed amount plus a variable amount depending of success achieved in the market. Allowances play an important factor in the salary owing to continuous travel and market visits.

Managing Sales Force

Integral part for success of marketing strategy is management of the sales force. The management of sales consists of following:

Recruitment is at the centre of an effective sales force. One approach in the selection is asking a customer what characteristics they look for in a sales representative. Companies develop selection procedure where behavioral and management skills are tested.

Training is essential to remain ahead of the competition. Sales force needs training before entering the market as well as training at different stage of the product life cycle.

Supervision on sales force is decided on the profile of product portfolio. A general supervision is maintained with respect to sales people dealing with potential clients. Another supervision is related to efficient time management from preparation of client call to closing of the deal.

Motivation is a key aspect for management of the sales force. Here compensation plays an important in driving up the motivational level. Compensation can be assigned based on sales quota. Other motivational tools are social gathering and family outing.

Evaluation is essential to management of a sales force. Sales reports sent by the sales force serve a good starting point of evaluation.

Art of negotiation and relationship marketing these two are the important aspects of successful sales representative and long term benefit for the company.

SERVICE MARKETING

Managing Service Quality and Brands

The intention of the 2015 revision is to keep ISO 9001 relevant, reflect changes in its environment, and ensure it continues to deliver "confidence in the organization's ability to consistently provide product that meets customer and applicable statutory and regulatory requirements."

According to ISO's Technical Committee, the revised standard should (among other things):

- Remain generic, and relevant to all sizes and types of organization operating in any sector;
- Maintain the current focus on effective process management to produce desired outcomes;
- Take account of changes in quality management systems practices and technology since the last major revision in 2000;
- Reflect changes in the increasingly complex, demanding and dynamic environments in which organizations operate;
- Apply Annex SL of the ISO Directives to enhance compatibility and alignment with other ISO management system standards;
- Facilitate effective organizational implementation and effective conformity assessment by first, second and third parties;
- Use simplified language and writing styles to aid understanding and consistent interpretations of its requirements; and,
- Provide a stable core set of requirements for the next 10 years or more.

A Primer for Quality

With these intentions met as a whole, global commerce should see a bump in overall quality levels going forward, but no one should panic that "everything is about to change." For example, let's focus on the last bullet point. The core set of requirements within the revised ISO 9001 standard will not differ from the current requirements. However, the language will be standardized, as will the approaches to management, based on the introduction of eight major quality management principles.

These principles were developed in the mid-1990s by a small group of experts who were familiar with the teachings and philosophies of the well-known quality gurus of the last century.

The eight principles are:

1. **Customer focus.** Organizations can establish this focus by trying to understand and meet their customers' current and future requirements and expectations.
2. **Leadership.** Organizations succeed when leaders establish and maintain the internal environment in which employees can become fully involved in achieving the organization's unified objectives.
3. **Involvement of people.** Organizations succeed by retaining competent employees, encouraging continuous enhancement of their knowledge and skills, and empowering them, encouraging engagement and recognizing achievements.
4. **Process approach.** Organizations enhance their performance when leaders manage and control their processes, as well as the inputs and outputs that tie these processes together.
5. **System approach to management.** Organizations sustain success when processes are managed as one coherent quality management system.
6. **Continuous improvement.** Organizations will maintain current levels of performance, respond to changing conditions, and identify, create and exploit new opportunities when they establish and sustain an ongoing focus on improvement.

7. **Factual approach to decision making.** Organizations succeed when they have established an evidence-based decision making process that entails gathering input from multiple sources, identifying facts, objectively analyzing data, examining cause/effect, and considering potential consequences.
8. **Mutually beneficial supplier relationships.** Organizations that carefully manage their relationships with suppliers and partners can nurture positive and productive involvement, support and feedback from those entities.

These principles form the conceptual foundation for the ISO portfolio of quality management standards and serve as the basis for the Good Manufacturing Practices (GMP), Good Clinical Practices (GCP), and Good Laboratory Practices (GLP) required by most government regulatory bodies. But these principles are not just the backbone of quality systems; they're also simply good business principles to put into practice across an enterprise. The standardization of management approach based on them will be driving global improvement and process excellence for at least the next 10 years.

MARKETING STRATEGIES OF A SERVICE FIRM

Developing a strong marketing plan is vital to the success of any business. Service firms can face challenges in their marketing strategies as they often don't offer physical products that can be demonstrated for customers. These companies therefore depend on delivering high levels of professionalism and efficiency. A comprehensive marketing strategy can help service providers highlight capabilities and attract clients.

Customer Referrals

Qualified sales leads can usually be found in the existing customer base. When a professional service firm deals with their current crop of satisfied customers, its sales staff should find out if those clients have business associates that would benefit from their services. These referrals come with an instant connection to the prospect and remove much of the anxiety often associated with making a cold call.

More Options

Professional networking opportunities give service firm chapters an additional avenue to implement their marketing strategies. Networking groups allow companies to conduct face-to-face interactions with potential clients and industry leaders. Gatherings that mix business with pleasure, such as conventions, charitable functions and civic events, give sales staffers additional chances to spread the word about the company. They can also interact with important contacts in ways that leave personal impressions.

Industry Specialization

With so many service firms competing for a limited number of potential clients, their respective marketing plans must include methods on how to stand out from their rivals. Since no firm can meet every customer's every need, each company must determine which skill sets it possesses and emphasize those skills. For instance, a law firm specializing in bankruptcy law will stress its abilities to clients seeking help in reorganizing their debts.

Social Media

Social media has quickly become one of the most effective marketing tools for service firms. Sites such as Facebook, Twitter and Tumblr give companies new outlets to spread their messages to a worldwide audience. Professional networking sites such as LinkedIn allow marketers and sales staff to connect with prospective customers based on work experience and industry status.

CUSTOMER RELATIONSHIP MARKETING

Customer relationship marketing (CRM) is a technique based on client relationships and customer loyalty. Using customer data and feedback, companies utilizing this marketing strategy develop long-term relationships with customers and develop laser-focused brand awareness. Customer relationship marketing varies greatly from the traditional transactional marketing approach that focuses on increasing individual sale numbers.

Companies that prioritize customer relationships, on the other hand, strive to create strong customer connections, which may be emotional, to their brand to promote customer loyalty and increase customer lifetime value. They benefit from word-of-mouth promotion and develop brand ambassadors.

Customer Relationship Marketing Strategies

Customer relationship marketing builds upon customer experience management and puts improving customer interactions to foster brand loyalty at the core of marketing activities and efforts. There are several ways that companies go about customer relationship marketing, including providing excellent customer service at all times, getting to know individual customers to anticipate their needs, and offering loyalty program perks and rewards for repeat customers. Companies typically turn to the internet and social media to pursue customer relationship marketing initiatives, which means that small businesses also can benefit from it by inviting customers to visit their websites, read and comment on blog posts, and communicate via social media platforms like Twitter and Instagram.

The goal of customer relationship marketing is to build trust with and engage customers to build brand loyalty and reduce customer churn. One of the best strategies for building relationships with customers is focusing on emotion. Brands who excel in CRM use nostalgia in their campaigns because it is one of the most powerful connections consumers can have to a brand, according to BDA CEO Jay Deutsch. That's why branded merchandising is becoming part of some of the most successful marketing campaigns.

Other strategies in customer relationship marketing include:

- **Show customers you value them with every interaction.** Consider spontaneously recognizing them and delighting them in unexpected ways
- **Listen to customers and respond.** Use social media monitoring tools to reply to comments and complaints and address customers' concerns
- **Give customers free information.** Identify topics and interests customers have and then create content to address them and give customers free access to it, such as informational videos on products they recently purchased or newsletters that highlight individual customers and share their stories
- **Expanded loyalty rewards.** Any company can offer perks and rewards, but you need to expand beyond the typical reward program and give people stuff they love or recognize them in unexpected ways
- **Communicate frequently.** A relationship is nothing without communication, so make sure you communicate with customers often via social media, email, messages, etc. (just be sure the communication provides value to customers and does not become intrusive or too frequent)

Benefits of Customer Relationship Marketing

When companies implement customer relationship marketing, they make good use of their customer data and identify customers that will be of more value to the company itself. With customer relationship marketing campaigns, companies save time and money by focusing on customers that will not be as costly in terms of maintaining relationships with them; they also make better decisions about which customers have underdeveloped potential.

Another advantage of utilizing customer relationship marketing is that it increases customer satisfaction and communication levels. Customers who have strong relationships with companies interact with them more frequently, which makes it easier to learn more about

customers via customer data platforms. These companies also save money by building relationships with existing customers rather than spending to attract new customers.

Other benefits of using a customer relationship marketing strategy include:

- **Delivering a consistent customer experience.** By becoming customer-centric and focusing on customer relationships, companies align their touchpoints and work across the organization to meet customer needs, improve satisfaction, and deliver an exceptional experience.
- **Gathering customer feedback.** Building strong relationships with customers requires communication, and companies put more stock in gathering feedback and analyzing it to make better business decisions to build stronger relationships.
- **Improving customer profitability.** Customers that are loyal to brands spend more with them; in fact, consumers are now putting customer experience ahead of cost when making purchasing decision.
- **Creating customer advocates.** The happier your customers are, the better the chances they will spread the word about you to others; when you build a strong relationship with them and deliver a consistent experience, they have better reviews to share.

RETAIL MARKETING

RECENT TRENDS IN INDIA

Retailing today is the fastest growing sectors in the global economy and is under transition phase; not only in South Asian countries like India and China but throughout the world. The increased popularity of organized retailing is mainly because of the consumers' changing behavior. This change has become possible due to double income families, breakup of joint family concept, changing lifestyles and favorable demographic patterns. Today consumers prefer to shop at places where they can get grocery, food, entertainment and others daily routine items under one roof. This has made retailing the most attractive sector of the Indian economy.

Following are the recent trends that have stood out in recent years and continue to grow further:

1. New retail formats and combinations are emerging and have opened a new world of opportunities for Indian youth. Due to huge amounts of new investments and decreasing charm for 'kirana' stores, the retail sector is expected to grow. Bank branches, bill counters, saloons, internet cafe have opened in the malls. The 'cash and carry' activities are expected to grab majority of attention.
2. Internet age, increased computer awareness and shrinking usage charges have made people enabled buy things online resulting in growth of non-store retailing. Retailers are informing about new arrivals/fresh stock through e-mails, television, SMS and telephones to which anyone can respond to through toll-free 16 digit numbers.
3. Specialty stores like 'Reliance Digital', 'Music World' 'Metal Junctions', 'Nokia World' and 'Pantaloons' have their presence in most of the malls in the country. Departmental stores have given way to malls, having a mixture of large and small retailers offering varied brands for each and every section of the society.

4. Sales promotion channels are increasingly becoming professional and targeting differently to different lifestyle groups. Newer and newer promotional techniques are emerging. Event managers are hired and visual merchandising professionals are consulted.

   Today retailers are not sticking to traditional methods of promoting a sale but personal selling door-to-door selling, free home delivery and payment through plastic money have emerged and is being widely used. Use of advanced technology is not the matter of affordability but is the reason for survival. Retailers are using computers, electronic devices, check out scanning systems, tag guns, vending machines, money counters and digital signage to enhance store's productivity. CCTVs, cameras, sensors and theft alarms are being used to prevent store theft.
5. Today retail organizations are not only targeting big cities but are considering tier II and tier III cities like Jaipur, Pune, Shimla, Karnal, Panipat, Coimbatore, Baroda, Chandigarh etc also. The South Indian states are one step ahead when it comes to shopping in the supermarkets for day-to-day needs and also have been influencing other states where supermarkets are being established.

   However, the main center of organized retailing is undeniably Chennai, which once was considered as a 'conservative', 'traditional' and cost-sensitive' market. The success of Chennai as retail hub has surprised all but list of factors contributed to its success. Reasonable real estate prices, double household income, increased presence of MNCs and industrial boom has led to the emergence of new residential societies resulting in increased purchasing power and demands for day- to-day goods under one roof.
6. **Use of Plastic Money.** Use of credit and debit cards for buying merchandise is relatively a new phenomenon but is gaining popularity immensely. Credit and debit cards are commonly known as 'plastic money'. Today, especially in metros, retail spending is mainly done by plastic cards, accounting for over 45 percent and is likely to touch 65 percent over the next five years.
7. **Distance – No bar.** Thanks to increased public transportation, better roads, highways and an overall improvement in the transportation infrastructure that has enabled customers to visit from one place to another smoothly than ever before. Now for want of quality goods, a customer can travel several kilometers to reach a particular store.
8. Partnerships and tie-ups among retailers, real estate developers, brands, franchisees, and financers have become the fashion of the day to spread risk related to huge investments and uncertainty.
9. The government infrastructure support, relaxation on foreign direct investments further has accelerated the growth of Indian organized retail sector. Consequently, the shopping malls are coming up throughout the country in a big way.
10. **Sophisticated customers.** Due to Internet revolution, customers are becoming conversant about the products they are interested in buying. For example, over thirty percent of Indian consumers collect information from the Internet about prices, features, guarantee/warranty options before visiting any store for the actual purchase.

    This is particularly true in case of automobiles, cell phones, consumer electronics, hotel bookings, travel packages etc. This suggested the retailers that they need to respond to varying consumer needs and growing assortment.
11. The gap between organized and unorganized (traditional 'kirana' shopping) retailing is coming close due to mall revolution and increasing Indian middle class in terms of size and income. According to a study conducted by 'Deloitte Haskins and Sells', one of the four largest accounting firms in the world, Indian retailing is growing at a faster pace as was expected from it and could constitute 25% of the total retail sector by 2011.

The study further reveals that new malls, increased disposable income and easy access to credit facilities have led to organized retailing to record all time high rate of growth of 50% per annum in 2007. The traditional 'kirana' stores by introducing modern retailing concepts such as self service, free home delivery system, credit facility and other value added services have been trying to reshape themselves.

12. **Need for retailing skills.** Undoubtedly, retailing in India is still in nascent stage. The success of organized retailing is yet to be proved. The success will be felt once an equitable stage is achieved. This requires enough store size, traffic flow, and revenue earned, but besides these factors, retailers have started concentrating on recruiting qualified and trained retail staff.

TYPES OF RETAIL OUTLETS

1. **Speciality store.** Speciality stores carry very limited product lines with deep assortment. They offer a wide choice in terms of models, size, style, colour and other important attributes in the assortment carried.
2. **Department store.** A departmental store is a large retail outlet that handles a wide variety of lines of product. It has a wide assortment in each line and is organized into separate departments for purposes of buying, promotion, services and control. It is sometimes called mass merchandising departmental store e.g., military canteens.
3. **Super markets.** A supermarket is designed to serve the total needs for food, laundry and household maintenance products. It is relatively large in size. Its operation is low cost, low margin, high volume and self service in nature.
4. **Convenience store.** A convenience store is located near residential area. It is relatively small. It is kept open for long hours. A limited lines of convenience products are offered for sale. The prices charged are slightly higher.
5. **Discount store.** A discount store sells standard merchandise at lower prices. Higher volumes of sales compensate lower margins and increase the overall profitability. Discount retailing has moved into speciality merchandise stores such as sport goods stores, electronics stores and book shops.
6. **Off price retailer.** An off-price retailer sells left over goods, over runs, and irregulars obtained at reduced prices from manufactures or other retailers. Off price retailers may be of three types.
7. **Factory outlets.** These are owned and operated by manufacturers. They carry the manufacturer's surplus, discontinued or irregular goods. e.g., dinner ware, shoes, upscale apparel, etc.
8. **Independent off price retailer.** Independent off-price retailers are owned and run by entrepreneurs or by divisions of larger retail corporations.
9. **Warehouse clubs.** These are otherwise known as wholesale clubs. They sell a limited selection of brand-name grocery items, appliances, clothing etc.
10. **Super store.** Super stores meet consumers' total needs for routinely purchased food and nonfood items.
11. **Hyper Markets.** Hyper markets originated in France. Hyper markets combine speciality stores, limited line stores in a single level store. Product assortment goes beyond routinely purchased goods. It includes furniture, large and small appliances, clothing items, etc.

    Bulk display and minimum handling by store personnel are the other features present in the hyper markets. Discount is offered to customers who are willing to carry heavy appliances and furniture out of the store.
12. **Catalogue showroom.** Customers order goods from a catalogue in the showroom. Then, they pick these goods up at a merchandise pickup area in the store.

EMERGING TRENDS IN MARKETING

CONCEPT OF E-MARKETING

Business, at least in part, is forced to move into the electronic space. It is due to spread of the Internet, competition rise and globalisation of business. In order to attract more customers and survive in the global market entrepreneurs have also had to change means of advertising. It is not enough to have high quality products to operate successfully in the market; high quality service and successful introduction of new methods of competition are vital.

Online marketing (e-marketing) – is an interactive process, when using information technologies long-term relations between the company and customers are developed. In the broad sense, marketing comprises strategic and tactic planning processes which are to meet customers' needs and bring maximum profit. E- marketing can be of two types:

- As a marketing strategy component of a whole organisation.
- As a standalone system, which contains all traditional marketing components, but they are transferred into e-space.

In e-marketing customers are not grouped into segments by the traditional demographic method but by their behaviour. To provide more and better quality information sales advertising is used. The number of distribution channels grows and the number of intermediaries increases as manufactures discover new ways of delivering the product to the buyer directly. Companies have to introduce a different type of marketing to be able to adjust to new circumstances.

E-marketing is associated more with an external perspective, how the Internet can be used to liaise with traditional environment, providing services to customers and reducing costs (administrative, etc.).

The impact of information technology on e-marketing:

- **A customer is the most important.** In today's business world conditions are dictated by consumers who determine competition conditions. Increased buying power, constantly changing needs and expectations lead to a shortened product life cycle.
- **Speed.** Information on the Internet is changing at a high speed, so the customer has to constantly monitor the process.
- **Distance abolition.** With the emergence of the Internet geographical barriers have disappeared. Companies communicate with their clients from various parts of the world. Attainability on a global scale is the factor which allows reaching markets which previously were not available. Therefore, the Internet is regarded as the global market with no limits.
- **Lack of time constraints.** It is non-stop activity, that is twenty-four hours a day, seven days a week (24/7)
- **The intellect-based capital** – imagination, creativity and entrepreneurship are more important resources that financial capital.

The impacts of electronic technology mentioned above let us conclude that e-marketing is a complex process designed for marketing purposes using the Internet and other digital technologies related to it.

Impact of the virtual environment on traditional marketing:

- Increases effectiveness of traditional marketing functions.
- Provides flexibility for marketing solutions (abolition of physical limits, access to information about products and services, transformation from a passive customer's state to an active).

DIRECT MARKETING

Direct marketing is a form of advertising in which companies provide physical marketing materials to consumers to communicate information about a product or service. Direct marketing does not involve advertisements placed on the internet, on television or over the radio. Types of direct marketing materials include catalogs, mailers and fliers.

Direct marketing removes the "middle man" from the promotion process, as a company provides a message directly to a potential customer. Companies with smaller advertising budgets typically use this type of marketing since they cannot afford to pay for advertisements on television and often do not have the brand recognition of larger firms.

Direct-marketing messages generally include a call to action, encouraging the recipient to respond via a toll-free phone number or a reply card or by clicking on a link in an email promotion. Companies are able to measure the effectiveness of their direct-marketing campaigns by tracking responses. Direct marketing is more effective when companies use targeted lists of prospects developed using available marketing data that can segment them into identifiable groups that are likely to have an interest in a product or service.

Over the years direct marketing has developed a bad reputation for cluttering up people's mail boxes with junk mail or generating spam in email inboxes. Many companies engage in opt-in or permission marketing, which limits their mailing or emailing to only those willing to receive it. Companies select communication channels they consider most effective for a particular market. For instance, a new gym may find more success distributing flyers, while a new grocery store prefers to mail promotional coupons to the residents of nearby neighborhoods.

Companies that use direct marketing benefit from being able to focus limited resources on a targeted promotion, which also allows them to personalize the marketing message. Because it is easy to measure responses, companies can test different marketing messages for improving the response rate. Direct marketing can be cost-effective if the customer database is well-managed.

The downside of direct marketing is that response rates can vary widely making the flow of prospects unpredictable. Ineffective campaigns can be costly, especially if they occur frequently. Companies that send blanket direct mail or email promotions have to overcome the negative image of junk mail and email spam. The key to effective direct marketing is an accurate database, which can be expensive to maintain.

DIGITAL MARKETING

Digital marketing is the use of the internet, mobile devices, social media, search engines, and other channels to reach consumers. Some marketing experts consider digital marketing to be an entirely new endeavor that requires a new way of approaching customers and new ways of understanding how customers behave compared to traditional marketing.

Understanding Digital Marketing

Digital marketing targets a specific segment of the customer base and is interactive. Digital marketing is on the rise and includes search result ads, email ads and promoted tweets – anything that incorporates marketing with customer feedback or a two-way interaction between the company and customer.

Internet (a.k.a. online) marketing differs from digital marketing. Internet marketing is advertising that is solely on the Internet, whereas digital marketing can take place over the telephone, on a subway platform, in a video game or via a smartphone app.

In the parlance of digital marketing, advertisers are commonly referred to as sources, while members of the targeted ads are commonly called receivers. Sources frequently target highly specific, well-defined receivers. For example, after extending the late-night hours of many of its locations, McDonald's needed to get the word out. It targeted shift workers and travelers with digital ads, because the company knew that these people made up a large segment of its late night business. McDonald's encouraged them to download a new Restaurant Finder app, targeting them with ads placed at ATMs and gas stations, as well as on websites that it new its customers frequented at night.

Digital Marketing Channels

- **Website Marketing.** A website is the centerpiece of all digital marketing activities. Alone, it is a very powerful channel, but it's also the medium needed to execute a variety of online marketing campaigns. A website should represent a brand, product and services in a clear and memorable way. It should be fast, mobile friendly, and easy to use.
- **Pay-Per-Click (PPC) Advertising.** PPC advertising enables you to reach internet users on a number of digital platforms through paid ads. You can setup PPC campaigns on Google, Bing, Linkendin, Twitter, Pinterest, or Facebook and show your ads to people searching for terms related to your products or services. PPC campaigns can segment users based on their demographic characteristics (age, gender etc) or even their particular interests or location. The most popular PPC platforms are Google Ads and Facebook.
- **Content Marketing.** The goal of a content marketing is to reach potential customers through the use of content. Content is usually published on a website and then promoted through social media, email marketing, SEO, or even PPC campaigns. The tools of content marketing include: blogs, ebooks, online courses, infographics, podcasts, and webinars.
- **Email Marketing.** Email marketing is still one of the most effective digital marketing channels. Many people confuse email marketing with spam email messages we all receive per day, but that's not what email marketing is all about. Email marketing is the medium to get in touch with your potential customers or the people interested in your brand. Many digital marketers use all other digital marketing channels to add leads to their email lists and then, through email marketing, they create customer acquisition funnels to turn those leads into customers.
- **Social Media Marketing.** The primary goal of a social media marketing campaign is brand awareness and establishing social trust but as you go deeper into social media marketing, you can use it to get leads or even as a direct sales channel.
- **Affiliate Marketing.** Affiliate marketing is one of the oldest forms of marketing, and the internet has brought new life to this old stand-by. With affiliate marketing, you promote other people's products, and you get a commission every time you make a sale or introduce a lead. Many well-known companies like Amazon have affiliate programs that pay out millions of dollars per month to websites that sell their products.
- **Video Marketing.** YouTube has become the second most popular search engine and a lot of users are turning to YouTube before they make a buying decision, to learn something or just to relax. There are several video marketing platforms, including Facebook Videos, Instagram, Vimeo to use to run a video marketing campaign. Companies find the most success with video by integrating it with SEO, content marketing, and social media marketing campaigns.
- **SMS Messaging.** Political parties and candidates use SMS messages to send positive information about their candidates and negative messages about their opponents.

GREEN MARKETING

Green marketing is the marketing of environmentally friendly products and services. It is becoming more popular as more people become concerned with environmental issues and decide that they want to spend their money in a way that is kinder to the planet.

Green marketing can involve a number of different things, such as creating an eco-friendly product, using eco-friendly packaging, adopting sustainable business practices, or focusing marketing efforts on messages that communicate a product's green benefits.

This type of marketing can be more expensive, but it can also be profitable due to the increasing demand. For example, products made locally in North America tend to be more expensive than those made overseas using cheap labor, but they have a much smaller carbon footprint because they don't have to fly across the globe to get here. For some consumers and business owners, the environmental benefit outweighs the price difference.

LOHAS

Consumers who prefer to purchase green products even though they might be more expensive fall into the 'LOHAS' category. LOHAS stands for Lifestyles of Health and Sustainability. According to Wikipedia:

"LOHAS describes an integrated, rapidly growing market for goods and services that appeal to consumers whose sense of environmental and social responsibility influences their purchase decisions."

These consumers are active supporters of environmental health and are the heaviest purchasers of green and socially responsible products. They also have the power to influence other consumers.

Green Marketing Methods

Beyond making an environmentally friendly product, business owners can do other things as part of their green marketing efforts. The following can all be part of a green marketing strategy:

- Using eco-friendly paper and inks for print marketing materials.
- Skipping the printed materials altogether and option for electronic marketing.
- Having a recycling program and responsible waste disposal practices.
- Using eco-friendly product packaging.
- Using efficient packing and shipping methods.
- Using eco-friendly power sources.
- Taking steps to offset environmental impact.

Greenwashing

Some marketers try to capitalize on the growing number of green consumers by simply taking a green marketing approach to products that might not otherwise be considered green. They try to position their products as a better choice for the environment when they're really not. An example of this is when a company uses the color green in their packaging, or the word green somewhere in their messaging, when there isn't anything particularly eco-friendly about their product, nor it's not more eco-friendly than competing products. Greenwashing is not only misleading, but it can also be damaging to a company's reputation.

If consumers want to be certain they are indeed buying a green product, they should look for official certifications listed on the product packaging.

INTERNATIONAL MARKETING

International marketing is the application of marketing principles by industries in one or more than one country. It is possible for companies to conduct business in almost any country around the world, thanks to the advances in international marketing.

In simple words, international marketing is trading of goods and services among different countries. The procedure of planning and executing the rates, promotion and distribution of products and services is the same worldwide.

In recent times, companies are not restricted to their national borders, but are open for international marketing. With the increasing change in customers' demands, choices, preferences and tastes, the economies are expanding and giving way to more competitive marketing. Thus, organizations need to respond rapidly to the demands of the customers with well-defined marketing strategies.

The word 'International Marketing' is defined as the exchange of goods and services across national borders to meet the requirements of the customers. It includes customer analysis in foreign countries and identifying the target market.

The **major participants** in international marketing are as follows :

- **Multinational Corporations (MNCs).** A multinational corporation (MNC) is an organisation that ensures the production of goods and services in one or more countries other than its home country. Such organizations have their offices, help desks or industrial set-up across nations and usually have a centralized head office where they co-ordinate global management.
- **Exporters.** They are the overseas sellers who sell products, and provide services across their home country by following the necessary jurisdiction.
- **Importers.** They are the overseas buyers who buy products and services from exporters by complying with the jurisdiction. An import by one nation is an export from the other nation.
- **Service companies.** A service company generates revenue by trading on services and not on physical commodities. A public accounting company is the best example of a service company. Revenue here is generated by preparing returns of income tax, performing audit services, and by maintaining financial records.

ENTRY MODE DECISIONS, PLANNING MARKETING MIX FOR INTERNATIONAL MARKETS

Market Selection Decision

Once a firm has decided to enter the international market, the next important marketing decision is market selection. As per company's present product mix, production capacity, and proposed expansion strategy, it selects one or more countries to operate in. In the same way, it has to decide on type of foreign buyers to be served.

Market segmentation and target market selection are two basic issues in the decision. Initially, a firm targets the most attractive and comparatively easy international markets. Global marketing research can help a company to study international consumer behaviour, segment international market, and select a few most profitable markets.

To assess international markets, following criteria may be used:

1. Present market opportunities
2. Future market opportunities
3. Market share

4. Uncertainties and challenges
5. Cost-profit estimates
6. Return on investment

Market Entry Decision

A firm has selected international markets to operate in. Now, the next imperative marketing decision is market entry, i.e., how to enter the market; which of the options to be used for foreign market entry. There are several options to choose an appropriate entry strategy.

1. Exporting

Exporting involves selling domestic products in foreign markets. It is easier and common entry option. Exporting consists of producing the products in home country and selling or exporting the same in the international market. There are two options in exporting, the first, company itself exports products in foreign markets, and, the second, company exports through intermediate agency or agent.

Some entry options in exporting, as suggested by Philip Kotler, include:

(i) **Export Department.** A company maintains a full-fledged export department to sell its products in foreign markets. The department is responsible for searching export opportunities, promotion and selling products, and performing all activities related to export business.

(ii) **Opening Branch in Foreign Market.** Some companies open their branches or shops in foreign markets to serve consumers. The head of the branch is responsible for all activities related to promotion and distribution of the company's products.

(iii) **Appointing Traveling Salesmen.** Some companies appoint salesmen to search customers in foreign market and serve them. They collect orders and manage necessary procedures. They can help develop relations with foreign agencies, retailer, and customers.

(iv) **Appointing Distributors.** In this entry option, a firm appoints agents, representatives, or middlemen in foreign markets. They are responsible to carry out all activities to promote and sell the company's products.

2. Direct Foreign Investment

A company sets up its own factory in other countries. Its carries out all production and marketing activities in foreign land. But, the option depends on a lot of factors such as market stability, costs of production and marketing, competition, government policies, and other factors determining favourableness of situation. Company should select this strategy carefully as there are considerable risk and uncertainties in some countries.

3. Joint Venture

The joint venture is jointly owned and managed by host and foreign companies, by two companies of two nations. A foreign company holds necessary equity to get voice in management but not enough to completely dominate the venture. Structure of joint venture depends on government policies and approach of host country.

In underdeveloped and developing countries, many multinational corporations are operating as joint ventures. For example, HMT represent joint venture with Swiss Machines and Tools, Proctor and Gamble has joint venture with Godrej, Suzuki of Japan has with Maruti Udyog, etc.

At present Indian governments and companies operate with more than 50 countries as joint ventures. When a giant company invests directly in many countries, it is called multinational companies (MNCc). There are several forms of joint venture, such as mixed companies, joint ownership companies, licensed companies, contract manufacturing, management contract, etc.

Marketing Mix Decision

Marketing mix decision involves preparing marketing mix (strategies) for international market. Marketing mix consists of 4P's – product decisions, pricing decisions, promotion decisions, and place or distribution decisions.

Marketing mix decisions remain same as domestic market except the target market. Here, all marketing mix decisions are taken with reference to foreign customers and global marketing environment.

Organisation Decision

Organisation for global marketing is an important decision. In order to implement, direct, and control international marketing efforts, a company must adopt an appropriate organization structure. The organisation is responsible to regulate foreign trade.

It is same as domestic marketing organisation; the only difference is that it is prepared to administer international marketing operations and activities. Structure depends on a lot of factors such as type of products, number of countries, type of buyers, etc. Sometimes, it is treated as the department or part of main organisation, for example, foreign trade department.

There are different types of organisation structures suit with international marketing such as:

(i) Product-wise Organisation
(ii) Country-wise Organisation,
(iii) Customer-wise Organisation
(iv) Place-wise organisation
(v) Matrix or Mix Organisation, etc.

MULTIPLE CHOICE QUESTIONS

1. Which theory of consumer behavior suggests that individuals seek to maximize their utility and make rational decisions based on their preferences and budget constraints?
   (a) Cognitive dissonance theory
   (b) Theory of planned behavior
   (c) Utility theory
   (d) Maslow's hierarchy of needs theory
2. According to the Elaboration Likelihood Model (ELM), consumers process information through two different routes. What are these two routes called?
   (a) Central route and peripheral route
   (b) Rational route and emotional route
   (c) Impulsive route and thoughtful route
   (d) Conformity route and independence route
3. The Theory of Reasoned Action (TRA) emphasizes the role of which two key factors in predicting and explaining consumer behavior?
   (a) Attitude and intention
   (b) Belief and perception
   (c) Social class and culture
   (d) Budget and price
4. In the Hierarchy of Effects Model, what is the sequence that consumers typically follow when making a purchasing decision?
   (a) Awareness, interest, desire, action
   (b) Action, interest, desire, awareness
   (c) Desire, awareness, interest, action
   (d) Action, awareness, interest, desire
5. According to Maslow's Hierarchy of Needs, which of the following is considered the most basic and fundamental human need?
   (a) Self-actualization
   (b) Safety and security
   (c) Social belongingness
   (d) Esteem and recognition
6. The Theory of Cognitive Dissonance, proposed by Leon Festinger, suggests that consumers are motivated to reduce dissonance or inconsistency between
   (a) Their beliefs and attitudes
   (b) Their perceived value and the product price
   (c) Their needs and wants
   (d) Their cultural background and societal norms
7. Which model of consumer behavior emphasizes the role of cultural, social, and personal factors in influencing consumer choices?
   (a) Hierarchy of Effects Model
   (b) Cognitive Dissonance Model
   (c) Howard-Sheth Model
   (d) Utility Model
8. The Information Processing Model of consumer behavior views consumers as
   (a) Passive recipients of marketing messages
   (b) Rational decision-makers who process information sequentially
   (c) Emotion-driven individuals who make impulsive choices
   (d) Largely influenced by external factors, such as peer pressure
9. According to the Diffusion of Innovation theory, what is the term for the early adopters who are willing to take risks and try new products or ideas?
   (a) Laggards
   (b) Early Majority
   (c) Innovators
   (d) Late Majority
10. The Fishbein Model, an extension of the Theory of Reasoned Action, includes the concept of
    (a) Normative beliefs
    (b) Cognitive dissonance
    (c) Social class
    (d) Consumer perception
11. According to the Behavioral Influence Model, which of the following is NOT one of the four main types of consumer decision-making?
    (a) Routine response behavior
    (b) Limited decision-making

(c) Extensive decision-making
(d) Impulse buying

12. The Theory of Selective Exposure suggests that consumers are more likely to pay attention to information that
(a) Supports their existing beliefs and attitudes
(b) Challenges their beliefs and attitudes
(c) Is delivered through traditional advertising channels
(d) Is presented in a humorous way

13. The Elaboration Likelihood Model (ELM) was proposed by
(a) Abraham Maslow
(b) Leon Festinger
(c) Philip Kotler
(d) Richard Petty and John Cacioppo

14. In the Howard-Sheth Model of consumer behavior, the term "perceptual screens" refers to
(a) The physical barriers consumers use to block out advertising
(b) Mental filters that screen out irrelevant information
(c) Electronic devices that filter online content
(d) Retail displays that block access to products

15. The concept of "perceived risk" in consumer behavior refers to the
(a) Actual financial risk associated with a purchase
(b) Potential social risks involved in a purchase
(c) Belief that a product will meet expectations
(d) Consumer's perception of the uncertainty or negative consequences associated with a purchase

16. According to the Extended Self Model, consumers often extend their self-concept by
(a) Reducing their consumption of material possessions
(b) Purchasing products that align with their self-identity
(c) Rejecting all forms of branding and labeling
(d) Minimizing the emotional connection with products

17. The Model of Ethical Consumer Behavior emphasizes the role of
(a) Advertising and promotional strategies
(b) Personal beliefs and values in consumer choices
(c) Peer pressure and social influence
(d) Economic factors and pricing strategies

18. The Hype Cycle Model suggests that new technologies or products go through a cycle that includes stages such as "Peak of Inflated Expectations" and "Trough of Disillusionment." This model is often used to explain
(a) The impact of economic factors on consumer behavior
(b) The adoption and perception of emerging technologies
(c) The role of emotional appeals in advertising
(d) The effects of celebrity endorsements

19. The Consumer Decision Journey model, developed by McKinsey & Company, proposes that consumers go through four key stages in their decision-making process. What are these stages?
(a) Awareness, interest, desire, action
(b) Need recognition, information search, evaluation, purchase
(c) Attention, interest, desire, action (AIDA)
(d) Cognitive, affective, conative, evaluative

20. The Regret Theory suggests that consumers experience regret when they believe they have made a suboptimal choice. This regret is often triggered by
(a) Overestimating the benefits of a product
(b) Underestimating the value of a product
(c) The availability of alternative choices
(d) The level of consumer satisfaction

21. What is the primary role of a brand in the context of marketing?
(a) To increase production efficiency
(b) To reduce consumer choices
(c) To differentiate products and create customer value
(d) To minimize advertising expenses

22. Brand equity represents
(a) The financial value of a brand
(b) The total assets of a company
(c) The brand's value to the customer
(d) The brand's market share

23. Which brand equity model focuses on customer-based brand equity and includes four key components brand salience, brand imagery, brand judgments, and brand feelings?

(a) Keller's CBBE model
(b) The Cost-Based Model
(c) The Production Efficiency Model
(d) The Brand Loyalty Model

24. Brand resonance, in the context of brand equity, refers to
(a) The feeling of detachment from a brand
(b) The depth and intensity of customer relationships with the brand
(c) A decrease in brand awareness
(d) The decline in brand loyalty

25. Brand leverage refers to a brand's ability to
(a) Minimize advertising expenses
(b) Expand into new markets and product categories
(c) Reduce brand loyalty
(d) Decrease the brand's visibility

26. Which of the following is NOT a characteristic of an effective brand name?
(a) Simplicity (b) Uniqueness
(c) Lengthiness (d) Memorability

27. The process of creating a new brand name is called
(a) Brand dilution
(b) Brand extension
(c) Brand development
(d) Brand naming or brand naming process

28. What type of brand name is created by blending two or more words to create a unique, catchy, and memorable name?
(a) Descriptive brand name
(b) Experiential brand name
(c) Coined brand name
(d) Generic brand name

29. In the context of brand names, what does the term "genericide" refer to?
(a) The process of creating a generic brand name
(b) The loss of trademark protection due to a brand name becoming synonymous with the product category
(c) The naming process of a brand extension
(d) The naming process of a line extension

30. A brand extension occurs when a brand
(a) Launches a completely new and unrelated brand
(b) Expands into a new market without any connection to the original brand
(c) Introduces a new product or service under an existing brand name
(d) Abandons the original brand name

31. What is the primary benefit of using brand extensions in brand management?
(a) Reducing customer loyalty
(b) Minimizing production costs
(c) Leveraging the brand's existing equity to enter new product categories
(d) Increasing advertising expenses

32. In the context of brand loyalty, what does the term "brand evangelists" refer to?
(a) Consumers who are indifferent to the brand
(b) Consumers who occasionally purchase the brand's products
(c) Highly loyal customers who passionately advocate for the brand
(d) Consumers who consistently switch brands

33. Brand loyalty can lead to
(a) A decrease in sales and market share
(b) Higher customer acquisition costs
(c) Repeat business, positive word-of-mouth, and resistance to competitor influences
(d) Decreased brand equity

34. What type of brand loyalty occurs when a customer purchases a brand out of habit or convenience without much emotional attachment?
(a) Behavioral loyalty
(b) Emotional loyalty
(c) Brand indifference
(d) Brand resistance

35. Co-branding is a strategy in which
(a) A company uses a single brand name for all its products
(b) Two or more brands are combined in a marketing campaign
(c) Two or more brands collaborate to create a new product or service
(d) A brand targets a single, specific market segment

36. The Aaker Model of brand equity includes which four brand dimensions?
(a) Brand awareness, brand preference, brand purchase intention, and brand memory
(b) Brand salience, brand imagery, brand judgments, and brand feelings
(c) Brand loyalty, brand recognition, brand personality, and brand awareness

(d) Brand price, brand quality, brand distribution, and brand promotion

37. In the context of branding, what is "brand salience"?
   (a) The extent to which a brand is recognized and associated with a product category
   (b) The brand's emotional connection with customers
   (c) The brand's quality and performance
   (d) The brand's promotional efforts

38. The "brand judgments" dimension in the Aaker Model of brand equity focuses on
   (a) Customers' emotional connection to the brand
   (b) How customers assess the brand's quality and credibility
   (c) The price of the brand's products
   (d) The brand's distribution channels

39. A key element in developing a successful branding strategy is to
   (a) Constantly change the brand's name to keep it fresh and relevant
   (b) Maintain a consistent brand image and message across all touchpoints
   (c) Avoid advertising and promotion to reduce expenses
   (d) Underprice the competition to gain market share

40. In the context of branding strategy, what does "brand resonance" refer to?
   (a) The immediate recognition of a brand name
   (b) The depth and intensity of customer relationships with the brand
   (c) The brand's aggressive promotional efforts
   (d) The brand's financial value

41. What is the primary role of a brand in the context of marketing?
   (a) To increase production efficiency
   (b) To reduce consumer choices
   (c) To differentiate products and create customer value
   (d) To minimize advertising expenses

42. Brand equity represents
   (a) The financial value of a brand
   (b) The total assets of a company
   (c) The brand's value to the customer
   (d) The brand's market share

43. Which brand equity model focuses on customer-based brand equity and includes four key components brand salience, brand imagery, brand judgments, and brand feelings?
   (a) Keller's CBBE model
   (b) The Cost-Based Model
   (c) The Production Efficiency Model
   (d) The Brand Loyalty Model

44. Brand resonance, in the context of brand equity, refers to
   (a) The feeling of detachment from a brand
   (b) The depth and intensity of customer relationships with the brand
   (c) A decrease in brand awareness
   (d) The decline in brand loyalty

45. Brand leverage refers to a brand's ability to
   (a) Minimize advertising expenses
   (b) Expand into new markets and product categories
   (c) Reduce brand loyalty
   (d) Decrease the brand's visibility

46. Which of the following is NOT a characteristic of an effective brand name?
   (a) Simplicity (b) Uniqueness
   (c) Lengthiness (d) Memorability

47. The process of creating a new brand name is called
   (a) Brand dilution
   (b) Brand extension
   (c) Brand development
   (d) Brand naming or brand naming process

48. What type of brand name is created by blending two or more words to create a unique, catchy, and memorable name?
   (a) Descriptive brand name
   (b) Experiential brand name
   (c) Coined brand name
   (d) Generic brand name

49. In the context of brand names, what does the term "genericide" refer to?
   (a) The process of creating a generic brand name
   (b) The loss of trademark protection due to a brand name becoming synonymous with the product category
   (c) The naming process of a brand extension
   (d) The naming process of a line extension

50. A brand extension occurs when a brand
   (a) Launches a completely new and unrelated brand

(b) Expands into a new market without any connection to the original brand
(c) Introduces a new product or service under an existing brand name
(d) Abandons the original brand name

51. What is the primary benefit of using brand extensions in brand management?
(a) Reducing customer loyalty
(b) Minimizing production costs
(c) Leveraging the brand's existing equity to enter new product categories
(d) Increasing advertising expenses

52. In the context of brand loyalty, what does the term "brand evangelists" refer to?
(a) Consumers who are indifferent to the brand
(b) Consumers who occasionally purchase the brand's products
(c) Highly loyal customers who passionately advocate for the brand
(d) Consumers who consistently switch brands

53. Brand loyalty can lead to
(a) A decrease in sales and market share
(b) Higher customer acquisition costs
(c) Repeat business, positive word-of-mouth, and resistance to competitor influences
(d) Decreased brand equity

54. What type of brand loyalty occurs when a customer purchases a brand out of habit or convenience without much emotional attachment?
(a) Behavioral loyalty
(b) Emotional loyalty
(c) Brand indifference
(d) Brand resistance

55. Co-branding is a strategy in which
(a) A company uses a single brand name for all its products
(b) Two or more brands are combined in a marketing campaign
(c) Two or more brands collaborate to create a new product or service
(d) A brand targets a single, specific market segment

56. The Aaker Model of brand equity includes which four brand dimensions?
(a) Brand awareness, brand preference, brand purchase intention, and brand memory
(b) Brand salience, brand imagery, brand judgments, and brand feelings
(c) Brand loyalty, brand recognition, brand personality, and brand awareness
(d) Brand price, brand quality, brand distribution, and brand promotion

57. In the context of branding, what is "brand salience"?
(a) The extent to which a brand is recognized and associated with a product category
(b) The brand's emotional connection with customers
(c) The brand's quality and performance
(d) The brand's promotional efforts

58. The "brand judgments" dimension in the Aaker Model of brand equity focuses on
(a) Customers' emotional connection to the brand
(b) How customers assess the brand's quality and credibility
(c) The price of the brand's products
(d) The brand's distribution channels

59. A key element in developing a successful branding strategy is to
(a) Constantly change the brand's name to keep it fresh and relevant
(b) Maintain a consistent brand image and message across all touchpoints
(c) Avoid advertising and promotion to reduce expenses
(d) Underprice the competition to gain market share

60. In the context of branding strategy, what does "brand resonance" refer to?
(a) The immediate recognition of a brand name
(b) The depth and intensity of customer relationships with the brand
(c) The brand's aggressive promotional efforts
(d) The brand's financial value

61. In the context of logistics and supply chain management, what does the term "lead time" refer to?
(a) The time it takes for a product to reach the end consumer
(b) The time it takes to manufacture a product
(c) The time it takes to unload goods from a container
(d) The time it takes to place an order with a supplier

62. Which of the following is NOT a primary driver of supply chain management?
(a) Cost reduction
(b) Customer satisfaction
(c) Inventory optimization
(d) Marketing promotions

63. Value creation in logistics and supply chain management can be achieved by
(a) Increasing lead times
(b) Reducing transportation efficiency
(c) Decreasing collaboration with suppliers
(d) Minimizing operational costs

64. What does the term "supply chain design" encompass in supply chain management?
(a) The physical layout of warehouses
(b) The creation of marketing campaigns
(c) The configuration and coordination of supply chain processes
(d) The design of product packaging

65. In supply chain management, the "bullwhip effect" refers to
(a) A type of transportation delay
(b) A phenomenon where small fluctuations in demand can lead to significant variations in orders upstream in the supply chain
(c) A shortage of raw materials
(d) A communication breakdown in the supply chain

66. What is the primary goal of designing and managing a sales force in an organization?
(a) Maximizing production efficiency
(b) Achieving synergy between marketing and sales
(c) Increasing customer acquisition costs
(d) Reducing the sales team's compensation

67. In designing a sales force, what does "territory management" involve?
(a) Assigning sales representatives to specific geographic areas
(b) Creating promotional materials
(c) Setting sales quotas
(d) Managing inventory levels

68. What is the primary responsibility of a "sales manager" in an organization?
(a) Identifying potential customers
(b) Supervising and directing the sales team
(c) Managing production facilities
(d) Setting advertising budgets

69. Which type of sales force compensation plan is based on a fixed salary with no additional performance-based incentives?
(a) Commission-based plan
(b) Salary-plus-bonus plan
(c) Straight salary plan
(d) Incentive-based plan

70. What is the term for the practice of assessing a salesperson's performance based on specific criteria and providing regular feedback and coaching?
(a) Sales team collaboration
(b) Sales force design
(c) Sales performance management
(d) Marketing management

71. In the context of personal selling, what does the term "prospecting" refer to?
(a) The act of analyzing financial statements
(b) The process of identifying and qualifying potential customers
(c) The negotiation of price and terms
(d) The delivery of products to customers

72. What is the primary purpose of a "sales presentation" in personal selling?
(a) To close a sale immediately
(b) To collect customer feedback
(c) To educate and persuade potential customers
(d) To request referrals

73. In personal selling, the "trial close" is a technique used to
(a) Conclude the sales presentation and finalize the sale
(b) Gather feedback from the customer
(c) Present a trial version of the product to the customer
(d) Negotiate the price

74. The "objection-handling" phase in personal selling involves
(a) Avoiding customer objections
(b) Acknowledging and addressing customer concerns and objections
(c) Raising objections to test the customer's commitment
(d) Redirecting the conversation away from objections

75. What is the term for the stage in personal selling where the salesperson asks the customer for the order or commitment to purchase?

(a) Closing the sale
(b) Qualifying the prospect
(c) Making the initial contact
(d) Developing a rapport

76. What is the primary goal of service quality management in service marketing?
(a) Minimizing customer expectations
(b) Reducing customer satisfaction
(c) Delivering consistent and exceptional service experiences
(d) Increasing service costs

77. Which of the following dimensions is NOT part of the SERVQUAL model for assessing service quality?
(a) Tangibles (b) Responsiveness
(c) Reliability (d) Availability

78. The "moments of truth" concept in service marketing refers to
(a) The critical points in a customer's journey where they interact with the service provider
(b) The moments of interaction between employees
(c) The moments when customers make a purchase decision
(d) The moments of conflict in customer interactions

79. Which service quality gap is related to the difference between management's perceptions of customer expectations and actual customer expectations?
(a) Gap 1 Knowledge Gap
(b) Gap 2 Policy Gap
(c) Gap 3 Delivery Gap
(d) Gap 4 Communication Gap

80. The "zone of tolerance" in service quality management represents
(a) The area where customers have very high expectations
(b) The range within which customers are willing to accept variations in service quality
(c) The area where service providers have complete control over quality
(d) The zone of optimal customer satisfaction

81. In service marketing, what does the term "brand equity" refer to in the context of service brands?
(a) The financial value of the brand
(b) The brand's unique symbol or logo
(c) The value and strength of the brand as perceived by customers
(d) The number of employees in the service organization

82. Which of the following statements about service branding is true?
(a) Service branding is not as important as product branding.
(b) Service branding is primarily focused on physical attributes.
(c) Service branding is essential for differentiating services and creating customer loyalty.
(d) Service branding is only relevant for large service firms.

83. What does the term "brand promise" represent in service branding?
(a) The price of the service
(b) A commitment to deliver specific benefits and experiences to customers
(c) The brand's logo
(d) The brand's financial value

84. In service marketing, "service blueprinting" is a technique used to
(a) Create a physical layout for service facilities
(b) Develop marketing campaigns
(c) Map the customer journey and identify critical service elements
(d) Set pricing strategies

85. Which of the following is NOT one of the dimensions of brand personality often used in service branding?
(a) Sincerity (b) Competence
(c) Convenience (d) Excitement

86. The "four Ps" of service marketing include all of the following EXCEPT
(a) Product (b) Place
(c) Promotion (d) People

87. What is the primary goal of relationship marketing in service firms?
(a) Maximizing short-term profits
(b) Building long-term customer relationships and loyalty
(c) Reducing advertising expenses
(d) Expanding into new markets

88. "Service recovery" strategies in service marketing are focused on
(a) Avoiding customer complaints

(b) Addressing and resolving service failures to regain customer trust
(c) Reducing service costs
(d) Improving the speed of service delivery

89. In service marketing, what is the term for the practice of encouraging existing customers to make additional purchases or use additional services?
(a) Cross-selling
(b) Advertising
(c) Product development
(d) Market segmentation

90. "Internal marketing" in service firms involves
(a) Targeting external customers through advertising
(b) Creating a positive work environment and ensuring that employees understand and support the brand promise
(c) Setting prices for services
(d) Reducing employee training costs

91. In customer relationship marketing, what is the primary goal of relationship building?
(a) Maximizing short-term profits
(b) Building long-term and mutually beneficial relationships with customers
(c) Reducing advertising expenses
(d) Focusing on one-time transactions

92. What is the term for the process of identifying and selecting the most valuable customers to focus on in relationship marketing?
(a) Customer segmentation
(b) Mass marketing
(c) One-size-fits-all approach
(d) Short-term marketing

93. The practice of "customer onboarding" in relationship marketing refers to
(a) Terminating customer relationships
(b) Acquiring new customers
(c) Welcoming and orienting new customers to the company's products and services
(d) Managing customer complaints

94. In relationship marketing, what does the term "churn rate" refer to?
(a) The rate at which customers become more profitable
(b) The rate at which customers refer new customers
(c) The rate at which customers terminate their relationship with the company
(d) The rate at which customers make repeat purchases

95. What is the primary goal of relationship "bonding" in relationship marketing?
(a) Creating strong, emotional connections with customers
(b) Maximizing short-term profits
(c) Reducing customer loyalty
(d) Expanding the customer base

96. In relationship marketing, what does the term "relationship marketing mix" encompass?
(a) The product, price, place, and promotion elements
(b) The short-term marketing strategies
(c) The relationship-building techniques
(d) The financial goals of the company

97. What is the primary objective of "personalization" in relationship marketing?
(a) Treating all customers the same
(b) Delivering mass marketing campaigns
(c) Customizing interactions, offers, and communication for individual customers
(d) Reducing customer loyalty

98. Which of the following relationship marketing strategies involves offering customers a range of products or services to meet their needs and preferences?
(a) Relationship continuity
(b) Cross-selling
(c) Mass marketing
(d) Short-term promotions

99. What is the term for the practice of monitoring and measuring the health and quality of customer relationships over time in relationship marketing?
(a) Customer satisfaction
(b) Customer churn
(c) Relationship analytics
(d) Market research

100. "Customer advocacy" in relationship marketing refers to
(a) Customers who frequently complain
(b) Customers who engage in fraudulent activities
(c) Customers who actively promote and recommend the company's products or services to others
(d) Customers who request discounts

101. Which of the following is NOT a key value of customer relationship marketing?
(a) Customer-centric approach
(b) Long-term customer relationships
(c) One-time transactions
(d) Customer satisfaction

102. What does the term "lifetime value of a customer" represent in relationship marketing?
(a) The total revenue generated from a customer throughout their entire relationship with the company
(b) The initial purchase amount made by a customer
(c) The number of times a customer visits the company's website
(d) The number of customers acquired in a single marketing campaign

103. "Touchpoints" in relationship marketing refer to
(a) Physical locations where customers interact with the company
(b) The act of making direct contact with customers
(c) The points of interaction between customers and the company, including digital and physical channels
(d) Short-term customer engagements

104. The customer relationship marketing process typically includes the stages of
(a) Acquisition, conversion, and profit maximization
(b) Market segmentation, advertising, and sales
(c) Product development, pricing, and promotion
(d) Awareness, interest, and desire

105. "Customer retention" in relationship marketing is focused on
(a) Acquiring new customers
(b) Increasing churn rate
(c) Keeping and nurturing existing customers
(d) Delivering short-term promotions

106. In the context of retail marketing in India, what does "omnichannel retailing" refer to?
(a) Operating a single physical store
(b) Selling products exclusively through online channels
(c) Providing a seamless shopping experience across multiple channels, including physical stores, websites, and mobile apps
(d) Focusing on traditional marketing methods

107. Which of the following is a recent trend in Indian retail marketing, involving partnerships with local artisans and small-scale producers to promote unique and locally-made products?
(a) Hypermarket retailing
(b) Franchising
(c) Sustainable retailing
(d) Collaborative retailing

108. "Smart retail" in India includes the integration of technology for various purposes, such as
(a) Increasing physical store size
(b) Reducing customer interaction
(c) Enhancing customer experience, personalization, and efficiency
(d) Eliminating the need for physical stores

109. In recent Indian retail marketing trends, what is the concept of "dark stores" or "fulfillment centers" related to?
(a) Stores with limited lighting
(b) Stores that only operate at night
(c) Facilities used for online order fulfillment, not open to the public
(d) Specialty stores selling dark-colored products

110. The practice of "phygital retail" in India refers to
(a) Retail stores operating exclusively through phone apps
(b) Combining physical and digital elements to create a blended shopping experience
(c) Traditional retail stores without any digital integration
(d) Geographical expansion of retail stores

111. In India, what is the primary characteristic of a "department store" as a type of retail outlet?
(a) Specializes in a narrow product category
(b) Offers a wide range of products and services under one roof
(c) Primarily sells discounted products
(d) Operates in rural areas

112. A "specialty store" in India typically focuses on
(a) Selling a variety of unrelated products
(b) Offering a wide range of discounted products
(c) Selling a narrow range of related products within a specific category
(d) Operating in large hypermarkets

113. What does the term "franchise retail" refer to in the Indian retail context?
(a) Selling products without any brand association
(b) Operating a single, independent store
(c) Establishing multiple stores under a licensing agreement with a parent company
(d) Selling products at a fixed price

114. "Discount stores" in India are known for
(a) Selling products at premium prices
(b) Offering high-end luxury goods
(c) Providing products at lower prices and with limited service
(d) Selling only through online channels

115. A "hypermarket" in India is typically characterized by
(a) A small store size
(b) Focusing on niche and specialty products
(c) Offering a wide range of products, including groceries, clothing, electronics, and more
(d) Operating exclusively online

116. What is the primary objective of e-Marketing?
(a) Maximizing traditional marketing efforts
(b) Promoting physical store locations
(c) Leveraging digital channels for marketing products and services
(d) Reducing customer engagement

117. Which term describes the process of increasing a website's visibility in search engine results pages (SERPs)?
(a) Content marketing
(b) Search Engine Optimization (SEO)
(c) Social media marketing
(d) Viral marketing

118. What does the acronym "SEM" stand for in e-Marketing?
(a) Social Engagement Metrics
(b) Search Engine Marketing
(c) Social Media Engagement
(d) Site Engagement Management

119. In e-Marketing, what is the primary focus of "content marketing"?
(a) Creating content for entertainment purposes
(b) Distributing any content without a strategy
(c) Generating and distributing valuable, relevant content to attract and engage a target audience
(d) Producing content without considering the audience

120. What is the term for the percentage of people who receive an email and take a desired action, such as making a purchase or signing up for a newsletter?
(a) Open rate
(b) Conversion rate
(c) Bounce rate
(d) Click-Through Rate (CTR)

121. In e-Marketing, what does "affiliate marketing" primarily involve?
(a) Promoting products directly to consumers
(b) Earning commissions by promoting other companies' products or services
(c) Focusing on viral marketing campaigns
(d) Ignoring digital marketing channels

122. What is the term for testing two versions of a webpage or campaign to determine which one performs better in e-Marketing?
(a) Split testing
(b) Viral marketing
(c) Behavioral targeting
(d) Social media optimization

123. What is the primary purpose of a "landing page" in e-Marketing?
(a) Providing general information about a company
(b) Serving as the homepage of a website
(c) Collecting customer information and encouraging a specific action
(d) Reducing customer interactions

124. In e-Marketing, what does the term "influencer marketing" involve?
(a) Creating content that appeals to a wide audience
(b) Collaborating with individuals who have a significant online following to promote products or services
(c) Ignoring the role of individuals in marketing
(d) Maximizing paid advertising campaigns

125. What is the term for targeting customers based on their online behavior and interactions in e-Marketing?
(a) Demographic targeting
(b) Behavioral targeting
(c) Psychographic targeting
(d) Geographic targeting

126. In e-Marketing, what is the term for targeting customers based on their physical location or geographic regions?
(a) Behavioral targeting
(b) Psychographic targeting
(c) Demographic targeting
(d) Geographic targeting

127. What does "retargeting" or "remarketing" involve in e-Marketing?
(a) Targeting new customers who have never visited a website
(b) Targeting customers who have previously visited a website but did not complete a desired action
(c) Ignoring past website visitors
(d) Targeting customers who have never used social media

128. In e-Marketing, what is the term for providing information about a product's environmental impact, such as its carbon footprint or energy efficiency?
(a) Green marketing
(b) Eco-labeling
(c) Environmental branding
(d) Sustainable advertising

129. Which term describes the practice of falsely promoting a product as environmentally friendly in e-Marketing?
(a) Green branding
(b) Eco-labeling
(c) Greenwashing
(d) Sustainability marketing

130. What is the term for creating and sharing online content, such as blogs, videos, and social media posts, to attract and engage a target audience in e-Marketing?
(a) Content marketing
(b) Video marketing
(c) Social media marketing
(d) Viral marketing

131. In e-Marketing, what does "CTA" stand for?
(a) Content Tracking Analysis
(b) Click-Through Activity
(c) Content Test and Analysis
(d) Call to Action

132. "PPC" in e-Marketing stands for
(a) Pay-Per-Click
(b) Post-Purchase Conversion
(c) Promotional Price Cuts
(d) Product Promotion Campaign

133. In e-Marketing, what is the term for targeting a specific group of customers based on their demographics, such as age, gender, or income?
(a) Behavioral targeting
(b) Psychographic targeting
(c) Geographic targeting
(d) Demographic targeting

134. "Bounce rate" in e-Marketing refers to
(a) The percentage of people who open an email
(b) The percentage of website visitors who leave the site without taking any action
(c) The number of clicks on a website
(d) The percentage of people who complete an online purchase

135. What is the term for designing products that can be easily disassembled and recycled in e-Marketing?
(a) Circular economy design
(b) Built-in obsolescence
(c) Linear product design
(d) Disposable product design

136. In e-Marketing, what does the term "ROI" stand for?
(a) Rate of Interest
(b) Return on Investment
(c) Revenue and Opportunity Index
(d) Reporting and Optimization Insights

137. "Geo-fencing" in e-Marketing involves
(a) Designing geo-specific advertising campaigns
(b) Focusing on global marketing efforts
(c) Targeting customers based on their physical location or proximity to a specific geographic area
(d) Ignoring geographic targeting

138. What is the term for the practice of providing information on the responsible use and disposal of a product in e-Marketing?
(a) Green labeling
(b) Sustainable branding
(c) End-of-life instructions
(d) Environmental messaging

139. "KPI" in e-Marketing stands for
(a) Key Performance Indicator
(b) Keyword Performance Insights
(c) Knowledge of Product Implementation
(d) Kiosk Placement Index

140. In e-Marketing, what is the term for promoting the use of public transportation, carpooling, or biking as a way to reduce environmental impact?
(a) Eco-friendly transportation
(b) Sustainable branding
(c) Green mobility marketing
(d) Maximizing individual car usage

141. What is the primary goal of Direct Marketing?
(a) Maximizing traditional advertising
(b) Promoting products through physical stores
(c) Targeting and engaging specific customers with personalized messages
(d) Reducing marketing budgets

142. In Direct Marketing, what does the term "direct response" refer to?
(a) Receiving feedback from customers
(b) Making purchases through a retail store
(c) Interacting with customers in a physical location
(d) Conducting market research

143. Which marketing channel is commonly used for sending direct mail to customers in Direct Marketing?
(a) Email
(b) Social media
(c) Television advertising
(d) Radio promotions

144. What is the term for a personalized message or offer sent to a specific customer in Direct Marketing?
(a) Mass marketing
(b) Direct mail
(c) Telemarketing
(d) One-to-one marketing

145. In Direct Marketing, what does the acronym "ROI" stand for?
(a) Return on Investment
(b) Rate of Inquiry
(c) Revenue from Online Interactions
(d) Reporting and Optimization Insights

146. What is the term for a marketing database that stores customer information and can be used for segmentation and personalization in Direct Marketing?
(a) CRM (Customer Relationship Management)
(b) Mass marketing database
(c) Generic contact list
(d) Sales lead database

147. In Direct Marketing, what is the primary objective of "telemarketing"?
(a) Conducting market research
(b) Generating sales through telephone interactions
(c) Sending promotional emails
(d) Collecting customer feedback

148. "Direct mail" in Direct Marketing refers to
(a) Sending unsolicited messages to potential customers
(b) Sending physical promotional materials, such as brochures and catalogs, to a targeted list of recipients
(c) Sending generic marketing emails
(d) Conducting market research through postal surveys

149. In Direct Marketing, what does the term "response rate" indicate?
(a) The number of marketing emails sent
(b) The number of customers in a mass marketing campaign
(c) The percentage of recipients who take a desired action in response to a marketing message
(d) The time it takes to develop a marketing campaign

150. What is the term for a marketing technique that encourages customers to take an immediate action, such as making a purchase, in Direct Marketing?
(a) Delayed marketing
(b) Direct response marketing
(c) Long-term engagement
(d) Customer retention

151. "Opt-out" in Direct Marketing allows customers to
(a) Opt-in to receive marketing messages
(b) Request more marketing messages
(c) Unsubscribe or decline further marketing communications
(d) Report spam emails

152. What is the primary purpose of "customer segmentation" in Direct Marketing?
(a) Targeting all customers with the same message
(b) Personalizing marketing messages based on customer behavior

(c) Sending generic marketing materials to all customers
(d) Maximizing marketing expenses

153. In Direct Marketing, what does the term "call to action" (CTA) refer to?
(a) A request for customer feedback
(b) A promotional phone call
(c) A specific action or response that the marketer wants the customer to take
(d) An informational webinar

154. "RFM analysis" in Direct Marketing stands for
(a) Rapid Feedback Measurement
(b) Relationship Forming Metrics
(c) Recency, Frequency, and Monetary Value
(d) Response Focus Method

155. What is the term for marketing materials that are sent to customers who have not requested them, often in bulk, in Direct Marketing?
(a) Permission marketing
(b) Opt-in marketing
(c) Unsolicited marketing
(d) Customer relationship marketing

156. In Direct Marketing, what does the term "multi-channel marketing" involve?
(a) Using a single marketing channel to reach all customers
(b) Using multiple marketing channels, such as email, social media, and direct mail, to engage customers
(c) Focusing solely on in-person marketing
(d) Ignoring marketing channels

157. What does the term "cross-selling" mean in Direct Marketing?
(a) Selling products to customers from different regions
(b) Selling products related to a customer's recent purchase
(c) Selling unrelated products to the same customer
(d) Selling products to customers without their consent

158. In Direct Marketing, what is the term for a type of marketing message sent to customers who have explicitly given permission to receive such messages?
(a) Inbound marketing
(b) Permission marketing
(c) Generic marketing
(d) Outbound marketing

159. "Landing page" in Direct Marketing refers to
(a) The homepage of a website
(b) A specific webpage designed to capture leads or prompt a specific action
(c) A page with general information about a company
(d) The contact page of a website

160. In Direct Marketing, what is the term for a communication sent to a customer with the aim of maintaining a positive relationship and encouraging repeat business?
(a) Customer acquisition
(b) Customer retention
(c) Generic marketing
(d) Product promotion

161. What is the term for a message or offer that is tailored to an individual customer's preferences and behavior in Direct Marketing?
(a) Segmented marketing
(b) Mass marketing
(c) Customized marketing
(d) Blanket marketing

162. In Direct Marketing, what does the term "opt-in" mean for customers?
(a) Customers are automatically subscribed to marketing messages
(b) Customers have no choice in receiving marketing communications
(c) Customers have given explicit consent to receive marketing messages
(d) Customers have chosen to unsubscribe from marketing messages

163. What is the term for the practice of sending marketing messages that are relevant to a customer's location or physical surroundings in Direct Marketing?
(a) Geotargeting
(b) Demographic targeting
(c) Behavioral targeting
(d) Mass marketing

164. "Lifetime value" in Direct Marketing refers to
(a) The total number of customers acquired in a given period
(b) The total revenue generated from a customer throughout their entire relationship with a company
(c) The cost of acquiring a new customer
(d) The number of leads generated in a marketing campaign

165. What is the term for marketing messages that are sent to a broad audience, often without specific targeting or personalization in Direct Marketing?
(a) Permission marketing
(b) Generic marketing
(c) Targeted marketing
(d) One-to-one marketing

166. What is the term for the process of optimizing a website to improve its visibility in search engine results pages?
(a) Content marketing
(b) Social media marketing
(c) Search engine optimization (SEO)
(d) Email marketing

167. In digital marketing, what does the acronym "PPC" stand for?
(a) Pay-Per-Click
(b) Public Profile Count
(c) Product Promotion Campaign
(d) Premium Product Catalog

168. Which digital marketing strategy involves creating valuable content to attract and engage a target audience, ultimately driving profitable customer action?
(a) Social media marketing
(b) Content marketing
(c) Affiliate marketing
(d) Mobile marketing

169. "CTR" in digital marketing stands for
(a) Click-Through Rate
(b) Conversion Tracking Ratio
(c) Content Test and Response
(d) Customer Targeting and Retention

170. In email marketing, what is the term for the percentage of people who receive an email and take a desired action, such as making a purchase or signing up for a newsletter?
(a) Bounce rate
(b) Open rate
(c) Click-through rate (CTR)
(d) Conversion rate

171. What is the primary goal of "affiliate marketing" in the digital marketing context?
(a) Selling products directly to customers
(b) Promoting a company's own products
(c) Earning commissions by promoting other company's products or services
(d) Reducing advertising expenses

172. "A/B testing" in digital marketing involves
(a) Creating a digital advertising campaign
(b) Testing two versions of a webpage or campaign to determine which one performs better
(c) Targeting all potential customers simultaneously
(d) Ignoring customer feedback

173. What is the primary purpose of a "landing page" in digital marketing?
(a) Serving as the homepage of a website
(b) Collecting customer information
(c) Redirecting users to social media profiles
(d) Providing general information about a company

174. "Influencer marketing" in digital marketing involves collaborating with individuals who have a significant following on
(a) Print media
(b) Television
(c) Social media and online platforms
(d) Radio

175. What does the term "retargeting" or "remarketing" mean in digital marketing?
(a) Targeting new customers
(b) Targeting customers who have previously visited a website but did not make a desired action
(c) Targeting competitors
(d) Reducing marketing budgets

176. Which digital marketing channel is primarily known for its "stories" feature, short-lived content, and real-time engagement with audiences?
(a) Search engine marketing
(b) Email marketing
(c) Social media marketing
(d) Affiliate marketing

177. "SERPs" in digital marketing stands for
(a) Social Engagement Ratio and Performance Score
(b) Search Engine Results Pages
(c) Site Engagement and Retention Statistics
(d) Sales and Revenue Prediction System

178. In digital marketing, what does the term "KPI" stand for?
(a) Key Performance Indicator
(b) Keyword Performance Insights
(c) Knowledge of Product Implementation
(d) Kiosk Placement Index

179. Which type of digital advertising is characterized by the format of brief video clips that play before, during, or after online video content?
(a) Social media advertising
(b) Display advertising
(c) Video advertising
(d) Email advertising

180. What is the term for the practice of creating and sharing online content, such as blogs, videos, and social media posts, to attract and engage a target audience?
(a) Video marketing
(b) Content marketing
(c) Email marketing
(d) Affiliate marketing

181. In digital marketing, what does "UGC" typically refer to?
(a) Unwanted Global Campaigns
(b) User-Generated Content
(c) Universal Growth Calculator
(d) Underlying Graphic Components

182. What is the term for the practice of segmenting a target audience into smaller, more specific groups based on various characteristics for more personalized marketing efforts?
(a) Mass marketing
(b) Niche marketing
(c) Customer profiling
(d) Market segmentation

183. In digital marketing, what does the term "CTA" stand for?
(a) Customer Testimonials and Awards
(b) Content Tracking Analysis
(c) Call to Action
(d) Customer Targeting Approach

184. "SMM" in digital marketing stands for
(a) Social Media Management
(b) Search Marketing Metrics
(c) Sales and Market Management
(d) Site Mapping and Monitoring

185. Which digital marketing channel is primarily focused on promoting products and services through email messages to a targeted list of recipients?
(a) Search engine marketing
(b) Social media marketing
(c) Email marketing
(d) Affiliate marketing

186. What does the term "ROI" stand for in the context of digital marketing?
(a) Return on Investment
(b) Reach of Interest
(c) Rate of Inquiry
(d) Revenue Over Internet

187. In digital marketing, what is the term for the practice of targeting potential customers based on their online behavior, such as website visits and interactions?
(a) Behavioral targeting
(b) Demographic targeting
(c) Geographic targeting
(d) Psychographic targeting

188. "Geo-fencing" in digital marketing involves
(a) Building virtual boundaries to track customer locations
(b) Focusing on global marketing efforts
(c) Targeting customers based on their demographic profile
(d) Ignoring geographic location in marketing campaigns

189. What is the term for the practice of using data to analyze and predict customer behavior and preferences in digital marketing?
(a) Data mining
(b) Data encryption
(c) Data obfuscation
(d) Data manipulation

190. "PPV" in digital marketing stands for
(a) Pay-Per-Visit
(b) Popular Product Videos
(c) Public Product Views
(d) Page Post Views

191. What is the primary focus of Green Marketing?
(a) Maximizing profits
(b) Promoting environmentally friendly products and practices
(c) Reducing marketing expenses
(d) Ignoring customer preferences

192. Which of the following is a key principle of Green Marketing?
(a) Wasteful consumption
(b) Disregard for sustainability
(c) Eco-friendly product development
(d) High energy consumption

193. In Green Marketing, what does the term "sustainable development" refer to?

(a) Focusing solely on short-term economic gains
(b) Meeting the needs of the present without compromising the ability of future generations to meet their own needs
(c) Ignoring environmental regulations
(d) Maximizing resource depletion

194. "Biodegradable packaging" in Green Marketing refers to
(a) Packaging that lasts indefinitely in landfills
(b) Packaging that is harmful to the environment
(c) Packaging that can naturally decompose and return to the environment
(d) Packaging made from non-renewable resources

195. What is the term for the practice of providing information about a product's environmental impact, such as its carbon footprint or energy efficiency?
(a) Greenwashing
(b) Eco-labeling
(c) Environmental obfuscation
(d) Sustainable branding

196. In Green Marketing, what does "cradle-to-cradle" design aim to achieve?
(a) Maximizing waste
(b) Designing products with a limited lifespan
(c) Designing products that can be recycled or repurposed at the end of their life cycle
(d) Minimizing environmental regulations

197. What is the term for a product's ability to be repaired and maintained, thus extending its useful life?
(a) Planned obsolescence
(b) Disposable design
(c) Built-in durability
(d) Product longevity

198. "Carbon footprint" in Green Marketing refers to
(a) The amount of carbon dioxide emitted by a company's marketing efforts
(b) The environmental impact of a product, particularly related to its greenhouse gas emissions
(c) The carbon content of packaging materials
(d) The amount of carbon found in marketing campaigns

199. What is the term for the practice of making a product with fewer materials or using materials that have a lower environmental impact?
(a) Resource depletion
(b) Green design
(c) Excessive consumption
(d) Unsustainable production

200. In Green Marketing, what is the term for promoting the use of public transportation or carpooling as a way to reduce environmental impact?
(a) Greenwashing
(b) Sustainable branding
(c) Promoting eco-friendly transportation
(d) Maximizing individual car usage

201. What is the term for the practice of falsely promoting a product as environmentally friendly when it is not?
(a) Green labeling
(b) Eco-hype
(c) Greenwashing
(d) Environmental branding

202. "Renewable energy sourcing" in Green Marketing refers to
(a) Using energy sources that are not replenished by nature
(b) Focusing on non-renewable energy sources
(c) Obtaining energy from sources like wind, solar, or hydropower
(d) Ignoring energy conservation

203. Which of the following is a primary aim of Green Marketing?
(a) Maximizing waste production
(b) Promoting energy-intensive manufacturing processes
(c) Promoting responsible and sustainable consumer behavior
(d) Ignoring environmental concerns

204. In Green Marketing, what is the term for the practice of reducing the amount of packaging used for a product?
(a) Excessive packaging
(b) Eco-labeling
(c) Minimal packaging
(d) Over-packaging

205. "Eco-efficiency" in Green Marketing involves
(a) Maximizing resource use
(b) Minimizing environmental impact while

optimizing economic performance
(c) Ignoring economic considerations
(d) Focusing on waste generation

206. What does the term "closed-loop supply chain" mean in Green Marketing?
(a) A supply chain that is unsustainable
(b) A supply chain that produces excessive waste
(c) A supply chain designed to minimize waste and promote recycling
(d) A supply chain with no environmental considerations

207. In Green Marketing, what does the term "green pricing" involve?
(a) Charging higher prices for eco-friendly products
(b) Reducing product prices to encourage consumption
(c) Promoting environmentally harmful pricing strategies
(d) Ignoring price considerations

208. "Biodiversity conservation" in Green Marketing refers to
(a) Encouraging the extinction of species
(b) Promoting the preservation of various species and ecosystems
(c) Focusing on practices harmful to the environment
(d) Ignoring the natural world

209. In Green Marketing, what is the term for the practice of providing information on the responsible use and disposal of a product?
(a) Greenwashing
(b) Sustainable branding
(c) End-of-life instructions
(d) Environmental labeling

210. "Green branding" in Green Marketing involves
(a) Promoting eco-unfriendly products
(b) Using environmental themes in brand identity and promotion
(c) Ignoring branding considerations
(d) Focusing on traditional branding strategies

211. What is the term for the practice of designing products to be easily recycled and used as materials for new products?
(a) Material inefficiency
(b) Single-use product design
(c) Circular economy design
(d) Unsustainable design

212. In Green Marketing, what does the term "LOHAS" stand for?
(a) Lasting Order and Harmony in Sales
(b) Lifestyle of Health and Sustainability
(c) Luxury Offerings for High-end Audiences
(d) Limited Opportunities for High Sales

213. What is the term for the practice of reusing and refurbishing products to extend their lifespan, reducing waste and environmental impact?
(a) Disposable product design
(b) Planned obsolescence
(c) Product reengineering
(d) Product upcycling

214. "Triple bottom line" in Green Marketing considers
(a) Profit as the sole measure of success
(b) Three key factors profit, people, and the planet, as measures of success
(c) Ignoring financial performance
(d) Reducing business operations

215. What is the term for the practice of incorporating environmental concerns and social responsibility into a company's core mission and values?
(a) Greenwashing
(b) Sustainable branding
(c) Green mission integration
(d) Ignoring corporate values

216. What does "entry mode" refer to in international marketing?
(a) The mode of transportation for exporting goods
(b) The process of launching a new product in the domestic market
(c) The strategy used to enter a foreign market
(d) The selection of advertising channels

217. In international marketing, which entry mode is characterized by a domestic firm granting the right to use its brand, product, or technology to a foreign firm for a fee or royalty?
(a) Exporting
(b) Licensing
(c) Joint venture
(d) Direct investment

218. What is a "joint venture" in international marketing?

(a) A type of export agreement
(b) A collaborative business arrangement between a domestic and foreign firm
(c) A one-time international marketing campaign
(d) An exclusive distribution agreement

219. Which entry mode in international marketing involves a firm establishing its presence in a foreign market by setting up a wholly-owned subsidiary?
(a) Exporting
(b) Franchising
(c) Direct investment
(d) Licensing

220. In international marketing, what is the "exporting" entry mode primarily associated with?
(a) Selling goods or services to a foreign market without establishing local operations
(b) Collaborative partnerships with foreign firms
(c) Local production and distribution
(d) Licensing of intellectual property

221. Which entry mode in international marketing allows a firm to offer its products or services through a foreign firm's distribution network?
(a) Licensing
(b) Exporting
(c) Franchising
(d) Strategic alliance

222. In international marketing, what does "franchising" involve?
(a) Exporting products to a foreign market
(b) Licensing the use of a brand and business model to a foreign firm
(c) Setting up wholly-owned subsidiaries in a foreign market
(d) Forming a joint venture with a foreign partner

223. Which international marketing entry mode involves selling products or services directly to foreign customers via the internet?
(a) Exporting
(b) Licensing
(c) E-commerce
(d) Direct investment

224. What is the term for the practice of adapting a company's products or services to meet the specific needs and preferences of a foreign market?
(a) Global standardization
(b) Market aggregation
(c) Product localization
(d) Export orientation

225. In international marketing, what is the "global standardization" approach?
(a) Adapting products and services to the preferences of each local market
(b) Developing a consistent global marketing strategy and product offering
(c) Exporting products without any changes to foreign markets
(d) Focusing on local marketing efforts exclusively

226. "Market aggregation" in international marketing refers to
(a) Tailoring marketing efforts to meet local market preferences
(b) Combining multiple markets into a single market segment
(c) Creating unique marketing strategies for each market
(d) Ignoring the importance of market diversity

227. What is the term for the systematic process of gathering, recording, and analyzing data about a foreign market and its consumers in international marketing?
(a) Market entry mode
(b) Export planning
(c) Market research
(d) Licensing strategy

228. In international marketing, "global marketing mix" typically includes which of the following elements?
(a) A standardized marketing strategy for all markets
(b) Customized marketing strategies for each market
(c) Local production of goods and services
(d) Focusing exclusively on the domestic market

229. In international marketing, what is the term for a strategy that combines global standardization with some degree of customization to meet local preferences?
(a) Market aggregation
(b) Product localization
(c) Global orientation
(d) Export standardization

230. Which element of the marketing mix in international marketing deals with pricing strategies tailored to each specific foreign market?
(a) Product (b) Promotion
(c) Place (d) Price

231. In international marketing, "cultural adaptation" refers to
(a) Ignoring cultural differences in marketing efforts
(b) Modifying marketing strategies and products to align with local cultural norms
(c) Using a single marketing approach across all cultures
(d) Exporting products without any consideration of culture

232. What is the term for adjusting a product's design and features to meet the requirements and preferences of a specific foreign market in international marketing?
(a) Market adaptation
(b) Product standardization
(c) Export strategy
(d) Marketing mix alignment

233. "Geographic diversification" in international marketing involves
(a) Focusing on a single geographic market
(b) Expanding operations to multiple geographic markets
(c) Adapting marketing strategies to local culture only
(d) Creating global marketing strategies

234. Which of the following is an element of the "promotion" component of the marketing mix in international marketing?
(a) Adapting product design to meet local preferences
(b) Adjusting pricing strategies
(c) Advertising and communication efforts
(d) Determining distribution channels

235. In international marketing, what does "country-of-origin effect" refer to?
(a) The preference of consumers for products originating from their own country
(b) The impact of a product's origin on its quality and value perception
(c) The practice of targeting specific countries in marketing campaigns
(d) Ignoring the influence of a product's origin

236. In international marketing, what is the "grey market" or "parallel import"?
(a) The market for products not officially authorized for sale in a particular country
(b) The authorized distribution channel for a product in a foreign market
(c) A type of licensing agreement
(d) A market segment for elderly consumers

237. What does the term "product bundling" refer to in international marketing?
(a) Offering a single product at multiple price points
(b) Combining several products or services into a single package
(c) Selling products without any additional services
(d) Adjusting product features to meet local regulations

238. In international marketing, what is the "ethnocentric approach" to marketing?
(a) Focusing exclusively on the domestic market
(b) Adapting products to meet local preferences
(c) Using a standardized global marketing strategy
(d) Prioritizing a single foreign market over all others

239. Which of the following is an example of an indirect export strategy in international marketing?
(a) Selling products directly to foreign customers
(b) Establishing a wholly-owned subsidiary in a foreign market
(c) Using a local intermediary to sell products to foreign customers
(d) Licensing a foreign firm to use a brand

240. In international marketing, what is the term for establishing local production facilities in a foreign market?
(a) Exporting
(b) Licensing
(c) Direct investment
(d) Indirect export

ANSWER KEY

1. (c)	**2.** (a)	**3.** (a)	**4.** (a)	**5.** (b)	**6.** (a)	**7.** (c)	**8.** (b)	**9.** (c)	**10.** (a)
11. (d)	**12.** (a)	**13.** (d)	**14.** (b)	**15.** (d)	**16.** (b)	**17.** (b)	**18.** (b)	**19.** (b)	**20.** (c)
21. (c)	**22.** (c)	**23.** (a)	**24.** (b)	**25.** (b)	**26.** (c)	**27.** (d)	**28.** (c)	**29.** (b)	**30.** (c)
31. (c)	**32.** (c)	**33.** (c)	**34.** (a)	**35.** (c)	**36.** (c)	**37.** (a)	**38.** (b)	**39.** (b)	**40.** (b)
41. (c)	**42.** (c)	**43.** (a)	**44.** (b)	**45.** (b)	**46.** (c)	**47.** (d)	**48.** (c)	**49.** (b)	**50.** (c)
51. (c)	**52.** (c)	**53.** (c)	**54.** (a)	**55.** (c)	**56.** (c)	**57.** (a)	**58.** (b)	**59.** (b)	**60.** (b)
61. (a)	**62.** (d)	**63.** (d)	**64.** (c)	**65.** (b)	**66.** (b)	**67.** (a)	**68.** (b)	**69.** (c)	**70.** (c)
71. (b)	**72.** (c)	**73.** (b)	**74.** (b)	**75.** (a)	**76.** (c)	**77.** (d)	**78.** (a)	**79.** (a)	**80.** (b)
81. (c)	**82.** (c)	**83.** (b)	**84.** (c)	**85.** (c)	**86.** (d)	**87.** (b)	**88.** (b)	**89.** (a)	**90.** (b)
91. (b)	**92.** (a)	**93.** (c)	**94.** (c)	**95.** (a)	**96.** (c)	**97.** (c)	**98.** (b)	**99.** (c)	**100.** (c)
101. (c)	**102.** (a)	**103.** (c)	**104.** (a)	**105.** (c)	**106.** (c)	**107.** (d)	**108.** (c)	**109.** (c)	**110.** (b)
111. (b)	**112.** (c)	**113.** (c)	**114.** (c)	**115.** (c)	**116.** (c)	**117.** (b)	**118.** (b)	**119.** (c)	**120.** (b)
121. (b)	**122.** (a)	**123.** (c)	**124.** (b)	**125.** (b)	**126.** (d)	**127.** (b)	**128.** (b)	**129.** (c)	**130.** (a)
131. (d)	**132.** (a)	**133.** (d)	**134.** (b)	**135.** (a)	**136.** (b)	**137.** (c)	**138.** (c)	**139.** (a)	**140.** (c)
141. (c)	**142.** (a)	**143.** (a)	**144.** (d)	**145.** (a)	**146.** (a)	**147.** (b)	**148.** (b)	**149.** (c)	**150.** (b)
151. (c)	**152.** (b)	**153.** (c)	**154.** (c)	**155.** (c)	**156.** (b)	**157.** (b)	**158.** (b)	**159.** (b)	**160.** (b)
161. (c)	**162.** (c)	**163.** (a)	**164.** (b)	**165.** (b)	**166.** (c)	**167.** (a)	**168.** (b)	**169.** (a)	**170.** (d)
171. (c)	**172.** (b)	**173.** (b)	**174.** (c)	**175.** (b)	**176.** (c)	**177.** (b)	**178.** (a)	**179.** (c)	**180.** (b)
181. (b)	**182.** (d)	**183.** (c)	**184.** (a)	**185.** (c)	**186.** (a)	**187.** (a)	**188.** (a)	**189.** (a)	**190.** (a)
191. (b)	**192.** (c)	**193.** (b)	**194.** (c)	**195.** (b)	**196.** (c)	**197.** (d)	**198.** (b)	**199.** (b)	**200.** (c)
201. (c)	**202.** (c)	**203.** (c)	**204.** (c)	**205.** (b)	**206.** (c)	**207.** (a)	**208.** (b)	**209.** (c)	**210.** (b)
211. (c)	**212.** (b)	**213.** (d)	**214.** (b)	**215.** (c)	**216.** (c)	**217.** (b)	**218.** (b)	**219.** (c)	**220.** (a)
221. (d)	**222.** (b)	**223.** (c)	**224.** (c)	**225.** (b)	**226.** (b)	**227.** (c)	**228.** (a)	**229.** (c)	**230.** (d)
231. (b)	**232.** (a)	**233.** (b)	**234.** (c)	**235.** (b)	**236.** (a)	**237.** (b)	**238.** (a)	**239.** (c)	**240.** (c)

UNIT 8

SYLLABUS

- Statistics for Management: Concept, Measures of Central Tendency and Dispersion, Probability Distribution – Binominal, Poison, Normal and Exponential
- Data Collection & Questionnaire Design
- Sampling – Concept, Process and Techniques
- Hypothesis Testing – Procedure; T, Z, F, Chi-square tests
- Correlation and Regression Analysis
- Operations Management – Role and Scope
- Facility Location and Layout – Site Selection and Analysis, Layout – Design and Process
- Enterprise Resource Planning – ERP Modules, ERP implementation
- Scheduling; Loading, Sequencing and Monitoring
- Quality Management and Statistical Quality Control, Quality Circles, Total Quality Management – KAIZEN, Benchmarking, Six Sigma; ISO 9000 Series Standards
- Operation Research – Transportation, Queuing Decision Theory, PERT / CPM

STATISTICS FOR MANAGEMENT

MEASURES OF CENTRAL TENDENCY

We have studied how to collect raw data, its classification and tabulation in a useful form, which contributes in solving many problems of statistical concern. Yet, this is not sufficient, because practical purposes, there is need for further condensation, particularly when we want to compare two or more different distributions. We may reduce the entire distribution to one number which represents the distribution.

A single value which can be considered as typical or representative of a set of observations and around which the observations can be considered as centered is called an 'Average' (or average value) or a center of location. Since such typical values tends to lie centrally within a set of observations when arranged according to magnitudes, averages are called measures of central tendency.

In fact the distribution have a typical value (average) about which, the observations are more or less symmetrically distributed. This is of great importance, both theoretically and practically. Dr. A.L. Bowley correctly stated, "Statistics may rightly be called the science of averages."

The word average is commonly used in day-to-day conversations. For example, we may say that Vinod is an average boy of my class; we may talk of an average Indian, average income, etc. When it is said, "Vinod is an average student," it means is that he is neither very good nor very bad, but a mediocre student. However, in statistics the term average has a different meaning.

The fundamental measures of tendencies are:

(1) Arithmetic mean
(2) Median
(3) Mode
(4) Geometric mean
(5) Harmonic mean
(6) Weighted averages

However, the most common measures of central tendencies or Locations are Arithmetic mean, median and mode.

Arithmetic Mean

This is the most commonly used average which you have also studied and used in lower grades. Here are two definitions given by two great masters of statistics.

Horace Sacrist. "Arithmetic mean is the amount secured by dividing the sum of values of the items in a series by their number."

W.I. King. "The arithmetic average may be defined as the sum of aggregate of a series of items divided by their number."

Thus, the students should add all observations (values of all items) together and divide this sum by the number of observations (or items).

Ungrouped Data

Suppose, we have 'n' observations (or measures) x_1, x_2, x_3, ..., x_n then the Arithmetic mean is obviously $\frac{x_1 + x_2 + x_3 + \ldots + x_n}{n}$.

We shall use the symbol x (pronounced as x bar) to denote the Arithmetic mean. Since, we have to write the sum of observations very frequently, we use the usual symbol 'Σ' (pronounced as sigma) to denote the sum. The symbol x_i will be used to denote, in general the 'ith' observation. Then the sum, $x_1 + x_2 + x_3 + \ldots\ldots + x_n$ will be represented by $\sum_{i=1}^{n} x_i$ or $\sum x_i$ simply.

Therefore, the Arithmetic Mean of the set $x_1 + x_2 + x_3 + \ldots\ldots + x_n$ is given by,

$$\overline{x} = \frac{\sum x_i}{n} = \frac{x_1 + x_2 + x_3 + \ldots + x_n}{n}$$

This method is known as the "Direct Method".

Indirect Method (Assumed Mean Method)

The assumed mean is used to compute the arithmetic mean and standard deviation for a grouped data. In other words, by assuming the mean for the grouped data, the actual mean can be obtained easily. Thus, the method of calculating the mean by assuming the mean is known as assumed mean method.

$$\bar{u} = \frac{\sum u_i}{n} \text{ where } u = x_i - A$$

A = Assumed Mean = A + $\bar{u}$

Short-cut Method

Sometimes the values of x are very big and in that case, to simplify the calculation the short-cut method is used. For this, first you assume a mean (called as the assumed mean). Let it be A. Now find the deviations of all the values of x from A. We now get a new variable $u_i = x_i - A$

Now find

$$\bar{u} = \frac{\sum u_i}{n} \text{ then } \bar{x} = \frac{\sum u_i}{n}$$

or $\bar{x} = A + \bar{u}$

Discrete Series

There is a difference in the methods for finding the arithmetic means of the individual series and a discrete series. In the discrete series, every term (*i.e.* value of x) is multiplied by its corresponding frequency ($f_i x_i$) and then their total (sum) is found ($\Sigma f_i x_i$). The arithmetic mean is then obtained by dividing the total frequency (Σf) by the above sum so obtained.

Therefore, if the observations $x_1 + x_2 + x_3 + ... + x_n$ are repeated $f_1 + f_2 + f_3 + ... + f_n$ times, then we have:

$$\text{Arithmetic mean } (\bar{x}) = \frac{\sum f_i x_i}{\sum f_i} \text{ i.e. } \frac{f_1 x_1 + f_2 x_2 + f_3 x_3 + ... + f_n x_n}{f_1 + f_2 + f_3 + ... + f_n}$$

The formula for arithmetic mean by direct method and by the short-cut methods are as follows:

Direct Method Short-cut Method

$$\bar{x} = \frac{\sum f_i x_i}{\sum f_i} \Rightarrow \bar{x} = A + \bar{u} \text{ where } \bar{u} = \frac{\sum f_i u_i}{\sum f_i}$$

and $u = x_i - A$

$$\text{Therefore, } \bar{x} = A + \frac{\sum f_i u_i}{\sum f_i}$$

Arithmetic Mean for Grouped Data

Continuous Series. The procedure of finding the arithmetic mean in this series, is the same as we have used in the discrete series. The only difference is that in this series, we are given class-intervals, whose mid-values (class-marks) are to be calculated first.

$$\text{Formula, Arithmetic mean } (\bar{x}) = \frac{\sum f_i x_i}{\sum f_i}$$

where x = mid-value

Step-Deviation Method. Here, all class intervals are of the same width say 'c'. This method is employed in place of the Short-cut method. We measure all the class-marks (mid values) from some convenient value, say 'A', which generally should be taken as the class-mark of a class of maximum frequency or of a class which is the middle one. All the class marks happen to be multiples of c, since all class intervals are equal. We consider class frequencies as if they are centered at the corresponding class-marks.

Theorem. If $x_1, x_2, x_3, ..., x_n$ are n values of the class marks with frequencies $f_1, f_2, f_3, ...f_n$ respectively and if each x_i is expressed in terms of the new variable u_i by the relation $x_i = A + cu_i$ then, with the usual notation, we have $\bar{x} = A + c\bar{u}$

where, $\bar{u} = \dfrac{\sum f_i u_i}{\sum f_i}$ and $u_i = \dfrac{x_i - A}{c}$

This method is also known as the "Coding method."

Properties of Arithmetic Mean

1. The sum of the deviations, of all the values of x, from their arithmetic mean, is zero.

   Justification: $\sum f_i(x_i - \bar{x}) = \sum f_i x_i - \bar{x}\sum f_i = 0$

   Since $\bar{x}$ is a constant, $\bar{x} = \dfrac{\sum f_i x_i}{\sum f_i}$ $\quad \therefore \sum f_i x_i = \bar{x}\sum f_i$

2. The product of the arithmetic mean and the number of items gives the total of all items.

   Justification: $\bar{x} = \dfrac{\sum f_i x_i}{\sum f_i} \Rightarrow \sum f_i x_i = \bar{x}\sum f_i$

   or $\bar{x} = \dfrac{\sum x_i}{N} \Rightarrow \bar{x} \cdot N = \sum x_i$

3. If $\bar{x}_1$ and $\bar{x}_2$ are the arithmetic mean of two samples of sizes n_1 and n_2 respectively then, the arithmetic mean $\bar{x}$ of the distribution combining the two can be calculated as

   $$\bar{x} = \frac{n_1\bar{x}_1 + n_2\bar{x}_2}{n_1 + n_2}$$

   This formula can be extended for more groups or samples.

   $$\bar{x}_1 = \frac{\sum x_{1i}}{n_1} \Rightarrow \sum x_{1i} = n_1\bar{x}_1$$

   Justification: $\bar{x}_1 = \dfrac{\sum x_{1i}}{n_1} \Rightarrow \sum x_{1i} = n_1\bar{x}_1$ = total of the observations of the first sample

   Similarly, $\sum x_{2i} = n_2\bar{x}_2$ = total of the observations of the first sample

   The combined mean of the two samples

   $$= \frac{\text{combined mean}}{n_1 + n_2}$$

   $$\bar{x} = \frac{n_1\bar{x}_1 + n_2\bar{x}_2}{n_1 + n_2}$$

Merits

1. It is rigidly defined. Its value is always definite.
2. It is easy to calculate and easy to understand. Hence, it is very popular.

3. It is based on all the observations; so that it becomes a good representative.
4. It can be easily used for comparison.
5. It is capable of further algebraic treatment such as finding the sum of the values of the observations, if the mean and the total number of the observations are given; finding the combined arithmetic mean when different groups are given etc.
6. It is not affected much by sampling fluctuations.

Demerits

1. It is affected by outliers or extreme values. For example, the average (A.) mean of 10, 15, 25 and 500 is $\bar{x} = \dfrac{10+15+25+500}{4} = 137.5$

   Now, observe first three values whose arithmetic. mean is $\dfrac{10+15+25}{3} = 16.67$ (approx.)

   Due to the outlier 500 the arithmetic. mean of the four numbers is raised to 137.5. In such a case arithmetic. mean is not a good representative of the given data.
2. It is a value which may not be present in the given data.
3. Many a times it gives absurd results like 4.4 children per family.
4. It is not possible to take out the average of ratios and percentages.
5. We cannot calculate it when open-end class intervals are present in the data.

Median

It is the value of the size of the central item of the arranged data (data arranged in the ascending or the descending order). Thus, it is the value of the middle item and divides the series in to equal parts.

In **Connor's words** – "The median is that value of the variable which divides the group into two equal parts, one part comprising all values greater and the other all values lesser than the median." For example, the daily wages of 7 workers are 5, 7, 9, 11, 12, 14 and 15 dollars. This series contains 7 terms. The fourth term *i.e.* 11 is the median.

Median in Individual Series (Ungrouped Data)

Steps

1. Set the individual series either in the ascending (increasing) or in the descending (decreasing) order, of the size of its items or observations.
2. If the total number of observations be 'n' then

   A. If 'n' is odd,

   $$\text{The median} = \text{size of} \left(\frac{n+1}{2}\right)^{\text{th}} \text{observation}$$

   B. If 'n' is even, the median

   $$= \frac{1}{2}\left[\begin{array}{l} \text{size of} \left(\dfrac{n}{2}\right)^{\text{th}} \text{observations} \\ + \text{size of} \left(\dfrac{n+1}{2}\right)^{\text{th}} \text{observations} \end{array}\right]$$

Median in Discrete Series

Steps :

1. Arrange the data in ascending or descending order of magnitude.

2. Find the cumulative frequencies
3. Apply the formula :

   A. If 'n' = $\sum f_i$ (odd) then,

   $$\text{Median} = \text{size of} \left(\frac{n+1}{2}\right)^{\text{th}} \text{item}$$

   B. If 'n' = $\sum f_i$ (even) then,

   $$\text{Median} = \frac{1}{2}\left[\begin{array}{l}\text{size of} \left(\frac{n}{2}\right)^{\text{th}} \text{item} \\ + \text{size of} \left(\frac{n+2}{2}\right)^{\text{th}} \text{item}\end{array}\right]$$

Median in Continuous Series (Grouped Data)

Steps :

1. Determine the particular class in which the value of the median lies. Use $n/2$ as the rank of the median and not $\left(\frac{n+1}{2}\right)$.
2. After ascertaining the class in which median lies, the following formula is used for determining the exact value of the median.

   $$\text{Median} = l_1 + \left(\frac{N/2 - c.f.}{f}\right)(l_2 - l_1)$$

   where, l_1 = lower limit of the median class, the class in which the middle item of the distribution lies.

   l_2 = upper limit of the median class

   $c.f.$ = cumulative frequency of the class preceding the median class

   f = sample frequency of the median class

   It should be noted that while interpolating the median value of frequency distribution it is assumed that the variable is continuous and that there is an orderly and even distribution of items within each class.

> The median is the value that is the mid-point of a group of values, having an equal number of items in the group above and below it. For instance, in a room with five people aged 23, 25, 37, 44 and 87, the median age is 37, as there are an equal number of persons older and younger than 37. The median is used where strong outliers may skew the representation of the group, such as with incomes. If you have one person who earns $1 billion a year and nine other people who earn under $100,000 a year, the mean income for people in the group would be around $100 million, a gross distortion. The median income would be under $100,000, more closely representing the situation of the majority of the group.

Note that, while calculating the median of a series, it must be put in the 'exclusive class-interval' form. If the original series is in inclusive type, first convert it into the exclusive type and then find its median.

Merits

1. It is rigidly defined.

2. It is easy to calculate and understand.
3. It is not affected by extreme values like the arithmetic mean. For example, 5 persons have their incomes Rs 2000, Rs 2500, Rs 2600, Rs 3000, Rs 5000. The median would be Rs 2600 while the arithmetic mean would be Rs 3020.
4. It can be found by mere inspection.
5. It is fully representative and can be computed easily.
6. It can be used for qualitative studies.
7. Even if the extreme values are unknown, median can be calculated if one knows the number of items.
8. It can be obtained graphically.

Mode

It is the size of that item which possesses the maximum frequency. According to Professor Kenney and Keeping, the value of the variable which occurs most frequently in a distribution is called the mode.

It is the most common value and point of maximum density.

Ungrouped Data (Individual Series)

The mode of this series can be obtained by mere inspection. The number which occurs most often is the mode.

Grouped Data

Steps :

1. Determine the modal class which as the maximum frequency.
2. By interpolation the value of the mode can be calculated as -

$$\text{Mode} = l_1 - \left(\frac{f_1 - f_0}{2f_1 - f_0 - f_2}\right)(l_2 - l_1)$$

where

l_1 = lower limit of the modal class
l_2 = upper limit of the modal class
f_1 = frequency of the modal class
f_0 = frequency of the class preceding to the modal class
f_2 = frequency of the class succeeding the modal class

Merits

1. It is simple to calculate.
2. In an individual or discrete distribution it can be located by mere inspection.
3. It is easy to understand. Everyone is used to the idea of average size of a garment, an average American etc.
4. It is not isolated like the median as it is the most common item.
5. Like the Average mean, it is not a value which cannot be found in the series.
6. It is not necessary to know all the items. What we need in the point of maximum density frequency.
7. It is not affected by sampling fluctuations.

Demerits

1. It is ill defined.
2. It is not based on all observations.
3. It is not capable of further algebraic treatment.
4. It is not a good representative of the data.
5. Sometimes there are more than one values of mode.

Empirical Relation between Mean, Median and Mode

A distribution in which the values of mean, median and mode coincide (*i.e.* mean = median = mode) is known as a symmetrical distribution. Conversely, when values of mean, median and mode are not equal the distribution is known as asymmetrical or skewed distribution. In moderately skewed or asymmetrical distribution a very important relationship exists among these three measures of central tendency. In such distributions the distance between the mean and median is about one-third of the distance between the mean and mode. Karl Pearson expressed this relationship as:

Mode = mean – 3 [mean – median]

Mode = 3 median – 2 mean

and Median = mode + $\frac{2}{3}$ [mean – mode]

Knowing any two values, the third can be computed.

Geometric Mean

Geometric Mean is a measure of central tendency which is generally used to compare two set of values. It is evaluated by finding product of all the numbers and then taking their n^{th} root. Geometric mean is different from arithmetic mean because it uses product of the observations rather than sum.

Formula for evaluating geometric mean is as follows, if we have n number of observations, then

$$\text{Geometric Mean} = \sqrt[n]{x_1 x_2 x_3 \ldots x_n}$$

Harmonic Mean

Harmonic Mean is also one of the different kinds of average and it is applied for the situations when you have a desired rate of average.

The reciprocal of the arithmetic mean is called as Harmonic Mean. It is calculated by dividing the number of observations by the sum of reciprocal of the observation.

The formula to find the harmonic mean is given by:

$$\text{Harmonic Mean (H)} = \frac{n}{\frac{1}{x_1} + \frac{1}{x_2} + \frac{1}{x_3} + \ldots \frac{1}{x_n}}$$

where, n = Total number of numbers or terms.

$x_1, x_2, x_3, \ldots x_n$ = Individual terms or individual values.

Weighted Mean (Averages)

Weighted Mean is a measurement of central tendency. It represents the average of a given data. Weighted mean is similar to arithmetic mean or sample mean. Weighted mean is calculated when data is given in a different way than in arithmetic mean or sample mean.

Sometimes, there are frequencies assigned to each term in the given data, then we can no longer use simple arithmetic mean formula. Few values may occur more frequently than others, therefore corresponding frequencies are allotted to each value. These frequencies are often referred as weights. In this case, weighted mean formula is used.

Weighted mean formula is as follows:

$$\bar{x} = \frac{\sum f_i x_i}{\sum f_i}$$

Where, $\bar{x}$ = weighted mean.

$x_i = x_1, x_2, x_3, ...$ = Items given.

and $f_i = f_1, f_2, f_3, ...$ = Frequencies corresponding to the given items

MEASURES OF DISPERSION

Range

In any statistical series, the difference between the largest and the smallest values is called as the range.

Thus Range (R) = L – S $\begin{cases} \text{L = Largest value of the series} \\ \text{S = Smallest value of the series} \end{cases}$

Coefficient of Range

The relative measure of the range. It is used in the comparative study of the dispersion co-efficient of

$$\text{Range} = \frac{L - S}{L + S}$$

Mean Deviation

Average deviations (mean deviation) is the average amount of variations (scatter) of the items in a distribution from either the mean or the median or the mode, ignoring the signs of these deviations by Clark and Senkade.

Individual Series

Steps :

(1) Find the mean or median or mode of the given series.

(2) Using and one of three, find the deviations (differences) of the items of the series from them. *i.e.* $x_i - x$, x_i – Me and x_i – Mo.
Me = Median and Mo = Mode.

(3) Find the absolute values of these deviations *i.e.* ignore there positive (+) and negative (–) signs.
i.e. $|x_i - x|$, $|x_i - \text{Me}|$ and $|x_i - \text{Mo}|$.

(4) Find the sum of these absolute deviations.
i.e. $\Sigma |x_i - x| +$, $\Sigma |x_i - \text{Me}|$, and $\Sigma |x_i - \text{Mo}|$.

(5) Find the mean deviation using the following formula.

M.D = $(\partial x) = \Sigma x_i - x$, $\partial(\text{Me}) = \Sigma x_i - \text{Me}$
or $\partial(\text{Mo}) = x_i \text{ Mo}$

Note that :

(i) generally M. D. obtained from the median is best for the practical purpose.

(ii) co-efficient of M. D. = $\frac{\partial \bar{x}}{x} = \frac{\partial(\text{Me})}{\text{Me}} = \frac{\partial(\text{Mo})}{\text{Mo}}$

Variance

The term variance was used to describe the square of the standard deviation R.A. Fisher in 1913. The concept of variance is of great importance in advanced work where it is possible to split the total into several parts, each attributable to one of the factors causing variations in their original series. Variance is defined as follows:

$$\text{Variance} = \frac{\Sigma(x_i - \overline{x})^2}{n}$$

Standard Deviation (S.D.)

It is the square root of the arithmetic mean of the square deviations of various values from their arithmetic mean. It is denoted by s.d. or σ.

Thus, s.d. $(\sigma_x) = \sqrt{\dfrac{\Sigma(x_i - \overline{x})^2}{n}}$ for the ungrouped data

$= \sqrt{\dfrac{\Sigma f_i(x_i - \overline{x})^2}{n}}$ for the grouped data

where $n = \Sigma f_i$

Merits

(1) It is rigidly defined and based on all observations.

(2) It is amenable to further algebraic treatment.

(3) It is not affected by sampling fluctuations.

(4) It is less erratic.

Demerits

(1) It is difficult to understand and calculate.

(2) It gives greater weight to extreme values.

Note that variance $V(x) = \dfrac{\Sigma(x_i - \overline{x})^2}{n}$ and

and s. d. (σ_x) = and $\sqrt{\dfrac{\Sigma(x_i - \overline{x})^2}{n}}$ and $\sqrt{\dfrac{\Sigma f_i(x_i - \overline{x})^2}{n}}$

Then $V(x) = \sigma_x^{\,2}$

Coefficient of Variation (C.V.)

To compare the variations (dispersion) of two different series, relative measures of standard deviation must be calculated. This is known as coefficient of variation or the coefficient of s.d. It's formula is

$$\text{C.V.} = \frac{\sigma_x}{\overline{x}} \times 100$$

Thus it is defined as the ratio s. d. to its mean.

Remark: It is given as a percentage and is used to compare the consistency or variability of two more series. The higher the C.V., the higher the variability and lower the C.V., the higher is the consistency of the data.

Combined Standard Deviation. If two sets containing n_1 and n_2 items having means x_1 and x_2 and standard deviations 1 and 2 respectively are taken together then,

(1) Mean of the combined data is $\bar{x} = \dfrac{n_1\bar{x}_1 + n_2\bar{x}_2}{n_1 + n_2}$

(2) s.d. of the combined set is $\sigma = \sqrt{\dfrac{n_1(\sigma_1^2 + d_1^2) + n_2(\sigma_2^2 + d_2^2)}{n_1 + n_2}}$

where $d_1 = \bar{x}_1 - \bar{x}$ and $d_2 = \bar{x}_2 - \bar{x}$

Percentile

The nth percentile is that value (or size) such that n% of values of the whole data lies below it. For example, a score of 7% from the topmost score would be 93th percentile as it is above 93% of the other scores.

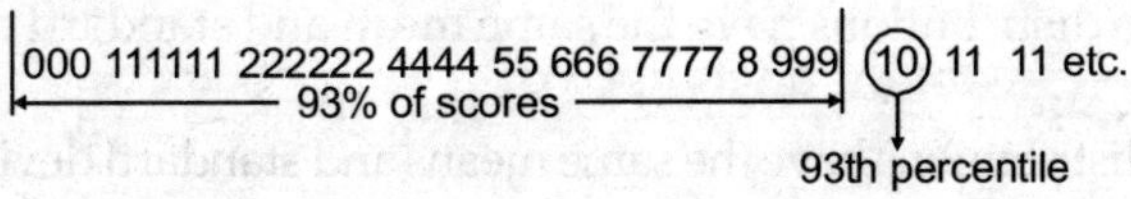

Percentile Range

It is used as one of the measure of dispersion. It is a set of data and is defined as $= P_{90} - P_{10}$ where P_{90} and P_{10} are the 90th and 10th percentile respectively. The semi - percentile range,

i.e. $\left(\dfrac{P_{90} - P_{10}}{2}\right)$ can also be used but it is not common in use.

Quartiles and Interquartile Range

If we concentrate on two extreme values (as in the case of range), we don't get any idea about the scatter of the data within the range (*i.e.* the two extreme values). If we discard these two values the limited range thus available might be more informative. For this reason the concept of interquartile range is developed. It is the range which includes middle 50% of the distribution. Here 1/4 (one quarter) of the lower end and 1/4 (one quarter) of the upper end of the observations are excluded.

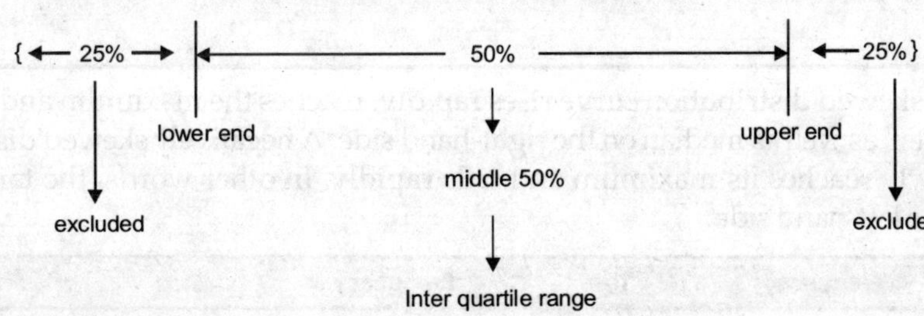

Now, the lower quartile (Q_1) is the 25th percentile and the upper quartile (Q_3) is the 75th percentile. It is interesting to note that the 50th percentile is the middle quartile (Q_2) which is in fact what you have studied under the title ' Median ". Thus, symbolically

Inter quartile range $= Q_3 - Q_1$

If we divide $(Q_3 - Q_1)$ by 2 we get what is known as Semi-Inter quartile range.

i.e. $\dfrac{Q_3 - Q_1}{2}$. It is known as Quartile deviation (Q. D or SI QR).

Therefore Q. D. (SI QR) $= \dfrac{Q_3 - Q_1}{2}$

MEASURES OF SKEWNESS, MOMENTS AND KURTOSIS

The voluminous raw data cannot be easily understood. Hence, we calculate the measures of central tendencies and obtain a representative figure. From the measures of variability, we can know that whether most of the items of the data are close to our away from these central tendencies. But these statical means and measures of variation are not enough to draw sufficient inferences about the data. Another aspect of the data is to know its symmetry. For "Graphic display" a frequency may be symmetrical about mode or may not be. This symmetry is well studied by the knowledge of the "Skewness." Still one more aspect of the curve that we need to know is its flatness or otherwise its top. This is understood by what is known as " Kurtosis."

Skewness

It may happen that two distributions have the same mean and standard deviations. For an example, see the below diagram.

Although the two distributions have the same means and standard deviations they are not identical. Where do they differ ?

They differ in symmetry. The left-hand side distribution is symmetrical one where as the distribution on the right-hand is asymmetrical or skewed. For a symmetrical distribution, the values, of equal distances on either side of the mode, have equal frequencies. Thus, the mode, median and mean - all coincide. Its curve rises slowly, reaches a maximum (peak) and falls equally slowly (Fig. 1). But for a skewed distribution, the mean, mode and median do not coincide. Skewness is positive or negative as per the positions of the mean and median on the right or the left of the mode.

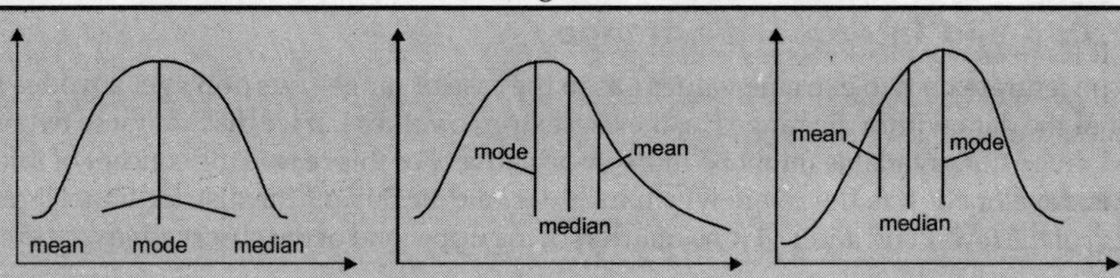

Fig. (1) Fig. (2) Fig. (3)

A positively skewed distribution curve rises rapidly, reaches the maximum and falls slowly. In other words, the tail as well as median on the right-hand side. A negatively skewed distribution curve (Fig. 3) rises slowly reaches its maximum and falls rapidly. In other words, the tail as well as the median are on the left-hand side.

Size	Frequency	Size	Frequency	Size	Frequency
1	12	1	4	1	3
2	13	2	6	2	7
3	14	3	12	3	8
4	15	4	10	4	10
5	14	5	8	5	12
6	13	6	7	6	6
7	12	7	3	7	4

Tests of Skewness

1. The values of mean, median and mode do not coincide. The more the difference between them, the more is the skewness.

2. Quartiles are not equidistant from the median, *i.e.* $(Q_3 - Me)$ $(Me - Q_1)$.
3. The sum of positive deviations from the median are not equal to the sum of the negative deviations.
4. Frequencies are not equally distributed at points of equal deviation from the mode.
5. When the data is plotted on a graph they do not give the normal bell-shaped form.

Measure of Skewness

First measure of skewness has been given by Karl Pearson.

Co-efficient of skewness

$$S_{kp} = \text{Mean} - \text{Mode} \quad J = \frac{\bar{x} - Mo}{\bar{x}}$$

i.e. $S_{kp} = - Mo$

Pearson has suggested the use of this formula if it is not possible to determine the mode (Mo) of any distribution,

(Mean – Mode) = 3 (mean – median)

$$S_{kp} = 3\,(-Mo) \text{ Thus } J = \frac{3(\bar{x} - Me)}{\sigma_{\bar{x}}}$$

Note :

(i) Although the co-efficient of skewness is always within ± 1, but Karl Pearson's co-efficient lies within ± 3.
(ii) If J = 0, then there is no skewness
(iii) If J is positive, the skewness is also positive.
(iv) If J is negative, the skewness is also negative.

Unless and until no indication is given, you must use only Karl Pearson's formula.

Moments

Moment is a familiar mechanical term for the measure of a force with reference to it's tendency to produce rotation. In statistics moments these are used to describe the various characteristics of a frequency distribution like center tendency, variation, skewness and kurtosis.

Moments are calculated using the arithmetic mean. According to Waugh, the arithmetic mean of the various powers of these deviations in any distribution are called the moments of the distribution. Let 'x' be the deviation of any item in a distribution from the arithmetic mean of that distribution. The arithmetic mean of the various powers of these deviations is the moments of the distribution. If we take the mean of the 1st power of the deviations, we get the 1st moment about the mean, the mean of the squares of the deviations gives the second moment about the mean, the mean of the cubes gives the third moment about the mean and so on. The moments about mean are called the "central moment" and are denoted by $\mu_1, \mu_2, \mu_3, \mu_4$ ....

Symbolically, $\mu_1 = \dfrac{\Sigma(x - \bar{x})}{n}$ or $\dfrac{\Sigma x}{n}$ ..... 1st central moment = 0

Since, sum of deviations of items from the arithmetic mean is always zero.

$$\mu_2 = \frac{\Sigma f(x - \bar{x})^2}{n} \text{ or } \frac{\Sigma x^2}{n} \quad (\mu_2 = \sigma^2 \text{ or } \sigma = \sqrt{\mu_2})$$

$$\mu_3 = \frac{\Sigma(x - \bar{x})^3}{n} \text{ or } \frac{\Sigma x^3}{n} \text{ and so on}$$

For frequency distribution,

$$\mu_1 = \frac{\Sigma f(x-\bar{x})}{n} \text{ or } \frac{\Sigma fx}{n} \qquad \mu_2 = \frac{\Sigma f(x-\bar{x})^2}{n} \text{ or } \frac{\Sigma fx^2}{n}$$

$$\mu_3 = \frac{\Sigma f(x-\bar{x})^3}{n} \text{ or } \frac{\Sigma fx^3}{n} \qquad \mu_4 = \frac{\Sigma f(x-\bar{x})^4}{n} \text{ or } \frac{\Sigma fx^4}{n}$$

where $n = \Sigma f$ and so on

In many cases it is very difficult to calculate moments about actual moment, particularly when actual mean is in fractions. In such case we first compute moments about an arbitrary origin 'A' and then convert these moments into moments about actual mean. These are called ' raw moments ' which are denoted by ν.

Thus we have

$$\nu_1 = \frac{\Sigma f(x-A)}{n}, \ \nu_2 = \frac{\Sigma f(x-A)^2}{n}$$

$$\nu_3 = \frac{\Sigma f(x-A)^3}{n}, \ \nu_4 = \frac{\Sigma f(x-A)^4}{n} \text{ and so on.}$$

For frequency distribution

$$\nu_1 = \frac{\Sigma f_i(x-A)}{n}, \ \nu_2 = \frac{\Sigma f_i(x-A)^2}{n}$$

$$\nu_3 = \frac{\Sigma f_i(x-A)^3}{n}, \ \nu_4 = \frac{\Sigma f_i(x-A)^4}{n} \text{ and so on}$$

Now, to obtain the central moment as

$$\mu = \nu - \nu = \sigma$$

$$\mu = \nu - 3\nu.\nu + 2\nu$$

$$\mu = \nu - 4\nu.\nu + 6\nu - 3\nu$$

Pearson's β and ν coefficients. Karl Pearson defined the following four coefficients, based upon four moments about the mean:

β coefficients
$$\beta_1 = \frac{\mu_3^3}{\mu_2^3} = \frac{\mu_3^2}{\sigma^6}$$
$$\beta_2 = \frac{\mu_4}{\mu_2^2} = \frac{\mu_4}{\sigma^4}$$

ν coefficient
$$\nu_1 = \sqrt{\beta_1} = \frac{\mu_3}{\sigma^3}$$
$$\nu_2 + \beta_2 - 3 = \frac{\mu_4}{\mu^2} - 3 = \frac{\mu_4 - 3\sigma^2}{\sigma^4}$$

These are pure numbers and they provide information about the shape of the curve obtained from the frequency distribution.

For symmetrical distribution, the moments of odd order about the mean vanish and therefore $\beta_3 = 0$ rendering $\beta_1 = 0$ thus β_1 gives the measure of departure from symmetry and also defines a measure of skewness. Also $\beta_2 = \frac{\mu_4}{\mu^2}$ gives the measure of flatness of the mode and also defines the measure of Kurtosis or convexity of the curve.

Note :

(1) If $\beta_2 = 3$ *i.e.* $\nu_2 = 0$ then the curve is normal which is neither flat nor peaked *i.e.* Meso kurtic.
(2) If $\beta_2 > 3$ *i.e.* $\nu_2 > 0$ then the curve is more peaked than a normal curve and is called Lepto kurtic.
(3) If $\beta_2 < 3$ *i.e.* $\nu_2 <> 0$ then curve is flatter than a normal curve and is called Platy kurtic.

Kurtosis

It has its origin in the Greek word "Bulginess." In statistics it is the degree of flatness or 'peakedness' in the region of mode of a frequency curve. It is measured relative to the 'peakedness' of the normal curve. It tells us the extent to which a distribution is more peaked or flat-topped than the normal curve. If the curve is more peaked than a normal curve it is called 'Lepto Kurtic.' In this case items are more clustered about the mode. If the curve is more flat-topped than the more normal curve, it is Platy-Kurtic. The normal curve itself is known as "Meso Kurtic."

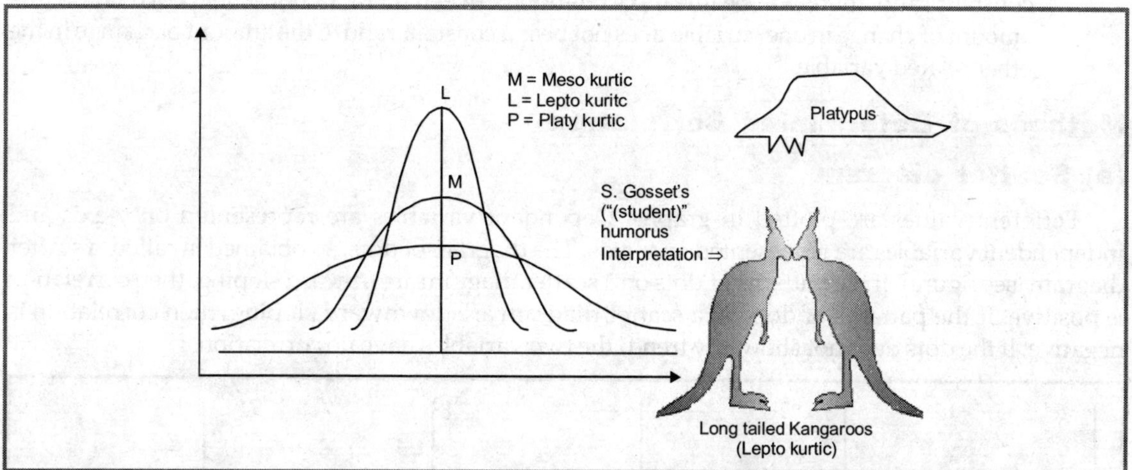

CORRELATION AND REGRESSION OF TWO VARIABLES

It is a statistical method to determine the relationship between two or more variables. Its values can lie between +1 and –1. The direction of the relation is determined by sign. If increase in one variable leads to increase in dependent variable, then relation is positive. On the other hand, if increase in one variable leads to decrease in dependent variable, then value will be negative. In case no relation exists between two variables, correlation will be zero.

Uses of Correlation

1. Decision maker will come to know the nature of relationship between variables and the degree of the relation.
2. Getting a quantitative figure for correlation makes the decision making process objective.
3. It helps in forecasting and planning because changes in variables and its impact can be estimated beforehand.
4. It helps the researcher in identifying such factors which can stabilize the economy.

Precautions in Applying Correlation

1. It is difficult to distinguish between dependent variables and independent variables.
2. Both the correlated variables are affected by a third variable, which has not been taken into consideration by the researcher.

3. The correlation may be due to chance.
4. Very high degree of correlation between two variables does not necessarily indicate a cause and effect relationship between them.

Types of Correlation

1. **Single and Multiple Correlation.** Only two variables are considered in single correlation, *i.e.*, one independent and another dependent variable. In case of multiple correlation, the relation between more than two variables is judged.
2. **Partial and Total Correlation.** In the case of partial correlation, relation of the two or more variables are considered assuming other variables to be constant. Total correlation is based on all the variables without assuming any variable to be constant.
3. **Linear and Non-linear Correlation.** When variation in the values of two variables have a constant ratio, there will be linear correlation between them. In non-linear correlation, the amount of change in one variable does not bear a constant ratio to the amount of change in the other related variable.

Methods of Determining Correlation

(a) Scatter diagram

Different values are plotted in graphs. Dependent variables are represented on y-axis and independent variables are represented on x-axis. The diagram of dots, so obtained is called a scatter diagram (see figure). If the patterns of dots on a scatter diagram are upward sloping, then correlation is positive. If the patterns of dots on a scatter diagram are downward sloping, then correlation is negative. If the dots does not show any trend, the two variables have no correlation.

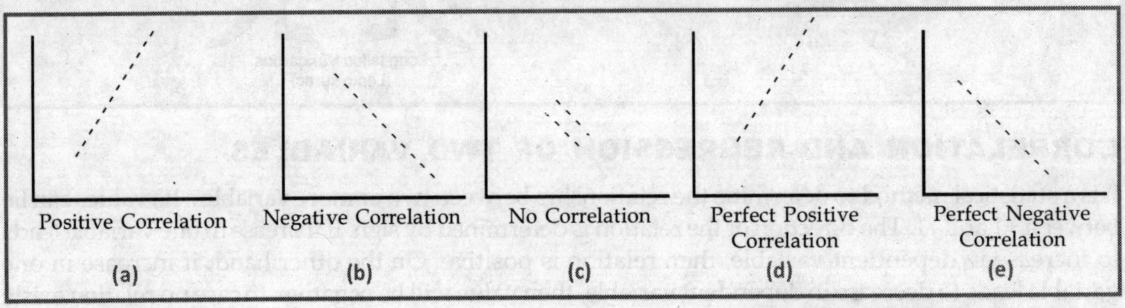

Scatter diagram

(i) **Merits of Scatter Diagram.** Scatter diagram is easy to understand. Even a layman who is not trained in mathematics or statistics can understand scattered diagram. If the relation is fairly apparent, then it can be shown through scattered diagram rather than by calculating through mathematical formula.

(ii) **Demerits of Scattered Diagram.** This method does not give any quantitative figure of the degree of correlation. Hence comparison of different data and their correlation are not possible. Scattered diagram is not an objective method of measuring correlation.

(b) Karl Pearson's Coefficient of Correlation

(i) **Measure from Mean**

$$r = \frac{\sum (x-\bar{x})(y-\bar{y})}{\sqrt{\sum (x-\bar{x})^2 \sum (y-\bar{y})^2}}$$

where x and y are the values of the variates.

If σx and σy denotes the standard deviation of the variates then r will be

$$r = \frac{\frac{1}{n}\sum(x-\bar{x})(y-\bar{y})}{\sqrt{\frac{1}{n}\sum(x-\bar{x})^2}\sqrt{\frac{1}{n}\sum(y-\bar{y})^2}}$$

$$= \frac{\text{cov } x, y}{\sigma_x \sigma_y}$$

where,

$$\text{Cov}(x, v) = \frac{1}{n}\Sigma(y-\bar{y})(x-\bar{x})$$

$$= \frac{1}{n}\Sigma xy - \bar{x}\frac{\Sigma y}{n} - \bar{y}\frac{\Sigma x}{n} + \bar{x}\,\bar{y}$$

(ii) **Change of Origin and Scale**

Let $u = \frac{x-a}{h}$, $v = \frac{y-b}{k}$

So that $x = a + hu$, $y = b + kv$

$\bar{x} = a + h\bar{u}$, $\quad \bar{y} = b + k\bar{v}$

$$r = \frac{\Sigma(x-\bar{x})(y-\bar{y})}{\sqrt{\Sigma(x-\bar{x})^2(y-\bar{y})^2}} = \frac{\Sigma(hu-h\bar{u})(kv-k\bar{v})}{\sqrt{h^2k^2\Sigma(u-\bar{u})^2\Sigma(v-\bar{v})^2}}$$

$$= \frac{\Sigma(u-\bar{u})(v-\bar{v})}{\sqrt{\Sigma(u-\bar{u})^2(v-\bar{v})^2}}$$

Correlation coefficient is independent of the change of origin and scale.

Example:

A: 105 104 102 101 100 99 98 96 93 92

B: 101 103 100 98 95 96 104 92 97 94

Let x and y denote the values in the series A and B respectively and let $u = x - 100$, $v = y - 96$.

Sl. No.	x	y	u	v	uv	u^2	v^2
1	105	101	5	5	25	25	25
2	104	103	4	7	28	16	49
3	102	100	2	4	8	4	16
4	101	98	1	2	2	1	4
5	100	95	0	–1	0	0	1
6	99	96	–1	0	0	1	0
7	98	104	–2	8	–16	4	64
8	96	92	–4	–4	16	16	16
9	93	97	–7	+1	–7	49	1
10	92	94	–8	–2	16	64	4
N = 10			–10	20	72	180	180

$$r = \frac{72 - \frac{1}{10}(-10)20}{\sqrt{180 - \frac{(-10)^2}{10}}\sqrt{180 - \frac{(20)^2}{10}}} = 0.596$$

(iii) **Short-cut Method**

$$\frac{\Sigma dx \cdot dy - \frac{\Sigma dx \cdot dy}{N}}{\sqrt{\left[\Sigma dx^2 - \frac{(\Sigma dx)^2}{N}\right] \times \left[\Sigma dy^2 - \frac{(\Sigma dy)^2}{N}\right]}}$$

In the formula,

$\sum dx$ and $\sum dy$ are sum of deviations from the assumed mean of x and y respectively.

$\sum dx^2$ and $\sum dy^2$ are sum of square of the deviations from the assumed mean in x and y series respectively.

(iv) **Correlation with Frequency Distribution**

$$r = \frac{N\sum f dx.dy - \sum f dx.\sum f dy}{\sqrt{\left[N\sum f dx^2 \left(\sum f dx\right)^2\right]\left[N\sum f dy^2 \left(\sum f.dy\right)^2\right]}}$$

Properties of the coefficient of correlation

1. The 'value of r' will lie between +1 and –1.
2. The 'value of r' is independent of change of scale and origin of the variable x and y.
3. The ' value of r' is the geometric mean of two regression coefficients.

   $r = \sqrt{b_{xy} . b_{yx}}$

4. Probable error can be calculated

   $$\text{P.E.} = 0.6745 \frac{1 - r^2}{\sqrt{N}}$$

   where 0.6745 is a constant number

   r is Pearson coefficient of correlation

   N is number of items.

5. Standard error can be calculated

   $$SE = \frac{1 - r^2}{\sqrt{N}}$$

Merits of Coefficient of Correlation

1. In one figure of r, both the degree of correlation and its direction can be calculated.
2. It can be derived from the use of standard deviation.
3. It is closely related to regression analysis.
4. Probable error and standard error can be calculated from coefficient of correlation.

Limitations of Coefficient of Correlation

1. It assumes a linear relationship between independent and dependent variables, which may not always be true.

2. It is applicable only if the distribution is normal.
3. The value of the coefficient is unduly affected by the extreme items.
4. It is difficult to calculate.
5. It is difficult to understand.

(c) Spearman's Rank Difference Method

Under this method, original values are not taken into account. Instead, the values are ranked.

(i) **Formula.** Formula of Spearman's rank-correlation coefficient is

$$r = 1 - \frac{6\sum d^2}{n(n^2-1)}$$

Where 'd' is the difference between the ranks of paired items of x and y variables.

(ii) **Correction for tied ranks.** In Spearman's rank-correlation method, the biggest item gets the first rank, the next to it gets second rank and so on. But, difficulty may be encountered where two or more items are of equal value. In such cases, correction has to be applied. $\frac{m(m^2-1)}{12}$ has to be added to $\sum d^2$. 'm' is the number of times a particular value of x and y has been repeated. Separate correction has to be applied for each separate case of repetition of ranks.

(iii) **Values of Spearman's Rank-Correlation.** If the value of d is zero for each individual, then the correlation is positive and will be equal to one.

If $6\sum d^2 = n(n^2-1)$ or, $\sum d^2 = \frac{n(n^2-1)}{6}$ then the correlation is zero, which means that there is no correlation at all between the two variables.

Example:

			Rank			
Sl. No.	x	y	x	y	d	Σd^2
1	105	101	1	3	−2	4
2	104	103	2	2	0	0
3	102	100	3	4	−1	1
4	101	98	4	5	−1	1
5	100	95	5	8	−3	9
6	99	96	6	7	−1	1
7	98	104	7	1	+6	36
8	96	92	8	10	-2	4
9	93	97	9	6	+3	9
10	92	94	10	9	+1	1
					0	$\Sigma d^2 = 66$

$$r = 1 - \frac{6\Sigma d^2}{n(n^2-1)} = 1 - \left[\frac{6(66)}{990}\right] = 1 - \frac{396}{990}$$

$$r = 1 - 0.4 = 0.6$$

Regression Analysis

Regression analysis is based on the relation-ship between two or more variables. The known variable is called as 'independent variable' and the variable we are trying to predict is called as 'dependent variable'. Regression analysis shows us how to determine both the nature and the strength of a relationship between independent variable and dependent variable.

According to M. M. Blair, "Regression analysis is a mathematical measure of the average relationship between two or more variables in terms of the original units of the data."

The term 'Regression' was first used by Sir Francis Galton in 1877 in the study of heredity. Galton made a study that showed that the height of sons born to tall parents will tend to move back, or 'Regress' towards the mean height of the population. In statistics the term 'Regression' is used to denote backward tendency which means going back to average. In Economics regression analysis is used as the basic technique for measuring or estimating the relationship among economic variables that constitute the essence of economic theory and economic life.

Before developing the methods of regression it is necessary to distinguish between two types of relationships, linear and non-linear :

1. If the relationships between two (or more) variables is best described by means of a straight line (or a plane), it is called linear. Linear relationship implies a constant change in the dependent variable with respect to changes in the independent variables. It is extensively used for predictive purposes.
2. If the underlying relationship between two (or more) variables is best described by a curve the relationship is called non-linear. A non-linear relationship implies a varying absolute change in the dependent variable with respect to changes in the independent variable. Its predictive value is limited.

Types of Regression

1. **Simple Regression.** The regression analysis for studying only two variables at a time, is called the Simple Regression.
2. **Multiple Regression.** The regression analysis for studying more than two variables at a time is known as Multiple Regression.
3. **Linear Regression.** The task of bringing out linear relationships consists of developing methods of fitting a straight line or the regression line, as is often called, to the data on two variables.
4. **Non-linear Regression.** If the curve of regression is not a straight line, then it is called a Non-linear Regression.

Utility of Regression Analysis

Today, the regression analysis technique plays a vital role in managerial decisions. The importance of this technique can be stated through the following points:

1. This technique helps in determining the coefficient of correlation.
2. This technique establishes the rate of change in one variable, in terms of the changes in another variable.
3. Regression analysis helps prediction and thus it can estimate the value of unknown quantities.

4. This technique helps in economic and business investigations.
5. The study of regression analysis indicates the cause and effect relationship.

Difference between Correlation and Regression Analysis

1. In correlation, we cannot say that one variable is the cause and other the effect. While in regression analysis one variable is taken as dependent and the other is independent – thus making it possible to study the cause and effect relationship.
2. Correlation coefficient is independent of change of scale and origin but regression coefficients are independent of change of origin but not of scale.
3. Correlation indicates the quantity of relation between to variables but regression analysis indicate the nature of two variables.

Precautions in the Use of Regression Analysis

As the regression analysis has a predictive value, its limitations must be recognised and it must be used with caution. Regression Analysis suffers from the following limitations :

1. A value of Y cannot be predicted if the value of X is beyond the values on which the regression equation is based. For example, if the various values of X range from 200 to 1400, then a value of Y corresponding to X = 1500 should not be estimated.
2. In case of a time series, the value of Y which involves the prediction of a result for 'X', a future event, may not be relevant. For example, if the data relate to years 1971 to 1979 and a prediction for 1980 or any later date is desired, regression analysis may not be used satisfactorily.
3. The analysis is confined to data where the distribution of Y is normal.

ELEMENTARY THEORY OF PROBABILITY

The theory of probability was developed towards the end of the 18th century and its history suggests that it developed with the study of games and chance, such as rolling a dice, drawing a card, flipping a coin etc. Apart from these, uncertainty prevailed in every sphere of life. For instance, one often predicts: "It will probably rain tonight." "It is quite likely that there will be a good yield of cereals this year" and so on. This indicates that, in layman's terminology the word 'probability' thus connotes that there is an uncertainty about the happening of events. To put 'probability' on a better footing we define it. But before doing so, we have to explain a few terms."

Trial

A procedure or an experiment to collect any statistical data such as rolling a dice or flipping a coin is called a trial.

Random Trial or Random Experiment

When the outcome of any experiment can not be predicted precisely then the experiment is called a random trial or random experiment. In other words, if a random experiment is repeated under identical conditions, the outcome will vary at random as it is impossible to predict about the performance of the experiment. For example, if we toss a honest coin or roll an unbiased dice, we may not get the same results as our expectations.

Sample Space

The totality of all the outcomes or results of a random experiment is denoted by Greek alphabet Ω or English alphabets and is called the sample space. Each outcome or element of this sample space is known as a sample print.

Event

Any subset of a sample space is called an event. A sample space S serves as the universal set for all questions related to an experiment 'S' and an event A w.r.t. It is a set of all possible outcomes favourable to the event A.

For example,

A random experiment :- flipping a coin twice

Sample space : Ω or S = {(HH), (HT), (TH), (TT)}

The question : "both the flipps show same face"

Therefore, the event A : { (HH), (TT) }

Equally Likely Events

All possible results of a random experiment are called equally likely outcomes and we have no reason to expect any one rather than the other. For example, as the result of drawing a card from a well shuffled pack, any card may appear in draw, so that the 52 cards become 52 different events which are equally likely.

Mutually Exclusive Events

Events are called mutually exclusive or disjoint or incompatible if the occurrence of one of them precludes the occurrence of all the others. For example in tossing a coin, there are two mutually exclusive events viz turning up a head and turning up of a tail. Since both these events cannot happen simultaneously. But note that events are compatible if it is possible for them to happen simultaneously. For instance in rolling of two dice, the cases of the face marked 5 appearing on one dice and face 5 appearing on the other, are compatible.

Exhaustive Events

Events are exhaustive when they include all the possibilities associated with the same trial. In throwing a coin, the turning up of head and of a tail are exhaustive events assuming of course that the coin cannot rest on its edge.

Independent Events

Two events are said to be independent if the occurrence of any event does not affect the occurrence of the other event. For example in tossing of a coin, the events corresponding to the two successive tosses of it are independent. The flip of one penny does not affect in any way the flip of a nickel.

Dependent Events

If the occurrence or non-occurrence of any event affects the happening of the other, then the events are said to be dependent events. For example, in drawing a card from a pack of cards, let the event A be the occurrence of a king in the 1st draw and B be the occurrence of a king in the 1st draw and B be the occurrence of a king in the second draw. If the card drawn at the first trial is not replaced then events A and B are independent events.

Note:

(1) If an event contains a single simple point *i.e.* it is a singleton set, then this event is called an elementary or a simple event.

(2) An event corresponding to the empty set is an "impossible event."

(3) An event corresponding to the entire sample space is called a 'certain event'.

Complementary Events

Let S be the sample space for an experiment and A be an event in S. Then A is a subset of S. Hence $\bar{A}$, the complement of A in S is also an event in S which contains the outcomes which are not favourable to the occurrence of A *i.e.* if A occurs, then the outcome of the experiment belongs to A, but if A does not occur, then the outcomes of the experiment belongs to $\bar{A}$.

It is obvious that A and $\bar{A}$ are mutually exclusive. $A \cap \bar{A} = \phi$ and $A \cup \bar{A} = S$.

If S contains n equally likely, mutually exclusive and exhaustive points and A contains m out of these n points then $\bar{A}$ contains $(n - m)$ sample points.

Mathematical (or A Priori or Classic) Definition

If there are 'n' exhaustive, mutually exclusive and equally likely cases and m of them are favourable to an event A, the probability of A happening is defined as the ratio m/n

Expressed as a formula:

$$P(A) = \frac{m}{n} = \frac{\text{Number of favourable outcomes}}{\text{Total number of possible outcomes}}$$

$$P(A) = \frac{n(A)}{n(S)}$$

This definition is due to 'Laplace.' Thus probability is a concept which measures numerically the degree of certainty or uncertainty of the occurrence of an event.

For example, the probability of randomly drawing taking from a well-shuffled deck of cards is 4/52. Since 4 is the number of favourable outcomes (*i.e.* 4 kings of diamond, spade, club and heart) and 52 is the number of total outcomes (the number of cards in a deck).

If A is any event of sample space having probability P, then clearly, P is a positive number (expressed as a fraction or usually as a decimal) not greater than unity. $0 \le P \le 1$ *i.e.* 0 (no chance or for impossible event) to a high of 1 (certainty). Since the number of cases not favourable to A are $(n - m)$, the probability q that event A will not happen is, $\frac{n-m}{n} = q$ or $q = 1 - m/n$ or $q = 1 - p$.

Now note that the probability q is nothing but the probability of the complementary event A *i.e.* $\bar{A}$

Thus $p(\bar{A}) = 1 - p$ or $p(\bar{A}) = 1 - p(\bar{A})$

so that $p(A) + p(\bar{A}) = 1$ *i.e.* $p + q = 1$

Relative Frequency Definition

The classical definition of probability has a disadvantage *i.e.* the words 'equally likely' are vague. In fact, since these words seem to be synonymous with "equally probable". This definition is circular as it is defining (in terms) of itself. Therefore, the estimated or empirical probability of an event is taken as the relative frequency of the occurrence of the event when the number of observations is very large.

Van Mise's Statistical (or Empirical) Definition

If trials are to be repeated a great number of times under essentially the same condition then the limit of the ratio of the number of times that an event happens to the total number of trials, as the number of trials increases indefinitely is called the probability of the happening of the event.

It is assumed that the limit exists and finite uniquely. Symbolically $p(A) = p = \lim_{n \to \infty} \frac{m}{n}$ provided it is finite and unique.

The two definitions are apparently different but both of them can be reconciled the same sense.

The Laws of Probability

So far we have discussed probabilities of single events. In many situations we come across two or more events occurring together. If event A and event B are two events and either A or B or both occurs, is denoted by $A \cap B$ or $(A + B)$ and the event that both A and B occurs is denoted by $A \cap B$ or AB. We term these situations as compound event or the joint occurrence of events. We may need probability that A or B will happen.

It is denoted by $P(A \cap B)$ or $P(A + B)$. Also we may need the probability that A and B (both) will happen simultaneously. It is denoted by $P(A \cap B)$ or $P(AB)$.

Consider a situation, you are asked to choose any 3 or any diamond or both from a well shuffled pack of 52 cards. Now you are interested in the probability of this situation.

Now see the following diagram.

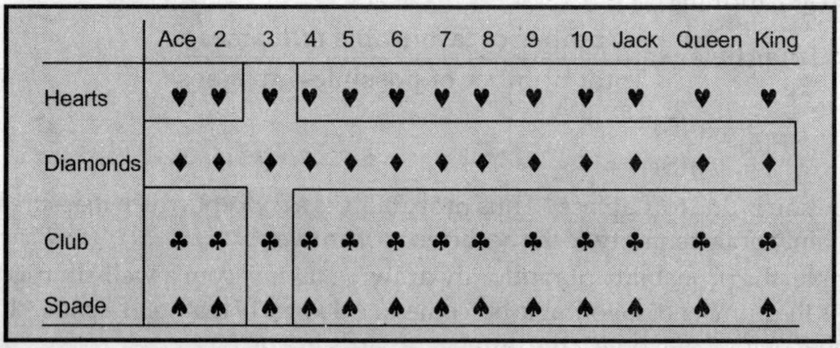

It is denoted by $P(A \cup B)$ or $P(A + B)$. Also we may need the probability that A and B (both) will happen simultaneously. It is denoted by $P(A \cap B)$ or $P(AB)$.

Consider a situation, you are asked to choose any 3 or any diamond or both from a well shuffled pack of 52 cards. Now you are interested in the probability of this situation.

Now count the dots in the area 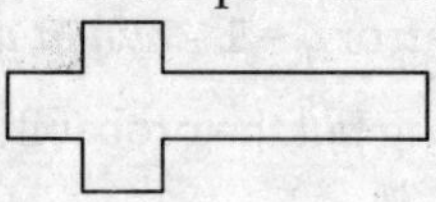 which fulfills the condition any 3 or any diamond or both. They are 16.

Thus the required probability

$$= \frac{\text{No. of favourable outcomes}}{\text{Total no. of outcomes}}$$

$$= \frac{16}{52} \text{ or } 0.31$$

In the language of set theory, the set any 3 or any diamond or both is the union of the sets 'any 3 which contains 4 cards' and 'any diamond' which contains 15 cards. The number of cards in their union is equal to the sum of these numbers minus the number of cards in the space where they overlap. Any points in this space, called the intersection of the two sets, is counted here twice (double counting), once in each set. Dividing by 52 we get the required probability.

$$= P(\text{any } 3) + P(\text{any diamond}) - P(3 \text{ of diamond})$$

$$= \frac{4}{52} + \frac{13}{52} - \frac{1}{52} = \frac{16}{52} \text{ or } 0.31$$

Thus P (any 3 or any diamond or both)

In general, if the letters A and B stands for any two events, then

$$\left.\begin{array}{c} (P \cup B) = P(A) + P(B) - P(A \cap B) \\ \text{or} \\ P(A + B) = P(A) + P(B) - P(AB) \end{array}\right\} \text{Addition Law}$$

Clearly, the outcomes of both A and B are non-mutually exclusive.

Odds in Favour and Against

If P is the probability that an event will occur and $q\ (= 1 - p)$ is the probability of the non-occurrence of the event; then we say that the odds in favour of the event occurring are $p : q$ (p to q) and the odds against its occurring are $q : p$.

For example, if the event consists of drawing a card if club from the deck of 52 cards, then the odds in favor are $\frac{13}{52} : \frac{39}{52}$ *i.e.* $\frac{1}{4} : \frac{3}{4}$ *i.e.* 1 : 3.

Similarly the odds against a card of diamond would be 3 : 1. The odds in favor of 4 or 6 in a single toss of a fair die are $\frac{1}{3} : \frac{2}{3}$; *i.e.* 1 : 2 and the odds against are 2 : 1.

Multiplication Law of Probability

If there are two independent events; the respective probability of which are known, then the probability that both will happen is the product of the probabilities of their happening respectively

$$P(AB) = P(A) \times P(B)$$

To compute the probability of two or even more independent event all occurring (joint occurrence) extent the above law to required number.

For example, first flip a penny, then the nickle and finally flip the dime.

On landing, probability of heads is $\frac{1}{2}$ for a penny

probability of heads is $\frac{1}{2}$ for a nickle

probability of heads is $\frac{1}{2}$ for a dime

Thus the probability of landing three heads will be $\frac{1}{2} \times \frac{1}{2} \times \frac{1}{2} = \frac{1}{8}$ or 0.125. (Note that all three events are independent)

Conditional Probability

In many situations you get more information than simply the total outcomes and favourable outcomes you already have and, hence you are in position to make yourself more informed to make judgements regarding the probabilities of such situations. For example, suppose a card is drawn at random from a deck of 52 cards. Let B denotes the event 'the card is a diamond' and A denotes the event 'the card is red'. We may then consider the following probabilities.

(i) $P(B) = \frac{^{13}C_1}{^{52}C_1} = \frac{13}{52}$

(ii) $P(A) = \frac{^{26}C_1}{^{52}C_1} = \frac{26}{52}$

(iii) P(AB) = The probability that the card is both a diamond and a red card

$$= \frac{^{13}C_1}{^{52}C_1} = \frac{13}{52}$$

(iv) The probability that the card is a diamond knowing that it is red.

Since there are 26 red cards of which 13 are diamonds, the probability that the card is diamond is $\frac{13}{26}$. In other words the probability of event B knowing that A has occurred is $\frac{13}{26}$.

The probability of B under the condition that A has occurred is known as condition probability and it is denoted by P (B/A). Thus $P(B/A) = \frac{13}{26}$. It should be observed that the probability of the event B is increased due to the additional information that the event A has occurred.

Conditional probability found using the formula $P(B/A) = \frac{P(AB)}{P(A)}$

Justification :- $P(A/B) = \frac{P(AB)}{P(A)} = \frac{13}{26} = \frac{13/52}{26/52} = \frac{P(AB)}{P(B)}$

Similarly $P(A/B) = \frac{P(AB)}{P(A)}$

In both the cases if A and B are independent events then P (A/B) = P (A) and P(B/A) = P(B)

Therefore $P(A) = \frac{P(AB)}{P(B)} \Rightarrow P(AB) = P(A) . P(B)$

or $P(B) = \frac{P(AB)}{P(A)} \Rightarrow P(AB) = P(A) . P(B)$

Propositions

(1) If A and B are independent events then A and B' are also independent where B' is the complementary event B.

(2) If A and B are independent events then A' and B' are also independent events.

(3) Two independent events cannot be mutually exclusive.

(4) De Morgan's Laws: $P(A \cup B)' = P(A' \cap B')$

$P(A \cap B)' = P(A' \cup B')$

Theoretical Distributions

Random Variables

When we assign a number to each point of a sample space, we have a function which is defined on the sample space. This function is called a random variable (or stochastic variable).

It is usually denoted by bold letters like **X** or **Y**.

Consider two independent tosses of a fair coin

$\therefore$ S = { (HH), (HT), (TH), (TT) }

Let X denote the number of heads.

Then X (HH) = 2, X (HT) = 1, X(TH) = 1 and X(TT) = 0

i.e. X = 0, 1, 2. Here X is known as a random variable. Thus a random variable is one, which denotes the numerical value of an outcome, of a random experiment.

(1) If the random variable X takes only finite values or countably infinite values, then X is known as a 'discrete variable'.

(2) If the random variable takes the uncountably infinite values between a specified range or limit, it is called as 'continuous random variable'.
For example: X denotes the age of a person.

Discrete Probability Distribution

Return to the above given example of tossing of a fair coin twice.

$$S = \{ (HH), (HT), (TH), (TT) \}$$

Then X (HH) = 2, X (HT) = 1, X (TH) = 1 and X(TT) = 0

Also $P(HH) = \frac{1}{4}, P(HT) = \frac{1}{4}, P(TH) = \frac{1}{4}$ and $P(HH) = \frac{1}{4}$

The probability distribution: Number of Heads

X P(x)

$$0 \rightarrow \frac{1}{4} \text{ or } 0.25$$

$$1 \rightarrow \frac{1}{4} + \frac{1}{4} = \frac{1}{2} \text{ or } 0.50$$

$$2 \rightarrow \frac{1}{4} \text{ or } 0.25$$

The probability graph can be obtained by using a bar chart as shown in figure (I) or a Histogram as shown in figure (II).

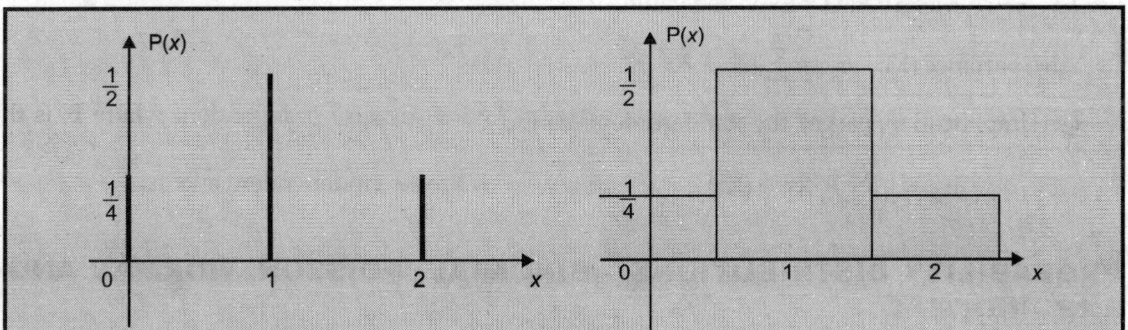

(I) (II)

Total of Probabilities of Discrete Random Variables

As you have noted from the probability distribution table or from the bar chart (in which the sum of ordinates *i.e.* heights of bar is:

(1) and from the Histogram (in which sum of the rectangular area is 1), the sum (total) of probabilities of all values of X always equal to 1.

Thus, if the random variable $X = X_1, X_2, X_3, \ldots\ldots X_i, \ldots\ldots X_n$ and X_i each is associated with a number P_i *i.e.* X_1 with P_1, X_2 with P_2 ...., $X_n = P_n$. Then P_i is called probabilities of X_i and is denoted by $P(X_i)$ or simply P(X) which satisfies (1) $P(X_i) > 0$

(2) $\sum_{i=1}^{n} P(X_i) = 1$ then $P(X_i)$ or P(X) is called the probability mass function of the discrete random variable X.

i.e. $X \; X_1 \; X_2 \; X_3 \; .... \; X_n$

$P(X) \; P_1 \; P_2 \; P_3 \; .... \; P_n$

Mathematical Expression of a Discrete Random Variable

If $X = x_i$ is a discrete random variable.

Taking $X = x_1, x_2, ..., x_n$ with respective probabilities

$P_i = P_1, P_2, ..., P_n$ then

The mathematical expression of X is denoted by E(X) and denoted by,

$$E(X) = P_1X_1 + P_2X_2 + ... + P_nX_n = \sum_{i=1}^{n} P_i X_i$$

Mean and Standard Deviation. If the random variable X, assumes the values $x_1, x_2, ..., x_n$ with associated probabilities as $P_1, P_2, ... P_n$ respectively then,

$$\text{Mean } (X \text{ or } \mu) = \frac{\sum_{i=1}^{n} P_i X_1}{\sum_{i=1}^{n} P_i}$$

$$\text{Therefore } \bar{X} \text{ or } \mu = \sum_{i=1}^{n} P_i X_i = E(X)$$

i.e. Mean = E(X) = Expected value.

$$\text{Also variance } (X) = \sigma_x 2 = \sum_{i=1}^{n} (X_i - \bar{X})^2 \; P_i$$

On simplification, we get, the standard deviation,

$$i.e. \quad \sigma_x 2 = \sqrt{\sum_{i=1}^{n} P_i X_i^2 = (\bar{X})^2}$$

PROBABILITY DISTRIBUTIONS - BINOMIAL, POISSON, NORMAL AND EXPONENTIAL

There is a more scientific way of drawing inferences about the population characteristics *i.e.*, through the study of theoretical distributions. In the population, the values of the variable may be distributed according to some definite probability law which can be expressed mathematically and the corresponding probability distribution laws may be based on 'a priori' considerations or 'a posteriori' inferences. These distributions are based on expectations on the basis of previous experience. Theoretical distributions also enable us to fit a mathematical model or a function of the form $y = p(x)$ to the given data.

The following probability distributions are:

A. Binomial Distribution

It is also known as the 'Bernoulli distribution' which was discovered by the Swiss mathematician in 1700. This distribution is used in following cases:

(i) The random experiment is performed repeatedly a finite and fixed number of times. In other words n, the number of trials, is finite and fixed.

(ii) The outcome of the random experiment (trial) results in the dichotomous classification of events. In other words, the outcome of each trial may be classified into two mutually disjoint categories, called success (the occurrence of the event) and failure (the non-occurrence of the event).

(iii) All the trials are independent, *i.e.*, the result of any trial, is not affected in any way by the proceeding trials and doesn't affect the result of succeeding trials.

(iv) The probability of success (happening of an event) in any trial is p and is constant for each trial. $q = 1 - p$, is then termed as the probability of failure (non-occurrence of the event) and is constant for each trial.

For example, if we toss a fair coin n times (which is fixed and finite) then the outcome of any trial is one of the mutually exclusive events, viz., head (success) and tail (failure). Further, all the trials are independent, since the result of any throw of a coin does not affect and is not affected by the result of other throws. Moreover, the probability of success (head) in any trial is ½, which is constant for each trial. Hence the coin tossing problems will give rise to Binomial distribution.

Similarly dice throwing problems will also conform to Binomial distribution.

Binomial distributions can also be used under the following conditions:

(i) n, the number of trials is finite.

(ii) Trials are independent.

(iii) p, the probability of success is constant for each trial.

Then $q = 1 - p$, is the probability of failure in any trial.

B. Poisson Distributions

It was derived by a French mathematician Simeon D. Poisson in 1837. It is used in following circumstances.

(i) n, the number of trials is indefinitely large *i.e.*, $n \to \infty$.

(ii) p, the constant probability of success for each trial is indefinitely small *i.e.*, $p \to 0$.

(iii) $np = m$, (say), is finite.

Poisson distribution has found application in a variety of fields such as Queuing Theory (Waiting time problem), Insurance, Business, Economics and Industry. Most of the Temporal Distributions (dealing with events which are supposed to occur in equal intervals of time) and the spatial Distributions (dealing with events which are supposed to occur in intervals of equal length along a straight line) follow the Poisson Probability Law.

Examples :

(i) Number of telephone calls arriving at a telephone switch board in unit time (say, per minute).

(ii) Number of customers arriving at the super market; say per hour.

(iii) The number of defects per unit of manufactured product (This is done for the construction of control chart for c in Industrial Quality Control).

(iv) To count the number of radio-active disintegrations of a radio-active element per unit of time (Physics).

(v) To count the number of bacterias per unit (Biology).

(vi) The number of defective material say, pins, blades etc. in a packing manufactured by a good concern.

(vii) The number of suicides reported in a particular day or the number of casualties (persons dying) due to a rare disease such as heart attack or cancer or snake bite in a year.

(viii) Number of accidents taking place per day on a busy road.

The Poisson distribution appears frequently in the literature of management science and finds a large number of managerial applications. It is used to describe a number of managerial situations including the arrivals of patients at a health clinic, the distribution of telephone calls going through a central switching system, the arriving of vehicles at a toll booth, the number of accidents at a crossing, and the number of looms in a textile will watching for service. All these examples have a common characteristics. They can all be described by a discrete random variable that takes on non-negative integer (whole number) values 0, 1, 2, 3, 4, 5 and so on the number of patients who how arrive at a health clinic in a given interval of time will be 0, 1, 2, 3, 4, 5 and so on.

Characteristics

Suppose we use the number of patients arriving at a health clinic during the busiest part of the day as an illustration of Poisson Probability Distribution characteristics.

(i) The average arrival of patients per 15-minute interval can be estimated from past office data.

(ii) If we divide the 15-minute interval into smaller intervals of, say, one second each, we will see that these statements are true.

(a) The probability that exactly one patient will arrive per second is a very small number and is constant for every second interval.

(b) The probability that two or more patients will arrive within a one second interval is so small that we can safely assign it a 0 probability.

(c) The number of patients who arrive in a one second interval is independent of where that one second interval is within the larger 15 minute interval.

(d) The number of patients who arrive in any one second interval is not dependent on the number of arrivals in any other one second interval.

It is acceptable to generalize from these conditions and to apply them to other processes of interest to management. If these processes melt the same conditions, then it is possible to use a Poisson Probability to describe them.

Calculating probabilities using Poisson Distribution. The probability of exactly x occurrences in a Poisson distribution is calculated using the relation.

$$P(x) = \frac{m^x . e^{-m}}{x!}$$

m = the average (mean) of the distribution

x = the specific value of the discrete random variable in which we are interested.

e = 2.718, the base of natural logarithms.

C. Normal Distribution

Normal probability distribution or commonly called the normal distribution is one of the most important continuous theoretical distributions in Statistics. Most of the data relating to economic and business statistics or even in social and physical sciences conform to this distribution.

The normal distribution was first discovered by English Mathematician De-Moivre in 1733. It is also known as Gaussian Distribution after Karl Friedrish Gauss who used this distribution to describe the theory of accidental errors of measurements involved in the calculations of orbits of heavenly bodies.

Statistically, A continuous variable X is said to follow normal distribution if it takes values from $-\infty$ to $+\infty$ with probabilities given by the function.

$$Y_x = Y_0 e^{-1/2} \frac{(X-\overline{X})^2}{\sigma} \text{ where}$$

$\overline{X}$ = Mean of the distribution

σ = Standard deviation of the distribution

e = is the base of natural law (e = 2.7183)

Y_0 = is the height of the ordinate corresponding to mean of distribution

$Y_0 = P(X - \overline{X})$

Y_x = is the height of the ordinate at distance x from $\overline{X}$

$Y_x = P(X = \overline{X} + X)$

$Y_x = P(X = \overline{X} - X)$

PROPERTIES OF NORMAL DISTRIBUTION

1. Normal distribution is a continuous probability distribution
2. Range of normal distribution is from $-\infty$ to $+\infty$. It means normal curve will never touch X-axis.
3. For normal distribution $\overline{X}$, M, Z coincide with each other.
4. Normal distribution is perfectly symmetrical.

   In other words left hand side of the distribution is perfectly similar to right hand side of the distribution. In other words weight of the ordinate at the distance x from origin is same on the left hand side as well as on the right hand side.

   $P(X = \overline{X} + x) \quad (x = \overline{X} - x)$
5. Total area under the normal curve will be equal to one, because of symmetry, it is 0.5 on the left hand side and 0.5 on the right hand side.

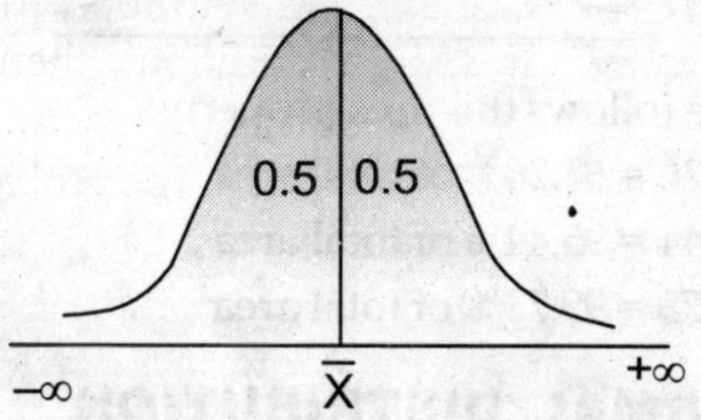

6. Normal distribution has two parameters $\overline{X}$ and σ. In other words

   $X \sim N.D.(\overline{X}, \sigma)$

   X follows normal distribution
7. Normal distribution is without skewness.

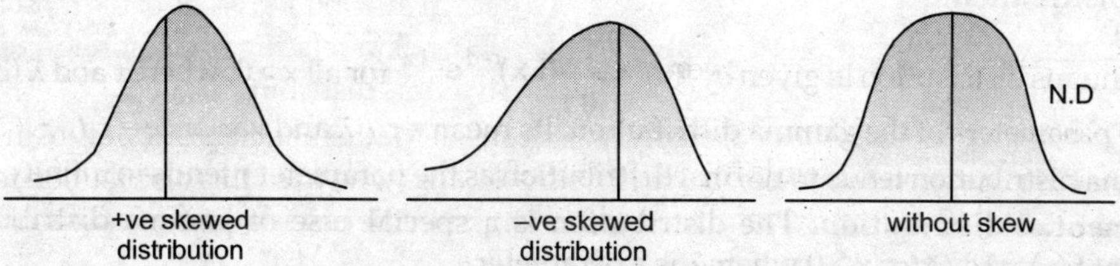

8. Normal distribution is Mesokotte

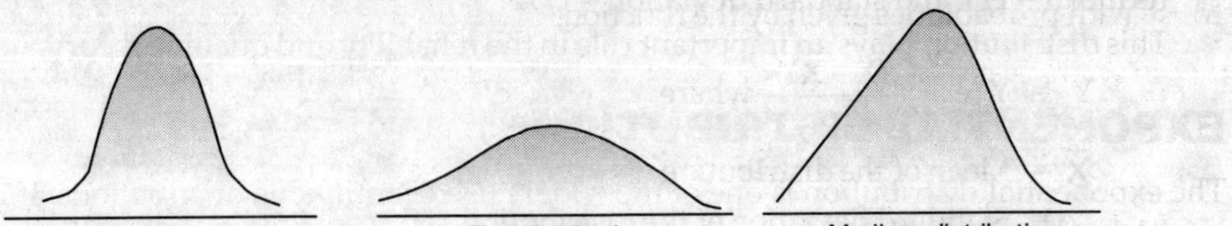

peaked distribution leptokotic | Flat distribution plasykotic | Medium distribution Neither too flat nor peaked Measokotic

9. Area property of Normal Distribution

$P = [\bar{x} - \sigma \le x \le \bar{x} + \sigma] = 0.6826$

$P = [\bar{x} - 2\sigma \le x \le \bar{x} + 2\sigma] = 0.9544$

$P = [\bar{x} - 3\sigma \le x \le \bar{x} + 3\sigma] = 0.9973$

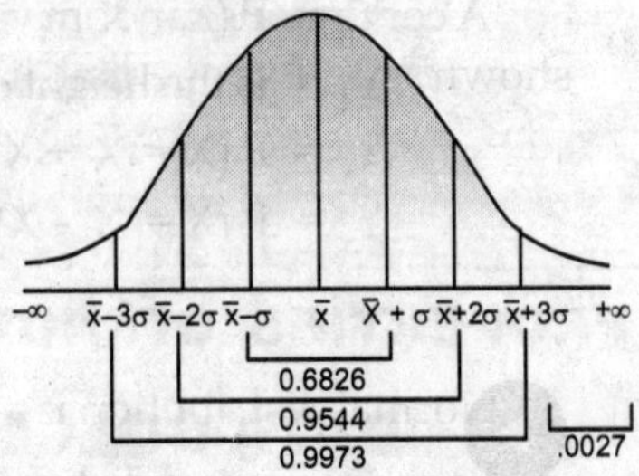

10. $x \sim N[\bar{X}, \sigma]$

$Z \sim N[0, 1]$

If X follows normal distribution with $\bar{X} = 0, \sigma = 1$

$\therefore$ Variable Z = Standard Normal Variable.

$Z = \dfrac{X - \bar{X}}{\sigma} \sim N[0, 1]$

Probability tables are available for this distribution

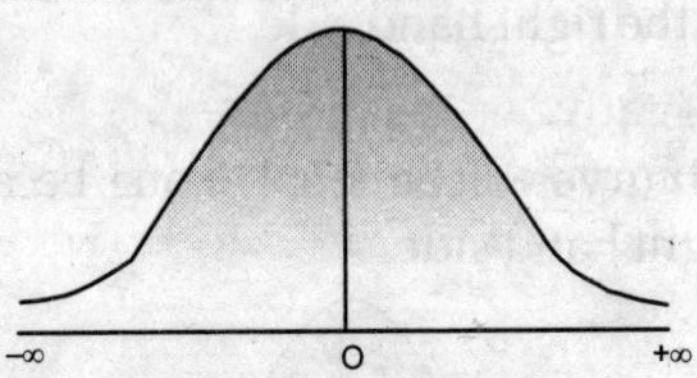

11. Standard normal variable follows this area property

$P = [-1 \le Z \le +1] = 0.6826 = 68.26\%$ of total area

$P = [-2 \le Z \le +2] = 0.9544 = 95.44\%$ of total area

$P = [-3 \le Z \le +3] = 0.9973 = 99.73\%$ of total area

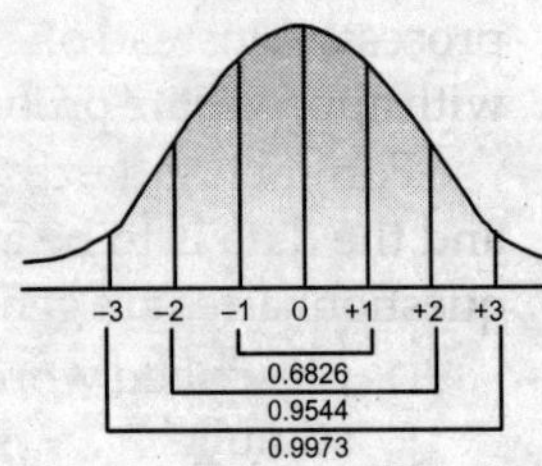

APPLICATION OF NORMAL DISTRIBUTION

(i) Calculation of errors made by chance in experimental measurements.

(ii) Computation of hit probability of a shot.

(iii) Statistical inference in almost every branch of science.

Gamma Distribution

This continuous distribution in given by $f(x) = \frac{1}{\lceil(r)}(1x)^{r-1}e^{-1x}$ for all $x \ge 0$, where r and λ (both > 0) are called the parameters of the gamma distribution. Its mean = r / λ and variance = r / λ^2.

Gamma distribution tends to normal distribution as the parameter r tends to infinity.

Exponential distribution. The distribution is a special case of gamma distribution when $r = 1$ so that $f(x) = \lambda e^{-\lambda x}$ for $x > 0$ where λ is a parameter.

Its mean = $1/\lambda$ and standard deviation = $1/\lambda$.

This distribution plays an important role in the reliability and queuing theory.

EXPONENTIAL DISTRIBUTION

The exponential distribution is one of the widely used continuous distributions. It is often used to model the time elapsed between events. We will now mathematically define the exponential distribution, and derive its mean and expected value. Then we will develop the intuition for the distribution and discuss several interesting properties that it has.

A continuous random variable X is said to have an exponential distribution with parameter $\lambda > 0$, shown as X~Exponential, if its PDF is given by

$$f X(x) = \begin{cases} \lambda e^{-\lambda x} & x > 0 \\ 0 & \text{otherwise} \end{cases}$$

DATA COLLECTION & QUESTIONNAIRE DESIGN

The design of a questionnaire will depend on whether the researcher wishes to collect exploratory information (i.e. qualitative information for the purposes of better understanding or the generation of hypotheses on a subject) or quantitative information (to test specific hypotheses that have previously been generated).

Exploratory Questionnaires

If the data to be collected is qualitative or is not to be statistically evaluated, it may be that no formal questionnaire is needed. For example, in interviewing the female head of the household to find out how decisions are made within the family when purchasing breakfast foodstuffs, a formal questionnaire may restrict the discussion and prevent a full exploration of the woman's views and processes. Instead one might prepare a brief guide, listing perhaps ten major open-ended questions, with appropriate probes/prompts listed under each.

Formal standardised questionnaires: If the researcher is looking to test and quantify hypotheses and the data is to be analysed statistically, a formal standardised questionnaire is designed. Such questionnaires are generally characterised by:

- prescribed wording and order of questions, to ensure that each respondent receives the same stimuli.
- prescribed definitions or explanations for each question, to ensure interviewers handle questions consistently and can answer respondents' requests for clarification if they occur.
- prescribed response format, to enable rapid completion of the questionnaire during the interviewing process.

SAMPLING

Sampling Theory: Sampling Distributions

Sampling is a tool which enables us to draw conclusions about the characteristics of the population after studying only those objects or items that are included in the sample.

In any statistical investigation the interest usually lies in studying the various characteristics relating to items or individuals belonging to a particular group. This group of individuals under study is known as the *population* or *universe.* For example, if an enquiry is intended to determine the average per capita income of the people in a particular city, the population will comprise all the earning people in that city. On the other hand if we want to study the expenditure habits of the families in that city, then the population will consist of all the households in that city.

The main objectives of the sampling theory are:

(i) To obtain the optimum results, *i.e.,* the maximum information about the characteristics of the population with the available sources at our disposal in terms of time, money and manpower by studying the sample values only.

(ii) To obtain the best possible estimates of the population parameters.

Sampling Distribution. If we draw a sample of size *n* from a given finite populations of size N, then the total number of possible samples is :

$$^{N}C_n = \frac{N!}{n!\ (N-n)!} = k, \text{ (say)}$$

For each of these *k* samples we can compute some statistic $t = t(x_1, x_2, \ldots, x_n)$, in particular the mean $\bar{x}$, the variance s^2, etc., as given below:

Sample Number	Statistic		
	t	$\bar{x}$	s^2
1	t_1	$\bar{x}_1$	s_1^2
2	t_2	$\bar{x}_2$	s_2^2
3	t_3	$\bar{x}_3$	s_3^2
⋮	⋮	⋮	⋮
⋮	⋮	⋮	⋮
k	t_k	$\bar{x}_k$	s_k^2

The set of the values of the statistic so obtained, one for each sample, constitutes what is called the *sampling distribution* of the statistic. For example, the values $t_1, t_2, t_3, \ldots, t_k$ determine the sampling distribution of the statistic t. In other words, statistic *t* may be regarded as a random variable which can take the values $t_1, t_2, t_3, \ldots, t_k$ and we can compute the various statistical constants like mean, variance, skewness, kurtosis, etc., for its distribution. Sample is defined as that part of the population which is drawn from the population to give judgement about the population. Suppose to make a statistical enquiry of housing industry of Ludhiana from the total population we draw 100 units. These 100 units will be called sample. Number of individuals or objects which are taken in the sample is called as size of the sample and is denoted by the symbol ***n***. If $n < 30$ it is called as small sample if on the other hand $n \geq 30$ it is called large sample.

Different sampling techniques are available. Important of them are random sampling, purposive sampling, stratified sampling, systematic sampling, multistage sampling etc. All these techniques have their own merits and demerits.

Two methods are explained below:

(a) **Sampling with replacement.** If while drawing a sample, out of a given population, drawn unit is replaced back before the next draw, sampling is called as sampling with replacement. If size of the population is N and size of the sample is n the number of possible samples is N^n.

(b) **Sampling without replacement.** If in the sampling process drawn unit is not replaced back, sampling is called as sampling without replacement. If size of the population is N and size of sample is n, the number of samples possible without replacement is NC_n.

Sampling Plans. Sampling plans using attribute or variables are :-

(a) **Single Sampling Plan.** A lot is accepted or rejected on the basis of a single sample drawn from that lot.

Characteristics of Single Sampling Plan

(i) A single sampling plan is easy to design, explain and administer.

(ii) It is the only practical type of sampling plan under conveygorized production conditions when duly one sample can be selected.

(iii) It involves a lower cost of training and supervising employees, transporting and sorting samples, etc.

(iv) It very accurately estimates lot quality.

(v) It is more economical than double sampling plan.

(vi) It involves a bigger sample size than the double sampling plan.

(vii) It involves record keeping less than that of double and multiple sampling plans.

(viii) A single sampling plan provides maximum information concerning the lot quality because each sample can be plotted on the control chart.

(b) **Double Sampling Plans.** If it is not possible to decide the fate of the lot on the basis of first sample, a second sample is drawn and the decision is taken on the basis of the combined results of first and second sample.

Characteristics of Double Sample Plan

(i) A double sampling plan is more expensive to administer than a composable single sampling plan.

(ii) It involves less inspection than that required for a single sampling plan

(iii) Double sampling plan is easier to sell to the personnel because psychologically the idea of giving a second chance to a lot before rejecting it exercises popular appeal.

(iv) It permits a smaller first sample than the sample size of the corresponding single sampling plan.

(v) A double sampling plan involves more overheads than a single sampling plan.

(vi) It involves more record keeping than a single sampling plan.

(c) **Multiple Sampling Plans.** A lot is accepted or rejected based upon the results obtained from several samples (of parts) drawn from the lot.

Characteristics

(i) A multiple Sampling Plan involves smaller first samples than single or double sampling plans.

(ii) A multiple sampling plan is comparatively difficult to design and explain, and expensive to administer.

(iii) It involves a higher overhead cost as compared to single and double sampling plans.
(iv) It involves more record keeping.
(v) In theory, multiple sampling may often permit lower total inspection than double sampling for a given degree of protection because of smaller sample sizes required.
(vi) New methods, which simplify multiple sampling, such as automatic sampling boxes may result in greatly improved efficiency in administering multiple sampling plans.
Multiple Sampling Plan Procedure.

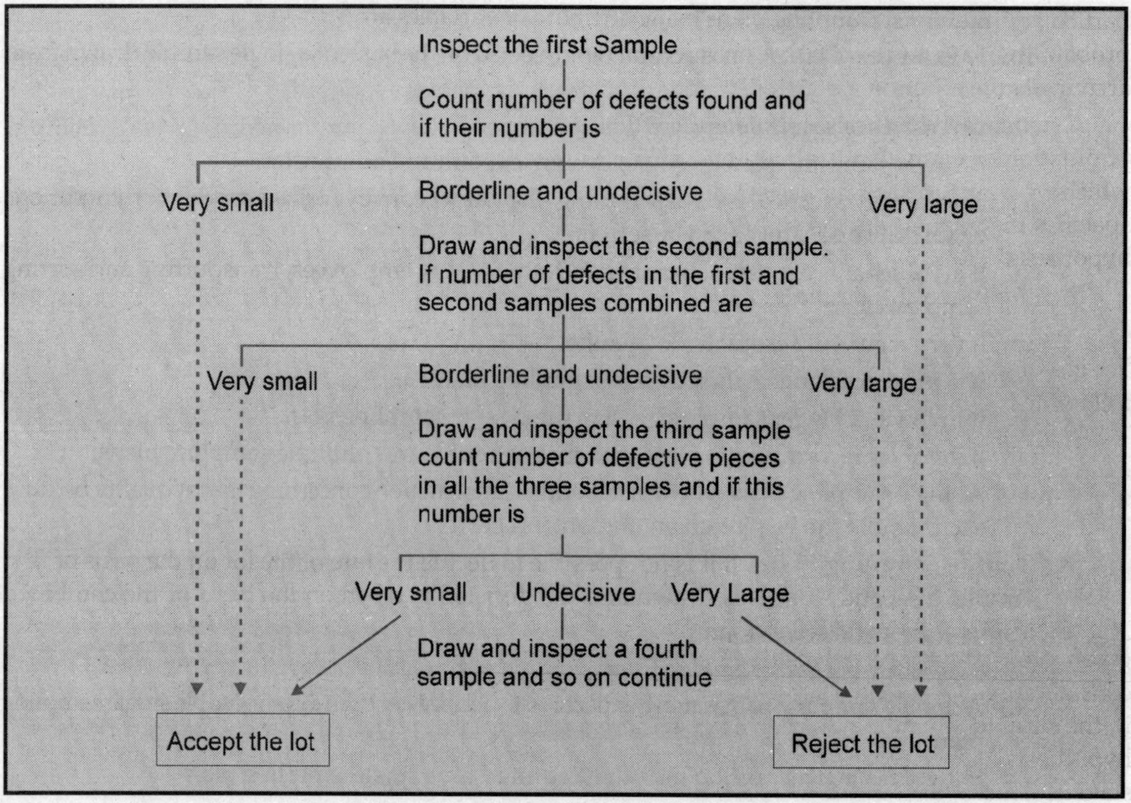

D. Sequential Sampling Plan (Item by item analysis). It involves increasing the sample size by one part at a time till the sample becomes large enough and contains sufficient number of defective pieces to decide intelligently whether to accept or reject the lot.

Characteristics

(i) It is easy to design, but more expensive to administer than a comparable multisampling plan, since more steps are needed to take a decision.
(ii) Since sample size is increased by one at a time, sample results are analysed much faster than in a simple or double sampling plan.
(iii) Sampling costs are least.
(iv) Overhead cost is maximum
(v) It is seldom used in lot acceptance control but is important because multiple sampling is based on it.

Testing of Hypothesis

This theory was initiated by J. Neyman and E.S. Pearsan and it employs statistical techniques to arrive at decisions in certain situations where there is an element of uncertainty on the basis of a sample whose size is fixed in advance.

Example. A pharmaceutical concern may be interested to find if a new drug is really effective for the particular ailment, say, in reducing blood pressure or inducing sleep; we may want to decide whether a given foodstuff is really effective in increasing weight; or which of the two brands of a particular product, say, foodstuffs, fertilisers, etc., is more effective. It is here that the modern theory of probability plays a very vital role in decision making and the branch of statistics which helps us in arriving at the criterion for such decisions is known as testing of hypothesis.

A statistical hypothesis is some assumption or statement, which may or may not be true, about a population or equivalently about the probability distribution characterising the given population, which we want to test on the basis of the evidence from a random sample. If the hypothesis completely specifies the population, then it is known as simple hypothesis, otherwise it is known as composite hypothesis.

In sampling from a normal population $N(\mu, \sigma^2)$, the hypothesis

$$H : \mu = \mu_0 \text{ and } \sigma^2 = \sigma_0^2$$

is a simple hypothesis since it completely specifies the distribution. On the other hand, each of the following hypothesis is a composite hypothesis :

(i) $\mu = \mu_0$, (Nothing known about σ^2)
(ii) $\sigma^2 = \sigma_0$, (μ not specified)
(iii) $\mu < \mu_0$, $\sigma^2 = \sigma_0^2$
(iv) $\mu > \mu_0$, $\sigma^2 = \sigma_0^2$
(v) $\mu = \mu_0$, $\sigma^2 > \sigma_0^2$ and so on.

A test of a statistical hypothesis is a two-action decision after observing a random sample from the given population, the two actions being the acceptance or rejection of the hypothesis under consideration. The truth or falsity of a statistical hypothesis is thus based on the information contained in the sample which may be consistent or inconsistent with the hypothesis and accordingly, the hypothesis may be accepted or rejected. It should be clearly borne in mind that the acceptance of a statistical hypothesis is due to insufficient evidence provided by the sample to reject it and does not necessarily imply that it is true.

HYPOTHESIS TESTING

Steps Involved in Hypothesis Testing

1. **Framing of hypothesis.** In all the problems of hypothesis testing, we frame a set of hypothesis. First of the two hypothesis is called as a Null hypothesis and is denoted by the symbol H_0. The other hypothesis is called as alternative Hypothesis and is denoted by the symbol H_0. The concept of null hypothesis is similar to the legal principle., 'Man is innocent until he is proved guilty.' To test whether one procedure is better than another, we assume that there is no difference between the procedures. Similarly to test whether there is a relationship between two variates, we take H_0 that there is no relationship. By accepting a null hypothesis, we mean that on the basis of the statistic calculated from the sample, we do not reject the hypothesis. It

however, does not imply that the hypothesis is proved to be true. Nor its rejection implies that it is disproved.

In hypothesis testing we assume that difference is insignificant unless and until it is proved that difference is significant. As clear null hypothesis will always be in the form of equality and alternative hypothesis will always be in the form of inequality.

Suppose we are to list the claim that on an average life of bulbs produced by Philips company is 500 hrs., our set of hypothesis will be

$H_0 = \mu = 500$ hours.

$H_1 = \mu \neq 500$ hours.

Similarly if we are to test the claim that on an average the bulb produced by philips company has a better life than the bulb produced by Bajaj Company, our act of hypothesis will be

$H_0 = \mu_1 = \mu_2$

$\mu_1 - \mu_2 = 0$

$H_1 = \mu_1 > \mu_2$

or $\mu_1 - \mu_2 > 0$

2. **Deciding the level of significance.** While testing hypothesis, two types of errors are possible

Ho	True	False
Accepted	✓	Type II Error
Rejected	Type I Error	✓

As clear Type I error is the error rejecting null hypothesis when it is true and should have been accepted. Type II error, on the other hand, is the error accepting null hypothesis when it is false and should have been rejected. In reality both of these errors are serious and efforts should be made to keep them at the lowest possible level. Unfortunately, it is not possible to reduce them simultaneously. If we try to reduce Type I error, probability of committing Type II error gets increased and vice-versa. It is universally accepted that Type I error is more serious than Type II error. For *e.g.*, in law, it is tried that innocent should not be punished, guilty may be set free. It is assumed that declaring innocent person a guilty is more serious than describing guilty person an innocent. Level of significance is defined as the probability of committing Type I Error. In other words, level of significance is the probability of rejecting null hypothesis when it is true and should have been accepted. In all practical problems because of its serious nature, probability of committing Type II error is kept at 1% level, 2% level or at the most 5% level. Suppose it is decided that probability of committing Type I error is to be kept at 5% level of significance, it means rejection region or shaded area should be 0.025 in the right tail and 0.025 on the left tail. And unshaded area in the right hand side as well as in the left hand side should be equal to 0.475. From Z tables it is clear that critical values of Z will be ± 1.96. If calculated value of Z is more than 1.96 or is less than –1.96, null hypothesis is true but we will reject it. The region is called acceptance region. The region in which if Z falls will lead to the rejection of null hypothesis is called as rejection region and the region in which if Z falls with result in the acceptance region.

3. **To select between single tail test or two tail test.** In hypothesis testing the third decision is regarding the selection between one tail test or two tail test. If we test the hypothesis that population mean is equal to μ against the alternative hypothesis then population mean is not equal to μ, it is a two tail test. If on the other hand, we are to test the hypothesis that population mean is equal to μ against the hypothesis that it is more than μ, it requires single tail test. It involves only right tail test. If we are to test hypothesis that population mean is equal to μ against the hypothesis that is less than μ, it will be single tail test and will involve only left tail.

LOS / Types of test	5%	2%	1%
Two tail	1.96	2.33	2.58
Right tail	+1.645	+2.05	+2.33
Left tail	-1.645	-2.05	-2.33

4. **Selection of appropriate test.** Last decision is to select appropriate test. They are many tests for the purpose of hypothesis testing like z test, t test, F test and Chi square (χ^2) test. Selection of test depends upon :

(a) Size of the sample

(b) Nature of the hypothesis

(c) Nature of distribution of the population from which sample is taken.

Large and Small Samples

On the basis of size of sampling, theory of sampling is divided into two categories : Large and small sampling. If size of the sample is 30 or more, sampling is said to be large sampling. If size of the sample is less than 30, it is said to be small sample. In all the problems of large sampling, we apply z test which is based on normal distribution.

z test has four applications:

(a) **To test hypothesis related with population mean** - Suppose we are to test any hypothesis regarding population $\bar{x} = \mu$ or not. For this purpose the following set of hypothesis is constructed.

H_0 = Population mean = μ

H_1 = Population mean ≠ μ

If we draw a large sample of size n and sample mean is denoted by the symbol $\bar{x}$. According to the central limit theorem, whatever is the form of parent population, sample $\bar{x}$ will be distributed normally as below.

Sample mean ~ N [Pop. mean, S.D. ($\bar{x}$)]

If null hypothesis is correct.

$$\bar{x} \sim N(\mu, \sigma_{\bar{x}})$$

$$\text{or } Z = \frac{\bar{x} - \mu}{\sigma/\sqrt{n}}$$

$$\sigma_{\bar{x}} = \frac{\sigma}{\sqrt{n}}$$

Where σ = Standard Deviation of the population

n = size of the sample

Calculated value of z is compared with its critical value at a given level of significance. If calculated value of z falls in the rejection region null hypothesis may be rejected otherwise accepted.

(b) **To test hypothesis related with difference of population means.** Z test can also be used for studying the significance of the difference between the two population means. For this purpose, following set of hypothesis is prepared:-

$H_0 : \mu_1 = \mu_2$

or $\mu_1 - \mu_2 = 0$ or Difference is insignificant

$H_1 : \mu_1 \neq \mu_2$

or $\mu_1 - \mu_2 \neq 0$ or Difference is significant

Suppose we draw large samples of sizes n_1 and n_2 from the two populations. The symbol $\bar{x}_1$ denotes means of the first sample and $\bar{x}_2$ denotes mean of the second sample. If samples are large, difference between two samples means will be distributed normally as below.

$$\bar{x}_1 - \bar{x}_2 \sim N\,[\mu_1 - \mu_2, \sigma_{\bar{x}_1 - \bar{x}_2}]$$

$$z = \frac{(\bar{x}_1 - \bar{x}_2) - (\mu_1 - \mu_2)}{\sigma_{\bar{x}_1 - \bar{x}_2}}$$

If null hypothesis is true then z is

$$z = \frac{\bar{x}_1 - \bar{x}_2}{\sigma_{\bar{x}_1 - \bar{x}_2}}$$

(c) **To test hypothesis related with proportion.** Sometimes investigator is dealing with a population which can be divided into two categories – (i) possessing the characteristic (ii) not possessing the characteristic. The possession of characteristic is called as success and its absence is called as failure. This type of sampling is called as sampling of attributes.

Suppose it is to be seen that the hypothesis population proportion of success is equal to P or not. Following set of hypothesis is prepared.

H_0 : Population proportion = P

H_1 : Population proportion $\neq$ P

If null hypothesis is true

$p \sim N\,[P, \sigma_p]$

$$z = \frac{p - P}{\sigma_p}$$

$$\sigma_p = \sqrt{\frac{PQ}{n}}$$

$$z = \frac{p - P}{\sqrt{\frac{PQ}{n}}}$$

P = Proportion of success

Q = Proportion of failure

We may estimate population proportion of success from sample proportion. For this purpose we will find various confidence limits.

95% confidence limit for population proportion will be

$p \pm 1.96\,\sigma_p$

98%

$p \pm 2.33\,\sigma_p$

99%

$p \pm 2.58\,\sigma_p$

(d) To test the significance of difference of proportion. For this purpose, following set of hypothesis is prepared

$H_0 : \sigma$ = difference is insignificant

$P_1 = P_2$ or $P_1 - P_2 = 0$

H_1 : difference is significant

$P_1 \neq P_2$ or $P_1 - P_2 \neq 0$

If sample of sizes = n_1 and n_2

No. of success in Ist sample = x_1

No. of success in IInd sample = x_2

$$p_1 = \frac{x_1}{n_1} \quad p_2 = \frac{x_2}{n_2}$$

If samples are large, difference of proportions will be distributed normally as below :

$$p_1 - p_2 \sim N\,[p_1 - p_2, \sigma_{p_1 - p_2}]$$

$$\sigma_{p_1 - p_2} = \sqrt{\frac{P_1Q_1}{n_1} + \frac{P_2Q_2}{n_2}}$$

$$p_1 - p_2 \sim N\,[p_1 - p_2, \sqrt{\frac{P_1Q_1}{n_1} + \frac{P_2Q_2}{n_2}}\,]$$

$$z = \frac{[p_1 - p_2] - [P_1 - P_2]}{\sqrt{\frac{P_1Q_1}{n_1} + \frac{P_2Q_2}{n_2}}}$$

If null hypothesis is true

$$z = \frac{[p_1 - p_2] - 0}{\sqrt{\frac{PQ}{n_1} + \frac{PQ}{n_2}}}$$

p_1 = sample proportion of test

n_1 = size of sample

Value of P and Q are calculated as below

$$p = \frac{n_1p_1 + n_2p_2}{n_1 + n_2}$$

$$\text{or } p = \frac{n_1\left(\frac{x_1}{n_1}\right) + n_2\left(\frac{x_2}{n_2}\right)}{n_1 + n_2}$$

Cancelling n_1 by n_1, n_2 by n_2, we get

$$p = \frac{x_1 + x_2}{n_1 + n_2}$$

$$Q = 1 - p$$

SMALL SAMPLING

t–test. When size of the sample is less than 30, theory of sampling is called as small sample. In Z test we assumed that sample statistics is distributed normally.

If size of sample is small, normality can not be applied. As a result a separate test or new test to deal with small samples is t-test.

Prof. Gosset developed 't' test under his pen name student. Therefore, it is also known as student's 't' test.

It is defined as :

If from a normal population with $\bar{x} = \mu$ the sample of size n is drawn, t is defined as

$$t = \frac{\bar{x} - \mu}{\frac{\sigma_s}{\sqrt{n-1}}}$$

where

$$\bar{x} = \frac{\Sigma x}{N}$$

$$\sigma_s = \frac{\sqrt{\Sigma(x-\bar{x})^2}}{n}$$

or

$$t = \frac{\bar{x} - \mu}{\frac{s}{\sqrt{n}}} \quad \text{where } \bar{x} = \frac{\Sigma x}{N}, s = \frac{\sqrt{\Sigma(x-\bar{x})^2}}{n-1}$$

Where s is called as unbiased estimate of population standard deviation.

Assumptions

1. Parent population is normal in nature
2. Sample is random in nature
3. Population standard deviation is not given.

USES OF 'T' TEST

1. To test hypothesis related with population mean

H_0 : Population mean = μ

H_1 : Population mean $\neq \mu$.

If we are to test the hypothesis that the population mean equal to μ or not. For this purpose, we will prepare the following set of hypothesis.

H_0 : pop. mean = μ.

H_1 : pop. mean $\neq \mu$

and t is calculated as

$$t = \frac{\bar{x} - \mu}{\frac{\sigma_s}{\sqrt{n-1}}}$$

Calculated value of 't' is compared with its tabulated value at a given level of significance for n-1 degrees of freedom. If 't' calculated is greater than 't' tabulated, null hypothesis may be rejected otherwise accepted.

2. To test hypothesis related with difference of population means

Ist case – Non Paired samples. To test whether the difference between two population means is significant or not. Following is the SET of hypothesis

$H_0 : \mu_1 = \mu_2$ or $\mu_1 - \mu_2 = 0$

or Difference is insignificant

$H_1 : \mu_1 \neq \mu_2$ or $\mu_1 - \mu_2 \neq 0$

or Difference is significant

Suppose $\bar{x}_1$ = mean of sample from 1st population

$\bar{x}_2$ = mean of sample from 2nd population

$$\therefore t = \frac{\bar{x}_1 - \bar{x}_2}{\sqrt{s^2\left[\frac{1}{n_1} + \frac{1}{n_2}\right]}}$$

n_1 = size of 1st sample

n_2 = size of 2nd sample

$$s^2 = \text{compiled pooled variance} = \frac{n_1\sigma_{s_1}^2 + n_2\sigma_{s_2}^2}{n_1 + n_2 - 2}$$

$$s^2 = \frac{n_1\frac{\left[\sum(x_1 - \bar{x}_1)^2\right]}{n_1} + n_2\frac{\left[\sum(x_2 - \bar{x}_2)^2\right]}{n_2}}{n_1 + n_2 - 2}$$

Cancelling n_1 by n_1, n_2 by n_2, we get

$$s^2 = \frac{\sum(x_1 - \bar{x}_1)^2 + \sum(x_2 - \bar{x}_2)^2}{n_1 + n_2 - 2}$$

Calculated value of t is compared with its critical value at a given Los for $n_1 + n_2 - 2$ degree of freedom and the decision is taken.

IInd case – Paired Samples. If the two samples are of the same size and the data are paired, then t is defined by

$$t = \frac{\bar{d} - 0}{(\sigma/\sqrt{n})}$$

where, $$s^2 = \frac{1}{n-1}\sum_1^n (d_i - \bar{d})^2$$

d_i = difference of the ith members of the samples;

$\bar{d}$ = mean of the difference

$$= \frac{\Sigma d_i}{n}$$

and the number of degree of freedom = n – 1

F-TEST

F- test is a small sample test given by Prof. Snedicor. It is defined as, if from two normal populations with equal variance, we draw independent random samples of sizes n_1 and n_2 respectively and $s_1^2 = \frac{\Sigma(x_1 - \bar{x}_1)^2}{n_1 - 1}$ is the unbiased estimate of variance of Ist population and $s_2^2 = \frac{\Sigma(x_2 - \bar{x}_2)^2}{n_2 - 1}$ is the unbiased estimate of variance of 2nd population, then statistic 'F' is defined as

$$F = \frac{s_1^2}{s_2^2} \text{ if } s_1^2 > s_2^2$$

$$\text{or } F = \frac{s_2^2}{s_1^2} \text{ if } s_2^2 > s_1^2$$

Assumptions

1. Parent population from which samples are drawn are normal in nature
2. Both the population have same variance.
3. Samples are random and independent.

Uses

1. To test the significance of the difference between the two population variance we can check that whether the populations from which samples are drawn have some variance or not. Following is the set of hypothesis.

$H_0 = \sigma_1^2 = \sigma_2^2$ or difference in two population variances is insignificant.

$H_1 = \sigma_1^2 \neq \sigma_2^2$ or difference is significant. Suppose, from the two population, we draw two samples of sizes n_1 and n_2 the unbiased estimates of population variances will be calculated as below.

$$s_1^2 = \frac{\Sigma(x_1 - \bar{x}_1)^2}{n_1 - 1}, \quad s_2^2 = \frac{\Sigma(x_2 - \bar{x}_2)^2}{n_2 - 1}$$

$$\text{Then } F = \frac{s_1^2}{s_2^2} \text{ if } s_1^2 > s_2^2 \qquad v_1 = n_1 - 1 ; v_2 = n_2 - 1$$

$$\text{or } F = \frac{s_2^2}{s_1^2} \text{ if } s_2^2 > s_1^2 \qquad v_1 = n_2 - 1 ; v_2 = n_1 - 1$$

Calculated value of 'F' is compared with its critical value at a given Los for v_1, v_2 degree of freedom and decision is taken.

F-TEST MAKES BASIS OF ANOVA

Analysis of variance is that technique of data analysis which is used for analysing total variations in the variable under study. Total variations are divided into variations because of chance factor. In the end by calculating 'F' ratio it is decided whether variations because of different treatments are significantly higher than variations because of chance factor.

The concept of ANOVA was developed by Prof. Fisher and is based upon 'F' test. Students 't' test can be used to study the difference of means if number of samples is two. If no. of samples is 3 or more, 't' test fails to study the significance of the difference between population means. In such cases, we apply ANOVA.

CHI-SQUARE TEST

When a fair coin is tossed 80 times, we expect from theoretical considerations that heads will appear 40 times and tail 40 times. But this never happens in practice i.e., the results obtained in an experiment do not agree exactly with the theoretical results. The magnitude of discrepaney between observation and theory is given by the quantity χ^2 (pronounced as chi-square). If $\chi^2 = 0$, the observed and theoretical frequencies completely agree. As the value of χ^2 increases, the discrepancy between the observed and theoretical frequencies increases.

If $O_1, O_2, ...O_n$ be a set of observed (experimental) frequencies and $E_1, E_2, ..., E_n$ be the corresponding set of expected (theoretical) frequencies, then χ^2 is defined by the relation.

$$\chi^2 = \frac{(O_1 - E_1)^2}{E_1} + \frac{(O_2 - E_2)^2}{E_2} + ... + \frac{(O_n - E_n)^2}{E_n}$$

$$= \sum \frac{(O_i - E_i)^2}{E_i}$$

with n -1 degree of freedom.

$[\Sigma O_i = \Sigma E_i = n$ the total frequency$]$

Uses

1. To test the significance of difference or to test the goodness of fit.
2. To test the association of attributes or characteristics

APPLICATIONS

(i) In two by two table if any cell frequency is less than 5, it will make the applicability of χ^2 test impossible. In the process of pooling degree of freedom will be lost. In '2×2' contingency table degree of freedom (2–1) (2–1) = 1. After pooling is done degree of freedom will be lost and correct degree of freedom will be zero for which χ^2 distribution does not exist. Hence χ^2 test cannot be applied. For this purpose Prof. F.C. Yates has give a correction called as Yates correction for continuity. After the application of this correction χ^2 is calculated as below.

$$\chi^2 = \frac{N\left[(ad - bc) - \frac{1}{2}N\right]^2}{(a+c)(b+d)(a+b)(c+d)}$$

Pooling will not be required and therefore χ^2 test can be applied.

(ii) Suppose we are to test hypothesis related with population variance. For this purpose we shall frame the following set of hypothesis.

H_0 : Population variance = σ^2

H_1 : Population variance ≠ σ^2

The value of χ^2 is calculated as below: $\chi^2 = \frac{(n)(\sigma_s^2)}{\sigma_0^2}$

where n = size of the sample: $\sigma_s^2 = \frac{\Sigma(x - \bar{x})^2}{n}$

σ_0^2 = Population variance claimed under null hypothesis.

Calculated value of χ^2 is compared with its critical value at a given level of significance for n-1 degree of freedom. If χ^2 (calculated) is greater than χ^2 (tab) null hypothesis may be rejected or otherwise accepted.

OPERATIONS MANAGEMENT

ROLE AND SCOPE OF PRODUCTION MANAGEMENT

Production may be defined as conversion of inputs – men, machine, materials, money, methods and management (6 Ms) into output through a transformation process. Output may be goods produced or services rendered. Production function has assumed a great importance as a key function in all industrial undertakings. All other functions revolve around this function. The activities of production are independent of the size of the undertaking. In a small concern one person may be undertaking this function whereas in large organisations this activity may be undertaken by various individuals or separate teams. The success or failure of an enterprise is dependent upon the extent of care and accuracy with which production function is managed.

Production with management activity can be described as an art of securing maximum prosperity with a minimum of effort so as to secure maximum prosperity and happiness of both employer and employee and give the public the best possible service.

Different aspects of production function:

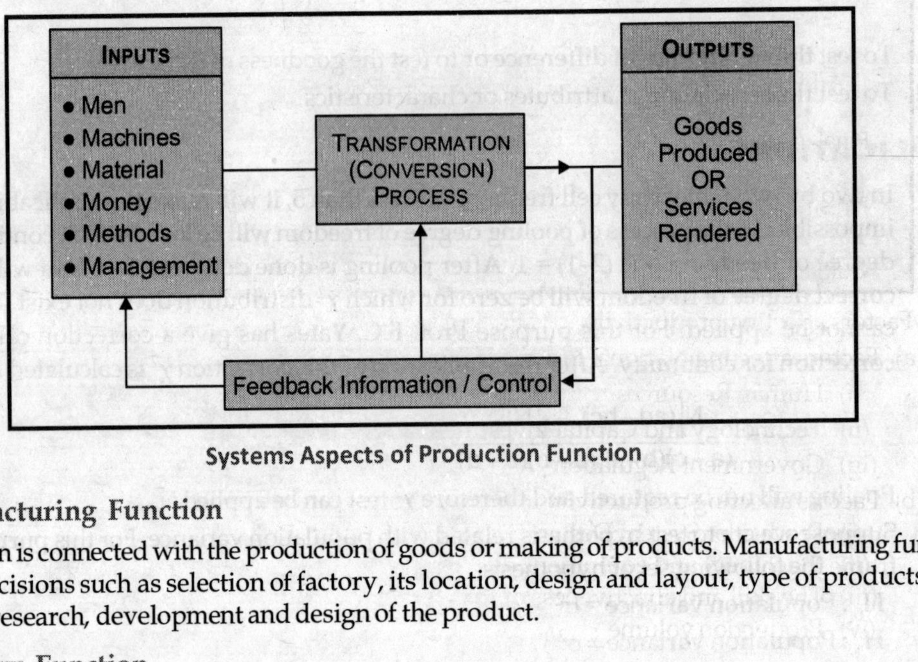

Systems Aspects of Production Function

1. Manufacturing Function

This function is connected with the production of goods or making of products. Manufacturing function includes decisions such as selection of factory, its location, design and layout, type of products to be produced; research, development and design of the product.

2. Ancillary Function

This function includes all those activities which support or smoothen production function. Ancillary function is related to production planning and control, maintenance, purchasing, store-keeping and materials handling.

3. Advisory Function

It helps in improving production function. It includes work study, method study, operational research, inspection and quality control.

There are four recognized factors of production

(a) Nature (land and other natural resources)

(b) Labour (human efforts)

(c) Capital (factory building, machinery, tools, raw materials, etc.)

(d) Enterprise (activity that organises other factors of production into an operating unit).

Related to production, an always difficult managerial decision is regarding the selection of plant site and then plant layout. Plant location should be such that production and distribution costs are minimum but the profit is maximum. After locating the site, the facilities (equipments, etc.) have to be laid out. A good plant layout permits the materials to move at the desired speed and at minimum cost.

Before starting the actual production, one has to plan the same. Production planning and control, considers the determination and regulation of production processes and has different functions like routing, scheduling, dispatching, progress, control, etc.

Production system can be shown as follows:

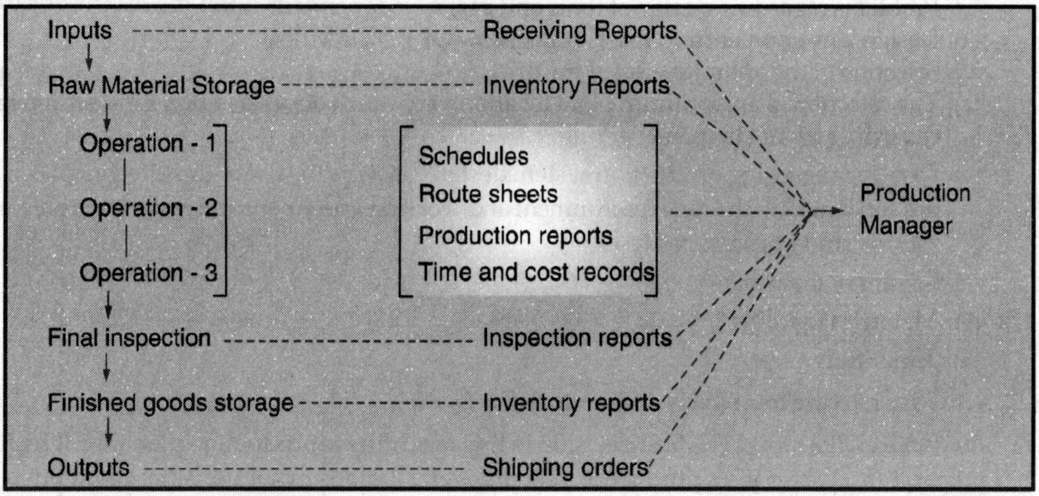

Factors affecting productivity

(a) Factors affecting National Productivity
   (i) Human Resources
   (ii) Technology and Capital Investment.
   (iii) Government Regulation

(b) Factors affecting productivity in manufacturing and services.
   (i) Product or System Design
   (ii) Machinery and equipment
   (iii) The skill and effectiveness of the worker
   (iv) Production volume

Kinds of Productivity Measures

(i) **Labour Productivity.** The resource inputs are aggregated in terms of labour hours. Hence the index is relatively free of changes caused by wage rates and labour mix.

(ii) **Direct Labour Cost productivity.** The resource inputs are aggregated in terms of direct labour costs. This will reflect the effect of both wage rates and changes in the labour mix.

(iii) **Capital Productivity.** Several formulations are possible. In one, the resource inputs may be the charges during the period of depreciation; in another, the inputs may be the book value of capital investment.

(iv) **Direct Cost Productivity.** In this formulation, all terms of direct cost associated with resources used are aggregated on a monetary value basis.

(v) **Energy Productivity.** In this formulation the only resource considered is the amount of energy consumed.

(vi) **Raw Material Productivity.** In this formulation, the numerators are usually weight of product, the denominators are the weight of raw material consumed.

Scope of Production. Scope of production management are :

(1) **Activities relating to Production system Design.** Decision relating to the production system design is the firm and fore-most activity of the production management. This activity concerns the:

- (i) Production engineering.
- (ii) Problems regarding design of tools and jigs.
- (iii) Design, development and INSTALLATION OF EQUIPMENT
- (iv) Selection of the optimum size of the firm.
- (v) The selection of an optimum plant location very much depends upon the decision taken regarding production engineering.
- (vi) Decision regarding production system design concerns the use of those techniques which are concerned with work environment and work measurement and includes problem like motion study process analyses.
- (vii) Layout of the plant.
- (viii) Material Handling
- (ix) Time Study.

(2) **Activities relating to analysis and control of activities.**

(a) **Production Planning.** The first decision in this regarding is production planning. It includes preparation of short term production schedules etc. Various major decisions required in production management are as follows :

- (i) **Production Design.** To lead in research and engineering competitions in all areas of our primary business, designing and producing products and services with outstanding quality and inherent customer value.
- (ii) **Process designing and equipment selection.** To determine and design the production process and equipment that will be compatible with low cost and high quality.
- (iii) **Layout.** To achieve production efficiency and effectiveness through skills, imagination and resourcefulness in plan layout and work method.
- (iv) **Location and Facility Engineering.** To locate, design and build efficiency and economic facilities that will yield high value to the company.
- (v) **Human Resource Management.** To provide good quality of work life with well designed, safe rewarding jobs, stable employment and equitable pay in exchange for outstanding individual contribution from employees at all levels.
- (vi) **Maintenance.** To achieve high utilization of equipment.
- (vii) **Quality Assurance Control.** To attain exceptional quality that is consistent with company policy and marketing objective.
- (viii) **Material Management.** To cooperate with supplies and sale control to develop stable, effective and efficient sources of supply for those components that are to be processed from outside sources.

(ix) **Inventory Control.** To achieve low investment through scientific inventory control such as:

- ABC Analysis
- VED Analysis
- Economic Order Quantity
- Inventory Turnover Ratio etc.

And through appropriate customer service levels and high facility utilization.

(b) **Production Control.** After planning the next step is production control because production plan cannot be activated unless they are properly guided and controlled. For this purpose, production manager has to regulate work assignment, service work progress and check and remove discrepancies, if any, in the actual and planned performances of production manager has to look after the production control activity through:

(i) Control on inventory such as raw materials purchased parts, finished goods etc.

(ii) Control on work-in-progress through production control.

(iii) Control of quality through process control.

FACILITY LOCATION AND LAYOUT

An important decision which has a bearing on efficiency of production management relates to the suitable location of plant. The chief object of an industrial concern is to maximise profit through the minimisation of cost of production. This is possible when the firm is of the right (*i.e.*, optimum) size and is located at a place which provides economies of all kinds in production. In other words, optimum size has to be combined with optimum location if profit is to be maximised. It must be clearly understood at this stage that optimum location does not necessarily imply the most favourable location where labour costs are lowest, transportation costs are minimum, and the water is the best, "bur rather where the entire group of considerations is optimised."

Situation give Rise to the Problem of Location

1. At the time of starting a business unit.
2. The increase volume of its business and the extent of its market requirement.
3. The facilities provided for in the original location plan are no longer sufficient for the expanding business and therefore expansion of the existing plant or a new location is necessary.
4. The lease for the site has expired, owner of the property is not prepared to renew the lease agreement.
5. The existing power or water supply at the site is no longer sufficient for the purpose of production.

The various factors which usually determine the location of industries may be described as under:

(A) Primary Factors

1. **Raw Material.** From the point of view of minimization of transport costs, the nature of raw material is of great importance. Certain raw materials are of weight-losing character, say sugarcane. Such materials lose much of their weight while passing through the process of production. As a result, the finished product is lighter than the raw materials used in its manufacture.

Therefore, a good deal of economy in transport costs can be achieved if industries which use weight-losing materials are located near the source of materials. Other things which are taken into consideration are :-

(a) whether the raw materials are home produced or imported – in the latter case the unit must be established near ports,

(b) if there is financial linkage with raw material supplies so that the raw material may be available below market prices at some specific points,

(c) reliability and continuity of the source of supply, and

(d) the security of means of transport.

2. **Market.** The industries which use 'pure' raw materials, that is say, materials which do not lose much of their weight while being converted into finished goods, are generally located near the markets. Cotton is a good example. Up to ginning, cotton is a weight-losing material; therefore, ginning factories are generally found near cotton *mandis* or markets. After ginning cotton becomes non-weight-losing, because out of a hundred pounds of cotton about 95 pounds of cloth can be obtained. This is the chief reason why the cotton textile industry is located near markets.
3. **Fuel and Power.** The problem of fuel and power can also be solved with reference to the nature of raw materials. The industries which use very large quantities of coal are generally located near the coal mines. The development of electric and diesel power has reduced the importance of coal. Many industries which were previously attached by coal are now located at other convenient centres. The development of paper industry in South India is an important example.
4. **Transport.** The facilities for transport available in a particular region and the policy of freight rates are also of great importance.
5. **Labour.** Another important factor influencing the location of industries is labour. Industry can be started only at a place where the right type of labour is abundantly available at reasonable wages.

(B) Secondary Factors

1. **Momentum of an Early Start.** Another factor of some importance has been the momentum of an early start. There are a number of places where, to begin with, only one or two factories were started. With the passage of time these places gained importance and attracted industries.
2. **Industrial Atmosphere.** The industrial atmosphere of a place cannot be measured in tangible terms, but it has a very important advantage. Industrial atmosphere may be said to exist where people living at a place think instinctively of industry and learn the intricacies of machines without much effort. This helps the growth of even new industries.
3. **Soil and Climate.** The question of soil and climate is important particularly for agricultural products like tea, coffee and rubber, but due to scientific inventions and developments it is becoming less important for most of the manufactured goods.
4. **Personal Factors.** The initial location of an industry may, be prompted more by the personal likes and dislikes than purely economic considerations.
5. **Historical Factors.** Factors like personal fancies of entrepreneurs or historical accidents may in many cases lead to the development of a place as the centre of an industry.
6. **Political Stability.** The lack of political stability in a state makes for uncertainty in the attitude of State Governments to industry. In locating a plant, it must be seen as to whether the State has a record of political and economic stability.

Types of Facilities

1. **Heavy Manufacturing.** Heavy manufacturing facilities are primarily plants that are relatively large and require a lot of space and as a result, are expensive to construct.

   Examples. Automobile Plants, Steel Mills and Oil Refineries. Sites for manufacturing plants are normally selected where construction and land cost can be kept at minimum and raw material sources are near by in order to reduce transportation costs.

2. **Light Industry.** Light industry facilities are typically perceives as smaller, cleaner plants that produce electronic equipment as components, parts used in assemblies or assembled products. Environmental issues are less important in light industry. Important factors affecting these types of industries are :
   - Labour Pool
   - Especially the availability of skilled workers
   - The Community Environment
   - Government regulation
   - Land Use Requirements.

   Examples. Examples might include plants making stereos. TVs or Computers etc.

3. **Warehouses and Distribution Centres.** Warehouses are a category of their own. Products are not manufactured or assembled with in their confines, nor are they sold from them. They represent an intermediate point in the logistical inventory system where products are held in storage.

4. **Retail and Service.** Retail and service operations generally require the smallest and least costly facilities.

   Examples. It includes such service facilities as restaurants, banks hotel cleaners, clinics and law offices ad retail facilities such as groceries and department stores.

Layout Planning and Analysis

Plant layout refers to the arrangement of the physical facilities including production centres for the manufacture of a product.

Objectives of Facilities Layout. The objectives of facilities layout are :

1. Minimize investment in equipment
2. Minimize overall production time.
3. Utilize existing space most effectively.
4. Provide for employee convenience, safety and comfort.
5. Maintain flexibility of arrangement and operations.
6. Minimize materials handling cost.
7. Facilitate the manufacturing process.
8. Facilitate the organisational structure.

The layout of new plant is determined by taking into consideration the following factors :-

(A) **Basic managerial policies and decisions.** The type of layout suitable for a particular plant will depend basically on the policies formulated by the management with regard to size of plant, the kind and quality of products, the scope for the expansion to be provided for, the extent to which the plant is to be integrated; amount of stocks to be carried at any time, the kind of employee facilities to be provided, etc.

(B) **Nature of plant location.** The size, shape and topography of the site at which the plant is located will naturally affect the arrangement of the general layout for receiving and shipping and for the best flow of production in and out of the plant.

(C) **Type of industry and process.** This is one of the most important factors influencing the choice of a certain plan of layout for a plant. Generally, the type of layout particularly the arrangement of machines at work centres and the location of workmen varies according to the peculiar nature of the industry to which the plant belongs.

There are three types of plant layout:

1. **Product or Line Layout.** Product or line layout means the arrangement of the machines in a line in the order in which they would be used in the process of manufacture of the product. It is suitable for the continuous mass production of goods as it makes it possible for the raw materials to be fed into the plant at one end and taken out as finished products on the other.

   In the line type of layout, there will be a separate production line for each type of product. Each line may have the same machines though these may be arranged differently or the machines for each line may be different.

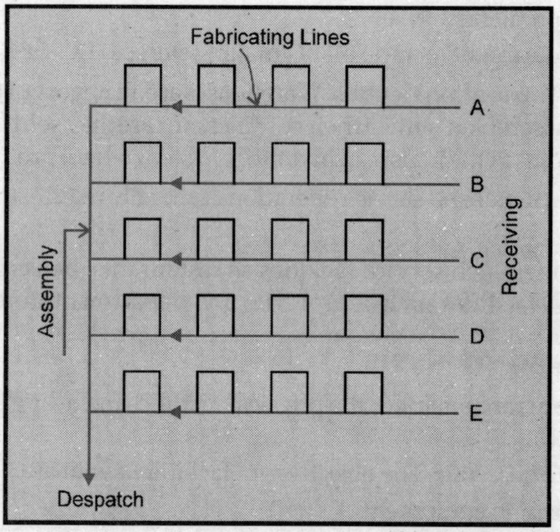

LINE LAYOUT

(The boxes along fabricating lines stand for machines)

Advantages of Product Layout

(i) The flow of product will be smooth and logical in flow lines.
(ii) In process inventory is less.
(iii) Throughput time is less.
(iv) Material handling cost is minimum.
(v) Operators need not be skilled.
(vi) Simple production planning and control system are possible.
(vii) Less space is occupied by work in transit and for temporary storage.

Limitations of Product Layout

(i) A breakdown on one machine in a product line may cause stoppages of machines in the downstream of the line.
(ii) A change in product design may require major alterations in the layout.
(iii) Comparatively high investment in equipments is required.

2. **Process or Functional Layout.** Process layout means the arrangement of similar machines in a group in one department according to the functions they perform in the plant. Thus, welding equipment may be placed in a separate welding department for the benefit of all lines of department.

   This type of layout is generally adopted for job order production under which different varieties of goods are produced in comparatively smaller quantities at irregular intervals. It can be shown as below:

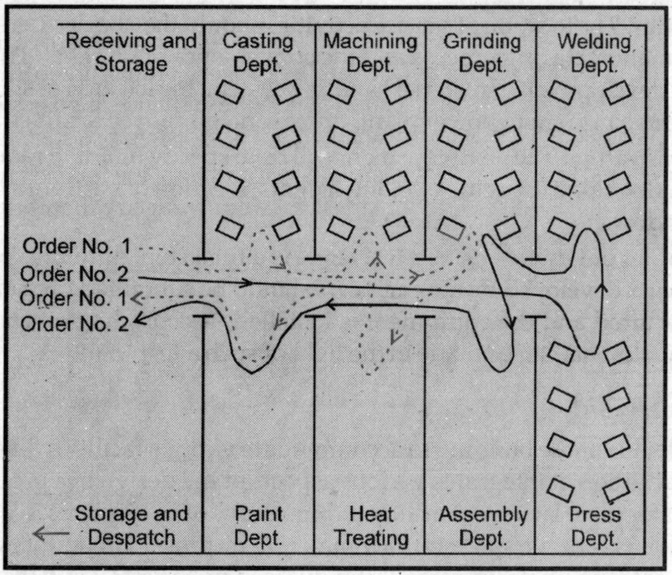

Advantages of Process Layout

(a) Machines are better utilized, fewer machines are required.
(b) A high degree of flexibility in terms of task allocation to machines exists.
(c) Comparatively low investment in machines is required.
(d) The diversity of tasks offers a more interesting and satisfying occupation for the operation.

Limitations of Process Layout

(a) Materials handling cost will be high.
(b) Production planning and control systems are more involved.
(c) Large amount of in-process inventory will results.
(d) Space and capital are tied up by work in process.
(e) Higher grades of skill are required.

3. **Combined Layout.** In practice, plants are generally laid out neither on the pure line pattern nor on the pure functional basis. It is usual for industries engaged in repetitive processes manufacturing standardized products to group expensive machines of a certain type for intensive use. Machine groupings of this type are then integrated into the 'line'. Likewise special service facilities like heavy cranes and fabrication stages calling for flexibility (say, welding) may be grouped for use on a number of different parts of a standard product.

Following steps have to be taken to develop a layout plan for a new establishment:

1. **Fixing the objectives and compilation of data.** This will include fixation of layout goals with respect to capacity, production flexibility and plants for future expansion. This may be followed by the preparation of operation process chart, machine data cards and templates of production machinery and material handling equipment.

2. **Formulation of an overall plan.** The next step in the development of a layout will be to prepare an overall plan including the flow of production, the arrangement of service activities and the best suited type of building. A floor plan may be prepared by grouping the machinery on line, or functional basis. Then, the type of building that will be most economical to construct keeping in view the layout plan and the location of the plant may be chosen.
3. **Arrangement of templates.** Templates representing machines and equipment may then be arranged on the floor plan according to the sequence indicated in the operation process chart.
4. **Service activities.** The location of service activities should then be decided keeping in view the facility of the manufacturing process and the convenience of workers. This will include decision about the development of material handling system, the location of shipping and receiving areas, the maintenance shop, power plant, offices and employee facilities and conveniences.
5. **Building specification.** The next step, then, will be to specify building requirements in respect of floor space, floor load capacities, ceiling heights, location of partitions, size and location of doors and windows.
6. **Preparation of layout drawings and test run.** As a final step, drawings of the layout and the supporting charts developed by the engineers should be submitted to management. When the building is acquired and the equipment is installed, test production runs should be made. Necessary adjustments can be made in the light of such a test - run.

Methods of Plant Layout

A layout furnishes details of the building to accommodate various facilities (like workers, material, machinery, etc.). In addition, it integrates various aspects of the design of a production system. The information required for plant laying out includes, dimensions of work places, sequence of operations, flow pattern of materials, storage space for raw material, in-process inventory and finished goods, offices, toilets, etc. There is no single universal technique leading to best layout; the different techniques independently or in conjunction with other techniques may be employed at different stages involved in plant or factory layout. The words plant and factory can be taken more or less as synonyms.

During different development stages of a layout, the following methods may be used.

(i) **Process flow charts.** They show, how different component parts assemble, in sequence of operations to form sub-assemblies which in turn lead to assemblies (finished products).

(ii) **Material Movement patterns.** The flow pattern of materials-in-process is traced and layout is built around it.

(iii) **Layout Analogues.** They cover two-dimensional cutouts or templates and three-dimensional models.

(a) **Templates.** They are used to develop plant layout. They are two-dimensional or block templates made up of cardboard, coloured paper or celluloid. They are made to scale and are placed on the scaled outline plan of the building. Templates or customs show the plan of the various facilities and the building. They show the actual floor space utilisation. The templates can be placed and attached with a tape either on a board or on a cross-hatched surface or on a graph paper and thus being known as Graphic technique. These templates have flexibility in use and can be moved on the graph paper from place to place in order to evaluate various feasible positions for different machines. It is better to photograph a layout before shifting the templates to try another layout of facilities. Templates save a lot of time and labour which otherwise would be spent in making drawings for each alternative plant layout arrangement.

A two-dimensional template gives machine outline and its details whereas a block template shows the boundary of the maximum projected area of the machine.

(b) **Three-Dimensional Models.** They are scale models of a facility, and, more near to the real situations as besides length and width they shows the height of the facility also. Models are especially suitable for persons who are not familiar with plant layout practice. Models are made up of wood or diecast plastic. They show minor details and can be mounted on a thick plastic sheet acting as the floor plan. Models are used mainly to develop floor plans and elevations. Models can be made for production machines, workers, material handling equipments or any other facility. Models are much more effective and fast as compared to drawings or templates especially when multi-storey plant layout is to be designed.

(iv) **The correlation chart.** It involves drawing a grid with rows presenting alternative solutions. Plant items can be ground floor, first floor or other floors of a multi-storey building.

(v) **Travel chart.** A travel chart as the name suggests is a chart or record of the amount of travel by the material in process while going from machine to machine a from one department to another. The amount of travel depends upon the frequency of movements between sections or departments. A travel chart helps improving the existing plant layout.

(vi) **Lord Path Matrix Method.** This method aims at reducing the transportation of in-process inventory from section to section. Like travel chart it also helps deciding the position of one department in relation to the other. The ultimate purpose is to modify the existing layout or the preliminary plant layout made by other techniques. The departments having mass flow of material or goods are placed close to each other.

ENTERPRISE RESOURCE PLANNING – ERP MODULES, ERP IMPLEMENTATION

Enterprise resource planning (ERP) is a process used by companies to manage and integrate the important parts of their businesses. Many ERP software applications exist to help companies implement resource planning by integrating all of the processes it needs to run a company with a single system. An ERP software system can integrate planning, purchasing inventory, sales, marketing, finance, human resources, and more.

Understanding Enterprise Resource Planning

You can think of an enterprise resource planning system as the glue that binds together the different computer systems for a large organization. Without an ERP application, each department would have its own system optimized for that division's particular tasks. With ERP software, each department still has its own system, but all of the systems can be accessed through one application with one interface.

ERP applications also allows the different departments to communicate and share information more easily with the rest of the company. It collects information about the activity and state of different divisions, making this information available to other parts, where it can be used productively.

ERP applications can help a corporation become more self-aware by linking information about production, finance, distribution, and human resources together. Because it connects different technologies used by each individual part of a business, an ERP application can eliminate costly duplicate and incompatible technology. The process often integrates accounts payable, stock-control systems, order-monitoring systems, and customer databases into one system.

ERP offerings have evolved over the years from traditional software models that make use of physical client servers to cloud-based software that offers remote, web-based access.

A company could experience cost overruns if its ERP system is not implemented carefully.

Special Considerations

An ERP system doesn't always eliminate inefficiencies within the business. The company needs to rethink the way it's organized, or else it will end up with incompatible technology.

ERP systems usually fail to achieve the objectives that influenced their installation because of a company's reluctance to abandon old working processes that are incompatible with the software. Some companies are also reluctant to let go of old software that worked well in the past. The key is to prevent ERP projects from being split into many smaller projects, which can result in cost overruns.

ERP Solutions Providers

Some familiar names are leaders in ERP software. Oracle Corp. (ORCL) originally supplied a relational database that integrated with ERP software developed by SAP (SAP) before entering the broader enterprise market in a big way in the early 2000's. Microsoft (MSFT) has long been an industry leader, with many customers using multiple software applications from the company.

As cloud-based solutions have grown in popularity in recent years, the traditional ERP industry leaders have seen challenges from upstarts such as Bizowie and WorkWise.

SCHEDULING

Production Scheduling

Once the planning (work) to meet sales is complete and a set of decisions have been formulated, the next step is the implementation of the decisions through detailed plans and schedules.

Schedule and control of production focus attention on the following :

(a) Knowing the total overall production targets – how to determine the amount of each product to be manufactured if there are products of different kinds and sizes ?

(b) How to decide about and deploy work force (different types of workers and kinds of skills) and equipment to achieve the target production rate ?

(c) How to determine individual work assignments ?

(d) What should be the information system to feed back quickly and accurately the actual output duly compared with the scheduled one ?

Scheduling means – when and in what sequence the work will be done. It involves deciding as to when the work will start and in a certain duration of time how much work will be finished. Scheduling deals with orders and machines, *i.e.*, it determines which order will be taken up on which machine and in which department by which operator. While doing so, the aim is to schedule as large amount of work as the plant facilities can conveniently handle by maintaining a free flow of material along the production line.

A production schedule is a statement of target dates for all orders or operations in hand and reveals their starting and finishing dates. Scheduling finalises the planning phase of production planning and control system.

Principles of Scheduling

1. **The principle of optimum task size.** Scheduling tends to achieve maximum efficiency when the task sizes are small, and all tasks of same order of magnitude.
2. **Principle of optimum production plan.** The planning should be such that it imposes an equal load on all plants.

3. **Principle of optimum sequence.** Scheduling tends to achieve the maximum efficiency when the work is planned so that work hours are normally used in the same sequence.

Inputs to Scheduling

1. **Performance standards.** The information regarding the performance standards (standard times for operations) helps to know the capacity in order to assign required machine hours to the facility.
2. Units in which loading and scheduling is to be expressed.
3. Effective capacity of the work centre.
4. Demand pattern and extent of flexibility to be provided for rush orders.
5. Overlapping of operations.
6. Individual job schedules.

Factors Affecting Scheduling

(a) External factors
   (i) Customer's demands.
   (ii) Customer's delivery dates.
   (iii) Stock of goods already lying with the dealers and retailers.

(b) Internal factors
   (i) Stock of finished goods with the firm.
   (ii) Time interval to process finished goods from raw material. In other words – how much time will be required to manufacture each component.
   (iii) Availability of equipment and machinery, their total capacity and specifications.
   (iv) Availability of materials; their quantity and specifications.
   (v) Availability of manpower (number, type and kind of skills).
   (vi) Additional manufacturing facilities if required.
   (vii) Feasibility of economic production runs.

Scheduling Procedure and Techniques

Scheduling normally starts with the Master Schedule. A Master Schedule resembles central office which possesses information about all the orders in hand. Master schedule is a weekly breakdown of the production requirements. The total capacity in any week is of 100 hours of work in the foundry shop.

As the orders are received, depending upon their delivery dates, they are marked on the master schedule. When the shop capacity is full for the present week the newly acquired orders are carried over to the next week and so on. A master schedule is thus updated continuously, it depicts a running total of the production requirements and shows the work ahead yet to be completed.

Advantages

1. It is simple and easy to understand
2. It can be kept running (i.e. current)
3. It involves less cost to make it and maintain it;
4. It can be maintained by non-technical staff
5. A certain percentage of total weekly capacity can be allocated for rush orders.

Disadvantages

1. It provides only overall pictures
2. It does not give detailed information

Applications

It finds applications:

1. In big firms, for the purpose of loading the entire plant.
2. In Research and Development organisations.
3. For the overall planning in foundries, computer centres, repair shops, etc.

After framing the overall picture of production requirements through a Master Schedule Chart, the detailed schedules are thought of and made for each component and subassemblies so that all parts are available at the time of assembly. There are number of usual aids and techniques, both in the form of conventional charts and commercially available boards, which aid in detailed scheduling. The technique to be employed for scheduling purposes depends upon the type of production, type and frequency of tasks, demand patterns etc. A useful scheduling device normally portrays planned production, actual performance and their comparison.

Some of the techniques employed for scheduling purposes are :

(a) **Perpetual Scheduling.** Like master scheduling, it is also simple and easy to understand, is kept current, involves less costs and can be maintained by clerical staff. But the information which it provides is very gross and at the same time it is not clear from the chart-when the work will take place.

(b) **Order Scheduling.** It is a most elaborate technique. The information required to generate an order schedule is, regarding the number of parts to be manufactured, name of the machines, their setup times, total production time and the date of completion of the order.

(c) **Loading by Schedule Period.** The task is broken into different operations which will be required to turn raw material into finished product. This type of scheduling involves a layer in-process (total) time because only one operation is to be performed in one time period. However, this makes it more flexible as an operation can be taken up at the most convenient time within the specified time period.

(d) **Commercial Devices.** Some of the commercial devices are : (i) Board master, (ii) Magnetic boards, (iii) Role charts.

Scheduling Strategies

Scheduling strategies very widely among firms and range from 'no scheduling' to very sophisticated approaches. These strategies are grouped into four classes :

1. **Detailed scheduling.** Detailed scheduling for specific jobs that are arrived from customers is impracticable in actual manufacturing situation. Changes in orders, equipment breakdown and unforeseen events deviate the plans.
2. **Cumulative scheduling.** Cumulative scheduling of total work load is useful especially for long range planning of capacity needs. This may load the current period excessively and under load future periods. It has some means to control the jobs.
3. **Cumulative detailed.** Cumulative detailed combinations is both feasible and practical approach. If master schedule has fixed and flexible portions.

4. **Priority decision rules.** Priority decision rules are scheduling guides that are used independently and in conjunction with one of the above strategies, *i.e.,* first come first serve. These are useful in reducing Work-In Process (WIP) inventory.

Types of Scheduling

Types of scheduling can be categorized as forward scheduling and backward scheduling:

1. **Forward scheduling** is commonly used in job shops where customers place their order on "needed as soon as possible" basis. Forward scheduling determines start and finish times of next priority job by assigning it the earliest available time slot and from that time, determines when the job will be finished in that work centre. Since the job and its components start as early as possible, they will typically be completed before they are due at the subsequent work centres in the routing. The forward method generates in the process inventory that are needed at subsequent work centres and higher inventory cost. Forward scheduling is simple to use and it gets jobs done in shorter lead times, compared to backward scheduling.
2. **Backward scheduling** is often used in assembly type industries and commit in advance to specific delivery dates. Backward scheduling determines the start and finish times for waiting jobs by assigning them to the latest available time slot that will enable each job to be completed just when it is due, but done before. By assigning jobs as late as possible, backward scheduling minimizes inventories since a job is not completed until it must go directly to the next work centre on its routing. Forward and backward scheduling methods are shown in Fig.

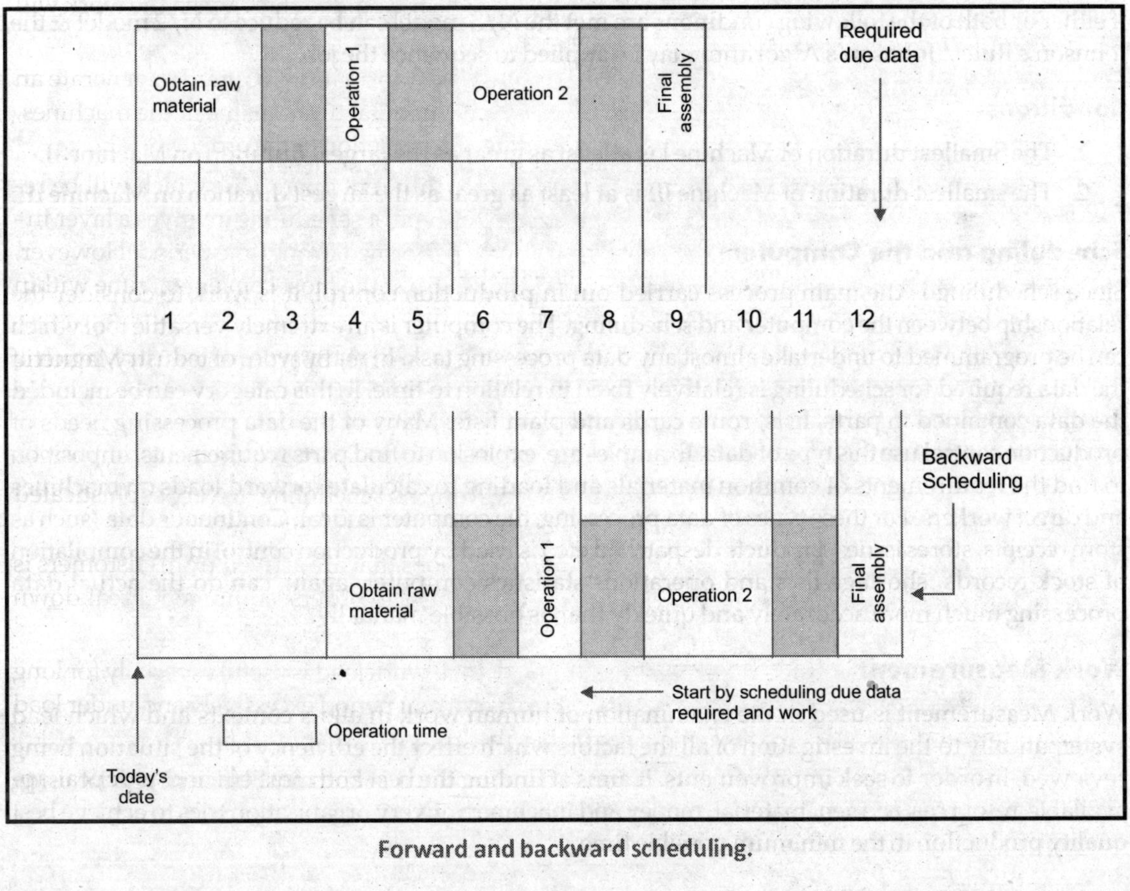

Forward and backward scheduling.

Job Scheduling Steps

Steps in "N Jobs, Two Machines in Series"?

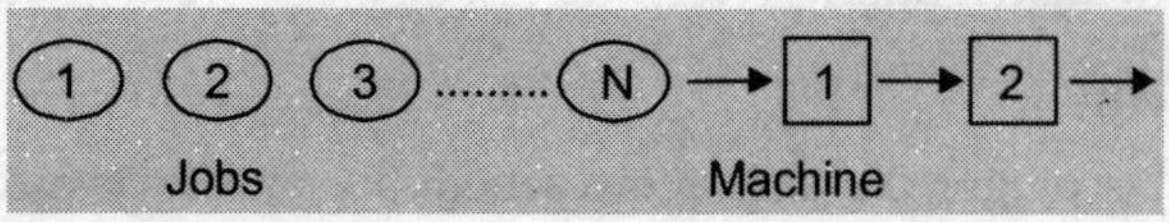

Steps

1. Select the Shortest operation duration.
2. If the Shortest duration requires the first machine schedule the job in the first available position in the sequence and if the shortest duration is one the second machine scheduled the job in the last available position in the sequence.
3. Remove the assigned job in the further consideration & return to step. I until all the jobs are assigned.

Procedure & Conditions in "N Jobs 3 Machines in Series"?

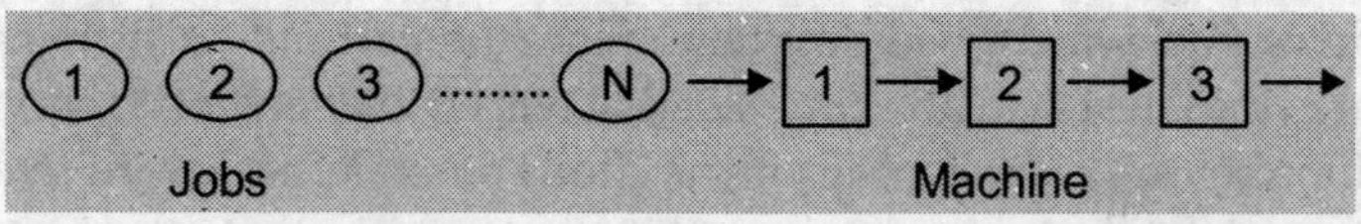

Procedure

If either or both of the following conditions are met the N/3 model can be reduce to N/2 model & the Johnson's Rule / Johnson's Algorithm may be applied to sequence the job.

Conditions

1. The Smallest duration of Machine I is atleast as great as the largest duration on Machine II.
2. The smallest duration of Machine III is at least as great as the largest duration on Machine III.

Scheduling and the Computer

Since scheduling is the main process carried out in production control, it is work to consider the relationship between the computer and scheduling. The computer is an extremely versatile tool which can be programmed to undertake almost any data processing task. In many types of industry, much of the data required for scheduling is relatively fixed in relation to time. In this category can be included the data contained in parts, lists, route cards and plant lists. Many of the data processing needs of production control use this type of data. Examples are, explosion to find parts requirements, imposition to find the requirements of common materials and loading to calculate forward loads on machines and direct workers. For these types of data processing, the computer is ideal. Continuous data (such as store receipts, stores issues, products despatched etc.) is used by production control in the compilation of stock records, shortage lists and operations statistics computer, again, can do the actual data processing much more accurately and quickly than is possible manually.

Work Measurement

Work Measurement is used in the examination of human work in all its contexts and which lead systematically to the investigation of all the factors which effect the efficiency of the situation being reviewed, in order to seek improvements. It aims at finding the best and most efficient way of using available resources, *i.e.* men, material, money and machinery. Every organisation tries to achieve best quality production in the minimum possible time.

Work measurement finds applications into

(a) Industries (Production operations, research and development)
(b) Marketing sales and distribution
(c) Offices stores and warehouses
(d) Material handling
(e) Design
(f) Building and other constructions
(g) Transport
(h) Hospital
(i) Army
(j) Agriculture, etc.

Objectives of work Measurement

Work Measurement

1. Determines the time required to do a job; thus it compares alternative methods and establishes the fastest method
2. Decides equipment requirements
3. Decides man power required for a job; it helps in man power economy.
4. Provides information for effective production planning and maintenance procedures.
5. Aids in calculating exact delivery dates;
6. Results in effective labour control.
7. Decides realistic labour budgeting and provides a basis for standard costing system
8. Provides a basis for fair and sound incentive schemes.

Procedure under work measurement. The various steps involved are :

1. Select the work worth studying and define the objectives to be achieved. An objective may be to reduce the manufacturing cost, or to reduce bottlenecks or to reduce fatigue incurred by the workers in order to increase their efficiency.
2. Record all the relevant information pertaining to the existing method in details and in the form of a chart to obtain a more clear picture about the same. Recording can be done with the help of following aids:

(a) Process charts:
   (i) Outline process chart
   (ii) Flow process chart; Man type, Material type and equipment type.
   (iii) Two handed process chart
   (iv) Multiple activity chart

(b) Diagrams
   (i) Flow diagrams
   (ii) String diagrams
   (iii) Cyclegraph
   (iv) Chronocyclegraph

(c) Motion and film Analysis (Micromotion and Menomotion Studies).
   (i) Simo chart

(d) Models, etc.

3. Examine the recorded events critically and in sequence. Critical examination involves answer to a number of questions. An activity can be eliminated, simplified or combined with another. The basic questions are
   Purpose – What is done ?
   Person – Who does it ?
   Place – Where it is done ?
   Means – How is it done ?
   Sequence – When is it done ?
   The above mentioned five basic questions, individually are further subjected to enquires like,
   Why – Why is it necessary, why he does it, why is it done there, why is it done by that method and why is it done at that time ?
   Alternative ways of doing. What else could be done, who else could do it, where else it could be done, how else it could be done.
   Best Method of Doing. What should be done, who should do it, where it should be done, how it should be done, and when it should be done.
4. Develop the best method as resulted from critical examination and record it. The developed method should be,
   (i) Practical and feasible
   (ii) Safe and effective
   (iii) Economical, and
   (iv) Acceptable to design, production control, quality control and sales departments.
5. Install the best developed method or the improved method. Installation involves three phases, namely-planning arranging and implementing. During first two stages the programme of installations (phase-wise) and a time-table, are planned and the necessary arrangements of resources, equipments, tools and instructions to workers, over-time etc. are made. The implementation or actual installation involves the introduction of developed method as standard practice. Problems associated with the developed method should be carefully studied and remedied, if necessary. Installation phase is complete as soon as the new method starts working smoothly and satisfactorily and gives encouraging results (the saving in time, scrap reduction) etc.
6. Maintain the new method i.e. ensure the proper functioning of the installed method by periodic checks and verifications. The purpose of checks and reviews is to find if the method being practised is the same or it has deviated from the authorised one. Reasons for deviation if any should be explored and the necessary changes may be made in the procedure being practised so that it reverts to the authorised one. Views of the workers, supervisor and other persons related with the authorised method can be of much help in exploring further improvements.

Statistical Quality Control

Control Charts. Control charts show the performance of a process from two points of view :

(i) First, they show a snap shot of the process at the moment the data are collected.

(ii) Second, they show the process trend as time progresses. Process trends are important because they help in identifying the out of control status if it actually exists. Also, they help to detect variations outside the normal operational limits, and to identify the causes of variations.

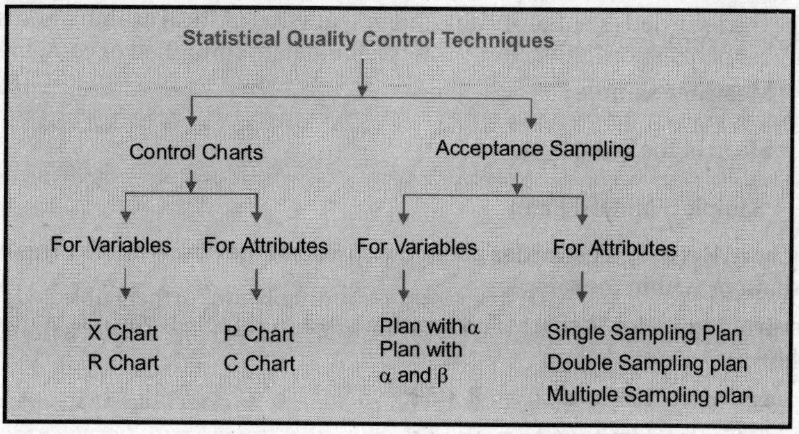

Generalized Representation of Control Chart

In this figure, the x-axis shows observation number in sequence. The y-axis shows the sample value of the observations. There are three namely, upper control limit, lower control limit and central line. The central line is with respect to the average of the observations.

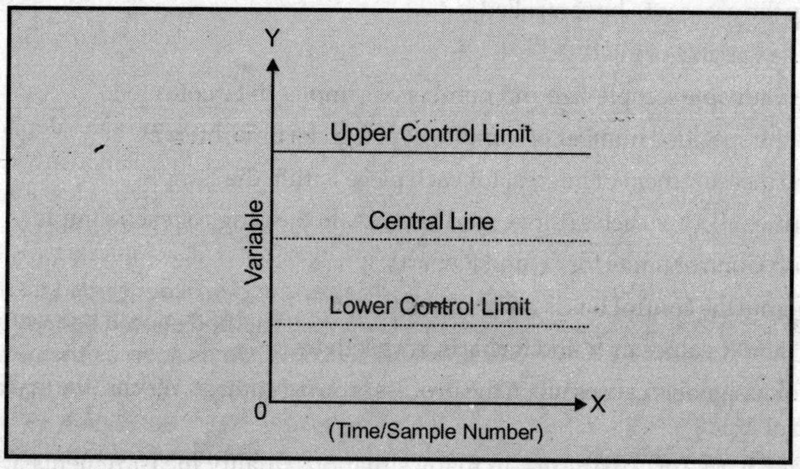

The Upper control limit and lower control limit jointly specify the range over which each sample observation can lie. After plotting all the sample observations on the chart, we should look for the pattern of those plots. If any sample observation is outside of these two limits, then we conclude that the process is out of control, and definitely requires corrective action.

Classification of Control Charts. Control chart may be classified as follows :

1. **Control Charts for Variables.** As the name indicates, these charts will use variable data of a process. Control charts for variables are further classified into two categories :

(i) **$\bar{X}$ Chart.** This chart gives an idea of the central tendency of the observations. These charts will reveal the variations between sample observations.

Control Limits for $\bar{X}$ Chart. The formulas used to establish various control limits are as follows :

Upper Control Limit, UCL $\bar{X} = \bar{\bar{X}} + 3\sigma$

Lower Control Limit, LCL $\bar{X} = \bar{\bar{X}} - 3\sigma$

$\bar{X}$ = Mean of a sample

$\bar{\bar{X}}$ = Mean of the Sample means

$\sigma_{\bar{X}}$ = Sample Standard Error

(ii) **R Chart.** R chart gives an idea about the spread of the observations. This chart shows the variations within the samples.

Control Limits for R chart. The formula used to establish various control limits are as follows :

Upper Control Limit, $UCL_R = R + 3\,s_R$

Lower Control Limit, $LCL_R = R - 3\,s_R$

Where R = Range of a sample observations

s_R = Standard deviation of R

Procedure to construct X chart and R chart

(i) Identify the process to be controlled.

(ii) Select the variable of interest.

(iii) Decide a suitable sample size and number of samples to be collected.

(iv) Collect the specified number of samples over a given time interval.

(v) Find the measurement of interest for each piece within the sample.

(vi) Obtain mean ($\bar{X}$) of each sample. And also obtain the range of each sample.

(vii) Establish Control limits for $\bar{X}$ and R charts.

(viii) Incorporate the control limits on $\bar{X}$ and R Charts.

(ix) Plot $\bar{X}$ and R values in $\bar{X}$ and R charts, respectively.

(x) Hunt for assignable causes when the process is out of control. We can say that a process is out of control.

2. **Control Charts for Attributes.** In many situations quality measurements are expressed as attributes (good or bad etc.). In such situations, the percent defective chart (P-chart) or the number of defective per sample area (C-chart) are considered to be more suitable control charts to control the quality.

(i) **P-chart.** The other name for P-chart is percent defective chart. P-chart is based on a normal distribution.

Purpose of P-chart. The purposes of this chart are summarized below :

(a) To discover the average proportion of non conforming articles or parts submitted for inspection over a period of time.

(b) To bring to the management attention, if there is any change in average quality level.

Control Limits for P-Chart. The formulas for control limits are as follows :

Upper Control Limit, $UCL_P = P + 3\,s_P$

Lower Control Limit, $LCL_P = P - 3s_P$

P = Process percent defective of a sample = (Number of defective items in a sample)/n

$\overline{p}$ = Process mean percent defective.

N = Sample Size

s_v = Standard deviation of percent defectives

(ii) **C-Chart.** This is based on the Poisson distribution. Some applications of C-chart are listed below :

- To control the number of nonconforming rivets in an aircraft wing.
- To control the number of defects in final assemblies (like, TV, radio, Computer, etc.)

Control Limits for C-chart

Upper Control Limit, $UCL_C = \overline{c} + 3\sqrt{\overline{c}}$

Upper Control Limit, $UCL_C = \overline{c} - 3\sqrt{\overline{c}}$

Where c is the mean number of non-conformities. Also, this is the central line in the control chart.

Acceptance Sampling. The objective of acceptance sampling is to take decision whether to accept or reject a lot based on sample's characteristics. The lot may be incoming materials or finished parts.

An accurate method to check the quality of lots is to do 100% inspection. But, 100% inspection will have the following limitations.

(i) The cost of inspection is high.

(ii) Destructive methods of testing will result in 100% spoilage of the parts.

(iii) Time taken for inspection will be too long.

(iv) When the population is large or infinite, it would be impossible or impracticable to inspect each unit.

Types of Acceptance Sampling

There are two types of acceptance sampling :

1. **Attribute Acceptance Sampling.** Here decision regarding acceptance or rejection is based on number of defectives found in a sample. A sample is taken from a lot and good items and defective items are separated. Then the number of defective items is compared with the allowable limit stated in sampling also. If the number of defective items is less than the allowable limit, the lot is accepted, otherwise rejected. This type of sampling is used widely because of its simplicity.

   (i) **Single Sampling Plan.** In such type of plan decision to accept or reject a lot is taken on the basis of the results of the first sample. The design of single sampling plan with a specified producer's risk and consumer's risk is demonstrated. The required data for designing such plan are as follows :

   (a) Producer's risk

   (b) Consumer's risk

   (c) Acceptable Quality Level

   (d) Lot Tolerance Percent Defectives

(ii) **Double Sampling Plan.** In the single sampling plan, based on the outcome of the sample, we either accept or reject the lot. But in double sampling plan, at the maximum, two samples will be drawn before accepting/rejecting a lot. If the outcome of the first sample is not to accept the lot, then one more sample is drawn. Based on the combined quality level of the sample, final decision will be made. The plan is explained with the following input.

- n_1 = size of the first sample
- n_2 = size of the second sample
- A_1 = Acceptance number for sample 1.
- A_2 = Acceptance number for sample 2
- R_1 = Rejection number for sample 1.
- R_2 = Rejection number for sample 2.

Procedure for Double Sampling Plan. The procedure for double sampling plan is summarized below :

Step 0. Input sample sizes, n_1 and n_2. Acceptance numbers, A_1 and A_2. Rejection numbers, R_1 and R_2.

Step 1. Take and inspect a sample of size n_1.

Step 2. If the number of defective pieces X_1 in the first sample is

(a) Less than or equal to A_1, then accept the lot and stop.

(b) Greater than or equal to R_1, then reject the lot and stop.

(c) In between A_1 and R_1 but excluding A_1 and R_1, then go to step 3.

Step 3. Take and inspect a second sample of size n_2. Let the number of defective pieces in the second sample to X_2.

Step 4. If the number of defectives founds in both the sample $(X_1 + X_2)$ is less than or equal to A_2, then accept the lot and stop, otherwise reject the lot and stop.

(iii) **Multiple Sampling Plan.** Under this plan, several samples are taken until a decision to accept or reject a lot is reached. It is known as sequential sampling plan also.

2. **Acceptance Sampling by Variables.** In practice, acceptance sampling by variables is most widely used. This is mainly because, most of the attributes are either reject/accept type. Also, the cost of data collection for such measure is less. But, acceptance sampling by variable may yield the desired result with less number of samples. This plan also uses producer's risk and consumer's risk.

QUALITY MANAGEMENT

A quality circle is a participatory management technique that enlists the help of employees in solving problems related to their own jobs. Circles are formed of employees working together in an operation who meet at intervals to discuss problems of quality and to devise solutions for improvements. Quality circles have an autonomous character, are usually small, and are led by a supervisor or a senior worker. Employees who participate in quality circles usually receive training in formal problem-solving methods—such as brain-storming, pareto analysis, and cause-and-effect diagrams—and are then encouraged to apply these methods either to specific or general company problems. After completing an analysis, they often present their findings to management and then handle implementation of approved solutions. Pareto analysis, by the way, is named after the Italian economist,

Vilfredo Pareto, who observed that 20 percent of Italians received 80 percent of the income—thus the principle that most results are determined by a few causes.

The interest of U.S. manufacturers in quality circles was sparked by dramatic improvements in the quality and economic competitiveness of Japanese goods in the post-World War II years. The emphasis of Japanese quality circles was on preventing defects from arising in the first place rather than through culling during post-production inspection. Japanese quality circles also attempted to minimize the scrap and downtime that resulted from part and product defects. In the United States, the quality circle movement evolved to encompass the broader goals of cost reduction, productivity improvement, employee involvement, and problem-solving activities.

TOTAL QUALITY MANAGEMENT

Now-a-days, customers demand products/services with greater durability and reliability at the most economic price. This forces producers to strictly follow quality procedures right from design till shipment and installation of the products. So that goal of any competitive industry is to provide a product or service at the most economical costs, ensuring full customer satisfaction. This can be achieved through Total Quality Management (TQM), because, quality is not a technical function, but a systemic process extending throughout all phases of the business, *e.g.*, marketing, design, development, engineering, purchasing, production/operations.

Benefits of TQM

The benefits of TQM can be classified into the following two categories :

1. **Customer satisfaction oriented benefits.**
   (a) Improvement in product quality.
   (b) Improvement in product design.
   (c) Improvement in production flow.
   (d) Improvement in employee morale and quality consciousness.
   (e) Improvement of product service.
   (f) Improvement in market place acceptance.
2. **Economic Improvements oriented benefits.** The benefits under this category are as follows :
   (a) Reductions in operating costs.
   (b) Reductions in operating losses.
   (c) Reduction in field service costs.
   (d) Reductions in liability exposure.

ISO 9000 SERIES

ISO stands for International Organization for Standardization.

1. ISO 9000 – Quality management and Quality assurance standards.
2. ISO 9001 – Quality systems : Quality in design
3. ISO 9002 – Quality systems : Production and Installation
4. ISO 9003 – Quality systems : Final inspection and test.
5. ISO 9004 – Quality management and systems.

Objectives of ISO 9000 Series

The objectives of ISO 9000 series is listed in Table :

Standard	Objectives/Tasks
ISO 9000	This provides guidelines on selection and use of quality management and quality assurance standards.
ISO 9001	It has 20 elements covering design, development, production, installation and servicing.
ISO 9002	It has 18 elements convering production and installation. It is same as ISO 9001 without the first two tasks, viz., design and development. This is applicable for the units excluding R & D functions.
ISO 9003	It has 12 elements covering final inspection and testing for laboratories and warehouses etc.
ISO 9004	This provides guidelines to interpret the quality management and quality assurance. This also has suggestions which are not mandatory.

Benefits of ISO 9000 Series

ISO 9000 series provides several tangible and intangible benefits which are listed below :

1. This gives competitive advantage in the global market.
2. Consistency in quality, since ISO helps in detecting non-conformity early which makes it possible to take corrective action.
3. Documentation of quality procedures adds clarity to quality system.
4. ISO 9000 ensures adequate and regular quality training for all members of the organization.
5. ISO helps the customers to have cost effective purchase procedure.
6. The customers while making purchases from companies with ISO certificate need not spend much on inspection and testing. This will reduce the quality cost and lead-time.
7. This will help in increasing productivity.
8. This will aid to improved morale and involvement of workers.
9. The level of job satisfaction would be more.

Steps in ISO 9000 Registration

1. Selection of appropriate standard from ISO 9001, ISO 9002 and ISO 9003 using the guidelines given in ISO 9000.
2. Preparation of quality manual to cover all the elements in the selected model.
3. Preparation of procedure and shop floor instruction which are used at the time of implementing the system. Also document these items.
4. Self-auditing to check compliance of the selected model.
5. Selection of a registrar and making application to obtain certificate for the selected model.

The registrar, on successful verification and assessment will register the company. Before selecting a registrar, one should know the following :

1. Accreditors of the registrar.
2. Background and credibility of the registrar.
3. Cost of registration through the proposed registrar.

4. Expected harmony between the company and the potential registrar while working towards implementing ISO model in the company.

Application ISO 9000 : ISO 14000 Series

Overview

The ISO 14000 series of environmental management standards are intended to assist organizations manage the environmental effect of their business practices. The ISO 14000 series is similar to the ISO 9000 series published in 1987. The purpose of the ISO 9000 deals with the overall management of an organization and ISO 14000 deals with the management of the environmental effects of an organization, both standards are concerned with processes, and there is talk of combining the two series into one.

Some of the standards in the ISO 14000 series are :

- ISO 14001–Specification of Environmental Management Systems
- ISO 14004–Guideline Standard
- ISO 14010 through ISO 14015–Environmental Auditing and Related Activities
- ISO 14020 through ISO 14024–Environmental Labelling
- ISO 14031 through ISO 14032–Environmental Performance Evaluation
- ISO 14040 through ISO 14043–Life Cycle Assessment
- ISO 14050–Terms and Definitions.

KAIZEN

Kaizen is a Japanese term meaning "change for the better" or "continuous improvement." It is a Japanese business philosophy regarding the processes that continuously improve operations and involve all employees. Kaizen sees improvement in productivity as a gradual and methodical process.

The concept of kaizen encompasses a wide range of ideas. It involves making the work environment more efficient and effective by creating a team atmosphere, improving everyday procedures, ensuring employee satisfaction, and making a job more fulfilling, less tiring, and safer.

How Kaizen Works?

Some of the key objectives of the kaizen philosophy include quality control, just-in-time delivery, standardized work, the use of efficient equipment, and the elimination of waste. The overall goal of kaizen is to make small changes over a period of time to create improvements within a company. That doesn't mean alterations happen slowly; it simply recognizes that small changes now can have huge impacts in the future. Improvements can come from any employee at any time. The idea is that everyone has a stake in the company's success and everyone should strive, at all times, to help make the business model better.

Many companies have adopted the kaizen concept. Most notably, Toyota employs the kaizen philosophy within its organization and has esteemed it as one of its core values. Within its production system, Toyota encourages and empowers all employees to identify areas of potential improvement and create viable solutions.

BENCHMARKING

Benchmarking is a process of measuring the performance of a company's products, services, or processes against those of another business considered to be the best in the industry, aka "best in class." The point of benchmarking is to identify internal opportunities for improvement. By studying companies with superior performance, breaking down what makes such superior performance possible, and then comparing those processes to how your business operates, you can implement changes that will yield significant improvements.

That might mean tweaking a product's features to more closely match a competitor's offering, or changing the scope of services you offer, or installing a new customer relationship management (CRM) system to enable more personalized communications with customers.

There are two basic kinds of improvement opportunities: continuous and dramatic. Continuous improvement is incremental, involving only small adjustments to reap sizeable advances. Dramatic improvement can only come about through reengineering the whole internal work process.

Step-by-Step Benchmarking

Benchmarking is a simple, but detailed, five-step process:

- Choose a product, service, or internal department to benchmark
- Determine which best-in-class companies you should benchmark against – which organizations you'll compare your business to
- Gather information on their internal performance, or metrics
- Compare the data from both organizations to identify gaps in your company's performance
- Adopt the processes and policies in place within the best-in-class performers

Benchmarking will point out what changes will make the most difference, but it's up to you to actually put them in place.

SIX SIGMA

Six Sigma is a system of statistical tools and techniques focused on eliminating defects and reducing process variability. The Six Sigma process includes measurement, improvement and validation activities. The designation, or title, Six Sigma, relates to the connection between the number of defects per million opportunities and the number of standard deviations found within a process specification. Within statistics, sigma is a reference to the intervals under a normal or "Gaussian" curve. Each interval is equal to one standard deviation or sigma. Therefore, Six Sigma refers to the plus or minus three sigma from the mean of the data under the curve. In the case of a normal distribution, 68.26% of the data points are within plus or minus one sigma from the mean, 95.46% are within two sigma and 99.73% are within three sigma. A process variation exceeding ± 3 sigma should be improved. With a Six Sigma capable process, only a very small number of possible failures could fall outside specification limits.

Highly skilled personnel trained in the use of the statistical tools and the techniques of Six Sigma implement the Six Sigma methodologies. The Six Sigma training and certification levels are borrowed from the martial arts. The certification or belt levels include white, yellow, green, black and master black belt designations.

How to Implement Six Sigma?

A typical Six Sigma project measures the current state and increases the performance of the business process to a new and statistically significant improved state using statistical tools. Standard Six Sigma capability refers to a very small number of possible failures that can exist outside the specification.

The method most frequently associated with Six Sigma is DMAIC, which stands for Define, Measure, Analyze, Improve and Control. Before beginning any Six Sigma improvement project, it is necessary to select a process that, if improved, would result in reduced cost, superior quality or increased efficiency. The process also must possess measurable data because what you cannot measure you cannot improve.

The process selected may currently be experiencing quality problems or generating a large amount of scrap.

A Black Belt or Master Black Belt will usually initiate Six Sigma projects through the creation of a charter. The charter typically includes details of the proposed improvement project, a business case and information regarding how the project fits into the company's goals or business strategy.

OPERATIONS RESEARCH

TRANSPORTATION MODEL

Transportation methods of solving linear programming problem aim at minimizing cost of (material handling) sending goods from dispatch stations to receiving ends. Generally, specific quantities of goods are shipped from several dispatch stations to a number of receiving centres. Linear programming approach in such situations tends to find, how many goods may be transported from which despatch station to which receiving end in order to make the shipment most economical (least costly). Transportation technique in such problems gives a feasible solution which is improved in a number of subsequent steps till the optimum (best) feasible solution is arrived at.

Assumptions

1. **Availability of quantity.** Quantity available for distribution at different sources or depots is equal to total requirement of different consumption centres.

$$\sum_{i=1}^{m} a_i = \sum_{j=1}^{n} b_j$$

quantity available = quantity required.

2. **Transportation of items.** Items can be conveniently transported from every production centre to every consumption centre.
3. **Cost per unit.** The per unit transportation cost of items from one production centre to another consumption centre is certain.
4. **Independent cost.** The per unit cost of transportation is independent of the quantity despatched.
5. **Objective.** The objective of such an arrangement is to minimise the total cost of transportation for the organisation as a whole.

Few basic terms with reference to the transportation problem

1. **Feasible Solution (FS).** A set of non-negative individual allocations ($x_{ij} \geq 0$) which simultaneously removes deficiencies is called a feasible solution.
2. **Basic feasible solution (BFS).** A feasible solution to a m-origin, n-destination problem is said to be basic if the number of positive allocations are m + n – 1 *i.e.*, one less than the sum of rows and columns.
3. **Optimal solution.** A feasible solution is said to be optimal if it minimizes the total transportation cost. The optimal solution itself may or may not be a basic solution. This is done through successive improvements to the initial basic feasible solution until no further decrease in transportation cost is possible.

There are two methods for solving transportation problems.

(a) **Vogel's approximate method**. It was developed by W.R. Vogel and gives good approximation to the solution. It provides optimum solution in simple problems. In complex transportation problems also, the first solution is obtained using Vogel's method which is further worked upon and tested for optimality by stepping stone method or modified distribution method.

(b) **North west corner method**. It derives its name from the fact that initial allocation of resources is started from the north - west corner of the matrix. Ignoring other things (*i.e.* cost) and simply considering the factory capacity and dealer's requirements, the minimum of the two is placed in north – west corner.

QUEUING THEORY

Queuing theory was started by A.K. Erlang. He started, in the year 1905, to explore the effect of fluctuating service demand on the utilization of automatic dial equipment.

A queue or a waiting line is something very common in everyday routine. There is a queue for bus, queue at ration shop, for cinema ticket and where not. Standing in queue wastes a lot of otherwise useful time. Besides everyday experience, queues can be seen on the shop floor, where in-process goods wait for next operation or inspection or wait for getting moved to another place. Such delays in the production lines naturally, increases production cycle duration, add to the product cost, may upset the whole system and it may not be possible to meet the specified delivery dates thereby annoying the customers.

Waiting lines cannot be completely eliminated, they can atleast be reduced by optimizing the number of service stations, or by adjusting the service times in one or more service stations.

Queuing theory analyses the feasibility of adding facilities (equipment, manpower) and assess the amount and cost of waiting times. In general, this theory can be applied wherever congestion occurs and a waiting line or a queue is formed. The purpose in such situations is to determine the optimum amount of facilities. Queuing theory helps finding lack of balance between items coming and going. It gives information about peak loads. It mathematically relates the length of queue and waiting time and the controllable factors, such as number of service stations or the time taken to process each article. It can also tell, how often and how long the times or persons in queue will probably have to wait.

Queuing theory mathematically predicts the way in which the waiting line will develop over given periods and in turn helps allocating facilities to deal the situation efficiently. In order to build a mathematical model for a queue forming situation *i.e.*, where items or persons arrive in a random manner, are processed or treated and then leave, following information is required:

(a) Distribution of gaps between the arrival of times. Say a telephone call comes after every ten minutes.

(b) Distribution of service times. Say every time a telephone talk continues for three minutes.

(c) The priority system.

(d) The processing facilities.

Assumptions

(a) There is only one type of queue discipline – that is first come, first served. A unit in queue will immediately go to the service station as soon as the station is free.

(b) There are steady state (stable) conditions *i.e.*, the probability that n items are in queue at any time, remains the same with the passage of time. In other words at all times the number of items in the queue remain same, the queue does not lengthen indefinitely with time.

(c) Both, the number of items in queue at any instant and the waiting time experience by a particular item are random variables. They are not functionally dependent on time. The problem thus reduces to estimate the average length of the queue at any instant, etc.

(d) Arrival rates follow Poisson distribution and service times follow exponential distribution. This situation referred as Poisson Arrivals and Exponential service times, holds goods in number of actual operating situations.

(e) Mean service rate n is greater than mean arrival rate m.

DECISION THEORY

Decision theory may be defined as a set of general concepts and techniques that assist a decision maker in choosing among alternatives. Decision theory problems are commonly cast in a standard framework, termed as a decision matrix which consists of the following components.

(a) Strategies or alternatives (S), available to the decision maker. For example, make or buy would be two strategies in a make - or - buy decision problem. Strategies are within control of the decision maker.

(b) States of Nature (N), which are characteristics of the environment and are beyond the control of decision maker. The term derives from the weather, where we might say, three states of nature; sunshine, rain or snow.

In business decisions, states of nature might be various levels of demand for a product, the number of competitors, government actions etc.

Decision Matrix

Strategies (s)	States of nature (N) and Probabilities of Occurrence (Pr)				
	N_1 Pr_1	N_2 Pr_2	N_3 Pr_3	- -	N_n Pr_n
S_1	O_{11}	O_{12}	O_{13}	-	O_{1n}
S_2	O_{21}	O_{22}	O_{23}	-	O_{2n}
S_m	O_{m1}	O_{m2}	O_{m3}	-	O_{mn}

(c) Predictions of likelihood (Pr) or the probability associated with the occurrence of each state. If a particular state of nature is sure to occur (Pr = 1.0), the decision situation is termed one of certainty.

If the decision maker can assign probability of occurrence to one or more states of nature, with no one state given a value of 1.0, it is termed as risk situation.

Finally, if the decision maker has no idea of the probabilities of occurrence of any state of nature, the situation is defined as decision making under uncertainty.

Thus in the decision matrix above, there would be an entry for probability if the situation is one of certainty or risk and no entry if it is one of uncertainty.

(d) Pay offs or outcomes (O), which represent the value associated with each combination of strategy and state of nature. The value may be stated in terms of utility, cost profit, satisfaction etc.

Solving a decision theory problem obviously requires some choice to be made from among the alternatives, and thus some rule or decision criterion must be selected for this purpose. For *e.g.*, in certainty situations, the decision criterion is to select the single strategy with the highest pay off.

Since only one state of nature is relevant, this entails a simple scanning of the pay off column under the certain N and picking the best one.

A. Decision making under certainty

Certainty implies that all facts are known for sure. It is assumed that there is complete and accurate knowledge of the consequences of each choice (or of the nature of future conditions). In other words, it means that for each alternative there is one and only one value of the pay off. A pay off matrix is a logical grouping of possible outcomes in a problem.

B. Decision making under risk

It refers to the situations where there are number of states of nature, and the manager knows the probability of occurrence for each of these states of nature (based upon past experience) etc.

C. Decision making (or Problem solving) under uncertainty

With decision making under uncertainty, one can expect to enumerate a finite number of states of nature. There is a total inability to estimate the likelihood of occurrence for each of these states of nature. The consequences of each choice cannot be defined by a correspondence relationship even within a probabilistic framework. In this type, it requires that the person responsible for making decisions should use his judgement. He must make sure that which outcomes are more likely than others and combine this knowledge with the consequences associated with the various decisions.

PERT / CPM

CRITICAL PATH METHOD (CPM)

In 1957, DuPont developed a project management method designed to address the challenge of shutting down chemical plants for maintenance and then restarting the plants once the maintenance had been completed. Given the complexity of the process, they developed the Critical Path Method (CPM) for managing such projects.

CPM provides the following benefits :

- Provides a graphical view of the project.
- Predicts the time required to complete the project.
- Shows which activities are critical to maintaining the schedule and which are not.

STEPS IN CPM PROJECT PLANNING

1. **Specify the individual activities.** From the work breakdown structure, list the activities in the project. The project (made up of several tasks) should have only a single start activity and a single finish activity.
2. **Determine the sequence of those activities.** Develop the relationship among the activities. Decide which activities must precede and which must follow others.
3. **Draw a network diagram.** Draw the 'Network' once all the activities and their sequencing have been defined. Network diagram originally was developed as an *activity on node* (AON) network, but some project planners prefer to specify the *activities on the arrow*.
4. **Estimate the completion time for each activity.** Assign time and/or cost estimates to each activity using past experience or the estimates of knowledgeable persons.

   CPM is a *deterministic model* that does not take into account variation in the completion time, so one fixed time is used for an activity.

5. **Identify the critical path.** The critical path is the longest-duration path through the network. The significance of the critical path is that the activities that lie on it cannot be delayed without delaying the project. Because of its impact on the entire project, critical path analysis is an important aspect of project planning.

   The critical path can be identified by determining the following four parameters for each activity.

   - ES – Earliest start time: the earliest time at which the activity can start given that its precedent activities must be completed first.
   - EF – Earliest finish time : equal to the earliest start time for the activity plus the time required to complete the activity.
   - LF – Latest finish time : the latest time at which the activity can be completed without delaying the project.
   - LS – Latest start time, equal to the latest finish time required to complete the activity.

   The total float (*slack time)* for an activity is the time between its earliest and latest start time, or between its earliest and latest finish time. Slack is the amount of time that an activity can be delayed past its earliest start or earliest finish without delaying the project.

   The critical path is the path through the project network in which none of the activities have slack, that is, the path for which ES = LS and EF = LF for all activities in the path. A delay in the critical path delays the project. Similarly, to accelerate the project it is necessary to reduce the total time required for the activities in the critical path.

6. **Update the CPM diagram.** As the project progresses, the actual task completion times will be known and the network diagram can be updated to include this information. A new critical path may emerge, and structural changes may be made in the network if project requirements change.

   Example. Illustration of CPM.

   WBS of a project is given in Table.

WBS for a Project

Activity	Immediate Predecessor	Completion Time (weeks)
A	–	5
B	–	6
C	A	4
D	A	3
E	A	1
F	E	4
G	D,F	14
H	B,C	12
I	G,H	2

The information in WBS indicates that the total time required to complete activities is 51 weeks. However, it can be seen from the network that several of the activities can be conducted simultaneously (A and B, for example). It is necessary to calculate critical path of the network.

EARLIEST START TIME AND EARLIEST FINISH TIME

We can do a forward pass calculation. Starting at the network's origin (node 1) and using a starting time of 0, we compute an *earliest start* (ES) and *earliest finish* (EF) time for each activity in the network. The expression EF = ES + t can be used to find the earliest finish time for a given activity. The completion time or the duration of an activity is represented as *t*.

For example, for activity A, ES = 0 and *t* = 5; thus the earliest finish time for activity A is EF = 0 + 5 = 5. Refer Figure.

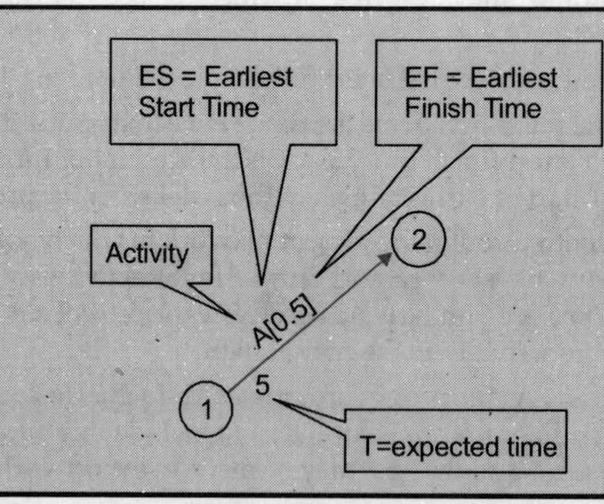

Early Start Time and Early Finish Time.

Completing the network from start based on above (Forward pass), we can calculate all ES and EF time as shown in figure.

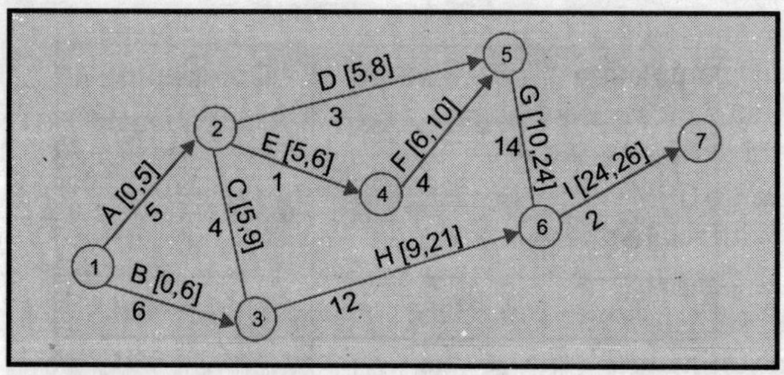

Network with ES and EF time in Forward Pass.

Earliest start time rule. *The earliest start time for an activity leaving a particular node is equal to the largest of the earliest finish times for all activities entering the node.*

Similarly, we can do a backward pass calculation. Starting at the completion point (node 7) and using a latest finish time (LF) of 26 for activity I, we trace back through the network computing a *latest start* (LS) and latest finish time for each activity.

The expression **LS = LF – t** can be used to calculate latest start time for each activity. For example, for activity I, LF = 26 and *t* = 2, thus the latest start time for activity I is LS = 26 – 2 = 24.

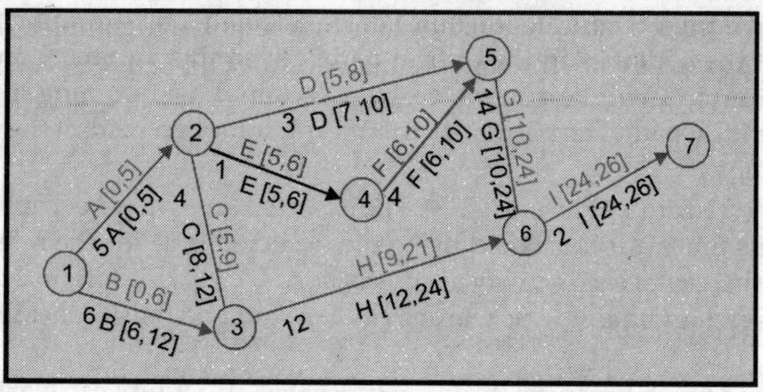

Network with LS and LF time in Backward Pass.

Latest finish time rule : *The latest finish time for an activity entering a particular node is equal to the smallest of the latest start times for all activities leaving the node.*

Float or Slack or Free Time

Slack is the length of time an activity can be delayed without affecting the completion date for the entire project. For example, slack for C = 3 weeks, i.e. Activity C can be delayed up to 3 weeks (LS (8 weeks) – ES (5 weeks) of LF (12 weeks) – EF (9 weeks) = 3 weeks) as given in Figure.

Float or slack shows how much allowance each activity has *i.e.* how long it can be delayed without affecting the completion date of the project. Critical path is a sequence of activities from start to finish with zero slack. Critical activities are activities on the critical path.

Critical path identifies the minimum time to complete project. If any activity on the critical path is shortened or extended, project time will be shortened or extended accordingly. If resources have to be spent to speed up some activities, it should be only for critical activities. Such shortening or project in critical path by adding resources is called project crashing. If resources have to be saved by lengthening some activities, it should be only for non-critical activities, up to the limit of float.

PROGRAM EVALUATION AND REVIEW TECHNIQUE (PERT)

The Program Evaluation and Review Technique (PERT) is a probabilistic network, model that allows for randomness in activity completion times. PERT was developed in the late 1950 for the U.S. Navy's Polaris project having thousands of contractors. It has the potential to reduce both the time and cost required to complete a project.

PERT steps are similar to CPM with only difference as to the estimation of time. Unlike CPM where times can be estimated with relative certainty, confidence, PERT uses 3 time estimates.

T_m = most likely time estimate

T_o = optimistic time estimate

T_p = pessimistic time estimate

PERT assumes a normal bell-shaped distribution (beta probability distribution) for the time estimates. For a beta distribution, the expected time for each activity can be approximated using the following weighted average :

Expected time = (Optimistic + 4x Most likely + Pessimistic) / 6

Expected Time $(T_e) = (T_o + 4T_m + T_p) / 6$

Standard Deviation $(s) = (T_p - T_o) / 6$

Variance $(V) = ((T_p - T_o) / 6)^2$

The variance in the project completion time can be calculated by summing the variances in the completion times of the activities in the critical path. Given this variance, one can calculate the probability that the project will be completed by a certain date assuming a normal probability distribution for the critical path. The normal distribution assumption holds if the number of activities in the path is large enough.

The calculation procedure is similar to CPM. The expected times may be displayed on the network diagram. The various times are calculated using the expected time for the relevant activities. The earliest start and finish times of each activity are determined by working forward through the network and determining the earliest time at which an activity can start and finish considering its predecessor activities.

The latest start and finish times are the latest times that an activity can start and finish without delaying the project, LS and LF are found by working backward through the network. The difference in the latest and earliest finish or latest and earliest start of each activity is that activity's slack. The critical path then is the path through the network in which none of the activities have slack.

Example. Illustration of PERT

For the following project details (Table), PERT has to be prepared.

Activity	Immediate Prede-cessor	Optimistic Time T_0	Most Likely Time T_m	Pessimistic Time T_p	Expected Time T_e	Σ	V
a	-	10	22	22	20	2	4
b	-	20	20	20	20	0	0
c	-	4	10	16	10	2	4
d	a	2	14	32	15	5	25
e	b,c	8	8	20	10	2	4
f	b,c	8	14	20	14	2	4
g	b,c	4	4	4	4	0	0
h	c	2	12	16	11	2.32	5,4
i	g,h	6	16	38	18	5.33	28.4
j	d,e	2	8	14	8	2	4

PERT Network diagram showing activities, ES, EF in forward pass in shown in Figure.

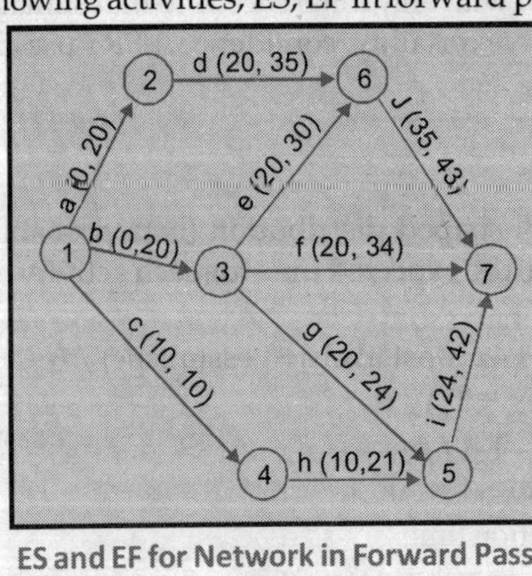

ES and EF for Network in Forward Pass.

PERT Network diagram showing LS, LF in backward pass is shown in the Figure.

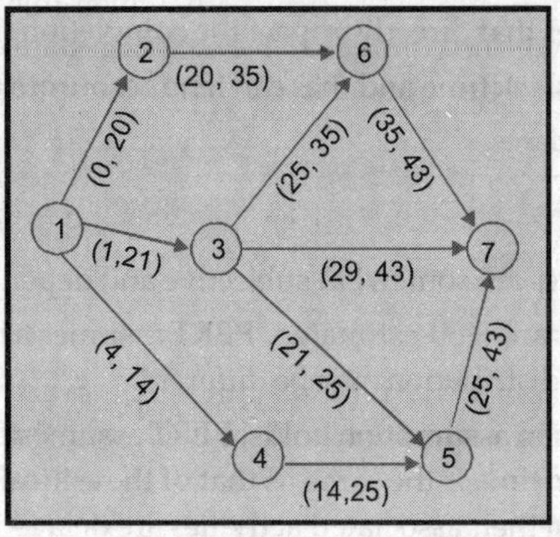

LS and LF for Network in Backward Pass.

The details of network calculations from forward and backward pass are summarised in Table.

Summary of Project Calculations

Activity	Expected Time	Earliest Start ES	Earliest Finish EF	Latest Start LS	Latest Finish LF	Float of Slack LS-ES or LF-EF	Critical Path
a	20	0	20	0	20	0	yes
b	20	0	20	1	21	1	
c	10	0	10	4	14	4	
d	15	20	35	20	35	0	Yes
e	10	20	30	25	35	5	
f	14	20	34	29	43	9	
g	4	20	24	21	25	1	
h	11	10	21	14	25	4	
i	18	24	42	25	43	1	
j	8	35	43	35	43	0	Yes

Critical path : a, d, j = 43 days.

Such PERT chart is not final. It may be necessary to make adjustment in PERT chart as project progresses. As the project unfolds, the estimated times can be replaced with actual times. In cases where there are delays, additional resources may be needed to stay on schedule and the PERT chart may be modified to reflect the new situation.

Benefits of PERT

PERT is useful because it provides the following information :

- Expected project completion time.

- Probability of completion before a specified date.
- The critical path activities that directly impact the completion time.
- The activities that have slack time and that can lend resources to critical path activities.
- Activities start and end dates.

Limitations of PERT

- The activity time estimates are somewhat subjective and depend on judgement.
- Even if the activity times are well-estimated, PERT assumes a beta distribution for these time estimates, but the actual distribution may be different.
- Even if the beta distribution assumption holds, PERT assumes that the probability distribution of the project completion time is the same as that of the critical path. Because other paths can become the critical path if their associated activities are delayed, PERT consistently underestimates the expected project completion time.

MULTIPLE CHOICE QUESTIONS

1. Which of the following is not a measure of central tendency?
   (a) Mean (b) Median
   (c) Mode (d) Variance
2. What is the primary goal of statistical analysis in management?
   (a) Describing data
   (b) Making predictions
   (c) Identifying causation
   (d) Developing strategies
3. In statistics, what is the definition of "population"?
   (a) A group of people
   (b) A subset of a sample
   (c) The entire set of items or individuals of interest
   (d) A random collection of data
4. Which of the following is not a measure of dispersion?
   (a) Range (b) Standard Deviation
   (c) Mean (d) Variance
5. In a normally distributed dataset, approximately what percentage of data falls within one standard deviation of the mean?
   (a) 25% (b) 50%
   (c) 68% (d) 95%
6. The measure of central tendency that is least affected by outliers is
   (a) Mean (b) Median
   (c) Mode (d) Variance
7. If a dataset has an even number of values, how is the median typically calculated?
   (a) By taking the average of the two middle values
   (b) By selecting the value that occurs most frequently
   (c) By finding the highest value in the dataset
   (d) By calculating the mean of all values
8. The median is the best measure of central tendency when
   (a) The data is skewed
   (b) The data is normally distributed
   (c) The data is unimodal
   (d) The data is discrete
9. The range of a dataset is calculated as
   (a) The difference between the maximum and minimum values
   (b) The sum of all values in the dataset
   (c) The variance divided by the mean
   (d) The square root of the variance
10. Which measure of dispersion is sensitive to outliers?
    (a) Range
    (b) Interquartile Range
    (c) Variance
    (d) Standard Deviation
11. The Interquartile Range (IQR) measures the spread of data between
    (a) The mean and the median
    (b) The first and third quartiles
    (c) The maximum and minimum values
    (d) The variance and standard deviation
12. In a binomial distribution, the number of trials is denoted by
    (a) n (b) p
    (c) x (d) q
13. In a binomial distribution, what is the probability of success on a single trial denoted by?
    (a) n (b) p
    (c) x (d) q
14. In a binomial distribution, the variance is calculated as
    (a) np (b) npq
    (c) nq (d) n^2p^2
15. In a binomial distribution, what is the probability of failure on a single trial denoted by?
    (a) n (b) p
    (c) x (d) q
16. The Poisson distribution is commonly used to model

(a) Continuous data
(b) Discrete data with a fixed number of trials
(c) The number of events occurring in a fixed interval of time or space
(d) Data with a normal distribution

17. In a Poisson distribution, what parameter represents the average rate of occurrence for an event?
(a) λ (lambda) (b) p
(c) μ (mu) (d) σ (sigma)

18. In a Poisson distribution, as the rate parameter » increases, what happens to the shape of the distribution?
(a) It becomes more negatively skewed
(b) It becomes more positively skewed
(c) It becomes more symmetrical
(d) It becomes taller and narrower

19. The area under the normal distribution curve between two z-scores represents
(a) The probability of a specific value occurring
(b) The cumulative probability
(c) The standard deviation
(d) The variance

20. In a standard normal distribution (mean = 0, standard deviation = 1), what is the value of the z-score for the 50th percentile?
(a) 0 (b) 1
(c) –1 (d) 0.5

21. In a normal distribution, approximately what percentage of data falls within two standard deviations of the mean?
(a) 34% (b) 68%
(c) 95% (d) 99.7%

22. The exponential distribution is often used to model
(a) The time between events in a Poisson process
(b) The number of successes in a binomial process
(c) The number of occurrences in a fixed interval
(d) Continuous data with a normal distribution

23. The parameter that characterizes the exponential distribution is
(a) λ (lambda) (b) p
(c) μ (mu) (d) α (sigma)

24. In the exponential distribution, as the rate parameter » increases, what happens to the probability density function?
(a) It becomes taller and narrower
(b) It becomes flatter and wider
(c) It remains unchanged
(d) It becomes a uniform distribution

25. The exponential distribution is often used to model waiting times between events. Which of the following events is an example of such a scenario?
(a) Number of cars passing through a toll booth
(b) Number of items in a grocery store shopping cart
(c) Number of goals scored in a soccer match
(d) Number of pages in a book

26. Which of the following measures is not a measure of central tendency?
(a) Variance (b) Median
(c) Mode (d) Mean

27. The coefficient of variation (CV) is a measure of relative
(a) Variation (b) Skewness
(c) Kurtosis (d) Central tendency

28. Which probability distribution is used to model the number of successes in a fixed number of independent Bernoulli trials?
(a) Normal distribution
(b) Poisson distribution
(c) Exponential distribution
(d) Binomial distribution

29. In the context of statistics, what does the term "kurtosis" refer to?
(a) A measure of the spread or dispersion of data
(b) A measure of the skewness of data
(c) A measure of the peakedness or flatness of a distribution
(d) A measure of the central tendency of data

30. The Chebyshev's inequality provides an upper bound on the proportion of data within how many standard deviations of the mean?
(a) 1 (b) 2
(c) 3 (d) 4

31. What is the primary purpose of data collection in research?
(a) To make predictions
(b) To prove a hypothesis

(c) To gather information
(d) To select a sample

32. Which of the following is not a method of data collection?
(a) Survey
(b) Experiment
(c) Observation
(d) Hypothesis

33. A questionnaire is a tool primarily used for
(a) Observing participants
(b) Experimentation
(c) Collecting self-report data
(d) None of the above

34. In questionnaire design, what is the purpose of a "pilot study"?
(a) To test the research hypothesis
(b) To collect the final dataset
(c) To test the questionnaire on a small sample before the main study
(d) To analyze the data

35. Open-ended questions in a questionnaire
(a) Allow for a limited range of responses
(b) Require a simple "yes" or "no" answer
(c) Encourage respondents to provide detailed responses in their own words
(d) Are used for demographic information

36. Which of the following is a disadvantage of using telephone surveys for data collection?
(a) Limited reach and difficulty in reaching specific target groups
(b) High cost
(c) Limited sample size
(d) Bias in responses

37. When conducting face-to-face interviews, what is an advantage of using structured interviews?
(a) Flexibility in question wording
(b) The ability to gather in-depth responses
(c) Standardization of questions and responses
(d) No need for trained interviewers

38. In survey research, what is a "sampling frame"?
(a) The list of questions in the questionnaire
(b) A statistical technique for selecting a sample
(c) The population from which a sample is drawn
(d) The data analysis process

39. When designing a questionnaire, what is the term for ensuring that the questions are clear and easily understood by respondents?
(a) Reliability (b) Validity
(c) Clarity (d) Pilot testing

40. In survey research, what is "non-response bias"?
(a) A bias introduced by the researcher's expectations
(b) Bias caused by the way questions are worded
(c) Bias resulting from differences between respondents and non-respondents
(d) Bias caused by the selection of a biased sample

41. When designing a questionnaire, what does it mean to use a Likert scale?
(a) Include Likert's biography in the questionnaire
(b) Use a scale ranging from 1 (Strongly Disagree) to 5 (Strongly Agree) for respondents to express their opinions
(c) Include only "yes" or "no" questions
(d) Avoid using scales of any kind

42. Which of the following is not a common mode of survey administration?
(a) Mail surveys
(b) Face-to-face interviews
(c) Random sampling
(d) Online surveys

43. A researcher wants to gather data about the behavior of customers in a retail store. Which data collection method is most suitable?
(a) Mail surveys
(b) Observational study
(c) Telephone interviews
(d) Online surveys

44. In survey research, what is the term for a questionnaire that is sent to a large number of people and filled out by respondents themselves?
(a) Self-administered questionnaire
(b) Face-to-face interview
(c) Structured interview
(d) Open-ended questionnaire

45. Which of the following is not a potential source of bias in questionnaire design?
(a) Wording of questions
(b) Order of questions

(c) Sample size
(d) Response options

46. Which of the following is a disadvantage of using online surveys for data collection?
(a) Speed of data collection
(b) Ability to reach a diverse sample
(c) Limited control over the sample
(d) High cost

47. In survey research, what is "sampling error"?
(a) The error caused by non-response bias
(b) The error introduced by the researcher's biases
(c) The error due to the random variability between a sample and the population it represents
(d) The error introduced by using Likert scales

48. Which of the following sampling techniques is used when you want to ensure that subgroups within the population are represented proportionally in the sample?
(a) Convenience sampling
(b) Cluster sampling
(c) Stratified sampling
(d) Quota sampling

49. A researcher wants to study the behavior of a specific group of individuals who have a common characteristic, such as age or income. Which type of sampling is most appropriate?
(a) Simple random sampling
(b) Convenience sampling
(c) Stratified sampling
(d) Snowball sampling

50. What is the primary advantage of using quota sampling in survey research?
(a) It ensures a representative sample from the population.
(b) It is easy to implement and cost-effective.
(c) It reduces non-response bias.
(d) It is based on random selection.

51. In questionnaire design, the term "double-barreled question" refers to
(a) A question that uses Likert scales
(b) A question that contains two separate inquiries in one
(c) A question that is too long
(d) A question that is unclear

52. Which of the following is not a common method of survey administration?
(a) Face-to-face interviews
(b) Content analysis
(c) Telephone surveys
(d) Self-administered questionnaires

53. In questionnaire design, what does it mean to use "skip patterns"?
(a) It refers to the order in which questions are asked.
(b) It involves skipping every second question.
(c) It is a type of question that should be avoided.
(d) It directs respondents to skip certain questions based on their previous answers.

54. When designing a questionnaire, what is the term for ensuring that the questionnaire measures what it is intended to measure?
(a) Clarity
(b) Reliability
(c) Validity
(d) Pilot testing

55. Which of the following is a potential disadvantage of using face-to-face interviews for data collection?
(a) High cost
(b) Limited control over the sample
(c) Limited access to respondents
(d) Anonymity of respondents

56. What is sampling in the context of research?
(a) Collecting the entire population data
(b) Collecting a representative subset of the population
(c) Conducting a complete census
(d) Collecting data from a non-representative group

57. What is the primary goal of sampling in research?
(a) To ensure 100% accuracy in data collection
(b) To reduce the cost of data collection
(c) To obtain a sample that accurately represents the population
(d) To avoid collecting data entirely

58. Which of the following is NOT a probability sampling technique?
(a) Simple random sampling
(b) Convenience sampling
(c) Systematic sampling
(d) Stratified sampling

59. In simple random sampling, every item in the population has
   (a) An equal chance of being included in the sample
   (b) A chance of zero for being included in the sample
   (c) A chance proportional to its size in the population
   (d) A chance based on its position in the population
60. What is stratified sampling?
   (a) Selecting every nth item from the population
   (b) Dividing the population into subgroups and then sampling from each subgroup
   (c) Selecting items based on their proximity to a fixed point
   (d) Selecting items without any specific pattern
61. Which sampling technique is most suitable when the population is too large to survey in its entirety, and a random sample is desired?
   (a) Stratified sampling
   (b) Cluster sampling
   (c) Systematic sampling
   (d) Judgment sampling
62. In systematic sampling, the first item is selected
   (a) Randomly
   (b) Using a fixed pattern
   (c) Based on the researcher's judgment
   (d) By stratifying the population
63. Which of the following is a non-probability sampling technique?
   (a) Systematic sampling
   (b) Convenience sampling
   (c) Stratified sampling
   (d) Cluster sampling
64. What is the main disadvantage of convenience sampling?
   (a) It is time-consuming
   (b) It can be costly
   (c) It often results in biased samples
   (d) It requires advanced statistical software
65. When is purposive or judgment sampling typically used?
   (a) When the population is very large
   (b) When randomness is essential
   (c) When the researcher selects specific individuals or items based on their expertise
   (d) When using a systematic sampling approach
66. What is the formula for calculating the sample size in a simple random sampling design?
   (a) N/n (b) N * n
   (c) N - n (d) (N-1)/(n-1)
67. What is the purpose of stratifying a population in stratified sampling?
   (a) To make the sampling process more complex
   (b) To create subgroups with equal sizes
   (c) To ensure that every element in the population has an equal chance of being selected
   (d) To ensure that every subgroup is adequately represented in the sample
68. When using systematic sampling, if the researcher chooses every 10th item from a population of 1000 items, what would be the sampling interval?
   (a) 1 (b) 10
   (c) 100 (d) 1000
69. What is the term for a list of all the items or individuals in a population from which a sample will be selected?
   (a) Sampling bias
   (b) Sampling frame
   (c) Population parameter
   (d) Sampling error
70. What is the purpose of cluster sampling?
   (a) To select a random sample from subgroups within the population
   (b) To select a random sample of individuals within a defined area or cluster
   (c) To select a sample based on the researcher's judgment
   (d) To ensure that every item in the population has an equal chance of being selected
71. When using stratified sampling, how are the strata defined?
   (a) Based on proximity to the researcher's location
   (b) Based on the items' sizes
   (c) Based on characteristics shared by items within each stratum
   (d) Based on the items' alphabetical order
72. Which of the following is a potential disadvantage of cluster sampling?
   (a) It is less efficient than other sampling methods

(b) It often results in a more representative sample
(c) It is suitable for small populations only
(d) It is easy to implement

73. In quota sampling, the categories are determined based on
(a) Random selection
(b) Researcher's judgment
(c) Population size
(d) Alphabetical order

74. Which of the following is a key advantage of using quota sampling?
(a) It ensures a truly random sample
(b) It is cost-effective
(c) It is based on a random selection process
(d) It allows for the inclusion of specific groups in the sample

75. What is the primary advantage of probability sampling methods?
(a) They are simple to implement
(b) They result in representative samples
(c) They do not require a sampling frame
(d) They are based on the researcher's judgment

76. In sampling, what is the term for the degree to which the sample statistics accurately represent the population parameters?
(a) Sampling error
(b) Sampling frame
(c) Sampling bias
(d) Sample size

77. Which of the following statements about random sampling is true?
(a) It guarantees that the sample will be free from bias.
(b) It guarantees that the sample will be representative of the population.
(c) It requires selecting items from the population in a specific order.
(d) It is the same as convenience sampling.

78. What is the formula for calculating the sample size needed for a proportion estimate in a simple random sample?
(a) N/n (b) N - n
(c) pq / E^2 (d) N + n

79. When conducting research, what is the term for the potential for certain items or individuals to be systematically overrepresented or underrepresented in the sample?
(a) Sampling error
(b) Sampling frame
(c) Sampling bias
(d) Sample size

80. What is the goal of using sampling techniques in research?
(a) To guarantee a 100% accurate sample
(b) To eliminate sampling error
(c) To minimize the cost of data collection
(d) To obtain a sample that accurately represents the population

81. What is the first step in hypothesis testing?
(a) Calculate the test statistic
(b) State the null and alternative hypotheses
(c) Collect the data
(d) Choose the significance level

82. In a hypothesis test, the null hypothesis is typically denoted as
(a) H0 (b) H1
(c) Ha (d) μ

83. The alternative hypothesis (Ha) represents
(a) The hypothesis the researcher wants to support
(b) The null hypothesis
(c) The level of significance
(d) The sampling distribution

84. What is the significance level (α) in hypothesis testing?
(a) The probability of making a Type II error
(b) The probability of making a Type I error
(c) The probability of rejecting the null hypothesis when it is true
(d) The confidence level

85. In a two-tailed hypothesis test, how is the critical region divided?
(a) Into the lower tail only
(b) Into the upper tail only
(c) Into both tails
(d) There is no critical region in a two-tailed test

86. The test statistic measures the difference between
(a) The null hypothesis and the population parameter
(b) The null hypothesis and the alternative hypothesis
(c) The sample statistic and the population parameter

(d) The sample statistic and the null hypothesis

87. What is the formula for the test statistic in a Z-test?
(a) $(\overline{x} - \mu) / (\sigma / \sqrt{n})$
(b) $(\overline{x} - \mu) / (\sigma)$
(c) $(\overline{x} - \mu) / (s / \sqrt{n})$
(d) $(\overline{x} - \mu) / (s)$

88. When conducting a Z-test for a population mean, which parameter is known?
(a) The sample mean ($\overline{x}$)
(b) The population mean (¼)
(c) The sample standard deviation (s)
(d) The sample size (n)

89. The critical value in a hypothesis test is determined based on the
(a) Sample size
(b) Level of significance
(c) Population parameter
(d) Sample mean

90. In a one-sample t-test for a population mean, the sample size is typically denoted as
(a) n (b) μ
(c) Ã (d) $\overline{x}$

91. Which statistical distribution is used for the critical values in a t-test?
(a) Normal distribution
(b) Chi-square distribution
(c) T-distribution
(d) F-distribution

92. The degrees of freedom in a t-test depend on
(a) The population size
(b) The sample size
(c) The level of significance
(d) The population mean

93. The F-statistic is used in which type of hypothesis test?
(a) Z-test (b) T-test
(c) Chi-square test
(d) Analysis of Variance (ANOVA)

94. What does the Chi-square (χ^2) test evaluate in hypothesis testing?
(a) Population means
(b) Independence between categorical variables
(c) Population variances
(d) The difference between two proportions

95. In a Chi-square (χ^2) test, the null hypothesis assumes
(a) Independence between categorical variables
(b) A significant difference between categorical variables
(c) Normality of data distribution
(d) A relationship between the categorical variables

96. The null hypothesis in a Chi-square test for independence states that
(a) There is no association between the variables
(b) There is a significant association between the variables
(c) The variables are normally distributed
(d) The variables have equal means

97. What is the formula for the test statistic in a Chi-square (χ^2) test for independence?
(a) $\Sigma(O - E)^2 / E$
(b) $\Sigma(O - E)^2 / O$
(c) $\Sigma(O - E) / E$
(d) $\Sigma(O - E) / O$

98. In a one-sample Z-test, the null hypothesis typically states that
(a) The sample mean is not equal to the population mean
(b) The sample mean is less than the population mean
(c) The sample mean is greater than the population mean
(d) The sample size is too small

99. The formula for the F-statistic in ANOVA is based on the ratio of
(a) Variance within groups to variance between groups
(b) The sample mean to the population mean
(c) The sample size to the population size
(d) The correlation coefficient

100. What is the critical value used in a Chi-square (χ^2) test determined by?
(a) The sample size
(b) The level of significance
(c) The population parameter
(d) The sample mean

101. The null hypothesis in a one-sample Z-test states that the sample mean is equal to the population mean. What is the alternative hypothesis (Ha)?

(a) The sample mean is less than the population mean
(b) The sample mean is greater than the population mean
(c) The sample mean is not equal to the population mean
(d) There is no alternative hypothesis

102. What is the formula for the test statistic in a one-sample Z-test for a population proportion (p)?
(a) $(\bar{p} - p)$ / "(p * (1 - p) / n)
(b) $(\bar{x} - \mu)$ / (Ã / √n)
(c) $(\bar{x} - \mu) / (s / \sqrt{n})$
(d) $(\bar{p} - p) / (\sigma / \sqrt{n})$

103. In hypothesis testing, a Type I error occurs when
(a) The null hypothesis is rejected when it is true
(b) The null hypothesis is accepted when it is true
(c) The alternative hypothesis is rejected when it is true
(d) The sample size is too small

104. Which of the following is a non-parametric test used for hypothesis testing when dealing with categorical data?
(a) T-test
(b) Chi-square test
(c) F-test
(d) Z-test

105. What is the purpose of conducting a post-hoc test in an analysis of variance (ANOVA)?
(a) To determine the sample size
(b) To test the null hypothesis
(c) To compare specific group means when the ANOVA reveals a significant difference
(d) To calculate the F-statistic

106. What does a correlation coefficient measure in statistical analysis?
(a) Strength and direction of a linear relationship between two variables
(b) Causation between two variables
(c) Variability of a single variable
(d) Relationship between three or more variables

107. The correlation coefficient can range between
(a) –1 and 1 (b) 0 and 1
(c) $-\infty$ and ∞ (d) –1 and 0

108. In a scatterplot, what does it mean if points cluster around a line with a positive slope?
(a) There is a strong positive correlation
(b) There is a strong negative correlation
(c) There is no correlation
(d) The relationship is non-linear

109. What does a correlation coefficient of 0.7 indicate?
(a) A perfect positive correlation
(b) A strong positive correlation
(c) A moderate positive correlation
(d) A weak positive correlation

110. In regression analysis, what is the dependent variable?
(a) The variable that is being predicted
(b) The variable that is held constant
(c) The variable that is independent of others
(d) The variable that is controlled by the researcher

111. What is the main goal of multiple regression analysis?
(a) To determine causation between variables
(b) To predict a dependent variable based on two or more independent variables
(c) To find the correlation coefficient
(d) To calculate the mean of a variable

112. In simple linear regression, the relationship between the dependent variable (Y) and the independent variable (X) is typically represented as
(a) $Y = aX + b$
(b) $Y = X^2$
(c) $Y = X + a$
(d) $Y = X - a$

113. What is the slope (a) of the regression equation $Y = aX + b$?
(a) The rate of change in Y for a one-unit change in X
(b) The Y-intercept
(c) The correlation coefficient
(d) The coefficient of determination

114. In multiple regression analysis, how are the coefficients for the independent variables estimated?
(a) Using the method of least squares
(b) By multiplying the variables together
(c) By taking the square root of the independent variables
(d) By dividing the variables by each other

115. What does a coefficient of determination (R^2) value of 0.85 indicate?

(a) 85% of the variance in the dependent variable is explained by the independent variables
(b) 15% of the variance in the dependent variable is explained by the independent variables
(c) There is no relationship between the variables
(d) R^2 values cannot exceed 1

116. Which of the following regression models is appropriate when the dependent variable is binary (e.g., 0 or 1)?
(a) Linear regression
(b) Multiple regression
(c) Logistic regression
(d) Polynomial regression

117. In correlation analysis, if the correlation coefficient is close to –1, it indicates
(a) A strong positive correlation
(b) A strong negative correlation
(c) No correlation
(d) A linear relationship

118. What is the range of the correlation coefficient (r) in correlation analysis?
(a) –1 to 1 (b) 0 to 1
(c) $-\infty$ to ∞ (d) –1 to 0

119. In regression analysis, what is the Y-intercept (b) of the regression equation $Y = aX + b$?
(a) The rate of change in Y for a one-unit change in X
(b) The slope of the regression line
(c) The predicted value of Y when X is zero
(d) The correlation coefficient

120. What does a p-value in regression analysis represent?
(a) The strength of the correlation
(b) The probability that the regression coefficients are not zero
(c) The coefficient of determination
(d) The Y-intercept of the regression equation

121. Which type of correlation coefficient is appropriate when dealing with non-linear relationships?
(a) Pearson's correlation coefficient (r)
(b) Spearman's rank correlation coefficient (ρ)
(c) Point-biserial correlation coefficient (rpb)
(d) Biserial correlation coefficient (rb)

122. When performing linear regression analysis, what does the residual represent?
(a) The predicted values of the dependent variable
(b) The independent variable
(c) The difference between the observed and predicted values of the dependent variable
(d) The Y-intercept of the regression equation

123. Which of the following is not a type of correlation coefficient?
(a) Pearson's correlation coefficient (r)
(b) Spearman's rank correlation coefficient (ξ)
(c) Chi-square correlation coefficient (ξ^2)
(d) Point-biserial correlation coefficient (rpb)

124. In regression analysis, multicollinearity refers to
(a) A high correlation between independent and dependent variables
(b) A high correlation among independent variables
(c) A high correlation between the sample and population
(d) A high correlation between the Y-intercept and the slope

125. Which regression model is used when the dependent variable is continuous, and the relationship between variables is non-linear?
(a) Simple linear regression
(b) Polynomial regression
(c) Logistic regression
(d) Multiple regression

126. In regression analysis, the coefficient of determination (R^2) measures
(a) The strength and direction of the relationship
(b) The correlation between two variables
(c) The proportion of variance in the dependent variable explained by the independent variables
(d) The slope of the regression line

127. What does a negative correlation coefficient (r) indicate?
(a) A strong positive correlation
(b) A strong negative correlation
(c) No correlation
(d) A non-linear relationship

128. In correlation analysis, if the correlation coefficient is close to 0, it indicates
(a) A strong positive correlation
(b) A strong negative correlation
(c) No correlation
(d) A non-linear relationship

129. In regression analysis, what does the term "heteroscedasticity" refer to?
(a) A non-linear relationship between variables
(b) A perfect positive correlation
(c) The violation of the assumption of constant variance of residuals
(d) The absence of multicollinearity

130. In logistic regression, what is the logistic function used to model?
(a) The linear relationship between variables
(b) The probability of an event occurring
(c) The variance of the dependent variable
(d) The coefficient of determination

131. What is the primary focus of operations management in an organization?
(a) Marketing and sales
(b) Human resources management
(c) Efficient production and delivery of products and services
(d) Financial management

132. Which of the following is NOT a typical role of operations management?
(a) Capacity planning
(b) Quality control
(c) Employee training and development
(d) Inventory management

133. Operations management is concerned with the design, planning, and control of which of the following?
(a) Marketing strategies
(b) Financial transactions
(c) Production and operations processes
(d) Legal regulations

134. The scope of operations management includes managing
(a) Only manufacturing processes
(b) Both manufacturing and service operations
(c) Only marketing activities
(d) Only financial transactions

135. Which of the following is NOT a key objective of operations management?
(a) Reducing costs
(b) Maximizing profitability
(c) Enhancing employee satisfaction
(d) Improving product or service quality

136. Lean production and Six Sigma are examples of techniques used in operations management to
(a) Increase production capacity
(b) Improve product quality and reduce defects
(c) Maximize financial profits
(d) Enhance marketing strategies

137. What does the term "Supply Chain Management" refer to in operations management?
(a) The production of goods and services
(b) The management of employees
(c) The entire network of organizations and activities involved in delivering a product or service to customers
(d) The process of financial management

138. Which of the following is NOT a component of the supply chain?
(a) Suppliers (b) Customers
(c) Competitors (d) Distributors

139. In operations management, the term "forecasting" is used for
(a) Predicting the future demand for products or services
(b) Calculating the production costs
(c) Managing the workforce
(d) Conducting quality control inspections

140. Operations managers are responsible for ensuring that production processes are
(a) As complex as possible
(b) As fast as possible
(c) As efficient and cost-effective as possible
(d) As unpredictable as possible

141. Just-in-Time (JIT) inventory management aims to
(a) Maximize inventory levels to avoid stock-outs
(b) Minimize lead times in the supply chain
(c) Store a large surplus of inventory
(d) Minimize production efficiency

142. Which of the following is a key performance indicator (KPI) often used in operations management to measure the efficiency of production processes?
(a) Return on investment (ROI)
(b) Customer satisfaction
(c) OEE (Overall Equipment Effectiveness)
(d) Sales revenue

143. Which of the following is a technique used in operations management to identify and eliminate waste in production processes?
(a) Total Quality Management (TQM)

(b) Inventory control
(c) Six Sigma
(d) Advertising

144. Which of the following operations management approaches focuses on providing the highest level of value to customers with the least amount of waste?
(a) Mass production
(b) Lean production
(c) Agile manufacturing
(d) Custom manufacturing

145. Operations managers often use a Gantt chart to
(a) Forecast demand for products
(b) Schedule and monitor project tasks over time
(c) Calculate manufacturing costs
(d) Perform quality control inspections

146. The role of operations management in managing capacity involves
(a) Controlling the speed of production
(b) Ensuring that capacity meets customer demand
(c) Maximizing capacity at all times
(d) Ignoring capacity constraints

147. In operations management, "total quality management" (TQM) focuses on
(a) Minimizing customer satisfaction
(b) Maximizing production costs
(c) Improving product or service quality and customer satisfaction
(d) Reducing lead times

148. Which of the following is an example of a service operation in operations management?
(a) Manufacturing automobiles
(b) Providing healthcare
(c) Producing consumer goods
(d) Mining natural resources

149. Benchmarking is a technique used in operations management to
(a) Set unrealistic performance goals
(b) Compare an organization's performance to industry best practices
(c) Increase production lead times
(d) Ignore customer feedback

150. Operations management can be described as the management of
(a) Human resources
(b) Marketing strategies
(c) Resources and processes used to produce and deliver products and services
(d) Financial investments

151. Which of the following is NOT a key element of operations management?
(a) Product design
(b) Facility layout
(c) Employee benefits
(d) Quality control

152. In operations management, the term "sustainability" refers to
(a) Maximizing profits at any cost
(b) The responsible use of resources to minimize environmental impact
(c) Ignoring the impact of operations on society
(d) Focusing solely on financial returns

153. What is the main goal of capacity planning in operations management?
(a) To reduce production costs
(b) To match production capacity to customer demand
(c) To maximize lead times
(d) To minimize customer satisfaction

154. In operations management, what does the term "lead time" refer to?
(a) The time it takes for a product to wear out
(b) The time it takes for a customer to place an order
(c) The time it takes to manufacture a product
(d) The time it takes for an order to be fulfilled, from initiation to delivery

155. Which of the following is NOT a technique used in operations management for quality control?
(a) Six Sigma
(b) Total Quality Management (TQM)
(c) Lean production
(d) Mass production

156. Facility location decisions involve determining the
(a) Type of facility to be built
(b) Location of the facility
(c) Size of the facility
(d) Cost of the facility

157. What is the primary objective of facility location analysis?
(a) Minimizing facility size
(b) Minimizing transportation costs

(c) Maximizing facility capacity
(d) Maximizing facility design

158. Which method is often used to select a facility location based on minimizing transportation costs?
(a) Factor rating method
(b) Center-of-gravity method
(c) Break-even analysis
(d) Pareto analysis

159. In facility location analysis, what does the "center of gravity" represent?
(a) The midpoint of the facility's perimeter
(b) The point where transportation costs are minimized
(c) The center of a geographic region
(d) The highest point in a facility

160. A facility location that minimizes transportation costs is especially important for businesses dealing with
(a) High-quality products
(b) Local customers
(c) Perishable goods
(d) Low-cost products

161. In facility layout, the objective of a "process layout" is to
(a) Group machines and equipment by function
(b) Minimize transportation time
(c) Maximize production capacity
(d) Reduce equipment costs

162. Which of the following is an advantage of a "product layout" in facility design?
(a) Flexibility in changing product lines
(b) Reduced setup times
(c) Lower equipment costs
(d) Enhanced employee satisfaction

163. A "fixed-position layout" is most commonly used in which type of industry?
(a) Manufacturing
(b) Healthcare
(c) Retail
(d) Information technology

164. In facility layout design, what does the term "workstation" refer to?
(a) A specialized facility for training employees
(b) A location for storing equipment
(c) A specific area where tasks are performed
(d) An administrative office

165. The process of arranging departments, workstations, machines, and equipment to improve workflow and productivity is known as
(a) Facility location analysis
(b) Process optimization
(c) Facility layout design
(d) Cost analysis

166. Which facility layout design focuses on arranging workstations to minimize transportation time and increase efficiency?
(a) Product layout
(b) Process layout
(c) Cellular layout
(d) Fixed-position layout

167. What is the primary objective of a "cellular layout" in facility design?
(a) Reducing setup times
(b) Maximizing equipment utilization
(c) Minimizing transportation costs
(d) Grouping machines and equipment to produce similar products

168. Which of the following is an advantage of a "hybrid layout" in facility design?
(a) Simplified maintenance
(b) Lower manufacturing costs
(c) Enhanced quality control
(d) Improved worker satisfaction

169. The "U-shaped" layout is often used in which type of facility design?
(a) Process layout
(b) Product layout
(c) Cellular layout
(d) Fixed-position layout

170. Facility layout decisions involve determining the arrangement of
(a) Raw materials
(b) Employee work schedules
(c) Departments, workstations, and equipment
(d) Accounting systems

171. In facility location analysis, the "factor rating method" involves
(a) Calculating transportation costs
(b) Assigning scores to potential locations based on multiple factors
(c) Identifying the center of gravity
(d) Designing the layout of a facility

172. The "break-even analysis" is often used to
(a) Determine the optimal facility layout

(b) Identify the center of gravity for a facility
(c) Determine the production capacity of a facility
(d) Analyze the point at which costs and revenues are equal

173. A facility location that minimizes transportation costs is especially important for businesses dealing with
(a) High-quality products
(b) Local customers
(c) Perishable goods
(d) Low-cost products

174. In facility layout, the "line balancing" technique is used to
(a) Arrange workstations in a straight line
(b) Optimize the layout of a product line
(c) Ensure that tasks at each workstation have similar cycle times
(d) Calculate the center of gravity

175. What is the goal of "balanced production" in facility layout design?
(a) To maximize production capacity
(b) To minimize facility size
(c) To ensure that workstations have equal tasks and cycle times
(d) To reduce employee training

176. The "space requirements method" in facility location analysis is used to
(a) Calculate the square footage of a facility
(b) Minimize facility costs
(c) Analyze transportation routes
(d) Determine the layout of departments and workstations

177. Which of the following facility location factors is typically related to the availability of labor and workforce skills?
(a) Market proximity
(b) Transportation costs
(c) Labor factors
(d) Government regulations

178. The "random-number method" is a technique used in facility location analysis to
(a) Assign scores to potential locations
(b) Determine the center of gravity
(c) Simulate various scenarios
(d) Calculate transportation costs

179. In facility location analysis, what is the "service area" of a facility?
(a) The area where customers are served
(b) The center of gravity
(c) The location of raw materials
(d) The size of the facility

180. Facility layout design plays a crucial role in determining the
(a) Number of employees
(b) Cost of materials
(c) Efficiency and productivity of operations
(d) Marketing strategies

181. What is the primary purpose of an ERP system?
(a) Managing customer relationships
(b) Managing enterprise resources and processes
(c) Managing financial transactions
(d) Managing external communication

182. Which of the following is NOT a typical module of an ERP system?
(a) Human Resources (HR)
(b) Customer Relationship Management (CRM)
(c) Supply Chain Management (SCM)
(d) Sales and Marketing

183. The module of an ERP system that focuses on managing employee information, payroll, and benefits is
(a) Financial Management
(b) Supply Chain Management
(c) Human Resources (HR)
(d) Inventory Management

184. In ERP terminology, what does "SCM" stand for?
(a) Sales and Customer Management
(b) Supply Chain Management
(c) System Control Module
(d) Service and Communication Management

185. Which ERP module is responsible for managing an organization's financial transactions, including accounting and budgeting?
(a) Customer Relationship Management (CRM)
(b) Production Planning and Control (PPC)
(c) Financial Management
(d) Inventory Management

186. What is the purpose of the "Production Planning and Control (PPC)" module in an ERP system?
(a) Managing employee information
(b) Managing manufacturing processes and schedules

(c) Managing customer relationships
(d) Managing financial transactions

187. ERP modules that focus on managing an organization's interactions with customers, sales, and marketing are often grouped under the abbreviation
(a) ERP-CRM (b) ERP-SCM
(c) ERP-PPC (d) ERP-HR

188. In the context of ERP, what is a "module"?
(a) A hardware component of an ERP system
(b) A software component that focuses on specific business functions
(c) A form of external communication
(d) A financial statement

189. What is the role of the "Inventory Management" module in an ERP system?
(a) Managing the organization's customer relationships
(b) Managing the procurement, storage, and tracking of inventory
(c) Managing financial transactions
(d) Managing production schedules

190. The "Supplier Relationship Management (SRM)" module in an ERP system focuses on
(a) Managing customer relationships
(b) Managing interactions with suppliers and vendors
(c) Managing employee information
(d) Managing production processes

191. The process of selecting an appropriate ERP system for an organization is known as
(a) ERP customization
(b) ERP implementation
(c) ERP evaluation and selection
(d) ERP training

192. The stage of ERP implementation that involves configuring the software to align with an organization's specific business processes is known as
(a) ERP evaluation (b) ERP customization
(c) ERP selection (d) ERP training

193. What is the primary goal of ERP implementation?
(a) Replacing all existing software systems in the organization
(b) Achieving process efficiency and effectiveness through the use of an integrated software solution
(c) Reducing the organization's workforce
(d) Focusing on individual business units

194. The phase of ERP implementation that involves ensuring that the ERP system works properly and meets the organization's requirements is known as
(a) ERP evaluation (b) ERP customization
(c) ERP testing (d) ERP training

195. What is "change management" in the context of ERP implementation?
(a) The process of selecting an ERP system
(b) The process of implementing ERP modules
(c) The process of managing the organizational and cultural changes that result from ERP implementation
(d) The process of customizing ERP software

196. What is the "pilot phase" of ERP implementation?
(a) The phase in which all employees are trained on the ERP system
(b) The phase in which the entire organization switches to the ERP system at once
(c) The phase in which a small group or department within the organization tests the ERP system before full implementation
(d) The phase in which the ERP system is evaluated for selection

197. Which of the following is NOT a key challenge in ERP implementation?
(a) Resistance to change from employees
(b) Inadequate training and user support
(c) Rapid and smooth transition without any disruptions
(d) High implementation costs

198. The phase of ERP implementation that involves training employees on how to use the ERP system is known as
(a) ERP evaluation (b) ERP customization
(c) ERP testing (d) ERP training

199. The "Big Bang" approach to ERP implementation involves
(a) Gradually implementing the ERP system department by department
(b) Implementing the entire ERP system for the entire organization at once
(c) Implementing the ERP system without any customization
(d) Implementing the ERP system only for certain customer-related processes

200. What is the role of an ERP project manager during the implementation process?

(a) Managing all financial transactions
(b) Customizing the ERP system
(c) Overseeing and coordinating the entire ERP implementation project
(d) Managing customer relationships

201. Which phase of ERP implementation involves migrating data from existing systems to the new ERP system?
(a) ERP evaluation (b) ERP customization
(c) ERP data migration
(d) ERP training

202. In ERP implementation, "post-implementation support" refers to
(a) The phase in which the ERP system is evaluated for selection
(b) The ongoing support, maintenance, and troubleshooting of the ERP system after it has been implemented
(c) The customization of ERP software
(d) The pilot phase of ERP testing

203. The process of evaluating the ERP system's performance, identifying issues, and making necessary improvements after implementation is known as
(a) ERP testing (b) ERP evaluation
(c) ERP customization (d) ERP selection

204. In ERP implementation, what is the purpose of a "gap analysis"?
(a) To identify differences between the organization's existing processes and the desired state with the ERP system
(b) To customize the ERP software
(c) To select the ERP system that best fits the organization's needs
(d) To test the ERP system

205. The stage of ERP implementation that involves deciding whether to build custom functionality or use standard ERP features is known as
(a) ERP evaluation (b) ERP customization
(c) ERP testing (d) ERP training

206. What is the primary goal of scheduling in operations management?
(a) Maximizing resource utilization
(b) Minimizing lead times
(c) Reducing production costs
(d) Maximizing sales revenue

207. Loading, in the context of production scheduling, refers to
(a) Assigning jobs or tasks to workstations or machines
(b) Storing raw materials in inventory
(c) Monitoring employee performance
(d) Managing customer relationships

208. Which of the following is NOT a scheduling criterion commonly used in operations management?
(a) Makespan (b) Setup time
(c) Employee satisfaction
(d) Due date

209. Sequencing, in production scheduling, involves determining the order in which jobs or tasks should be
(a) Delayed (b) Cancelled
(c) Completed (d) Started

210. The process of tracking and controlling the progress of production jobs in real-time is known as
(a) Loading (b) Sequencing
(c) Monitoring (d) Scheduling

211. Which of the following is NOT a common scheduling method used in operations management?
(a) First-Come-First-Served (FCFS)
(b) Earliest Due Date (EDD)
(c) Last-In-First-Out (LIFO)
(d) Shortest Processing Time (SPT)

212. In the context of job shop scheduling, which scheduling method is used when the priority is given to the job with the shortest processing time?
(a) First-Come-First-Served (FCFS)
(b) Earliest Due Date (EDD)
(c) Shortest Processing Time (SPT)
(d) Last-In-First-Out (LIFO)

213. Which scheduling method prioritizes jobs based on their due dates, with the job having the earliest due date scheduled first?
(a) First-Come-First-Served (FCFS)
(b) Earliest Due Date (EDD)
(c) Shortest Processing Time (SPT)
(d) Last-In-First-Out (LIFO)

214. The "makespan" in scheduling refers to
(a) The maximum time it takes to complete all jobs in a schedule
(b) The time it takes to set up a machine
(c) The due date for a job
(d) The time it takes to load a workstation

215. Which of the following scheduling methods is also known as "first-come-first-served" and schedules jobs in the order they arrive?

(a) Earliest Due Date (EDD)
(b) Shortest Processing Time (SPT)
(c) Last-In-First-Out (LIFO)
(d) First-Come-First-Served (FCFS)

216. The Gantt chart is a tool commonly used in scheduling for
(a) Calculating the makespan
(b) Visualizing the schedule of jobs over time
(c) Assigning due dates to jobs
(d) Loading workstations

217. In job shop scheduling, what is the "flow time" of a job?
(a) The time it takes to process a job
(b) The time it takes to transport a job from one workstation to another
(c) The total time a job spends in the production process
(d) The time it takes to load a job

218. Which of the following is NOT a common approach to monitoring and controlling the progress of production jobs?
(a) Using visual cues and Kanban boards
(b) Real-time tracking through software
(c) Randomly assigning due dates
(d) Regularly updating Gantt charts

219. Which scheduling method focuses on minimizing the total flow time of all jobs in the schedule?
(a) Shortest Processing Time (SPT)
(b) Earliest Due Date (EDD)
(c) First-Come-First-Served (FCFS)
(d) Last-In-First-Out (LIFO)

220. In a job shop environment, what is the "Johnson's rule" used for?
(a) Scheduling jobs in the order they arrive
(b) Prioritizing jobs based on due dates
(c) Sequencing jobs on machines to minimize makespan
(d) Monitoring employee performance

221. What is the primary objective of quality management?
(a) Maximizing profits
(b) Reducing workforce
(c) Ensuring customer satisfaction
(d) Minimizing production costs

222. Statistical Quality Control (SQC) involves
(a) Reducing defects in the final product
(b) Eliminating the need for quality inspections
(c) Increasing production speed
(d) Maximizing the use of raw materials

223. Which of the following tools is commonly used in Statistical Quality Control (SQC) for process control and identifying variations?
(a) Histogram (b) Pareto chart
(c) Fishbone diagram (d) Scatter plot

224. Quality Circles are groups of employees who
(a) Focus on marketing strategies
(b) Work on various assembly lines
(c) Collaborate to identify and solve quality-related issues
(d) Manage financial transactions

225. Total Quality Management (TQM) emphasizes continuous improvement in
(a) Reducing production speed
(b) Employee turnover
(c) Customer satisfaction and processes
(d) Equipment maintenance

226. KAIZEN is a Japanese term that refers to
(a) Continuous improvement
(b) Rapid production
(c) Reducing waste
(d) Strict quality control

227. Benchmarking is a process that involves
(a) Ignoring industry best practices
(b) Comparing an organization's performance to industry best practices
(c) Maximizing defects in products
(d) Reducing employee satisfaction

228. Which of the following is a key principle of Six Sigma methodology?
(a) Reducing the customer base
(b) Increasing process variability
(c) Reducing defects to a minimum
(d) Ignoring quality control

229. The ISO 9000 Series Standards primarily focus on
(a) Environmental management
(b) Quality management and quality assurance
(c) Occupational health and safety
(d) Financial management

230. Which ISO 9000 standard provides guidelines for auditing the quality management system of an organization?
(a) ISO 9001 (b) ISO 9002
(c) ISO 9003 (d) ISO 9004

231. The concept of "Continuous Improvement" is a fundamental principle of which quality management approach?
(a) Quality Circles
(b) Six Sigma
(c) Benchmarking
(d) Total Quality Management (TQM)

232. Which statistical tool is often used to analyze the causes of a problem and identify its root causes?
(a) Histogram (b) Pareto chart
(c) Control chart (d) Scatter plot

233. In Six Sigma, what is the typical goal for the "process sigma level"?
(a) 1 sigma (b) 3 sigma
(c) 6 sigma (d) 10 sigma

234. Which phase of the DMAIC (Define, Measure, Analyze, Improve, Control) process in Six Sigma involves the development and testing of potential solutions?
(a) Measure (b) Analyze
(c) Improve (d) Define

235. The "fishbone diagram" is also known as
(a) Pareto chart (b) Ishikawa diagram
(c) Scatter plot (d) Histogram

236. Which of the following is a key aspect of Total Quality Management (TQM)?
(a) Focusing solely on the bottom line (profits)
(b) Ignoring customer feedback
(c) Involving employees at all levels in decision-making and problem-solving
(d) Minimizing process efficiency

237. The "Plan-Do-Check-Act" (PDCA) cycle is commonly associated with which quality management concept?
(a) KAIZEN (b) Benchmarking
(c) Six Sigma
(d) TQM (Total Quality Management)

238. In benchmarking, what does the term "best-in-class" refer to?
(a) The highest possible quality standards
(b) The organization with the most employees
(c) The industry leader in a particular performance category
(d) The organization with the lowest profits

239. Which of the following is a key principle of Quality Circles?
(a) Excluding employees from decision-making
(b) Limiting employee involvement
(c) Encouraging employees to participate in problem-solving and decision-making
(d) Minimizing employee training

240. Which of the following is NOT a typical tool or technique used in Six Sigma methodology?
(a) DMAIC (b) Lean principles
(c) SWOT analysis (d) Control charts

241. The "voice of the customer" is a central concept in which quality management approach?
(a) Six Sigma (b) Benchmarking
(c) Quality Circles
(d) TQM (Total Quality Management)

242. The "black belt" and "green belt" designations in Six Sigma refer to
(a) The color coding of production areas
(b) Employee uniforms
(c) Levels of expertise and training in Six Sigma methodology
(d) Marketing strategies

243. Which of the following is NOT a key aspect of ISO 9000 Series Standards?
(a) Establishing a quality management system
(b) Continual improvement
(c) Environmental management
(d) Customer focus

244. Which of the following quality management tools is used to monitor and control the quality of a process over time?
(a) Control chart (b) Ishikawa diagram
(c) Pareto chart (d) Scatter plot

245. The term "zero defects" is closely associated with which quality management approach?
(a) Benchmarking
(b) Total Quality Management (TQM)
(c) Quality Circles
(d) Six Sigma

246. The "Kaizen Blitz" or "Rapid Improvement Event" is a technique used in
(a) Quality Circles (b) Benchmarking
(c) Six Sigma (d) KAIZEN

247. In the context of quality management, what does "CTQ" stand for?
(a) Critical to Quality
(b) Customer Tracking and Quality
(c) Continuous Total Quality
(d) Control the Quantity

248. Which of the following is NOT a phase in the DMAIC (Define, Measure, Analyze, Improve, Control) process in Six Sigma?
(a) Define (b) Audit
(c) Measure (d) Control

249. The primary purpose of a "quality policy" in an organization is to
(a) Define environmental standards
(b) Outline financial goals
(c) Communicate the organization's commitment to quality
(d) Describe marketing strategies

250. In the context of quality management, what is the primary purpose of a "SWOT analysis"?
(a) Identifying internal strengths and weaknesses, as well as external opportunities and threats
(b) Monitoring employee performance
(c) Setting up a quality management system
(d) Determining the organization's budget

251. The "5 Whys" technique is a problem-solving method commonly associated with which quality management approach?
(a) Total Quality Management (TQM)
(b) Quality Circles
(c) Benchmarking (d) Six Sigma

252. The term "champion" in Six Sigma refers to
(a) A high-level executive who provides support and resources for Six Sigma projects
(b) The lead person responsible for data collection
(c) The final inspector in the production process
(d) The chief financial officer

253. Which ISO 9000 standard provides guidelines for the certification of a quality management system?
(a) ISO 9001 (b) ISO 9002
(c) ISO 9003 (d) ISO 9004

254. The "House of Quality" is a tool commonly used in which quality management approach?
(a) Total Quality Management (TQM)
(b) Quality Circles
(c) Benchmarking (d) Six Sigma

255. In benchmarking, what is the term "best practice" often used to describe?
(a) Any practice employed by the organization
(b) The organization's standard operating procedures
(c) The most effective and efficient practices in the industry or field
(d) Practices that are unique to a specific organization

256. What is the primary objective of the transportation problem in operations research?
(a) Maximizing profits
(b) Minimizing transportation costs
(c) Reducing workforce
(d) Maximizing production speed

257. In the transportation problem, what does the term "supply" refer to?
(a) Demand for goods at a destination
(b) Cost of transportation
(c) Availability of goods at a source
(d) Production speed

258. The Queuing theory is primarily concerned with the study of
(a) Inventory management
(b) Waiting lines and service systems
(c) Transportation costs
(d) Quality control

259. In Queuing theory, what does "arrival rate" represent?
(a) The rate at which customers arrive at a service facility
(b) The time it takes to complete a service
(c) The capacity of the service facility
(d) The maximum waiting time

260. Decision Theory is concerned with
(a) Finding the optimal solution in deterministic situations
(b) Making decisions in uncertain situations
(c) Maximizing profits
(d) Reducing production speed

261. In Decision Theory, the term "payoff" refers to
(a) The cost of decision-making
(b) The result or outcome associated with a decision
(c) Inventory levels
(d) Service times

262. PERT stands for
(a) Program for Evaluation and Review Techniques
(b) Probability Evaluation and Risk Tolerance
(c) Project Evaluation and Resource Tracking
(d) Product Efficiency and Resource Testing

263. In PERT/CPM, what does the "critical path" represent?

(a) The path that takes the longest time to complete
(b) The path that requires the most resources
(c) The path with the highest risk
(d) The shortest path

264. Which of the following is a common objective in the transportation problem?
(a) Maximizing production speed
(b) Maximizing the number of routes
(c) Minimizing transportation costs
(d) Minimizing the number of facilities

265. In the context of Queuing theory, what is "service rate"?
(a) The rate at which customers arrive at a service facility
(b) The maximum waiting time
(c) The rate at which customers are served
(d) The number of customers in the queue

266. Decision Theory helps decision-makers deal with
(a) Certainty
(b) Risk and uncertainty
(c) Probability theory
(d) Inventory management

267. The PERT/CPM techniques are commonly used in
(a) Inventory management
(b) Production speed optimization
(c) Project planning and scheduling
(d) Queuing theory

268. What is the primary purpose of the "objective function" in the transportation problem?
(a) To maximize production speed
(b) To represent the total cost of transportation
(c) To minimize the number of facilities
(d) To track resources

269. In the Queuing model, what does "arrival rate" represent?
(a) The rate at which customers arrive at a service facility
(b) The time it takes to complete a service
(c) The capacity of the service facility
(d) The maximum waiting time

270. Decision Theory often involves evaluating various decision alternatives using
(a) Random selection
(b) Decision trees and decision criteria
(c) Waiting lines (d) Queuing models

271. Which of the following is NOT a common component of a PERT/CPM analysis?
(a) Activity time estimates
(b) Project network diagram
(c) Waiting time
(d) Critical path determination

272. In the transportation problem, what does the "demand" refer to?
(a) The cost of transportation
(b) The capacity of the service facility
(c) Customer satisfaction
(d) Demand for goods at a destination

273. In Queuing theory, the term "service discipline" refers to
(a) The rate at which customers arrive at a service facility
(b) The time it takes to complete a service
(c) The rules that determine the order in which customers are served
(d) Inventory management

274. What is the primary purpose of the "decision matrix" in Decision Theory?
(a) To maximize profits
(b) To minimize waiting times
(c) To provide a structured approach to evaluate decision alternatives
(d) To determine the critical path

275. In PERT/CPM analysis, "slack" or "float" refers to
(a) The amount of time an activity can be delayed without delaying the project
(b) The capacity of the service facility
(c) The probability of success
(d) The number of decision alternatives

26. Which of the following is NOT a common assumption in the transportation problem?
(a) The cost of transportation is linear
(b) The supply and demand constraints are always equal
(c) Transportation costs are constant
(d) Transportation costs are known

277. The "queue discipline" in Queuing theory refers to
(a) The rate at which customers arrive at a service facility
(b) The rules that determine the order in which customers are served
(c) The maximum waiting time
(d) The service rate

278. Decision Theory often involves the use of decision trees to

(a) Determine the critical path

(b) Represent decision alternatives and their outcomes

(c) Calculate transportation costs

(d) Create project network diagrams

279. In PERT/CPM analysis, what does the "earliest start time" of an activity represent?

(a) The latest time an activity can start without delaying the project

(b) The earliest time an activity can start without delaying the project

(c) The maximum waiting time

(d) The cost of transportation

280. The transportation problem aims to minimize transportation costs while satisfying

(a) Customer demand constraints

(b) The critical path

(c) Waiting times

(d) Inventory levels

ANSWER KEY

1. (d)	**2.** (b)	**3.** (c)	**4.** (c)	**5.** (c)	**6.** (b)	**7.** (a)	**8.** (a)	**9.** (a)	**10.** (a)
11. (b)	**12.** (a)	**13.** (b)	**14.** (b)	**15.** (d)	**16.** (c)	**17.** (a)	**18.** (c)	**19.** (b)	**20.** (a)
21. (c)	**22.** (a)	**23.** (a)	**24.** (a)	**25.** (a)	**26.** (a)	**27.** (a)	**28.** (d)	**29.** (c)	**30.** (d)
31. (c)	**32.** (d)	**33.** (c)	**34.** (c)	**35.** (c)	**36.** (a)	**37.** (c)	**38.** (c)	**39.** (c)	**40.** (c)
41. (b)	**42.** (c)	**43.** (b)	**44.** (a)	**45.** (c)	**46.** (c)	**47.** (c)	**48.** (c)	**49.** (c)	**50.** (a)
51. (b)	**52.** (b)	**53.** (d)	**54.** (c)	**55.** (a)	**56.** (b)	**57.** (c)	**58.** (b)	**59.** (a)	**60.** (b)
61. (b)	**62.** (a)	**63.** (b)	**64.** (c)	**65.** (c)	**66.** (a)	**67.** (d)	**68.** (b)	**69.** (b)	**70.** (b)
71. (c)	**72.** (a)	**73.** (b)	**74.** (d)	**75.** (b)	**76.** (a)	**77.** (b)	**78.** (c)	**79.** (c)	**80.** (d)
81. (b)	**82.** (a)	**83.** (a)	**84.** (b)	**85.** (c)	**86.** (c)	**87.** (c)	**88.** (b)	**89.** (b)	**90.** (a)
91. (c)	**92.** (b)	**93.** (d)	**94.** (b)	**95.** (a)	**96.** (a)	**97.** (a)	**98.** (a)	**99.** (a)	**100.** (b)
101. (c)	**102.** (a)	**103.** (a)	**104.** (b)	**105.** (c)	**106.** (a)	**107.** (a)	**108.** (a)	**109.** (c)	**110.** (a)
111. (b)	**112.** (a)	**113.** (a)	**114.** (a)	**115.** (a)	**116.** (c)	**117.** (b)	**118.** (a)	**119.** (c)	**120.** (b)
121. (b)	**122.** (c)	**123.** (c)	**124.** (b)	**125.** (b)	**126.** (c)	**127.** (b)	**128.** (c)	**129.** (c)	**130.** (b)
131. (c)	**132.** (c)	**133.** (c)	**134.** (b)	**135.** (c)	**136.** (b)	**137.** (c)	**138.** (c)	**139.** (a)	**140.** (c)
141. (b)	**142.** (c)	**143.** (c)	**144.** (b)	**145.** (b)	**146.** (b)	**147.** (c)	**148.** (b)	**149.** (b)	**150.** (c)
151. (c)	**152.** (b)	**153.** (b)	**154.** (d)	**155.** (d)	**156.** (b)	**157.** (b)	**158.** (b)	**159.** (b)	**160.** (c)
161. (a)	**162.** (b)	**163.** (a)	**164.** (c)	**165.** (c)	**166.** (a)	**167.** (d)	**168.** (d)	**169.** (c)	**170.** (c)
171. (b)	**172.** (d)	**173.** (c)	**174.** (c)	**175.** (c)	**176.** (d)	**177.** (c)	**178.** (c)	**179.** (a)	**180.** (c)
181. (b)	**182.** (d)	**183.** (c)	**184.** (b)	**185.** (c)	**186.** (b)	**187.** (a)	**188.** (b)	**189.** (b)	**190.** (b)
191. (c)	**192.** (b)	**193.** (b)	**194.** (c)	**195.** (c)	**196.** (c)	**197.** (c)	**198.** (d)	**199.** (b)	**200.** (c)
201. (c)	**202.** (b)	**203.** (b)	**204.** (a)	**205.** (b)	**206.** (a)	**207.** (a)	**208.** (c)	**209.** (c)	**210.** (c)
211. (c)	**212.** (c)	**213.** (b)	**214.** (a)	**215.** (d)	**216.** (b)	**217.** (c)	**218.** (c)	**219.** (a)	**220.** (c)
221. (c)	**222.** (a)	**223.** (a)	**224.** (c)	**225.** (c)	**226.** (a)	**227.** (b)	**228.** (c)	**229.** (b)	**230.** (d)
231. (d)	**232.** (b)	**233.** (c)	**234.** (c)	**235.** (b)	**236.** (c)	**237.** (d)	**238.** (c)	**239.** (c)	**240.** (c)
241. (a)	**242.** (c)	**243.** (c)	**244.** (a)	**245.** (d)	**246.** (d)	**247.** (a)	**248.** (b)	**249.** (c)	**250.** (a)
251. (d)	**252.** (a)	**253.** (a)	**254.** (d)	**255.** (c)	**256.** (b)	**257.** (c)	**258.** (b)	**259.** (a)	**260.** (b)
261. (b)	**262.** (a)	**263.** (a)	**264.** (c)	**265.** (c)	**266.** (b)	**267.** (c)	**268.** (b)	**269.** (a)	**270.** (b)
271. (c)	**272.** (d)	**273.** (c)	**274.** (c)	**275.** (a)	**276.** (b)	**277.** (b)	**278.** (b)	**279.** (b)	**280.** (a)

UNIT

9

SYLLABUS

- International Business – Managing Business in Globalization Era; Theories of International Trade; Balance of payment
- Foreign Direct Investment – Benefits and Costs
- Multilateral regulation of Trade and Investment under WTO
- International Trade Procedures and Documentation; EXIM Policies
- Role of International Financial Institutions – IMF and World Bank
- Information Technology – Use of Computers in Management Applications; MIS, DSS
- Artificial Intelligence and Big Data
- Data Warehousing, Data Mining and Knowledge Management – Concepts
- Managing Technological Change

INTERNATIONAL BUSINESS

International Business conducts business transactions all over the world. These transactions include the transfer of goods, services, technology, managerial knowledge, and capital to other countries. International business involves exports and imports.

International Business is also known, called or referred as a *Global Business* or an *International Marketing*.

An international business has many options for doing business, it includes,

1. Exporting goods and services.
2. Giving license to produce goods in the host country.
3. Starting a joint venture with a company.
4. Opening a branch for producing & distributing goods in the host country.
5. Providing managerial services to companies in the host country.

Features of International Business

The nature and **characteristics** or features of international business are:

1. Large scale operations. In international business, all the operations are conducted on a very huge scale. Production and marketing activities are conducted on a large scale. It first sells its goods in the local market. Then the surplus goods are exported.

2. **Integration of economies.** International business integrates (combines) the economies of many countries. This is because it uses finance from one country, labour from another country, and infrastructure from another country. It designs the product in one country, produces its parts in many different countries and assembles the product in another country. It sells the product in many countries, i.e., in the international market.
3. **Dominated by developed countries and MNCs.** International business is dominated by developed countries and their multinational corporations (MNCs). At present, MNCs from USA, Europe and Japan dominate (fully control) foreign trade. This is because they have large financial and other resources. They also have the best technology and research and development (R & D). They have highly skilled employees and managers because they give very high salaries and other benefits. Therefore, they produce good quality goods and services at low prices. This helps them to capture and dominate the world market.
4. **Benefits to participating countries.** International business gives benefits to all participating countries. However, the developed (rich) countries get the maximum benefits. The developing (poor) countries also get benefits. They get foreign capital and technology. They get rapid industrial development. They get more employment opportunities. All this results in economic development of the developing countries. Therefore, developing countries open up their economies through liberal economic policies.
5. **Kéen competition.** International business has to face keen (too much) competition in the world market. The competition is between unequal partners i.e. developed and developing countries. In this keen competition, developed countries and their MNCs are in a favourable position because they produce superior quality goods and services at very low prices. Developed countries also have many contacts in the world market. So, developing countries find it very difficult to face competition from developed countries.
6. **Special role of science and technology.** International business gives a lot of importance to science and technology. Science and Technology (S & T) help the business to have large-scale production. Developed countries use high technologies. Therefore, they dominate global business. International business helps them to transfer such top high-end technologies to the developing countries.
7. **International restrictions.** International business faces many restrictions on the inflow and outflow of capital, technology and goods. Many governments do not allow international businesses to enter their countries. They have many trade blocks, tariff barriers, foreign exchange restrictions, etc. All this is harmful to international business.
8. **Sensitive nature.** The international business is very sensitive in nature. Any changes in the economic policies, technology, political environment, etc. has a huge impact on it. Therefore, international business must conduct marketing research to find out and study these changes. They must adjust their business activities and adapt accordingly to survive changes.

Various explanations have been put forward to explain the reasons as to why international trade takes place and which country should export and import which products. Economic theories have moved a long way from mercantilism to the present day of globalization. Mercantilism prevailed in the seventeenth and eighteenth centuries. Mercantilism supported self sufficiency and advocated countries to increase export and decrease import so that maximum foreign exchange in the form of gold could be accumulated within the country. They held that country should become powerful by accumulating gold. Mercantilism supported regulations of foreign trade and opposed free trade policy.

THEORIES OF INTERNATIONAL TRADE

Comparative Advantage Theory

Ricardo explained the advantages of international trade if one country is more productive than another country in all lines of production. If USA can produce all goods with less labour cost than India, does it still benefit the country to trade ? The answer is yes, so long as India is not equally less productive in all lines of production, it still pays both countries to trade.

Cost Comparison
Labour Cost of Production (in hours)

	1 Unit of Goods A	1 Unit of Goods B
USA	80	90
India	120	100

USA has an absolute advantage in the production of goods A and B, because the labour cost of production for each unit of the two commodities is less in USA than in India.

In order to explain the trade between USA and India, concept of opportunity cost is used. The opportunity cost for a good A is the amount of other goods which have to be given up in order to produce one (additional) unit of A.

Opportunity cost
Opportunity costs for

	Good A	Good B
USA	80/90=8/9	90/80=9/8
India	120/100=12/10	100/120=10/12

A country has a comparative advantage in producing a good if the opportunity cost for producing the good is lower at home than in the other country. USA has the lower opportunity cost of the two countries in producing good A, while India has the lower opportunity cost in producing good B. Thus, USA has a comparative advantage in the production of good A and India has a comparative advantage in the production of cloth.

In order to use the concept of comparative advantage, there must be at least two countries and two goods. As long as the two countries opportunity costs for one good differ, one country has comparative advantage in the production of the other goods. As long as this is the case, both countries will gain from trade, regardless of the fact that one of the countries might have an absolute disadvantage in both lines of production.

(i) Assumptions of Comparative Cost Theory

1. There is only one factor of production.
2. The cost of production is payment to labour.
3. Labour is homogeneous and can be used to produce either goods A or goods B.
4. No training of labour is required.
5. No Government interference.
6. No barrier to trade by foreign country.
7. No transport cost.
8. Production takes place under constant returns to scale.
9. Both the countries under consideration are assumed to be of equal economic strength. Hence, gain from trade is equally shared by both the countries.
10. Unlimited demand for the product at the prevailing prices.

(ii) Flaws in the Theory of Comparative Cost

1. Empirical evidence shows that labour cost is a small portion of the total cost. In most of the successful companies, it is only 8%. To base a theory on labour cost will provide wrong predictions.
2. This theory ignores demand. Even if opportunity cost of goods A is low in USA, its price may be higher than in India, if the demand for the product is high in USA. Such products may be exported by India even if opportunity cost of the product is lower in India.
3. This theory does not explain the reason why opportunity cost in one country producing a good is lower or higher than in the other countries.

Heckscher-Ohlin theory of International Trade

Comparative advantage theory of international trade took only one factor of production *i.e.* labour. Hecksher-Ohlin argued that it is caused because different countries have different factor endowments. This theory studies the relationship between commodity and factor prices and relationship between input and output. It takes a general equilibrium approach to the study of international trading relationship between countries.

Country with capital abundance will be able to produce capital intensive products efficiently and the country with labour abundance will be able to produce labour intensive products efficiently. This is because the cost of capital *i.e.* rate of interest will be low in countries with abundant capital while salaries & wages will be low in countries with abundant labour. Hence a product which requires more capital than labour will be cheaper in capital abundant country. Taking the example of USA and India, it can be said that India, which is abundant in manpower but lacks capital resources will be able to produce good-efficiently, which uses relatively more labour. USA, which has abundant capital relative to manpower will be able to produce good efficiently, which uses relatively more capital.

(i) Assumptions of Heckscher-Ohlin theory

1. There is perfect competition in commodity as well as factor market.
2. The technology for producing a good is different for different countries but it will be same for a product produced in different countries.
3. Factors of production are mobile within the country but are unable to move from one country to another.

(ii) Limitations of Heckscher-Ohlin Theory

1. Labour in India is not of the same quality as in USA, Japan or Europe. Labour is trained in developed countries with at least fifteen years' duration, while most of the labour in underdeveloped country is illiterate and untrained. Hence labour is not homogeneous.
2. As the capital intensity increases, the quality of labour required to operate it should also be high. Hence it is not possible for a product to be produced by same production technique in two different countries with different level of development.
3. Cost of production is not just a function of cost of factors of production but also of the rate of improvement in technology in different countries. USA is spending lot more on Research & Development than India. Therefore, cost of production decreases at greater rate in USA than India.
4. Factor endowment of a country may change over time.

Overlapping Product Ranges (Linder – 1960s)

1. primarily concerned with DEMAND
2. trade in natural resources is, indeed, dictated by factor endowments and relative costs of production
3. But trade in manufactured goods is more dependent on similarities in product demand across countries
   a. as per-capita income rises the complexity and quality level of products, and range of product sophistication also rises
   b. entrepreneurs directing the firms that produce these goods are more knowledgeable about their domestic market than about foreign markets, so they cannot effectively serve markets that are significantly different from what they know
   c. thus international trade is influenced by similarities of demand and similar per-capita income
   d. Example – US and Canada would do more trade than US and Mexico because of greater similarities
4. Linder's theory is the basis for "market segmentation" a now widely accepted theory used by all international businesses

Product Cycle Theory (Raymond Vernon – 1966)

Raymond Vernon developed the international product life cycle theory in the 1960s. The international product life cycle theory stresses that a company will begin to export its product and later take on foreign direct investment as the product moves through its life cycle. Eventually a country's export becomes its import. Although the model is developed around the U.S, it can be generalised and applied to any of the developed and innovative markets of the world.

The product life cycle theory was developed during the 1960s and focused on the U.S since most innovations came from that market. This was an applicable theory at that time since the U.S dominated the world trade. Today, the U.S is no longer the only innovator of products in the world. Today companies design new products and modify them much quicker than before. Companies are forced to introduce the products in many different markets at the same time to gain cost benefits before its sales declines. The theory does not explain trade patterns of today.

Internal and External Economies-of-Scale (Paul Krugman - 1980's)

1. Primarily concerned with MONOPOLIES
2. Internal Economies-of-Scale
   a. when the cost-per-unit depends on the size of the firm, the larger the firm the greater the scale of benefits.
   b. a firm possessing internal economies-of-scale can theoretically monopolize an industry if it produces more, lowering costs, it can then lower the market price by setting the market price.
   c. if, by comparative advantage, nations foster such giants, they will take up a lot of the workforce, allowing other countries to specialize in the remaining industries.
   d. this helps explain trading between countries in a single good, inconsistent with previous theories if a monopoly is gaining share by specializing and standardizing then other companies in the same industry can find a niche due to product differentiation.
3. External Economies-of-Scale
   a. if cost-per-unit depends on the size of the industry as opposed to the size of the company, then a country can dominate in a product without having a monopoly.

b. Countries can build up a "critical-mass" of small competitive firms (German fine crystal as opposed to Boeing).
c. industry dominance internationally without necessarily aggravating market imperfections.

Competitive Advantage of Nations (Michael Porter)

1. Primarily concerned with NATIONS.
2. National Competitive Advantage Diamond: four main attributes of a country that determine its competitive advantage:
   a. **Factor Endowments.** A nation's wealth in terms of factors of production like skilled labor or infrastructure. Porter identifies that it is the more advanced factors (communications infrastructure, sophisticated and skilled labor, research facilities and expertise), more than basics like demographics and natural resources that best determine the competitive advantage of the nation. He also claimed that it is in these advanced resources that individuals, companies and governments can invest.
   b. **Demand Conditions.** The nature of demand for a product in the home market. If the domestic consumers are sophisticated and demanding, it pushes a company to continuing improvements in efficiency, leading to competitive advantage.
   c. **Related and Supporting Industries.** Do supplier or related industries exist and are they internationally competitive. For example, US strength in computers is partially a result of earlier US strength in semiconductors. Since this is true, many strong industries in countries are clustered.
   d. **Firm Strategy, Structure, and Rivalry.** The social norms of a country, government controls on the industry and domestic rivalry within the industry. In a country that places greater emphasis on engineering strength, you will see strong engineering firms. Porter argues that in America, the emphasis on finance, and having financial people in top management has lead to an overemphasis on short term financial returns rather than long-term investment. Heavy domestic rivalry creates incentives to innovate and upgrade.

BALANCE OF PAYMENTS

The balance of payments is rarely a way of listing receipts and payments in international transactions for a country. Balance of payment is an application of double-entry book keeping and if entry is done in a proper way, debits and credits will always balance; hence in a way, the balance of payment will always be in equilibrium. It is important to understand in what way the balance of payments can be in disequilibrium and in what sense it will always be in equilibrium.

Account of a Country's Balance of Payments

I.	**Credits**	
1.	Exports of goods	1100
2.	Exports of services	300
3.	Unrequired receipts (Gifts, indemnities, *etc.*) from foreigners	200
4.	Capital receipts (borrowing from capital, repayment by or sale of assets to, foreigners)	400
	Total Receipts	**2000**

II. Debits

5.	Imports of goods	1600
6.	Imports of services	100
7.	Unrequired payments (gifts, indemnities, *etc.* to foreigners)	160
8.	Capital payments (lending to, capital repayments to or purchase of assets from foreigners)	140
	Total Payments	**2000**

Credit entries show all the ways in which a country can acquire foreign currency. Debit entries show all the ways in which a country can spend the foreign exchange.

Items (1), (2), (3), (5), (6), and (7) enumerate all the payments and receipts made for the current period of time; they all have a flow dimension and refer to a certain value of exports per time period. The balance of payments of a country always refer to a certain time period, usually a calendar year.

Items (4) and (8) express changes in stock and refer to capital receipts and payments. Government, corporation and individuals borrow money from abroad, which leads to inflow of foreign currencies, and these transactions will be entered as items in (4). Similarly, Government, corporation and individuals lend money abroad, leading to outflow of foreign currencies and these transactions will be entered as items in (8).

Total of Credit side of Balance of payment should always equal debit side.

Various Balances

(i) **Balance of Trade.** It is difference between item (1) and (5) of above Table 1. In case exports of goods is Rs. 1100 crore and imports of goods is Rs 1600 crore, balance of trade will be 1100–600= –500. Balance of trade is the difference in the revenue through exports and foreign currency spent on imports. Balance of trade need not always balance. If the country exports more goods than it imports, it is said to have a favourable balance or surplus in its balance of trade. If it imports more goods than it exports, it has a deficit or unfavourable balance of trade. Even though the country had a deficit in its balance of trade, this might be offset by items on other accounts.

(ii) **Balance of services.** It is the difference between export of services and import of services. From above Table, balance of services is calculated from differences between item (2) and item (6). In case export of services is Rs. 300 crore and import of services is Rs. 100 crore, balance of trade will be Rs. 300 crore –Rs. 100 crore = Rs. 200 crore.

(iii) **Balance of unrequited transfers.** It is the difference between unrequired receipts and unrequited payments. From Table 1, balance of unrequited transfer is calculated from differences between item (3) and item (7). In case of unrequited receipts of Rs. 200 crore and unrequited payment of Rs. 160 crore, balance of unrequited transfers will be: Rs. 200 crore minus Rs. 160 crore is equal to Rs. 40 crore.

(iv) **Balance on current account.** It shows the flow aspect of a country's international transactions. Balance on current account can be calculated by adding up the balance of trade, services and unrequited transfers. All the goods and services produced within the country and exported during the time period in question, are entered on the credit side of the balance of current account, and all the goods and services imported and consumed within the country during the same period are entered on the debit side of the balance of current account. All the international transactions entering a country's system of national accounting should be listed on the country's balance of current account.

Balance on current A/C = -500 + 200 + 40 = -360

(v) **Balance on capital account.** All items of a flow nature should be included in the balance of current account and that all items expressing changes in stock should enter the balance of capital account. If a country has a deficit on the balance of current account, the country has spent more abroad during the period than it has earned. A way to settle this is by a transaction on the capital account. The country can deplete part of its stock to an amount equal to the deficit on the balance of current account. This can be done by borrowing from abroad, selling assets or by depleting its reserves of foreign currency. Balance on current account can be calculated by deriving the difference between item (4) and item (6). If capital receipts is Rs 400 crore and capital payment is Rs 140 ,then balance on capital account is: Rs 400 crore minus Rs 140 crore is equal to Rs 260 crore. Balance of capital account should be equal to balance on current account, but of opposite sign. Adding up of balances of capital account and current account leads to balance of payments which should always be zero.

(vi) **Various balances calculated from Table.**

1.	Balance of Trade items (1) minus (5)	1100 – 1600 = –500
2.	Balance of services items (2) minus (6)	300 – 100 = +200
3.	Balance of unrequited transfers items (3) minus (7)	200 – 160 = + 40
4.	Balance of current account items (1) + (2) + (3) – [(5)+(6)+(7)]	= 1600 – 1860 = –260
5.	Balance of capital account item (4) minus (8)	= +260
6.	Balance of payments + 260+(–260) balance of current account plus balance of capital account	= 0

Disequilibrium in the Balance of Payment

Balance of payment will always be in equilibrium because two sides of the balance of payment are based on double entry system of accountancy. In this book keeping sense, the balance of payment will always balance.

In economic sense, balance of payment will be in disequilibrium when country borrows from abroad or depletes its foreign currency reserves unwillingly. If on the other hand, the country's reserves of foreign currency were plentiful and the depletion of these reserves were a consequence of a deliberate policy, then this is not the case of a deficit in its balance of payment. In order to analyse the nature of problem in the external sector, it is necessary to study the nature of its international capital flows and the nation's economic policy.

(i) **Autonomous capital flows.** These are capital flow which has no connection with the country's balance of payment situation. Autonomous capital flow takes place regardless of other items in the balance of payment. Such types of capital flow are planned capital movements and depend on the rate of return available in the country where capital is being invested. Autonomous capital flow is influenced by rate of interest in the economy, taxation policy and political climate of the country. The different decision units – the individual, firms, Government may engage in capital transaction with the rest of the world for different reasons. These autonomous capital flows have consequences on the balance of payment situation of the country but capital flow is not affected by balance of payment problem.

(ii) **Accommodating capital flows.** These are capital flows that take place specifically to equalize the balance of payment in the book keeping. They are unplanned and unforeseen capital flows. Accommodating capital flows are ex-post in nature. Only at the end of the period can one discover whether accommodating capital inflow or outflow is needed. Mostly Government is involved in case of accommodating capital flows.

(iii) **Economic Policy.** In order to balance the balance of payment, country can either concentrate on current account or capital account. To reduce deficit on current account, Government may devalue its currency which will increase price of imports and decrease price of exports. Government can increase capital flow by increasing the rate of interest. Government can also take direct action. It may resort to protection by raising tariff or by quantitative restriction and canalisation.

FOREIGN DIRECT INVESTMENT

Advantages and Disadvantages of Foreign Direct Investment

Foreign direct investment (FDI) is made into a business or a sector by an individual or a company from another country. It is different from portfolio investment, which is made more indirectly into another country's economy by using financial instruments, such as bonds and stocks.

There are various levels and forms of foreign direct investment, depending on the type of companies involved and the reasons for investment. A foreign direct investor might purchase a company in the target country by means of a merger or acquisition, setting up a new venture or expanding the operations of an existing one. Other forms of FDI include the acquisition of shares in an associated enterprise, the incorporation of a wholly owned company or subsidiary and participation in an equity joint venture across international boundaries.

If you are planning to engage in this kind of venture, you should determine first if it provides you and the society with maximum benefits. One good way to do this is evaluating its advantages and disadvantages.

Advantages of Foreign Direct Investment

1. Economic Development Stimulation

Foreign direct investment can stimulate the target country's economic development, creating a more conducive environment for you as the investor and benefits for the local industry.

2. Easy International Trade

Commonly, a country has its own import tariff, and this is one of the reasons why trading with it is quite difficult. Also, there are industries that usually require their presence in the international markets to ensure their sales and goals will be completely met. With FDI, all these will be made easier.

3. Employment and Economic Boost

Foreign direct investment creates new jobs, as investors build new companies in the target country, create new opportunities. This leads to an increase in income and more buying power to the people, which in turn leads to an economic boost.

4. Development of Human Capital Resources

One big advantage brought about by FDI is the development of human capital resources, which is also often understated as it is not immediately apparent. Human capital is the competence and knowledge of those able to perform labor, more known to us as the workforce. The attributes gained by training and sharing experience would increase the education and overall human capital of a country. Its resource is not a tangible asset that is owned by companies, but instead something that is on loan. With this in mind, a country with FDI can benefit greatly by developing its human resources while maintaining ownership.

5. Tax Incentives

Parent enterprises would also provide foreign direct investment to get additional expertise, technology and products. As the foreign investor, you can receive tax incentives that will be highly useful in your selected field of business.

6. Resource Transfer

Foreign direct investment will allow resource transfer and other exchanges of knowledge, where various countries are given access to new technologies and skills.

7. Reduced Disparity Between Revenues and Costs

Foreign direct investment can reduce the disparity between revenues and costs. With such, countries will be able to make sure that production costs will be the same and can be sold easily.

8. Increased Productivity

The facilities and equipment provided by foreign investors can increase a workforce's productivity in the target country.

9. Increment in Income

Another big advantage of foreign direct investment is the increase of the target country's income. With more jobs and higher wages, the national income normally increases. As a result, economic growth is spurred. Take note that larger corporations would usually offer higher salary levels than what you would normally find in the target country, which can lead to increment in income.

Disadvantages of Foreign Direct Investment

1. Hindrance to Domestic Investment

As it focuses its resources elsewhere other than the investor's home country, foreign direct investment can sometimes hinder domestic investment.

2. Risk from Political Changes

Because political issues in other countries can instantly change, foreign direct investment is very risky. Plus, most of the risk factors that you are going to experience are extremely high.

3. Negative Influence on Exchange Rates

Foreign direct investments can occasionally affect exchange rates to the advantage of one country and the detriment of another.

4. Higher Costs

If you invest in some foreign countries, you might notice that it is more expensive than when you export goods. So, it is very imperative to prepare sufficient money to set up your operations.

5. Economic Non-Viability

Considering that foreign direct investments may be capital-intensive from the point of view of the investor, it can sometimes be very risky or economically non-viable.

6. Expropriation

Remember that political changes can also lead to expropriation, which is a scenario where the government will have control over your property and assets.

7. Negative Impact on the Country's Investment

The rules that govern foreign exchange rates and direct investments might negatively have an impact on the investing country. Investment may be banned in some foreign markets, which means that it is impossible to pursue an inviting opportunity.

8. Modern-Day Economic Colonialism

Many third-world countries, or at least those with history of colonialism, worry that foreign direct investment would result in some kind of modern day economic colonialism, which exposes host countries and leave them vulnerable to foreign companies' exploitations.

MULTILATERAL REGULATION OF TRADE AND INVESTMENT UNDER WTO

World Trade Organization (WTO)

GATT was an international body having its headquarters at Geneva and was founded in 1947 by 23 member countries including India. The body now comprises of 164 member countries of which around two-thirds are developing nations.

According to the approved GATT accord, a Preparatory Committee would be set up, which in turn would set up the World Trade Organization (WTO), to become operational in early 1995. The WTO will act as a permanent watchdog on the International Trade and will enjoy the status similar to that of UNIDO wherein each member nation will have single voting right.

GATT was converted from a provisional agreement into a formal international organisation called World Trade Organization (WTO) with effect from January 1, 1995. WTO will serve as a single institutional framework encompassing GATT and all the result of the Uruguay Round.

It will be directed by a Ministerial Conference that will meet at least once every two years and its regular business will be overseen by a General Council. The WTO is a more powerful body with enlarged functions than the GATT and is envisaged to play a major role in the world economic affairs.

Role of WTO in International Trade

(i) WTO's aim is to liberalise international trade.

(ii) WTO establishes rules regarding international trade and sees that these rules are obeyed.

(iii) 153 countries of the world are currently members of the WTO.

(iv) It is seen that the developed countries have unfairly retained trade barriers. On the other hand, WTO rules have forced developing countries to remove trade barriers.

Functions of WTO

The former GATT was not really an organisation; it was merely a legal arrangement. On the other hand, the WTO is a new international organisation set up as a permanent body. It is designed to play the role of a watchdog in the spheres of trade in goods, trade in services, foreign investment, intellectual property rights, etc. Article III has set out the following five functions of WTO;

(i) The WTO shall facilitate the implementation, administration and operation and further the objectives of this Agreement and of the Multilateral Trade Agreements, and shall also provide the frame work for the implementation, administration and operation of the Plurilateral Trade Agreements.

(ii) The WTO shall provide the forum for negotiations among its members concerning their multilateral trade relations in matters dealt with under the Agreement in the Annexes to this Agreement.

(iii) The WTO shall administer the Understanding on Rules and Procedures Governing the Settlement of Disputes.

(iv) The WTO shall administer Trade Policy Review Mechanism.

(v) With a view to achieving greater coherence in global economic policy making, the WTO shall cooperate, as appropriate, with the international Monetary Fund (IMF) and with the International Bank for Reconstruction and Development (IBRD) and its affiliated agencies.

Objectives of WTO

Important objectives of WTO are mentioned below:

(i) to implement the new world trade system as visualised in the Agreement;

(ii) to promote World Trade in a manner that benefits every country;

(iii) to ensure that developing countries secure a better balance in the sharing of the advantages resulting from the expansion of international trade corresponding to their developmental needs;

(iv) to demolish all hurdles to an open world trading system and usher in international economic renaissance because the world trade is an effective instrument to foster economic growth;

(v) to enhance competitiveness among all trading partners so as to benefit consumers and help in global integration;

(vi) to increase the level of production and productivity with a view to ensuring level of employment in the world;

(vii) to expand and utilize world resources to the best;

(viii) to improve the level of living for the global population and speed up economic development of the member nations.

India and WTO

India is one of the founding members of the World Trade Organisation (WTO) and participation in the WTO rule based system implies greater stability, transparency and predictability in the governance of international trade.

The importance of WTO in promoting multilateral trade is being increasingly acknowledged. The WTO rules envisage non-discrimination in the form of national treatment and most favoured nation (MFN) treatment to our exports in the markets of other WTO members.

National treatment ensures that our exports to other member countries would not be discriminated vis-a-vis their domestic products. MFN treatment likewise ensures non-discrimination among various members in their tariff regimes and also other rules and regulations.

Emerging from continued discussions in various multilateral for a , developmental issues along with trade related issues are being increasingly focused at the international level. Poverty concerns of developing countries along with development and trade policies are also being given cognisance.

Need has been felt for integration of trade policies with development strategies, increasing support to areas of finance and debt relief, recognising the importance of technology for development, improvement in market access for developing countries in sectors like textiles, clothing and agriculture, and providing better access to the dispute settlement mechanisms for these countries.

The issue of abuse of the anti-dumping procedure, the problems of rules of origin criteria, technical barriers to trade, regional trading blocs, etc., are also being considered at various levels in the WTO.

The Government of India has taken several steps to implement the policy commitments made under some of the agreements, particularly under the Agreement on Tariffs and Quantitative Restrictions Agreement on Agriculture (AoA), Trade Related Intellectual Property Rights (TRIPs), Trade Related Investment Measures (TRIMs), General Agreement on Trade in Services (GATS), apart from others. A strategy for tariff negotiations is, however, required.

The additional 'non-trade' issues relating to transparency in government procurement practices trade and competition policy, trade and environment, and trade and labour standards proposed in the Singapore and the Geneva Ministerial need to be addressed for negotiations.

The commitments regarding the technical barriers to trade, social agenda covering labour standards and environmental and phyto-sanitary issues also require establishment of certain national standards and technical regulations in a standardised and transparent system.

At the same time, there are some issues on which India has expressed certain reservations. These are:

During the implementation of WTO agreements in the last six years, India has experienced certain imbalances and inequities in the WTO agreements. It is found that some developed countries have not fulfilled their obligations in letter and spirit of the WTO agreements, and many of the Special and Differential Treatment clauses, in favour of developing countries, added in various WTO agreements have remained in operational.

Taking advantage of the exception clauses provided in the WTO, most industrialised countries are still enforcing various regulations on foreign producers and suppliers.

Extending the scope of the investment regime in WTO beyond Trade Related Investment Measures and General Agreements on Trade in Services, is not appropriate.

A multilateral framework cannot guarantee an increase in FDI inflows although it threatens to adversely affect the quality of the inflows.

There are also other asymmetries present, as the WTO does not address the responsibilities of corporations which often impose trade restrictive clauses on their subsidiaries.

WTO has not been able to ensure abolition of non-trade barriers being imposed on labour and environmental considerations, including the linkage in certain Generalised System of Preferences (GSP) schemes to these issues.

The present negotiations strategy is based on the decisions taken at the Doha Ministerial in November 2001. The Doha Declaration focused mainly on TRIPs agreement, public health, trade and environment and the implementation related issues and concerns. Elaborate timetables on work programme for current negotiations in agriculture and services and other issues have been worked out.

The Doha Conference presented mixed results for India. India's main concern was to speed up implementation of various agreements and to undo the imbalances and inequities present in some WTO agreements. From India's point of view, faster removal of the textile quotas maintained by developed countries like the USA was the most important implementation issue, which was, however, met with limited success. As far as environmental issues are concerned, the Doha declaration has mandated negotiations to clarify WTO rules in the light of multilateral environmental agreements. These negotiations could lead to developed countries raising barriers against goods from developing countries on the pretext of environmental protection.

India had also reservations on starting negotiations on four new 'non-trade' areas, namely, multilateral investment, global rules on competition, transparency in government procurement and trade facilitation, i.e., framing of uniform custom's procedures for clearance of goods. India could secure only a two-year respite and the study process would continue for two more years, i.e. up to the Fifth Ministerial Conference, when a decision about negotiations will be taken on the basis of an explicit consensus.

Apart from mandated negotiations in agriculture and services where the process has already started, negotiations on market access for non- agricultural products is quite important for India, as reduction or elimination of tariffs, tariff peaks and tariff escalation as well as removal of non-tariff barriers will be quite helpful in exports. India would, of course, have to make offers even though the negotiations will be carried out under less than full reciprocity as far as developing countries are concerned.

The other area where action is required is in regard to extension of protection of geographical indications to products other than wines and spirits under Article 23 of TRIPs and the relationship between TRIPs and the Convention on Biological Diversity (CBD), and Traditional Knowledge (TK) under Article 71.1. The process of legislation in regard to geographical indications needs to be completed. In the area of TRIPs and access to medicine, where additional flexibility is provided in separate ministerial declarations in terms of compulsory licensing and parallel imports, India can benefit in terms of lower prices of crucial life saving drugs and even promoting exports of pharmaceutical products.

India and other developing countries should now ensure an average balance of reciprocity in these negotiations. There is need for a continued effort to handle some of the complex issues, as per international requirements as well as our domestic resources and other constraints, during the Tenth Five Year Plan.

INTERNATIONAL TRADE PROCEDURES AND DOCUMENTATION; EXIM POLICIES

International Economic Institution

At the Bretton Woods Conference in 1944 it was decided to establish a new monetary order that would expand international trade, promote international capital flows and contribute to monetary stability. The IMF and the World Bank were borne out of this Conference of the end of World War II. The World Bank was established to help the restoration of economies disrupted by War by facilitating the investment of capital for productive purposes and to promote the long-range balanced growth of international trade. On the other hand, the IMF is primarily a supervisory institution for coordinating the efforts of member countries to achieve greater cooperation in the formulation of economic policies. It helps to promote exchange stability and orderly exchange relations among its member countries. It is in this context that the present chapter reviews the purpose and working of some of the international financial institutions and the contributions made by them in promoting economic and social progress in developing countries by helping raise standards of living and productivity to the point of which development becomes self-sustaining.

International Sources of Finance

One major source of financing is international non-profit agencies. There are several regional development banks such as the Asian Development Bank, the African Development Bank and Fund and the Caribbean Development Bank. The primary purpose of these agencies is to finance productive development projects or to promote economic development in a particular region. The Inter-American Development Bank, for example, has the principal purpose of accelerating the economic development of its Latin American member countries. In general, both public and private entities are eligible to borrow money from such agencies as long as private funds are not available at reasonable rates and terms. Although the interest rate can vary from agency to agency, these loan rates are very attractive and very much in demand.

Of all the international financial organisations, the most familiar is the World Bank, formally known as the International Bank for Reconstruction and Development (IBRD). The World Bank has two affiliates that are legally and financially distinct entities, the International Development Association (IDA) and the International Finance Corporation (IFC). All three organisations have the same central goals: to promote economic and social progress in poor or developing countries by helping raise standards of living and productivity to the point at which development becomes self-sustaining.

Toward this common objective, the World Bank, IDA and IFC have three interrelated functions and these are to lend funds, to provide advice and to serve as a catalyst in order to stimulate investments by others. In the process, financial resources are channelled from developed countries to the developing world with the hope that developing countries, through this assistance, will progress to a level that will permit them, in turn, to contribute to the development process of other less fortunate countries. Japan is a prime example of a country that has come full circle. From being a borrower, Japan is now a major lender to these three organisations. South Korea is moving in a direction similar to that of Japan nearly a quarter of a century ago.

EXIM POLICIES

Exim Policy, also known as the Foreign Trade Policy is announced every 5 years by Ministry of Commerce and Industry, Government of India. It is updated every year on the 31st of March and all the amendments and improvements in the scheme are effective from the 1st of April. Exim policy deals in general provisions pertaining to exports and imports, promotional measures, duty exemption schemes, export promotion schemes, special economic zone programs and other details for different sectors. The Government announces a supplement to this policy each year. The Government of India also releases the Hand Book of Procedures detailing the procedures to be followed for each of the schemes mentioned in the Exim Policy.

The new EXIM policy has been formulated focusing increase in export scenario, boosting production and supporting the concepts like Make in India and Digital India.

Salient Features

- Two new schemes namely "Merchandise Exports from India Scheme (MEIS)" and "Service Exports from India Scheme has been introduced replacing multiple schemes existing earlier.
- MEIS to promote export of notified goods to notified markets and SEIS for benefit of all exporters in India.
- Reduce export obligations by 25% and give boost to domestic manufacturing supporting the "Make in India" concept.
- Both MEIS and SEIS firm will get subsidized office spaces in SEZs, along with other benefits.
- As a step to Digital India concept, online procedure to upload digitally signed document by CA/CS/Cost Accountant are developed and further mobile app for filing tax, stamp duty has been developed.

- Benefits of MEIS would be eligible for e-commerce of handicrafts, handlooms, books etc. Exports up to 25000 per consignment will get SEIS benefit.
- Duty Credit scrips to be freely transferable and usable for payments of custom duty, excise duty and service tax.
- Recognition of status holder has been changed from Rupees to US Dollars earning. The position status holder will recognize and reward those entrepreneurs who helped in India to become a major export player.
- Manufacturers who are also status holders will be enable to self-certify their manufactured goods as originating from India.
- Repeatedly submission of physical copies of documents available on Exporter Importer Profile is not required.
- Agricultural and village industry products to be supported across the globe at rates of 3% and 5% under MEIS.
- Export obligation period for export items related to defense, military store, aerospace and nuclear energy to be 24 months. Certificate of independent Chartered Engineer for redemption of EPGG authorization is no longer required.

ROLE OF INTERNATIONAL FINANCIAL INSTITUTIONS

INTERNATIONAL MONETARY FUND (IMF)

The International Monetary Fund (IMF) came into official existence on December 27, 1945, when 29 countries signed its Articles of Agreement (its Charter) agreed at a conference held in Bretton Woods, New Hampshire, USA, from July 1-22, 1944. The IMF commenced financial operations on March 1, 1947. Its current membership is 189 countries. Its Total Quotas are SDR 476 billion (about US$ 755.7 billion at the exchange rate), following a 45 per cent quota increase effective from January 22, 1999.

- **Staff.** Approximately 2,700 from 110 countries.
- **Accounting Unit.** Special Drawing Right (SDR). As of August 23, 1999, SDR I equalled US $1.370280.

IMF is a cooperative institution that 182 countries have voluntarily joined because they see the advantage of consulting with one another on this forum to maintain a stable system of buying and selling their currencies so that payments in foreign currency can take place between countries smoothly and without delay. Its policies and activities are guided by its Charter known as the Articles of Agreement.

IMF lends money to members having trouble meeting financial obligations to other members, but only on the condition that they undertake economic reforms to eliminate these difficulties for their own good and that of the entire membership. Contrary to widespread perception, the IMF has no effective authority over the domestic economic policies of its members. What authority the IMF does possess is confined to requiring the member to disclose information on its monetary and fiscal policies and to avoid, as far as possible, putting restrictions on exchange of domestic for foreign currency and on making payments to other members.

There are several major accomplishments to the credit of the International Monetary System. For example, it

- sustained a rapidly increasing volume of trade and investment;
- displayed flexibility in adapting to changes in international commerce;
- proved to be efficient (even when there were decreasing percentages of reserves to trade);

- proved to be hardy (it survived a number of pre-1971 crises, speculative and otherwise, and the down-and-up swings of several business cycles);
- allowed for a growing degree or international cooperation;
- established a capacity to accommodate reforms and improvements.

To an extent, the fund served as an international central bank to help countries during periods of temporary balance of payments difficulties by protecting their rates of exchange. Because of that, countries did not need to resort to exchange controls and other barriers to restrict world trade.

Origins of IMF

The need for an organisation like the IMF became evident during the great depression that ravaged the world economy in the 1930s. A widespread lack of confidence in paper money led to a spurt in the demand for gold and severe devaluation in the national currencies. The relation between money and the value of goods became confused as did the relation between the value of one national currency and another.

In the 1940s, Harry Dexter (US) and John Maynard Keynes (UK) put forward proposals for a system that would encourage the unrestricted conversion of one currency into another, establish a clear and unequivocal value for each currency and eliminate restrictions and practices such as competitive devaluations. The system required cooperation on a previously unattempted scale by all nations in establishing an innovative monetary system and an international institution to monitor it. After much negotiations in the difficult war time conditions, the international community accepted the system and an organisation was formed to supervise it.

The IMF began operations in Washington DC in May 1946. It then had 39 members. The IMF's membership now is 189.

Members and Administration

On joining the IMF, each member country contributes a certain sum of money called a 'quota subscription', as a sort of credit union deposit. Quotas serve various purposes.

- They form a pool of money that the IMF can draw from to lend to members in times of financial difficulty.
- They form the basis of determining the Special Drawing Rights (SDR).
- They determine the voting power of the member.

Statutory Purposes

The purposes of the International Monetary Fund are:

- To promote international monetary cooperation through a permanent institution that provides the machinery for consultation and collaboration on international monetary problems.
- To facilitate the expansion and balanced growth of international trade and to contribute, thereby, to the promotion and maintenance of high levels of employment and real income and to the development of the productive resources of all members as primary objectives of economic policy.
- To promote exchange stability, to maintain orderly exchange arrangements among members and to avoid competitive exchange depreciation.
- To assist in the establishment of a multilateral system of payments in respect of current transactions between members and in the elimination of foreign exchange restrictions which hamper the growth of world trade.

- To give confidence to members by making the general resources of the Fund temporarily available to them under adequate safeguards, thus providing them with opportunity to correct maladjustment in their balance of payments without resorting to measures destructive to national or international prosperity.
- In accordance with the above, to shorten the duration and lessen the degree of disequilibrium in the international balances of payments of members.

Financial Assistance

The IMF lends money only to member countries with balance of payments problems. A member country with a payments problem can immediately withdraw from the IMF the 25 per cent of its quota. A member in greater difficulty may request for more money from the IMP and can borrow up to three times its quota provided the member country undertakes to initiate a series of reforms and uses the borrowed money effectively. The frequently used mechanisms by the IMF to lend money are

1. Standby Arrangements
2. Extended Arrangements
3. Structural Adjustment Mechanism (With low interest rates)

Regular IMF Facilities

- Standby Arrangements (SBA) are designed to provide short-term balance of payments assistance for deficits of a temporary or cyclical nature, such arrangements are typically for 12 to 18 months. Drawings are phased on a quarterly basis, with their release made conditional on meeting performance criteria and the completion of periodic programme reviews. Repurchases are made 31/4 to 5 years after each purchase.
- Extended Fund Facility (EFF) is designed to support medium-term programmes that generally run for three years. The EFF aims at overcoming balance of payments difficulties stemming from macroeconomic and structural problems. Performance criteria are applied, similar to those in standby arrangements and repurchases are made in 4½ to 10 years.

Concessional IMF Facility

- Enhanced Structural Adjustment Facility (ESAF) was established in 1987 and enlarged and extended in 1994. Designed for low-income member countries with protracted balance of payments problems, ESAF drawings are loans and not purchases of other members' currencies. They are made in support of three year programmes and carry an annual interest rate of 0.5 per cent, with a 5th year grace period and a 10 year maturity. Quarterly benchmarks and semiannual performance criteria apply; 80 low income countries are currently eligible to use the ESAF.

SDRs

As time passed, it became evident that the Fund's resources for providing short-term accommodation to countries in monetary difficulties were not sufficient. To resolve the situation, the Fund, after much debate and long deliberations, created new drawing rights in 1969. Special Drawing Rights (SDRs), sometimes called paper gold, are special account entries on the IMF books designed to provide additional liquidity to support growing world commerce. Although SDRs are a form of money not convertible to gold, their gold value is guaranteed, which helps to ensure their acceptability. Initially, SDRs worth $9.5 billion were created.

Participant nations may use SDRs as a source of currency in a spot transaction, as a loan for clearing a financial obligation, as a security for a loan, as a Swap against currency, or in a forward exchange operation. A nation with a balance of payments need may use its SDRs to obtain usable currency from another nation designated by the fund. A participant also may use SDRs to make payments to the Fund, such as repurchases. The Fund itself may transfer SDRs to a participant for various purposes including the transfer of SDRs instead of currency to a member using the Fund's resources.

By providing a mechanism for international monetary cooperation, working towards reducing restrictions to trade and capital flows and helping members with their short-term balance of payments difficulties, the IMF makes a significant and unique contribution to human welfare and improved living standards throughout the world.

Services

Besides supervising the international monetary system and providing financial support to member countries, the IMF assists its members by:

- Providing technical assistance in certain areas of its competence.
- Running an educational institute in Washington and offering training courses abroad.
- Issuing wide variety of publications containing valuable information and statistics that are useful not only to the member countries but also to banks, research institutes, university and the media.

THE WORLD BANK

The World Bank group is a multinational financial institution established at the end of World War II (1944) to help provide long-term capital for the reconstruction and development of member countries. The group is important to multinational corporations because it provides much of the planning and financing for economic development projects involving billions of dollars for which private businesses can act as contractors and suppliers of goods and engineering related services.

The purpose for the setting up of the Bank are :

- To assist in the reconstruction and development of territories of members by facilitating the investment of capital for productive purposes, including the restoration of economies destroyed or disrupted by war, the reconversion of productive facilities to peacetime needs and encouragement of the development or productive facilities and resources in less developed countries.
- To promote private foreign investment by means of guarantees or participation in loans and other investments made by private investors; and when private capital is not available on reasonable terms, to supplement private investment by providing, on suitable conditions, finance for productive purposes out of its own capital, funds raised by it and its other resources.
- To promote the long-range balanced growth of international trade and the maintenance of equilibrium in balance of payments by encouraging international investment for the development of the productive resources of members, thereby assisting in raising productivity, the standard of living and condition of labour in their territories.
- To arrange the loans made or guaranteed by it in relation to international loans through other channels so that the more useful and urgent projects, large and small alike, can be dealt with first.
- To conduct its operations with due regard to the effect of international investment on business conditions in the territories of members and, in the immediate post-war years, to assist in bringing about a smooth transition from a wartime to a peacetime economy.

The World Bank is the International Bank for Reconstruction and Development (IBRD) and the International Development Association (IDA). The IBRD has two affiliates, the International Finance Corporation (IFC) and the Multilateral Investment Guarantee Agency (MIGA). The Bank, the IFC and the MIGA are sometimes referred to as the "World Bank Group".

INFORMATION TECHNOLOGY

USE OF COMPUTERS IN MANAGEMENT APPLICATIONS

Computers do more than help businesses create professional looking slides and print sales reports. Because computers can often automate time-consuming tasks that humans perform, software developers create programs that solve a variety of problems. Whether you're a sole proprietor selling jewelry or a global conglomerate such as Sony, you'll benefit by learning to use computers to help you manage your business.

Data Management

Data management activities form the foundation for many activities that businesses perform. Computers make it possible for companies to organize and manipulate massive amounts of information productively. Larger corporations may use multiple SQL Server databases to oversee data operations while smaller businesses might take advantage of the data manipulation features in applications such as Microsoft Access. Regardless of your business's size, you probably work with information and need to store it. Business websites also use database software to sell products and even give people the ability to join their sites. If you a have a website, you can set up data management software yourself or hire a company to manage it for you.

Office and Supply Management

Companies make money by buying and selling products at a profit, and computers help them manage inventory and supplies efficiently. Wal-Mart, for example, uses a sophisticated NeoVista inventory management software system that enables the company to keep products available in stores when people need them. Computers are also useful for helping smaller businesses track and manage basic supplies, such as printer paper, pencils and even cups for the water cooler.

People Management

Communicating with a coworker who is sitting in the next cubicle is rarely a problem, but coordinating and managing meetings where people reside in different states can be a challenge. Computer software enables businesses to conduct virtual meetings where people meet over the Internet and makes it possible for everyone in the business to view a common calendar. Some companies strive to increase productivity by monitoring the computers that people use. Monitoring enables companies to track billable hours and identify activities that may be unprofitable. If you do any kind of time tracking or meeting planning, scheduling and calendar software can help you.

Record Keeping and Accounting

When tax time arrives, you can be prepared by accessing financial records that you've kept during the year on a computer. Accounting software helps people manage money, create budgets, track sales and monitor resource usage. Products such as QuickBooks, Quicken and NetSuite provide accounting solutions for businesses of all sizes. Look for accounting programs that can access the Web if members in your organization need to access and share accounting information from multiple locations. You'll also find spreadsheet programs useful for doing everything from creating time sheets to managing payroll.

MANAGEMENT INFORMATION SYSTEM (MIS)

We know Transaction Processing Systems are operations oriented. In contrast Management Information System (MIS) assist managers in decision making and problem solving. They use results produced by the Transaction processing systems, but they may also use other information. In any Organization, decisions must be made on many issues that recur regularly and require a certain amount of information because the decision making process is well understood, the manager can identify the information that will be needed for the purpose. In turn, the information systems can be developed so that reports are prepared regularly to support these recurring decisions.

Thomas R. Prince defines MIS as a "Computer based network containing one or more operating systems, provides relevant data to management for decisions making purposes and also containing the necessary mechanism for implementing changes of responses made by management in the decision making.

Characteristics of an effective MIS:

1. Management Oriented
2. Management Directed
3. Integrated
4. Common data flows
5. Heavy Planning element
6. Sub System Concept
7. Common Database
8. Computerised

Prerequisites of an effective MIS. The main pre-requisites of an effective MIS are as follows:

(a) **Database.** It can be defined as a "Super file" which consolidates data records formerly stored in many data files. The data in database in organized in such a way that accesses to the data is improved and redundancy is reduced. Normally database is sub-divided into major information sub-sets needed to run a business. These sub-sets are:

(a) Customer and sale file. (b) Vendor File
(c) Personnel File (d) Inventory File
(e) Central Ledger Accounting File.

The main characteristics of database is that each sub-system utilises some data & information kept in the same file to satisfy its information needs.

The other important characteristics of data base are as follows:

(i) It is user-oriented.
(ii) It is capable of being used as a common data source, to various users, helps in avoiding duplication of efforts in storage and retrieval of data and information.
(iii) It is available to authorised persons only.
(iv) It is controlled by a separate authority established for the purpose, known as Data Base Management System (DBMS).

The maintenance of data in database requires computer hardware, software and experienced computer professionals. In addition it requires a good data collection system equipped with experts who have first-hand knowledge of the operations of the company and its information needs.

(b) Qualified system and management staff. The second pre-requisite of effective MIS is that it should be manned by qualified officers. These officers who are expert in the field should understand clearly the views of their fellow officers. For this, the organisational management base should comprise of two categories of officers viz. (1) Systems and Computer experts and (2) Management experts.

Systems and Computer experts in addition to their expertise in their subject area should also be capable of understanding management concepts to facilitate the understanding of problems faced by the concern. They should also be clear about the process of decision making and information requirements for planning and control functions.

This pre-requisite is confronted with a problem viz., procurement of suitable experts. The problem is dealt by recruiting fresh candidates and developing them to meet specific requirements. Also, its is difficult to retain such experts on long term basis as their scope in the job market is quite high.

(c) **Support of Top Management.** The management information system to be effective, should receive the full support of top management. The reasons for this and as follows:

1. Subordinate managers are usually lethargic about activities, which do not receive the support of their superiors (top management).
2. The resources involved in computer-based information systems are large and are growing larger in view of importance gained by management information system.

To gain the support of top management, the officers should place before top management all the supporting facts and state clearly the benefits, which will accrue from it to the concern. This step will certainly enlighten management, and will change their attitude towards MIS. Their wholehearted support and cooperation will help in making MIS an effective one.

(d) **Control and maintenance of MIS.** Control of the MIS means the operation of the system as it was designed to operate. Some time, users develop their own procedures or short cut methods to use the system, which reduce its effectiveness. To check such habits of users, the management at each level in the organization should devise checks for the information system control.

Maintenance is closely related to control. There are times when the need for improvements to the system will be discovered. Formal methods for changing and documenting changes must be provided.

(e) **Evaluation of MIS.** An effective MIS should be capable of meeting the information requirements of its executives in future as well. This capability can be maintained by evaluating the MIS and taking appropriate timely action. The evaluation of MIS should take into account the following points.

1. Examining whether enough flexibility exists in the system, to cope with any expected or unexpected information requirement in future.
2. Ascertaining the views of users and the designers about the capabilities and deficiencies of the system.
3. Guiding the appropriate authority about the steps to be taken to maintain effectiveness of MIS.

Evaluation of DSS. The concept of Decision Support Systems (DSS) evolved in the 1960's from studies of decision making in Organizations. These studies noted that managers required flexible systems to respond to less well defined questions than those addressed by operational employees. Advances in hardware technology, interactive computing design, graphic capabilities and programming languages contributed to this evolution. Decision support systems have achieved broad use in accounting and auditing today.

The main purpose of emphasized in DSS philosophy is the recognition of the central role played by decision maker a human manager. The salutary importance of this philosophy indirectly removed by the possible threat posed by some early passionate MIS professionals who proposed that large corporate wide databases would replace the managers. So the evolution of DSS disapproved such a myth thereby creating a clearer picture of the role of the machine Vs. man.

DECISION SUPPORT SYSTEMS (DSS)

Systems that support decisions are simply the Decision Support System (DSS). DSS represents both a philosophy and a set of tools. At the philosophical level, it is the next stage of evolution of EDP & MIS. While EDP concentrated on accurate and timely processing of data, MIS emphasized the value added components of data, namely information. DSS goes one step further in emphasizing the Organization and presentation of information in a manner that has direct relevance to the supporting phase of decision maker. So the objective is to improve the quality of decision making through information. In other words Decision Support System is information systems frequently used by accountants, managers & auditors to assist them in the decision-making process.

Characteristics of Decision Support System

Although decision support system applications vary widely in their level of sophistication and specific purpose, they possess several characteristics is common.

(1) Decision support system support management decision making.
(2) Decision support systems solve relatively unstructured problems.
(3) Finally a "friendly" computer interface is also a characteristic of a decision support system.

Components of Decision Support

A Decision support system has four basic components :

(i) The user
(ii) One or more databases
(iii) Planning Languages
(iv) the model base.

ARTIFICIAL INTELLIGENCE AND BIG DATA

AI is a branch of computer science which deals with the study and creation of computer systems that show some form of intelligence systems that learn new concepts and tasks, systems that can understand a natural language or perceive and comprehend and systems that perform other types of facts that require human types of intelligence.

UNDERSTANDING OF THE ARTIFICIAL INTELLIGENCE (AI)

Requires an understanding of related terms such as intelligence, knowledge, reasoning, thought, cognition learning and number of computer related terms. According to dictionaries, Intelligence as the ability to acquire, understand and apply knowledge or the ability to exercise thought and reason. Of course intelligence is more than, this. It collects all the knowledge and facts, both conscious and unconscious, which we have acquired through study and experiences.

Intelligence is the integrated sum of those which gives us the ability to remember a face that seen thirty or more years before or to build and send rocket on moon and the food for this intelligence is knowledge.

We have several systems that perform many types of intelligence tasks.

We have

- systems which can solve complex problems in mathematics.
- systems that can help in finding optimal system configuration.
- systems that can be used for scheduling for many diverse tasks.
- systems that can be used for the military & for business.
- systems that is used for diagnosing medical diseases.
- systems which can see well enough to recognize objects from photographs, video cameras & other sensors.

In spite of these achievements, we still have not been able to produce coordinated & autonomous systems which possess some of the basis abilities of a three years old child. These include the ability to recognize and remember numerous diverse objects in a scene, to learn new sounds and associate them with objects and concepts and to adopt readily to many diverse new situations. These are the challenges that are facing by researches in AI.

What are NOT AI?

AI is not study & creation of conventional computer systems, even though one can argue that all program show some degree of intelligence but AI program will go beyond this in demonstrating a high level of intelligence to a degree that equals or exceeds the intelligence required of a human in performing some tasks.

AI is not study of mind, nor of body, nor of languages or linguistics.

But the goal of AI is to develop the working computer systems that are truly capable of performing tasks that require high levels of intelligence. The important point is that the systems all be capable of performing intelligent tasks effectively & efficiently.

For the better understanding of AI, we study

robotics
memory organization
knowledge representation
storage & recall
learning models
inference techniques
common sense reasoning

AI is coming of an age where practical Commercial products are now available including a variety of robotic device. Vision systems that recognize shapes and objects, expert systems that perform many difficult tasks as well as or their human expert counter parts.

- intelligent systems that help pace a student's learning and monitor the students' progress.
- intelligent editors that assist users in building special knowledge bases, & systems which can learn to improve their performance.

AI & Related Fields. AI is closely related with fields like engineering, particularly Electrical and Mechanical Engineering, Linguistics, Psychology, Cognitive Science and Philosophy. Robotics is also regarded by some researchers as a branch of AI but this view is not common.

AI & Robotics. Robotics is also related with AI by some researches. They said it is a branch of AI but this view is not common. Because many researches consider Robotics as a separate inter disciplinary field which combines concepts & techniques from AI, electrical & mechanical & optical engineering.

AI & EE (Electrical Engineering). AI has much in common with engineering particularly Electrical and Mechanical Engineering. AI & EE are both interested in computational processes and systems, and how they relate to senses of perception such as vision and speech.

ME (Mechanical Engineering) & AI share common interests in their desire to build intelligent robots. Their goals are to build robots that can see & move around, perform mechanical tasks and understand human speech.

AI & linguistics. The field of linguistics shares an interest in the theory of grammars & languages with AI. Both fields have a desire to build a well-founded theory, & to see the development of systems that understand natural languages, that can synthesize speech & that are capable of language translations.

AI and Psychologists are concerned with workings of mind, the mental and emotional processes that drive human behaviour. As such, we should not be surprised to learn that researches in AI have much in common with psychologists during last 20 years. AI has adopted models of thinking & learning form psychology. AI has given psychologists fresh ideas and enhances their ability to model human cognitive functions as computer.

AI and Cognitive Science. Researches from AI & psychology have joined together at some universities to form a separate discipline known as cognitive science. Like AI researchers, cognitive scientists are interested in the computation processes required to perform certain human functions & in the mental & computational states related to such processes like computer science, cognitive science is still searching for a theory & foundation that will qualify it as a science.

Big Data

Artificial Intelligence (AI), mobile, social and Internet of Things (IoT) are driving data complexity, new forms and sources of data. Big data analytics is the use of advanced analytic techniques against very large, diverse data sets that include structured, semi-structured and unstructured data, from different sources, and in different sizes from terabytes to zettabytes.

Big data is a term applied to data sets whose size or type is beyond the ability of traditional relational databases to capture, manage, and process the data with low-latency. And it has one or more of the following characteristics – high volume, high velocity, or high variety. Big data comes from sensors, devices, video/audio, networks, log files, transactional applications, web, and social media - much of it generated in real time and in a very large scale.

Analyzing big data allows analysts, researchers, and business users to make better and faster decisions using data that was previously inaccessible or unusable. Using advanced analytics techniques such as text analytics, machine learning, predictive analytics, data mining, statistics, and natural language processing, businesses can analyze previously untapped data sources independent or together with their existing enterprise data to gain new insights resulting in better and faster decisions.

DATA WAREHOUSE

A data warehouse is a technique for collecting and managing data from varied sources to provide meaningful business insights. It is a blend of technologies and components which allows the strategic use of data.

Data Warehouse is electronic storage of a large amount of information by a business which is designed for query and analysis instead of transaction processing. It is a process of transforming data into information and making it available to users for analysis.

DATA MINING

Data mining is looking for hidden, valid, and potentially useful patterns in huge data sets. Data Mining is all about discovering unsuspected/ previously unknown relationships amongst the data.

It is a multi-disciplinary skill that uses machine learning, statistics, AI and database technology.

The insights extracted via Data mining can be used for marketing, fraud detection, and scientific discovery, etc.

Why use Data Warehouse?

Some most Important reasons for using Data warehouse are:

- Integrates many sources of data and helps to decrease stress on a production system.
- Optimized Data for reading access and consecutive disk scans.
- Data Warehouse helps to protect Data from the source system upgrades.
- Allows users to perform master Data Management.
- Improve data quality in source systems.

Why use Data mining?

Some most important reasons for using Data mining are:

- Establish relevance and relationships amongst data. Use this information to generate profitable insights
- Business can make informed decisions quickly
- Helps to find out unusual shopping patterns in grocery stores.
- Optimize website business by providing customize offers to each visitor.
- Helps to measure customer's response rates in business marketing.
- Creating and maintaining new customer groups for marketing purposes.
- Predict customer defections, like which customers are more likely to switch to another supplier in the nearest future.
- Differentiate between profitable and unprofitable customers.
- Identify all kind of suspicious behavior, as part of a fraud detection process.

Summary

- A data warehouse is a blend of technologies and components which allows the strategic use of data. It is a process of centralizing data from different sources into one common repository.
- Data mining is looking for hidden, valid, and potentially useful patterns in huge data sets.
- Data Warehouse helps to protect Data from the source system upgrades.
- Data warehouses are used by data scientists, business intelligence developers, to analyze data.
- Data mining technology helps businesses to reach closer to their objectives.

KNOWLEDGE MANAGEMENT

There are many definitions of Knowledge Management, but the one we prefer is the simplest - "Knowledge Management is the way you manage your organisation, when you understand the value of your knowledge". In other words, it is the management framework (of Roles and Accountabilities, Processes, Technologies and Governance) that you put in place to maximise the value and application of your knowledge, and which provide a managed approach to building, developing and retaining know-how, in service of business goals.

Knowledge Management is about systematically making use of the knowledge in the organization, and applying it to your business problem; tapping into "What your company knows"; to help you deliver your business results. It consists of never making the same mistake once (let along twice), and making every decision in the light of the full knowledge base of the company. The management of knowledge needs to be part of your business practices, just like the management of finance and the management of safety.

What is Knowledge?

Knowledge is the ability to make effective decisions, and take effective action (based on a definition by Peter Senge).

Part of the confusion between Knowledge Management and Information Management is almost certainly the lack, in the English language, of any distinction between Know-How, and Know-What. We use the word "knowledge" for both of these forms of knowing.

However Knowledge management has always delivered its real value when applied to "Know-How" – to improving the competence of the organisation by giving people access to the knowledge they need to make the correct decisions.

The implication of this definition, is that it allows you to align Knowledge Management with Decision Support. At a recent Knowledge Management planning workshop, for example, the project leader asked that the KM plan be focused entirely in the upcoming decision to select the project concept. We then had a great discussion as a team about "what do we need to know, to make an effective decision on concept selection?" The knowledge needs inventory that emerged from this discussion was then used to plan the project learning actions.

KM Technologies

Knowledge management (KM) technology can be categorised:

- **Groupware.** Software that facilitates collaboration and sharing of organisational information. Such applications provide tools for threaded discussions, document sharing, organisation-wide uniform email, and other collaboration-related features.
- **Workflow systems.** Systems that allow the representation of processes associated with the creation, use and maintenance of organisational knowledge, such as the process to create and utilise forms and documents.
- **Content management and document management systems.** Software systems that automate the process of creating web content and/or documents. Roles such as editors, graphic designers, writers and producers can be explicitly modeled along with the tasks in the process and validation criteria. Commercial vendors started either to support documents or to support web content but as the Internet grew these functions merged and vendors now perform both functions.
- **Enterprise portals.** Software that aggregates information across the entire organisation or for groups such as project teams.
- **eLearning.** Software that enables organisations to create customised training and education. This can include lesson plans, monitoring progress and online classes.
- **Planning and scheduling software.** Software that automates schedule creation and maintenance. The planning aspect can integrate with project management software.
- **Telepresence.** Software that enables individuals to have virtual "face-to-face" meetings without assembling at one location. Video conferencing is the most obvious example.

MANAGING TECHNOLOGY CHANGE

1. **Understand Your Existing Environment.** By understanding your business processes and how data fuels your operations, you will see where and how to apply the new technology to accelerate revenue, efficiency, quality and overall customer experience. Gain a clear picture of

your existing technology landscape to determine key points of integration between systems, people and processes.

2. **Consider Multiple Options.** The technology marketplace moves fast and over time migrates to common ground. Do your research and consider several options and vendors. You'll need to conduct thorough due diligence to determine which option best aligns with your current needs, while providing the flexibility to meet your organization's future needs.
3. **Engage End-Users Early and Often.** While not all organizations are comfortable with Agile methods, they've proven that collaborating with the real end users is important to success. Engaging end users early and often during the technology selection, implementation and adoption process increases your chances for success exponentially. Your users will feel a sense of ownership, commitment and accountability right from the start, helping you achieve best and highest adoption rates.
4. **Plan for Change & Manage Expectations.** You need a disciplined approach for planning and managing your implementation. By managing user and stakeholder expectations and helping them understand how they can change, they will see the full advantage of the technology.
5. **Build the Best Team.** Sure, you want expertise in a number of exciting technologies, whether it be mobile, cloud computing or big data. However, the real key to success is building a team with multi-disciplinary expertise in the specific technology, your business processes, data and existing technology landscape.

The benefits of technology innovation are attainable if the evaluation, implementation and adoption are properly planned for and expectations are clearly set and managed.

MULTIPLE CHOICE QUESTIONS

1. What is one of the key challenges faced by businesses in the era of globalization?
   (a) Reduced international competition
   (b) Increased protectionism
   (c) Limited access to global markets
   (d) Rapid changes in technology and markets
2. Which theory of international trade suggests that countries should specialize in the production of goods in which they have an absolute advantage?
   (a) Theory of Comparative Advantage
   (b) Mercantilism
   (c) Factor Proportions Theory
   (d) Theory of Absolute Advantage
3. The Theory of Comparative Advantage was formulated by
   (a) Adam Smith (b) David Ricardo
   (c) John Maynard Keynes
   (d) Karl Marx
4. What is the primary objective of the World Trade Organization (WTO)?
   (a) To promote protectionism
   (b) To regulate international finance
   (c) To facilitate international trade and resolve trade disputes
   (d) To control currency exchange rates
5. Which theory of international trade suggests that countries should specialize in the production of goods that make the most efficient use of their abundant factors of production?
   (a) Theory of Absolute Advantage
   (b) Theory of Comparative Advantage
   (c) Mercantilism
   (d) Product Life Cycle Theory
6. In the context of international business, what does the term "FDI" stand for?
   (a) Foreign Direct Investment
   (b) Free Trade Agreement
   (c) Foreign Debt Index
   (d) Federal Development Initiative
7. Which of the following is NOT a phase of the International Product Life Cycle?
   (a) Introduction
   (b) Growth
   (c) Maturity
   (d) Decline
8. What is the primary focus of the "Porter's Diamond Model" in international business?
   (a) The role of government in international trade
   (b) The importance of currency exchange rates
   (c) Determining the competitive advantage of nations in specific industries
   (d) The impact of cultural factors on international business
9. Which organization is responsible for issuing the "World Investment Report"?
   (a) United Nations Conference on Trade and Development (UNCTAD)
   (b) World Health Organization (WHO)
   (c) International Monetary Fund (IMF)
   (d) United Nations Educational, Scientific and Cultural Organization (UNESCO)
10. What does the "BoP" acronym represent in the context of international business?
   (a) Balance of Payments
   (b) Business Operating Profit
   (c) Bill of Purchases
   (d) Balance of Products
11. Which component of the Balance of Payments records international transactions related to the import and export of goods and services?
   (a) Current Account
   (b) Capital Account
   (c) Financial Account
   (d) Official Reserve Account
12. In the Balance of Payments, the "Capital Account" primarily includes transactions related to
   (a) Imports and exports of goods and services

(b) Investments in fixed assets, such as factories and infrastructure
(c) The purchase and sale of financial assets, such as stocks and bonds
(d) Foreign exchange rate movements

13. Which of the following is considered a credit item in the Balance of Payments?
(a) Imports of goods and services
(b) Exports of goods and services
(c) Capital outflows
(d) Income earned from foreign investments

14. A trade deficit in the Current Account of the Balance of Payments indicates that
(a) A country is exporting more than it is importing
(b) A country is importing more than it is exporting
(c) There is a balance in international trade
(d) The country's currency is overvalued

15. The "Official Reserve Account" in the Balance of Payments records transactions related to
(a) Government revenues and expenditures
(b) The exchange rate of the national currency
(c) Changes in a country's foreign exchange reserves
(d) Income from tourism

16. Which theory of international trade suggests that the factors of production, such as labor and capital, are the key determinants of a country's comparative advantage in trade?
(a) Theory of Comparative Advantage
(b) Theory of Absolute Advantage
(c) Heckscher-Ohlin Theory (Factor Proportions Theory)
(d) Theory of Mercantilism

17. What is the primary goal of the "Export-Import Bank" in international trade?
(a) To promote protectionism
(b) To provide export financing and insurance
(c) To regulate currency exchange rates
(d) To control trade deficits

18. What does the term "exchange rate" refer to in international finance?
(a) The rate at which goods are exchanged in international trade
(b) The rate at which currencies of different countries are exchanged
(c) The rate at which international investments are made
(d) The rate at which interest is exchanged

19. In the context of international trade, what is the purpose of a "tariff"?
(a) To promote free trade
(b) To discourage imports and protect domestic industries
(c) To facilitate foreign direct investment
(d) To encourage exports

20. The "Economic Espionage Act" of the United States primarily deals with
(a) Import regulations
(b) Intellectual property protection and prevention of economic espionage
(c) Export controls
(d) Currency exchange rates

21. Which of the following trade theories suggests that countries should engage in international trade by specializing in producing goods for which they have the lowest opportunity cost?
(a) Theory of Absolute Advantage
(b) Mercantilism
(c) Theory of Comparative Advantage
(d) Product Life Cycle Theory

22. The "Trade-Related Aspects of Intellectual Property Rights" (TRIPS) agreement is administered by
(a) World Trade Organization (WTO)
(b) United Nations (UN)
(c) World Health Organization (WHO)
(d) United Nations Educational, Scientific and Cultural Organization (UNESCO)

23. Which type of foreign exchange rate system is characterized by the central bank actively intervening to stabilize the national currency's value?
(a) Fixed exchange rate system
(b) Floating exchange rate system
(c) Managed floating exchange rate system
(d) Pegged exchange rate system

24. What is the primary focus of "Greenfield investments" in foreign direct investment (FDI)?
(a) Acquiring existing foreign companies
(b) Investing in new facilities and projects in a foreign country
(c) Trading in the foreign currency market
(d) Obtaining loans from foreign banks

25. Which organization is responsible for issuing the "Global Investment Trends Monitor" report?

(a) International Monetary Fund (IMF)
(b) World Trade Organization (WTO)
(c) United Nations Conference on Trade and Development (UNCTAD)
(d) World Health Organization (WHO)

26. What does "FDI" stand for in the context of international business?
(a) Foreign Domestic Integration
(b) Free Data Implementation
(c) Foreign Direct Investment
(d) Fiscal Development Initiative

27. Which of the following is a key benefit of Foreign Direct Investment for host countries?
(a) Reduced competition
(b) Increased domestic investment
(c) Higher unemployment rates
(d) Reduced economic growth

28. What is the primary motivation for a multinational corporation to engage in FDI?
(a) Maximizing domestic employment
(b) Minimizing foreign competition
(c) Expanding market access and seeking higher returns
(d) Reducing international trade barriers

29. The "horizontal FDI" model involves
(a) Investing in a similar business abroad
(b) Investing in unrelated industries abroad
(c) Exporting goods and services
(d) Focusing on domestic operations only

30. Which factor contributes to the increased flow of FDI?
(a) Strict trade barriers
(b) Political instability
(c) Lack of infrastructure
(d) Globalization and liberalization

31. What is the primary concern regarding the "resource curse" in the context of FDI?
(a) Overinvestment in technology
(b) Overreliance on natural resources
(c) Inadequate infrastructure
(d) Lack of government intervention

32. FDI often leads to the transfer of
(a) Human rights violations
(b) Pollution control technology
(c) Cultural homogeneity
(d) Resource depletion

33. Which of the following is a potential cost of FDI for host countries?
(a) Enhanced technological transfer
(b) Increased competition
(c) Reduced foreign exchange reserves
(d) Economic growth and employment

34. "Vertical FDI" primarily involves
(a) Expanding into new industries
(b) Investing in a similar business abroad
(c) Integrating different stages of the production process
(d) Collaborating with domestic competitors

35. In the context of FDI, what does "capital flight" refer to?
(a) A surge in domestic investment
(b) A sudden outflow of foreign capital from a country
(c) Attracting foreign investment
(d) A rise in the exchange rate

36. What is one of the key benefits of FDI for host countries related to technology transfer?
(a) Limited access to global markets
(b) Reduced competition
(c) Enhanced technological capabilities and innovation
(d) Decreased domestic investment

37. "Greenfield FDI" typically involves
(a) Mergers and acquisitions
(b) Investing in existing businesses abroad
(c) Starting new operations or projects in a foreign country
(d) Focusing on the domestic market only

38. Which type of FDI often leads to concerns about cultural homogenization and the loss of cultural diversity?
(a) Horizontal FDI
(b) Vertical FDI
(c) Resource-seeking FDI
(d) Market-seeking FDI

39. The "crowding-out effect" in the context of FDI refers to
(a) Increased investment in domestic industries
(b) Decreased investment in domestic industries due to foreign competition
(c) Government subsidies for foreign investors
(d) Export promotion policies

40. What is the primary concern regarding "deindustrialization" in the context of FDI?

(a) Enhanced technological capabilities
(b) Increased domestic production
(c) The decline of domestic manufacturing industries
(d) Reduced capital flight

41. Which of the following is a common benefit of FDI for host countries?
(a) Reduced foreign competition
(b) Increased government regulations
(c) Enhanced export capabilities
(d) Loss of intellectual property rights

42. What is the primary motivation for a country to restrict FDI through regulations and restrictions?
(a) To encourage FDI
(b) To promote economic growth
(c) To protect domestic industries and national interests
(d) To reduce unemployment rates

43. Which theory suggests that countries may restrict FDI in industries that are considered crucial for national security or economic stability?
(a) Theory of Comparative Advantage
(b) Theory of Nationalization
(c) Theory of FDI Regulation
(d) Theory of Strategic Trade Policy

44. The "spillover effect" in the context of FDI refers to
(a) Enhanced economic growth in the host country
(b) Increased competition from foreign firms
(c) Technology transfer to domestic firms
(d) A decrease in government regulation

45. Which of the following is a potential cost of FDI for host countries related to labor standards?
(a) Improved working conditions
(b) Reduced labor exploitation
(c) Lower wages and poor working conditions
(d) Enhanced labor rights protection

46. The "race to the bottom" in the context of FDI refers to
(a) Intense competition among domestic firms
(b) Competition among host countries to attract foreign investors by lowering labor and environmental standards
(c) A rapid increase in FDI
(d) Enhanced domestic labor standards

47. Which of the following is a common benefit of FDI for host countries related to infrastructure development?
(a) Reduced investment in transportation and utilities
(b) Enhanced infrastructure development
(c) Increased reliance on foreign infrastructure
(d) Overcrowding in urban areas

48. The "infant industry argument" suggests that
(a) Established industries should receive government subsidies
(b) New industries need protection from foreign competition until they become competitive
(c) Foreign investors should focus on mature industries
(d) Domestic industries are invulnerable to competition

49. What does the "locational advantage" refer to in the context of FDI?
(a) The strategic location of a country
(b) The advantage of being located near key suppliers
(c) The benefits of hosting foreign investors
(d) The advantages of being located in an economic free zone

50. In the context of FDI, the "host country" refers to
(a) The country where the investing firm is headquartered
(b) The country that provides foreign aid to developing nations
(c) The country that receives foreign investment from a multinational corporation
(d) A country with no foreign trade relations

51. What does "WTO" stand for?
(a) World Tariff Organization
(b) World Trade Organization
(c) World Taxation Organization
(d) World Technology Organization

52. The primary goal of the WTO is to
(a) Promote fair and equal distribution of wealth
(b) Regulate international taxation
(c) Facilitate international trade and resolve trade disputes
(d) Regulate global climate change

53. Which agreement forms the foundation of the WTO's rules on international trade in goods?
(a) TRIPS Agreement
(b) GATT Agreement
(c) TRIMS Agreement
(d) GATS Agreement

54. The "TRIPS Agreement" pertains to
(a) Tariffs on industrial products
(b) International trade in services
(c) Intellectual property rights
(d) Environmental protection

55. What is the purpose of the "TRIMS Agreement" under the WTO?
(a) Regulating trade in textiles and clothing
(b) Promoting agricultural trade
(c) Regulating trade-related investment measures
(d) Facilitating trade in educational services

56. The "GATS Agreement" primarily deals with
(a) Trade in industrial products
(b) Trade in agricultural products
(c) Trade in services
(d) Trade in intellectual property

57. The "Agreement on Agriculture" under the WTO aims to
(a) Promote fair labor practices
(b) Regulate labor unions
(c) Reform trade in agricultural products
(d) Enhance environmental protection

58. The WTO's "Trade Policy Review Mechanism" (TPRM) serves to
(a) Promote trade in weapons
(b) Monitor and review the trade policies of member countries
(c) Regulate international tourism
(d) Establish uniform taxation policies

59. The WTO's principle of "most-favored-nation (MFN) treatment" means that
(a) Members must provide special benefits to their trading partners
(b) Members must treat all other members equally in terms of trade privileges
(c) Members must engage in preferential trade agreements
(d) Members must reduce their tariffs to zero

60. What is the central purpose of the "Doha Development Agenda" in the WTO?
(a) Regulating climate change
(b) Promoting environmental protection
(c) Advancing the development objectives of developing countries through trade
(d) Restricting trade in agricultural products

61. The "Trade Facilitation Agreement" under the WTO focuses on
(a) Promoting free trade zones
(b) Reducing trade barriers and simplifying customs procedures
(c) Regulating foreign direct investment
(d) Regulating trade in services

62. Which of the following WTO agreements addresses trade in environmental goods and services?
(a) GATT Agreement
(b) GATS Agreement
(c) GSP Agreement
(d) ITA Agreement

63. The "Trade-Related Investment Measures" (TRIMS) Agreement prohibits certain investment-related measures that
(a) Encourage foreign investment
(b) Regulate intellectual property rights
(c) Distort trade and lead to discrimination against foreign products
(d) Promote technology transfer

64. What does "GSP" stand for in the context of the WTO?
(a) Global Sustainability Partnership
(b) General Services Program
(c) Generalized System of Preferences
(d) Global Security Protocol

65. The WTO's "Safeguards Agreement" allows member countries to impose temporary import restrictions when they face a surge in imports that
(a) Promotes domestic industries
(b) Damages domestic industries
(c) Benefits foreign competitors
(d) Reduces trade barriers

66. The "WTO Dispute Settlement Understanding" provides a framework for
(a) Promoting trade in agricultural products
(b) Resolving trade disputes among member countries
(c) Regulating foreign exchange rates
(d) Regulating labor standards

67. The principle of "national treatment" in the WTO means that foreign products and services should be treated

(a) More favorably than domestic products and services
(b) Less favorably than domestic products and services
(c) Equally to domestic products and services
(d) With preferential trade benefits

68. The WTO's "Trade-Related Aspects of Intellectual Property Rights" (TRIPS) Agreement deals with issues related to
(a) Environmental protection
(b) Labor standards
(c) Intellectual property rights, including patents and trademarks
(d) Agricultural trade

69. What does "TBT" stand for in the context of the WTO?
(a) Trade-Related Business Techniques
(b) Technical Barriers to Trade
(c) Trade-Based Tariff
(d) Trade and Business Technology

70. The "Precautionary Principle" in the WTO allows countries to take protective measures when
(a) They have scientific evidence to support such measures
(b) They want to promote free trade
(c) They face no environmental risks
(d) They engage in unfair trade practices

71. Which round of WTO negotiations focused on the reduction of tariffs, non-tariff barriers, and agricultural subsidies?
(a) Doha Development Round
(b) Uruguay Round
(c) Cancún Round
(d) Bali Round

72. The "Trade-Related Investment Measures" (TRIMS) Agreement prohibits which of the following practices?
(a) Export subsidies
(b) Voluntary export restraints
(c) Discriminatory trade measures that favor domestic industries
(d) Environmental protection regulations

73. The "Bali Package" under the WTO included agreements on issues related to
(a) Agriculture, trade facilitation, and development
(b) Intellectual property rights and investment
(c) Services and labor standards
(d) Environmental protection and climate change

74. The "DSU" in the WTO refers to the
(a) Development and Sustainability Unit
(b) Dispute Settlement Understanding
(c) Domestic Subsidy Unit
(d) Development Support Unit

75. Which WTO round was launched with the primary goal of advancing trade liberalization and development?
(a) Bali Round
(b) Doha Development Round
(c) Uruguay Round
(d) GATT Round

76. What does "EXIM" stand for in the context of international trade?
(a) Export-Import
(b) Extra-International Markets
(c) Exchange and Import
(d) External Importation

77. In international trade, what is the primary purpose of a "proforma invoice"?
(a) To finalize the sale of goods
(b) To confirm the order for goods
(c) To request payment for goods
(d) To provide an estimate of the cost of goods and shipping

78. Which document is used to provide a detailed description of the goods being exported and their value for customs clearance purposes?
(a) Commercial invoice
(b) Bill of lading
(c) Certificate of origin
(d) Proforma invoice

79. What does an "INCOTERM" specify in international trade?
(a) Import duties and taxes
(b) Payment terms and conditions
(c) Quality standards for goods
(d) Packaging requirements

80. In the context of international trade, what is the purpose of a "Certificate of Origin"?
(a) To determine the quality of the goods
(b) To specify the payment terms

(c) To declare the country where the goods were produced
(d) To provide insurance coverage for the goods

81. Which international trade term represents an agreement between a buyer and a seller regarding the delivery of goods, cost, and risk?
(a) CIF (b) FOB
(c) LCL (d) TCO

82. The "Bill of Lading" is a document primarily used for
(a) Providing a detailed description of the goods
(b) Declaring the country of origin
(c) Confirming the terms of payment
(d) Acknowledging the receipt of goods for shipment

83. What does "CIF" stand for in international trade terms?
(a) Cost, Insurance, and Freight
(b) Customs, Importation, and Fees
(c) Certificate of Insurance and Freight
(d) Cash in Hand and Financing

84. The "Harmonized System (HS) Code" is a standardized classification system used for
(a) Packaging and labeling goods
(b) Determining payment terms
(c) Classifying products for customs and trade purposes
(d) Providing insurance coverage for goods

85. Which of the following documents certifies that the goods have been inspected and are in conformity with the buyer's requirements?
(a) Certificate of origin
(b) Bill of lading
(c) Inspection certificate
(d) Proforma invoice

86. What is the primary purpose of a "Packing List" in international trade?
(a) To list the items included in a shipment
(b) To specify payment terms
(c) To declare the country of origin
(d) To request payment for goods

87. Which international trade term represents an agreement where the seller assumes all costs and risks until the goods reach the buyer's premises?
(a) CFR (b) EXW
(c) DDP (d) DDU

88. The "Letter of Credit" (LC) is a financial instrument used in international trade to
(a) Insure shipments against damage or loss
(b) Request a refund for defective goods
(c) Provide payment security for the seller
(d) Specify the quality standards for goods

89. What is the primary purpose of a "Certificate of Inspection" in international trade?
(a) To certify the authenticity of a product
(b) To specify the payment terms
(c) To declare the country of origin
(d) To verify the quality, quantity, and condition of goods

90. In international trade, what is the primary purpose of a "Dock Receipt"?
(a) To acknowledge the receipt of goods for shipment
(b) To specify the payment terms
(c) To declare the country of origin
(d) To list the items included in a shipment

91. The "Export License" is typically required for the export of
(a) All goods and services
(b) Only high-value goods
(c) Goods with restricted or controlled export status
(d) Agricultural products

92. Which international trade term represents an agreement where the seller is responsible for all costs and risks until the goods are delivered to the buyer's premises?
(a) DDP
(b) FCA
(c) DAT
(d) CPT

93. The "EXIM Bank" in a country primarily provides support and financing for
(a) Domestic infrastructure projects
(b) Importers and exporters engaged in international trade
(c) International tourism
(d) Environmental protection initiatives

94. What is the purpose of an "ATA Carnet" in international trade?
(a) To provide insurance coverage for goods
(b) To specify payment terms

(c) To facilitate the temporary importation of goods for exhibitions and trade fairs
(d) To certify the country of origin

95. Which of the following is an international organization that aims to facilitate the flow of global trade by streamlining customs procedures and documentation?
(a) ICC (International Chamber of Commerce)
(b) IMF (International Monetary Fund)
(c) WTO (World Trade Organization)
(d) UNCTAD (United Nations Conference on Trade and Development)

96. What is the primary objective of the "Generalized System of Preferences" (GSP) in international trade?
(a) To promote environmental protection
(b) To regulate payment terms
(c) To provide customs clearance services
(d) To grant preferential trade treatment to developing countries

97. Which international trade document is often required by customs authorities to assess and collect duties and taxes on imported goods?
(a) Certificate of Origin
(b) Bill of Lading
(c) Customs Declaration Form
(d) Proforma Invoice

98. The "Insurance Certificate" is a document used in international trade to provide coverage for
(a) Damaged or lost goods during transit
(b) Export subsidies
(c) Labor standards
(d) Environmental protection

99. What is the primary function of a "Shipping Order" in international trade?
(a) To list the items included in a shipment
(b) To request payment for goods
(c) To specify payment terms
(d) To authorize the carrier to transport the goods

100. Which international trade term represents an agreement where the seller bears all costs and risks until the goods are placed alongside the vessel at the named port of shipment?
(a) CIP (b) CFR
(c) DAT (d) DDP

101. What does "IMF" stand for in the context of international financial institutions?
(a) International Monetary Foundation
(b) International Military Force
(c) International Monetary Fund
(d) International Management Facility

102. The primary purpose of the IMF is to
(a) Promote international trade
(b) Provide development aid to poor countries
(c) Maintain global peace and security
(d) Ensure stability in the international monetary system

103. The IMF's primary tool for providing financial assistance to member countries in need is
(a) Grants
(b) Loans with low-interest rates
(c) Direct investments in member countries
(d) Aid packages

104. What is the primary focus of the World Bank in terms of development assistance?
(a) Promoting international trade
(b) Providing emergency relief in conflict zones
(c) Reducing poverty and promoting economic development
(d) Supporting international peacekeeping missions

105. The World Bank primarily provides financial support to
(a) Developed countries
(b) Low- and middle-income countries
(c) Emerging markets
(d) Military organizations

106. The IMF's Special Drawing Rights (SDRs) are a form of
(a) Currency exchange rates
(b) Subsidies for agriculture
(c) International currency
(d) Stock market shares

107. What does the IMF's "Structural Adjustment Program" (SAP) typically involve?
(a) Providing direct financial assistance to countries
(b) Promoting international trade agreements
(c) Implementing economic policy reforms in exchange for financial support
(d) Funding large infrastructure projects

108. The World Bank consists of two main institutions. What are they?
(a) United Nations Development Program (UNDP) and World Trade Organization (WTO)
(b) International Development Association (IDA) and International Monetary Fund (IMF)
(c) International Finance Corporation (IFC) and International Bank for Reconstruction and Development (IBRD)
(d) World Health Organization (WHO) and United Nations Educational, Scientific and Cultural Organization (UNESCO)

109. The World Bank's "International Development Association" (IDA) primarily focuses on providing assistance to
(a) Middle-income countries
(b) Low-income countries
(c) Developed countries
(d) High-income countries

110. Which of the following is a key objective of the IMF's surveillance activities?
(a) Promoting international trade agreements
(b) Monitoring global military developments
(c) Assessing the economic and financial health of member countries
(d) Providing emergency relief in natural disasters

111. The World Bank's "International Finance Corporation" (IFC) primarily focuses on
(a) Providing loans to low-income countries
(b) Supporting educational initiatives in developing countries
(c) Promoting private sector development in emerging markets
(d) Maintaining global peace and security

112. Which of the following is a core function of the IMF in assisting member countries in financial crises?
(a) Funding large infrastructure projects
(b) Providing grants for education
(c) Offering technical assistance and policy advice
(d) Facilitating international trade agreements

113. The IMF's "Article IV Consultations" refer to
(a) Meetings of heads of state
(b) Bilateral trade agreements
(c) Regular assessments of a country's economic and financial developments
(d) Special Drawing Rights (SDRs)

114. What is the primary role of the IMF's "Bretton Woods Institutions"?
(a) Providing disaster relief assistance
(b) Promoting global peacekeeping missions
(c) Regulating international currency exchange rates
(d) Providing financial and economic stability

115. The IMF's "Quota" system is used to determine
(a) The number of member countries
(b) Voting rights and financial contributions of member countries
(c) The exchange rates between different currencies
(d) The interest rates on loans

116. Which international organization is responsible for maintaining international monetary and financial cooperation?
(a) World Health Organization (WHO)
(b) World Trade Organization (WTO)
(c) International Monetary Fund (IMF)
(d) United Nations Educational, Scientific and Cultural Organization (UNESCO)

117. The "Poverty Reduction Strategy Papers" (PRSPs) are primarily associated with which international financial institution?
(a) United Nations Development Program (UNDP)
(b) World Trade Organization (WTO)
(c) International Monetary Fund (IMF)
(d) World Bank

118. The IMF's "Balance of Payments" is a record of a country's
(a) Government budget expenditures
(b) Trade deficit or surplus
(c) Military spending
(d) Foreign aid contributions

119. The IMF's "General Resources Account" (GRA) provides financial assistance to member countries with
(a) No conditions attached
(b) Low-interest loans
(c) Strict policy conditionality
(d) Trade concessions

120. Which of the following is a key function of the World Bank's "International Bank for Reconstruction and Development" (IBRD)?
(a) Providing loans to low-income countries
(b) Focusing on private sector development
(c) Offering grants for education
(d) Supporting infrastructure projects in middle-income countries

121. The World Bank's "IDA Blend" countries are characterized by
(a) High-income status
(b) Low-income status
(c) Middle-income status
(d) Strong economic growth

122. The World Bank's "International Bank for Reconstruction and Development" (IBRD) provides loans to member countries primarily for
(a) Emergency relief in conflict zones
(b) Private sector development
(c) Large infrastructure projects
(d) Poverty reduction

123. What is the primary objective of the IMF's "Financial Assistance for Low-Income Countries" program (FALC)?
(a) Promoting international trade agreements
(b) Reducing poverty and promoting economic development
(c) Providing humanitarian aid in conflict zones
(d) Offering low-interest loans to all member countries

124. The World Bank's "Concessional Finance" window provides financial assistance to
(a) High-income countries
(b) Middle-income countries
(c) Low-income countries on highly concessional terms
(d) Emerging markets

125. Which international financial institution focuses on promoting economic stability and monetary cooperation among its member countries?
(a) World Trade Organization (WTO)
(b) International Monetary Fund (IMF)
(c) United Nations Development Program (UNDP)
(d) World Health Organization (WHO)

126. What is the primary purpose of a Management Information System (MIS)?
(a) To process transactions
(b) To support decision-making at various levels of management
(c) To automate routine tasks
(d) To manage hardware and software

127. Which of the following best describes a Decision Support System (DSS)?
(a) A system for automating routine tasks
(b) A system for processing transactions
(c) A system for supporting complex decision-making tasks
(d) A system for managing software development

128. In a typical Management Information System (MIS), data is processed and transformed into information through a process known as
(a) Data analysis
(b) Data mining
(c) Data manipulation
(d) Data transformation

129. Which of the following is a common application of a Decision Support System (DSS)?
(a) Record-keeping
(b) Automating customer service
(c) Analyzing sales data to determine future strategies
(d) Managing employee schedules

130. In an MIS, what is the role of a "Database Management System (DBMS)"?
(a) Managing hardware components
(b) Providing decision support
(c) Storing and retrieving data efficiently
(d) Processing financial transactions

131. Which type of information system provides support for operational and tactical decision-making?
(a) Transaction Processing System (TPS)
(b) Management Information System (MIS)
(c) Decision Support System (DSS)
(d) Enterprise Resource Planning (ERP) System

132. What is the primary goal of a Transaction Processing System (TPS)?
(a) Providing support for strategic decision-making

(b) Capturing and processing routine business transactions
(c) Analyzing historical data
(d) Managing customer relationships

133. In the context of an MIS, what does the term "data warehousing" refer to?
(a) A technique for data mining
(b) A repository for storing large volumes of historical data
(c) Real-time transaction processing
(d) A process for automating customer service

134. What is the key function of a Decision Support System (DSS) in supporting decision-makers?
(a) Capturing and processing routine transactions
(b) Automating data entry tasks
(c) Providing interactive tools and models for analysis
(d) Managing hardware resources

135. The main focus of a Transaction Processing System (TPS) is on
(a) Analyzing historical data
(b) Supporting strategic decision-making
(c) Capturing and processing day-to-day business transactions
(d) Managing hardware and software resources

136. What is the primary output of a Management Information System (MIS)?
(a) Raw data
(b) Decision models
(c) Information reports
(d) Hardware components

137. Which information system integrates various business functions and processes to improve overall efficiency and effectiveness?
(a) Management Information System (MIS)
(b) Decision Support System (DSS)
(c) Enterprise Resource Planning (ERP) System
(d) Transaction Processing System (TPS)

138. The primary data source for a Transaction Processing System (TPS) is
(a) External databases
(b) Historical data
(c) Day-to-day business transactions
(d) Decision support models

139. Which of the following is a characteristic of a Decision Support System (DSS)?
(a) Focus on historical data analysis
(b) Automated data entry
(c) User-friendly interfaces for complex queries and analysis
(d) Routine transaction processing

140. In the context of MIS, what does "drill-down" mean?
(a) Analyzing historical data
(b) Browsing through large datasets
(c) Investigating details of data at different levels
(d) Automating customer service

141. A Management Information System (MIS) typically provides information to which level of management?
(a) Top-level management
(b) Middle-level management
(c) Operational management
(d) All levels of management

142. What is the primary purpose of a "Dashboard" in the context of information systems?
(a) Real-time data entry
(b) Providing decision support
(c) Presenting key performance indicators and data visually
(d) Capturing business transactions

143. A "Data Warehouse" is designed to
(a) Process financial transactions
(b) Store and manage large volumes of historical data
(c) Provide real-time decision support
(d) Automate routine tasks

144. What is the primary role of a "Model" in a Decision Support System (DSS)?
(a) Storing and retrieving data
(b) Providing real-time transaction processing
(c) Supporting decision-makers in analyzing and solving problems
(d) Automating customer service

145. Which type of information system focuses on providing support for the day-to-day operations of an organization?
(a) Decision Support System (DSS)
(b) Enterprise Resource Planning (ERP) System

(c) Management Information System (MIS)
(d) Transaction Processing System (TPS)

146. In an MIS, what is the purpose of "Data Mining"?
(a) Presenting information visually
(b) Discovering patterns and relationships in data
(c) Capturing routine transactions
(d) Managing hardware and software resources

147. Which of the following is a key function of an Enterprise Resource Planning (ERP) System?
(a) Capturing and processing routine transactions
(b) Automating data analysis
(c) Integrating various business functions and processes
(d) Providing real-time decision support

148. What is the primary output of a Transaction Processing System (TPS)?
(a) Decision support models
(b) Information reports
(c) User interfaces
(d) Hardware components

149. The primary users of a Decision Support System (DSS) are typically
(a) Operational staff
(b) Top-level executives and managers
(c) Middle-level managers
(d) Data entry clerks

150. What is the primary function of a "User Interface" in an information system?
(a) Storing and retrieving data
(b) Analyzing historical data
(c) Facilitating interaction between users and the system
(d) Managing hardware resources

151. What is the primary goal of Artificial Intelligence (AI)?
(a) To create machines that mimic human intelligence
(b) To replace human workers with automated systems
(c) To process large amounts of data quickly
(d) To improve data security

152. Machine Learning is a subfield of AI that focuses on
(a) Processing large datasets
(b) Mimicking human behavior
(c) Teaching computers to learn from data
(d) Developing hardware for AI systems

153. What is "Big Data" in the context of information technology?
(a) Large physical data storage devices
(b) Datasets too large to be processed by traditional methods
(c) High-speed internet connections
(d) Advanced data visualization techniques

154. Which of the following is a key component of a Big Data ecosystem?
(a) AI algorithms
(b) Data centers
(c) Data visualization tools
(d) Virtual reality devices

155. In the context of Big Data, what is the "3V" model?
(a) Volume, Visualization, and Velocity
(b) Variety, Velocity, and Veracity
(c) Validity, Visualization, and Value
(d) Volume, Value, and Validity

156. What is the primary purpose of data preprocessing in Big Data analytics?
(a) Reducing the variety of data
(b) Enhancing data quality and consistency
(c) Increasing data volume
(d) Eliminating data velocity

157. Which AI technique involves training a model to make predictions or decisions based on data?
(a) Deep learning
(b) Reinforcement learning
(c) Natural language processing
(d) Expert systems

158. Natural Language Processing (NLP) is a subfield of AI that focuses on
(a) Teaching computers to understand and generate human language
(b) Analyzing large datasets
(c) Developing hardware for AI systems
(d) Processing numerical data

159. Which of the following is an example of supervised learning in machine learning?
(a) Clustering
(b) Classification
(c) Reinforcement learning
(d) Unsupervised learning

160. Which technology is commonly used for storing and managing large volumes of data in Big Data applications?
(a) Relational databases
(b) NoSQL databases
(c) Data warehouses
(d) Spreadsheets

161. In the context of Big Data, what does the term "MapReduce" refer to?
(a) A data visualization technique
(b) A distributed computing framework for processing large datasets
(c) A machine learning algorithm
(d) A natural language processing tool

162. Which of the following is a characteristic of "Dark Data"?
(a) Data that is easily accessible and well-organized
(b) Data that is actively being used in business operations
(c) Data that is unstructured and underutilized
(d) Data that is publicly available on the internet

163. In the context of Big Data, what is "Hadoop"?
(a) A programming language for machine learning
(b) A type of NoSQL database
(c) An open-source framework for distributed data processing
(d) A data visualization tool

164. Which of the following is a common challenge in handling Big Data?
(a) Lack of data security
(b) Slow internet connectivity
(c) Limited data storage capacity
(d) Difficulty in data integration and analysis

165. Which type of machine learning is used for optimizing decisions based on trial and error?
(a) Supervised learning
(b) Reinforcement learning
(c) Unsupervised learning
(d) Semi-supervised learning

166. In the context of Big Data, what is the "Veracity" aspect of the 3V model?
(a) The volume of data
(b) The value of data
(c) The variety of data
(d) The quality and trustworthiness of data

167. What is the primary objective of "Data Mining" in Big Data analytics?
(a) Storing and retrieving data
(b) Discovering patterns and relationships in data
(c) Increasing data volume
(d) Enhancing data quality

168. Which AI technique focuses on teaching computers to understand and generate human language?
(a) Reinforcement learning
(b) Deep learning
(c) Natural Language Processing (NLP)
(d) Expert systems

169. Which type of machine learning involves clustering data points into groups based on their similarities?
(a) Supervised learning
(b) Unsupervised learning
(c) Reinforcement learning
(d) Semi-supervised learning

170. The process of "Feature Engineering" in machine learning involves
(a) Selecting the most important data features
(b) Creating new features from existing data
(c) Removing irrelevant data
(d) Storing data in a warehouse

171. What is the primary role of "Data Lakes" in Big Data management?
(a) Storing data in structured formats
(b) Reducing data volume
(c) Storing vast amounts of raw, unstructured data
(d) Enhancing data veracity

172. Which of the following is a common use of AI in healthcare?
(a) Predictive maintenance for manufacturing
(b) Optimizing supply chain logistics
(c) Disease diagnosis and personalized treatment recommendations
(d) Analyzing social media trends

173. Which technology is used to store and manage large volumes of structured data efficiently?
(a) Hadoop
(b) Data lakes
(c) Relational databases
(d) Data visualization tools

174. What is the primary advantage of using "Ensemble Learning" in machine learning?
(a) Simplifies the model-building process
(b) Reduces the need for feature engineering
(c) Combines multiple models to improve predictive accuracy
(d) Increases data velocity

175. In the context of AI, what is a "Neural Network"?
(a) A type of data visualization tool
(b) A type of machine learning algorithm
(c) A database management system
(d) A human-like robot

176. What is the primary purpose of a data warehouse?
(a) Real-time data processing
(b) Storing and managing large volumes of historical data
(c) Handling transactional data
(d) Automating customer service

177. Data mining is a process that involves
(a) Storing data in a centralized repository
(b) Extracting valuable patterns and knowledge from data
(c) Real-time data processing
(d) Creating data visualizations

178. Which of the following is a common task in knowledge management?
(a) Data warehousing
(b) Data integration
(c) Capturing and sharing organizational knowledge
(d) Data visualization

179. In data warehousing, what is the role of Extract, Transform, Load (ETL) processes?
(a) Data storage
(b) Data visualization
(c) Data integration and transformation
(d) Real-time data processing

180. The process of "Data Cleansing" in data warehousing refers to
(a) Storing data securely
(b) Removing inconsistencies and errors from data
(c) Capturing data from external sources
(d) Data visualization

181. What is the primary focus of "Data Mart" in the context of data warehousing?
(a) Storing all enterprise data
(b) Storing data for a specific department or business unit
(c) Data integration
(d) Data visualization

182. Data mining algorithms are used to
(a) Create data warehouses
(b) Discover hidden patterns and trends in data
(c) Store large volumes of data
(d) Manage data security

183. In knowledge management, what does "tacit knowledge" refer to?
(a) Explicit, codified knowledge
(b) Knowledge that is difficult to articulate or transfer
(c) Historical data
(d) Data visualization techniques

184. The "OLAP" acronym in the context of data warehousing stands for
(a) Online Analytical Processing
(b) Online Learning and Automation Platform
(c) Operational Logistics and Analysis Protocol
(d) Open-source Library for Algorithmic Processing

185. In data mining, what is "Association Rule Mining" primarily used for?
(a) Discovering patterns in spatial data
(b) Identifying frequent itemsets and relationships in data
(c) Real-time data processing
(d) Data visualization

186. What is the primary objective of "Decision Support" in data mining?
(a) Storing data securely
(b) Enhancing data quality and consistency
(c) Assisting decision-makers with insights from data
(d) Real-time data processing

187. In knowledge management, what is the role of a "Community of Practice"?
(a) Data warehousing
(b) Sharing knowledge and expertise among a group of people with common interests
(c) Data integration
(d) Data visualization

188. The process of "Clustering" in data mining involves
(a) Storing data securely
(b) Grouping data points with similar characteristics
(c) Real-time data processing
(d) Creating data visualizations

189. In data warehousing, what does "Data Aggregation" refer to?
(a) Capturing data from external sources
(b) Data integration and transformation
(c) Storing large volumes of historical data
(d) Summarizing data at a higher level

190. "Explicit knowledge" in knowledge management is best described as
(a) Knowledge that is difficult to articulate or transfer
(b) Knowledge that is widely known and documented
(c) Data integration techniques
(d) Real-time data processing

191. The process of "Text Mining" in data mining involves
(a) Analyzing and extracting information from unstructured text data
(b) Creating data visualizations
(c) Real-time data processing
(d) Data warehousing

192. In data warehousing, what is the primary goal of "Data Partitioning"?
(a) Enhancing data quality
(b) Data integration and transformation
(c) Storing data securely
(d) Improving query performance by dividing data into smaller units

193. The "Data Warehouse Schema" defines
(a) Data integration techniques
(b) The structure and organization of data in the data warehouse
(c) Real-time data processing
(d) Data visualization techniques

194. In knowledge management, what is the primary role of a "Knowledge Repository"?
(a) Data integration and transformation
(b) Storing and organizing knowledge assets
(c) Data warehousing
(d) Data visualization

195. "Sequential Pattern Mining" in data mining is primarily used for
(a) Detecting fraudulent activities
(b) Analyzing data in real-time
(c) Discovering patterns in sequential data
(d) Data visualization techniques

196. Which of the following is a common tool used for data visualization in knowledge management?
(a) OLAP
(b) ETL
(c) Data visualization software
(d) Data integration

197. In data warehousing, what is the role of "Data Mart" in relation to the central data warehouse?
(a) Data integration and transformation
(b) Data visualization
(c) Storing data for a specific department or business unit
(d) Real-time data processing

198. In knowledge management, what is the primary function of a "Knowledge Map"?
(a) Summarizing data at a higher level
(b) Data warehousing
(c) Visualizing the organization's knowledge assets and connections
(d) Data integration

199. "Predictive Analytics" in data mining is primarily concerned with
(a) Analyzing historical data
(b) Making future predictions based on data patterns
(c) Storing and retrieving data
(d) Data integration

200. In the context of knowledge management, what does the term "Knowledge Transfer" refer to?
(a) The process of capturing and sharing knowledge within an organization
(b) Data integration and transformation
(c) Data warehousing
(d) Real-time data processing

201. What is the primary driver for technological change in organizations?
(a) Cost reduction
(b) Innovation and competitive advantage
(c) Employee satisfaction
(d) Regulatory compliance

202. Which stage in the technology adoption lifecycle typically represents the early enthusiasts who are willing to try and adopt new technologies?
(a) Laggards
(b) Early Majority
(c) Innovators
(d) Late Majority

203. Which of the following is a common resistance factor to technological change in organizations?
(a) Effective communication
(b) Supportive leadership
(c) Fear of job loss
(d) Employee empowerment

204. The "Kotter's Eight-Step Model for Leading Change" includes steps such as creating a sense of urgency, forming a powerful guiding coalition, and
(a) Implementing quick fixes
(b) Consolidating gains
(c) Maintaining the status quo
(d) Avoiding employee involvement

205. In the context of technological change, what does "pilot testing" involve?
(a) Launching a new technology without prior testing
(b) Testing a technology on a limited scale to assess its feasibility
(c) Conducting market research
(d) Terminating an ongoing project

206. The "Technology Acceptance Model (TAM)" focuses on understanding
(a) The cost of technology adoption
(b) Factors that influence user acceptance of technology
(c) The history of technology development
(d) Technological obsolescence

207. What is the primary objective of "Change Management" in the context of technological change?
(a) Avoiding any changes in the organization
(b) Ensuring a smooth transition and adoption of new technologies
(c) Retaining outdated technologies
(d) Isolating employees from the change process

208. Which of the following is a benefit of involving employees in the technological change process?
(a) Increased resistance to change
(b) Decreased job satisfaction
(c) Enhanced ownership and commitment to the change
(d) Faster adoption without employee involvement

209. What is the term for the stage in the technology adoption lifecycle where a significant portion of the target population has adopted the new technology, and it becomes more widely accepted?
(a) Innovators
(b) Early Majority
(c) Late Majority
(d) Laggards

210. In the context of technological change, what is a "Change Champion"?
(a) Someone who resists change and encourages others to do the same
(b) A technology consultant
(c) An individual who actively promotes and supports the change within the organization
(d) A technology vendor

211. Which of the following is a key element in "Lewin's Three-Step Model" for managing change?
(a) Maintaining the status quo
(b) Refreezing to stabilize the change
(c) Ignoring employee concerns
(d) Implementing change abruptly

212. In technology adoption, what does "relative advantage" refer to?
(a) The cost of the technology
(b) The degree to which a new technology is perceived as better than the one it replaces
(c) Employee resistance
(d) The availability of technical support

213. Which type of organizational change is characterized by incremental improvements to existing technologies and processes?
(a) Radical change
(b) Disruptive change
(c) Continuous improvement
(d) Status quo

214. In the context of technological change, what is "Change Readiness"?
(a) The willingness to avoid any change in the organization
(b) The degree of employee resistance
(c) The state of preparedness and willingness to adopt new technologies
(d) The rate of technology obsolescence

215. The "ADKAR Model" for change management focuses on which elements?
(a) Awareness, Design, Knowledge, Action, Resistance
(b) Analysis, Deployment, Key Stakeholders, Advancement, Results
(c) Awareness, Desire, Knowledge, Ability, Reinforcement
(d) Adoption, Documentation, Key Performance Indicators, Analysis, Review

216. What is the primary goal of a "Change Impact Assessment" in managing technological change?
(a) To prevent any change in the organization
(b) To assess the financial implications of the change
(c) To understand how the change will affect the organization and its employees
(d) To eliminate employee resistance

217. Which type of change management strategy involves making incremental improvements to existing technologies and processes?
(a) Adaptive change
(b) Radical change
(c) Continuous improvement
(d) Avoidance

218. What is the primary purpose of a "Change Control Board" in managing technological change?
(a) To promote employee resistance to change
(b) To oversee the implementation of technology projects
(c) To avoid all technological changes
(d) To review and approve proposed changes and their impact on the organization

219. In technology adoption, what is the "Chasm"?
(a) A physical barrier to technology adoption
(b) The gap between early adopters and the early majority
(c) A term for employee resistance
(d) A technology assessment tool

220. What is the primary focus of a "Change Vision" in the context of managing technological change?
(a) Promoting employee resistance
(b) Outlining the desired future state and benefits of the change
(c) Avoiding change
(d) Eliminating employee involvement

221. Which of the following is a key factor in technology adoption and change management?
(a) Avoiding communication with employees
(b) Employee involvement and communication
(c) Employee isolation
(d) Rapid implementation without planning

222. In the context of technological change, what does the term "Change Agent" refer to?
(a) A technology vendor
(b) Someone who promotes employee resistance to change
(c) An individual or group responsible for guiding and facilitating the change process
(d) An external consultant

223. Which of the following is a common approach to managing resistance to change?
(a) Isolating employees from the change process
(b) Ignoring employee concerns
(c) Addressing employee concerns through open communication and involvement
(d) Promoting employee resistance

224. "Technology Obsolescence" refers to
(a) The tendency of employees to resist technology
(b) The need for continuous employee training
(c) The process of technology becoming outdated and no longer useful
(d) Rapid technology implementation

225. Which technology adoption curve stage is characterized by a slow and cautious approach to adopting new technologies?
(a) Early Majority (b) Late Majority
(c) Laggards (d) Innovators

226. Which term refers to the process of gathering and storing data from various sources for analytical processing?
(a) Data Warehousing
(b) Data Mining
(c) Knowledge Management
(d) Technological Change

227. What is the primary objective of data mining?
(a) To store and manage large volumes of data
(b) To extract meaningful patterns and insights from data
(c) To facilitate collaboration and knowledge sharing
(d) To manage technological changes in data systems

228. Which concept focuses on the effective utilization of organizational knowledge to achieve strategic objectives?
(a) Data Warehousing
(b) Data Mining
(c) Knowledge Management
(d) Technological Change

229. What does data warehousing primarily involve?
(a) Storing and managing data in a structured manner
(b) Analyzing data to extract patterns and trends
(c) Implementing technological changes in data systems
(d) Facilitating knowledge sharing among employees

230. Which process involves transforming raw data into a structured format suitable for analysis and reporting?
(a) Data Warehousing
(b) Data Mining
(c) Knowledge Management
(d) Technological Change

231. What is the main goal of knowledge management?
(a) To develop advanced data storage techniques
(b) To promote effective decision-making through data analysis
(c) To enhance organizational learning and innovation
(d) To implement technological changes in information systems

232. Which concept focuses on discovering hidden patterns and relationships within large datasets?
(a) Data Warehousing
(b) Data Mining
(c) Knowledge Management
(d) Technological Change

233. Which aspect of managing technological change involves upgrading hardware and software systems?
(a) Data Warehousing
(b) Data Mining
(c) Knowledge Management
(d) Technological Change

234. What is the primary role of data warehousing in organizations?
(a) To promote collaboration among employees
(b) To facilitate data analysis and decision-making
(c) To manage organizational knowledge assets
(d) To implement technological changes in data systems

235. Which process involves capturing, storing, and sharing organizational knowledge for future use?
(a) Data Warehousing
(b) Data Mining
(c) Knowledge Management
(d) Technological Change

236. What does data mining primarily focus on?
(a) Managing data storage systems
(b) Extracting knowledge from data
(c) Facilitating communication within organizations
(d) Implementing technological changes

237. Which concept involves identifying, acquiring, and using internal and external resources to achieve organizational goals?
(a) Data Warehousing
(b) Data Mining
(c) Knowledge Management
(d) Technological Change

238. What is the main purpose of data warehousing?
(a) To automate business processes

(b) To store and manage large volumes of data
(c) To facilitate employee training
(d) To implement technological changes

239. Which process involves preserving organizational knowledge and expertise?
(a) Data Warehousing
(b) Data Mining
(c) Knowledge Management
(d) Technological Change

240. What is the primary function of data mining in organizations?
(a) Storing and organizing data
(b) Sharing information with stakeholders
(c) Discovering hidden patterns in data
(d) Implementing technological changes

241. Which aspect of technological change management involves assessing the impact of new technologies on business processes?
(a) Data Warehousing
(b) Data Mining
(c) Knowledge Management
(d) Technological Change

242. Which concept involves the design and implementation of systems for storing and managing structured data?
(a) Data Warehousing
(b) Data Mining
(c) Knowledge Management
(d) Technological Change

243. What is the primary goal of data warehousing?
(a) To facilitate real-time data analysis
(b) To improve data security
(c) To provide a single source of truth for organizational data
(d) To implement technological changes

244. Which process involves transforming data into actionable insights for decision-making?
(a) Data Warehousing
(b) Data Mining
(c) Knowledge Management
(d) Technological Change

245. Which aspect of managing technological change involves training employees to use new systems effectively?
(a) Data Warehousing
(b) Data Mining
(c) Knowledge Management
(d) Technological Change

ANSWER KEY

1. (d)	**2.** (d)	**3.** (b)	**4.** (c)	**5.** (d)	**6.** (a)	**7.** (d)	**8.** (c)	**9.** (a)	**10.** (a)
11. (a)	**12.** (c)	**13.** (b)	**14.** (b)	**15.** (c)	**16.** (c)	**17.** (b)	**18.** (b)	**19.** (b)	**20.** (b)
21. (c)	**22.** (a)	**23.** (c)	**24.** (b)	**25.** (c)	**26.** (c)	**27.** (b)	**28.** (c)	**29.** (a)	**30.** (d)
31. (b)	**32.** (b)	**33.** (b)	**34.** (c)	**35.** (b)	**36.** (c)	**37.** (c)	**38.** (a)	**39.** (b)	**40.** (c)
41. (c)	**42.** (c)	**43.** (d)	**44.** (c)	**45.** (c)	**46.** (b)	**47.** (b)	**48.** (b)	**49.** (a)	**50.** (c)
51. (b)	**52.** (c)	**53.** (b)	**54.** (c)	**55.** (c)	**56.** (c)	**57.** (c)	**58.** (b)	**59.** (b)	**60.** (c)
61. (b)	**62.** (d)	**63.** (c)	**64.** (c)	**65.** (b)	**66.** (b)	**67.** (c)	**68.** (c)	**69.** (b)	**70.** (a)
71. (a)	**72.** (c)	**73.** (a)	**74.** (b)	**75.** (b)	**76.** (a)	**77.** (d)	**78.** (a)	**79.** (d)	**80.** (c)
81. (a)	**82.** (d)	**83.** (a)	**84.** (c)	**85.** (c)	**86.** (a)	**87.** (c)	**88.** (c)	**89.** (d)	**90.** (a)
91. (c)	**92.** (a)	**93.** (b)	**94.** (c)	**95.** (a)	**96.** (d)	**97.** (c)	**98.** (a)	**99.** (d)	**100.** (b)
101. (c)	**102.** (d)	**103.** (b)	**104.** (c)	**105.** (b)	**106.** (c)	**107.** (c)	**108.** (c)	**109.** (b)	**110.** (c)
111. (c)	**112.** (c)	**113.** (c)	**114.** (d)	**115.** (b)	**116.** (c)	**117.** (d)	**118.** (b)	**119.** (c)	**120.** (d)
121. (b)	**122.** (c)	**123.** (b)	**124.** (c)	**125.** (b)	**126.** (b)	**127.** (c)	**128.** (d)	**129.** (c)	**130.** (c)
131. (b)	**132.** (b)	**133.** (b)	**134.** (c)	**135.** (c)	**136.** (c)	**137.** (c)	**138.** (c)	**139.** (c)	**140.** (c)
141. (d)	**142.** (c)	**143.** (b)	**144.** (c)	**145.** (d)	**146.** (b)	**147.** (c)	**148.** (b)	**149.** (b)	**150.** (c)
151. (a)	**152.** (c)	**153.** (b)	**154.** (c)	**155.** (b)	**156.** (b)	**157.** (a)	**158.** (a)	**159.** (b)	**160.** (b)
161. (b)	**162.** (c)	**163.** (c)	**164.** (d)	**165.** (b)	**166.** (d)	**167.** (b)	**168.** (c)	**169.** (b)	**170.** (b)
171. (c)	**172.** (c)	**173.** (c)	**174.** (c)	**175.** (b)	**176.** (b)	**177.** (b)	**178.** (c)	**179.** (c)	**180.** (b)
181. (b)	**182.** (b)	**183.** (b)	**184.** (a)	**185.** (b)	**186.** (c)	**187.** (b)	**188.** (b)	**189.** (d)	**190.** (b)
191. (a)	**192.** (d)	**193.** (b)	**194.** (b)	**195.** (c)	**196.** (c)	**197.** (c)	**198.** (c)	**199.** (b)	**200.** (a)
201. (b)	**202.** (c)	**203.** (c)	**204.** (b)	**205.** (b)	**206.** (b)	**207.** (b)	**208.** (c)	**209.** (c)	**210.** (c)
211. (b)	**212.** (b)	**213.** (c)	**214.** (c)	**215.** (c)	**216.** (c)	**217.** (a)	**218.** (d)	**219.** (b)	**220.** (b)
221. (b)	**222.** (c)	**223.** (c)	**224.** (c)	**225.** (c)	**226.** (a)	**227.** (b)	**228.** (c)	**229.** (a)	**230.** (a)
231. (c)	**232.** (b)	**233.** (d)	**234.** (b)	**235.** (c)	**236.** (b)	**237.** (c)	**238.** (b)	**239.** (c)	**240.** (c)
241. (d)	**242.** (a)	**243.** (c)	**244.** (b)	**245.** (d)					

UNIT 10

SYLLABUS

- Entrepreneurship Development – Concept, Types, Theories and Process, Developing Entrepreneurial Competencies
- Intrapreneurship – Concept and Process
- Women Entrepreneurship and Rural Entrepreneurship
- Innovations in Business – Types of Innovations, Creating and Identifying Opportunities, Screening of Business Ideas
- Business Plan and Feasibility Analysis – Concept and Process of Technical, Market and Financial Analysis
- Micro and Small Scale Industries in India; Role of Government in Promoting SSI
- Sickness in Small Industries – Reasons and Rehabilitation
- Institutional Finance to Small Industries – Financial Institutions, Commercial Banks, Cooperative Banks, Micro Finance.

Entrepreneurship

Doing new things or doing things that are already being done, is a simple definition of entrepreneurship. It can be described as a creative and innovative response to the environment. Such responses can take place in any field of social endeavour - business, agriculture, education, social work and the like. Knowledge about the economic-political environment, more particularly about the economic policies of the government and the financial as well as commercial institutions, is important for the entrepreneur.

An entrepreneur is one who organises, manages and assumes the risk of an enterprise. An entrepreneur visualizes a business, takes bold steps to establish undertaking, coordinates the various factors of production and gives it a start. They are the owners of the business who contribute the capital and bear the risk of uncertainties in business life. Entrepreneur is action - oriented and highly motivated. He has the ability to evaluate business opportunities, to gather the necessary resources to take advantage of them and to initiate appropriate action to ensure success.

He is associated with innovations. He is the main factor of production. He takes decision regarding what to produce, how to produce, where to produce and for whom to produce. He mobilizes other factors of production namely, land, labour, capital, organisation and initiates production process. He is responsible for both the profit or the loss.

ENTREPRENEURIAL DEVELOPMENT

The main objective of the entrepreneurial development schemes is to motivate and assist prospective and potential entrepreneurs to set up small scale units of their own and thereby become self - employed and continue to contribute significantly to production and employment in the country. Entrepreneurial development programmes increase entrepreneurial spirit and provide scope for self-development by focusing attention on the self and on self-directed motivational change.

With the new thrust for the development of Industries in backward areas and for promoting the weaker sections Small Industries Development Organisation (SIDO) diversified its entrepreneurship training programmes in the year 1978-79 to serve new categories of entrepreneurs like rural artisans, educated unemployed, weaker sections of the society, women entrepreneurs, students and physically handicapped persons and Defence personnel.

There can be entrepreneurial failure also.

Different factors are:

1. Poor Management
   (a) Incompetence
   (b) Unbalanced experience
   (c) Inexperience in management
   (d) Inexperience in line
2. Production Problems
   (a) Lack of production planning and control
   (b) Frequent machine breakdown
   (c) Poor raw material
   (d) Power cuts
   (e) Labour Problems
   (f) Lack of technical know how
   (g) Insufficient quality control
   (h) Wastage in material
   (i) High rate of rejection, etc.
3. High fixed cost
   (a) Heavy investment in land and building
   (b) Increased administrative and other overheads
   (c) Market borrowing at high interest rate
4. Marketing problems
   (a) Competition from larger and already established units
   (b) Insufficient sales force
   (c) Low quality of finished goods
   (d) Recession, etc.
5. Financial Problems
   (a) Allowing long credits to the purchasers of finished goods
   (b) Diversion of short term funds into long term uses
   (c) Wilful diversions of funds for investments in assets not connected with production
6. Neglect of business
7. Fraud
8. Disaster

Through careful analysis of entrepreneurs' successes and failures, economists have identified key factors for up and coming business owners to consider closely. Taking them into account can reduce risk. In contrast, paying them no attention can precipitate in downfall of a new enterprise.

- **Motivation.** What is the incentive for starting a business? Is it money alone? True, many entrepreneurs achieve great wealth. However, money is almost always tight in the startup and early phases of a new business. Many entrepreneurs do not even take salary until they can do so and still leave the firm with a positive cash flow.

- **Strategy.** What is the strategy for distinguishing the product or service? Is the plan to compete solely on the basis of selling price? Price is important, but most economists agree that it is extremely risky to compete on price alone. Large firms that produce huge quantities have the advantage in lowering costs.
- **Realistic Vision.** Is there a realistic vision of the enterprises potential? Insufficient operating funds are the cause of many failed businesses. Entrepreneurs often underestimate start-up costs and overestimate sales revenues in their business plans. Some analysts advise adding 50 percent to final cost estimates and reducing sales projections. Only then can the entrepreneur examine cash flow projections and decide if he or she is ready to launch a new business.

Small Business – Concepts, Government Policy for Promotion of Small and Tiny Enterprises

The term 'small-scale industries' has been defined in three ways.

1. The conventional definition includes cottage and handicraft industries which employ traditional labour-intensive methods to produce traditional products, largely in village households. They employ none or almost a few hired hands. The handloom textile industry is an example. Though once famous, this sector has been steadily declining.
2. The operational definition for policy purposes includes all those undertakings having an investment in fixed assets in plant and machinery, whether held on ownership terms or by lease or by hire-purchase, not exceeding Rs. 60 lakh. A tiny unit is one whose investment in fixed assets in plant and machinery does not exceed Rs. five lakh. An ancillary undertaking is one whose investment in plant and machinery does not exceed Rs. 75 lakh and is engaged in
   (a) the manufacture of parts, components, sub-assemblies, toolings or intermediate; or
   (b) rendering of services or supplying 1/3 per cent of their total service or production, as the case maybe, to other units for production of other articles. The investment ceiling has been raised recently to Rs. 3 crore for SSI units and to Rs. 25 lakh for tiny units. (The government has decided to lower the ceiling from Rs. 3 crore to Rs. 1 crore).
3. The third definition of small-scale industries relates to national income accounting. This includes all manufacturing and processing activities, including maintenance and repair services, undertaken by both household and non-household small-scale manufacturing units, which are not registered under the Factories Act, 1948.

The strengths and weaknesses of these small businesses can be seen by the SWOT analysis.

Strengths : Flexibility in production volumes and design changes
: Faster decision making
: Lower labour costs
: Lower overheads.

Weaknesses : Often lack of management, marketing or financial skills
: Technological obsolescence
: Poor financing
: Lack of marketing strength.

Opportunities : Large companies are outsourcing more to reduce their own costs
: Promising export markets
: Higher investment limits mean companies can expand and modernise
: Big companies can take a larger equity stake in small ones.

Threats	:	With concessions disappearing, inefficient units will die
	:	With dereservation, competition will come from large companies
	:	With import liberalisation, competition will come from MNCs and cheap inputs
	:	Smaller, less aggressive companies will suffer.

The government announced its policy toward small and tiny enterprises. The primary objective of the policy was to impart more vitality and growth impetus to the sector to enable it to contribute its mite fully to the economy particularly in terms of growth of output, employment and exports.

The features of the policy are :

1. Tiny Enterprises

The Government has already announced an increase in the investment limits in plant and machinery of small-scale industries, ancillary units and export-oriented units to Rs. 60 lakh and 75 lakh respectively. Such limits in respect of 'tiny' enterprises would now be increased from the present Rs. 2 lakh to Rs. 5 lakh, irrespective of locations of the unit.

Service sub-sector is a fast growing area and there is need to provide support to it in view of its recognised potential for generating employment. Hence, all industry related service and business enterprises, irrespective of their location, would be recognised as small-scale industries and their investment ceilings would correspond to those of any enterprises.

It has also been decided to widen the scope of the National Equity Fund Scheme to cover projects upto Rs. 10 lakh for equity support (upto 15 per cent). Single Window Loan Scheme has been enlarged to cover projects upto Rs. 20 lakh with working capital margin upto Rs. 10 lakh. Composite loans under Single Window Scheme, now available only through State Financial Corporation (SFCs) and State Small Industries Development Corporation (SSIDCs) would also be chanelised through commercial banks. This would facilitate access to a larger number of entrepreneurs.

2. Financial Support Measures

Inadequate access to credit-both short term and long term, remains a perennial problem facing the small-scale sector. Emphasis would henceforth shift from subsidised/cheap credit, except for specified target groups, and efforts would be made to ensure both adequate flow of credit on a normative basis and the quality of its delivery for viable operations of this sector.

To provide access to the capital market and to encourage modernisation and technological upgradation it has been decided to allow equity participation by other industrial undertakings in the SSI, not exceeding 24 per cent of the total shareholding. This would also provide a powerful boost to ancillarisation and sub-contracting, leading to the expansion of employment opportunities.

A beginning has been made towards solving the problem of delayed payments to small industries by setting up of 'factoring' services through Small Industries Development Bank of India (SIDBI). Network of such services would be set up throughout the country and operated through commercial banks. A suitable legislation will be introduced to ensure prompt payment of small industries bills.

3. Infrastructural Facilities

Adequacy and equitable distribution of indigenous and imported raw materials would be ensured to the small-scale sector, particularly the tiny sub-sector.

A Technology Development Cell (TDC) would be set up in the Small Industries Development Organisation (SIDO) which would provide technology inputs to improve productivity and competitiveness of the products of the small-scale sector. The TDC would coordinate the activities of the Tool Rooms, Process-cum-Product Development Centres (PPDs), existing as well as to be established under SIDO, and would also interact with the other industrial research and development organisations to achieve its objectives.

4. Marketing and Exports

Though the SSI sector is making significant contribution to total exports, both direct and indirect, a large potential remains untapped. The SIDO has been recognised as the nodal agency to support the small scale industries in export promotion.

National Small Industries Corporation (NSIC) would concentrate on the marketing of mass consumption items under a common brand name and organic links between NSIC and SSIDs would be established.

5. Handicraft Sector

Scheme for training and design development and for production and marketing assistance will be given encouragement. The key areas in handicrafts that could contribute towards a faster pace of rural industrialization are production and marketing.

6. Other Village Industries

The activities of the Khadi and Village Industries Commission and the State Khadi and Village Industries Boards will be expanded and the organisations strengthened to discharge their responsibilities more effectively.

The programmes of intensive development of KVI through area approach with tie-up with DRDA, TRYSEM and ongoing development programmes relating to weaker sections like Scheduled Castes, Scheduled Tribes and women would be extended throughout the country.

7. Promotion of Entrepreneurship

The Government will continue to support the first generation entrepreneurs through training and will support their efforts. Large number of EDP trainers and motivators will be trained to significantly expand the Entrepreneurship Development Programmes (EDP). Women entrepreneurs will receive support through special training programmes.

8. Modernisation, Technology and Quality Upgradation

Industry associations would be encouraged and supported to establish quality counselling and common testing facilities. Technology and markets would be established.

A reoriented programme of modernisation and technological upgradation aimed at improving productivity, efficiency and cost effectiveness in the small-scale sector would be pursued.

Indian Institutes of Technology (IITs) and selected regional/other engineering colleges will serve as technological information, design and development centres in their respective command areas.

In the Indian context, micro, small and medium enterprises as per the Micro, Small and Medium Enterprises (MSME) Development Act, 2006 are defined based on their investment in plant and machinery (for manufacturing enterprise) and on equipments for enterprises providing or rendering services. According to the Micro, Small and Medium Enterprises (MSME) Development Act of 2006, (India) a micro enterprise is where the investment in plant and machinery does not exceed twenty five lakh rupees. A medium enterprise is where the investment in plant and machinery is more than five crore rupees but does not exceed ten crore rupees. A small enterprise is where the investment in plant and machinery is more than twenty five lakh rupees but does not exceed five crore rupees. In the case of the enterprises engaged in providing or rendering of services, as

(a) a micro enterprise is where the investment in equipment does not exceed ten lakh rupees.

(b) a small enterprise is where the investment in equipment is more than ten lakh rupees but does not exceed two crore rupees.

(c) a medium enterprise is where the investment in equipment is more than two crore rupees but does not exceed five crore rupees.

According to the Ministry of Micro, Small and Medium Enterprises, recent ceilings on investment for enterprises to be classified as micro, small and medium enterprises are as follows:

Classification	Manufacturing Enterprises*	Service Enterprises**
Micro	Rs. 2.5 million/ Rs. 25 lakh (US$ 50,000)	Rs. 1 million/ Rs. 10 lakh (US$ 20,000)
Small	Rs. 50 million/ Rs. 5 crore (US$ 1 million)	Rs. 20 million/ Rs. 2 crore (US$ 40,00,000)
Medium	Rs. 100 million/ Rs. 10 crore (US$ 2 million)	Rs. 50 million/ Rs. 5 crore (US$ 1 million)

* Investment limit in Plant & Machinery

** Investment limit in equipments

*** Rs 50 = 1 USD

It is important to mention some of the organisations that are associated with small-scale industry/ MSMEs:

Small Industries Development Organisation (SIDO), Small Scale Industries Board (SSIB), National Small Industries Corporation Ltd. (NSIC), Confederation of Indian Industry (CII), Federation of Indian Chamber of Commerce and Industry (FICCI), PHD Chamber of Commerce and Industry (PHDCCI), Associated Chamber of Commerce and Industry of India (ASSOCHAM), Federation of Indian Exporters Organisation (FIEO), World Association for Small and Medium Enterprises (WASME), Federation of Associations of Small Industries of India (FASII), Consortium of Women Entrepreneurs of India (CWEI), Laghu Udyog Bharti (LUB), Indian Council of Small Industries (ICSI), Indian Institute of Entrepreneurship (IIE), National Institute of Small-Industry Extension Training (NISIET), National Backward Caste Finance Development Corporation, National Institute for Entrepreneurship and Small Business Development (NIESBUD), Small Entrepreneurs Promotion and Training Institute (SEPTI), Small Industries Development Bank of India (SIDBI) etc.

Factors affecting MSMEs

Some of the key constraints that are being faced by the Indian MSMEs are:

(a) Accessing adequate and timely financing on competitive terms, particularly longer tenure loans.

(b) Accessing credit on easy terms has become difficult in the backdrop of current global financial crisis and the resultant liquidity constraints in the Indian financial sector, which has held back the growth of SMEs and impeded overall growth and development.

(c) The financing constraints faced by Indian SMEs are attributable to a combination of factors that include policy, legal/regulatory framework (in terms of recovery, bankruptcy and contract enforcement), institutional weaknesses (absence of good credit appraisal and risk management/ monitoring tools), and lack of reliable credit information on SMEs.

(d) It has become difficult for lenders to be able to assess risk premiums properly, creating differences in the perceived versus real risk profiles of SMEs.

(e) Access to skilled manpower, R&D facilities and marketing channels is limited.

(f) Availability of finance at cheaper rates, skills about decision-making and good management and accounting practices, and access to modern technology.

PROCESS OF BUSINESS OPPORTUNITY IDENTIFICATION (INTRAPRENEURSHIP)

Entrepreneurship is different from management. Paul H. Wilken explains that entrepreneurship involves *initiating changes* in production, whereas management involves the ongoing coordination of the production process. He states, "entrepreneurship is a discontinuous phenomenon, appearing to initiate changes in the production process ... and then disappearing unit it reappears until it reappears to initiate another change."

Entrepreneurship is, above all, about change. "Entrepreneurs see change as the norm and as healthy. Usually, they do not bring about the change themselves (that is, they are usually not inventors). But – and this defines entrepreneur and entrepreneurship – *the entrepreneur always searches for change, responds to it, and exploits it as an opportunity.*" These words were written by Peter Drucker, a well-known contemporary management writer, but they might just as easily have come from the pen of Schumpeter, the economist quoted earlier, who popularized the term "entrepreneurship." For Schumpeter, indeed, the whole process of economic change depended on the person who makes it happen – the entrepreneur.

The function that is specific to entrepreneurs is the ability to take the factors of production – land, labour, and capital – and use them to produce *new* goods or services. The entrepreneur perceives opportunities that other business executives do not see or do not care about.

Some entrepreneurs use information that is generally available to produce something new. Henry Ford, for example, invented neither the automobile nor the division of labour, but he applied the division of labour to the production of automobiles in a new way – the assembly line. Other entrepreneurs see new business opportunities. Akio Morita, the president of Sony, the Japanese consumer electronics giant, saw that his company's existing products could be adapted to create a new one – the Walkman personal stereo. "Basically, the entrepreneur sees a need and then brings together the manpower, materials, and capital required to meet that need." Grinding coffee beans and selling brewed coffee are not new. What is new is the quality and ambience that Starbucks gives to these activities. Essentially an entrepreneur creates an organisation as a way of offering something new to customers, employees, or other stakeholders.

The greeting card industry offers an example of how entrepreneurs can find a niche by offering something different. In the $5.3 billion retail card market, the biggest three companies – Hallmark Cards, American Greeting, and Gibson Greeting – have 85 percent of the sales. However, more than a thousand smaller publishers are trying to outdo each other with creativity and innovation for the remaining 15 percent. Responding to complains of the sometimes boring nature of traditional cards, some start-ups target particular niches in the market. One such greeting card companies. The founder, Mark Norris, started his company in response to frustration with the quality and variety of greeting cards available to ethnic consumers. His cards are solid in card shops, museums, and up-scale retailers on four continents, and he has plans to expand the company's focus to include the general market. Cardthartic of Chicago is a company aimed at the gay and lesbian market. Its first line of cards addresses such occurrences as adoptions by same-sex couples of the loss of someone to AIDS. Its president, Jodee Stevens, launched the venture with $90,000 in personal funds and posted first year revenues of less than $100,000. Stevens expects the company to break even in two three years.

WOMEN ENTREPRENEURSHIP

Women entrepreneurship has been recognised as an important source of economic growth. Women entrepreneurs create new jobs for themselves and others and also provide society with different solutions to management, organisation and business problems. However, they still represent a minority of all entrepreneurs. Women entrepreneurs often face gender-based barriers to starting and growing their businesses, like discriminatory property, matrimonial and inheritance laws and/or cultural practices; lack of access to formal finance mechanisms; limited mobility and access to information and networks, etc.

Women's entrepreneurship can make a particularly strong contribution to the economic well-being of the family and communities, poverty reduction and women's empowerment, thus contributing to the Millennium Development Goals (MDGs). Thus, governments across the world as well as various developmental organisations are actively undertaking promotion of women entrepreneurs through various schemes, incentives and promotional measures.

Women entrepreneurs in the four southern states and Maharashtra account for over 50% of all women-led small-scale industrial units in India

Policies and Schemes for Women Entrepreneurs in India

In India, the Micro, Small & Medium Enterprises development organisations, various State Small Industries Development Corporations, the Nationalised banks and even NGOs are conducting various programmes including Entrepreneurship Development Programmes (EDPs) to cater to the needs of potential women entrepreneurs, who may not have adequate educational background and skills. The Office of DC (MSME) has also opened a Women Cell to provide coordination and assistance to women entrepreneurs facing specific problems.

There are also several other schemes of the government at central and state level, which provide assistance for setting up training-cum-income generating activities for needy women to make them economically independent. Small Industries Development Bank of India (SIDBI) has also been implementing special schemes for women entrepreneurs.

In addition to the special schemes for women entrepreneurs, various government schemes for MSMEs also provide certain special incentives and concessions for women entrepreneurs. For instance, under **Prime Minister's Rozgar Yojana (PMRY)**, preference is given to women beneficiaries. The government has also made several relaxations for women to facilitate the participation of women beneficiaries in this scheme. Similarly, under the **MSE Cluster Development Programme** by Ministry of MSME, the contribution from the Ministry of MSME varies between 30-80% of the total project in case of hard intervention, but in the case of clusters owned and managed by women entrepreneurs, contribution of the M/o MSME could be upto 90% of the project cost. Similarly, under the **Credit Guarantee Fund Scheme for Micro and Small Enterprises**, the guarantee cover is generally available upto 75% of the loans extended; however the extent of guarantee cover is 80% for MSEs operated and/or owned by women.

RURAL ENTREPRENEURSHIP

India is a country of villages. About three-fourth of India's population are living in rural areas out of which 75% of the labour force is still earning its livelihood from agriculture and its allied activities. Land being limited is unable to absorb the labour force in agriculture. Therefore, there is a need to develop rural industries to solve rural unemployment and rural migration to cities. Growth and development of rural economy is an essential pre-condition to development of the nation as a whole. The gap between rural urban disparities should be lessened.

The standard of living of the rural people should be increased. Entrepreneurship in rural sector provides an answer to the above problems. Indian rural sector is no longer primitive and isolated. Therefore, entrepreneurship in the rural and tribal areas looms large to solve the problems of poverty, unemployment and backwardness of Indian economy. Rural industrialisation is viewed as an effective means of accelerating the process of rural development. Government of India has been continuously assigning increasing importance and support for the promotion and growth of rural entrepreneurship.

Meaning

Rural entrepreneurs are those who carry out entrepreneurial activities by establishing industrial and business units in the rural sector of the economy. In other words, establishing industrial and business units in the rural areas refers to rural entrepreneurship. In simple words, rural entrepreneurship implies entrepreneurship emerging in rural areas. Or, say, rural entrepreneurship implies rural industrialisation. Thus, we can say, entrepreneurship precedes industrialization.

Definition

Rural industries and business organisations in rural areas generally associated with agriculture and allied activities to agriculture. According to KVIC (Khadi and Village Industry Commission), "village industries or Rural industry means any industry located in rural areas, population of which does not exceed 10,000 or such other figure which produces any goods or renders any services with or without use of power and in which the fixed capital investment per head of an artisan or a worker does not exceed a thousand rupees".

The modified definition of rural industries has been given by Government of India in order to enlarge its scope. According to Government of India, "Any industry located in rural area, village or town with a population of 20,000 and below and an investment of Rs. 3 crores in plant and machinery is classified as a village industry."

Types of Rural Industries

All the village industries come under the following broad categories :

Agro Based Industries like sugar industries, jaggery, oil processing from oil seeds, pickles, fruit juice, spices, diary products etc.

Forest Based Industries like wood products, bamboo products, honey, coir industry, making eating plates from leaves.

Mineral based industry like stone crushing, cement industries, red oxide making, wall coating powders etc.

Textile Industry like spinning, weaving, colouring, bleaching.

Engineering and Services like agriculture equipments, tractors and pumpsets repairs etc.

INNOVATIONS IN BUSINESS

Everyone can innovate. Innovation means coming up with new ways of doing things. Bringing innovation into your business can help you save time and money, and give you the competitive advantage to grow and adapt your business in the marketplace.

Innovation generally refers to changing processes or creating more effective processes, products and ideas.

For businesses, this could mean implementing new ideas, creating dynamic products or improving your existing services. Innovation can be a catalyst for the growth and success of your business, and help you to adapt and grow in the marketplace.

Being innovative does not only mean inventing. Innovation can mean changing your business model and adapting to changes in your environment to deliver better products or services. Successful innovation should be an in-built part of your business strategy, where you create a culture of innovation and lead the way in innovative thinking and creative problem solving.

Innovation can increase the likelihood of your business succeeding. Businesses that innovate create more efficient work processes and have better productivity and performance.

Key steps towards Business Innovation

Find areas and ways to innovate in your business through research and planning:

1. Conduct an analysis of the trends in the market environment, your customers' wants and needs and your competitors.
2. Consult with customers and employees for ideas on improving processes, products and services both internally and externally. Find out more about connecting with customers for ideas.
3. Seek advice. Use available resources such as business advisors, grants and assistance to drive innovation in your business. This may include seeking Intellectual Property (IP) protection to commercialise your ideas. Learn more about local collaboration and international collaboration with researchers.
4. Be open to new ideas and adaptive to change.
5. Develop a strategic, responsive plan, which promotes innovation as a key business process across the entire business. Learn about creating an innovative business culture and developing a strategy for innovation.
6. Train and empower your employees to think innovatively from the top down.

BUSINESS PLAN AND FEASIBILITY ANALYSIS

Entrepreneurs face many challenges when creating a new venture. Although the business plan is one of the most well-known documents, the feasibility study may be just as important. Before the entrepreneur can seek funding, he or she must demonstrate that the idea is truly a good one.

Rochester.edu explained that a feasibility study, "can be defined as a controlled process for identifying problems and opportunities, determining objectives, describing situations, defining successful outcomes, and assessing the range of costs and benefits associated with several alternatives for solving a problem."

In order to create a feasibility study, entrepreneurs need to define dimensions of business viability including: market viability, technical viability, business model viability, management model viability, economic and financial model viability, and exit strategy viability.

A good outline for a feasibility study includes:

- Introduction
- Product or Service
- Technology
- Market Environment
- Competition
- Industry
- Business Model
- Market and Sales Strategy
- Production Operations Requirements
- Management and Personnel Requirements

- Regulations and Environmental Issues
- Critical Risk Factors
- Financial Predictions Including: Balance Sheet, Income Statement, Cash Flow Statement, Break Even Analysis, and Capital Requirements.

A feasibility study is not the same thing as a business plan. The feasibility study would be completed prior to the business plan. The feasibility study helps determine whether an idea or business is a viable option. The business plan is developed after the business opportunity is created. StrategicBusinessTeam.com explained, "A feasibility study is carried out with the aim of finding out the workability and profitability of a business venture. Before anything is invested in a new business venture, a feasibility study is carried out to know if the business venture is worth the time, effort and resources. A feasibility study is filled with calculations, analysis and estimated projections while a business plan is made up of mostly tactics and strategies to be implemented in other to grow the business."

While it may seem the feasibility study is similar in many ways to the business plan, it is important to keep in mind that the feasibility study is developed prior to the venture. StrategicBusinessStream pointed out that "a feasibility study can readily be converted to a business plan." It's important to think of the business plan in terms of growth and sustainability and the feasibility study in terms of idea viability.

SICKNESS IN SMALL ENTERPRISES

According to the SICA, a sick industrial company means an industrial company (being a company registered for not less than five years) which has at the end of any financial year accumulated losses equal to or exceeding its entire networth.

Sickness can be any. It can be actual or potential sickness.

Actual Sickness

(i) Erosion of net worth by 50 per cent or more.
(ii) Units being closed for a total period of six months and more during the last year, and
(iii) Default in payment of loan instalment.

Incipient Sickness or Potential Sickness

Capacity utilisation is less than 50 per cent of the highest achieved during the preceding five years.

According to State Financial Corporation (SFCs), any unit which fails to pay three consecutive installments (half-yearly) of interest and / or principal is sick.

In the small-scale sector, a unit is treated as sick (according to the RBI), if it has

(a) incurred cash loss in the previous accounting year, is likely to continue to incur cash loss in the current accounting year and has an erosion in its networth to the extent of 50 percent or more and / or
(b) has defaulted on any interest payment for consecutive four quarters / installments of principal for consecutive two quarters, with persistent irregularity in the operation of its cash credit limit.

Causes for Sickness

Sickness can be caused by two factors :

Internal factors mainly relate to the poor quality of the top management. Poor quality of top management may take one of several forms: excessive conservatism, excessive complacency, growth-mania, poor financial control, excessive centralisation and authoritarianism, weak board and a weak watchdog function, excessive commitment to policies that worked well once but no longer appropriate, poor financial or marketing management and the like.

External causes can be further classified into:

- industry-specific factors;
- government-related factors;
- financial institutions-related factors.

The external causes have been explained as follows:

1. **Industry-Specific Factors.** These relate to stagnation or recession in the industry (*e.g.*, the textile industry), competition faced by the unit (*e.g.*, small units, rayon grade, pulp units) and excess capacity in the industry (*e.g.*, the type of industry).

   Entry of MNCs and strict quality and hygiene specifications prescribed and enforced by them have contributed to the sickness of several firms, particularly in the SSI sector.
2. **Government-Related Factors.** These include tax burden on the unit, especially import duties, excise duties and sales tax; legal restrictions on the units; expansion/ diversification (as with FERA and MRTP companies); frequent changes in government policies affecting the unit; liberal imports that compete with the unit's products; the government or its agencies going back on its promises made to the unit (such as promised price performance to the joint sector units); poor law and order situation (as in parts of North and Eastern India) political interference in the unit's affairs (as in the public sector units and agro-based industry); unhelpful government machinery (*e.g.*, in supplying power or in clearing a project) and the like.
3. **Financial Institutions - Related Factors.** These include harshness in dealing with the unit; delay in providing finance to the unit; inadequate working and/ or long-term capital provided by them and their inexpert assessment of the client's finance proposal.

Others. Other external factors include customer resistance to the unit's products; erratic availability of raw materials / components/ power / fuel to the unit (e.g., paper and sugar industries, aluminum units); inadequate transport facilities available to the unit (e.g., for transporting coal) and the like.

Rehabilitation of Sick Enterprises

In order to tackle the problem of sickness, there are three agencies.

1. **Role of the Government.** Government's efforts at creating infrastructural facilities, specialised industrial and financial institutions, package of incentives for entrepreneurs etc. have borne rich fruit. The government's vacillating policies, incompetence in managing the core sector, excessive protection to domestic units has helped a lot. Under the Sick Industrial Companies (Special Provisions) Act, 1985, the government has set up a Board for Industrial and Financial Reconstruction (BIFR) which will have to be notified by the management of companies of their potential sickness.

   A second area where the government can be helpful is vis-a-vis industrial licensing. The very existence of licensing and monopoly regulation legislation implies that there is a stampede to 'get in', whenever licensing is liberalised for an industry or the economy as a whole.
2. **Role of Financial Institutions.** The apex financial institutions like IDBI, IFCI, ICICI and nationalised commercial banks are in an extremely favourbale position to prevent industrial sickness. The following are the ways by which sickness can be prevented.

A. Continuous Monitoring of Unit

(i) Periodic financial reports.
(ii) Desk officer for client unit
(iii) Institutional nominee(s) on the board.
(iv) Periodic inspections.
(v) Institutional adviser deputed to the unit, especially to monitor project implementation in risky ventures.
(vi) Inter-institutional reviews of unit.
(vii) Market intelligence and industry cells.

B. Careful Project Appraisal

(i) Independent verification of sales, profits etc., projections of the client.
(ii) Careful scrutiny of technology and plant size, choices of location, government-related contingencies and quality of management.
(iii) Use of external consultants for appraising large or risky projects.

C. Professional Institutional Response to Unit's Problems

(i) Training of desk officers and reputed advisers in professional management.
(ii) Discretionary authority to monitoring desk officers to commit the institutions (up to some limits) to immediate contingency reliefs.
(iii) Better coordination and faster response by financial institutions through a smaller consortium.
(iv) Lead agency concept.

D. Required Systems at Client Units

(i) Approval of financial institutions for appointing (or removing) internal and statutory auditors, etc.
(ii) Professional Management training for promoters.

E. Incentives to Units to Remain Healthy

(i) Interest relief if there is no sickness.
(ii) Penal interest for avoidable project cost escalation, careless or false sales and profit projections.

3. **Role of Industry Associations.** The industry association could have some sort of a first aid cell. This could consist of professional who could go to the aid of a unit that is beginning to fall, with the offer of managerial and technical help. These professionals would be particularly useful since they would be conversant with the nature of the industry and with practices that have effectively worked in the industry.

The industry association can perform a professionalising function by conducting training programmes for managers, technocrats etc. The programmes could be quite useful since they would be tailored to suit the needs of the industry. Suitable industry association periodicals could also disseminate case studies of effective practices.

The industry associations would facilitate acquisitions of weaker units by stronger units and other contractual arrangements to help out ailing units, such as loan of managers from stronger units, sharing of marketing or production facilities, sharing of import of technology, a fair sharing of imported inputs, collaboration in mounting export campaigns etc.

A good practical review by each industry association of installed and usable capacity in the industry, capacity utilisation, growth trends, problems and opportunities etc., should be useful for the potential new entrants for deciding whether to enter the industry or not, and for existing firms for taking strategic diversification, expansion and project-mix decisions. This should also help the financial institutions to formulate industry-specific guidelines about funding project finance requests and the government to formulate industry-specific licensing guidelines.

There are few agencies being set up for the prevention of sickness. These are :

(i) **Industries Development and Regulation Act, 1951,** which provides for takeover of a sick unit by the Govt. of India. Before resorting to a takeover, other alternatives like rehabilitation through the concerned state government and financial institutions or for the merger of a sick unit with a healthy unit could be explored. This is necessary because too many sick units have been taken over by the government invoking the provisions of the Act converting the public sector into virtually a 'hospital bed for sick private units.'

(ii) **Sick Industrial Companies (Special provisions) Act, 1985.** The Act was passed by the Parliament and received the assent of the President in January 1986. It was amended in December 1991 so as to bring government companies within the purview of the Act. The Act provides for the setting up of a Board for Industrial and Financial Reconstruction (BIFR). With the establishment of the BIFR, with effect from January 12, 1987, medium and large-scale companies whose networth has been eroded by 50 per cent or more, will be obliged to report this fact to the Board. The Board has been given wide-ranging powers in respect of the approval of rehabilitation packages for sick industrial companies, including their reconstruction and revival as well as the change of managements or amalgamation with any other company or sale or lease of a part or whole of the industrial undertaking or even winding up of the company.

(iii) **Industrial Reconstruction Bank of India.** It came into being on March 20, 1985 by converting the erstwhile Industrial Reconstruction Corporation of India. The IRBI is a principal reconstruction agency which provides assistance for the reconstruction and rehabilitation of sick industrial units. In addition to granting of loans and advances to industrial concerns, underwriting of shares and debentures, guarantee of loans and deferred payments, IRBI's wide spectrum of activities also include such developmental activities as providing infrastructural facilities, raw materials, consultancy, managerial and merchant banking services, machinery and other equipment on lease or hire-purchase basis for the purpose of reconstruction and the development of industrial concerns.

(iv) **State Finance Corporations and Commercial Banks.** These banks will be asked to devise a scheme for the rehabilitation of sick units in the small-scale sector, and the assistance given by them for the revival of such units will be eligible for refinancing by the IRBI at a concessional rate of interest.

MICRO AND SMALL SCALE INDUSTRIES IN INDIA

For a country to grow, the government should actively promote business enterprises. Among business enterprises, the Micro, Small and Medium Enterprises (MSME) deserve special attention. Though MSMEs are small investment enterprises, but their contribution to the Indian economy is very significant.

What are MSMEs?

Micro, Small and Medium Enterprises Development (MSMED) Act, 2006 which was notified on October 2, 2006, deals with the definition of MSMEs. The MSMED Act, 2006 defines the Micro, Small and Medium Enterprises based on:

1. the investment in plant and machinery for those engaged in manufacturing or production, processing or preservation of goods.
2. the investment in equipment for enterprises engaged in providing or rendering of services.

What is the Importance and role of MSMEs in Indian Economy?

To Generate Large Scale Employment

In India, capital is scarce and labor abundant. MSMEs are thought to have lower capital-output and capital-labour ratios than large-scale industries, and therefore, better serve growth and employment objectives. The MSME sector in India has grown significantly since 1960 - with an average annual growth rate of 4.4% in the number of units and 4.62% in employment (currently employing 30 million). Not only do MSMEs generate the highest employment per capita investment, they also go a long way in checking rural-urban migration by providing people living in isolated areas with a sustainable source of employment.

Non-traditional products account for more than 95% of the MSME exports (dominating in the export of sports goods, readymade garments, plastic products etc.). Since these products are mostly handcrafted and hence eco-friendly, there exists a tremendous potential to expand the quantum of MSME led exports. Also, MSMEs act as ancillary industries for Large Scale Industries providing them with raw materials, vital components and backward linkages e.g. large scale cycle manufacturers of Ludhiana rely heavily on the MSMEs of Malerkotla which produce cycle parts.

Making Growth Inclusive

MSMEs are instruments of inclusive growth which touch upon the lives of the most vulnerable and marginalized. For many families, it is the only source of livelihood. Thus, instead of taking a welfare approach, this sector seeks to empower people to break the cycle of poverty and deprivation. It focuses on people's skills and agency. However, different segments of the MSME sector are dominated by different social groups.

The Twelfth Plan has listed the following as the objectives for the MSME sector:

- Promoting competitiveness and productivity in the MSME space.
- Making the MSME sector innovative, improving technology and depth.
- Enabling environment for promotion and development of MSMEs.
- Strong presence in exports.
- Improved managerial processes in MSMEs.

Policy Towards Small-Scale Industries

- Though MSMEs were recognised as important for employment generation and equitable distribution of income from the earliest days of Indian Independence, it appears that the objectives of policies stressing the role of MSMEs are not being realised.
- Since independence in 1947, especially since the late 1950s, development has been wide-ranging, both in terms of programs and regions. Policy measures included inter-alia fiscal concessions, subsidized and directed bank credit, and technical and marketing support, along with reservations of products for exclusive production by the MSME sector.

- These policy measures were in tune with the other policies such as the domestic investment and foreign trade policies that became more restrictive over the years.
- Since the mid-1980s there has been a gradual turnaround in policy, including reforms in the tax system and liberalization of import policy.
- The shift in MSME policy emphasis from protection to the promotion of competitiveness began with the introduction of an exclusive policy for MSME in 1991. Since then, the policy support in the 1990s and early 2000s has been large to enable the MSMEs to overcome key challenges to their performance and growth, namely, finance, technology, and marketing, among others.
- To operate these programs and to monitor their progress, new agencies and institutions have been set up, and the existing ones strengthened at the national, regional, state, and lower levels. There is also a special bank for MSMEs - SIDBI. The SSIs have their own associations and are also represented in the national and state level associations of large-scale industries.

Recent Initiatives

- As part of the National Manufacturing Competitiveness Programme (NMCP) - 10 specific initiatives were taken to enhance the competitiveness of the entire value chain of the MSME sector.
- Limited Liability Partnership (LLP) Act, 2008 was introduced to enable early corporatization of MSMEs and tap the capital market for fund raising. Accordingly, MSME platforms are created in BSE and NSE in 2012.
- To develop a roadmap for the development and promotion of MSMEs, a task force was created by the Prime Minister of India in 2009. The Task Force, which comprised, among others, six specific theme-based sub-groups (on credit, marketing, infrastructure, technology, skill development, exit policy, labor, and taxation) submitted its report in 2010 suggesting: (1) Immediate policy measures (2) Medium-term institutional measures (3) Legal and regulatory structures to create a conducive environment for entrepreneurship and growth of MSMEs.
- The Inter-Ministerial Committee for Accelerating Manufacturing in Micro, Small and Medium Enterprises made recommendations on: (a) the promotion of start-ups (b) facilitating operation and growth (covering credit, technology, and marketing) (c) closure and exit (d) labour laws and regulations.
- These policy initiatives are clear and consistent, aimed at transforming the ecosystem for the MSMEs sector by influencing: (1) Birth (encouraging Start-Ups) (2) Operations and growth (by simplifying laws and regulations, and facilitating their access to credit. Better technology and dynamic markets, apart from skilled labour and reliable infrastructure) (3) Orderly and easy exit.
- Thus, the emerging focus of India's MSME policy aims at covering the entire lifecycle of MSMEs to ensure a healthy, vibrant and competitive MSME sector.

INSTITUTIONAL FINANCE TO SMALL INDUSTRIES

The government at both central and state level established various financial institutions to provide non-financial and financial assistances to small-scale industries. As the small-scale industries are weak financial structure, they require non-financial assistances, so that, they could compete with large scale industries. The government established various institutions to provide non-financial assistances exclusively to the small-scale industries. In the same way there are institutions in addition to commercial banks which cater to the financial requirements of small scale industries. In this chapter an attempt has been made to present the various institutions involved in providing financial and non-financial assistances to small-scale industries.

Small industries continue to remain an important sector of the Indian economy. On seeing the contribution of this sector the government is extending various non-financial assistances to these industries. In the era of globalization small industries have to face the competition directly from the large industries. In this process some of the small units become unviable and sick. As the governments is always for strengthening small-scale industries it not only ensures regular supply of credit but also extends various non-financial assistances by establishing different specialized institutions.

The small industries development organisation (SIDO) functions as an apex body concerned with planning the policy and co-ordinating the institutional activities both at the central and state level for implementing programmes for the development of small-scale industries.

SIDO is the nodal agency for formulating, co-ordinating and monitoring the policies and programmes for promotion and development of small-scale industries in the country. It maintains close liaison with the central ministries, Planning Commission, State Governments, financial institutions, voluntary organisations and other agencies concerned with the development of small-scale industries. It provides comprehensive range of facilities and services including, consultancy in tecno-economic managerial aspects, training, common facility services, common processing and testing facilities, cooling facilities, and marketing assistance to small scale units. It provides these services through a network of small industrial services institute.

The SIDO provides a comprehensive range of common facilities, technology support services, marketing assistance, entrepreneurial development support, and the here, through its network of 30 Small Industries Service Institutes (SISIs), 28 branches of SISIs, four Regional Testing Centre's (RTCs), seven Field Testing Stations (FTSs), two Small Entrepreneur Promotion and Training Institution (SEPTIs) and one hand tool design development and training centre. The SIDO also has a network of tool rooms and process-cum product development centers (PPDCs) to provide technology and training support. These institutions are run as autonomous bodies, registered as societies under the Societies Act. Over the last 52 years, the SIDO has served a very useful purpose as a catalyst of growth of the micro, small and medium enterprises through its vast network of field organisations spread all over the country

Small Industries Service Institutes (SISIs) were set up to provide consultancy and training to small-scale enterprises-both existing and prospective. There are 30 SISIs and 28 branches of SISIs in the state capital and other places all over the country. The important functions performed by SISIs are interface between central and state governments, dissemination of economic information, technical support services, preparation of project profiles, holding of entrepreneurship development programmes, management and skill development programmes, providing advisory services on energy conservation, pollution control, quality control export promotion, market surveys, and the like.

The Small-Scale Industries (SSI) board was setup by central Government in 1954 to facilitate co-ordination and inter-institutional linkages and to render advice to the government on various policy matters concerning the development of SSI sector. The term of the SSI Board is for two years. Industry Associations provide support to the SSI sector and boards provide common platform to raise industry related issues.

The Small Enterprise Information and Research Centre Network (SENET), was launched in April 1997. SENET has been awarded the golden icon national award 2005 for "Best Documented Knowledge Resource" under professional category by the Department of Administrative Reforms and Public

Grievances (DARPG), Government of India. The scheme of SENET was modified and its scope enlarged to include office automation.

- To pioneer, create and promote web-based data base of all relevant information, data, and the like, for the benefit of small scale sector;
- To facilitate easier on–line access to information seekers, especially the small scale sector, by networking to the extent possible, all relevant data from central and state governments, government agencies engaged directly or indirectly in the promotion, development, etc, of the MSME sector, national and state level industry associations, NGOs, etc.

The entrepreneurship development and training is one of the key elements for the promotion of micro, small and medium enterprises (MSMEs), especially for creation of new enterprises by the first generation entrepreneurs. In order to inculcate the entrepreneurial culture amongst the first generation of entrepreneurs on a regular basis, the Ministry has set up three national entrepreneurship development Institutes namely, National Institute for Micro, Small and Medium Enterprises (NI-MSME) at Hyderabad, National Institute for Entrepreneurship and Small Business Development (NIESBUD) at Noida (Uttar Pradesh) and Indian Institute of Entrepreneurship (IIE) at Guwahati, as autonomous societies. These institutes are engaged in developing training modules; undertaking research and training; and providing consultancy services for entrepreneurship development and promotion of MSMEs, including enhancement of their competitiveness.

The NISIET, formerly known as Central Industrial Extension Training Institute (CIETI), was set up in 1960 at New Delhi as a department of central government under the Ministry of Commerce and Industry. Its main objective was to provide training to the personnel of the central small industries organisation as well as the departments of industries of the state government. Subsequently, in 1962, it was shifted to Hyderabad and converted into an autonomous society. In 1984, the institute was renamed as National Institute of Small Industry Extension Training (NISIET). NISIET's role has largely benefited the India a micro, small and medium enterprises (MSMEs) but also in other the different activities:

(i) he role of the Ministry of Micro, Small and Medium Enterprises is mainly to assist the States in their effort to promote growth and development of MSMEs and to address common concerns of enterprises.
(ii) The formulation and implementation of policies and programmes projects/schemes are undertaken by the Ministry with the assistance of its attached office, public sector enterprise, statutory bodies and autonomous organisations.
(iii) The aim of this Ministry is to provide prompt service to citizens through its attached office, public sector enterprises, statutory bodies and autonomous organisations, for accelerating the growth of MSMEs and also to enhance their competitiveness.
(iv) The Ministry seeks to fulfill its mission by formulating appropriate policies and designing/implementing support measures in the fields of credit, technological up gradation, marketing, entrepreneurship development and undertaking effective advocacy for these purposes.

Financial Support

For the successful starting, sustenance and development of any SSIs unit, several critical inputs are essential. The foremost is the environment in which the unit function (invigorating/stimulating depressing), the economic system and administrative culture access to essential raw materials, right technology, trained personal and training opportunities and existence of market. The most critical input, however, that has remained is, access to finance both for investment in fixed assets and for working capital. It is now accepted increasingly and universally that there is need for ensuring relatively easier access to credit, timely and adequate, need based at affordable rate of interest. Credit being the most important input in the development process, the need for effective delivery and management of the same is given high priority .

It is generally recognized that in developing countries and to some extent in industrialized countries. SSI has limited access to financial sources from banks and other financial institutions. Even today major financing of SSI is done from sources other than institutional mechanism. Financing from own sources and borrowings.

Reserve Bank of India

In a country's credit system, the central bank plays a very important role. This is especially so in developing countries, where the role of a central bank is not merely that of regulation of credit, but also one of establishment of an adequate institutional machinery for the provision of credit to the various sectors of the economy. The Reserve Bank of India also played an active role in the establishment of institutions which provide credit to agriculture and industry. In the field of credit for industry, the bank played a vital role in the establishment of the Industrial Finance Corporation of India in 1948, the State Financial Corporation in 1952 and the Industrial Development Bank of India in 1964. In all these institutions, the bank's contribution has been in the form of share capital, loans and management.

An important development which has assisted in the expansion of the flow of credit to small-scale industries was the institution of Credit Guarantee Scheme in July 1960, for loans advanced by banks and other credit institutions. While the risk was borne by the Central Government, the formulation of the scheme and its administration was responsibility of the Reserve Bank of India. The Reserve Bank of India monitors the advances to the priority sector (agriculture, small-scale industries and small road and water transport operators, retail trade and small business, education housing and export) and issues policy guidelines regarding this from time to time.

The Industrial Development Bank of India (IDBI)

The Industrial Development Bank of India limited, now more popularly known as IDBI Bank, was established as a wholly-owned subsidiary of Reserve Bank of India. The foundation of the bank was laid down under an Act of Parliament, in July 1964. The main aim behind the setting up of IDBI was to provide credit and other facilities for the Indian industry, which was still in the initial stages of growth and development. In February 1976, the ownership of IDBI was transferred to Government of India.

The IDBI became the main institution, through which the institutes engaged in financing, promoting and developing industry were to be coordinated. In January 1992, IDBI accessed domestic debt market for the first time, with innovative deep discount bonds, and registered path-breaking success. In the following year, it set up the IDBI Capital Market Services ltd., as it wholly-owned subsidiary, to offer a broad range of financial services, including bond trading, equity broking, client asset management and depository services.

In September 1994, in response to RBI's policy of opening up domestic banking sector to private participation, IDBI Bank limited, in association with SIDBI. In July 1995, public issue of the bank was taken out, after which the government's shareholding came down (though it still retains majority of the shareholding in the bank). In September 2003, IDBI took over Tata Home Finance Ltd. Renamed as 'IDBI Home finance limited', it diversified its business domain and entering the area of retail finance sector.

The year 2005 witnessed the merger of IDBI Bank with the Industrial Development Bank of India Ltd. The new entity continued to its development finance role, while providing an array of wholesale and retail banking products (and does so till date). The following year, IDBI bank acquired United Western Bank (which at that, time had 230 branches spread over 47 districts in 9 states). In the financial year of 2008, IDBI bank had a net income of Rs. 9415.9 crores and total assets of Rs. 120601 crores.

In order to make the IDBI's co-coordinating role more effective, the Narasimhan Committee has suggested that the IDBI should give up its direct financing and perform only promotional apex and refinancing role in respect of other institutions like SFCs. The direct lending function should be entrusted to a separate finance company especially set up for this purpose.

To help the small-scale industries overcome the problem, IDBI has come up with a scheme, called Seed Capital Scheme. It is operated through the agency of notified SIDCs and SFCs. In Tamil Nadu it is operated through TIIC. Projects assisted by commercial banks are also eligible for seed capital assistance. The amount of seed capital assistance per concern shall not exceed 20 per cent of the project cost, subject to a ceiling of Rs. 15 lakhs. The assistance will be in the form of soft loans. The soft loan would be interest free which will carry a service charge of one per cent per annum. No security except the personal guarantee of the promoter is stipulated.

In the case of small-scale industries, requirement of seed capital assistance upto the first Rs. 4 lakhs is expected to be financed by State Financial Corporations from their special capital scheme and only the excess if any, over this amount would be met out of the present scheme.

Small Industries Development Bank of India (SIDBI)

The Small Industries Development Bank of India (SIDBI), a whollyowned subsidiary of Industrial Development Bank of India (IDBI), set up by an Act of Parliament, is the principal financial institution for the promotion, financing and development of industry in the small, tiny and cottage sectors and for co-co-ordinating the functions of the institutions engaged in similar activities. The outstanding portfolio and activities of IDBI pertaining to the small-scale sector and has emerged, over the years as the main purveyor of credit to small, tiny and cottage sector .

The SIDBI discounts and rediscounts bills arising from the sale of machinery or manufactured by, industrial concerns in the small-scale sector. It also provides seed capital/soft loan assistance under national equity fund, Mahila Udyam Nidhi and seed capital schemes through specified lending agencies.

The SIDBI further grants direct assistance as well as undertakes refinancing of loans extended by primary lending institutions for financing export of products manufactured by industrial concerns in the small-scale sector.

The SIDBI extends financial support to the National Small Industries Development Corporation for providing scarce raw materials to SSI units and marketing their end products. It also extends financial support to national small industries corporations for providing leasing hire purchase and marketing support to SSI units.

The financial assistance of the SIDBI to the small-scale units scattered through out the country is channeled through the existing credit delivery mechanism comprising of state financial corporations, commercial banks, cooperative banks and Regional Rural Banks which have a vast network of branches in the country.

State Financial Corporations (SFCs)

The Central Government passed in 1951 the State Financial Corporation Act along the lines of the IFC Act provide at the state level long term finance to medium and small scale industries. This is of course a permissive legislation enabling each state government to set up its own state financial corporations.

Industrial Finance Corporation of India was set up in 1948 to cater to the needs of large industrial concerns. After its introduction in August 1952, the first corporation was registered in Punjab in

February 1953. They can render financial assistance only to limited companies and co-operative societies.

The main function of SFCs is to provide finance by way term loans, direct subscriptions to equity, debenture, seed capital and discounting of bills of exchange the functioning of these state level financial institutions are beset with problems on account of political interference, non-performing loans and inefficient huge non-performing assets putting their efficient management in jeopardy. The SFCs Amendment Act (2000) becomes effective from September 2000 to improve functioning of SFCs. The amended act infuses greater flexibility to cope with the challenges post by the deregulated financial systems.

The governments also setup a committee under D.O. Gupta to look into the functioning of the State Financial Corporations. This was a sequel to the observations of the Abid Hussein Committee to strengthen the role of State Financial Corporations and to examine ways for restructuring and revitalization. The Committee in its report submitted in January 2001 indicated that future business of the SFCs would be affected by stiff competition emerging in the financial system and suggested various measures for restructuring and recapitalization. The SIDBI also suggested ways for restructuring operations of State Financial Corporations.

Financing of SSI by commercial banks

Until the 1970's conventional Development Finance Corporations were considered as a main vehicles for channeling loan funds to small industries. But these institutions were found to be too centralized, the access to finance on a widely dispersed basis from commercial banks, with their vast network of branches, naturally emerged as an important alternate institutional source of SSI financing. The commercial banks are able to attract local domestic saving and respond quickly to the demand of the SSI units by offering greater variety of services. However, with the strengthening of capital base of development financial institution by the government, commercial banks started referring long term loans to them and remained content in financing working capital needs.

For a long period, commercial banks did not come forward to extend financial assistance to the small-scale industries because of the SSIs weak economic base. The first lead in this regard was taken by the State Bank of India, in consultation with the Reserve Bank of India in March 1956 by setting up a pilot scheme for the provision of credit for small-scale industries. In the beginning, the scheme was confined to 9 branches of the SBI, which was later extended to all the branches of the SBI. The commercial banks started taking initiation in financing SSI's in a greater way only after the bank nationalization in July 1969.

Normally, the commercial banks provide assistance for working capital requirements of the SSI's over the years. They have also started providing 'term' finance as is indicated by the data complied by the RBI that of all the advances given to the SSI's by the commercial banks, the share of the term loan accounted for nearly 30 per cent. A notable feature in the financing of SSI's has been the introduction of the "Lead Bank Scheme", by the RBI. Under this scheme each district has been allotted to one scheduled commercial bank for the intensive development of banking facilities. The introduction of "Credit Guarantee Scheme", in 1960, was a big fillip in the filed of commercial banks' financing to SSI's initially, this scheme was introduced in 22 district on an experimental basis. Latter, it was extended to all over the country.

The availability of credit to the SSI sector improved further with the stipulation on foreign banks to extend at least 10 per cent of their net bank credit to the SSI sector and to deposit the shortfall, if any, with the small industries development bank of India (SIDBI).

The small-scale industry is considered to be one of the priority sectors. Banks are expected to lend small-scale industries just as they finance agriculture. Over the period of years, the share of advance to small scale industries in total priority sector advances has been on the increase.

Microfinance

Microfinance is a very popular term in today's financial market scenario. As the name suggests, microfinance refers to microcredit or micro-loan. Microfinance refers to a banking or financial service that is offered by banks or other financial institutions to individuals who belong to the low-income or underprivileged sections of the society. Microfinance can be in the form of loans, insurance, and savings deposits.

It is very helpful to small-sized enterprise owners as well as entrepreneurs with low capital. There are many people across the world, especially in India, who do not have access to proper financial assistance. They live in rural areas as well as in urban areas of India and do not have sufficient knowledge and access to take help from conventional sources of finance such as banks and investors.

Microfinancing is a great way to help poor individuals to be financially independent. They can use these funds offered by banks at very low rates of interest to start their own small venture or to make their other dreams come true. Many of the underprivileged people in the nation do not have any idea about saving money or managing their finances. When they acquire microfinance from a reliable institution, they will get exposure to managing money on their own and also about utilising funds in a sensible manner.

Microfinance is also offered to people who are interested in purchasing equipment or vehicles of high value that are required for carrying out their business activities. These can be tractors for agriculture, machines for manufacturing textiles, trucks for transportation of the goods created by the small entrepreneurs, etc.

Definition of Microfinancing

Microfinancing is typically defined as the process of providing loans, credit, savings, and other necessary financial services and products to individuals who are extremely poor to get access to the regular sources of finance such as banks or other financial institutions.

Microfinance is provided to the underprivileged people with the belief that charity or philanthropy is not the solution to poverty.

How does Microfinance Work in India?

Both banks and non-banking financial corporations (NBFCs) offer microfinance in India. There are also microfinance institutions in the country that are exclusively dedicated to offering microfinance to people. Microfinance institutions aim at getting people out of poverty and improving poor people's financial conditions. Microfinance institutions target poor people who are unemployed, who are or want to be entrepreneurs, and who are into farming.

Microfinance is usually procured by loan applicants through 3 modules and they include:

- Through banks, non-banking financial corporations, and microfinance institutions.
- By establishing good relations with banks or other financial institutions.
- By getting together as a group with a common goal of obtaining finance to create and develop new small business ventures or to make a living.

List of Few Microfinance Institutions in India

In our country, there are a number of institutions that offer microfinance exclusively. We will take a look at only a few select microfinance institutions in the country:

1. Annapurna Microfinance Pvt Ltd.
2. BSS Microfinance Pvt Ltd.
3. Asirvad Microfinance Pvt Ltd.

4. Disha Microfin Pvt Ltd.
5. Fusion Microfinance Pvt Ltd.
6. Arohan Financial Services Pvt Ltd.
7. Cashpor Micro Credit
8. Grama Vidiyal Micro Finance Ltd.
9. ESAF Microfinance and Investments Pvt Ltd.
10. Equitas Microfinance Pvt Ltd.
11. Madura Micro Finance Ltd.
12. Satin Creditcare Network Ltd.
13. S.M.I.L.E Microfinance Ltd.
14. Grameen Financial Services Pvt Ltd.
15. Janalakshmi Financial Services Pvt Ltd.
16. SKS Microfinance Ltd.
17. ASA International India Pvt Ltd.
18. Sonata Finance Pvt Ltd.
19. Shree Kshetra Dharmasthala Rural Development Project
20. RGVN (North East) Microfinance Limited
21. Swadhaar FinServe Pvt Ltd.
22. Belstar Investment & Finance Pvt Ltd.
23. Suryoday Micro Finance Pvt Ltd.
24. SV Creditline Pvt Ltd.
25. Future Financial Services Ltd.
26. Ujjivan Financial Services Pvt Ltd.
27. Utkarsh Micro Finance Pvt Ltd.
28. Adhikar Microfinance Pvt Ltd.
29. Uttrayan Financial Services Pvt Ltd.
30. Chaitanya India Fin Credit Pvt Ltd.
31. Indian Cooperative Network for Women Ltd.
32. Growing Opportunity Finance (India) Pvt Ltd.
33. M Power Micro Finance Pvt Ltd.
34. Rashtriya Seva Samithi
35. IDF Financial Services Pvt Ltd.
36. Mahasemam Trust.

Features of Microfinance

- Microfinance is typically offered to anyone who does not have a stable source of income due to unemployment. It is also given to those who are involved in contract labour or who work part-time.
- It is also given to anyone who does not have a proper credit history that can be verified. Lack of credit history will be mostly due to lack of access to acquire credit.
- There are also some applicants who may have a poor credit history due to high debts. They may have entered into debt situations due to shortage of funds to repay. They may also have got into debt troubles due to scams planned by unregistered moneylenders who tend to take advantage of poor people since they do not have much financial knowledge.

- Microfinance typically does not require loan applicants to submit any collateral while applying for the loan. These loans are usually unsecured in nature. Even if a microfinance institution does ask for a collateral, they are very reasonable. They understand the financial condition of the applicant.
- Microfinance is also offered to people living below poverty line (BPL) since they do not have access to other forms of financing.
- Microfinancing promotes simplified and small savings among poor people. It encourages them to build their funds step-by-step.
- Microfinancing offers repeat loans to applicants. This helps borrowers repay their loan promptly as the repayment tenure is very short. Once the small loan is repaid on time, the applicants will receive their next loan. A repeat loan is always offered to someone who has already borrowed and shown their capability in repaying it on time.
- Microfinance also intends to assist to individuals in securing good medical treatment when they have health issues.
- Generally, microfinance institutions approach clients instead of waiting for clients to approach them. They want impoverished people to be aware that there are inexpensive forms of financing.
- Microfinance institutions have easy and quick loan application processes.
- The interest rate for microfinance is very low.
- When a micro loan is offered, the lender does not ask the applicant for the purpose of lending. The loan can be utilised for any purpose.
- Some microfinance options also come with micro insurance. Micro insurance is offered as it helps the borrower in protecting his or her credit extensively. The micro insurance facility is very reasonably priced.
- Microfinance aims at developing financial sustainability among economically downtrodden people.
- Microfinance helps in creating more and more jobs. It enables uneducated people to be involved in some source of employment instead of staying idle.
- Microfinance institutions aim to eliminate interest rate ceilings as they believe that these ceilings can restrict poor people from securing finance.
- Microfinance focuses on offering financial transparency by offering loans to individuals without any hidden costs or fees or charges.
- Microfinance believes that poor people need a broad set of financial services apart from just loans. It also holds that these financial services should be simplified, easily accessible, economical, and flexible in nature. These services include cash transfer facilities, savings schemes with minimal or zero deposit, and micro insurance.

Different Microfinance Models in India

India has a number of institutions that offer microfinance exclusively. Each institution uses a particular model or a blend of different models in order to provide microfinance to applicants. These microfinance institutions have embraced both conventional and advanced ideas of lending in order to distribute credit evenly in the society without uneven accumulation of credit among the rich people. There are many microfinance models in the country and this could be because of the high number of social and cultural groups, the large geographical size of the nation, the presence of multiple economic classes, and a solid existence of non-governmental organisations that are dedicated to uplifting the socio-economic condition of the disadvantaged people of the country.

The main six categories of microfinance models that are followed in India include:

1. Self-help group model

A self-help group (SHG) is described as a group of 5 to 20 individuals who belong to the low-income class. Each group member typically contributes funds from their own savings and then this money is pooled in together. These funds are then utilised to support their common goal of improving their lifestyles and to make themselves financially secure.

2. Grameen model

The Grameen model to distribute microfinance originated in Bangladesh. After seeing the success of the model in Bangladesh, many institutions in India started to adopt it by making some adjustments. A few of the institutions that acquired the principles of the Grameen model are CASHPOR Financial and Technical Services Limited, SHARE Microfinance Limited, Activists for Social Alternatives (ASA).

This particular model believes in providing a mandatory training course to the group members for at least 7 days. The model will offer microfinance to an applicant without asking for any collateral at low costs. The loan application process has minimum or zero paperwork and is processed very quickly keeping in mind the urgency for funds.

3. Co-operative credit union model

These organisations apply the co-operative model to offer microfinance in rural areas. The Cooperative Development Forum (CDF), Hyderabad has applied the co-operative credit union model successfully by giving primary importance to savings. The main entities in the CDF are women's or men's thrift co-operatives (WTCs and MTCs). They have small groups of individuals wherein each group has a particular leader who heads group meetings, accumulates the savings of each group member, and looks into the repayment of loans. The group leader is responsible for making sure all small loans are repaid promptly by each member.

4. Federated self-help groups (SHGs) or SHG Federation model

A normal self-help group (SHG) is typically consistent of a few members with the aim of making each member self-sufficient with adequate funds and high-quality equipment to produce first-class output. It is usually small in size. Due to the success of these groups, there was a need for a large-scale self-help group. This led to the establishment of federated self-help groups. A federated self-help group refers to a large scale self-help group with a large number of members. It is a federation of multiple self-help groups. A federation of self-help groups will have around 1000 to 2000 members whereas a single self-help group will have only up to 20 members.

5. Rotating Savings and Credit Associations (ROSCAs) model

Under this model, funds are offered to groups of individuals through unconventional means. The members of such associations include individuals who have certain common features such as ethnicity, community, language, professions, occupations, etc. These members contribute funds on a regular basis and utilise them for attaining a common goal.

The whole model works according to a systematic way where every member receives funds within a particular time frame and he or she is required to repay it before the deadline. After this member, another member will start the whole micro loan process. It functions in the form of a cycle. Unless one member completes the repayment cycle on time, a new member cannot procure a loan. Hence, with the help of peer pressure and efficient monitoring skills from the association's leaders, each member will make sure that the loan is repaid promptly without any delay. Due to fear if the loan cycle will stop because of any one person, every member ensures that each loan is repaid on time.

Chit fund companies in India carry out their lending operations just like ROSCAs. They encourage the underprivileged people of the society to save money and accumulate lump sums for the purpose of purchasing high-value products. A chit fund scheme will have a fixed tenure and a fixed value. Every member will be required to pool in money on a monthly basis and this will be utilised for the goals of a company. These ROSCAs or chit fund models help in eliminating the gap between different sections of the society that is present due to conventional banking ways.

6. Microfinance companies

In India, microfinance companies can be registered as a non-banking financial company (NBFC) under Companies Act or Reserve Bank of India (RBI). An NBFC engages in accumulating funds and using them for offering credit and other financial services to other people. An NBFC generally provides personal loans, car loans, two-wheeler loans, crop loans, agricultural loans, and lots more. Non-banking financial companies can offer both regular loans as well as micro loans to the less fortunate people of the society. These NBFCs can be regulated by the Reserve Bank of India (RBI) or the Companies Act.

MULTIPLE CHOICE QUESTIONS

1. What is the primary focus of entrepreneurship development?
(a) Encouraging established businesses
(b) Fostering innovation and new ventures
(c) Promoting corporate mergers
(d) Regulating existing industries

2. Which of the following is a common type of entrepreneurship?
(a) Intrapreneurship
(b) Extraterrestrial entrepreneurship
(c) Extravagant entrepreneurship
(d) Inexpensive entrepreneurship

3. Who proposed the "Entrepreneurial Traits Theory," which suggests that certain personality traits are associated with successful entrepreneurs?
(a) Karl Marx
(b) Abraham Maslow
(c) David McClelland
(d) Sigmund Freud

4. What is the initial step in the entrepreneurial process?
(a) Business expansion
(b) Market research and analysis
(c) Financial planning
(d) Legal documentation

5. In entrepreneurship, the term "Start-up" typically refers to
(a) A well-established, mature business
(b) An innovative venture in its early stages
(c) A business in decline
(d) A government-owned enterprise

6. Which theory of entrepreneurship suggests that entrepreneurs possess unique skills and abilities that enable them to recognize opportunities and act on them?
(a) Resource-Based Theory
(b) Trait Theory
(c) Psychological Theory
(d) Innovation Theory

7. In the entrepreneurial process, what does the term "Business Plan" refer to?
(a) A formal document outlining the company's vision, goals, and strategies
(b) The first stage of marketing a new product
(c) The legal registration of the business
(d) Employee training programs

8. Which of the following is a characteristic of an entrepreneurial opportunity?
(a) Limited market demand
(b) Low risk
(c) Innovative solutions to problems or needs
(d) High employee turnover

9. What is the term for an entrepreneur who starts a business based on an innovative product or service?
(a) Imitative entrepreneur
(b) Innovative entrepreneur
(c) Repetitive entrepreneur
(d) Traditional entrepreneur

10. What is the process of identifying, evaluating, and exploiting opportunities called in the context of entrepreneurship development?
(a) Business expansion
(b) Intrapreneurship
(c) Entrepreneurship
(d) Opportunity recognition

11. Which theory of entrepreneurship suggests that entrepreneurs play a critical role in the economy by allocating resources and creating value?
(a) Resource-Based Theory
(b) Innovation Theory
(c) Economic Theory
(d) Trait Theory

12. In entrepreneurship, what is the term for the ability to take calculated risks and manage uncertainty?
(a) Risk aversion
(b) Risk management

(c) Risk tolerance
(d) Risk elimination

13. The "Intrapreneurship" concept involves
(a) Starting a new venture outside an existing organization
(b) Entrepreneurial activities within an established organization
(c) Government regulation of entrepreneurial ventures
(d) Exporting products to international markets

14. In the entrepreneurial process, what is the term for the stage where a business idea is transformed into a tangible product or service?
(a) Idea generation
(b) Opportunity recognition
(c) Business planning
(d) Product development

15. Which type of entrepreneur is often focused on copying or imitating successful business models?
(a) Imitative entrepreneur
(b) Innovative entrepreneur
(c) Serial entrepreneur
(d) Social entrepreneur

16. What is the term for the legal registration of a business entity?
(a) Market analysis
(b) Business plan
(c) Business registration
(d) Risk assessment

17. In entrepreneurship, "Serial Entrepreneurs" are individuals who
(a) Only start one business in their lifetime
(b) Start and manage multiple businesses over their career
(c) Focus on non-profit ventures
(d) Work as employees within established organizations

18. Which stage of the entrepreneurial process involves obtaining the necessary resources and funding to start the business?
(a) Market analysis
(b) Opportunity recognition
(c) Financial planning
(d) Business expansion

19. In entrepreneurship, what is the term for the process of monitoring and adjusting a business's activities to achieve its goals?
(a) Opportunity recognition
(b) Business registration
(c) Business plan
(d) Business management

20. The "Social Entrepreneurship" concept is primarily concerned with
(a) Maximizing profits for shareholders
(b) Addressing social or environmental issues through business ventures
(c) Importing and exporting goods
(d) Government regulation of businesses

21. Which theory of entrepreneurship emphasizes the role of innovation and creativity in entrepreneurial success?
(a) Resource-Based Theory
(b) Innovation Theory
(c) Psychological Theory
(d) Economic Theory

22. In the entrepreneurial process, what does the term "Scaling" refer to?
(a) Reducing the size of a business
(b) Expanding the business to achieve growth
(c) Legal registration of the business
(d) Business closure

23. "Entrepreneurial Competencies" typically include skills such as
(a) Risk aversion and compliance
(b) Resource management and regulation
(c) Opportunity recognition and innovation
(d) Employee turnover and cost control

24. Which of the following is an essential aspect of "Entrepreneurial Ecosystem" development?
(a) Fostering risk aversion
(b) Restricting access to funding
(c) Supporting and connecting entrepreneurs with resources and networks
(d) Promoting conformity

25. What is the term for the process of developing entrepreneurial skills, knowledge, and behaviors?
(a) Business registration
(b) Opportunity recognition
(c) Entrepreneurship development
(d) Risk management

26. What is the primary focus of intrapreneurship?
(a) Starting a new business venture
(b) Promoting entrepreneurial activities within an established organization

(c) Government regulation of business operations
(d) Importing and exporting goods

27. Intrapreneurs are individuals who
(a) Start and manage multiple businesses over their career
(b) Work as employees within established organizations but exhibit entrepreneurial behaviors
(c) Focus on social entrepreneurship
(d) Avoid any involvement in business activities

28. Which of the following is a key characteristic of intrapreneurs?
(a) Risk aversion
(b) Resistance to change
(c) Innovation and creativity
(d) Compliance with established processes

29. The term "Corporate Entrepreneurship" is often used interchangeably with
(a) Intrapreneurship
(b) Entrepreneurship
(c) Social entrepreneurship
(d) Government regulation

30. Intrapreneurs typically operate within the framework of an existing organization and are encouraged to
(a) Promote conformity
(b) Avoid any changes
(c) Innovate and take calculated risks
(d) Follow rigid rules and regulations

31. What is the primary goal of intrapreneurship within an organization?
(a) Maintain the status quo
(b) Minimize employee involvement
(c) Foster innovation and new ideas
(d) Ensure government compliance

32. Intrapreneurship often involves employees taking the initiative to
(a) Resist change
(b) Follow instructions without question
(c) Develop and implement new projects or ventures within the organization
(d) Avoid any risks

33. What is the term for an intrapreneurial project that is separate from the organization's core business but still benefits the organization?
(a) Intrapreneurial spin-off
(b) Corporate spin-off
(c) Outsourcing
(d) Government regulation

34. Intrapreneurs are often granted the autonomy to
(a) Avoid taking risks
(b) Innovate and make decisions related to their projects
(c) Comply with all existing rules and procedures
(d) Restrict their activities to routine tasks

35. The concept of intrapreneurship was first introduced by
(a) Peter Drucker (b) Sigmund Freud
(c) Karl Marx (d) Abraham Maslow

36. Intrapreneurship is often encouraged as a way to
(a) Stifle employee creativity
(b) Avoid change
(c) Generate new ideas and drive organizational growth
(d) Limit innovation

37. Intrapreneurs are individuals who exhibit entrepreneurial behaviors such as creativity, innovation, and risk-taking, but they operate within the context of an
(a) Established organization
(b) Independent business venture
(c) International trade environment
(d) Unregulated industry

38. What is the primary reason for organizations to promote intrapreneurship?
(a) To maintain a stagnant work environment
(b) To avoid change and innovation
(c) To foster creativity and generate new opportunities
(d) To minimize employee involvement

39. Intrapreneurs are often granted the flexibility to
(a) Follow rigid rules and regulations
(b) Conform to established practices
(c) Innovate and take calculated risks
(d) Avoid any form of decision-making

40. The concept of intrapreneurship can be traced back to the philosophy of
(a) Karl Marx
(b) Abraham Maslow
(c) Sigmund Freud
(d) Joseph Schumpeter

41. Intrapreneurs are typically motivated by a desire to
(a) Avoid taking any initiative
(b) Maintain the status quo
(c) Create value and make a difference within the organization
(d) Resist change

42. The term "Intrapreneurial Culture" refers to an organizational environment that
(a) Discourages innovation and creativity
(b) Promotes conformity and routine tasks
(c) Encourages and supports intrapreneurial activities
(d) Fosters resistance to change

43. What is the primary role of the "Intrapreneurial Champion" within an organization?
(a) To resist intrapreneurial activities
(b) To support and advocate for intrapreneurial initiatives
(c) To follow established procedures and processes
(d) To avoid any risks

44. Intrapreneurs often work on projects that aim to
(a) Conform to industry standards
(b) Maintain the status quo
(c) Generate new opportunities or solve existing problems
(d) Avoid any form of creativity

45. Which term refers to the process of creating a separate entity within an organization to develop and implement new projects or ventures?
(a) Intrapreneurial spin-off
(b) Outsourcing
(c) Intrapreneurial resistance
(d) Bureaucracy

46. Intrapreneurship is often viewed as a way to counteract
(a) Employee engagement
(b) Bureaucracy and stagnation
(c) Government regulation
(d) Resistance to change

47. What is the term for the financial and logistical support provided by organizations to intrapreneurs to help them develop and implement their projects?
(a) Intrapreneurial spin-off
(b) Intrapreneurial resistance
(c) Intrapreneurial incubation
(d) Outsourcing

48. Intapreneurs are often driven by a strong desire to
(a) Maintain the status quo
(b) Avoid change and innovation
(c) Challenge the existing norms and create value
(d) Avoid any risks

49. The term "Intrapreneurial Project" typically refers to
(a) Routine tasks assigned to employees
(b) Innovation and creativity within an established organization
(c) Government-mandated initiatives
(d) Financial audits and compliance activities

50. Intrapreneurs are often encouraged to take calculated risks and
(a) Avoid any form of innovation
(b) Follow rigid rules and regulations
(c) Innovate, create, and implement new ideas within the organization
(d) Promote employee resistance to change

51. What challenges do women entrepreneurs often face in the business world?
(a) Lack of gender equality
(b) Limited access to capital and resources
(c) Reduced government regulations
(d) Gender-neutral opportunities

52. Which organization promotes and supports women's entrepreneurship in India?
(a) National Aeronautics and Space Administration (NASA)
(b) National Rural Employment Guarantee Act (NREGA)
(c) National Commission for Women (NCW)
(d) Women's Entrepreneurship Development Program (WEDP)

53. What is a common form of support provided to women entrepreneurs to help them start and grow their businesses?
(a) Gender-based discrimination
(b) Entrepreneurship training and development programs
(c) Excessive government regulations
(d) High-interest loans

54. Rural entrepreneurship often focuses on businesses related to
(a) Heavy industry and manufacturing

(b) Agriculture, agri-business, and cottage industries
(c) Urban services
(d) High-tech startups

55. What is the term for a government program that provides financial support to women entrepreneurs and small business owners?
(a) International trade
(b) Women Entrepreneurship Development Program (WEDP)
(c) Rural entrepreneurship
(d) Urbanization

56. In rural entrepreneurship, what is the role of "Self-Help Groups" (SHGs)?
(a) Encouraging urbanization
(b) Supporting women's entrepreneurship in rural areas
(c) Promoting heavy industry and manufacturing
(d) Discouraging economic activities

57. What is the primary goal of promoting women's entrepreneurship?
(a) Maintaining gender-based discrimination
(b) Encouraging gender inequality
(c) Empowering women and enhancing their economic independence
(d) Reducing access to education

58. Which type of support is often provided to rural entrepreneurs to promote agriculture and agri-business ventures?
(a) Import restrictions
(b) Subsidies, training, and access to markets
(c) High-interest loans
(d) Heavy taxation

59. What is the term for the use of Information and Communication Technology (ICT) to promote rural entrepreneurship and provide access to information and markets?
(a) Digital divide (b) Urbanization
(c) E-commerce (d) E-governance

60. Which organization in India is dedicated to supporting and promoting women entrepreneurs and rural entrepreneurship?
(a) National Aeronautics and Space Administration (NASA)
(b) National Rural Employment Guarantee Act (NREGA)
(c) National Commission for Women (NCW)
(d) National Institute for Entrepreneurship and Small Business Development (NIESBUD)

61. What is the term for the phenomenon where women entrepreneurs create and run businesses that address the unique needs and preferences of women consumers?
(a) Gender-sensitive entrepreneurship
(b) Gender-neutral entrepreneurship
(c) Women's exclusion
(d) Gender-based discrimination

62. In the context of women's entrepreneurship, what is "Microfinancing"?
(a) Large-scale loans for women entrepreneurs
(b) Small loans and financial services provided to women entrepreneurs, especially in rural areas
(c) High-interest loans
(d) Gender-neutral financing

63. What is the term for businesses that operate in rural areas and are often focused on agricultural and agri-business activities?
(a) Cottage industries (b) Heavy industries
(c) Urban enterprises (d) Urbanization

64. What is the primary objective of "Skill Development Programs" for women entrepreneurs in rural areas?
(a) Discouraging economic activities
(b) Promoting heavy industry and manufacturing
(c) Enhancing the skills and capabilities of women for entrepreneurship and economic independence
(d) Increasing gender inequality

65. In rural entrepreneurship, what is the role of "Cluster Development"?
(a) Concentrating all economic activities in urban areas
(b) Promoting rural industrialization
(c) Supporting the growth of agri-businesses
(d) Promoting the development of business clusters and networks in rural areas

66. Which government body in India plays a significant role in promoting and supporting women's entrepreneurship and rural entrepreneurship?
(a) National Aeronautics and Space Administration (NASA)
(b) National Rural Employment Guarantee Act (NREGA)
(c) National Commission for Women (NCW)
(d) Ministry of Micro, Small and Medium Enterprises

67. What is the primary role of "National Bank for Agriculture and Rural Development (NABARD)" in the context of rural entrepreneurship?
   (a) Providing heavy industry loans
   (b) Promoting urbanization
   (c) Providing financial support and resources to rural entrepreneurs, especially in agriculture
   (d) Discouraging rural economic activities
68. What is the term for the phenomenon where women entrepreneurs often face difficulties accessing financial resources and credit due to gender-based discrimination?
   (a) Gender-sensitive entrepreneurship
   (b) Gender-based discrimination
   (c) Gender-neutral entrepreneurship
   (d) Urbanization
69. In rural entrepreneurship, what is the role of "Rural Marketing"?
   (a) Promoting urbanization
   (b) Focusing on international trade
   (c) Marketing products and services in rural areas and creating demand
   (d) Restricting access to markets
70. What is the primary goal of "Rural Entrepreneurship Development Programs"?
   (a) Reducing gender inequality
   (b) Promoting gender-based discrimination
   (c) Enhancing entrepreneurship and income generation in rural areas
   (d) Encouraging urbanization
71. In rural entrepreneurship, what is the role of "Agripreneurship"?
   (a) Discouraging agricultural activities
   (b) Promoting heavy industry and manufacturing
   (c) Promoting entrepreneurship in agriculture and related sectors
   (d) Reducing access to rural markets
72. What is the term for businesses and startups located in rural areas that leverage local resources, culture, and traditions for economic growth?
   (a) Urban enterprises
   (b) Rural enterprises
   (c) Cottage industries
   (d) International trade
73. In the context of women's entrepreneurship, what is the term for businesses that cater to the unique needs and preferences of women, such as fashion, beauty, and wellness?
   (a) Cottage industries
   (b) Gender-sensitive entrepreneurship
   (c) Urban enterprises
   (d) Heavy industries
74. What is the term for innovations that involve incremental improvements in existing products or processes?
   (a) Disruptive innovations
   (b) Radical innovations
   (c) Sustaining innovations
   (d) Blue ocean innovations
75. Which type of innovation aims to create entirely new markets or industries by addressing unmet needs?
   (a) Disruptive innovations
   (b) Incremental innovations
   (c) Product innovations
   (d) Process innovations
76. The concept of "Blue Ocean Strategy" is associated with
   (a) Creating new markets by making competition irrelevant
   (b) Focusing on red ocean markets with intense competition
   (c) Restricting innovation to incremental changes
   (d) Avoiding risk and maintaining the status quo
77. What is the term for the process of identifying and evaluating opportunities for innovation and new business ventures?
   (a) Idea generation
   (b) Opportunity recognition
   (c) Market research
   (d) Risk assessment
78. In the context of innovation, what does the term "Open Innovation" refer to?
   (a) Keeping all innovation processes within the organization
   (b) Collaborating with external partners, including customers and suppliers, to develop new ideas and products
   (c) Avoiding external influence on innovation
   (d) Restricting innovation to internal research and development
79. What is the primary goal of "Design Thinking" in the innovation process?

(a) Minimizing the role of customers in product development
(b) Focusing on cost reduction
(c) Solving complex problems and creating user-centric solutions
(d) Avoiding market research

80. The process of "Screening Business Ideas" involves
(a) Rejecting all new ideas to maintain the status quo
(b) Evaluating and selecting the most promising business ideas
(c) Avoiding risk and change
(d) Implementing every new idea without analysis

81. Which of the following is a common technique for screening business ideas in the innovation process?
(a) Idea generation
(b) SWOT analysis
(c) Blue Ocean Strategy
(d) Avoiding customer feedback

82. What is the term for the process of gathering information to assess the feasibility and potential of a business idea?
(a) Idea generation
(b) Opportunity recognition
(c) Market research
(d) Risk assessment

83. In the innovation process, what is the term for the analysis of an idea's strengths, weaknesses, opportunities, and threats?
(a) SWOT analysis
(b) Blue Ocean Strategy
(c) Design thinking
(d) Risk assessment

84. What is the primary goal of conducting a "Feasibility Study" when screening business ideas?
(a) To discourage innovation and new ventures
(b) To assess the viability and potential risks of a business idea
(c) To avoid external partnerships
(d) To implement every idea without analysis

85. Which of the following factors is typically considered during the screening of business ideas?
(a) Ignoring customer feedback
(b) Market demand, competition, and financial feasibility
(c) Avoiding external partnerships
(d) Restricting innovation to internal research and development

86. "Proof of Concept" in the innovation process refers to
(a) The rejection of innovative ideas
(b) Demonstrating the technical and economic feasibility of an idea
(c) Avoiding the testing of new products
(d) Rejecting customer feedback

87. In the context of innovation, what is the term for the process of testing a product or idea in a controlled environment before launching it in the market?
(a) Prototype testing
(b) Avoiding customer feedback
(c) Blue Ocean Strategy
(d) Idea generation

88. "Pilot Testing" is a phase in the screening of business ideas that involves
(a) Avoiding market research
(b) Launching a product directly to the mass market
(c) Testing a product in a limited market segment before a full-scale launch
(d) Rejecting all new ideas

89. In the innovation process, what is the term for the launch of a new product or service to a small group of early adopters to gather feedback and make improvements?
(a) Market research (b) Prototype testing
(c) Beta testing (d) SWOT analysis

90. Which of the following is an example of a radical innovation?
(a) Introducing a new flavor of an existing soft drink
(b) Inventing a completely new type of transportation
(c) Improving the packaging of an existing product
(d) Expanding a successful retail chain to new locations

91. What is the term for innovations that involve changes to the way a product is produced or delivered?
(a) Product innovations
(b) Process innovations
(c) Incremental innovations
(d) Disruptive innovations

92. "Crowdsourcing" is a method used to
(a) Reject external feedback
(b) Avoid customer involvement
(c) Gather ideas, feedback, or solutions from a large group of people or the online community
(d) Limit innovation to internal resources

93. Which type of innovation focuses on improving or enhancing an existing product or service?
(a) Blue Ocean innovations
(b) Incremental innovations
(c) Radical innovations
(d) Disruptive innovations

94. "Entrepreneurial Alertness" refers to
(a) The ability to avoid new business opportunities
(b) The ability to identify and recognize new business opportunities
(c) Rejecting customer feedback
(d) Focusing on existing products and services

95. What is the term for a new business opportunity that has the potential to create economic value?
(a) Risk assessment
(b) Opportunity recognition
(c) Idea generation
(d) Avoiding external partnerships

96. Which of the following is a step in the innovation process for creating and identifying opportunities?
(a) Ignoring customer feedback
(b) Avoiding market research
(c) Generating, screening, and evaluating ideas
(d) Restricting innovation to internal resources

97. "Risk Assessment" in the screening of business ideas involves
(a) Minimizing all risks to avoid change
(b) Identifying and analyzing potential risks associated with a business idea
(c) Ignoring customer feedback
(d) Avoiding external partnerships

98. In the context of innovation, "Idea Generation" is the first step in the process and involves
(a) Avoiding market research
(b) Developing a detailed business plan
(c) Creatively generating new business ideas
(d) Rejecting all external feedback

99. What is the primary purpose of a business plan?
(a) To provide detailed financial statements
(b) To outline the legal structure of the business
(c) To define the business concept and its feasibility
(d) To create marketing materials for the business

100. What is the term for the process of assessing the potential for a business idea to become a successful venture?
(a) Market analysis
(b) Business plan development
(c) Feasibility analysis
(d) Technical analysis

101. The technical analysis component of a feasibility study focuses on
(a) Legal requirements for the business
(b) Market demand for the product or service
(c) The technical and operational aspects of the business idea
(d) Financial projections

102. What does the term "Proof of Concept" refer to in the context of business feasibility analysis?
(a) A formal business plan
(b) Demonstrating the technical and economic feasibility of the business idea
(c) Market research findings
(d) An intellectual property assessment

103. The market analysis component of a feasibility study involves
(a) Analyzing the production process
(b) Identifying the target market and demand for the product or service
(c) Creating financial projections
(d) Outlining the legal structure of the business

104. In a feasibility analysis, what does the term "Competitive Analysis" involve?
(a) Evaluating the potential for profits
(b) Analyzing the competition in the market and the business's competitive advantage
(c) Technical assessment of the business idea
(d) Legal requirements and regulations

105. "SWOT analysis" in a feasibility study assesses
(a) The legal structure of the business
(b) Strengths, weaknesses, opportunities, and threats related to the business idea
(c) Technical aspects of the business
(d) Market demand for the product

106. What is the term for assessing the legal and regulatory requirements that impact the business idea in a feasibility study?
(a) Market analysis (b) Technical analysis
(c) Legal analysis (d) Economic analysis

107. The financial analysis component of a feasibility study involves
(a) Analyzing the competition in the market
(b) Identifying the target market and demand for the product
(c) Developing financial projections and assessing the financial feasibility of the business
(d) Creating marketing materials

108. In a business plan, what does the term "Income Statement" represent?
(a) A summary of the legal structure of the business
(b) A list of the company's strengths and weaknesses
(c) A financial statement that shows revenue, expenses, and profit or loss over a specific period
(d) An analysis of the technical aspects of the business idea

109. "Break-even analysis" in a business plan helps determine
(a) The technical feasibility of the business idea
(b) The legal structure of the business
(c) The point at which total revenue equals total costs, indicating when the business becomes profitable
(d) Market demand for the product

110. What does the term "Cash Flow Statement" represent in a business plan?
(a) A summary of the legal structure of the business
(b) A list of the company's strengths and weaknesses
(c) A financial statement that tracks the inflow and outflow of cash over a specific period
(d) An analysis of the technical aspects of the business idea

111. The "Payback Period" in a business plan refers to
(a) The time it takes to recover the initial investment through net cash flows
(b) The analysis of competition in the market
(c) The legal requirements and regulations for the business
(d) Technical assessment of the business idea

112. "Net Present Value (NPV)" in a business plan assesses
(a) Market demand for the product
(b) The technical feasibility of the business idea
(c) The financial feasibility by comparing the present value of cash inflows and outflows
(d) Legal requirements for the business

113. In a business plan, the term "Sensitivity Analysis" is used to
(a) Analyze the competitive advantage of the business
(b) Assess the impact of changes in key assumptions on financial outcomes
(c) Evaluate the technical aspects of the business idea
(d) Examine the legal and regulatory requirements

114. What is the primary goal of a "Feasibility Report"?
(a) To outline the legal structure of the business
(b) To provide a detailed business plan
(c) To present an analysis of the technical aspects of the business idea
(d) To present the findings of a feasibility analysis, including technical, market, and financial assessments

115. What is the term for an analysis that considers the economic factors that might impact the success of a business idea, such as inflation, interest rates, and economic trends?
(a) Technical analysis (b) Legal analysis
(c) Economic analysis (d) Market analysis

116. Which of the following statements is true about the "Technical Analysis" in a feasibility study?
(a) It focuses on assessing the legal and regulatory requirements.
(b) It analyzes the competition in the market.
(c) It evaluates the technical and operational aspects of the business idea.
(d) It creates marketing materials for the business.

117. "Market Segmentation" in a feasibility study involves
(a) Analyzing the legal and regulatory requirements.

(b) Identifying and dividing the target market into smaller, distinct groups.
(c) Assessing the technical feasibility of the business idea.
(d) Developing financial projections.

118. "Break-even analysis" is an essential financial assessment in a feasibility study because it helps determine
(a) The competitive advantage of the business.
(b) The point at which total revenue equals total costs, indicating when the business becomes profitable.
(c) The technical feasibility of the business idea.
(d) Legal and regulatory requirements.

119. In a feasibility study, "Cash Flow Statement" is crucial for assessing
(a) The competitive advantage of the business.
(b) The inflow and outflow of cash over a specific period.
(c) The technical feasibility of the business idea.
(d) Legal and regulatory requirements.

120. "Payback Period" is important in a feasibility study because it helps determine
(a) The competitive advantage of the business.
(b) The time it takes to recover the initial investment through net cash flows.
(c) The technical feasibility of the business idea.
(d) Legal and regulatory requirements.

121. "Net Present Value (NPV)" in a feasibility study is used to assess
(a) The competitive advantage of the business.
(b) The financial feasibility by comparing the present value of cash inflows and outflows.
(c) The technical feasibility of the business idea.
(d) Legal and regulatory requirements.

122. What is the term for the analysis that examines how changes in key assumptions affect financial outcomes in a feasibility study?
(a) Technical analysis
(b) Sensitivity analysis
(c) Economic analysis (d) Market analysis

123. A "Feasibility Report" typically includes findings related to
(a) The legal and regulatory requirements.
(b) Detailed financial projections.
(c) Technical and operational aspects of the business idea.
(d) The results of a feasibility analysis, including technical, market, and financial assessments.

124. In the context of industries, what does "SSI" stand for?
(a) Small Scale Investments
(b) Small Scale Innovations
(c) Small Scale Industries
(d) Small Scale Implementation

125. What is the primary characteristic that defines a Small Scale Industry in India?
(a) Low production capacity
(b) Limited geographic scope
(c) A minimum number of employees
(d) Low investment in machinery and equipment

126. Which government body in India is responsible for formulating policies and providing support for the development of small scale industries?
(a) Ministry of Heavy Industries and Public Enterprises
(b) Ministry of Micro, Small, and Medium Enterprises
(c) Ministry of Finance
(d) Ministry of Commerce and Industry

127. The "Khadi and Village Industries Commission" (KVIC) in India primarily promotes
(a) Large-scale industries
(b) Traditional handicrafts and rural industries
(c) Urbanization
(d) Medium-sized enterprises

128. What is the primary goal of promoting Micro and Small Scale Industries (MSMEs) in India?
(a) To discourage entrepreneurship
(b) To promote large-scale industries
(c) To generate employment and foster economic development
(d) To restrict innovation

129. Which financial institution in India provides financial support to MSMEs by offering various credit schemes and services?
(a) Reserve Bank of India (RBI)
(b) Small Industries Development Bank of India (SIDBI)
(c) National Stock Exchange (NSE)
(d) Central Board of Direct Taxes (CBDT)

130. The "District Industries Centers" (DICs) play a crucial role in promoting MSMEs by providing various support services at the district level. Which government ministry oversees the DICs?
(a) Ministry of External Affairs
(b) Ministry of Home Affairs
(c) Ministry of Micro, Small, and Medium Enterprises
(d) Ministry of Agriculture and Farmers Welfare

131. Which government scheme offers financial support to MSMEs for the modernization of their production equipment and techniques?
(a) Pradhan Mantri Jan Dhan Yojana (PMJDY)
(b) National Rural Employment Guarantee Act (NREGA)
(c) Credit Guarantee Fund Scheme for Micro and Small Enterprises (CGMSE)
(d) Technology Upgradation Fund Scheme (TUFS)

132. In the context of MSMEs, what does the term "Credit Guarantee Fund Trust for Micro and Small Enterprises" (CGTMSE) do?
(a) It provides loans to large-scale industries.
(b) It offers credit support and collateral-free loans to MSMEs.
(c) It manages the foreign trade policy.
(d) It promotes rural employment.

133. What is the primary purpose of the "National Small Industries Corporation" (NSIC) in India?
(a) To restrict innovation in small-scale industries
(b) To promote large-scale industries
(c) To facilitate marketing support and technology upgradation for MSMEs
(d) To control the financial market

134. Which government initiative aims to provide training and skill development to entrepreneurs and workers in the MSME sector?
(a) Pradhan Mantri Jan Dhan Yojana (PMJDY)
(b) National Rural Employment Guarantee Act (NREGA)
(c) Prime Minister's Employment Generation Programme (PMEGP)
(d) Skill India

135. The "Prime Minister's Employment Generation Programme" (PMEGP) primarily focuses on
(a) Promoting large-scale industries
(b) Providing employment opportunities in urban areas
(c) Generating self-employment through the establishment of micro-enterprises
(d) Discouraging entrepreneurship

136. What is the primary goal of the "Make in India" campaign?
(a) To encourage the import of foreign goods
(b) To promote large-scale industries
(c) To boost domestic manufacturing and attract foreign investment
(d) To limit the production capacity of MSMEs

137. The government's "Startup India" initiative primarily aims to
(a) Promote the growth of large corporations
(b) Support the establishment and growth of startups and small businesses
(c) Discourage entrepreneurship
(d) Provide training to government employees

138. Which government scheme focuses on the development of common infrastructure and facilities in industrial clusters to promote MSMEs?
(a) Pradhan Mantri Jan Dhan Yojana (PMJDY)
(b) Credit Guarantee Fund Scheme for Micro and Small Enterprises (CGMSE)
(c) Scheme of Fund for Regeneration of Traditional Industries (SFURTI)
(d) National Rural Employment Guarantee Act (NREGA)

139. "Zero Defect, Zero Effect" is an initiative associated with the promotion of MSMEs in India. What does it aim to achieve?
(a) To reduce product quality to save costs
(b) To encourage pollution and environmental damage
(c) To ensure that products have zero defects and do not have an adverse effect on the environment
(d) To minimize employment opportunities in the MSME sector

140. The "Micro Units Development and Refinance Agency Ltd" (MUDRA) primarily provides
(a) Training and skill development for entrepreneurs
(b) Collateral-free loans to micro-enterprises
(c) Support for large corporations
(d) Export promotion services

141. In the context of MSMEs, what does the term "Udyog Aadhar" represent?
(a) A government department responsible for industrial growth
(b) A national festival to promote entrepreneurship
(c) An online registration process for MSMEs
(d) A tax scheme for large corporations

142. What is the primary objective of "Cluster Development Programs" for MSMEs?
(a) To isolate MSMEs from each other
(b) To promote large-scale industries
(c) To enhance the competitiveness of MSMEs by promoting the development of industrial clusters
(d) To discourage entrepreneurship

143. The "Rajiv Gandhi Udyami Mitra Yojana" aims to provide
(a) Financial support to large corporations
(b) Collateral-free loans to MSMEs
(c) Export promotion services
(d) Employment opportunities in the agricultural sector

144. The "National Small Industries Day" is celebrated in India on
(a) January 26 (b) August 15
(c) October 2 (d) August 30

145. What is the primary function of the "Credit Linked Capital Subsidy Scheme" (CLCSS) for MSMEs?
(a) To discourage the use of credit for business growth
(b) To provide direct financial assistance to MSMEs
(c) To promote large-scale industries
(d) To provide financial support to startups

146. Which ministry is responsible for the "Zero Defect, Zero Effect" (ZED) certification scheme for MSMEs?
(a) Ministry of Home Affairs
(b) Ministry of Micro, Small, and Medium Enterprises
(c) Ministry of Finance
(d) Ministry of External Affairs

147. In the context of MSMEs, what does the term "Lean Manufacturing Competitiveness Scheme" (LMCS) aim to promote?
(a) A reduction in manufacturing efficiency
(b) Adoption of Lean manufacturing practices to enhance competitiveness
(c) Heavy reliance on labor-intensive processes
(d) Promotion of large-scale industries

148. Which government initiative focuses on the digital empowerment of MSMEs and provides support for technology adoption and capacity building?
(a) Pradhan Mantri Jan Dhan Yojana (PMJDY)
(b) Credit Guarantee Fund Scheme for Micro and Small Enterprises (CGMSE)
(c) Digital MSME Scheme
(d) National Rural Employment Guarantee Act (NREGA)

149. In the context of small industries, what does "sickness" refer to?
(a) Physical health issues of the workers
(b) An industrial unit's inability to operate profitably and meet its financial obligations
(c) A government program for healthcare
(d) An organization's focus on well-being

150. What is the primary reason for sickness in small industries?
(a) Excessive production capacity
(b) Inadequate demand for products
(c) High-profit margins
(d) Over-employment

151. Which of the following is a common external factor contributing to the sickness of small industries?
(a) Efficient management
(b) Access to skilled labor
(c) Economic policies and regulations
(d) High demand for products

152. What is the term for a situation in which an industrial unit is unable to meet its financial obligations and repay loans?
(a) Profitability (b) Solvency
(c) Efficiency (d) Growth

153. What is "Technological Obsolescence" in the context of small industries?
(a) The use of outdated technology in production
(b) High demand for products
(c) Efficient management practices
(d) Low competition

154. The "Bottleneck Sickness" in small industries is typically caused by
(a) Access to abundant resources

(b) Smooth production processes
(c) A single problem or bottleneck affecting the entire production
(d) Efficient management

155. "Cash Flow Sickness" in small industries is characterized by
(a) Adequate cash reserves
(b) A surplus of funds
(c) A lack of funds to meet daily operating expenses
(d) High profitability

156. What is the term for a situation where small industries are unable to compete with larger counterparts due to economies of scale?
(a) Scale inefficiency
(b) Economic disparities
(c) Large-scale competition
(d) Small-scale competition

157. The term "Sick Industries Companies (Special Provisions) Act" provides legal provisions for the
(a) Promotion of small industries
(b) Rehabilitation and winding up of sick industrial companies
(c) Taxation of large corporations
(d) Efficient management of large industries

158. Which government institution plays a key role in the rehabilitation of sick small industries in India?
(a) Ministry of Finance
(b) Small Industries Development Bank of India (SIDBI)
(c) Ministry of External Affairs
(d) National Stock Exchange (NSE)

159. "Board for Industrial and Financial Reconstruction" (BIFR) in India primarily deals with the
(a) Promotion of small industries
(b) Rehabilitation and revival of sick industrial companies
(c) Taxation of large corporations
(d) Efficient management of large industries

160. What is the primary role of "Industrial Sickness"?
(a) To encourage industrial growth
(b) To analyze the reasons for sickness in small industries
(c) To provide healthcare services
(d) To promote large corporations

161. What is the term for the situation in which a company's liabilities exceed its assets, and it is unable to meet its financial obligations?
(a) Solvency
(b) Profitability
(c) Technological obsolescence
(d) Cash flow sickness

162. The "Overdues Sickness" in small industries is related to
(a) Timely repayment of loans
(b) Efficient management
(c) Delayed payments and overdue bills
(d) Scale efficiency

163. The "Multiplicity Sickness" in small industries is characterized by
(a) Simple and streamlined production processes
(b) A lack of competition
(c) An over-diversified product range
(d) Efficient management

164. "Debtor Sickness" in small industries results from
(a) Efficient management of accounts receivable
(b) Timely payment of bills by customers
(c) Delayed payments from debtors or customers
(d) Scale efficiency

165. The term "Liquidity Sickness" refers to a situation in which small industries face
(a) A surplus of liquid assets
(b) Difficulty in converting assets into cash to meet short-term obligations
(c) High profitability
(d) Efficient management

166. In the context of sick small industries, what is "Neglect Sickness"?
(a) Neglecting opportunities for growth
(b) Efficient management
(c) A situation where government policies and banks neglect the needs of sick units
(d) A surplus of funds

167. The "Operating Sickness" in small industries is primarily related to
(a) Timely repayment of loans
(b) Efficient management of resources
(c) Operational inefficiencies and losses
(d) High demand for products

168. "Real Sickness" in small industries occurs when
(a) Production capacity exceeds demand
(b) Efficient management is in place
(c) Production processes are smooth
(d) A company is unable to operate profitably and meet its financial obligations

169. What is the primary goal of the "Rehabilitation of Sick Industrial Companies" (RISIC) policy in India?
(a) To promote the growth of large corporations
(b) To rehabilitate and revive sick small industrial companies
(c) To discourage entrepreneurship
(d) To provide financial support to startups

170. The "Asset Reconstruction Companies" (ARCs) in India are involved in the
(a) Promotion of small industries
(b) Rehabilitation of sick industrial companies
(c) Taxation of large corporations
(d) Efficient management of large industries

171. What is the term for a situation in which small industries are unable to access credit and financial resources for their operations?
(a) Financial sufficiency
(b) Credit sickness
(c) Efficient management
(d) Over-employment

172. The term "Efficiency Sickness" in small industries indicates
(a) Efficient management practices
(b) A lack of competition
(c) Over-employment
(d) A situation where production processes are inefficient

173. Which government body is responsible for implementing and monitoring the rehabilitation of sick small industries in India?
(a) Ministry of Finance
(b) Board for Industrial and Financial Reconstruction (BIFR)
(c) Ministry of External Affairs
(d) National Stock Exchange (NSE)

174. What is the primary purpose of providing institutional finance to small industries?
(a) To promote large corporations
(b) To create a surplus of funds
(c) To encourage entrepreneurship and support the growth of small enterprises
(d) To restrict competition

175. Small industries often require financial assistance for various purposes. Which institution primarily provides long-term finance to them?
(a) Commercial banks
(b) Cooperative banks
(c) Microfinance institutions
(d) Development financial institutions

176. Which institution was established to promote and develop small industries in India by providing financial and non-financial support?
(a) Reserve Bank of India (RBI)
(b) Small Industries Development Bank of India (SIDBI)
(c) National Stock Exchange (NSE)
(d) Ministry of Finance

177. The term "Refinance" in the context of institutional finance refers to
(a) Providing credit to large corporations
(b) Providing funding to microfinance institutions
(c) Financial assistance provided by development financial institutions to primary lending institutions
(d) Microfinance support for women entrepreneurs

178. Commercial banks play a crucial role in providing financial assistance to small industries. What type of finance do commercial banks typically offer?
(a) Short-term and long-term loans
(b) Grants and subsidies
(c) Equity investments
(d) Skill development programs

179. "Priority Sector Lending" is a mandate by the Reserve Bank of India (RBI) that requires commercial banks to allocate a certain percentage of their total lending to which sector, including small industries?
(a) Large corporations
(b) Agriculture and allied activities
(c) Export-oriented businesses
(d) Information technology

180. Cooperative banks, often established at the grassroots level, primarily serve
(a) Large corporations
(b) Urban areas
(c) Rural and semi-urban areas
(d) Export-oriented businesses

181. What is the primary function of cooperative banks in providing institutional finance to small industries?
(a) To provide long-term loans
(b) To encourage urban development
(c) To promote large corporations
(d) To provide credit to the rural and agricultural sectors

182. The "Self-Help Group (SHG) Bank Linkage Program" is associated with
(a) Commercial banks
(b) Cooperative banks
(c) Microfinance institutions
(d) Development financial institutions

183. Microfinance institutions primarily focus on providing financial services to
(a) Large corporations
(b) Urban businesses
(c) Low-income individuals, including small entrepreneurs
(d) Export-oriented businesses

184. What is the term for the practice of lending small amounts of money to individuals or microenterprises to help them establish or expand their businesses?
(a) Equity financing (b) Venture capital
(c) Microfinance
(d) Cooperative banking

185. The "Micro Units Development and Refinance Agency Ltd" (MUDRA) primarily focuses on providing financial support to
(a) Large corporations
(b) Micro and small enterprises
(c) Urban businesses
(d) Export-oriented businesses

186. The "Pradhan Mantri Mudra Yojana" (PMMY) is a government scheme aimed at providing access to credit for
(a) Large corporations
(b) Rural and semi-urban businesses
(c) Women entrepreneurs
(d) Micro and small businesses

187. In the context of institutional finance, what does "SIDO" stand for?
(a) Small Industries Development Organization
(b) Special Institutional Development Order
(c) Securities and Investment Development Office
(d) Self-Help and Innovation Development Organization

188. The "Credit Guarantee Fund Trust for Micro and Small Enterprises" (CGTMSE) primarily provides
(a) Grants and subsidies to large corporations
(b) Collateral-free credit to micro and small enterprises
(c) Skill development programs for urban businesses
(d) Support for export-oriented businesses

189. "SIDO" is an organization under the Ministry of Micro, Small, and Medium Enterprises (MSME) responsible for
(a) Providing financial assistance to large corporations
(b) Promoting cooperative banks
(c) Coordinating and implementing programs for the development of small industries
(d) Export promotion

190. Which financial institution was established to support and promote the development of export-oriented businesses, including small industries?
(a) Reserve Bank of India (RBI)
(b) Export-Import Bank of India (EXIM Bank)
(c) National Stock Exchange (NSE)
(d) Small Industries Development Bank of India (SIDBI)

191. The "Rajiv Gandhi Shilpi Swasthya Bima Yojana" is an insurance scheme for
(a) Large corporations
(b) Rural and semi-urban businesses
(c) Health coverage for artisans and weavers
(d) Export-oriented businesses

192. The term "Equity Financing" refers to
(a) Loans provided by commercial banks
(b) Investment in a business in exchange for ownership shares
(c) Collateral-free loans to micro-enterprises
(d) Financing for large corporations

193. What is the primary goal of the "Cluster Development Program" in the context of institutional finance for small industries?
(a) To encourage competition among small enterprises
(b) To promote large corporations

(c) To enhance the competitiveness of small industries by promoting the development of industrial clusters
(d) To provide skill development programs

194. The term "Credit Suisse" is often associated with
(a) Commercial banking
(b) Development financial institutions
(c) Export financing
(d) Microfinance

195. In the context of institutional finance, what is "Village Industries"?
(a) Large corporations based in rural areas
(b) Small enterprises engaged in traditional and handicraft activities in rural areas
(c) Urban businesses
(d) Development financial institutions

196. What is the primary objective of the "Credit Linked Capital Subsidy Scheme" (CLCSS) for small industries?
(a) To provide grants to large corporations
(b) To encourage urban development
(c) To promote large corporations
(d) To provide financial assistance to micro and small enterprises for technology upgradation

197. The term "Venture Capital" is often associated with
(a) Collateral-free credit
(b) Microfinance institutions
(c) Equity financing for startups and high-growth businesses
(d) Cooperative banks

198. Which government institution provides training and skill development programs for entrepreneurs in the small industries sector?
(a) National Stock Exchange (NSE)
(b) Ministry of Finance
(c) Ministry of External Affairs
(d) National Institute for Entrepreneurship and Small Business Development (NIESBUD)

199. Which financial institution primarily focuses on providing financial services to individuals within small industries?
(a) Commercial Banks
(b) Cooperative Banks
(c) Microfinance Institutions
(d) Development Banks

200. In which sector are Cooperative Banks more prevalent in providing financial assistance?
(a) Urban Industries
(b) Large-scale Enterprises
(c) Rural Communities
(d) Export-oriented Businesses

201. Which financial entity is known for offering a wider array of financial products and services tailored to the needs of small industries?
(a) Commercial Banks
(b) Development Banks
(c) Microfinance Institutions
(d) Investment Banks

202. Which institution typically charges higher interest rates on loans to small industries due to higher risk?
(a) Cooperative Banks
(b) Development Banks
(c) Commercial Banks
(d) Microfinance Institutions

203. In which type of institution are financial literacy programs commonly offered to small industries?
(a) Development Banks
(b) Commercial Banks
(c) Investment Banks
(d) Microfinance Institutions

204. Which institution often acts as an intermediary connecting small industries with potential investors?
(a) Development Banks
(b) Cooperative Banks
(c) Commercial Banks
(d) Microfinance Institutions

205. Which type of bank is more likely to require extensive documentation and collateral for loan approvals from small industries?
(a) Cooperative Banks
(b) Development Banks
(c) Commercial Banks
(d) Microfinance Institutions

206. In which sector do Cooperative Banks primarily serve the financial needs of the community?
(a) Export-oriented Businesses
(b) Urban Industries
(c) Large-scale Enterprises
(d) Rural Communities

207. Which financial institution plays a critical role in providing access to capital for small industries?
(a) Investment Banks
(b) Microfinance Institutions
(c) Commercial Banks
(d) Development Banks

208. Which entity primarily offers long-term financing options tailored to the capital needs of small industries?
(a) Microfinance Institutions
(b) Commercial Banks
(c) Cooperative Banks
(d) Development Banks

209. Which institution is more inclined to provide low-interest loans to small industries?
(a) Development Banks
(b) Microfinance Institutions
(c) Cooperative Banks
(d) Commercial Banks

210. In which type of institution are financial services primarily targeted towards women entrepreneurs within small industries?
(a) Commercial Banks
(b) Development Banks
(c) Microfinance Institutions
(d) Cooperative Banks

211. Which financial entity is known for offering collateral-free financing options to small industries?
(a) Microfinance Institutions
(b) Development Banks
(c) Cooperative Banks
(d) Commercial Banks

212. Which institution typically requires higher documentation and collateral from small industries due to risk mitigation?
(a) Cooperative Banks
(b) Development Banks
(c) Microfinance Institutions
(d) Commercial Banks

213. In which type of bank are financial literacy programs less commonly offered to small industries?
(a) Commercial Banks
(b) Development Banks
(c) Microfinance Institutions
(d) Cooperative Banks

214. Which financial institution plays a crucial role in connecting small industries with potential investors?
(a) Microfinance Institutions
(b) Commercial Banks
(c) Development Banks
(d) Cooperative Banks

215. Which entity is less likely to offer flexible repayment options to small industries?
(a) Microfinance Institutions
(b) Development Banks
(c) Cooperative Banks
(d) Commercial Banks

216. In which type of bank are financial services primarily aimed at promoting rural development?
(a) Development Banks
(b) Microfinance Institutions
(c) Commercial Banks
(d) Cooperative Banks

217. Which institution primarily offers short-term financing solutions to small industries?
(a) Development Banks
(b) Commercial Banks
(c) Microfinance Institutions
(d) Cooperative Banks

218. Which financial entity balances social impact with financial sustainability in its operations?
(a) Commercial Banks
(b) Cooperative Banks
(c) Microfinance Institutions
(d) Development Banks

ANSWER KEY

1. (b) **2.** (a) **3.** (c) **4.** (b) **5.** (b) **6.** (b) **7.** (a) **8.** (c) **9.** (b) **10.** (d)
11. (c) **12.** (c) **13.** (b) **14.** (d) **15.** (a) **16.** (c) **17.** (b) **18.** (c) **19.** (d) **20.** (b)
21. (b) **22.** (b) **23.** (c) **24.** (c) **25.** (c) **26.** (b) **27.** (b) **28.** (c) **29.** (a) **30.** (c)
31. (c) **32.** (c) **33.** (a) **34.** (b) **35.** (a) **36.** (c) **37.** (a) **38.** (c) **39.** (c) **40.** (d)
41. (c) **42.** (c) **43.** (b) **44.** (c) **45.** (a) **46.** (b) **47.** (c) **48.** (c) **49.** (b) **50.** (c)
51. (b) **52.** (d) **53.** (b) **54.** (b) **55.** (b) **56.** (b) **57.** (c) **58.** (b) **59.** (d) **60.** (d)
61. (a) **62.** (b) **63.** (a) **64.** (c) **65.** (d) **66.** (d) **67.** (c) **68.** (b) **69.** (c) **70.** (c)
71. (c) **72.** (b) **73.** (b) **74.** (c) **75.** (a) **76.** (a) **77.** (b) **78.** (b) **79.** (c) **80.** (b)
81. (b) **82.** (c) **83.** (a) **84.** (b) **85.** (b) **86.** (b) **87.** (a) **88.** (c) **89.** (c) **90.** (b)
91. (b) **92.** (c) **93.** (b) **94.** (b) **95.** (b) **96.** (c) **97.** (b) **98.** (c) **99.** (c) **100.** (c)
101. (c) **102.** (b) **103.** (b) **104.** (b) **105.** (b) **106.** (c) **107.** (c) **108.** (c) **109.** (c) **110.** (c)
111. (a) **112.** (c) **113.** (b) **114.** (d) **115.** (c) **116.** (c) **117.** (b) **118.** (b) **119.** (b) **120.** (b)
121. (b) **122.** (b) **123.** (d) **124.** (c) **125.** (d) **126.** (b) **127.** (b) **128.** (c) **129.** (b) **130.** (c)
131. (d) **132.** (b) **133.** (c) **134.** (d) **135.** (c) **136.** (c) **137.** (b) **138.** (c) **139.** (c) **140.** (b)
141. (c) **142.** (c) **143.** (d) **144.** (d) **145.** (b) **146.** (b) **147.** (b) **148.** (c) **149.** (b) **150.** (b)
151. (c) **152.** (b) **153.** (a) **154.** (c) **155.** (c) **156.** (a) **157.** (b) **158.** (b) **159.** (b) **160.** (b)
161. (a) **162.** (c) **163.** (c) **164.** (c) **165.** (b) **166.** (c) **167.** (c) **168.** (d) **169.** (b) **170.** (b)
171. (b) **172.** (d) **173.** (b) **174.** (c) **175.** (d) **176.** (b) **177.** (c) **178.** (a) **179.** (b) **180.** (c)
181. (d) **182.** (a) **183.** (c) **184.** (c) **185.** (b) **186.** (d) **187.** (a) **188.** (b) **189.** (c) **190.** (b)
191. (c) **192.** (b) **193.** (c) **194.** (a) **195.** (b) **196.** (d) **197.** (c) **198.** (d) **199.** (c) **200.** (c)
201. (b) **202.** (d) **203.** (d) **204.** (a) **205.** (c) **206.** (d) **207.** (d) **208.** (d) **209.** (a) **210.** (c)
211. (a) **212.** (d) **213.** (a) **214.** (c) **215.** (d) **216.** (d) **217.** (b) **218.** (c)

ADDITIONAL MULTIPLE CHOICE QUESTIONS

1. From the following determinants of the price elasticity of demand, indicate the correct code for the determinants having a positive relationship with the degree of the price elasticity of demand :

(a) Range of substitutes of the commodity
(b) Extent of the different uses of the commodity
(c) Portion of the income of the buyer spent on the commodity
(d) Income group of buyers purchasing the commodity

Code :
(1) (a) and (b) only
(2) (c) and (d) only
(3) (a), (b) and (c) only
(4) (b), (c) and (d) only

2. Match the items given in List - I with those given in the List - II and suggest the correct code :

List - I	**List - II**
(a) Marginal Productivity/Average Productivity	(i) Isoquant curve
(b) Substitutability of inputs	(ii) Isocost line
(c) Constant Negative Slope	(iii) Production Function
(d) Convex to origin	(iv) Elasticity of Production

Codes:

	(a)	**(b)**	**(c)**	**(d)**
(1)	(i)	(ii)	(iii)	(iv)
(2)	(ii)	(i)	(iv)	(iii)
(3)	(iv)	(iii)	(ii)	(i)
(4)	(iii)	(iv)	(i)	(ii)

3. From the following two statements of Assertion (A) and Reasoning (R) suggest the correct code :

Assertion (A) : The equilibrium price is decided at the level where the quantity demanded equals the quantity supplied.

Reasoning (R) : At this level excess of demand and excess of supply both remain zero.

Code :
(1) (A) is correct but (R) is incorrect.
(2) (A) is incorrect but (R) is correct.
(3) (A) and (R) both are correct but (R) is not right explanation of (A).
(4) (A) and (R) both are correct and (R) is right explanation of (A).

4. Despite differences in cost of production the oligopolists will not vary the prices of their products as per which combination of the following models ?

(a) Collusion model
(b) Cournot's model
(c) Kinked Demand model
(d) Price Leadership model

Select the correct code.
(1) (a) and (b) only
(2) (c) and (d) only
(3) (a) and (d) only
(4) (a), (b) and (c) only

5. For the following two statements of Assertion (A) and Reasoning (R) suggest the correct code:

Assertion (A) : Low initial price regarded as the principal means for entering into mass market for some new products.

Reasoning (R) : Firms generally enter into production of new products with excess capacity of the plant initially.

Code :

(1) (A) is correct but (R) is not correct.
(2) (A) is not correct but (R) is correct.
(3) (A) and (R) both are correct and (R) is right explanation of (A).
(4) (A) and (R) both are correct but (R) is not right explanation of (A).

6. The firm may go for defensive advertising as per which one of the following approaches ?
(1) Percentage to sales approach
(2) Return on investment approach
(3) Competitive parity approach
(4) Objective and task approach

7. Indicate the correct code from the following that does not represent the Profitability Index for an investment proposal of a firm :
(a) Average annual net income earned divided by the investment
(b) Equating annual net cash inflows to investment
(c) Ratio of present value of future cash inflows to investment making it equal to zero
(d) Ratio of present value of future cash inflows to present cash outflows

Code :
(1) (a), (b) and (c) only
(2) (a) and (c) only
(3) (b) and (d) only
(4) (a), (b) and (d) only

8. Match the items of List II with the items of List I and indicate the code of correct matching.

List I	**List II**
(a) Organisation Man	(i) Maximising self interest.
(b) Self-actualising Man	(ii) Using capabilities to develop a sense of creatingcertain things.
(c) Complex Man	(iii) Sacrificing individuality for the sake of group.
(d) Rational-Economic Man	(iv) Understanding human needs may not be the final step in understanding human behaviour.

Codes:

	(a)	**(b)**	**(c)**	**(d)**
(1)	(iv)	(i)	(iii)	(ii)
(2)	(iii)	(ii)	(iv)	(i)
(3)	(i)	(iv)	(ii)	(iii)
(4)	(ii)	(i)	(iv)	(iii)

9. Who proposed the Balance Theory of attitude formation ?
(1) Festinger
(2) Fritz Heider
(3) Charles Osgood and Percy Tannenbaum
(4) Rosenberg

10. Which one of the following is an element of motivation according to Vroom's Vector Valence theory ?
(1) Involvement (2) Equity
(3) Instrumentality (4) Existence

11. Which one of the following is not a component of Bass' Theory of Transformational Leadership ?
(1) Idealized influence
(2) Inspirational motivation
(3) Intellectual stimulation
(4) Team consideration

12. **Assertion (A) :** Under stressful situations, a person is unable to listen to and understand the message correctly.
Reasoning (R) : During stressful situations, the psychological frame of mind changes and the message gets distorted due to the beliefs, experiences, goals and values held by the receiver of the message.

Code :
(1) (A) and (R) both are correct and (R) is the correct explanation of (A).
(2) (A) and (R) both are correct but (R) is not the correct explanation of (A).
(3) (A) is correct whereas (R) is incorrect.
(4) (R) is correct whereas (A) is incorrect.

13. Match the items of List-II with the items of List-I and suggest the correct code :

List-I (Source of resistance)	**List-II (Coping mechanisms)**
(a) Perceived peripherality of change	(i) Role redefinition and re-orientation
(b) Fear of loss of power	(ii) Participation and involvement

(c) Fear of obsolescence (iii) Participation in diagnosis
(d) Fear of imposition (iv) Development of skills

Codes:

	(a)	(b)	(c)	(d)
(1)	(iv)	(i)	(iii)	(ii)
(2)	(ii)	(i)	(iv)	(iii)
(3)	(iii)	(i)	(iv)	(ii)
(4)	(i)	(iii)	(iv)	(ii)

14. Match the items of List-II with the items of List-I and indicate the code of correct matching.

List-I (Model of Organisational Behaviour)	List-II (Employee Orientation)
(a) Autocratic	(i) Responsible behaviour
(b) Custodial	(ii) Security and benefits
(c) Supportive	(iii) Job performance
(d) Collegial	(iv) Obedience

Codes:

	(a)	(b)	(c)	(d)
(1)	(iv)	(ii)	(iii)	(i)
(2)	(iv)	(iii)	(i)	(ii)
(3)	(i)	(iv)	(iii)	(ii)
(4)	(iv)	(i)	(ii)	(iii)

15. Which one of the following types of strike is without the consent of official of union ?
(1) Jurisdictional strike
(2) Wild cat strike
(3) Sympathy strike
(4) Slow down strike

16. Which one of the following describes the metamorphosis stage of employee socialisation?
(1) Employee joins organisation with his values, attitudes and expectations.
(2) Employee studies the organisation culture.
(3) Employee evaluates the dichotomy between expectations and reality.
(4) Employee becomes comfortable with organisation and internalises its norms.

17. When employees work longer days in exchange for longer weekends or other days off, it is called :
(1) Flexy time (2) Job sharing
(3) Compressed work week
(4) Extended timing

18. 'Employee relations' include which of the following ?
(a) Organisation's efforts to manage relationships between employer and employees.
(b) The programs to prevent and resolve problems arising from work situations.
(c) Relations between management and trade unions.
(d) Organisation's structure of managing rapport between boss and staff.

Code :
(1) (a) and (c)
(2) (a), (b) and (d)
(3) (b) and (c)
(4) (c) only

19. In which of the following, the payment of bonus is linked to performance of specific employees or group of employees ?
(a) Profit sharing
(b) Gain sharing plans
(c) Social system plans

Code :
(1) (a) only
(2) (b) only
(3) Both (a) and (b)
(4) (a), (b) and (c)

20. Which one of the following is a contract made through collusion between management and labour representatives and contains terms beneficial to management and unfavourable to union workers ?
(1) Unilateral contract
(2) Aleatory contract
(3) Sweetheart contract
(4) Invalid contract

21. When an employee is willing to go above and beyond what is typically expected in his or her role, it is known as :
(1) Employee Empowerment
(2) Employee Engagement
(3) Employee Enhancement
(4) Employee Encouragement

22. Indicate the correct code for the following types of decisions to be incorporated within financial decisions.
(a) Investment decisions
(b) Financing decisions
(c) Pricing decisions
(d) Profit distribution decisions

Code :

(1) (a) and (b) only
(2) (a), (b) and (c) only
(3) (a), (b) and (d) only
(4) (b), (c) and (d) only

23. In case the profitability index of an investment is equal to one(=1), the net present value of the investment will be :

(1) More than one (>1)
(2) Equal to one (=1)
(3) Less than one (<1)
(4) Equal to zero (=0)

24. For the following two statements of Assertion (A) and Reasoning (R) select the correct code :

Assertion (A) : Risk analysis of capital investment is the most complex and controversial area in finance.

Reasoning (R) : Capital investment decisions are based on estimates of future cash inflows.

Code :

(1) (A) is incorrect but (R) is correct.
(2) (A) is correct but (R) is incorrect.
(3) (A) and (R) both are correct and (R) is right explanation of (A).
(4) (A) and (R) both are correct but (R) is not right explanation of (A).

25. Acquisition of firms is the same as :

(a) a merger (b) an amalgamation
(c) a takeover (d) an absorption

Select the correct code.

(1) (a), (b) and (c) only
(2) (b), (c) and (d) only
(3) (a) and (b) only
(4) (c) and (d) only

26. M-M Hypothesis for capital structure is based on which code of the following assumptions ?

(a) Capital markets are perfect
(b) Firms belong to equal risk class
(c) There is 100% dividend payout ratio
(d) There are nominal corporate taxes

Select the correct code.

(1) (a) and (b) only
(2) (a), (b) and (c) only
(3) (b), (c) and (d) only
(4) (a), (b) and (d) only

27. The formula $P_0 = \frac{D}{K} + \frac{\frac{R}{K}(E-D)}{K}$ (where P_0 is market price of shares, E is earning per share, D is dividend per share. R is rate of Return and K is cost of equity) for determining the dividend of the firm has been given by :

(1) Myron Gordon
(2) James E Walter
(3) Modigliani - Miller
(4) David Durrand

28. Indicate the correct code for the following two statements of Assertion (A) and Reasoning (R) :

Assertion (A) : Invertors in capital market now have higher inclination for investment in debentures.

Reasoning (R) : Debentures have active secondary markets now.

Code :

(1) Both (A) and (R) are correct ; and (R) is the right explanation of (A).
(2) Both (A) and (R) are correct ; but (R) is not the right explanation of (A).
(3) (A) is correct but (R) is incorrect.
(4) Both (A) and (R) are incorrect.

29. Which one of the following expresses the tendency of consumers to interpret information in a way that fits one's preconceptions in the consumer buying behaviour ?

(1) Selective Attention
(2) Selective Distortion
(3) Selective Retention
(4) Subliminal Perception

30. Which one of the following is not a factor that reduces price sensitivity of a product ?

(1) The product is more distinctive.
(2) Buyers are fully aware of substitutes.
(3) Buyers cannot store the product.
(4) The product is assumed to have more quality, prestige, or exclusiveness.

31. Attributes or benefits that consumers strongly associate with a brand, positively evaluate, and believe they could not find to the same extent with a competitive brand is known as :

(1) Competitive points-of-parity
(2) Relational points-of-parity
(3) Correlational points-of-parity
(4) Points-of-difference

32. Which one of the following represents 'Penetrated market' ?
(1) The part of the qualified available market the company decides to pursue.
(2) The set of consumers who are buying the company's product.
(3) The set of consumers who have interest, income, and access to a particular offer.
(4) The set of consumers with a sufficient level of interest in a market offer.

33. Match the items of List - II with the items of List - I and suggest the correct code :

List - I (Components of holistic marketing)	List - II (Key constituent / Dimension)
(a) Internal marketing	(i) Brand and customer equity
(b) Performance marketing	(ii) Stakeholder
(c) Integrated marketing	(iii) Marketing department
(d) Relationship marketing	(iv) Communications

Codes:

	(a)	(b)	(c)	(d)
(1)	(iii)	(i)	(iv)	(ii)
(2)	(iii)	(ii)	(i)	(iv)
(3)	(ii)	(i)	(iii)	(iv)
(4)	(i)	(iii)	(iv)	(ii)

34. Match the items of List - II with the items of List - I and suggest the correct code :

List - I	List - II
(a) Style	(i) That comes quickly into public view, are adopted with great zeal, peak early, and decline very fast.
(b) Fashion	(ii) Basic and distinctive mode of expression appearing in a field of human endeavour.
(c) Fad	(iii) Currently accepted or popular style in a given field.

Codes:

	(a)	(b)	(c)
(1)	(ii)	(iii)	(i)
(2)	(iii)	(i)	(ii)
(3)	(i)	(ii)	(iii)
(4)	(ii)	(i)	(iii)

35. The following are the statements relating to the new product development. Indicate the statements being correct or incorrect.
Statement (I) : Most established companies do not focus on incremental innovation for new product development.
Statement (II) : Most established companies enter new markets by tweaking products for new customers.
Code :
(1) Both the statements are correct.
(2) Both the statements are incorrect.
(3) Statement (I) is correct while Statement (II) is incorrect.
(4) Statement (I) is incorrect while Statement (II) is correct.

36. Match the items of List II with List I and select the correct code :

List I	List II
(a) H.M.L. classification	(i) To determine the criticality of an item and its effect on production and other services. It is specially used for classification of spare parts.
(b) V.E.D. classification	(ii) Based on the pat tern of issues from stores and is useful in controlling obsolescence and helpful in identifying active items and surplus items.
(c) SDE classification	(iii) The classification unit value is the criterion and not the annual consumption.
(d) FSN classification	(iv) Based on problems faced in procurements, availability of items and useful in the context of scarcity of supply.

Codes:

	(a)	(b)	(c)	(d)
(1)	(ii)	(iii)	(iv)	(i)
(2)	(iv)	(i)	(ii)	(iii)
(3)	(ii)	(iv)	(i)	(iii)
(4)	(iii)	(i)	(iv)	(ii)

37. **Statement (I) :** The critical path has been defined as the longest duration path between the first and the last nodes of a project.

Statement (II) : The duration of a project is not always the same as the duration of its critical path.

Statement (III) : The Earliest start and finish times of an activity are based on the condition that every activity will not be started and finished as early as possible.

Find the correct code for given statements being correct or incorrect.

(1) Statement (I) and (II) are correct but (III) is not correct.

(2) Statement (I) and (III) are correct but (II) is not correct.

(3) Statement (I) is correct but (II) and (III) are not correct.

(4) Statement (II) is correct but (I) and (III) are not correct.

38. **Statement (I) :** Internal failure costs are generated after the product is dispatched as a result of non-performance to requirements.

Statement (II) : External failure costs are generated before the product is dispatched as a result of non-conformance to requirements.

Which of the following code is correct related to above statements being correct or incorrect ?

(1) Both Statements (I) and (II) are correct.

(2) Both Statements (I) and (II) are not correct.

(3) Statement (I) is correct but (II) is not correct.

(4) Statement (II) is correct but (I) is not correct.

39. Which of the following code is correct for the given statements being correct or incorrect ?

Statement (I) : Method analysis is a technique in job design in which job is considered as a whole.

Statement (II) : Principles of motion economy aim at minimizing the fatigue of workers due to repetitive motion of the different parts of body.

Statement (III) : Work sampling is a method used to determine the idle time of machine or workers as a whole during the day.

Code :

(1) Statement (I) and (III) are not correct but Statement (II) is correct.

(2) Statement (I) and (II) are not correct but Statement (III) is correct.

(3) Statement (II) and (III) are not correct but (I) is correct.

(4) Statement (I), (II) and (III) all are correct

40. 'Just In Time' originally developed in 1970s by a Japanese company was initially known as :

(1) Honda Manufacturing system

(2) Isuzu Manufacturing system

(3) Mitsubishi Manufacturing system

(4) Toyota Manufacturing system

41. Match the items of List - II with List - I to find the correct code :

List - I	List - II
(a) Technological Processes	(i) Building Design, Facility Layout
(b) Facilities	(ii) Vendor Capabilities, Acquisition Decision
(c) Personnel Estimates	(iii) Process Design, Process Linkage
(d) Vertical Integration Studies	(iv) Skill Requirements, Supervision Requirements

Codes:

	(a)	(b)	(c)	(d)
(1)	(iii)	(i)	(iv)	(ii)
(2)	(i)	(iii)	(iv)	(ii)
(3)	(ii)	(i)	(iv)	(iii)
(4)	(i)	(iii)	(ii)	(iv)

42. Following statements are given for plant location strategies :

Statement (I) : White goods manufacturing companies have separate plants for colour TVs, washing machines, microwave ovens, etc.; for avoiding confusion and bringing about economies of scale.

Statement (II) : Pepsi and Coke have bottling plants scattered all over the country which cater to different regions to avoid confusion at the main manufacturing set-up rather than reducing overall transportation costs and the lead time for supplying goods in the markets.

Find the correct code of the above statements being correct or incorrect.

(1) Statement (I) is not correct but (II) is correct.
(2) Statements (I) and (II) both are correct.
(3) Statement (I) is correct but (II) is not correct.
(4) Statements (I) and (II) both are not correct.

43. The following are the two statements relating to the theory of probability. Indicate the statements being correct or incorrect.

Statement (I) : The probability of the joint occurrence of independent events A and B is equal to the probability of A multiplied by the probability of B or vice versa.

Statement (II) : The probability of the joint occurrence of independent event A and dependent event B is equal to the probability of event A multiplied by the conditional probability of B when A has occurred or vice versa.

Code :
(1) Both the statements are correct.
(2) Both the statements are incorrect.
(3) Statement (I) is correct while Statement (II) is incorrect.
(4) Statement (I) is incorrect while Statement (II) is correct.

44. Which one of the following possibilities leads to Type I error in hypothesis testing?
(1) The hypothesis is true but our test leads to its rejection.
(2) The hypothesis is false but our test leads to its acceptance.
(3) The hypothesis is true and our test leads to its acceptance.
(4) The hypothesis is false and our test leads to its rejection.

45. Which one among the following relates to the probability-based sampling technique?
(1) Quota sampling
(2) Snow-ball sampling
(3) Stratified sampling
(4) Judgement sampling

46. Which of the following statements relating to Correlation and Regression are true ?
(a) The Coefficient of Correlation is independent of change of origin and scale.
(b) The Coefficient of Correlation between the two variables is the arithmetic average of the two Regression Coefficients.
(c) The probable error of the Coefficient Correlation is 0.6745 times of its standard error.
(d) Coefficient of Correlation multiplied by the ratio between the standard deviations of the two variables denotes the slope of the regression line.

Code :
(1) (a), (b) and (c)
(2) (a), (c) and (d)
(3) (b) and (d)
(4) (b), (c) and (d)

47. In which one of the following probability distributions, the mean value of the distribution is the sole parameter of the distribution ?
(1) Normal distribution
(2) Binomial distribution
(3) Exponential distribution
(4) Poisson distribution

48. Match the items of List-II with the items of List-I and denote the code of correct matching

List - I	List - II
(a) Testing the goodness of fit of a distribution	(i) Z-test
(b) Testing the significance of the differences among the average performance of more than two sample groups	(ii) Chi-square test
(c) Testing the significance of the difference between the average performance of two sample groups (Large-sized)	(iii) F-test

Codes:

	(a)	(b)	(c)
(1)	(iii)	(i)	(ii)
(2)	(ii)	(iii)	(i)
(3)	(ii)	(i)	(iii)
(4)	(i)	(ii)	(iii)

49. What is "Block Chain" in the field of information technology ?
(1) Motherboard protection device.
(2) Protection of details of electronic transaction.
(3) Taking random snaps of electronic transactions.

(4) Blocking continuous electronic transactions.

50. When the organizational requirements advocate tight cost control ; frequent, detailed control reports ; structured organization and responsibilities and incentives based on meeting strict quantitative targets then it is called :

(1) Differentiation strategy
(2) Focus strategy
(3) Diversification strategy
(4) Overall cost leadership

51. Statement (I) : Strategic turn around is a more serious form of internal retrenchment and leads to divestment or liquidation.

Statement (II) : Divestment is usually a part of rehabilitation or restructuring plan and is adopted when a turn around has been attempted but has proven to be unsuccessful.

Statement (III) : Combination strategies are the simple solutions that strategists have to offer when faced with the challenges of real life business.

Select the correct code for above mentioned statements being correct or incorrect.

(1) Statements (I) and (II) are correct but statement (III) is not correct.
(2) Statement (II) and (III) are correct but statement (I) is not correct.
(3) Statement (I) is correct but statements (II) and (III) are not correct.
(4) Statement (II) is correct but statements (I) and (III) are not correct.

52. According to Weighted-factor Approach to strategic incentive management, if for any strategic business unit, return on assets is 25%, cash flow is 25%, strategic funds programs (developmental expenses) is 25% and market share increase is also 25%, then this will fall in which category ?

(1) High Growth
(2) Medium Growth
(3) Low Growth
(4) Very High Growth

53. A concept given for diversified corporations which advocates (a) What businesses should a diversified corporation own and why ; and (b) What organizational structure, management processes, and philosophy will foster superior performance from the corporation's individual business units, is known as :

(1) Corporate Portfolio Analysis
(2) Strategic Alternative Analysis
(3) Corporate Parenting Analysis
(4) S.B.U. Analysis

54. A company in packaged tea business provides special service to its institutional buyers, apart from its consumer sales through market intermediaries, in order to encourage bulk buying and thus improving marketing efficiency, is an example of :

(1) No change strategy
(2) Profit strategy
(3) Stability strategy
(4) Pause/Proceed-with-caution strategy

55. Match the items of List II with List I and select the correct code :

List I	**List II**
(a) Mission	(i) Aspiration expressed as strategic intent
(b) Vision	(ii) Activities needed to accomplish plan
(c) Objectives	(iii) Accomplishing results at certain time
(d) Programs	(iv) Reason for existence

Codes:

	(a)	**(b)**	**(c)**	**(d)**
(1)	(iv)	(i)	(iii)	(ii)
(2)	(ii)	(iii)	(i)	(iv)
(3)	(iii)	(iv)	(ii)	(i)
(4)	(iv)	(iii)	(i)	(ii)

56. The willingness to reject unfamiliar as well as negative information is called :

(1) Marketing Myopia
(2) Vision Myopia
(3) Strategic Myopia
(4) Environmental Myopia

57. Timely and adequate assistance and rehabilitation efforts to MSEs should begin on a proactive basis when early signs of sickness are detected. This stage is termed as :

(1) Supporting Stage
(2) Handholding Stage
(3) Sustaining Stage
(4) Recovery Stage

58. Which one among the following is not a factor external to an entrepreneur ?

(1) Machinery on hire purchase
(2) Accommodation in industrial estates

(3) Financial assistance from non-government sources
(4) Business experience in the same or related line

59. Assertion (A) : When an industrial unit falls sick, those who depend on it have to face an uncertain future.

Reasoning (R) : The sick units continue to operate below the break-even point and are, thus, forced to depend on external sources for funds of their long-term survival.

Code :

(1) (A) and (R) both are correct ; and (R) is the right explanation of (A).
(2) Both (A) and (R) are correct ; but (R) is not the right explanation of (A).
(3) Both (A) and (R) are incorrect.
(4) (A) is correct but (R) is incorrect.

60. Individuals who are the founders of the business and conceptualize a business plan by putting efforts to make the plan a success are known as :

(1) Quasi entrepreneurs
(2) Bold entrepreneurs
(3) Pure entrepreneurs
(4) Owner-manager

61. Match the items of List (II) with the items of List (I) :

List (I)	List (II)
(a) Entrepreneurship is essentially a creative activity.	(i) Fransis A. Walker
(b) An entrepreneur is an organizer and coordinator of various factors of production.	(ii) Peter F. Drucker
(c) An entrepreneur is one who always searches for change, responds to it, and exploits it as an opportunity.	(iii) Joseph Schumpeter

Codes:

	(a)	(b)	(c)
(1)	(iii)	(i)	(ii)
(2)	(iii)	(ii)	(i)
(3)	(ii)	(i)	(iii)
(4)	(ii)	(iii)	(i)

62. In which one of the following years, the Government of India did not bring an Industrial Policy Resolution ?

(1) 1948 (2) 1956
(3) 1965 (4) 1977

63. Who among the following bridges the gap between inventors and managers ?

(1) Investor (2) Entrepreneur
(3) Industrialist (4) Intrapreneur

64. Which one among the following is not a true statement ?

(1) Accountability and transparency is not visible in less developed countries.
(2) A disciplined and controlled corporate governance can considerably reduce financial turmoil.
(3) A good corporate citizenship is a sort of national pride.
(4) A good corporate governance can considerably reduce corporate frauds.

65. Ethics are moral principles and values which :

(1) are legally enforceable
(2) guide a firm's behaviour
(3) provide employees with rules on how to behave
(4) govern the actions of an individual

66. Match the items of List-(II) with those of List-(I) ; and choose the correct code of combination :

List-(I)	List-(II)
(a) Procedural Justice	(i) Justice to a particular community which has been suffering in the past from injustice.
(b) Commutative Justice	(ii) Treat equal people equally and unequal people unequally.
(c) Communitarian	(iii) Justice is ensured at the beginning and all people are treated Justice equally.
(d) Distributive Justice	(iv) Actions performed complying to the law.

Codes:

	(a)	(b)	(c)	(d)
(1)	(iv)	(iii)	(ii)	(i)
(2)	(iv)	(iii)	(i)	(ii)
(3)	(iv)	(i)	(ii)	(iii)
(4)	(iii)	(i)	(ii)	(iv)

67. **Statement (I) :** According to Plato, a capitalist system is unjust because of many reasons including distributive injustice.

Statement (II) : Capitalism leads to alienation of workers.

Code :

(1) Statement (I) is correct but (II) is incorrect.
(2) Statement (II) is correct but (I) is incorrect.
(3) Both the Statements (I) and (II) are incorrect.
(4) Both the Statements (I) and (II) are correct.

68. The "Polluters must pay" principle is commonly accepted practice that those who produce pollution should bear the cost of managing it to prevent damage to human health or the environment. This principle was adopted in :

(1) 1996 Manila Declaration
(2) 2002 Kyoto Declaration
(3) 1992 Rio Declaration
(4) 2007 Paris Declaration

69. **Statement (I) :** For the improvement in the corporate governance, the Department of Company Affairs (DCA) proposed a code of behaviour for the public sector companies in the year 1998.

Statement (II) : The Clause 49 of SEBI was amended on August 2001, which had made it mandatory for every public company listed on Indian stock exchanges to sign it.

Code :

(1) Statement (I) is correct but (II) is incorrect.
(2) Statement (II) is correct but (I) is incorrect.
(3) Both the Statements (I) and (II) are correct.
(4) Both the Statements (I) and (II) are incorrect.

70. Who among the following has not given a model on Corporate Social Responsibility (CSR) ?

(1) Walker (2) Friedman
(3) Ackerman (4) Carroll

71. The following statements relate to Badli workman. Indicate the correct code.

Statement (I) : A 'Badli Workman' is employed in an industrial establishment in place of another workman whose name is borne on muster rolls of the establishment.

Statement (II) : A 'Badli workman' ceases to be regarded as such if he has completed three month's service in the establishment.

Code :

(1) Statement (I) is right, (II) is wrong.
(2) Statement (I) is wrong, (II) is right.
(3) Both the statements are right.
(4) Both the statements are wrong.

72. Co-determination is used for :

(1) Collective bargaining
(2) Industrial democracy
(3) Industrial action
(4) Union leadership

73. **Statement (I) :** Employee leasing is a contractual arrangement in which the leasing company is called Professional Employer Organisation (PEO).

Statement (II) : In employee leasing contract, the leasing company provides employees for non-specialised areas of work.

Code :

(1) Statement (I) is correct but (II) is incorrect.
(2) Statement (I) is incorrect but (II) is correct.
(3) Both the statements are correct.
(4) Both the statements are incorrect.

74. Who among the following relatives of a deceased insured person is not "dependent" under the Employees' State Insurance Act, 1948 ?

(1) Widow
(2) Widowed mother
(3) Legitimate son who has attained the age of twenty five
(4) Widowed daughter-in-law

75. **Assertion (A) :** One of the trends to build a sustainable competitive advantage are innovations and innovations management.

Reasoning (R) : Human Resource Management has to be able to connect innovations with the traditional change management to design a true powerful weapon against competitors in the market.

Code :

(1) Both (A) and (R) are correct ; and (R) is the right explanation of (A).
(2) Both (A) and (R) are correct ; but (R) is not the right explanation of (A).

(3) (A) is correct but (R) is incorrect.
(4) (R) is correct but (A) is incorrect.

76. Which of the following is not a principle of 'Hot Stove Rule' ?
(1) Prior Warning
(2) Immediate Response
(3) Consistent Action
(4) Personal Approach

77. In India, tripartite bodies of industrial relations began on the recommendations of which one of the following commissions ?
(1) Law Commission of India
(2) Whitley Commission
(3) National Statistical Commission
(4) Kothari Commission

78. The extrinsic properties of the product or service, including the ways in which the brand attempts to meet customers' psychological or social needs is known as :
(1) Brand judgments
(2) Brand resonance
(3) Brand imagery
(4) Brand performance

79. Which one of the following is an example of 'Real needs' of a customer ?
(1) The customer wants an inexpensive mobile phone.
(2) The customer wants a car whose operating cost, not initial price, is low.
(3) The customer expects good service from the dealer.
(4) The customer wants friends to see him as a savvy consumer.

80. The following statements relate to the functions of the marketing channel members. Indicate the statements being correct or incorrect.

Statement (I) : Channel members do not gather information about potential and current customers, competitors and other actors and forces in the marketing environment.

Statement (II) : Channel members acquire the funds to finance inventories at different levels in the marketing channel.

Code :
(1) Both the statements are correct.
(2) Both the statements are incorrect.
(3) Statement (I) is correct while Statement (II) is incorrect.
(4) Statement (I) is incorrect while Statement (II) is correct.

81. Which one of the following attributes of advertising regarding launching of a new product calls for spending all the advertising budget in a single period ?
(1) Pulsing (2) Continuity
(3) Concentration (4) Flighting

82. Select the correct code of the Assertion (A) and Reasoning (R) :

Assertion (A) : Companies should measure the profitability of their products, territories, customer groups, segments, trade channels and order sizes.

Reasoning (R) : Measure of profitability helps companies determine whether to expand, reduce, or eliminate any product or marketing activities to ensure profitability control.

Code :
(1) Both (A) and (R) are correct and (R) is the right explanation of (A).
(2) Both (A) and (R) are correct but (R) is not the right explanation of (A).
(3) (A) is correct but (R) is incorrect.
(4) (R) is correct but (A) is incorrect.

83. In which one of the following types of store retailers, large, low-cost, low margin, high-volume, self-service store attributes are designed to meet total needs for food and household products ?
(1) Supermarket
(2) Superstore
(3) Discount store
(4) Convenience store

84. Match the items of List-II with the items of List-I and suggest the correct code :

List-I (Marketing and Business Practices)	List-II (Meaning)
(a) Customer partnering	(i) Working more closely with customers to add value to their operations.
(b) Uncovering	(ii) Using data mining and other analytical methods to develop deep insights into customers and how they behave.

(c) Broadening		(iii)	Studying "best practice companies" to improve performance.
(d) Benchmarking		(iv)	Factoring the interests of customers, employees, shareholders, and other stakeholders into the activities of the enterprice.

Codes:

	(a)	(b)	(c)	(d)
(1)	(i)	(ii)	(iii)	(iv)
(2)	(i)	(ii)	(iv)	(iii)
(3)	(iv)	(ii)	(i)	(iii)
(4)	(iv)	(ii)	(iii)	(i)

85. A firm earns return on investment at the rate of 20%, earning per share is ₹ 15, payout ratio is 50%, cost of equity is 12%; the market price per share as per Walter's model is :

(1) ₹ 300 (2) ₹ 240
(3) ₹ 75 (4) ₹ 166.67

86. Consider the below mentioned statements and state the correct code of the statements being true or false.

Statement (I) : A debt-equity ratio of 2 : 1 indicates that for every 1 unit of equity, the company has raised 2 units of debt.

Statement (II) : The cost of floating an equity issue is lesser than the cost of floating a debt

Code :

(1) Both the Statements (I) and (II) are false.
(2) Both the Statements (I) and (II) are true.
(3) Statement (I) is false and Statement (II) is true.
(4) Statement (I) is true and Statement (II) is false.

87. Debt Service Coverage Ratio indicates which one of the following ?

(1) Effective utilisation of assets.
(2) Number of times fixed assets cover borrowed funds.
(3) Excess of Current Assets over Current Liabilities.
(4) Number of times surplus covers interest and instalments of Term Loans.

88. Authorised capital of a company is ₹ 5 lacs; 40% of it is paid up. Loss incurred during the year is ₹ 50,000. Accumulated loss carried from last year is ₹ 2 lac. The company has a Tangible Net Worth of :

(1) ₹ 2 lacs (2) ₹ 2.50 lacs
(3) ₹ (-)50,000 (4) ₹ 7,50,000

89. Match the items of List-II with the items of List-I and select the correct matching.

List-I	**List-II**
(a) Liquidity Risk	(i) Refers to the chance that the firm will be unable to recover its dues from its debtors.
(b) Financial Risk	(ii) Refers to the possibility of adverse effect on firm's assets, liabilities and income due to movement of interest rates.
(c) Exchange Risk	(iii) Refers to the firm's inability to pay its dues towards creditors.
(d) Default Risk	(iv) Refers to the inability of the firm to meet its financial obligations on time owing to non-availability of ready cash.

Codes:

	(a)	(b)	(c)	(d)
(1)	(i)	(ii)	(iii)	(iv)
(2)	(i)	(iii)	(iv)	(ii)
(3)	(iv)	(iii)	(ii)	(i)
(4)	(iv)	(iii)	(i)	(ii)

90. Which one of the following is related to control function of the financial manager ?

(1) To negotiate with bankers for a loan.
(2) To analyse variance between standard costs and actual costs.
(3) To estimate the future cash flows from a proposed project.
(4) To advertise the public issue of the firm.

91. A firm is currently earning ₹ 50,000 and its one share has a present market value of ₹ 175. It has 5,000 shares outstanding. The earnings of the firm is expected to remain stable and it has a payout ratio of 100%. The cost of equity is :

(1) 10% (2) 5.71%
(3) 100% (4) 23.50%

92. With project cost of ₹ 300 lacs, profits after depreciation (straight line method) and tax for its lifetime of 5 years are estimated at ₹ 10 lacs, ₹ 10 lacs, ₹ 30 lacs, ₹ 40 lacs and ₹ 50 lacs respectively. The cost of capital is 12% and discount factors @ 12%, for the first five years are 0.89, 0.80, 0.71, 0.64 and 0.57 respectively. The Net present value of project is :

(1) ₹ 8.90 lacs (2) ₹ 140 lacs
(3) ₹ (–)207.70 lacs (4) ₹ 308.90 lacs

93. Match the items of List (II) with those of List (I) and choose the correct code of combination.

List (I) (Credit Rating Agency)	**List (II) (Year of Establishment)**
(a) CRISIL	(i) 1860
(b) Moody's Investors Service	(ii) 1909
(c) Standard and Poor	(iii) 1914
(d) Fitch Ratings	(iv) 1987

Codes:

	(a)	**(b)**	**(c)**	**(d)**
(1)	(iv)	(iii)	(i)	(ii)
(2)	(i)	(iii)	(ii)	(iv)
(3)	(iv)	(ii)	(i)	(iii)
(4)	(ii)	(i)	(iii)	(iv)

94. Which of the following statements are true ? Select the correct code.

(a) WTO rules are mainly applied to trade in goods but other areas such as services, intellectual property, etc., are not covered by them.
(b) GATT had contracting parties, whereas WTO has members.
(c) The dispute settlement system under WTO is much more efficient, speedy and transparent unlike the GATT system which was highly susceptible to blockages.

Code :

(1) (a) and (b) (2) (b) and (c)
(3) (a), (b) and (c) (4) (a) and (c)

95. Which trade group, among the following holds 'Tamil' as one of its official language ?

(1) ASEAN (2) SAARC
(3) BRICS (4) MINT

96. Arrange the following steps involved in choosing the target market in sequence, starting from the first step

(A) Profile the traits of each segment: characteristics, needs, benefits sought, preferences and buying behavior.
(B) Look for segments which are relatively less satisfied by the current offers of competing brands in the market.
(C) Identify the segment(s), look at each segment as a distinct marketing opportunity and grasp what makes each segment unique.
(D) Evaluate whether the segment meets all the attributes of 'effective segments'. Check which one presents the best opportunity.
(E) Finally, select the best segments - those segments that are most appropriate for the firm - as the target.

Choose the correct answer from the options given below:

(1) A, B, C, D, E (2) B, C, D, E, A
(3) C, A, B, D, E (4) D, A, B, C, E

97. Which of the following is a benchmarking tool to measure performance along the logistics supply chain among countries ?

(1) Logistics Preparedness Index
(2) Supply Chain Performance Index
(3) Logistics Performance Index
(4) Supply Chain Preparedness Index

98. Which of the following is/are not true about linear shipping ?

(a) It is used for cargo with higher unit value and manufactured or semi-manufactured goods.
(b) Its shipping lines offer slower shipping services.
(c) It operates regularly on a fixed schedule.
(d) Its document of transport contract is called 'Charter Party'.

Code :

(1) (a) and (c) (2) (a), (b) and (d)
(3) (d) only (4) (b) and (d)

99. The statements relate to International Financial Environment. Denote the code of the statements being correct or incorrect.

Statement (I) : Foreign exchange risk denotes the variance of domestic currency value of assets, liabilities, or operating income attributable to anticipated changes in exchange rates.

Statement (II) : Foreign exchange exposures denote the sensitivity of the real value of assets, liabilities and operating income to unanticipated changes in exchange rates expressed in its functional currency.

Code :

(1) Both the statements are correct.
(2) Both the statements are incorrect.
(3) Statement (I) is correct while Statement (II) is incorrect.
(4) Statement (I) is incorrect while Statement (II) is correct.

100. Which among the following firms having foreign trade qualifies for financial assistance under the Market Development Assistance (MDA) Scheme ?
(1) Having annual turnover upto ₹ 10 crore.
(2) Having annual turnover upto ₹ 20 crore.
(3) Having annual turnover upto ₹ 25 crore.
(4) Having annual turnover upto ₹ 30 crore.

101. Match the items of the List - I with those of the List - II and indicate the correct code :

List - I	List - II
(a) Positive income elasticity	(i) Substitute goods
(b) Negative income elasticity	(ii) Complementary goods
(c) Positive cross elasticity	(iii) Inferior goods
(d) Negative cross elasticity	(iv) Superior goods

Codes:

	(a)	(b)	(c)	(d)
(1)	(ii)	(i)	(iv)	(iii)
(2)	(i)	(ii)	(iii)	(iv)
(3)	(iv)	(iii)	(i)	(ii)
(4)	(i)	(iv)	(ii)	(iii)

102. For the following two statements of Assertion (A) and Reasoning (R), indicate the correct code:
Assertion (A) : Ridge Lines in isoquat map set the limits for the positive productivities of the respective inputs used in the production process.
Reasoning (R) : Isoquants will slope positively if the use of an input is increased beyond the limit set by the ridge lines.
Code :
(1) Both (A) and (R) are correct and (R) is correct explanation of (A)
(2) Both (A) and (R) are correct but (R) is not correct explanation of (A)
(3) (A) is correct but (R) is not correct
(4) (A) is not correct but (R) is correct

103. For perfect competition, indicate the correct code for essential conditions from the following :
(a) Large number of buyers and sellers
(b) Perfect knowledge of the market
(c) Homogeneous product for sale
(d) Absence of transportation cost
(e) Freedom of entry and exit of buyers and sellers from the market
(f) Rational Behaviour of buyers and sellers
Code :
(1) (a), (b), (c), (d) and (f)
(2) (b), (c), (d), (e) and (f)
(3) (a), (b), (c), (d), (e) and (f)
(4) (a), (c), (d), (e) and (f)

104. Match the items of the List - I with those of List - II and suggest the correct code from the following :

List - I	List - II
(a) GDP	(i) National income
(b) GDP at factor cost	(ii) NDP plus Net flow of income from abroad
(c) NNP at factor cost	(iii) Money value of final goods and services produced
(d) NNP	(iv) Total gross value added by all enterprises in the economy

Codes:

	(a)	(b)	(c)	(d)
(1)	(i)	(iii)	(ii)	(iv)
(2)	(iii)	(iv)	(i)	(ii)
(3)	(iv)	(iii)	(ii)	(i)
(4)	(ii)	(i)	(iv)	(iii)

105. When an individual is motivated to approach two or more positive but mutually exclusive goals, he is facing which one type of the following conflicts ?
(1) Approach - Approach Conflict
(2) Approach - Avoidance Conflict
(3) Avoidance - Avoidance Conflict
(4) Person-Role Conflict

106. 'Contact Hypothesis' is based on the belief that:
(1) the more we interact with someone, the less prejudiced or perceptually biased we will be against that person

(2) familiarity breeds contempt
(3) contact among group members leads to conflict
(4) mutual discussion leads to reframing of problems

107. According to Vroom's theory of motivation, which one of the following is correct ?
(1) Valence = Force × Expectancy
(2) Expectancy = Force × Valence
(3) Valence= Motivation × Force
(4) Force = Valence × Expectancy

108. The process by which sensory information is actively organised and interpreted by brain, is called :
(1) Attitude (2) Learning
(3) Perception (4) Training

109. An interview, in which the applicant is interviewed sequentially by several persons and each rates the applicant on a standard form, is called :
(1) Unstructured Sequential Interview
(2) Structured Sequential Interview
(3) Job - related Interview
(4) Mass Interview

110. Which of the following are tripartite bodies?
(a) Indian Labour Conference
(b) Standing Labour Committee
(c) State Level Advisory Boards

Code:
(1) Both (a) and (b)
(2) Both (a) and (c)
(3) Both (b) and (c)
(4) (a), (b) and (c)

111. Which one of the following theories of labour welfare believes that workers are becoming more and more aware of their rights and welfare measures can appease them ?
(1) Philanthropic theory
(2) Placating theory
(3) Public Relations theory
(4) Functional theory

112. Which one of the following is not a characteristic of the 'Hot - Stove Rule' of disciplinary action ?
(1) Discipline is directed against the act and not against anybody else.
(2) Rules and regulations fore-warn regarding consequences of indiscipline.
(3) Consistency of disciplinary action is certain.
(4) Discipline is personal.

113. Which combination of the following statements about the net present value method of the investment project appraisal is correct ?
(a) It considers all the cash flows from the project
(b) It gives more weightage to distant flows than near-term flows
(c) It considers the time value of money

Code :
(1) (a) and (b) only
(2) (b) and (c) only
(3) (a) and (c) only
(4) (a), (b) and (c) all

114. Capital structure of a business unit consists of:
(1) Equity and preference share capital
(2) Equity, long-term debt and short-term loan
(3) Equity capital and debt capital
(4) Equity, preference and debt capital

115. In the formula $k_d = \frac{1}{B_0}$ used for computation of the cost of debt capital, B_0 denotes as which one of the following ?
(1) Net cash inflow at the time of issue
(2) Market price of debenture
(3) Face value of debenture
(4) Probable net cash inflow to debenture holder on sale of the debenture in near future

116. In computation of the weighted average cost of capital, weights are assigned as per :
(1) Proportion of fixed and current assets
(2) Proportion of different sources of finance
(3) Proportion of long-term and short term debts
(4) Proportion of the various components of equity in the business

117. "The customer wants an inexpensive car". This is an example of which one of the following type of needs ?
(1) Stated needs (2) Real needs
(3) Unstated needs (4) Secret needs

118. **Assertion (A) :** Marketers are increasingly asked to justify their investments in financial and profitability terms and rarely in terms of building the brand and customer base.

Reasoning (R) : Organizations recognize that little of their market value comes from intangible assets.

Code :

(1) Both (A) and (R) are correct.
(2) Both (A) and (R) are incorrect.
(3) (A) is correct and (R) is the right explanation of (A).
(4) (A) is correct but (R) is not the right explanation of (A).

119. Which one of the following is a false statement?

(1) The most attractive market segment is one in which entry barriers are low and exit barriers are high.
(2) A market segment is unattractive when there are actual or potential substitutes for the product.
(3) A market segment is unattractive if buyers possess strong or growing bargaining power.
(4) A segment is unattractive if the company's suppliers are concentrated or organized.

120. Match the items of List - I with that of List - II and suggest the correct code :

List - I (Pricing Strategies)	**List - II (Explanations)**
(a) Customary pricing	(i) Ending a price with 99 paise
(b) Skimming	(ii) pricing a product based on perceived expectations of customers
(c) Penetration pricing	(iii) Setting a high price which gradually reduces as competitors enter the market
(d) Psychological pricing	(iv) Offering at a low price for a new product during its initial offering

Codes:

	(a)	(b)	(c)	(d)
(1)	(i)	(iii)	(iv)	(ii)
(2)	(ii)	(iii)	(iv)	(i)
(3)	(iv)	(ii)	(iii)	(i)
(4)	(i)	(ii)	(iii)	(iv)

121. Which one of the following OR Models is appropriate for project planning and scheduling operations ?

(1) Games Models
(2) Inventory Models
(3) Network Models
(4) Queuing Models

122. While obtaining the optimal solution to the linear programming problem, by using graphical method, which one of the following is contradictory to the essential requirements ?

(1) Collection of all feasible solutions entails the use of a convex set
(2) There are infinite number of basic feasible solutions within the solution space
(3) In the convex set of the feasible solutions, atleast one of the extreme points gives an optimal solution
(4) The value of the objective function will be the same for all convex combinations of the extreme points if such points are more than one in the feasible solution space

123. For calculating Economic Order Quantity (EOQ), you are given the following formula:

$$EOQ = \sqrt{\frac{2DC_O}{Ch}}$$

When Let D = Demand
R = Rate of replenishment
L = Lead time
C_p = Unit purchase price
C_h = Unit holding cost
C_o = Unit ordering cost
C_s = Shortage cost
Q = Quantity to be ordered

This inventory model is suitable for which one of the following situations ?

(1) Economic Order Quantity Model with uniform demand
(2) Economic Order Quantity Model with variable demand
(3) Economic Order Quantity Model when shortages are permitted
(4) Economic Order Quantity Model with gradual replenishment

124. While using Markov Analysis, which one of the following assumptions is incompatible ?

(1) The system has an infinite set of possible outcomes
(2) Transition probabilities are constant over a given length of time
(3) The condition of the system in any given period depends on preceding period condition

(4) Changes in the system may occur only once during each period

125. Statement - I : A hypothesis test for comparing the variances of two independent populations with the help of variances of two small samples is known as chi-square test.

Statement - II : To test the hypothesis that the population standard deviation has a specific value on the basis of the values of sample standard deviation of small sized sample, F-test is relevant.

Code :

(1) Both the statements are correct
(2) Both the statements are incorrect
(3) Statement - I is correct while Statement - II is incorrect
(4) Statement - I is incorrect while Statement - II is correct

126. Statement-I : A sampling distribution of mean, prepared on the basis of small sized samples from a population which is not normally distributed, is not normally distributed.

Statement-II : To test the significance of the difference between means of two small sized samples when the parameter values of the standard deviations are given, Z-test can be applied.

Code :

(1) Both the statements are correct
(2) Both the statements are incorrect
(3) Statement - I is correct while Statement - II is incorrect
(4) Statement - I is incorrect while Statement - II is correct

127. Which one of the following is restricted non-probability based sampling method ?

(1) Stratified sampling
(2) Quota sampling
(3) Cluster sampling
(4) Systematic sampling

128. Statement-I : When a null hypothesis is true but as per the hypothesis- testing, it is rejected; it is known as Type II error in hypothesis-testing.

Statement-II : For testing the significance of the differences among the performance of more than two sample groups when the data are non-parametric, Kruskal-Wallis (H) test is appropriate.

Code :

(1) Both the statements are correct
(2) Both the statements are incorrect
(3) Statement - I is correct while Statement - II is incorrect
(4) Statement - I is incorrect while Statement - II is correct

129. Match the items of List - I with those of List - II and choose the correct code :

List - I	List - II
(a) Greenfield Investments	(i) Unique product or services sold in domestic market targeting international markets through its customers
(b) Turnkey Projects	(ii) Typical North-American-process for rapid market expansion
(c) Piggy Backing	(iii) It is the most costly investments and holds the highest risk
(d) Franchising	(iv) A project where the facility is built from the ground and turned over to the client ready to go

Codes:

	(a)	(b)	(c)	(d)
(1)	(iii)	(iv)	(i)	(ii)
(2)	(iii)	(iv)	(ii)	(i)
(3)	(iii)	(ii)	(i)	(iv)
(4)	(iv)	(iii)	(ii)	(i)

130. Which of the following statements is not correct about strategic management ?

(1) It involves formulation and implementations of minor goals
(2) It involves initiatives taken by the top management
(3) It is based on consideration of resources
(4) It includes assessment of internal and external environment of organization

131. Which one among the following is not a correct statement ?

(1) ANZ Grindlays merged with American Express Bank to emerge competatively
(2) Apple computers uses differentiation competitive strategy to emphasize innovative product
(3) Operating strategies are implemented at departmental level

(4) Corporate strategy describes a company's overall direction towards growth by managing business and product line

132. Statement - I : Trade Policy Review Body is a forum for the entire membership to review the trade policies of all WTO members.

Statement - II : The WTO administers the "Trade Review Mechanism".

Code :

(1) Statement I is correct but II is incorrect
(2) Statement II is correct but I is incorrect
(3) Both the statements I and II are correct
(4) Both the statements I and II are incorrect

133. A transportation problem with m origins and n destinations becomes a trans-shipment problem with

(1) (m + n) sources and (m + n) destinations
(2) (m + n – 1) sources and equal number of destinations
(3) (m – n) sources and (m – n) destinations
(4) (m + n – 2) sources and (m + n – 2) destinations

314. The support for Entrepreneurial and Managerial Development of Small and Medium Enterprises (incubator) scheme of the National Manufacturing Competitiveness Programme (NMCP) aims to which one of the following?

(1) To provide Startup financial support to new ventures.
(2) To provide financial support to existing MSMEs.
(3) To provide supporting and nourishing business based new ideas in knowledge institutions.
(4) To build awareness on intellectual property rights for the MSMEs

135. The relationship between subsidy and incentive can appropriately be brought out by which one of the following propositions?

(1) Incentives are concessions, bounties offered to borrow money to set up a production activity, while subsidy is a non cash concession given to translate idea into productive action
(2) Incentives and subsidies are cash disbursement only to the intrapreneur
(3) Incentives and subsidies are non-cash motivating factor to promote a new enterprise
(4) Incentives are financial as well as non financial stimuli encouraging to undertake productive activities ; while subsidy pertains to a single lumpsum payment given by the government to an entrepreneur for compensating him for the excess cost over administered price of a product or service

136. Industrial parks fall under which one of the following categories ?

(1) General industrial clusters
(2) Specialised industrial clusters
(3) Conglomeration of heterogenous group of enterprises under one umbrella
(4) Integrated comprehensive business centres

137. Which one among the following countries does not favour gender equality ?

(1) Sweden (2) USA
(3) Denmark (4) Saudi Arabia

138. Assertion (A) : Bad corporate governance can cast doubt on a company's reliability.

Reasoning (R) : Companies that do not cooperate sufficiently with auditors can publish non-compliant financial results.

Code :

(1) Both (A) and (R) are correct and (R) is the right explanation of (A).
(2) Both (A) and (R) are correct but (R) is not the right explanation of (A).
(3) (A) is correct but (R) is incorrect.
(4) (R) is correct but (A) is incorrect.

139. Which one among the following is not a part of Corporate Social Initiatives ?

(1) Socially-responsible business practices
(2) Corporate social marketing
(3) Cause-related marketing
(4) Corporate ambience building

140. Which among the following are also called Corporate Social Responsibility ?

(a) Corporate Conscience
(b) Corporate Citizenship
(c) Responsible Business

Code :

(1) (a) and (b) (2) (a), (b) and (c)
(3) (a) and (c) (4) (b) and (c)

141. Which one of the following consists of both vertical sequence of jobs and a series of horizontal opportunities ?

(1) Network Career Path

(2) Cafeteria Career Path
(3) Transitory Career Path
(4) Spiral Career Path

142. Arrange the following steps of disciplinary actions in correct sequence.
(a) Complaint
(b) Issue of charge sheet
(c) Preliminary fact finding
(d) Consideration of explanation
(e) Suspension pending enquiry
(f) Holding of enquiry
(g) Order of punishment
(h) Appeal

Code :
(1) (a), (c), (b), (d), (e), (f), (g), (h)
(2) (a), (b), (c), (d), (e), (f), (g), (h)
(3) (a), (e), (b), (c), (d), (f), (g), (h)
(4) (a), (d), (b), (c), (e), (f), (g), (h)

143. Who among the following is known for application of Psychology to industry and management ?
(1) Thomas Peters (2) Chester Barnard
(3) Mary Parker Follett
(4) Hugo Munsterberg

144. The Right to strike is a __________.
(1) Fundamental right
(2) Legal right
(3) Right under directive principles of state policy
(4) Social right of employee

145. Which one of the following is not an unfair labour practice ?
(1) Use of force to prevent a worker from attending work
(2) Staging demonstration at residence of managerial staff members
(3) Damaging property of employer
(4) Going on unauthorised leave

146. Who was the founder of Madras Labour Union ?
(1) N.M. Joshi (2) N.M . Lokhande
(3) B.P. Wadia (4) V.V. Giri

147. Who said that wages always tend to be equivalent to subsistence level ?
(1) Keynes (2) Ricardo
(3) Walker (4) Pigou

148. 'Kanban' refers to which one of the following ?
(1) Employing sufficient manpower
(2) An ideal state in which production quantities are equal to delivery quantities
(3) Promotion of right people
(4) Both (1) and (3)

149. Which one of the following represents a system where by an employer regularly deducts a portion of employee's wage to pay subscription fee of trade union ?
(1) Checkout (2) Checkin
(3) Settlement (4) Checkoff

150. According to Five-Stage Model of the Consumer Buying Process, which one of the following sequence is followed ?
(1) Purchase Decision→Problem Recognition → Information Search → Post Purchase Behaviour → Evaluation of Alternatives
(2) Evaluation of Alternatives → Purchase Decision → Information Search → Post Purchase Behaviour → Problem Recognition
(3) Information Search → Evaluation of Alternatives → Purchase Decision → Problem Recognition → Post Purchase Behaviour
(4) Problem Recognition → Information Search → Evaluation of Alternatives → Purchase Decision → Post Purchase Behaviour

151. Match the items of List - I with the items of List - II and select the correct code of matching

List - I (E - Commerce Companies)	**List - II (Product Categories)**
(a) Voylla Retail	(i) Kids and baby products
(b) Limeroad	(ii) Imitation Jewellery
(c) First cry.com	(iii) Furniture and home decor
(d) Pepperfry	(iv) Fashion and life style

Codes:

	(a)	(b)	(c)	(d)
(1)	(i)	(iii)	(ii)	(iv)
(2)	(iii)	(iv)	(i)	(ii)
(3)	(ii)	(iv)	(i)	(iii)
(4)	(ii)	(i)	(iv)	(iii)

152. Which one of the following refers to the use of online and offline promotion techniques to increase the audience of a site ?

(1) Search-engine optimization
(2) Traffic building campaign
(3) Search-engine marketing
(4) Quality score

153. Match the items of List - I with the items of List - II and select the correct code of matching

List - I (Type of store Retailers)	List - II (Formats)
(a) Speciality store	(i) Broad selection of high-mark up, fast moving, brand-name goods sold by a list
(b) Drug store	(ii) Narrow product line
(c) Super store	(iii) Prescription and pharmacies
(d) Catalogue showroom	(iv) Huge selling space

Codes:

	(a)	(b)	(c)	(d)
(1)	(iv)	(iii)	(i)	(ii)
(2)	(ii)	(i)	(iv)	(iii)
(3)	(iii)	(ii)	(iv)	(i)
(4)	(ii)	(iii)	(iv)	(i)

154. On which one of the following, the corporate advertising concentrates ?
(1) Brand Personality
(2) Product Personality
(3) Organizational Personality
(4) Recruitment

155. Which one of the following represents Poly-centric orientation of the management ?
(1) Each host country is unique
(2) Home country is superior
(3) Sees similarities and differences in markets and countries
(4) Sees similarities and differences in a world region

156. Which one of the following refers to "attributes or benefits that consumers strongly associate with a brand, positively evaluate, and believe they could not find to the same extent with a competitive brand" ?
(1) Points-of-attributes
(2) Points-of-difference
(3) Points-of-parity
(4) Points-of-purchase

157. Match the items of List - I with the items of List - II and select the correct code of matching

List - I (Advertising Agencies)	List - II (Clients)
(a) Ogilvy and Mather Ltd	(i) HDFC
(b) JWT Hindustan Thompson Associates	(ii) Coca-Cola
(c) Mudra Communications	(iii) Vodafone
(d) McCann- Erikson India Ltd	(iv) Nestle

Codes:

	(a)	(b)	(c)	(d)
(1)	(ii)	(i)	(iii)	(iv)
(2)	(iii)	(i)	(ii)	(iv)
(3)	(iv)	(iii)	(i)	(ii)
(4)	(iii)	(iv)	(i)	(ii)

158. For the following two statements indicate the correct code :

Statement - I : Advertising is any paid form of personal presentation and promotion of ideas, goods, or services by an identified sponsor.

Statement - II : Sales promotion consists of most long-term incentive tools, designed to stimulate greater purchase of particular products or services by consumers or the trade.

Code :
(1) Both the statements are correct
(2) Both the statements are incorrect
(3) Statement I is correct but statement II is incorrect
(4) Statement II is correct but Statement I is incorrect

159. Vertical merger is the merger of two firms which are involved in which one of the following forms ?
(1) Similar line of business
(2) Different stages of distribution and production in same business activity
(3) Different and unrelated business activities
(4) Partly similar line of business and partly in different unrelated business activities

160. The cost arising out of the failure of the customers to meet their obligations when payment on credit sales become due after the expiry of the credit period, may be attributed to which one of the following ?
(1) Collection Cost
(2) Default Cost
(3) Delinquency Cost
(4) Attrition Costs

161. In derivative contract, settlement by offset, denotes which one of the following ?

(1) Settlement of a maturing futures contract by cash payment in order to offset the mutual obligation on the contract
(2) Closing out a futures contract before maturity with an offsetting trade
(3) Terminating a futures contract by executing a new contract by way of payment of cash in a mutually agreed proportion
(4) A fresh contract is entered into by discarding the earlier contract outside the exchange

162. Purchasing power parity theory signifies which one of the following ?

(1) Ability to exchange one currency for another at a given conversion rate and in terms of the usability of a currency for foreign transactions
(2) Which states that exchange rates between currencies are in equilibrium when their purchasing power is the same in each of the two countries
(3) When one party of an economic transaction has equal degree of information in currency market about it and shared equally to arrive at uniform foreign exchange selection decision
(4) No one party can significantly influence foreign exchange rate in the market and all will be guided by asymmetric information

163. When a direct quote of the home currency or any other currency is not available in the forex market, it is computed with the help of exchange quotes of other pairs of currencies, is referred to by which one of the following ?

(1) Cross rate
(2) Arbitrage rate
(3) Transaction rate
(4) Translation rate

164. In a derivative transaction, the term margin denotes to which one of the following ?

(1) Cash or collateral provided by a customer to a broker to protect the broker from loss on a contract
(2) Cash or collateral provided by a broker to a customer to protect the customer from loss on contract
(3) A broker's request for more collateral to bring a customer's margin requirement to a premium margin level
(4) A customer's request for more collateral to bring a broker's margin requirement to a minimum standard level

165. In the area of corporate risk management, systematic risk fulfils which one of the following conditions ?

(1) Systematic risk is unavoidable; this is the contribution of an individual asset to the risk of market portfolio.
(2) Systematic risk is avoidable by an investor, and it can be eliminated by diversification.
(3) The level of systematic risk in an asset cannot be measured by the beta coefficient.
(4) The expected return-beta relationship is referred to as Systematic Market Line (SML).

166. The difference between a forward trade and a derivative may be attributed to which one of the following ?

(1) The position of owning a good that one plans to sell in the future, the position of expecting to purchase the good in the future
(2) The parties agree to trade at a specified time in the future, at a price set now; a derivative involves only payments of money, with no delivery of any commodity or assets
(3) The parties agree to trade at a future time, at a price to be decided in future; a derivative involves payments at a future specified time along with physical delivery of any commodity or asset
(4) The parties agree to trade and the amounts to be paid or received will not depend on the value at that time

167. Multilateral Investment Guarantee Agency (MIGA), an affiliate of World Bank, aims to address which one of the following ?

(1) To promote comparative advantage among the trading nations to foster international trade
(2) To promote a platform for dispute settlement mechanism in world trade guarantee
(3) To encourage foreign direct investment in developing countries by protecting investors from non-commercial risk

(4) To promote international trade in goods and intelligence services

168. Under foreign exchange risk measurement, economic risk emerges out of which of the following ?

(a) Riskiness of company's foreign exchange positions resulting from its business activities.

(b) The holding period or length of time over which the foreign exchange position is planned to be held.

(c) A change in the present value of the future after tax cash flows due to changes in exchange rates.

(d) The unit of currency to be used for the denomination of the value of currency.

Code :

(1) (a) only (2) Both (a) and (b)
(3) (c) only (4) (d) only

169. Regional trading block agreement among USA, Canada and Mexico is formed and named by which one of the following ?

(1) North American Free Trade Region
(2) North American Free Trade Agreement
(3) North and Central American Free Trade Agreement
(4) North American Free and Tariff Trade Agreement

170. If a bank in India, SBI, has an account with citibank, Newyork, and another Indian Bank, Allahabad Bank, wants to refer to that account while corresponding with citibank, Newyork, the Allahabad Bank would refer to which one of the following accounts ?

(1) Loro account
(2) Mirror account
(3) Vostro account
(4) Mix of Nostro and Vostro account

171. Treaties of Rome (1957) was responsible for creation of which one of the following ?

(1) European Economic Community (EEC)
(2) General Agreement on Tariffs and Trade (GATT)
(3) WTO
(4) General Agreement on Trade in Services (GATS)

172. Agreement on Trade Related Investment Measures (TRIMS) under WTO regime aims to address which one of the following measures?

(1) Protection of investment in creation of Intellectual Property Rights (IPRs)
(2) No member shall apply any measures in violation of the national treatment principles of GATT and discriminate against foreigners or foreign products
(3) It does not prohibit investment measures that place a restriction on quantities and measures requiring a certain percentage of local procurement
(4) It encourages measures which limit imports or set targets for exports and trade balancing requirements

173. In international marketing, export documentation framework engulfs which one of the following ?

(1) Export census documents compiled by the department of commerce
(2) Shipper's Export Declarations (SEDs)
(3) Foreign commercial service including websites of individual countries
(4) All of the above

174. In dispute resolution mechanism of the WTO regime, the collapse of the Doha Round talks at Cancun in September 2003 has been attributed to which one of the following ?

(1) Subsidies in agriculture and agricultural domestic support policies of developed nations
(2) Measures on protecting intellectual property rights of innovators
(3) Agreement on Textiles and Clothing (ATC) under Multi-Fibre Arrangement
(4) Trade in the shape of individuals travelling to foreign countries to supply services

175. In international financial environment for settlement of debts there is a practice known as netting practice. The netting practice pertains to which one of the following ?

(1) A practice by which subsidiaries of affiliates within the TNC network settle inter-subsidiary debts for the net amount owed during the post-transaction period.
(2) A practice involving the sale of export accounts receivable to a third party within the TNC network.
(3) A practice of purchasing an account receivable where the credit term exceeds the permissible limit within the TNC network.

(4) Where the difference between international transaction of gross capital account receivables and payables are settled against current account receivables and payables.

176. Managerial economics is concerned with which combination of the following ?
(a) Investment Analysis and Decisions
(b) Production Behaviour and Cost Analysis
(c) Input Reward Analysis and Decisions
(d) Economic Environment Analysis

Codes:
(1) (a), (b) and (c) (2) (b), (c) and (d)
(3) (a), (b) and (d) (4) (a), (c) and (d)

177. When P_0 and P_1 and Q_0 and Q_1 denote before and after change in the price and quantity respectively and in both the situations, total outlay remains the same, which of the following formulae give the similar value of the arc price - elasticity of demand ?

(a) $\dfrac{Q_0 - Q_1}{P_0 - P_1} \times \dfrac{P_0 + P_1}{Q_0 + Q_1}$

(b) $\dfrac{Q_0 - Q_1}{P_0 - P_1} \times \dfrac{P_0}{Q_1}$

(c) $\dfrac{Q_0 - Q_1}{P_0 - P_1} \times \dfrac{P_0}{Q_0}$

(d) $\dfrac{Q_0 - Q_1}{P_0 - P_1} \times \dfrac{P_1}{Q_1}$

Code :
(1) (b), (c) and (d) (2) (a), (b) and (d)
(3) (a), (c) and (d) (4) (b), (c) and (d)

178. In case the producer's equilibrium shifts to a higher isoquant due to decrease in price of an input, the curve combining the successive equilibrium positions is known as :
(1) Product Possibility Curve
(2) Price Factor Curve
(3) Expansion Path
(4) Product Line

179. Which one of the following statements is not correct ?
(1) Marginal cost declines at a faster rate as compared to the average cost.
(2) Marginal cost rises at a faster rate as compared to the average cost.
(3) Marginal cost equals average cost where average cost is minimum.
(4) Average cost equals marginal cost where marginal cost is minimum.

180. Cost - Plus pricing is not suitable for :
(1) Product Tailoring
(2) Profit Maximising
(3) Monopsony Pricing
(4) Public Utility Pricing

181. Match the following and select the correct code of matching :

List - I	List - II
(a) F.W. Taylor	(i) Fair day's pay for fair day's work
(b) Henry L. Gantt	(ii) Motion study
(c) Frank and Lillian Gilbreth	(iii) Graphic scheduling for planning and controlling of work
(d) Max Weber	(iv) Bureaucratic organisation

Codes:

	(a)	(b)	(c)	(d)
(1)	(i)	(ii)	(iii)	(iv)
(2)	(i)	(iii)	(ii)	(iv)
(3)	(iv)	(iii)	(ii)	(i)
(4)	(iv)	(i)	(ii)	(iii)

182. The achievement of goals with the least amount of resources is :
(1) Effectiveness
(2) Efficiency
(3) Productivity
(4) Both (1) and (2)

183. Which one of the following is the fundamental rethinking and radical redesign of business processes to achieve improvements in performance ?
(1) Reengineering (2) Reorganising
(3) Revisiting (4) Rescheduling

184. Match the following and select the code of correct matching :

List - I	List - II
(a) Motivating through rewards and penalties	(i) Charismatic leadership
(b) Changing organisation by creating and communicating a vision	(ii) Situational leader ship
(c) Influencing by dint of personality and charm	(iii) Transactional leadership

(d) Modifying style with respect to readiness of followers		(iv) Transformational leadership	

Codes:

	(a)	(b)	(c)	(d)
(1)	(iii)	(i)	(ii)	(iv)
(2)	(iii)	(iv)	(i)	(ii)
(3)	(iii)	(iv)	(ii)	(i)
(4)	(iv)	(iii)	(ii)	(i)

185. Which one of the following is not a 'hygiene factor' of Herzberg's Two Factor theory ?
(1) Interpersonal relations
(2) Working conditions
(3) Responsibility
(4) Job security

186. Assertion (A) : Promotion is a move within the organisation to a higher position that has greater responsibilities and requires more advanced skills.

Reasoning (R) : Promotion may not involve a raise in status but a hike in salary is a must.

Code :
(1) (A) and (R) both are correct.
(2) (A) and (R) both are incorrect.
(3) (A) is correct whereas (R) is incorrect.
(4) (A) is incorrect whereas (R) is correct.

187. Match the following and select the code of correct matching :

List - I	List - II
(a) Identification of leadership potential	(i) Vocational Tests
(b) Finding most suitable area of working	(ii) Aptitude Tests
(c) Discovering interest and potential for acquiring skills	(iii) Intelligence Tests
(d) Measuring capacity to think, learn and draw relationships	(iv) Personality Tests

Codes:

	(a)	(b)	(c)	(d)
(1)	(iv)	(iii)	(ii)	(i)
(2)	(i)	(ii)	(iii)	(iv)
(3)	(iv)	(i)	(ii)	(iii)
(4)	(i)	(iii)	(ii)	(iv)

188. Which one of the following is a facility to file anonymous complaints ?
(1) Juke Box (2) Wide Box
(3) Gripe Box (4) Hard Box

189. Which of the following is/are not gainsharing plan(s) ?
(a) Scanlon Plan
(b) Rucker Plan
(c) Employee Stock Option Plan
(d) Improshare Plan

Code :
(1) (c) only (2) (d) only
(3) (c) and (d) both (4) (b), (c) and (d)

190. In which one of the following methods of performance appraisal, predetermined percentages of rates are placed in various performance categories ?
(1) Alternation Ranking Method
(2) Forced Distribution Method
(3) Paired Comparison Method
(4) Check - list Method

191. Indicate the correct code for the combination from the following regarding the superiority of the wealth maximisation over the profit maximisation objective of the financial management :
(a) It takes into account long term stability and survival of the firm.
(b) It takes care of all other objectives of the firm like exploring and expanding markets, etc.
(c) It is based on the assumption of perfect competition in the market.
(d) It considers risk alongwith returns.

Code :
(1) (a), (b), (c) and (d)
(2) (b), (c) and (d)
(3) (a), (b) and (d)
(4) (a), (c) and (d)

192. The controller function of the financial management concerns with :
(1) advertising the public issue of the firm
(2) negotiating with banks for loans
(3) analysing variance between standard costs and actual costs
(4) estimating the future cash flows from certain project

193. Capital Asset Pricing Model (CAPM) for risk measurement has been given by :

(1) Sharpe and Lintner
(2) Lintner and Treynor
(3) Sharpe, Lintner and Treynor
(4) Lintner, Modigliani and Miller

194. Beta (β) is a measure of :
(1) Systematic Risk
(2) Unsystematic Risk
(3) Total Risk
(4) Business Risk

195. Capital budgeting is concerned with :
(1) Arranging cash resources for the project.
(2) Managing the working capital of the firm.
(3) Managing the fixed assets through repairs and renewals.
(4) Evaluating the returns and investment in projects.

196. Which one of the following is the demand state where "Consumers dislike the product and may even pay to avoid it" ?
(1) Unwholesome demand
(2) Declining demand
(3) Negative demand
(4) Latent demand

197. Evaluate the statements according to Brand Asset Valuator Model of Brand Equity :
Statement (I) : Knowledge measures the degree to which a brand is seen as different from others as well as its pricing power.
Statement (II) : Esteem measures perceptions of quality and loyalty or how well the brand is regarded and respected.
Code :
(1) Both the Statements are correct.
(2) Both the Statements are incorrect.
(3) Statement (I) is correct while Statement (II) is incorrect.
(4) Statement (I) is incorrect while Statement (II) is correct.

198. If a coaching institute provides some supporting study material along with teaching, then which one of the following service mix category would it be ?
(1) Hybrid offering
(2) Major service with accompanying minor goods and services
(3) Tangible good with accompanying services
(4) Pure service

199. **Statement (I) :** A low market - penetration index indicates substantial growth potential for all the firms.
Statement (II) : Generally, price competition increases and margins fall when the market - penetration index is already high.
Code :
(1) Both the Statements are correct.
(2) Both the Statements are incorrect.
(3) Statement (I) is correct while Statement (II) is incorrect.
(4) Statement (I) is incorrect while Statement (II) is correct.

200. Which one of the following is a system of partnerships and alliances that a firm creates to source, augment, and deliver its offerings ?
(1) Value network
(2) Omnichannel marketing
(3) Integrated marketing channel system
(4) Direct marketing channel

201. **Statement (I) :** Time study is an area of study whose fundamental purpose is to set time standards for work using different methods.
Statement (II) : Work measurement is a structured process of directly observing and measuring (using a timing device) human work in order to establish the time required for completion of the work by a qualified worker when working at a defined level of performance.
Code :
(1) Both the Statements are correct.
(2) Both the Statements are incorrect .
(3) Statement (I) is correct while Statement (II) is incorrect.
(4) Statement (I) is incorrect while Statement (II) is correct.

202. "Perquisites" or "perks" are
(1) Additional responsibilities assigned to employees
(2) Extra benefits or privileges provided to certain employees, such as company cars or club memberships
(3) Adhering to government regulations
(4) Ignoring the values and needs of colleagues

203. In the context of distinguishing between forecasting and prediction, which one of the following statements is false ?
(1) Forecasting is based on a theoretical model while prediction may be based on intuition.

(2) Forecasting reflects management's judgement after taking all available information into account; while prediction involves the projection of the past into the future.
(3) Error analysis is possible in the case of forecasting while no error analysis is done in the case of prediction.
(4) No objectivity is found in the case of prediction.

204. An activity that consumes no time but shows precedence among activities is known as :
(1) Slack activity
(2) Successor activity
(3) Dummy activity
(4) Critical activity

205. Which one of the following is not correct matching between level of facility planning and type of activity ?
(1) Global level and site location and selection
(2) Macro layout level and Site planning
(3) Micro layout level and Cell design
(4) Sub - Micro layout level and work station and Cell design

206. Which one of the following statements is false?
(1) Sample space refers to the collection of all favourable outcomes of an experiment.
(2) Collectively exhaustive events are those whose union is sample space.
(3) All the outcomes of an experiment are known as sample space.
(4) Two events are said to be independent if the happening of one does not affect the probability of happening of the other.

207. Which one of the following is a false statement?
(1) A binomial distribution involves infinite number of trials
(2) The mean and the variance of a Poisson distribution are equal
(3) The standard normal distribution has $\mu = 0$ and $\sigma = 1$
(4) The standard deviation of an exponential distribution is equal to its mean

208. In PERT/CPM analysis, what does the "earliest start time" of an activity represent?
(1) The latest time an activity can start without delaying the project
(2) The earliest time an activity can start without delaying the project
(c) The maximum waiting time
(d) The cost of transportation

209. Which one of the following statements is true ?
(1) If one of the regression coefficients is greater than one, the other must also be greater than one.
(2) The product of the two regression coefficients is always more than one.
(3) Correlation coefficient is the arithmetic mean of the two regression coefficients.
(4) The signs of the two regression coefficients are always the same.

210. In the absence of which of the following, SPSS can be used as an alternate ?
(1) MS Word (2) MS Excel
(3) MS Access (4) MS Datapro

211. Match the items of List - I with List - II and select the code of correct matching :

List - I	List - II
(a) Merger of Vodafone and Idea	(i) Business Strategy
(b) Launch of Apple iphone 7 plus	(ii) Operational Strategy
(c) Manufacturing Samsung mobile handsets in India	(iii) Corporate Strategy

Codes:

	(a)	(b)	(c)
(1)	(iii)	(i)	(ii)
(2)	(iii)	(ii)	(i)
(3)	(ii)	(iii)	(i)
(4)	(ii)	(i)	(iii)

212. Which among the following are 5 Ps of strategy as identified by Mintzberg ?
(a) Plan (b) Problem
(c) Pattern (d) Position
(e) Ploy (f) Perspective

Code :
(1) (a), (b), (c), (d) and (e)
(2) (a), (b), (d), (e) and (f)
(3) (b), (c), (d), (e) and (f)
(4) (a), (c), (d), (e) and (f)

213. Assertion (A) : A firm's relative position within its industry determines whether the firm's overall profitability is above or below the industry average.

Reasoning (R) : The fundamental basis of average profitability in the long run is sustainable competitive advantage.

Code :

(1) (A) and (R) both are correct and (R) is the right explanation of (A).

(2) (A) and (R) both are correct but (R) is not the right explanation of (A).

(3) (A) is correct but (R) is incorrect.

(4) (R) is correct but (A) is incorrect.

214. Statement (I) : A "Star" is the market leader in a high-growth market ; and it has sufficient cash to support other businesses.

Statement (II) : "Dogs" have weak market share in high - growth market.

Code :

(1) Statement (I) is correct but (II) is incorrect.

(2) Statement (II) is correct but (I) is incorrect.

(3) Both the Statements (I) and (II) are correct.

(4) Both the Statements (I) and (II) are incorrect.

215. Which among the following is not a generic strategy ?

(1) Unity Strategy

(2) Cost Leadership Strategy

(3) Differentiation Strategy

(4) Niche Strategy

216. Elements of entrepreneurial competencies, according to the theorist of the subject, pertain to which one of the following ?

(1) Body of knowledge, set of skills, cluster of appropriate motives and traits

(2) Ability to prepare viable project, executional skills and materialisation of group goals

(3) Ability to work in a group, enforce group dynamics and motivate employees

(4) Assigning priorities to hierarchy of Maslow's monetary needs and non-monetary needs

217. Under the new norms of Micro, Small and Medium Enterprises Development (MSMED) Act 2006, the criteria of investment limit in plant and machinery for MSME falls under which one of the following category ?

(1) Micro ₹ 25 lakh, small ₹ 5 crore, Medium ₹ 10 crore

(2) Micro ₹ 20 lakh, small ₹ 2.5 crore, Medium ₹ 5 crore

(3) Micro ₹ 20 lakh, small ₹ 6 crore, Medium ₹ 8 crore

(4) Micro ₹ 25 lakh, small ₹ 10 crore, Medium ₹ 15 crore

218. Entrepreneurial Judo strategy aims at which one of the following ?

(1) Filling holes left by others in the industry.

(2) Developing effectiveness in the industry.

(3) Mobilising finance and effective use to reduce NPAs.

(4) Creating competitive environment in the environment of SMMEs.

219. Preparation of a business plan as a pre-requisite to a promotion of a business enterprise, relates to which one of the following ?

(1) There is no flaws in the business idea, the fashion, conviction and tenacity of the entrepreneur.

(2) Make arrangement for finance and prevent occurrence of NPAs by business entity.

(3) Ensure that business entity works at break even level.

(4) Make plan to raise finance from market and alternative investment opportunities.

220. Federation of Associations of Small Industries of India (FASII) promoted in 1959 is whichone of the following type ?

(1) Government organisation

(2) Liaisoning organisation

(3) Small Scale unit

(4) SSI Board

221. Statement (I) : The science of ethics is a normative science.

Statement (II) : Normative sciences judge the value of the facts in terms of an idea ; concerned with judgements of 'what ought to be' but not with factual judgements.

Code :

(1) Statement (I) is correct but Statement (II) is incorrect.

(2) Statement (II) is correct but Statement (I) is incorrect.

(3) Both the Statements (I) and (II) are incorrect .

(4) Both the Statements (I) and (II) are correct.

222. Match the items of List (I) with those of List (II); and choose the correct combination :

List - I	List - II
(a) Ethics are the principles of conduct	(i) John Donaldson governing an individual or profession.
(b) Ethics is the discipline	(ii) Keith Davis is good and bad, or

	dealing with what		right and wrong, or with moral duty and obligation.
(c)	Ethics are a set of rules that defines right	(iii)	Shea and wrong conduct.
(d)	Business ethics, in short can be described	(iv)	R. Wayne Mondy as the systematic study of moral (ethical) matters pertaining to business, industry or related activities, institutions, or practicesand beliefs.

Codes:

	(a)	(b)	(c)	(d)
(1)	(iii)	(iv)	(i)	(ii)
(2)	(iii)	(iv)	(ii)	(i)
(3)	(iv)	(iii)	(ii)	(i)
(4)	(i)	(ii)	(iii)	(iv)

223. Assertion (A) : Decisions in small matters largely tend to set a pattern for the more important ones you may make as managers.

Reasoning (R) : A multi - industry survey conducted in the USA indicated that 40% of the managers said that their superiors had at some time told them to do certain things unethical.

Code :

(1) (A) and (R) both are correct and (R) is the right explanation of (A).
(2) (A) is correct whereas (R) is incorrect.
(3) (A) is incorrect whereas (R) is correct.
(4) (A) and (R) both are correct but (R) is not the correct explanation of (A).

224. Deontological theory of ethics is concerned with which of the following ?

(a) Duty ethics
(b) Obligation ethics
(c) Rule based ethics
(d) Classical ethics

Code :

(1) (a) and (b) (2) (a) and (c)
(3) (a) and (d) (4) (a), (b) and (c)

225. Utilitarianism theory of ethics refers to which one of the following ?

(1) Welfare (2) Duty
(3) Obligation (4) Rules

226. Assertion (A) : Every company should have a grievance redressal mechanism.

Reasoning (R) : Grievance is a feeling that should be expressed mandatorily, arising out of anything connected to company that employee thinks is inequitable or unfair.

Codes :

(1) (A) and (R) both are correct and (R) is the right explanation of (A).
(2) (A) and (R) both are correct, but (R) is not the right explanation of (A).
(3) (A) is correct and (R) is incorrect.
(4) (A) is incorrect and (R) is correct.

227. Assertion (A) : Integrative Bargaining is a type of win-loose strategy.

Reasoning (R) : In integrative bargaining, productivity aspects are considered in mutualproblem solving to increase gains.

Codes :

(1) (A) is correct, but (R) is incorrect.
(2) (A) is incorrect, but (R) is correct.
(3) (A) is correct and (R) is right explanation of (A).
(4) (A) is correct, but (R) is not the right explanation of (A).

228. Match the List – I with List – II relating to approaches to Industrial Relations.

List – I	**List – II**
(a) Systems approach	(i) Peaceful co-existence of capital and labour.
(b) V.V. Giri approach	(ii) Developed by John. T. Dunlop.
(c) Gandhian approach	(iii) Preference to voluntary arbitration.
(d) Socio-ethical approach	(iv) Assuming moral responsibility of understanding each other.

Codes:

	(a)	(b)	(c)	(d)
(1)	(ii)	(iii)	(i)	(iv)
(2)	(iii)	(ii)	(iv)	(i)
(3)	(i)	(ii)	(iv)	(iii)
(4)	(iv)	(i)	(iii)	(ii)

229. Consider the following statements :

Statement I : Union grievance procedures can differ from firm to firm.

Statement II : Peaceful picketing during a strike of workers is lawful.

Statement III : The National Labour Relations Board (NLRB) is an agency created by the Wagner Act to investigate about the minimum wages in all business units.

Codes :

(1) Only statements I and II are correct.
(2) Only statement I is correct.
(3) Only statement II is correct.
(4) Only statement III is correct.

230. **Assertion (A) :** General business conditions can greatly modify the number and type of middlemen available.

Reasoning (R) : Technological advances have made a significant effect on increase in online purchase and vending machines.

Codes :

(1) (A) is incorrect and (R) is correct.
(2) (A) and (R) both are incorrect.
(3) (A) and (R) both are correct and (R) is the right explanation of (A).
(4) (A) and (R) both are correct, but (R) is not the right explanation of (A).

231. Which of the following describe the four set of variables determining buyer behaviour as per Howard Sheth Theory ?

(1) Physical input variable, external variable, exogenous variable, output variable.
(2) Personality attitudes, perception of consumer, learning variable of consumer, brand variable.
(3) Social input variable, purchasing attitudinal behaviour, selection behaviour, Brand effect variable.
(4) Stimulus input variable, internal behaviour of buyer, exogenous variables, response output variables.

232. Which of the following is the consumer behaviour model which conceives the person (consumer) as a system with outputs (behaviour) in response to inputs ?

(1) The Thorndike's Theory
(2) The Engel Kollet Blackwell Theory
(3) Buying Theory by Drucker
(4) Comprehensive Theory of consumer behaviour

233. The Facebook, popularly used for online marketing, was founded in which year and by whom ?

(1) 2004, Peter Corbett
(2) 2005, Peter Corbett
(3) 2004, Mark Zuckerberg
(4) 2005, Mark Zuckerberg

234. Which of the following is a form of online word of mouth that encourages consumers to pass along company developed products and services or any other information online?

(1) Viral Marketing
(2) Microsites
(3) Interstitials
(4) Contextual placements

235. Consider the following statements relating to online marketing :

Statement I : Online communities and forums come in only one shape and size.

Statement II : In paid search, marketers bid in a continuous auction on search terms that serve as a proxy for the consumer's product or consumption interest.

Statement III : Marketers must recognize that only some consumers want to engage with some brands.

Codes :

(1) Only statements I and II are correct.
(2) Only statements II and III are correct.
(3) Only statements I and III are correct.
(4) All the statements are correct.

236. Which one of the following is informal workplace, sometimes garage, where intrapreneurial teams work to develop new products ?

(1) Garage teams
(2) Venture teams
(3) Skunk works
(4) Communities of practice

237. Match the items of List – I with the items of List – II.

List – I	List – II
(a) A moderate approach to current asset financing.	(i) Continually recurring short-term liabilities.
(b) Short-term credit.	(ii) Some permanent current assets and even some fixed assets, are financed with shortterm debt.
(c) Accrued liabilities.	(iii) Involves matching the maturities of assets and liabilities.

(d) Aggressive approach to current assets financing.	(iv) Any liability originally scheduled for payment within one year.

Codes:

	(a)	(b)	(c)	(d)
(1)	(iv)	(ii)	(iii)	(i)
(2)	(iii)	(iv)	(i)	(ii)
(3)	(ii)	(iii)	(i)	(iv)
(4)	(i)	(iii)	(ii)	(iv)

238. Debt management ratios do not include
(1) Times-interest-earned ratio
(2) EBITDA coverage ratio
(3) Debt ratio
(4) Price/Cash flow ratio

239. The current market price of a company's share is ₹ 90 and the expected dividend per share next year is ₹ 4.50. If the dividends are expected to grow at a constant rate of 8%, the share holder's required rate of return is
(1) 8.88% (2) 13%
(3) 5% (4) 4.5%

240. A project costs ₹ 3,000 now is expected to generate year-end cash inflows of ₹ 500, ₹ 1,000, ₹ 1,000 and ₹ 1,100 in years first through four. The discounting factor for these 4 years at project's opportunity cost of 10% is 0.91, 0.83, 0.75 and 0.68 respectively. The Net present Value of project is.
(1) + ₹ 310 (2) – ₹ 310
(3) – ₹ 217 (4) + ₹ 600

241. Which one is false statement ?
(1) Net operating working capital is the difference between the current assets necessary to operate the business and those current liabilities on which no interest is charged (generally accounts payable and accruals).
(2) Operating assets are current assets and fixed assets necessary to operate the business.
(3) Economic value added is the difference between after-tax operating profit and the total cost of capital, including the cost of equity capital.
(4) Economic value added does not differ from accounting profit.

242. Which statement is false ?
(1) Capital Asset pricing Model (CAPM) is based on the proposition that any stock's required rate of return is equal the risk-free rate of return plus a risk premium that reflects only the risk remaining after diversification.
(2) The relevant riskiness of an individual stock is its contribution to the riskiness of a well-diversified portfolio.
(3) A stock's relevant risk is greater than its stand-alone risk.
(4) Different stocks will affect the portfolio differently, so different securities have different degrees of relevant risk.

243. From the following particulars, determine funds from operations :

	₹
Salaries & Wages expenses	7,000
Profit on sale of land	25,000
Loss on sale of building	13,000
Net loss as per P & L a/c.	3,200
Depreciation on machinery	16,000
Amortization of goodwill	8,000
Stationery expenses	5,000

(1) ₹ 77,200 (2) ₹ 8,800
(3) ₹ 3,200 (4) ₹ 25,000

244. The stand point of Exchange rates which seeks to define the relationship between currencies based on relative inflation, is called ______
(1) Fixed Rate
(2) Floating Rate
(3) Purchasing Power
(4) Interest Rate

245. Changing Global Marketing Communication for each local market is called ______.
(1) International Marketing
(2) Communication Linkage
(3) Communication Adaption
(4) International Deal

246. In a market economy, when consumers influence the allocation of resources through their demand for products, it is popularly called as what ?
(1) Cultural dynamics
(2) Customer psychology
(3) Consumer sovereignty
(4) Principle of maximization

247. How to enter in the Global Market ? Arrange serially.
A – Deciding wether to go abroad.
B – Deciding on the marketing organization.

C – Deciding how to enter the market.
D – Deciding on Marketing programme.
E – Deciding in which market to enter.

Codes :

(1) A, D, C, E, B (2) A, B, C, D, E
(3) A, E, C, D, B (4) B, D, C, E, A

248. When the two countries are having the gold standard, their currency units are either made of gold specified purity and weight or freely convertible into gold of given purity at fixed rate, this theory known as ________.

(1) Purchasing power parity
(2) Mint parity theory
(3) Balance of payment theory
(4) Stable Foreign Exchange Rate

249. Which among the following is associated with high-income economic and Human Development Index (HDI) ?

(1) TRID (2) TRIM
(3) GATT (4) OECD

250. In commodity market, the foreign exchange rate is determined as per ________.

(1) Equilibrium Rate of Foreign Exchange
(2) Comparative Price of Foreign Currency
(3) Demand and Supply of Foreign Currency
(4) SDR

251. From the following two statements of Assertion (A) and Reasoning (R), indicate the correct code :

Assertion (A) : The quantity of a product demanded invariably changes inversely to changes in its price.

Reason (R) : The price effect is the net result of the positive substitution effect and negative income effect.

Codes :

(1) (A) and (R) both are correct.
(2) (A) is incorrect but (R) is correct.
(3) (A) is correct but (R) is incorrect.
(4) (A) and (R) both are incorrect.

252. Match the items of the List – I with that of the List – II and suggest the correct code from the following :

List – I	List – II
i. Cost function	a. Kinked demand
ii. Supply function	b. Isoquants
iii. Production function	c. Engineering method
iv. Oligopoly	d. Factor prices

Codes :

	i	ii	iii	iv		i	ii	iii	iv
(1)	c	d	a	b	(2)	b	a	c	d
(3)	a	b	d	c	(4)	d	c	b	a

253. Which one of the following combinations may not render the investment multiplier inapplicable ?

(1) Net imports, undistributed profits and taxation.
(2) Excess stocks of consumption goods, debt cancellation and savings.
(3) Price inflation, public investment programmes and strong liquidity preference.
(4) Closed economy, unemployment in the economy, constant marginal propensity to consume.

254. Match the items of the List – I with that of the List – II and suggest the correct code from the following :

List – I	List – II
i. Competitive Parity	a. Variations in Advertising
ii. Promotional Elasticity of Market	b. Level advertising
iii. Optimal promotional mix	c. Advertising expenditure decision
iv. Contra-cycle advertising	d. Marginal equivalency of media outlay

Codes :

	i	ii	iii	iv		i	ii	iii	iv
(1)	b	c	a	d	(2)	a	b	c	d
(3)	b	a	d	c	(4)	d	a	b	c

255. Match the following and indicate the code of correct matching :

List – I	List – II
a. Classical conditioning	i. Response-Stimulus learning
b. Operant conditioning	ii. Stimulus-Response learning
c. Cognitive theory	iii. Stimulus-Stimulus learning
d. Social learning	iv. Modelling process

Codes :

	a	b	c	d		a	b	c	d
(1)	ii	iii	iv	i	(2)	ii	i	iii	iv
(3)	i	ii	iii	iv	(4)	iv	iii	ii	i

256. Boss offers an employee a promotion which has huge increase in salary along with a new title. It also requires employee to work ten

hours more per week along with shifting to a remote place. It is an example of which one of the following ?
(1) Approach conflict
(2) Approach – Approach conflict
(3) Approach – Avoidance conflict
(4) Avoidance – Avoidance conflict

257. Which one of the following is not an example of semantic barrier ?
(1) Poorly chosen words and phrases
(2) Faulty translation
(3) Use of symbols that have various meanings
(4) Guarding against certain type of information

258. **Assertion (A) :** Equity theory of work motivation is based on social exchange process, in which individuals make contributions (inputs) and expect certain rewards (outcomes).
Reason (R) : Individuals decide whether or not a particular exchange is satisfactory by comparing their inputs and outcomes with those of others and try to rectify inequality.
Codes :
(1) (A) is correct but (R) is not correct.
(2) (A) is not correct but (R) is correct.
(3) Both (A) and (R) are correct and (R) is right explanation of (A).
(4) Both (A) and (R) are correct but (R) is not the right explanation of (A).

259. Which one of the following methods of performance appraisal involves ranking employees from best to worst in a particular trait ?
(1) Graphic Rating Scale method
(2) Forced Distribution method
(3) Paired Comparison method
(4) Alternation Ranking method

260. Which one of the following is not a basic feature of 'Scanlon Plan' ?
(1) Philosophy of competition
(2) Identity
(3) Competence
(4) Involvement system

261. A union of electricians working in different industries is called by which one of the following ?
(1) Craft Union (2) Industrial Union
(3) General Union (4) National Union

262. Which one of the following is not correct about voluntary retirement scheme in public enterprises ?
(1) It was designed to help enterprises rationalise their surplus manpower.
(2) Salary for the purpose of VRS consists of basic pay only.
(3) Benefits are in addition to money that has accrued to provident fund.
(4) Benefit is tax-free severance payment.

263. In case Mutual Funds invest in the securities whose price variations suggest the general price movement, it is called
(1) Hedge Fund (2) Index Fund
(3) Growth Fund (4) Balanced Fund

264. Indicate the correct code of the combinations of the following methods commonly used for capital budgeting
a. Payback Period
b. Profitability Index
c. Utility theory
d. Internal rate of return

Codes :
(1) a, b and c (2) b, c and d
(3) a, b and d (4) a, c and d

265. Match the items of List – I with those of List– II and indicate the correct code from the following :

List – I	List – II
i. Sale of existing firm to the management	a. Reverse synergy
ii. Financing acquisition with substantial secured borrowings	b. Management buyout
iii. Firms demerged worth more to other firms	c. Reverse capital budgeting
iv. Cash inflows on demerger at present at the sacrifice in form of cash out-flow on transfer of division/asset	d. Leveraged buyout

Codes :

	i	ii	iii	iv
(1)	a	b	c	d
(2)	c	a	b	d
(3)	b	d	a	c
(4)	b	a	d	c

266. NPV and IRR methods of investment evaluation may give divergent accept-reject decisions on account of which of the following?
a. Varying initial investment

b. Divergent cash flows from the investment projects
c. Disparity in the lives of the investment projects Indicate the correct code of their combinations

Codes :

(1) a and b only (2) b and c only
(3) a and c only (4) a, b and c all

267. Match the items of List – I with the items of List – II and select the code of correct matching :

List – I	**List – II**
a. Latent demand	i. More consumers would like to buy the product than can be satisfied.
b. Full demand	ii. Consumers may be attracted to products that have undesirable social consequences.
c. Overfull demand	iii. Consumers may share a strong need that cannot be satisfied by an existing product.
d. Unwholesome demand	iv. Consumers are adequately buying all products put into the market place.

Codes :

	a	b	c	d		a	b	c	d
(1)	iii	i	iv	ii	(2)	iii	iv	i	ii
(3)	iv	iii	i	ii	(4)	i	ii	iii	iv

268. Match the items of List – I with the items of List – II and select the code of correct matching :

List – I (Medium of Mass Communication)	**List – II (Limitations)**
a. Outdoor	i. Relative high cost; increasing consumer resistance
b. Yellow pages	ii. Over production could lead to runaway costs
c. Brochures	iii. High competition; long ad purchase lead time; creative limitations
d. Telephone	iv. Limited audience selectivity; creative limitations

Codes :

	a	b	c	d		a	b	c	d
(1)	iv	iii	ii	i	(2)	i	ii	iii	iv
(3)	iii	ii	iv	i	(4)	iv	ii	i	iii

269. "The manufacturer threatens to withdraw a resource or terminate a relationship if intermediaries fail to cooperate", refers to which one of the following channel power?

(1) Referent power (2) Coercive power
(3) Legitimate power (4) Reward power

270. Assertion (A) : A company's positioning and differentiation strategy must change over the product life cycle.

Reason (R) : A company's product, market and competitors change over the product life cycle.

Codes :

(1) (A) is correct, but (R) is incorrect.
(2) (A) is incorrect but (R) is correct.
(3) Both (A) and (R) are correct, but (R) is not the right explanation of (A).
(4) Both (A) and (R) are correct, and (R) is the right explanation of (A).

271. The following information is given :
Expected usage of 50,000 units in a period of 250 days
Cost of processing an order ₹ 20 per order
Carrying cost per unit ₹ 0.50 for the period
lead time on an order : 5 days
Company wants to keep a reserve supply of two day's usage.
How many units will be included in the reorder point ?

(1) 2000 (2) 1000
(3) 400 (4) 1400

272. Statement – I : A variable in the Linear Programming problem representing the unused quantity of an input resource is called surplus variable.

Statement – II : Values of the variables in the objective function of the dual of a primary problem denote shadow prices of the variables.

Codes :

(1) Both the Statements are correct.
(2) Both the statements are incorrect.
(3) Statement – I is correct while Statement– II is incorrect.
(4) Statement – I is incorrect while Statement – II is correct.

273. The least amount of time an activity is expected to consume. Which one of the following relates to the above expression as per PERT language ?

(1) Expected time (2) Most likely time
(3) Optimistic time (4) Pessimistic time

274. Which one of the following is not covered while considering the types of costs involved in quality control ?
(1) Preventive costs
(2) Manufacturing costs
(3) Inspection costs (4) Failure costs

275. Match the items of List – I with the items of List–II and indicate the code of correct matching :

List – I	List – II
a. The parameters of the distribution are n and p	i. Normal distribution
b. The mean and the variance of the distribution are identical	ii. Exponential distribution
c. The mean and the standard deviation of the distribution determines central location and spread respectively.	iii. Binomial distribution
d. The graph of the probability density function of the distribution slopes downward to the right from its maximum mean value	iv. Poisson distribution

Codes :

	a	b	c	d		a	b	c	d
(1)	iii	iv	i	ii	(2)	i	ii	iii	iv
(3)	iv	iii	i	ii	(4)	iii	i	iv	ii

276. When a researcher wants to select a representative sample to assess different parameters from a large sized finite heterogeneous population, which one of the following sampling techniques is the most appropriate ?
(1) Judgemental sampling
(2) Simple random sampling
(3) Stratified random sampling
(4) Quota sampling

277. Statement – I : The mean of the sampling distribution of mean is equal to the parameter value of the population mean.
Statement – II : Stratified sampling technique is unrestricted probability (random) sampling technique.
Codes :
(1) Both the Statements are correct.
(2) Both the Statements are incorrect.
(3) Statement – I is correct while Statement – II is incorrect.
(4) Statement – I is incorrect while Statement – II is correct.

278. You are given the following information about advertising expenditure and sales :

(₹ in lakh)

	Advertisement (X)	Sales (Y)
Arithmetic mean	10	90
Standard Deviation	3	12

Correlation coefficient between advertising expenditure and sales = 0.80. What is the likely sales for advertising budget of ₹ 15 lakh ?
(1) 120 lakh (2) 106 lakh
(3) 58 lakh (4) 48 lakh

279. Assertion (A) : McDonald's India Pvt. Ltd., the wholly-owned subsidiary of the US based fast-food giant McDonald's Corporation, along with Coca-Cola, is developing a fruit based beverage, to be retailed exclusively at McDonald's outlets.
Reason (R) : Organizations rightly try to diversify in order to spread their risks across several industries.
Codes :
(1) (A) and (R) both are correct and (R) is the right explanation of (A).
(2) (A) and (R) both are correct but (R) is not the right explanation of (A).
(3) (A) is correct but (R) is incorrect.
(4) (R) is correct but (A) is incorrect.

280. Statement – I : Competitors analysis begins with identification of potential competitors.
Statement – II : An industry analysis gives information regarding probable sources of competition.
Codes :
(1) Statement – I is correct but II is incorrect.
(2) Statement – II is correct but I is incorrect.
(3) Both the Statements are correct.
(4) Both the Statements are incorrect.

281. Strategic management consists of which one of the following combinations :
(a) Environmental scanning
(b) Strategy for outplay
(c) Strategy formulation
(d) Strategy implementation
(e) Evaluation and control
Codes :
(1) (a), (b), (c) and (d) only

(2) (b), (c), (d) and (e) only
(3) (a), (c), (d) and (e) only
(4) (b), (c) and (d) only

282. Michael Porter's Five Forces Model includes which one of the following combinations ?
(a) Threat of new potential entrants
(b) Threat of substitute product / service
(c) Bargaining power of suppliers
(d) Bargaining power of buyers
(e) Rivalry among current competitors
(f) Rivalry among prospective competitors
Codes :
(1) (a), (c), (d), (e) and (f)
(2) (a), (b), (d), (e) and (f)
(3) (a), (b), (c), (e) and (f)
(4) (a), (b), (c), (d) and (e)

283. Which one of the following is not a common motivation of an entrepreneur ?
(1) Desire to maintain the status quo
(2) Search for more rewarding work
(3) Search for personal and professional growth
(4) Desire for independence

284. The SFURTI programme of the government is to boost production in which one of the following industries ?
(1) Auto-components industry
(2) Industries using renewable energy
(3) Khadi and village industry
(4) Construction industry

285. Match the items of List – I with the items of List – II and identify the correct code of combination :

List – I	List – II
a. Entrepreneurship and Dynamic Capitalism	i. A.D. Chandler Jr.
b. The Affluent Society	ii. J.K. Galbraith
c. Theory of Economic Development	iii. Joseph Schumpeter
d. The Dynamics of Industrial Capitalism	iv. B.A. Kirchhoff

Codes :

	a	b	c	d		a	b	c	d
(1)	i	iii	ii	iv	(2)	i	ii	iii	iv
(3)	iv	iii	ii	i	(4)	iv	ii	iii	i

286. **Statement – I :** Entrepreneurs recognize opportunities where others see chaos or confusion.
Statement – II : Entrepreneurs bring aggressive capital for the existing business in traditional market place.
Codes :
(1) Statement – I is correct but II is not correct.
(2) Statement – II is correct but I is not correct.
(3) Both the Statements are correct.
(4) Both the Statements are incorrect.

287. Social responsibility of business while appropriating natural resources by a corporate entity has been recommended in which one of the following ?
(1) Montreal Protocol of 1987
(2) Millennium Development Goals 2008
(3) Sustainable Development Goals 2015 in Global Sustainability Report
(4) UNDP Human Development Report

288. Disclosure of corporate governance practice and its compliance has been stipulated in which one of the following ?
(1) Directors' Responsibility Statement under Section 134 of the Companies Act 2013.
(2) Auditor's Report
(3) C.A.G. Report
(4) Report of the SEBI and MCA 21

289. Kumar Mangalam Birla Committee Report, Ramesh Chandra Committee Report, Cadbury Committee Report primarily focus on which one of the following ?
(1) ethical issues in business practice and marketing practice
(2) health programme of the employees in an organisation
(3) issues relating to corporate governance practice
(4) gender issues in management and equality for all

290. 'The continuing commitment by business to behave ethically and contribute to economic development while improving the quality of life of the workforce and their families as well as of the local community and society at large. This may be attributed rightly to which one of the following ?
(1) ethical responsibility of business
(2) corporate social responsibility
(3) commitment towards employee welfare
(4) compliance with the provisions of the Plantation Workers Act.

291. Arrange the steps of diagnostic model of human resource management in the correct sequence from the first to the last. Select the code of correct sequence :

a. Evaluate b. Prescribe
c. Diagnose d. Implement

Codes :

(1) c, b, a, d (2) c, b, d, a
(3) a, c, d, b (4) a, c, b, d

292. Which one of the following is a training technique in which trainees act out parts in a realistic management situation ?
(1) Action learning (2) Role playing
(3) Behaviour modelling
(4) Case study

293. Match the following and indicate the code of correct matching :

List – I	**List – II**
a. INTUC	i. Bhartiya Janta Party
b. AITUC	ii. Communist Party of India
c. BMS	iii. Indian National Congress
d. CITU	iv. Communist Party of India (Marxist)

Codes :

	a	b	c	d		a	b	c	d
(1)	iii	ii	i	iv	(2)	iii	i	ii	iv
(3)	iii	iv	ii	i	(4)	iii	iv	i	ii

294. The agreement arrived at during the course of conciliation proceeding in industrial disputes is known as
(1) Settlement (2) Award
(3) Reward
(4) Accord and sanction

295. Results of a period that may occur at the initial career entry when the new employee's high job expectations confront the reality of a boring, unchallenging job.
This may rightly be attributed to which one of the following ?
(1) Reality Shock (2) Mentoring Shock
(3) Mental upcharge (4) Career upset

296. The two dominant aspects of industrial relations scene in the modern industrial society are covered in which one of the following ?
(1) Conflict and conciliation
(2) Cooperation and conciliation
(3) Conflict and cooperation
(4) Cooperation and codetermination

297. The decision of the adjudication authority and arbitrator in disputes is termed as
(1) Settlement (2) Award
(3) Reward (4) Accord and approval

298. In case of a domestic enquiry, which one of the following is not correct about enquiry officer ?
(1) He has to follow the principles of natural justice.
(2) He can recommend punishment alongwith the report of findings.
(3) He is generally an officer of the establishment but in some cases enquiry is also held by some outside agency.
(4) He can take final decision about punishment and issue an order inflicting punishment.

299. Match the items of List – I with the items of List – II and select the code of correct matching:

List – I	**List – II**
a. Core benefit	i. Bed, bathroom, towel, desk and closet
b. Basic product	ii. Clean bed sheet
c. Expected product	iii. Rest and sleep

Codes :

	a	b	c		a	b	c
(1)	i	ii	iii	(2)	iii	ii	i
(3)	iii	i	ii	(4)	ii	i	iii

300. Select the correct sequence of steps in setting a pricing policy :
(a) Determining Demand
(b) Analyzing competitors' Costs, Prices and Offers
(c) Selecting the Final Price
(d) Selecting the Pricing Objective
(e) Estimating costs
(f) Selecting a pricing method

Codes :

(1) (d), (a), (e), (b), (f) and (c)
(2) (a), (e), (b), (d), (f) and (c)
(3) (a), (b), (e), (d), (f) and (c)
(4) (a), (b), (c), (d), (e) and (f)

301. Which one of the following is a digital communications technique that involves improving visibility and monitoring sentiment within social networks and blogs ?
(1) Email marketing
(2) Display advertising
(3) E-PR
(4) Search engine optimization

302. Which one of the following is the report of the company's strengths and weaknesses relative to various competitors ?
(1) Competitor value analysis
(2) Customer value analysis

(3) Customer profitability analysis
(4) Customer perceived value

303. A company prices a 2 litre bottle of its mineral water at ₹ 30 but 60 ml of the same water in a moisturizer spray for ₹ 75. This is an example of which one of the following pricing practices?
(1) Product-Form pricing
(2) Customer-segment pricing
(3) Image pricing
(4) Location pricing

304. **Assertion (A) :** Companies must manage service quality by understanding the effects of each service encounter.
Reason (R) : Customer's expectations play a critical role in their service experiences and evaluations.
Select the correct codes :
Codes :
(1) Both (A) and (R) are correct, but (R) is not the right explanation of (A).
(2) Both (A) and (R) are correct and (R) is the right explanation of (A).
(3) (A) is correct but (R) is incorrect.
(4) (R) is correct but (A) is incorrect.

305. **Statement – I :** Direct marketing is a non-interactive marketing system.
Statement – II : Direct marketing uses one or more media to effect a measurable response or transaction at any location.
Select the correct code :
Codes :
(1) Both the Statements are correct.
(2) Both the Statements are incorrect.
(3) Only Statement – I is correct.
(4) Only Statement – II is correct.

306. Which one of the following refers to "two or more unrelated companies put together resources or programmes to exploit an emerging market opportunity" ?
(1) Holistic marketing
(2) Horizontal marketing system
(3) Hub and spoke system
(4) Co-branding

307. Credit sales of a firm in a certain year amounted to ₹ 12,00,000 and the sundry debtors outstanding at the beginning and the end of the year amounted to ₹ 1,20,000 and ₹ 80,000 respectively. Indicate the correct code for the debtors turnover ratio and the average collection period from the following :
(1) 10 and 1.2 months (2) 12 and 1 month
(3) 15 and 0.8 month (4) 6 and 2 months

308. In international marketing, what is the term for establishing local production facilities in a foreign market?
(1) Exporting
(2) Licensing
(3) Direct investment
(4) Indirect export

309. The credit policy of a firm is not decided for which combination of the following ?
a. Maximisation of sales
b. Minimisation of bad debt losses
c. Maximisation of shareholder's wealth
d. Minimisation of adverse effect on the volume of sales
Codes :
(1) a, b and c (2) b, c and d
(3) a, c and d (4) a, b and d

310. Match the items of List – I with those in List– II and indicate the correct code for the following :

List – I	**List – II**
i. Concentration Banking	a. William J. Baumol
ii. Optimum cash balance under certainty	b. Cash collection technique
iii. Playing the float	c. Miller M.H. and Orr D
iv. Optimum cash balance under uncertainty	d. Cash disbursement technique

Codes :

	i	ii	iii	iv		i	ii	iii	iv
(1)	a	c	b	d	(2)	b	a	d	c
(3)	c	d	a	b	(4)	d	b	c	a

311. Indicate the correct code for the liquidity ratios from the following :
a. Current Ratio
b. Acid Test/Quick Ratio
c. Total Assets Turnover Ratio
d. Defensive-Interval Ratio
Codes :
(1) a, b and c (2) b, c and d
(3) a, b and d (4) a, c and d

312. Non-payment by solvent debtor till due date involves which one type of cost from the following ?
(1) Default cost
(2) Delinquency cost
(3) Capital cost
(4) Extra collection cost

313. Banks normally provide working capital finance in forms of which combination of the following ?

a. Term loans b. Discounting of bills
c. Overdrafts d. Cash credits

Codes :

(1) a, b and c (2) b, c and d
(3) a, b and d (4) a, c and d

314. In case a product's selling price (per unit) is ₹ 20, the variable cost (per unit) is ₹ 14, fixed factory overheads, (per year) is ₹ 5,40,000 and fixed selling overheads is ₹ 2,52,000, the break-even in terms of sales volume and the number of units to be sold to earn a profit of ₹ 60,000 will be which one of the following ?

Break-even Volume of Sales and Units to be sold for the desired profits

(1) ₹ 24,60,000 and 1,36,000 units
(2) ₹ 25,40,000 and 1,40,000 units
(3) ₹ 26,40,000 and 1,42,000 units
(4) ₹ 28,60,000 and 1,48,000 units

315. Anti dumping duty is levied on which one of the following :

(1) The goods exported from home country to encourage more export to a sovereign.
(2) The goods imported into the home country for the purpose of re-export to another sovereign.
(3) The dumped imports which is causing damage to the domestic industry in the importing country.
(4) The dumped imports which are meant for re-entry into a sovereign for further trade.

316. Assertion (A) : Export Processing Zones (EPZs) were set up as an enclave separated from the Domestic Tariff Area (DTA) and converted into SEZs.

Reason (R) : The Export Oriented Units (EOUs) scheme is complimentary to the EPZ and is introduced to enable exporters enjoy liberal package of incentives.

Codes :

(1) (A) is correct but (R) is incorrect
(2) (A) is incorrect but (R) is correct.
(3) Both (A) and (R) are correct but (R) is not the right explanation of (A).
(4) Both (A) and (R) are correct and (R) is the right explanation of (A).

317. Challenges before international business such as base erosion and profit shifting (BEPs), tax avoidance and shifting between a holding company and a subsidiary located in two different tax sovereigns may be resolved by which one of the following ?

(1) Mandate of Viena convention
(2) Montreal protocol
(3) Technology transfer transactions, cyber space
(4) Kyoto protocol

318. An efficient dispute settlement mechanism under WTO was brought in by which one of the following :

(1) The Uruguay Round Agreement
(2) Doha Round
(3) UNDP Human Development Report 2000
(4) The Uruguay and Geneva Round of Negotiation

319. The undernoted items may be categorized into which one of the following ?

Export quota, exchange control, profit remittance restrictions, subsidies, government procurement

(1) Tariffs
(2) Unrestricted tariffs
(3) Non-tariff barriers
(4) Hybrid of tariff and no-tariff barriers

320. The undernoted items are categorized into which one of the following international product decisions for global business ?

Straight extension, product adaptation, communication extension, communication adaptation, product extension, dual adaptation and innovation

(1) Product diversification
(2) Product market segmentation
(3) Product communication strategies
(4) Market segmentation and product promotion

321. Match the items given in List – I with the items of List – II and indicate the code of correct matching :

List – I	List – II
a. CIP	i. Carriage
b. CPT	ii. Insurance and carriage
c. DAF	iii. Freight, cost, insurance
d. CIF	iv. Frontier

Codes :

	a	b	c	d		a	b	c	d
(1)	ii	i	iv	iii	(2)	i	ii	iii	iv
(3)	iii	ii	iv	i	(4)	iv	iii	ii	i

322. To comply with the requirement of TRIPS agreement and to protect products of Indian origin, which one of the following was enacted?

(1) WTO Compliance Act 1999

(2) Geographical Indication of Goods (Registration and Protection) Act 1999
(3) The Patents Act
(4) The Copyright Act

323. Which one of the following transactions can be carried on without any restriction or regulation of the RBI under the FEMA ?
(1) Transfer or issue of any foreign security by a person resident in India.
(2) Transfer or issue of any security by a person resident outside India.
(3) Drawal of foreign exchange for payments due on account of amortization of loans or for depreciation of direct investment.
(4) Export, import or holding of currency notes.

324. How does Green HRM contribute to fostering a culture of environmental responsibility in the workplace?
(1) By ignoring the impact of HR practices on the environment
(2) By promoting wasteful practices among employees
(3) By integrating sustainability values into HR policies and encouraging eco-friendly behavior
(4) By discouraging employees from engaging in environmental initiatives

325. Which of the following statements are true in context of customer value and satisfaction concept?
(A) Value perceptions increase with quality, service and price
(B) Customer value triad is primarily a combination of quality, service and price
(C) Marketing is the identification, creation, communication, delivery and monitoring of customers value
(D) If the perceived performance of the product matches with perceived expectations, the customer is delighted
(E) Satisfaction reflects a person's judgement of a products perceived performance in relation to expectations

Choose the correct answer from the options given below:
(1) (A), (B) and (C) only
(2) (B), (C) and (D) only
(3) (A), (D) and (E) only
(4) (B), (C) and (E) only

326. Statements given below are related to analysis of variance. Identify the statement/s that are **true :**

Statement (I): The shape of 'F' distribution depends on the number of degrees of freedom in both the numerator and the denominator of the 'F' ratio.

Statement (II): In analysis of variance, sample sizes should be equal.

Statement (III): Analysis of variance may be used to test whether the means of more than two populations are equal.

Codes :
(1) **Statements (I), (II)** and **(III)** are true
(2) **Statements (I)** and **(II)** are true
(3) **Statements (I)** and **(III)** are true
(4) Only **statement (III)** is true

327. From the following statements choose the **correct** statement/s :

Statement (I): A statistic is a characteristic of a population.

Statement (II): The standard error of mean is the standard deviation of the sampling distribution.

Statement (III): The standard error of mean decreases in direct proportion to sample size.

Codes :
(1) Only (I) and (II) is true
(2) Only (II) and **(III)** are true
(3) Only (II) is true
(4) Only **(III)** is true

328. Which among the following are the examples of key less interfaces ?
(1) Mouse, OCR, pen and voice recognition
(2) Keyboard, OCR, pen and voice recognition
(3) Bar coding, OCR, pen and voice recognition
(4) None of the above

329. Which of the following are the inputs of marketing information system ?
(a) Marketing research data
(b) Marketing intelligence data
(c) External environment data
(d) Strategic plan

Choose the **correct** option :
(1) Only (a) and (b)
(2) Only (a), (b) and (c)
(3) Only (a), (c) and (d)
(4) (a), (b), (c) and (d)

330. The Uruguay round provided 'Sunset' clause to control :
(1) Customs valuation

(2) Dumping
(3) Technical barriers to trade
(4) Dispute settlement

331. In order to promote domestic capital goods manufacturing industry, Specific Export Obligation under EPCG scheme, in case capital goods are procured from indigenous manufacturers, has been reduced from 90% to
(1) 50% (2) 60%
(3) 75% (4) 80%

332. International banking dealing with non-residents only and not in the currency of the country where they are located is called
(1) Non-resident Banking
(2) Offshore Banking
(3) Euro Currency Banking
(4) London Discount House

333. Exporter's 'Export risk insurance' is covered by
(1) Insurance Companies
(2) Export Credit Guarantee Corporation
(3) Reserve Bank of India
(4) Export Development Authorities

334. Match List I with List II

	List I (Theory)		List II (What Nation's do)
a.	Mercantilism	I.	The range of products made or grown for export would depend upon the relative availability of different factors in each country
b.	Theory of Absolute Advantage	II.	Gold and silver are the mainstay of national wealth
c.	Theory of Comparative Advantage	III.	Countries should specialize in the production of goods for which they have absolute advantage
d.	Factor Endowment	IV.	Nations should produce those goods for which they have the greatest relative advantage

Choose the correct answer from the options given below:
(1) a-I, b-II, c-III, d-IV
(2) a-II, b-III, c-IV, d-I
(3) a-III, b-II, c-I, d-IV
(4) a-IV, b-III, c-II, d-I

335. Member Countries of NAFTA are
(1) Brazil, USA and Canada
(2) Canada, USA and Mexico
(3) USA, Argentina and Canada
(4) Panama, USA and Canada

336. Presently in India, rupee convertability in foreign exchange is
(1) Restricted (2) Partial
(3) Full (4) None of the above

337. A country can improve its balance of payment through contribution both to current account and capital account by way of
(1) Export promotion
(2) Foreign Direct Investment
(3) Import of Capital
(4) Export of Capital

338. "_____ is a statement showing a Country's Commercial Transaction with the rest of the world . It shows inflow and outflow of foreign exchange. It is divided into current and capital accounts. The former records the transaction in goods and services."
(1) Foreign Direct Investment
(2) Balance of Payment
(3) Movement of Foreign Exchange
(4) International Commitments

339. The activity of making profit through buying a Currency cheap in one market and selling it dear in the other market at a particular point of time is known as
(1) Forward currency
(2) Currency arbitrage
(3) Speculation of currency
(4) Depreciated currency

340. Match the items of **List - I** with **List - II** with regards to the causes of sickness in small scale industry.

List - I	List - II
(a) Internal causes of sickness	(i) Own financing by banks
(b) External problems	(ii) Red tapism
(c) Sickness because of government policies	(iii) Faulty project selection

Codes:

	(a)	(b)	(c)
(1)	(i)	(ii)	(iii)
(2)	(i)	(iii)	(ii)
(3)	(ii)	(i)	(iii)
(4)	(iii)	(i)	(ii)

341. **Assertion (I):** A sick industry is one which is not healthy in terms of its financial management.

Assertion (II): A unit which has incurred cash losses for one year and it is likely to continue to incur cash loss for current year as well as for following year is considered to be a sick unit.

(1) **Assertion (I)** only is correct.
(2) **Assertion (II)** only is correct.
(3) **Assertion (I)** and **(II)** both are incorrect.
(4) **Assertion (I)** and **(II)** both are correct.

342. Which of the following is/are eligible to get the benefit under the scheme of "Rehabilitation of Sick Enterprises" by the Government of India ?

(1) Micro sick unit
(2) Small sick unit
(3) Medium sick unit
(4) All of the above

343. Match the items of **List - I** with **List - II** with regards to phases of entrepreneurial process:

List - I	List - II
(a) Identify and evaluate the opportunity	(i) Executive summary
(b) Develop business plan	(ii) Develop access to needed resources
(c) Determine the required resources	(iii) Implement control system
(d) Manage the enterprise	(iv) Assess the com petitive environment

Codes:

	(a)	(b)	(c)	(d)
(1)	(iv)	(ii)	(iii)	(i)
(2)	(iv)	(i)	(ii)	(iii)
(3)	(i)	(iii)	(ii)	(iv)
(4)	(iv)	(iii)	(i)	(ii)

344. Which among the following is **not** a scheme by the MSME ?

(1) Assistance to Training Institutions (ATI)
(2) Credit Linked Capital Subsidy (CLCS)
(3) Credit Linked Assets Subsidy (CLAS)
(4) ISO 9000/ISO 14001 Certification Reimbursement

345. The enforcement mechanisms followed in respect of implementation of corporate governance practices are indicated below. Choose any one of the mechanism which is **not** included in corporate governance practice.

(1) Clause 49 of the Listing Agreement
(2) Directors responsibility statement, appointment of independent directors, audit committee and internal check
(3) Corporate governance compliance certificate, audit committee report, appointment of woman director
(4) Formulation of mission statement, appointment of a whistleblower, contents of red herring prospectus

346. There is a provision in the Companies Act, 2013 regarding related party transactions to ensure ethical standards in managerial decisions. From the following options identify who is **not** a related party as per the Companies Act, 2013.

(1) A person on whose advice, directions or instructions (except given in professional capacity) a director or manager is accustomed to act.
(2) A private company in which a director or manager is a director or holds along with his relatives less than 2% of its paid up share capital.
(3) A firm in which a director, manager or his relative is a partner.
(4) A holding/subsidiary or associate company, subsidiary's subsidiary and such person as would be prescribed.

347. Ethics deals with ideals, it is regarded as a normative science. Choose any one from the following options which is **not** a part of ethics as a normative science.

(1) It tells what a human conduct ought to be.
(2) It determines norms, ideals, standards or values.
(3) It passes judgements of value stating whether a particular conduct is in conformity with the moral ideal or the ideal of goodness.
(4) It passes judgements regarding facts and events as they are and state the laws governing them.

348. Value formulation is a combination of several factors indicated below. Which one of them is the appropriate option ?

(1) Biological source, medical source, legal mandate, organisational mission and vision
(2) Legal source, moral source, spiritual source, philanthropic source
(3) Organisational culture, command from higher authorities, judicial pronouncements
(4) Genetic source, environmental source (culture, education, religious faith), influence of superiors, multimedia source

349. In the sphere of ethics in decision making, for determining morally correct action, there are specific stages providing rationale for moral action. Choose any one appropriate option from the following.
(1) Actions that avoid punishment, actions that serve one's needs, actions that gain approval from others, actions that abide laws and authority, social contracts and actions supported by universal principles.
(2) Actions that impose punishment, actions that are not followed by feedback response, actions beyond moral approbation, approved by judicial pronouncement, supported by universal principles.
(3) Actions that are morally right, legally enforceable, is used on external believes that events are controlled by destiny, fate or luck, not supported by social contracts, supported by universal principles.
(4) Actions that are morally wrong but supported by hierarchy and organisational goal of profit maximisation, individual judgement about ethicality of the decision is ignored.

350. Assertion (A): According to David Fritzsche, business ethics is the process of evaluating decisions, either pre or post, with respect to the moral standards of society's culture.

Reason (R): Managers need not evaluate the moral dimensions of a decision before making it, because they are to carry out the order of the higher authority to maximise commercial gain for the entity.

Codes :
(1) Both (A) and (R) are correct.
(2) (A) is correct and (R) is the right explanation of (A).
(3) (A) is correct but (R) is not the right explanation of (A).
(4) Both (A) and (R) are incorrect.

351. Indicate the correct code for the scope of managerial economics from the following :
a. Demand Analysis
b. Production and Cost Analysis
c. Pricing and Investment Decisions
d. Factor pricing Decisions
e. Economic Environmental Analysis

Codes :
(1) a, b, c, d (2) b, c, d, e
(3) a, b, c, e (4) a, c, d, e

352. Price elasticity of demand for a product is measured by
(1) $Ed = \frac{\Delta Q}{Q} \times \frac{\Delta P}{P}$ (2) $Ed = \frac{\Delta Q}{Q} \div \frac{\Delta P}{P}$
(3) $Ed = \frac{\Delta P}{Q} \times \frac{Q}{P}$ (4) $Ed = \frac{\Delta P}{P} \div \frac{\Delta Q}{Q}$
(Where Ed = elasticity of demand, Q = Quantity, P = Price and Δ = represents change)

353. Which one of the following will be the appropriate pricing strategy for a new product expecting an expanding market ?
(1) Monopoly pricing
(2) Skimming pricing
(3) Penetrating pricing
(4) Differential pricing

354. Match the items of the List – I with those of the List – II and suggest the correct code from the following :

List – I	List – II
i. Loss Leader	a. Locational price differentials
ii. Unchanged Pricing	b. Products with high initial demands
iii. Basing Point Pricing	c. Product line pricing
iv. Skimming Pricing	d. Oligopoly pricing

Codes :

	i	ii	iii	iv		i	ii	iii	iv
(1)	a	b	c	d	(2)	c	d	a	b
(3)	d	b	a	c	(4)	c	a	b	d

355. In case the firm makes varying investments on the different investment projects, the appropriate project evaluation technique would be, which one of the following ?
(1) Average annual rate of return technique
(2) Pay back period technique
(3) Net present value technique
(4) Profitability index technique

356. According to Henry Fayol, which one of the following combinations of qualities are required in a manager ?
(1) Physical, mental, experience, educational and conceptual
(2) Technical, human, conceptual, mental and moral
(3) Physical, mental, moral, educational, technical and experience
(4) Mental, moral, conceptual, educational, technical and experience

357. Neo-classical organisation theory emphasises on which one of the following ?
(1) Flat structure of organisation
(2) Tall structure of organisation
(3) Coordination by hierarchy
(4) Unity of command

358. According to Graicuna's formula of span of management, if a superior has three subordinates, what number of cross-relationships would be ?
(1) three (2) six
(3) nine (4) eighteen

359. In Reddin's 'Tridimensional Grid', which one of the following is a less effective style of leadership ?
(1) Developer (2) Missionary
(3) Executive (4) Bureaucrat

360. **Assertion (A) :** Attribution theory is based on relationship between personal perception and interpersonal behaviour.
Reasoning (R) : Since most 'whys' are not directly observable, people must depend upon cognitions, particularly perception.
Codes :
(1) (A) is right but (R) is wrong.
(2) (A) is wrong but (R) is right.
(3) Both (A) and (R) are right but (R) does not explain (A).
(4) Both (A) and (R) are right and (R) explains (A).

361. Arrange the following steps of training and development process in the right sequence :
a. Need analysis b. Validation
c. Evaluation
d. Implement the programme
e. Instructional design
(1) a, e, d, c, b (2) a, e, c, b, d
(3) a, e, b, d, c (4) a, b, e, c, d

362. Which one of the following is related to 'Standard of Personnel' ?
(1) Job Specification (2) Job Description
(3) Job Design (4) Job Evaluation

363. If an employee desires to pay more than the minimum required contribution under the Employees' Provident Fund and Miscellaneous Provisions Act, 1952, then
(1) employer shall also pay an amount equal to the total contribution of employee.
(2) employer shall pay only half of the additional contribution of employee.
(3) employer is under no obligation to pay the additional contribution.
(4) the act is silent regarding this matter.

364. Under the Employees' State Insurance Act, 1948, sickness benefit can be paid for which one of the following maximum periods ?
(1) 45 days in two consecutive benefit periods.
(2) 66 days in two consecutive benefit periods.
(3) 91 days in two consecutive benefit periods.
(4) 180 days in two consecutive benefit periods.

365. Which one of the following laws is enacted by the Central Government and enforced by the State Governments ?
(1) The Employees State Insurance Act, 1948
(2) The Employees' Provident Fund and Miscellaneous Provisions Act, 1952
(3) Factories Act, 1948
(4) The Mines Act, 1952

366. The cost of external equity can be most appropriately computed as per the
(1) Earnings price ratio
(2) Dividend price ratio
(3) Dividend price plus growth ratio
(4) Capital assets pricing model

367. For the following items in List – I and List – II, indicate the correct code after matching them :

List – I	List – II
i. Net income approach for capital structure	a. Modigliani, M. and Miller M.H.
ii. Net operating income approach for capital structure	b. Robert Bruner

iii. Irrelevance of capital structure for the value of the firm. — c. Ezra Soloman

iv. FRICT analysis for capital structure — d. David Durand

Codes :

	i	ii	iii	iv		i	ii	iii	iv
(1)	a	b	c	d	(2)	d	c	a	b
(3)	d	c	b	a	(4)	b	a	d	c

368. Which one of the following is not a feature of 'Preference Shares'?

(1) Prior claim on income/assets of the company over equity shareholders.
(2) Redeemability after certain period.
(3) Possessing voting rights on important issues of the company.
(4) May possess the right to participate in surplus profits of the company.

369. The basic consideration for dividend pay-out for a company excludes which one of the following ?

(1) Investment opportunities for the company
(2) Expectations of the shareholders of the company
(3) Legal and financial restrictions for the company
(4) Stability of the dividend considerations

370. For the following two statements of Assertion (A) and Reasoning (R) indicate the correct code:

Assertion (A) : Shareholders Wealth Maximization (SWM) and not the profit maximisation is an appropriate and operationally feasible financial management goal.

Reasoning (R) : There exists a principal-agent relationship between the shareholders and the management of the company.

Codes :

(1) (A) and (R) both are correct.
(2) (A) is correct but (R) is incorrect.
(3) (A) is incorrect but (R) is correct.
(4) (A) and (R) both are incorrect

371. Which one of the following components is not the part of broad marketing environment?

(1) Technological environment
(2) Task environment
(3) Demographic environment
(4) Natural environment

372. The Coco Cola Company markets a wide range of different beverage products including bottled water, soft-drinks, juices and sports drinks. Each product appeals to a different segment. This is an example of which type of market offering ?

(1) Differentiated marketing
(2) Target marketing
(3) Undifferentiated marketing
(4) Intensified marketing

373. Temporarily reducing prices to increase short-run sales is an example of which one of the following ?

(1) Segmented pricing
(2) Promotional pricing
(3) Dynamic pricing
(4) Geographical pricing

374. Match the items of List – I with the items of List – II and indicate the code of correct matching :

List – I	List – II
a. Brand elements	i. The marketer's vision of what the brand must be and do for consumers.
b. Brand line	ii. All products, original as well as line and category extensions, sold under a particular brand name.
c. Brand personality	iii. Those trademark able devices that serve to identify and differentiate the brand.
d. Brand promise	iv. The specific mix of human traits that may be attributed to a particular brand.

Codes :

	a	b	c	d		a	b	c	d
(1)	iii	ii	iv	i	(2)	i	ii	iii	iv
(3)	iii	i	iv	ii	(4)	iv	iii	ii	i

375. Statement – I : In developing advertising programme marketing managers must always start by identifying the target market and buyer motives.

Statement – II : A company may run multiple ad campaigns at the same time, each emphasizing different aspects of its brand and service.

(1) Only Statement – I is correct.
(2) Only Statement – II is correct.
(3) Both Statements – I and II are correct.
(4) Both Statements – I and II are incorrect.

376. Match the items of List – I with the items of List – II and select the code of correct matching with regard to forecasting models for operations :

List – I (Model Type (name))	List – II (Description)
a. Delphi technique	i. Causal quantitative model
b. Economic modeling	ii. Quantitative model (Naive)
c. Exponential Smoothing	iii. Qualitative model

Codes:

	a	b	c		a	b	c
(1)	i	ii	iii	(2)	iii	i	ii
(3)	iii	ii	i	(4)	ii	iii	i

377. In which one of the following situations, a product-oriented layout is appropriate ?
(1) A medical clinic
(2) An automated carwash
(3) A work centre for welding, heat treating and painting
(4) A home plumbing repair business.

378. A graphic tool to trace the interaction of several workers with one machine is termed as
(1) Gang process chart
(2) Flow process chart
(3) Activity chart
(4) Operation chart

379. Which one of the following is a technique of statistical quality control used for product control ?
(1) R-chart (2) Sampling plan
(3) np-chart (4) control-chart

380. The decision-criterion in which a decision-maker selects an alternative that maximizes H (criterion of realism) = [a × (maximum in column)] + [(1 – a) × (minimum in column)] is called
(1) Laplace criterion
(2) Hurwicz criterion
(3) Wald's criterion
(4) Bayesian criterion

381. Which one of the following expressions relates to an event which represents the occurrence of either A or B or both ?
(1) $A \cup B$ (2) $A \cap B$
(3) $\bar{A} \cap \bar{B}$ (4) $(A \cap \bar{B}) \cup (\bar{A} \cap B)$

382. A Bernoulli process has all but which one of the following properties ?
(1) Each trial has two possible outcomes.
(2) The probability of a success on any trial remains fixed over time.
(3) The probability of success on any trial is equal to the probability of failure.
(4) Trials are statistically independent.

383. Statement – I : The product of coefficient of correlation, standard deviation of variable 'X' and Standard deviation of variable 'Y' gives the measure of covariance between X and Y variables.

Statement – II : The product of coefficient of correlation between X and Y variables and the ratio between standard deviation of X variable to standard deviation of Y variable measures the slope of the regression line of X on Y variable.

Codes :
(1) Both the Statements are correct.
(2) Both the Statements are incorrect.
(3) Statement – I is correct while Statement – II is incorrect.
(4) Statement – I is incorrect while Statement – II is correct.

384. Statement – I : Both the probable error and standard error of the coefficient of correlation are different.

Statement – II : When a sampling distribution of mean is prepared by taking small sized samples from a normally distributed population, the distribution takes the shape of normal distribution.

Codes :
(1) Both the Statements are correct.
(2) Both the Statements are incorrect.
(3) Statement – I is correct while Statement– II is incorrect.
(4) Statement – I is incorrect while Statement – II is correct.

385. Which one of the following is not the major characteristics of internet ?
(1) Open (2) Expensive
(3) Global (4) Untrusted

386. Assertion (A) : Private foreign capital lends to flow to the high profit areas rather than to the priority sectors.

Reasoning (R) : One of the important limitations to utilize the foreign capital is the absorptive capacity of the recipient country.

Codes :
(1) (A) and (R) both are correct and (R) is the correct explanation of (A).
(2) (A) and (R) both are correct but (R) is not the correct explanation of (A).

(3) (A) is correct whereas (R) is incorrect.
(4) (R) is correct whereas (A) is incorrect.

387. Consider the following statements and identify the correct code of true statements :

(a) When an organization's survival is threatened and it is not competing effectively, retrenchment strategies are often needed.
(b) Turnaround strategy is used when an organization is performing well but has not yet reached a critical stage.
(c) Divestment strategy involves selling the business or setting it up as a separate corporation.
(d) Liquidation strategy involves closure of business which is no longer profitable.

Codes :
(1) Only (a), (b) and (c) are correct.
(2) Only (b), (c) and (d) are correct.
(3) Only (a), (c) and (d) are correct.
(4) Only (a) and (d) are correct.

388. **Statement – I :** Most businesses start off as "Question Marks", in that they enter a highgrowth market in which there is already a market leader.

Statement – II : A "Star" is the market leader in a high-growth market, but it does not necessarily provide much cash.

(1) Statement – I is correct but Statement – II is incorrect.
(2) Statement – II is correct but Statement – I is incorrect.
(3) Both the Statements are incorrect.
(4) Both the Statements are correct.

389. Match the items of List – I with List – II and identify the code of correct matching :

List – I	List – II
a. Consistent actions one time	i. A perspective
b. It reflects the decision of the firm to offer particular products or services in particular markets.	ii. A ploy
c. A manoeuvre intended to outwit competitor	iii. A position
d. A view of what the organization is to become	iv. A pattern

Codes:

	a	b	c	d		a	b	c	d
(1)	iv	iii	i	ii	(2)	iv	i	ii	iii
(3)	iv	iii	ii	i	(4)	iii	iv	ii	i

390. Apple computers uses a differentiation competitive strategy that emphasizes innovative product with creative design. This is an example of

(1) Functional strategy
(2) Business strategy
(3) Operating strategy
(4) Product strategy

391. Match the items of List – I with the items of List – II and select the code of correcting matching :

List – I	List – II
a. Richard Cantillon	i. Entrepreneur must accept the challenge and should be willing hard to achieve something
b. Joseph A. Schumpeter	ii. Entrepreneurs are all those persons who are engaged in economic activity.
c. J.K. Golbraith	iii. Entrepreneur is a person who introduces innovation and change.

Codes:

	a	b	c		a	b	c
(1)	iii	i	ii	(2)	i	iii	ii
(3)	ii	iii	i	(4)	ii	i	iii

392. Total Quality Management, job redesigning, new techniques of doing things and management by consensus are the examples of which one of the following ?

(1) Opportunistic entrepreneurship
(2) Administrative entrepreneurship
(3) Incubative entrepreneurship
(4) Mass entrepreneurship

393. Under technology and quality upgradation support to help manufacturing MSMEs buy energy efficient technologies for production, what percentage of the actual expenditure is provided as financial support by the Government of India ?

(1) 75% (2) 60%
(3) 50% (4) 25%

394. Which one of the following is not a personal characteristic of an entrepreneur ?
(1) Innovative
(2) Hardworking
(3) Practical
(4) Submissive

395. Which one of the following is the most insignificant reason for sickness in SSI sector?
(1) Power shortage
(2) Lack of demand
(3) Management problems
(4) Equipment problems

396. **Statement – I :** Ethical principles tend to be broader than legal principles.
Statement – II : Laws and ethics are closely related.
Codes :
(1) Statement – I is correct but Statement – II is incorrect.
(2) Statement – II is correct but Statement – I is incorrect.
(3) Both the Statements are correct.
(4) Both the Statements are incorrect.

397. **Assertion (A) :** The state shall endeavour to protect and improve the environment and to safeguard the forest and wildlife of the country.
Reasoning (R) : The Directive principles of state policy of the Indian Constitution Command the State to ensure protection and improvement of environment and to safeguard forest and wildlife.
Codes :
(1) (A) is correct but (R) is not correct.
(2) (R) is correct but (A) is not correct.
(3) Both (A) and (R) are correct and (R) is the right explanation of (A).
(4) Both (A) and (R) are correct but (R) is not the right explanation of (A).

398. Match the items of List – I with List – II and identify the code of correct matching :

List – I (CSR Models)	List – II (Emphasis)
a. Ethical Model	i. Corporate responsibilities limited to private owners.
b. Statist Model	ii. Voluntary commitment by companies to public welfare
c. Liberal Model	iii. State ownership and legal requirements determine corporate responsibilities.
d. Stakeholder Model	iv. Companies respond to the need of customers, communities, etc

Codes :

	a	b	c	d		a	b	c	d
(1)	ii	iii	i	iv	(2)	ii	i	iii	iv
(3)	ii	i	iv	iii	(4)	i	iii	ii	iv

399. Which one among the following is not correct about J. J. Irani Committee's recommendations on Company Law (2005) :
(1) 2/5th of the board of a listed company should comprise of independent directors.
(2) Introduce the concept of One Person Company (OPC).
(3) Allow corporations to self-regulate their affairs.
(4) Disclose proper and accurate compilation of financial information of a corporation.

400. A business should act ethically for which of the following reasons ?
(a) To prevent harm to the general public
(b) To meet stake-holder expectations
(c) To protect their own employees
(d) To maximize profit of the business
Codes :
(1) (a), (b) and (c) only
(2) (b), (c) and (d) only
(3) (a), (c) and (d) only
(4) (a) and (d) only

ANSWER KEY

1. (3)	2. (3)	3. (4)	4. (2)	5. (3)	6. (3)	7. (1)	8. (2)	9. (2)	10. (3)
11. (4)	12. (1)	13. (3)	14. (1)	15. (2)	16. (4)	17. (3)	18. (2)	19. (2)	20. (3)
21. (2)	22. (3)	23. (4)	24. (3)	25. (2)	26. (2)	27. (2)	28. (1)	29. (2)	30. (2)
31. (4)	32. (2)	33. (1)	34. (1)	35. (4)	36. (4)	37. (1)	38. (3)	39. (4)	40. (4)
41. (1)	42. (3)	43. (1)	44. (1)	45. (3)	46. (2)	47. (3)	48. (2)	49. (2)	50. (4)
51. (1)	52. (1)	53. (3)	54. (4)	55. (1)	56. (3)	57. (2)	58. (4)	59. (1)	60. (3)
61. (1)	62. (3)	63. (2)	64. (1)	65. (4)	66. (1)	67. (4)	68. (3)	69. (3)	70. (1)
71. (1)	72. (2)	73. (1)	74. (3)	75. (1)	76. (4)	77. (2)	78. (3)	79. (2)	80. (4)
81. (3)	82. (1)	83. (2)	84. (2)	85. (1)	86. (4)	87. (4)	88. (1)	89. (3)	90. (2)
91. (2)	92. (1)	93. (3)	94. (2)	95. (1)	96. (3)	97. (3)	98. (3)	99. (1)	100. (3)
101. (3)	102. (1)	103. (3)	104. (2)	105. (1)	106. (1)	107. (4)	108. (3)	109. (2)	110. (4)
111. (2)	112. (4)	113. (3)	114. (4)	115. (2)	116. (2)	117. (1)	118. (3)	119. (1)	120. (1)
121. (3)	122. (2)	123. (1)	124. (1)	125. (4)	126. (3)	127. (2)	128. (4)	129. (1)	130. (1)
131. (1)	132. (3)	133. (1)	134. (3)	135. (4)	136. (2)	137. (4)	138. (1)	139. (4)	140. (2)
141. (4)	142. (1)	143. (4)	144. (2)	145. (4)	146. (3)	147. (2)	148. (2)	149. (4)	150. (4)
151. (3)	152. (2)	153. (4)	154. (3)	155. (1)	156. (2)	157. (4)	158. (3)	159. (2)	160. (2)
161. (2)	162. (2)	163. (1)	164. (1)	165. (1)	166. (2)	167. (3)	168. (3)	169. (2)	170. (1)
171. (1)	172. (2)	173. (4)	174. (1)	175. (1)	176. (3)	177. (2)	178. (3)	179. (4)	180. (2)
181. (2)	182. (2)	183. (1)	184. (2)	185. (3)	186. (3)	187. (2)	188. (3)	189. (1)	190. (2)
191. (3)	192. (3)	193. (3)	194. (1)	195. (4)	196. (3)	197. (4)	198. (2)	199. (1)	200. (1)
201. (1)	202. (2)	203. (2)	204. (3)	205. (1)	206. (1)	207. (1)	208. (2)	209. (4)	210. (2)
211. (1)	212. (4)	213. (1)	214. (1)	215. (1)	216. (1)	217. (1)	218. (1)	219. (1)	220. (2)
221. (4)	222. (4)	223. (4)	224. (4)	225. (1)	226. (1)	227. (2)	228. (1)	229. (1)	230. (3)
231. (4)	232. (2)	233. (3)	234. (1)	235. (2)	236. (3)	237. (2)	238. (4)	239. (2)	240. (1)
241. (4)	242. (3)	243. (1)	244. (3)	245. (3)	246. (3)	247. (3)	248. (2)	249. (4)	250. (3)
251. (3)	252. (1)	253. (4)	254. (2)	255. (2)	256. (3)	257. (4)	258. (3)	259. (4)	260. (1)
261. (1)	262. (2)	263. (2)	264. (3)	265. (3)	266. (4)	267. (1)	268. (4)	269. (2)	270. (4)
271. (4)	272. (4)	273. (3)	274. (2)	275. (1)	276. (3)	277. (3)	278. (2)	279. (1)	280. (3)
281. (3)	282. (4)	283. (1)	284. (3)	285. (4)	286. (1)	287. (3)	288. (1)	289. (3)	290. (2)
291. (2)	292. (2)	293. (1)	294. (1)	295. (1)	296. (3)	297. (2)	298. (4)	299. (3)	300. (1)
301. (3)	302. (2)	303. (1)	304. (2)	305. (4)	306. (2)	307. (2)	308. (3)	309. (3)	310. (1)
311. (3)	312. (2)	313. (2)	314. (2)	315. (3)	316. (4)	317. (3)	318. (1)	319. (3)	320. (3)
321. (1)	322. (2)	323. (3)	324. (3)	325. (4)	326. (3)	327. (2)	328. (1)	329. (2)	330. (2)
331. (1)	332. (2)	333. (2)	334. (2)	335. (2)	336. (2)	337. (1)	338. (2)	339. (2)	340. (4)
341. (4)	342. (4)	343. (2)	344. (3)	345. (4)	346. (2)	347. (4)	348. (4)	349. (1)	350. (3)
351. (3)	352. (1)	353. (3)	354. (2)	355. (3)	356. (3)	357. (1)	358. (3)	359. (4)	360. (4)
361. (3)	362. (1)	363. (3)	364. (3)	365. (1)	366. (4)	367. (2)	368. (3)	369. (4)	370. (1)
371. (2)	372. (1)	373. (2)	374. (1)	375. (3)	376. (2)	377. (2)	378. (1)	379. (2)	380. (2)
381. (1)	382. (3)	383. (1)	384. (1)	385. (2)	386. (2)	387. (3)	388. (4)	389. (1)	390. (2)
391. (3)	392. (2)	393. (3)	394. (4)	395. (1)	396. (3)	397. (3)	398. (1)	399. (1)	400. (1)

MODEL PAPERS (Revised Pattern)

MODEL PAPER-1

Note : This paper contains **hundred** (100) Objective type questions, each carrying **two** (2) marks.

1. Which one of the following approaches stresses that there are no universal rules for managers to follow in order to perform the job?
   (A) Contingency (B) System
   (C) Mathematical (D) Empirical

2. Match List I with List II and select the correct answer using the codes given below:

List I (Type of Assets)	List II (Example of Assets)
a. Fixed Assets	I. Discount on shares or debentures, preliminary expenses
b. Intangible Assets	II. Timberlands, mineral deposits, oil (reserves)
c. Wasting Assets	III. Goodwill, patents, trade marks etc.
d. Fictitious Assets	IV. Plant and machinery, building

Codes:

	a	b	c	d
(A)	IV	III	II	I
(B)	I	II	III	IV
(C)	II	I	III	IV
(D)	IV	III	I	II

3. Which of the following is the condition of equilibrium for the monopolist ?
   (A) MR = MC (B) MC = AR
   (C) AR = MC = Price (D) AC = AR

4. Which company first developed the 360 degree system of appraisal?
   (A) Wipro in 1990
   (B) Godrej Soaps in 1991
   (C) General Electric, US in 1992
   (D) None of the above

5. If both supply and demand increase by the same proportion,
   (A) Quantity remains constant
   (B) Price remains constant
   (C) Price increases
   (D) Quantity increases

6. What leads to rationing and black marketing under perfect competition ?
   (A) Price support
   (B) Excess demand
   (C) Decrease in supply
   (D) Price control

7. In Maslow's need hierarchy theory, which of the following is not high order needs ?
   (A) Safety
   (B) Social
   (C) Esteem
   (D) Self-Actualisation

8. Feeling arising out of inadequate definition of roles is known as
   (A) Role ambiguity
   (B) Role conflict
   (C) Role perception
   (D) Role expectation

9. A type of group discussion process in which members of the group are encouraged to

generate as many imaginative and creative ideas in a relatively short period of time is known as

(A) Brain storming (B) Group working
(C) Simulation (D) Group effect

10. The amount of satisfaction an individual anticipates from a particular outcome is known as

(A) Theory Y (B) Theory Z
(C) Valence (D) Stress

11. A personality characteristic indicating one's willingness to do whatever it takes to get one's own way is known as

(A) Locus of control
(B) Machiavellism
(C) Job characteristic model
(D) Personality legitimacy

12. The process of studying and collecting information relating to a specific job is known as

(A) Motion study
(B) Job analysis
(C) Job specification
(D) Job enrichment

13. The horizontal expansion of jobs is termed as

(A) Job enlargement
(B) Job enrichment
(C) Job sharing
(D) Job involvement

14. A bargaining which is based upon zero-sum game is known as

(A) Integrative bargaining
(B) Principled bargaining
(C) Distributive bargaining
(D) None of these

15. The final link in the communication process that puts the message back into the system as a check against misunderstandings is described as

(A) Decoding
(B) Feedback
(C) Feedback Loop (D) None of these

16. In the 'Managerial grid' 9, 1 style is termed as

(A) Team Management
(B) Country Club Management
(C) Authority Obedience
(D) Improvised Management

17. Which of the following is not one of the 5s of housekeeping?

(A) Sort (B) Systemize
(C) Specialize (D) Shine

18. Internal rate of return method applied for capital budgeting decision

(A) allows to take different discount factors.
(B) uses cost of capital as discount factor.
(C) may give more than one IRR.
(D) distinguishes between the IRR for lending and borrowing decision.

19. Beta in the context of security analysis indicates

(A) Systematic risk (B) Unsystematic risk
(C) Total risk (D) All of the above

20. Assuming constant rate of growth of dividend, value of share will be equal to

(A) $P_0 = \frac{D_0}{r-g}$ (B) $P_0 = \frac{D_1}{r-g}$
(C) $P_1 = \frac{D_0}{r+g}$ (D) $P_1 = \frac{D_0}{r} + g$

21. Theoretically, with the issue of rights share the value of existing shares

(A) will increase
(B) will not change
(C) will reduce
(D) may increase or decrease

22. When the cash flow outcomes of succeeding period depends on what has happened before, the probabilities of succeeding period are known as

(A) joint probabilities
(B) conditional probabilities
(C) simple probabilities
(D) decision tree

23. A high risk, high-yield often unsecured bond rated below investment grade is known as
(A) Income-bond
(B) Subordinated debentures
(C) Junk bond
(D) Serial bond

24. Who coined the term 4 Ps ?
(A) Philip Kotler (B) Stanton
(C) Peter Drucker (D) Mc Carthy

25. In the buying decision process, what is the term used for a person who first suggests buying the product ?
(A) Consumer (B) Decider
(C) Initiator (D) Influencer

26. Which of the following is in order ?
(A) Product, place, price and promotion.
(B) Price, product, promotion and place.
(C) Promotion, place, product and price.
(D) Product, price, place and promotion.

27. Which of the demographic variable is not used by marketers for demographic segmentation ?
(A) Income (B) Gender
(C) Family life cycle (D) Poverty

28. Which of the following indicates the distinction between Advertising and Publicity?
(A) Advertising is expensive, publicity is less expensive.
(B) Advertising is through T.V., publicity is through print media.
(C) Advertising is a paid form of communication, Publicity is not a paid form of communication.
(D) Advertising is through film stars, Publicity is through cricketers.

29. Which of the following order about product life cycle is correct ?
(A) Introduction, Maturity, growth and decline.
(B) Introduction, growth, maturity and decline.
(C) Introduction, decline, maturity and growth.
(D) Growth, maturity, decline and introduction.

30. Companies that attack other firms including market leader in an attempt to build market share are called
(A) Market followers
(B) Market challengers
(C) Market penetrators
(D) Market Nichers

31. Tactical production planning decision includes
(A) Layout planning
(B) Machine loading
(C) Production process
(D) Plant location

32. Which of the following is not to be considered for plant location decision ?
(A) Availability of labour
(B) Availability of power
(C) Availability of raw material
(D) Brand image

33. Moving average forecasting is used to
(A) establish the trend of the past
(B) forecast the current demand
(C) forecast market competition
(D) forecast Quasi demand

34. To which practice is the term "corporate governance" given?
(A) Organising (B) Management
(C) Control (D) Forecasting

35. The communication that takes place through facial expression, body position, eye contact and other facial expression is
(A) Oral or verbal Communication
(B) Written Communication
(C) Non verbal Communication
(D) All of these

36. A company is producing steel rods. Assuming that the length of steel rods follows normal distribution with mean 10 inches & variance equal to 0.04 sq. inches. The standard error of mean, when a random sample of 16 is taken, will be

(A) 4/10 (B) 2/20
(C) 2/40 (D) None of these

37. Judgement sampling to select the sampling units from population is termed as
(A) Probability sampling
(B) Non-probability sampling
(C) Systematic sampling
(D) None of these

38. Wide area network is
(A) Network of computers spread over a small geographical area.
(B) Network of computers spread over a large geographical area.
(C) Network of computers in a room.
(D) None of these.

39. Correlation coefficient between two variables X & Y is calculated as 0.63. If the measurements of X & Y are changed to $U = \frac{X-10}{5}$ & $V = \frac{X+5}{10}$ the new value of correlation coefficient will be
(A) 0.063 (B) 0.315
(C) 0.63 (D) None of these

40. A person appears in an interview for a job in the two companies say X and Y. The chances of selection in company X is 0.7 and chances of selection in Y is 0.6. The probability of his selection in either of the two companies will be
(A) 0.42 (B) 0.88
(C) 0.50 (D) None of these

41. Which of the following helps a manager to identify the opportunities and threats in the competitive industry environment ?
(A) Analysis of organisational structure.
(B) Analysis of competitive forces.
(C) Analysis of operations.
(D) Market Research

42. Essence of strategy at strategic Business Unit level is
(A) How to build core competency
(B) How to gain competitive advantage
(C) How to gain market share
(D) All of the above

43. Which one of the following is a primary activity in a value chain ?
(A) Operations
(B) Firm infrastructure
(C) Technology development
(D) Procurement

44. Business unit which holds a large market share in a mature and slow growing industry is called
(A) Star (B) Dog
(C) Question Mark (D) Cash cow

45. Which strategy requires a company to concentrate its efforts in one or more narrow segments instead of broad based strategy ?
(A) Cost leadership (B) Focus
(C) Differentiation (D) None of the above

46. Which of the following is an example of an external threat ?
(A) New trade regulations
(B) Global sales potential
(C) Economies of scale
(D) Decreased competition

47. Which of the following has been entrusted with the responsibility of developing and supporting small business ?
(A) IDBI (B) RBI
(C) NABARD (D) SIDBI

48. "Innovation and entrepreneurship" is a book written by
(A) Philip Kotler
(B) C. K. Prahlad
(C) Pradeep Khandwala
(D) Peter F. Drucker

49. Strategising within value frame work is an approach of
(A) Management
(B) Administration
(C) Governance
(D) Stake holders

50. Social responsibility means that a business
(A) Functions efficiently without harming the society

(B) Abjures the profit motive
(C) Keeps pollution under check
(D) Pays its Taxes to Government

51. During last five years per capita income of India is increasing, that means
(A) National income growth of India is more than growth of population.
(B) Growth in population is more than the growth in National income of India.
(C) National income of India & population of India have grown at the uniform rate.
(D) All of the above

52. In the short run firm considers the minimum of its average variable cost curve as
(A) Break-even point
(B) Shutdown point
(C) Economies of scope
(D) None of the above

53. The positive cross elasticity of demand between two products means
(A) two products are substitutes
(B) two products are complementary
(C) two products are neither substitutes nor complementary
(D) none of the above

54. A monopolist always operates in the
(A) Inelastic segment of its demand curve
(B) Elastic segment of its demand curve
(C) Unitary elastic segment of its demand curve
(D) None of the above

55. The price elasticity of demand for any product in the long run
(A) is more than it's short run value.
(B) is less than its short run value.
(C) is same as its short run value.
(D) None of the above.

56. Earnings foregone in the context of the best alternative is termed as
(A) Past cost
(B) Historical cost
(C) Opportunity cost
(D) Sunk cost

57. A situation where management is unable to provide employment due to non-availability of work is called
I. Lock out   II. Lay off
III. Termination   IV. Closure
Find the correct combination according to the code.
(A) I & II   (B) II & III
(C) I & III   (D) II & IV

58. Which one of the settlement methods is not relevant here for disputes ?
(A) Collective Bargaining
(B) Compulsory Adjudication
(C) Voluntary Arbitration
(D) Reference to Civil Court

59. Which of the following shows a situation of Trade Union rivalries in India ?
(A) Different Unions in different organisations.
(B) More unions in the same organisation having affiliation with different political parties and representing the same type of workers.
(C) More unions in the same organisation all representing different types of workers.
(D) None of the above.

60. Reduction of Labour Force is called
(A) Termination   (B) Retrenchment
(C) Lay-off   (D) Right sizing

61. The process of establishing the value of jobs in a job hierarchy is known as
(I) Job analysis
(II) Job requirement
(III) Job evaluation
(IV) Performance evaluation
Find the correct combination according to the code.
(A) I & II   (B) II & III
(C) III & IV   (D) I & IV

62. Which of the following is the meaning of Human Resource Planning ?
(A) Evaluation of job

(B) Satisfaction of the employees on the job

(C) Appraising the performance of employees

(D) It is the process by which an organisation ensures that it has the right number and kind of people at the right place, at the right time.

63. Green HRM is the use of HRM policies to promote the cause of

(A) staff welfare

(B) management salaries

(C) environmental sustainability

(D) brotherhood

64. Micro-finance is also called

(A) micro-insurance

(B) micro-credit

(C) start-up capital

(D) collatual finance

65. An Artificial intelligence technique that allows computers to understand associations and relationships between objects and events is called

(A) heuristic processing

(B) cognitive science

(C) relative symbolism

(D) pattern matching

66. Which of the following formula is used to calculate Pay Back Period when cash inflows are constant?

(A) Fixed Assets/Current Assets

(B) Fixed Assets/Current Liabilities

(C) Initial Investment cost/Annual cash inflows

(D) None of the above

67. The P/E ratio approach to stock valuation is also known as

(A) Earnings multiplier approach

(B) Dividend discounting approach

(C) Required rate of return

(D) None of the above

68. The capital structure theories which argue that capital structure is relevant to the value of firm contain

I. Net Income Approach

II. Net Operating Income Approach

III. Traditional Approach

IV. Modigliani and Miller Approach

Find the correct combination according to the code :

(A) I & II are correct.

(B) I & III are correct.

(C) III & IV are correct.

(D) II & IV are correct.

69. Short term financing instruments may contain

I. Commercial Paper

II. Public Deposits

III. Term Loans

IV. Trade Credit

Find the correct combination according to the code.

(A) I, II & III are correct.

(B) II, III & IV are correct.

(C) III & IV are correct.

(D) I, II & IV are correct.

70. For calculating weighted average cost of capital, cost of each source of capital is multiplied by proportion applicable to it. The proportions may be based on

(A) Book values only

(B) Target capital structure only

(C) Market values only

(D) All of the above

71. Which of the following is not included in 7 P's of services marketing?

(A) Process

(B) People

(C) Pricing

(D) Public relations

72. Which of the following is not a stage in the new product development?

(A) Generation of ideas

(B) Business analysis

(C) Market segmentation

(D) Test marketing

73. Industrial marketing involves

(A) Business to Business

(B) Business to Customer
(C) Customer to Customer
(D) Retailer to Consumer

74. The concept of Marketing Myopia is propounded by
(A) Philip Kotler
(B) C.K. Prahalada
(C) Peter Drucker
(D) Theodore Levitt

75. In which stage of product life cycle, the company takes decision whether to maintain, harvest or drop the product ?
(A) Introduction
(B) Growth
(C) Maturity
(D) Decline

76. Which of the following is the best technique to manage the existing products ?
(A) Ansoff Matrix
(B) Balanced score card
(C) BCG Matrix
(D) Product life cycle analysis

77. Which of the following is not an element of production management ?
(A) Plant (B) Profit
(C) Process (D) People

78. Production Management Tactical Planning decisions include
(A) Establishing parameters for measuring operational efficiency and productivity.
(B) Establishing quality specifications and test details.
(C) Determining starting and finishing time of each job in the work stations.
(D) None of the above

79. Work study refers to
(A) Analysis of work into smaller parts followed by re-arrangement of these parts to give the same effectiveness at lesser cost.
(B) Analytical investigation of the methods involved in the work.
(C) Developing new methods to give work effectiveness.
(D) All of the above

80. Economic lot size is known as
(A) the lot size for which the total cost per time period is minimum.
(B) the ordering cost and carrying cost are minimum.
(C) the lot size that strikes a balance between ordering cost and carrying cost.
(D) the quantity to be ordered each time is fixed.

81. Objective of Value Engineering is
(A) Reduce cost without reducing the quality.
(B) Increase value without increasing the cost.
(C) Reduce cost by reducing the quality.
(D) None of the above

82. Probable error is
(A) $.6745\left(\frac{1-r^2}{\sqrt{N}}\right)$
(B) $6340\sqrt{\frac{dxdy}{N}\times dx^2dy^2}$
(C) $.6745\sqrt{\frac{N}{\Sigma dx}}$
(D) $.6340\times\frac{N}{\sqrt{\Sigma dx}}$

83. The weak law of large numbers is another version of
(A) convergence in probability
(B) random number generation
(C) financial probability law
(D) poisson probability law

84. The basic assumptions underlying the t-test for the difference of two sample means are that the parent populations are ________ and population variances are ________.
(A) of any shape; equal and known
(B) normal; equal and known
(C) normal; equal but unknown
(D) normal; unequal but known

85. LAN stands for

(A) Large Area Network
(B) Local Area Network
(C) Long Accurate Network
(D) Lay Access Network

86. Match the following

List-I (Indicator)	List-II (Application)
(a) r	1. Correlation Analysis
(b) $\overline{X}$	2. Mean
(c) σ	3. Deviation
(d) Z	4. Mode
	5. Economic Order Processing

Codes :

	(a)	(b)	(c)	(d)
(A)	3	1	4	2
(B)	3	4	1	2
(C)	1	2	3	4
(D)	1	4	2	3

87. What enables the management to find out whether the strategic management process are appropriate, compatible and functioning in the desirable direction ?

(A) Implementation control
(B) Special alert control
(C) Premise control
(D) Strategic control

88. Which one is not the part of Michael Porter's five forces model ?

(A) Threat of substitutes
(B) Firm's core competence
(C) Rivalry among existing players
(D) Threat of new entrants

89. Which of the following strategy is regarded unfair ?

(A) Collusion
(B) Strategic alliance
(C) Differentiation
(D) Turn around strategy

90. Which of the following relationship strategies result into forming of a new organisation ?

(A) Strategic alliance
(B) Partnership
(C) Joint venture
(D) None of the above

91. A growth strategy is designed to increase

(A) the scale and scope of the Business operations.
(B) the corporate image of the business.
(C) corporate social responsibility of business.
(D) none of the above.

92. Cost leadership strategy is related to

(A) Functional strategy
(B) SBU strategy
(C) Corporate strategy
(D) Global strategy

93. Countries derive their competitive advantage in international trade through their

(A) Comparative cost advantage
(B) Contribution to the World trade
(C) Natural endowments
(D) All of the above

94. Which analysis helps to understand the strength and weaknesses of a firm ?

(A) Environment analysis
(B) Business analysis
(C) SWOT analysis
(D) None of the above

95. Which one of the following is not the social responsibility of business ?

(A) Adopting village for development.
(B) Providing drinking water and medical facilities in remote villages.
(C) Construction of Temples.
(D) Opening in House R & D department.

96. Match the following :

List – I (Concept)	List – II (Term)
a. An ongoing and formalised effort that focuses on developing	i. Direction phase

enriched and more capable workers

b.	A career development activity in which managers make decisions regarding the advancement potential of subordinates	ii.	Career development
c.	A career development activity that focuses on preparing people to fill executive positions	iii.	Promotability forecast
d.	Determining the type of career that employees want and the steps they must take to realise their career goals	iv.	Succession planning

Codes:

	a	b	c	d
(A)	i	ii	iii	iv
(B)	ii	iii	iv	i
(C)	ii	iii	i	iv
(D)	i	iii	ii	iv

97. A formal explanation of the knowledge, skills, abilities, traits and other characteristics necessary for effective job performance is known as

(A) Job Description
(B) Job Analysis
(C) Job Specification
(D) Job Enrichment

98. ________ aims to reduce reliance on arbitrary methods of pay determination by introducing an element of objectivity in the way jobs are compared.

(A) Performance appraisal
(B) Job evaluation
(C) Job enrichment
(D) Attrition

99. Match the following :

	List – I		List – II
a.	The process of examining how work creates or adds value to the ongoing processes in a business	i.	Job Enrichment
b.	A fundamental rethinking and radical redesign of business processes to achieve dramatic improvements in cost, quality, service and speed	ii.	Job Design
c.	The process of organising work into the tasks required to perform a specific task	iii.	Work flow analysis
d.	The process of putting specialised tasks back together so that one person is responsible for producing a whole product or an entire service	iv.	Business process reengineering (BPR)

Codes:

	a	b	c	d
(A)	i	ii	iii	iv
(B)	ii	i	iv	iii
(C)	iii	iv	i	ii
(D)	iii	iv	ii	i

100. ______ involves creating a brand identity based on heritage or nostalgia for a company's past products.

(A) Niche Marketing
(B) Online Marketing
(C) Online Marketing
(D) Direct Marketing

ANSWER KEY

1. (A)	**2.** (A)	**3.** (A)	**4.** (C)	**5.** (B)	**6.** (C)	**7.** (A)	**8.** (D)	**9.** (A)	**10.** (C)
11. (B)	**12.** (B)	**13.** (B)	**14.** (C)	**15.** (C)	**16.** (B)	**17.** (C)	**18.** (C)	**19.** (A)	**20.** (B)
21. (C)	**22.** (B)	**23.** (C)	**24.** (D)	**25.** (C)	**26.** (D)	**27.** (B)	**28.** (B)	**29.** (B)	**30.** (B)
31. (C)	**32.** (D)	**33.** (C)	**34.** (B)	**35.** (C)	**36.** (A)	**37.** (A)	**38.** (B)	**39.** (B)	**40.** (A)
41. (D)	**42.** (D)	**43.** (D)	**44.** (D)	**45.** (B)	**46.** (A)	**47.** (D)	**48.** (D)	**49.** (A)	**50.** (A)
51. (C)	**52.** (D)	**53.** (B)	**54.** (B)	**55.** (D)	**56.** (C)	**57.** (B)	**58.** (C)	**59.** (B)	**60.** (C)
61. (C)	**62.** (D)	**63.** (C)	**64.** (B)	**65.** (C)	**66.** (C)	**67.** (D)	**68.** (C)	**69.** (C)	**70.** (D)
71. (D)	**72.** (C)	**73.** (A)	**74.** (D)	**75.** (D)	**76.** (D)	**77.** (D)	**78.** (B)	**79.** (D)	**80.** (C)
81. (A)	**82.** (A)	**83.** (A)	**84.** (B)	**85.** (B)	**86.** (C)	**87.** (A)	**88.** (B)	**89.** (A)	**90.** (B)
91. (A)	**92.** (C)	**93.** (D)	**94.** (C)	**95.** (C)	**96.** (B)	**97.** (C)	**98.** (B)	**99.** (D)	**100.** (B)

MODEL PAPER-2

Note : This paper contains **hundred** (100) Objective type questions, each question carrying **two** (2) marks.

1. Retailer cooperatives belong to which of the following distribution channel systems?

(A) Contractual (B) Administered

(C) Horizontal (D) Corporate

2. Rearrange the steps in appraisal process.

a. Objectives of performance appraisal

b. Establish job expectations

c. Design in appraisal programme

d. Performance Management

e. Appraise performance

f. Performance interview

g. Archive appraisal data

h. Use appraisal data for appropriate purposes

(A) dchgfabe (B) hgfedbca

(C) abcfghde (D) abcdefgh

3. In a mixed economy, the central problems are solved through which of following ?

(A) Price mechanism

(B) Regulated market mechanism

(C) Market mechanism and economic planning

(D) Economic planning and control

4. Indicate the correct code matching the items in List – I with those in List – II as follows :

List – I	List – II
a. Excess of aggregate investment over aggregate savings, at full employment level	i. Stability of National Income
b. Equality of aggregate income and savings	ii. Recessionary gap
c. Comparatively greater decrease in income following a decrease in investment	iii. Multiplier effect
d. Aggregate expenditure being less than national income at full employment level	iv. Inflationary gap

Codes:

	a	b	c	d
(A)	ii	iv	i	iii
(B)	iv	i	iii	ii
(C)	iii	ii	iv	i
(D)	i	iii	ii	iv

5. The study of gestures and body postures for their impact on communication is known as

(A) Kinesics

(B) Proximics

(C) Semantics

(D) Informal channels

6. Production can be measured in terms of which of the following ?

(A) Total productivity

(B) Marginal productivity

(C) Average productivity

(D) All of the above

7. Which of the following is an objective of human resource management ?

(A) Productivity
(B) Quality of work life
(C) Organisational change
(D) All the above

8. Motivation implies that the employees in an organisation
(A) Exert more effort to accomplish the desired goals of the organisation.
(B) Exert more effort to accomplish the individual goals.
(C) Exert more effort to accomplish the common goals of employees.
(D) Exert more effort to accomplish the desired goals of the employer, employees and the Government.

9. Communication can be
(A) Oral
(B) Written
(C) Oral and Written
(D) None of the above

10. Which of the following is not considered as a leadership style ?
(A) Autocratic style (B) Paternalistic style
(C) Futuristic style (D) Free reign style

11. Organisational elements of job design are concerned with
(A) Cost Techniques
(B) Organisational Efficiency
(C) Firm
(D) Cost Approach

12. What are the operative functions of HRM ?
(A) Organising (B) Directing
(C) Controlling (D) All of the above

13. Which one is not a performance appraisal method ?
(A) 360° performance appraisal
(B) Balanced score card
(C) Rank method
(D) Interview method

14. Selection of persons in an organisation is the responsibility of
(A) Security Dept. (B) Personnel Dept.
(C) Trade Unions (D) Canteen Dept.

15. Labour Welfare facilities were incorporated in which legislation ?
(A) MRTP Act
(B) Essential Commodities Act
(C) Consumer Protection Act
(D) Factories Act

16. Job analysis involves
(A) Job description and job specification
(B) Job order and job description
(C) Job specification and job order
(D) Job satisfaction and job description

17. Which one of the following represents number of years required to recover the initial investment ?
(A) Accounting rate of return
(B) Pay back period
(C) Internal rate of return
(D) Net present value

18. Other things being equal, stocks which are highly liquid command
(A) Higher dividend payout ratio
(B) Lower dividend payout ratio
(C) Higher P/E multiples
(D) Lower P/E multiples

19. Weighted Average Cost of Capital may contain
I. Cost of Equity
II. Cost of Debt
III. Cost of goods purchased
IV. Cost of initial investment Find the correct combination according to the code:
(A) I, II & III are correct.
(B) II, III & IV are correct.
(C) III & IV are correct.
(D) I & II are correct

20. Long term sources of finance may contain
I. Retained earnings
II. Inter corporate deposits
III. Debentures
IV. Preference share capital Find the correct combination according to the code :
(A) I, III & IV are correct
(B) II, III & IV are correct

(C) II & III are correct
(D) II & IV are correct

21. What are the benefits of human resource planning ?
(A) Achieve economy in hiring new workers.
(B) Match personnel activities and future organization objectives efficiently.
(C) Improve the utilization of human resources.
(D) All of the above

22. Human Resource Management includes
1. Employee Grievance
2. Organizational climate
3. Job incentives
4. Recruitment
5. Selection

Select the correct answer from the following :
(A) 1, 2, 3 and 4
(B) 1, 3, 4 and 5
(C) 1 and 5
(D) All of the above

23. Match the following :

a.	Job Analysis	1.	Determining worth of a job.
b.	Job Evaluation	2.	Examining how work adds value to the ongoing process.
c.	Job Design	3.	Determining the pertinent facts about the job.
d.	Work Flow Analysis	4.	Organizing work into the tasks required to perform a specific job.

Code:

	a	b	c	d
(A)	1	2	3	4
(B)	4	3	2	1
(C)	3	1	4	2
(D)	2	3	1	4

24. Which ratio explains that how much portion of earning is distributed in the form of dividend ?
(A) Dividend – Debt Ratio
(B) Equity – Debt Ratio
(C) Pay-out Ratio
(D) Earning – Yield Ratio

25. Modern approach to financial management is
I. The total fund requirement of the firm.
II. The asset to be acquired.
III. Payment of dividend to shareholders.
(A) I only (B) II only
(C) II & III only (D) I, II & III

26. If a company uses its company name for its entire range of products offered, then it is called
(A) Private branding
(B) Corporate branding
(C) Product-line branding
(D) Specific product branding

27. One-level channel of distribution consists of
(A) Producer - consumer
(B) Producer - dealer - consumer
(C) Producer - dealer - retailer - consumer
(D) Producer - dealer - wholesaler - retailer - consumer

28. The primary role of a production manager is
(A) To meet the production target and delivery schedule
(B) To produce goods/services of right quality
(C) To produce goods/services by right quantity at the predetermined time
(D) All of the above

29. Fixed Position Layout is used when
(A) the operation requires heavy tools and equipments.
(B) the operation requires only hand tools and simple equipments.
(C) the continuity of production process is to be maintained.
(D) none of the above

30. Critical Path Method (CPM) is concerned with estimation of
(A) Optimistic time
(B) Production lead time
(C) Pessimistic time
(D) None of the above

31. In a normal distribution, mean (m) ± 3s(3 standard deviation) limits contains approximately
(A) 99.73% of the observations
(B) 99.27% of the observations
(C) 96% of the observations
(D) 95% of the observations

32. Firms choose a focus strategy to serve the needs of which of the following ?
(A) Buyers group
(B) Different-segment of a product line
(C) Different geographical market
(D) All of the above

33. Which of the following is not the component of work study ?
(A) Work measurement
(B) Case study
(C) Time study
(D) Motion study

34. The incidence of occupational disease in an industry in such that the workmen have 20% chance of suffering from it. What is the probability that out of 6 workmen 4 or more will contact disease?
(A) $\frac{160}{3}$ (B) $\frac{39}{139}$
(C) $\frac{53}{3125}$ (D) $\frac{3}{69}$

35. If X is a random variable normally distributed with mean u and variance σ^2, then the mean deviation about mean is given by
(A) $\frac{1}{\sqrt{2\pi}}$ (B) $\sqrt{\frac{2}{\pi}}\sigma$
(C) $\frac{\sigma}{\sqrt{2\pi}}$ (D) $\sqrt{2\sigma}$

36. The level of significance is the probability of committing
(A) type I error (B) type II error
(C) standard error (D) probable error

37. When the relationship is of quantitative nature, the appropriate statistical tool for discovering and measuring the relationship and expressing it, in brief formula is known as
(A) Sampling Theory
(B) Regression Analysis
(C) Average
(D) Correlation

38. Mean and variance of Binomial Distribution are
(A) m and σ^2 (B) m and nq
(C) m and np (D) np and npq
(Where the terms have usual statistical meaning)

39. Which of the following is the characteristic of a strategic business unit ?
(A) It serves a homogenous set of markets.
(B) It serves a unique set of products.
(C) It owns responsibility for its own profitability.
(D) All of the above.

40. Which one of the following is not a generic strategy ?
(A) Cost Leadership
(B) Product Differentiation
(C) Focus strategy
(D) Innovation

41. A retrenchment strategy is designed to reduce
(A) technical losses
(B) manpower
(C) the scale and scope of the business operation
(D) all of the above

42. World Trade Organisation provides
(A) Rule based multilateral trading system.
(B) Equity and social justice to the people.
(C) Rule based regional trading system
(D) All of the above

43. Sick enterprise is referred to
(A) CII (B) RBI
(C) SIDBI (D) BIFR

44. Ethical values are derived from
(A) Corporate philosophy
(B) Organisational culture
(C) Corporate objectives
(D) The religious books

45. Which of the following is not related to business ethics ?
(A) Social responsibility of business
(B) Environmental ethics
(C) Ecological consciousness
(D) Profiteering

46. Which of the following is the cause of sickness of an enterprise ?
(A) Lack of adequate capital
(B) Lack of demand for the products
(C) Lack of raw material
(D) All of the above

47. Value driven companies are
(A) sure to be successful in the long run.
(B) sure to be unsuccessful as they are not maximising profits.
(C) sure to become charitable institutions.
(D) none of the above

48. Which of the following is not a tool of corporate governance ?
(A) Preparation of financial statements
(B) Appointment of independent directors.
(C) Compulsory audit of financial statements.
(D) Time bound promotion of employees.

49. Which of the following is not the social responsibility of the business ?
(A) Promotion of Markets
(B) Promotion of Green Environment
(C) Promotion of Education
(D) Promotion of Public Health

50. The Business Code of Conduct provides guidance to managers and employees
(A) when they encounter an ethical dilemma.
(B) for improving their technical skills.
(C) for pursuing their business goals.
(D) All of the above

51. In the case of an inferior commodity, the income elasticity of demand is
(A) Positive (B) Unitary
(C) Negative (D) Infinity

52. The slope of the iso-cost line is determined by
(A) Prices of the two factors
(B) Productivity of the two factors
(C) Degree of substitutability of the two factors
(D) None of these

53. Which one of the following statements is correct or more nearly correct ?
(A) An increase in the price of commodity represents a fall in its value
(B) Value has nothing to do with the price
(C) If the price of a commodity falls, its value relative to other goods does not change
(D) The price of a good is its value measured in terms of money

54. The important macro-economic aggregates are
(A) Aggregate Consumption
(B) Gross Domestic Capital Formation
(C) Gross Domestic Savings and GNP
(D) All of the above

55. Match the following

	List – I	List – II
I.	For a given 10 per cent change in price, demand changes by zero per cent	1. $e > 1$
II.	For a given 10 per cent change in price demand changes by 5 per cent	2. $e = 1$
III.	For a given 10 per cent change in price demand changes by 10 per cent	3. $e < 1$

IV. For a given 10 per cent change in price, demand changes by 20 per cent — 4. $e = 0$

Code :

	I	II	III	IV
(A)	3	1	2	4
(B)	4	3	2	1
(C)	1	2	3	4
(D)	2	3	1	4

56. Long – lasting beliefs about what is important in a variety of situations, that guide our decisions and actions are :

(A) values
(B) ethical dimensions
(C) priorities
(D) desires

57. Figure – Ground Theory explains the process of

(A) Cognition (B) Sensation
(C) Perception (D) Motivation

58. Successive re-inforcements resulting in desired behaviour are

(A) mentoring
(B) motivation
(C) shaping
(D) behaviour-modification

59. Psychological contract is related to

(A) job – person fit
(B) role – person fit
(C) organisation – person fit
(D) none of the above

60. Equity is called as

(A) equality of all
(B) standard performance
(C) comparative sense of justice to self
(D) none of the above

61. The distinction between 'job enrichment' and 'job enlargement' is

(A) semantics
(B) 'job enrichment' is vertical loading while 'job enlargement' is horizontal loading
(C) 'job enrichment' is the outgrowth of Hertzberg's theory while 'job enlargement' is of Maslow's orientation.
(D) 'job enrichment' is more for the individual and the other is more of organisation making

62. In 'delegation'

(A) Only authority is delegated not responsibility
(B) Both authority and responsibility are delegated
(C) Only responsibility is delegated, not authority
(D) Neither responsibility, nor authority is delegated

63. Cross-functional groups that operate across space, time and organisational boundaries with members who communicate mainly through information technologies are

(A) telecomputers
(B) virtual teams
(C) teleworkers
(D) telemarketers

64. Career resilience means

(A) Ability to switch careers
(B) Ability to remain with same competencies refining suitably for organizations
(C) Lack of capacity to remain in career
(D) None of the above

65. Lock out means

(A) An antithesis of strike
(B) Refusal to employ any person in employment
(C) the temporary closing of a place of employment
(D) Illegal strike

66. Which is the task of a finance manager ?

(A) Investment decision
(B) Dividend decision
(C) Management of income
(D) All of the above

67. Which method of capital budgeting focuses on liquidity of a project ?

(A) Net present value
(B) Profitability index
(C) Payback period
(D) Internal rate of returns

68. Which statement is true about deep discount bonds ?
(A) These are in the form of low interest bonds
(B) These bonds are sold at a discounted value and on maturity face value of the bond is paid to the investors
(C) There is no interest payout during lock-in period
(D) None of the above

69. Financial leverage is
(A) $\frac{\text{EBIT}}{\text{Sales}} \times 100$ (B) $\frac{\text{EBIT}}{\text{EBT}}$
(C) $\frac{\text{Sales}}{\text{Fixed Assets}}$ (D) $\frac{\text{Profit}}{\text{Sales}} \times \text{Capital}$

70. Match the following

List–I (items /method)	List – II (used / Application)
I. Rate of return method	1. Capital budgeting
II. Purchase consideration	2. Merger
III. Diminishing Balance Method	3. Depreciation
IV. Fifo Method	4. Stock valuation

Code :

	I	II	III	IV
(A)	1	3	2	4
(B)	3	2	4	1
(C)	1	2	3	4
(D)	1	4	3	2

71. Arrange the following steps of a five-stage model of the consumer buying process :
I. Evaluation of Alternatives
II. Need Arousal
III. Information search
IV. Purchase Decision
V. Post Purchase behaviour

Code

(A)	IV	II	III	I	V
(B)	III	II	I	IV	V
(C)	I	II	IV	III	V
(D)	II	III	I	IV	V

72. It refers to the total number of items in the Product Mix. It is known as following.
(A) The width of product mix
(B) The length of product mix
(C) The depth of product mix
(D) The consistency of product mix

73. Given below are two statements, one labelled as Assertion (A), and the other labelled as Reason (R). State the correct answer from code given below.

Assertion (A). Pure-click companies can be search engines, Internet service providers, commerce sites, transaction sites, content sites and enabler sites.

Reason (R) : Pure-click companies are those companies that have launched a website without any previous existence as a firm.

Code :
(A) (A) is correct, but (R) is wrong.
(B) Both (A) and (R) are correct.
(C) (A) is wrong, but (R) is correct.
(D) Both (A) and (R) are wrong.

74. Match List-I and List-II.

List – I (Characteristics of Services)	List – II (Marketing Strategy applied considering a characteristic of service)
I. Intangibility	1. Preparing a service blue print showing each service and process in a flow chart.
II. Inseparability	2. Tangiblize the intangible
III. Variability	3. To train more service providers and build up client confidence.

IV. Perishability		4.	Use differential pricing

Code :

	I	II	III	IV
(A)	2	1	3	4
(B)	2	3	1	4
(C)	1	3	2	4
(D)	2	1	4	3

75. A diverse collection of incentive tools designed to stimulate quicker buying of a particular product or service by consumers or the trade is known as
(A) Advertising
(B) Personal selling
(C) Publicity
(D) Sales promotion

76. Which of the following departments is not directly affected by the facilities location decision ?
(A) Production / operations
(B) Marketing
(C) Personnel
(D) Finance

77. Ship building and construction of dams and bridges are typical examples of
(A) Fixed position layout
(B) Functional layout
(C) Product layout
(D) Project type layout

78. If unit item cost = Rs. 10, monthly carrying charge = 3 per cent, monthly demand = 100 units and ordering cost = Rs. 20 per order, the EOQ is :
(A) 11.45 (B) 400
(C) 115.4 (D) 33.3

79. In managing a project, a network is better suited than Gantt chart because
(A) It can be updated more easily
(B) It clearly brings out the interdependencies between the different activities
(C) Both (A) and (B)
(D) None of the above

80. The aggregate production plan spans
(A) Short time horizon
(B) Intermediate time horizon
(C) Long time horizon
(D) None of the above

81. The probability that a contractor will get a plumbing contract is $\frac{2}{3}$ and that he will get an electric contract is $\frac{5}{9}$. If the probability of his getting at least one of the two contracts is $\frac{4}{5}$, then the probability that he will get both contracts is
(A) 10/45 (B) 8/27
(C) 14/45 (D) 26/45

82. If a random variable X follows Poisson distribution such that P(X = 1) = P(X = 2), then the mean of the distribution is
(A) 1 (B) 2
(C) 3 (D) 4

83. The value of R1.23 lies between
(A) –1 and +1 (B) –1 and 0.0
(C) 0.0 and +1 (D) – 0.5 and + 0.5

84. A source programme is
(A) a programme written in machine language
(B) a programme to be translated into machine language
(C) the machine language translation of a programme written in high-level language
(D) none of the above

85. Processing data in groups collected over periods of time is known as
(A) Time - sharing
(B) Batch processing
(C) Real – time processing
(D) Multi – processing

86. "We must forget to learn and learn forgetting" is ascribed to
(A) Tom Peters
(B) Peter F. Drucker
(C) Abraham S. Maslow

(D) Garry Hamel

87. In highly competitive environment an organization to achieve sustained success should be
(A) Better
(B) Bigger
(C) Resilient
(D) None of the above

88. Corporate governance is about
(A) Crafting the strategy
(B) Compliance with regulatory regime
(C) Satisfying the stakeholders
(D) governing the company in the interest of government in power

89. Strategic planning is about
(A) Strategic thinking
(B) Strategic programming
(C) Tactical Planning
(D) Portfolio Planning

90. If two or more companies are merged and only one of them survives while others loose their independent entity, it is referred to as
(A) Merger (B) Absorption
(C) Amalgamation (D) Combination

91. The MSMED Act, 2006 classified enterprises broadly into
(A) Two categories
 (i) Manufacturing enterprises and
 (ii) Service enterprises
(B) Three categories
 (i) Micro enterprises
 (ii) Small enterprises
 (iii) Medium enterprises
(C) Four categories
 (i) Micro enterprises
 (ii) Small enterprises
 (iii) Tiny enterprises
 (iv) Medium enterprises
(D) Four categories
 (i) Tiny enterprises
 (ii) Micro enterprises
 (iii) Small business enterprises
 (iv) Medium enterprises

92. Which sector is called as Primary Sector in India ?
(A) Industrial sector
(B) Service sector
(C) External sector
(D) Agricultural sector

93. How many times the census of registered Micro, small and medium Enterprises (MSMEs) have been made by Small Industries Development Organisation (SIDO) ?
(A) 1 (B) 2
(C) 3 (D) 4

94. EDII is situated at
(A) New Delhi (B) Ahmedabad
(C) Patna (D) Kolkata

95. Industrial Policy of which year contained for the very first time a special thrust on measures for promoting and strengthening small tiny and village enterprises
(A) 1956 (B) 1991
(C) 1948 (D) 1977

96. Members of organizations are increasingly finding themselves facing situations in which they are required to define right and wrong conduct. It is most aptly called as following
(A) Environmental issues of ethics
(B) Social responsibilities of business
(C) Corporate governance & ethics
(D) Ethical Dilemmas of business

97. Significant feature of Kaizen Budgeting is
(A) employee suggestion
(B) customer suggestion
(C) cost suggestion
(D) price suggestion

98. Arrange the following steps of a simple ethics programme
I. Walk the talk
II. Size up your company's current ethics
III. Train your people

IV. Solicit feedback from your employees
V. Create a code of conduct

Code :

(A) V, I, IV, II, III
(B) II, V, IV, III, I
(C) II, V, III, IV, I
(D) II, IV, III, II, I

99. Who is involved in 'Shoplifting' from the following ?
(A) Producer
(B) Seller
(C) Consumer & or a customer
(D) None of the above

100. Budgeting method, which incorporates an improvement anticipated in budgeting period into budget numbers, can be classified as
(A) anticipated budgeting
(B) number budgeting
(C) predict budgeting
(D) kaizen budgeting

ANSWER KEY

1. (A)	**2.** (D)	**3.** (C)	**4.** (B)	**5.** (A)	**6.** (D)	**7.** (D)	**8.** (D)	**9.** (C)	**10.** (C)
11. (B)	**12.** (D)	**13.** (D)	**14.** (B)	**15.** (D)	**16.** (A)	**17.** (B)	**18.** (D)	**19.** (D)	**20.** (A)
21. (D)	**22.** (B)	**23.** (C)	**24.** (C)	**25.** (D)	**26.** (B)	**27.** (A)	**28.** (D)	**29.** (B)	**30.** (A)
31. (A)	**32.** (D)	**33.** (B)	**34.** (C)	**35.** (B)	**36.** (A)	**37.** (C)	**38.** (D)	**39.** (D)	**40.** (D)
41. (C)	**42.** (D)	**43.** (D)	**44.** (D)	**45.** (D)	**46.** (D)	**47.** (A)	**48.** (D)	**49.** (A)	**50.** (A)
51. (C)	**52.** (B)	**53.** (A)	**54.** (D)	**55.** (B)	**56.** (A)	**57.** (C)	**58.** (D)	**59.** (A)	**60.** (D)
61. (B)	**62.** (B)	**63.** (B)	**64.** (B)	**65.** (C)	**66.** (D)	**67.** (C)	**68.** (B)	**69.** (D)	**70.** (C)
71. (D)	**72.** (C)	**73.** (D)	**74.** (B)	**75.** (D)	**76.** (D)	**77.** (D)	**78.** (C)	**79.** (C)	**80.** (C)
81. (C)	**82.** (C)	**83.** (A)	**84.** (C)	**85.** (D)	**86.** (A)	**87.** (C)	**88.** (C)	**89.** (B)	**90.** (A)
91. (C)	**92.** (D)	**93.** (D)	**94.** (B)	**95.** (D)	**96.** (C)	**97.** (A)	**98.** (A)	**99.** (C)	**100.** (D)

PREVIOUS YEARS' PAPERS

JUNE, 2019

MANAGEMENT

PAPER-II

Note : This paper contains **hundred (100)** objective type questions of **two (2)** marks each. **All** questions are **compulsory**.

1. As a newly appointed marketing manager of a firm, you have been asked to determine if a special Point-of-Purchase (POP) display causes the purchase of the product on display. What type of research design will be needed?
   (A) Exploratory
   (B) Descriptive
   (C) Experimental
   (D) Normative

2. Transactional Analysis does NOT help in
   (A) Problem solving
   (B) Higher social status
   (C) Improved communication within the organisation
   (D) Better leadership

3. Linux is the most well-known and Widely used
   (A) Open source operating system
   (B) Java platform
   (C) Communication software
   (D) System software

4. Match List-I with List-II :

Set I(Decision making Bias)	Set II (Explanation)
(a) Anchoring Bias	(i) Represents a case of selective perception
(b) Escalation of commitment	(ii) Refers to our staying with a decision even if there is clear evidence it's wrong
(c) Confirmation Bias	(iii) Tendency to believe falsely, after the outcome is known
(d) Hindsight Bias	(iv) Tendency to fixate on initial information and fail to adequately adjust for subsequent information

Choose the correct option from those given below

Code:
(A) (a)-(ii); (b)-(iii); (c)-(i); (d)-(iv)
(B) (a)-(iv); (b)-(ii); (c)-(i); (d)-(iii)
(C) (a)-(iv); (b)-(ii); (c)-(iii); (d)-(i)
(D) (a)-(iii); (b)-(i); (c)-(iv); (d)-(ii)

5. Which one of the following is NOT an integral part of credit policy of a business firm?
   (A) Credit standards
   (B) Credit terms
   (C) Collection policy
   (D) Creclitrating

6. The mistake of paying more attention to the specific products of a company offers than to the benefits and experience produced by these products is known as
   (A) Marketing phobia
   (B) Marketing trivia
   (C) Marketing myopia
   (D) Marketing inertia

7. What is the payoff at maturity of a long call below the strike price?

(A) In the money
(B) Zero
(C) Greater than zero
(D) Out of money

8. The correlation coefficient is the _______ of two regression coefficients.
(A) Geometric mean
(B) Arithmetic mean
(C) Harmonic mean
(D) Median

9. Following are two statements with regard to product life cycle (PLC):

Statement I : Product sales pass through distinct stages of PLC, each posing different challenges, opportunities and problems to the seller.

Statement II : A company's positioning and differentiation strategy must change as its product, market and competitors change over the product life cycle. Which of the following options is correct?
(A) Statement I is correct, but II is incorrect
(B) Statement II is correct, but I is incorrect
(C) Both the statements I and II are correct
(D) Both the statements I and II are incorrect

10. The technology advancements in the banking sector posed a challenge for the old players in the industry. The public sector banks lagged in modernization because of the traditional and bureaucratic banking norms that were in force. In the face of competition, public sector banks had to hire new talent and keep an open mind about evolving norms as per the market requirements.

Which of the following analysis/methods can help banks to identify jobs and duties of employees as well as what kinds of people to hire for different jobs?
(A) Job evaluation
(B) Work-force Analysis
(C) Job Analysis
(D) Work-load Analysis

11. An airline offering special lounge for waiting is an example of which one of the following differentiations of the service offer?
(A) Differentiation through special constituents
(B) Differentiation through the experience
(C) Differentiation through brand image
(D) Differentiation through pricing

12. The scheme, which has been launched by the MSME Ministry to access the capabilities and creditworthiness of the micro and small enterprises (MSEs), is called :
(A) Performance and credit rating scheme
(B) Zero defect Zero effect certification
(C) Performance and economic rating scheme
(D) Technology upgradation scheme

13. AB Ltd. manufactures filing cabinets. For the current year, the company expects to sell 4,000 cabinets involving a loss of Rs. 2,00,000. Only 40 percent of the plant's normal capacity is being utilised during the current year. The fixed costs for the year are Rs. 10,00,000 and fully variable costs are 60 percent of the sales value. What is the break-even point in terms of sales value?
(A) Rs. 25,00,000
(B) Rs. 20,00,000
(C) Rs. 16,66,667
(D) Rs. 30,00,000

14. According to which of the following approaches of decision making, a manager picks up a course of action that is satisfactory or good enough under the circumstances?
(A) The Behavioral Approach
(B) The Bounded Rationality Approach
(C) The 'Garbage Can' Approach
(D) The Cooperative Social Systems Approach

15. What is the market price per share (face value = 100) as per Walter model if the profitability rate of the company is 16 percent, payout ratio is 80 percent and the cost of capital is 10 percent?

(A) 169.20 (B) 182.90
(C) 179.20 (D) 180.90

16. Which out of the following is NOT true about consumer satisfaction?
(A) Consumer satisfaction is a post consumption phenomenon
(B) Consumer satisfaction is a mild, positive emotional state resulting from a favourable appraisal of a consumption outcome
(C) Consumer satisfaction results from a cognitive appraisal
(D) Consumer satisfaction is not different from consumer loyalty. Both are same concepts

17. Which of the following approaches was added by Quinn to the Mintzberg's modes of strategic decision making?
(A) Entrepreneurial approach
(B) Logical incrementalism approach
(C) Adaptive approach
(D) Planning approach

18. Study the data given below :
Net profit for the year ending 31-12-17 after preference dividend and tax ⟶ Rs. 1,00,000
No. of equity shares as on 1-1-2017 ⟶ Rs. 50,000
No. of 12% convertible debentures of Rs. 100 each ⟶ Rs. 1,00,000
Each debenture is convertible into 10 equity shares. The tax rate applicable to the company is 30%.
The diluted earning per share will be
(A) Rs. 3.06 (B) Rs. 2.00
(C) Rs. 3.68 (D) Rs. 4.40

19. Balassa Index is often used as a tool to measure the
(A) Relative trade performance of individual countries in particular commodities
(B) Comparative cost advantage of nations
(C) Product life cycle for different commodities
(D) National competitive advantage

20. The ratio between customer's perceived benefits and the resources they use to obtain those benefits is known as
(A) Customer satisfaction
(B) Customer value
(C) Customer retention
(D) Customer loyalty

21. Respondents of a recent sample survey provided names of friends they thought would be likely users of a new product. These friends were contacted, completed a survey, and asked to supply names of other Likely users. Which method of sampling has been used in this survey?
(A) Judgemental
(B) Snowball
(C) Expert
(D) Quota

22. Match List-I with List-II:

List-I	List-II
(a) Propitious niche	(i) It focuses on improving the competitive position within specific industry that the business unit serves
(b) Strategic window	(ii) An extremely favourable market situation so well suited to the firm's competitive advantage that other organizations are not likely to challenge it
(c) Mission	(iii) A unique market opportunity that is available only for a particular time
(d) Business strategy	(iv) It is an objective and measurable common thread to highlight and

focus the energy of everyone in the direction that the management believes is the best for the best

Choose the correct option from these given below:

(A) (a)-(iv); (b)-(i); (c)-(iii); (d)-(ii)
(B) (a)-(i); (b)-(ii); (c)-(iv); (d)-(iii)
(C) (a)-(iii); (b)-(iv); (c)-(ii); (d)-(i)
(D) (a)-(ii); (b)-(iii); (c)-(iv); (d)-(i)

23. Which one of the following is true for a monopoly firm that operates at the level of output where MR = MC?

(A) If AR > AC, there is abnormal profit for the firm
(B) If AR = AC, there is abnormal profit for the firm
(C) If AR > AC, the firm earns only normal profit
(D) If AR < AC, the firm earns only normal profit

24. Name the human resource demand (need) forecasting technique, which solicits estimates of personnel needs from a group of experts, usually managers. The HRP experts act as intermediaries, summarise the various responses and report the findings back to the experts. The experts are surveyed again after they receive this feedback. Summaries and surveys are repeated until the experts' opinions begin to agree. The agreement reached is the forecast of the personnel needs.

Select the correct option :

(A) Ratio-trend Analysis
(B) Regression Analysis
(C) Delphi Technique
(D) Venture Analysis

25. Which are the asset-related covenants adopted by financial institutions while granting a loan?

(A) Maintenance of working capital position in terms of a minimum current ratio
(B) Prohibition on disposal of promoters' shareholding
(C) Restriction on creation of further charge on asset
(D) Ban on sale of fixed assets without the lender's concurrence

Which one of the following options is most appropriate?

(A) (a), (c), (d)
(B) (a), (b)
(C) (a), (d)
(D) (b), (c), (d)

26. The DuPont approach breaks down the earnings power on the shareholders' book value (RoE) as

(A) Net Profit Margin X Total Assets Turnover X Equity Multiplier
(B) Total Assets Turnover X Gross Profit Margin X Debt Ratio
(C) Total Assets Turnover X Net Profit Margin
(D) Total Assets Turnover X Gross Profit Margin X Equity Multiplier

27. A large firm operating over a wide geographical area can speed up its collection by

(A) Concentration banking
(B) Centralised collection
(C) Playing the float
(D) Discretionary payment

28. For which of the following types of goods the demand increases rapidly with the increase in consumer's income but slows down with further increases in income?

(A) Inferior goods
(B) Essential consumer goods
(C) Normal goods
(D) Luxury and prestige goods

29. A firm's competitive advantage over its competitor is best described by the

(A) Difference between buyers' willingness to pay (WTP) and suppliers' willingness to sell (WTS) is greater than the competitor's difference between the WTP and WTS

(B) Combined valuation of businesses more than the individual sum of businesses
(C) Winner businesses Win more than the loser's lose
(D) Superiority of the corporate strategy over its business strategy

30. The income or gain expected from the second best use of resources lost due to the best use of the scarce resources is known as
(A) Marginality principle
(B) Opportunity cost
(C) Incremental principle
(D) Equi-marginal principle

31. Which national institute has set up/established a 'Centre for Research in Entrepreneurship Education and Development (CREED)' with the objective to broaden the frontier of entrepreneurship research?
(A) Indian Institute of Management, Ahmedabad
(B) Entrepreneurship Development Institute of India
(C) Delhi University
(D) Institute of Rural Management, Anand

32. The following statements relate to Mudra Yojana :

Statement I : Mudra is an NBFC supporting development scheme of micro enterprise sector in the country. It provides refinance support to Bank/MFIs for lending to micro units having loan requirement up to Rs. 10 lakh.

Statement II : Mudra has created different products/schemes for refinancing loans. These interventions have been named 'Shishu', 'Kishore' and 'Tarun' to signify the state of growth/development and funding needs of the beneficiary micro unit/entrepreneur.

Which of the following options is correct?
(A) Statement I is correct, but II is incorrect
(B) Statement II is correct, but I is incorrect
(C) Both the statements I and II are correct
(D) Both the statements I and II are incorrect

33. The credit of taking portfolio theory from abstraction to reality goes to
(A) Harry Markowitz
(B) William Sharpe
(C) Jack Trepnor
(D) Eugene Fama

34. The Industrial Disputes Act 1947 has provided a machinery for settlement of industrial disputes. Which amongst the following machinery has NOT been provided under the Act?
(A) Works Committee
(B) Collective Bargaining
(C) National Tribunal
(D) Voluntary Arbitration

35. Evaluate the statements according to Aaker model of defining brand identity/equity :

Statement I : A particularly important concept for building brand equity is brand identity that represents what the brand stands for and promises to customers.

Statement II : The core identity is most likely to change as the brand travels to new markets and products.

Which of the following options is correct?
(A) Both the statements are correct
(B) Both the statements are incorrect
(C) Statement (I) is correct while Statement (II) is incorrect
(D) Statement (I) is incorrect while Statement (II) is correct

36. Today's new generation knowledge workers and professionals competing for career advancement and ready to work longer hours and work almost seven days a week is called
(A) Hard working employees
(B) Bonded labour
(C) Willing Slaves
(D) Forced workers

37. Feasibility analysis is the process of determining if a business idea is viable. It consists of four areas of feasibility analysis. Identify the correct combination

(A) Product/service feasibility; Industry/target market feasibility; Organizational feasibility; Human resource feasibility
(B) Industry/target market feasibility, Organisational feasibility, Human resource feasibility; Leadership feasibility
(C) Financial feasibility, Product/service feasibility; Industry/target market feasibility, Organizational feasibility
(D) Industry/target market feasibility, Organizational feasibility; Financial feasibility, Leadership feasibility

38. Singapore Airlines offer personalised service at airport, excellent service in flight, menu of customer's choice, personal TV etc. It is an example of
(A) Functional brand
(B) Justified brand
(C) Image brand
(D) Experience brand

39. Assertion (A): Corporate governance is an important instrument of investor protection.
Reason (R) : Strong corporate governance is indispensable to resilient and vibrant capital markets.
Which one of the following options is correct?
(A) Both (A) and (R) are correct and (R) is the right explanation of (A)
(B) Both (A) and (R) are correct but (R) is not the right explanation of (A)
(C) (A) is correct but (R) is incorrect
(D) Both (A) and (R) are incorrect

40. The process for enabling employees to better understand and develop their career skills and interests and to use these skills and interests most effectively both within the company and after they leave the firm, is known as
(A) Career development
(B) Career planning
(C) Career management
(D) Career counselling

41. When prices are rising, the LIFO produces
(A) Highest cost flow and lowest inventory
(B) Lowest cost flow and highest inventory
(C) Highest cost flow and highest inventory
(D) Lowest cost flow and lowest inventory

42. Firm A acquires firm B. Market price of shares of B is 20 per share and BPS is 5. For an exchange ratio of 1.5 : 1, what was the P/E ratio used in acquiring firm B?
(A) 4 (B) 5
(C) 6 (D) 2.67

43. The term 'The War for Talent' was coined by
(A) McKinsey (B) T. V. Rao
(C) Udai Pareek (D) D. Ulrich

44. What refers to the stock of employee skills, knowledge and capabilities that may not show up in a balance sheet but have significant impact on a firm's performance?
(A) Human Resource Planning
(B) Human Resource Management
(C) Human Capital
(D) Number of Employees

45. Which of the following statements is true?
(A) The Spearman correlation coefficient is a measure of the association between two interval variables.
(B) The Pearson correlation coefficient is designed to capture the extent of linear association between variables.
(C) In regression analysis, the dependent variable is treated as a fixed variable, While the independent variable is random.
(D) The Pearson correlation coefficient can range from +2.0 to –2.0.

46. What is the one-month forward price of crude oil trading at \$70 a barrel when annual interest rate is 6 percent and monthly storage cost amounts to \$0.60?
(A) \$69.75
(B) \$70.25
(C) \$70.95
(D) \$69.05

47. **Statement I :** All ideas are opportunities.
Statement II : An opportunity is an idea that has the qualifies of being attractive, durable and timely.
Which of the following options is correct?
(A) Both the statements are correct
(B) Both the statements are incorrect
(C) Statement I is correct while statement II is incorrect
(D) Statement I is incorrect while statement II is correct

48. The money spent for repairs of a motor car used by the business is a
(A) Revenue Expenditure
(B) Capital Expenditure
(C) Deferred Revenue Expenditure
(D) Contingent Expenditure

49. NITI Aayog, GOI, has launched a scheme to develop ecosystem for women entrepreneurship in India. Identify the scheme out of the following :
(A) Women Empowerment Agency
(B) Women Entrepreneurship Platform
(C) Naari Shakti Aayog
(D) Women Knowledge Center

50. Organisations encounter many different forces for change which may be external or internal. Which among the following does NOT come under the external forces of change?
(A) Technological advancement
(B) Workforce diversity
(C) Change in leadership
(D) Competition in the market

51. Which of the following institutions is known as the 'soft loan window' of the World Bank?
(A) International Monetary Fund
(B) International Development Agency
(C) International Finance Corporation
(D) Asian Development Bank

52. Match List-I with List-II:

List-I	List-II
(a) Expatriates	(i) Citizens of the country in which the multinational company has its headquarters
(b) Home-country	(ii) Non citizens of nationals the countries in which employees are working
(c) Third-country nationals	(iii) Citizens of a country other than the parent or the host country
(d) Host-country nationals	(iv) Citizens of the countries in which employees are working

Choose the correct option from those given below :
(A) (a)-(ii); (b)-(i); (c)-(iv); (d)-(iii)
(B) (a)-(ii); (b)-(i); (c)-(iii); (d)-(iv)
(C) (a)-(i); (b)-(ii); (c)-(iv); (d)-(iii)
(D) (a)-(iv); (b)-(i); (c)-(ii); (d)-(iii)

53. For a situation where 100 misprints are distributed randomly throughout the 100 pages of a book, the probability that a page selected at random will contain at most one misprint will be
(A) 0.724 (B) 0.728
(C) 0.732 (D) 0.736

54. A specific category of information system serving middle managers by providing reports on the organization's current performance is called
(A) MIS (B) TPS
(C) DSS (D) ESS

55. In which Amendment of the Constitution, the Government of India made a pioneering attempt to provide for 'workers' participation in management in industry', by suitable legislation in the Directive Principles of State Policy?
(A) The Constitution (42 Amendment Act), 1976
(B) The Constitution (41 Amendment Act), 1975

(C) The Constitution (46 Amendment Act), 1977

(D) The Constitution (40 Amendment Act), 1972

56. In most of the cases 'cessation of work', refusal to continue to work or refusal to accept employment is called strike. Which of the following does NOT come under the form of strike?

(A) Sit-down strike (B) Hunger strike

(C) Gherao (D) Work-to-rule

57. Which of the following institutions prepares and publishes FDI confidence index annually?

(A) UNCTAD (B) WTO

(C) A.T. Kearney (D) MSCI

58. Entering a foreign market by developing foreign-based assembly or manufacturing facilities is known as

(A) Exporting

(B) Licensing

(C) Joint ownership

(D) Direct investment

59. Indicate the correct answer for the combination from the following regarding the conditions for the applicability of a binominal distribution :

(a) There are independent trials

(b) Each trial has only two possible outcomes

(c) The probabilities of two outcomes do not remain constant

(d) The trials are independent

Which of the following options is correct'?

(A) (a), (b) and (c)

(B) (a), (c) and (d)

(C) (a), (b) and (d)

(D) (b), (c) and (d)

60. Two friends are on WhatsApp discussing a holiday plan immediately, Uber pops up within WhatsApp to help book a ride and provide an estimate. This is known as

(A) Contextual digital marketing

(B) Direct mail marketing

(C) Mail order marketing

(D) Telemarketing

61. Which one of the following demand forecasting methods is NOT a survey method?

(A) Delphi method

(B) End use method

(C) Graphical method

(D) Complete enumeration method

62. The following statements relate to organisational culture :

Statement I : Culture is the cumulative preference of some states of life and some organized Ways of dealing with basic concerns by members of a society.

Statement II : There are various ways of making employees aware about the organization's culture. These include stories, language, rituals, organizational structure and physical layout and rules and policies.

Which of the following options is correct?

(A) Statement I is correct, but II is incorrect

(B) Statement II is correct, but I is incorrect

(C) Both the statements I and II are correct

(D) Both the statements I and II are incorrect

63. Which of the following were two major criteria for the first official definition of small scale industry coined, in the year 1950?

(A) the size of gross investment in fixed assets and the strength of the work force

(B) the size of gross investment in fixed assets and the annual turnover

(C) the strength of the workforce and the annual turnover

(D) the annual turnover and the annual profit

64. Cash Flow Analysis is an important financial tool for the management. Its chief advantages are

(a) Helps in cash management

(b) Helps in external financial management

(c) Helps in internal financial management

(d) Discloses the movements of cash

Which of the following options is correct?
(A) (a), (c) and (d) only
(B) (a), (b) and (d) only
(C) (a) and (d) only
(D) (a), (b), (c) and (d)

65. Match List-I with List-II:

List-I	List-II
(a) Product line	(i) Total number of items under each product/brand in the line
(b) Depth of product	(ii) Number of products/brands in the line
(c) Width of product mix	(iii) Group of closely related products
(d) Length of product line	(iv) Number of product lines

Choose the correct option from those given below:
(A) (a)-(iii); (b)-(i); (c)-(iv); (d)-(ii)
(B) (a)-(iii); (b)-(iv); (c)-(ii); (d)-(i)
(C) (a)-(iv); (b)-(i); (c)-(ii); (d)-(iii)
(D) (a)-(ii); (b)-(i); (c)-(iii); (d)-(iv)

66. Which one of the following is NOT correct for National Income?
(A) Gross National Product (GNP) > Gross National Income (GNI)
(B) Gross Domestic Product (GDP) = GNP less Net Income from Abroad
(C) Net National Product (NNP) = GNP less Depreciation
(D) Net Domestic Product (NDP) = NNP less Net Income from Abroad

67. Which out of the following is the principal financial institution for the promotion, financing and development of industries in the small scale sector and to coordinate the functions of other institutions engaged in similar activities?
(A) Infrastructure Development Finance Company Limited
(B) Industrial Finance Corporation of India Limited
(C) Industrial Development Bank of India
(D) Small Industries Development Bank of India

68. The following statements relate to marketing:

Statement I : "For any business enterprise there are two and only two basic functions : marketing and innovation. These two produce results; all the rest are costs"

Statement II : "The product concept of marketing holds that business can be managed by maximisation of production and the resultant lower unit cost and low price."

Which of the following options is correct?
(A) Statement I is correct but II is incorrect
(B) Statement II is correct, but I is incorrect
(C) Both the statements I and II are correct
(D) Both the statements I and II are incorrect

69. The system of collective bargaining as a method of settlement of industrial disputes has been adopted and provided under
(A) The Industrial Disputes Act, 1947
(B) The Trade Unions Act, 1926
(C) The Industrial Employment (Standing Orders) Act, 1946
(D) The Taft-Hartley Act, 1947

70. Which one amongst the following is NOT social security legislation?
(A) Employees' Compensation Act, 1923
(B) Employees' State Insurance Act, 1948
(C) Payment of Wages Act, 1936
(D) Payment of Gratuity Act, 1972

71. Which one of the following involves selling at a loss to gain access to a market and perhaps to drive competition?
(A) Persistent dumping
(B) Predatory dumping
(C) Reverse dumping
(D) Sporadic dumping

72. The ethical decision 'Same Job, Same Wage' is used under which criterion?
(A) Rights (B) Utilitarianism
(C) Justice (D) Culture

73. The cooperative bank came into existence with the enactment of the Co-operative Credit Societies Act, 1912. Which among the following does not come under the structure of co-operative bank?
(A) State Co-operative Bank
(B) Land Development Bank
(C) Regional Rural Bank
(D) Primary Agricultural Credit Societies

74. Re-engineering, a radical redesign of business processes, is an essential and integral to which of the following strategies?
(A) Expansion strategy
(B) Diversification strategy
(C) Growth strategy
(D) Turnaround strategy

75. If actual production of units are lower than the budgeted level of production, which of the following costs would be lower than the budgeted costs?
(A) Variable cost per unit
(B) Total variable cost
(C) Total fixed cost
(D) None of the above

76. Match List-I with List-II :

List-I	List-II
(a) Gate keeper	(i) Encourages silent or shy members to contribute to the discussion
(b) Supporter	(ii) Explores with the group if all group members agree with the decision
(c) Consensus tester	(iii) Reduces tension in the group, reconciles differences and explores opportunities
(d) Harmonizer	(iv) Invites all group members one by one to speak and encourages people to participate

Choose the correct option from those given below:
(A) (a)-(ii); (b)-(i); (c)-(iv); (d)-(iii)
(B) (a)-(ii); (b)-(iv); (c)-(i); (d)-(iii)
(C) (a)-(iv); (b)-(i); (c)-(iii); (d)-(ii)
(D) (a)-(iv); (b)-(i); (c)-(ii); (d)-(iii)

77. Exponential distribution comprises which of the following characteristics?
(a) It is discrete distribution
(b) It is a family of distributions
(c) It is skewed to the left
(d) The x values range from zero to infinity
Which one of the following options is most appropriate?
(A) (a), (b), (c) and (d) (B) (b), (c) and (d)
(C) (c) and (d) (D) (b) and (d)

78. Name the theory/concept/thought concerned with designing and shaping jobs to fit the physical abilities and characteristics of individuals so that they can perform their jobs effectively.
(A) Economics (B) Physiology
(C) Ergonomics (D) Psychology

79. Four distinctive service characteristics greatly affect the design of marketing program for services. The appropriate combination is
(A) Intangibility, inseparability, variability and touchability
(B) Intangibility, inseparability, variability and perishability
(C) Inseparability, variability, perishability and touchability,
(D) Variability, perishability, intangibility and touchability

80. If Mr. X pays a well-known fashion innovator such as Calvin Klein for the right to use its name on his apparel and accessories, then Mr. X is using which type of branding?
(A) Co-branding
(B) Private branding
(C) Manufacturer's branding
(D) Licensed branding

81. If risk-free return is 8 percent and the expected return on a market portfolio is 12 percent, the required return on a stock is 15 percent. What is stock beta?
(A) 0.75 (B) 1.75
(C) 1.25 (D) 2.75

82. Read the following regarding PERT and CPM:
(a) PERT is probabilistic in nature and CPM is deterministic in nature.
(b) PERT is most suitable for new as well as old projects but CPM is of great value for projects that are repetitive.
(c) PERT focuses primarily on time element and attaches lesser significance to the cost. On the contrary, the CPM puts strong emphasis on cost.
(d) PERT is activity-oriented and CPM is event-oriented.

Which one of the following options is most appropriate?
(A) (a) and (d) (B) (a), (c) and (d)
(C) (a), (b), (c) and (d) (D) (a) and (c)

83. Which of the following institutions is responsible for the execution of the India's import-export policies?
(A) Chief Controller of Imports and Exports
(B) Federation of Indian Export Organizations
(C) Export Promotion Councils and Commodity Boards
(D) Director General of Foreign Trade (DGFT)

84. Which of the following modules is NOT a part of a typical ERP system?
(A) The Corporate Management (CM) Module
(B) The Asset Management (AM) Module
(C) The Human Resource (HR) Module
(D) The Project System (PS) Module

85. Fine speciality store falls into
(A) High-mark up, lower volume group
(B) High-mark up, higher volume group
(C) Low-mark up, lower volume group
(D) Low-mark up, higher volume group

86. MM Hypothesis for capital structure is based on which of the following assumptions?
(a) Investors are rational and have homogeneous expectations
(b) Perfect capital market
(c) 100% retention of profits
(d) No taxes

Which of the following options is most appropriate?
(A) (a), (b), (d) (B) (a), (c), (d)
(C) (b), (c), (d) (D) (a), (b), (c), (d)

87. Authority is the right to make decisions to direct the Work of others and to give orders. In this context match List-I with List-II:

List-I	List-II
(a) Line Authority	(i) Gives a manager the right to advice other managers or employees
(b) Staff Authority	(ii) Traditionally gives managers the right to issue orders to other managers or employees
(c) Line Manager	(iii) A manager who assists and advises the manager
(d) Staff Manager	(iv) A manager who is authorised to direct the work of subordinates is responsible for accomplishing the organisation's tasks

Choose the correct option from those given below:
(A) (a)-(i); (b)-(iv); (c)-(iii); (d)-(ii)
(B) (a)-(ii); (b)-(i); (c)-(iv); (d)-(iii)
(C) (a)-(iv); (b)-(ii); (c)-(iii); (d)-(i)
(D) (a)-(ii); (b)-(iii); (c)-(i); (d)-(iv)

88. A company's share is currently selling for Rs. 50 and is expecting a dividend of Rs. 3 per share after one year which is expected

to grow at 8% indefinitely. What is the equity capitalisation rate?

(A) 9 per cent (B) 17 per cent
(C) 14 per cent (D) 24 per cent

89. John Dunning argued that FDI is attracted because of unique advantage of
(A) Firms seeking to establish a dominant market presence
(B) Product life cycle advantages
(C) Ownership, location and internalisation
(D) Market imperfection

90. Data scrubbing is
(A) A process to reject data from the data warehouse and to create the necessary indexes.
(B) A process to load the data in the data warehouse and to create necessary indices.
(C) A process to upgrade the quality of data before it is moved into a data warehouse.
(D) A process to upgrade the quality of data after it is moved into a data warehouse.

91. India's Trade Policy, 2015-20 stipulates to raise India's share in world exports to
(A) 5.0 percent (B) 2.5 percent
(C) 3.5 percent (D) 4.5 percent

92. Which among the following is a correct statement?
(A) Entrepreneur is an employee and intrapreneur is free and the leader of the operation.
(B) Intrapreneur is an employee and entrepreneur is free and the leader of the operation.
(C) Entrepreneurship is the change initiative taken within a going concern by the people working in the organisation.
(D) Intrapreneurship is the change initiative taken by a group of independent people.

93. International Fisher Effect suggests that a home currency will
(A) Appreciate if the current home interest rate exceeds the current foreign interest rate
(B) Depreciate if the current home interest rate exceeds current foreign interest rate
(C) Appreciate if the current home inflation rate exceeds the current foreign inflation rate
(D) Depreciate if the current home inflation rate exceeds the current foreign inflation rate

94. Depreciation charged on fixed assets in the Funds Flow Statement is/are
(a) Source of funds
(b) An application of funds
(c) Sources of funds in limited sense
(d) Added back to the operating profit to find out funds from operations

Which one of the following options is correct?
(A) (a) and (d) only (B) (b) only
(C) (d) only (D) (c) and (d) only

95. Which of the following statistical techniques should be used when you wish to examine the association between two nominal variables?
(A) Multiple regression analysis
(B) Simple correlation coefficient
(C) Chi-square contingency test
(D) Pearson correlation coefficient

96. Match List-I with List-II:

List-I (Training Need Assessment Technique)	List-II (Advantages/ Merits)
(a) Observation	(i) Questions can be modified
(b) Questionnaires	(ii) Generates data relevant to Work environment
(c) Online technology	(iii) Inexpensive
(d) interviews	(iv) Objective

Choose the correct option from those given below :

(A) (a)-(i); (b)-(iii); (c)-(ii); (d)-(iv)

(B) (a)-(ii); (b)-(iii); (c)-(iv); (d)-(i)

(C) (a)-(iii); (b)-(ii); (c)-(iv); (d)-(i)

(D) (a)-(iv); (b)-(iii); (c)-(i); (d)-(ii)

97. Match List-I with List-II :

List-I	List-II
(a) Goal	(i) Basic function or task of an organisation
(b) Strategy	(ii) End towards which an activity is directed
(c) Mission	(iii) Adoption of course of action to achieve long term objectives
(d) Rule	(iv) Actions or non-actions allowing no discretion

Choose the correct option from those given below:

(A) (a)-(i); (b)-(iv); (c)-(ii); (d)-(iii)

(B) (a)-(iv); (b)-(i); (c)-(ii); (d)-(iii)

(C) (a)-(ii); (b)-(iii); (c)-(i); (d)-(iv)

(D) (a)-(iv); (b)-(iii); (c)-(i); (d)-(ii)

98. Which of the following invalidates informal persuasions to boycott China imported goods?

(A) Plurilateral agreement

(B) Protection through tariffication

(C) National treatment rule

(D) Most favoured nation principle

99. Match List-I with List-II:

List-I (Market structure)	List-II (Feature)
(a) Perfect competition	(i) Product is differentiated
(b) Monopoly	(ii) Homogeneous or differentiated products
(c) Monopolistic competition	(iii) Factors of production are freely mobile between firms
(d) Oligopoly	(iv) Legal restrictions on entry of new firms

Choose the correct option from those given below :

(A) (a)-(i); (b)-(ii); (c)-(iv); (d)-(iii)

(B) (a)-(iii); (b)-(iv); (c)-(i); (d)-(ii)

(C) (a)-(ii); (b)-(iv); (c)-(iii); (d)-(i)

(D) (a)-(ii); (b)-(iv); (c)-(i); (d)-(iii)

100. According to BCG matrix, for which one of the following positions of SBU the firm should decide to curtail losses by divesting?

(A) Star (B) Question mark

(C) Cash cow (D) Dog

ANSWER KEY

1. (C)	**2.** (B)	**3.** (A)	**4.** (B)	**5.** (D)	**6.** (C)	**7.** (B)	**8.** (A)	**9.** (C)	**10.** (C)
11. (A)	**12.** (A)	**13.** (A)	**14.** (B)	**15.** (C)	**16.** (D)	**17.** (B)	**18.** (B)	**19.** (A)	**20.** (B)
21. (B)	**22.** (D)	**23.** (A)	**24.** (C)	**25.** (A)	**26.** (A)	**27.** (A)	**28.** (C)	**29.** (A)	**30.** (B)
31. (B)	**32.** (C)	**33.** (B)	**34.** (B)	**35.** (C)	**36.** (C)	**37.** (C)	**38.** (D)	**39.** (A)	**40.** (C)
41. (A)	**42.** (C)	**43.** (A)	**44.** (C)	**45.** (B)	**46.** (C)	**47.** (D)	**48.** (A)	**49.** (B)	**50.** (C)
51. (B)	**52.** (B)	**53.** (D)	**54.** (A)	**55.** (A)	**56.** (C)	**57.** (C)	**58.** (D)	**59.** (C)	**60.** (A)
61. (C)	**62.** (C)	**63.** (A)	**64.** (A)	**65.** (A)	**66.** (A)	**67.** (D)	**68.** (A)	**69.** (A)	**70.** (C)
71. (B)	**72.** (B)	**73.** (C)	**74.** (D)	**75.** (B)	**76.** (D)	**77.** (D)	**78.** (C)	**79.** (B)	**80.** (D)
81. (B)	**82.** (D)	**83.** (D)	**84.** (A)	**85.** (A)	**86.** (A)	**87.** (B)	**88.** (C)	**89.** (C)	**90.** (C)
91. (C)	**92.** (B)	**93.** (B)	**94.** (D)	**95.** (C)	**96.** (B)	**97.** (C)	**98.** (C)	**99.** (B)	**100.** (D)

DECEMBER, 2019

MANAGEMENT

PAPER-II

Note : This paper contains **hundred (100)** objective type questions of **two (2)** marks each. **All** questions are **compulsory**.

1. Mergers and acquisitions are example of which strategy of Ansoff (2 × 2) matrix'?

(1) Present Product — Present market
(2) Present Product — New market
(3) New Product — Present market
(4) New Product — New market

2. Which one of the following statements is true?

(1) The desire for a commodity backed by ability and Willingness to pay is demand
(2) Decrease in input prices causes a leftward shift in supply curve
(3) Demand for car and price of petrol are inversely related
(4) Most demand functions are of the form, D = a + bP

3. In micro economics which among the following sequence in respect of internal issues of the business firms is correct?

(1) What to produce, how to produce, how much to produce, how to determine price of product
(2) What to produce, how much to produce, how to produce, how to determine price of the product
(3) How much to produce, What to produce, how to produce, how to determine the price of the product
(4) What to produce, how much to produce, how to determine price of the product, how to produce

4. Which one of the following is the sequence of selection?

(1) Application blank, initial interview, employment tests, final interview, checking references, physical examination
(2) Application blank, employment tests, initial interview, checking references, physical examination, final interview
(3) Employment tests, initial interview, checking references, physical examination, final interview
(4) Employment tests, initial interview, checking references, final interview, physical examination

5. Which one of the following is closest to the nature of decision making'?

(1) Decision on a particular course of action
(2) Too self evident requiring an answer
(3) Deciding on a choice after a series of brain storming
(4) The process of identifying problems and opportunities and then resolving them

6. A forecasting technique in which the group consists of persons who are physically dispersed and are anonymous to one another is called

(1) Delphi Technique
(2) Brain Storming Technique
(3) Heuristic Ideation Technique
(4) Decision Tree Technique

7. Which one of the following is NOT correct in case of indifference curves?

(1) Indifference curves slope downward to right

(2) Indifference curves of imperfect substitutes are convex to the origin
(3) Indifference curves neither intersect nor are tangent to one another
(4) Lower indifference curves indicate a higher level of satisfaction

8. Human Resource selection is concerned with
(1) The activity to select a suitable pool of candidates
(2) Always being simulated by the departure of an employee
(3) Always ascertaining a candidates personality to ensure a suitability fit
(4) Applying appropriate technique to select a candidate

9. Human Resource Management (HRM) helps build successful cross border alliances by ensuring that
(1) Organisation spends 20 percent of their HR budgets on cross border alliances
(2) A strategy is in place before embarking on a cross border alliance
(3) Organisations that export their ideas to other societies and cultures
(4) International joint ventures are staffed by high quality managers

10. Which one of the following is NOT a forecasting technique for assessing human resource requirement in an organisation?
(1) Ratio analysis
(2) Trend analysis
(3) Gaps analysis
(4) Replacement charts

11. Why has the bureaucratic form of organization been fundamentally questioned?
(1) Pressure of Globalization has rendered it unsuitable
(2) Organizations are experiencing acute pressure to change and pursue innovation as a means of securing business growth
(3) Organizations have grown so large that it is almost impossible to create an effective bureaucracy to manage them
(4) Information Technology has made it redundant.

12. Which one of the following countries is NOT the member of the Shanghai Cooperation Organization (SCO)?
(1) China (2) Pakistan
(3) India (4) Japan

13. Human Resource (HR) procedures provide for an important element of consistency in which managerial perspective'?
(1) Direction
(2) Strategy
(3) Decision Making
(4) Recruitment

14. In Queuing Theory. statistical pattern by which customers arrive over a period of time follows
(1) Binomial distribution
(2) Normal distribution
(3) Poisson distribution
(4) Long-normal distribution

15. Which of the following is a correct description of attitude?
(1) Attitudes are learned.
(2) Attitudes are organized and are core to an individual.
(3) Attitudes are the major determinants of human behaviour.
(4) Attitud..s are beliefs, feelings and action tendencies of individual toward objects, ideas and people.

16. Homogenous subsets in the sampling are called
(1) Clusters
(2) Samples
(3) Sample sizes
(4) Strata

17. Customer Life Time Value (CLV) in the first year is

(1) $CLV(1) = m \times \frac{r}{(1+d)}$

(2) $CLV(1) = m + \frac{r}{(1+d)}$

(3) $CLV(1) = m - \frac{r}{(1-d)}$

(4) $CLV(1) = m \times \frac{r}{(1-d)}$

18. When an activity is not connected to any of intermediate or end event. and has no bearing on the project, completion, is known as

(1) Dangling (2) Looping
(3) Dummy (4) Slack

19. According to which of the following concept, it is presumed that business will continue its operations for longtime?

(1) Accounting period concept
(2) Realization concept
(3) Going concern concept
(4) Separate entity concept

20. Sale of long term investment shows

(1) Application of funds
(2) Source of funds
(3) Change in current assets
(4) Change in current liabilities

21. The Total Asset Turnover Ratio and Total Assets to Networth Ratio of Kuber Ltd. are 1.75 and 2, respectively. If the Net Profit Margin of this company is 8%. What is the Return on Equity (ROE)?

(1) 0.20 (2) 0.2-5
(3) 0.22 (4) 0.28

22. Net Income approach to valuation is based on which of the following assumption?

(1) There are taxes and cost of debt is less than cost of equity
(2) There are taxes and use of debt does not change the risk perception of investors
(3) There are no taxes and use of debt changes the risk perception of investors
(4) There are no taxes and cost of debt is less than the cost of equity and the use of debt does not change the risk perception of investors.

23. Which of the following is aptly described by '2/10, net 30'?

(1) Credit policy
(2) Credit standards
(3) Credit terms
(4) Collection policy

24. The major factor that allowed Portfolio Theory to develop into Capital Market Theory is

(1) Risk free asset
(2) Homogenous expectations
(3) Infinite divisibility of assets
(4) Absence of taxes and transaction costs

25. When managers commit errors of over optimism in evaluating merger opportunities due to excessive pride or animal spirit is termed as

(1) Managerialism
(2) Information Signaling
(3) Hubris Hypothesis
(4) Sitting on gold mine

26. Which of the following methods of capital budgeting is best suited for leveraged projects?

(1) Net present value
(2) Internal rate of return
(3) Accounting rate of return
(4) Profitability index

27. When each coupon payment and the redemption value of bond are detached and are issued as separate and independent instruments are called

(1) Coupons
(2) Strips
(3) Certificates
(4) Warrants

28. The effect of continuous compounding is captured by
    (1) Present Value × e^{rt}
    (2) Present Value × e^{-rt}
    (3) Present Value/ × e^{rt}
    (4) Future Value × e^{rt}
29. Public Relations as a part of promotion in marketing refers to
    (1) Management of reputation of the company
    (2) Promoting products/brands of the company
    (3) Managing an event of the company
    (4) Conducting publicity campaigns around relevant issues
30. Which of the following is NOT the characteristic of "Hyper Competition"?
    (1) Competitions get bold, aggressive and hostile with dynamic movements
    (2) Shorter Product and design life cycles
    (3) Uncertainty in business environment increases along with heterogenicity
    (4) Financing cost becomes high
31. Concept testing, test marketing and product testing are parts of which of the following?
    (1) Innovation – Diffusion process
    (2) Product life cycle
    (3) New Product development
    (4) Market development
32. Modern organised retail business has a multitude of formats. These formats can be classified according to the following :
    (1) Merchandise offered only
    (2) Size of the store area only
    (3) Customer groups only
    (4) Merchandise offered and size of the store area
33. In Service Quality GAPS model proposed by Parasuraman et.al., Gap 4 refers to
    (1) Difference between the service level expected by the customer and the service level received by customer
    (2) Difference between the service delivered and the promise made to t-he customer
    (3) Difference between the service specifications adopted and service quality actually delivered
    (4) Difference between the service expectations and service specifications given by the customers
34. The system that provides an organisation with sophisticated planning and control functionalities, greater connectivity to its suppliers, business partners and customers is described as
    (1) Customer Relationship Management (CRM)
    (2) Manufacturing Resource Planning (MRP)
    (3) Enterprise Resource Planning (ERP)
    (4) Economic Order Quantity (EOQ)
35. The situation of simultaneous satisfaction of row minima and column minima rule is termed as
    (1) Unboundedness
    (2) Infeasibility
    (3) Degeneracy
    (4) Post-optimality analysis
36. Which of the following information systems at the management level of an organisation serves the functions of planning. controlling and decision making by providing routine summary and exception reports?
    (1) Management Information Systems
    (2) Artificial Intelligence Systems
    (3) Executive Support Systems
    (4) Decision Support Systems.
37. Theory of Comparative Advantage given by David Ricardo in 1817 is
    (1) Two Commodity and One Factor theory
    (2) Two Commodity and Two Factor theory
    (3) Two Country, Two Commodity and Two Factor theory
    (4) Two Country, Two Commodity and One Factor theory

38. SIP in Market Targeting refers to
(1) Systematic Investment Planning
(2) Short Input Processing
(3) Segment Investing Portfolio
(4) Segment Invasion Plan

39. Who propounded the 'Force-Field theory' of change process'?
(1) Kurt Lewin
(2) Peter Drucker
(3) Joseph A. Schumpeter
(4) David C. McClelland

40. Which one of the following is NOT a source of opportunity identification'?
(1) Employees and ex-employees
(2) Dealers and Distributors
(3) Policy Documents
(4) Friends and relatives

41. Pearl Ltd. Company purchased a van for Rs. 12,000 making a down payment of Rs. 5,000 cash and signing a Rs. 7,000 note payable in 60 days. As a result of this transaction :
(a) Total assets will increase by Rs. 12,000
(b) Total liabilities will increase by Rs. 7,000
(c) This transactions will not have immediate effect on owner's equity in the business
(d) From the point of view of short-term creditor, this transaction will make business more liquid
Choose the correct option :
(1) (a) and (c)
(2) (b) and (d)
(3) (a) and (b)
(4) (b) and (c)

42. The combined leverage
(a) is the summation of the degree of operating leverage and the financial leverage
(b) measures total risk of the firm
(c) is the difference between the degree of operating leverage and financial leverage
(d) indicates the effect that changes in sales Will have on earning per share
Choose the correct option
(1) (a) and (b)
(2) (b) and (c)
(3) (b) and (d)
(4) (c) and (d)

43. As per RBI guidelines (2008), an WISME IS considered to have reached the stage of incipient sickness if the following events are triggered
(a) When there are cost overruns because of delay in commencement of commercial production by more than 6 months
(b) The enterprise incurs losses for 2 years or cash loss for one year
(c) The capacity utilisation is less than 50 percent of the projected level in term of sales
(d) There is an errosion in the net worth due to accumulated cash losses to the extent of 50 percent of net worth during the previous accounting year
(1) (a) and (b) only
(2) (a), (b) and (c) only
(3) (b) and (c) only
(4) (b), (c) and (d)

44. Which of the following fully capture foreign exchange risk exposure of an manufacturing enterprise?
(a) Transaction exposure
(b) Economic exposure
(c) Translation exposure
(d) Currency exposure
Choose the correct option :
(1) (a) and (b) only
(2) (b) and (c) only
(3) (c) and (d) only
(4) (a), (b) and (c) only

45. According to Mintzberg's model of strategic decision making. its modes are :
(a) Entrepreneurial, adaptation and planning

(b) Managerial, incrementalisation and judgmental
(c) Entrepreneurial, planning and incrementalisation
(d) Judgemental, managerial and leadership

Which of the following options is correct'?
(1) (a), (b) and (d) only
(2) (a) and (c) only
(3) (b) and (c) only
(4) (b), (c) and (d) only

46. 'Collusion' is one of the co operative strategies in business combination that
(a) may be explicit
(b) may be tacit
(c) may reduce technological risk
(d) may be illegal in many countries

Which of the following option is correct'?
(1) only (a) and (b)
(2) (b), (c) and (d)
(3) (a), (b) and (c)
(4) (a), (b) and (d)

47. To keep the brand live, contemporary and relevant, marketer uses a variety of measures such as
(a) Brand extension
(b) Brand rejuvenation
(c) Brand relaunch
(d) Brand proliferation

Which of the following is correct?
(1) (a) and (b) only
(2) (a) and (c) only
(3) (a), (b) and (d) only
(4) (a), (b), (c) and (d)

48. Direct marketing is carried out in variety of ways. Some of the main forms of direct marketing are
(a) Mail order marketing
(b) Telemarketing
(c) Online marketing
(d) Direct selling

Which of the following option is correct?
(1) (a), (b) and (c) only
(2) (a), (b), (c) and (d)
(3) (a), (b) and (d) only
(4) (a) and (c) only

49. The strategic issues to which a retailing firm has to respond are :
(a) Location decisions
(b) Brand building decisions
(c) Merchandise mix decisions
(d) Target market selection

Which of the following option is correct?
(1) (a), (b) and (c) only
(2) (a) and (c) only
(3) (a), (b), (c) and (d)
(4) (a), (c) and (d) only

50. Grounds for market segmentation based behaviour are :
(a) Benefit sought
(b) Life style
(c) Purchase occasion
(d) Usage rate

Which of the following option is correct'?
(1) (a) and (b) only
(2) (a), (c) and (d) only
(3) (a), (b) and(c) only
(4) (a), (b), (c) and (d)

51. Which of the following describes a combination of manufacturing systems designed to ensure that, theoretically, 100 percent good units flow to subsequent operations?
(a) Autonomation
(b) Automation
(c) Bakayoke
(d) Kaizen

Select correct option :
(1) (a) and (b) only
(2) (b) and (c) only
(3) (a) and (c) only
(4) (c) and (d) only

52. Identify the correct combination of properties of point estimates from the options given below :

(a) Efficiency
(b) Consistency
(c) Adequacy
(d) Unbiasedness

Choose correct option :

(1) (a), (b) and (d)
(2) (b), (c) and (d)
(3) (a), (c) and (d)
(4) (a), (b) and (d)

53. At a given significance level, sample results in the rejection region are called

(a) Statistically significant
(b) Statistically insignificant
(c) Statistically critical
(d) Confidence interval

Select correct option :

(1) (a) and (c) only
(2) (b) and (c) only
(3) (a) and (b) only
(4) (a) and (d) only

54. The difference between the point estimate and the true value of population parameter being estimated is known as

(a) Sampling error
(b) Estimation error
(c) Probable error
(d) Standard error

Choose the correct option from the options given below :

(1) (a) and (c) only
(2) (c) and (d) only
(3) (a) and (b) only
(4) (a), (b) and (c) only

55. Identify the right combination of primary data collection methods from the following:

(a) Observation
(b) Experimentation
(c) Corporate database
(d) Survey method

Choose the correct option :

(1) (a) and (d) only
(2) (c) and (d) only
(3) (a), (b) and (d)
(4) (a), (b) and (c)

56. Gains to corporate restructuring originates and derived from

(a) Resource re-allocation
(b) Market power
(c) Macro conditioning
(d) Operating synergy

Which option is correct?

(1) (a) and (b) only
(2) (b) and (d) only
(3) (a), (b) and (d)
(4) (a), (b) and (c)

57. The reasons behind the growth of financial markets globally are

(a) Currency fluctuations
(b) Deregulation
(c) International Banks
(d) Information Technology

Select correct option :

(1) Only (a) and (b)
(2) Only (c) and (d)
(3) (a), (b) and (c)
(4) (b), (c) and (d)

58. Entrepreneurs are motivated to start business enterprise because of various factors

(a) Ambitious factors
(b) Compelling factors
(c) Facilitating factors
(d) Family factors

Which of the following options is correct?

(1) (a), (b) and (c) only
(2) (a) and (c) only
(3) (a) and (d) only
(4) (a), (b), (c) and (d)

59. Whistle blowing is normally unjustified in case of the following :

(a) Ulterior motive, Breach of trust

(b) To protect public interest
(c) Insufficient evidence
(d) To inspire other employees
Choose the correct option :
(1) (a) and (b)
(2) (a) and (c)
(3) (b) and (c)
(4) (b) and (d)

60. On which of the following principles is Andrew Carnegie's view on Corporate Social Responsibility, as reflected in his book, 'The Gospel of Wealth' based?
(a) Peter Principle
(b) Sealer Principle
(c) Charity Principle
(d) Steward Principle
Choose the correct option from the following :
(1) (a) and (b) only
(2) (b) and (c) only
(3) (c) and (d) only
(4) (a) and (d) only

61. Which one of the following is NOT the prominent objective of human resource planning?
(1) To prevent overstaffing and under-staffing
(2) To ensure employee availability
(3) To provide direction to all HR activities
(4) To evaluate the performance of the employees

62. **Assertion (A) :** Foreign trade policy is an important instrument that incentivise the exporters of the country.
Reasons (R) : It is important for exporters of our country to have knowledge of foreign trade policy
Which of the following option is correct?
(1) Both (A) and (R) are correct and (R) is the correct explanation of (A)
(2) Both (A) and (R) are correct but (R) is not the correct explanation of (A)
(3) (A) is correct but (R) is not correct
(4) Both (A) and (R) are incorrect

63. Methods of off-the-job training are
(a) lectures, simulations and laboratory training
(b) role playing, vestibule training and video presentation
(c) job rotation and coaching
(d) job instruction training
Choose the correct option :
(1) (a) and (c) (2) (a) and (b)
(3) (b) and (d) (4) (b) and (c)

64. Psychological barriers in communication take place due the following reasons :
(a) Premature evaluation, lack of attention
(b) Organizational facilities, status relationships
(c) Poor retention, lack of reliance
(d) Hierarchy, organization policies
Choose the correct option :
(1) (a) and (b) (2) (a) and (c)
(3) (b) and (c) (4) (b) and (d)

65. Novation, a feature of future exchanges stipulates
(1) Future contracts are traded in an exchange
(2) Exchange becomes a counter-party for all trades
(3) Futures contracts delivery dates are standardised
(4) Credit risk using intricate system of margins

66. Match the following approaches of moral reasoning with their propounders :

Moral Reasoning	Proponder(s)
(a) Consequentialism Approach	(i) Thomas Hobbes, Ayow Rand
(b) Deontological Approach	(ii) Aristotle
(c) Natural law theory	(iii) Ronald F. White
(d) Theological Approach	(iv) W.D. Ross, John Rawls

Choose the correct option from the following:

(1) (a)-(i), (b)-(iv), (c)-(iii), (d)-(ii)
(2) (a)-(ii), (b)-(iii), (c)-(i), (d)-(iv)
(3) (a)-(i), (b)-(iv), (c)-(ii), (d)-(iii)
(4) (a)-(i), (b)-(ii), (c)-(iv), (d)-(iii)

67. Match the terms With the statement given below:

(a) Human behaviour results from a continuous and multidirectional interaction between the person and the situation — (i) Interactionalism
(b) People are central to the organization and they must be developed to their potential — (ii) Productivity Approach
(c) Manager's efficiency depends on optimum utilization of resources — (iii) Contingency Approach
(d) The belief that there is no one best option available for an organization — (iv) HR Approach

Select the correct option:

(1) (a)-(i), (b)-(iv), (c)-(ii), (d)-(iii)
(2) (a)-(i), (b)-(ii). (c)-(iii), (d)-(iv)
(3) (a)-(i), (b)-(iii), (c)-(ii), (d)-(iv)
(4) (a)-(ii), (b)-(i), (c)-(iii), (d)-(iv)

68. Match the following according to their definition:

(a) Career Planning — (i) A process whereby an individual sets career goals and identifies means to achieve them
(b) Career development — (ii) A process of enabling employees to better understand and develop their skill and interest and use them for the interest of organization and self
(c) Career management — (iii) The process of analysis and identifying the need and availability of human resources so that organization can meet its objectives
(d) Human resource planning — (iv) Refers to a formal approach used by the firm to ensure that people with proper qualification and experience are available when needed

Choose the correct option:

(1) (a)-(ii), (b)-(iv), (c)-(iii), (d)-(ii)
(2) (a)-(i), (b)-(iv), (c)-(ii), (d)-(iii)
(3) (a)-(ii), (b)-(iii), (c)-(iv), (d)-(i)
(4) (a)-(iii), (b)-(i), (c)-(ii), (d)-(iv)

69. Match the following constructs of asset pricing with its propagators.

Asset Pricing Constructs	Proposer(s)
(a) Mean-Variance portfolio criterion	(i) Black and Scholes
(b) Size and Book to market value portfolios	(ii) Sharpa, Lintner and Mossin
(c) Capital Asset Pricing model	(iii) Fama & French
(d) Derivative (option) pricing	(iv) Markowitze, Harry

Choose the correct match from options given below:

(1) (a)-(iii), (b)-(i), (c)-(iv), (d)-(ii)

(2) (a)-(iv), (b)-(iii), (c)-(ii), (d)-(i)
(3) (a)-(ii), (b)-(iv), (c)-(i), (d)-(iii)
(4) (a)-(iv), (b)-(i), (c)-(iii), (d)-(ii)

70. Match the following constructs With underlying theories on dividend decisions :

List I Dividend Constructs	List II Theories on Dividend
(a) Bird-in-the hand argument	(i) M-M theory
(b) Irrelevance of dividends	(ii) Walter Model
(c) Interdependence of investment and dividend decisions	(iii) Lintner model
(d) Tax considerations in dividend decisions	(iv) Gordon model

Choose the correct options from those given below :
(1) (a)-(ii), (b)-(i), (c)-(iii), (d)-(iv)
(2) (a)-(iv), (b)-(iii), (c)-(i), (d)-(ii)
(3) (a)-(iii), (b)-(ii), (c)-(i), (d)-(iv)
(4) (a)-(iv), (b)-(i), (c)-(ii), (d)-(iii)

71. Match List I with List II

List I (Strategy)	List II (Example)
(a) Merger	(i) HUL-TOMCO
(b) Acquisition	(ii) Kelvinator-Whirlpool
(c) Takeover	(iii) Diamlerchrysler-AG
(d) Hostile bid	(iv) L & T Technology-Mind Tree

Choose the correct option from the given below :
(1) (a)-(i), (b)-(ii), (c)-(iii), (d)-(iv)
(2) (a)-(iii), (b)-(ii), (c)-(iv), (d)-(i)
(3) (a)-(ii), (b)-(iv), (c)-(i), (d)-(iii)
(4) (a)-(iii), (b)-(i), (c)-(ii), (d)-(iv)

72. Match List I with List II :

List I (Branding Strategy)	List II (Meaning)
(a) Line Extension	(i) New product category and existing brand name
(b) Brand Extension	(ii) Existing product category and existing brand name
(c) Multi Brands	(iii) Existing product category and new brand names
(d) Co-branding	(iv) Putting two established brand names of different companies on the same product

Choose the correct option from the given below :
(1) (a)-(i), (b)-(ii), (c)-(iii), (d)-(iv)
(2) (a)-(ii), (b)-(i)- (c)-(iii), (d)-(iv)
(3) (a)-(iii), (b)-(i), (c)-(ii), (d)-(iv)
(4) (a)-(i), (b)-(iii), (c)-(ii), (d)-(iv)

73. Match the following product categories and quality certification mark(s).

Product Categories	Quality Certification Marks
(a) Gold and silver jewellery	(i) ISI Mark
(b) Agricultural products	(ii) FPO Mark
(c) Industrial products	(iii) BIS Hallmark
(d) Processed food products	(iv) AGMARK

Choose the correct match from the options given below :
(1) (a)-(i), (b)-(ii), (c)-(iv), (d)-(iii)
(2) (a)-(i), (b)-(iv), (c)-(iii), (d)-(ii)
(3) (a)-(iii), (b)-(ii), (c)-(i), (d)-(iv)
(4) (a)-(iii), (b)-(iv), (c)-(i), (d)-(ii)

74. Match List I with List II

List I (Theories of International Trade)	List II (Propounder (s))
(a) Theory of Absolute Advantage	(i) Raymond Vernon

(b) Factor Proportion Theory (ii) Steffan Linder

(c) Country Similarity Theory (iii) Heckscher Ohlin

(d) Product Life Cycle Theory (iv) Adam Smith

Choose the correct opt-ion from the given below:

(1) (a)-(i), (b)-(ii), (c)-(iii), (d)-(iv)
(2) (a)-(iv), (b)-(ii) (c)-(iii), (d)-(i)
(3) (a)-(iv), (b)-(m), (c)-(ii), (c)-(i)
(4) (a)-(iii), (b)-(ii), (c)-(iv), (d)-(i)

75. An MNC Wants to invest in India. Of the following entry modes, select the right order in terms of increasing risk?

(a) Co-operative joint venture
(b) Branch office
(c) Portfolio investment
(d) Wholy owned subsidiary
(e) Equity joint venture

Select correct option:

(1) (d), (c), (e), (a) and (b)
(2) (b), (a), (e), (c) and (d)
(3) (a), (b), (e), (d) and (c)
(4) (c), (a), (e), (b) and (d)

76. Budgeting is closely related to planning in an organisation. It involves four stages and their correct sequence is

(1) Setting the objectives, specifying the goals, laying down the strategies, preparation of budget
(2) Setting the objectives, laying down the strategies, specifying the goals, preparation of budget
(3) Laying down the strategies, setting the objectives, specifying the goals, preparation of budget
(4) Specifying the goals, setting the objectives, laying down the strategies, preparation of budget

77. A global manager has cultural predisposition as follows:

(a) Regiocentricisin
(b) Geocentricisin
(c) Polycentricism
(d) Ethnocentricism

Which one of the following sequence is correct?

(1) (a), (b), (c) and (d)
(2) (c), (d), (a) and (b)
(3) (b), (a), (c) and (d)
(4) (d), (c), (a) and (b)

78. The steps followed in developing a global pay system in right sequence are:

(1) Set strategy, identify crucial executive behaviour, global philosophy framework, identify gaps, systematize pay system, adopt pay policies
(2) Set strategy, global philosophy framework, identify gaps, identify crucial executive behaviour, adopt pay policies, systematize pay system
(3) Identify crucial executive behavior, set strategy, global philosophy framework, identify gaps, systeinatize pay system, adopt pay policies
(4) Adopt pay policies, identify crucial executive behaviour, set strategy, global philosophy framework, identify gaps, systematize pay system.

79. The right sequence in respect of stages of group development is

(1) Forming, storming, norming, performing, adjourning
(2) Storming, forming, norming, adjourning, performing
(3) Norming, performing, storming, forming, adjourning
(4) Storming, forming, norming, performing, adjourning

80. There are 7 elements of personal selling which are followed in certain sequence at the time of making sales to customers by salesperson. The correct sequence is

(1) Prospecting, approach, pre-approach, presentation, overcoming objections, follow-up, closing
(2) Pre-approach, approach, prospecting, presentations, overcoming objections, follow-up, closing
(3) Prospecting, pre-approach, approach, presentation, overcoming objections, closing, follow-up
(4) Approach, prospecting, pre-approach, overcoming objections, presentation, closing, follow-up

81. These are five distinct International Expansion Entry modes which are followed by businesses for entering international markets. Their correct sequence is

(1) Licensing, Franchising, Exporting, Partnering, Strategic Alliance
(2) Strategic Alliance, Exporting, Licensing, Partnering, Franchising
(3) Exporting, Strategic Alliance, Partnering, Licensing, Franchising
(4) Exporting, Licensing, Franchising, Partnering, Strategic Alliance

82. Which of the following sequence are the steps of 'QUEST' technique of external economic analysis?

(1) Conceptualization Phase —> Evaluation Phase —> Feedback Phase —> Analysis Phase
(2) Preparation Phase —> Divergent Planning Phase —> Option identification Phase —> Scenario Development Phase
(3) Development Phase —> Scanning Phase —> Evaluation Phase —> Strategic Implementation Phase
(4) Scanning Phase —> Segmentation Phase —> Generative Phase —> Review Phase

83. International negotiation is a seven step process comprising of the following

(a) Information exchange and offer
(b) Concession
(c) Preparation
(d) Building a relationship
(e) Strategy
(f) Persuasion
(g) Agreement

Which of the following sequence is in the light order?

(1) (e), (c), (a), (f), (g), (b) and (d)
(2) (c), (e), (d), (a), (f), (b) and (g)
(3) (g), (c), (e), (f), (d), (a) and (b)
(4) (d), (a), (c), (e), (f), (g) and (b)

84. Marketing feasibility of any idea includes the following aspects :

(a) Current and future demand estimates
(b) Market segmentation and identification of target markets
(c) Competition analysis
(d) Market testing

Which of the following option are correct?

(1) (a), (b) and (c) only
(2) (b), (c) and (d) only
(3) (a) and (b) only
(4) (a), (b), (c) and (d)

85. For marketing the products of MSME, marketing strategy has to be formulated which consists of 4Ps

(a) Product (b) Promotion
(c) Place (d) Price

Which one of the following sequence is correct?

(1) (a), (b), (c) and (d)
(2) (a), (b), (c) and (d)
(3) (a), (d), (c) and (b)
(4) (a), (c), (d) and (b)

86. Given below are two statements labelled as Assertion (A) and Reason (R).

Assertion (A) : Every product or service should be branded otherwise they will be treated as commodity.

Reasons (R) : If the product or service is branded then it always commands a higher price.

Read the statements and choose the correct answer from the options given below :

(1) Both (A) and (R) are correct and (R) is the right explanation of (A)
(2) Both (A) and (R) are correct and (R) is not the right explanation of (A)
(3) (A) is correct but (R) is incorrect
(4) Both (A) and (R) are correct

87. Given below are two statements labelled as Assertion (A) and Reason (R). Read the statements and answer the question that follows:

Assertion (A) : International product standardisation is least costly in terms of both manufacturing and marketing costs for the company. So companies should bring uniformity in their marketing mix elements

Reasons (R) : No change in the product itself is required for marketing overseas but many items may require some adaptation for making them suitable to the foreign markets.

Which of the following options is correct?

(1) Both the statements (A) and (R) are correct and (R) is the correct explanation of (A)
(2) Both (A) and (R) are correct but (R) is not the correct explanation of (A)
(3) Statement (A) is correct but (R) is incorrect
(4) Both statements (A) and (R) are incorrect

88. Given below are two statements labelled as Assertion (A) and Reason (R). Read the statements and answer the question that follows:

Assertion (A) : The basic thrust of strategic decision making in the process of strategic management is to make a choice regarding the courses of action to adopt, which is the primary task of the senior management.

Reasons (R) : This is so because the basic concern in strategic management is to seek answers to questions. What is our business? What will it be? and What should it be?

Which of the following options is correct'?

(1) Both the statements (A) and (R) are correct and (R) is the right explanation of (A)
(2) Both the statements (A) and (R) are correct but (R) is not the right explanation of (A)
(3) Statement (A) is correct but statement (R) is incorrect
(4) Both statements (A) and (R) are incorrect

89. Two statements given below are labelled as Assertion (A) and Reason (R). Read the statements and answer the question that follows.

Assertion (A) : Plant location is often oriented toward dominant factors such as raw material sources While Warehouse location is definitely distribution oriented.

Reason (R) : Plant location decision is driven by the competition and competitor While the Warehouse location decision is exclusively driven by the cost considerations.

Which of the following options is the correct?

(1) Both statements are correct and statement (R) is the correct explanation of statement (A)
(2) Both the statements are correct and statement (R) is not the correct explanation of (A)
(3) Statement (A) is correct and statement (R) is not correct
(4) Statement (R) is correct and statement (A) is not correct

90. Given below are two statements labelled as Assertion (A) and Reason (R). Read the statements and answer the question that follows:

Assertion (A) : The addition of independent variable(s) causes the predictions error to become smaller

Reasons (R) : With addition of independent variable, R^2 becomes larger to cause smaller prediction error

Which of the following options is correct?

(1) Both statements are correct and (R) is the correct explanation of (A)

(2) Both statements are true and (R) is not the correct explanation of (A)

(3) Statement (A) is correct and Statement (R) is incorrect

(4) Statement (R) is correct» and Statement (A) is incorrect

Question Numbers : (91 to 95).

Question Label Comprehension

Based on the information given below, answer the questions which follow.

Kruger Corporation has recently implemented a standard cost system. The management has obtained the following information for variance analysis :

(a) Standard cost information :

Direct materials	=	Rs. 5 per kg.
Quantity allowed per unit	=	100 kg per unit
Direct labour rate	=	Rs. 20 per hour
Hours allowed per unit	=	2 hours per unit
Fixed overhead budget	=	Rs. 12.000 per month
Normal level of production	=	1.200 units
Fixed overhead application rate	=	Rs. 10 per unit
Variable overhead applicable rate	=	Rs. 2 per unit
Total overhead applicable rate	=	Rs. 12 per unit

(b) Actual cost information :

Cost of material purchased and consumed	=	Rs. 4.68.000
Quantity of material purchased and consumed	=	Rs. 1.04.000 kg
Cost of direct labour	=	Rs. 46.480
Hours of direct labour	=	2240 Hrs.
Cost of variable overhead	=	Rs. 2.352
Cost of fixed overhead	=	Rs. 12.850
Volume of production	=	1000 units

Sub questions

91. What is the direct materials price variance, given an actual price of Rs. 4.00 per kg?

(1) Rs. 20,600 unfavourable

(2) Rs. 52,600 favourable

(3) Rs. 48,600 favourable

(4) Rs. 52.000 unfavourable

92. What is the material quantity variance?

(1) Rs. 26.000 favourable

(2) Rs. 20,000 unfavourable

(3) Rs. 28,000 favourable

(4) Rs. 29,000 unfavourable

93. What is the labour efficiency variance?

(1) Rs. 4,800 unfavourable

(2) Rs. 4,200 favourable

(3) Rs. –1,800 favourable

(4) Rs. 1,200 unfavourable

94. Obtain the overhead spending variance.

(1) Rs. 29,202 unfavourable

(2) Rs. 1.202 unfavourable

(3) Rs. 1,200 favourable

(4) Rs. 15.202 favourable

95. What is the overhead volume variance?

(1) Rs. 4,600 favourable

(2) Rs. 2,200 unfavourable

(3) Rs. 4,000 unfavourable

(4) Rs. 2,000 unfavourable

Question Numbers : (96 to 100).

Question Label : Comprehension

Read the passage and attempt the questions that follow :

Dinesh, a young executive, joined Softech Co. three months back. Coming with a brilliant academic record, he played key role to revamp the company's finance and management procedures for which he was recognized by the management. But now his performance has come down with mistakes found in most of his actions. Several things transpired against him. His only son turned spastic and he was overlooked for promotion against a new comer. This witnessed him becoming less popular among staff. Adding to that, a mild flirtation with a female employee was blown out of proportion.

Dinesh has became emotionally and professionally depressed with morale down and seemed loosing self-confidence badly.

Sub questions

96. As HR Manager which life positions in Transactional Analysis would you expect Dinesh to have?

(1) I'm Ok, You are Ok
(2) I'm Ok, You are not Oh
(3) I'm not Ok, You are Ok
(4) I'm not Ok, You are not Ok

97. Which type of promotion policy would you recommend to Softech Co ?

(a) Career ladder
(b) Merit Based
(c) Accretion of duties
(d) Competitive and non-competitive

Choose the correct option from the following

(1) (a) and (b)
(2) (b) and (c)
(3) (c) and (d)
(4) (a) and (c)

98. As HR Manager, which counseling mode would you choose for Dinesh?

(1) Developmental mode
(2) Disciplinary mode
(3) Open ended mode
(4) Unbiased mode

99. The HR Manager should impart which of the following skills to Dinesh'?

(1) Technical skills
(2) Peoples skills
(3) Communication skills
(4) Negotiating skills

100. Which management approach should the HR Manager deploy for Dinesh here?

(1) HR Approach
(2) Contingency Approach
(3) Systems Approach
(4) Interactionalism Approach

ANSWER KEY

1. (4)	**2.** (1)	**3.** (1)	**4.** (1)	**5.** (4)	**6.** (1)	**7.** (4)	**8.** (4)	**9.** (4)	**10.** (4)
11. (2)	**12.** (4)	**13.** (3)	**14.** (3)	**15.** (4)	**16.** (4)	**17.** (1)	**18.** (1)	**19.** (3)	**20.** (2)
21. (4)	**22.** (4)	**23.** (3)	**24.** (1)	**25.** (3)	**26.** (1)	**27.** (2)	**28.** (1)	**29.** (1)	**30.** (4)
31. (3)	**32.** (4)	**33.** (2)	**34.** (3)	**35.** (3)	**36.** (3)	**37.** (4)	**38.** (4)	**39.** (1)	**40.** (3)
41. (4)	**42.** (3)	**43.** (2)	**44.** (4)	**45.** (2)	**46.** (4)	**47.** (3)	**48.** (1)	**49.** (4)	**50.** (2)
51. (3)	**52.** (4)	**53.** (1)	**54.** (3)	**55.** (3)	**56.** (3)	**57.** (4)	**58.** (4)	**59.** (2)	**60.** (3)
61. (4)	**62.** (2)	**63.** (2)	**64.** (2)	**65.** (2)	**66.** (1)	**67.** (1)	**68.** (2)	**69.** (2)	**70.** (4)
71. (4)	**72.** (2)	**73.** (4)	**74.** (3)	**75.** (2)	**76.** (1)	**77.** (4)	**78.** (1)	**79.** (1)	**80.** (3)
81. (4)	**82.** (2)	**83.** (2)	**84.** (1)	**85.** (3)	**86.** (3)	**87.** (2)	**88.** (1)	**89.** (2)	**90.** (1)
91. (4)	**92.** (2)	**93.** (1)	**94.** (2)	**95.** (4)	**96.** (1)	**97.** (2)	**98.** (1)	**99.** (2)	**100.** (4)

SEPTEMBER, 2020

MANAGEMENT

PAPER-II

Note : This paper contains **hundred (100)** objective type questions of **two (2)** marks each. **All** questions are **compulsory**.

1. Which of the following oligopoly firms architectural framework is often described as the First-Mover Advantage Model?
   (1) The Cournot Model
   (2) Stackelberg Model
   (3) The Bertrand Model
   (4) The Kinked Demand Curve Model
2. What is NOT an assumption underpinning the rational decision-making model?
   (1) Incomplete information
   (2) An agreed goal
   (3) A structured problem
   (4) High level of certainty regarding the environment
3. The problems arising from expression in communication are called?
   (1) Spatial barriers
   (2) Semantic problems
   (3) Wrong Assumptions
   (4) Selecting perception
4. What is a paradigm?
   (1) A theoretical assumption
   (2) An illustration
   (3) An example sewing as a model
   (4) A theoretical model
5. Which one of the following comprises people with complementary skills committed to a common purpose, common performance goals and an approach for which they hold themselves mutually accountable?
   (1) Group (2) Team
   (3) Organisation (4) Firm
6. Demonstration type of training method is used to train
   (1) Supervisors (2) Workers
   (3) Managers
   (4) Senior Executives
7. One trait that dominates a personality so much that it influences nearly everything a person does is a
   (1) Global Trait (2) Specific Trait
   (3) Cardinal Trait (4) Central Trait
8. Personality tests are given to measure a prospective employee's motivation to function in a particular working environment. There are various tests designed to assess a candidate's personality. Name the test which measures one's self-sufficiency, neurotic tendency, sociability introversion and extroversion, locus of control and self-confidence
   (1) The Bernreuter Personality Inventory
   (2) The Thematic Apperception Test
   (3) The Thurstone Temperament Survey
   (4) Minnesota Multiphasic Personality Test
9. Which one of the following is a position from which someone is unlikely to move to a higher level of work responsibility?
   (1) Career Goals (2) Career Path
   (3) Career Progression
   (4) Career Plateau
10. The balanced scorecard developed by Kaplan and Norton contains four dimensions. Which one out of the following is one of the dimensions of the balanced scorecard?

(1) Competitor-Analysis
(2) Customer service
(3) Human Resources
(4) Production Management

11. Which one of the following means a mandatory settlement of an industrial dispute by a labour court or a tribunal?
(1) Collective bargaining
(2) Arbitration
(3) Conciliation
(4) Adjudication

12. Who among the following has developed the Institutional Theory of Work-life Initiative?
(1) Daft and Weick
(2) Milliken et al
(3) Dimaggio and Powell
(4) Pfeffer and Salancik

13. As a regulatory norm in India, a listed company in ordinary course is required to report quarterly results within how many days of the end of the quarters?
(1) 45 (2) 15
(3) 30 (4) 90

14. Which of the following is excluded from the responsibility of the International Accounting Standards Board (IASB)?
(1) Harmonization and convergence of Accounting Standards.
(2) Promulgation and adaption of Generally Accepted Accounting Principles (GAAP).
(3) Promulgation of International Accounting Standards.
(4) Promulgation and gaining acceptance of International Financial Reporting Standards (IFRS)

15. A firm's current asset and current liabilities are Rs.1600 and Rs.1000, respectively. How much can it borrow on a short-term basis without reducing the current ratio below 1.25?
(1) Rs 2000 (2) Rs 1280
(3) Rs 1400 (4) Rs 1080

16. From the information given below, find out the efficiency ratio of the firm's operations: Budgeted production: 880 Units, Actual production: 750 Units
Standard hours per unit: 10 hours, Actual working hours: 6000 hours
(1) 125% (2) 80%
(3) 75% (4) 120%

17. Given the interest rate on a 1-year loan is 14.5 per cent and inflation is expected to be 6.5 per cent in India. What should be the interest rate on a 1-year maturity loan in Thailand when the expected inflation rate is 8.5 per cent?
(1) 18.35 per cent
(2) 14.65 per cent
(3) 16.65 per cent
(4) 16.35 per cent

18. The linear relation between the excess return on individual securities and the overall market at every point in time is known as
(1) Capital Market Line (CML)
(2) Security Market Line (SML)
(3) Security Characteristic Line (SCL)
(4) Market Specification Bias (MSB)

19. What should be Economic Order Quality (EOQ) for procurement of 20000 units annually at a price of Rs.12 per unit for consumption in production, when the cost per order is Rs.2000 and the inventory carrying cost is 25 per cent of inventory value?
(1) 6000 units (2) 5164 units
(3) 6145 units (4) 5416 units

20. Which one of the following describes the relationship between the market value of a firm's securities and the replacement cost of its physical assets?
(1) Tobin's q-ratio
(2) Residual analysis
(3) Retention ratio
(4) Book to price ratio

21. What are the segmentation variables used to segment the market for toothpaste as a product?

(1) Demographic Segmentation Bases
(2) Psychological Segmentation Bases
(3) Behavioural Segmentation Bases
(4) Geographical Segmentation Bases

22. The stages of a turnaround process are
(1) Realignment, Retrenchment, Recovery
(2) Realignment, Stabilize, Recovery
(3) Reassess, Stabilize, Survival
(4) Reassess, Retrenchment, Survival

23. In Porter's Generic Strategies Model, a focus strategy involves
(1) Selling a limited range of products.
(2) Selling to a narrow customers segment.
(3) Selling to one region only.
(4) Selling simple products that are cheap to produce.

24. This system of distribution channel consists of producers, wholesalers and retailers acting as a unified system. One channel member owns the others, has contracts with them, or wields so much power that they must cooperate. Name this system of channel distribution
(1) Conventional distribution channel.
(2) Vertical marketing system (VMS).
(3) Consumer distribution system.
(4) National marketing distribution system.

25. Complex Buying Behaviour is characterised by
(1) Products are of low risk but the involvement level is high.
(2) When the level of involvement is high and the significant difference between brands is low.
(3) When the level of involvement is low and significant difference among brands is high.
(4) When the level of Involvement is high and significant difference among brands is high.

26. A Brand Extension Strategy refers to
(1) Extending existing brand names to new forms of an existing product category.
(2) Extending an existing brand name to a new or modified product in a new category.
(3) Coming out with different brands in a given product category.
(4) All the above

27. Coke has started coke parlours - the Red Lounge - for tech crazy adolescents called experience outlet. What type of differentiation strategy can this be called?
(1) Differentiating the service utilizing Brand Image.
(2) Differentiating through People.
(3) Differentiating through Process.
(4) Differentiating through Physical Evidence.

28. The CRM Strategy adopted by Big Bazar in India is all about
(1) Frequency Marketing Program.
(2) Club Membership Program.
(3) Structural Relationship Program.
(4) Experiential Relationship Program

29. Six Sigma level of Quality management results in
(1) 34 defects per one million.
(2) 3.4 defects per million.
(3) 3.0 defects per million.
(4) 3.2 defects per million.

30. Automobile Assembly or Manufacturing follows which one of the following types of layout?
(1) Process Layout.
(2) Fix d—Position Layout.
(3) Product-Focused Layout.
(4) Cellular Layout

31. Which one of the following is NOT a method of primary data collection?
(1) Interview (2) Questionnaire
(3) Delphi method
(4) Documents

32. One use of a regression line is
(1) To determine if any x values are outliers.

(2) To determine if any y values are outliers.
(3) To determine if a change in x causes a change in y.
(4) To estimate the change in y for a one-unit change in x.

33. Which of the following international Trade theories, the 'Leontief Paradox' pertains to
(1) Comparative Advantage theory.
(2) Product life cycle theory.
(3) Heckscher-Ohlin theory.
(4) Absolute Advantage theory.

34. FDI in multi-brand retailing in India is
(1) Capped to 49 per cent and had to approach the Department of Industrial Policy and Promotion (DIPP) for permission.
(2) Capped to 51% but not under Automatic Route in India.
(3) Capped to 51% but under Automatic Route.
(4) Capped to 51% but under Automatic Route with few strings attached.

35. The current Foreign Trade Policy (FTP) announced by Government of India covers the policy period
(1) 1995 - 2000 (2) 2000 - 2005
(3) 1996 - 2001 (4) 2015 - 2020

36. An Information system that captures and records fundamental business events is a(n)
(1) Transaction Processing System.
(2) Executive Information System.
(3) Decision Support System.
(4) Expert System.

37. Under the Sick Industrial Companies (Special Provision) Act, 1985, a sick Industrial company means
(1) Being a company registered for not less than 10 years which has at the end of any financial year accumulated losses equal to 50% of its net worth.
(2) Being a company registered for not less than 5 years which has at the end of any financial year accumulated losses equal to or exceeding its entire net worth.
(3) Being a company which has accumulated losses equal to its entire net worth.
(4) Being a company which immediately after start, has accumulated losses which eat up 50% of its net worth.

38. Disruptive innovations in business are those that
(1) Create a new market by offering value products.
(2) Involve often, new technology or a new business model to offer value to the market.
(3) Displace established market-leading firms, products and alliances.
(4) All of the above.

39. Marketing Support/Assistance to MSMEs for Bar Code allows
(1) Reimbursement of 80% of the one-time registration fee and 80% of the annual recurring fee for first three years paid by MSMEs to GS1 India for bar coding.
(2) Reimbursement of 75% of the one-time registration fee only paid by MSMEs to GS1 India for barcoding.
(3) Reimbursement of 75% of the recurring fee for first three years paid to GS1 by MSMEs for barcoding.
(4) Reimbursement of 75% of the one-time registration fee and 75% of the annual recurring fee for first three years paid by MSMEs to GS1 India for barcoding.

40. The MSMED Act to cover micro, small and medium Industries in India was introduced in
(1) June, 2006 (2) June, 2005
(3) June, 2007 (4) August, 2008

41. The approaches to management thinking which were developed during the first half of the 20th century are:
(A) Scientific management, general administrative, quantitative and contingency approach.

(B) Scientific management, general administrative, quantitative and organizational behaviour.
(C) General administrative, globalization, organizational behaviour and quantitative.
(D) System approach, scientific management, General administrative and organizational behaviour.

Choose the correct answer from the options given below:

(1) A and B (2) B and C
(3) B only (4) D only

42. In a rising income scenario, the obvious decision choices of firms having very low-income elasticity for their products would be
(A) Search for new markets
(B) Product innovation
(C) Discontinuation of product line
(D) Product line extension
(E) Exporting

Choose the most appropriate answer from the options given below:

(1) A, B and C only
(2) C, D and E only
(3) B and D only
(4) B and E only

43. The underlying principles of the Combined Code of Corporate Governance and Conduct are:
(A) Acceptability (B) Openness
(C) Integrity
(D) Accountability and Responsibility

Choose the correct answer from the options given below:

(1) A only (2) A and C
(3) B and D (4) D only

44. Which of the following HR decisions can be influenced by HR analytics?
(A) HR Planning
(B) Succession Planning
(C) Hiring
(D) Performance
(E) Compensation and Rewards

Choose the most appropriate answer from the options given below:

(1) A, C, D only
(2) C, E only
(3) C, D, E only
(4) A, B, C, D and E

45. Which of the following should be avoided by interviewers?
(A) Establish an easy and informal relationship.
(B) Analyze career and interests to reveal strengths, weaknesses, patterns of behaviour.
(C) Ask leading questions.
(D) Plunge too quickly into demanding questions.
(E) Encourage the candidate to talk.

Choose the most appropriate answer from the options given below:

(1) A, C, D only
(2) C, D only
(3) C, D, E only
(4) B, C only

46. What out of the following are the involvements of the Strategic Human Resource Management in Corporate Strategy?
(A) Human Resources Management is fully integrated with the strategy and the strategic needs of the firm.
(B) Human resource policies cohere both across policy areas and across hierarchies.
(C) Human Resource practices are adjusted, accepted and used by line managers and employees as part of their daily work.
(D) Human Resources architecture is composed of the systems, practices, competencies, and employee performance behaviours that reflect the development and management of the firm's human resources.

Choose the most appropriate answer from the options given below:

(1) A, B, C only (2) B, C, D only
(3) A, B, C and D (4) A, C, D only

47. 'Award' under the Industrial Dispute Act. 1947 is:
(A) Interim determination of Labour court.
(B) Not an arbitration award under section 10A.
(C) Final determination of labour court.
(D) Not final determination of arbitration award under section 10A.
Choose the most appropriate answer from the options given below:
(1) A and C only (2) A and B only
(3) A, B and C only (4) B and D only

48. Which of the following labour laws are related to working hours, conditions of services and employment?
(A) The Payment of Wages Act. 1936.
(B) The Trade Union Act. 1926.
(C) The Factories Act, 1948.
(D) The Mines Act, 1952.
Choose the most appropriate answer from the options given below:
(1) A and C only (2) A and D only
(3) C and D only (4) B, C and D only

49. Which of the following statements are included in financial statements?
(A) Cash flow statement.
(B) Funds flow statement.
(C) Balance sheet.
(D) Statement of change in equity.
(E) Income statement.
Choose the most appropriate answer from the options given below:
(1) A, B, C and D only
(2) A, C, D and E only
(3) B, C, D and E only (4) B, C and E only

50. Which of the following cause conflicting ranking of an investment opportunity under the NPV and IRR criteria?
(A) Cash flow pattern disparity.
(B) Investment size disparity.
(C) Investment life disparity.
(D) Product life cycle disparity.
Choose the most appropriate answer from the options given below:
(1) A, B and C only
(2) B, C and D only
(3) A, C and D only
(4) A, B and D only

51. For which of the following considerations, investors prefer current (near) cashflows over the future (distant) cashflows?
(A) Inflation and value erosion.
(B) Risk aversion and avoidance.
(C) Liquidity preferences.
(D) Return generation and value protection.
(E) Risk appetite and tolerance.
Choose the most appropriate answer from the options given below:
(1) A, B and E only (2) B, D and E only
(3) A, D and E only (4) A, B, C and D only

52. Based on asymmetric information, managers prefer to finance firms' capital structure in which order as postulated in the Pecking Order Theory?
(A) Retained earnings and internal sources.
(B) External debt financing.
(C) Hybrid security and convertible bonds.
(D) New issue of Equity shares.
Choose the correct order from the options given below:
(1) A, D, C and B (2) A, B, C and D
(3) B, C, A and D (4) C, D, A and B

53. Which of the following are integral dimensions of a firm's credit policy?
(A) Credit Standards
(B) Credit appraisal
(C) Credit period
(D) Cash discount
(E) Collection policy
Choose the most appropriate answer from the options given below:
(1) A, B, C and D only
(2) A, C, D and E only
(3) A, B, D and E only
(4) A, B, C and E only

54. According to Ansoff Product-Market Expansion Grid, intensification can be achieved through three distinct strategies. Identify them out of the following:

(A) Market Attractiveness.

(B) Market Penetration.

(C) Market Development.

(D) Product Development.

Choose the correct answer from the options given below:

(1) A, B and C only (2) B, C and D only

(3) A, B and D only (4) A, C and D only

55. Under the cost-based pricing, the following methods/approaches are commonly used:

(A) Marginal cost pricing.

(B) Markup pricing (cost-plus pricing).

(C) Absorption cost pricing (full cost pricing).

(D) Return on Investment pricing.

Choose the correct answer from the options given below:

(1) A, B and C only (2) B, C and D only

(3) A, C, and D only

(4) A, B, C and D - All

56. Planning, implementing and controlling the physical flow of materials, final goods and related information from points of origin to points of consumption to meet customer requirements at a profit is known as:

(A) Inventory Management.

(B) Marketing Logistics.

(C) Physical Distribution.

(D) Selling Management.

Choose the correct answer from the options given below:

(1) A and B only (2) B and C only

(3) C and D only (4) A and D only

57. Customer Relationship Management (CRM) performs several tasks and brings several benefits.

Identify them out of the following:

(A) Support cross-selling and upselling to existing customers.

(B) Manages customer interaction and customer service.

(C) Serves as a sustainable competitive advantage.

(D) Helps convert buyers into profitable customers, build enduring relations with them and retain them as customers for life.

Choose the correct answer from the options given below:

(1) A, B and C only

(2) B, C and D only

(3) A, C, and D only

(4) A, B, C and D - All

58. Identify the most important types of retail stores:

(A) Convenience store.

(B) Online store.

(C) Departmental store.

(D) Direct-selling store.

(E) Superstore.

Choose the correct answer from the options given below:

(1) A, B and C only (2) A, C and E only

(3) B, C and D only (4) A, D and E only

59. For calculating arithmetic mean for a grouped data set, assumptions are:

(A) The class intervals must be closed.

(B) The width of each class interval should be equal.

(C) The mid-value of each class interval must represent the average of all values in that class.

(D) All values of observations can not be evenly distributed.

Choose the most appropriate answer from the options given below:

(1) A and B only (2) A, B and C only

(3) A and C only (4) A, B, C and D

60. The function which states the determinants of the quality to be either maximized or minimized is called as:

(A) Feasible function.

(B) Optimal function.

(C) Criterion function.
(D) Sustainability function.
(E) Objective function.
Choose the correct answer from the options given below:
(1) A, B and C only (2) C and D only
(3) C and E only (4) C, D and E only

61. What is a social enterprise concerned with?
(A) Profit Maximization.
(B) Maximizing Market Share.
(C) Providing Public Service.
(D) Running a business to create social benefits.
(E) To maximize improvements in financial, social and environmental well-being.
Choose the most appropriate answer from the options given below:
(1) A, D and E only (2) C, D and E only
(3) D and E only (4) A, B, D and E only

62. At the time of exporting goods from India, what documents are to be filed for custom clearance of goods?
(A) Shipping bill.
(B) Airway bill.
(C) Invoice (Commercial Invoice).
(D) Packing list
(E) Marine Insurance Policy.
Choose the correct answer from the options given below:
(1) A, C, D only (2) A, B, C, D only
(3) A, C, D, E only (4) A, C, E only

63. Identify the techniques of Artificial intelligence from the following:
(A) Artificial Neural Networks.
(B) Heuristics
(C) Fuzzy models.
(D) Support Vector.
(E) Genetic Algorithms.
Choose the most appropriate answer from the options given below:
(1) A, C, D only (2) A, C, E only
(3) C, D, E only (4) A, B, C only

64. International Cooperation Scheme under marketing promotion scheme to MSME entrepreneurs is available for what type of activities?
(A) Participation in international exhibitions, trade fairs.
(B) Giving advertisements in international trade journals.
(C) Participation in buyer-seller meets in foreign countries.
(D) For meeting overseas agents and negotiating business.
(E) For availing overseas grants and aids.
Choose the most appropriate answer from the options given below:
(1) A, and C only (2) A, B and C only
(3) A, C and D only (4) A and D only

65. The statement "Entrepreneurship is a mother of foresight and willingness to assume risks in undertakings particularly a new one". Who has said above the underlined portion of the statement?
(A) Richard Cantillon.
(B) Leon Walras.
(C) William Diamond.
(D) Peter F. Drucker.
(E) J.A. Schumpeter.
Choose the correct answer from the options given below:
(1) A, C only (2) B, C only
(3) D, E only (4) C, E only

66. Match List I with List II

List I	List II
(A) Consumer clinics	I. Consumers shop in a store screen and purchasing it by touching the picture of a shopping cart.
(B) Market experiments	II. It is the simulation of consumer behaviour using computer models based on the theory of

	complexity to assess the impact of managerial decisions.
(C) Virtual shopping	III. These are conducted in the actual market place with similar socio-economic characteristics to record consumer responses consequent to given change(s) in demand determinants.
(D) Virtual management	IV. These are laboratory experiments in which the participants are given a sum of money and asked to spend it in a simulated store to see how they react to changes.

Choose the correct answer from the options given below:

(1) A-II, B-III, C-I, D-IV
(2) A-IV, B-III, C-I, D-II
(3) A-III, B-I, C-II, D-IV
(4) A-IV, B-III, C-II, D-I

67. Match List I with List II

List I	List II
(A) I am OK, you are OK	I. Avoidant
(B) I am OK, you are not OK	II. Bossing
(C) I am not OK, you are OK	III. Competent
(D) I am not OK, you are not OK	IV. Diffident

Choose the correct answer from the options given below:

(1) A-III, B-I, C-IV, D-II
(2) A-III, B-II, C-IV, D-I
(3) A-II, B-III, C-IV, D-I
(4) A-II, B-IV, C-III, D-I

68. Match List I with List II

List I	List II
(A) Labour welfare is a desirable state of existence comprehending physical, mental, moral and emotional health or well being.	I. Relative concept
(B) In planning for welfare, the individual alone should not be taken into consideration.	II. Positive concept
(C) Welfare work differs over time and place.	III. Social concept
(D) Welfare connotes at least minimum desirable conditions of existence biologically and socially determined.	IV. Total concept

Choose the correct answer from the options given below:

(1) A-II, B-IV, C-III, D-I
(2) A-III, B-II, C-I, D-IV
(3) A-IV, B-I, C-II, D-III
(4) A-IV, B-III, C-I, D-II

69. Match List I with List II

List I	List II
(A) Ind. AS 8	I. Statement of cash flows.
(B) Ind. AS 110	II. Accounting Policies, Changes in Accounting Estimates and Errors.
(C) Ind. AS 7	III. Related Party Disclosure.
(D) Ind. AS 24	IV. Consolidated Financial Statements.

Choose the correct answer from the options given below:

(1) A-III, B-IV, C-II, D-I
(2) A-II, B-IV, C-III, D-I

(3) A-II, B-IV, C-I, D-III
(4) A-IV, B-II, C-I, D-III

70. Match List I with List II

List I	List II
(A) Value creation	I. Time value of money
(B) Value protection	II. Options and futures
(C) Asset pricing	III. Merger and Acquisitions
(D) Price discovery	IV. CAPM and APT

Choose the correct answer from the options given below:
(1) A-III, B-I, C-IV, D-II
(2) A-II, B-IV, C-I, D-III
(3) A-I, B-II, C-III, D-IV
(4) A-IV, B-III, C-II, D-I

71. Match List I with List II

List I	List II
(A) Corporate Strategy	I. Turnaround Strategy
(B) Directional Strategy	II. Parenting Strategy
(C) Retrenchment Strategy	III. Pause/Proceed with Caution Strategy
(D) Stability Strategy	IV. Growth Strategy

Choose the correct answer from the options given below:
(1) A-IV, B-III, C-II, D-I
(2) A-II, B-IV, C-I, D-III
(3) A-I, B-III, C-II, D-IV
(4) A-IV, B-I, C-III, D-II

72. Match List I with List II

List I	List II
(A) Product	I. Click and mortar companies
(B) Price	II. Disintermediation
(C) Place	III. EDLP
(D) Promotion	IV. Brand

Choose the correct answer from the options given below:
(1) A-I, B-II, C-III, D-IV
(2) A-III, B-IV, C-II, D-I
(3) A-IV, B-III, C-II, D-I
(4) A-II, B-IV, C-I, D-III

73. Match List I with List II

List I	List II
(A) Coefficient of range	I. $\frac{\sigma}{\bar{x}} \times 100$
(B) Coefficient of QD	II. $\frac{\text{mean absolute deviation}}{\bar{x} \text{ or Me}}$
(C) Coefficient of MAD	III. $\frac{Q_3 - Q_1}{Q_3 + Q_1}$
(D) Coefficient of variation (CV)	IV. $\frac{H-L}{H+L}$

Choose the correct answer from the options given below:
(1) A-IV, B-III, C-II, D-I
(2) A-III, B-IV, C-I, D-II
(3) A-I, B-II, C-III, D-IV
(4) A-II, B-I, C-IV, D-III

74. Match List I with List II

List I	List II
(A) Bali Package	I. United Nations Conference, 1944
(B) Doha Declaration	II. (9th Ministerial Conference), 2013
(C) Uruguay Round	III. (4th Ministerial Conference), 2001
(D) Bretton woods Conference	IV. (Within GATT), 1986

Choose the correct answer from the options given below:
(1) A-II, B-III, C-I, D-IV
(2) A-I, B-IV, C-III, D-II
(3) A-III, B-II, C-IV, D-I
(4) A-II, B-III, C-IV, D-I

75. Match List I with List II

List I **Business Strategy**	List II **Compensation Strategy**
(A) Invest to grow	I. Reward Personal Growth

(B) Manage Earnings - Protect Market	III. Stress on Cost Control
(C) Harvest Earnings - Reinvest elsewhere	III. Reward Managerial Skills
(D) Total Reward Strategy	IV. Stimulate entrepreneurship

Choose the correct answer from the options given below:

(1) A-II, B-IV, C-I, D-III
(2) A-IV, B-III, C-II, D-I
(3) A-III, B-IV, C-I, D-II
(4) A-I, B-III, C-IV, D-II

76. Find the correct sequence of management theories in their origin:

(A) Bertalanffy's Systems Theory.
(B) Elton Mayo - Human Relations Management Theory.
(C) Max Weber - Bureaucracy Management Theory.
(D) F.W. Taylor - Scientific Management Theory.
(E) Henri Fayol - Administrative Management Theory.

Choose the correct answer from the options given below:

(1) A – B – C – D – E
(2) E – D – A – B – C
(3) C – B – D – A – E
(4) D – E – C – B – A

77. Logically, arrange in sequence the following activities to create the architecture of the ideal manufacturing firm.

(A) Seamlessly integrates the physical and the virtual resources
(B) Operates extremely efficient factories and plants
(C) Concentrates on core competencies and outsources all other operations
(D) Real-time enterprise to respond instantaneously to changes in its business
(E) Learning organization facilitating cross-fertilization of ideas

Choose the correct answer from the options given below:

(1) B, C, A, D, E (2) D, E, C, A, B
(3) C, E, B, A, D (4) C, B, A, E, D

78. Arrange in sequence the following accounting constructs and principles in order of their precedence.

(A) Conservatism
(B) Full disclosure
(C) Separate entity and Going concern
(D) Matching principle
(E) Revenue recognition

Choose the correct answer from the options given below:

(1) A, B, D, C, E (2) C, A, E, D, B
(3) C, D, E, B, A (4) A, D, C, E, B

79. Arrange in sequence the following steps in the construction of the optimum portfolios as per the Sharpe Single Index Model

(A) Ranking of investment opportunities
(B) Determining investment weightages
(C) Identification of investment opportunities
(D) Ascertaining the cut-off point
(E) Allocation and commitment of financial resources

Choose the correct sequence from the options given below:

(1) C, A, D, B, E (2) A, B, C, D, E
(3) C, B, A, D, E (4) C, D, A, B, E

80. Consumers pass through five stages with every purchase. Arrange the stages mentioned below in the correct sequence starting from the first stage.

(A) Information search
(B) Evaluation of alternatives
(C) Post-purchase behaviour
(D) Need recognition
(E) Purchase decision

Choose the correct answer from the options given below:

(1) A, B, C, D, E (2) B, C, D, E, A
(3) D, A, B, E, C (4) D, E, A, B, C

81. Arrange the following in descending order of importance
(A) Free Trade Area
(B) Customs union
(C) Economic cooperation
(D) Economic union
(E) Common markets
Choose the correct answer from the options given below:
(1) C – D – A – E – B
(2) A – C – D – B – E
(3) C – A – D – E – B
(4) C – A – B – E – D

82. The correct sequence in a business plan can be
(A) Executive summary
(B) Details about the Entrepreneur
(C) Marketing and Economic Details
(D) Financial Details
(E) Human Resources Details
Choose the correct answer from the options given below:
(1) A – B – C – D – E
(2) B – C – E – D – A
(3) B – C – A – E – D
(4) A – B – E – D – C

83. Arrange the following group task performances according to the ascending stages of group development.
(A) Clarify all misunderstandings
(B) Termination of task
(C) Highly productive
(D) Work output is low, focused on defining the goals and tasks
(E) Issues are resolved, group norms develop
Choose the correct answer from the options given below:
(1) A, D, E, C, B (2) D, A, C, E, B
(3) D, A, E, C, B (4) D, A, E, B, C

84. Choose the correct set of options in defining the process of 'Six Sigma' in strategic implementation
(A) Define (B) Measure
(C) Establish (D) Improve
(E) Analyze
Choose the correct answer from the options given below:
(1) C – D – B – E – A
(2) D – B – A – E – C
(3) E – D – B – A – C
(4) A – B – E – D – C

85. Arrange the following steps involved in choosing the target market in sequence, starting from the first step
(A) Profile the traits of each segment: characteristics, needs, benefits sought, preferences and buying behavior.
(B) Look for segments which are relatively less satisfied by the current offers of competing brands in the market.
(C) Identify the segment(s), look at each segment as a distinct marketing opportunity and grasp what makes each segment unique.
(D) Evaluate whether the segment meets all the attributes of 'effective segments'. Check which one presents the best opportunity.
(E) Finally, select the best segments - those segments that are most appropriate for the firm - as the target.
Choose the correct answer from the options given below:
(1) A, B, C, D, E (2) B, C, D, E, A
(3) C, A, B, D, E (4) D, A, B, C, E

86. Given below are two Statements: one is labelled as Assertion A and the other is labelled as Reason R
Assertion A: At some point, a product's sales growth will slow down, and it will enter the maturity stage.
This maturity stage normally lasts longer than the previous stages of PLC and it poses strong challenges to marketing management.
Reason R: Slow down in sales growth is due to the acceptance of the product by most potential buyers. It is also due to the entry of

competing firms in the market and price competition stiffening.

In light of the above statements, choose the correct answer from the options given below.

(1) Both A and R are true and R is the correct explanation of A
(2) Both A and R are true but R is NOT the correct explanation of A
(3) A is true but R is false
(4) A is false but R is true

87. Given below are two Statements: one is labelled as Assertion A and the other is labelled as Reason R

Assertion A: Investors around the world are demanding socially and environmentally conscious options in equities, bonds, ETF or hedge funds.

Reason R: Climate change and environment have become 'defining factors' in companies' long-term prospects with a significant reallocation of capital as the shortage of clean water and air have become existential questions.

In light of the above statements, choose the correct answer from the options given below.

(1) Both A and R are true and R is the correct explanation of A
(2) Both A and R are true but R is NOT the correct explanation of A
(3) A is true but R is false
(4) A is false but R is true

88. Given below are two statements:

Statement I: Power of the employee to remove dissatisfaction is low when his position in the organization is extremely important.

Statement II: The more the employees believe that a union can obtain positive work aspects, the more instrumental the union is for the employees.

In light of the above statements, choose the correct answer from the options given below.

(1) Both Statement I and Statement II are true
(2) Both Statement I and Statement II are false
(3) Statement I is correct but Statement II is false
(4) Statement I is incorrect but Statement II is true

89. Given below are two statements:

Statement I: In psychographic segmentation of the market, the science of psychology is used for understanding and segmenting the consumers.

Statement II: Segmenting consumers based on psychographics rests on identifying consumers' state of mind, and hence helps in piecing together with a more incisive profile of the target consumers.

In light of the above statements, choose the most appropriate answer from the options given below.

(1) Both Statement I and Statement II are true
(2) Both Statement I and Statement II are false
(3) Statement I is correct but Statement II is false
(4) Statement I is incorrect but Statement II is true

90. Given below are two statements:

Statement I: Quota sampling is the non-random method of selecting a sample from a population.

Statement II: The standard error of the estimate is inversely proportional to the square root of the sample size.

In light of the above statements, choose the correct answer from the options given below

(1) Both Statement I and Statement II are true
(2) Both Statement I and Statement II are false
(3) Statement I is correct but Statement II is false

(4) Statement I is incorrect but Statement II is true

Question Numbers : (91 to 95)
Question Label : Comprehension
Read the passage and attempt the questions that follow:

Marketing plays a critical role in organizations. It is considered as an entrepreneurial and strategic function of the business. Marketing's main function is to meet customer needs. At the same time, it also needs to generate profit and build a "relationship" with customers. Marketing is different from and larger than selling.

Many different concepts of marketing such as the exchange concept, production concept, product concept, sales concept and marketing concept have been in vogue over the years. Concepts other than the marketing concept result in, 'marketing myopia', which signifies a narrow perception of marketing and a short-sighted view of the business. In fact, all the concepts in vogue turn out to be inadequate, to varying degrees. Marketers are unable to secure the needed practical guidance on the core of marketing from any of them. None of them is centred on the idea of value delivery when value delivery ought to take the centre stage in marketing. There is thus a need for a more concrete perspective on marketing.

In the marketing context, 'value' has certain unique ramifications. 'Benefits' translate into 'value'. People do not buy products, they buy 'value'. The 'value-delivery' process involves selecting the value to be offered, creating the value and capturing the value back from the market through pricing, enhancing and sustaining the value. And 'value delivery' has to be a corporate-level concern.

91. What is the role played by marketing in an organization?
(1) It is considered as an entrepreneurial function of business.
(2) It is considered as a strategic function of business.
(3) It is considered as an entrepreneurial and strategic function of business.
(4) It is considered as sub-ordinate role of business.

92. The main function of the marketing is to
(1) Generate profit
(2) Build relationships with customers
(3) Meet customer needs
(4) Meet customer needs, build relationships with customers and also generate profit

93. Which one of the following different concepts of marketing holds that generating customer satisfaction is the main task of marketing?
(1) Exchange concept
(2) Product concept
(3) Selling concept
(4) Marketing concept

94. Name the process which involves selecting the value to be offered, creating the value, communicating the value, delivering the value and capturing the value back from the market
(1) Product-delivery process
(2) Corporate brand delivery process
(3) Value-delivery process
(4) Marketing process

95. 'Marketing Myopia' concept of marketing refers to
(1) A narrow perception of marketing and a short-sighted view of business.
(2) The value concept of marketing.
(3) Social marketing concept of marketing.
(4) Green marketing concept of marketing.

Question Numbers : (141 to 145)
Question Label : Comprehension
Read the passage and answer the questions that follow:

Mr Mohan, an MBA with specialisation in Human Resources joined a company XYZ into the business of garments in Delhi. Before joining the company XYZ, he had prior experience of working in corporates for 5 years. He has worked in the area of compensation dealing with workers and employees. In the company XYZ, Mr Mohan was entrusted with the work of dealing with both workers and executives and look towards their compensation and remuneration. Mr Mohan has to be abreast with the latest rules of compensation both in theory and as prescribed by the government of Delhi. The company XYZ believed in both types of benefits to be given to their employees – both workers and executives – fringe benefits and non-fringe benefits. For executives, the company XYZ believes in equity both within the company and outside also. All policies of the company XYZ relating to compensation management were told to Mr Mohan and he has to follow them objectively.

96. Executives ask the company XYZ to give them perquisites and Mr Mohan has to decide. Out of the following which one is the prerequisite?
(1) Group Insurance
(2) Medical Allowance
(3) Club Membership
(4) Provident Fund

97. If you were Mr Mohan, which of the following is an example of payment that is consistent from period to period despite the number of hours worked?
(1) Wage (2) Salary
(3) Reward (4) Incentive

98. Management of XYZ company asks Mr Mohan to answer the question that. 'A behaviour which has a rewarding experience is likely to be repeated' is postulated by
(1) Behaviourial theory
(2) Reinforcement and expectancy theory
(3) Agency theory
(4) Contingency theory

99. From the knowledge acquired by Mr Mohan during the MBA program, he has to explain to the management of the company XYZ, that out of the following, which one is not a part of the Remuneration Model?
(1) Job Description (2) Job Analysis
(3) Job Hierarchy (4) Job Evaluation

100. Mr Mohan, HR Executive of XYZ company, has to design a compensation plan that must be
(1) Understandable, Workable, Acceptable
(2) Reasonable, Workable, Acceptable
(3) Understandable, Feasible, Acceptable
(4) Understandable, Workable, Compensable

ANSWER KEY

1. (2)	**2.** (1)	**3.** (2)	**4.** (3)	**5.** (2)	**6.** (2)	**7.** (3)	**8.** (1)	**9.** (4)	**10.** (2)
11. (4)	**12.** (3)	**13.** (1)	**14.** (2)	**15.** (3)	**16.** (1)	**17.** (3)	**18.** (3)	**19.** (2)	**20.** (1)
21. (3)	**22.** (1)	**23.** (2)	**24.** (2)	**25.** (4)	**26.** (2)	**27.** (4)	**28.** (1)	**29.** (2)	**30.** (3)
31. (4)	**32.** (4)	**33.** (3)	**34.** (4)	**35.** (4)	**36.** (1)	**37.** (2)	**38.** (4)	**39.** (4)	**40.** (1)
41. (3)	**42.** (3)	**43.** (*)	**44.** (4)	**45.** (2)	**46.** (3)	**47.** (1)	**48.** (3)	**49.** (2)	**50.** (1)
51. (4)	**52.** (2)	**53.** (2)	**54.** (2)	**55.** (1)	**56.** (2)	**57.** (4)	**58.** (2)	**59.** (2)	**60.** (3)
61. (3)	**62.** (2)	**63.** (2)	**64.** (1)	**65.** (1)	**66.** (2)	**67.** (2)	**68.** (4)	**69.** (3)	**70.** (1)
71. (2)	**72.** (3)	**73.** (1)	**74.** (4)	**75.** (2)	**76.** (4)	**77.** (3)	**78.** (2)	**79.** (1)	**80.** (3)
81. (4)	**82.** (2)	**83.** (3)	**84.** (4)	**85.** (3)	**86.** (1)	**87.** (1)	**88.** (4)	**89.** (1)	**90.** (1)
91. (3)	**92.** (4)	**93.** (4)	**94.** (3)	**95.** (1)	**96.** (3)	**97.** (4)	**98.** (2)	**99.** (2)	**100.** (1)

NOVEMBER, 2021

MANAGEMENT

PAPER-II

Note : This paper contains **hundred (100)** objective type questions of **two (2)** marks each. **All questions are compulsory**.

1. Which one of the following information type is NOT included in a skill inventory?
(1) Employee's personal data
(2) Organization's training schedule
(3) Employee's potential
(4) Salary and Job history

2. Which one of the following approaches stresses that there are no universal rules for managers to follow in order to perform the job?
(1) Contingency (2) System
(3) Mathematical (4) Empirical

3. The best level of output for a perfectly competitive firm in short run is a point where P = MR = MC, provided that
(1) $P < AVC/P < AVC$
(2) $P > AVC/P > AVC$
(3) $P = AVC/P = AVC$
(4) $P \geq AVC/P \geq AVC$

4. What is the role of advertisements and selling costs in perfectly competitive markets?
(1) Informative to intimate product/service availability
(2) Enlarging market size
(3) Very essential for survival of the firm
(4) Influencing buyer behaviour

5. It is believed that employees' attitude influence their perception of work, but the employees' experience at work may also modify or shape their attitudes. This is an example of
(1) Contingency Approach
(2) Democratic Approach
(3) Interactional Approach
(4) Socio-technical system Approach

6. Which one of the following employee behaviour is NOT true in case of high stress level?
(1) Anxiety
(2) Careless mistakes
(3) Nervousness
(4) Low and bad judgemental ability

7. Information regarding 'personal job demands (human expenditure involved in work, such as energy expenditure)' collected in job analysis falls in which one of the following?
(1) Work Activities
(2) Worker-Oriented Activities
(3) Personal Requirements
(4) Job Context

8. Which one of the following orientation programmes seek to ratify the usefulness of the characteristics that the person brings to the new job?
(1) Serial Orientation
(2) Disjunctive Orientation
(3) Investiture Orientation
(4) Divestiture Orientation

9. In which one of the following motives, relevant for organizational climate, there is an urge to be relevant and useful to large groups including society as a whole?
(1) Affiliation (2) Influence
(3) Extension (4) Achievement

10. If the market price of PQR Ltd. is 44, EPS is 3.75 and the retention ratio is 60%, then the

multiplier according to Graham and Dodd Model of Dividend policy is

(1) 15 (2) 19.5
(3) 16 (4) 18.7

11. The holistic, integrated and goal-oriented process of planning, recruiting, selecting, developing, managing, and compensating employees is known as
(1) Human Resource Management
(2) Strategic Human Resource Management
(3) Talent Management
(4) Human Resource Planning

12. Which one of the following performance appraisal methods prevents supervisors from rating all or most employees "satisfactory" or "high"?
(1) Critical Incident Method
(2) Forced Distribution Method
(3) Paired Comparison Method
(4) Alternation Ranking Method

13. In case of agency problem, the actions of managers are very likely to be directed towards the goal of
(1) Profit maximisation
(2) Wealth maximisation
(3) Survival and self-sufficiency
(4) Self-sufficiency

14. Which one of the following measures better explains inflation in an economic ecosystem?
(1) GNP deflator
(2) Wholesale Price Index (WPI)
(3) Consumer Price Index (CPI)
(4) Rate of change in GNP deflator

15. Du Pont analysis formula involves which financial elements for computation of earning power?
(1) Net profit margin, Total assets turnover and Equity multiplier
(2) Total assets turnover and sales turnover profitability
(3) Profit margin, Sales turnover and Asset-use efficiency
(4) Total assets turnover and Equity multiplier

16. Following information is available for the year 2018 and 2019 of ABC Ltd:

Year	2018	2019
Sales	Rs. 32,00,000	Rs. 57,00,000
Profit/(Loss)	(Rs. 3,00,000)	Rs. 7,00,000

Calculate P/V ratio
(1) 40% (2) 16%
(3) 28% (4) 12%

17. Which methods of risk analysis better serve lender's perspective in the capital budgeting decisions?
(1) Risk Adjusted Discount Rate
(2) Certainty Equivalent approach
(3) Simulation and Sensitivity analyses
(4) Decision Analysis

18. As per Walter's model, the market value of a growing firm will increase if the dividend payout ratio is
(1) Increased (2) Decreased
(3) Constant (4) 100%

19. In the absence of covariance among securities in the portfolio, if each security has an average standard deviation of 20%, the portfolio of 100 securities would have a standard deviation of
(1) 2% (2) Zero
(3) 20% (4) 5%

20. The relationship between an investor's expectation of return on bonds with respect to the investment horizon is called
(1) Bond yield
(2) Yield to maturity
(3) Risk immunization
(4) Term structure of interest rates

21. ___________ usually have intensive distribution because sales of these products tend to have a direct relationship to their availability
(1) Convenience Goods
(2) Speciality Goods
(3) Shopping Goods
(4) Unsought Goods

22. Which phrase best completes the statement below?
One of the key tasks of a marketer is to _______ and to create a perception among consumers that the product is worth purchasing.
(1) Make products easily visible and available
(2) Promote sales of products
(3) Differentiate their products from those of competitors
(4) Do market surveys

23. When companies offer products in small packages or charge on a pay-per-use basis, then such strategies are part of:
(1) Regionalisation strategies
(2) Strategies for the Bottom-of-the Pyramid
(3) Strategies for competing with global companies
(4) Strategies for internationalisation

24. At the business level, organisations need to position their business as being Low-cost leaders or Differentiated. The position when cost leadership is high in terms of lower prices/lower costs and differentiation is low, is called:
(1) Focused Cost Leaders
(2) Cost Leaders
(3) Differentiators
(4) Focused differentiators

25. The process of converting a non-productive, inactive asset into a productive asset by selling receivables to a company that specialises in their collection and administration, is described as
(1) Credit administration
(2) Factoring
(3) Receivables management
(4) Credit rating

26. "Moments of Truth" in services marketing was given by:
(1) Jan Carlzon
(2) Rosser Reeves
(3) Parasuraman and Zeithamal
(4) Gary Armstrong

27. Which one of the following tasks is NOT expected to be performed in Sales Management?
(1) Formulating sales policies
(2) Designing sales territories
(3) Selecting and recruitment of salesforce
(4) Determining the selling price of the firm's products

28. In the retail industry, a 'Category Killer' is referred to as:
(1) A multi-category large discount store that is famous for its wide selection of products
(2) A speciality store wedded to discounting and domination of a product category
(3) A store in a residential area and offers all household goods and fresh groceries
(4) A unique 24/7 store located on major highways and also located in fuel stations

29. When is the finite population multiplier expected to be approximately equal to one?
(1) $N \geq 20n / N \geq 20n$
(2) $N \geq 30n / N \geq 30n$
(3) $N \geq 10n / N \geq 10n$
(4) $N \geq 40n / N \geq 40n$

30. Which of the following is true with regard to method of least squares used in simple regression analysis?
(1) It minimises the sum of the squared values of the independent variable
(2) It minimises the sum of squared differences between the values of independent variable and their mean
(3) It minimises the sum of the squared differences between the actual values of dependent variable and the estimated values of the dependent variable as per regression equation
(4) It minimises the sum of squared values of the dependent variable

31. In statistical quality control, the expected process variation (natural tolerance) is commonly taken to be

(1) $\mu \pm 1\sigma / \mu \pm 1\sigma$ (2) $\mu \pm 2\sigma / \mu \pm 2\sigma$

(3) $\mu \pm 3\sigma / \mu \pm 3\sigma$ (4) $\mu \pm s/\sqrt{n} / \mu \pm s/\sqrt{n}$

32. Who is widely credited for placing Japan as a world leader in the quality of its manufactured products?

(1) Schonberger R. J.
(2) Deming W.E.
(3) Juran J.M
(4) Goddard. W

33. A transportation problem with m origins and n destinations becomes a trans-shipment problem with

(1) (m + n) sources and (m + n) destinations
(2) (m + n − 1) sources and equal number of destinations
(3) (m − n) sources and (m − n) destinations
(4) (m + n − 2) sources and (m + n − 2) destinations

34. When is a firm not expected to prefer FDI to licensing?

(1) The firm has valuable know how that cannot be adequately protected by a contract
(2) The firm needs tight control over a foreign entity in order to maximise its market share and earnings in that country
(3) The firm faces high transportation costs and tariffs
(4) The firm's skills and capabilities are difficult to replicate in a foreign market

35. In the context of Data Mining, which one of the following is a method of Data Reduction?

(1) Normalization
(2) Data Compression
(3) Multiple Regression
(4) Outlier Analysis

36. In the context of the International Monetary System, the case for a fixed exchange rate regime claims:

(1) The need to maintain a fixed exchange rate imposes monetary discipline on a country
(2) The goods and service manufactured in the country become more competitive in international markets
(3) Floating exchange rate regimes are vulnerable to speculative pressure
(4) Far from correcting trade imbalance, depreciating a currency in the foreign exchange market tends to cause price inflation

37. The computer system most likely to be used by a large bank for the savings account of a customer would be:

(1) An on-line, real-time system
(2) A generalized utility system
(3) A batch processing system
(4) A direct access database system

38. Which one of the following is NOT desirable while handling a grievance?

(1) The union will identify specific contractual provisions allegedly being violated
(2) Make arrangement with individual employees that are inconsistent with the labour agreement
(3) Hold the grievance discussions privately
(4) Examine the grievant personnel's record

39. Entrepreneurs who are characterised by a refusal to adopt opportunities and make changes in production systems even if it affects the returns of the organisation are called

(1) Fabian Entrepreneurs
(2) Life timers entrepreneurs
(3) Imitative entrepreneurs
(4) Drone entrepreneurs

40. Which one of the following is NOT a part of the current account of a country's balance of payments?

(1) Import of Goods
(2) Portfolio Investment
(3) Investment income
(4) Export of Goods

41. A price ceiling below the equilibrium price of a commodity leads to

(A) Commodity glut in market
(B) Shortage of commodity
(C) Demand erosion
(D) Black marketing

Choose the correct answer from the options given below:

(1) A and B only (2) B and C only
(3) B and D only (4) A and D only

42. The essential conditions for price discrimination practice to succeed in different markets are

(A) Firms must have strong interdependence per se
(B) Firm must have some control over the price of the product
(C) Differentiated products and strong entry restrictions
(D) Price elasticity of demand must differ in different markets
(E) Markets for the products must be separable

Choose the correct answer from the options given below:

(1) A, B and C only
(2) B, C and D only
(3) C, D and E only
(4) B, D and E only

43. Which of the following are creative problem solving characteristics of effective managers?

(A) Cognitive style
(B) Conceptual blocks
(C) Divergent thinking
(D) Activity balance

Choose the correct answer from the options given below:

(1) A and C only (2) B and C only
(3) A, C and D only
(4) B, C and D only

44. The term 'Flexible Manufacturing Technology' or 'Lean Production', covers a range of manufacturing technologies designed to:

(A) Become compliant with government regulations
(B) Reduce setup times for complex equipment
(C) Increase utilization of individual machines through better scheduling
(D) Improve quality control at all stages of the manufacturing process

Choose the correct answer from the options given below:

(1) A, C and D only
(2) B, C and D only
(3) A and D only
(4) B and C only

45. Theory of international trade promotes

(A) Increase in demand for exportable products
(B) Rise in prices and volumes
(C) Improvement in quality of products
(D) Reduction in prices and increase in quality for consumers

Choose the correct answer from the options given below:

(1) A, B and C only
(2) A, C and D only
(3) B, C and D only
(4) A and B only

46. To achieve its aims in Strategic Human Resource Management, organization's formulate and execute Human Resources

(A) Policies (B) Behaviours
(C) Practices (D) Competencies

Choose the correct answer from the options given below:

(1) A and B only (2) A and C only
(3) B and C only (4) A, B, C and D

47. The salient features of Zero Base Budgeting are:

(A) It is a decision oriented approach
(B) The decision unit is broken into understandable decision packages which are ranked according to importance
(C) The responsibility is shifted from top management to the manager of the decision unit
(D) It is an accounting oriented approach

(E) Top management decides why a particular amount of money should be spent on a particular decision unit

Choose the correct answer from the options given below:

(1) A, B and C only
(2) D and E only
(3) A and B only
(4) C, D and E only

48. The formula for calculating Degree of Operating Leverage (DOL) are:

(A) $\text{DOL} = \frac{\text{\% change in EBIT}}{\text{\% Change in sales}}$

(B) $\text{DOL} = \frac{\text{Contribution}}{\text{EBIT}}$

(C) $\text{DOL} = \frac{\text{EBIT+Fixed cost}}{\text{EBIT}}$

(D) $\text{DOL} = \frac{\text{EBIT}}{\text{Contribution}}$

Choose the correct answer from the options given below:

(1) A, C and D only
(2) B, C and D only
(3) A, B and C only
(4) A and B only

49. Funds flow and Cash flow statements are important managerial tools and help the firm to know:

(A) Liquidity position
(B) Capital expenditure incurred
(C) Dividend paid
(D) Extent of external financing

Choose the correct answer from the options given below:

(1) A, B and C only
(2) B, C and D only
(3) A and D only
(4) A, B, C and D

50. Portfolio theory provides a normative approach to investing based on which of the following assumptions?

(A) Risk-return spread is uniform for all asset classes
(B) Investors are risk-averse
(C) Market risk pricing is identical for all investors
(D) Return on assets are normally distributed
(E) Uniform investment horizon

Choose the correct answer from the options given below:

(1) A, B and C only
(2) B, C and D only
(3) C, D and E only
(4) A, C and E only

51. Out of the following, which are the most common error committed by Entrepreneurs?

(A) To anticipate roadblocks
(B) No commitment or dedication
(C) Proposing market niche (Segment)
(D) Lack of demonstrated experience
(E) No realistic goals

Choose the correct answer from the options given below:

(1) A, B and C only
(2) B, D and E only
(3) C, D and E only
(4) B, C, D and E only

52. Identify the drivers for increased Foreign Institutional Investment flows in Indian stock markets in recent times

(A) Covid-19 pandemic driven liquidity outflows from the western capital markets
(B) Geopolitical supply chain relocations
(C) Increased India weightage in MSCI Emerging Market Index
(D) Steep decline in interest rates in large market friendly economies
(E) Favourable risk-reward ratios in Indian stock markets

Choose the correct answer from the options given below:

(1) A, B and C only
(2) C, D and E only
(3) B, C and D only
(4) A, B, C and D only

53. Notable myths about Entrepreneurs and Entrepreneurship are

(A) Entrepreneurs are academics and social misfits
(B) Entrepreneurs must fit into an ideal profile
(C) Entrepreneurs are doers and thinkers
(D) All Entrepreneurs need is money
(E) Entrepreneurs are not born but made
Choose the correct answer from the options given below:
(1) A, B, C and D only
(2) B, C, D and E only
(3) A, B and D only
(4) C, D and E only

54. The reasons why firms enter into strategic alliances are:
(A) Enter new markets
(B) Abide by government regulations
(C) Reduce manufacturing costs
(D) Developing and diffusing technology
Choose the correct answer from the options given below:
(1) A, B and C only (2) B, C and D only
(3) A, B and D only (4) A, C and D only

55. Out of the following, which are the CORRECT forms of Product Life Cycle:
(A) Bell-shaped PLC
(B) Scalloped PLC
(C) Cycle-Recycle PLC
(D) Growth-Slump PLC
Choose the correct answer from the options given below:
(1) A, B, C and D
(2) B, C and D only
(3) A, C and D only
(4) A, B and C only

56. Which of the following denote the CORRECT set of unrecognised form of organisational justice?
(A) Procedural justice
(B) Shareholder justice
(C) Collateral justice
(D) Interactional justice
Choose the correct answer from the options given below:
(1) A and C only (2) B and C only
(3) A and B only (4) A and D only

57. Once a company has appointed dealers, the main elements of dealer motivation then are:
(A) Territory of operation
(B) Trade discount
(C) Special incentives
(D) Effective communication
Choose the correct answer from the options given below:
(1) A, B and C only
(2) B, C and D only
(3) A, C and D only
(4) A and B only

58. In consumer markets, for a market segment to be an effective and viable target, the segment should be:
(A) Identifiable
(B) Reachable
(C) Transcending International boundaries
(D) Sizeable
Choose the correct answer from the options given below:
(1) A and B only
(2) A, B and D only
(3) B, C and D only
(4) C and D only

59. To gain sustainable competitive advantage in low cost manufacturing, Indian businesses are expected to
(A) Reduce production cost, sacrifice profits and advertise more
(B) Support MSMEs, to strengthen the supply chain
(C) Adopt product differentiation and focus more on innovations
(D) Bridge trust deficit and gain support from the public, workers and policy markers
Choose the correct answer from the options given below:
(1) A and B only (2) B and C only
(3) A, B and C only (4) B, C and D only

60. Which of the following are necessary conditions for applying Siméon Denis Poisson distribution in the field of managerial decision making?
   (A) Each occurrence of an event is independent of the occurrence of the other event
   (B) The probability of an occurrence is the same for any two intervals of equal length
   (C) Poisson distribution describes continuous occurrences over a specific time interval
   (D) In each interval, occurrences can range from zero to infinity

   Choose the correct answer from the options given below:
   (1) A and B only
   (2) A, C and D only
   (3) A, B and D only
   (4) A, B and C only

61. An outlier does NOT affect which of the following statistical measures?
   (A) Quartile range
   (B) Standard deviation
   (C) Median
   (D) Regression coefficients

   Choose the correct answer from the options given below:
   (1) A and C only (2) A, C and D only
   (3) A and B only (4) B and D only

62. Out of the following, which are the IMF facilities available to member countries?
   (A) Extended Fund Facility (EFF)
   (B) Structural Adjustment Lending (SAL)
   (C) Compensatory Financing Facility (CFF)
   (D) Stand-by Arrangements (SBA)

   Choose the correct answer from the options given below:
   (1) A and B only
   (2) A, B and C only
   (3) A, C and D only
   (4) B, C and D only

63. Which of the following are types of foreign exchange risks or exposures?
   (A) Translation Exposure
   (B) Transaction Exposure
   (C) Social Exposure
   (D) Economic Exposure

   Choose the correct answer from the options given below:
   (1) A and B only (2) A, B and D only
   (3) A, B, C and D (4) A and D only

64. Out of the following, the examples of radical innovations are:
   (A) Personal Computers
   (B) Frozen Yogurt
   (C) Disposable diapers
   (D) Overnight mail delivery
   (E) Microwave popcorn

   Choose the correct answer from the options given below:
   (1) B, D and E only
   (2) A, B and C only
   (3) A, C and E only
   (4) A, C and D only

65. Technical feasibility analysis will include which of the following?
   (A) Crucial technical specifications with respect to the design and product safety
   (B) Engineering requirements
   (C) Product development
   (D) Product testing
   (E) Plant location

   Choose the correct answer from the options given below:
   (1) A, B, C and D only
   (2) B, C, D and E only
   (3) A, B, C, D and E
   (4) A, C, D and E only

66. Match List I with List II

List I (Concept(s))	List II (Description(s))
(A) Annuity	I. Process of application of interest over interest, period after period, on a given sum at specific rate for specified time

(B) Time value of money	II. A fixed and equal amount of money payable or receivable at periodic intervals of time equal to the amount of loan (Principal) and interest at a given rate
(C) Compounding	III. Widely used in the field of finance in determination of equated monthly installments for recovery of loans in a specified time period at a given rate of interest
(D) EMI	IV. A fixed and equal amount of money payable or receivable at periodic intervals evenly spaced over time

Choose the correct answer from the options given below:

(1) A-IV, B-III, C-I, D-II

(2) A-IV, B-I, C-II, D-III

(3) A-II, B-III, C-I, D-IV

(4) A-III, B-IV, C-II, D-I

67. Match List I with List II

List I	List II
(A) Snob effect	I. If firms are disproportionately powerful, the market leader makes the first move and captures two-third, of the market
(B) Smallworld model	II. When some people demand a smaller quantity of a commodity as more people consume it, in order to be different and exclusive
(C) Stackelberg model	III. Oligopolistic firms seek to maximize sales after an adequate rate of profit has been earned to satisfy stockholders
(D) Sales maximisation model	IV. Theory that a corporate giant can be made to operate as a small firm by linking well connected individuals from each level of the organisation to one another

Choose the correct answer from the options given below:

(1) A-IV, B-II, C-I, D-III

(2) A-II, B-IV, C-I, D-III

(3) A-III, B-I, C-II, D-IV

(4) A-II, B-III, C-IV, D-I

68. Match List I with List II

List I	List II
(A) Simple structure	I. A structure that supports an organization's capacity to continuously adapt and change
(B) Functional structure	II. A structure in which the entire organization is made up of workgroups
(C) Team structure	III. It is an organisational design that groups similar occupational specialties together
(D) Learning organization structure	IV. It is an organizational design with low departmentalization, wide span of control and little formalization

Choose the correct answer from the options given below:

(1) A-IV, B-III, C-II, D-I
(2) A-III, B-II, C-IV, D-I
(3) A-II, B-III, C-I, D-IV
(4) A-IV, B-I, C-III, D-II

69. Match List I with List II

List I	List II
(A) Ind AS 11	I. Revenue Recognition
(B) Ind AS 2	II. Effect of change in exchange rate
(C) Ind AS 3	III. Valuation of Inventories
(D) Ind AS 9	IV. Cash flow statement

Choose the correct answer from the options given below:

(1) A-I, B-II, C-III, D-IV
(2) A-IV, B-II, C-I, D-III
(3) A-III, B-II, C-IV, D-I
(4) A-II, B-III, C-IV, D-I

70. Match List I with List II

List I Option strategies	List II Description(s)
(A) Protective put	I. Buying an asset along with a put on it
(B) Covered call	II. Buying a call as well as put options on an asset at the same exercise price
(C) Long straddle	III. Combining two or more options on the same asset with differing exercise prices or times to maturity
(D) Spread	IV. Writing a call position on an asset along with buying the asset

Choose the correct answer from the options given below:

(1) A-II, B-IV, C-I, D-III
(2) A-I, B-IV, C-II, D-III
(3) A-III, B-II, C-IV, D-I
(4) A-I, B-III, C-IV, D-II

71. Match List I with List II

List I Brand concept	List II Meaning
(A) Brand image	I. Customer's emotional response and reactions with respect to Brand
(B) Brand feelings	II. Image of the Brand in the customer's mind, meeting their social/psychological needs
(C) Brand position	III. How customers think of the Brand under various purchase situations
(D) Brand salience	IV. Deliberate attempt on the part of marketer of the Brand to create a unique position in the mind of customer

Choose the correct answer from the options given below:

(1) A-I, B-II, C-III, D-IV
(2) A-II, B-I, C-III, D-IV
(3) A-III, B-II, C-I, D-IV
(4) A-II, B-I, C-IV, D-III

72. Match List I with List II

List I	List II
(A) Erratic levels of customs service	I. Inventory is in the wrong place at the wrong time
(B) No vision of future demand and its impact on production	II. Lack of agreement between different departments i.e. Customer service, Distribution and Manufacturing

(C) Too many changeovers in production	III. Production lacks confidence in marketing department's forecast
(D) Too many stockouts	IV. Inventory is either too high or too low

Choose the correct answer from the options given below:

(1) A-IV, B-I, C-III, D-II
(2) A-IV, B-III, C-II, D-I
(3) A-II, B-III, C-I, D-IV
(4) A-III, B-I, C-IV, D-II

73. Match List I with List II

List I	List II
(A) Markovian property	I. Rule of determining the order in which members of the queue are selected to begin service
(B) Waiting time in system	II. The time of next arrival is completely uninfluenced by when the last arrival occurred
(C) Steady state condition	III. The queueing is in after operating for some time with a fixed utilisation factor less than one
(D) Queue discipline	IV. Elapsed time that an individual customer spends in queue, both before service and during service

Choose the correct answer from the options given below:

(1) A-II, B-I, C-III, D-IV
(2) A-II, B-IV, C-III, D-I
(3) A-II, B-I, C-III, D-IV
(4) A-III, B-IV, C-II, D-I

74. Match List I with List II

List I Terms relate to	List II Organisation
(A) Bali Package	I. UNCTAD
(B) To assist developing countries in the area of trade and capital	II. IMF
(C) International monetary cooperation among member countries	III. World Bank
(D) Providing loans for building capital infrastructure of a country	IV. WTO

Choose the correct answer from the options given below:

(1) A-IV, B-II, C-III, D-I
(2) A-IV, B-I, C-II, D-III
(3) A-II, B-III, C-IV, D-I
(4) A-III, B-IV, C-I, D-II

75. Match List I with List II

List I Entrepreneur type	List II Features based on Entrepreneurial Competency
(A) Passenger	I. Ability to do and no will to do
(B) Star/Ideal	II. No ability to do and no will to do
(C) Dead wood	III. Ability to do and will to do
(D) May run	IV. No ability to do and will to do

Choose the correct answer from the options given below:

(1) A-I, B-II, C-III, D-IV
(2) A-IV, B-III, C-II, D-I
(3) A-IV, B-III, C-I, D-II
(4) A-III, B-IV, C-I, D-II

76. Arrange the following economic identities in a sequential evolution to understand consumer demand.

(A) Law of Demand
(B) Utility analyses
(C) Demand Elasticity analysis
(D) Indifference curve analysis
(E) Demand Forecasting

Choose the correct answer from the options given below:

(1) A, B, D, C, E (2) B, D, A, C, E
(3) B, C, D, E, A (4) C, D, B, E, A

77. Arrange the team member's behaviour in the group building process in the proper sequence

(A) Lot of competition and hostilities
(B) Upset and depressed
(C) Eager, anxious, gather impressions and data about the similarities and differences among members
(D) Interdependence in personal relations
(E) Less dissatisfied and a feeling of belongingness to the group

Choose the correct answer from the options given below:

(1) B, C, A, D, E (2) B, C, A, D, E
(3) C, A, D, B, E (4) C, A, E, D, B

78. Arrange the following key roles in the inverse order of their involvement in the process of organizational change

(A) Chief implementer
(B) Task forces
(C) Corporate management
(D) Implementation team
(E) Consultant

Choose the correct answer from the options given below:

(1) A, E, C, B, D (2) C, E, A, D, B
(3) C, A, E, D, B (4) E, A, C, B, D

79. Sequence the following to draw a logical timeline for dividend payment.

(A) Payment date
(B) Declaration date
(C) Ex-dividend date
(D) Record date
(E) Notice to stock exchanges

Choose the correct answer from the options given below:

(1) E, A, B, D, C (2) B, D, A, C, E
(3) B, D, A, E, C (4) E, B, C, D, A

80. Arrange the following to describe the sequence involved in Cost Volume Profit Analysis (CVP)

(A) Establishing the fixed and variable costs related to the product
(B) Drawing up break even charts which establish the point at which sales start to produce profit
(C) Working out P/V ratio by calculating contribution as a proportion of sales revenue
(D) Determining the cumulative effect of each product on profitability to assess the effects of change in product mix
(E) Calculating the relationship between sales volume and sales revenue by actual or assumed unit prices

Choose the correct answer from the options given below:

(1) A, E, C, B, D (2) A, B, E, C, D
(3) A, C, B, E, D (4) A, E, B, C, D

81. The product hierarchy stretches from basic needs to particular items in some sequence. Identify the CORRECT sequence or levels of the product hierarchy

(A) Product type (B) Product family
(C) Product class (D) Need family
(E) Product line

Choose the correct answer from the options given below:

(1) A, B, C, D, E (2) E, D, C, B, A
(3) D, B, C, E, A (4) D, E, C, A, B

82. As per the Anglo-Saxon Model of Corporate Governance, the authority lies with the following. Arrange these in decreasing order of authority.

(A) Board of Directors
(B) Managers
(C) Shareholders

(D) Employees (Company)
(E) Trade unions
Choose the correct answer from the options given below:
(1) A, C, B, E, D (2) A, B, C, D, E
(3) C, B, E, A, D (4) C, A, B, D, E

83. Sequence the innovation adoption process that consists of five stages which potential consumers pass through while attempting to arrive at a decision to try or not to try an innovative product.
(A) Consumer tries the innovation
(B) Consumer undertakes a "mental trial" of the innovation
(C) Consumer decides to use the innovation repeatedly
(D) Consumer becomes interested in the innovative product
(E) Consumer gets aware about the existence of the innovation
Choose the correct answer from the options given below:
(1) C, A, B, E, D (2) D, B, A, C, E
(3) B, D, A, E, C (4) E, D, B, A, C

84. In theory, several levels of economic integration are possible. Arrange the following from the least to the most integrated:
(A) Common Market
(B) Free Trade Area
(C) Economic Union
(D) Political Union
(E) Customs Union
Choose the correct answer from the options given below:
(1) A, B, C, D, E (2) B, E, A, C, D
(3) A, C, D, E, B (4) C, B, A, E, D

85. Creativity is the process of generating a novel idea. The five steps of the creative process in sequence are:
(A) Elaboration
(B) Preparation
(C) Evaluation
(D) Insight
(E) Incubation
Choose the correct answer from the options given below:
(1) B, E, D, C, A (2) D, E, A, B, C
(3) B, D, E, A, C (4) E, D, C, B, A

86. Given below are two statements, one is labelled as Assertion A and the other is labelled as Reason R
Assertion A: An oligopolist firm cannot decide the price it wishes to charge as well as the quantity it wishes to sell, both at the same time.
Reason R: An oligopolist firm takes into consideration the competitors' actions and counter actions because of a strong interdependence among the competitive firms
In light of the above statements, choose the most appropriate answer from the options given below
(1) Both A and R are correct and R is the correct explanation of A
(2) Both A and R are correct but R is NOT the correct explanation of A
(3) A is correct but R is not correct
(4) A is not correct but R is correct

87. Given below are two statements
Statement I: The Transactional Analysis Model is an effective tool to understand why people behave in certain ways.
Statement II: The Transactional Analysis Model cannot be used to improve communication
In light of the above statements, choose the correct answer from the options given below
(1) Both Statement I and Statement II are true
(2) Both Statement I and Statement II are false
(3) Statement I is true but Statement II is false
(4) Statement I is false but Statement II is true

88. Given below are two statements
Statement I: A satisfied employee may be highly disengaged.

Statement II: It is possible to feel engaged by the organisation and not the job.

In light of the above statements, choose the most appropriate answer from the options given below

(1) Both Statement I and Statement II are true
(2) Both Statement I and Statement II are false
(3) Statement I is true but Statement II is false
(4) Statement I is false but Statement II is true

89. Given below are two statements, one is labelled as Assertion A and the other is labelled as Reason R

Assertion A: Acquiring firms often are willing to pay a price higher than the status quo value of assets for the right to control management of target firms.

Reason R: The value of control stems from the changes that can be made to improve performance by debottlenecking capacity, streamlining and strengthening operations, managerial systems and processes.

In light of the above statements, choose the correct answer from the options given below

(1) Both A and R are correct and R is the correct explanation of A
(2) Both A and R are correct but R is NOT the correct explanation of A
(3) A is correct but R is not correct
(4) A is not correct but R is correct

90. Given below are two statements, one is labelled as Assertion A and the other is labelled as Reason R

Assertion A: The main reason for companies to move to global markets is to take advantages of the economies of scope.

Reason R: Economies of production arise due to the Competitiveness Index of the country in which the companies produce.

In light of the above statements, choose the correct answer from the options given below

(1) Both A and R are correct and R is the correct explanation of A
(2) Both A and R are correct but R is NOT the correct explanation of A
(3) A is correct but R is not correct
(4) A is not correct but R is correct

Read the following passage and answer the questions

Well before the pandemic, some companies had already adopted the work from anywhere system. But the large-scale implementation happened in 2012 when the US federal government across departments including Agriculture, NASA and the US patent office allowed remote work for employees. The pandemic however has accelerated this phenomenon by 10 years. The acceptance of remote work by several companies globally, is one of the few blessings of an otherwise incredibly hard time. The companies pioneering its adoption will be the 'magnets for talent' as it enables them to attract the best as it grows.

The employees are expected to greatly benefit from remote work as their control over their own time increases. They do not have to commute and are able to work either in the day or at night, depending on their personal style, while enjoying geographical flexibility to live wherever they want. People could save more if they move to smaller towns. They could choose to move to a better climate or to a culturally preferred location.

Companies with a remote work system can hire talent globally with ease and increase productivity. In the US patent office, productivity went up by 4.4% when it moved to work from anywhere. Employees felt more loyal to the organization for giving them such flexibility and put more effort into their work.

Work from anywhere has the power to reshape our old understanding of work. Employees and companies connecting now in meetings of the mind have more fusion of creativity rather than continuing with the previous approach of physical attendance, hierarchical communication with all the hours spent inside office buildings.

Managers will however, need to be sensitive to bias against remote working. Even loneliness could be addressed by augmented reality. It is of significance that the pandemic does not represent normal times when schools, day cares and help will be available.

Remote work actually suits women employees as many women forego career opportunities if these involve relocation which is their family life constrain.

Work from anywhere system though adopted in stress, has in fact worked out so well that post-pandemic too, the world Economic Forum finds employers are ready to give at least 44% of employees a work from anywhere option.

91. Which of the following best describes the title of the given passage?
(1) Manifestations of productivity
(2) Remote working challenges
(3) Work from anywhere
(4) Remote working for women employees

92. Faced with double shift of official and domestic work, in which perspective working women benefited from remote working?
(1) Bridges gender diversity
(2) Offers equal opportunity
(3) Offers work-life balance
(4) Favours their soft-skill disposition

93. Which one of the following best describes the benefits of remote working for employees?
(1) Temporal flexibility
(2) Cultural cohesiveness
(3) Climate conditioning
(4) Family bonding

94. According to the passage, which one of the following is the most significant challenge to employees working from remote places?
(1) Cloud data security
(2) Augmented reality
(3) Work life constraints
(4) Promotional bias

95. Which one of the following is the most incipient benefit of adoption of work anywhere system?
(1) Productivity improvement
(2) Better gender diversity
(3) Increased employee royalty
(4) Lesser employee engagement cost

Read the given passage and answer the questions that follow

XYZ company is in the business of FMCG products focusing on items like Atta, Besan, Maida etc. They are presently operating outside Delhi, in the state of Haryana. Looking at demand in Delhi, they want to market their products in Delhi, covering the entire Delhi. After going through various market reports and market surveys, they found that competition is very high in Delhi. They want to focus on the quality of their products and still want to fight the competition. They want to create a marketing strategy for their business at the time of entering the Delhi market. For doing so, they have appointed you as Manager Marketing (Incharge Delhi) to design a marketing strategy for them.

96. As the Marketing Manager of XYZ company, what type of pricing strategy would you recommend?
(1) Image pricing
(2) Complementary pricing
(3) Captive pricing strategy
(4) Loss leader strategy

97. What basis can be used for segmenting the market for FMCG products like Atta, Besan, Maida etc.?
(1) Demographic bases segmentation
(2) Geographic segmentation
(3) Psychographic segmentation
(4) Behavioral segmentation

98. Once the market for FMCG products like Atta, Besan, Maida etc. has been segmented, what targeting approach will you advocate?

(1) Single segment concentration
(2) Selective specialisation
(3) Market specialisation
(4) Product specialisation

99. For distribution of FMCG products like Atta, Baisan, Maida etc., what type of distribution strategy will you recommend?
(1) Intensive distribution
(2) Selective distribution
(3) Exclusive distribution
(4) Dual level of distribution

100. As a manufacture of FMCG range of products such as Atta, Suzi, Maida, Baisan etc., what type of trade promotion will you recommend for Dealer / Distributors of your products?
(1) Trade discounts
(2) Bundle pricing
(3) On pack coupons
(4) Free samples

ANSWER KEY

1. (2)	**2.** (1)	**3.** (2)	**4.** (2)	**5.** (3)	**6.** (2)	**7.** (2)	**8.** (3)	**9.** (3)	**10.** (3)
11. (3)	**12.** (2)	**13.** (3)	**14.** (4)	**15.** (1)	**16.** (1)	**17.** (2)	**18.** (2)	**19.** (1)	**20.** (4)
21. (1)	**22.** (3)	**23.** (2)	**24.** (1)	**25.** (2)	**26.** (1)	**27.** (4)	**28.** (2)	**29.** (1)	**30.** (3)
31. (3)	**32.** (2)	**33.** (1)	**34.** (3)	**35.** (2)	**36.** (2)	**37.** (1)	**38.** (2)	**39.** (4)	**40.** (2)
41. (3)	**42.** (4)	**43.** (2)	**44.** (2)	**45.** (4)	**46.** (2)	**47.** (1)	**48.** (3)	**49.** (4)	**50.** (2)
51. (2)	**52.** (4)	**53.** (3)	**54.** (4)	**55.** (4)	**56.** (2)	**57.** (2)	**58.** (2)	**59.** (4)	**60.** (3)
61. (1)	**62.** (3)	**63.** (2)	**64.** (4)	**65.** (3)	**66.** (1)	**67.** (2)	**68.** (1)	**69.** (4)	**70.** (2)
71. (4)	**72.** (2)	**73.** (2)	**74.** (2)	**75.** (2)	**76.** (2)	**77.** (4)	**78.** (2)	**79.** (4)	**80.** (1)
81. (3)	**82.** (4)	**83.** (4)	**84.** (2)	**85.** (1)	**86.** (1)	**87.** (3)	**88.** (4)	**89.** (1)	**90.** (3)
91. (3)	**92.** (3)	**93.** (1)	**94.** (4)	**95.** (1)	**96.** (3)	**97.** (4)	**98.** (3)	**99.** (1)	**100.** (1)

OCTOBER, 2022

MANAGEMENT

PAPER-II

Note : This paper contains **hundred (100)** objective type questions of **two (2)** marks each. **All questions are compulsory.**

1. Which one of the following factor is not a factor in case of wide span of wide span of management?
   (1) Fast changes external and internal environment
   (2) Well-defined plans for repetitive operation
   (3) Effective interaction between superior and subordinate
   (4) Thorough training of subordinate

2. Which one of the following principles of management states that for a group of activity having the same objective, there should be one head and one plan?
   (1) Unity of command
   (2) Division of work
   (3) Unity of direction
   (4) Centralization

3. In which of the following situation(s), a competitive firm is advised to shut down operations temporarily?
   (1) P < AVC (2) P < ATC
   (3) P < MC (4) P < MR

4. Percentage of output lost for each one point reduction in the inflation rate is called
   (1) Input and output ratio
   (2) Capital-output ratio
   (3) Sacrifice ratio
   (4) Technological quotient

5. Which one of the following is a taxable perquisite?
   (1) Insurance premium
   (2) Salary of servant employed by an employee
   (3) Loan to employees
   (4) Accommodation provided by the employee

6. Which one of the following is the characteristic of organizational climate?
   (1) There are policies that set forth the organization's beliefs about how employee and/or customers are to be treated
   (2) Standards of behaviour exist
   (3) When organizational participant interact with one another, they use common language
   (4) This is an overall "feeling" that is conveyed by the physical layout and the way participants interact

7. Which one of the following is organizational process related Job stress?
   (1) Little performance feed back
   (2) Role ambiguity
   (3) No opportunity for advancement
   (4) Rotating work shifts

8. Which one of the following is not a characteristic of a manager?
   (1) Does the right thing (2) Imitates
   (3) Asks how and when
   (4) Accepts the status quo

9. According to the Economic Times study, which one of the following is India's best company to work for in 2021?
   (1) Blue Dart Express Limited
   (2) DHL Express India Private Limited
   (3) NTPC Limited
   (4) Max Life Insurance Company Limited

10. Which one of the following is the most significant factor according to the Dunlop Model of Industrial Relation?

(1) External forces (2) Management
(3) Labour (4) Government

11. Which one of the following is not an intra-mural function of trade unions?
(1) Hike in wages
(2) Extension of medical facilities during sickness and casualties
(3) Job security
(4) Providing more benefits

12. Which one of the following is a disadvantage of MBO as a performance appraisal tool?
(1) Difficult to develop
(2) Time-consuming
(3) Difficult to rate or rank employees relative to one another
(4) Can cause disagreements among employees

13. Marston company sells a single product at a price of Rs. 50 per unit, its fixed costs total Rs. 15.000 and variable costs amount to Rs. 20 per unit. If management reduces the sales price of this product by Rs. 5 per unit the sales volume needed for the company to break even will:
(1) Increase by Rs. 5,000
(2) Increase by Rs. 4,500
(3) Increase by Rs. 2,000
(4) Remain unchanged

14. Nobel Laureate (2013) Robert Shiller advocates price earning ratio based on:
(1) Trailing twelve months earnings
(2) Latest four quarters earnings
(3) Analysts' forward earnings forecast
(4) Cyclically adjusted 10 years' earnings

15. The traditional accounting practice of resolving uncertainty by choosing the solution that leads to the lower amount of income being recognized in the current accounting period is based on which of the following accounting principles?
(1) Realization (2) Matching
(3) Conservatism (4) Materiality

16. If a company's current ratio declined in a year during which its quick ratio improved, which of the following is the most likely explanation?
(1) Inventory is increasing
(2) Inventory is declining
(3) Receivables are being collected more rapidly than in the past
(4) Receivables are being collected more slowly than in the past

17. Earnings per share of a company is Rs. 5 and the rate of return required by its shareholders is 16 per cent. Assuming Gordon valuation model, what rate of return should be earned on investment to ensure that the market price of its share is Rs. 50 and the dividend pay out is 40 per cent?
(1) 20 per cent (2) 16.67 per cent
(3) 33.33 per cent (4) 25 per cent

18. In which of the following methods of capital budgeting, cash flows are reinvested at the cost of capital?
(1) Internal rate of return (ERR)
(2) Net Present Value (NPV)
(3) Payback period
(4) Accounting rate of return (ARR)

19. Which of the following is a pre-offer takeover defence employed by target companies in hostile takeovers?
(1) Green mail (2) Pacman defence
(3) Poison pills
(4) Liability restructuring

20. In the absence of transactions costs, if a stock plots above the security market line (SML), it is
(1) Overpriced (2) Underpriced
(3) Fairly priced (4) Efficiently priced

21. Retailer cooperatives belong to which of the following distribution channel systems?
(1) Contractual (2) Administered
(3) Horizontal (4) Corporate

22. Which of the following is the correct explanation of resource-based approach?
(1) Internal sources are more important for a firm than internal forces for competitive advantage
(2) Process whereby a firm determines the costs associated with organizational activities

(3) External factors are more important than internal factors for competitive advantage
(4) Effective integration of both external and internal factors is the key to competitive advantage

23. A copier machine company provides better after sales service to its existing customer to improve its (company) and product image and increase sales of accessories and consumables. Above given statement is an example of :
(1) Stability strategy aimed at customer functions
(2) Stability strategy aimed at customer groups
(3) Expansion strategy aimed at customer groups
(4) Expansion strategy aimed at customer functions

24. Concept of 'fit' is central to which of the following schools of thought on strategy formulation?
(1) The positioning school
(2) The cognitive school
(3) The planning school
(4) The design school

25. How often and how easily customers think of the brand under various purchase or consumption situations, is known as:
(1) brand salience (2) brand resonance
(3) brand feelings (4) brand imagery

26. Huge stores that combine supermarket, discount and warehouse retailing are called:
(1) Discount store (2) Category killer
(3) Hyper market (4) Off-price retailer

27. Central focus of which of the following models is five-stage consumer decision process?
(1) Nicosia Model
(2) Hovard-Sheth Model
(3) Engel-Kollat Blackwell model
(4) Sheth-Newman-Gross Model

28. A salesperson who relies on creative methods for selling products and services is called:
(1) Demand creator
(2) Missionary
(3) Solution vendor
(4) Deliverer

29. Customers arrive at a reception counter at an average interval rate of 10 minutes and the receptionist takes an average of 6 minutes for one customer. The average queue length is:
(1) 3/10 (2) 9/10
(3) 11/10 (4) 7/10

30. Which of the following is not an advantage of implementing a quality system that conform to ISO standards?
(1) Improvement in employee involvement
(2) Improvement in house keeping
(3) Improvement in customer satisfaction
(4) Inefficient decision making

31. A technique of building up a List or a sample of a special population by using an initial set of members as informants is called:
(1) Quota sampling
(2) Convenience sampling
(3) Snowball sampling
(4) Purposive sampling

32. Which of the following is true for the coefficient of correlation?
(1) It is not dependent on the change of scale
(2) It is not dependent on the change of origin
(3) It is not dependent on both the change of scale and change of origin
(4) It is dependent upon change of scale, but not dependent upon change of origin

33. Which one of the following is not the disadvantage of international licensing?
(1) Inviting a potential competitor in third country markets
(2) High agency costs
(3) Possible loss of quality control
(4) No detailed involvement with foreign customers

34. Which one of the following is not the assumption of Theory of Absolute and Comparative advantage?

(1) Countries are driven only by maximization of production and consumption
(2) Only two countries are engaged in the production and consumption of just two goods
(3) There are transportation costs for shipping goods from one country to another
(4) Labour is the only factor of production that helps in converting the raw materials into finished products

35. Which one of the following factor does not influence the flow of FDI under Demand factors?
(1) Customer access
(2) Follow rivals
(3) Resource availability
(4) Exploitation of competitive advantage

36. Which of the following constitutes Foreign Direct Investment?
(1) A speculator trying to make a profit by buying company shares on a foreign stock exchange
(2) Indian energy company buying territory abroad where it expects to find oil reserve
(3) A tourist purchasing foreign currency to spend on a holiday abroad
(4) A company signing an agreement with a wholesaler to distribute its products in foreign markets

37. Diffusion of innovation theory is associated with:
(1) Peter Drucker (2) Schumpeter
(3) Everett Rogers (4) Fredrick Taylor

38. Currently, the country with the highest level of entrepreneurial activity, represented by Global Entrepreneurship Index is:
(1) Korea (2) Norway
(3) US (4) Australia

39. The first and foremost important feature for a project to be successful is:
(1) It should have a legal support
(2) It should have adequate financing
(3) It should have a market
(4) It should benefit society

40. Which scheme on performance and credit rating has been launched by Union MSME Ministry to assess the credit worthiness and capabilities of industries in the sector?
(1) Zero Defect Scheme
(2) Certification Performance and Economy Rating Scheme
(3) Performance and Credit Rating Scheme
(4) Industrial Incentive Scheme

41. What are the problems commonly associated with the scientific management?
(A) Managers often implement only the increased output part of the plan
(B) Manager's allow Workers to share the benefit thus increased labour costs
(C) Jobs become over-simplified and repetitive, often replaced by new technology
(D) Workers feel comfortable due to job security and practiced work
(E) Workers do not feel comfortable because of heavy pressure of work
Choose the correct answer from the options given below:
(1) (A), (C) and (D) only
(2) (B), (C) and (D)
(3) (C) and (D) only
(4) (A) and (C) only

42. The assumptions of rational decision making are:
(A) Preferences are not clear
(B) Preferences are not constant and stable
(C) Problem is clear and unambiguous
(D) No time or cost constraint exist
(E) Final choice will maximize pay off
Choose the correct answer from the options given below:
(1) (A), (C), (D), (E) only
(2) (A), (B), (C) only
(3) (C), (D), (E) only
(4) (A), (B), (D), (E) only

43. Efficacy of written communication depends upon:
(A) Lengthy presentation
(B) Editing after writing
(C) Brevity in sentences

(D) Use of strong Words
(E) Effective use of words

Choose the most appropriate answer from the options below:
(1) (B), (C) and (E) only
(2) (D) and (E) only
(3) (B), (C),(D) only
(4) (A), (C), (D), (E) only

44. An approach of managing international operations in which nationality is downplayed and the firm actively searches on world-wide or regional basis for the best people to fill key positions, is known as:
(A) Geocentric approach
(B) Ethnocentric approach
(C) Polycentric approach

Choose the most appropriate answer from the options below:
(1) (A) and (B) only (2) (A) only
(3) (B) and (C) only (4) (C) only

45. Which of the following are the examples of need for status?
(A) Being in a position of authority over others
(B) Having executive privileges
(C) Participating in pleasant social activities
(D) Working for the right company in the right job
(E) Living in the right neighbourhood

Choose the most appropriate answer from the options below:
(1) (A), (B), (C) only
(2) (B), (D), (E) only
(3) (A), (D), (E) only
(4) (A), (B), (C), (D) only

46. Talent management process include(s):
(A) Human resource planning
(B) Selection of employees
(C) Development of employees
(D) Employee compensation
(E) Employee separation

Choose the most appropriate answer from the options below:
(1) (A), (B) only (2) (B), (C), (D) only
(3) (C), (D) (E) only
(4) (A), (B), (C), (D) only

47. Which of the following focus of OD interventions are relevant if the nature of intervention is structured?
(A) Reorganization
(B) Team development
(C) Counselling
(D) Work review
(E) MBO

Choose the most appropriate answer from the options below:
(1) (A), (B) only
(2) (A), (D), (E) only
(3) (B), (C), (E) only
(4) (A), (B), (C), (E) only

48. Which of the following technologies am fast changing the accounting ecosystems?
(A) Blockchain technology
(B) Enterprise Resource planning (ERP)
(C) Cloud computing
(D) Robotics
(E) Machine learning

Choose the correct answer from the options below:
(1) (A), (B) and (C) only
(2) (C), (D) and (E) only
(3) (A), (D), and (E) only
(4) (A), (C) and (E) only

49. Which of the following are the underlying assumptions of cost-volume profit (CVP) analysis?
(A) Number of units produced and sold are equal
(B) Cost inputs and the output produced are linearly related
(C) Sales price and sales mix remain constant
(D) Zero base budgeting underlay costs and pricing decision
(E) Total fixed costs and variable cost per unit are constant

Choose the correct answer from the options given below:
(1) (A), (B), and (C) only

(2) (C), (D) and (E) only
(3) (A), (C), and (E) only
(4) (B), (C) and (D) only

50. While preparing a budget, which of the following activities enable managers to do a better job of managing:
(A) Advance warning of and assignment of responsibility for conditions that require corrective action
(B) Develop new policy to improve control of inventory management
(C) Adjusting the budget to reflect different levels of sales or production
(D) Coordination of activities among all departments within the organization
(E) Creation of standards for evaluating performance
Choose the correct answer from the options given below:
(1) (A), (B) and (C) only
(2) (C), (D) and (E) only
(3) (A), (D) and (E) only
(4) (B), (C) and (D) only

51. Which of the following tests/studies are related to testing of the weak form stock market efficiency?
(A) Event studies (B) Size effect
(C) Runs test
(D) Price - Earnings (P/E) ratios
(E) Autocorrelation tests
Choose the most appropriate answer from the options given below:
(1) (A), (B) and (C) only
(2) (C), (D) and (E) only
(3) (A) and (C) only
(4) (C) and (E) only

52. Which of the following are essential characteristics of financial markets?
(A) Price continuity and depth
(B) Liquidity and marketability
(C) Normative governance and regulation
(D) Timely and accurate information flow
(E) Minimum transaction cost and informational efficiency
Choose the most appropriate answer from the options given below:
(1) (A), (B) and (C) only
(2) (C), (D) and (E) only
(3) (B), (C) and (D) only
(4) (A), (B), (D) and (E) only

53. Which of the following statements are true in context of customer value and satisfaction concept?
(A) Value perceptions increase with quality, service and price
(B) Customer value triad is primarily a combination of quality, service and price
(C) Marketing is the identification, creation, communication, delivery and monitoring of customers value
(D) If the perceived performance of the product matches with perceived expectations, the customer is delighted
(E) Satisfaction reflects a person's judgement of a products perceived performance in relation to expectations
Choose the correct answer from the options given below:
(1) (A), (B) and (C) only
(2) (B), (C) and (D) only
(3) (B), (C) and (E) only
(4) (A), (D) and (E) only

54. Which of the following statements characterise the growth phase of product life cycle?
(A) Build intensive distribution
(B) Maximize profit while defending market share
(C) Build awareness and interest in the mass market
(D) Diversify brand and items models
(E) Price to penetrate market
Choose the most appropriate answer from the options given below:
(1) (A), (B) and (C) only
(2) (A), (C) and (E) only
(3) (C), (D) and (E) only
(4) (A), (D) and (E) only

55. Which of the following statements are true in the context of CRM (Customer Relationship Management) 2.0?

(A) Customer interactions are not pre planned but happen in real time
(B) Software as a service is the dominant CRM model particularly in small and medium-sized businesses
(C) Customer data is typically stored on corporate servers only
(D) Means available for analytics are only standard multivariate statistical procedures such as cluster analysis and logistic regression
(E) CRM 2.0 uses massive amounts of structured and unstructured data

Choose the most appropriate answer from the options given below:
(1) (A), (C) and (D) only
(2) (B), (C) and (E) only
(3) (A), (B) and (E) only
(4) (C), (D) and (E) only

56. Penetration price strategy is followed under which of the following conditions?
(A) Where there is a high degree of price elasticity of demand
(B) When strong competition is expected soon after product introduction
(C) When company wants to recoup its research and development expenditure
(D) When company must keep demand within its production capacity

Choose the most appropriate answer from the options given below:
(1) (A) and (C) only
(2) (B) and (D) only
(3) (A) and (B) only
(4) (A) and (D) only

57. Which of the following are the myths of brand communities?
(A) Build the brand and the community will follow
(B) Focus on opinion leaders to build a strong community
(C) Brand communities exist to serve the business
(D) Online social networks are the best way to build community
(E) Social networks are one community tool, but the tool is not the strategy

Choose the most appropriate answer from the options given below:
(1) (A) and (E) only
(2) (B), (E) and (D) only
(3) (A), (B) and (C) only
(4) (A), (B), (C) and (D) only

58. Which of the following statements are true?
(A) A good measure of dispersion" is not duly affected by extreme observations
(B) Standard deviation incorporates the effect of extreme values thus making it most reliable measure of dispersion
(C) Co-efficient of determination (R^2) is always positive and less than one
(D) Non parametric tests do not require us to make restrictive assumptions about shape of population distribution
(E) Z-test cannot be applied when population is normal

Choose the correct answer from the options given below:
(1) (A), (C), (D) only (2) (B), (D), (E) only
(3) (D), (E) only (4) (A), (D), (E) only

59. Indicate correct options of the following statements on data collection and questionnaire design.
(A) In order to ensure sufficiency of data, the field questionnaire must be 10% above the required number
(B) In structured interviews, interviewers attributes can significantly affect the respondent's replies
(C) Presentation of closed-ended questions and the general layout constitute important considerations in preparing a self administrated questionnaire
(D) In computer assisted data collection, degree of control over the interview process is high
(E) Description of important terminologies/jargons helps to improve the efficiency of respondent in filling the questionnaire.

Choose the most appropriate answer from the options given below:
(1) (A), (B), (C), (D) only
(2) (A), (C), (D), (E) only

(3) (B), (C), (D), (E) only
(4) (C), (D), (E) only

60. Which of the following statement(s) are true in the context of quality standards?
(A) KAIZEN approach deals with continuous improvement
(B) BIS represents India in ISO
(C) TQM cannot applied to crude oil refining
(D) Six sigma allows 3.4 defects per one million cases
(E) Statistical quality control applications are limited to manufacturing industries
Choose the most appropriate answer from the options given below:
(1) (C), (D), (E) only
(2) (B), (C), (D) only
(3) (A), (B), (D) only
(4) (A), (D), (E) only

61. Business intelligence is to improve the timeliness and quality of the input for decision making, It helps the managers to understand which of the following:
(A) Internal capabilities of the organization
(B) Trends and future directions in the markets
(C) External environment such as economic, political, social and demographic environment
(D) Behaviour of the competitors
(E) External capabilities of the organization
Choose the most appropriate answer from the options given below:
(1) (A), (B), (C) and (D) only
(2) (A), (D), (E) only
(3) (A), (B), (D), (E) only
(4) (A), (C) and (E) only

62. Data warehousing has various characteristics including :
(A) Focuses on modelling and analysis of data relating to a specific area
(B) Data warehouse is an integration of data from various systems Like CRM system, SCM system, etc.
(C) The time variant for a data warehouse has a historical perspective for example, past 10-20 years
(D) It is stored permanently i.e. data once stored cannot be updated
(E) It is stored temporarily i.e. data once stored can be updated
Choose the most appropriate answer from the options given below:
(1) (B), (D), (E) only
(2) (A), (B), (D) only
(3) (A), (C), (D) only
(4) (C), (E) only

63. In regression model, assumptions of error term are:
(A) Zero-mean assumption
(B) Constant-variance assumption
(C) Dependence assumption
(D) Independence assumption
(E) Normality assumption
Choose the correct answer from the options given below:
(1) (A), (C), (D), (E) only
(2) (A), (B), (C) only
(3) (B), (C), (D), (E) only
(4) (A), (B), (D), (E) only

64. Reason(s) for sickness in small industries in India are:
(A) Minimal use of artificial intelligence in business
(B) Inability to cope up with large market size
(C) Lack of innovation and technology focus
(D) Direct and indirect competition from foreign players
(E) Absence of regulatory support
Choose the most appropriate answer from the options given below:
(1) (B), (D), (E) only
(2) (A), (D), (E) only
(3) (A), (B), (C) only
(4) (B), (C), (D) only

65. Innovative small firms are more likely to be in existence in which of the following sectors?
(A) Knowledge - based services
(B) Biotechnology

(C) Information technology
(D) Automobiles
(E) Cement

Choose the most appropriate answer from the options given below:

(1) (D), (E) only (2) (C), (D), (E) only
(3) (A), (C) only (4) (B), (E) only

66. Match List I with List II

List I Management concepts and theories	List II Description
(A) System theory	(I) Customer oriented approach emphasizing human resources and quantitative methods to continuously improve
(B) Contingency theory	(II) Concerned with formal patterns of arrangements and relationship developed by management
(C) Organization design	(III) Based on open-systems theory and recognizes that there are many, internal and external factors that influence organizational behaviour
(D) Total Quality Management	(IV) All parts of an organization are interrelated and dependent on one another

Choose the correct answer from the options given below:

(1) (A)-(IV), (B)-(III), C-(II), D-(I)
(2) (A)-(II), (B)-(III), C-(I), D-(IV)
(3) (A)-(I), (B)-(II), C-(IV), D-(III)
(4) (A)-(III), (B)-(I), C-(II), D-(IV)

67. Match List I with List II

List I – Big Five Personality Traits	List II – Descriptive characteristics
(A) Agreeableness	(I) Assertive
(B) Emotional stability	(II) Imaginative
(C) Extroversion	(III) Trusting
(D) Openness to experience	(IV) Secure

Choose the correct answer from the options given below:

(1) (A)-(III), (B)-(I), C-(IV), D-(II)
(2) (A)-(III), (B)-(IV), C-(I), D-(II)
(3) (A)-(IV), (B)-(III), C-(I), D-(II)
(4) (A)-(III), (B)-(IV), C-(II), D-(I)

68. Match List I with List II

List I – Life Cycle of an MNC	List II – Staffing approach
(A) Setting up the host unit	(I) Polycentric approach is preferred
(B) Establishing the technology team to begin core operational activities	(II) Distinctly polycentric approach
(C) Full blown operations of the host unit with significant role in establishing global objectives and targets	(III) Distinctly polycentric approach; could get to geocentric approach
(D) Strong operational leadership at the unit level while globally consolidating with parent company	(IV) Usually an ethnocentric or a geocentric approach

Choose the correct answer from the options given below:

(1) (A)-(IV), (B)-(II), C-(I), D-(III)
(2) (A)-(IV), (B)-(II), C-(II), D-(III)
(3) (A)-(I), (B)-(IV), C-(III), D-(II)
(4) (A)-(II), (B)-(I), C-(III), D-(IV)

69. Match List I with List II

List I – Costs and Financial Concepts	List II – Mechanism and Measures
(A) Financial leverage	(I) Contribution margin ÷ EBIT

(B) Contribution margin	(II) (EBIT) ÷ (EBIT – interest)
(C) Operating leverage	(III) Contribution margin) ÷ (EBIT -- interest)
(D) Combined leverage	(IV) Sales – variable costs

Choose the correct answer from the options given below:

(1) (A)-(II), (B)-(I), C-(IV), D-(III)
(2) (A)-(III), (B)-(IV), C-(I), D-(II)
(3) (A)-(I), (B)-(III), C-(IV), D-(II)
(4) (A)-(II), (B)-(IV), C-(I), D-(III)

70. Match List I with List II

List I Characteristic based price factors	**List II Descriptions**
(A) Volatility (VOL)	(I) Captures deviations from linearity in the relationship between returns and firm size
(B) Momentum (MOM)	(II) Uses returns to firms outside the equity universe to account for risk dimensions not captured by the other risk factors
(C) Size Non Linearity (SNL)	(III) Differentiates between stocks with positive and negative excess returns in the recent past
(D) Non Estimation Indicator (NEI)	(IV) Captures both long term and short term dimensions of relative returns variability

Choose the correct answer from the options given below:

(1) (A)-(I), (B)-(III), C-(IV), D-(II)
(2) (A)-(IV), (B)-(III), C-(I), D-(II)
(3) (A)-(IV), (B)-(I), C-(II), D-(III)
(4) (A)-(III), (B)-(IV), C-(I), D-(II)

71. Match List I with List II

List I Company	**List II Nature of business**
(A) Alliance air	(I) Swiss travel group
(B) Delhivery	(II) Online travel company
(C) Ixigo	(III) State owned regional carrier
(D) Kuoni	(IV) New age logistic and supply chain start up

Choose the correct answer from the options given below:

(1) (A)-(I), (B)-(IV), C-(III), D-(II)
(2) (A)-(III), (B)-(IV), C-(II), D-(I)
(3) (A)-(III), (B)-(II), C-(IV), D-(I)
(4) (A)-(II), (B)-(IV), C-(I), D-(III)

72. Match List I with List II

List I – Possible level of customer expectations	**List II – Example**
(A) Normative expectations	(I) I expect this restaurant to serve me in an adequate manner
(B) Acceptable expectations	(II) I expect terrible service from this restaurant but came because price is low
(C) Minimum trouble expectations	(III) Most of the times this restaurant is very good, but when it gets busy the service is slow
(D) Experience-based expectations	(IV) As expensive as this restaurant is, it ought to have excellent food and service

Choose the correct answer from the options given below:

(1) (A)-(IV), (B)-(II), C-(I), D-(III)
(2) (A)-(IV), (B)-(I), C-(III), D-(II)
(3) (A)-(IV), (B)-(I), C-(II), D-(III)
(4) (A)-(I), (B)-(IV), C-(II), D-(III)

73. Match List I with List II

List I Symbol	List II Process charty activity
(A) D	(I) Storage
(B) ⇒	(II) Input
(C) △	(III) Delay
(D) □	(IV) Transport

Choose the correct answer from the options given below:

(1) (A)-(IV), (B)-(III), C-(I), D-(II)

(2) (A)-(I), (B)-(III), C-(II), D-(IV)

(3) (A)-(III), (B)-(I), C-(II), D-(IV)

(4) (A)-(III), (B)-(IV), C-(I), D-(II)

74. Match List I with List II

List I Trade concepts and terminology	List II Description
(A) GATS	(I) Extends multilateral rules and disciplines to service
(B) TRIPS	(II) The agreement requires compliance with the provisions of Bern convention of 1886 to which India is a signatory
(C) TRIMS	(III) Refers to certain conditions imposed by a government in respect of foreign investment in the country
(D) MFN	(IV) Prevents countries from discriminating among foreign suppliers of services

Choose the correct answer from the options given below:

(1) (A)-(I), (B)-(II), C-(III), D-(IV)

(2) (A)-(II), (B)-(I), C-(IV), D-(II)

(3) (A)-(III), (B)-(IV), C-(II), D-(I)

(4) (A)-(IV), (B)-(III), C-(I), D-(II)

75. Match List I with List II

List I Concepts	List II Institution/Schemes
(A) Entrepreneurship and innovation	(I) Atal Tinkering lab
(B) Gaps in value chains	(II) Pradhan Mantri Matsya Sampada Yojana
(C) Think Tank	(III) Atal Innovation Mission
(D) Machine learning	(IV) Niti Aayog

Choose the correct answer from the options given below:

(1) (A)-(II), (B)-(IV), C-(I), D-(III)

(2) (A)-(I), (B)-(IV), C-(III), D-(II)

(3) (A)-(IV), (B)-(III), C-(I), D-(II)

(4) (A)-(III), (B)-(II), C-(IV), D-(I)

76. Arrange the following goods in the ascending order of the underlying income elasticity of demand.

(A) Necessities (B) Inferior goods

(C) Normal goods (D) Luxury goods

(E) Giffen goods

Choose the correct answer from the options given below:

(1) (E), (B), (A), (C), (D)

(2) (D), (C), (B), (A), (E)

(3) (E), (B), (C), (D), (A)

(4) (A), (D), (C), (B), (E)

77. Arrange the following steps of organizational socialization in the proper sequence:

(A) Select a good first supervisor to be incharge of socialization

(B) Provide a challenging first job

(C) Design a relaxed orientation program

(D) Provide timely and consistent feed back

(E) Provide relevant training

Choose the correct answer from the options given below:

(1) (C), (E), (D), (B), (A)

(2) (C), (D), (E), (A), (B)

(3) (B), (E), (D), (A), (C)

(4) (D), (A), (E), (B), (C)

78. Arrange the given stages of process of organisational change in the correct sequence

(A) Information collection

(B) Diagnosis

(C) Motivation

(D) Action proposal
(E) Stabilization

Choose the correct answer from the options given below:
(1) (C), (B), (A), (D), (E)
(2) (A), (C), (D), (E), (B)
(3) (D), (A), (C), (B), (E)
(4) (A), (B), (C), (D), (E)

79. Arrange the following bond issues in increasing order of the underlying risk:
(A) Convertible bonds
(B) Callable bonds
(C) Mortgage bonds
(D) Unsecured bond
(E) Junk bonds

Choose the correct answer from the options given below:
(1) (C), (B), (A), (D), (E)
(2) (B), (C), (A), (D), (E)
(3) (A), (C), (B), (E), (D)
(4) (C), (A), (B), (D), (E)

80. Arrange the following in the ascending order in terms of their equity market capitalisation:
(A) India
(B) United States (USA)
(C) Hong Kong
(D) Japan
(E) China

Choose the correct answer from the options given below:
(1) (B), (E), (A), (C), (D)
(2) (D), (B), (C), (E), (A)
(3) (B), (E), (D), (C), (A)
(4) (A), (C), (D), (E), (B)

81. Arrange the following steps in the segmentation process in sequential order:
(A) Determine which demographics, life styles and usage behaviour make the segment distinct and actionable
(B) Create a "value proposition" and product-price positioning strategy for each segment
(C) Group customers into segments based on needs and benefits sought by them
(D) Determine overall attractiveness of each segment based on some predetermined criteria
(E) Create "segment story board" to list the attractiveness of each segments positioning strategy

Choose the correct answer from the options given below:
(1) (C), (A), (D), (E), (B)
(2) (C), (A), (D), (B), (E)
(3) (A), (C), (D), (B), (E)
(4) (A), (D), (C), (B), (E)

82. Arrange the following modes of entry in foreign markets starting with the mode of entry having least commitment, risk, control and profit potential:
(A) Company hires a local manufacturer to produce the product.
(B) Company starts exports working through domestic export agents and exports management companies.
(C) Company joins hands with local investor and forms a company in which both share ownership and control.
(D) Company starts export using domestic export department and overseas sales branch.
(E) Company offers a complete brand concept and operating system to an investor in return of certain fee.

Choose the correct answer from the options given below:
(1) (D), (B), (E), (C), (A)
(2) (B), (D), (E), (A), (C)
(3) (B), (D), (A), (E), (C)
(4) (D), (B), (A), (E), (C)

83. What is the correct sequence of steps involved in the master production schedule preparation?
(A) Obtaining the net requirement of materials
(B) Revising the preliminary master production schedule to accommodate the inadequacy of materials
(C) Obtaining the specification on required production
(D) Assessing the inventory in hand and on order
(E) Determining the gross requirements of materials using MRP

Choose the correct answer from the options given below:
(1) (A), (D), (C), (B), (E)
(2) (A), (E), (C), (D), (B)
(3) (B), (C), (A), (D), (E)
(4) (C), (E), (D), (A), (B)

84. The main processing functions of information system are given below. Arrange them in sequencing order:
(A) Process transaction
(B) Maintain master file
(C) Process enquiry
(D) Process report
(E) Process interactive supper applications
Choose the correct answer from the options given below:
(1) (A), (B), (C), (D), (E)
(2) (A), (C), (D), (B), (E)
(3) (A), (D), (C), (B), (E)
(4) (A), (B), (D), (C), (E)

85. The steps involved in development of a project are given below. Arrange them in proper sequence.
(A) Selection of business idea for a detailed analysis from the competing ideas
(B) Project installation and initiation
(C) Feasibility analysis
(D) Identification of investment opportunity
(E) Arrangements for financing
Choose the correct answer from the options given below:
(1) (D), (A), (C), (E), (B)
(2) (A), (C), (E), (D), (B)
(3) (B), (C), (A), (E), (D)
(4) (C), (D), (E), (B), (A)

86. Given below are two statements:
Statements I: Employers use human resource management activities to help employees realize their full career potential.
Statements II: Employers do this just because they gain by making better utilization of employee's potential.
In the light of the above statements, choose the most appropriate answer from the options given below :
(1) Both Statement I and Statement II are correct
(2) Both Statement I and Statement II are incorrect
(3) Statement I is correct but Statement II is incorrect
(4) Statement I is incorrect but Statement II is correct

87. Given below are two statements
Statement I: Effective channel management calls for selecting intermediaries and training and motivating them in order to build long term partnership,
Statement II: Channel integration must recognize the distinctive strengths of online and offline selling and maximize their joint contributions.
In the light of the above statements, choose the most appropriate answer from the options given below :
(1) Both Statement I and Statement II are correct
(2) Both Statement I and Statement II are incorrect
(3) Statement I is correct but Statement II is incorrect
(4) Statement I is incorrect but Statement II is correct

88. Given below are two statements
Statement I: Interest coverage ratio indicates how many times fixed interest charges are earned, based on the earnings available to pay these expenses.
Statement II: One minus the reciprocal of interest coverage ratio indicates how far earnings could decline before it would be impossible to pay the interest charges from current earnings.
In the light of the above statements, choose the most appropriate answer from the options given below :
(1) Both Statement I and Statement II are true
(2) Both Statement I and Statement II are false
(3) Statement I is true but Statement II is false

(4) Statement I is false but Statement II is true

89. Given below are two statements : One is labelled as Assertion A and the other is labelled as Reason B.

Assertion (A): Sustained current account surplus encourages the government to liberalize imports and capital Movements.

Reasons (R): The current account and balance of payments positions of a country can significantly influence its economic policies,

In the light of the above statements, choose the correct answer from the options given below :

(1) Both (A) and (R) are true and (R) is the correct explanation of (A)

(2) Both (A) and (R) are true but (R) is NOT the correct explanation of (A)

(3) (A) is true but (R) is false

(4) (A) is false but (R) is true

90. Given below are two statements : One is labelled as Assertion A and the other is labelled as Reason R.

Assertion A: Median is the middle most item in the set of numbers.

Reasons (R): Mode is not unduly affected by extreme values.

In the light of the above statements, choose the most appropriate answer from the options given below :

(1) Both (A) and (R) are true and (R) is the correct explanation of (A)

(2) Both (A) and (R) are true but (R) is NOT the correct explanation of (A)

(3) (A) is true but (R) is false

(4) (A) is false but (R) is true

Read the following paragraph and answer the five questions that follow :

Digital transformation has been a key theme of the Union Budget 2022 with announcements ranging from infrastructure status to data centers to taking fibre to all panchayats under the Bharat-net program Introduction of a, block chain based sovereign digital currency and setting up of 75 digital banking units, constitution of task force for animation, visual effects, gaming and comics (AVGC), launch of a digital university., digitalization of school education platforms and support for the Production Linked Incentive (PLI) scheme for large scale electronics manufacturing and IT hardware were also part of the overall focus.

Announced in 2015 with the goal of ushering in digitally driven transformation in governance, economy and society, it has already led to the launch of new schemes as well as the expansion of others like Unified Payments Interface (UPI) the digital literacy program (PMGDISHA), e-hospital, Digilocker, Common Service Centers (CSCs) and the number of internet users has also grown to over 83 crores. It needs to ensure world class digital infrastructure including high speed broadband connectivity and 5-G network, hyperscale data centers to make India a global hub for data centers and cloud, With increased focus on privacy, security and the need for storing data within the country, there are strong demand drivers in place for making investments in data centers attractive,

Whole govt. approach and creation of new public digital platforms in major domains such as education, health, agriculture and logistics need to undergo a paradigm shift, There also needs to be strong focus on standard interoperability and using common technology platforms such as Aadhaar, UPI, Singlesign-on to make the development of new applications easier and faster, Creation of a vibrant startup ecosystem in artificial intelligence, machine learning, internet of things holds the key to achieving trillion-dollar digital economy goal.

Further, there is an equally strong need tu modernise digital laws in India to support growth of digital economy and address concerns on accountability of online platforms and increasing cyber security to create trust and confidence amongst the users in the online world, which is crucial for digital inclusion and to bring the remaining population into the digital world. A national policy on data governance is the need of hour so that access to data is made easier for research apart from a strong push for skilling and capacity building in digital technologies at all levels in partnership with the industry and academia to make India skill and talent capital of the world.

91. Which of the following could be the most appropriate title of the passage?

(1) Digital Transformation
(2) Digital India: Way Ahead
(3) India: Digital and Skill Capital
(4) Vishava Guru Bharat: Digital Challenge

92. According to the passage, which one is the most crucial for the universalization of digital inclusion?

(1) Artificial intelligence, machine learning and internet of things
(2) New Laws to promote accountability, cyber security and privacy
(3) Digital promotion in education, health, agriculture and logistics
(4) Digital skilling and capacity building

93. Given below are two statements : One is labelled as Assertion A and the other is labelled as Reason R.

India needs to modernize its digital Laws to support the rapid growth of the digital economy.

Reasons (R) : New digital Laws are needed for digital inclusion and bringing more people to the digital world thus to increase digital users.

In the light of the above statements, choose the correct, answer from the options given below:

(1) Both (A) and (R) are true and (R) is the correct explanation of (A)
(2) Both (A) and (R) are true but (R) is NOT the correct explanation of (A)
(3) (A) is true but (R) is false
(4) (A) is false but (R) is true

94. What has been the focus for digital transformation in the India Union Budget, 2022?

(A) High speed broadband connectivity
(B) Accountability of online platforms
(C) Infrastructure status to data centres
(D) Increasing data and intellectual property security
(E) Task force for Animation, Visual effects, Gaming and Comics (AVGC)

Choose the correct answer from the options given below :

(1) (A), (B) and (C) Only
(2) (A), (D) and (E) only
(3) (B) and (D) only
(4) (C) and (E) only

95. Which of the following initiatives have already initiated India's digital transformation process in governance, economy and society?

(1) Aadhaar, UPI and Common Service Centers (CSCs)
(2) Production Linked Incentive Scheme
(3) PM Gati Shakti Initiatives
(4) Industry academia participation for digital technologies

Read the following paragraph and answer the five questions that follow :

ABG Global Ltd. is a large size cereal manufacturing company that markets its morning cereals products to various countries of the world. In order to cater to the local markets, the company makes small changes in its product like sweetness and flavours. The core product, branding and packaging are all standardised. The sales of products have witnessed an unexpected rise in various Asian markets including India in the past few years. In response to this growing demand, the company has pursued an aggressive strategy of marketing and producing its products by doubling its capacity. Last year, the company suffered a jolt, when its sales declined sharply. A careful analysis of market revealed that the market segment which adopted the company's product were upper-middle class representing families where both spouses are working, Initially it was glamorous to adopt cereals as alternative breakfast option, But, after certain time, they reverted back to traditional Indian breakfast, India, being a highly conventional market offers less scope for standardized global products, In a volatile demand structure wherein huge marketing efforts are required, inhouse doubling of production capacity can result in large unrecoverable investment, thus hinting towards alternative strategies, The CEO of the company is now laying emphasis on product positioning strategies, Replacing a full meal with a non-Indian food has a lower success rate calling for customization. As such brand equity may not work.

96. ________ is a combination of standardization and differentiation, where the core strategy remains same, but ________ is made to take into account specific customer group requirement.

(1) Positioning, effort
(2) Evaluation, segmentation
(3) Penetration improvement
(4) Focus, differentiation

97. A strategy aimed at reducing uncertainty faced by consumers when choosing products with unknown product quality is termed as

(1) Standardization
(2) Internationalization
(3) Customization
(4) Improvisation

98. ________ is a set of consumers who evince interest in the marketers offer.

(1) Target market
(2) Potential market
(3) Loyal market
(4) Skimmed market

99. While expanding business to new markets, analysis of following is required as a first step

(1) Need for product improvement
(2) Analysis of current market position
(3) Need for technological infrastructure
(4) Possibilities of marketing tie-ups

100. In times of marker uncertainties and low brand loyalties, the international firms should respond to spurt in demand for its products through

(1) Flexible inhouse capacities
(2) Balancing local and global production
(3) Outsourcing
(4) Customized pricing

ANSWER KEY

1. (1)	**2.** (3)	**3.** (1)	**4.** (3)	**5.** (2)	**6.** (4)	**7.** (1)	**8.** (1)	**9.** (2)	**10.** (1)
11. (2)	**12.** (2)	**13.** (3)	**14.** (4)	**15.** (3)	**16.** (2)	**17.** (1)	**18.** (2)	**19.** (3)	**20.** (2)
21. (1)	**22.** (1)	**23.** (2)	**24.** (1)	**25.** (1)	**26.** (3)	**27.** (3)	**28.** (1)	**29.** (2)	**30.** (4)
31. (3)	**32.** (3)	**33.** (4)	**34.** (3)	**35.** (3)	**36.** (2)	**37.** (3)	**38.** (3)	**39.** (3)	**40.** (3)
41. (4)	**42.** (3)	**43.** (1)	**44.** (2)	**45.** (2)	**46.** (4)	**47.** (2)	**48.** (4)	**49.** (3)	**50.** (3)
51. (4)	**52.** (4)	**53.** (3)	**54.** (2)	**55.** (3)	**56.** (3)	**57.** (4)	**58.** (1)	**59.** (3)	**60.** (3)
61. (1)	**62.** (2)	**63.** (4)	**64.** (4)	**65.** (3)	**66.** (1)	**67.** (2)	**68.** (2)	**69.** (4)	**70.** (2)
71. (2)	**72.** (3)	**73.** (4)	**74.** (1)	**75.** (4)	**76.** (1)	**77.** (3)	**78.** (1)	**79.** (1)	**80.** (4)
81. (2)	**82.** (3)	**83.** (4)	**84.** (4)	**85.** (1)	**86.** (3)	**87.** (1)	**88.** (1)	**89.** (1)	**90.** (2)
91. (2)	**92.** (2)	**93.** (2)	**94.** (4)	**95.** (1)	**96.** (4)	**97.** (1)	**98.** (2)	**99.** (2)	**100.** (3)

MARCH 2023

MANAGEMENT

PAPER-II

Note : This paper contains **hundred (100)** objective type questions of **two (2)** marks each. **All** questions are **compulsory**.

1. What kind of elasticity of demand is faced by the oligopolistic firm?
   (1) Low elasticity for price rise and more elasticity for price cuts.
   (2) High elasticity for both whether there is price rise or price cuts.
   (3) Low elasticity for both whether there is price rise or price cuts.
   (4) High elasticity for price rise but less elasticity for price cuts.

2. Which of the following correctly explains the notion of consumer surplus?
   (1) The difference between what consumers are willing to pay for a given quantity of goods and services and the amount they actually pay.
   (2) The difference between what consumers are willing to buy given quantity of goods and services and the quantity they actually buy.
   (3) The difference between what consumers are willing to plan to buy given quantity of goods and services and the quality they actually buy.
   (4) The difference between total utility and addition to total utility from goods and services the consumers buy.

3. The market-demand and supply equation for a product are:
   $Q_D = 30 - 3P$
   $Q_S = 20 + 2P$
   Here Q for quantity; P for price. What is the equilibrium demand?
   (1) 18 (2) 16
   (3) 24 (4) 20

4. "Corporate governance is to conduct the business in accordance with the owner's (shareholders) desires" is conceptualized by:
   (1) Henry Fayol (2) Milton Friedman
   (3) Peter Drucker (4) Lord Cadbury

5. According to Maslow's hierarchy of needs, which one of the following organizational aspects will not be included in the self-actualization needs?
   (1) Advancement (2) Job challenge
   (3) Status (4) Self-image

6. Which one of the following is not a job-related performance data to identify the performance of an employee?
   (1) Attitude Surveys
   (2) Late deliveries
   (3) Grievances
   (4) Absenteeism

7. Which one of the following is not an effect on performance, behaviour and health when stress level of an employee is high?
   (1) Feeling sleepy all the time
   (2) Poor performance
   (3) Exhaustion (4) Nervousness

8. Which one of the following methods of forecasting human resource demand is not a qualitative method?
   (1) Delphi technique
   (2) Markov analysis
   (3) Nominal group technique
   (4) Group brain storming

9. Which one of the following is NOT a characteristic of Performance Management?

(1) Owned by human resource department
(2) Does not have direct link to reward
(3) Continuous review with one or more formal reviews in a year
(4) Joint or participative process

10. Which one of the following is not an advantage of staffing international operations of an MNC using Parent Country Nationals (PCN)?
(1) Proper linkage between foreign subsidiary and the headquarters.
(2) Familiar with the local norms and culture.
(3) Use of PCN helps develop global capabilities in the organisation.
(4) Knowledgeable about how the parent company operates.

11. Which one of the following can be the coping mechanism if the source of resistance to change is the fear of loss of power?
(1) Active support from the top
(2) Participation and involvement
(3) Role clarity and definition
(4) Role redefinition and re-orientation

12. If the employers' attitude towards trade unions is of acceptance, their behaviour will be
(1) Dictatorial (2) Paternal
(3) Business-like (4) Participative

13. Accounting principles are generally based on:
(1) Practicability (2) Subjectivity
(3) Convenience in recording
(4) Legal framework

14. ABC Ltd. produces two products X and Y in its production unit. Each unit of X and Y takes 5 hours and 10 hours as production time respectively. 1000 units of X and 600 units of Y were produced in a month. Actual man-hours in this production were 10,000. Yearly budgeted hours are 96,000. The activity ratio is
(1) 125% (2) 137.50%
(3) 108.33% (4) 125.50%

15. Computation of overhead absorption rates should be based on
(1) Maximum capacity
(2) Practical capacity
(3) Idle capacity
(4) Normal capacity

16. Operating budget consists of two parts, called as ______ budget and _____ budget.
(1) Cash, Expense (2) Flexible, Master
(3) Programme, Responsibility
(4) Master, Utilisation

17. As per CAPM model, the required rate of return on a security is
(1) Return on Treasury Bonds + Market Risk Premium
(2) Return on individual securities + Beta Premium
(3) Return on Government Securities + Unsystematic Risk Premium
(4) Return on Corporate Securities + Systematic Risk Premium

18. A firm can delay and favourably affect the control of its cash disbursements through the use of
(1) Bootstrapping payables
(2) Zero balance accounts
(3) Yield sensing for marketable securities
(4) Hedging of intangibles

19. Firm A wants to acquire Firm B and the financial details of the firms are:

	A	B
Market Price per share	Rs. 50	Rs. 20
Number of shares	1,000,000	500,000
Market value of the firm	Rs. 50 million	Rs. 10 million

If the merger is expected to bring gains which have a present value of Rs. 10 million and Firm A offers one share for every two shares of Firm B to the shareholders of Firm B, the apparent cost of acquiring firm B is
(1) Rs. 3,500,000 (2) Rs. 5,000,000
(3) Rs. 7,692,516 (4) Rs. 2,500,000

20. Which of the following forms of purchasing power parity states that changes in spot rates over a period of time reflect the changes in price levels over the same period in the currencies of the concerned economies?

(1) Relative form (2) Absolute form
(3) Expectations form (4) Contango form

21. Which of the following marketing channel function helps to fulfill the completed transactions?

(1) Gathering and distributing information about consumers.
(2) Reaching an agreement on price and other terms.
(3) Communicating with prospective buyers.
(4) Assuming the risks of carrying out the channel work.

22. A portion of a market that is so well suited to a firm's internal and external environment that other firms are not likely to challenge and dislodge it, is called

(1) Core competency
(2) Propitious niche
(3) Market segment
(4) Product positioning

23. An approach to corporate strategy in which top management views its product lines and business units as a series of investments from which it expects a profitable return is called

(1) business mix (2) integrated strategy
(3) portfolio analysis
(4) scenario analysis

24. The total combined customer lifetime values of all of the company's customers is known as

(1) Customer equity
(2) Customer-perceived value
(3) Customer Lifetime value
(4) Customer share

25. Which of the following indicates "Perishability" aspect of service characteristics?

(1) Customers participate in and affect the transaction.
(2) Service delivery and customer satisfaction depend on employee actions.
(3) Customers affect each other.
(4) It is difficult to synchronize supply and demand with services.

26. Which of the following are the distinctive features of "Big data" being used in Analytical CRM?

(1) Volume, Variety, Velocity, Veracity
(2) Volume, Variability, Variety, Veracity
(3) Valence, Variety, Volume, Variance
(4) Variance, Valence, Velocity, Veracity

27. "A tennis player slams his tennis racket to the ground when disappointed with his/her game". In above example, tennis player exhibits which of the following defense mechanism to handle frustration?

(1) Aggression (2) Regression
(3) Projection (4) Rationalization

28. "An outlet which starts as a general retailer grows into a specialized retailer and in course of time becomes even a bigger general retailer".
Above statement corresponds to which of the following theory of Retail?

(1) Wheel of Retailing Theory
(2) Retail Accordion Theory
(3) Theory of Natural Selling
(4) Retail Life Cycle Theory

29. A cold drink bottling plant fills bottles of 500 ml. capacity with mean of 500 ml and a standard deviation of 5. At least what percentage of bottles would contain cold drink between 490 ml and 510 ml?

(1) 75 per cent (2) 95 per cent
(3) 67 per cent (4) 81 per cent

30. Karl Pearson co-efficient of variation (CV) measures which of the following characteristics?

(1) Homogeneity (2) Unbiasedness
(3) Consistency (4) Efficiency

31. For a project activity, the optimistic, the pessimistic and the most likely times are 4, 14 and 6 days respectively. Its average time is:

(1) 10 days (2) 7 days
(3) 12 days (4) 9 days

32. In decision analysis, the expected value of perfect information is calculated as:
(1) Expected payoff with perfect information minus Expected payoff without experimentation.
(2) Expected value of sample information minus expected payoff with perfect information.
(3) Maximum payoff for each state of nature multiplied by the prior probability of that state of nature.
(4) Expected increase in the payoff minus the cost of the experimentation.

33. Which one of the following is NOT a non-tariff barrier?
(1) Quota
(2) Customs and entry procedures
(3) Combined rates
(4) Exchange control

34. Which of the following marketing strategy falls under Geocentric kind of international orientation?
(1) Extension of domestic strategy to foreign markets
(2) Global standardisation
(3) Localisation
(4) Trade-off between localization and standardisation

35. Which of the following events contributed most to the disruption in the Bretton Woods system?
(1) Introduction of Special Drawing Rights.
(2) Western dominance over the system.
(3) Suspension of convertibility of dollar into gold in 1971.
(4) Oil price shock of 1973.

36. Which of the following integrations is related to supernational organizational structure?
(1) Free Trade Area (2) Economic Union
(3) Common Market
(4) Economic Integration

37. L.C. Gupta's sickness prediction model primarily focused on which of the following?
(1) Earnings Before Interest and Tax
(2) Sales and Working capital levels
(3) EBIT and operating cash flows
(4) Market value of equity and debt

38. 'Entrepreneur is an innovator playing the role of a dynamic businessman adding material growth to economic development', is articulated by:
(1) Porter (1990)
(2) Lichtenstein and Lyons (2010)
(3) Joseph Schumpeter (1883-1950)
(4) Shane (2008)

39. String of activities that moves a product from the raw material stage through manufacturing and distribution, and ultimately to the end user is called
(1) Business model
(2) Business verticals
(3) Value chain
(4) Business concept

40. A metaphor describing the time period in which a firm can realistically enter a new market is called
(1) Opportunity fall
(2) Opportunity gap
(3) Window of opportunity
(4) Opportunity recognition

41. According to Max Weber, in an ideal bureaucracy
a. Jobs are broken down into simple, routine and well-defined tasks
b. Offices/Positions are organized in a hierarchy
c. All organizational members are to be selected on the basis of technical qualifications
d. Rules and Regulations are applied uniformly, avoiding involvement with personalities and personal preferences of employees
e. The interests of any one employee or group of employees should not take precedence over the interests of the organization as a whole

Choose the most appropriate answer from the options given below:

(1) a, b, c, d only (2) b, c, d, e only
(3) a, b, d, e only (4) a, b, c, e only

42. Which of the following are Feedforward control measures for reducing workplace violence?

a. Investigate incidences and take appropriate action
b. Train employees about how to avoid danger if situation arises
c. Review company policies and change these policies, if necessary
d. Clearly communicate policies to employees
e. Observe how employees treat and interact with each other

Choose the most appropriate answer from the options given below:

(1) a and c only (2) c and e only
(3) b and d only (4) b, d and e only

43. Which of the following are the sources of ethical problems in organizations'?

a. Failure of personal character
b. Organisational goals Vs Social values
c. Psychological egoism and rationalism
d. Virtue and common good conflict
e. Conflict of personal values and organizational goals

Choose the correct answer from the options given below:

(1) a, b and c only (2) c, d and e only
(3) a, b and e only (4) b, d and e only

44. Psychological factors of individual behaviour will include which of the following:

a. Perception b. Emotional intelligence
c. Values d. Economic status
e. Attitudes

Choose the most appropriate answer from the options given below:

(1) a, b, c only (2) a, c, e only
(3) b, d, e only (4) b, c, e only

45. Which of the following are the traits of successful leaders?

a. Creative b. Assertive
c. Persuasive d. Decisive
e. Self-confident

Choose the most appropriate answer from the options given below:

(1) a, c, d only (2) a, b, e only
(3) b, c, d, e only (4) b, d, e only

46. Which of the following will fall under the grievances relating to promotion category?

a. Supersession b. Increments
c. Acting promotions d. Seniority
e. Pay fixation

Choose the most appropriate answer from the options given below:

(1) a, c, d only (2) b, d, e only
(3) a, c, e only (4) a, c, d, e only

47. Which of the following are constituents of trade unions'?

a. Members b. Employers
c. Political Party d. Government
e. Society

Choose the most appropriate answer from the options given below:

(1) a, b only (2) a, c, d only
(3) b, c, e only (4) a, b, d, e only

48. Which of the following are benefits for the organization of career management?

a. Improved performance
b. Improved productivity
c. Increased retention of high talent employees
d. Development of competencies and personal skills
e. Better individual-organization match

Choose the correct answer from the options given below

(1) a, b, c only (2) b, c, e only
(3) a, b, c, d only (4) a, d, e only

49. Which of the following are three levels of training in the six-sigma quality system'?

a. Blue Belts b. Yellow Belts
c. Black Belts d. Red Belts
e. Green Belts

Choose the most appropriate answer from the options given below

(1) a, b and c only (2) c, d and e only
(3) a, d and e only (4) b, c and e only

50. Which of the following statements are true in context of efficient market'?

a. Equilibrium rates of return will prevail
b. Investor cannot earn a positive return
c. Volatility will be very high
d. Securities of listed firms sell at their fair values
e. Investors are generally risk-averse

Choose the most appropriate answer from the options given below:

(1) a, d only (2) b, c only
(3) d, e only (4) b, e only

51. Which of the following are considered interlocking elements of a versatile business model"

a. Regulatory support and promoter experience
b. Customer value proposition
c. Financial resources and cost sheets
d. Key resources and processes
e. Profit formula

Choose the most appropriate answer from the options given below:

(1) a, b and c only (2) c, d and e only
(3) a, c and d only (4) b, d and e only

52. Which of the following are construed for government intervention to support entrepreneurship and small firms'?

a. Stimulate demand and new venture creation in the emerging sectors
b. Decentralised asset ownership and people participation
c. Help firms to adopt new technology to avoid market failure
d. Supporting women participation in business and high-tech firms
e. Export promotion and currency stabilization

Choose the most appropriate answer from the options given below:

(1) a, b and c only (2) c, d and e only
(3) a, c and d only (4) b, d and e only

53. Indian national strategy for financial inclusion, 2019-24 aims at

a. Broadening and deepening of financial inclusion
b. Digitisation and seamless facilitation of financial transactions
c. Access to formal financial services in an affordable manner
d. Women empowerment and strengthening Self-Help Group (SHG) ecosystems
e. Promoting financial literacy and consumer protection

Choose the most appropriate answer from the options given below:

(1) a, b and c only (2) c, d and e only
(3) a, b and d only (4) a, c and e only

54. Which of the following statements are applicable to value-based pricing concept?

a. Design product to deliver desired value at target price
b. Set target price to match customer perceived value
c. Determine costs that can be incurred
d. Convince buyers of products value
e. Assess customer needs and value perceptions

Choose the most appropriate answer from the options given below:

(1) a, b, c and e only (2) a, b, c and d only
(3) b, c, d and e only (4) a, d and e only

55. Which of the following criteria core competencies must meet in order to create value and provide a viable basis for synergy among the businesses in a corporation

a. Core competencies must be difficult for competitors to imitate.
b. Different businesses in the corporation must be similar in at least one important way.
c. Core competence must enhance competitive advantage by creating superior customer value

d. Core competencies must facilitate business diversification through shared activities with competing firms.

e. Core-competencies must leverage business resources with competing firm to reduce business costs.

Choose the most appropriate answer from the options given below:

(1) a, b and c only (2) c, d and e only
(3) a, d and e only (4) b, c and d only

56. Which of the following Digital marketing statements are correct?

a. Click through Rate is calculated by dividing the total number of clicks by the total number of ad impressions.

b. Long tail keywords are general key words which draw lower customer traffic.

c. Adwords is Google's earned search marketing programme.

d. Search Engine Marketing includes both search engine optimization and paid search.

e. Ad Auction is the process that Google runs for every Google search to decide which ad must appear for that specific search and in which order these set of ads will be displayed.

Choose the most appropriate answer from the options given below:

(1) a, b and c only (2) b, c and d only
(3) a, b and e only (4) a, d and e only

57. Which of the following circumstances favour "Sprinkle Approach" for launching products in international markets?

a. The life cycle of the product is relatively short.

b. The competitive intensity of the market is very high with strong and fierce competitors.

c. Cost of entry in markets is relatively high.

d. Finn has large resources to manage simultaneous product launch in multiple markets.

e. The size of the target market is small with low growth potential.

Choose the most appropriate answer from the options given below:

(1) a, b and d only (2) a, c and e only
(3) b, d and e only (4) c, d and e only

58. Which of the following characteristics of a data set are understood using the Karl Pearson coefficient of variation?

a. Disparity b. Consistency
c. Uniformity d. Homogeneity
e. Unbiasedness

Choose the correct answer from the options given below:

(1) a, b and c only (2) c, d and e only
(3) a, b and e only (4) b, c and e only

59. Which of the following statistical tests examines the equality of two means?

a. F-test b. 't'-test
c. Chi-square (χ^2) test
d. Mann-Whitney 'U' test
e. Kolmogorov-Smirnov test

Choose the correct answer from the options given below:

(1) a and c only (2) b and d only
(3) a, b and c only (4) c, d and e only

60. Which of the following comprises the interdependent troika of waste, overburden and unevenness in the 'lean' manufacturing?

a. Muri: Unreasonable work stress on men and machines.

b. Deviations from quality, productivity and breakdowns.

c. Muda: Non-value adding work.

d. Uncertainty in task times, in demand and customer's role.

e. Mura: Inconsistency and variation in workflow, speed and quality.

Choose the most appropriate answer from the options given below:

(1) a, b and c only (2) c, d and e only
(3) a, c and d only (4) a, c and e only

61. Identify the correct statement(s) about Data Warehousing (DW):

a. DW system must be acceptable to regulators and business community.
b. DW system must not be based on open-source platforms.
c. DW system must present information attractive to users.
d. DW system must be secure bastion that protects the information.
e. DW system must be adaptive to change.

Choose the correct answer from the options given below:

(1) a, c only (2) e, b only
(3) a, d, e only (4) b, c, d only

62. Identify the incorrect statement(s) from the following:

a. Technology is a differentiator among similar business enterprises.
b. Technology cannot create value for' not-for-profit' organisations.
c. Pace of technology affects the business model of modem enterprises.
d. Needs and Goals be defined before acquisition of technology.
e. Organisations pay little attention to the process of change once a decision to acquire technology has been taken.

Choose the correct answer from the options given below:

(1) b only (2) c, b only
(3) a, c only (4) d, e only

63. Which of the following are considered as the 'principal standards' in the ISO series developed by the International Organization for Standardization?

a. ISO 9000 b. ISO 9001
c. ISO 9002 d. ISO 9003
e. ISO 9004

Choose the correct answer from the options given below:

(1) a, b and c only (2) b, c and d only
(3) c, d and e only (4) a and e only

64. Identify the correct statements in context of equity financing.

a. Borrowing limit increases as a consequence of increase in number of shares.
b. Ordinary shares are generally not redeemable.
c. Issue of new shares dilutes the EPS if the profits do not increase immediately in proportion to increase in number of shares.
d. A company is not legally obliged to pay dividend.
e. Ordinary shares are less riskier from investor's perspective.

Choose the correct answer from the options given below:

(1) c, e only (2) a, b, c, d only
(3) b, c, d only (4) a, e only

65. As per Du Pont equation for ROE, other things remaining constant, which of the following statements is false?

a. An increase in the net profit margin will increase the ROE.
b. A decrease in debt to asset ratio will increase the ROE.
c. A decrease in return on assets will decrease the ROE.
d. An increase in the average asset turnover will increase the ROE.
e. An increase in equity multiplier will increase the ROE.

Choose the correct answer from the options given below:

(1) b only (2) c, d only
(3) a, e only (4) a, c Only

66. Match List I with List II:

List I	List II
a. Directive style	I. High tolerance for ambiguity and an intuitive way of thinking.
b. Analytic style	II. Low tolerance for ambiguity and an intuitive way of thinking
c. Conceptual style	III. Low tolerance for ambiguity.
d. Behavioural style	IV. High tolerance for ambiguity and

rational way of thinking.

Choose the correct answer from the options given below:

(1) a-III, b-IV, c-I, d-II (2) a-III, b-IV, c-II, d-I
(3) a-IV, b-III, c-II, d-I (4) a-II, b-I, c-IV, d-III

67. Match List I with List II:

List I (Cattell's Personality Factors)	**List II (Bipolar dimensions)**
a. Social boldness	I. Imaginative Vs. Practical
b. Abstractedness	II. Shrewd Vs. Forthright
c. Private	III. Controlled Vs. Casual
d. Perfectionism	IV. Venturesome Vs. Timid

Choose the correct answer from the options given below:

(1) a-III, b-I, c-II, d-IV (2) a-I, b-IV, c-II, d-III
(3) a-IV, b-II, c-I, d-III (4) a-IV, b-I, c-II, d-III

68. Match List I with List II:

List I (VRIO Framework criteria)	**List II (Domain (HR) Applications)**
a. Value	I. Edge in terms of skills, knowledge and abilities
b. Rareness	II. Teamwork
c. Imitability	III. Empowerment programs
d. Organisation	IV. Unique history or culture

Choose the correct answer from the options given below:

(1) a-III, b-I, c-IV, d-II (2) a-I, b-IV, c-III, d-II
(3) a-II, b-IV, c-I, d-III (4) A-III, b-I, c-II, d-IV

69. Match List I with List II

List I (Investment Decision rule)	**List II (Feature)**
A. NPV	I. Insufficiently consistent
B. Payback	II. Highly Inflexible
C. Cash Returns	III. Balance between flexibility and consistency
D. Accounting Returns	IV. Relatively consistent

Choose the correct answer from the options given below:

(1) a-III, b-IV, c-I, d-II (2) a-I, b-II, c-IV, d-III
(3) a-III, b-II, c-IV, d-I (4) a-II, b-III, c-I, d-IV

70. Match List I with List II

List I (Theory)	**List II (What Nation's do)**
a. Mercantilism	I. The range of products made or grown for export would depend upon the relative availability of different factors in each country
b. Theory of Absolute Advantage	II. Gold and silver are the mainstay of national wealth
c. Theory of Comparative Advantage	III. Countries should specialize in the production of goods for which they have absolute advantage
d. Factor Endowment	IV. Nations should produce those goods for which they have the greatest relative advantage

Choose the correct answer from the options given below:

(1) a-I, b-II, c-III, d-IV
(2) a-III, b-II, c-I, d-IV
(3) a-II, b-III, c-IV, d-I
(4) a-IV, b-III, c-II, d-I

71. Match the following.

List I (Acquisition 'Play')	**List II (Strategy to achieve performance premium)**
a. Acquire synergistic product/ market position.	I. Use borrowing capacity and other financial strengths to

			achieve an immediate performance premium.
b.	Acquire a company with under-utilized financial strength.	II.	Anticipate shortages and price increases in the physical assets' value. Invest to exploit the resource, using distribution capacity.
c.	Acquire an under-skilled company in a related industry.	III.	Achieve scale economies of distribution, production and technology.
d.	Acquire an underexploited physical asset.	IV.	Apply superior marketing, technology and production expertise to enhance the competitive position and performance of the acquisition candidate.

Choose the correct answer from the options given below:

(1) a-III, b-I, c-IV, d-II (2) a-IV, b-II, c-I, d-III
(3) a-III, b-IV, c-II, d-I (4) a-II, b-III, c-I, d-IV

72. Match the following.

	List I (Buyer's Need Assessment Question)		List II (Example)
a.	Problem Impact Queen	I.	How much inventory of the product do you carry?
b.	Problem discovery question	II.	Have you experienced any delays in getting those materials from your current suppliers?
c.	Solution value question	III.	What effects do the delays in receiving the materials have on your production costs?
d.	Situational question	IV.	If the rejection rate on your quality inspection is reduced to under 1%, how much would that save you?

Choose the correct answer from the options given below:

(1) a-II, b-I, c-IV, d-III
(2) a-II, b-IV, c-III, d-I
(3) a-I, b-III, c-II, d-IV
(4) a-III, b-II, c-IV, d-I

73. Match List I with List II:

	List I		List II
a.	Crashing an activity	I.	Length of the longest path through the project network.
b.	Project Network	II.	It shows the time and cost when the activity is fully crashed.
c.	Critical path	III.	It consists of a number of nodes and a number of arcs that connects two different nodes.
d.	Crash point	IV.	Taking special (costly) measures to reduce the duration of an activity below its normal value.

Choose the correct answer from the options given below:

(1) a-II, b-IV, c-III, d-I
(2) a-IV, b-III, c-I, d-II
(3) a-IV, b-III, c-II, d-I
(4) a-III, b-I, c-IV, d-II

74. Match List I with List II:

List I (KM Model)	List II (Approach)
a. Von Krogh and Roos	I. Sense-making
b. Wiig	II. Semantic Network
c. Monaka and Takeuchi	III. Organisational epistemology
d. Choo and Weick	IV. Spiralling

Choose the correct answer from the options given below:

(1) a-II, b-I, c-III, d-IV
(2) a-I, b-III, c-II, d-IV
(3) a-III, b-II, c-IV, d-I
(4) a-I, b-II, c-III, d-IV

75. Match the following.

List I (Entrepreneurship Thinkers)	List II (Entrepreneurial manifestations)
a. Bamoul (2002)	I. Innovating firms are more profitable than the non-innovators.
b. Geroski et.el. (1993) and Leiponen (2000)	II. Entrepreneur is a marriage broker between what is desirable from an economic point of view and what is profitable from technological point of view.
c. Timmons and Spinelli (2007)	III. Entrepreneurship is a way of thinking, reasoning and acting that is opportunity obsessed, holistic in approach and leadership balanced.
d. Burton Klein (1917)	IV. In free market economies, innovation is a necessity if a firm wants to survive.

Choose the correct answer from the options given below:

(1) a-IV, b-I, c-III, d-II
(2) a-II, b-IV, c-III, d-I
(3) a-I, b-IV, c-II, d-III
(4) a-III, b-I, c-IV, d-II

76. Arrange the following steps of developing an organizational structure in sequence.

a. Enumerate and group the activities of the enterprise consistent with the determined objectives.
b. Assign the grouped activities to personnel. Similar functions should be combined into one position.
c. Clearly define the objectives to determine the type, stability and basic characteristics of the Organization.
d. Determine the span of supervision, the types of organization, the basis of departmentation and pattern of authority structure.
e. Assess the capacities and abilities of human and other resources at the disposal of enterprise. Adapt the organization in sync with the reality.

Choose the correct answer from the options given below:

(1) c, a, b, d, e (2) a, c, b, e, d
(3) c, b, a, e, d (4) e, d, c, a, b

77. Arrange the following steps of Strategic Human Resource Management in the logical sequence.

a. Improve participative management.
b. To promote teamwork.
c. Shift focus from statutory participation to total participation.
d. Achieve group cohesiveness by inculcating participative management.
e. To achieve excellence in human resource management.

Choose the correct answer from the options given below:

(1) e, d, b, a, c (2) e, b, d, a, c
(3) b, a, d, e, c (4) a, c, e, b, d

78. Sequence the following steps in the preparation of a versatile and seasoned business plan.

a. Industry and market analysis.

b. Operations, marketing plan and financing.

c. Company and management team profiling.

d. Risk and contingency analysis.

e. Executive summary.

Choose the correct answer from the options given below:

(1) a, b, d, c, e (2) c, b, a, d, e

(3) e, c, a, b, d (4) d, a, c, b, e

79. Arrange the following in the increasing (higher) order of employee participation in decision-making.

a. Joint management councils

b. Workers' representative in the board

c. Works Committees

d. Workers' participation in management

e. Workers' share in equity

Choose the correct answer from the options given below:

(1) c, a, e, d, b (2) a, c, d, b, e

(3) c, a, b, d, e (4) c, a, d, e, b

80. Following are the steps followed by finance manager in procurement of a loan for working capital. Arrange them in a proper sequence.

a. Co-ordinating the verification of assets

b. Submission of loan proposal

c. Estimation of Working Capital Requirements

d. Creation of charge on Assets

e. Document Execution

Choose the correct answer from the options given below:

(1) a, d, b, c, e (2) c, b, a, e, d

(3) a, b, e, c, d (4) b, a, e, c, d

81. Identify the correct sequence of activities involved in the process of buy back of shares.

a. Letter of offer to the shareholders

b. Opening of bank account

c. Approval for Extra-ordinary General Meeting

d. Convening board meeting

e. Declaration of Solvency

Choose the correct answer from the options given below:

(1) e, a, b, c, d (2) c, b, a, e, d

(3) d, c, e, a, b (4) b, c, a, e, d

82. Arrange the following steps of six sigma process in a sequence.

a. Discover variation relationship for the vital variables and establish operating tolerances on each of the vital variables.

b. Validate measurement system, methods and procedures, establish the current processes' capability.

c. Validate the measurement system's ability to produce repeatable data; determine the capability of the process to control the vital variables, implement statistical process control on the vital variables.

d. Select the critical-to-quality characteristics and define the required performance standards.

e. Define upper and lower performance limits; identify sources of variation; screen potential causes of variation to identify the vital variables needing control.

Choose the correct answer from the options given below:

(1) d, e, b, a, c (2) e, d, b, a, c

(3) d, b, a, e, c (4) d, b, e, a, c

83. Arrange the following steps of personal selling process in a sequence.

a. Making an appointment with customer to establish rapport.

b. Gathering relevant information about the prospects and their needs to plan sales presentation.

c. Handling customer's objections related to price/value/functionality of the product.

d. Discovering, clarifying and understanding the buyer's needs.
e. Gaining buyer's commitment to action.

Choose the correct answer from the options given below

(1) d, a, b, c, e (2) a, b, c, d, e
(3) b, a, d, c, e (4) e, a, b, c, d

84. Sequence the following in order to eliminate waste and inefficiencies in the lean manufacturing.

a. Seiso b. Shitsuke
c. Seiri d. Seiketsu
e. Seiton

Choose the correct answer from the options given below:

(1) b, c, e, d, a (2) c, a, d, b, e
(3) e, d, b, c, a (4) c, e, a, d, b

85. Identify the correct sequence of steps involved in decision making for change of technology.

a. Conducting initial comparisons of alternative technologies.
b. Evaluating the state of present technology.
c. Listing down the probable post implementation issues
d. Financial feasibility analysis of proposed technology.
e. Identifying the learning requirements.

Choose the correct answer from the options given below:

(1) d, c, a, e, b (2) b, a, e, d, c
(3) a, b, c, e, d (4) d, e, a, b, c

86. Given below are two statements:

Statement I: When I say that I like my organization, I am expressing an attitude towards my organization.

Statement II: We can control our behaviour in a way that does not reflect our beliefs and values.

In the light of the above statements, choose the correct answer from the options given below :

(1) Both Statement I and Statement II are correct.
(2) Both Statement I and Statement II are incorrect.
(3) Statement I is correct but Statement II is incorrect.
(4) Statement I is incorrect but Statement II is correct.

87. Given below are two statements: One is labelled as Assertion 'A' and the other is labelled as Reason 'R'.

Assertion 'A': The objective functions in business organizations are complex requiring the processing of large volume of data.

Reason 'R': AI based non-linear models can solve the problems of arriving at a dynamic solution to business problems.

In the light of the above statements, choose the most appropriate answer from the options given below.

(1) Both A and R are correct and R is the correct explanation of A.
(2) Both A and R are correct but R is NOT the correct explanation of A.
(3) A is correct but R is incorrect.
(4) A is incorrect but R is correct.

88. Given below are two statements:

Statement I: The product of two regression co-efficient, b_{xy} and b_{yx} equals r_2 and cannot exceed 1.

Statement II: The average of two regression coefficients $\left(\frac{(b_{xy}+b_{yx})}{2}\right)$ is always greater than the correlation coefficient, r_{xy}.

In the light of the above statements, choose the correct answer from the options given below:

(1) Both Statement I and Statement II are correct.
(2) Both Statement I and Statement II are incorrect.
(3) Statement I is correct but Statement II is incorrect.
(4) Statement I is incorrect but Statement II is correct.

89. Given below are two statements:

One is labelled as Assertion A and the other is labelled as Reason R.

Assertion 'A': If the securities with less than perfect negative correlation between their price movements are combined, portfolio risk can be reduced significantly.

Reason 'R': The term with negative correlation has the effect of reducing the computed value of total portfolio risk, given other terms that are positive.

In the light of the above statements, choose the most appropriate answer from the options given below:

(1) Both A and R are correct and R is the correct explanation of A.
(2) Both A and R are correct but R is NOT the correct explanation of A.
(3) A is correct but R is incorrect.
(4) A is incorrect but R is correct.

90. Given below are two statements:

One is labelled as Assertion 'A' and the other is labelled as Reason 'R'.

Assertion 'A': Entrepreneurship has emerged as a focal point of policy in the majority of countries.

Reason 'R': Entrepreneurship contributes to job generation, innovation and promotes social cohesion.

In the light of the above statements, choose the most appropriate answer from the options given below.

(1) Both A and R are correct and R is the correct explanation of A.
(2) Both A and R are correct but R is NOT the correct explanation of A.
(3) A is correct but R is incorrect.
(4) A is incorrect but R is correct.

Read the following passage carefully and answer the questions that follow:

There has been much froth and foam across rooms and boardrooms regarding the ethics, legality and appropriateness of the practice of working for one organization while also taking up extra responsibilities and jobs with another. As a trend, it is becoming commonplace in the IT and ITeS space. This is welcome. It makes sense to encourage more flexibility to employees if these firms want to move up the value chain. So, employers should accept the reality and use it to their advantage.

But genuine concerns against 'side-hustles' must be addressed. During the pandemic, the IT sector swiftly adapted to Work from home (WFH), and professionals furthered their professional practice. Many preferred continuing WFH. But that raised the suspicion of many employers about workers taking up a second job to earn more. Meanwhile, a sharp rise in demand for IT professionals with new skills, and their shortage, widened the demand supply gap. Those who could not cope with the expectations - at the entry or middle levels - were fired. But the gig economy provides choices and added competition to both employer and employee. Trust is a core issue. Conflicts of interest and intellectual property rights violations are non-negotiable. Other aspects - fatigue impacting productivity, short-term vs long-term engagements in two jobs, skill acquisition, difficulty in monitoring beyond delivery of a defined output, the challenge to objectively measure output for a given compensation, peer-pressure, industry trends in employment contracts - also influence the attitude towards moonlighting.

But IT professionals can't be treated as captives. The industry must set the bar for high performance and productivity, yet in trusted working conditions that rewards fairly and recognizes performance and skills in a transparent way. A fair and broad-based definition of moonlighting must be included in the employment contract. A sound HR policy anchored in ethical management principles will ensure that there is no need to howl at moonlighting.

91. The practice of working for one organization while also taking up extra responsibilities and job with another requires:

a. Trust
b. Conflict of interest
c. Stagnation of employee growth
d. Employees adding limited value to their parent organization
e. Intellectual property rights

Choose the most appropriate answer from the options given below:

(1) a, b, e only (2) a, c, d only
(3) b, d, e only (4) a, b, c only

92. Given below are two statements:

Statement I: The practice of moonlighting is increasing because IT professionals are not being rewarded fairly.

Statement II: The contents of employee contract have precisely defined the moonlighting.

In the light of the above statements, choose the correct answer from the options given below:

(1) Both Statement I and Statement II are correct.
(2) Both Statement I and Statement II are incorrect.
(3) Statement I is correct but Statement II is incorrect.
(4) Statement I is incorrect but Statement II is correct.

93. As per the given passage, those employees who could not meet the skill gap were:

(1) Demoted (2) Trained
(3) Transferred (4) Discharged

94. Moonlighting encourages:

a. Commitment for the organization.
b. Flexibility to employees.
c. Adding skills.
d. Employee turnover rate.
e. Work from home.

Choose the most appropriate answer from the options given below:

(1) a, b, c only (2) b, c, d only
(3) a, d, e only (4) b, c, e only

95. The practice of 'moonlighting' is

(1) Equally applicable in all industries
(2) Ethical
(3) Adds value to the organization
(4) Legal and enforceable

Read the following passage carefully and answer the questions that follow:

Indian aviation will fly out of pandemic-induced fare bands with some of its heaviest losses behind it. Indian fliers have also been through a bout of technical glitches that the authorities have traced back to aircraft not having enough certifying manpower and flying with the minimum permissible list of defective equipment. A strong festive demand could reverse the sequential declines in air travel during the ongoing lean season. The removal of airfare caps coincides with a recent softening of jet fuel prices which, however, remain elevated. Freedom to pass on the biggest cost component to fliers should improve the financial metrics of airlines. One is keeping one's fingers crossed and seat belts buckled.

The industry is witnessing a round of capital infusion that also affects the competitive intensity. The Tatas are consolidating the splintered market share of the group's various airlines, and SpiceJet is considering a stake sale to raise funds. Market leader Indigo expects its strong revenue performance will lead it back into profits soon. Although the industry's air traffic yields have surpassed pre-pandemic levels, fuel costs and a declining rupee could subdue earnings. Newly opened up foreign routes are likely to witness stiff competition. Tire launch of Akasa Air and resumption of operations by Jet Airways will increase demand for airline employees. Air India is restoring salaries to pre-Covid levels.

Industry-wide losses are expected to fall sharply this year as Indian aviation enters another phase of growth. India is among the fastest growing aviation markets in the world and has a lot of catching up to do in terms of the size of its commercial aircraft fleet. Given the country's traffic growth projections, Indian airlines are likely to acquire more clout as aircraft buyers. The government, on its part, has a high budget for decongesting airports and is encouraging the development of the domestic aircraft maintenance industry. As India's airlines fly out of the current cloud bank, sunny skies await.

96. The factor adversely affecting Indian aviation is
(1) Removal of airfare caps
(2) Softening of jet fuel prices
(3) Declining value of rupee against US dollar
(4) Indian airlines acquiring clout as aircraft buyers

97. The future of Indian aviation industry is likely to be
(1) Favourable (2) Unfavourable
(3) Uncertain (4) Challenged

98. Given below are two statements:
One is labelled as Assertion 'A' and the other is labelled as Reason 'R'.
Assertion 'A': Pandemic is not the only reason for the losses in the aviation industry.
Reason 'R': Large number of technical reasons have resulted into the cancellation of flights.
In the light of the above statements, choose the most appropriate answer from the options given below :
(1) Both A and R are correct and R is the correct explanation of A.
(2) Both A and R are correct but R is NOT the correct explanation of A.
(3) A is correct but R is incorrect.
(4) A is incorrect but R is correct.

99. Which one of the following will impair the competitive intensity of the industry?
(1) Capital infusion
(2) Consolidation of market share
(3) Launch of Akasa Airline
(4) Turbulence in fuel prices

100. Which of the following are the initiatives taken by the Government to promote aviation industry?
a. Big budget for decongesting airports.
b. Encouraging domestic aircraft maintenance industry.
c. Capital infusion to expand capacity.
d. Reducing the permissible list of defective equipment.
e. Removal of airfare caps.
Choose the most appropriate answer from the options given below:
(1) a, b only (2) a, b, e only
(3) c and d only (4) a, b, c only

ANSWER KEY

1. (4)	**2.** (1)	**3.** (3)	**4.** (2)	**5.** (3)	**6.** (1)	**7.** (1)	**8.** (2)	**9.** (1)	**10.** (2)
11 (4)	**12.** (3)	**13.** (1)	**14.** (2)	**15.** (4)	**16.** (3)	**17.** (1)	**18.** (2)	**19.** (4)	**20.** (1)
21. (4)	**22.** (2)	**23.** (3)	**24.** (1)	**25.** (4)	**26.** (1)	**27.** (1)	**28.** (2)	**29.** (2)	**30.** (1)
31. (2)	**32.** (1)	**33.** (3)	**34.** (2)	**35.** (3)	**36.** (2)	**37.** (3)	**38.** (3)	**39.** (3)	**40.** (3)
41. (1)	**42.** (3)	**43.** (3)	**44.** (2)	**45.** (4)	**46.** (4)	**47.** (1)	**48.** (2)	**49.** (4)	**50.** (1)
51. (4)	**52.** (3)	**53.** (4)	**54.** (1)	**55.** (1)	**56.** (4)	**57.** (1)	**58.** (1)	**59.** (2)	**60.** (4)
61. (3)	**62.** (1)	**63.** (2)	**64.** (2)	**65.** (1)	**66.** (1)	**67.** (4)	**68.** (1)	**69.** (3)	**70.** (3)
71. (1)	**72.** (4)	**73.** (2)	**74.** (3)	**75.** (1)	**76.** (1)	**77.** (2)	**78.** (3)	**79.** (4)	**80.** (2)
81. (3)	**82.** (4)	**83.** (3)	**84.** (4)	**85.** (2)	**86.** (1)	**87.** (2)	**88.** (1)	**89.** (1)	**90.** (1)
91. (1)	**92.** (2)	**93.** (4)	**94.** (4)	**95.** (3)	**96.** (3)	**97.** (1)	**98.** (1)	**99.** (1)	**100.** (2)

DECEMBER 2023

MANAGEMENT

PAPER-II

Note : This paper contains **hundred (100)** objective type questions of **two (2)** marks each. **All** questions are **compulsory**.

1. The variety of approaches to management analysis, the amount of research and the number of different views have resulted in much confusion as to what management is, what management theory and science is and how managerial events should be analysed. Who called this situation 'the management theory jungle ?
(1) Chester Barnard (2) Elton Mayo
(3) Harold Koontz (4) Henry L. Gantt

2. Who is known as the "Father of brainstorming?
(1) Alex F. Osborn (2) Frank Gilbreelh
(3) Elton Mayo (4) Peter Drucker

3. In the case of an Executive Chairman, what is the minimum percentage of independent Directors required on the Board?
(1) At least one-third
(2) At least half
(3) At least one-fourth
(4) At least two-thirds

4. What is the minimum prescribed net profit threshold for Companies to be required to undertake Corporate Social Responsibility activities under clause 135 of the Companies Act, 2013 ?
(1) 1% of net profit (2) 2% of net profit
(3) 3% of net profit (4) 5% of net profit

5. Who argued that 'Attitude follow behavior'?
(1) Leon Festinger (2) Elton Mayo
(3) Mary P. Follet (4) F. Herzberg

6. What represents basic convictions that 'a specific mode of conduct or end-state of existence is personally or socially preferable to an opposite or converse mode of conduct or end-state of existence' ?
(1) Ethics (2) Belief
(3) Values (4) Personality

7. "Demonstrating statistically a relationship between scores on a selection procedure and job performance of a sample of workers" is called:
(1) Content Validity
(2) Construct Validity'
(3) Criterion Validity
(4) Test Validity

8. Likert had proposed only six dimensions of organisational climate. Who proposed seven steps of organisational climate ?
(1) Litwin and Stringer
(2) Schein
(3) Kluckhohn and strodtbeck
(4) Hofstede

9. Which types of employees are included in the definition of HRM by P. Morgan ?
(A) Host-Country Nationals
(B) Parent Country Nationals
(C) Third Country Nationals
(D) Domestic Country Nationals
Choose the correct answer from the options given below :
(1) (A), (B) Only
(2) (A), (B), (C) Only
(3) (B), (C), (D) Only
(4) (A), (B), (C), (D) Only

10. What should be the maximum size of numbers of representatives in the Joint Management Council?

(1) Six only (2) Twelve only
(3) Sixteen only (4) Twenty only

11. Performance appraisal too often degenerates into a dishonest annual rituals," who stated this ?

(1) Armstrong and Murlis
(2) Newton and Findlay
(3) Barlow (4) Grint

12. Who has authored the book "the Third Wave" ?

(1) Hammel and Prahlad
(2) Toffler
(3) Aldrich
(4) Nilkant and Ram Narayan

13. Which one of the following is correct Accounting Equation ?

(1) Assets = Liabilities – Capital
(2) Capital = Assets + Liabilities
(3) Liabilities = Capital + Assets
(4) Liabilities – Assets – Capital

14. Which is the value of P/V Ratio ?

	Period I	Period II
Sales (Rs.)	700000	900000
Profit (Rs.)	–10000	10000

(1) 10% (2) 20%
(3) 30% (4) 25%

15. If Current Ratio = 25, Liquid Ratio = 1.5, Working Capital = Rs. 90,000. What is the value of Inventory ?

(1) Rs. 60,000 (2) Rs. 90,000
(3) Rs. 1,50,000 (4) Rs. 2,10,000

16. In case of financial enterprises, cash flow arisen from flow dividend received and paid is shown in cash statement under-which one of the following activities ?

(1) Operating Activities.
(2) Financing Activities.
(3) Investing Activities.
(4) Dividend received is operating activities and divided paid is financing activities.

17. Which one of the following is correct about NPV and IRR of project (A) and project (B) ?

(1) NPV (A) + NPV (B) = NPV of (A + B)
(2) NPV (A) = NPV (B) $\neq$ NPV of (A + B)
(3) IRR (A) + IRR (B) = IRR of (A + B)
(4) IRR (A) $\times$ IRR (B) $\neq$ IRR(A – B)

18. Which one of the following is characterised in the interest rate parity ?

(1) The exchange rate between the currencies of two countries equal the ratio between the price of goods in these countries.
(2) The forward rate must be equal to the expected future spot rate.
(3) Nominal interest rate differential must be equal to the expected inflation rate differential in the two countries.
(4) The relationship between interest rates and exchange rate of two countries.

19. Company's current price of share is Rs 60 and dividend per share is Rs. 4. If its capitalisation rate is 12 percents. What is dividend growth rate ?

(1) 10% (2) 20%
(3) 3.2% (4) 5%

20. Gross working Capital refers to firms :

(1) Total Current Assets
(2) The difference between current assets and current liabilities.
(3) Total liquid assets
(4) Total investment in the firms

21. As per Henry Mintsberg, which of the following is NOT a part of his conception of types of strategies ?

(1) Intended Strategy
(2) Unrealised Strategy
(3) Contingency Strategy
(4) Emergent Strategy

22. As per Ries and Trout, which one of the following is NOT a standard criteria for successful positioning ?

(1) Competitiveness (2) Consistency
(3) Credibility (4) Commitment

23. The Parenting Fit Matrix related to Strategy Formulation was proposed by -

(1) T.L Wheelan, T D Hunger & K Ranganjan
(2) M. Alexander, A Cambell & M Goold
(3) G.D. Harrell, R.O Kieper & A Cambell
(4) G Hammel, L Segel & A C Inkpen

24. Which of the following is one of the five main factors given by E. M. Rogers that influence adoption of an innovation ?
(1) Accountability (2) Trialibility
(3) Flexibility (4) Salability

25. Consumers who are open to new ideas and are among the first to try new products, services or practices are called as -
(1) Dogmatic (2) Laggards
(3) Innovators (4) Early Majority

26. 'Making the brand a meaningful part of consumers conversations and likes by fostering direct and continuous customer involvement in shaping brand conversations, experiences and community'.
The above description pertains to which of the following concepts ?
(1) Customer Generated Marketing
(2) Societal Marketing Concept
(3) Customer Relationship Management
(4) Customer Engagement Marketing

27. 'A channel structure in which producers, wholesalers, and retailers act as a unified system One channel member owns the others, has contracts with them or has so much power that they all cooperate.' ?
The above description pentains to which of the following concepts ?
(1) Conventional Distribution Channel
(2) Vertical Marketing System
(3) Franchise System
(4) Horizontal Marketing System

28. 'A furnishing retailer company opens a new generation of furniture galleries that are part store, part ulterior design studio and part restaurant'.
This is an example of winch of the following ?
(1) Franchise Retailing
(2) Experiential Retailing
(3) Departmental Store Retailing
(4) Mega Retailing

29. The Contingency table in statistics is one:
(1) That consists of rows and columns that is used to classify data on two dimensions.
(2) That summarizes the number of measurements which are less than the upper-class boundary of each class.
(3) That summarizes the percentage of items (or measurement) in each of several non-overlapping classes.
(4) That displays points representing each class frequency above their class midpoints.

30. The primary difference between CPM and PERT is that:
(1) PERT lias one time estimate and CPM has three time estimates.
(2) PERT has two time estimates and CPM has three time estimates.
(3) PERT has three time estimates and CPM requires only one time factor for each activity.
(4) PERT makes the assumption that activities time are known with certainty and CPM employs three time estimates to compute expected values.

31. What is the major assumption we make when computing a mean form Grouped data:
(1) All values are discrete.
(2) Even value in a class is equal to the midpoint.
(3) Each class contains exactly the same number of values,
(4) No value occurs more than once.

32. What shall be the transportation cost if a researcher uses North-West Corner Rule to get the basic feasible solution to the following:

Distribution Centers					
Sources	DI	D2	D3	D4	Supply
SI	2	3	11	7	6
S2	1	0	6	1	1
S3	5	3	15	9	10
Requirements	7	5	3	2	

(1) 112 (2) 102
(3) 105 (4) 116

33. Which of the following Industry 4.0 technologies shall detect temperature, humidity and vibration changes, enabling avoidance of system malfunction and human protection in Oil and Gas Industry ?
(1) Artificial Intelligence (AI)
(2) Internet of Things (IOT)
(3) Big Data
(4) Machine Learning (ML)

34. To support Indian Artificial Intelligence (AI) Startups, which technological infrastructure is expected to be developed by Government of India ?
(1) Creation of EPZ
(2) Creation of GPU Clusters
(3) Creation of SPZ Clusters
(4) Creation of IT Parks

35. After 10 years of deadlock, European Union (EU) is ready to negotiate with India in WTO on which issue related to food security ?
(1) Public Stockholding Norms
(2) Climate Change
(3) Non-tariff barriers to trade
(4) Sanitary & Phytosanitarv measures

36. G20 Summit (2023) Proposed which Economic corridor including shipping and rail lines ?
(1) IMEE (India Middle East Europe Economic Corridor)
(2) BRI (Bolt and Road Initiative)
(3) CMREC (China Mongolia Russia Economic Corridor)
(4) NELB (New Eurasian Land Bridge (Corridor)

37. "Innovation is the specific instruments of entrepreneurship-the act that endows resources with a new capacity to create wealth" who said this?
(1) Peter Drucker
(2) J. A. Shumpeter
(3) Frank H. Knight
(4) Frank W. Young

38. In which institutions of women entrepreneurship Jyoti Jeevan Naik was associated?
(1) Shri Mahila Griha Udyog Lijjat Papad
(2) Sahkari Mahila Gram Samittee
(3) Jivika
(4) Self-employed Women's Association

39. Which type of Intrapreneur is known for generating innovative ideas and seeking ways to improve processes ?
(1) Employee Intrapreneur
(2) Doers Intrapreneur
(3) Creator Intrapreneur
(4) Implemented Intrapreneur

40. Fixing the zero date is important step in establishing a project -
(1) Preliminary steps (2) Secondary steps
(3) Definition steps (4) Last steps

41. What is NOT a misuse of committees?
(A) Authority
(B) Membership
(C) Replacement for a manager
(D) For decisions beyond participants authority
(1) (C) and (D) only (2) (A) and (B) only
(3) (C) and (A) only (4) (A) and (D) only

42. Two sets of theories are popular in the organisational behavior literature - The Behavioral and Cognitive. Behavioral theory constitutes of:
(A) Classical conditioning
(B) Operant conditioning
(C) Perceived consequences
(D) Social learning
(E) Prior learning
(1) (A), (B) arid (C) only

(2) (A), (B) and (D) only
(3) (B), (C) and (E) only
(4) (B), (C) and (D) only

43. The techniques for appraising performance include :
(A) Graphic Rating Scale Method
(B) Potential Rating
(C) Alternation Ranking Method
(D) Diversity Counts
(E) Paired Comparison Method
Choose the correct answer from the options given below
(1) (A), (B) and (D) only
(2) (B), (C) and (D) only
(3) (C), (D) and (E) only
(4) (A), '(C) and (E) only

44. Which of the following are four stages of Psychosexual Development for personality development according to Freud?
(A) Oral (B) Anal
(C) Phallic (D) Meticulous
(E) Genital
Choose the correct answer from the options given below:
(1) (A), (B),(C), (D) Only
(2) (A), (B), (C), (E) Only
(3) (B), (C), (D), (E) Only
(4) (A), (C), (D), (E) Only

45. Which of the following consists of broad model of HRM/HRD ?
(A) Hard variant of HRM (Matching Model of HRM)
(B) Soft valiant of HRM (Harvard Model HRM)
(C) 5P Model of HRM (Model of strategic HRM)
(D) Business Strategic Model of HRM (Business School Model)
(1) (A) and (B) only
(2) (B) and (C) only
(3) (A), (B) and (C) only
(4) (B), (C) and (D) only

46. Which of the following summarised under three Cs for human resource development ?
(A) Competence (B) Communication
(C) Commitment (D) Culture
(1) (A), (B) and (C) only
(2) (A), (C)and (D) only
(3) (B), (C) and (D) only
(4) (A), (B) and (D) only

47. Which of thee following are cash from financing activities of ?
(A) Cash receipt from issue of share
(B) Cash payment for buy-back of share
(C) Brokerage paid for acquisition of fixed assets
(D) Payment of cash dividend
(E) Cash receipt of interest and dividend on Long-term investment
Choose the correct answer from the options given below :
(1) (A), (B) and (C) only
(2) (A), (C) and (D) only
(3) (B), (C) and (D) only
(4) (A), (B) and (D) only

48. Which of the following related to Combined Leverage (CL)
(A) $CL = \frac{\text{Contribution}}{\text{PBT}}$
(B) $CL = \frac{\text{EBIT}}{\text{EBT}}$
(C) $CL = \frac{\text{Contribution}}{\text{EBT}}$
(D) $CL = \frac{\text{\% Change in EPS}}{\text{\% Change in sales}}$
(E) CL = Operating leverage × Financial leverage
Choose the correct answer from the options given below :
(1) (A), (B) and (E) only
(2) (B), (C) and (E) only
(3) (A), (D) and (E) only
(4) (A), (B) and (C) only

49. Which of the following are assumption of Net Operating Income Approach of Capital Structure ?
(A) There is no Corporate Tax

(B) Cost of debt remain constant at all level
(C) The Business risk remain constant every level of debt and equity mix
(D) The cost of Debt is less than cost of equity
(E) Overall cost of Capital remain constant

Choose the correct answer from the options given below:
(1) (A), (B) and (C) only
(2) (A) and (B) only
(3) (C), (D) and (E) only
(4) (A), (B), (C) and (E) only

50. Which of the following reasons may be attributed to the individuals time preference for money ?
(A) Risk
(B) Value of money would be increased
(C) Future uncertainties
(D) Preference for consumption
(E) Investment opportunities

Choose the correct answer from the options given below :
(1) (A), (B), and (C) Only
(2) (B), (C), and (D) Only
(3) (A), (C), (D) and (E) Only
(4) (A), (D), and (E) Only

51. Which of the following assumptions are based on Walter's Model of dividend ?
(A) Internal Financing
(B) 100 percent pay out ratio
(C) The firm has a short term life
(D) Constant EPS and dividend per Share (DIV)
(E) Increasing return and minimise cost of Capital

Choose the correct answer from the options given below :
(1) (A), (B) and (C) Only
(2) (A), (C) and (D) Only
(3) (B), (D) and (E) Only
(4) (A), (B) and (D) Only

52. Which of the following strategies are types of combination strategies ?
(A) No change strategies
(B) Pause/Proceed with caution strategies
(C) Term around strategies
(D) Profit strategies
(E) Concentration strategies
(1) (B) and (C) Only (2) (E) and (D) Only
(3) (A) and (B) Only (4) None of these

53. Which of the following are the important principles of Re-engineering according to Michael Hammer ?
(A) Develop value added jobs to balance out job elimination.
(B) Take specific actions to make the program operational.
(C) Subsume information processing work into the real work that produces the information.
(D) Develop action plan of activities needed to achieve the objectives.
(E) Treat geographically dispersed resources as though they were centralised,

Choose the correct answer from the options given below:
(1) (A) and (C) Only
(2) (B) and (D) Only
(3) (C) and (E) Only
(4) (B) and (E) Only

54. Which of the following are unique features of services ?
(A) Services are non-perishable.
(B) Services have inseparability of production and consumption.
(C) Services have the quality of perfect standardization.
(D) Services have the characteristic of Variability.
(E) Services are highly tangible so can be touched.

Choose the correct answer from the options given below :
(1) (A) and (D) Only
(2) (A) and (C) Only
(3) (C) and (D) Only
(4) (A) and (E) Only

55. Which of the following are the main issues to be tackled by the conceptual component of Customer Relationship Management Programme?
(A) Processing all customer requests coming in through multiple channels.
(B) Setting out the CRM objectives in clear terms.
(C) Creating a good product and mass marketing it.
(D) Putting customers first.
(E) Segmenting the market on die basis of occupations.
Choose the correct answer from the options given below :
(1) (B) and (D) Only
(2) (A) and (E) Only
(3) (C) and (D) Only
(4) (D) and (E) Only

56. Creating a seamless cross-channel buying experience that integrates in-stone, online, and mobile shopping.
The above is the description of which of the following?
(A) In store Marketing
(B) Direct Marketing
(C) Omni Channel Retailing
(D) Online Marketing
(E) Digital Marketing
Choose the correct answer from the options given below :
(1) (D) Only (2) (C) Only
(3) (A) and (B) Only
(4) (D) and (E) Only

57. The location focus for service firms should be on determining the volume of Customers and Revenue.
The major determinants of volume of Customers and Revenue are:
(A) Service and image compatibility with demographics of the customer drawing area.
(B) Proximity to raw materials arid suppliers.
(C) Quality of the competitor.
(D) Uniqueness of die firm's and competitor's location.
(E) Operating Policies of the competitor
Choose the correct answer from the options given below :
(1) (A), (C) and (E) Only
(2) (C), (D) and (E) Only
(3) (A), (C) and (D) Only
(4) (B), (D) and (E) Only

58. Six Sigma is:
(A) a strategy that focuses on total customer satisfaction.
(B) a mathematical function that connects quality lost and cost.
(C) a program to reduce defects.
(D) a disciplines that follows DMAIC model.
Choose the correct answer from the options given below :
(1) (A) and (D) Only
(2) (B) and (C) Only
(3) (A), (C) and (D) Only
(4) (B), (C) and (D) Only

59. For making a single-channel, single-phase queuing models, which of die following assumption are involved -
(A) Every arrival waits to be served regardless of the length of the time.
(B) Arrival are independent of preceding arrivals, but the average number of arrivals does not change over time.
(C) Arrival come from a finite or very small population on LIFO basis
(D) Service times follow the negative expantial distribution or are constant.
(E) The average service rate is greater than the average arrival rate.
Choose the correct answer from the options given below :
(1) (A), (B) and (C) Only
(2) (A), (B), (C) and (D) Only
(3) (A), (B), (D) and (E) Only
(4) (B), (C), (D) and (E) Only

60. Conditions under which companies may find more advantages to locate production in foreign countries than export to them are:

(A) When production abroad is costlier than at home ?

(B) When transportation costs are too high for moving goods or services internationally ?

(C) When companies lack domestic capacity ?

(D) When government inhibit the import of foreign products ?

(E) When products and services need not be altered substantially to gain sufficient consumer demand abroad ?

Choose the correct answer from the options given below :

(1) (A), (B) and (D) Only

(2) (B), (C) and (D) Only

(3) (C), (D) and (E) Only

(4) (E), (A) and (B) Only

61. Which of the following statements are correct about International Trade Theories ?

(A) According to mercantilism, countries should import more than they export.

(B) A country that practices neo-mercantilism attempts to run, export surplus to achieve a social or political objective.

(C) Theory of absolute advantage reasoned that restricted trade would lead country to specialize in those products that gave it a competitive advantage.

(D) According to theory of comparative advantage gains from trade will occur even in a country that has absolute advantage in all products because the country must give up less efficient output to produce more efficient output.

Choose the correct answer from the options given below:

(1) (A) and (C) Only

(2) (B) and (C) Only

(3) (C) and (D) Only

(4) (B) and (D) Only

62. Which of the followings are the national financial institutions ?

(A) Industrial Development Bank of India

(B) Industrial Finance Corporation of India

(C) The Stale Industrial Development Corporation

(D) United Nations Development Programme

(E) State Financial Corporations,

Choose the correct answer from the options given below :

(1) (A), (B) and (C) Only

(2) (B), (C) and (D) Only

(3) (A), (B), (C) and (E) Only

(4) (A), (C), (D) and (E) Only

63. Cooperative credit system in India mainly consists of :

(A) the short-term agricultural credit institutions.

(B) the long term agricultural credit institutions.

(C) the non-agricultural credit cooperatives.

(D) the short term industrial credit institutions.

Choose the correct answer from the options given below :

(1) (A), (B) Only

(2) (A), (B) and (C) Only

(3) (B), (C) and (D) Only

(4) (A), (C) and (D) Only

64. Which of the following are methods of assessment of economic viability of the project?

(A) Pay Back Period (PBP)

(B) Return on Investment (ROI)

(C) Net Present Value (NPV)

(D) Benefit cost Ratio (BCR)

(E) Critical Path Method (CPM)

Choose the correct answer from the options given below :

(1) (A), (B) and (C) Only

(2) (A), (B), (C) and (D) Only

(3) (B), (C), (D) and (E) Only

(4) (A), (C), (D) and (E) Only

65. Given below are two statements:

Statement (I): The adaptation of leadership styles to different contingencies has been well characterised by Robert Tannenbaum and Warren H. Schmidt, developers of leadership continuum concept.

Statement (II): They see leadership as involving variety of styles, ranging from one that is highly boss-oriented to one that is highly subordinate centered.

In the light of the above statements, choose the most appropriate answer from the options given below:

(1) Both Statement I and Statement II are correct
(2) Both Statement I and Statement II are incorrect
(3) Statement I is correct but Statement II is incorrect
(4) Statement I is incorrect but Statement II is correct

66. Match List–I with List–II.

List–I Theory/Approach	**List–II Proponders**
(A) Operational Management	(I) Mekinsey
(B) Behavioral Approach	(II) Wilfredo Pareto
(C) Social Systems Approach	(III) Henri Fayol
(D) 7-S Approach	(IV) Elton Mayo

Choose the correct answer from the options given below:

(1) (A)-(III), (B)-(II), (C)-(IV), (D)-(I)
(2) (A)-(I), (B)-(II), (C)-(III), (D)-(IV)
(3) (A)-(III), (B)-(IV), (C)-(II), (D)-(I)
(4) (A)-(I), (B)-(IV), (C)-(III), (D)-(II)

67. Match List–I with List–II.

List–I Motivational Theory	**List–II Proponder**
(A) Need Hierarchy Theory	(I) Fedrick Herzberg
(B) Two-Factor Theory	(II) Abraham H. Maslow
(C) Expectancy Theory	(III) Douglas MC Gregar
(D) Theory of X vs Y	(IV) V.H. Vroom

Choose the correct answer from the options given below:

(1) (A)-(I), (B)-(III), (C)-(II), (D)-(IV)
(2) (A)-(II), (B)-(I), (C)-(IV), (D)-(III)
(3) (A)-(III), (B)-(I), (C)-(II), (D)-(IV)
(4) (A)-(IV), (B)-(II), (C)-(I), (D)-(III)

68. Match List–I with List–II.

List–I Employers Attitude

(A) My Boat Attitude
(B) Shared Boat Attitude
(C) Our Boat Attitude
(D) Your Boat Attitude

List–II Appropriate Meaning

(I) Get off, if you do not like it.
(II) It is our own common enterprise, Let us combine our efforts to better it.
(III) We Sail together. Do not rock the boat.
(IV) With a sense of ownership and pride, the purpose is to let employees whole heartedly contribute to the cause of the enterprise.

Choose the correct answer from the options given below:

(1) (A)-(I), (B)-(III), (C)-(II), (D)-(IV)
(2) (A)-(II), (B)-(III), (C)-(I), (D)-(IV)
(3) (A)-(IV), (B)-(III), (C)-(II), (D)-(I)
(4) (A)-(II), (B)-(III). (C)-(IV), (D)-(I)

69. Match List–I with List–II.

List–I Accounting Standard	**List–II Related Concept**
(A) Ind AS -1	(I) Cash Flow Statement
(B) Ind AS – 7	(II) Presentation of Financial Statement
(C) Ind AS -16	(III) Revenue recognition
(D) Ind AS -18	(IV) Property Plant and Equipment

Choose the correct answer from the options given below:

(1) (A)-(I), (B)-(II), (C)-(III), (D)-(IV)
(2) (A)-(II), (B)-(I), (C)-(IV), (D)-(III)
(3) (A)-(II), (B)-(I), (C)-(III), (D)-(IV)
(4) (A)-(I), (B)-(III), (C)-(IV), (D)-(III)

70. Match List–I with List–II.

List–I Meaning	List–II Concept
(A) Divestitures	(I) The parent firm no longer exists.
(B) Pac-man defence	(II) Does not bring any cash to the parent company.
(C) Spin-off	(III) Selling of some of assets of the firm.
(D) Split-up	(IV) Target company making a counter bid for raiders company.

Choose the correct answer from the options given below:

(1) (A)-(IV), (B)-(III), (C)-(II), (D)-(I)
(2) (A)-(III), (B)-(IV), (C)-(II), (D)-(I)
(3) (A)-(III), (B)-(IV), (C)-(I), (D)-(II)
(4) (A)-(I), (B)-(II), (C)-(III), (D)-(IV)

71. Match List–I with List–II.

List–I Tools	List–II Proposed by
(A) Balance Score Card	(I) Heing weitrich
(B) TOWS Matrix	(II) C.W. Hofer
(C) Product/Marke Evolution Matrixt	(III) Roberts Kaplan and David P. Norton
(D) VRIO Frame Work	(IV) Jay Barney

Choose the correct answer from the options given below:

(1) (A)-(II), (B)-(I), (C)-(IV), (D)-(III)
(2) (A)-(III), (B)-(I), (C)-(II), (D)-(IV)
(3) (A)-(II), (B)-(III), (C)-(IV), (D)-(I)
(4) (A)-(IV), (B)-(II), (C)-(III), (D)-(I)

72. Match List–I with List–II.

List–I Decision Rule	List–II Rationale for applying the decision Rule to Down App.
(A) Conjunctive	(I) "I bought the Smartphone App with the highest over all rating".
(B) Disjunctive	(II) "I downloaded the Smartphone App that had the most downloads".
(C) Affect Referred	(III) "I selected the Smart Phone App that had no bad features".
(D) Majority vote	(IV) "I picked the Smart Phone App that excelled in at least one attribute

Choose the correct answer from the options given below:

(1) (A)-(IV), (B)-(III), (C)-(II), (D)-(I)
(2) (A)-(II), (B)-(III), (C)-(IV), (D)-(I)
(3) (A)-(III), (B)-(IV), (C)-(I), (D)-(II)
(4) (A)-(I), (B)-(IV), (C)-(II), (D)-(III)

73. Match List–I with List–II.

List–I Inspection Process	List–II Inspection Type
(A) Operator doing his job properly and self check at the point of production or purchase.	(I) Poka-Yoke
(B) That classifies items as being either good or defective.	(II) Source Inspection
(C) Assisted by the use of check list and controls such as fail - safe device that ensures production of a good unit every time.	(III) Variable Inspection

(D) Classification of items as falling continuum scale such as dimension or strength — (IV) Attribute Inspection

Choose the correct answer from the options given below:

(1) (A)-(III), (B)-(II), (C)-(IV), (D)-(I)
(2) (A)-(III), (B)-(II), (C)-(I), (D)-(IV)
(3) (A)-(II), (B)-(IV), (C)-(I), (D)-(III)
(4) (A)-(II), (B)-(III), (C)-(I), (D)-(IV)

74. Match List–I with List–II.

List–I

Data Warehouse Types Concept

(A) Data Marts
(B) Operational Data Store
(C) Enterprise Data Warehouse
(D) Metadata

List–II

Functions Meaning of Data Ware Houses

(I) Provides a fairly recent form of customer information file and is used as interim Staging area.
(II) Provides integration of data from many sources into a standard format.
(III) Describe the structure and some meaning about data
(IV) Subset of a data warehouse, typically consisting of a single subject area

Choose the correct answer from the options given below:

(1) (A)-(IV), (B)-(I), (C)-(II), (D)-(III)
(2) (A)-(IV), (B)-(I), (C)-(III), (D)-(II)
(3) (A)-(I), (B)-(IV), (C)-(II), (D)-(III)
(4) (A)-(II), (B)-(III), (C)-(I), (D)-(IV)

75. Match List–I with List–II.

List–I **Name of Theories of Entrepreneurship**	**List–II** **Proponder**
(A) Theory of Opportunities and Innovation.	(I) Frank W. Young
(B) Theory of Change.	(II) Peter F. Drucker
(C) Theory of Religious Beliefs.	(III) John H. Kunkel
(D) Theory of Entrepreneurship Supply.	(IV) Max Weber

Choose the correct answer from the options given below:

(1) (A)-(II), (B)-(I), (C)-(IV), (D)-(III)
(2) (A)-(I), (B)-(II), (C)-(III), (D)-(IV)
(3) (A)-(IV), (B)-(III), (C)-(1I), (D)-(I)
(4) (A)-(II), (B)-(III), (C)-(I), (D)-(IV)

76. Arrange the steps of process of learning in proper order

(A) Acquiring Knowledge
(B) internalization of new knowledge
(C) Using learning on all situation
(D) Assimilation or retention
(E) Application of new learning
(F) Self-monitored learning

Choose the correct answer from the options given below

(1) (A), (D), (B), (E), (C), (F)
(2) (A), (B), (C), (D), (E), (F)
(3) (A), (C), (B), (D), (E), (F)
(4) (B), (D), (F), (C), (A), (E)

77. There exists certain requirements for effective control Arrange the requirements from later to initial as proposed by Koontz and Weihrich.

(A) Tailoring controls to individual managers.
(B) Fitting the control system to the organisational culture.
(C) Making sure that control point up exceptions at critical point
(D) Seeking objectivity of controls.

Choose the correct answer from the options given below :

(1) (B), (A), (C), (D) (2) (B), (C), (D), (A)
(3) (B), (A), (D), (C) (4) (B), (D), (C), (A)

78. Arrange the Indian Trade Unions/Associations according to their formation/establishment from earlier to latter.

(A) Madras Labour Union

(B) Bhartiya Mazdoor Sangh
(C) The Indian National Trade Union Congress
(D) All India Trade Union Congress
(E) The Red Trade Union Congress

Choose the correct answer from the options given below :

(1) (A), (C), (B), (D), (E) Only
(2) (A), (D), (E), (C), (B) Only
(3) (B), (A), (C), (D), (E) Only
(4) (D), (A), (E), (C), (B) Only

79. Arrange the following steps of the Budgeting process in the proper sequence

(A) Obtaining estimates
(B) Communicating Budget
(C) Reporting Interim Progress towards budget objectives
(D) Implementing the budget plan
(E) Co-ordinating estimate

Choose the correct answer from the options given below :

(1) (B), (A), (E), (D), (C) Only
(2) (A), (E), (C), (B), (D) Only
(3) (A), (E), (B), (C), (D) Only
(4) (A), (E), (B), (D), (C) Only

80. Arrange the following process of working capital cycle of manufacturing concern in a proper sequence:

(A) Raw material
(B) Cash
(C) Debtors
(D) Finish goods
(E) Work in progress

Choose the correct answer from the options given below:

(1) (B), (A), (E), (D), (C) Only
(2) (A), (E), (B), (C), (D) Only
(3) (A),(E),(D),(B),(C) Only
(4) (A), (E), (D), (C), (B) Only

81. Arrange the following stages of international development in sequential ascending order.

(A) Primarily domestic company with international division
(B) Domestic company
(C) Multinational corporation with global emphasis
(D) Multinational corporation with multidomestic emphasis
(E) Domestic company with export division

Choose the correct answer from the options given below:

(1) (E), (B), (C), (A), (D) Only
(2) (B), (E), (A), (D), (C) Only
(3) (B), (E), (A), (C), (D) Only
(4) (B), (A), (E), (D), (C) Only

82. Put in sequence the four steps to convert the raw real-world data into minable data sets

(A) Data Cleaning
(B) Data Reduction
(C) Data Transformation
(D) Data Consolidation

Choose the correct answer from the options given below

(1) (B), (A), (C), (D) Only
(2) (D), (A), (C), (B) Only
(3) (A), (D), (C), (B) Only
(4) (B), (C), (A), (D) Only

83. Arrange the Project Life Cycle Phases in proper order :

(A) Concept Phase
(B) Planning and Organising Phase
(C) Definition Phase
(D) Implementation Phase
(E) Project Clean-up Phase

Choose the correct answer from the options given below :

(1) (A), (C), (B), (D), (E) Only
(2) (A), (B), (C), (D), (E) Only
(3) (C), (A), (B), (D), (E) Only
(4) (A), (D), (C), (B), (E) Only

84. The objective of Scheduling is to allocate and prioritize demand to available facilities, the Scheduling decisions ranges from years to minutes/hours/days. Arrange the following Scheduling decisions:

(A) Aggregate Planning

(B) Short-term Scheduling
(C) Master Schedule
(D) Capacity Planning

Choose the correct answer from the options given below:

(1) (B), (A), (C), (D) Only
(2) (D), (A), (C). (B) Only
(3) (A),(D),(C),(B) Only
(4) (B), (C), (A), (D) Only

85. Arrange the following components of Value-Delivery Process in proper sequence from 1st to 6th step.

(A) Communicating the Value
(B) Enhancing the Value (including sustaining the value)
(C) Capturing the value back from the market (through pricing)
(D) Delivering the value
(E) Selecting the value (including exploring the value)
(F) Creating the Value

Choose the correct answer from the options given below :

(1) (E), (F), (A), (D), (C), (B) Only
(2) (F), (B), (D), (E), (A), (C) Only
(3) (E), (F), (C), (D), (A), (B) Only
(4) (A), (E), (F), (B), (C), (D) Only

86. Given below are two statements:

Statement (I): Planning premises are defined as the anticipated environment in which plans are expected to operate. They include assumptions or forecasts of the future ans known conditions that will affect the operation of plans.

Statement (II): No distinction should be drawn between forecasts that are planning premises and forecasts that are translated into future expectancies, usually in financial terms, from actual plans developed.

In the light of the above statements, choose the most appropriate answer from the options given below:

(1) Both Statement I and Statement II are correct
(2) Both Statement I and Statement II are incorrect
(3) Statement I is correct but Statement II is incorrect
(4) Statement I is incorrect but Statement II is correct

87. Given below are two statements:

Statement (I): Organisation Development Interventions are sets structured activities in which selected organisational units engage in a sequence of tasks that will lead to organisational improvement.

Statement (II): The range of Organisation Development interventions is quite extensive. Interventions have been developed to solve most problems related to the human side of organisations.

In the light of the above statements, choose the most appropriate answer from the options given below:

(1) Both Statement I and Statement II are correct
(2) Both Statement I and Statement II are incorrect
(3) Statement I is correct but Statement II is incorrect
(4) Statement I is incorrect but Statement II is correct

88. Given below are two statements:

Statement (I): Economic exposure refers to the change in the value of firm caused by unexpected changes in the exchange rate.

Statement (II): Transaction exposure refers to long term cash flow exposure.

In the light of the above statements, choose the most appropriate answer from the options given below:

(1) Both Statement I and Statement II are correct
(2) Both Statement I and Statement II are incorrect
(3) Statement I is correct but Statement II is incorrect
(4) Statement I is incorrect but Statement II is correct

89. Given below tire two statements: one is labelled as Assertion (A) and the other is labelled as Reason (R).

Assertion (A): A brand is an important corporate resource.

Reason (R): A brand embodies all of the characteristics of a company's product in the mind of the consumer.

In the light of the above statements, choose the most appropriate answer from the options given below:

(1) Both (A) and (R) are correct and (R) is the correct explanation of (A)
(2) Both (A) and (R) are correct but (R) is not the correct explanation of (A)
(3) (A) is correct but (R) is not correct
(4) (A) is not correct but (R) is correct

90. Given below are two statements: one is labelled as Assertion (A) and the other is labelled as Reason (R).

Assertion (A): The failure of the international market to connect firms as collaborators will entice a company to enter with wholly owned operations or wholly owned FDI.

Reason (R): The company perceives having operating advantages to overcome its liability of foreignness.

In the light of the above statements, choose the most appropriate answer from the options given below:

(1) Both (A) and (R) are correct and (R) is the correct explanation of (A)
(2) Both (A) and (R) are correct but (R) is not the correct explanation of (A)
(3) (A) is correct but (R) is not correct
(4) (A) is not correct but (R) is correct

Read the following passage carefully, and answer question.

In this modern digitalized world, business are required to be mindful both in terms of what they are doing and how they are doing it. The company's brand is not just dependent on the quality of products they are offering to people but on the overall impact of the company's operations on the society, environment and the economy.

Their sense of social responsibility provides them with a competitive edge over their competitors in a crowded marketplace. CSR is a holistic and integrated management concept whereby companies integrate their social and environmental objectives with their business objectives. It companies integrate their social and environmental objectives with their business objectives. It works on a Triple Bottom Line Approach i.e. Company focuses on 3P's; People, Planet and Profit while addressing all the expectations of its stakeholders. The majority of policy initiatives in the country are driven by the objectives of equal opportunities, minimizing poverty and human deprivation, focus on fundamental rights, etc. thereby leading to strong human development.

The choices that we make today will be going to affect and influence our future generations.

Despite all this, inequality and disparity still exists. This year, the Indian Government implemented new CSR guidelines. These guidelines require Indian companies to spend 2 percent of their net profit on CSR. India is the first country in the world to make CSR mandatory, including the CSR mandate in Companies Act, 2013, is a great step of engaging the corporate sector in the equitable development of the country. Earlier companies were required to spend 2 percent of tire profits towards CSR and in case of failure to do so; they were required to give reasons. But as per the present amendment, companies are required to spent 2 percent of profit towards CSR in the given time limit or are required to turn over this amount of profits in the funds which are run by the government.

The new amendment will require all the companies which qualify the provisions under CSR guidelines to spend the specified part of their profits towards Corporate Social Responsibility without failing.

91. Given below are two statements:

Statement (I): CSR is a holistic and integrated management concept whereby companies integrate their industrial and future objectives with their business objectives.

Statement (II): In this modern digitalized world, business are required to be mindful both in terms of what they the doing and how they are doing.

In the light of the above statements, choose the most appropriate answer from the options given below:

(1) Both Statement I and Statement II are correct

(2) Both Statement I and Statement II are incorrect

(3) Statement I is correct but Statement II is incorrect

(4) Statement I is incorrect but Statement II is correct

92. According to the passage, what is the significance of a company's Social responsibility in the modern digitalized world ?

(1) It has no impact on the company's brand.

(2) It depends solely on the quality of products.

(3) It provides a competitive edge in the crowded market place.

(4) It leads to higher profits.

93. What is the 'Triple Bottom Line Approach' in CSR as mentioned in the passage ?

(1) Focus on customer satisfaction, revenue and profit.

(2) Focus on people, planed and profit.

(3) Focus on shareholder's interest, environmental sustainability and innovation.

(4) Focus on reducing costs, increasing production and market share.

94. Given below are two statements: one is labelled as Assertion (A) and the other is labelled as Reason (R).

Assertion (A): Companies are required to spend 2% of profits towards CSR in the given time limit.

Reason (R): The Government of India has made stringent provisions for CSR in the Companies Act, 2013.

In the light of the above statements, choose the most appropriate answer from the options given below:

(1) Both (A) and (R) are correct and (R) is the correct explanation of (A)

(2) Both (A) and (R) are correct but (R) is not the correct explanation of (A)

(3) (A) is correct but (R) is not correct

(4) (A) is not correct but (R) is correct

95. What is the consequence for companies that fail to most the CSR spending requirement as per the new amendments ?

(1) Companies may file a suitable explanation.

(2) Companies may seek grace from the Government.

(3) Companies may get it done from the Sister Companies.

(4) Companies are required to turn over the profits to government - run funds.

Read the following passage carefully, and answer question.

Introduction of Corporate Governance in a company brings order and methods in decision making process and fixes who should own the responsibility'. The company will focus on its mission, vision and not any personal likes dislikes of a few top officers. The benefits of corporate governance are difficult to quantify in short range.

Accounting jugglery and showing profits give a company's short term gains but they are not long term policies for financial credibility. True financial performance of a company, openness and governance policies give investor's confidence.

The unethical policies or mismanagement by CEO or director of a company will be exposed by adhering to corporate governance principles. Corporate governance will throw light on excessive remunerations given to directors or CEOs. It improves investors confidence and relations.

The occurrence of frauds and mismanagement can be detected early for remedial actions. It is also agreed that no system can remove fraudulent practices fully. Corporate governance is an open democratic system. They may appear long winded or time consuming or individual decision making is hindered.

96. What is one of the primary goals of including corporate governance in a company ?
(1) Maximizing short-term profits.
(2) Discouraging personal likes and dislikes of top management.
(3) Bringing order and method to decision making.
(4) Enhancing competition in the market.

97. According to the passage, what is the benefit of adhering to corporate governance for investors ?
(1) Short term gains
(2) Confidence in true financial performance
(3) Higher rates of dividend
(4) Possibilities of rights issues

98. How does corporate governance help in exposing unethical policies or mismanagement in a company?
(1) By promoting company's flag ship brand.
(2) By enhancing employees productivity.
(3) By fixing responsibilities and promoting openness.
(4) By encouraging accounting Jugglery.

99. How does the passage describe corporate governance as system ?
(1) Time ensuring but effective.
(2) Hinding the risk of fraud.
(3) An open democratic system with some drawbacks.
(4) A system capable of removing fraudulent activities 100%.

100. Which one of the following is one of the advantages of corporate governance mentioned in lire passage ?
(1) Hiding excessive remuneration of directors and CEOs.
(2) Discouraging individual decision making.
(3) Improving investors confidence and relations.
(4) Avoiding competition.

ANSWER KEY

1. (3)	**2.** (1)	**3.** (2)	**4.** (2)	**5.** (1)	**6.** (3)	**7.** (3)	**8.** (1)	**9.** (2)	**10.** (2)
11 (1)	**12.** (2)	**13.** (4)	**14.** (1)	**15.** (1)	**16.** (4)	**17.** (1)	**18.** (4)	**19.** (4)	**20.** (1)
21. (3)	**22.** (4)	**23.** (2)	**24.** (2)	**25.** (3)	**26.** (4)	**27.** (2)	**28.** (2)	**29.** (1)	**30.** (3)
31. (2)	**32.** (4)	**33.** (2)	**34.** (2)	**35.** (1)	**36.** (1)	**37.** (1)	**38.** (1)	**39.** (3)	**40.** (4)
41. (1)	**42.** (2)	**43.** (4)	**44.** (2)	**45.** (3)	**46.** (2)	**47.** (4)	**48.** (1,3)	**49.** (4)	**50.** (3)
51. (4)	**52.** (4)	**53.** (3)	**54.** (1)	**55.** (1)	**56.** (2)	**57.** (3)	**58.** (3)	**59.** (3)	**60.** (2)
61. (4)	**62.** (3)	**63.** (2)	**64.** (2)	**65.** (1)	**66.** (3)	**67.** (2)	**68.** (1)	**69.** (2)	**70.** (2)
71. (2)	**72.** (3)	**73.** (3)	**74.** (1)	**75.** (1)	**76.** (1)	**77.** (4)	**78.** (2)	**79.** (4)	**80.** (4)
81. (2)	**82.** (2)	**83.** (1)	**84.** (2)	**85.** (1)	**86.** (3)	**87.** (1)	**88.** (2)	**89.** (1)	**90.** (1)
91. (4)	**92.** (3)	**93.** (2)	**94.** (1)	**95.** (4)	**96.** (3)	**97.** (2)	**98.** (3)	**99.** (3)	**100.** (3)

OOO

SEPTEMBER 2024

MANAGEMENT

PAPER-II

Note : This paper contains **hundred (100)** objective type questions of **two (2)** marks each. **All questions are compulsory.**

1. Robert L Katz identified three kinds of skills for administrators. Which among the following skills was NOT identified by Katz?
(1) Technical skill (2) Human skill
(3) Design skill (4) Conceptual skill

2. "The right that is delegated to an individual or department to control specified processes, practices, policies, or other matters relating to activities undertaken by person in other departments" is called:
(1) Product authority
(2) Functional authority
(3) Temporary authority
(4) Service authority

3. When we measure what type of demand we assume that effects of other variables is constant?
(1) Revenue and price elasticity of demand
(2) Gross elasticity of demand
(3) Income elasticity of demand
(4) Promotional elasticity of demand

4. The structuralist theory of inflation was proposed by :
(1) G. Myrdal and P. Streeten
(2) V.N Pandit
(3) Milton Fredman
(4) Fritz Machlup

5. A sum total of ways in which an individual reacts and interacts with others is called:
(1) Perception (2) Attitude
(3) Personality (4) Values

6. Whistle blowing is:
(1) The choices made from among two or more alternatives
(2) A discrepancy between some current state of affairs and some desired state
(3) Reporting unethical practices by their employer to outsiders
(4) Refers to choices that are consistent and value maximising

7. A phenomenon in which the norm for consensus overrides that realistic appraisal of alternative course of action is:
(1) Groupshift
(2) Groupthink
(3) Brainstorming
(4) Nominal group technique

8. The procedure for determining the duties and skill requirements of a job and the kind of person who should be hired for it is :
(1) Job description (2) Job analysis
(3) Job specification (4) Job evaluation

9. "Formulating and executing human resource policies and practices that produce the employee competencies and behaviours the company needs to achieve its strategic aims" is called?
(1) Strategic human resource Management
(2) Strategic human resource Planning
(3) Strategic human resource Auditing
(4) Strategic human resource Evaluation

10. Who has developed the HRD scorecard?
(1) T.V. Rao (2) Peter F. Drucker
(3) J. Friedman (4) J. Bright

11. "The process for enabling employees to better understand and develop their career and interests more effectively" is termed as ?
(1) Career Planning

(2) Career Management
(3) Career Development
(4) Career Counselling

12. What is the belief among pluralists regarding conflict in organisation?
(1) Conflict is unnecessary and should be avoided at all cost
(2) Conflict is necessary and should be ignored
(3) Conflict is necessary but it can be managed and resolved
(4) Conflict should be eliminated through strict rules

13. What is the value of cost of capital after tax in a perpetual bond sold at par, coupon rate of interest being 7 per cent. Assuming that firm pay tax at a 50 per cent rate?
(1) 7% (2) 35%
(3) 5% (4) 3.5%

14. If profit before interest and tax is Rs.10000, provision for Tax=Rs.5000, No. of Equity Share = 3000. Preference dividend = 2000. Dividend per equity share=0.40, what is the value of payout ratio?
(1) 10% (2) 20%
(3) 50% (4) 40%

15. Prepaid salary is which type of account ?
(1) Personal Account
(2) Real Account
(3) Nominal Account
(4) Both Personal and Real Account

16. From the following information :

Year	2021	2022
Sales	Rs. 32,00,000	Rs. 57, 00,000
Profit Loss	Rs. 3,00,000	Rs. 7,00,000

What is the value of P/V ratio?
(1) 16% (2) 40%
(3) 12.5% (4) 25%

17. If $R_f = 10\%$, $R_m = 18\%$ and $B_i = 1.35$, What is the expected rate of return for security?
(1) 28.8% (2) 18.8%
(3) 8.8% (4) 20.8%

18. Which one of the following cost arises due to the failure of the customers to meet their obligations when payment on credit sales become due after the expiry of the credit period?
(1) Collection costs
(2) Capital costs
(3) Delinquency costs
(4) Default costs

19. A company paid a dividend of ₹3.70 in the previous year. The dividends in the future are expected to grow perpetually at a rate of 8 per cent. What is the share price today if the market captalises dividend at 12 per cent?
(1) ₹ 40 (2) ₹ 33
(3) ₹ 100 (4) ₹ 200

20. Which one of the following is Walter's formula to determine the market price per share?
(1) $p = \frac{D/V}{K} + \frac{r}{K}(EPS - D/V)$
(2) $p = D/V + \frac{r(EPS - D/V)/K}{K}$
(3) $p = \frac{D/V}{K} + \frac{r(EPS - D/V)/K}{K}$
(4) $p = \frac{D/V}{K} + \frac{r(EPS - D/V)}{K}$

21. "Dividing a market into smaller segments of buyers with distinct needs, characteristics or behaviours that might require separate marketing strategies or mixes" is termed as?
(1) Market Targeting
(2) Market Segmentation
(3) Market Differentiation
(4) Market Positioning

22. "Consumer buying behaviour in situations characterised by high consumer involvement in a purchase and significant prescribed differences among brands" is termed as:
(1) Complex buying behaviour
(2) Dissonance-reducing buying behaviour

(3) Habitual buying behaviour
(4) Veriety-seeking buying behaviour

23. Who has propounded the 'Diamond of National Competitive Advantages' model of corporate level strategies?
(1) M. E. Porter (2) H. I. Ansoff
(3) J. B. Barney (4) Peter F. Drucker

24. Who has suggested the 7-S framework for organisational change?
(1) Mckinsey (2) Peter Drucker
(3) Dale Yoder (4) Mintzberg

25. Which one of the following is true about service marketing?
(1) Services can be seen, tasted, felt, heard or smelled before purchase
(2) Services can be separated from the service providers
(3) Quality of services depends on who provides them and when, where and how
(4) Services can be stored for later sale or use

26. Which of the following movement of products clearly defines the term "Inbound Logistics"?
(1) Suppliers to company
(2) Company to Reseller
(3) Reseller to Customer
(4) Customers to Suppliers

27. Which of the following is a type of off-price retailer?
(1) Super store
(2) Category killer
(3) Factory outlet
(4) Discount store

28. Which one of the following is true about the role of sales force personal selling?
(1) Personal selling consists largely of non-personal communication with large group of customers
(2) Personal selling is interpersonal arm of promotion mix
(3) Personal selling is less effective than advertising in more complex selling situations
(4) Personal selling sales force is not allowed to adjust marketing offer and presentation to fit each customer's special needs

29. Which of the following is true about the term "KAIZEN"?
(1) KAIZEN is dramatic, a real attention getter. It is like magma that appears in abrupt eruptions from time to time
(2) KAIZEN involves all the activities directed towards maintaining current technological, managerial and operating standards and improving current standards
(3) KAIZEN is subtle and its results are seldom immediately visible. It is an ongoing process and involves entire organisation
(4) KAIZEN is seen as major changes in the wake of technological break throughs or the introduction of latest management concepts or production techniques

30. The mean of binomial distribution is 40 and standard deviation 6. What is the value of n?
(1) 36 (2) 360
(3) 400 (4) 40

31. Which one of the following is a non-parametric test?
(1) χ^2-test (2) t- test
(3) z-test (4) F-test

32. Find the initial feasible solution of the following transportation problem by Vogel's Approximation Method (VAM).

From \ To	W_1	W_2	W_3	Supply
F_1	16	20	12	200
F_2	14	8	18	160
F_3	26	24	16	100
Demand	180	130	150	460 / 460

(1) ₹ 6060 (2) ₹ 6660
(3) ₹ 6000 (4) ₹ 6600

33. Which one of the following is a type of Foreign Direct Investment?
(1) Greenfield Investment
(2) Foreign Portfolio Investment
(3) Qualified Foreign Investment
(4) Commercial loans

34. Which one of the following in NOT a technique of foreign trade financing?
(1) Discounting
(2) Banker's Acceptance
(3) Factoring
(4) Forfeiting

35. Which one of the following is NOT a component of Balance of Payments?
(1) Official Reserves Account
(2) Current Account
(3) Deficit Account
(4) Capital Account

36. Which of the following helps in Business decision making in ill-structured decision situation often using complex spreadsheet by creating "what if" models for manager?
(1) Management Information System (MIS)
(2) Decision Support System (DSS)
(3) Knowledge Work System (KWS)
(4) Executive Support System (ESS)

37. Which type of Intrapreneur is known for generating innovative ideas and seeking ways to improve process?
(1) Employee Intrapreneur
(2) Doers Intrapreneur
(3) Creator Intrapreneur
(4) Implementers Intrapreneur

38. In which of the following Association organisation Ela Bhatt is associated?
(1) Mukta Services
(2) Lijjat Papad
(3) Self employed women's Association
(4) Avya Global connect

39. What can lead to the withdrawal of status respect according to Hagen's theory of Entrepreneurship?
(1) Increased recognition from the group
(2) Perception that efforts and purposes are highly valued
(3) Belief in the stability of status symbols
(4) Perception that efforts and purposes are not valued by others

40. What is the primary objective of a feasibility study?
(1) To persuade investors to fund a project
(2) To assess the historical background of a business
(3) To uncover strength and weakness of a business idea
(4) To outline the technical development process

41. Arrange the steps in demand forecasting from beginning to end
A. Specifying objectives
B. Making choice of methods
C. Determing the perspective
D. Estimation and interpretation of results
E. Collection of data and data adjustment
Choose the *correct* answer from the options given below:
(1) A, B, D, C, E (2) C, A, E, D, B
(3) C, B, A, D, E (4) A, C, B, E, D

42. Arrange the major steps of Luthan's O.B. Mod approach to behavioral performance management from earlier to later
A. Measure B. Identity
C. Intervene D. Analyse
E. Evaluate
Choose the *correct* answer from the options given below:
(1) A, B, C, D, E (2) B, C, D, E, A
(3) A, C, B, E, D (4) B, A, D, C, E

43. Arrange the Five Stages of Conflict Process in proper sequence from beginning to end
A. Potential opposition or incompatibility
B. Intentions
C. Cognition and personalisation
D. Outcomes
E. Behaviour
Choose the *correct* answer from the options given below:

(1) A, C, E, B, D (2) A, C, B, E, D
(3) A, B, C, D, E (4) A, D, E, C, B

44. Arrange the career management process in proper sequence from beginning to end.

A. Assessment
B. Strategy
C. Career planning
D. Career evaluation
E. Career Development

Choose the *correct* answer from the options given below:

(1) A, B, C, D, E (2) B, A, C, E, D
(3) A, B, D, C, E (4) B, A, D, C, E

45. Arrange the Repatriation process in proper order as given by Peter J Dowling.

A. Preparation
B. Transition
C. Physical relocation
D. Re-adjustment

Choose the *correct* answer from the options given below:

(1) A, B, C, D (2) A, C, B, D
(3) B, A, C, D (4) A, D, B, C

46. Arrange the following components of cost sheet in proper sequence starting from first to last,

A. Cost of sale
B. Cost of production
C. Raw material consumed
D. Factory cost
E. Prime cost

Choose the *correct* answer from the options given below:

(1) A, B, C, D, E (2) C, D, E, B, A
(3) C, D, E, A, B (4) C, E, D, B, A

47. Arrange the following developments in International monetary system in the order of sequence starting from oldest to newest; -

A. Gold standard
B. Smithsonian arrangement
C. Specie commodity standard
D. Floating Rate Regime
E. Fixed Party System

Choose the *correct* answer from the options given below:

(1) A, C, B, E, D (2) B, A, C, E, D
(3) E, C, A, D, B (4) C, A, E, B, D

48. Arrange the Hambrick and Fredrickson model of strategic management in proper sequence from beginning to end.

A. Vision and mission
B. Goals and objectives
C. Internal and external strategic analysis
D. Implementation Levers and strategic leadership
E. Strategy arenas vehicles differentiators staging economic logic

Choose the *correct* answer from the options given below:

(1) A, C, B, D, E (2) A, B, E, C, D
(3) A, B, C, D, E (4) B, A, C, D, E

49. Arrange the following Buyer-Readiness stages in correct sequence from starting to end.

A. Knowledge B. Awareness
C. Preference D. Conviction
E. Liking

Choose the *correct* answer from the options given below:

(1) B, A, E, C, D (2) A, B, C, D, E
(3) B, E, A, C, D (4) E, A, B, D, C

50. Arrange the following Historical Events in operations management in the order of sequence starting from oldest to newest.

A. Quality Revolution
B. Scientific Management
C. Industrial Revolution
D. Operations Research
E. Human Relations

Choose the *correct* answer from the options given below:

(1) C, B, E, D, A (2) B, C, D, E, A
(3) A, B, D, C, E (4) E, C, B, A, D

51. Arrange the following procedures of testing hypotheses in proper sequence.

A. Making decisions
B. Setting a test criterion

C. Set up hypothesis
D. Set up suitable significance level
E. Doing computations
Choose the *correct* answer from the options given below:
(1) C, D, B, E, A (2) B, C, D, A, E
(3) C, D, A, B, E (4) D, C, B, E, A

52. Arrange the following Trade Negotiation Rounds of World Trade Organisation in the order of their occurrence from oldest to latest:
A. Bali Conference
B. Geneva Conference
C. Hong Kong Conference
D. Cancun Conference
E. Doha Conference
Choose the *correct* answer from the options given below:
(1) A, B, C, E ,D (2) B, C, D, E, A
(3) A, B, C, D, E (4) E, D ,C, B, A

53. Arrange the following stages/elements of technology management in proper sequence starting from first TO fast:
A. Technology Adaptation
B. Technology Abandonment
C. Technology Advancement
D. Technology Acquisition
E. Technology Awareness
Choose the *correct* answer from the options given below:
(1) A, C, D, B, E (2) B, C, D, A, E
(3) E, D, A, C, B (4) D, C, A, B, E

54. Arrange the Project Life Cycle phase in proper sequence from starting to end.
A. Definition phasc
B. Conception phase
C. Implementation phase
D. Planning and organising phase
E. Project clean-up phase
Choose the *correct* answer from the options given below:
(1) A, B, D, E, C (2) B, A, D, C,E
(3) B, A, C, D, E (4) E, A, C, D, B

55. Arrange the financial institutions according to their formation from latest to earliest
A. Industrial Finance Corporation of India
B. Regional Rural Bank
C. National Bank for Agriculture and Rural Development
D. National Industrial Development Corporation
E. The Reserve Bank of Lidia.
Choose the *correct* answer from the options given below:
(1) B, C, A, D, E (2) C, B, D, A, E
(3) B, D, E, C, A (4) A, B, C, D, E

56. The major strategies and policies, for a business enterprise, that give an overall direction to operations are likely to be in which of the following areas?
A. Growth B. Finance
C. Needs D. Personnel
E. Marketing
Choose the *correct* answer from the options given below:
(1) A, B, C and D Only
(2) B, C, D and E Only
(3) A, B, D and E Only
(4) A, C, D and E only

57. John Challenger suggested that we should consider certain things in acting more ethically in downsizing. What things he suggested?
A. Planning
B. Pessimism about the future of the company
C. Emotions
D. Timing
E. Stakeholder perception
Choose the *correct* answer from the options given below:
(1) A, C, D and E Only
(2) A, B, C and D Only
(3) B, C, D and E Only
(4) A, B, D and E Only

58. In Flow Model, associated with forecasting personnel needs, the forecaster will-

A. Determine the time that should be covered.
B. Establish categories to which employees can be assigned.
C. Will not estimate the probability of transition.
D. Will solicit estimate of personnel needed from group of exports.
E. Count annual movements among states for several time period.

Choose the *correct* answer from the options given below:
(1) A, B and C Only
(2) A, B and D Only
(3) A, B and E Only
(4) B, C and D Only

59. Arrange the Model of Organisation Development Process of H.M.F Rush in proper sequence from beginning to end.
A. Problem Recognition
B. Organization diagnosis
C. Feed back for change strategy
D. Interventions
E. Measurement and Evaluation

Choose the *correct* answer from the options given below:
(1) A, B, C, D, E (2) A, B, C, E, D
(3) B, A, C, D, E (4) C, A, D, B, E

60. Which of the followings are Career Development Initiatives?
A. Career Planning workshops.
B. Mentoring
C. Career Counselling
D. Coaching
E. Personal Development Plans

Choose the *correct* answer from the options given below:
(1) A, B, C and D Only
(2) A, B, C and E Only
(3) B, C, D and E Only
(4) A, C, D and E Only

61. Which of the following are settlement machineries of industrial disputes under Industrial Disputes Act, 1947?
A. Works Committee
B. Collective Bargaining
C. Conciliation
D. Adjudication
E. Voluntary Arbitration

Choose the *correct* answer from the options given below:
(1) A, B, C and D Only
(2) A, C, D and E only
(3) B, C, D and E Only
(4) C, A and D Only

62. In which of the following cases there will be Flow of Funds?
A. Purchase of Building for cash
B. Cash collection from debtors
C. Cash payment to creditors
D. Issue of share for cash
E. Payment of creditors by issue of shares

Choose the *correct* answer from the options given below:
(1) A, B and C Only
(2) B and C Only
(3) A, C and D Only
(4) A, D and E Only

63. Which of the following are correct formulas of combined leverage?

A. $DCF = \frac{\%\text{Change in EPS}}{\%\text{Change in Sales}}$

B. $DCF = \frac{\text{Contribution}}{\text{Profit before Tax}}$

C. $DCF = \frac{\text{Contribution}}{\text{Profit after Tax}}$

D. $DCF = \frac{\text{EBIT} + \text{Fixed Cost}}{\text{PBT}}$

E. $DCF = \frac{\text{Change in EBIT}}{\text{Change in Sales}}$

Choose the *correct* answer from the options given below:
(1) A, B and C Only
(2) B, C and D Only
(3) A, C and D Only
(4) A, B and D Only

64. Which of the following are correct with respect to foreign exchange market?

A. Short position = Supply of a currency < demand for currency.

B. Short position = Supply of a currency > demand for currency.

C. Long position = supply of a currency > demand for currency

D. Long position = supply of a currency < demand for currency

E. Square position = Supply of a currency= demand for currency

Choose the *correct* answer from the options given below:

(1) A, C and E Only
(2) B, D and E Only
(3) B, C and E Only
(4) A, D and E Only

65. Which of the following are merits of Internal Rate of Return Method of Capital Budgeting?

A. Consider all cash flows

B. Satisfies the value additivity principle

C. Generally consistent with wealth maximization principle

D. It considers the time value of money

E. It never fails to indicate correct choice between mutually exclusive projects.

Choose the *correct* answer from the options given below:

(1) A, B and E Only
(2) A, C and E Only
(3) B, C and D Only
(4) A, C, and D only

66. Which of the following are the modes of strategic decision making according to Miztzberg?

A. Entrepreneurial Mode

B. Adaptive Mode

C. Planning Mode

D. Logical Incrementallisation Mode

Choose the *correct* answer from the options given below:

(1) A and B Only
(2) C and D Only
(3) A, B and C Only
(4) A, B, C and D Only

67. Which of the following terms are associated with the VRIO framework of Internal Analysis?

A. Valuable

B. Rare

C. Intimitable

D. Organised for usage

E. Innovative

Choose the *correct* answer from the options given below:

(1) A and B Only
(2) A, B and C Only
(3) A, B and E Only
(4) A, B, C and D Only

68. Which among the following characteristics influence consumer buying behavior strongly?

A. Cultural

B. Social

C. Personal

D. Psychological

E. Technological

Choose the *correct* answer from the options given below:

(1) A, B, C and D Only
(2) B, C, D and E Only
(3) A, C, D and E Only
(4) A, B, D and E Only

69. Under Brand Sponsorship, store brands are also known as which other names from the following?

A. National Brands

B. Generic Brands

C. Private Brands

D. Distributor Brands

E. Manufacturers Brands

Choose the *correct* answer from the options given below:

(1) B, C and D Only
(2) A, B and C Only

(3) C, D and E Only
(4) A, D and E Only

70. Which of the following are positional averages?

A. Geometric mean
B. Harmonic mean
C. Mode
D. Median
E. Percentiles

Choose the *correct* answer from the options given below:

(1) A, B and E Only
(2) C and D Only
(3) D and E Only
(4) C, D and E Only

71. Which of the following are properties of regression coefficients?

A. $r = \sqrt{b_{yx} \times b_{xy}}$
B. Change in origin are not affected
C. Change in scale are not affected
D. If both the regression coefficient have negative sign, the correlation coefficient will have negative sign
E. If one regression coefficient is greater than one then other regression coefficient must be less than one.

Choose the *correct* answer from the options given below:

(1) B, C, D and E Only
(2) A, D and E Only
(3) A, B, D and E Only
(4) A, B and C only

72. Which of the following are the main objectives of establishment of International Monetary Fund (IMF)?

A. To provide long-term hinds at concession rates to the poorest member countries.
B. To promote the development of Private enterprises in member countries.
C. To regulate the exchange rates and enforce the rules.
D. To promote exchange stability, maintaining orderly exchange arrangements and avoiding competitive exchange devaluation.
E. To assist in establishment of a multilateral system of payments in respect of current transaction between members.

Choose the *correct* answer from the options given below:

(1) A, B and C Only
(2) B, C and D Only
(3) A, C and E Only
(4) C, D and E Only

73. Which among the following are true about World Trade Organisation (WTO)?

A. The WTO is a simple extension of General Agreement of Tariffs and Trade (GATT)
B. The WTO is a permanent institution with its own secretariat
C. The agreements which constitute the WTO are almost all plurilateral and thus involve commitments for the entire members
D. The WTO includes Trade in Services and trade-related aspects of intellectual property rights
E. The WTO dispute settlement system is faster, more automatic and thus much less susceptible to blockages, titan old GATT system

Choose the *correct* answer from the options given below:

(1) B, D and E Only
(2) A, B and C Only
(3) C, D and E Only
(4) B, C and D Only

74. Which of the following are operational methodology of Self Help Group?

A. Village meeting of women in villages by MFI
B. Group formation
C. Group Training for 5-7 days on procedures and business development skills

D. Group meeting once in a week for mobilizing saving, disbursing and repaying loans.

E. Lending money for long term loans

Choose the *correct* answer from the options given below:

(1) A, B and C Only
(2) B, C and D Only
(3) A, B, C and D Only
(4) B, C, D and E Only

75. Which of the following Institutions are providing micro finance services to the poors?

A. Conventional weaker section lending banks.
B. Microfinance Institution.
C. Self Help Group-bank linkage programme
D. EXIM banks

Choose the *correct* answer from the options given below:

(1) A and B Only
(2) B and C Only
(3) C and D Only
(4) A, B and C Only

76. Match the List-I with List-II

LIST I Approaches of Management	LIST II Explanation
A. Decision theory approach	I. Managing is seen as mathematical process
B. Management science approach	II. Managerial practice depends on circumstances
C. Operational approach	III. Focus is on making decisions
D. Contingency approach	IV. Draws together concepts, principles, techniques and knowledge from other fields of managerial approach

Choose the *correct* answer from the options given below:

(1) A-III, B-I, C-IV, D-II
(2) A-I, B-II, C-III, D-IV
(3) A-III, B-IV, C-II, D-I
(4) A-IV, B-III, C-I, D-II

77. Match the List-I with List-II

LIST I Macro level Organisational stressors	LIST II Causative factor in organisation
A. Rotating work shifts	I. Organisational structure and design
B. Line-staff conflicts	II. Administrative policies and strategies
C. Appraisal system	III. Working conditions
D. Polluted air	IV. Organisational process

Choose the *correct* answer from the options given below:

(1) A-I, B-II, C-III, D-IV
(2) A-II, B-III, C-IV, D-I
(3) A-II, B-I, C-IV, D-III
(4) A-I, B-IV, C-II, D-III

78. Match the List-I with List-II

LIST I Conflict	LIST II Appropriate view
A. The Traditional view	I. The belief that conflict is a natural and inevitable outcome in any group
B. The Human Relations view	II. The belief that all conflict is harmful and must be avoided
C. The Interactionist View	III. Conflict that supports the goals of the group and improves its performance

D. Functional conflict	IV. The belief that conflict is not a positive force in a group but that it is absolutely necessary for a group to perform effectively

Choose the *correct* answer from the options given below:

(1) A-II, B-I, C-III, D-IV
(2) A-II, B-I, C-IV, D-III
(3) A-I, B-II, C-IV, D-III
(4) A-I, B-III, C-II, D-IV

79. Match the List-I with List-II

LIST I Forms of Strikes	LIST II Appropriate Meaning
A. Economic strike	I. A strike aimed at protesting illegal conduct by the employer.
B. Unfair labour practice strike	II. A strike that results from a failure to agree on the terms of a contract that involves wages, benefits and other conditions of employment.
C. Wild cat strike	III. A strike that takes place when one union strikes in support of the strike of another.
D. Sympathy strike	IV. An unauthorized strike occurring during the term of a contract.

Choose the *correct* answer from the options given below:

(1) A-I, B III, C-II, D-IV
(2) A-II, B-I, C-IV, D-III
(3) A-III, B-I, C-II, D-IV
(4) A-I, B-II, C III, D-IV

80. Match the List-I with List-II

LIST I Ind A.S	LIST II Related to
A. IndAS-12	I. Earning per share
B. IndAS-16	II. Intangible assets
C. IndAS-33	III. Property plant and equipment
D. IndAS-38	IV. Income Taxes

Choose the *correct* answer from the options given below:

(1) A-I, B-III, C-IV, D-II
(2) A-IV, B-III, C-I, D-II
(3) A-IV, B-III, C-II, D-I
(4) A-III, B-IV, C-I, D-II

81. Match the List-I with List-II

LIST I Types of Variance	LIST II Formula
A. Material Cost Variance	I (Standard Quantity - Actual Quantity) × standard price
B. Material Price Variance	II. (Standard price - Actual price) × Actual Quantity
C. Material Usage Variance	III. Standard cost of actual quantity of actual mixture-Standard cost of actual quantity of standard mixture
D. Material Mix Variance	IV. (Standard price × standard quantity) - (Actual price × Actual Quantity)

Choose the *correct* answer from the options given below:

(1) A-I, B-II, C-III, D-IV
(2) A-IV, B-I, C II, D-III
(3) A-II, B-IV, C-I, D-III
(4) A-IV, B-II, C-I, D-III

82. Match the List-I with List-II

LIST I Corporate Restructuring	LIST II Meaning
A. Leveraged Buyouts	I. Company sells a part of its business to third party
B Divestment	II. Company create a new company from the existing single entity
C. Sell-off	III. Sale of a company's assets or division to the outsiders
D. Spin-off	IV. An acquisition of a company in which the acquisition is substantially financed through debt

Choose the *correct* answer from the options given below:

(1) A-IV, B-III, C-I, D-II
(2) A-III, B-IV, C-I, D-II
(3) A-I, B-II, C-III, D-IV
(4) A-IV, B-III, C-II, D-I

83. Match the List-I with List-II

LIST I Derivative type	LIST II Their Explanation
A. Call Option	I. An agreement to buy or sell an asset on a specific date for a specified price, settlement happens at the end of the period.
B. Put option	II. An agreement between two parties to buy or sell an asset at a certain time in future at certain price, through standardized contracts and traded through stock exchange.
C. Future Contract	III. A contract that gives the holder the right but not the obligation to buy specified securities at a specified exercise date.
D. Forward Contract	IV. A contract that gives the holder the right but not the obligation to sell securities on or by a certain date at a fixed exercise price.

Choose the *correct* answer from the options given below:

(1) A-IV, B-III, C-I, D-II
(2) A-III, B-II, C-I, D-IV
(3) A-II, B-I, C-III. D-IV
(4) A-III, B-IV, C-II, D-I

84. Match the List-I with List-II

LIST I Pricing situation	LIST II Description
A. Product line Pricing	I. Pricing optional or accessory products sold with the main product
B. Optional product pricing	II. Setting prices across an entire product line
C. Captive product Pricing	III. Pricing low value by product to get rid of or make money on them.
D. By-Product Pricing	IV. Pricing products that must be used with the main product.

Choose the *correct* answer from the options given below:

(1) A-I, B-III, C-IV, D-II
(2) A-II, B-III, C-IV, D-I
(3) A-II, B-I, C-IV, D-III
(4) A-III, B-IV; C-II, D-I

85. Match the List-I with List-II

LIST I Model/ Framework	LIST II Developed By
A. VRIO Framework	I. J.B. Barney
B. Value Chain Analysis	II. M.E. Porter
C. Product Market Matrix	III. H.I. Ansoff
D. PEST Analysis	IV. Johnson and Scholes

Choose the *correct* answer from the options given below:

(1) A-I, B-II, C-III, D-IV
(2) A-I, B-III, C-II, D-IV
(3) A-III,B-I, C-II, D-IV
(4) A-II, B-I, C-IV, D-III

86. Match the List-I with List-II

LIST I Types of Buying Decision Behaviour	LIST II Their Explanation
A. Complex Buying Behaviour	I. Highly involved in a purchase and perceive significant difference among brands
B. Dissonance-reducing buying behaviour	II. Low consumer involvement and little significant brand difference
C. Habitual Buying Behaviour	III. Low consumer involvement but significant perceived brand differences
D. Variety seeking buying behaviour	IV. Highly involved with an expensive, infrequent, or risky purchase but see little difference among brands.

Choose the *correct* answer from the options given below:

(1) A-III, B-II, C-I, D-IV
(2) A-I, B-IV, C-III, D-II
(3) A-II, B-III, C-I, D-IV
(4) A-IV, B-III, C-I, D-II

87. Match the List-I with List-II

LIST I Societal classification of products	LIST II Degree of long-run consumer benefit and immediate consumer satisfaction
A. Deficient Products	I. Low long-run consumer benefit and high immediate satisfaction
B. Pleasing Products	II. High long-run consumer benefit and high immediate satisfaction
C. Salutary Products	III. High long-run consumer benefit and low immediate satisfaction
D. Desirable Products	IV. Low long-run consumer benefit and low immediate satisfaction

Choose the *correct* answer from the options given below:

(1) A-IV, B-I, C III, D-II
(2) A-I, B-II, C-III, D-IV
(3) A-II, B-III, C-I, D-IV
(4) A-III, B-IV, C-II, D-I

88. Match the List-I with List-II

LIST I Nature of Study	LIST II Choice of Sampling Method
A. Size of all strata is equal	I. Quota sampling
B. Information can be provided by few respondents	II. Convenience sampling
C. Information is required from particular strata of population	III. Judgement sampling
D. To obtain quick information	IV. Startified random sampling

Choose the *correct* answer from the options given below:

(1) A-IV, B-III, C-I, D-II
(2) A-IV, B-III, C-II, D-I
(3) A-III, B-IV, C-II, D-I
(4) A-I, B-II, C-III, D-IV

89. Match the List-I with List-II

LIST I International Business Orientation	LIST II Explanation
A. Ethnocentric Orientation	I. A Global marketing strategy is followed

	across all the countries considering the world as a global village without any boundaries
B. Polycentric	II.. Common marketing strategy is applied in a group of foreign countries having similarities in terms of consumers and business environment
C. Regio centric Orientation	III. Marketing strategies are modified as per the needs of local consumer of the foreign market
D. Geocentric Orientation	IV. Marketing strategy of Domestic market is applied in the foreign country's market

Choose the *correct* answer from the options given below:

(1) A-III, B-IV, C-I, D-II

(2) A-IV, B-III, C-II, D-I

(3) A-I. B-II, C-III, D-IV

(4) A-II, B-III, C-I, D-IV

90. Match the List-I with List-II

LIST I **Name of Theories**	**LIST II** **Propounder**
A. Theory of Opportunities and Innovation	I. Frank H Knight
B. Theory of profit	II. Peter F Drucker
C. Theory of Entrepreneurial Supply	III. Sigmund Feud
D. Psychoanalytic Theory	IV. Thomas Cochran

Choose the *correct* answer from the options given below:

(1) A-II, B-III, C-IV, D-I

(2) A-II, B-I, C-IV, D-III

(3) A-I, B-III, C-II, D-IV

(4) A-III, B-II, C-I, D-IV

Read the passage carefully and answer the Question that follow:

Organizational culture refers to qualities of the workplace itself that influence its employees, whereas Organizational behavior refers to the resulting behavior of the people within it. Organizational culture includes factors such as core values, the company's mission statement and expectations of the employees. It defines the identity and how it wants to be perceived.

For the instance, if a company has a mission statement focused on providing the highest quality of customer service, then the core values may be centered around communication, professionalism and customer satisfaction. This will shape the employees expectations, such as expecting them to be willing and courteous to go the extra mile to serve the customer.

Organizational behavior is the resulting behavior of the people within the organization based on the culture they're immersed in. if the company culture is one that promotes customer service, then the employees are likely to display behavior such as friendliness and helpfulness when dealing with customers.

The opposite may be true if the company's culture revolves around a competitive environment and employees are expected to go above and beyond to be the most successful. In this case, employees may display behavior such as aggressiveness and competitiveness in order to achieve the highest results.

Organizational culture works as the foundation for the employee's behavioral exhibit, and the two are closely intertwined. If a company wishes to create a positive working environment, it is essential to establish an organizational culture that promotes a healthy behavioral environment among its employees.

91. Which of the following is NOT a factor included in organisational culture?

(1) Core values

(2) Companies mission

(3) Employee's salary

(4) Expectations of employees

92. In a company with a culture focused on customer service, employees are expected to demonstrate behaviors such as:
(1) Competitiveness and aggression
(2) Friendliness and helpfulness
(3) Independence and autonomy
(4) Innovation and Creativity

93. What might employees in a competitive organisational culture display?
(1) Cooperation and teamwork
(2) Friendliness and helpfulness
(3) Indifference and passiveness
(4) Aggressiveness and Competitiveness

94. Which statement best describes the relationship between organisational culture and organisational behavior?
(1) Organisational culture influences the resulting behavior of employees
(2) Organisational culture is the result of organisational behavior
(3) Organisational behavior is solely determined by external factors
(4) Organisational behavior is independent of organisational culture

95. What role does organisational behavior play in the workplace?
(1) It defines organisational goals
(2) It represents resultant employee actions
(3) It determines managerial decisions
(4) It outlines employee training programmes

Read the passage carefully and answer the Questions:

AI's impact on the workforce is multifaceted. It involves the automation of repetitive and routine tasks, changing skill requirements and job displacement. This can be beneficial for employees as it frees them up to focus on more complex and creative work, but it can also create concerns about job displacement and changes in the demand for certain types of jobs. However, AI is also creating new job opportunities, especially in data analytics machine learning and AI development.

Despite these potential benefits, there are also concerns about the drawbacks of implementing AI on a larger scale in the workforce. One potential concern is job displacement, which can lead to unemployment and the need for re skilling and upskilling. Another concern is the potential for bias and discrimination in algorithms, which can have negative consequences for marginalized individuals and communities.

Privacy and security are also major concerns regarding the impact of AI on the workforce. As AI becomes more advanced, it is important to ensure that personal data is protected, and AI system are secure against cyberattacks. Nonetheless, AI can also enhance efficiency and productivity, and its advancements may lead to new job opportunities for workers with the right skills and knowledge.

96. What is one potential benefit of AI in the workforce mentioned in the passage?
(1) Increased job displacement
(2) Automation of repetitive tasks
(3) Reduced need for creativity
(4) Decreased demand for data analysis

97. Which potential drawback of AI in the workforce is associated with algorithmic decision- making
(1) Reduced efficiency
(2) Increased job satisfaction
(3) Bias and Discrimination
(4) Enhanced security measures

98. Which skill is likely to become increasingly important in light of AI's impact on the workforce?
(1) Manual Labour
(2) Routine administrative task
(3) Following predefined procedures
(4) Creative thinking and problem-solving

99. According to the passage, what must be ensured as AI becomes more advanced in the workforce?
(1) Protection of personal data and cybersecurity
(2) Improved job security for all workers

(3) Increased bias in decision making
(4) Decreased efficiency in operations

100. Which statement summarieses a potential outcome of advancement in workforce according to the passage?
(1) AI will eliminate all job roles that require creativity
(2) AI will benefit workers in specialised technical field
(3) AI advancement may create new job opportunities
(4) AI will lead to a decrease in overall workforce productivity

ANSWER KEY

1. (3)	**2.** (2)	**3.** (3)	**4.** (1)	**5.** (5)	**6.** (3)	**7.** (2)	**8.** (2)	**9.** (1)	**10.** (1)
11. (2)	**12.** (3)	**13.** (4)	**14.** (4)	**15.** (1)	**16.** (1)	**17.** (4)	**18.** (3)	**19.** (3)	**20.** (3)
21. (2)	**22.** (1)	**23.** (1)	**24.** (1)	**25.** (3)	**26.** (3)	**27.** (3)	**28.** (2)	**29.** (3)	**30.** (3)
31. (1)	**32.** (1)	**33.** (1)	**34.** (1)	**35.** (3)	**36.** (3)	**37.** (3)	**38.** (3)	**39.** (4)	**40.** (3)
41. (4)	**42.** (4)	**43.** (2)	**44.** (2)	**45.** (2)	**46.** (2)	**47.** (4)	**48.** (2)	**49.** (1)	**50.** (1)
51. (1)	**52.** (4)	**53.** (3)	**54.** (2)	**55.** (2)	**56.** (2)	**57.** (1)	**58.** (3)	**59.** (2)	**60.** (2)
61. (2)	**62.** (4)	**63.** (4)	**64.** (1)	**65.** (4)	**66.** (4)	**67.** (4)	**68.** (1)	**69.** (1)	**70.** (4)
71. (3)	**72.** (4)	**73.** (1)	**74.** (3)	**75.** (4)	**76.** (4)	**77.** (3)	**78.** (2)	**79.** (2)	**80.** (2)
81. (4)	**82.** (1)	**83.** (4)	**84.** (3)	**85.** (1)	**86.** (1)	**87.** (1)	**88.** (1)	**89.** (2)	**90.** (2)
91. (3)	**92.** (2)	**93.** (4)	**94.** (1)	**95.** (2)	**96.** (2)	**97.** (3)	**98.** (4)	**99.** (1)	**100.** (3)

❍❍❍

JUNE 2025

MANAGEMENT

PAPER-II

Note : This paper contains **hundred (100)** objective type questions of **two (2)** marks each. **All** questions are **compulsory**.

1. Match List - I with List - II:

List – I	**List – II**
Item	**Concept**
A. Furniture	I. Process costing
B. Cement	II. Job costing
C. Petroleum	III. Output costing
D. Interior Decoration	IV. Operating costing

Choose the **correct** answer from the options given below :

(1) A-I, B-II, C-III, D-IV
(2) A-IV, B-III, C-II, D-I
(3) A-II, B-III, C-I, D-IV
(4) A-II, B-I, C-III, D-IV

2. Which of the following are characteristics of a Normal probability distribution?

A. The two tails of normal curve extend to infinity in both directions and never touch horizontal axis.
B. Normal curve is symmetrical around vertical line.
C. The values of mean, median and mode are equal.
D. Mean and variance of the distribution are equal.
E. Mean and standard deviation are equal.

Choose the **correct** answer from the options given below :

(1) A, B, D Only (2) C, D, E Only
(3) A, B, E Only (4) A, B, C Only

3. Idle capacity costs due to avoidable causes are transferred to which of the following heads/accounts?

(1) Prime Cost
(2) Factory Overhead
(3) Cost of Production
(4) Costing Profit and Loss A/c

4. Which of the following are implications of e-HRM?

A. PERT B. CPM
C. Recruitment D. Selection
E. Training

Choose the **correct** answer from the options given below :

(1) C, D, E Only (2) A, B, C Only
(3) B, C, D Only (4) A, B, E Only

5. Match List - I with List - II:

List – I	**List – II**
Ratio	**Purpose**
A. Liquidity	I. Assessing the operating performance
B. Activity	II. Assessing the ability to meet maturing obligation
C. Profitability	III. Assessing the effectiveness of utilization of assets
D. Debt	IV. Assessing the management of fixed financial change

Choose the **correct** answer from the options given below :

(1) A-II, B-III, C-I, D-IV
(2) A-I, B-II, C-III, D-IV
(3) A-III, B-I, C-IV, D-II
(4) A-IV, B-III, C-II, D-I

6. Arrange the steps of creative process for an idea.

A. Preparation B. Incubation
C. Germination D. Verification
E. Illumination

Choose the **correct** answer from the options given below :

(1) A, B, C, D, E (2) C, A, B, E, D
(3) E, D, C, B, A (4) C, B, A, D, E

7. Receipts of interest on foreign investments and royalties on trade marks held abroad are reflected in which of the following part of the Balance of Payment?

(1) Balance of Trade
(2) Capital Account
(3) Balance of Invisibles
(4) Official Reserves Account

8. The error arising from the treatment of revenue expenditure as capital expenditure and vice-versa, is termed as:

(1) Error of Omission
(2) Error of Principle
(3) Error of Compensation
(4) Error of Recognition

9. Which of the followings are the examples of current liabilities :

A. Current investments
B. Short-term borrowings
C. Bills receivables
D. Bills payables
E. Accrued income

Choose the **correct** answer from the options given below :

(1) A and E Only (2) B and D Only
(3) C and E Only (4) A and C Only

10. Arrange the following steps of buyer decision making.

A. Information research
B. Evaluation of alternatives
C. Need recognition
D. Purchase decision
E. Post purchase behaviour

Choose the **correct** answer from the options given below :

(1) A, B, C, D, E (2) C, A, B, D, E
(3) A, C, D, E, B (4) B, A, D, C, E

11. General statements that guide or channelize thinking in decision making are:

(1) Policies (2) Goals
(3) Strategy (4) Rules

12. A relatively large, low cost, high volume, self-service operation designed to serve the consumer's needs for household products is:

(1) Department Store
(2) Convenience Store
(3) Super Store
(4) Super Market

13. Arrange the stages of group development in proper sequence.

A. Performing B. Norming
C. Storming D. Forming
E. Adjourning

Choose the **correct** answer from the options given below :

(1) A, B, C, D, E (2) B, C, D, E, A
(3) C, D, E, A, B (4) D, C, B, A, E

14. Which of the following are not directly financing small scale industries?

A. Small Industries Development Bank of India (SIDBI)
B. World Bank
C. Industrial Development Bank of India (IDBI)
D. International Monetary Fund (IMF)
E. National Small Industries Corporation Ltd. (NSIC)

Choose the **most appropriate** answer from the options given below :

(1) B, C and D Only
(2) A and B Only
(3) A and C Only
(4) A and E Only

15. Which of the following is the condition where χ^2 (chi-square) should not be applied?

(1) If there are only two cells, expected frequency in each cell should be 5 or more.
(2) Samples of at least 50 observations must be drawn randomly from the population.

(3) If number of cells are more than two and more than 20% of the cells have expected frequencies less than 5.

(4) Data should be expressed in original units rather than ratio or percentage.

16. Match List - I with List - II:

List – I Methods	List – II Description
A. Net present value	I. Ratio of PV of inflows to investment
B. Internal rate of return	II. Rate where NPV = 0
C. Profitability index	III. Present value of inflows Present value of outflows
D. Payback period	IV. Time to recover initial cost

Choose the **correct** answer from the options given below :

(1) A-III, A-II, C-I, D-IV
(2) A-I, B-II, C-III, D-IV
(3) A-III, B-IV, C-II, D-I
(4) A-II, B-I, C-IV, D-III

17. Which of the following Acts were meant for labour welfare?

A. The Factory Act, 1948
B. The Employee Insurance Act, 1948
C. The Payment of Gratuity Act, 1972
D. The Consumer Protection Act, 2019
E. The Companies Act, 2013

Choose the **correct** answer from the options given below :

(1) A, B and C Only
(2) C, D and E Only
(3) A, C and D Only
(4) C, D, and A Only

18. Expatriates are:

(1) Noncitizens of the countries in which employee are working
(2) Host Country Nationals
(3) Home Country Nationals
(4) Third Country Nationals

19. Which of the following behaviour corresponds to the statement "Discretionary behaviour that contributes to the psychological and social environment of the workplace"?

(1) Individual Behaviour
(2) Group Behaviour
(3) Organizational Citizenship Behaviour
(4) Group Dynamics

20. Which of the followings are the types of personality according to Holland's Typology?

A. Realistic
B. Investigative
C. Social
D. Extrovert
E. Introvert

Choose the **correct** answer from the options given below :

(1) C, D and E Only
(2) B, C and D Only
(3) A, B and C Only
(4) D, E and B Only

21. Arrange the following steps in the correct logical sequence to explain how indifference curves are derived ?

A. The consumer plots combination of goods that provide the same satisfaction
B. The consumer ranks preferences over combination of two goods
C. A downward-sloping, convex indifference curve is formed
D. The consumer reaches equilibrium where the budget line is tangent to the indifference curve

Choose the correct answer from the options given below :

(1) A, B, C, D
(2) B, A, C, D
(3) A, C, B, D
(4) D, B, A, C

22. Arrange the steps in rational decision making.

A. Evaluate the alternatives
B. Develop the alternatives
C. Allocate weights to the criteria
D. Identify the decision criteria
E. Define the problem

Choose the **correct** answer from the options given below :

(1) E, D, C, B, A (2) A, B, C, D, E

(3) B, C, D, E, A (4) C, D, E, A, B

23. Encouraging customer switching to a brand is :

(1) Sales Promotion

(2) Publicity

(3) Informative Advertising

(4) Persuasive Advertising

24. Which of the following is NOT a part of 4Ps of the marketing mix ?

(1) Product (2) Price

(3) Place

(4) Producer services

25. Which of the following is not the advantage of merger?

(1) Increased Market Share

(2) Synergy

(3) Diversification

(4) Increased Competition

26. Finance function involves :

(1) Procurement of finance only

(2) Expenditure of funds only

(3) Safe custody of funds only

(4) Procurement and effective utilization of funds

27. Which of the following is characterized by the use of small, intermittent assault on different market segments held by the competitors ?

(1) Encirclement

(2) Flanking Maneuver

(3) Guerrilla Warfare

(4) Frontal Assault

28. According to MM theory, the market price of the share will:

(1) Changes after the payment of dividend.

(2) Changes after payment of interest and tax.

(3) Will change due to market fluctuations.

(4) Remains unchanged even after the payment of dividend.

29. Match List - I with List - II:

List – I Theory	List – II Description
A. Trait theory of leadership	I. Focuses of followers readiness
B. Behavioural theory of leadership	II. Stress unfavourly affects a situation that can reduce influence of the leader
C. Cognitive resource theory	III. Specific behaviour differentiates leaders from non leaders
D. Situational leadership theory	IV. Personal qualities and characteristics that differentiates from non leaders

Choose the **correct** answer from the options given below :

(1) A-I, B-II, C-III, D-IV

(2) A-IV, B-III, C-II, D-I

(3) A-III, B-I, C-IV, D-II

(4) A-IV, B-II, C-1, D-III

30. Extending an existing brand name to new forms, colours, sizes or flavours of an existing product category is:

(1) Co-branding

(2) Line extension

(3) Brand extension

(4) Brand sponsorship

31. Arrange the process of capital budgeting in proper sequence.

A. Identification of potential investment opportunities

B. Decision making

C. Assembling of proposed investments

D. Preparation of capital budget and appropriation

E. Implementation

Choose the **correct** answer from the options given below :

(1) B, A, C, D, E (2) E, A, C, B, D
(3) D, B, A, E, C (4) A, C, B, D, E

32. Arrange the following five steps of resource-based approach to strategy analysis proposed by Grant.

A. Identify resource gaps and invest in upgrading weaknesses.
B. Select the strategy that best exploits the firms' capabilities relative to external opportunities.
C. Appraise the profit potential of these capabilities in terms of their potential for sustainable competitive advantage.
D. Combine the firm's strength into specific capabilities.
E. Identify and classify the firm's resources in terms of strength and weaknesses.

Choose the **correct** answer from the options given below :

(1) C, D, E, A, B (2) B, A, C, D, E
(3) A, B, C, D, E (4) E, D, C, B, A

33. Which of the followings imply Flat Organisation?

A. High level of Decentralization
B. Narrow span of control
C. Impersonality
D. Less extended communication lines
E. Distance from top to bottom

Choose the **correct** answer from the options given below :

(1) A, B and C Only
(2) B, C and D Only
(3) A, D and E Only
(4) A and D Only

34. Match List - I with List - II:

List – I Item	List – II Description
A. Par value	I. Specified interest rate
B. Maturity period	II. Number of years after which the value is payable to bond holders
C. Coupon rate	III. Amount by which a bond sells at a value higher than the par value
D. Premium	IV. Value on the face of the bond

Choose the **correct** answer from the options given below :

(1) A-III, B-I, C-IV, D-II
(2) A-II, B-IV, C-I, D-III
(3) A-I, B-IV, C-III, D-II
(4) A-IV, B-II, C-I, D-III

35. Which of the following is the right sequence of Employability Skills Matrix (ESM) ?

(1) Critical thinking, Communication, Collaboration, Knowledge and Social responsibility
(2) Communication, Collaboration, Knowledge, Social responsibility and Critical thinking
(3) Collaboration, Knowledge, Social responsibility, Critical thinking and Communication
(4) Knowledge, Social responsibility, Critical thinking, Communication and Collaboration

36. Arrange the following steps in the correct sequence in the budgetary control system.

A. Preparation of budgets for different departments.
B. Comparison of actual performance with budgeted figures
C. Establishment of objectives and budget key factors
D. Analysis of variances
E. Taking correlative actions

Choose the **correct** answer from the options given below :

(1) C, B, D, A, E (2) C, A, B, D, E
(3) C, B, A, D, E (4) A, C, D, B, E

37. Which of the following is not a basis for behavioural segmentation?

A. Purchase Occasion
B. Digital Divide

C. Usage rate of the product
D. Benefit sought from the product
E. Lifestyle of consumer

Choose the **most appropriate** answer from the options given below :

(1) A, B and D Only
(2) B and C Only
(3) A and E Only
(4) B and E Only

38. Match List - I with List - II:

List – I Term	List – II Description
A. Monopoly	I. Free entry and exit
B. Perfect competition	II. Single seller and no close substitute
C. Monopolistic competition	III. Differentiated products and many sellers
D. Oligopoly	IV. Strategic interdependence among firms

Choose the **correct** answer from the options given below :

(1) A-I, B-II, C-III, D-IV
(2) A-II, B-I, C-III, D-IV
(3) A-III, B-IV, C-I, D-II
(4) A-III, B-II, C-IV, D-I

39. A barrier to the matching of expected and perceived service levels caused by the unwillingness of services providers to provide the necessary resources is:

(1) Misconception barrier
(2) Inadequate resources barrier
(3) Inadequate delivery barrier
(4) Exaggerated promise's barrier

40. Real-factor demand-pull inflection can be caused by:

A. Increase in investment
B. Decrease in consumer demand
C. Decrease in imports given the exports
D. Decrease in exports given the imports
E. Decrease in government expenditure without change in tax revenue.

Choose the **correct** answer from the options given below :

(1) B and E Only (2) E and B Only
(3) A and C Only (4) A and D Only

41. Advantages of decentralization are :

A. No duplication of efforts or resources.
B. Reduces problem of communication and red tape.
C. Strong central leadership develops which may required in crisis.
D. Coordination of activities of subordinates are better achieved.
E. Ensures the development of employees.

Choose the **correct** answer from the options given below :

(1) C and D Only (2) B and E Only
(3) D and E Only (4) A and E Only

42. When NPV and IRR give different rankings, which of the following problem is the cause of disparity that arises when the initial investment in mutually exclusive projects is different ?

(1) Time-Disparity Problem
(2) Size-Disparity Problem
(3) Unequal Expected Lives
(4) Conventional Equivalent Problem

43. Which of the following assumptions are central to the pecking order theory of capital structure ?

A. Managers have more information about their firm's value than investors
B. Asymmetric information exist between managers and the investors
C. Issuing equity indicates that the current share price is overvalued
D. Firms always aim for well-defined debt equity target
E. Equity is cheaper than debt as free source of raising finance

Choose the **correct** answer from the options given below :

(1) A, D, E Only (2) A, B, C Only
(3) A, B, E Only (4) A, C, D Only

44. Which one of the following is not the HR audit?
(1) Job Descriptions
(2) Recruitment and Selection
(3) Mandated Benefits
(4) Balanced Scorecard

45. Which transactions are classified as operating activities?
A. Sold manufacturing plant
B. Collected bills receivables from customers
C. Purchase of building
D. Paid to suppliers
E. Issued equity shares at a premium
Choose the **most appropriate** answer from the options given below :
(1) A and C Only (2) B and C Only
(3) B and D Only (4) A and E Only

46. Which of the following are direct sellers in India ?
A. Herbalife International India
B. Lakme products India
C. Modicare
D. Amway India enterprises
E. Avon beauty products India
Choose the **most appropriate** answer from the options given below :
(1) A, B, C, D, E (2) A, C, D, E Only
(3) A, B, C, D Only (4) A, D, C, E Only

47. When the responsibility, scope and challenges in work is deliberately upgraded, it is known as:
(1) Job Description
(2) Job Enrichment
(3) Job Rotation
(4) Job Assignment

48. Match List - I with List - II:

List – I **Data tool**	List – II **Applications**
A. OLAP	I. Breaks a big data problem down into sub-problems, distributes them among upto thousands of inexpensive computer processing nodes, and that combines result into smaller datasets
B. Hadoop	II. Finds hidden pattern in large data bases and inferring rules from them to predict future behaviour
C. Data mart	III. A summarized or highly focused portion of organization's database is placed for a separate database for a specific population of users
D. Data mining	IV. Supports multidimensional data and enables users to view the same data in different ways using multiple dimensions

Choose the **correct** answer from the options given below :
(1) A-I, B-II, C-IV, D-III
(2) A-III, B-IV, C-II, D-I
(3) A-IV, B-I, C-III, D-II
(4) A-I, B-III, C-I, D-IV

49. Match List - I with List - II:

List – I **Concept**	List – II **Description**
A. Personnel management	I. Focuses on profit maximization by contributing by the people
B. Human Resource management	II. Managing employee, employer relations amicably
C. Industrial relation	III. Managing Human resource challenges of international operations

D. International HRM	IV. Developing attitude of the people for their best contribution

Choose the **correct** answer from the options given below :

(1) A-I, B-III, C-IV, D-I
(2) A-II, B-II, C-III, D-IV
(3) A-I, B-IV, C-II, D-III
(4) A-IV, B-III, C-II, D-I

50. Type II error occurs when :

(1) H (Null hypothesis) is true and is accepted
(2) H (Null hypothesis) is true and is rejected
(3) H (Null hypothesis) is false and is accepted
(4) H (Alternate hypothesis) is false and is rejected

51. Which of the following is not a non-probability method of selecting samples from a population?

(1) Judgement sampling
(2) Convenience sampling
(3) Multistage sampling
(4) Purposive sampling

52. Match List - I with List - II:

List – I **Term**	**List – II** **Description**
A. Transparency	I. Protection of stakeholder's interests
B. Accountability	II. Clear and accurate disclosure of material facts
C. Responsibility	III. Answerability for decision and actions
D. Fairness	IV. Ethical conduct and compliance with law

Choose the **correct** answer from the options given below :

(1) A-II, B-III, C-IV, D-I
(2) A-III, B-II, C-I, D-IV
(3) A-II, B-I, C-III, D-IV
(4) A-IV, B-II, C-I, D-III

53. Arrange the steps involved in the case-based reasoning

A. System finds closest fit and retrieves solution
B. System asks user additional questions to narrow search
C. System modifies the solution to better fit the problem and got successful
D. System searches data base for similar cases
E. User describes the problem

Choose the **correct** answer from the options given below :

(1) D, B, A, C, E (2) E, B, D, A, C
(3) E, D, B, A, C (4) B, A, C, E, D

54. Sequence the following activities in the process of standard costing.

A. Establishing standard cost
B. Measurement of actual cost
C. Identifying variance and causes of variance
D. Disposing the variance to cost and profit centres
E. Comparison of actual and standard costs

Choose the **correct** answer from the options given below :

(1) A, B, E, C, D (2) A, B, C, D, E
(3) A, B, E, D, C (4) A, B, D, C, E

55. Match List - I with List - II:

List – I **Theories**	**List – II** **Propounder**
A. Hierarchy of need theory	I. Abraham Maslow
B. Theory X and Theory Y	II. Douglas McGregor
C. Two factor theory	III. Frederick Herzberg
D. Expectancy theory	IV. Victor Vroom

Choose the **correct** answer from the options given below :

(1) A-I, B-II, C-III, D-IV
(2) A-IV, B-III, C-II, D-I
(3) A-II, B-III, C-IV, D-I
(4) A-III, B-II, C-I, D-IV

56. Match List - I with List - II:

List – I Term	List – II Description
A. R-chart	I. Chart of averages to plot location values
B. P-chart	II. Chart of variability to plot sample ranges
C. X-chart	III. Chart showing proportion of defectives per sample
D. C-chart	IV. Chart showing number of defectives per item/unit

Choose the **correct** answer from the options given below :

(1) A-I, B-II, C-III, D-IV
(2) A-I, B-III, C-IV, D-II
(3) A-I, B-III, C-II, D-IV
(4) A-IV, B-III, C-II, D-I

57. Match List - I with List - II:

List – I Types	List – II Description
A. Predatory pricing	I. A geographical pricing strategy where seller designates same city and charges all customers the freight cost from that city
B. Deceptive pricing	II. Where a firm reduces its prices with the aim of driving out of competitions
C. Price unbundling	III. When consumers are mislead by price deals offered by companies
D. Basing point pricing	IV. Pricing each element in the offering so that the price of the total package is raised

Choose the **correct** answer from the options given below :

(1) A-I, B-II, C-III, D-IV
(2) A-II, B-III, C-IV, D-I
(3) A-IV, B-III, C-II, D-I
(4) A-III, B-II, C-I, D-IV

58. Which of the following is not the type of start up firms?

(1) Salary-substitute firms
(2) Life style firms
(3) Entrepreneurial firms
(4) Ordinance firms

59. Match List - I with List - II:

List – I Women Entrepreneur	List – II Enterprise
A. Richa Kar	I. Zivame
B. Kiran Mazumdar Shaw	II. Kamani Tubes
C. Kalpana Saroj	III. Biocon Limited
D. Falguni Nayar	IV. Nykaa

Choose the **correct** answer from the options given below :

(1) A-I, B-III, C-II, D-IV
(2) A-I, B-II, C-III, D-IV
(3) A-I, B-III, C-IV, D-II
(4) A-I, B-IV, C-II, D-III

60. Which one of the following is not the Central Trade Union of India ?

(1) INTUC (2) The AFL-CIO
(3) CITU (4) BMS

61. In designing an agent in AI, PEAS stands for:

(1) Performance, Environment, Actuators, Sensors
(2) Performance, Extractor, Actions, Security
(3) Problem, Effort, Action, Sensor
(4) Program, Environment, Architecture, Sensors

62. Countries try to hold the value of their currencies within some range against an important reference currency or a 'basket of currencies, is referred to as:

(1) Dirty-float system
(2) Pegged exchange rate
(3) Fixed exchange rate
(4) Extended exchange facility

63. Which of the following is not essential for nurturing Intrapreneurs ?
(1) Building culture and climate
(2) Building Competence
(3) Building relationship
(4) Learning Sign language

64. Which of the following is the example of Social Entrepreneurship?
(1) PFL
(2) Sulabh International
(3) Hyundai
(4) HUL

65. The 'Leontiff Paradox' is in contradiction of which of the following theory ?
(1) Theory of Comparative Advantage
(2) Factor Endowments Theory
(3) Theory of Absolute Advantage
(4) Neo-Mercantilism Theory

66. Match List - I with List - II:

List – I Description	**List – II Term**
A. Goodwill associated with a brand name, which adds tangible value and more profits	I. Brand extension
B. The use of an established brand name as a new brand within same brand market	II. Brand authenticity
C. The use of an established brand name for brands in unrelated market	III. Brand stretching
D. The extent to which consumers perceive a brand to be faithful to its essence	IV. Brand equity

Choose the **correct** answer from the options given below :
(1) A-I, B-II, C-III, D-IV
(2) A-II, B-I, C-IV, D-III
(3) A-IV, B-I, C-III, D-II
(4) A-IV, B-III, C-II, D-I

67. Arrange the steps for calculating portfolio expected return.
A. Multiply weight of each asset with its expected return
B. Add all the weighted return
C. Identifying weights of individual securities
D. Compute expected return of the portfolio

Choose the **correct** answer from the options given below :
(1) C, A, B, D (2) A, B, C, D
(3) C, B, A, D (4) B, A, C, D

68. A channel structure in which producers, wholesalers and retailers act as a unified system is:
(1) Conventional Distribution Channel
(2) Direct Marketing Channel
(3) Vertical Marketing System Channel
(4) Indirect Marketing Channel

69. Which of the following is incorrect?
(1) bxy = 0.8, byx = 0.8
(2) bxy = 1.2, byx = 1.2
(3) bxy = 1.2, byx = 0.8
(4) bxy = 0.8, byx = 1.2

70. Which of the following are components of Agile supply chain ?
A. Virtual
B. Market sensitive
C. Pickup fulfillment
D. Process integration
E. Store based fulfillment

Choose the **most appropriate** answer from the options given below :
(1) A, B, C, D Only (2) A, B, D Only
(3) A, C, D Only (4) A, B, C, E Only

71. Which of the followings are the risks associated with the Generic competitive strategies suggested by Porter ?

A. Risk of Human Resources
B. Risk of Cost leadership
C. Risk of strategic rollup
D. Risk of differentiation
E. Risk of focus

Choose the **most appropriate** answer from the options given below :
(1) A, C, D and E Only
(2) B, D and E Only
(3) B, C, D and E Only
(4) A and B Only

72. Arrange the steps in implementing an HRIS.
A. Inception of Idea
B. Feasibility study
C. Selecting a project team
D. Vendor analysis
E. Defining requirements

Choose the **correct** answer from the options given below :
(1) A, B, C, D, E (2) A, B, C, E, D
(3) B, C, D, E, A (4) C, D, E, A, B

73. Sequence the steps for Vogel's approximation method.
A. Assign largest quantity as per rim requirements to the cell in the row/column with smallest cost.
B. Select largest difference of rows/columns
C. Find difference between the two unallocated least cost cells from each row and each column
D. Eliminate the row/column that has been satisfied
E. Check all rim requirement conditions are met

Choose the **correct** answer from the options given below :
(1) C, B, A, D, E (2) A, B, C, D, E
(3) A, C, D, E, B (4) C, A, D, B, E

74. Which of the following is NOT the characteristic of strategic decisions that deals with the long-run future of an entire organization ?
(1) Invariability (2) Consequential
(3) Rare (4) Directive

75. Which one of the following is not the method of performance appraisal?
(1) 360° Degree Appraisal
(2) MBO
(3) Halo effect
(4) BARS

76. The Cost of Capital is:
(1) The fee required to sell stock using financial institution.
(2) The amount you pay to be an investor.
(3) The required rate of return to appease the supplier of a certain kind of funding to be utilized in the organization.
(4) The sum required to finance a specific purchase.

77. Which of the following types of entrepreneurs are based on personality traits?
A. Franchises
B. The real manager
C. The achiever
D. Industrial entrepreneur
E. Owner-cum-manager

Choose the **most appropriate** answer from the options given below:
(1) A, B, C Only (2) B and C Only
(3) B, C, D Only (4) C and E Only

78. Which of the following concept relates to the statement "A process by which individuals organize and interpret their sensory impressions to give meaning to their environment"?
(1) Attitude (2) Aptitude
(3) Perception (4) Intuition

79. Which one is not the form of discrimination?
(1) Sexual Harassment
(2) Exclusion
(3) Intimidation
(4) Group Cohesiveness

80. Which of the following is not a determinant of demand?

(1) Price of Goods
(2) Consumer Income
(3) Cost of Production
(4) Consumer Preferences

81. Which of the following are the new organization structure ?

A. The team structure
B. The virtual structure
C. Boundary less structure
D. The Matrix structure
E. The sample structure

Choose the **correct** answer from the options given below :

(1) A, B, C Only (2) B, C, D Only
(3) C, D, E Only (4) A, B, E Only

82. Which of the following statements are True?

A. Preference capital represents a hybrid form of financing.
B. Preference capital carries definite legal obligation.
C. Retained earnings represent the profits ploughed back in the business.
D. Disadvantages of equity capital are that it represents a permanent source of finance.
E. Equity share holders do not have right to claim over assets in the event of liquidation.

Choose the **correct** answer from the options given below :

(1) B and E Only (2) A and C Only
(3) B and D Only (4) A and C Only

83. Which of the following are methods of dispersion?

A. Median
B. Mean
C. Mean deviation
D. Standard deviation
E. Range

Choose the **correct** answer from the options given below :

(1) A and E Only (2) A, C and E Only
(3) B, C and D Only (4) C, D and E Only

84. Match List - I with List - II:

List – I Term	List – II Description
A. The probability of both success and failure remains constant	I. Binomial Distribution
B. The mean of distribution may be negative or positive	II. Poisson Distribution
C. The sum of all probabilities is equal to 1	III. Normal Distribution
D. The probability of occurrence of an outcome within a very small time period is very small	IV. Random Variable

Choose the **correct** answer from the options given below :

(1) A-I, B-III, C-IV, D-II
(2) A-I, B-II, C-III, D-IV
(3) A-IV, B-III, C-II, D-I
(4) A-I, B-II, C-IV, D-III

85. Which ratio measures the amount that investors are willing to pay for each rupee of earnings; where higher the ratio, the larger the investors confidence in the firm's future?

(1) Price/Earning Ratio
(2) Earning per Share
(3) Dividend Payout Ratio
(4) Return of Capital Employed

86. According to eclectic theory of foreign direct investment, foreign direct investment will occur on which of the following conditions when they are to be uniquely combined?

A. Ownership
B. Location
C. Market power
D. Internationalization
E. Vertical integration

Choose the **most appropriate** answer from the options given below :

(1) B, C, D and E Only
(2) A, C, D and E Only
(3) D and E Only
(4) A, B and D Only

87. Which of the following institute is not promoting entrepreneurship in India?
(1) National Institute for Entrepreneurship and Small Business Development (NIESBUD)
(2) Entrepreneurship Development Institute (EDI)
(3) Institute for Design of Electrical Measuring Instruments (IDEMI)
(4) National Small Industries Corporation (NSIC)

88. Arrange the steps of designing a distribution logistics system.
A. Finding out what the customers and channels want in product delivery
B. Articulating the distribution objectives and prescribing the minimum service level to be ensured in product delivery.
C. Optimizing the costs of the system and tackling the cost-service tussle
D. Finding out what competitors do
E. Providing for flexibility in the system

Choose the **correct** answer from the options given below:

(1) A, B, C, D, E (2) B, A, C, D, E
(3) C, A, B, E, D (4) B, A, D, C, E

89. Find out the correct options from the following.
A. A future contract is custom designed.
B. Buying a put option is equivalent to buying insurance.
C. The cost of carry is not the cost of holding a security.
D. The difference between the spot price and the future price is called the basis.
E. An American option can be exercised only at its expiration date

Choose the **most appropriate** answer from the options given below :

(1) A and E Only (2) B and D Only
(3) B and E Only (4) A and C Only

90. Cross elasticity of demand refers to:
(1) Change in demand due to change in price.
(2) Change in demand due to change in income.
(3) Change in demand due to change in price of another goods.
(4) Change in demand due to less availability of goods.

Read the following paragraph and answer the questions:

Teresa worked as a caregiver for years and when her husband passed away she was completely lost. Fighting grief and housing instability, she turned into a junior assistant cum typist (FACT) at a university. She initially felt shame, wondering if she was worth anything. One day, her Section Officer made her as a 'custodian' for people and places. After that she felt noticed and appreciated, and so began 18 rewarding years in position.

This is the focal point of mattering - that feeling of being valued and recognition creates value. It's even more deeper than belonging and is critical to motivation, mental well-being, and retention. But currently, many employees feel invisible and undervalued, which leads to disengagement, burnout and low morale. In spite of investments in the workplace, a 'mattering deficit' persists because mattering is constructed through everyday human interactions, not perks or policies.

To engage mattering, leaders need to look and listen to their teams, notice difficulties, listen and ask substantive questions. Compassionate acts and follow-ups create trust. Affirming people's strength, narrative and purpose reinforce their distinct value. Sharing impact stories, such as how JACT made spaces joyful, moves the purpose deeper. Individuals also believe that they matter when they see how small efforts relate to larger goals -such as NASA employees connecting what they do to landing a man on moon. Essentially, building a culture of mattering means leaders to consistently demonstrate to people they are noticed, heard, valued and required. Its easy to talk about in theory, but not common practice- but revolutionary when it is executed correctly.

91. Which of the following statement is NOT supported by the passage?
(1) Individuals remain longer in the work environment where they feel mattering.
(2) Perks alone can ensure emotional connection.
(3) Seeing and hearing employees can create profound trust.
(4) Mattering stems from human interactions, rather than policy.

92. What leadership behaviour most directly foster mattering in the long term, according to the passage?
(1) Awarding employees publicly during ceremonies.
(2) Setting regular one-on-one feedback sessions.
(3) Continually affirming employee's purpose and distinctness within daily tasks.
(4) Awarding annual bonuses based on company profitability.

93. What contributes to 'mattering' in the workplace ?
A. Acts of compassion
B. Personal connection
C. Perks and policies
D. Daily human interactions
E. Feel competition
Choose the most appropriate answer from the options given below :
(1) A, B, C and E Only
(2) B, C and E Only
(3) A, B and D Only
(4) C, D and E Only

94. Which of the following are least effective in producing a sense of mattering?
A. Providing health insurance benefits
B. Changing uniform
C. Celebrating birthdays
D. Ignoring JACT suggestion
E. Weekly department meetings
Choose the **most appropriate** answer from the options given below :
(1) A, B and C Only
(2) D and E Only
(3) A and B Only
(4) A, B, C and E Only

95. What does the term 'mattering' mean in the passage?
(1) Doing your job well
(2) Following rules
(3) Competing with others
(4) Feeling valued and knowing you add value

Read the following paragraph and answer the questions:

One of numerous executive orders of the President aims to achieve global price parity for prescription drugs sold in the Country X. This move offers hope to many citizen's burdened by high healthcare costs. Enforcing this rule in practice, however, might be challenging because it might entail into import-export rules that don't align with existing legislation of Country X. Similar to President's previous attempts to lower drug prices during his first term, this move could also encounter legal challenges. However, the government can take some action against large pharmaceutical companies, commonly referred to as 'Big Pharma', by encouraging less expensive generic drugs and putting an end to unfair practices that delays their release. Perhaps, the Country X pharmaceutical companies have not yet responded negatively to it possibly because the new order has little effect on their profits.

The majority of Indian pharmaceutical exports to Country X fall into the low profit generic drugs market, which is less vulnerable to President's regulations of Country X. Indian businesses might not receive preferential treatment for their branded medicines as the Country X might prefer to purchase them from developed countries like Germany, UK or France. Additionally, as evidenced by trade negotiation with China, the Country X views pharmaceuticals as a sensitive area and might continue imposing special import duties on them. Generic medications from India are currently free from import duties in the Country X. However it might now insist on the same tariff-free treatment for its own Pharmaceutical exports to India. Meanwhile, India has established a solid international reputation as a supplier of affordable medications. It can bargain for better trade conditions by using this image.

96. What conclusion can be drawn regarding the present position of the Country X pharmaceutical industry with regard to executive order?
(1) Actively encouraging
(2) Indifferent as their margins remain unaffected
(3) Strongly opposed
(4) Already implementing it

97. Match List - I with List - II:

List – I Country	List – II Role
A. India	I. Where to find branded medications
B. Germany	II. Attempting to regulate the cost of drugs
C. China	III. Provider of inexpensive generic medicines
D. Country X	IV. Taking part in pharmaceutical discussions about tariffs

Choose the **correct** answer from the options given below :
(1) A-IV, B-III, C-II, D-I
(2) A-III, B-IV, C-I, D-II
(3) A-III, B-I, C-IV, D-II
(4) A-II, B-III, C-I, D-IV

98. Which of the following best sums up the significance of Indian generics for the affordability of healthcare in the Country X?
A. They are less expensive
B. Country X import duties do not apply to them
C. They are mainly used to treat life-threatening diseases.
D. They contribute to lower overall healthcare costs.
E. They serve as alternatives to branded drugs.

Choose the most appropriate answer from the options given below :
(1) A, B, C and D Only
(2) A, B, D and E Only
(3) C, D and E Only
(4) A, C and D Only

99. What is the central irony in President's push for drug price in the Country X?
(1) It benefits only non-Country X companies
(2) It depends on low cost imports from nations the Country X wants to restrict
(3) It runs counter to his endorsement of big pharma
(4) It will reduce worldwide healthcare expenditures

100. Which of the following statement is correct as per the paragraph?
(1) Country X attempted to restrict supply of drugs from china and avoiding negotiations with it.
(2) President had never attempted to lower drug prices in Country X
(3) India being a supplier of affordable medicines can bargain its trade conditions
(4) Country X is currently imposing import duties on generic medicines from India

ANSWER KEY

1. (4)	**2.** (4)	**3.** (4)	**4.** (1)	**5.** (1)	**6.** (2)	**7.** (3)	**8.** (2)	**9.** (2)	**10.** (2)
11. (1)	**12.** (4)	**13.** (4)	**14.** (1)	**15.** (3)	**16.** (1)	**17.** (1)	**18.** (1)	**19.** (3)	**20.** (3)
21. (2)	**22.** (1)	**23.** (4)	**24.** (4)	**25.** (4)	**26.** (4)	**27.** (3)	**28.** (4)	**29.** (2)	**30.** (2)
31. (4)	**32.** (4)	**33.** (4)	**34.** (4)	**35.** (1)	**36.** (2)	**37.** (4)	**38.** (2)	**39.** (2)	**40.** (4)
41. (2)	**42.** (2)	**43.** (2)	**44.** (4)	**45.** (3)	**46.** (2,4)	**47.** (2)	**48.** (3)	**49.** (3)	**50.** (3)
51. (3)	**52.** (1)	**53.** (3)	**54.** (1)	**55.** (1)	**56.** (3)	**57.** (2)	**58.** (4)	**59.** (1)	**60.** (2)
61. (1)	**62.** (1)	**63.** (4)	**64.** (2)	**65.** (2)	**66.** (3)	**67.** (1)	**68.** (3)	**69.** (2)	**70.** (2)
71. (2)	**72.** (2)	**73.** (1)	**74.** (1)	**75.** (3)	**76.** (3)	**77.** (2)	**78.** (3)	**79.** (4)	**80.** (3)
81. (1)	**82.** (2,4)	**83.** (4)	**84.** (1)	**85.** (1)	**86.** (4)	**87.** (3)	**88.** (4)	**89.** (2)	**90.** (3)
91. (2)	**92.** (3)	**93.** (3)	**94.** (3)	**95.** (4)	**96.** (2)	**97.** (3)	**98.** (2)	**99.** (2)	**100.** (3)

JANUARY 2026

MANAGEMENT

PAPER-II

Note : This paper contains **hundred (100)** objective type questions of **two (2)** marks each. **All** questions are **compulsory**.

1. Which of the following are Non Random Sampling?

A. Cluster Sampling
B. Systematic Sampling
C. Quota Sampling
D. Purposive Sampling
E. Multi-Stage Sampling

Choose the **correct** answer from the options given below :

(1) A and B only (2) C and D only
(3) A, B and C only (4) B, C and E only

2. Which of the following strategy is generally adopted by a market challenger firm ?

(1) Follow at a distance
(2) Indirect attack
(3) Multiple Niching
(4) Protect Market Share

3. Given below are two statements one is labelled as Assertion (A) and the other is labelled as Reason (R).

Assertion (A): Liberal credit policies increase the probability of defaults and the associated bad debt losses.

Reason (R): Relaxing credit standards will generally increase sales but may reduce the quality of receivables.

In the light of the above statements, choose the **most appropriate** answer from the options given below:

(1) Both (A) and (R) are correct and (R) is the correct explanation of (A)
(2) Both (A) and (R) are correct but (R) is not the correct explanation of (A)
(3) (A) is correct but (R) is not correct
(4) (A) is not correct but (R) is correct

4. Identify the correct sequence of entrepreneurial process:

A. Establish vision
B. Identify an opportunity
C. Gather resources
D. Persuade others
E. Create New venture/product/market

Choose the correct answer from the options given below :

(1) B, A, D, C, E (2) B, D, A, C, E
(3) A, B, D, C, E (4) B, E, D, C, A

5. Based on the Data Mining Process used in Business Analytics arrange the following in sequence:

A. Pre-Processing the data selecting attributes of interest and checking the outliers
B. Assess the degree to which the selected model make company understood variability/similarity in behaviour and generate segments
C. Understanding "What are the common characteristics of the customers, that the company has lost to its competitors"
D. Identify the spending behaviour of shoppers understanding the most relevant variables and use of descriptive statistics.
E. Modeling technique are selected and applied on dataset.

Choose the **correct** answer from the options given below :

(1) B, E, C, D, A (2) C, E, B, A, D
(3) D, E, B, A, C (4) C, D, A, E, B

6. The kinked demand curve theory of oligopoly suggests that:
   (1) Firms can freely raise prices without losing demand
   (2) Price cuts are matched by rivals, but price increases are not
   (3) Price increases are matched, but price cuts are not
   (4) Demand is perfectly elastic at prevailing price

7. Which of the following is not the type of Data Warehouse?
   (1) Data Marts (DMs)
   (2) Operational Data Stores (ODS)
   (3) Enterprise Data Warehouses (EDW)
   (4) Data Integration Houses (DIH)

8. The process by which people's emotions are caused by the emotions of others is called ?
   (1) Emotion Regulation
   (2) Emotion Contagion
   (3) Emotional Dissonance
   (4) Emotional Labour

9. As per Accounting Standard - 22, Deferred Tax Liability arises when :
   (1) Accounting income is less than taxable income
   (2) Accounting income is more than taxable income
   (3) Accounting income is equal to taxable income
   (4) There is an accounting loss but a taxable income

10. Entries into the cells of a contingency table should be :
    (1) Frequencies
    (2) Mean Values
    (3) Percentages
    (4) Degrees of Freedom

11. String of activities that moves a firm's product from the raw material stage through manufacturing, distribution and ultimately to the end user is called:
    (1) Product Life Cycle
    (2) Value Chain
    (3) New Product Development
    (4) Product Value Continuum

12. Given below are two statements one is labelled as Assertion (A) and the other is labelled as Reason (R).
    Assertion (A): Generally, the customers consider the sales force as the representative of the company.
    Reason (R): Often, the company's sale force works directly with the customers.
    In the light of the above statements, choose the **most appropriate** answer from the options given below:
    (1) Both (A) and (R) are correct and (R) is the correct explanation of (A)
    (2) Both (A) and (R) are correct but (R) is not the correct explanation of (A)
    (3) (A) is correct but (R) is not correct
    (4) (A) is not correct but (R) is correct

13. HR managers usually employ a systematic process when undertaking Human Resource Planning. Arrange the process in correct sequence:
    A. The Formulation of staffing strategies to meet organisational needs.
    B. Labour supply analysis (including both internal and external sources).
    C. Labour demand forecasting.
    D. Environmental scanning.
    E. Balancing supply and demand consideration
    Choose the **correct** answer from the options given below:
    (1) A, C, B, E, D (2) D, C, B, E, A
    (3) D, A, C, B, E (4) A, D, C, E, B

14. In Production & Operations Management, the abbreviation CNC (its a machine) stands for:
    (1) Computer Number Centered
    (2) Computer Numerically Controlled
    (3) Customer Number Center
    (4) Case Numerically Controlled

15. Match **List - I** with **List - II**.

List - I	**List - II**
Term	**Description**
A. Price Earnings to Growth Ratio (PEG)	I. Net margin × Assets turnover × Financial Leverage

B.	Altman's Z score	II.	A tool for predicting corporate bankruptcy using ratio analysis
C.	Return on Equity - DuPont analysis	III.	A ratio which is used as an indication of fair pricing of a stock
D.	Market capitalization	IV.	No. of shares × current market price

Choose the **correct** answer from the options given below :

(1) A-III, B-II, C-I, D-IV
(2) A-II, B-III, C-I, D-IV
(3) A-I, B-III, C-II, D-IV
(4) A-IV, B-II, C-I, D-III

16. Match **List - I** with **List - II**.

List - I Concept	**List - II Description**
A. Marketing Concept	I. Qualitative, performing and innovative products
B. Selling Concept	II. Large-scale sales and promotion effort
C. Production Concept	III. Customer focus and values
D. Product Concept	IV. Available and affordable products

Choose the **correct** answer from the options given below :

(1) A-I, B-II, C-III, D-IV
(2) A-II, B-III, C-I, D-IV
(3) A-IV, B-III, C-II, D-I
(4) A-III, B-II, C-IV, D-I

17. Identify the correct sequence of stages in the sales process:

A. Initial contact
B. Gather the sales Lead
C. Meeting objections and concerns
D. Qualifying the Lead
E. Sales presentation

Choose the **correct** answer from the options given below:

(1) B, A, D, E, C (2) A, B, C, D, E
(3) B, D, A, C, E (4) A, C, B, D, E

18. Which of the following is not an example of systematic risk?

(1) Strike by factory workers
(2) Interest rate risk
(3) Purchasing power risk
(4) Economic recession

19. A transaction that takes place when a large firms that has a small equity stake in a small firm decided to acquire a 100% interest in the firm is called:

(1) Spin out
(2) Spin in
(3) Link Joint Venture
(4) Scale Joint Venture

20. Match **List - I** with **List - II**.

List - I Strategy	**List - II Description**
A. Protective Put	I. Combining two or more call options (or two or more put options) on the same stock with differing exercise prices or times to maturity.
B. Spread	II. Writing a call position on an asset along with buying the asset. Buying an asset along with a put on it.
C. Covered call	III. Buying a call as well as put on a stock at the same exercise price.
D. Long straddle	IV. Choose the correct answer from the options given below:

Choose the **correct** answer from the options given below:

(1) A-II, B-III, C-I, D-IV
(2) A-III, B-I, C-II, D-IV
(3) A-III, B-II, C-IV, D-I
(4) A-I, B-III, C-IV, D-II

21. Match **List - I** with **List - II**.

List - I (Leverage)	**List - II (Interpretation)**
A. Operating Leverage	I. Sensitivity of EPS to EBIT changes
B. Financial Leverage	II. Sensitivity of EBIT to sales changes
C. Combined Leverage	III. Sensitivity of EPS to Sales changes
D. Degree of Leverage	IV. Ratio-based quantitative measure

Choose the **correct** answer from the options given below:

(1) A-II, B-I, C-III, D-IV
(2) A-I, B-II, C-III, D-IV
(3) A-I, B-II, C-IV, D-III
(4) A-III, B-I, C-II, D-IV

22. Arrange the following step of pricing process in a logical order :

A. Analyse competitors' price
B. Estimate demand and revenue
C. Select pricing method
D. Assess pricing objectives
E. Determine Cost

Choose the **correct** answer from the options given below:

(1) A, C, D, B, E (2) D, A, B, C, E
(3) D, B, E, A, C (4) A, D, E, B, C

23. Match **List - I** with **List - II**.

List - I Industry Structure	**List - II Opportunities**
A. Declining Industry	I. Product Refinement
B. Emerging Industry	II. First mover advantage
C. Mature Industry	III. Harvest
D. Fragmented Industry	IV. Consolidation

Choose the **correct** answer from the options given below:

(1) A-II, B-III, C-I, D-IV
(2) A-III, B-II, C-I, D-IV
(3) A-I, B-II, C-III, D-IV
(4) A-IV, B-II, C-I, D-III

24. The tendency to draw a negative general impression about an individual based on a single characteristic refers to which of the following?

(1) Selective perception (2) Halo effect
(3) Horns effect (4) Stereotyping

25. Identify Emotion Regulation techniques from among the following:

A. Emotional Suppression
B. Cognitive reappraisal
C. Social sharing
D. Emotional Intelligence
E. Emotional Labour

Choose the **correct** answer from the options given below:

(1) A, B and C only (2) A, C and D only
(3) B, C and D only (4) A, B and E only

26. The "Vs" that define the Big Data are:

A. Volume B. Variety
C. Velocity D. Validity
E. Veracity

Choose the **correct** answer from the options given below:

(1) A, B and C only
(2) B, C and E only
(3) A, B, C and E only
(4) B, C, D and E only

27. Given below are two statements one is labelled as Assertion (A) and the other is labelled as Reason (R).

Assertion (A): Reality shock occurs when a new employee's high expectations and enthusiasm confront the reality of a boring, unchallenging job.

Reason (R): Providing realistic job interview, challenging first job, and experienced mentors can help preventing reality shock.

In the light of the above statements, choose the **most appropriate** answer from the options given below:

(1) Both (A) and (R) are correct and (R) is the correct explanation of (A)
(2) Both (A) and (R) are correct but (R) is not the correct explanation of (A)
(3) (A) is correct but (R) is not correct
(4) (A) is not correct but (R) is correct

28. Match **List - I** with **List - II**.

List - I **Organizations**	**List - II** **Management tools and Techniques**
A. World Bank	I. Trade Policy Review Mechanism (TPRM)
B. WTO	II. International Commodity Agreements (ICAs)
C. CFC	III. Global System of Trade Preferences (GSTP)
D. UNCTAD	IV. The Logistics Performance Index (LPI)

Choose the **correct** answer from the options given below:

(1) A-II, B-I, C-IV, D-III
(2) A-III, B-IV, C-I, D-II
(3) A-IV, B-III, C-II, D-I
(4) A-IV, B-I, C-II, D-III

29. Which of the following techniques of enhancing strategic thinking is most similar to Devil's Advocacy ?

(1) Brains storming
(2) Dialectical inquiry
(3) Nominal group technique
(4) Delphi method

30. Given below are two statements one is labelled as Assertion (A) and the other is labelled as Reason (R).

Assertion (A): In monopolistic competition, firms face a downward-sloping demand curve that is more elastic than under monopoly.

Reason (R): In monopolistic competition, close substitutes of the product are available in the market.

In the light of the above statements, choose the **most appropriate** answer from the options given below:

(1) Both (A) and (R) are correct and (R) is the correct explanation of (A)
(2) Both (A) and (R) are correct but (R) is not the correct explanation of (A)
(3) (A) is correct but (R) is not correct
(4) (A) is not correct but (R) is correct

31. Five jobs are to be scheduled in two machines in a manufacturing shop. All the five jobs undergo processing in both machines as per table.

		Processing Time	
		Machine 1	Machine 2
A.	Job 1	4	7
B.	Job 2	6	3
C.	Job 3	2	3
D.	Job 4	7	7
E.	Job 5	8	6

Identify the best sequence using Johnson's rule.

Choose the **correct** answer from the options given below:

(1) A, B, C, D, E
(2) B, E, D, A, C
(3) C, A, D, E, B
(4) D, C, B, A, E

32. Given below are two statements: one is labelled as Assertion (A) and the other is labelled as Reason (R).

Assertion (A): It is possible for almost everyone to become a leader if circumstances allow him/her to perform functions dictated by the situation.

Reason (R): The qualities, characteristics and skill required in a leader are determined to a large extent by the demands of the situation in which he/she is to function as a leader.

In the light of the above statements, choose the **most appropriate** answer from the options given below:

(1) Both (A) and (R) are correct and (R) is the correct explanation of (A)
(2) Both (A) and (R) are correct but (R) is not the correct explanation of (A)
(3) (A) is correct but (R) is not correct
(4) (A) is not correct but (R) is correct

33. The sampling procedure in which committees are formed by choosing people from various departments in an organization to help making decisions on product development, budget allocations and marketing strategies is known as:

(1) Stratified Sampling
(2) Multistage Sampling

(3) Systematic Sampling
(4) Cluster Sampling

34. Identify the steps involved in the creative process:

A. Preparation
B. Opportunity Recognition
C. Incubation
D. Insight
E. Feasibility analysis

Choose the **correct** answer from the options given below:

(1) A, B and E only (2) A, C and D only
(3) B, D and E only (4) A, E and C only

35. Match **List - I** with **List - II**.

List - I (Term)	List - II (Description)
A. Law of Diminishing Marginal Utility	I. On each successive unit consumed, the utility derived goes on falling
B. Consumer Surplus	II. The rate at which consumer is ready to compromise goods X for another goods Y, holding the level of satisfaction constant
C. Marginal Rate of Substitution	III. Difference between what a consumer is ready to pay for a commodity and what he actually pays for it
D. Budget Line	IV. All those combinations of two goods which consumer can buy spending his given money income and their given prices.

Choose the **correct** answer from the options given below:

(1) A-II, B-III, C-I, D-IV
(2) A-III, B-II, C-I, D-IV
(3) A-I, B-III, C-II, D-IV
(4) A-IV, B-II, C-I, D-III

36. Which of the following best describes an American call option?

(1) It gives the holder the right to sell the underlying asset at a specified price within a specified period.
(2) It assists the holder to purchase the underlying asset at the market price on expiry only.
(3) It gives the holder the right to buy the underlying asset at a specified price within a specified period.
(4) It is a contract that guarantees a fixed return irrespective of market movements.

37. The difference between the standard quantity of a material specified for actual production and the actual quantity of material used at standard price is known as:

(1) Material Cost Variance
(2) Material Usage Variance
(3) Material Price Variance
(4) Material Yield Variance

38. Which of the following are the assumptions of Modigliani and Miller's Dividend Irrelavance Theory?

A. Perfect Capital Market
B. No taxes
C. No transaction Cost and no time lag
D. Fixed Investment Policy
E. Investors behave irrationally

Choose the **correct** answer from the options given below:

(1) A, B, C, D and E (2) C, D and E only
(3) A, B, C and D only (4) A, B and E only

39. Which of the following perceive pluralistic approach to Industrial Relation:

A. Work place conflict is seen as a temporary aberration, resulting from poor management, from employees who don't mix with organisation's culture.
B. Trade Unions as legitimate representatives of employees interest.
C. Stability in industrial relations as the product of concession and compromises between management and union.

D. Organisations as coalitions of competing interest, where the management role is to mediate amongst the different interest groups.

E. Conflict arises not just because of competing interests within the organisation but because of division within the society between those who own resources and those who have only labour to offer.

Choose the **correct** answer from the options given below:

(1) A, C and E only (2) C, D and E only
(3) B, C and D only (4) A, B and D only

40. An entrepreneur whose aim is to maximise the economic returns at a level consistent with the survival of the firm, with or without the element of growth is called :

(1) Fabian entrepreneur
(2) First generation entrepreneur
(3) Modern entrepreneur
(4) Classical entrepreneur

41. Generally, a supermarket in classified by which of the following category ?

(1) Relative prices (2) Ownership
(3) Product line sold (4) Service provided

42. Which of the following statements is not correct?

(1) Unsystematic risk can be eliminated through diversification.
(2) Systematic risk can be eliminated through diversification.
(3) The Capital Market Line is an efficient set of risk free and risky securities, and it shows the risk return trade-off in the market equilibrium.
(4) In CAPM model, the market risk of a security is measured in terms of its sensitivity to the market movements which is referred as securities B.

43. In case of cost-push inflation :

(1) Demand curve shifts to the right
(2) Demand curve shifts to the left
(3) Supply curve shifts to the left
(4) Supply curve shifts to the right

44. Arrange the logical steps under the Net Income (IN) approach of capital structure:

A. Increase in financial leverage reduces the overall cost of capital.
B. Reduced overall cost of capital increases the value of the firm.

Assumes cost of equity and cost of debt remain constant.

C. Concludes that value of firm can be maximized by using as much debt as possible.
D. Choose the correct answer from the options given below:

(1) C, A, B, D (2) A, C, D, B
(3) B, A, C, D (4) C, B, D, A

45. Put the given steps in sequence to solve the Transportation Model problem in Operations Research:

A. Test for Optimality
B. Perform Optimality Test
C. Make a Transportation Table
D. Find the basic feasible solution
E. Iterate towards an optimal solution

Choose the **correct** answer from the options given below:

(1) A, C, B, D, E (2) C, D, B, E, A
(3) D, E, B, A, C (4) E, D, A, B, C

46. In the VRIO framework, the V stands for which one of the following questions?

(1) Is a resource currently controlled by only a small number of competing firms?
(2) Do firms without a resource face a cost disadvantage in obtaining or developing it ?
(3) Are a firm's other policies organised to support the exploitation of its resources?
(4) Does a resource enable a firm to exploit an environmental opportunity and/or neutralize an environment threat?

47. Fixed manufacturing overhead costs are recognised as:

(1) Period costs under absorption costing
(2) Product costs under variable costing
(3) Part of ending inventory costs under both absorption and variable costing
(4) Product costs under absorption costing

48. Given below are two statements one is labelled as Assertion (A) and the other is labelled as Reason (R).

Assertion (A): Most fast growth entrepreneurial ventures organise as corporations or limited liability companies rather than as sole proprietorship or partnership.

Reason (R): Business losses of corporations can be deducted against the shareholder's other sources of income.

In the light of the above statements, choose the **most appropriate** answer from the options given below:

(1) Both (A) and (R) are correct and (R) is the correct explanation of (A)

(2) Both (A) and (R) are correct but (R) is not the correct explanation of (A)

(3) (A) is correct but (R) is not correct

(4) (A) is not correct but (R) is correct

49. Foreign exchange quotation when expressed in a manner that reflects the exchange of a specified number of foreign currencies vis-à-vis one unit of local currency is expressed as:

(1) Direct Quotation

(2) European Quotation

(3) Indirect Quotation

(4) Geographical Arbitrage

50. Match **List - I** with **List - II**.

List - I Concept	**List - II Model**
A. The concept advocates the view that "where data lives"	I. Saas
B. Infrastructure resources like networks, storage, servers are provided to clients.	II. Daas
C. Allows consumers to use applications and software that run on distant computers in the cloud infrastructure	III. Iaas
D. Companies can deploy their software and applications in the cloud so that their customers can use them.	IV. Pass

Choose the **correct** answer from the options given below:

(1) A-II, B-III, C-I, D-IV

(2) A-III, B-II, C-I, D-IV

(3) A-II, B-I, C-IV, D-III

(4) A-IV, B-III, C-II, D-I

51. Which of the following strategies are commonly used by a firm to win a "Format War"?

A. Killer Applications

B. Cooperate with Competitors

C. Tapered Integration

D. Transfer Pricing

E. Divestment Strategy

Choose the **correct** answer from the options given below:

(1) A and E only (2) B and C only

(3) C and D only (4) A and B only

52. Arrange the following steps in the correct order of Controlling Process:

A. Comparison of actual performance with the standards

B. Measurement of actual performance

C. Corrective action wherever required

D. Establishment of standards

Choose the **correct** answer from the options given below:

(1) B, A, C, D (2) D, B, A, C

(3) B, C, A, D (4) A, C, B, D

53. Which of the following statements are correct for computing the Cost of Equity?

A. If dividend is expected to be constant, then dividend price approach should be used.

B. If earnings per share is expected to be constant, then earnings price approach should be used.

C. If earnings and dividend are expected to grow at a constant rate, then realized yield should be used.

D. If it is difficult to forecast future, then Growth approach (Gordon's model) should be used which looks into the past.

E. When the cost of equity or expectation of the investor is dependent on risk, then Capital Assets Pricing Model (CAPM) should be used.

Choose the **correct** answer from the options given below:

(1) A, B and C only (2) A, B and D only
(3) B, C and D only (4) A, B and E only

54. The positive model is applied to planned change through an approach is called appreciative inquiry (AI). Which of the following is not the cyclical step of AI?

(1) Discovery (2) Dreaming
(3) Design (4) Dedication

55. 'Horizontal FDI' means:

(1) When a firm invests in a foreign country in similar production activity as carried out in home country exploiting its competitive advantage in the host country.
(2) Foreign firm takes control over domestic assets
(3) Direct investment made overseas with aim to provide inputs for the firm's production processes in the home country.
(4) Direct investment in industries abroad so as to either provide inputs for the firm's domestic operations or sell its domestic output overseas.

56. Arrange the following steps of implementation of corporate diversification in the logical order:

A. Allocate resources and authority to divisions
B. Establish coordination & monitor performance
C. Design appropriate organizational structure
D. Identify core competencies and market opportunities
E. Select diversification strategy

Choose the **correct** answer from the options given below:

(1) A, B, D, C, E (2) E, C, B, A, D
(3) D, E, C, A, B (4) C, D, E, B, A

57. Which one of the following theory of corporate governance focuses on the principal-agent conflict, where managers may prioritize their own interests over those of shareholders, thereby necessitating monitoring, incentives, and control mechanism?

(1) Stewardship Theory
(2) Agency Theory
(3) Stakeholder Theory
(4) Resource Dependence Theory

58. Match **List - I** with **List - II**.

List - I (Name of Study)	**List - II (Name)**
A. Time and motion study	I. Koontz and Donnell
B. Hawthorne experiments	II. Elton Mayo
C. Universalist approach	III. F.W. Taylor
D. Bureaucracy	IV. Max Weber

Choose the **correct** answer from the options given below:

(1) A-II, B-III, C-I, D-IV
(2) A-III, B-II, C-I, D-IV
(3) A-I, B-III, C-II, D-IV
(4) A-IV, B-II, C-I, D-III

59. Generally, consumers undertake complex buying behaviour in situations characterized by which one of the followings?

(1) High involvement in purchase and few perceived difference among brands
(2) Low involvement in purchase and significant perceived difference among brands
(3) High involvement in purchase and significance perceived difference among brands
(4) Low involvement in purchase and few significant perceived difference among brands

60. Arrange the following steps of Global marketing process in a correct order:

A. Implement the marketing strategy
B. Decide on market entry strategy
C. Monitor and control
D. Identify and evaluate marketing opportunities
E. Develop a marketing program

Choose the **correct** answer from the options given below:

(1) A, B, C, D, E (2) D, B, E, A, C
(3) B, E, D, A, C (4) E, B, D, A, C

61. Given below are two statements one is labelled as Assertion (A) and the other is labelled as Reason (R).

Assertion (A): Various sub-assemblies in the 2-wheeler plant need to be configured to match the production rate. Similarly, the final assembly stations also need to have the required number of resources at each station to meet the targeted demand.

Reason (R): In such a scenario, to arrive at a balanced flow of components on the shop floor, the company need to group machines together based on their functionality and jobs will move from one functional department to other.

In the light of the above statements, choose the **most appropriate** answer from the options given below:

(1) Both (A) and (R) are correct and (R) is the correct explanation of (A)
(2) Both (A) and (R) are correct but (R) is not the correct explanation of (A)
(3) (A) is correct but (R) is not correct
(4) (A) is not correct but (R) is correct

62. Arrange the basic process of HR strategy in correct orders:

A. Identify people issues
B. Communicate HR strategy
C. Identify strategic Business issues
D. Scan External Environment
E. Develop HR strategy

Choose the **correct** answer from the options given below:

(1) E, A, C, D, B (2) C, D, E, A, B
(3) A, C, D, B, E (4) D, C, A, E, B

63. 'Human Capacity' under Building Trade Capacity as per efforts made by WTO to meet special requirements of developing countries refers to help on which of the following:

(1) Roads and Ports
(2) National Standards Authorities
(3) Customs
(4) Trade Lawyers

64. Arrange the following steps in fixed income portfolio process in order:

A. Drafting guideline for investment policy
B. Setting up objective
C. Selection of securities and other assets
D. Evaluation of performance with benchmark
E. Selection of portfolio strategy

Choose the **correct** answer from the options given below:

(1) B, A, C, E, D (2) B, A, E, C, D
(3) C, D, E, B, A (4) A, B, C, E, D

65. Match **List - I** with **List - II.**

List - I Leadership Style	**List - II Maturity level of Subordinates**
A. Telling	I. Moderate to high
B. Selling	II. High
C. Participating	III. Low
D. Delegating	IV. Low to moderate

Choose the **correct** answer from the options given below:

(1) A-III, B-IV, C-I, D-II
(2) A-III, B-IV, C-II, D-I
(3) A-IV, B-III, C-I, D-II
(4) A-II, B-IV, C-III, D-I

66. In Collective Bargaining, an 'impasse' refers to:

(1) The combined refusal by employees to buy employer's product
(2) A refusal by the employer to provide opportunities to work
(3) A situation that occurs when the parties are not able to move further towards settlement, usually because one party is demanding more than the other will offer.
(4) A situation where employees carry sign announcing their concerns near the employer's place of business.

67. According to which of the following theories of International Business, the pattern of FDI is determined by combination of Core Competency, locational advantage and entry mode?

(1) International Product Life Cycle Theory
(2) Market Imperfection Theory

(3) Internalization Theory
(4) Eclectic Theory

68. A conscious belief that only the host-country managers can ever really understand the culture and behaviour of the host-country market. It refers to which of the following top executives' values:

(1) Ethnocentric (2) Geocentric
(3) Polycentric (4) Egocentric

69. Low nurturing and low regulating leader behaviour is called:

(1) Consulting style (2) Supporting style
(3) Delegating style (4) Directive style

70. Match **List - I** with **List - II**.

List - I Steps to generate creative ideas	**List - II Description**
A. Incubation	I. Idea is subject to scrutiny
B. Insight	II. Idea transformed to something of value
C. Evaluation	III. Thinks about a problem
D. Elaboration	IV. Idea is born

Choose the **correct** answer from the options given below:

(1) A-III, B-IV, C-I, D-II
(2) A-III, B-I, C-IV, D-II
(3) A-IV, B-III, C-I, D-II
(4) A-IV, B-III, C-II, D-I

71. Given below are two statements one is labelled as Assertion (A) and the other is labelled as Reason (R).

Assertion (A): Margin of safety can be negative if actual sales are less than break even sales.

Reason (R): Negative Margin of safety means losses equal fixed costs minus contribution.

In the light of the above statements, choose the **most appropriate** answer from the options given below:

(1) Both (A) and (R) are correct and (R) is the correct explanation of (A)
(2) Both (A) and (R) are correct but (R) is not the correct explanation of (A)
(3) (A) is correct but (R) is not correct
(4) (A) is not correct but (R) is correct

72. Identify the correct sequence of activities involved in Quality Circle Development:

A. Constitution of QC
B. Start-up phase
C. Presentation and approval of suggestions
D. Initial problem solving
E. Implementation

Choose the **correct** answer from the options given below:

(1) B, A, D, C, E (2) B, A, C, D, E
(3) A, B, D, E, C (4) A, D, E, B, C

73. Which of the following statements are correct?

A. Gross Domestic Product at Market Price = Gross National Product at Market Price + Net Factor Income From Abroad
B. Gross Domestic Product at factor Cost-Gross Domestic Product at Market Price – Indirect Taxes + Subsidies
C. Net Domestic Product at Market Price = Net National Product at Market Price-Net Factor Income From Abroad
D. Gross Domestic Product at Market Price = Net Domestic Product at Market Price + Depreciation
E. Net National Product at Market Price = Gross Domestic Product at Market Price + Net Factor Income From Abroad + Depreciation

Choose the **correct** answer from the options given below:

(1) A, B and C only (2) A, B and D only
(3) B, C and D only (4) A, B and E only

74. Match **List - I** with **List - II**.

List - I Purpose of Tool (Quality Related)	**List - II Quality Management Tool**
A. Identifying Specific Improvement opportunities	I. Control Charts
B. Analysing problems and their root causes	II. Pareto Diagrams
C. Highlighting Problems	III. Pokya Yoke

D. Operational Planning for building quality into products/services — IV. Fish Bone Diagram

Choose the **correct** answer from the options given below:
(1) A-II, B-III, C-IV, D-I
(2) A-III, B-II, C-I, D-IV
(3) A-IV, B-II, C-III, D-I
(4) A-II, B-IV, C-I, D-III

75. The number of new orders received by the company over last 25 working days are as follows 3, 0, 1, 4, 4, 4, 2, 5, 3, 6, 4, 5, 1, 4, 2, 3, 0, 2, 4, 5, 4, 2, 3, 3, 1. The average orders received during these working days:
(1) 2 orders (2) 3 orders
(3) 4 orders (4) 5 orders

76. Match **List - I** with **List - II**.

List - I Strategic Business Unit	**List - II Features**
A. Dogs	I. Used to find other developing businesses
B. Stars	II. Can be converted into stars
C. Cash Cows	III. Need heavy investment, to finance their rapid growth
D. Question Mark	IV. Harvested or divested from portfolio

Choose the **correct** answer from the options given below:
(1) A-I, B-II, C-III, D-IV
(2) A-II, B-I, C-IV, D-III
(3) A-IV, B-III, C-I, D-II
(4) A-III, B-II, C-I, D-IV

77. Under which of the following conditions, a brand is said to have a negative brand equity ?
(1) Consumers are unaware of the brand's existence
(2) Consumers react less favorably to the brand than to an unbranded version
(3) The brand is unable to differentiate itself in the market place
(4) The financial value of the brand decreases below its market price

78. Arrange the following features of adopter groups of new products in the correct order of stages of adoption process:
A. Skeptical B. Deliberate
C. Venturesome D. Tradition bound
E. Opinion leaders

Choose the **correct** answer from the options given below:
(1) A, C, D, B, E (2) B, D, C, E, A
(3) C, E, B, A, D (4) D, C, B, A, E

79. Which of the following best describes the 4 A's from the buyer's viewpoint ?
A. Adjustability B. Awareness
C. Accessibility D. Affordability
E. Acceptability

Choose the **correct** answer from the options given below:
(1) A, B, C only (2) B, C, D, E only
(3) B, C, D only (4) A, C, D, E only

80. Which of the following organisational structure is generally adopted by firms to realise the full potential of cost leadership strategies?
(1) M - form structure
(2) U - form structure
(3) A - form structure
(4) H - form structure

81. Which of the following include the target firm's responses to acquisition efforts, that do not affect the wealth of equity holders?
(1) Search for white knights
(2) Golden parachutes
(3) Shark repellants
(4) Poison pills

82. Given below are two statements one is labelled as Assertion (A) and the other is labelled as Reason (R).

Assertion (A): In the related diversification, a firm acquires a new business whose value chain possesses competitively valuable cross-business strategic fits.

Reason (R): Related diversification strategies mainly aimed to realise financial, managerial and/or operational synergies.

In the light of the above statements, choose the **most appropriate** answer from the options given below:

(1) Both (A) and (R) are correct and (R) is the correct explanation of (A)
(2) Both (A) and (R) are correct but (R) is not the correct explanation of (A)
(3) (A) is correct but (R) is not correct
(4) (A) is not correct but (R) is correct

83. When the supervisor keeps a log of positive and negative examples of a subordinate's work-related bevaviour, it refers to which one of the following methods of performance appraisal?

(1) Paired Comparison Method
(2) Critical Incident Method
(3) Forced Distributive Incidence Method
(4) Alternation Ranking Method

84. The rate at which a company is spending its capital until it reaches profitability is called:

(1) Burn rate (2) Indifference rate
(3) Break even rate (4) Spin off rate

85. Match **List - I** with **List - II**.

List - I	**List - II**
Category	**Strategic Description**
A. Defenders	I. Highly competitive and slave of their environment
B. Prospectors	II. Exploit niches in the market place
C. Analyzer	III. Cost control as primary focus
D. Reactor	IV. Innovation

Choose the **correct** answer from the options given below:

(1) A-III, B-IV, C-II, D-I
(2) A-II, B-I, C-III, D-IV
(3) A-II, B-III, C-I, D-IV
(4) A-I, B-III, C-II, D-IV

86. Given below are two statements one is labelled as Assertion (A) and the other is labelled as Reason (R).

Assertion (A): For exports of goods, the exporter has to apply to the nominated export inspection agency for conducting the pre-shipment and quality control inspection for the export consignment and obtain Export Credit Certificate conforming to the prescribed specifications.

Reason (R): This inspection certificate would be required for customs clearance of cargo before shipment.

In the light of the above statements, choose the **most appropriate** answer from the options given below:

(1) Both (A) and (R) are correct and (R) is the correct explanation of (A)
(2) Both (A) and (R) are correct but (R) is not the correct explanation of (A)
(3) (A) is correct but (R) is not correct
(4) (A) is not correct but (R) is correct

87. Which of the following is true:

(1) The role of Central bank in the foreign exchange market is commercial in nature.
(2) Forward exchange rate is the rate of that day on which the transaction has taken place
(3) Cross rate is the rate of exchange of two currencies on the basis of exchange quotes of other pairs of currencies.
(4) The rate at which a foreign exchange dealer is ready to sell a currency is called bid rate.

88. If two goods are perfect substitutes for each other, Cross elasticity of demand between them will be:

(1) Zero (2) Positive
(3) Negative (4) Infinity

89. Match **List - I** with **List - II**.

List - I	**List - II**
Social Scientists	**Framework Theory**
A. McGuire	I. Balance Theory of attitude change
B. Rokeach	II. Framework of cultural dimensions
C. Hofstede	III. Framework of values
D. Heider	IV. Matrix of attitudinal change

Choose the **correct** answer from the options given below:

(1) A-IV, B-III, C-II, D-I
(2) A-IV, B-II, C-III, D-I
(3) A-III, B-IV, C-II, D-I
(4) A-IV, B-I, C-III, D-II

90. Which among the following is not a hygiene factor ?
(1) Salary
(2) Supervision
(3) Company Policy
(4) Responsibility

Read the following passage and answer the questions:

The Chairman astonished HR leaders by announcing the company's discontinuation of annual reviews, substituting them with immediate feedback, goal-oriented coaching and weekly incentives. This transformation, once considered heretical, has gained widespread acceptance: around one-third of U.S. companies, including Adobe, Deloitte, GE, Microsoft and PwC, have transitioned from inflexible annual evaluations to regular, informal assessments. Conventional performance evaluations, previously effective for determining compensation and recognizing talent, have evolved into expensive, bureaucratic processes that are unpopular among both employees and managers. Critics contend that they prioritize historical conduct over prospective development, hinder collaboration and do not fulfill commercial requirements. Originating from the military's merit rating system, performance appraisals have transitioned between accountability and development, influenced by variables including inflation, compulsory ranking at GE, executive compensation reforms and the competitive pursuit of talent. Currently, low inflation, streamlined organizational structures, agile work methodologies and the necessity for ongoing innovation have made annual reviews redundant. Organizations are currently emphasizing agility, collaboration, and personnel development, concentrating on continuous dialogue and immediate objective. Despite ongoing challenges-such as bias, salary discrepancies and inadequate supervisor training-organizations that implement continuous feedback mechanisms experience enhanced satisfaction, superior coaching and greater alignment with corporate objectives. The transition signifies a necessity: performance management must adapt to cultivate future talent.

91. Match **List - I** with **List - II**.

	List - I		**List - II**
A.	Origin of performance appraisals	I.	Compulsory ranking at GE
B.	Bureaucratic evolution	II.	Expensive and unpopular processes
C.	Factors influencing appraisal changes	III.	Military's merit rating system
D.	Current organizational focus	IV.	Agility, collaboration and continuous dialogue

Choose the **correct** answer from the options given below:
(1) A-II, B-III, C-I, D-IV
(2) A-I, B-II, C-III, D-IV
(3) A-III, B-IV, C-II, D-I
(4) A-IV, B-II, C-III, D-I

92. Why have annual reviews become redundant in organizations today?
(1) Because of compulsory ranking and bureaucracy
(2) Due to low inflation, agile work methodologies, streamlined structures and innovation needs
(3) Since employees demanded higher compensation
(4) Because military systems were abandoned

93. What replaced annual reviews in the company, as announced by the Chairman ?
(1) Only compensation-based incentives
(2) Historical performance records
(3) Immediate feedback, goal-oriented coaching and weekly incentives
(4) Executive compensation reforms

94. Which of the following statements are correct as per paragraph ?

A. Companies like Adobe, Deloitte, GE, Microsoft and PwC have shifted to informal assessments.
B. Annual reviews are now seen as promoting collaboration and innovation.
C. Continuous feedback improves satisfaction, coaching and corporate alignment.
D. Annual evaluations originated from executive compensation reforms.
E. Current organizations emphasize agility, collaboration and personnel development through continuous dialogue.

Choose the **correct** answer from the options given below :
(1) A, C, D and E only
(2) A, C and E only
(3) B, D and E only
(4) A, C and D only

95. Critics argue that conventional performance evaluations:
(1) Encourage collaboration and future-oriented growth
(2) Fulfill commercial requirements effectively
(3) Prioritize historical conduct over development, hinder-collaboration and fail to meet business needs
(4) Motivate employees through transparent ranking

Read the following passage and answer the questions:

Jensen examines the dynamics of corporate takeovers and challenges prevailing misconceptions surrounding them. He argues that takeovers are not merely hostile disruptions but serve as a crucial mechanism of the market for corporate control. According to Jensen, inefficient management teams often fail to maximize shareholder value and takeovers act as disciplinary tool by transferring control to more competent managers. He emphasizes that while popular belief portrays takeovers as destructive to employees and communities, empirical evidence suggests that they frequently generate significant economic gains by reallocating resources to more productive uses. Jensen distinguishes between the folklore-emotional and political arguments against takeovers depicting as harmful to employees and society and the science, which demonstrates their role in improving efficiency and shareholder wealth. He also addresses concerns about debt financing in leveraged buyouts, contending that high leverage can impose financial discipline on managers by reducing wasteful spending. Ultimately, Jensen frames takeovers as an essential corrective force within capitalism, countering managerial inefficiency and aligning corporate behavior with shareholder interests. His analysis laid the groundwork for modern corporate finance debates on governance, agency costs and the value-creating potential of mergers and acquisitions.

96. Jensen emphasizes that while popular belief portrays takeovers as destructive, empirical evidence shows they:
(1) Reduce corporate efficiency
(2) Increase wasteful spending
(3) Produce substantial economic benefits
(4) Neutralize shareholder interests

97. Match **List - I** with **List - II**.

List - I Term	**List - II** Description
A. Folklore view	I. Portrayed as destructive to employees and communities
B. Scientific evidence	II. Generates significant economic gains by reallocating resources
C. Inefficient management	III. Fails to maximize shareholder value
D. Debt financing	IV. Imposes financial discipline by reducing wasteful spending

Choose the **correct** answer from the options given below:
(1) A-II, B-IV, C-III, D-I
(2) A-I, B-III, C-II, D-IV
(3) A-I, B-II, C-III, D-IV
(4) A-II, B-III, C-I, D-IV

98. Which of the following reflect Jensen's "Science" of takeovers ?

A. Improve shareholder wealth
B. Reallocate resources productively
C. Impose financial discipline through debt
D. Operate as hostile disruptions
E. Function as an essential corrective force in capitalism

Choose the **correct** answer from the options given below :
(1) B, C, D and E only
(2) A, B, C and E only
(3) C and E only
(4) A, B and C only

99. In the paragraph, inefficient management teams are described as those who:
(1) Fail to enhance shareholder value
(2) Encourage political influence
(3) Maximize community welfare
(4) Eliminate market competition

100. According to the paragraph, takeovers are not merely hostile disruptions but serve as :
(1) A way of destroying communities
(2) An extension of political arguments
(3) A pivotal mechanism of the market for corporate control
(4) A reduction in shareholder rights

ANSWER KEY

1. (2)	**2.** (2)	**3.** (1)	**4.** (1)	**5.** (4)	**6.** (2)	**7.** (4)	**8.** (2)	**9.** (2)	**10.** (1)
11. (2)	**12.** (1)	**13.** (2)	**14.** (2)	**15.** (1)	**16.** (4)	**17.** (1)	**18.** (1)	**19.** (2)	**20.** (2)
21. (1)	**22.** (3)	**23.** (2)	**24.** (3)	**25.** (1)	**26.** (3)	**27.** (1)	**28.** (4)	**29.** (2)	**30.** (1)
31. (3)	**32.** (1)	**33.** (4)	**34.** (2)	**35.** (3)	**36.** (3)	**37.** (2)	**38.** (3)	**39.** (3)	**40.** (4)
41. (3)	**42.** (2)	**43.** (3)	**44.** (1)	**45.** (2)	**46.** (4)	**47.** (4)	**48.** (3)	**49.** (3)	**50.** (1)
51. (4)	**52.** (2)	**53.** (4)	**54.** (4)	**55.** (1)	**56.** (3)	**57.** (2)	**58.** (2)	**59.** (3)	**60.** (2)
61. (3)	**62.** (4)	**63.** (4)	**64.** (2)	**65.** (1)	**66.** (3)	**67.** (4)	**68.** (3)	**69.** (3)	**70.** (1)
71. (1)	**72.** (1)	**73.** (3)	**74.** (4)	**75.** (2)	**76.** (3)	**77.** (2)	**78.** (3)	**79.** (2)	**80.** (2)
81. (3)	**82.** (1)	**83.** (2)	**84.** (1)	**85.** (1)	**86.** (4)	**87.** (3)	**88.** (4)	**89.** (1)	**90.** (4)
91. (1)	**92.** (2)	**93.** (3)	**94.** (2)	**95.** (3)	**96.** (3)	**97.** (3)	**98.** (2)	**99.** (1)	**100.** (3)